UNITED NATIONS CONFERENCE ON TRADE AND DEVELOPMENT
CONFÉRENCE DES NATIONS UNIES SUR LE COMMERCE ET LE DÉVELOPPEMENT

UNCTAD
HANDBOOK
OF STATISTICS

MANUEL
DE STATISTIQUES
DE LA CNUCED

2006

DÉPÔT
DEPOSIT

UNITED NATIONS
NATIONS UNIES

PER
UNI
TD
453

TD/STAT.31

UNITED NATIONS PUBLICATION
Sales No. E/F.07.II.D.2
ISBN 978-92-1-012063-0 ISSN 0251-9461

The *UNCTAD Handbook of Statistics* provides essential data for analysing world trade, investment, international financial flows and development. Reliable statistical information is often the first step when preparing recommendations or taking decisions that will commit countries for many years as they strive to integrate into the world economy and improve the living standards of their citizens. Whether it be for research, consultation or technical cooperation, UNCTAD needs comparable, often detailed economic, demographic and social data, available if possible over several decades and for as many countries as possible.

In addition to collecting and checking data and calculating related indicators that facilitate the work of the secretariat's economists, the *UNCTAD Handbook of Statistics* provides an opportunity to share a rich statistical database with decision makers and research specialists – academics, officials from national governments or international organizations, executive managers or members of NGOs from developing, transition or developed countries. The *Handbook* further offers journalists comprehensive information in a presentation that meets their needs.

This edition of the *Handbook of Statistics* has been restructured to present data in a more coherent fashion and enhance their analytical value. Statistics are available for more groups of countries, some headings have been expanded, and new statistics on commodities have been introduced for the first time.

The publication is available in three complementary formats: printed copy, CD-ROM and online (www.unctad.org/statistics/handbook), in order to provide maximum benefit to all users.

Particular acknowledgement is due to the Statistics Division, Department of Economic and Social Affairs of the United Nations, as well to by other international organizations, for their help in preparing this publication.

Le but du *Manuel de Statistiques de la CNUCED* est de fournir les données statistiques essentielles à l'analyse du commerce mondial, de l'investissement des flux financiers internationaux et du développement. Une information statistique fiable est souvent le préalable à la formulation de recommandations et à la prise de décisions qui engageront les pays pour de longues années dans leur processus d'intégration dans l'économie mondiale et l'amélioration des conditions de leurs peuples. Que ce soit pour la recherche, la concertation ou la coopération technique, la CNUCED a besoin de données économiques, démographiques et sociales comparables et souvent détaillées, disponibles si possible sur plusieurs décennies et sur un maximum de pays.

Au-delà de la mobilisation et de la vérification des données, du calcul d'indicateurs dérivés qui alimentent les travaux des économistes du secrétariat, le *Manuel de Statistiques de la CNUCED* est l'occasion de partager une base statistique riche avec les décideurs et les chercheurs, qu'ils soient universitaires, fonctionnaires d'administrations nationales ou d'organisations internationales, cadres d'entreprises ou membres d'organisations non gouvernementales de pays en développement, en transition ou développés. Les journalistes trouvent aussi dans ce manuel une information synthétique dans une présentation bien adaptée à leurs préoccupations.

Cette édition du *Manuel de Statistiques* a été restructurée pour présenter les données d'une façon plus cohérente et accroître leur valeur analytique. Les statistiques sont disponibles au niveau d'un plus grand nombre de groupes de pays, certaines rubriques ont été étoffées et un premier pas a été fait avec l'introduction de nouvelles statistiques sur les produits de base.

La publication est disponible dans trois formats complémentaires, l'édition imprimée, le CD-ROM et la version en ligne (www.unctad.org/statistics/handbook), pour que chaque utilisateur, où qu'il soit, puisse en tirer le meilleur avantage.

Le secrétariat de la CNUCED tient à remercier la Division de statistique, Département des affaires économiques et sociales de l'ONU, et diverses organisations internationales du concours qu'elles ont apporté à la préparation de cette publication.

TABLE OF CONTENTS	TABLE DES MATIÈRES

PART ONE **International merchandise trade**	**PREMIÈRE PARTIE** **Commerce international des marchandises**

TABLE OF CONTENTS
TABLE DES MATIÈRES

PART FIVE
International trade in services

CINQUIÈME PARTIE
Commerce international des services

PART SIX
Commodities

SIXIÈME PARTIE
Produits de base

PART SEVEN
International finance

SEPTIÈME PARTIE
Flux financiers internationaux

PART EIGHT
Development indicators

TABLE DES MATIÈRES

7.4	Envois de fonds des travailleurs :	
	Recettes	356
	Paiements	357
7.5.1	Réserves internationales des économies en développement par pays et régions géographiques	358
7.5.2	Réserves internationales des économies en développement par groupements économiques	364
7.6.1	Flux financiers publics bilatéraux et multilatéraux à destination des économies en développement par pays et régions géographiques	366
7.6.2	Flux financiers publics bilatéraux et multilatéraux à destination des économies en développement par groupements économiques	379
7.7	Dette extérieure à long terme par catégories de prêt des :	
	A. Économies en développement	383
	B. Économies en développement : Afrique	384
	C. Économies en développement : Amérique	385
	D. Économies en développement : Asie	386
	E. Économies en développement : Océanie	387
	F. Principaux exportateurs de pétrole	388
	G. Principaux exportateurs d'articles manufacturés	389

HUITIÈME PARTIE
Indicateurs du développement

8.1.1	Produit intérieur brut nominal : Total et par habitant des pays et des régions géographiques	392
8.1.2	Produit intérieur brut nominal : Total et par habitant des groupements économiques	400
8.2.1	Taux de croissance annuels moyens du produit intérieur brut réel total et par habitant des pays et des régions géographiques	402
8.2.2	Taux de croissance annuels moyens du produit intérieur brut réel total et par habitant des groupements économiques	410
8.3.1	Produit intérieur brut par catégories de dépenses et par branches d'activité économique des pays et des régions géographiques	412
8.3.2	Produit intérieur brut par catégories de dépenses et par branches d'activité économique des groupements économiques	430
8.4.1	Population et main d'œuvre des pays et des régions géographiques	434
8.4.2	Population et main d'œuvre des groupements économiques	452
8.5.1	Indicateurs démographiques des pays et des régions géographiques	456
8.5.2	Indicateurs démographiques des groupements économiques	470

These notes summarize the content of each part of the *Handbook* according to the revised Table of Contents of the present issue of the *Handbook of Statistics*.

The tables included in this book represent analytical summaries of the full time series contained in the UNCTAD *Handbook of Statistics 2006-07* on CD-ROM and on the statistics portal of the UNCTAD website at www.unctad.org. In certain instances, the two electronic versions might contain different figures from the printed volume, as they are published somewhat later and may reflect more recent data.

PART ONE
International merchandise trade

Tables 1.1 show the value of total exports and imports, expressed in millions of dollars and percentages of the world total, of individual countries and geographical regions (1.1.1), economic groupings (1.1.2), and trade groups (1.1.3). The trade flows shown in table 1.1.1 refer to the General Trade System except for the countries which employ the Special Trade System and which are marked with an asterisk. The General Trade System is used when the statistical territory of a compiling country coincides with its economic territory. Consequently, imports include all goods entering the economic territory of a compiling country and exports include all goods leaving the economic territory of the compiling country. The Special Trade System is used when the statistical territory comprises only a particular part of the economic territory within which «goods may be disposed of without customs restriction». In such a case, imports include all goods entering the free circulation area of the compiling country, which means cleared through customs for home use, and exports include all goods leaving the free circulation area of a compiling country.

Average annual growth rates of international trade derived from table 1.1 are presented in tables 1.2.

Tables 1.3 contain trade balances (exports f.o.b. minus imports c.i.f.) and these balances, as a percentage of imports of individual countries, geographical regions and economic groupings.

Table 1.4 shows the relative importance of trade among group members as compared to the regional or total trade of that group.

PART TWO
International merchandise trade by region

Table 2.1 shows the export and import structure of individual countries by main regions of origin and destination. Data are presented for as many individual countries as possible, while trade partners are grouped in 14 major clusters.

Table 2.2 presents the structure of exports by destination and imports by origin by major commodity groups for 11 selected country groups. The table provides detailed information on the world trade network for 19 regions of origin and destination and six commodity groups.

Totals of international merchandise trade presented in the tables found in parts one and two are not strictly comparable due to complementary but different sources and remaining unallocated trade flows, despite efforts to distribute trade flows by destination, origin and commodity group.

Exports by destination may differ considerably in some cases from data on imports as reported by countries of destination for a variety of factors, among which the following may be of particular importance:

- Most import data are reported on a c.i.f. rather than an f.o.b. basis.
- Imports arrive at destination, and are registered with some time lag from the date they were recorded as exports.
- There may be considerable differences between the recorded destination of exports and the actual destination as shown in import statistics. Similarly, the classification used by the exporting country may differ from the one assigned by the importing country.

PART THREE
International merchandise trade by product

Table 3.1 shows the export and import structure of individual economies by commodity groups for selected years for eight commodity groups (all food items, agricultural raw materials, fuels, ores and metals, manufactured goods, chemical products, machinery and transport equipment and other manufactured goods).

Tables 3.2 (A, B and C, respectively) present the structure of exports for the world and for developed and developing economies, by product, at the SITC group (Revision 3, 3-digit) level. Each product share of world exports is calculated for each economic grouping as well as the average annual growth rate and the latter's deviation in relation to the world growth rate.

Table 3.2D establishes for each economy the list of main products exported (SITC group Revision 3, 3-digit level). Each product's share of total exports of individual countries, geographical regions and the world is also indicated.

Table 3.2E lists major exporters of 70 leading products among developing economies at the SITC group (Revision 3, 3-digit) level as well as corresponding shares in world trade.

Table 3.3 provides concentration indices and structural change indices for exports and imports by product group at SITC (Revision 3, 3-digit) level. The first indicator shows how a product market is concentrated in a few countries or homogeneously distributed among several countries. The structural change indicator shows whether the market share for a given product among export countries has changed significantly when compared with a reference year.

Totals of international merchandise trade presented in the tables of this third part may also differ from the data contained in the first and second parts for the above reasons, to which must be added margins of exports and imports not distributed by commodity group or the use of different product nomenclatures by the exporting and importing countries.

PART FOUR
International merchandise trade indicators

Tables 4.1 include calculation results of concentration and diversification indices for individual countries, geographical regions and economic groupings. This concentration index specifically shows how exports and imports of individual countries or country groupings are concentrated on several products or otherwise distributed in a more homogeneous manner among a series of products. The diversification indicator signals whether the structure of exports or imports by product of a given country or country grouping differs from the structure by product shown for the world.

Tables 4.2 contain volume indices and unit value indices of exports and imports, and derived terms of trade and purchasing power of exports calculated at the level of individual countries and geographical regions (4.2.1) and economic groupings (4.2.2).

To improve data coverage, especially for the latest periods, the following procedure was used:

- A set of average prices indices at SITC (Revision 3, 3-digit) group level was constructed using several sources: USA BLS external trade prices indices; Unit value indices of Japan Customs; UNCTAD *Commodity Price Statistics*.
- At the country level, unit value indices were calculated using previous year's trade values at the SITC 3-digit level available in table 3.2 as weights.

In some instances these indices may differ from the estimates published in official sources, since the main aim is to provide tentative estimates for most developing countries on a comparable basis.

Table 4.3 presents average applied import MFN tariff rates for major categories of non-agricultural and non-fuel products by individual markets.

PART FIVE
International trade in services

Tables 5.1.1, 5.1.2, and 5.1.3 present the value of total trade in services by individual country, geographical region, economic grouping and trade group. The tables show values of exports (credits) and imports (debits) of services that were derived from statistics on international service transactions as presented in the IMF's *Balance of Payments Statistics*. Services are defined as the economic output of intangible commodities that may be produced, transferred and consumed at the same time. However, services cover a heterogeneous range of intangible products and activities that are difficult to capture within a single definition and are sometimes hard to separate from goods. Services are outputs produced to order, and they typically include changes in the condition of the consumers realized through the activities of the producers at the demand of customers. Ownership rights over services cannot be established. By the time production of a service is completed, it must have been provided to a consumer.

Services figures shown here comprise 11 principal services categories according to the concepts and definitions of the IMF *Balance of Payments Manual* (BPM5, 1993). These categories cover: transport; travel; communications; construction; insurance; financial services; computer and information services; royalties and license fees; other business services; personal, cultural and recreational services; and government services n.i.e. Given the general difficulties involved in statistically capturing certain aspects of the trade in services, the balance-of-payments figures presented here may be somewhat downward-biased as compared with the actual value of the international trade in services. The aggregate data from tables 5.1 include the UNCTAD secretariat's estimates of missing values that are not shown separately.

Table 5.2 indicates 20 major exporters and importers, among developing economies, for each of the 10 principal services sectors as defined in the IMF *Balance of Payments Manual* (BPM5, 1993), which are transport; travel; communication; construction; computer and information services; insurance; financial services; royalties and licence fees; other business services; and personal, cultural and recreational services. Government services n.i.e. are not included.

Table 5.3 focuses on tourism services in individual countries in recent years. It presents the following statistics: value of total expenditure of visitors, value of visitors' expenditure excluding transportation, number of tourists' overnight stays, and number of arrivals of visitors. All figures refer to non-resident visitors (inbound tourism). The international (non-resident) visitor is an international traveller travelling to a place other than her/his usual environment for a stay of less than 12 months and whose main purpose of a trip is other than exercise an activity remunerated from within the place visited. This includes all persons who arrive in a particular economy to stay for less than a year for business purposes or personal reasons. Tourists are those who stay at least one night in a collective or private accommodation in the country visited. Same-day visitors are persons who do not stay overnight in a country visited.

Table 5.4 concerns international maritime transport. It contains data on the world merchant fleet by flag of registration and by type of ship by region and economy and puts in a special perspective the group of major open-registry countries. A ship owner who registers his or her vessel in an open-registry country does not need to have any connection with a country of registry. The number of open-registry countries has varied over the years, but five appear consistently: Bermuda, Bahamas, Cyprus, Liberia, and Panama. In this table, the group also includes Malta. The table contains consolidated time series from various issues of the UNCTAD *Review of Maritime Transport*, which is one of UNCTAD's flagship publications. It reports on the worldwide evolution of shipping, ports and multimodal transport related to the major traffics of liquid bulk, dry bulk and containers.

PART SIX
Commodities

Table 6.1 includes aggregated price indices for primary commodity groups such as food, tropical beverages, vegetable oilseeds and oils, agricultural raw materials and minerals, ores and metals, as well as an all groups price index in current US dollars. Also included are the annual and quarterly free-market price indices for selected commodities exported by developing economies. In order to reflect recent patterns for commodities exported by developing countries, price indices for the above mentioned commodity groups have been rebased onto 2000=100 and weights used for their construction have been revised. The new weights are based on the value of exports of developing countries from 1999 to 2001. The table is based on data from the UNCTAD *Commodity Price Statistics* database. Additional up-to-date figures on commodity prices are available on the statistics portal of the UNCTAD website.

Table 6.2 presents instability indices and trends in free-market prices for selected primary commodities that are of particular interest to developing economies.

Table 6.3 presents information on the production of aluminium and copper at different processing stages and consumption by individual country and by geographical region. Figures for the production of bauxite are expressed at gross volume, while those for copper ore production are shown in metal content.

PART SEVEN
International finance

Table 7.1 presents summaries of the current account of the balance of payments for individual countries and territories. Balance-of-payments current account data cover all transactions between residents and non-residents of a reporting economy, involving economic values and mainly concerning goods, services, income and current transfers. Data on these principal categories, with an additional detail on direct investment income, are covered in the table. For information about the concepts regarding the categories mentioned, please see the IMF *Balance of Payments Manual* (BPM5, 1993).

Table 7.2 contains summaries of the capital and financial account of the balance of payments for individual economies. Capital and financial account figures cover transactions in foreign assets and liabilities. Assets represent claims on non-residents, while liabilities are indebtedness to non-residents of the reporting economy. No valuation changes or other non-transaction modifications of net foreign assets are reflected in these accounts. Capital account includes capital transfers and acquisition and disposal of non-produced, non-financial assets. Financial account covers investments (direct, portfolio and other) and reserve assets (comprised of monetary gold, SDRs, foreign exchange and others). Statistics on these principal categories of the capital and financial account are included in the *Handbook*. Detailed notes with explanations of categories and terminology used are provided after the table. For more information, see the IMF *Balance of Payments Manual* (BPM5, 1993).

Tables 7.3.1, 7.3.2 and 7.3.3 contain information on foreign direct investment (FDI) inflows and outflows by individual country, geographical region, economic grouping and trade group. These figures correspond to the Statistical Annexes of the UNCTAD *World Investment Report 2006: FDI from Developing and Transition Economies: Implications for Development*. Foreign direct investment (FDI) is defined as an investment involving a long-term relationship and reflecting a lasting interest in and control by a resident entity in one economy (foreign direct investor or parent enterprise) of an enterprise resident in a different economy (FDI enterprise or affiliate enterprise or foreign affiliate). Such investment involves both the initial transaction between the two entities and all subsequent transactions between them and among foreign affiliates. A direct investment enterprise is defined as an incorporated or unincorporated

enterprise in which the direct investor, resident in another economy, owns 10 percent or more of the ordinary shares of voting power (or the equivalent).

Table 7.4 presents values of receipts and payments of workers' remittances for individual economies. It also shows workers' remittances as percentage of international trade (exports and imports, balance-of-payments data). According to the definition of the IMF *Balance of Payments Manual* (BPM5, 1993), workers' remittances are goods and financial instruments transferred by migrants living and working (being residents) in a new economy to residents of the economy in which the migrants formerly resided. A migrant must live and work in the new economy for more than one year to be considered a resident there. The BPM5 classifies workers' remittances separately from compensation of employees. Table 7.4 includes both categories in the values shown, in order to present a clearer picture of the flows that enter or exit economies via transfers by migrant or non-resident workers.

Table 7.5 presents data on international reserves (total reserves minus gold) of developing economies by country, region and economic grouping. Other calculations included show months of imports that these reserves could finance at current import levels, as well as the annual change in total reserves. According to the IMF definition, total reserves minus gold consist of the sum of the country's foreign exchange, their reserve position in the IMF and the US dollar value of SDR holdings by their monetary authorities.

Table 7.6 gives a summary of official financial flows to developing economies by type of flow, country, geographical region and economic grouping. Flows from bilateral and multilateral sources are shown as recorded by the Development Assistance Committee (DAC – OECD).

Table 7.7 presents time series, in millions of dollars, on the external long-term indebtedness of developing economies for major economic groupings. It also provides a detailed breakdown of public and publicly guaranteed debt by source of lending. External debt data in this table are based on the Debtor Reporting System (DRS) maintained by the World Bank.

PART EIGHT
Development indicators

Tables 8.1 provide information on total and per capita nominal GDP (in dollars) by individual country, geographical region and economic grouping. The GDP figures in dollars are derived from GDP data provided in national currencies. The prevailing annual average market exchange rates, as reported by IMF, have been used for the conversion from national currencies to dollars.

Tables 8.2 contain annual average growth rates of total and per capita real GDP by individual country, geographical region and economic grouping. The growth rates are based on GDP in constant 1990 dollars.

Tables 8.3 provide data on GDP by type of expenditure and kind of economic activity, by individual country, geographical region and economic grouping.

Tables 8.4 provide data on population and labour force: total population, urban population as a percentage of total population, total labour force, female labour force as a percentage of total labour force, total agriculture labour force and female labour force as a percentage of total agriculture labour force. The information is available by individual country, geographical region and economic grouping.

Table 8.5 focuses on selected demographic period indicators. All these period indicators (population growth rate, natural increase rate per 1000 inhabitants, net migration rate per 1000 inhabitants, crude birth and death rate per 1000 inhabitants, infant mortality rate per 1000 live births, life expectancy at birth) are estimates for both sexes combined by individual country, geographical region and economic grouping.

OTHER NOTES

Unless otherwise specified, country aggregates are the sums of the relevant country data by group. Calculations of aggregates may in some cases include data estimated by the UNCTAD secretariat that are not necessarily all reported separately.

Data were collected and checked to ensure that they matched the geographical coverage of the countries, as described at the beginning of the Handbook. However, some gaps could not be avoided due to data unavailability and are described in the notes at the end of tables.

Because of rounding, details and percentages in tables do not necessarily add up to totals.

Unless otherwise stated, dollars ($) refer to US dollars and data in dollars are expressed in current US dollars of the year to which they refer.

Average annual growth rates are defined as the coefficient b in the exponential trend function $y = ae^{bt}$ where t stands for time. This method takes all observations in a period into account. Therefore, the resulting growth rates reflect trends that are not unduly influenced by exceptional values.

EXPLANATION OF SYMBOLS
0   Zero means that the amount is nil or negligible.
_   The symbol underscore indicates that the item is not applicable.
.. Two dots indicate that the data are not available or are not separately reported.
-   Use of a hyphen between years (e.g. 1985-1990) signifies the full period involved, including the initial and final years.
(e) Estimate
(p) Provisional data
(r) Revised data
Some exceptions are indicated in footnotes.

The country distributions presented are for statistical convenience only and follow those used by the Statistics Division, Department of Economic and Social Affairs (DESA) of the United Nations. They are grouped by economic criteria or by adhesion to commercial agreements for the purpose of statistical analysis and research.

The term "economies", as used in this publication, describes regions, countries and territories.

Country-level data is included according to reported statistics or according to estimations which could be calculated.

This edition introduces modifications to the presentation of country groups as compared with those of the previous editions of the *Handbook*. These changes, intended to increase the analytical value of the publication, are detailed below.

1. Geographical regions, countries and territories

This section includes countries and territories according to three categories of development. Each category is further divided by geographical regions:

Developed economies:
This category is subdivided into geographical regions: America, Asia, Europe and Oceania. The following modifications supersede the preceding version:
- America: now includes Bermuda, Greenland, Saint Pierre and Miquelon;
- Europe: now includes all the countries of the geographical region. The European Union is now presented under «Trade Groups».

Economies in transition:
In previous editions, the Commonwealth of Independent States (CIS) and South-East Europe constituted a group. This edition groups together these economies under the name «Economies in transition», subdivided between Asia and Europe. The CIS is now presented under "Trade Groups".

Developing economies:
All countries and territories in America, Africa, Asia and Oceania not specified above. These geographical regions are further subdivided into subregions in order to present more detailed statistics. The exact composition of each subregion is shown on the following pages. Exceptions are specified in table footnotes.

2. Economic groupings of developing countries

The *Handbook* provides numerous and varied groups of countries and territories in order to provide easy access to the statistics necessary for socio-economic analysis and development research. Certain regional groupings of special interest are introduced, for example "Developing Economies, not including China" (referring to continental China) or "Northern Africa without Sudan" or "Sub-Saharan Africa" (including Sudan with and without South Africa). Latin America and Asia are also presented at various levels of aggregation.

"Least developed countries" and "Landlocked developing countries" are recognized by the United Nations as categories that require special attention from the international community. Since 1994, the United Nations recognizes the particular problems of the small island developing States (SIDS), even though the criteria to establish an official list of SIDS is not yet determined. The unofficial list is used by UNCTAD for analytical purposes only.

The category of "Heavily indebted poor countries" (those economies benefiting from the HIPC debt reduction initiative of the World Bank and the International Monetary Fund) now includes 40 countries, as compared with 38 presented in the last edition of the *Handbook*.

The group "Major petroleum exporters" consists of countries whose share of petroleum and petroleum products was not less than 50 per cent of their total exports, and whose exports of these products amounted to a minimum average of US$ 1.5 billion for the period 1999-2001. This group is divided into three geographical zones: Africa, America and Asia.

The group "Major exporters of manufactures", divided into two geographical zones, America and Asia, consists of the economies whose share of manufactured products was not less than 50 per cent of their total exports, and whose exports of these products amounted to a minimum average of US$ 20 billion for the period 1999-2001.

Two new groupings are added to this edition: "Emerging economies" (in America and Asia) and "Newly industrialized economies" (composed of first and second tier countries introduced by UNCTAD's *Trade and Development Report*).

All developing economies are categorized into three subgroups according to their per capita GDP in 2000: high-income, middle-income and low-income. The composition of these groups is unchanged. This breakdown is based on GDP and population data available in 2004 and was not revised in order to maintain the composition of the groups for several editions of the *Handbook of Statistics*.

3. Trade groups and interregional groups

Statistics of trade groups with special analytic interest are presented according to their pertinence. These groupings include all relevant economies and are subclassified by the geographical regions used in previous editions, with the exception of following interregional groups: African, Caribbean and Pacific States (ACP); Asia-Pacific Economic Cooperation (APEC); Black Sea Economic Cooperation (BSEC); and Commonwealth of Independent States (CIS).

DEVELOPED ECONOMIES

GEOGRAPHICAL REGIONS

America

Bermuda	Greenland	United States of America
Canada	Saint Pierre and Miquelon	including Puerto Rico

Asia

Israel
Japan

Europe

Andorra	Greece	Portugal
Austria	Holy See	San Marino
Belgium	Hungary	Slovakia
Cyprus	Iceland	Slovenia
Czech Republic	Ireland	Spain
Denmark	Italy	Sweden
Estonia	Latvia	Switzerland including
Faeroe Islands	Lithuania	Liechtenstein
Finland including Åland Islands	Luxembourg	United Kingdom of Great Britain
France including French Guiana,	Malta	and Northern Ireland including Channel
Guadeloupe, Martinique,	Netherlands	Islands and Isle of Man
Monaco and Réunion	Norway including Svalbard	
Germany	and Jan Mayen	
Gibraltar	Poland	

Oceania

Australia
New Zealand

ECONOMIES IN TRANSITION

GEOGRAPHICAL REGIONS

Asia

Armenia	Kazakhstan	Turkmenistan
Azerbaijan	Kyrgyzstan	Uzbekistan
Georgia	Tajikistan	

Europe

Albania	Croatia	Serbia and Montenegro
Belarus	Republic of Moldova	The former Yugoslav Republic
Bosnia and Herzegovina	Romania	of Macedonia
Bulgaria	Russian Federation	Ukraine

1. GEOGRAPHICAL REGIONS

Africa

Eastern Africa

British Indian Ocean Territory	Madagascar	Somalia
Burundi	Malawi	Uganda
Comoros	Mauritius	United Republic of Tanzania
Djibouti	Mayotte	Zambia
Eritrea	Mozambique	Zimbabwe
Ethiopia	Rwanda	
Kenya	Seychelles	

Middle Africa

Angola	Chad	Equatorial Guinea
Cameroon	Congo	Gabon
Central African Republic	Democratic Republic of the Congo	São Tomé and Principe

Northern Africa

Algeria	Morocco	Western Sahara
Egypt	Sudan	
Libyan Arab Jamahiriya	Tunisia	

Southern Africa

Botswana	Namibia	Swaziland
Lesotho	South Africa	

Western Africa

Benin	Guinea	Nigeria
Burkina Faso	Guinea-Bissau	Saint Helena
Cape Verde	Liberia	Senegal
Côte d'Ivoire	Mali	Sierra Leone
Gambia	Mauritania	Togo
Ghana	Niger	

America

Caribbean islands

Greater Caribbean	Small Caribbean islands	
Cuba	Anguilla	Montserrat
Dominican Republic	Antigua and Barbuda	Netherlands Antilles
Haiti	Aruba	Saint Kitts and Nevis
Jamaica	Bahamas	Saint Lucia
	Barbados	Saint Vincent and the Grenadines
	British Virgin Islands	Trinidad and Tobago
	Cayman Islands	Turks and Caicos Islands
	Dominica	United States Virgin Islands
	Grenada	

Central America

Belize	Guatemala	Nicaragua
Costa Rica	Honduras	Panama
El Salvador	Mexico	

South America

Argentina	Ecuador	Suriname
Bolivia	Falkland Islands (Malvinas)	Uruguay
Brazil	Guyana	Venezuela (Bolivarian Republic of)
Chile	Paraguay	
Colombia	Peru	

1. GEOGRAPHICAL REGIONS

Asia

Eastern Asia

China	Macao, Special Administrative
Democratic People's Republic	Region of China
of Korea	Mongolia
Hong Kong, Special Administrative	Republic of Korea
Region of China	Taiwan Province of China

Southern Asia

Afghanistan	India	Nepal
Bangladesh	Iran, Islamic Republic of	Pakistan
Bhutan	Maldives	Sri Lanka

South-Eastern Asia

Brunei Darussalam	Malaysia	Thailand
Cambodia	Myanmar	Timor-Leste
Indonesia	Philippines	Viet Nam
Lao People's Democratic Republic	Singapore	

Western Asia

Bahrain	Occupied Palestinian territory	Turkey
Iraq	Oman	United Arab Emirates
Jordan	Qatar	Yemen
Kuwait	Saudi Arabia	
Lebanon	Syrian Arab Republic	

Oceania

American Samoa	Micronesia, Federated States of	Samoa
Christmas Islands	Midway Islands	Solomon Islands
Cocos (Keeling) Islands	Nauru	Tokelau
Cook Islands	New Caledonia	Tonga
Fiji	Niue	Tuvalu
French Polynesia	Norfolk Island	Vanuatu
Guam	Northern Mariana Islands	Wake Island
Johnston Island	Palau	Wallis and Futuna Islands
Kiribati	Papua New Guinea	
Marshall Islands	Pitcairn	

2. ECONOMIC GROUPINGS

Least developed countries - LDCs (50)

	Year of inclusion in the group			Year of inclusion in the group			Year of inclusion in the group
Africa and Haiti							
Angola	1994	Gambia	1975	Niger			1971
Benin	1971	Guinea	1971	Rwanda			1971
Burkina Faso	1971	Guinea-Bissau	1981	Senegal			2001
Burundi	1971	Haiti	1971	Sierra Leone			1982
Central African Republic	1975	Lesotho	1971	Somalia			1971
Chad	1971	Liberia	1990	Sudan			1971
Democratic Republic of the Congo	1991	Madagascar	1991	Togo			1982
Djibouti	1982	Malawi	1971	Uganda			1971
Equatorial Guinea	1982	Mali	1971	United Republic of Tanzania			1971
Eritrea	1994	Mauritania	1986	Zambia			1991
Ethiopia	1971	Mozambique	1988				
Asia		**Islands**					
Afghanistan	1971	Cape Verde	1977	Tuvalu			1986
Bangladesh	1975	Comoros	1977	Vanuatu			1985
Bhutan	1971	Kiribati	1986				
Cambodia	1991	Maldives	1971				
Lao People's Democratic Republic	1971	Samoa	1971				
Myanmar	1987	São Tomé and Principe	1982				
Nepal	1971	Solomon Islands	1991				
Yemen	1971	Timor-Leste	2003				

Landlocked developing countries - LLDCs (31)

Afghanistan	Kazakhstan*	Rwanda
Armenia*	Kyrgyzstan*	Swaziland
Azerbaijan*	Lao People's Democratic Republic	Tajikistan*
Bhutan	Lesotho	The former Yugoslav Republic
Bolivia	Malawi	of Macedonia *
Botswana	Mali	Turkmenistan*
Burkina Faso	Mongolia	Uganda
Burundi	Nepal	Uzbekistan*
Central African Republic	Niger	Zambia
Chad	Paraguay	Zimbabwe
Ethiopia	Republic of Moldova*	

* These countries are classified as economies in transition (neither developed nor developing).
  However, as they are landlocked States, they are also members of this group.

Small island developing States - SIDS (29)

Antigua and Barbuda	Maldives	Samoa
Bahamas	Marshall Islands	São Tomé and Principe
Barbados	Mauritius	Seychelles
Cape Verde	Micronesia, Federated States of	Solomon Islands
Comoros	Nauru	Timor-Leste
Dominica	Palau	Tonga
Fiji	Papua New Guinea	Trinidad and Tobago
Grenada	Saint Kitts and Nevis	Tuvalu
Jamaica	Saint Lucia	Vanuatu
Kiribati	Saint Vincent and the Grenadines	

Heavily indebted poor countries - HIPCs (40)

Benin	Ghana	Nicaragua
Bolivia	Guinea	Niger
Burkina Faso	Guinea-Bissau	Rwanda
Burundi	Guyana	São Tomé and Principe
Cameroon	Haiti	Senegal
Central African Republic	Honduras	Sierra Leone
Chad	Kyrgyzstan	Somalia
Comoros	Liberia	Sudan
Congo	Madagascar	Togo
Côte d'Ivoire	Malawi	Uganda
Democratic Republic of the Congo	Mali	United Republic of Tanzania
Eritrea	Mauritania	Zambia
Ethiopia	Mozambique	
Gambia	Nepal	

2. ECONOMIC GROUPINGS

Major petroleum exporters (21)

Africa

Algeria	Congo	Libyan Arab Jamahiriya
Angola	Gabon	Nigeria

America

Netherlands Antilles	Venezuela (Bolivarian Republic of)
Trinidad and Tobago	

Asia

Bahrain	Iraq	Saudi Arabia
Brunei Darussalam	Kuwait	Syrian Arab Republic
Indonesia	Oman	United Arab Emirates
Iran, Islamic Republic of	Qatar	Yemen

Major exporters of manufactured goods (12)

America

Brazil
Mexico

Asia

China	Malaysia	Taiwan Province of China
Hong Kong, Special Administrative	Philippines	Thailand
Region of China	Republic of Korea	Turkey
India	Singapore	

Emerging economies (10)

America	**Asia**
Argentina	Malaysia
Brazil	Republic of Korea
Chile	Singapore
Mexico	Taiwan Province of China
Peru	Thailand

Newly industrialized economies (8)

First tier	**Second tier**
Hong Kong, Special Administrative	Indonesia
Region of China	Malaysia
Republic of Korea	Philippines
Singapore	Thailand
Taiwan Province of China	

2. ECONOMIC GROUPINGS

INCOME GROUPS

2000 per capita current GDP above US$ 4,500: High-income (42)

American Samoa	Hong Kong, Special Administrative	Saint Kitts and Nevis
Anguilla	Region of China	Saint Lucia
Antigua and Barbuda	Kuwait	Saudi Arabia
Argentina	Lebanon	Seychelles
Aruba	Libyan Arab Jamahiriya	Singapore
Bahamas	Macao, Special Administrative	Taiwan Province of China
Bahrain	Region of China	Trinidad and Tobago
Barbados	Mexico	Turks and Caicos Islands
British Virgin Islands	Montserrat	United Arab Emirates
Brunei Darussalam	Netherlands Antilles	United States Virgin Islands
Cayman Islands	New Caledonia	Uruguay
Chile	Northern Mariana Islands	Venezuela (Bolivarian Republic of)
Falkland Islands (Malvinas)	Oman	
French Polynesia	Palau	
Grenada	Qatar	
Guam	Republic of Korea	

2000 per capita current GDP between US$ 1,000 and US$ 4,500: Middle-income (50)

Algeria	Guatemala	Saint Vincent and the
Belize	Iran, Islamic Republic of	Grenadines
Bolivia	Jamaica	Samoa
Botswana	Jordan	South Africa
Brazil	Malaysia	Suriname
Cape Verde	Maldives	Swaziland
Colombia	Marshall Islands	Syrian Arab Republic
Cook Islands	Mauritius	Thailand
Costa Rica	Micronesia, Federated States of	Tokelau
Cuba	Morocco	Tonga
Dominica	Namibia	Tunisia
Dominican Republic	Nauru	Turkey
Ecuador	Niue	Tuvalu
Egypt	Occupied Palestinian territory	Vanuatu
El Salvador	Panama	Wallis and Futuna Islands
Equatorial Guinea	Paraguay	
Fiji	Peru	
Gabon	Saint Helena	

2000 per capita current GDP below US$ 1,000: Low-income (65)

Afghanistan	Ghana	Nicaragua
Angola	Guinea	Niger
Bangladesh	Guinea-Bissau	Nigeria
Benin	Guyana	Pakistan
Bhutan	Haiti	Papua New Guinea
Burkina Faso	Honduras	Philippines
Burundi	India	Rwanda
Cambodia	Indonesia	São Tomé and Principe
Cameroon	Iraq	Senegal
Central African Republic	Kenya	Sierra Leone
Chad	Kiribati	Solomon Islands
China	Lao People's Democratic Republic	Somalia
Comoros	Lesotho	Sri Lanka
Congo	Liberia	Sudan
Côte d'Ivoire	Madagascar	Timor-Leste
Democratic People's Republic	Malawi	Togo
of Korea	Mali	Uganda
Democratic Republic of the Congo	Mauritania	United Republic of Tanzania
Djibouti	Mongolia	Viet Nam
Eritrea	Mozambique	Yemen
Ethiopia	Myanmar	Zambia
Gambia	Nepal	Zimbabwe

Africa

Arab Maghreb Union - UMA (5)	*Year of accession*
Algeria	1989
Libyan Arab Jamahiriya	1989
Mauritania	1989
Morocco	1989
Tunisia	1989

Common Market for Eastern and Southern Africa - COMESA (19)

Angola	1994
Burundi	1994
Comoros	1994
Democratic Republic of the Congo	1994
Djibouti	1994
Egypt	1994
Eritrea	1994
Ethiopia	1994
Kenya	1994
Madagascar	1994
Malawi	1994
Mauritius	1994
Rwanda	1994
Seychelles	1994
Sudan	1994
Swaziland	1994
Uganda	1994
Zambia	1994
Zimbabwe	1994

Economic Community of Central African States - ECCAS (11)

	Year of accession
Angola	1999
Burundi	1983
Cameroon	1983
Central African Republic	1983
Chad	1983
Congo	1983
Democratic Republic of the Congo	1983
Equatorial Guinea	1983
Gabon	1983
Rwanda	1983
São Tomé and Principe	1983

Economic Community of the Great Lakes Countries - CEPGL (3)

Burundi	1976
Democratic Republic of the Congo	1976
Rwanda	1976

Economic Community of West African States - ECOWAS (15)

Benin	1975
Burkina Faso	1975
Cape Verde	1977
Côte d'Ivoire	1975
Gambia	1975
Ghana	1975
Guinea	1975
Guinea-Bissau	1975
Liberia	1975
Mali	1975
Niger	1975
Nigeria	1975
Senegal	1975
Sierra Leone	1975
Togo	1975

Economic and Monetary Community of Central Africa - CEMAC (6)

	Year of accession
Cameroon	1994
Central African Republic	1994
Chad	1994
Congo	1994
Equatorial Guinea	1994
Gabon	1994

Mano River Union - MRU (3)

Guinea	1973
Liberia	1973
Sierra Leone	1973

Southern African Development Community - SADC (14)

Angola	1992
Botswana	1992
Democratic Republic of the Congo	1992
Lesotho	1992
Madagascar	2005
Malawi	1992
Mauritius	1992
Mozambique	1992
Namibia	1992
South Africa	1994
Swaziland	1992
United Republic of Tanzania	1992
Zambia	1992
Zimbabwe	1992

West African Economic and Monetary Union - UEMOA (8)

Benin	1994
Burkina Faso	1994
Côte d'Ivoire	1994
Guinea-Bissau	1994
Mali	1994
Niger	1994
Senegal	1994
Togo	1994

America

Andean Community - ANCOM (5)	*Year of accession*
Bolivia	1996
Colombia	1996
Ecuador	1996
Peru	1996
Venezuela (Bolivarian Republic of)	1996

Caribbean Community CARICOM (15)

	Year of accession
Antigua and Barbuda	1974
Bahamas	1983
Barbados	1973
Belize	1974
Dominica	1974
Grenada	1974
Guyana	1973
Haiti	1997
Jamaica	1973
Montserrat	1974
Saint Kitts and Nevis	1974
Saint Lucia	1974
Saint Vincent and the Grenadines	1974
Suriname	1995
Trinidad and Tobago	1973

Central American Common Market - CACM (5)

	Year of accession
Costa Rica	1962
El Salvador	1961
Guatemala	1961
Honduras	1961
Nicaragua	1961

America

Free Trade Area of the Americas - FTAA (34)

	Year of accession
Antigua and Barbuda	1994
Argentina	1994
Bahamas	1994
Barbados	1994
Belize	1994
Bolivia	1994
Brazil	1994
Canada	1994
Chile	1994
Colombia	1994
Costa Rica	1994
Dominica	1994
Dominican Republic	1994
Ecuador	1994
El Salvador	1994
Grenada	1994
Guatemala	1994
Guyana	1994
Haiti	1994
Honduras	1994
Jamaica	1994
Mexico	1994
Nicaragua	1994
Panama	1994
Paraguay	1994
Peru	1994
Saint Kitts and Nevis	1994
Saint Lucia	1994
Saint Vincent and the Grenadines	1994
Suriname	1994
Trinidad and Tobago	1994
United States of America	1994
Uruguay	1994
Venezuela (Bolivarian Republic of)	1994

Latin American Integration Association - LAIA (12)

	Year of accession
Argentina	1980
Bolivia	1980
Brazil	1980
Chile	1980
Colombia	1980
Cuba	1999
Ecuador	1980
Mexico	1980
Paraguay	1980
Peru	1980
Uruguay	1980
Venezuela (Bolivarian Republic of)	1980

Mercado Común del Sur MERCOSUR (4)

	Year of accession
Argentina	1994
Brazil	1994
Paraguay	1994
Uruguay	1994

North American Free Trade Agreement - NAFTA (3)

	Year of accession
Canada	1992
Mexico	1992
United States of America	1992

Organization of Eastern Caribbean States - OECS (9)

	Year of accession
Anguilla	1995
Antigua and Barbuda	1981
British Virgin Islands	1984
Dominica	1981
Grenada	1981
Montserrat	1981
Saint Kitts and Nevis	1981
Saint Lucia	1981
Saint Vincent and the Grenadines	1981

Asia

Asia-Pacific Trade Agreement - APTA (6) *

	Year of accession
Bangladesh	1975
China	2001
India	1975
Lao People's Democratic Republic	1975
Republic of Korea	1975
Sri Lanka	1975

* Former Bangkok Agreement

Association of South-East Asian Nations - ASEAN (10)

	Year of accession
Brunei Darussalam	1984
Cambodia	1999
Indonesia	1967
Lao People's Democratic Republic	1997
Malaysia	1967
Myanmar	1997
Philippines	1967
Singapore	1967
Thailand	1967
Viet Nam	1995

Economic Cooperation Organization - ECO (10)

	Year of accession
Afghanistan	1992
Azerbaijan	1992
Iran, Islamic Republic of	1985
Kazakhstan	1992
Kyrgyzstan	1992
Pakistan	1985
Tajikistan	1992
Turkey	1985
Turkmenistan	1992
Uzbekistan	1992

Gulf Cooperation Council - GCC (6)

	Year of accession
Bahrain	1981
Kuwait	1981
Oman	1981
Qatar	1981
Saudi Arabia	1981
United Arab Emirates	1981

South Asian Association for Regional Cooperation - SAARC (7)

	Year of accession
Bangladesh	1985
Bhutan	1985
India	1985
Maldives	1985
Nepal	1985
Pakistan	1985
Sri Lanka	1985

Europe

European Free Trade Association - EFTA (3)

	Year of accession
Iceland	1960
Norway	1960
Switzerland	1960

European Union - EU (25)

	Year of accession
Austria	1995
Belgium	1957
Cyprus	2004
Czech Republic	2004
Denmark	1973
Estonia	2004
Finland	1995
France	1957
Germany	1957
Greece	1981
Hungary	2004
Ireland	1973
Italy	1957
Latvia	2004
Lithuania	2004
Luxembourg	1957
Malta	2004
Netherlands	1957
Poland	2004
Portugal	1986
Slovakia	2004
Slovenia	2004
Spain	1986
Sweden	1995
United Kingdom	1973

Euro Zone (12)

	Year of accession
Austria	2002
Belgium	2002
Finland	2002
France	2002
Germany	2002
Greece	2002
Ireland	2002
Italy	2002
Luxembourg	2002
Netherlands	2002
Portugal	2002
Spain	2002

TRADE GROUPS

Oceania

	Year of accession
Melanesia Spearhead Group - MSG (4)	
Fiji	1996
Papua New Guinea	1988
Solomon Islands	1988
Vanuatu	1988

Interregional groups

African, Caribbean and Pacific Group of States - ACP (79)

Angola	Gambia	Rwanda
Antigua and Barbuda	Ghana	Saint Kitts and Nevis
Bahamas	Grenada	Saint Lucia
Barbados	Guinea	Saint Vincent and the Grenadines
Belize	Guinea-Bissau	Samoa
Benin	Guyana	São Tomé and Principe
Botswana	Haiti	Senegal
Burkina Faso	Jamaica	Seychelles
Burundi	Kenya	Sierra Leone
Cameroon	Kiribati	Solomon Islands
Cape Verde	Lesotho	Somalia
Central African Republic	Liberia	South Africa
Chad	Madagascar	Sudan
Comoros	Malawi	Suriname
Congo	Mali	Swaziland
Cook Islands	Marshall Islands	Timor-Leste
Côte d'Ivoire	Mauritania	Togo
Cuba	Mauritius	Tonga
Democratic Republic of the Congo	Micronesia, Federated states of	Trinidad and Tobago
Djibouti	Mozambique	Tuvalu
Dominica	Namibia	Uganda
Dominican Republic	Nauru	United Republic of Tanzania
Equatorial Guinea	Niger	Vanuatu
Eritrea	Nigeria	Zambia
Ethiopia	Niue	Zimbabwe
Fiji	Palau	
Gabon	Papua New Guinea	

	Year of accession		Year of accession		Year of accession
Asia-Pacific Economic Cooperation - APEC (21)		Singapore	1989	**Commonwealth of Independent States - CIS (12)**	
		Taiwan Province of China	1991		
Australia	1989	Thailand	1989	Armenia	1991
Brunei Darussalam	1989	United States of America	1989	Azerbaijan	1991
Canada	1989	Viet Nam	1998	Belarus	1991
Chile	1994			Georgia	1993
China	1991	**Black Sea Economic Cooperation - BSEC (11)**		Kazakhstan	1991
Hong Kong, Special Administrative				Kyrgyzstan	1991
Region of China	1991	Albania	1992	Republic of Moldova	1991
Indonesia	1989	Armenia	1992	Russian Federation	1991
Japan	1989	Azerbaijan	1992	Tajikistan	1991
Malaysia	1989	Bulgaria	1992	Turkmenistan	1991
Mexico	1993	Georgia	1992	Ukraine	1991
New Zealand	1989	Greece	1992	Uzbekistan	1991
Papua New Guinea	1993	Republic of Moldova	1992		
Peru	1998	Romania	1992		
Philippines	1989	Russian Federation	1992		
Republic of Korea	1989	Turkey	1992		
Russian Federation	1998	Ukraine	1992		

ACP	African, Caribbean and Pacific Group of States
ANCOM	Andean Community
APEC	Asia-Pacific Economic Cooperation
APTA	Asia-Pacific Trade Agreement (Former Bangkok Agreement)
ASEAN	Association of South-East Asian Nations
BPM	*Balance of Payments Manual* (IMF)
BSEC	Black Sea Economic Cooperation
CACM	Central American Common Market
CARICOM	Caribbean Community
CEMAC	Economic and Monetary Community of Central Africa (formerly UDEAC)
CEPGL	Economic Community of the Great Lakes Countries
c.i.f.	cost, insurance and freight
CIS	Commonwealth of Independent States
COMESA	Common Market for Eastern and Southern Africa (formerly PTA)
DAC	Development Assistance Committee (of OECD)
DRS	Debtor Reporting System
ECCAS	Economic Community of Central African States
ECE	Economic Commission for Europe
ECO	Economic Cooperation Organization
ECOWAS	Economic Community of West African States
EFTA	European Free Trade Association
ESCAP	Economic and Social Commission for Asia and the Pacific
ESCWA	Economic and Social Commission for Western Asia
EU	European Union
excl.	excluding
FAO	Food and Agriculture Organization of the United Nations
FDI	foreign direct investment
f.o.b.	free on board
FTAA	Free Trade Area of the Americas
GATS	General Agreement on Trade in Services
GCC	Gulf Cooperation Council
GDP	gross domestic product
GFCF	gross fixed capital formation
GNP	gross national product
HIPC	heavily indebted poor countries
IEA	International Energy Agency
ILO	International Labour Organization
IMF	International Monetary Fund
KTOE	kilotons of oil equivalent
LAIA	Latin American Integration Association
LDC	least developed country
MERCOSUR	Mercado Común del Sur
MFN	most favoured nation
MRU	Mano River Union
MSG	Melanesia Spearhead Group
NAFTA	North American Free Trade Agreement
n.e.s.	not elsewhere specified
NIE	newly industrialized economies
n.i.e.	not included elsewhere
NPISHs	non-profit institutions serving households
OA	official aid
ODA	official development assistance
OE	oil equivalent
OECD	Organization for Economic Co-operation and Development
OECS	Organization of Eastern Caribbean States
OOF	other official flows
OPEC	Organization of the Petroleum Exporting Countries
SAARC	South Asian Association for Regional Cooperation
SADC	Southern African Development Community
SAR	Special Administrative Region
SDR	special drawing right
SITC	Standard International Trade Classification
TFYR	The former Yugoslav Republic of Macedonia
TNC	transnational corporation
TPES	total primary energy supply
UEMOA	West African Economic and Monetary Union
UMA	Arab Maghreb Union
UNAIDS	Joint United Nations Programme on HIV/AIDS
UNCTAD	United Nations Conference on Trade and Development
UN/DESA/SD	United Nations Department of Economic and Social Affairs, Statistics Division
UNESCO	United Nations Educational, Scientific and Cultural Organization
UNICEF	United Nations Children's Fund
UNWTO	World Tourism Organization
WHO	World Health Organization
WTO	World Trade Organization

Ces notes générales présentent le contenu de chaque tableau du *Manuel de statistiques* ainsi que les modifications introduites dans cette nouvelle édition.

Les tableaux inclus dans cette publication constituent un résumé analytique des séries chronologiques complètes publiées dans le *Manuel de statistiques 2006-07 de la CNUCED* sur CD-ROM et dans la version en ligne sur le portail des statistiques du site internet de la CNUCED à l'adresse suivante : www.unctad.org. Toutefois les données disponibles dans les versions électronique et imprimée pourront, dans certains cas, être différentes en raison de leur mise à jour et de leur publication à des dates différentes.

PREMIÈRE PARTIE
Commerce international des marchandises

Les tableaux 1.1 donnent la valeur des exportations et des importations totales de marchandises, exprimée en millions de dollars et en pourcentage du monde, des pays et régions géographiques (1.1.1), groupements économiques (1.1.2) et groupements commerciaux (1.1.3). Les flux du commerce présentés dans le tableau 1.1.1 se réfèrent au Système du Commerce Général, à l'exception des pays et territoires qui utilisent le Système du Commerce Spécial et qui sont munis d'un astérisque. Le Système du Commerce Général est utilisé lorsque le territoire statistique d'un pays coïncide avec son territoire économique, et en conséquence, les importations comprennent tous les biens admis sur le territoire du pays déclarant et les exportations tous les biens qui le quittent. Le Système du Commerce Spécial est utilisé lorsque le territoire statistique ne comprend qu'une partie du territoire économique à l'intérieur de laquelle « les biens peuvent être écoulés librement sans restriction douanière ». Dans ce cas, les importations comprennent tous les biens qui entrent dans la zone de libre circulation du pays déclarant, c'est-à-dire qui ont été dédouanés pour mise à la consommation et les exportations comprennent tous les biens qui quittent la zone de libre circulation du pays déclarant.

Les taux d'évolution annuels moyens du commerce international des marchandises, calculés à partir des valeurs des tableaux 1.1, figurent dans les tableaux 1. 2.

Les tableaux 1.3 présentent les balances commerciales (exportations f.a.b. moins importations c.a.f.), ainsi que ces mêmes balances en pourcentage des importations des pays, régions géographiques et groupements économiques.

Le tableau 1.4 indique l'importance des échanges entre pays membres de groupements commerciaux par rapport aux exportations régionales et totales de ces groupements.

DEUXIÈME PARTIE
Commerce international des marchandises par régions

Le tableau 2.1 présente la structure des exportations et des importations des pays par régions de destination et d'origine. Le plus grand nombre possible de pays en développement sont inclus tandis que les partenaires commerciaux sont regroupés en 14 groupes considérés comme particulièrement importants pour l'analyse du commerce international.

Le tableau 2.2 indique la structure des exportations par destination ainsi que des importations par origine et par groupes de produits pour le monde et une sélection de 11 groupements de pays. Le tableau fournit une information détaillée sur le réseau du commerce international avec le monde, 19 régions d'origine et de destination, et pour six différents groupes de produits.

Les totaux du commerce international des marchandises présentés dans les tableaux des première et deuxième parties ne sont pas strictement comparables en raison de sources complémentaires mais différentes et d'une marge d'exportations et d'importations non distribuées, en dépit des efforts déployés pour répartir les flux commerciaux par destinations et origines.

Les exportations ventilées par destinations peuvent accuser un écart parfois considérable par rapport aux importations déclarées par les pays destinataires en raison de divers facteurs dont les plus importants sont les suivants :

- Les importations sont déclarées en principe «valeur c.a.f.» plutôt que «valeur f.a.b».
- Les importations de marchandises peuvent arriver à destination et être enregistrées longtemps après la date de leur enregistrement à l'exportation.
- D'importantes différences peuvent exister entre la destination des exportations déclarée par les pays exportateurs et la destination réelle telle qu'indiquée dans les statistiques d'importation.

TROISIÈME PARTIE
Commerce international des marchandises par produits

Le tableau 3.1 fournit la structure des exportations et des importations des pays par produits classés en 8 groupes (produits alimentaires, matières premières d'origine agricole, combustibles, minerais et métaux, produits manufacturés, dont produits chimiques, machines et matériel de transport, articles manufacturés divers) pour plusieurs années.

Les tableaux 3.2A, B et C présentent respectivement les exportations du monde, des économies développées et en développement, par produits à un niveau très détaillé (CTCI révision 3, position à trois chiffres). Les parts que représente chaque produit dans les exportations du monde et de la région, sont calculées pour chaque groupe d'économies, ainsi que le taux annuel moyen de croissance et l'écart de ce dernier par rapport au taux de croissance mondial.

Le tableau 3.2D établit, pour chaque économie, la liste des principaux produits qu'elle exporte (CTCI révision 3, position à trois chiffres). La part de chaque produit dans le total des exportations du pays, de la région et du monde est également indiquée.

Le tableau 3.2E liste les plus gros exportateurs de 70 produits parmi les produits les plus exportés par les économies en développement (CTCI révision 3, position à trois chiffres), ainsi que les parts correspondantes dans le commerce mondial.

Le tableau 3.3 fournit les indices de concentration et de changements structurels des exportations et des importations des produits au niveau de la CTCI (révision 3, position à trois chiffres). Le premier indicateur a vocation à montrer comment le marché d'un produit est concentré sur quelques pays ou réparti de façon plus homogène entre les pays. L'indicateur de changement structurel indique si la répartition du commerce d'un produit entre les pays exportateurs ou importateurs a connu une évolution importante par rapport à une année de référence.

Les totaux du commerce international des marchandises présentés dans les tableaux de cette troisième partie peuvent aussi être différents des données des première et deuxième parties pour les raisons précédemment citées, auxquelles il convient d'ajouter des marges d'exportations et d'importations non distribuées par groupes de produits ou l'utilisation de nomenclatures différentes de produits par le pays exportateur et le pays importateur.

QUATRIÈME PARTIE
Indicateurs du commerce international des marchandises

Les tableaux 4.1 contiennent les résultats du calcul des indices de concentration et de diversification des pays, régions géographiques et groupements économiques. Cet indice de concentration a vocation à montrer comment les exportations et importations d'un pays ou groupe de pays sont concentrées sur quelques produits ou réparties de façon plus homogène sur une gamme de produits. L'indicateur de diversification indique si la structure par produits des exportations ou importations d'un pays ou groupe de pays diverge de la structure par produits observée au niveau du monde.

Les tableaux 4.2 fournissent les indices de volume des exportations et des importations complétant ainsi l'information en valeur disponible dans les tableaux 1.1 et 1.2, les indices de la valeur unitaire des exportations et importations et les indices de termes de l'échange et le pouvoir d'achat des exportations dérivés des indices de valeur unitaire, calculés au niveau des pays et régions géographiques (4.2.1) et des groupements économiques (4.2.2).

Afin d'améliorer la couverture des données et spécialement pour les années récentes, la méthode suivante a été utilisée pour le calcul des valeurs unitaires :
- Un ensemble d'indices de prix moyens au niveau des groupes de la CTCI (révision 3, position à 3 chiffres) a été construit en utilisant les sources suivantes : USA BLS external trade prices indices ; Unit value indices of Japan Customs et les *Statistiques de prix des produits de base* de la CNUCED.
- Au niveau des pays individuels, les indices de la valeur unitaire ont été calculés en utilisant comme pondération les valeurs des exportations et des importations de l'année précédente disponibles dans la table 3.2.

Dans certains cas ces indices peuvent différer des estimations publiées dans les sources officielles, le but principal étant de fournir des estimations approximatives et comparables pour la plupart des pays en développement.

Le tableau 4.3 contient les données sur les droits de douane NPF moyens appliqués à l'importation des principales catégories de produits non-agricoles et non-pétroliers, par marchés individuels.

CINQUIÈME PARTIE
Commerce international des services

Les tableaux 5.1.1, 5.1.2 et 5.1.3 présentent la valeur des exportations et des importations totales des services par pays, par régions géographiques, groupements économiques et groupements commerciaux. Les tableaux incluent les valeurs des exportations (crédits) et des importations (débits) des services qui proviennent des statistiques sur les transactions internationales de services, telles qu'elles sont présentées dans les *Statistiques de la balance des paiements* du FMI. Les services sont définis comme rendements économiques de produits intangibles qui peuvent être produits, transférés et consommés au même moment. Cependant, les services recouvrent un groupe large et hétérogène de produits et d'activités que l'on peut difficilement englober dans une définition. Parfois, la démarcation entre les services et les marchandises n'est pas aisée. Les services sont produits sur commande et ils ont généralement pour résultat un changement des conditions des consommateurs qui ont demandé les services. Pour que la production d'un service soit terminée, il doit être fourni au consommateur. Les chiffres couvrent les 11 catégories principales de services conformément à la définition du *Manuel de la balance des paiements* du FMI (MBP5, 1993). Ces catégories comprennent : transports ; voyages ; communications ; le bâtiment et les travaux publics ; assurances ; services financiers ; l'informatique et l'information ; redevances et droits de licence ; autres services aux entreprises ; services personnels, culturels et relatifs aux loisirs ; et les services fournis ou reçus par les administrations publiques. De manière générale, les difficultés à mesurer statistiquement la valeur du commerce des services persistent et les données de la balance des paiements sur les services peuvent être inférieures à la valeur des transactions réelles. Les agrégats inclus dans le tableau 5.1 comprennent les valeurs manquantes, estimées par le secrétariat de la CNUCED, qui ne sont pas présentées séparément.

Le tableau 5.2 liste, parmi les économies en développement, les 20 plus gros exportateurs et importateurs pour chacun des 10 secteurs principaux du commerce des services, c'est-à-dire les transports ; les voyages ; les communications ; le bâtiment et les travaux publics ; l'informatique et l'information ; les assurances ; les services financiers ; les redevances et droits de licence ; autres services aux entreprises ; et les services personnels, culturels et relatifs aux loisirs. Les services fournis ou reçus par les administrations publiques ne sont pas inclus.

Le tableau 5.3 fait apparaître les données sur les services liés au tourisme en présentant, par pays et pour les années récentes, les statistiques suivantes : valeur des dépenses totales des visiteurs, valeur des dépenses des visiteurs sans le coût du transport, nombre de nuitées des touristes et nombre d'arrivées des visiteurs. Tous les indicateurs se réfèrent aux visiteurs non-résidents (visiteurs internationaux). Le visiteur international est un voyageur voyageant dans une économie - où il n'est pas résident - pour y rester moins de 12 mois et dont le but principal du voyage est d'exercer une activité qui n'est pas rémunérée par une entité résidente dans l'économie visitée. Cela inclut des personnes qui arrivent sur le territoire d'une économie pour y rester moins d'une année pour affaires ou pour des raisons personnelles. Les touristes sont ceux qui séjournent dans le pays visité au moins une nuit dans un logement collectif ou privé. Les visiteurs d'une journée sont des personnes qui ne passent pas la nuit dans le pays visité.

Le tableau 5.4 concerne le transport maritime international. Il contient des données sur la flotte marchande mondiale par pavillons d'immatriculation et par types de navires et fait spécialement ressortir le groupe des principaux pays de libre immatriculation. Un propriétaire qui enregistre son navire dans un pays «libre d'immatriculation» ne doit avoir aucune relation avec ce pays. Le nombre de pays de libre immatriculation a changé au cours des années, mais néanmoins cinq d'entre eux apparaissent constamment : Bahamas, Bermudes, Chypre, Libéria et Panama. Dans ce tableau, Malte fait aussi partie du groupe. Ce tableau incorpore les informations consolidées provenant des différentes éditions de la publication *Review of Maritime Transport*, qui est une des publications phares de la CNUCED. Elle rend compte de l'évolution mondiale du transport multimodal, portuaire et maritime concernant les principaux trafics de vracs liquides, de vracs secs et de conteneurs.

SIXIÈME PARTIE
Produits de base

Le tableau 6.1 donne les indices annuels et trimestriels de prix sur le marché libre d'une sélection de produits de base exportés par les économies en développement. Ces indices sont aussi disponibles au niveau des groupes de produits de base suivants : produits alimentaires, boissons tropicales, huiles et graines oléagineuses, matières premières d'origine agricole, minéraux, minerais et métaux ainsi qu'un indice de l'ensemble. Afin de refléter l'évolution récente des produits de base exportés par les pays en développement, les indices ont été calculés en utilisant 2000=100 comme année de base et les pondérations ont été révisées en conséquence, à partir de la valeur des exportations des pays en développement de 1999 à 2001. Ce tableau a été établi à partir de données extraites de la base de données en ligne des statistiques de prix des produits de base accessible depuis le portail des statistiques du site web de la CNUCED.

Le tableau 6.2 complète l'information sur les prix des produits de base par les indices d'instabilité et les tendances de prix sur le marché libre d'une sélection de produits de base ayant une importance particulière pour les économies en développement.

Le tableau 6.3 présente la production d'aluminium et de cuivre à différents niveaux de transformation et leur consommation par pays et régions géographiques. Les chiffres de la production de bauxite sont exprimés en volume brut, alors que ceux de la production du minerai de cuivre sont indiqués en métal contenu.

SEPTIÈME PARTIE
Flux financiers internationaux

Le tableau 7.1 contient un état récapitulatif du «compte courant» de la balance des paiements des pays et territoires individuels. Les données du compte des transactions courantes de la balance des paiements recouvrent toutes les transactions, entre entités résidentes et non-résidentes, portant sur des valeurs économiques, concernant notamment les biens, les services, les revenus et les transferts courants. Ce tableau comprend les statistiques sur ces catégories principales, y compris le détail additionnel sur les revenus d'investissement direct étranger. Pour l'information sur les concepts concernant les catégories mentionnées, veuillez vous référer au *Manuel de la balance des paiements du FMI* (MBP5, 1993).

Le tableau 7.2 fait apparaître l'état récapitulatif du «compte de capital et d'opérations financières» de la balance des paiements des économies individuels. Les chiffres des comptes de capital

et des comptes financiers couvrent les transactions en avoirs et engagements étrangers. Les avoirs représentent des créances sur les non-résidents et les engagements des dettes envers les non-résidents. Toutes les réévaluations et autres variations d'avoirs et d'engagements qui ne reflètent pas des transactions sont exclues du compte de capital et d'opérations financières. Le compte de capital est subdivisé en transferts de capital et en acquisitions et cession d'avoirs non-financiers non-produits. Le compte financier recouvre les investissements (directs, de portefeuille et autres) et les avoirs de réserve (or monétaire, DTS, devises et autres créances). Ce tableau comprend les statistiques sur ces catégories principales du «compte de capital et d'opérations financières». Pour l'information sur les concepts concernant les catégories mentionnées, veuillez vous référer au Manuel de la balance des paiements du FMI (MBP5, 1993).

Les tableaux 7.3.1, 7.3.2 et 7.3.3 sont consacrés aux investissements directs en provenance de l'étranger (IDE). Ils présentent les flux entrants et sortants de l'IDE par pays et régions géographiques, groupements économiques et groupements commerciaux. Les chiffres correspondent aux données contenues dans l'Annexe statistique du World Investment Report 2006: FDI from Developing and Transition Economies: Implications for Development, de la CNUCED. L'investissement direct étranger (IDE) est un investissement impliquant une relation à long terme et témoignant de l'intérêt durable d'une entité résidant dans un pays (investisseur étranger direct ou société mère) à l'égard d'une entreprise résidant dans un autre pays (entreprise bénéficiaire, entreprise affiliée, ou encore filiale étrangère). Cet investissement englobe à la fois la transaction initiale entre les deux entités et toutes les transactions ultérieures entre elles et entre filiales étrangères, qu'elles soient constituées ou non en sociétés. L'entreprise d'investissement direct est définie comme une entreprise dotée ou non de la personnalité morale, dans laquelle un investisseur direct qui est résident d'une autre économie détient au moins 10% des actions ordinaires ou des droits de vote (ou l'équivalent).

Le tableau 7.4 fournit les informations sur les envois de fonds des travailleurs pour les principales économies en développement concernées. Ces données sont également communiquées en pourcentage du commerce international (total des exportations et importations). Selon la définition du Manuel de la balance des paiements du FMI (MBP5, 1993), les envois de fonds des travailleurs sont les transferts de biens ou d'actifs financiers effectués par les migrants qui vivent et travaillent (considérés résidents) dans une économie en faveur des résidents de leur ancien pays de résidence. Un migrant doit vivre et travailler dans une nouvelle économie durant plus d'une année pour y être considéré résident. Le MBP5 classifie séparément les envois de fonds des travailleurs de la rémunération des salariés. Les valeurs du tableau 7.4 incluent les deux catégories mentionnées, afin de mieux présenter les flux entrants dans ou sortants d'une économie à travers les transferts liés aux travailleurs migrants ou non-résidents.

Le tableau 7.5 fait apparaître les données relatives aux réserves internationales (les réserves totales moins l'or) des économies en développement par pays, par régions et par groupements économiques. Les mois d'importation que ces réserves peuvent financer, dans la situation actuelle du commerce international du pays, sont également indiqués, ainsi que la variation annuelle des réserves totales. Selon la définition du FMI, les réserves totales moins l'or représentent la somme des avoirs du pays en devises, leur position des réserves au FMI et la valeur en dollars E.U. des avoirs en DTS de leurs autorités monétaires.

Les flux financiers publics vers les économies en développement sont retracés dans tableaux 7.6 par catégories de flux, pays, régions géographiques et groupements économiques. La définition des flux bilatéraux et multilatéraux est conforme aux publications du Comité d'aide au développement (CAD – OCDE).

Le tableau 7.7 contient des données sur la dette extérieure à long terme des principaux groupes d'économies en développement, en particulier la ventilation détaillée de la dette publique ou garantie par l'état par sources d'emprunt. Les données de la dette extérieure

présentées dans ce tableau se basent sur le Système de notification des pays débiteurs (SNPD), géré par la Banque mondiale.

HUITIÈME PARTIE
Indicateurs du développement

Les tableaux 8.1 fournissent le Produit Intérieur Brut nominal total et par habitant (en dollars) des pays, régions géographiques et groupements économiques. Les données de PIB en dollars ont été obtenues à partir des valeurs de PIB exprimées à l'origine en monnaies nationales. Les taux de change moyens annuels sur le marché libre, obtenus des séries statistiques du FMI, ont été utilisés pour la plupart des pays lors de la conversion en dollars.

Les taux annuels moyens de variation du PIB réel total et du PIB réel par habitant des pays, régions géographiques et groupements économiques sont disponibles dans les tableaux 8.2. Les taux de croissance se basent sur le PIB en dollars constants de l'année 1990.

Le PIB total est décomposé par catégories de dépenses et la valeur ajoutée totale par branches d'activité économique dans les tableaux 8.3, pour les pays, régions géographiques et groupements économiques.

Les tableaux 8.4 fournissent des données sur la population et la main d'œuvre: population totale, population urbaine en pourcentage de la population totale, main-d'œuvre totale, main-d'œuvre féminine en pourcentage de la main d'œuvre totale, main-d'œuvre dans l'agriculture, main-d'œuvre féminine en pourcentage de la main-d'œuvre totale dans l'agriculture.

Les données de base sur la population et la main d'œuvre sont complétées par les indicateurs sur la démographie du tableau 8.5: taux d'accroissement de la population, taux d'évolution naturelle par 1000 habitants, taux net de migration par 1000 habitants, taux de natalité et de mortalité bruts pour 1000 habitants, taux de mortalité infantile pour 1000 naissances vivantes, espérance de vie à la naissance.

AUTRES NOTES

Sauf indication contraire, les agrégats de pays sont obtenus en sommant les données des pays composant le groupe. Les calculs d'agrégats peuvent dans certains cas inclure des données estimées par le secrétariat de la CNUCED qui ne sont pas nécessairement toutes rapportées séparément. Par ailleurs, la somme des chiffres et des pourcentages indiqués dans les tableaux ne correspond pas nécessairement aux totaux en raison des arrondis.

Les données ont été collectées et vérifiées pour qu'elles correspondent à la couverture géographique des pays, telle qu'elle est décrite en début de Manuel. Toutefois certains écarts n'ont pu être évités en fonction de la disponibilité des données. Ils sont alors décrits dans les notes de fin de tableau.

Sauf indication contraire, le terme «dollar» s'entend dollar des États-Unis d'Amérique et les données en dollars sont exprimées en dollars courants de l'année à laquelle elles se réfèrent.

Les taux moyens d'évolution annuelle sont définis par le coefficient b de la fonction exponentielle de tendance $y = ae^{bt}$, où t représente le temps. Cette méthode permet de prendre en compte toutes les observations concernant une période donnée sans que le taux de croissance obtenu ne soit trop affecté par des valeurs exceptionnelles.

SIGNIFICATION DES SYMBOLES
0 Un zéro signifie que le montant est nul ou négligeable.
_ Un tiret signifie que la rubrique est sans objet.
.. Deux points signifient que les données ne sont pas disponibles ou ne sont pas communiquées séparément.
- Le trait d'union entre deux millésimes (par exemple 1985-1990) indique qu'il s'agit de la période tout entière, y compris la première et la dernière année mentionnées.
(e) Estimation
(p) Donnée provisoire
(r) Donnée révisée
Les exceptions sont indiquées dans les notes de bas de page.

Les pays et territoires sont présentés suivant des critères géographiques conformes à ceux de la Division de statistique, Département des affaires économiques et sociales (DAES) de l'ONU. Les pays et territoires sont aussi regroupés suivant des critères économiques ou d'adhésion à des accords commerciaux à des fins d'analyse statistique et de recherche.

Dans cette publication, le terme «économie» couvre les régions, les pays et les territoires.

Les pays sont montrés dans les tableaux s'ils ont communiqué des données ou si des estimations ont pu être calculées.

La présente édition du *Manuel de Statistiques* comporte des modifications par rapport à l'année précédente dans la présentation des groupes de pays. Ces changements, destinés à augmenter la valeur analytique de la publication, sont détaillés ci-dessous.

1. Régions géographiques et pays et territoires

Les pays et territoires sont répartis dans trois catégories subdivisées en régions géographiques :

Économies développées :
Elles sont réparties entre 4 grandes régions : Amérique, Asie, Europe et Océanie. Par rapport à la version précédente, les changements concernent les deux régions suivantes :
- Amérique : ont été ajoutés les Bermudes, Groenland et Saint Pierre et Miquelon.
- Europe : le groupe englobe tous les pays de la région géographique et l'union européenne est désormais présentée avec les groupements commerciaux.

Économies en transition :
Dans l'édition précédente du *Manuel de Statistiques*, la Communauté des États indépendants (CEI) et l'Europe du Sud-Est constituaient un groupe. Dans cette nouvelle édition, ces économies, regroupées sous l'appellation d'économies en transition, sont partagées entre l'Asie et l'Europe. La CEI, quant à elle, est prise en compte dans les groupements commerciaux.

Économies en développement :
Cette catégorie regroupe tous les autres pays et territoires d'Afrique, d'Amérique, d'Asie et d'Océanie. Les grandes régions géographiques couvrant l'ensemble des économies en développement sont divisées en sous-régions pour permettre la présentation de statistiques plus détaillées. La composition de chaque région est décrite dans les pages suivantes. Les exceptions à ce classement que l'on retrouve dans certains tableaux spécifiques sont indiquées dans des notes.

2. Groupements économiques des économies en développement

Dans le *Manuel de statistiques de la CNUCED*, les regroupements des pays et territoires en développement sont nombreux et variés afin de disposer facilement des données statistiques nécessaires à l'analyse socio-économique et aux recherches sur le développement. Certains groupements régionaux spécifiques, présentant un intérêt supplémentaire, ont été introduits tel que le groupe des «Économies en développement, Chine non comprise», qui se réfère seulement à la Chine continentale, l'Afrique septentrionale sans le Soudan «l'Afrique subsaharienne» Soudan compris, avec et sans l'Afrique du Sud. L'Amérique latine et l'Asie sont également présentées à différents niveaux d'agrégation.

Les pays les moins avancés (PMA) et les pays en développement sans littoral sont des groupes de pays qui requièrent une attention particulière de la communauté internationale. Depuis 1994, les Nations Unies ont également pris en compte les problèmes particuliers des petits états insulaires en développement mais n'ont pas établi de liste officielle de ces états. La liste présentée dans le *Manuel de statistiques* est utilisée par la CNUCED à des fins analytiques uniquement.

Le groupe des «pays pauvres très endettés» (PPTE) inclut 40 pays au lieu des 38 présents dans la dernière version et la composition du groupe a légèrement changé. Ces pays bénéficient de l'initiative de désendettement de la Banque mondiale et du Fonds monétaire international.

Le groupement des «Principaux exportateurs de pétrole» comprend les pays dont la part du pétrole et des produits pétroliers ne représentait pas moins de 50% de leurs exportations totales, et les exportations de ces produits s'élevaient à au moins 1,5 milliards de dollars en 1999 - 2001 en moyenne. Les pays composant ce groupement sont répartis en trois zones géographiques : Afrique, Amérique et Asie.

Le groupement des «Principaux exportateurs d'articles manufacturés», répartis sur deux zones géographiques, Amérique et Asie, comprend les économies dont la part d'articles manufacturés ne représentait pas moins de 50% de leurs exportations totales, et leurs exportations d'articles manufacturés avaient une valeur moyenne d'au moins 20 milliards de dollars en 1999 - 2001.

Dans cette édition ont été ajoutés deux nouveaux groupements: les économies émergentes (en Amérique et Asie) et les économies nouvellement industrialisées (premier et deuxième tier). Leur composition est celle utilisée dans le *Rapport sur le commerce et le développement* de la CNUCED.

Les économies en développement sont aussi divisées en trois groupes de revenu en fonction du PIB par habitant en 2000 : revenu élevé, revenu intermédiaire et revenu faible. Cette répartition est basée sur les données de PIB et de population qui étaient disponibles en 2004 et elle n'a pas été révisée afin de maintenir la composition des groupes durant plusieurs éditions du *Manuel de Statistiques*.

3. Groupements commerciaux et interrégionaux

Les statistiques des groupements commerciaux sont présentées dès lors qu'elles sont pertinentes et présentent un intérêt analytique. Ces groupements englobent toutes les économies concernées et sont classés suivant les grandes régions géographiques utilisées précédemment, à l'exception des groupements interrégionaux suivants : le Groupe des États d'Afrique, des Caraïbes et du Pacifique (ACP), le groupe de Coopération économique de l'Asie et du Pacifique (CEAP), de Coopération économique de la Mer Noire (CEMN) et la Communauté des États indépendants (CEI).

ÉCONOMIES DÉVELOPPÉES

RÉGIONS GÉOGRAPHIQUES

Amérique

Bermudes	États-Unis d'Amérique y compris	Groenland
Canada	Porto Rico	Saint Pierre et Miquelon

Asie

Israël
Japan

Europe

Allemagne	Grèce	Pologne
Andorre	Hongrie	Portugal
Autriche	Îles Féroé	République Tchèque
Belgique	Irlande	Royaume-Uni de Grande-Bretagne
Chypre	Islande	et d'Irlande du Nord y compris les
Danemark	Italie	îles anglo-normandes et l'île de Man
Espagne	Lettonie	Saint-Marin
Estonie	Lituanie	Saint-Siège
Finlande y compris les îles d'Åland	Luxembourg	Slovaquie
France y compris la Guadeloupe,	Malte	Slovénie
la Guyane française, la Martinique,	Norvège y compris les îles Svalbard	Suède
Monaco et la Réunion	et Jan Mayen	Suisse y compris le Liechtenstein
Gibraltar	Pays-Bas	

Océanie

Australie
Nouvelle-Zélande

ÉCONOMIES EN TRANSITION

RÉGIONS GÉOGRAPHIQUES

Asie

Arménie	Kazakhstan	Tadjikistan
Azerbaïdjan	Kirghizstan	Turkménistan
Géorgie	Ouzbékistan	

Europe

Albanie	Croatie	République de Moldova
Bélarus	Ex-République yougoslave	Roumanie
Bosnie-Herzégovine	de Macédoine	Serbie-et-Monténégro
Bulgarie	Fédération de Russie	Ukraine

1. RÉGIONS GÉOGRAPHIQUES

Afrique

Afrique orientale

Burundi	Malawi	Seychelles
Comores	Maurice	Somalie
Djibouti	Mayotte	Territoire britannique de l'océan indien
Érythrée	Mozambique	Zambie
Éthiopie	Ouganda	Zimbabwe
Kenya	République-Unie de Tanzanie	
Madagascar	Rwanda	

Afrique centrale

Angola	Gabon	République démocratique du Congo
Cameroun	Guinée équatoriale	Sao Tomé-et-Principe
Congo	République centrafricaine	Tchad

Afrique septentrionale

Algérie	Maroc	Tunisie
Égypte	Sahara occidental	
Jamahiriya arabe libyenne	Soudan	

Afrique australe

Afrique du Sud	Lesotho	Swaziland
Botswana	Namibie	

Afrique occidentale

Bénin	Guinée	Nigéria
Burkina Faso	Guinée-Bissau	Sainte-Hélène
Cap-Vert	Libéria	Sénégal
Côte d'Ivoire	Mali	Sierra Leone
Gambie	Mauritanie	Togo
Ghana	Niger	

Amérique

Amérique centrale

Belize	Guatemala	Nicaragua
Costa Rica	Honduras	Panama
El Salvador	Mexique	

Amérique du Sud

Argentine	Équateur	Suriname
Bolivie	Guyana	Uruguay
Brésil	Îles Falkland (Malvinas)	Venezuela (République bolivarienne du)
Chili	Paraguay	
Colombie	Pérou	

Caraïbes

Grandes Antilles	**Petites Antilles**	
Cuba	Anguilla	Îles Turques et Caïques
Haïti	Antigua-et-Barbuda	Îles Vierges américaines
Jamaïque	Antilles néerlandaises	Îles Vierges britanniques
République dominicaine	Aruba	Montserrat
	Bahamas	Sainte-Lucie
	Barbade	Saint-Kitts-et-Nevis
	Dominique	Saint-Vincent-et-les Grenadines
	Grenade	Trinité-et-Tobago
	Îles Caïmanes	

ÉCONOMIES EN DÉVELOPPEMENT

1. RÉGIONS GÉOGRAPHIQUES

Asie

Asie orientale

Chine	Mongolie
Hong-Kong, région administrative spéciale de Chine	Province chinoise de Taiwan
	République de Corée
Macao, région administrative spéciale de Chine	République populaire démocratique de Corée

Asie méridionale

Afghanistan	Inde	Népal
Bangladesh	Iran, République islamique d'	Pakistan
Bhoutan	Maldives	Sri Lanka

Asie du Sud-Est

Brunéi Darussalam	Myanmar	Thaïlande
Cambodge	Philippines	Timor-Leste
Indonésie	République démocratique populaire lao	Viet Nam
Malaisie	Singapour	

Asie occidentale

Arabie saoudite	Koweït	Territoire palestinien occupé
Bahreïn	Liban	Turquie
Émirats arabes unis	Oman	Yémen
Iraq	Qatar	
Jordanie	République arabe syrienne	

Océanie

Fidji	Îles Salomon	Pitcairn
Guam	Île Wake	Polynésie française
Îles Christmas	Îles Wallis et Futuna	Samoa
Îles Cocos (Keeling)	Kiribati	Samoa américaines
Îles Cook	Micronésie, États fédérés de	Tokélaou
Île Johnston	Nauru	Tonga
Îles Mariannes septentrionales	Nioué	Tuvalu
Îles Marshall	Nouvelle-Calédonie	Vanuatu
Îles Midway	Palaos	
Île Norfolk	Papouasie-Nouvelle-Guinée	

2. GROUPEMENTS ÉCONOMIQUES

Pays les moins avancés - PMA (50)

	Année d'inclusion dans le groupe		*Année d'inclusion dans le groupe*		*Année d'inclusion dans le groupe*
Afrique et Haïti					
Angola	1994	Haïti	1971	République démocratique	
Bénin	1971	Lesotho	1971	du Congo	1991
Burkina Faso	1971	Libéria	1990	République-Unie de Tanzanie	1971
Burundi	1971	Madagascar	1991	Rwanda	1971
Djibouti	1982	Malawi	1971	Sénégal	2001
Érythrée	1994	Mali	1971	Sierra Leone	1982
Éthiopie	1971	Mauritanie	1986	Somalie	1971
Gambie	1975	Mozambique	1988	Soudan	1971
Guinée	1971	Niger	1971	Tchad	1971
Guinée équatoriale	1982	Ouganda	1971	Togo	1982
Guinée-Bissau	1981	République centrafricaine	1975	Zambie	1991
Asie		**Îles**			
Afghanistan	1971	Cap-Vert	1977	Vanuatu	1985
Bangladesh	1975	Comores	1977		
Bhoutan	1971	Îles Salomon	1991		
Cambodge	1991	Kiribati	1986		
Myanmar	1987	Maldives	1971		
Népal	1971	Samoa	1971		
République démocratique		Sao Tomé-et-Principe	1982		
populaire lao	1971	Timor-Leste	2003		
Yémen	1971	Tuvalu	1986		

Pays en développement sans littoral (31)

Afghanistan	Kazakhstan*	République centrafricaine
Arménie*	Kirghizistan*	République démocratique
Azerbaïdjan*	Lesotho	populaire lao
Bhoutan	Malawi	République de Moldova *
Bolivie	Mali	Rwanda
Botswana	Mongolie	Swaziland
Burkina Faso	Népal	Tadjikistan*
Burundi	Niger	Tchad
Éthiopie	Ouganda	Turkménistan*
Ex-République yougoslave	Ouzbékistan*	Zambie
de Macédoine*	Paraguay	Zimbabwe

* Ces pays font partie du groupement des économies en transition (ni développées, ni en développement).
Cependant, comme ce sont des pays sans littoral, ils appartiennent aussi à ce groupement.

Petits états insulaires en développement (29)

Antigua-et-Barbuda	Jamaïque	Saint-Vincent-et-les Grenadines
Bahamas	Kiribati	Samoa
Barbade	Maldives	Sao Tomé-et-Principe
Cap-Vert	Maurice	Seychelles
Comores	Micronésie, États fédérés de	Timor-Leste
Dominique	Nauru	Tonga
Fidji	Palaos	Trinité-et-Tobago
Grenade	Papouasie-Nouvelle-Guinée	Tuvalu
Îles Marshall	Sainte-Lucie	Vanuatu
Îles Salomon	Saint-Kitts-et-Nevis	

Pays pauvres très endettés - PPTE (40)

Bénin	Guyana	République centrafricaine
Bolivie	Haïti	République démocratique du Congo
Burkina Faso	Honduras	République-Unie de Tanzanie
Burundi	Kirghizstan	Rwanda
Cameroun	Libéria	Sao Tomé-et-Principe
Comores	Madagascar	Sénégal
Congo	Malawi	Sierra Leone
Côte d'Ivoire	Mali	Somalie
Érythrée	Mauritanie	Soudan
Éthiopie	Mozambique	Tchad
Gambie	Népal	Togo
Ghana	Nicaragua	Zambie
Guinée	Niger	
Guinée-Bissau	Ouganda	

2. GROUPEMENTS ÉCONOMIQUES

Principaux pays exportateurs de pétrole (21)

Afrique

Algérie	Congo	Jamahiriya arabe libyenne
Angola	Gabon	Nigéria

Amérique

Antilles néerlandaises	Venezuela (République bolivarienne du)
Trinité-et-Tobago	

Asie

Arabie saoudite	Indonésie	Oman
Bahreïn	Iran, République islamique d'	Qatar
Brunéi Darussalam	Iraq	République arabe syrienne
Émirats arabes unis	Koweït	Yémen

Principaux pays exportateurs d'articles manufacturés (12)

Amérique

Brésil
Mexique

Asie

Chine	Malaisie	
Hong-Kong, région administrative spéciale de Chine	Philippines	Singapour
	Province chinoise de Taiwan	Thaïlande
Inde	République de Corée	Turquie

Économies émergentes (10)

Amérique	**Asie**
Argentine	Malaisie
Brésil	Province chinoise de Taiwan
Chili	République de Corée
Mexique	Singapour
Pérou	Thaïlande

Économies nouvellement industrialisées (8)

Premier tier	**Deuxième tier**
Hong-Kong, région administrative spéciale de Chine	Indonésie
Province chinoise de Taiwan	Malaisie
République de Corée	Philippines
Singapour	Thaïlande

2. GROUPEMENTS ÉCONOMIQUES

GROUPES DE REVENU

PIB courant par habitant supérieur à 4500 dollars en 2000 : Revenu élevé (42)

Anguille
Antigua-et-Barbuda
Antilles néerlandaises
Arabie saoudite
Argentine
Aruba
Bahamas
Bahreïn
Barbade
Brunéi Darussalam
Chili
Émirats arabes unis
Grenade
Guam
Hong-Kong, région administrative
    spéciale de Chine

Îles Caïmanes
Îles Falkland (Malvinas)
Îles Mariannes du Nord
Îles Turques et Caïques
Îles Vierges américaines
Îles Vierges britanniques
Jamahiriya arabe libyenne
Koweït
Liban
Macao, région administrative
    spéciale de Chine
Mexique
Montserrat
Nouvelle-Calédonie
Oman
Palaos

Polynésie française
Province chinoise de Taiwan
Qatar
République de Corée
Sainte-Lucie
Saint-Kitts-et-Nevis
Samoa américaines
Seychelles
Singapour
Trinité-et-Tobago
Uruguay
Venezuela (République bolivarienne du)

PIB courant par habitant compris entre 1000 et 4500 dollars en 2000 : Revenu intermédiaire (50)

Afrique du Sud
Algérie
Belize
Bolivie
Botswana
Brésil
Cap-Vert
Colombie
Costa Rica
Cuba
Dominique
Égypte
El Salvador
Équateur
Fidji
Gabon
Guatemala

Guinée équatoriale
Îles Cook
Îles Marshall
Îles Wallis et Futuna
Iran, République islamique d'
Jamaïque
Jordanie
Malaisie
Maldives
Maroc
Maurice
Micronésie, États fédérés de
Namibie
Nauru
Nioué
Panama
Paraguay

Pérou
République arabe syrienne
République dominicaine
Sainte-Hélène
Saint-Vincent-et-les Grenadines
Samoa
Suriname
Swaziland
Territoire palestinien occupé
Thaïlande
Tokélaou
Tonga
Tunisie
Turquie
Tuvalu
Vanuatu

PIB courant par habitant inférieur à 1000 dollars en 2000 : Revenu faible (65)

Afghanistan
Angola
Bangladesh
Bénin
Bhoutan
Burkina Faso
Burundi
Cambodge
Cameroun
Chine
Comores
Congo
Côte d'Ivoire
Djibouti
Érythrée
Éthiopie
Gambie
Ghana
Guinée
Guinée-Bissau
Guyana
Haïti
Honduras

Îles Salomon
Inde
Indonésie
Iraq
Kenya
Kiribati
Lesotho
Libéria
Madagascar
Malawi
Mali
Mauritanie
Mongolie
Mozambique
Myanmar
Népal
Nicaragua
Niger
Nigéria
Ouganda
Pakistan
Papouasie-Nouvelle-Guinée
Philippines

République démocratique
    populaire lao
République centrafricaine
République démocratique
    du Congo
République populaire
    démocratique de Corée
République-Unie de Tanzanie
Rwanda
Sao Tomé-et-Principe
Sénégal
Sierra Leone
Somalie
Soudan
Sri Lanka
Tchad
Timor-Leste
Togo
Viet Nam
Yémen
Zambie
Zimbabwe

Afrique

Communauté de développement de l'Afrique australe - CDAA (14)

	Année d'adhésion
Afrique du Sud	1994
Angola	1992
Botswana	1992
Lesotho	1992
Madagascar	2005
Malawi	1992
Maurice	1992
Mozambique	1992
Namibie	1992
République démocratique du Congo	1992
République-Unie de Tanzanie	1992
Swaziland	1992
Zambie	1992
Zimbabwe	1992

Communauté économique des États de l'Afrique centrale - CEEAC (11)

Angola	1999
Burundi	1983
Cameroun	1983
Congo	1983
Gabon	1983
Guinée équatoriale	1983
République centrafricaine	1983
République démocratique du Congo	1983
Rwanda	1983
Sao Tomé-et-Principe	1983
Tchad	1983

Communauté économique et monétaire de l'Afrique centrale CEMAC (6)

Cameroun	1994
Congo	1994
Gabon	1994
Guinée équatoriale	1994
République centrafricaine	1994
Tchad	1994

Communauté économique des États de l'Afrique de l'Ouest - CEDEAO (15)

	Année d'adhésion
Bénin	1975
Burkina Faso	1975
Cap-Vert	1977
Côte d'Ivoire	1975
Gambie	1975
Ghana	1975
Guinée	1975
Guinée-Bissau	1975
Libéria	1975
Mali	1975
Niger	1975
Nigéria	1975
Sénégal	1975
Sierra Leone	1975
Togo	1975

Communauté économique des pays des Grands Lacs - CEPGL (3)

Burundi	1976
République démocratique du Congo	1976
Rwanda	1976

Marché commun des États de l'Afrique de l'Est et du Sud - COMESA (19)

Angola	1994
Burundi	1994
Comores	1994
Djibouti	1994
Égypte	1994
Érythrée	1994
Éthiopie	1994
Kenya	1994
Madagascar	1994
Malawi	1994
Maurice	1994
Ouganda	1994
République démocratique du Congo	1994
Rwanda	1994
Seychelles	1994
Soudan	1994
Swaziland	1994
Zambie	1994
Zimbabwe	1994

Union du fleuve Mano - UFM (3)

	Année d'adhésion
Guinée	1973
Libéria	1973
Sierra Leone	1973

Union du Maghreb arabe - UMA (5)

Algérie	1989
Jamahiriya arabe libyenne	1989
Maroc	1989
Mauritanie	1989
Tunisie	1989

Union économique et monétaire ouest-africaine - UEMOA (8)

Bénin	1994
Burkina Faso	1994
Côte d'Ivoire	1994
Guinée-Bissau	1994
Mali	1994
Niger	1994
Sénégal	1994
Togo	1994

Amérique

Accord de libre-échange nord-américain - ALENA (3)

	Année d'adhésion
Canada	1992
États-Unis d'Amérique	1992
Mexique	1992

Association latino-américaine d'intégration - ALADI (12)

Argentine	1980
Bolivie	1980
Brésil	1980
Chili	1980
Colombie	1980
Cuba	1999
Équateur	1980
Mexique	1980
Paraguay	1980
Pérou	1980
Uruguay	1980
Venezuela (République bolivarienne du)	1980

Communauté andine - ANCOM (5)

	Année d'adhésion
Bolivie	1996
Colombie	1996
Équateur	1996
Pérou	1996
Venezuela (République bolivarienne du)	1996

Communauté des Caraïbes CARICOM (15)

	Année d'adhésion
Antigua-et-Barbuda	1974
Bahamas	1983
Barbade	1973
Belize	1974
Dominique	1974
Grenade	1974
Guyana	1973
Haïti	1997
Jamaïque	1973
Montserrat	1974
Saint-Kitts-et-Nevis	1974
Saint-Vincent-et-les Grenadines	1974
Suriname	1995
Trinité-et-Tobago	1973

Amérique

Marché commun d'Amérique centrale - MCAC (5)	Année d'adhésion
Costa Rica	1962
El Salvador	1961
Guatemala	1961
Honduras	1961
Nicaragua	1961

Marché commun sud-américain - MERCOSUR (4)	Année d'adhésion
Argentine	1994
Brésil	1994
Paraguay	1994
Uruguay	1994

Organisation des États des Caraïbes orientales - OECO (9)	Année d'adhésion
Anguilla	1995
Antigua-et-Barbuda	1981
Dominique	1981
Grenade	1981
Îles Vierges britanniques	1984
Montserrat	1981
Sainte-Lucie	1981
Saint-Kitts-et-Nevis	1981
Saint-Vincent-et-les Grenadines	1981

Zone de libre échange des Amériques - ZLEA (34)	Année d'adhésion
Antigua-et-Barbuda	1994
Argentine	1994
Bahamas	1994
Barbade	1994
Belize	1994
Bolivie	1994
Brésil	1994
Canada	1994
Chili	1994
Colombie	1994
Costa Rica	1994
Dominique	1994
El Salvador	1994
Équateur	1994
États-Unis d'Amérique	1994
Grenade	1994
Guatemala	1994
Guyana	1994
Haïti	1994
Honduras	1994
Jamaïque	1994
Mexique	1994
Nicaragua	1994
Panama	1994
Paraguay	1994
Pérou	1994
République dominicaine	1994
Sainte-Lucie	1994
Saint-Kitts-et-Nevis	1994
Saint-Vincent-et-les Grenadines	1994
Suriname	1994
Trinité-et-Tobago	1994
Uruguay	1994
Venezuela (République bolivarienne du)	1994

Asie

Accord commercial de l'Asie et du Pacifique - ACAP (6) *	Année d'adhésion
Bangladesh	1975
Chine	2001
Inde	1975
République de Corée	1975
République démocratique populaire lao	1975
Sri Lanka	1975
* Ex-Accord de Bangkok	

Association de l'Asie du Sud pour la coopération régionale - SAARC (7)	Année d'adhésion
Bangladesh	1985
Bhoutan	1985
Inde	1985
Maldives	1985
Népal	1985
Pakistan	1985
Sri Lanka	1985

Association des nations de l'Asie du Sud-Est - ANASE (10)	Année d'adhésion
Brunéi Darussalam	1984
Cambodge	1999
Indonésie	1967
Malaisie	1967
Myanmar	1997
Philippines	1967
République démocratique populaire lao	1997
Singapour	1967
Thaïlande	1967
Viet Nam	1995

Conseil de coopération du Golfe - CCG (6)	Année d'adhésion
Arabie saoudite	1981
Bahreïn	1981
Émirats arabes unis	1981
Koweït	1981
Oman	1981
Qatar	1981

Organisation de coopération économique - OCE (10)	Année d'adhésion
Afghanistan	1992
Azerbaïdjan	1992
Iran, République islamique d'	1985
Kazakhstan	1992
Kirghizistan	1992
Ouzbékistan	1992
Pakistan	1985
Tadjikistan	1992
Turkménistan	1992
Turquie	1985

Europe

Association européenne de libre-échange - AELE (3)	Année d'adhésion
Islande	1960
Norvège	1960
Suisse	1960

Union européenne - UE (25)	Année d'adhésion
Allemagne	1957
Autriche	1995
Belgique	1957
Chypre	2004
Danemark	1973
Espagne	1986
Estonie	2004
Finlande	1995
France	1957
Grèce	1981
Hongrie	2004
Irlande	1973
Italie	1957
Lettonie	2004
Lituanie	2004
Luxembourg	1957
Malte	2004
Pays-Bas	1957
Pologne	2004
Portugal	1986
République tchèque	2004
Royaume-Uni	1973
Slovaquie	2004
Slovénie	2004
Suède	1995

Zone Euro de l'Union européenne (12)	Année d'adhésion
Allemagne	2002
Autriche	2002
Belgique	2002
Espagne	2002
Finlance	2002
France	2002
Grèce	2002
Irlande	2002
Italie	2002
Luxembourg	2002
Pays-Bas	2002
Portugal	2002

Océanie

Groupe Fer de lance mélanésien - MSG (4)

Fidji	1996
Îles Salomon	1988
Papouasie-Nouvelle-Guinée	1988
Vanuatu	1988

Groupements interrégionaux

Groupe des États d'Afrique, des Caraïbes et du Pacifique - ACP (79)

Afrique du Sud	Guinée équatoriale	République démocratique du Congo
Angola	Guyana	République dominicaine
Antigua-et-Barbuda	Haïti	République-Unie de Tanzanie
Bahamas	Îles Cook	Rwanda
Barbade	Îles Marshall	Sainte-Lucie
Belize	Îles Salomon	Saint-Kitts-et-Nevis
Bénin	Jamaïque	Saint-Vincent-et-les Grenadines
Botswana	Kenya	Samoa
Burkina Faso	Kiribati	Sao Tomé-et-Principe
Burundi	Lesotho	Sénégal
Cameroun	Libéria	Seychelles
Cap-Vert	Madagascar	Sierra Leone
Comores	Malawi	Somalie
Congo	Mali	Soudan
Côte d'Ivoire	Maurice	Suriname
Cuba	Mauritanie	Swaziland
Djibouti	Micronésie, États fédérés de	Tchad
Dominique	Mozambique	Timor-Leste
Érythrée	Namibie	Togo
Éthiopie	Nauru	Tonga
Fidji	Niger	Trinité-et-Tobago
Gabon	Nigéria	Tuvalu
Gambie	Nioué	Vanuatu
Ghana	Ouganda	Zambie
Grenade	Palaos	Zimbabwe
Guinée	Papouasie-Nouvelle-Guinée	
Guinée-Bissau	République centrafricaine	

Coopération économique de l'Asie et du Pacifique - CEAP (21)

Australie	1989
Brunéi Darussalam	1989
Canada	1989
Chili	1994
Chine	1991
États-Unis d'Amérique	1989
Fédération de Russie	1998
Hong-Kong, région administrative spéciale de Chine	1991
Indonésie	1989
Japon	1989
Malaisie	1989
Mexique	1993
Nouvelle-Zélande	1989
Papouasie-Nouvelle-Guinée	1993
Pérou	1998
Philippines	1989
Province chinoise de Taiwan	1991
République de Corée	1989
Singapour	1989
Thaïlande	1989
Viet Nam	1998

Coopération économique de la Mer Noire - CEMN (11)

Albanie	1992
Arménie	1992
Azerbaïdjan	1992
Bulgarie	1992
Fédération de Russie	1992
Géorgie	1992
Grèce	1992
République de Moldova	1992
Roumanie	1992
Turquie	1992
Ukraine	1992

Communauté des États indépendants - CEI (12)

Arménie	1991
Azerbaïdjan	1991
Bélarus	1991
Fédération de Russie	1991
Géorgie	1993
Kazakhstan	1991
Kirghizistan	1991
Ouzbékistan	1991
République de Moldova	1991
Tadjikistan	1991
Turkménistan	1991
Ukraine	1991

AASP	autres apports du secteur public
ACAP	Accord commercial de l'Asie et du Pacifique (Ex-Accord de Bangkok)
ACP	Groupe des États d'Afrique, des Caraïbes et du Pacifique
AELE	Association européenne de libre-échange
AGCS	Accord général sur le commerce des services
ALADI	Association latino-américaine d'intégration
ALENA	Accord de libre-échange nord-américain
ANASE	Association des nations de l'Asie du Sud-Est
ANCOM	Communauté andine
anc.	ancien, ancienne, anciennement
AP	aide publique
APD	aide publique au développement
ATEP	Approvisionnements totaux en énergie primaire
CAD	Comité d'aide au développement (OCDE)
CARICOM	Communauté des Caraïbes
CCG	Conseil de coopération du Golfe
CDAA	Communauté de développement de l'Afrique australe
CEAP	Coopération économique de l'Asie et du Pacifique
CEDEAO	Communauté économique des États de l'Afrique de l'Ouest
CEE	Commission économique pour l'Europe
CEEAC	Communauté économique des États de l'Afrique centrale
CEI	Communauté des États indépendants
CEMAC	Communauté économique et monétaire de l'Afrique centrale (anc. UDEAC)
CEMN	Coopération économique de la Mer Noire
CEPGL	Communauté économique des pays des Grands Lacs
CESAP	Commission économique et sociale pour l'Asie et le Pacifique
CESAO	Commission économique et sociale pour l'Asie occidentale
c.a.f.	coût, assurance, fret
CNUCED	Conférence des Nations Unies sur le commerce et le développement
COMESA	Marché commun d'Afrique de l'Est et du Sud
CTCI	Classification type pour le commerce international
DTS	droit de tirage spécial
EP	équivalent de pétrole
f.a.b.	franco à bord
FAO	Organisation des Nations Unies pour l'alimentation et l'agriculture
FBCF	formation brute de capital fixe
FMI	Fonds monétaire international
IDE	Investissement direct étranger
IEA	Agence internationale de l'énergie
ISBLM	institutions sans but lucratif au service des ménages
LERY	L'ex-République yougoslave de Macédoine
KTEP	kilo tonnes d'équivalent de pétrole
MBP	*Manuel de la balance des paiements* (FMI)
MCAC	Marché commun d'Amérique centrale
MERCOSUR	Marché commun sud-américain
MSG	Groupe Fer de lance mélanésien
n.c.a.	non classé ailleurs
n.d.a.	non dénommé ailleurs
NEI	nouvelles économies industrialisées
NPF	nation la plus favorisée
OCDE	Organisation de coopération et de développement économiques
OCE	Organisation de coopération économique
OECO	Organisation des États des Caraïbes orientales
OIT	Organisation internationale du travail
OMC	Organisation mondiale du commerce
OMS	Organisation mondiale de la santé
OMT	Organisation mondiale du tourisme
ONU/DAES/DS	Organisation des Nations Unies, Département des affaires économiques et sociales, Division de statistique
ONUSIDA	Programme commun des Nations Unies sur le VIH/SIDA
OPEP	Organisation des pays exportateurs de pétrole
PIB	produit intérieur brut
PMA	pays les moins avancés
PNB	produit national brut
PPTE	pays pauvres très endettés
RAS	région administrative spéciale
SAARC	Association de l'Asie du Sud pour la coopération régionale
SNPD	Système de notification des pays débiteurs
STN	société transnationale
UE	Union européenne
UEMOA	Union économique et monétaire des États de l'Afrique de l'Ouest
UFM	Union du fleuve Mano
UMA	Union du Maghreb arabe
UNESCO	Organisation des Nations Unies pour l'éducation, la science et la culture
UNICEF	Fonds des Nations Unies pour l'enfance
ZLEA	Zone de libre échange des Amériques

The *Handbook of Statistics* refers to the Standard International Trade Classification (SITC) Revision 3 detailed below.

Le *Manuel de statistiques* se réfère à la Classification type pour le commerce international (CTCI) révision 3 qui est détaillée ci-dessous.

Depending on the table, nomenclature of statistics is detailed at the 3-digit level or by broad product group as follows:

Les statistiques sont présentées, selon les tableaux, au niveau détaillé de la nomenclature (position à trois chiffres) ou par groupes de produits dont la composition est la suivante :

SITC codes

Codes CTCI	Product groups	Groupes de produits
0 + 1 + 22 + 4	Food items	Produits alimentaires
2 - (22 + 27 + 28)	Agricultural raw materials	Matières premières d'origine agricole
27 + 28 + 68	Ores and metals	Minerais et métaux
3	Fuels	Combustibles
(5 + 6 + 7 + 8) - 68	Manufactured goods:	Articles manufacturés :
5	- Chemical products	- Produits chimiques
7	- Machinery and transport equipment	- Machines et matériel de transport
(6 + 8) - 68	- Other manufactured goods	- Articles manufacturés divers

Codes	Standard International Trade Classification (SITC) Revision 3 (1 to 3 digits)	Classification type pour le commerce international (CTCI) révision 3 (positions de un à trois chiffres)
0	**Food and live animals**	**Produits alimentaires et animaux vivants**
00	**Live animals other than animals of division 03**	**Animaux vivants exclus ceux de la division 03**
001	Live animals other than animals of division 03	Animaux vivants autres que ceux aquatiques
01	**Meat and meat preparations**	**Viandes et préparations de viandes**
011	Meat of bovine animals, fresh, chilled or frozen	Viande des animaux de l'espèce bovine, frais, réfrigérés ou congelés
012	Other meat and edible meat offal	Autres viandes et abats comestibles
016	Meat, edible meat offal, salted, dried; flours, meals	Viandes et abats comestibles salés, fumés; farines et poudres
017	Meat, edible meat offal, prepared, preserved, n.e.s.	Préparations de viandes et d'abats, n.d.a.
02	**Dairy products and birds' eggs**	**Produits laitiers et oeufs d'oiseaux**
022	Milk, cream and milk products (excluding butter, cheese)	Lait et produits laitiers (sauf beurre, fromages)
023	Butter and other fats and oils derived from milk	Beurre et autres matières grasses du lait
024	Cheese and curd	Fromages et caillebotte
025	Birds' eggs, and eggs' yolks; egg albumin	Oeufs d'oiseaux et jaunes d'oeufs frais, blanc d'oeuf
03	**Fish (not marine mammals), crustaceans, molluscs and aquatic invertebrates and preparations thereof**	**Poissons, crustacés et mollusques et préparations de poisons, de crustacés et de mollusques**
034	Fish, fresh (live or dead), chilled or frozen	Poissons frais, vivants ou morts, réfrigérés ou congelés
035	Fish, dried, salted or in brine; smoked fish	Poissons séchés, salés, fumés
036	Crustaceans, molluscs and aquatic invertebrates	Crustacés, mollusques et invertébrés aquatiques
037	Fish, aqua. invertebrates, prepared, preserved, n.e.s.	Poissons, crustacés, mollusques, préparés ou conservés, n.d.a.
04	**Cereals and cereal preparations**	**Céréales et préparations à base de céréales**
041	Wheat (including spelt) and meslin, unmilled	Froment (dont épeautre) et méteil non moulus
042	Rice	Riz
043	Barley, unmilled	Orge non mondée
044	Maize (not including sweet corn), unmilled	Maïs non moulu
045	Cereals, unmilled (excluding wheat, rice, barley, maize)	Céréales non moulues (sauf froment, riz, orge, maïs)
046	Meal and flour of wheat and flour of meslin	Semoules
047	Other cereal meals and flour	Autres semoules et farines de céréales
048	Cereal preparations, flour of fruits or vegetables	Préparations; céréales, fécules de fruit ou légume
05	**Vegetables and fruits**	**Légumes et fruits**
056	Vegetables, roots, tubers, prepared, preserved, n.e.s.	Préparations ou conserves de légumes, n.d.a.
057	Fruits and nuts (excluding oil nuts), fresh or dried	Fruits (sauf oléagineux), frais ou secs
058	Fruit, preserved, and fruit preparations (no juice)	Préparations et conserves de fruits (sauf jus)
059	Fruit and vegetable juices, unfermented, no spirit	Jus de fruits, non fermentés, sans alcool
06	**Sugars, sugar preparations and honey**	**Sucres, préparations à base de sucre, et miel**
061	Sugars, molasses and honey	Sucres, mélasses et miel
062	Sugar confectionery	Sucreries
07	**Coffee, tea, cocoa, spices, and manufactures thereof**	**Café, thé, cacao, épices, et produits dérivés**
071	Coffee and coffee substitutes	Café et succédanés du café
072	Cocoa	Cacao
073	Chocolate, food preparations with cocoa, n.e.s.	Chocolat et autres préparations du cacao, n.d.a.
074	Tea and mate	Thé et maté
075	Spices	Épices
08	**Feeding stuff for animals (excluding unmilled cereals)**	**Nourriture destinée aux animaux (sauf céréales non moulues)**
081	Feeding stuff for animals (excluding unmilled cereals)	Nourriture destinée aux animaux (sauf céréales non moulues)
09	**Miscellaneous edible products and preparations**	**Produits et préparations alimentaires divers**

| 091 | Margarine and shortening | Margarine et graisses culinaires |
| 098 | Edible products and preparations, n.e.s. | Produits et préparations alimentaires, n.d.a. |

1	**Beverages and tobacco**	**Boissons et tabacs**
11	**Beverages**	**Boissons**
111	Non-alcoholic beverages, n.e.s.	Boissons non alcooliques, n.d.a.
112	Alcoholic beverages	Boissons alcooliques
12	**Tobacco and tobacco manufactures**	**Tabacs bruts et fabriqués**
121	Tobacco, unmanufactured; tobacco refuse	Tabacs bruts ou non fabriqués; déchets de tabac
122	Tobacco, manufactured	Tabacs fabriqués (dont succécanés de tabac)

2	**Crude materials, inedible, except fuels**	**Matières brutes non comestibles, sauf carburants**
21	**Hides, skins and furskins, raw**	**Cuirs, peaux et pelleteries, bruts**
211	Hides and skins (except furskins), raw	Cuirs et peaux (sauf pelleteries), bruts
212	Furskins, raw, other than hides and skins of group 211	Pelleteries brutes autres que ceux du groupe 211
22	**Oil seeds and oleaginous fruits**	**Graines et fruits oléagineux**
222	Oil seeds and oleaginous fruits (excluding flour)	Graines et fruits oléagineux (sauf farines)
223	Oil seeds & oleaginous fruits (incl. flour, n.e.s.)	Graines et fruits oléagineux (dont farines, n.d.a.)
23	**Crude rubber (including synthetic and reclaimed)**	**Caoutchouc brut (y compris synthétique et régénéré)**
231	Natural rubber and similar gums, in primary forms	Caoutchouc naturel, balata, guayule, etc., formes primaires.
232	Synthetic rubber; reclaimed rubber; waste and scrap	Caoutchouc synthétique; caoutchouc régénéré; déchets et débris
24	**Cork and wood**	**Liège et bois**
244	Cork, natural, raw and waste (incl. blocks, sheets)	Liège naturel brut et déchets (dont blocs, feuilles)
245	Fuel wood (excluding wood waste) and wood charcoal	Bois de chauffage (sauf déchets), charbon de bois
246	Wood in chips or particles and wood waste	Bois en plaquettes, particules, déchets de bois
247	Wood in the rough or roughly squared	Bois bruts ou équarris
248	Wood, simply worked, and railway sleepers of wood	Bois simplement travaillés, traverses de bois pour voies ferrées
25	**Pulp and waste paper**	**Pâtes à papier et déchets de papier**
251	Pulp and waste paper	Pâtes à papier et déchets de papier
26	**Textiles fibres and their wastes**	**Fibres textiles et leurs déchets**
261	Silk	Soie
263	Cotton	Coton
264	Jute and other textile bast fibre, n.e.s., not spun; tow, waste	Jute et autres fibres textiles libériennes, n.d.a., déchets
265	Vegetable textile fibres, not spun; waste of them	Fibres textiles végétales (sauf coton, jute); déchets
266	Synthetic fibres suitable for spinning	Fibres synthétiques discontinues, pour filature
268	Wool and other animal hair (including wool tops)	Laines et autres poils (dont rubans de laine)
27	**Crude fertilizers (excluding div. 56) & crude minerals**	**Engrais bruts saufs ceux de la division 56, et minéraux bruts**
272	Crude fertilizers (excluding those of division 56)	Engrais bruts (sauf ceux de la division 56)
273	Stone, sand and gravel	Pierres, sables et graviers
274	Sulphur and unroasted iron pyrites	Soufre et pyrite de fer non grillées
277	Natural abrasives, n.e.s. (including industrial diamonds)	Abrasifs naturels, n.d.a. (dont diamants industriels)
278	Other crude minerals	Autre minéraux bruts
28	**Metalliferous ores and metal scrap**	**Minerais métallifères et déchets de métaux**
281	Iron ore and concentrates	Minerais de fer et leurs concentrés
282	Ferrous waste and scrap; remelting ingots, iron, steel	Déchets et débris de fer, fonte, acier; lingots
283	Copper ores & concentrates; copper mattes, cement copper	Minerais de cuivre et concentrés; mattes de cuivre; cuivre de cément
284	Nickel ores & concentrates; nickel mattes, etc.	Minerais de nickel et concentrés; mattes, etc.
285	Aluminium ores and concentrates (including alumina)	Minerais d'aluminium et concentrés (dont alumine)
286	Ores and concentrates of uranium or thorium	Minerais d'uranium ou de thorium et concentrés
287	Ores and concentrates of base metals, n.e.s.	Minerais de métaux communs et concentrés, n.d.a.
288	Non-ferrous base metal waste and scrap, n.e.s.	Déchets et débris de métaux communs non ferreux, n.d.a.
289	Ores & concentrates of precious metals; waste, scrap	Minerais de métaux précieux et concentrés; débris et déchets
29	**Crude animal and vegetable materials, n.e.s.**	**Matières brutes d'origine animale ou végétale, n.d.a.**
291	Crude animal materials, n.e.s.	Matières brutes d'origine animale, n.d.a.
292	Crude vegetable materials, n.e.s.	Matières brutes d'origine végétale, n.d.a.

3	**Mineral fuels, lubricants and related materials**	**Combustibles minéraux, lubrifiants et produits connexes**
32	**Coal, coke and briquettes**	**Houilles, cokes et briquettes**
321	Coal, whether or not pulverized, not agglomerated	Houilles, même pulvérisées, mais non agglomérées
322	Briquettes, lignites and peat	Briquettes, lignite et tourbe
325	Coke & semi-cokes of coal, lignite or peat; retort carbon	Cokes et semi-cokes de houille lignite ou tourbe; charbon de cornue
33	**Petroleum, petroleum products and related materials**	**Pétrole et produits dérivés du pétrole et produits connexes**
333	Petroleum oils, oils from bituminous materials, crude	Huiles brutes de pétrole ou minéraux bitumineux
334	Petroleum oils or bituminous minerals > 70 % oil	Huiles de pétrole ou minéraux bitumineux > 70% huile
335	Residual petroleum products, n.e.s., related materials	Produits résiduels du pétrole, n.d.a.; produits connexes

34	**Gas, natural and manufactured**	**Gaz naturel et gaz manufacturé**
342	Liquefied propane and butane	Propane et butane liquéfiés
343	Natural gas, whether or not liquefied	Gaz naturel, même liquéfié
344	Petroleum gases, other gaseous hydrocarbons, n.e.s.	Gaz de pétrole et autres hydrocarbures gazeux, n.d.a.
345	Coal gas, water gas & similar gases (excl. hydrocarbons)	Gaz de houille, pauvre et similaires (sauf hydrocarbures)
35	**Electric current**	**Énergie électrique**
351	Electric current	Énergie électrique
4	**Animal and vegetable oils, fats and waxes**	**Huiles, graisses et cires d'origine animale ou végétale**
41	**Animal oils and fats**	**Huiles et graisses d'origine animale**
411	Animal oils and fats	Huiles et graisses d'origine animale
42	**Fixed vegetable oils and fats, crude, refined or** fractionated	**Huiles végétales fixes, douces, brutes, épurées ou raffinées**
421	Fixed vegetable oils and fats, 'soft', crude, refined or fractionated	Huiles végétales fixes, douces, brutes, épurées ou raffinées
422	Fixed vegetable fats & oils, crude, refined, fractionated, other than 'soft'	Huiles végétales fixes, brutes, épurées ou raffinées, autres que douces
43	**Animal and vegetable fats and oils, processed;** waxes of animal or vegetable origin	**Huiles et graisses animales et végétales, préparées et cires** d'origine animale et végétale
431	Animal or veg. oils & fats, processed, n.e.s.; waxes, mixt.	Huiles et graisses animales ou végétales, préparées, n.d.a.; cires
5	**Chemicals and related products, n.e.s.**	**Produits chimiques et produits connexes, n.d.a.**
51	**Organic chemicals**	**Produits chimiques organiques**
511	Hydrocarbons, n.e.s., & halogenated, nitr. derivative	Hydrocarbures, n.d.a. et dérivés halogènes, nitrosés, sulfonés, nitrés
512	Alcohols, phenols, and their derivatives	Alcools, phénols, et leurs dérivés halogénés
513	Carboxylic acids, anhydrides, halides, peroxides; derivatives	Acides carboxyliques, anhydrides, halogénures, péroxydes; dérivés
514	Nitrogen-function compounds	Composés à fonctions azotées
515	Organo-inorganic, heterocyclic compounds, nucl. acids	Composés organo-inorganiques et composés hétérocycliques; sels
516	Other organic chemicals	Autres produits chimiques organiques
52	**Inorganic chemicals**	**Produits chimiques inorganiques**
522	Inorganic chemical elements, oxides & halogen salts	Produits chimiques inorganiques : éléments, oxydes, sels
523	Metallic salts & peroxysalts, of inorganic acids	Sels et persels métalliques des acides inorganiques
525	Radioactive and associated materials	Matières radioactives et produits associés
53	**Dyeing, tanning and colouring materials**	**Produits pour teinture et tannage et colorants**
531	Synthetic organic colouring matter & colouring lakes	Matières colorantes organiques synthétiques; préparations, laques
532	Dyeing & tanning extracts, synthetic tanning materials	Extraits pour teinture et tannage
533	Pigments, paints, varnishes and related materials	Pigments, peintures, vernis et produits connexes
54	**Medicinal and pharmaceutical products**	**Produits médicinaux et pharmaceutiques**
541	Medicinal and pharmaceutical products, excluding 542	Produits médicinaux et pharmaceutiques (sauf 542)
542	Medicaments (including veterinary medicaments)	Médicaments pour médecine humaine ou vétérinaire
55	**Essential oils and resinoids & perfume materials;** toilet, polishing and cleansing preparations	**Huiles essentielles et produits utilisés en parfumerie;** préparations pour la toilette, produits d'entretien et détersifs
551	Essential oils, perfume & flavour materials	Huiles essentielles, produits pour la parfumerie, la confiserie
553	Perfumery, cosmetics or toilet preparations (soaps exclud.)	Produits de parfumerie ou de toilette; préparations (savons exclus)
554	Soaps, cleansing and polishing preparations	Savons, produits d'entretien et détersifs
56	**Fertilizers (other than those of group 272)**	**Engrais manufacturés (autres que ceux du groupe 272)**
562	Fertilizers (other than those of group 272)	Engrais (autres que ceux du groupe 272)
57	**Plastics in primary forms**	**Matières plastiques sous formes primaires**
571	Polymers of ethylene, in primary forms	Polymères de l'éthylène, sous formes primaires
572	Polymers of styrene, in primary forms	Polymères du styrène, sous formes primaires
573	Polymers of vinyl chloride or of halogenated olefins	Polymères du chlorure de vinyle ou d'autres oléfines halogènes
574	Polyacetals, other polyethers and epoxide resins, polyesters	Polyacetals, autres polyéthers et résines époxydes, polyesters
575	Other plastics, in primary forms	Autres matières plastiques, sous formes primaires
579	Waste, parings and scrap, of plastics	Déchets, rognures et débris de matières plastiques
58	**Plastics in non-primary forms**	**Matières plastiques sous formes autres que primaires**
581	Tubes, pipes and hoses of plastics	Tubes et tuyaux en matières plastiques
582	Plates, sheets, films, foil & strip, of plastics	Plaques, feuilles, rubans en matières plastiques
583	Monofilaments, of plastics, cross-section > 1mm	Monofilaments en plastiques (coupe transversale > 1mm)
59	**Chemical materials and products, n.e.s.**	**Matières et produits chimiques, n.d.a.**
591	Insecticides and similar products, for retail sale	Insecticides, produits similaires, conditionnés pour la vente au détail
592	Starches, wheat gluten; albuminoidal substances; glues	Amidons et fécules, gluten de froment; matières albuminoïdes; colles
593	Explosives and pyrotechnic products	Explosifs et articles de pyrotechnie
597	Prepared additives for mineral oils; lubricating preparations;	Additifs pour huiles minérales
598	Miscellaneous chemical products, n.e.s.	Produits chimiques divers, n.d.a.

6	**Manufactured goods classified chiefly by material**	**Articles manufacturés classés principalement d'après la matière première**
61	**Leather, leather manufactures and dressed furskins**	**Cuirs et peaux, préparés et apprêtés**
611	Leather	Cuirs et peaux préparés
612	Manufactures of leather, n.e.s.; saddlery & harness	Ouvrages en cuir, n.d.a.; articles de bourrellerie
613	Furskins, tanned or dressed, excluding those of 8483	Pelleteries tannées ou apprêtées (sauf 8483)
62	**Rubber manufactures, n.e.s.**	**Caoutchouc manufacturé, n.d.a.**
621	Materials of rubber (pastes, plates, sheets, etc.)	Produits en caoutchouc (pâtes, plaques, tubes, etc.)
625	Rubber tyres, tyre treads or flaps and inner tubes	Pneumatiques en caoutchouc
629	Articles of rubber, n.e.s.	Ouvrages en caoutchouc, n.d.a.
63	**Cork and wood manufactures (excluding furniture)**	**Ouvrages en liège et en bois (sauf meubles)**
633	Cork manufactures	Ouvrages en liège
634	Veneers, plywood, and other wood, worked, n.e.s.	Placage, contre-plaqué et autres bois travaillés, n.d.a.
635	Wood manufacture, n.e.s.	Ouvrages en bois, n.d.a.
64	Paper and paper manufactures	Papiers et préparations de papier
641	Paper and paperboard	Papiers et cartons
642	Paper and paperboard, cut to shape or size, articles	Papiers et cartons découpés
65	**Textile yarn, fabrics, made-up articles, n.e.s., and related products**	**Fils, tissus et articles textiles façonnés, n.d.a., et produits connexes**
651	Textile yarn	Fils textiles
652	Cotton fabrics, woven (excluded narrow or special fabrics)	Tissus de coton (sauf petites largeurs ou spéciaux)
653	Fabrics, woven, of man-made fabrics	Tissus en matières textiles synthétiques ou artificielles
654	Other textile fabrics, woven	Autres tissus
655	Knitted or crocheted fabrics, n.e.s.	Étoffes de bonneterie (dont velours), n.d.a.
656	Tulles, trimmings, lace, ribbons & other small wares	Tulles, dentelles et autres articles de mercerie
657	Special yarn, special textile fabrics & related	Fils spéciaux, tissus spéciaux et produits connexes
658	Made-up articles, wholly or chiefly of textile materials, n.e.s	Articles façonnés entièrement ou principalement en matières textiles, n.d.a.
659	Floor coverings, etc.	Revêtements de sols, etc.
66	**Non metallic mineral manufactures, n.e.s.**	**Articles minéraux non métalliques manufacturés, n.d.a.**
661	Lime, cement and fabricated construction materials (excluding glass and clay materials)	Chaux, ciments et matériaux de construction fabriqués (sauf argile et verre)
662	Clay construction and refractory construction materials	Matériaux de construction réfractaires, en argile
663	Mineral manufactures, n.e.s.	Articles minéraux manufacturés, n.d.a.
664	Glass	Verre
665	Glassware	Ouvrages en verre
666	Pottery	Poterie
667	Pearls, precious and semi-precious stones	Perles fines ou de culture, pierres gemmes et similaires
67	**Iron and steel**	**Fer et acier**
671	Pig iron & spiegeleisen, sponge iron, powder & granules	Fonte, fer spongieux, poudres de fer et d'acier
672	Ingots, primary forms, of iron or steel; semi-finished products	Lingots et autres formes primaires en fer ou acier;
673	Flat-rolled prod., iron, non-alloy steel, not coated	Produits laminés plats, en fer ou aciers non alliés
674	Flat-rolled prod., iron, non-alloy steel, coated, clad	Produits laminés plats, fer, aciers non alliés, zingués
675	Flat-rolled products of alloy steel	Produits laminés plats, en aciers alliés
676	Iron & steel bars, rods, angles, shapes & sections	Barres, profilés en fer ou acier (dont palplanches)
677	Rails & railway track construction mat., iron, steel	Rails et autres éléments de voies ferrées, fer, acier
678	Wire of iron or steel	Fils de fer ou d'acier
679	Tubes, pipes & hollow profiles, fittings, iron, steel	Tubes, profilés creux et accessoires, fer ou acier
68	**Non-ferrous metals**	**Métaux non ferreux**
681	Silver, platinum, other metals of the platinum group	Argent, platine et métaux de la mine du platine
682	Copper	Cuivre
683	Nickel	Nickel
684	Aluminium	Aluminium
685	Lead	Plomb
686	Zinc	Zinc
687	Tin	Étain
689	Miscellaneous non-ferrous base metals for metallurgy.	Autres métaux communs non ferreux utilisés en métallurgie
69	**Manufactures of metal, n.e.s.**	**Articles manufacturés en métal, n.d.a.**
690	Merchandises not classified according to kind	Marchandises non classées par catégorie
691	Structures & parts, n.e.s., of iron, steel, aluminium	Constructions et parties, n.d.a., en fonte, fer, acier
692	Metal containers for storage or transport	Récipients métalliques pour stockage ou transport
693	Wire products (excluding electrical) and fencing grills	Ouvrages en fils métalliques (sauf électriques), grillages
694	Nails, screws, nuts, bolts, rivets & the like, of metal	Pointes, vis, écrous, boulons, clous et similaires
695	Tools for use in the hand or in machine	Outils à main et outils pour machines
696	Cutlery	Coutellerie

697	Household equipment of base metal, n.e.s.	Articles d'économie domestique en métaux communs, n.d.a.
699	Manufactures of base metal, n.e.s.	Articles manufacturés en métaux communs, n.d.a.

	7	**Machinery and transport equipment**	**Machines et matériel de transport**
	71	**Power-generating machinery and equipment**	**Machines génératrices, moteurs et leur équipement**
	711	Vapour-generating boilers, auxiliary plant; parts	Chaudières à vapeur, auxiliaires, parties et pièces
	712	Steam turbines and other vapour turbines, parts, n.e.s.	Turbines à vapeur, parties, pièces détachées, n.d.a.
	713	Internal combustion piston engines, parts, n.e.s.	Moteurs à explosion ou à combustion interne, n.d.a.
	714	Engines and motors, non-electric; parts, n.e.s.	Moteurs et machines motrices, non électrique, n.d.a.
	716	Rotating electric plant and parts thereof, n.e.s.	Appareils électriques rotatifs, pièces détachées, n.d.a.
	718	Other power generating machinery and parts, n.e.s.	Moteurs et machines motrices, pièces, parties, n.d.a.
	72	**Machinery specialized for particular industries**	**Machines et appareils spécialisés pour les industries particulières**
	721	Agricultural machinery (excluding tractors) & parts	Machines agricoles (sauf tracteurs), parties, pièces
	722	Tractors (excluding those of 71414 & 74415)	Tracteurs (sauf 74414 et 74415)
	723	Civil ingineering & contractors' plant & equipment	Appareils, matériel de génie civil et construction
	724	Textile & leather machinery, & parts thereof, n.e.s.	Machines pour industrie textile, cuir et peaux, n.d.a.
	725	Paper mill, pulp mill machinery; paper articles man.	Machines pour pâte à papier et papier; parties, pièces
	726	Printing & bookbinding machinery, & parts thereof	Machines pour imprimerie, brochage, reliure; parties
	727	Food-processing machines (excluding domestic)	Machines pour industrie alimentaire
	728	Other machinery for particular industries, n.e.s.	Autres machines pour industries particulières, n.d.a.
	73	**Metal working machinery**	**Machines et appareils pour le travail des métaux**
	731	Machine-tools working by removing material	Machines-outils travaillant par enlèvement de matière
	733	Machine.-tools for working metal (exclud.removing material)	Machines pour travail des métaux (sans enlèvement)
	735	Parts, n.e.s., & accessories for machines of 731, 733	Pièces, n.d.a., des machines des groupes 731 et 733
	737	Metalworking machinery (excluding machine tools) & parts	Machines pour travail des métaux, n.d.a.; pièces détachées
	74	**Other industrial machinery and parts**	**Autres machines industrielles et pièces détachées**
	741	Heating & cooling equipment & parts thereof, n.e.s.	Appareils de chauffage et de réfrigération, n.d.a.
	743	Pumps (excluding liquid), air & gas compressors & fans; centrifuges	Pompes (sauf pour liquides), compresseurs; ventilateurs; centrifigeuses
	744	Mechanical handling equipment, & parts, n.e.s.	Équipement mécanique de manutention, pièces, n.d.a.
	745	Other non-electrical machinery, tools & mechanical apparatus, and parts thereof	Appareils et outils non électriques, pièces, n.d.a.
	746	Ball or roller bearings	Roulements à billes, galets, rouleaux ou aiguilles
	747	Appliances for pipes, boiler shells, tanks, vats, etc.	Articles de robinetterie, tuyauterie et similaires
	749	Non-electric parts & accessories. of machinery, n.e.s.	Parties, non électriques d'appareils mécaniques, n.d.a.
	75	**Office machines and automatic data processing machines**	**Machines et appareils de bureau ou pour le traitement automatique de l'information**
	751	Office machines	Machines et appareils de bureau
	752	Automatic data processing machines, n.e.s.	Machines automatiques de traitement de l'information, n.d.a.
	759	Parts, accessories for machines of groups 751, 752	Parties et pièces détachées pour groupes 751, 752
	76	**Telecommunications and sound recording apparatus and reproducing apparatus and equipment**	**Appareils et equipements de télécommunications et pour l'enregistrement et la reproduction du son**
	761	Television receivers, whether or not combined	Téléviseurs, même combinés à d'autres appareils
	762	Radio-broadcast receivers, whether or not combined	Appareils de radiodiffusion, même combinés à d'autres appareils
	764	Telecommunication equipment, n.e.s.; & parts, n.e.s.	Équipements de télécommunication, n.d.a., et parties
	77	Electrical machinery, apparatus and appliances, n.e.s.	Machines et appareils électriques, n.d.a.
	771	Electric power machinery, and parts thereof	Appareils pour production, transformation de l'énergie
	772	Apparatus for electrical circuits; switchboard, control panels	Appareils pour circuits électriques; tableaux de commande et parties
	773	Equipment for distributing electricity, n.e.s.	Équipement pour distribution d'électricité, n.d.a.
	774	Electro-diagnostic apparatus for medical or veterinary sciences and radiological apparatus	Appareils d'électrodiagnostic à usage médical ou vétérinaire et Appareils de radiologie
	775	Household type equipment, electrical or not, n.e.s.	Machines et appareils, à usage domestique, n.d.a.
	778	Electrical machinery & apparatus, n.e.s.	Machines et appareils électriques, n.d.a.
	78	**Road vehicles**	**Véhicules routiers**
	781	Motor vehicles for the transport of persons	Véhicules automobiles pour transport de personnes
	782	Motor vehicles for the transport of goods and special purposes	Véhicules automobiles pour le transport de marchandises et pour usages spéciaux
	783	Road motor vehicles, n.e.s.	Véhicules routiers, n.d.a.
	784	Parts & accessories of vehicles of 722, 781, 782, 783	Parties, pièces détachées des groupes 722, 781, 782, 783
	79	**Other transport equipment**	**Autres matériels de transport**
	791	Railway vehicles and associated equipment	Véhicules et matériel pour chemin de fer
	792	Aircraft and associated equipment; spacecraft and spacecraft launch vehicles, parts thereof	Aéronefs et matériels connexes; véhicules spatiaux et leurs véhicules lanceurs; leurs parties et pièces détachées
	793	Ships, boats and floating structures	Navires, bateaux et engins flottants

8	**Miscellaneous manufactured articles**	**Articles manufacturés divers**
81	**Prefabricated buildings, sanitary, heating and lighting fixtures, n.e.s.**	**Constructions préfabriquées, appareils sanitaires de chauffage et d'éclairage, n.d.a.**
811	Prefabricated buildings	Constructions préfabriquées
812	Sanitary, plumbing, heating fixtures, fittings, n.e.s.	Appareils sanitaires, plomberie, chauffage, n.d.a.
813	Lighting fixtures and fittings, n.e.s.	Appareillages d'éclairage, n.d a.
82	**Furniture and parts thereof**	**Meubles et leurs parties et pièces détachées**
821	Furniture and parts thereof	Meubles et leurs parties et pièces détachées
83	**Travel goods, handbags and similar containers**	**Articles de voyage, sacs à mains et contenants similaires**
831	Travel goods, handbags and similar containers	Articles de voyage, sacs à mains et contenants similaires
84	**Articles of apparel, and clothing accessories**	**Vêtements et accessoires du vêtement**
841	Men's clothing of textile fabrics, not knitted	Articles d'habillement en matières textiles pour hommes
842	Women's clothing, of textile fabrics	Articles d'habillement en matières textiles pour femmes
843	Men's or boy's clothing, of textile, knitted, crocheted	Articles d'habillement, en bonneterie pour hommes
844	Women's clothing, of textile, knitted or crocheted	Articles d'habillement, en bonneterie pour femmes
845	Articles of apparel, of textile fabrics, n.e.s.	Vêtements en matières textiles, n.d.a.
846	Clothing accessories, of textile fabrics	Accessoires du vêtement en matières textiles
848	Articles of apparel, clothing access., excluding textile	Vêtements et accessoires en matières non textiles
85	**Footwear**	**Chaussures**
851	Footwear	Chaussures
87	**Professional and scientific instruments, n.e.s.**	**Instruments professionnels et scientifiques, n.d.a.**
871	Optical instruments and apparatus, n.e.s.	Appareils et instruments d'optique, n.d.a.
872	Instruments & appliances, n.e.s., for medical, surgical, dental or veterinary purposes	Appareils, n.d.a. pour médecine, art dentaire, chirurgie ou pour usage vétérinaire
873	Meters & counters, n.e.s.	Compteurs et instruments de mesure, n.d.a.
874	Measuring, analysing & controlling apparatus, n.e.s.	Appareils et instruments de mesure, contrôle, n.d.a.
88	**Photographic apparatus, equipment and supplies and optical goods, n.e.s.; watches and clocks**	**Appareils et fournitures de photographie et d'optique, n.d.a.; montres et horloges**
881	Photographic apparatus and equipment, n.e.s.	Appareils et équipement photographiques, n.d.a.
882	Cinematographic and photographic supplies	Fournitures cinématographiques et photographiques
883	Cinematograph films, exposed & developed	Films cinématographiques, impressionnés, développés
884	Optical goods, n.e.s.	Éléments d'optique et articles de lunetterie, n.d.a.
885	Watches and clocks	Horlogerie
89	**Miscellaneous manufactured articles, n.e.s.**	**Articles manufacturés divers, n.d.a.**
890	Merchandises not classified according to kind	Marchandises non classées par catégorie
891	Arms & ammunition	Armes et munitions
892	Printed matter	Imprimés
893	Articles, n.e.s., of plastics	Ouvrages, n.d.a., en matières plastiques
894	Baby carriages, toys, games and sporting goods	Voitures pour le transport des enfants, jouets, jeux et articles pour divertissements et sports
895	Office & stationery supplies, n.e.s.	Articles de papeterie, fournitures de bureau, n.d.a.
896	Works of art, collectors' pieces & antiques	Objets d'art, de collection et d'antiquité
897	Jewellery & articles of precious material., n.e.s.	Articles de bijouterie et d'orfèvrerie, n.d.a.
898	Musical instruments, parts; records, tapes & similar	Instruments de musique; disques, bandes et similaires
899	Miscellaneous manufactured articles, n.e.s.	Autres articles manufacturés divers

9	**Commodities and transactions, not classified elsewhere in the SITC**	**Articles et transactions, non classés ailleurs dans la CTCI**
91	**Postal packages not classified according to kind**	**Colis postaux non classés par catégorie**
911	Postal packages not classified according to kind	Colis postaux non classés par catégorie
93	**Special transactions and commodities not classified**	**Transactions spéciales et articles non classés par catégorie**
931	Special transactions and commodities not classified	Transactions spéciales et articles non classés par catégorie
96	**Coin (other than gold coin), not being legal tender**	**Monnaies n'ayant pas cours légal**
961	Coin (other than gold coin), not being legal tender	Monnaies n'ayant pas cours légal
97	**Gold, non-monetary (excluding ores & concentrates)**	**Or, à usage non monétaire**
971	Gold, non-monetary (excluding ores & concentrates)	Or, à usage non monétaire

1

INTERNATIONAL **MERCHANDISE** TRADE

COMMERCE INTERNATIONAL DES **MARCHANDISES**

Region, country or territory	Exports (f.o.b.) - Exportations (f.a.b.) Millions of dollars							
	1980	1990	2000	2002	2003	2004	2005	2006
WORLD	**2 032 139**	**3 478 571**	**6 444 106**	**6 472 603**	**7 526 945**	**9 167 120**	**10 440 780**	**11 982 932**
DEVELOPED ECONOMIES	1 327 573	2 506 381	4 229 833	4 237 872	4 884 506	5 761 155	6 291 932	7 085 021
DEVELOPING ECONOMIES	597 559	842 883	2 044 590	2 052 444	2 410 557	3 090 696	3 750 526	4 408 951
ECONOMIES IN TRANSITION	107 007	129 307	169 683	182 287	231 882	315 269	398 322	488 960
Developed economies: America	**293 549**	**521 758**	**1 058 872**	**945 821**	**997 956**	**1 123 533**	**1 267 022**	**1 442 551**
Bermuda	37	60	51	55	60	73	49	(p)25
Canada	67 734	127 629	276 635	252 394	272 739	304 453	359 399	(p)404 791
Greenland	211	452	263	263	380	480	405	-
Saint Pierre and Miquelon	1	26	5	6	6	(e)7	(e)11	-
United States*	225 566	393 592	781 918	693 103	724 771	818 520	907 158	(p)1 037 320
Developed economies: Asia	**135 979**	**299 157**	**510 653**	**446 073**	**503 601**	**604 293**	**637 675**	**690 989**
Israel*	5 538	11 576	31 404	29 347	31 784	38 618	42 770	46 449
Japan	130 441	287 581	479 249	416 726	471 817	565 675	594 905	(e)644 541
Developed economies: Europe	**870 680**	**1 636 320**	**2 583 140**	**2 766 562**	**3 294 876**	**3 926 564**	**4 259 675**	**4 805 422**
Austria*	17 489	41 135	67 740	78 573	97 112	118 318	125 353	140 341
Belgium*				215 853	255 526	306 718	334 857	369 019
Belgium-Luxembourg*	64 656	118 294	196 834	–	–	–	–	–
Cyprus*(1)	532	957	951	770	834	1 081	1 303	(e)1 098
Czechoslovakia (former) (2)	14 891	11 906						
Czech Republic*	–	–	28 996	38 486	48 709	67 194	77 985	(e)94 643
Denmark*(3)	16 749	37 037	51 315	57 422	66 489	77 042	85 237	92 446
Estonia*(4)	–	–	3 830	4 336	5 622	5 540	7 710	(e)9 600
Faeroe Islands	187	400	474	539	595	614	598	(p)630
Finland	14 150	26 571	46 122	45 088	53 152	61 491	66 117	77 002
France*	116 409	217 265	327 753	331 298	391 901	451 888	464 061	489 357
Germany, Dem. Rep. (former)	17 312							
Germany, Federal Rep. (former)	192 860	–	–	–	–	–	–	–
Germany*	–	410 104	552 049	615 049	751 294	909 448	972 015	(e)1 127 677
Greece*	5 153	8 105	11 756	10 401	13 377	15 300	17 235	20 852
Hungary*	8 671	9 598	28 016	34 512	42 532	54 892	62 179	(p)72 782
Iceland*	918	1 592	1 891	2 228	2 385	2 896	2 944	3 453
Ireland*	8 398	23 747	77 447	88 153	92 723	104 738	109 887	112 442
Italy*	78 104	170 486	240 622	254 104	299 227	353 611	373 645	410 408
Latvia*	–	–	1 865	2 284	2 893	3 982	5 108	(e)5 752
Lithuania (4)	–	–	3 548	5 232	6 970	9 307	11 782	(p)14 109
Luxembourg*	–	–	–	10 201	13 292	16 242	18 823	22 836
Malta	483	1 130	2 443	2 225	2 467	2 627	2 224	(p)2 529
Netherlands*	84 948	131 775	233 231	243 749	295 908	357 245	406 928	462 127
Norway	18 543	34 049	60 058	59 702	67 479	81 750	101 937	121 624
Poland*	14 191	13 627	31 651	41 010	53 537	73 792	89 347	(p)109 108
Portugal*	4 640	16 422	24 374	25 875	31 746	35 770	38 202	43 305
Slovakia*	–	–	11 889	14 478	21 966	27 605	31 998	(p)41 407
Slovenia*	–	–	8 732	10 357	12 767	15 879	17 896	(p)20 989
Spain*	20 720	55 521	115 301	125 528	156 091	182 535	192 908	205 373
Sweden	30 906	57 538	87 170	81 396	102 068	123 207	130 467	147 358
Switzerland*	29 634	63 794	81 534	87 876	100 693	118 527	125 927	(p)141 665
United Kingdom*	110 137	185 268	285 549	279 840	305 519	347 326	385 002	445 491
Developed economies: Oceania	**27 365**	**49 146**	**77 168**	**79 416**	**88 073**	**106 765**	**127 561**	**146 058**
Australia*	21 944	39 752	63 870	65 033	71 546	86 420	105 832	(p)123 715
New Zealand	5 421	9 394	13 297	14 383	16 527	20 344	21 729	(e)22 343
Developing economies: Africa	**118 993**	**106 993**	**147 173**	**146 432**	**178 378**	**231 332**	**298 026**	**332 801**
Eastern Africa	*7 025*	*7 335*	*9 977*	*11 546*	*12 423*	*14 844*	*16 417*	*18 914*
Burundi*	65	75	50	31	38	48	57	(e)54
Comoros*	11	18	14	19	27	19	14	(e)17
Djibouti*	13	25	75	83	37	38	40	-
Ethiopia (former)	425	298	–	–	–	–	–	–
Eritrea	–	–	(e)19	(e)52	7	57	50	-
Ethiopia	–	–	486	480	496	678	883	(e)1 043
Kenya	1 245	1 032	1 734	2 116	2 411	2 684	3 293	(e)3 392
Madagascar*	401	318	824	486	856	1 039	763	(e)766
Malawi	295	417	379	407	525	483	497	(e)494
Mauritius	435	1 194	1 810	1 801	1 898	1 993	2 144	(e)2 322
Mozambique	281	126	364	810	1 044	1 504	1 745	(e)2 343
Rwanda	121	109	53	56	58	98	125	(e)115

For sources and notes, see end of table.

	Imports (c.i.f.) - Importations (c.a.f.) Millions de dollars							Régions, pays ou territoires
1980	1990	2000	2002	2003	2004	2005	2006	
2 073 685	**3 590 163**	**6 642 126**	**6 640 572**	**7 735 944**	**9 446 634**	**10 712 215**	**12 203 386**	**MONDE**
1 473 663	2 635 583	4 617 741	4 574 707	5 304 555	6 309 661	7 035 695	7 913 821	ÉCONOMIES DÉVELOPPÉES
492 931	800 081	1 904 395	1 911 101	2 232 262	2 877 627	3 359 059	3 915 401	ÉCONOMIES EN DÉVELOPPEMENT
107 091	154 499	119 990	154 764	199 127	259 345	317 462	374 164	ÉCONOMIES EN TRANSITION
320 210	**641 358**	**1 505 222**	**1 428 917**	**1 549 434**	**1 807 251**	**2 065 559**	**2 278 735**	**Économies développées : Amérique**
343	595	719	746	833	988	985	(e)1 095	Bermudes
62 544	123 244	244 786	227 499	245 021	279 912	331 565	(p)357 407	Canada
328	445	347	387	460	601	595	-	Groenland
10	86	70	55	69	(e)70	(e)63	-	Saint-Pierre-et-Miquelon
256 985	516 987	1 259 300	1 200 230	1 303 050	1 525 680	1 732 350	(p)1 919 574	Etats-Unis*
151 080	**252 162**	**410 915**	**372 711**	**419 233**	**497 406**	**562 064**	**625 314**	**Économies développées : Asie**
9 784	16 794	31 404	35 517	36 303	42 864	47 142	(p)47 228	Israël*
141 296	235 368	379 511	337 194	382 930	454 542	514 922	(e)578 086	Japon
974 502	**1 690 578**	**2 616 169**	**2 685 343**	**3 228 244**	**3 872 426**	**4 256 558**	**4 849 682**	**Économies développées : Europe**
24 444	49 088	72 426	78 200	99 496	119 848	127 501	140 202	Autriche*
			198 059	234 862	285 483	319 135	353 579	Belgique*
71 864	120 314	188 871	—	—	—	—	—	Belgique-Luxembourg*
1 202	2 568	3 846	3 863	4 283	5 659	6 282	(e)6 989	Chypre*(1)
12 774	13 106	—	—	—	—	—	—	Tchécoslovaquie (anc.) (2)
		33 852	42 773	53 801	71 619	76 340	(e)92 984	République tchèque*
19 340	33 248	45 577	50 256	57 408	68 124	75 684	86 085	Danemark*(3)
		4 236	4 810	6 480	8 336	10 109	(e)12 896	Estonie*(4)
219	333	533	485	693	625	748	(p)780	Îles Féroé
15 635	27 001	34 458	34 175	42 493	51 418	59 082	68 846	Finlande
137 554	240 753	339 086	328 844	398 699	470 718	504 813	534 046	France*
19 082	—	—	—	—	—	—	—	Allemagne, Rép. Dém. d' (anc.)
188 002								Allemagne, Rép. Fédérale d' (anc.)
—	346 153	497 413	489 660	604 398	715 396	775 127	(e)918 100	Allemagne*
10 548	19 777	33 494	31 530	44 836	52 734	54 141	63 211	Grèce*
9 245	8 671	31 955	37 788	47 602	59 637	65 783	(p)75 399	Hongrie*
999	1 680	2 591	2 275	2 789	3 553	4 558	5 991	Islande*
11 153	20 682	51 063	52 332	53 867	61 784	68 658	72 662	Irlande*
100 741	181 968	238 860	246 702	297 414	355 129	385 316	437 212	Italie*
—	—	3 184	4 053	5 242	7 048	8 592	(e)10 991	Lettonie*
—	—	5 219	7 526	9 668	12 386	15 511	(p)19 294	Lituanie (4)
			12 635	16 159	20 037	21 923	26 645	Luxembourg*
938	1 961	3 400	2 839	3 398	3 824	3 808	(p)3 881	Malte
88 419	126 475	218 361	218 986	264 611	319 515	364 320	415 887	Pays-Bas*
16 926	27 221	34 392	34 890	39 486	48 085	54 792	64 183	Norvège
16 690	8 413	48 940	55 113	68 004	87 909	100 903	(p)124 647	Pologne*
9 309	25 264	39 970	40 105	47 183	54 922	61 267	66 592	Portugal*
—	—	13 412	17 460	23 760	30 469	36 168	(p)44 468	Slovaquie*
		10 116	10 933	13 853	17 571	19 626	(p)22 920	Slovénie*
34 078	87 554	156 210	164 895	208 529	258 206	289 180	316 322	Espagne*
33 438	54 245	72 911	66 870	83 511	100 384	111 600	126 362	Suède
36 356	69 691	83 584	83 672	96 448	111 603	121 216	(p)132 347	Suisse*
115 545	224 412	348 208	363 613	399 260	470 406	514 375	606 162	Royaume-Uni*
27 871	**51 486**	**85 434**	**87 736**	**107 644**	**132 579**	**151 515**	**160 090**	**Économies développées : Océanie**
22 399	41 985	71 529	72 690	89 084	109 384	125 281	(p)133 613	Australie*
5 472	9 501	13 905	15 047	18 559	23 195	26 234	(e)26 477	Nouvelle-Zélande
93 788	**97 037**	**130 973**	**142 179**	**170 948**	**210 342**	**246 931**	**278 432**	**Économies en développement : Afrique**
10 759	*12 704*	*17 017*	*18 486*	*20 206*	*25 897*	*30 987*	*35 051*	*Afrique orientale*
168	231	148	129	157	176	267	(e)366	Burundi*
29	52	43	53	70	85	89	98	Comores*
213	215	270	284	238	261	277	-	Djibouti*
722	1 081	—	—	—	—	—	—	Ethiopie (anc.)
—	—	471	538	433	480	495	(e)562	Erythrée
		1 262	1 622	2 119	3 087	4 127	(e)4 710	Ethiopie
2 125	2 223	3 105	3 245	3 725	4 553	6 149	(e)7 175	Kenya
764	566	997	603	642	1 496	1 332	(e)1 404	Madagascar*
439	575	532	695	786	933	1 157	995	Malawi
614	1 618	2 207	2 159	2 363	2 771	3 160	(e)3 443	Maurice
800	878	1 162	1 543	1 753	2 035	2 408	(e)2 500	Mozambique
262	287	213	248	259	284	433	(e)515	Rwanda

Pour les sources et les notes, se reporter à la fin du tableau.

Region, country or territory	Exports (f.o.b.) - Exportations (f.a.b.) Millions of dollars							
	1980	1990	2000	2002	2003	2004	2005	2006
Seychelles	21	57	193	228	274	291	315	(e)188
Somalia	141	150	(e)193	(e)297	(e)322	(e)350	(e)420	-
Uganda	345	152	460	443	562	709	863	970
United Republic of Tanzania*	511	331	734	980	1 218	1 466	1 480	(e)1 728
Zambia*	1 305	1 309	666	930	981	1 461	1 852	(e)2 981
Zimbabwe	1 409	1 725	1 925	2 327	1 670	1 926	(e)1 877	(e)1 992
Middle Africa	*8 856*	*11 772*	*17 048*	*18 188*	*21 408*	*32 119*	*49 941*	*60 985*
Angola*	1 902	3 884	7 921	8 328	9 508	13 475	24 109	(e)31 155
Cameroon*(5)	1 384	2 002	1 833	1 802	2 246	2 478	3 104	(e)3 880
Central African Republic*(5)	116	120	161	147	121	125	128	
Chad*	71	188	183	185	601	2 191	3 032	-
Congo*(5)	911	981	2 489	2 289	2 630	3 900	4 774	(e)6 660
Dem. Rep. of the Congo*	2 269	2 326	760	1 132	1 374	1 850	2 190	-
Equatorial Guinea	14	62	1 097	(e)1 890	(e)2 095	4 596	7 136	-
Gabon*(5)	2 173	2 204	2 602	2 411	2 826	3 500	5 464	(e)6 800
São Tome and Principe*	17	4	3	5	7	4	3	(e)3
Northern Africa	*44 042*	*41 055*	*54 113*	*51 801*	*64 108*	*83 454*	*111 961*	*124 934*
Algeria*	13 871	14 707	21 650	18 820	24 105	32 342	46 538	-
Egypt*	3 046	4 957	4 689	4 708	6 311	7 530	10 672	(e)13 752
Libyan Arab Jamahiriya	21 910	13 225	12 689	11 604	14 344	20 203	28 884	(e)35 996
Morocco*	2 441	4 265	7 428	7 849	8 778	9 917	10 549	(e)12 064
Sudan*	543	374	1 807	1 949	2 542	3 778	4 824	(e)5 070
Tunisia	2 231	3 527	5 850	6 871	8 027	9 685	10 494	11 513
Southern Africa	*25 540*	*23 568*	*35 141*	*34 506*	*42 810*	*54 088*	*60 486*	*62 275*
Botswana*	..	..	2 713	2 319	3 024	3 467	4 395	(e)3 919
Lesotho	..	..	211	357	470	697	650	(e)727
Namibia	..	..	1 320	1 072	1 260	1 829	2 071	(e)2 642
South Africa	(a)25 540	(a)23 568	29 983	29 723	36 482	46 146	51 626	53 170
Swaziland	..	..	914	1 035	1 574	1 949	1 744	(e)1 818
Western Africa	*33 530*	*23 263*	*30 893*	*30 391*	*37 630*	*46 827*	*59 221*	*65 693*
Benin*	63	288	392	448	541	568	569	
Burkina Faso	90	152	206	245	321	479	347	(e)434
Cape Verde*	4	6	11	11	13	15	18	(e)21
Côte d'Ivoire*	3 135	3 072	3 888	5 275	5 788	6 919	7 488	8 148
Gambia	31	31	15	13	12	22	(e)22	-
Ghana	1 257	891	1 671	1 860	2 562	2 739	2 802	(e)3 599
Guinea	401	671	666	709	609	726	910	-
Guinea-Bissau	11	19	62	54	65	76	99	(e)108
Liberia*	600	2 207	329	176	109	104	132	-
Mali*	205	359	545	875	928	977	1 135	(e)1 354
Mauritania*	194	447	355	332	318	368	566	(e)717
Niger*	566	283	283	279	352	437	577	(e)610
Nigeria	25 934	13 671	21 174	18 573	24 047	31 148	42 277	(e)46 590
Senegal*	477	762	920	1 067	1 257	1 510	1 536	(e)1 645
Sierra Leone*	224	138	13	49	92	139	158	(e)225
Togo*	338	268	363	427	616	601	586	(e)610
Developing economies: America	**111 224**	**143 801**	**361 101**	**346 571**	**380 642**	**470 518**	**566 842**	**679 988**
Caribbean	*22 356*	*11 661*	*18 984*	*15 925*	*18 022*	*21 431*	*25 268*	*30 947*
Antigua and Barbuda*	26	21	50	45	48	45	(e)48	-
Aruba (6)	..	155	2 526	1 488	2 052	2 724	3 484	
Bahamas (7)	5 009	238	576	446	425	357	480	(e)510
Barbados	228	215	272	242	250	278	359	(e)311
Cuba*	5 577	4 910	1 676	1 422	1 677	2 332	(e)2 251	(e)2 758
Dominica*	10	55	54	43	40	40	41	41
Dominican Republic*	962	735	5 737	5 165	5 471	5 936	5 777	-
Grenada*	17	28	76	38	38	32	28	(e)21
Haiti	226	160	318	280	347	391	470	(e)494
Jamaica	963	1 158	1 295	1 114	1 180	1 390	1 500	(e)1 892
Montserrat*	1	2	1	1	2	4	1	(e)2
Netherlands Antilles*	(b)5 162	1 790	1 986	1 609	1 161	1 360	1 010	-
Saint Kitts and Nevis*	24	24	49	62	55	54	58	-
Saint Lucia*	58	127	47	49	62	80	64	(e)64
Saint Vincent and the Grenadines*	15	83	47	39	38	33	40	(e)42
Trinidad and Tobago*	4 077	1 960	4 274	3 882	5 178	6 374	9 657	(e)14 434
Central America	*23 271*	*45 538*	*179 353*	*172 543*	*178 367*	*203 147*	*229 728*	*268 540*
Belize	111	133	210	158	192	205	207	(e)264
Costa Rica*	1 002	1 448	5 850	5 264	6 102	6 301	7 026	(e)8 162
El Salvador*	967	582	1 332	1 238	1 255	1 381	1 572	(e)1 905

For sources and notes, see end of table.

Imports (c.i.f.) - Importations (c.a.f.) Millions de dollars								Régions, pays ou territoires
1980	1990	2000	2002	2003	2004	2005	2006	
99	187	343	422	412	497	505	(e)991	Seychelles
435	81	(e)343	(e)454	(e)459	(e)464	(e)610	-	Somalie
293	288	1 538	1 111	1 250	2 023	1 895	2 504	Ouganda
1 258	1 364	1 524	1 660	2 189	2 531	2 757	(e)3 760	République-Unie de Tanzanie*
1 088	1 220	993	1 253	1 574	2 017	2 575	(e)2 378	Zambie*
1 449	1 839	1 864	2 467	1 778	2 203	2 750	(e)2 763	Zimbabwe
5 884	*6 778*	*8 161*	*11 047*	*13 795*	*15 816*	*20 370*	*23 706*	*Afrique centrale*
1 328	1 578	3 040	3 760	5 480	5 832	8 353	(e)11 275	Angola*
1 602	1 400	1 484	1 868	2 163	2 406	2 891	(e)3 217	Cameroun*(5)
81	154	117	120	118	148	171	182	République centrafricaine*(5)
74	286	317	1 646	777	859	1 117	1 212	Tchad*
562	621	737	1 092	1 344	1 761	2 039	(e)1 871	Congo*(5)
1 519	1 739	1 035	1 081	1 594	1 986	2 270	-	Rép. dém. du Congo*
26	61	451	507	1 236	1 567	2 109	2 040	Guinée équatoriale
674	918	952	942	1 043	1 216	1 370	(e)1 572	Gabon*(5)
19	21	30	31	41	41	50	(e)66	Sao Tomé-et-Principe*
31 553	*44 952*	*48 945*	*53 318*	*58 405*	*72 879*	*86 564*	*94 422*	*Afrique septentrionale*
10 559	9 780	9 201	11 422	12 916	18 169	20 044	(p)21 005	Algérie*
4 860	16 783	14 010	12 552	11 139	12 859	19 851	(e)20 723	Égypte*
6 777	5 336	4 081	5 462	6 292	7 599	(e)7 853	(e)10 287	Jamahiriya arabe libyenne
4 255	6 922	11 534	11 864	14 250	17 849	20 341	(e)22 623	Maroc*
1 576	619	1 553	2 493	2 898	3 586	5 298	(e)4 920	Soudan*
3 526	5 513	8 567	9 526	10 910	12 818	13 177	14 865	Tunisie
19 700	*18 399*	*35 482*	*34 280*	*48 268*	*62 502*	*71 254*	*78 174*	*Afrique australe*
..	..	2 469	1 927	2 500	3 340	3 248	(e)2 945	Botswana*
..	..	717	832	1 081	1 399	1 317	1 460	Lesotho
..	..	1 550	1 310	1 980	2 420	2 336	(e)2 446	Namibie
(a)19 700	(a)18 399	29 695	29 267	41 084	53 466	62 304	69 185	Afrique du Sud
..	..	1 052	944	1 623	1 877	(e)2 049	(e)2 138	Swaziland
25 893	*14 203*	*21 368*	*25 048*	*30 273*	*33 248*	*37 755*	*47 079*	*Afrique occidentale*
331	265	613	725	892	894	894	880	Bénin*
359	536	611	739	925	1 272	1 279	1 356	Burkina Faso
68	136	230	275	350	386	438	571	Cap-Vert*
2 991	2 098	2 785	2 456	3 231	4 292	5 094	5 820	Côte d'Ivoire*
165	188	187	(e)161	156	229	237	(e)235	Gambie
1 129	1 199	2 973	2 707	3 233	4 297	5 345	(e)6 403	Ghana
270	699	612	667	640	690	820	-	Guinée
55	86	49	59	65	83	119	125	Guinée-Bissau
535	210	668	178	170	337	324	(e)340	Libéria*
439	602	806	928	1 252	1 291	1 612	(e)1 344	Mali*
286	220	454	357	387	557	750	-	Mauritanie*
594	389	395	468	622	750	800	760	Niger*
16 643	5 627	8 721	12 442	14 873	14 164	15 200	(e)22 596	Nigéria
1 052	1 220	1 553	2 031	2 399	2 839	3 498	3 671	Sénégal*
427	149	149	264	303	286	345	(e)397	Sierra Leone*
551	581	562	591	(e)775	(e)880	(e)1 000	(e)1 010	Togo*
123 588	**127 195**	**388 885**	**351 625**	**364 999**	**444 089**	**515 178**	**606 663**	**Économies en développement : Amérique**
27 362	*18 658*	*30 396*	*28 636*	*29 026*	*31 251*	*36 928*	*41 408*	*Caraïbes*
88	255	402	400	419	451	610	-	Antigua-et-Barbuda*
..	536	835	841	848	875	1 031	-	Aruba (6)
7 546	1 112	2 074	1 728	1 762	1 905	2 230	(e)2 794	Bahamas (7)
525	704	1 156	1 071	1 195	1 413	1 604	(e)1 507	Barbade
6 505	6 745	4 843	4 177	4 662	5 610	(e)7 592	(e)9 437	Cuba*
48	118	148	116	128	145	164	167	Dominique*
1 964	3 006	9 479	8 838	7 627	7 845	8 592	-	République dominicaine*
50	106	248	199	253	250	288	265	Grenade*
375	332	1 036	1 130	1 188	1 306	1 454	1 789	Haïti
1 171	1 928	3 301	3 533	3 639	3 772	4 460	(e)5 467	Jamaïque
12	48	22	25	28	25	30	(e)25	Montserrat*
(b)5 676	2 141	2 854	2 268	2 606	1 957	2 322	-	Antilles néerlandaises*
45	110	172	178	175	175	185	(e)190	Saint-Kitts-et-Nevis*
124	271	355	309	403	437	418	(e)436	Sainte-Lucie*
57	136	163	179	201	226	240	(e)263	Saint-Vincent-et-les Grenadines*
3 178	1 109	3 308	3 644	3 892	4 858	5 708	(e)6 513	Trinité-et-Tobago*
29 743	*51 772*	*206 620*	*202 242*	*206 055*	*237 807*	*257 784*	*298 117*	*Amérique centrale*
150	211	524	525	552	(e)511	593	(e)656	Belize
1 540	1 990	6 389	7 188	7 663	8 268	9 812	(e)11 764	Costa Rica*
966	1 263	3 795	3 902	4 375	4 871	5 362	(e)6 359	El Salvador*

Pour les sources et les notes, se reporter à la fin du tableau.

1.1.1 Exports and imports of countries
and geographical regions
Value

Region, country or territory	Exports (f.o.b.) - Exportations (f.a.b.) Millions of dollars							
	1980	1990	2000	2002	2003	2004	2005	2006
Guatemala*	1 520	1 163	2 711	2 473	2 632	2 939	3 477	(e)3 661
Honduras*	829	831	1 380	1 321	1 321	1 537	1 679	(p)1 930
Mexico	18 031	40 711	166 367	160 682	165 396	189 084	213 891	(p)250 292
Nicaragua	451	331	643	561	605	756	858	(p)1 027
Panama, excl.Canal-Zone (former)	361							
Panama*	–	340	859	846	864	944	1 018	(e)1 299
South America	**65 598**	**86 602**	**162 764**	**158 103**	**184 253**	**245 939**	**311 845**	**380 500**
Argentina*	8 021	12 353	26 341	25 650	29 566	34 576	40 106	(e)46 181
Bolivia	942	926	1 230	1 299	1 598	2 146	2 671	(p)4 223
Brazil	20 132	31 414	55 086	60 362	73 084	96 475	118 308	137 470
Chile*	4 705	8 373	19 210	18 180	21 664	32 215	40 574	58 996
Colombia	3 924	6 721	13 043	11 911	13 080	16 224	21 146	(p)24 391
Ecuador*	2 481	2 714	4 927	5 042	6 223	7 753	10 100	(e)12 378
Guyana*	389	251	502	495	513	593	553	(e)578
Paraguay	310	959	869	951	1 242	1 627	1 697	1 906
Peru*	3 898	3 231	6 955	7 714	9 091	12 617	16 587	(p)23 431
Suriname	514	472	505	157	187	782	1 212	-
Uruguay	1 059	1 693	2 295	1 861	2 206	2 931	3 405	(p)4 524
Venezuela (Bolivarian Republic of)	19 221	17 497	31 802	24 482	25 800	38 001	55 487	(p)65 210
Developing economies: Asia	**365 007**	**589 285**	**1 532 260**	**1 556 043**	**1 847 027**	**2 383 760**	**2 879 746**	**3 389 475**
Eastern Asia	**76 165**	**280 565**	**774 897**	**822 499**	**1 003 970**	**1 285 402**	**1 538 450**	**1 847 814**
China	18 099	62 091	249 203	325 591	438 228	593 326	761 953	(p)969 100
China, Hong Kong SAR	19 752	82 160	201 860	200 092	223 762	259 260	289 337	322 669
China, Macao SAR	613	1 701	2 547	2 357	2 581	2 812	2 476	(e)2 936
China, Taiwan Province of	19 786	67 079	147 777	130 457	143 900	173 909	197 779	(p)224 000
Korea, Dem. People's Rep. of	..	1 857	708	1 008	1 066	1 380	(e)1 422	-
Korea, Republic of (8)	17 512	65 016	172 267	162 470	193 817	253 845	284 419	(p)326 159
Mongolia	403	661	536	524	616	870	1 065	(p)1 529
Southern Asia	**26 127**	**47 033**	**92 735**	**100 185**	**118 171**	**149 772**	**192 495**	**222 570**
Afghanistan	670	235	137	100	144	314	340	-
Bangladesh	759	1 671	6 399	6 102	7 050	8 151	9 297	(e)12 277
Bhutan	17	70	103	113	154	183	304	-
India	8 586	17 969	42 379	50 372	58 963	76 649	99 474	(e)120 887
Iran, Islamic Republic of*	12 328	19 305	28 345	28 186	33 991	44 403	59 690	(p)64 514
Maldives	8	78	109	132	152	181	162	(p)225
Nepal	80	204	804	568	662	756	830	(e)817
Pakistan	2 618	5 589	9 028	9 913	11 930	13 379	16 051	16 470
Sri Lanka	1 062	1 912	5 430	4 699	5 125	5 757	6 347	(e)6 735
South-Eastern Asia	**73 957**	**144 152**	**429 192**	**406 502**	**452 280**	**567 906**	**651 340**	**759 071**
Brunei Darussalam*	4 581	2 213	(e)3 903	(e)3 702	(e)4 421	(e)5 057	(e)6 250	-
Cambodia	16	86	1 961	1 754	2 087	2 589	2 910	(e)3 372
Indonesia	23 950	25 675	62 124	58 120	62 631	71 585	85 660	(e)102 973
Lao People's Dem. Rep.*	28	79	330	298	378	361	506	(e)655
Malaysia (9)(10)	12 945	29 452	98 229	93 265	99 369	125 744	140 870	(p)160 490
Myanmar	477	328	1 646	3 046	2 483	2 380	3 813	(e)3 673
Philippines	5 741	8 117	39 783	36 502	36 229	39 680	39 879	(e)47 492
Singapore (11)	19 375	52 730	137 804	125 177	144 182	198 637	229 649	(p)270 570
Thailand*	6 505	23 068	68 963	68 108	80 324	96 248	110 178	(p)128 220
Viet Nam	339	2 404	14 449	16 530	20 176	25 625	31 625	(e)35 377
Western Asia	**188 758**	**117 535**	**235 436**	**226 857**	**272 606**	**380 679**	**497 461**	**560 020**
Bahrain	3 606	3 761	6 195	5 794	6 632	7 519	10 025	(e)12 006
Iraq*	26 349	10 314	20 603	13 157	9 711	18 490	24 027	(e)32 042
Jordan	574	1 064	1 899	2 770	3 082	3 922	4 302	5 167
Kuwait*	19 842	7 042	19 436	15 369	20 287	28 599	45 178	(e)58 227
Lebanon	955	494	715	1 046	1 524	1 748	1 837	(e)2 304
Oman	2 387	5 508	11 319	11 172	11 669	13 342	18 692	(e)22 028
Qatar*	5 680	3 529	11 424	10 771	13 382	18 685	25 762	-
Saudi Arabia*	101 577	44 416	77 481	72 464	93 245	125 997	166 398	-
Syrian Arab Republic*	2 108	4 212	4 633	6 536	5 731	5 383	(e)6 609	(e)7 144
Turkey*	2 910	12 959	27 775	34 561	46 576	61 683	71 928	(e)82 654
United Arab Emirates	21 967	23 544	49 878	49 596	56 833	90 639	116 290	(e)137 283
Yemen Arab Republic (former)	25	–	–	–	–	–	–	–
Yemen, Democratic (former)	777							
Yemen*	–	692	4 079	3 621	3 934	4 676	6 413	(e)9 005
Developing economies: Oceania	**2 335**	**2 803**	**4 057**	**3 397**	**4 509**	**5 087**	**5 911**	**6 688**
American Samoa*	127	311	346	388	460	446	374	(p)432
Cook Islands	4	5	7	7	9	7	5	-
Fiji	470	497	538	519	674	693	701	(p)695

For sources and notes, see end of table.

Imports (c.i.f.) - Importations (c.a.f.) Millions de dollars								Régions, pays ou territoires
1980	1990	2000	2002	2003	2004	2005	2006	
1 598	1 649	5 171	6 304	6 722	7 812	8 810	(e)10 187	Guatemala*
1 009	935	2 855	2 981	3 276	3 916	4 613	(p)5 418	Honduras*
22 144	43 548	182 702	176 607	178 503	206 623	221 819	(p)256 130	Mexique
887	637	1 805	1 754	1 879	2 212	2 595	(p)2 988	Nicaragua
1 449								Panama, sans la zone du canal (anc.)
–	1 539	3 379	2 982	3 086	3 594	4 180	(e)4 614	Panama*
66 482	**56 766**	**151 869**	**120 747**	**129 917**	**175 031**	**220 465**	**267 138**	**Amérique du Sud**
10 545	4 078	25 280	8 990	13 834	22 445	28 693	(e)34 288	Argentine*
665	687	1 830	1 770	1 616	1 844	2 341	2 821	Bolivie
24 961	22 522	59 053	49 716	50 859	66 410	77 633	91 384	Brésil
5 797	7 742	18 507	17 092	19 389	24 918	32 637	(e)38 129	Chili*
4 739	5 589	11 539	12 711	13 889	16 746	21 204	(p)26 162	Colombie
2 253	1 865	3 721	6 431	6 703	8 226	10 287	(e)12 109	Équateur*
396	311	653	576	576	651	787	(e)861	Guyana*
615	1 352	2 193	1 672	2 446	3 097	3 791	5 879	Paraguay
2 499	3 470	8 888	7 493	8 414	10 101	12 502	15 327	Pérou*
504	472	526	492	704	800	(e)975	-	Suriname
1 680	1 343	3 466	1 964	2 190	3 114	3 879	(p)4 775	Uruguay
11 827	7 335	16 213	11 840	9 298	16 679	25 736	(p)34 428	Venezuela (République bolivarienne du)
272 005	**570 895**	**1 379 148**	**1 411 527**	**1 689 030**	**2 215 148**	**2 588 149**	**3 020 951**	**Économies en développement : Asie**
85 536	**265 896**	**742 868**	**772 815**	**956 454**	**1 231 895**	**1 411 296**	**1 648 847**	**Asie orientale**
19 941	53 345	225 094	295 171	412 760	561 229	659 953	(p)791 600	Chine
22 447	82 490	212 805	207 644	231 896	271 074	299 533	335 754	Chine, Hong Kong RAS
543	1 533	2 261	2 531	2 755	3 478	3 913	(e)4 742	Chine, Macao RAS
19 764	54 831	139 927	112 758	127 366	168 090	182 571	(p)202 698	Chine, Taiwan Province de
..	2 930	1 686	1 894	2 049	2 540	(e)2 903	-	Corée, Rép. populaire dém. de
22 292	69 844	160 481	152 126	178 827	224 463	261 238	(e)309 660	Corée, République de (8)
548	924	615	691	801	1 021	1 184	(p)1 489	Mongolie
39 540	**57 416**	**95 548**	**110 028**	**135 459**	**178 603**	**232 627**	**271 667**	**Asie méridionale**
841	936	1 176	2 452	2 101	2 177	2 520		Afghanistan
2 599	3 618	8 360	7 914	9 516	12 599	13 889	(e)16 017	Bangladesh
50	81	175	197	249	411	(e)500	-	Bhoutan
14 864	23 580	51 523	56 517	72 558	99 775	139 360	(e)169 835	Inde
13 427	18 330	15 207	23 800	29 100	35 207	39 562	(p)40 507	Iran, Rép. islamique d'*
29	137	389	392	471	642	745	(p)927	Maldives
342	672	1 573	1 419	1 754	1 870	1 860	(e)2 604	Népal
5 350	7 376	10 864	11 233	13 038	17 949	25 357	28 405	Pakistan
2 037	2 685	6 281	6 105	6 672	7 973	8 834	(e)10 353	Sri Lanka
65 641	**162 292**	**370 591**	**355 116**	**398 759**	**508 996**	**593 708**	**667 883**	**Asie du Sud-Est**
572	1 001	(e)1 107	(e)1 556	(e)1 327	(e)1 422	(e)1 491		Brunéi Darussalam*
180	164	1 936	2 361	2 668	3 269	3 928	(e)4 527	Cambodge
10 834	21 837	33 515	31 285	42 078	54 874	69 498	(e)76 322	Indonésie
92	185	535	431	524	506	809	(e)980	Rép. dém. populaire lao*
10 779	29 258	81 963	79 869	81 948	105 298	114 411	(p)130 926	Malaisie (9)(10)
357	273	2 401	2 348	2 091	2 196	1 927	(e)1 906	Myanmar
8 291	13 004	37 027	37 180	39 502	42 345	46 964	(e)52 819	Philippines
24 007	60 774	134 545	116 441	127 934	173 585	200 047	(p)237 570	Singapour (11)
9 214	33 045	61 923	64 645	75 824	94 410	118 158	(p)125 975	Thaïlande*
1 314	2 752	15 638	19 000	24 863	31 091	36 476	(e)35 367	Viet Nam
81 289	**85 291**	**170 140**	**173 568**	**198 358**	**295 654**	**350 518**	**432 554**	**Asie occidentale**
3 483	3 712	4 633	5 011	5 657	6 584	7 540	(e)8 934	Bahreïn
8 707	6 526	13 384	9 477	7 871	19 814	23 532	(e)24 238	Iraq*
2 402	2 600	4 597	5 076	5 743	8 128	10 506	11 447	Jordanie
6 533	3 972	7 157	9 001	10 986	12 631	17 608	(e)15 288	Koweït*
3 650	2 525	6 230	6 447	7 171	9 400	9 359	(e)9 124	Liban
1 732	2 681	5 040	6 005	6 572	8 865	8 827	(e)10 585	Oman
1 447	1 695	3 252	4 052	4 897	6 004	10 061	(e)12 614	Qatar*
30 165	24 107	30 197	32 290	33 928	44 744	59 459	(e)63 478	Arabie saoudite*
4 124	2 400	3 815	4 488	5 111	7 049	(e)8 101	(e)8 843	République arabe syrienne*
7 910	22 302	54 503	49 663	65 637	96 368	98 998	(e)137 460	Turquie*
8 631	11 199	35 009	39 137	41 110	72 082	91 660	126 033	Émirats arabes unis
978								Rép. arabe du Yémen (anc.)
1 527	–	–	–	–	–	–	–	Yémen dém. (anc.)
–	1 571	2 324	2 921	3 675	3 986	4 867	(e)4 510	Yémen*
3 550	**4 954**	**5 389**	**5 770**	**7 285**	**8 047**	**8 801**	**9 356**	**Économies en développement : Océanie**
95	360	506	499	624	604	506	(p)342	Samoa américaines*
23	52	51	47	70	74	75	-	Îles Cook
562	754	856	906	1 209	1 446	1 607	(p)1 845	Fidji

Pour les sources et les notes, se reporter à la fin du tableau.

Region, country or territory	Exports (f.o.b.) - Exportations (f.a.b.) Millions of dollars							
	1980	1990	2000	2002	2003	2004	2005	2006
French Polynesia*	30	111	244	167	151	185	210	(p)236
Guam	61	82	74	60	76	50	(e)52	-
Kiribati	3	3	4	3	3	(e)2	4	(e)6
Nauru	65	60	28	9	9	(e)8	(e)7	-
New Caledonia*	409	480	606	498	788	977	1 114	(e)989
Papua New Guinea	1 031	1 144	2 095	1 641	2 207	2 558	3 280	(e)4 015
Samoa*	17	9	14	14	15	11	12	(p)68
Solomon Islands*	74	70	65	57	74	97	105	(e)135
Tonga	7	11	9	14	18	15	10	(e)10
Tuvalu	..	1	0	0	0	0	0	-
Vanuatu	36	19	26	19	27	37	38	-
Economies in transition: Asia	_	_	**17 782**	**19 187**	**24 864**	**34 854**	**45 370**	**58 973**
Armenia*	_	_	294	505	686	715	950	1 004
Azerbaijan*	_	_	1 745	2 167	2 590	3 615	4 347	6 372
Georgia (4)	_	_	323	346	461	647	867	(p)993
Kazakhstan*(4)	_	_	8 812	9 670	12 927	20 093	27 849	(p)38 250
Kyrgyzstan	_	_	505	486	582	719	672	(p)794
Tajikistan (4)	_	_	780	650	797	915	909	(p)1 399
Turkmenistan (4)	_	_	2 506	2 850	3 632	3 870	4 939	(e)5 324
Uzbekistan (4)	_	_	2 817	2 513	3 189	4 280	4 837	-
Economies in transition: Europe	**107 007**	**129 307**	**151 901**	**163 100**	**207 018**	**280 415**	**352 952**	**429 986**
Albania	..	224	258	340	448	605	658	793
Belarus	_	_	7 326	8 021	9 946	13 774	15 979	19 739
Bosnia and Herzegovina*(12)	_	_	1 067	1 110	1 477	2 087	2 590	(e)3 413
Bulgaria*	10 372	4 822	4 809	5 749	7 540	9 931	11 739	(p)14 981
Croatia*	_	_	4 432	4 904	6 187	8 024	8 773	10 376
Moldova, Republic of	_	_	472	644	789	980	1 091	(p)1 052
Macedonia, TFYR*	_	_	1 323	1 116	1 367	1 676	2 041	2 401
Romania*	11 209	5 775	10 367	13 876	17 619	23 485	27 730	32 336
Russian Federation (4)	_	_	105 565	107 110	135 929	183 207	243 569	(p)301 976
Serbia and Montenegro*	_	_	1 711	2 275	2 650	3 979	4 553	-
Yugoslavia, SFR (former)	8 978	14 308	_	_	_	_	_	_
USSR (former)	76 449	104 177	_	_	_	_	_	_
Ukraine (4)	_	_	14 573	17 957	23 067	32 666	34 228	38 368

Sources:
- UN, *Yearbook of International Trade Statistics*
- UN, *Monthly Bulletin of Statistics*
- UN, Economic Commission for Europe
- IMF, *International Financial Statistics*
- IMF, *Direction of Trade Statistics*
- World Trade Organization
- Eastern Caribbean Central Bank
- National sources
- UNCTAD secretariat estimates

Notes:
- Countries which use the Special Trade System as reporting system are marked with an asterisk (*).
(a) Data refers to South Africa Customs Union (Botswana, Lesotho, Namibia, South Africa and Swaziland).
(b) Including Aruba.
(1) Excluding military imports.
(2) From 1985 onwards, data are not comparable to those shown for prior periods due to revisions of the koruna-to-US dollar exchange rate.
(3) Prior to 1985, general trade.
(4) Prior to 1994, covers only trade with countries outside the CIS.
(5) Inter-trade between the member countries of CEMAC is excluded.
(6) Prior to 2000, data exclude imports into and exports from the free zone; mineral fuels are also excluded.
(7) From 1990 onwards, trade statistics exclude certain oil and chemical products.
(8) Excluding imports of goods financed through foreign aid.
(9) Inter-trade between the States of Malaysia included.
(10) Excluding military imports and offshore installations of petroleum industry.
(11) Including trans-shipments to and from peninsular Malaysia.
(12) Prior to 1998, data refer to the Federation of Bosnia and Herzegovina only. The other entity of Bosnia and Herzegovina, Republika Srpska, is not included.

Imports (c.i.f.) - Importations (c.a.f.) Millions de dollars								Régions, pays ou territoires
1980	1990	2000	2002	2003	2004	2005	2006	
547	928	1 072	1 268	1 568	1 480	1 702	(p)1 658	Polynésie française*
400	461	421	(e)342	(e)412	(e)524	(e)692	-	Guam
17	27	40	50	52	(e)63	76	(p)64	Kiribati
12	38	27	25	20	(e)15	(e)14	-	Nauru
456	883	922	1 012	1 532	1 641	1 774	(e)1 912	Nouvelle-Calédonie*
1 176	1 118	1 151	1 235	1 367	1 680	1 729	(e)1 987	Papouasie-Nouvelle-Guinée
63	81	90	128	129	155	187	(p)282	Samoa*
89	91	92	69	94	122	185	(e)220	Îles Salomon*
38	62	69	89	94	105	110	(e)117	Tonga
..	4	5	11	10	11	13	-	Tuvalu
73	96	87	90	105	128	131	(e)136	Vanuatu
–	–	**13 515**	**15 885**	**20 228**	**28 339**	**35 403**	**45 566**	**Économies en transition : Asie**
–	–	882	987	1 280	1 351	1 768	2 194	Arménie*
–	–	1 172	1 666	2 626	3 516	4 200	5 268	Azerbaïdjan*
–	–	709	796	1 141	1 847	2 491	(p)3 681	Géorgie (4)
–	–	5 040	6 584	8 409	12 781	17 353	(p)23 677	Kazakhstan*(4)
–	–	554	587	717	941	1 108	(p)1 718	Kirghizistan
–	–	675	721	881	1 191	1 330	(p)1 723	Tadjikistan (4)
–	–	1 786	2 120	2 512	3 320	3 443	3 595	Turkménistan (4)
–	–	2 697	2 425	2 662	3 392	(e)3 710	-	Ouzbékistan (4)
107 091	**154 499**	**106 474**	**138 879**	**178 900**	**231 006**	**282 059**	**328 598**	**Économies en transition : Europe**
..	423	1 090	1 503	1 864	2 309	2 618	3 057	Albanie
		8 646	9 092	11 558	16 491	16 708	22 323	Bélarus
–	–	3 894	4 416	5 613	6 650	7 577	7 587	Bosnie-Herzégovine*(12)
9 650	4 710	6 505	7 987	10 902	14 467	18 163	(p)23 001	Bulgarie*
		7 887	10 722	14 209	16 589	18 560	21 488	Croatie*
–	–	776	1 039	1 403	1 773	2 293	(p)2 693	Moldova, République de
–	–	2 094	1 995	2 306	2 932	3 228	3 763	Macédoine, LERY*
13 843	9 843	13 055	17 862	24 003	32 664	40 463	51 106	Roumanie*
		44 862	60 966	76 070	97 382	125 303	137 548	Fédération de Russie (4)
–	–	3 711	6 320	7 952	10 753	11 009	-	Serbie-et-Monténégro*
15 076	18 871	–	–	–	–	–	–	Yougoslavie, RSF (anc.)
68 522	120 651	–	–	–	–	–	–	URSS (anc.)
–	–	13 956	16 977	23 020	28 997	36 136	45 022	Ukraine (4)

Sources :
- ONU, *Annuaire statistique du commerce international*
- ONU, *Bulletin mensuel de statistique*
- ONU, Commission économique pour l'Europe
- FMI, *International Financial Statistics*
- FMI, *Direction of Trade Statistics*
- Organisation mondiale du commerce
- Banque centrale des Caraïbes orientales
- Sources nationales
- Estimations du secrétariat de la CNUCED

Notes :
- Les pays qui utilisent le système du commerce spécial en tant que système d'enregistrement sont marqués par un astérisque (*).
(a)   Donnée relative à l'Union Douanière d'Afrique du Sud (Afrique du Sud, Botswana, Lesotho, Namibie et Swaziland).
(b)   Y compris Aruba.
(1)   Non compris les importations militaires.
(2)   A partir de 1985, les chiffres ne sont pas comparables à ceux des années antérieures à cause des révisions du taux de change de la couronne par rapport au dollar des États-Unis.
(3)   Avant 1985, commerce général.
(4)   Avant 1994, concerne seulement le commerce avec les pays extérieurs à la CEI.
(5)   Non-compris le commerce entre les pays membres de CEMAC.
(6)   Avant 2000, les données excluent les importations en provenance et les exportations à destination de la zone de libre circulation; les combustibles minéraux sont également exclus.
(7)   A partir de 1990, certains produits pétroliers et chimiques ne sont plus inclus dans les statistiques du commerce.
(8)   Non-compris les biens d'importation financés par l'aide à l'étranger.
(9)   Y compris le commerce entre les États de la Malaisie.
(10)   Non-compris les importations militaires et l'installation près des côtes de l'industrie pétrolière.
(11)   Y compris les transbordements vers et en provenance de la Malaisie péninsulaire.
(12)   Avant 1998, les données se réfèrent uniquement à la Fédération de la Bosnie-Herzégovine. L'autre entité de la Bosnie-Herzégovine, Republika Srpska, n'est pas incluse.

Region, country or territory	Exports (f.o.b.) - Exportations (f.a.b.) Percentage - En pourcentage										
	1980	1985	1990	1995	2000	2001	2002	2003	2004	2005	2006
WORLD	100.000	100.000	100.000	100.000	100.000	100.000	100.000	100.000	100.000	100.000	100.000
DEVELOPED ECONOMIES	65.329	68.368	72.052	69.803	65.639	66.232	65.474	64.894	62.846	60.263	59.126
DEVELOPING ECONOMIES	29.405	25.365	24.231	27.582	31.728	31.000	31.710	32.026	33.715	35.922	36.794
ECONOMIES IN TRANSITION	5.266	6.267	3.717	2.615	2.633	2.769	2.816	3.081	3.439	3.815	4.080
Developed economies: America	**14.445**	**15.731**	**14.999**	**15.041**	**16.432**	**15.995**	**14.613**	**13.258**	**12.256**	**12.135**	**12.038**
Bermuda	0.002	0.001	0.002	0.001	0.001	0.001	0.001	0.001	0.001	0.000	(p)0.000
Canada	3.333	4.616	3.669	3.719	4.293	4.201	3.899	3.624	3.321	3.442	(p)3.378
Greenland	0.010	0.009	0.013	0.007	0.004	0.004	0.004	0.005	0.005	0.004	-
Saint Pierre and Miquelon	0.000	0.000	0.001	0.000	0.000	0.000	0.000	0.000	(e)0.000	(e)0.000	-
United States*	11.100	11.105	11.315	11.314	12.134	11.788	10.708	9.629	8.929	8.689	(p)8.657
Developed economies: Asia	**6.691**	**9.309**	**8.600**	**8.942**	**7.924**	**6.994**	**6.892**	**6.691**	**6.592**	**6.108**	**5.766**
Israel*	0.272	0.318	0.333	0.369	0.487	0.470	0.453	0.422	0.421	0.410	0.388
Japan	6.419	8.991	8.267	8.573	7.437	6.524	6.438	6.268	6.171	5.698	(e)5.379
Developed economies: Europe	**42.845**	**41.891**	**47.040**	**44.529**	**40.085**	**41.996**	**42.743**	**43.774**	**42.833**	**40.798**	**40.102**
Austria*	0.861	0.875	1.183	1.117	1.051	1.144	1.214	1.290	1.291	1.201	1.171
Belgium*	–	–	–	–	–	–	3.335	3.395	3.346	3.207	3.080
Belgium-Luxembourg*	3.182	2.727	3.401	3.599	3.054	3.235	–	–	–	–	–
Cyprus*(1)	0.026	0.024	0.028	0.024	0.015	0.016	0.012	0.011	0.012	0.012	(e)0.009
Czechoslovakia (former) (2)	0.733	0.604	0.342	–	–	–	–	–	–	–	–
Czech Republic*	–	–	–	0.420	0.450	0.540	0.595	0.647	0.733	0.747	(e)0.790
Denmark*(3)	0.824	0.867	1.065	0.985	0.796	0.836	0.887	0.883	0.840	0.816	0.771
Estonia*(4)	–	–	–	0.036	0.059	0.065	0.067	0.075	0.060	0.074	(e)0.080
Faeroe Islands	0.009	0.009	0.011	0.007	0.007	0.008	0.008	0.008	0.007	0.006	(p)0.005
Finland	0.696	0.691	0.764	0.784	0.716	0.699	0.697	0.706	0.671	0.633	0.643
France*	5.728	5.181	6.246	5.841	5.086	5.229	5.118	5.207	4.929	4.445	4.084
Germany, Dem. Rep. (former)	0.852	1.282	–	–	–	–	–	–	–	–	–
Germany, Federal Rep. (former)	9.490	9.335	–	–	–	–	–	–	–	–	–
Germany*	–	–	11.789	10.129	8.567	9.243	9.502	9.981	9.921	9.310	(e)9.411
Greece*	0.254	0.230	0.233	0.214	0.182	0.166	0.161	0.178	0.167	0.165	0.174
Hungary*	0.427	0.433	0.276	0.248	0.435	0.494	0.533	0.565	0.599	0.596	(p)0.607
Iceland*	0.045	0.041	0.046	0.035	0.029	0.033	0.034	0.032	0.032	0.028	0.029
Ireland*	0.413	0.526	0.683	0.865	1.202	1.339	1.362	1.232	1.143	1.052	0.938
Italy*	3.843	3.893	4.901	4.523	3.734	3.953	3.926	3.975	3.857	3.579	3.425
Latvia*	–	–	–	0.025	0.029	0.032	0.035	0.038	0.043	0.049	(e)0.048
Lithuania (4)	–	–	–	0.052	0.055	0.069	0.081	0.093	0.102	0.113	(p)0.118
Luxembourg*	–	–	–	–	–	–	0.158	0.177	0.177	0.180	0.191
Malta	0.024	0.020	0.032	0.037	0.038	0.032	0.034	0.033	0.029	0.021	(p)0.021
Netherlands*	4.180	3.952	3.788	3.931	3.619	3.733	3.766	3.931	3.897	3.897	3.857
Norway	0.912	1.014	0.979	0.812	0.932	0.957	0.922	0.897	0.892	0.976	1.015
Poland*	0.698	0.583	0.392	0.443	0.491	0.584	0.634	0.711	0.805	0.856	(p)0.911
Portugal*	0.228	0.289	0.472	0.441	0.378	0.390	0.400	0.422	0.390	0.366	0.361
Slovakia*	–	–	–	0.166	0.184	0.204	0.224	0.292	0.301	0.306	(p)0.346
Slovenia*	–	–	–	0.161	0.136	0.150	0.160	0.170	0.173	0.171	(p)0.175
Spain*	1.020	1.231	1.596	1.893	1.789	1.886	1.939	2.074	1.991	1.848	1.714
Sweden	1.521	1.546	1.654	1.557	1.353	1.223	1.258	1.356	1.344	1.250	1.230
Switzerland*	1.458	1.393	1.834	1.580	1.265	1.328	1.358	1.338	1.293	1.206	(p)1.182
United Kingdom*	5.420	5.144	5.326	4.604	4.431	4.409	4.323	4.059	3.789	3.687	3.718
Developed economies: Oceania	**1.347**	**1.437**	**1.413**	**1.292**	**1.197**	**1.247**	**1.227**	**1.170**	**1.165**	**1.222**	**1.219**
Australia*	1.080	1.147	1.143	1.028	0.991	1.025	1.005	0.951	0.943	1.014	(p)1.032
New Zealand	0.267	0.290	0.270	0.264	0.206	0.222	0.222	0.220	0.222	0.208	(e)0.186
Developing economies: Africa	**5.856**	**4.181**	**3.076**	**2.084**	**2.284**	**2.233**	**2.262**	**2.370**	**2.523**	**2.854**	**2.777**
Eastern Africa	*0.346*	*0.266*	*0.211*	*0.188*	*0.155*	*0.168*	*0.178*	*0.165*	*0.162*	*0.157*	*0.158*
Burundi*	0.003	0.006	0.002	0.002	0.001	0.001	0.000	0.000	0.001	0.001	(e)0.000
Comoros*	0.001	0.001	0.001	0.000	0.000	0.000	0.000	0.000	0.000	0.000	(e)0.000
Djibouti*	0.001	0.001	0.001	0.000	0.001	0.001	0.001	0.000	0.000	0.000	-
Ethiopia (former)	0.021	0.017	0.009	–	–	–	–	–	–	–	–
Eritrea	–	–	–	(e)0.002	(e)0.000	(e)0.000	(e)0.001	0.000	0.001	0.000	-
Ethiopia	–	–	–	0.008	0.008	0.007	0.007	0.007	0.007	0.008	(e)0.009
Kenya	0.061	0.049	0.030	0.036	0.027	0.031	0.033	0.032	0.029	0.032	(e)0.028
Madagascar*	0.020	0.014	0.009	0.010	0.013	0.015	0.008	0.011	0.011	0.007	(e)0.006
Malawi	0.015	0.012	0.012	0.008	0.006	0.007	0.006	0.007	0.005	0.005	(e)0.004
Mauritius	0.021	0.022	0.034	0.030	0.028	0.026	0.028	0.025	0.022	0.021	(e)0.019
Mozambique	0.014	0.004	0.004	0.003	0.006	0.012	0.013	0.014	0.016	0.017	(e)0.020
Rwanda	0.006	0.007	0.003	0.001	0.001	0.001	0.001	0.001	0.001	0.001	(e)0.001

For sources and notes, see end of table.

Imports (c.i.f.) - Importations (c.a.f.) Percentage - En pourcentage											Régions, pays ou territoires
1980	1985	1990	1995	2000	2001	2002	2003	2004	2005	2006	
100.000	100.000	100.000	100.000	100.000	100.000	100.000	100.000	100.000	100.000	100.000	MONDE
71.065	71.087	73.411	69.051	69.522	69.422	68.890	68.570	66.793	65.679	64.849	ÉCONOMIES DÉVELOPPÉES
23.771	22.996	22.285	28.598	28.671	28.415	28.779	28.856	30.462	31.357	32.085	ÉCONOMIES EN DÉVELOPPEMENT
5.164	5.918	4.303	2.351	1.806	2.163	2.331	2.574	2.745	2.964	3.066	ÉCONOMIES EN TRANSITION
15.442	21.347	17.864	18.005	22.662	22.004	21.518	20.029	19.131	19.282	18.673	Économies développées : Amérique
0.017	0.020	0.017	0.011	0.011	0.011	0.011	0.011	0.010	0.009	(e)0.009	Bermudes
3.016	3.968	3.433	3.219	3.685	3.553	3.426	3.167	2.963	3.095	(p)2.929	Canada
0.016	0.015	0.012	0.008	0.005	0.005	0.006	0.006	0.006	0.006	-	Groenland
0.000	0.002	0.002	0.001	0.001	0.001	0.001	0.001	(e)0.001	(e)0.001	-	Saint-Pierre-et-Miquelon
12.393	17.343	14.400	14.766	18.959	18.434	18.074	16.844	16.151	16.172	(p)15.730	États-Unis*
7.286	6.906	7.024	7.001	6.187	6.011	5.613	5.419	5.265	5.247	5.124	Économies développées : Asie
0.472	0.486	0.468	0.567	0.473	0.554	0.535	0.469	0.454	0.440	(p)0.387	Israël*
6.814	6.421	6.556	6.434	5.714	5.457	5.078	4.950	4.812	4.807	(e)4.737	Japon
46.994	41.265	47.089	42.604	39.388	40.200	40.438	41.730	40.993	39.736	39.740	Économies développées : Europe
1.179	1.033	1.367	1.269	1.090	1.167	1.178	1.286	1.269	1.190	1.149	Autriche*
_	_	_	_	_	_	2.983	3.036	3.022	2.979	2.897	Belgique*
3.465	2.765	3.351	3.347	2.844	2.986	_	_	_	_	_	Belgique-Luxembourg*
0.058	0.061	0.072	0.071	0.058	0.061	0.058	0.055	0.060	0.059	(e)0.057	Chypre*(1)
0.616	0.549	0.365	_	_	_	_	_	_	_	_	Tchécoslovaquie (anc.) (2)
_	_	_	0.505	0.510	0.599	0.644	0.695	0.758	0.713	(e)0.762	République tchèque*
0.933	0.898	0.926	0.880	0.686	0.708	0.757	0.742	0.721	0.707	0.705	Danemark*(3)
_	_	_	0.046	0.064	0.067	0.072	0.084	0.088	0.094	(e)0.106	Estonie*(4)
0.011	0.012	0.009	0.006	0.008	0.008	0.007	0.009	0.007	0.007	(p)0.006	Îles Féroé
0.754	0.651	0.752	0.565	0.519	0.510	0.515	0.549	0.544	0.552	0.564	Finlande
6.633	5.450	6.706	5.682	5.105	5.137	4.952	5.154	4.983	4.713	4.376	France*
0.920	1.153	_	_	_	_	_	_	_	_	_	Allemagne, Rép. Dém. d' (anc.)
9.066	7.798	_	_	_	_	_	_	_	_	_	Allemagne, Rép. Fédérale d' (anc.)
_	_	9.642	8.887	7.489	7.599	7.374	7.813	7.573	7.236	(e)7.523	Allemagne*
0.509	0.499	0.551	0.496	0.504	0.444	0.475	0.580	0.558	0.505	0.518	Grèce*
0.446	0.405	0.242	0.295	0.481	0.527	0.569	0.615	0.631	0.614	(p)0.618	Hongrie*
0.048	0.045	0.047	0.034	0.039	0.035	0.034	0.036	0.038	0.043	0.049	Islande*
0.538	0.493	0.576	0.619	0.769	0.790	0.788	0.696	0.654	0.641	0.595	Irlande*
4.858	4.315	5.069	3.946	3.596	3.693	3.715	3.845	3.759	3.597	3.583	Italie*
_	_	_	0.035	0.048	0.055	0.061	0.068	0.075	0.080	(e)0.090	Lettonie*
_	_	_	0.070	0.079	0.095	0.113	0.125	0.131	0.145	(p)0.158	Lituanie (4)
_	_	_	_	_	_	0.190	0.209	0.212	0.205	0.218	Luxembourg*
0.045	0.037	0.055	0.056	0.051	0.043	0.043	0.044	0.040	0.033	(p)0.032	Malte
4.264	3.598	3.523	3.548	3.288	3.262	3.298	3.421	3.382	3.401	3.408	Pays-Bas*
0.816	0.765	0.758	0.632	0.518	0.515	0.525	0.510	0.509	0.511	0.526	Norvège
0.805	0.583	0.234	0.556	0.737	0.786	0.830	0.879	0.931	0.942	(p)1.021	Pologne*
0.449	0.377	0.704	0.625	0.602	0.617	0.604	0.610	0.581	0.572	0.546	Portugal*
_	_	_	0.177	0.202	0.242	0.263	0.307	0.323	0.338	(p)0.364	Slovaquie*
_	_	_	0.182	0.152	0.159	0.165	0.179	0.186	0.183	(p)0.188	Slovénie*
1.643	1.474	2.439	2.175	2.352	2.418	2.483	2.696	2.733	2.700	2.592	Espagne*
1.613	1.405	1.511	1.246	1.098	0.988	1.007	1.080	1.063	1.042	1.035	Suède
1.753	1.512	1.941	1.535	1.258	1.315	1.260	1.247	1.181	1.132	(p)1.085	Suisse*
5.572	5.388	6.251	5.120	5.242	5.374	5.476	5.161	4.980	4.802	4.967	Royaume-Uni*
1.344	1.569	1.434	1.441	1.286	1.207	1.321	1.391	1.403	1.414	1.312	Économies développées : Océanie
1.080	1.274	1.169	1.174	1.077	0.999	1.095	1.152	1.158	1.170	(p)1.095	Australie*
0.264	0.295	0.265	0.267	0.209	0.208	0.227	0.240	0.246	0.245	(e)0.217	Nouvelle-Zélande
4.523	3.569	2.703	2.311	1.972	2.107	2.141	2.210	2.227	2.305	2.282	Économies en développement : Afrique
0.519	0.388	0.354	0.300	0.256	0.281	0.278	0.261	0.274	0.289	0.287	Afrique orientale
0.008	0.009	0.006	0.004	0.002	0.002	0.002	0.002	0.002	0.002	(e)0.003	Burundi*
0.001	0.002	0.001	0.001	0.001	0.001	0.001	0.001	0.001	0.001	0.001	Comores*
0.010	0.010	0.006	0.003	0.004	0.004	0.004	0.003	0.003	0.003	-	Djibouti*
0.035	0.049	0.030	_	_	_	_	_	_	_	_	Éthiopie (anc.)
_	_	_	0.009	0.007	0.007	0.008	0.006	0.005	0.005	(e)0.005	Érythrée
_	_	_	0.022	0.019	0.028	0.024	0.027	0.033	0.039	(e)0.039	Éthiopie
0.102	0.071	0.062	0.057	0.047	0.050	0.049	0.048	0.048	0.057	(e)0.059	Kenya
0.037	0.017	0.016	0.012	0.015	0.015	0.009	0.008	0.016	0.012	(e)0.012	Madagascar*
0.021	0.014	0.016	0.009	0.008	0.009	0.010	0.010	0.010	0.011	0.008	Malawi
0.030	0.026	0.045	0.038	0.033	0.031	0.033	0.031	0.029	0.029	(e)0.028	Maurice
0.039	0.021	0.024	0.013	0.017	0.017	0.023	0.023	0.022	0.022	(e)0.020	Mozambique
0.013	0.015	0.008	0.005	0.003	0.004	0.004	0.003	0.003	0.004	(e)0.004	Rwanda

Pour les sources et les notes, se reporter à la fin du tableau.

Region, country or territory	Exports (f.o.b.) - Exportations (f.a.b.) Percentage - En pourcentage										
	1980	1985	1990	1995	2000	2001	2002	2003	2004	2005	2006
Seychelles	0.001	0.001	0.002	0.001	0.003	0.004	0.004	0.004	0.003	0.003	(e)0.002
Somalia	0.007	0.005	0.004	(e)0.003	(e)0.003	(e)0.005	(e)0.005	(e)0.004	(e)0.004	(e)0.004	-
Uganda	0.017	0.020	0.004	0.009	0.007	0.007	0.007	0.007	0.008	0.008	0.008
United Republic of Tanzania*	0.025	0.013	0.010	0.013	0.011	0.014	0.015	0.016	0.016	0.014	(e)0.014
Zambia*	0.064	0.040	0.038	0.020	0.010	0.016	0.014	0.013	0.016	0.018	(e)0.025
Zimbabwe	0.069	0.056	0.050	0.041	0.030	0.020	0.036	0.022	0.021	(e)0.018	(e)0.017
Middle Africa	*0.436*	*0.411*	*0.338*	*0.221*	*0.265*	*0.255*	*0.281*	*0.284*	*0.350*	*0.478*	*0.509*
Angola*	0.094	0.117	0.112	0.072	0.123	0.106	0.129	0.126	0.147	0.231	(e)0.260
Cameroon*(5)	0.068	0.037	0.058	0.032	0.028	0.028	0.028	0.030	0.027	0.030	(e)0.032
Central African Republic*(5)	0.006	0.005	0.003	0.003	0.002	0.002	0.002	0.002	0.001	0.001	-
Chad*	0.003	0.003	0.005	0.005	0.003	0.003	0.003	0.008	0.024	0.029	
Congo*(5)	0.045	0.055	0.028	0.023	0.039	0.033	0.035	0.035	0.043	0.046	(e)0.056
Dem. Rep. of the Congo*	0.112	0.094	0.067	0.032	0.012	0.015	0.017	0.018	0.020	0.021	
Equatorial Guinea	0.001	0.001	0.002	0.002	0.017	(e)0.026	(e)0.029	(e)0.028	0.050	0.068	-
Gabon*(5)	0.107	0.099	0.063	0.052	0.040	0.041	0.037	0.038	0.038	0.052	(e)0.057
São Tome and Principe*	0.001	0.000	0.000	0.000	0.000	0.000	0.000	0.000	0.000	0.000	(e)0.000
Northern Africa	*2.167*	*1.683*	*1.180*	*0.697*	*0.840*	*0.810*	*0.800*	*0.852*	*0.910*	*1.072*	*1.043*
Algeria*	0.683	0.653	0.423	0.216	0.336	0.309	0.291	0.320	0.353	0.446	-
Egypt*	0.150	0.188	0.142	0.067	0.073	0.067	0.073	0.084	0.082	0.102	(e)0.115
Libyan Arab Jamahiriya	1.078	0.625	0.380	0.165	0.197	0.184	0.179	0.191	0.220	0.277	(e)0.300
Morocco*	0.120	0.110	0.123	0.133	0.115	0.116	0.121	0.117	0.108	0.101	(e)0.101
Sudan*	0.027	0.019	0.011	0.011	0.028	0.027	0.030	0.034	0.041	0.046	(e)0.042
Tunisia	0.110	0.088	0.101	0.106	0.091	0.107	0.106	0.107	0.106	0.101	0.096
Southern Africa	*1.257*	*0.829*	*0.678*	*0.539*	*0.545*	*0.554*	*0.533*	*0.569*	*0.590*	*0.579*	*0.520*
Botswana*	..	..	..	..	0.042	0.040	0.036	0.040	0.038	0.042	(e)0.033
Lesotho	..	..	..	..	0.003	0.005	0.006	0.006	0.008	0.006	(e)0.006
Namibia	..	..	..	..	0.020	0.019	0.017	0.017	0.020	0.020	(e)0.022
South Africa	(a)1.257	(a)0.829	0.678	0.539	0.465	0.473	0.459	0.485	0.503	0.494	0.444
Swaziland	..	..	..	..	0.014	0.017	0.016	0.021	0.021	0.017	(e)0.015
Western Africa	*1.650*	*0.992*	*0.669*	*0.439*	*0.479*	*0.447*	*0.470*	*0.500*	*0.511*	*0.567*	*0.548*
Benin*	0.003	0.008	0.008	0.008	0.006	0.006	0.007	0.007	0.006	0.005	-
Burkina Faso	0.004	0.004	0.004	0.005	0.003	0.004	0.004	0.004	0.005	0.003	(e)0.004
Cape Verde*	0.000	0.000	0.000	0.000	0.000	0.000	0.000	0.000	0.000	0.000	(e)0.000
Côte d'Ivoire*	0.154	0.151	0.088	0.074	0.060	0.064	0.081	0.077	0.075	0.072	0.068
Gambia	0.002	0.002	0.001	0.000	0.000	0.000	0.000	0.000	0.000	(e)0.000	-
Ghana	0.062	0.031	0.026	0.033	0.026	0.028	0.029	0.034	0.030	0.027	(e)0.030
Guinea	0.020	0.025	0.019	0.014	0.010	0.012	0.011	0.008	0.008	0.009	-
Guinea-Bissau	0.001	0.001	0.001	0.001	0.001	0.001	0.001	0.001	0.001	0.001	(e)0.001
Liberia*	0.030	0.022	0.063	0.016	0.005	0.002	0.003	0.001	0.001	0.001	-
Mali*	0.010	0.006	0.010	0.009	0.008	0.012	0.014	0.012	0.011	0.011	(e)0.011
Mauritania*	0.010	0.019	0.013	0.009	0.006	0.006	0.005	0.004	0.004	0.005	(e)0.006
Niger*	0.028	0.013	0.008	0.006	0.004	0.004	0.004	0.005	0.005	0.006	(e)0.005
Nigeria	1.276	0.665	0.393	0.237	0.329	0.286	0.287	0.319	0.340	0.405	(e)0.389
Senegal*	0.023	0.029	0.022	0.019	0.014	0.016	0.016	0.017	0.016	0.015	(e)0.014
Sierra Leone*	0.011	0.007	0.004	0.001	0.000	0.000	0.001	0.001	0.002	0.002	(e)0.002
Togo*	0.017	0.010	0.008	0.007	0.006	0.006	0.007	0.008	0.007	0.006	(e)0.005
Developing economies: America	**5.473**	**5.532**	**4.134**	**4.419**	**5.604**	**5.630**	**5.354**	**5.057**	**5.133**	**5.429**	**5.675**
Caribbean	*1.100*	*0.706*	*0.335*	*0.251*	*0.295*	*0.299*	*0.246*	*0.239*	*0.234*	*0.242*	*0.258*
Antigua and Barbuda*	0.001	0.001	0.001	0.001	0.001	0.001	0.001	0.001	0.000	(e)0.000	-
Aruba (6)	..	..	0.004	0.026	0.039	0.039	0.023	0.027	0.030	0.033	
Bahamas (7)	0.247	0.138	0.007	0.003	0.009	0.007	0.007	0.006	0.004	0.005	(e)0.004
Barbados	0.011	0.018	0.006	0.005	0.004	0.004	0.004	0.003	0.003	0.003	(e)0.003
Cuba*	0.274	0.304	0.141	0.031	0.026	0.027	0.022	0.022	0.025	(e)0.022	(e)0.023
Dominica*	0.000	0.001	0.002	0.001	0.001	0.001	0.001	0.001	0.000	0.000	0.000
Dominican Republic*	0.047	0.037	0.021	0.073	0.089	0.085	0.080	0.073	0.065	0.055	-
Grenada*	0.001	0.001	0.001	0.000	0.001	0.001	0.001	0.001	0.000	0.000	(e)0.000
Haiti	0.011	0.009	0.005	0.002	0.005	0.004	0.004	0.005	0.004	0.005	(e)0.004
Jamaica	0.047	0.029	0.033	0.028	0.020	0.020	0.017	0.016	0.015	0.014	(e)0.016
Montserrat*	0.000	0.000	0.000	0.000	0.000	0.000	0.000	0.000	0.000	0.000	(e)0.000
Netherlands Antilles*	(b)0.254	0.052	0.051	0.029	0.031	0.039	0.025	0.015	0.015	0.010	
Saint Kitts and Nevis*	0.001	0.001	0.001	0.000	0.001	0.001	0.001	0.001	0.001	0.001	-
Saint Lucia*	0.003	0.003	0.004	0.002	0.001	0.001	0.001	0.001	0.001	0.001	(e)0.001
Saint Vincent and the Grenadines*	0.001	0.003	0.002	0.001	0.001	0.001	0.001	0.001	0.000	0.000	(e)0.000
Trinidad and Tobago*	0.201	0.109	0.056	0.048	0.066	0.069	0.060	0.069	0.070	0.092	(e)0.120
Central America	*1.145*	*1.573*	*1.309*	*1.712*	*2.783*	*2.752*	*2.666*	*2.370*	*2.216*	*2.200*	*2.241*
Belize	0.005	0.006	0.004	0.003	0.003	0.003	0.002	0.003	0.002	0.002	(e)0.002
Costa Rica*	0.049	0.050	0.042	0.067	0.091	0.081	0.081	0.081	0.069	0.067	(e)0.068
El Salvador*	0.048	0.034	0.017	0.019	0.021	0.020	0.019	0.017	0.015	0.015	(e)0.016

For sources and notes, see end of table.

12

Imports (c.i.f.) - Importations (c.a.f.) Percentage - En pourcentage											Régions, pays ou territoires
1980	1985	1990	1995	2000	2001	2002	2003	2004	2005	2006	
0.005	0.005	0.005	0.004	0.005	0.007	0.006	0.005	0.005	0.005	(e)0.008	Seychelles
0.021	0.013	0.002	(e)0.005	(e)0.005	(e)0.007	(e)0.007	(e)0.006	(e)0.005	(e)0.006	-	Somalie
0.014	0.016	0.008	0.020	0.023	0.025	0.017	0.016	0.021	0.018	0.021	Ouganda
0.061	0.042	0.038	0.032	0.023	0.027	0.025	0.028	0.027	0.026	(e)0.031	République-Unie de Tanzanie*
0.052	0.036	0.034	0.013	0.015	0.020	0.019	0.020	0.021	0.024	(e)0.019	Zambie*
0.070	0.044	0.051	0.051	0.028	0.027	0.037	0.023	0.023	0.026	(e)0.023	Zimbabwe
0.284	*0.274*	*0.189*	*0.112*	*0.123*	*0.150*	*0.166*	*0.178*	*0.167*	*0.190*	*0.194*	*Afrique centrale*
0.064	0.069	0.044	0.028	0.046	0.050	0.057	0.071	0.062	0.078	(e)0.092	Angola*
0.077	0.057	0.039	0.021	0.022	0.029	0.028	0.028	0.025	0.027	(e)0.026	Cameroun*(5)
0.004	0.006	0.004	0.003	0.002	0.002	0.002	0.002	0.002	0.002	0.001	République centrafricaine*(5)
0.004	0.008	0.008	0.007	0.005	0.011	0.025	0.010	0.009	0.010	0.010	Tchad*
0.027	0.029	0.017	0.013	0.011	0.017	0.016	0.017	0.019	0.019	(e)0.015	Congo*(5)
0.073	0.061	0.048	0.020	0.016	0.013	0.016	0.021	0.021	0.021	-	Rép. dém. du Congo*
0.001	0.001	0.002	0.002	0.007	0.013	0.008	0.016	0.017	0.020	0.017	Guinée équatoriale
0.032	0.042	0.026	0.017	0.014	0.016	0.014	0.013	0.013	0.013	(e)0.013	Gabon*(5)
0.001	0.000	0.001	0.001	0.000	0.000	0.000	0.001	0.000	0.000	(e)0.001	Sao Tomé-et-Principe*
1.522	*1.595*	*1.252*	*0.934*	*0.737*	*0.782*	*0.803*	*0.755*	*0.771*	*0.808*	*0.774*	*Afrique septentrionale*
0.509	0.484	0.272	0.243	0.139	0.155	0.172	0.167	0.192	0.187	(p)0.172	Algérie*
0.234	0.546	0.467	0.225	0.211	0.199	0.189	0.144	0.136	0.185	(e)0.170	Égypte*
0.327	0.202	0.149	0.099	0.061	0.069	0.082	0.081	0.080	(e)0.073	(e)0.084	Jamahiriya arabe libyenne
0.205	0.189	0.193	0.192	0.174	0.173	0.179	0.184	0.189	0.190	(e)0.185	Maroc*
0.076	0.038	0.017	0.023	0.023	0.036	0.038	0.037	0.038	0.049	(e)0.040	Soudan*
0.170	0.136	0.154	0.151	0.129	0.149	0.143	0.141	0.136	0.123	0.122	Tunisie
0.950	*0.563*	*0.512*	*0.585*	*0.534*	*0.522*	*0.516*	*0.624*	*0.662*	*0.665*	*0.641*	*Afrique australe*
..	..	..	..	0.037	0.028	0.029	0.032	0.035	0.030	(e)0.024	Botswana*
..	..	..	..	0.011	0.010	0.013	0.014	0.015	0.012	0.012	Lesotho
..	..	..	..	0.023	0.024	0.020	0.026	0.026	0.022	(e)0.020	Namibie
(a)0.95	(a)0.563	0.512	0.585	0.447	0.442	0.441	0.531	0.566	0.582	0.567	Afrique du Sud
..	..	..	..	0.016	0.018	0.014	0.021	0.020	(e)0.019	(e)0.018	Swaziland
1.249	*0.749*	*0.396*	*0.381*	*0.322*	*0.373*	*0.377*	*0.391*	*0.352*	*0.352*	*0.386*	*Afrique occidentale*
0.016	0.016	0.007	0.014	0.009	0.010	0.011	0.012	0.009	0.008	0.007	Bénin*
0.017	0.016	0.015	0.009	0.009	0.010	0.011	0.012	0.013	0.012	0.011	Burkina Faso
0.003	0.004	0.004	0.005	0.003	0.004	0.004	0.005	0.004	0.004	0.005	Cap-Vert*
0.144	0.086	0.058	0.056	0.042	0.038	0.037	0.042	0.045	0.048	0.048	Côte d'Ivoire*
0.008	0.005	0.005	0.003	0.003	0.002	(e)0.002	0.002	0.002	0.002	(e)0.002	Gambie
0.054	0.043	0.033	0.037	0.045	0.046	0.041	0.042	0.045	0.050	(e)0.052	Ghana
0.013	0.018	0.019	0.016	0.009	0.009	0.010	0.008	0.007	0.008	-	Guinée
0.003	0.003	0.002	0.003	0.001	0.001	0.001	0.001	0.001	0.001	0.001	Guinée-Bissau
0.026	0.014	0.006	0.010	0.010	0.004	0.003	0.002	0.004	0.003	(e)0.003	Libéria*
0.021	0.015	0.017	0.015	0.012	0.015	0.014	0.016	0.014	0.015	(e)0.011	Mali*
0.014	0.011	0.006	0.008	0.007	0.007	0.005	0.005	0.006	0.007	-	Mauritanie*
0.029	0.018	0.011	0.007	0.006	0.006	0.007	0.008	0.008	0.007	0.006	Niger*
0.803	0.437	0.157	0.158	0.131	0.181	0.187	0.192	0.150	0.142	(e)0.185	Nigéria
0.051	0.041	0.034	0.027	0.023	0.027	0.031	0.031	0.030	0.033	0.030	Sénégal*
0.021	0.007	0.004	0.003	0.002	0.003	0.004	0.004	0.003	0.003	(e)0.003	Sierra Leone*
0.027	0.014	0.016	0.011	0.008	0.009	0.009	(e)0.010	(e)0.009	(e)0.009	(e)0.008	Togo*
5.960	**4.119**	**3.543**	**4.768**	**5.855**	**5.915**	**5.295**	**4.718**	**4.701**	**4.809**	**4.971**	**Économies en développement : Amérique**
1.319	*0.910*	*0.520*	*0.360*	*0.458*	*0.470*	*0.431*	*0.375*	*0.331*	*0.345*	*0.339*	*Caraïbes*
0.004	0.008	0.007	0.007	0.006	0.006	0.006	0.005	0.005	0.006	-	Antigua-et-Barbuda*
..	..	0.015	0.011	0.013	0.013	0.013	0.011	0.009	0.010	-	Aruba (6)
0.364	0.151	0.031	0.024	0.031	0.030	0.026	0.023	0.020	0.021	(e)0.023	Bahamas (7)
0.025	0.030	0.020	0.015	0.017	0.017	0.016	0.015	0.015	0.015	(e)0.012	Barbade
0.314	0.393	0.188	0.054	0.073	0.082	0.063	0.060	0.059	(e)0.071	(e)0.077	Cuba*
0.002	0.003	0.003	0.002	0.002	0.002	0.002	0.002	0.002	0.002	0.001	Dominique*
0.095	0.088	0.084	0.099	0.143	0.137	0.133	0.099	0.083	0.080	-	République dominicaine*
0.002	0.003	0.003	0.002	0.004	0.003	0.003	0.003	0.003	0.003	0.002	Grenade*
0.018	0.022	0.009	0.013	0.016	0.016	0.017	0.015	0.014	0.014	0.015	Haïti
0.056	0.055	0.054	0.054	0.050	0.053	0.053	0.047	0.040	0.042	(e)0.045	Jamaïque
0.001	0.001	0.001	0.001	0.000	0.000	0.000	0.000	0.000	0.000	(e)0.000	Montserrat*
(b)0.274	0.068	0.060	0.035	0.043	0.044	0.034	0.034	0.021	0.022	-	Antilles néerlandaises*
0.002	0.003	0.003	0.003	0.003	0.003	0.003	0.002	0.002	0.002	(e)0.002	Saint-Kitts-et-Nevis*
0.006	0.006	0.008	0.006	0.005	0.006	0.005	0.005	0.005	0.004	(e)0.004	Sainte-Lucie*
0.003	0.004	0.004	0.003	0.002	0.003	0.003	0.003	0.002	0.002	(e)0.002	Saint-Vincent-et-les Grenadines*
0.153	0.075	0.031	0.033	0.050	0.056	0.055	0.050	0.051	0.053	(e)0.053	Trinité-et-Tobago*
1.434	*1.266*	*1.442*	*1.752*	*3.111*	*3.133*	*3.046*	*2.664*	*2.517*	*2.406*	*2.443*	*Amérique centrale*
0.007	0.006	0.006	0.005	0.008	0.008	0.008	0.007	(e)0.005	0.006	(e)0.005	Belize
0.074	0.054	0.055	0.078	0.096	0.103	0.108	0.099	0.088	0.092	(e)0.096	Costa Rica*
0.047	0.047	0.035	0.055	0.057	0.060	0.059	0.057	0.052	0.050	(e)0.052	El Salvador*

Pour les sources et les notes, se reporter à la fin du tableau.

1.1.1   Exports and imports of countries
and geographical regions
Share

Region, country or territory	Exports (f.o.b.) - Exportations (f.a.b.) Percentage - En pourcentage										
	1980	1985	1990	1995	2000	2001	2002	2003	2004	2005	2006
Guatemala*	0.075	0.054	0.033	0.039	0.042	0.040	0.038	0.035	0.032	0.033	(e)0.031
Honduras*	0.041	0.040	0.024	0.024	0.021	0.021	0.020	0.018	0.017	0.016	(p)0.016
Mexico	0.887	1.358	1.170	1.539	2.582	2.563	2.482	2.197	2.063	2.049	(p)2.089
Nicaragua	0.022	0.015	0.010	0.009	0.010	0.010	0.009	0.008	0.008	0.008	(p)0.009
Panama, excl.Canal-Zone (former)	0.018										
Panama*	–	0.017	0.010	0.012	0.013	0.015	0.013	0.011	0.010	0.010	(e)0.011
South America	**3.228**	**3.252**	**2.490**	**2.456**	**2.526**	**2.578**	**2.443**	**2.448**	**2.683**	**2.987**	**3.175**
Argentina*	0.395	0.426	0.355	0.406	0.409	0.429	0.396	0.393	0.377	0.384	(e)0.385
Bolivia	0.046	0.032	0.027	0.021	0.019	0.021	0.020	0.021	0.023	0.026	(p)0.035
Brazil	0.991	1.301	0.903	0.900	0.855	0.941	0.933	0.971	1.052	1.133	1.147
Chile*	0.232	0.193	0.241	0.310	0.298	0.295	0.281	0.288	0.351	0.389	0.492
Colombia	0.193	0.180	0.193	0.196	0.202	0.199	0.184	0.174	0.177	0.203	(p)0.204
Ecuador*	0.122	0.147	0.078	0.083	0.076	0.076	0.078	0.083	0.085	0.097	(e)0.103
Guyana*	0.019	0.010	0.007	0.009	0.008	0.008	0.008	0.007	0.006	0.005	(e)0.005
Paraguay	0.015	0.015	0.028	0.018	0.013	0.016	0.015	0.016	0.018	0.016	0.016
Peru*	0.192	0.151	0.093	0.106	0.108	0.114	0.119	0.121	0.138	0.159	(p)0.196
Suriname	0.025	0.017	0.014	0.009	0.008	0.003	0.002	0.002	0.009	0.012	-
Uruguay	0.052	0.046	0.049	0.041	0.036	0.033	0.029	0.029	0.032	0.033	(p)0.038
Venezuela (Bolivarian Republic of)	0.946	0.733	0.503	0.357	0.494	0.443	0.378	0.343	0.415	0.531	(p)0.544
Developing economies: Asia	**17.962**	**15.554**	**16.940**	**20.992**	**23.778**	**23.081**	**24.040**	**24.539**	**26.003**	**27.582**	**28.286**
Eastern Asia	**3.748**	**6.096**	**8.066**	**10.885**	**12.025**	**11.845**	**12.707**	**13.338**	**14.022**	**14.735**	**15.420**
China	0.891	1.388	1.785	2.879	3.867	4.302	5.030	5.822	6.472	7.298	(p)8.087
China, Hong Kong SAR	0.972	1.532	2.362	3.362	3.132	3.070	3.091	2.973	2.828	2.771	2.693
China, Macao SAR	0.030	0.046	0.049	0.039	0.040	0.037	0.036	0.034	0.031	0.024	(e)0.025
China, Taiwan Province of	0.974	1.558	1.928	2.159	2.293	1.981	2.016	1.912	1.897	1.894	(p)1.869
Korea, Dem. People's Rep. of	..	..	0.053	0.019	0.011	0.013	0.016	0.014	0.015	(e)0.014	-
Korea, Republic of (8)	0.862	1.537	1.869	2.420	2.673	2.432	2.510	2.575	2.769	2.724	(p)2.722
Mongolia	0.020	0.035	0.019	0.009	0.008	0.008	0.008	0.008	0.009	0.010	(p)0.013
Southern Asia	**1.286**	**1.480**	**1.352**	**1.262**	**1.439**	**1.430**	**1.548**	**1.570**	**1.634**	**1.844**	**1.857**
Afghanistan	0.033	0.029	0.007	0.003	0.002	0.001	0.002	0.002	0.003	0.003	-
Bangladesh	0.037	0.051	0.048	0.072	0.099	0.098	0.094	0.094	0.089	0.089	(e)0.102
Bhutan	0.001	0.001	0.002	0.002	0.002	0.002	0.002	0.002	0.002	0.003	-
India	0.422	0.464	0.517	0.593	0.658	0.701	0.778	0.783	0.836	0.953	(e)1.009
Iran, Islamic Republic of*	0.607	0.719	0.555	0.355	0.440	0.386	0.435	0.452	0.484	0.572	(p)0.538
Maldives	0.000	0.001	0.002	0.002	0.002	0.002	0.002	0.002	0.002	0.002	(p)0.002
Nepal	0.004	0.008	0.006	0.007	0.012	0.012	0.009	0.009	0.008	0.008	(e)0.007
Pakistan	0.129	0.139	0.161	0.155	0.140	0.149	0.153	0.158	0.146	0.154	0.137
Sri Lanka	0.052	0.068	0.055	0.073	0.084	0.078	0.073	0.068	0.063	0.061	(e)0.056
South-Eastern Asia	**3.639**	**3.677**	**4.144**	**6.219**	**6.660**	**6.269**	**6.280**	**6.009**	**6.195**	**6.238**	**6.335**
Brunei Darussalam*	0.225	0.149	0.064	0.046	(e)0.061	(e)0.059	(e)0.057	(e)0.059	(e)0.055	(e)0.060	-
Cambodia	0.001	0.001	0.002	0.017	0.030	0.040	0.027	0.028	0.028	0.028	(e)0.028
Indonesia	1.179	0.943	0.738	0.879	0.964	0.913	0.898	0.832	0.781	0.820	(e)0.859
Lao People's Dem. Rep.*	0.001	0.003	0.002	0.006	0.005	0.005	0.005	0.005	0.004	0.005	(e)0.005
Malaysia (9)(10)	0.637	0.777	0.847	1.430	1.524	1.423	1.441	1.320	1.372	1.349	(p)1.339
Myanmar	0.023	0.016	0.009	0.017	0.026	0.038	0.047	0.033	0.026	0.037	(e)0.031
Philippines	0.283	0.234	0.233	0.339	0.617	0.528	0.564	0.481	0.433	0.382	(e)0.396
Singapore (11)	0.953	1.158	1.516	2.288	2.138	1.969	1.934	1.916	2.167	2.200	(p)2.258
Thailand*	0.320	0.361	0.663	1.092	1.070	1.050	1.052	1.067	1.050	1.055	(p)1.070
Viet Nam	0.017	0.035	0.069	0.105	0.224	0.244	0.255	0.268	0.280	0.303	0.295
Western Asia	**9.289**	**4.302**	**3.379**	**2.626**	**3.654**	**3.538**	**3.505**	**3.622**	**4.153**	**4.765**	**4.673**
Bahrain	0.177	0.147	0.108	0.080	0.096	0.090	0.090	0.088	0.082	0.096	(e)0.100
Iraq*	1.297	0.528	0.297	0.010	0.320	0.257	0.203	0.129	0.202	0.230	(e)0.267
Jordan	0.028	0.040	0.031	0.034	0.029	0.037	0.043	0.041	0.043	0.041	0.043
Kuwait*	0.976	0.538	0.202	0.247	0.302	0.262	0.237	0.270	0.312	0.433	(e)0.486
Lebanon	0.047	0.015	0.014	0.013	0.011	0.014	0.016	0.020	0.019	0.018	(e)0.019
Oman	0.117	0.200	0.158	0.117	0.176	0.179	0.173	0.155	0.146	0.179	(e)0.184
Qatar*	0.280	0.174	0.101	0.067	0.177	0.164	0.166	0.178	0.204	0.247	-
Saudi Arabia*	4.999	1.394	1.277	0.968	1.202	1.099	1.120	1.239	1.374	1.594	
Syrian Arab Republic*	0.104	0.083	0.121	0.069	0.072	0.085	0.101	0.076	0.059	(e)0.063	(e)0.060
Turkey*	0.143	0.404	0.373	0.419	0.431	0.507	0.534	0.619	0.673	0.689	(e)0.690
United Arab Emirates	1.081	0.749	0.677	0.564	0.774	0.789	0.766	0.755	0.989	1.114	(e)1.146
Yemen Arab Republic (former)	0.001	0.030									
Yemen, Democratic (former)	0.038	..									
Yemen*	–	–	0.020	0.038	0.063	0.054	0.056	0.052	0.051	0.061	(e)0.075
Developing economies: Oceania	**0.115**	**0.098**	**0.081**	**0.088**	**0.063**	**0.056**	**0.052**	**0.060**	**0.055**	**0.057**	**0.056**
American Samoa*	0.006	0.010	0.009	0.005	0.005	0.005	0.006	0.006	0.005	0.004	(p)0.004
Cook Islands	0.000	0.000	0.000	0.000	0.000	0.000	0.000	0.000	0.000	0.000	-
Fiji	0.023	0.016	0.014	0.012	0.008	0.009	0.008	0.009	0.008	0.007	(p)0.006

For sources and notes, see end of table.

1.1.1   Exportations et importations des pays
et des regions géographiques
Part
1

1980	1985	1990	1995	2000	2001	2002	2003	2004	2005	2006	Régions, pays ou territoires
Imports (c.i.f.) - Importations (c.a.f.) Percentage - En pourcentage												
0.077	0.058	0.046	0.063	0.078	0.088	0.095	0.087	0.083	0.082	(e)0.083	Guatemala*
0.049	0.044	0.026	0.031	0.043	0.046	0.045	0.042	0.041	0.043	(p)0.044	Honduras*
1.068	0.941	1.213	1.453	2.751	2.754	2.660	2.307	2.187	2.071	(p)2.099	Mexique
0.043	0.047	0.018	0.019	0.027	0.028	0.026	0.024	0.023	0.024	(p)0.024	Nicaragua
0.070											Panama, sans la zone du canal (anc.)
–	0.068	0.043	0.048	0.051	0.046	0.045	0.040	0.038	0.039	(e)0.038	Panama*
3.206	*1.943*	*1.581*	*2.656*	*2.286*	*2.312*	*1.818*	*1.679*	*1.853*	*2.058*	*2.189*	*Amérique du Sud*
0.509	0.188	0.114	0.385	0.381	0.318	0.135	0.179	0.238	0.268	(e)0.281	Argentine*
0.032	0.034	0.019	0.027	0.028	0.027	0.027	0.021	0.020	0.022	0.023	Bolivie
1.204	0.705	0.627	1.037	0.889	0.917	0.749	0.657	0.703	0.725	0.749	Brésil
0.280	0.151	0.216	0.305	0.279	0.272	0.257	0.251	0.264	0.305	(e)0.312	Chili*
0.229	0.204	0.156	0.265	0.174	0.201	0.191	0.180	0.177	0.198	(p)0.214	Colombie
0.109	0.087	0.052	0.080	0.056	0.084	0.097	0.087	0.087	0.096	(e)0.099	Équateur*
0.019	0.011	0.009	0.010	0.010	0.009	0.009	0.007	0.007	0.007	(e)0.007	Guyana*
0.030	0.025	0.038	0.060	0.033	0.034	0.025	0.032	0.033	0.035	0.048	Paraguay
0.121	0.090	0.097	0.178	0.134	0.114	0.113	0.109	0.107	0.117	0.126	Pérou*
0.024	0.015	0.013	0.011	0.008	0.007	0.007	0.009	0.008	(e)0.009	–	Suriname
0.081	0.035	0.037	0.055	0.052	0.048	0.030	0.028	0.033	0.036	(p)0.039	Uruguay
0.570	0.399	0.204	0.242	0.244	0.282	0.178	0.120	0.177	0.240	(p)0.282	Venezuela (République bolivarienne du)
13.117	**15.149**	**15.902**	**21.409**	**20.764**	**20.308**	**21.256**	**21.834**	**23.449**	**24.161**	**24.755**	**Économies en développement : Asie**
4.125	*6.155*	*7.406*	*10.870*	*11.184*	*10.910*	*11.638*	*12.364*	*13.041*	*13.175*	*13.511*	*Asie orientale*
0.962	2.079	1.486	2.530	3.389	3.807	4.445	5.336	5.941	6.161	(p)6.487	Chine
1.082	1.462	2.298	3.692	3.204	3.143	3.127	2.998	2.870	2.796	2.751	Chine, Hong Kong RAS
0.026	0.038	0.043	0.039	0.034	0.037	0.038	0.036	0.037	0.037	(e)0.039	Chine, Macao RAS
0.953	0.990	1.527	1.986	2.107	1.677	1.698	1.646	1.779	1.704	(p)1.661	Chine, Taiwan Province de
..	..	0.082	0.026	0.025	0.029	0.029	0.026	0.027	(e)0.027	–	Corée, Rép. populaire dém. de
1.075	1.532	1.945	2.588	2.416	2.206	2.291	2.312	2.376	2.439	(e)2.537	Corée, République de (8)
0.026	0.054	0.026	0.008	0.009	0.010	0.010	0.010	0.011	0.011	(p)0.012	Mongolie
1.907	*1.968*	*1.599*	*1.393*	*1.439*	*1.514*	*1.657*	*1.751*	*1.891*	*2.172*	*2.226*	*Asie méridionale*
0.041	0.059	0.026	0.007	0.018	0.027	0.037	0.027	0.023	0.024	–	Afghanistan
0.125	0.125	0.101	0.125	0.126	0.131	0.119	0.123	0.133	0.130	(e)0.131	Bangladesh
0.002	0.004	0.002	0.002	0.003	0.003	0.003	0.003	0.004	(e)0.005	–	Bhoutan
0.717	0.784	0.657	0.665	0.776	0.788	0.851	0.938	1.056	1.301	(e)1.392	Inde
0.647	0.591	0.511	0.245	0.229	0.284	0.358	0.376	0.373	0.369	(p)0.332	Iran, Rép. islamique d'*
0.001	0.003	0.004	0.005	0.006	0.006	0.006	0.006	0.007	0.007	(p)0.008	Maldives
0.017	0.022	0.019	0.026	0.024	0.023	0.021	0.023	0.020	0.017	(e)0.021	Népal
0.258	0.290	0.205	0.220	0.164	0.159	0.169	0.169	0.190	0.237	0.233	Pakistan
0.098	0.091	0.075	0.099	0.095	0.093	0.092	0.086	0.084	0.082	(e)0.085	Sri Lanka
3.165	*3.275*	*4.520*	*6.807*	*5.579*	*5.322*	*5.348*	*5.155*	*5.388*	*5.542*	*5.473*	*Asie du Sud-Est*
0.028	0.030	0.028	0.040	(e)0.017	(e)0.018	(e)0.023	(e)0.017	(e)0.015	(e)0.014	–	Brunéi Darussalam*
0.009	0.006	0.005	0.023	0.029	0.033	0.036	0.034	0.035	0.037	(e)0.037	Cambodge
0.522	0.505	0.608	0.778	0.505	0.485	0.471	0.544	0.581	0.649	(e)0.625	Indonésie
0.004	0.009	0.005	0.011	0.008	0.008	0.006	0.007	0.005	0.008	(e)0.008	Rép. dém. populaire lao*
0.520	0.603	0.815	1.488	1.234	1.155	1.203	1.059	1.115	1.068	(p)1.073	Malaisie (9)(10)
0.017	0.014	0.008	0.026	0.036	0.045	0.035	0.027	0.023	0.018	(e)0.016	Myanmar
0.400	0.268	0.362	0.543	0.557	0.546	0.560	0.511	0.448	0.438	(e)0.433	Philippines
1.158	1.293	1.693	2.385	2.026	1.813	1.753	1.654	1.838	1.867	(p)1.947	Singapour (11)
0.444	0.455	0.920	1.356	0.932	0.969	0.973	0.980	0.999	1.103	(p)1.032	Thaïlande*
0.063	0.091	0.077	0.156	0.235	0.250	0.286	0.321	0.329	0.347	(e)0.290	Viet Nam
3.920	*3.751*	*2.376*	*2.339*	*2.562*	*2.563*	*2.614*	*2.564*	*3.130*	*3.272*	*3.545*	*Asie occidentale*
0.168	0.153	0.103	0.071	0.070	0.067	0.075	0.073	0.070	0.070	(e)0.073	Bahreïn
0.420	0.519	0.182	0.013	0.202	0.206	0.143	0.102	0.210	0.220	(e)0.199	Iraq*
0.116	0.134	0.072	0.071	0.069	0.076	0.076	0.074	0.086	0.098	0.094	Jordanie
0.315	0.295	0.111	0.149	0.108	0.123	0.136	0.142	0.134	0.164	(e)0.125	Koweït*
0.176	0.108	0.070	0.139	0.094	0.114	0.097	0.093	0.100	0.087	(e)0.075	Liban
0.084	0.155	0.075	0.081	0.076	0.091	0.090	0.085	0.094	0.082	(e)0.087	Oman
0.070	0.056	0.047	0.065	0.049	0.059	0.061	0.063	0.064	0.094	(e)0.103	Qatar*
1.455	1.162	0.671	0.538	0.455	0.487	0.486	0.439	0.474	0.555	(e)0.520	Arabie saoudite*
0.199	0.195	0.067	0.090	0.057	0.071	0.068	0.066	0.075	(e)0.076	(e)0.072	République arabe syrienne*
0.381	0.558	0.621	0.684	0.821	0.647	0.748	0.848	1.020	0.924	(e)1.126	Turquie*
0.416	0.322	0.312	0.402	0.527	0.583	0.589	0.531	0.763	0.856	1.033	Emirats arabes unis
0.047	0.092										Rép. arabe du Yémen (anc.)
0.074	..	–	–	–	–	–	–	–	–	–	Yémen dém. (anc.)
–	–	0.044	0.035	0.035	0.039	0.044	0.048	0.042	0.045	(e)0.037	Yémen*
0.171	**0.159**	**0.138**	**0.109**	**0.081**	**0.084**	**0.087**	**0.094**	**0.085**	**0.082**	**0.077**	**Économies en développement : Océanie**
0.005	0.015	0.010	0.008	0.008	0.008	0.008	0.008	0.006	0.005	(p)0.003	Samoa américaines*
0.001	0.001	0.001	0.001	0.001	0.001	0.001	0.001	0.001	0.001		Îles Cook
0.027	0.022	0.021	0.017	0.013	0.014	0.014	0.016	0.015	0.015	(p)0.015	Fidji

Pour les sources et les notes, se reporter à la fin du tableau.

Region, country or territory	Exports (f.o.b.) - Exportations (f.a.b.) Percentage - En pourcentage										
	1980	1985	1990	1995	2000	2001	2002	2003	2004	2005	2006
French Polynesia*	0.001	0.002	0.003	0.004	0.004	0.003	0.003	0.002	0.002	0.002	(p)0.002
Guam	0.003	0.001	0.002	0.002	0.001	0.001	0.001	0.001	0.001	(e)0.000	-
Kiribati	0.000	0.000	0.000	0.000	0.000	0.000	0.000	0.000	(e)0.000	0.000	(e)0.000
Nauru	0.003	0.003	0.002	0.001	0.000	0.000	0.000	0.000	(e)0.000	(e)0.000	-
New Caledonia*	0.020	0.014	0.014	0.009	0.009	0.007	0.008	0.010	0.011	0.011	(e)0.008
Papua New Guinea	0.051	0.046	0.033	0.051	0.033	0.029	0.025	0.029	0.028	0.031	(e)0.034
Samoa*	0.001	0.001	0.000	0.000	0.000	0.000	0.000	0.000	0.000	0.000	(p)0.001
Solomon Islands*	0.004	0.004	0.002	0.003	0.001	0.001	0.001	0.001	0.001	0.001	(e)0.001
Tonga	0.000	0.000	0.000	0.000	0.000	0.000	0.000	0.000	0.000	0.000	(e)0.000
Tuvalu	..	0.000	0.000	0.000	0.000	0.000	0.000	0.000	0.000	0.000	-
Vanuatu	0.002	0.002	0.001	0.001	0.000	0.000	0.000	0.000	0.000	0.000	-
Economies in transition: Asia	–	–	–	**0.248**	**0.276**	**0.293**	**0.296**	**0.330**	**0.380**	**0.435**	**0.492**
Armenia*	–	–	–	0.005	0.005	0.006	0.008	0.009	0.008	0.009	0.008
Azerbaijan*	–	–	–	0.012	0.027	0.037	0.033	0.034	0.039	0.042	0.053
Georgia (4)	–	–	–	0.003	0.005	0.005	0.005	0.006	0.007	0.008	(p)0.008
Kazakhstan*(4)	–	–	–	0.102	0.137	0.140	0.149	0.172	0.219	0.267	(p)0.319
Kyrgyzstan	–	–	–	0.008	0.008	0.008	0.008	0.008	0.008	0.006	(p)0.007
Tajikistan (4)	–	–	–	0.014	0.012	0.011	0.010	0.011	0.010	0.009	(p)0.012
Turkmenistan (4)	–	–	–	0.038	0.039	0.044	0.044	0.048	0.042	0.047	(e)0.044
Uzbekistan (4)	–	–	–	0.066	0.044	0.044	0.039	0.042	0.047	0.046	-
Economies in transition: Europe	**5.266**	**6.267**	**3.717**	**2.367**	**2.357**	**2.475**	**2.520**	**2.750**	**3.059**	**3.381**	**3.588**
Albania	..	..	0.006	0.004	0.004	0.005	0.005	0.006	0.007	0.006	0.007
Belarus	–	–	–	0.093	0.114	0.120	0.124	0.132	0.150	0.153	0.165
Bosnia and Herzegovina*(12)	–	–	–	0.000	0.017	0.018	0.017	0.020	0.023	0.025	(e)0.028
Bulgaria*	0.510	0.677	0.139	0.104	0.075	0.083	0.089	0.100	0.108	0.112	(p)0.125
Croatia*	–	–	–	0.087	0.069	0.075	0.076	0.082	0.088	0.084	0.087
Moldova, Republic of	–	–	–	0.014	0.007	0.009	0.010	0.010	0.011	0.010	(p)0.009
Macedonia, TFYR*	–	–	–	0.023	0.021	0.019	0.017	0.018	0.018	0.020	0.020
Romania*	0.552	0.617	0.166	0.153	0.161	0.184	0.214	0.234	0.256	0.266	0.270
Russian Federation (4)	–	–	–	1.604	1.638	1.668	1.655	1.806	1.999	2.333	(p)2.520
Serbia and Montenegro*	–	–	–	0.030	0.027	0.031	0.035	0.035	0.043	0.044	-
Yugoslavia, SFR (former)	0.442	0.543	0.411	–	–	–	–	–	–	–	–
USSR (former)	3.762	4.430	2.995	–	–	–	–	–	–	–	–
Ukraine (4)	–	–	–	0.254	0.226	0.263	0.277	0.306	0.356	0.328	0.320

Sources:
- UN, *Yearbook of International Trade Statistics*
- UN, *Monthly Bulletin of Statistics*
- UN, Economic Commission for Europe
- IMF, *International Financial Statistics*
- IMF, *Direction of Trade Statistics*
- World Trade Organization
- Eastern Caribbean Central Bank
- National sources
- UNCTAD secretariat estimates

Notes:
- Countries which use the Special Trade System as reporting system are marked with an asterisk (*).
(a) Data refers to South Africa Customs Union (Botswana, Lesotho, Namibia, South Africa and Swaziland).
(b) Including Aruba.
(1) Excluding military imports.
(2) From 1985 onwards, data are not comparable to those shown for prior periods due to revisions of the koruna-to-US dollar exchange rate.
(3) Prior to 1985, general trade.
(4) Prior to 1994, covers only trade with countries outside the CIS.
(5) Inter-trade between the member countries of CEMAC is excluded.
(6) Prior to 2000, data exclude imports into and exports from the free zone; mineral fuels are also excluded.
(7) From 1990 onwards, trade statistics exclude certain oil and chemical products.
(8) Excluding imports of goods financed through foreign aid.
(9) Inter-trade between the States of Malaysia included.
(10) Excluding military imports and offshore installations of petroleum industry.
(11) Including trans-shipments to and from peninsular Malaysia.
(12) Prior to 1998, data refer to the Federation of Bosnia and Herzegovina only. The other entity of Bosnia and Herzegovina, Republika Srpska, is not included.

1980	1985	1990	1995	2000	2001	2002	2003	2004	2005	2006	Régions, pays ou territoires
				Imports (c.i.f.) - Importations (c.a f.) Percentage - En pourcentage							
0.026	0.027	0.026	0.019	0.016	0.017	0.019	0.020	0.016	0.016	(p)0.014	Polynésie française*
0.019	0.014	0.013	0.008	0.006	0.007	(e)0.005	(e)0.005	(e)0.006	(e)0.006	-	Guam
0.001	0.001	0.001	0.001	0.001	0.001	0.001	0.001	(e)0.001	0.001	(p)0.001	Kiribati
0.001	0.001	0.001	0.001	0.000	0.000	0.000	0.000	(e)0.000	(e)0.000	-	Nauru
0.022	0.017	0.025	0.018	0.014	0.015	0.015	0.020	0.017	0.017	(e)0.016	Nouvelle-Calédonie*
0.057	0.050	0.031	0.028	0.017	0.017	0.019	0.018	0.018	0.016	(e)0.016	Papouasie-Nouvelle-Guinée
0.003	0.003	0.002	0.002	0.001	0.002	0.002	0.002	0.002	0.002	(p)0.002	Samoa*
0.004	0.004	0.003	0.003	0.001	0.001	0.001	0.001	0.001	0.002	(e)0.002	Îles Salomon*
0.002	0.002	0.002	0.001	0.001	0.001	0.001	0.001	0.001	0.001	(e)0.001	Tonga
..	0.000	0.000	0.000	0.000	0.000	0.000	0.000	0.000	0.000	-	Tuvalu
0.004	0.003	0.003	0.002	0.001	0.001	0.001	0.001	0.001	0.001	(e)0.001	Vanuatu
–	–	–	0.202	0.203	0.246	0.239	0.261	0.300	0.330	0.373	**Économies en transition : Asie**
–	–	–	0.013	0.013	0.014	0.015	0.017	0.014	0.017	0.018	Arménie*
–	–	–	0.013	0.018	0.022	0.025	0.034	0.037	0.039	0.043	Azerbaïdjan*
–	–	–	0.008	0.011	0.012	0.012	0.015	0.020	0.023	(p)0.030	Géorgie (4)
–	–	–	0.073	0.076	0.101	0.099	0.109	0.135	0.162	(p)0.194	Kazakhstan*(4)
–	–	–	0.010	0.008	0.007	0.009	0.009	0.010	0.010	(p)0.014	Kirghizistan
–	–	–	0.016	0.010	0.011	0.011	0.011	0.013	0.012	(p)0.014	Tadjikistan (4)
–	–	–	0.015	0.027	0.035	0.032	0.032	0.035	0.032	0.029	Turkménistan (4)
–	–	–	0.056	0.041	0.044	0.037	0.034	0.036	(e)0.035	-	Ouzbékistan (4)
5.164	5.918	4.303	2.149	1.603	1.917	2.091	2.313	2.445	2.633	2.693	**Économies en transition : Europe**
..	..	0.012	0.014	0.016	0.021	0.023	0.024	0.024	0.024	0.025	Albanie
			0.107	0.130	0.130	0.137	0.149	0.175	0.156	0.183	Bélarus
–	–	–	0.018	0.059	0.064	0.067	0.073	0.070	0.071	0.062	Bosnie-Herzégovine*(12)
0.465	0.672	0.131	0.108	0.098	0.114	0.120	0.141	0.153	0.170	(p)0.188	Bulgarie*
			0.141	0.119	0.143	0.161	0.184	0.176	0.173	0.176	Croatie*
–	–	–	0.016	0.012	0.014	0.016	0.018	0.019	0.021	(p)0.022	Moldova, République de
–	–	–	0.033	0.032	0.026	0.030	0.030	0.031	0.030	0.031	Macédoine, LERY*
0.668	0.554	0.274	0.197	0.197	0.243	0.269	0.310	0.346	0.378	0.419	Roumanie*
–	–	–	1.167	0.675	0.840	0.918	0.983	1.031	1.170	1.127	Fédération de Russie (4)
–	–	–	0.051	0.056	0.076	0.095	0.103	0.114	0.103	-	Serbie-et-Monténégro*
0.727	0.601	0.526	–	–	–	–	–	–	–	–	Yougoslavie, RSF (anc.)
3.304	4.091	3.361	–	–	–	–	–	–	–	–	URSS (anc.)
–	–	–	0.297	0.210	0.247	0.256	0.298	0.307	0.337	0.369	Ukraine (4)

Sources :
- ONU, *Annuaire statistique du commerce international*
- ONU, *Bulletin mensuel de statistique*
- ONU, Commission économique pour l'Europe
- FMI, *International Financial Statistics*
- FMI, *Direction of Trade Statistics*
- Organisation mondiale du commerce
- Banque centrale des Caraïbes orientales
- Sources nationales
- Estimations du secrétariat de la CNUCED

Notes :
- Les pays qui utilisent le système du commerce spécial en tant que systeme d'enregistrement sont marqués par un astérisque (*).
(a) Donnée relative à l'Union Douanière d'Afrique du Sud (Afrique du Sud, Botswana, Lesotho, Namibie et Swaziland).
(b) Y compris Aruba.
(1) Non compris les importations militaires.
(2) A partir de 1985, les chiffres ne sont pas comparables à ceux des années antérieures à cause des révisions du taux de change de la couronne par rapport au dollar des États-Unis.
(3) Avant 1985, commerce général.
(4) Avant 1994, concerne seulement le commerce avec les pays extérieurs à la CEI.
(5) Non-compris le commerce entre les pays membres de CEMAC.
(6) Avant 2000, les données excluent les importations en provenance et les exportations à destination de la zone de libre circulation; les combustibles minéraux sont également exclus.
(7) A partir de 1990, certains produits pétroliers et chimiques ne sont plus inclus dans les statistiques du commerce.
(8) Non-compris les biens d'importation financés par l'aide à l'étranger.
(9) Y compris le commerce entre les États de la Malaisie.
(10) Non-compris les importations militaires et l'installation près des côtes de l'industrie pétrolière.
(11) Y compris les transbordements vers et en provenance de la Malaisie péninsulaire
(12) Avant 1998, les données se réfèrent uniquement à la Fédération de la Bosnie-Herzégovine. L'autre entité de la Bosnie-Herzégovine, Republika Srpska, n'est pas incluse.

Economic grouping	Exports (f.o.b.) - Exportations (f.a.b.) Millions of dollars							
	1980	1990	2000	2002	2003	2004	2005	2006
DEVELOPING ECONOMIES	**597 559**	**842 883**	**2 044 590**	**2 052 444**	**2 410 557**	**3 090 696**	**3 750 526**	**4 408 951**
Developing economies excluding China	579 446	780 735	1 795 345	1 726 819	1 972 297	2 497 343	2 988 544	3 439 820
Developing economies excluding LDCs	582 281	823 180	2 007 931	2 012 548	2 364 888	3 029 847	3 667 767	4 309 682
High-income countries	325 833	458 645	1 112 630	1 042 129	1 186 230	1 510 314	1 793 693	2 059 630
Middle-income countries	131 420	202 273	413 028	417 847	490 323	620 428	741 991	841 746
Low-income countries	140 306	181 965	518 933	592 467	734 005	959 954	1 214 842	1 507 576
Heavily indebted poor countries	19 722	21 587	26 565	29 316	34 851	44 800	51 465	60 891
Landlocked countries	7 463	8 318	32 497	34 568	43 072	58 847	73 210	90 877
Small island developing states	12 627	7 081	11 658	10 433	12 709	14 608	19 086	25 174
Least developed countries	*15 262*	*19 620*	*36 612*	*39 856*	*45 631*	*60 816*	*82 719*	*99 227*
Africa and Haiti	12 243	16 048	20 908	23 994	28 421	41 040	57 951	68 270
Asia	2 848	3 365	15 460	15 601	16 893	19 410	24 414	30 443
Islands	170	208	245	261	317	366	355	514
Major petroleum exporters	*320 338*	*220 130*	*406 006*	*370 486*	*432 066*	*584 675*	*789 194*	*898 025*
Africa	66 700	48 672	68 525	62 025	77 460	104 568	152 047	173 739
America	28 460	21 247	38 062	29 974	32 138	45 735	66 154	80 654
Asia	225 178	150 211	299 419	278 488	322 467	434 372	570 993	643 632
Major exporters of manufactured goods	*169 375*	*492 766*	*1 407 492*	*1 447 639*	*1 703 830*	*2 164 540*	*2 557 666*	*3 040 004*
America	38 163	72 125	221 453	221 044	238 480	285 559	332 199	387 762
Asia	131 212	420 642	1 186 040	1 226 596	1 465 350	1 878 981	2 225 467	2 652 242
Emerging economies	*130 912*	*333 426*	*898 998*	*852 064*	*960 392*	*1 213 350*	*1 392 362*	*1 625 810*
America	54 788	96 081	273 959	272 587	298 801	364 967	429 467	516 370
Asia	76 124	237 346	625 039	579 477	661 592	848 383	962 895	1 109 439
Newly industrialized economies	*125 567*	*353 297*	*928 806*	*874 191*	*984 214*	*1 218 908*	*1 377 771*	*1 582 572*
First tier	76 425	266 985	659 708	618 196	705 661	885 651	1 001 184	1 143 398
Second tier	49 141	86 312	269 098	255 995	278 553	333 257	376 587	439 174
Developing economies: Africa	**118 993**	**106 993**	**147 173**	**146 432**	**178 378**	**231 332**	**298 026**	**332 801**
Northern Africa excluding Sudan	43 500	40 681	52 306	49 852	61 566	79 676	107 137	119 864
Sub-Saharan Africa	75 494	66 312	94 867	96 580	116 813	151 655	190 889	212 937
Sub-Saharan Africa excluding South Africa	49 954	42 744	64 884	66 856	80 331	105 510	139 264	159 767
Developing economies: America	**111 224**	**143 801**	**361 101**	**346 571**	**380 642**	**470 518**	**566 842**	**679 988**
Central America and Greater Carribean Islands excluding Puerto Rico	30 998	52 501	188 378	180 524	187 041	213 197	239 726	279 461
Central America and Greater Carribean Islands excluding Mexico and Puerto Rico	12 967	11 790	22 011	19 842	21 645	24 113	25 835	29 169
South America and Central America	88 868	132 140	342 117	330 646	362 621	449 086	541 574	649 041
South America excluding Brazil	45 466	55 188	107 679	97 741	111 169	149 464	193 537	243 030
Developing economies: Asia	**365 007**	**589 285**	**1 532 260**	**1 556 043**	**1 847 027**	**2 383 760**	**2 879 746**	**3 389 475**
Eastern and South-Eastern Asia excluding China	132 023	362 626	954 886	903 410	1 018 022	1 259 982	1 427 838	1 637 785
Southern Asia excluding India	17 542	29 064	50 356	49 813	59 208	73 124	93 021	101 683

Sources:
- UN, *Yearbook of International Trade Statistics*
- UN, *Monthly Bulletin of Statistics*
- UN, Economic Commission for Europe
- IMF, *International Financial Statistics*
- IMF, *Direction of Trade Statistics*
- World Trade Organization
- Eastern Caribbean Central Bank
- National sources
- UNCTAD secretariat estimates

Imports (c.i.f.) - Importations (c.a.f.) Millions de dollars								Groupements économiques
1980	1990	2000	2002	2003	2004	2005	2006	
492 931	**800 081**	**1 904 395**	**1 911 101**	**2 232 262**	**2 877 627**	**3 359 059**	**3 915 401**	**ÉCONOMIES EN DÉVELOPPEMENT**
472 943	746 686	1 679 209	1 615 806	1 819 370	2 316 243	2 698 929	3 123 602	Économies en développement sans la Chine
469 038	775 101	1 860 369	1 860 905	2 173 347	2 806 174	3 274 504	3 821 782	Économies en développement sans les PMA
222 876	398 957	1 007 583	931 159	1 026 062	1 300 892	1 493 528	1 737 297	Pays à revenu élevé
144 621	223 828	430 440	429 952	490 149	627 650	721 587	834 284	Pays à revenu intermédiaire
125 435	177 296	466 373	549 990	716 051	949 085	1 143 944	1 343 820	Pays à revenu faible
24 549	23 477	37 223	40 788	46 680	57 838	68 857	76 252	Pays pauvres très endettés
9 121	12 326	36 808	41 885	49 106	63 782	76 236	90 761	Pays sans littoral
15 717	10 270	16 986	17 290	18 853	21 780	24 947	28 985	Petits états insulaires en développement
23 836	*24 844*	*43 864*	*50 018*	*58 714*	*71 228*	*84 314*	*93 357*	*Pays les moins avancés*
16 485	16 699	24 379	28 877	34 815	42 579	52 100	57 417	Afrique et Haïti
6 966	7 501	18 480	20 043	22 578	27 015	30 299	33 563	Asie
386	645	1 005	1 098	1 321	1 634	1 915	2 377	Îles
149 382	*133 476*	*203 745*	*221 895*	*250 057*	*345 496*	*430 831*	*504 713*	*Principaux exportateurs de pétrole*
36 542	23 860	26 731	35 120	41 948	48 740	54 859	68 606	Afrique
20 680	10 585	22 375	17 752	15 796	23 494	33 766	43 263	Amérique
92 160	99 031	154 639	169 023	192 312	273 261	342 206	392 843	Asie
206 615	*508 542*	*1 401 546*	*1 398 337*	*1 643 614*	*2 109 569*	*2 420 685*	*2 841 812*	*Principaux exportateurs d'articles manufacturés*
47 105	66 071	241 755	226 323	229 362	273 033	299 452	347 514	Amérique
159 510	442 471	1 159 791	1 172 014	1 414 252	1 836 636	2 121 233	2 494 298	Asie
152 003	*329 111*	*873 270*	*785 737*	*862 898*	*1 096 342*	*1 249 709*	*1 442 089*	*Économies émergentes*
65 947	81 360	294 430	259 897	270 998	330 497	373 284	435 259	Amérique
86 056	247 751	578 839	525 839	591 899	765 846	876 425	1 006 830	Asie
127 629	*365 082*	*862 187*	*801 948*	*905 375*	*1 134 138*	*1 292 420*	*1 471 725*	*Économies nouvellement industrialisées*
88 511	267 938	647 758	588 969	666 023	837 212	943 389	1 085 682	Premier tier
39 118	97 144	214 429	212 979	239 352	296 926	349 031	386 043	Deuxieme tier
93 788	**97 037**	**130 973**	**142 179**	**170 948**	**210 342**	**246 931**	**278 432**	**Économies en développement : Afrique**
29 977	44 333	47 392	50 826	55 508	69 293	81 267	89 502	Afrique septentrionale sans le Soudan
63 812	52 704	83 581	91 354	115 441	141 049	165 665	188 930	Afrique subsaharienne
44 112	34 305	53 886	62 087	74 357	87 583	103 360	119 745	Afrique sub-saharienne sans l'Afrique du Sud
123 588	**127 195**	**388 885**	**351 625**	**364 999**	**444 089**	**515 178**	**606 663**	**Économies en développement : Amérique**
39 759	63 783	225 280	219 920	223 171	256 340	279 882	323 402	Amérique centrale et Grandes Antilles sans Porto Rico
17 615	20 234	42 578	43 313	44 668	49 717	58 063	67 272	Amérique centrale et Grandes Antilles sans le Mexique et Porto Rico
96 226	108 537	358 489	322 989	335 972	412 839	478 249	565 255	Amérique du Sud et Amérique centrale
41 521	34 244	92 816	71 031	79 058	108 622	142 832	175 754	Amérique du Sud sans le Brésil
272 005	**570 895**	**1 379 148**	**1 411 527**	**1 689 030**	**2 215 148**	**2 588 149**	**3 020 951**	**Économies en développement : Asie**
131 235	374 843	888 365	832 760	942 453	1 179 662	1 345 051	1 525 130	Asie orientale et Asie du Sud-Est sans la Chine
24 675	33 836	44 025	53 511	62 901	78 828	93 267	101 832	Asie méridionale sans l'Inde

Sources :
- ONU, *Annuaire statistique du commerce international*
- ONU, *Bulletin mensuel de statistique*
- ONU, Commission économique pour l'Europe
- FMI, *International Financial Statistics*
- FMI, *Direction of Trade Statistics*
- Organisation mondiale du commerce
- Banque centrale des Caraïbes orientales
- Sources nationales
- Estimations du secrétariat de la CNUCED

Economic grouping	Exports (f.o.b.) - Exportations (f.a.b.) Percentage										
	1980	1985	1990	1995	2000	2001	2002	2003	2004	2005	2006
DEVELOPING ECONOMIES	**29.41**	**25.37**	**24.23**	**27.58**	**31.73**	**31.00**	**31.71**	**32.03**	**33.72**	**35.92**	**36.79**
Developing economies excluding China	28.51	23.97	22.44	24.70	27.86	26.70	26.68	26.20	27.24	28.62	28.71
Developing economies excluding LDCs	28.65	24.69	23.66	27.11	31.16	30.40	31.09	31.42	33.05	35.13	35.97
High-income countries	16.03	12.93	13.18	15.32	17.27	16.27	16.10	15.76	16.48	17.18	17.19
Middle-income countries	6.47	6.78	5.81	6.17	6.41	6.40	6.46	6.51	6.77	7.11	7.02
Low-income countries	6.90	5.66	5.23	6.09	8.05	8.32	9.15	9.75	10.47	11.64	12.58
Heavily indebted poor countries	0.97	0.79	0.62	0.47	0.41	0.44	0.45	0.46	0.49	0.49	0.51
Landlocked countries	0.37	0.31	0.24	0.47	0.50	0.53	0.53	0.57	0.64	0.70	0.76
Small island developing states	0.62	0.40	0.20	0.19	0.18	0.18	0.16	0.17	0.16	0.18	0.21
Least developed countries	*0.75*	*0.67*	*0.56*	*0.47*	*0.57*	*0.60*	*0.62*	*0.61*	*0.66*	*0.79*	*0.83*
Africa and Haiti	0.60	0.53	0.46	0.30	0.32	0.34	0.37	0.38	0.45	0.56	0.57
Asia	0.14	0.14	0.10	0.16	0.24	0.25	0.24	0.22	0.21	0.23	0.25
Islands	0.01	0.01	0.01	0.01	0.00	0.00	0.00	0.00	0.00	0.00	0.00
Major petroleum exporters	*15.76*	*8.76*	*6.33*	*4.64*	*6.30*	*5.85*	*5.72*	*5.74*	*6.38*	*7.56*	*7.49*
Africa	3.28	2.21	1.40	0.77	1.06	0.96	0.96	1.03	1.14	1.46	1.45
America	1.40	0.89	0.61	0.43	0.59	0.55	0.46	0.43	0.50	0.63	0.67
Asia	11.08	5.65	4.32	3.44	4.65	4.34	4.30	4.28	4.74	5.47	5.37
Major exporters of manufactured goods	*8.33*	*12.07*	*14.17*	*19.42*	*21.84*	*21.47*	*22.37*	*22.64*	*23.61*	*24.50*	*25.37*
America	1.88	2.66	2.07	2.44	3.44	3.50	3.42	3.17	3.12	3.18	3.24
Asia	6.46	9.41	12.09	16.98	18.41	17.96	18.95	19.47	20.50	21.32	22.13
Emerging economies	*6.44*	*8.82*	*9.59*	*12.65*	*13.95*	*13.20*	*13.16*	*12.76*	*13.24*	*13.34*	*13.57*
America	2.70	3.43	2.76	3.26	4.25	4.34	4.21	3.97	3.98	4.11	4.31
Asia	3.75	5.39	6.82	9.39	9.70	8.85	8.95	8.79	9.25	9.22	9.26
Newly industrialized economies	*6.18*	*8.10*	*10.16*	*13.97*	*14.41*	*13.37*	*13.51*	*13.08*	*13.30*	*13.20*	*13.21*
First tier	3.76	5.78	7.68	10.23	10.24	9.45	9.55	9.38	9.66	9.59	9.54
Second tier	2.42	2.32	2.48	3.74	4.18	3.91	3.96	3.70	3.64	3.61	3.66
Developing economies: Africa	**5.86**	**4.18**	**3.08**	**2.08**	**2.28**	**2.23**	**2.26**	**2.37**	**2.52**	**2.85**	**2.78**
Northern Africa excluding Sudan	2.14	1.66	1.17	0.69	0.81	0.78	0.77	0.82	0.87	1.03	1.00
Sub-Saharan Africa	3.71	2.52	1.91	1.40	1.47	1.45	1.49	1.55	1.65	1.83	1.78
Sub-Saharan Africa excluding South Africa	2.46	1.69	1.23	0.86	1.01	0.98	1.03	1.07	1.15	1.33	1.33
Developing economies: America	**5.47**	**5.53**	**4.13**	**4.42**	**5.60**	**5.63**	**5.35**	**5.06**	**5.13**	**5.43**	**5.67**
Central America and Greater Carribean Islands excluding Puerto Rico	1.53	1.95	1.51	1.85	2.92	2.89	2.79	2.48	2.33	2.30	2.33
Central America and Greater Carribean Islands excluding Mexico and Puerto Rico	0.64	0.59	0.34	0.31	0.34	0.33	0.31	0.29	0.26	0.25	0.24
South America and Central America	4.37	4.83	3.80	4.17	5.31	5.33	5.11	4.82	4.90	5.19	5.42
South America excluding Brazil	2.24	1.95	1.59	1.56	1.67	1.64	1.51	1.48	1.63	1.85	2.03
Developing economies: Asia	**17.96**	**15.55**	**16.94**	**20.99**	**23.78**	**23.08**	**24.04**	**24.54**	**26.00**	**27.58**	**28.29**
Eastern and South-Eastern Asia excluding China	6.50	8.38	10.42	14.23	14.82	13.81	13.96	13.53	13.74	13.68	13.67
Southern Asia excluding India	0.86	1.02	0.84	0.67	0.78	0.73	0.77	0.79	0.80	0.89	0.85

Sources:
- UN, *Yearbook of International Trade Statistics*
- UN, *Monthly Bulletin of Statistics*
- UN, Economic Commission for Europe
- IMF, *International Financial Statistics*
- IMF, *Direction of Trade Statistics*
- World Trade Organization
- Eastern Caribbean Central Bank
- National sources
- UNCTAD secretariat estimates

Imports (c.i.f.) - Importations (c.a.f.) En pourcentage											Groupements économiques
1980	1985	1990	1995	2000	2001	2002	2003	2004	2005	2006	
23.77	**23.00**	**22.29**	**28.60**	**28.67**	**28.41**	**28.78**	**28.86**	**30.46**	**31.36**	**32.08**	**ÉCONOMIES EN DÉVELOPPEMENT**
22.81	20.91	20.80	26.07	25.28	24.61	24.33	23.52	24.52	25.19	25.60	Économies en développement sans la Chine
22.62	22.02	21.59	27.95	28.01	27.67	28.02	28.09	29.71	30.57	31.32	Économies en développement sans les PMA
10.75	9.94	11.11	14.91	15.17	14.39	14.02	13.26	13.77	13.94	14.24	Pays à revenu élevé
6.97	6.50	6.23	7.54	6.48	6.44	6.47	6.34	6.64	6.74	6.84	Pays à revenu intermédiaire
6.05	6.56	4.94	6.15	7.02	7.58	8.28	9.26	10.05	10.68	11.01	Pays à revenu faible
1.18	0.92	0.65	0.59	0.56	0.61	0.61	0.60	0.61	0.64	0.62	Pays pauvres très endettés
0.44	0.45	0.34	0.55	0.55	0.62	0.63	0.63	0.68	0.71	0.74	Pays sans littoral
0.76	0.46	0.29	0.26	0.26	0.26	0.26	0.24	0.23	0.23	0.24	Petits états insulaires en développement
1.15	*0.98*	*0.69*	*0.64*	*0.66*	*0.74*	*0.75*	*0.76*	*0.75*	*0.79*	*0.77*	*Pays les moins avancés*
0.79	0.62	0.47	0.37	0.37	0.42	0.43	0.45	0.45	0.49	0.47	Afrique et Haïti
0.34	0.33	0.21	0.25	0.28	0.31	0.30	0.29	0.29	0.28	0.28	Asie
0.02	0.02	0.02	0.02	0.02	0.02	0.02	0.02	0.02	0.02	0.02	Îles
7.20	*5.88*	*3.72*	*3.38*	*3.07*	*3.38*	*3.34*	*3.23*	*3.66*	*4.02*	*4.14*	*Principaux exportateurs de pétrole*
1.76	1.26	0.66	0.56	0.40	0.49	0.53	0.54	0.52	0.51	0.56	Afrique
1.00	0.54	0.29	0.31	0.34	0.38	0.27	0.20	0.25	0.32	0.35	Amérique
4.44	4.08	2.76	2.51	2.33	2.51	2.55	2.49	2.89	3.19	3.22	Asie
9.96	*11.67*	*14.16*	*20.41*	*21.10*	*20.42*	*21.06*	*21.25*	*22.33*	*22.60*	*23.29*	*Principaux exportateurs d'articles manufacturés*
2.27	1.65	1.84	2.49	3.64	3.67	3.41	2.96	2.89	2.80	2.85	Amérique
7.69	10.02	12.32	17.92	17.46	16.75	17.65	18.28	19.44	19.80	20.44	Asie
7.33	*6.95*	*9.17*	*13.16*	*13.15*	*12.19*	*11.83*	*11.15*	*11.61*	*11.67*	*11.82*	*Économies émergentes*
3.18	2.07	2.27	3.36	4.43	4.38	3.91	3.50	3.50	3.48	3.57	Amérique
4.15	4.87	6.90	9.80	8.71	7.82	7.92	7.65	8.11	8.18	8.25	Asie
6.15	*7.11*	*10.17*	*14.82*	*12.98*	*11.99*	*12.08*	*11.70*	*12.01*	*12.06*	*12.06*	*Économies nouvellement industrialisées*
4.27	5.28	7.46	10.65	9.75	8.84	8.87	8.61	8.86	8.81	8.90	Premier tier
1.89	1.83	2.71	4.17	3.23	3.15	3.21	3.09	3.14	3.26	3.16	Deuxième tier
4.52	**3.57**	**2.70**	**2.31**	**1.97**	**2.11**	**2.14**	**2.21**	**2.23**	**2.31**	**2.28**	**Économies en développement : Afrique**
1.45	1.56	1.23	0.91	0.71	0.75	0.77	0.72	0.73	0.76	0.73	Afrique septentrionale sans le Soudan
3.08	2.01	1.47	1.40	1.26	1.36	1.38	1.49	1.49	1.55	1.55	Afrique subsaharienne
2.13	1.45	0.96	0.82	0.81	0.92	0.93	0.96	0.93	0.96	0.98	Afrique sub-saharienne sans l'Afrique du Sud
5.96	**4.12**	**3.54**	**4.77**	**5.85**	**5.92**	**5.30**	**4.72**	**4.70**	**4.81**	**4.97**	**Économies en développement : Amérique**
1.92	1.82	1.78	1.97	3.39	3.42	3.31	2.88	2.71	2.61	2.65	Amérique centrale et Grandes Antilles sans Porto Rico
0.85	0.88	0.56	0.52	0.64	0.67	0.65	0.58	0.53	0.54	0.55	Amérique centrale et Grandes Antilles sans le Mexique et Porto Rico
4.64	3.21	3.02	4.41	5.40	5.45	4.86	4.34	4.37	4.46	4.63	Amérique du Sud et Amérique centrale
2.00	1.24	0.95	1.62	1.40	1.40	1.07	1.02	1.15	1.33	1.44	Amérique du Sud sans le Brésil
13.12	**15.15**	**15.90**	**21.41**	**20.76**	**20.31**	**21.26**	**21.83**	**23.45**	**24.16**	**24.76**	**Économies en développement : Asie**
6.33	7.35	10.44	15.15	13.37	12.42	12.54	12.18	12.49	12.56	12.50	Asie orientale et Asie du Sud-Est sans la Chine
1.19	1.18	0.94	0.73	0.66	0.73	0.81	0.81	0.83	0.87	0.83	Asie méridionale sans l'Inde

Sources :
- ONU, *Annuaire statistique du commerce international*
- ONU, *Bulletin mensuel de statistique*
- ONU, Commission économique pour l'Europe
- FMI, *International Financial Statistics*
- FMI, *Direction of Trade Statistics*
- Organisation mondiale du commerce
- Banque centrale des Caraïbes orientales
- Sources nationales
- Estimations du secrétariat de la CNUCED

Trade group	Exports (f.o.b) - Exportations (f.a.b.) Millions of dollars							
	1980	1990	2000	2002	2003	2004	2005	2006
AFRICA								
CEPGL	2 455	2 510	863	1 219	1 469	1 996	2 372	2 359
COMESA	13 851	18 268	24 777	26 610	31 148	40 106	56 311	68 407
ECCAS	9 042	11 956	17 151	18 275	21 503	32 264	50 123	61 154
ECOWAS	33 336	22 816	30 538	30 060	37 312	46 459	58 655	64 976
MRU	1 225	3 016	1 008	933	810	968	1 200	1 267
SADC	34 349	35 197	50 523	51 706	61 884	79 286	97 143	108 245
CEMAC (UDEAC)	4 668	5 558	8 365	8 723	10 519	16 790	23 639	27 637
UEMOA	4 884	5 202	6 659	8 670	9 867	11 567	12 336	13 478
UMA	40 648	36 171	47 972	45 476	55 573	72 514	97 031	106 828
AMERICA								
ANCOM	30 467	31 089	57 956	50 447	55 791	76 740	105 991	129 634
CACM	4 768	4 354	11 916	10 856	11 915	12 915	14 613	16 685
CARICOM	11 669	4 927	8 276	7 052	8 554	10 660	14 718	19 972
FTAA	393 784	658 165	1 413 465	1 287 548	1 373 261	1 587 071	1 826 653	2 114 845
LAIA	88 302	131 500	329 800	319 553	350 626	435 980	526 223	631 761
MERCOSUR	29 522	46 418	84 591	88 823	106 097	135 608	163 516	190 081
NAFTA	311 331	561 932	1 224 920	1 106 179	1 162 906	1 312 057	1 480 448	1 692 403
OECS	152	340	324	277	283	288	281	277
ASIA								
APTA	46 045	148 738	476 009	549 532	703 561	938 088	1 161 996	1 435 813
ASEAN	73 957	144 152	429 192	406 502	452 280	567 906	651 340	759 071
ECO	18 527	38 088	82 450	91 097	116 358	153 271	191 562	220 955
GCC	155 060	87 800	175 733	165 166	202 048	284 779	382 344	421 704
SAARC	13 129	27 493	64 253	71 899	84 036	105 055	132 465	157 716
EUROPE								
EFTA	49 095	99 434	143 483	149 805	170 558	203 173	230 808	266 742
EU 25	821 398	1 536 486	2 439 183	2 616 219	3 123 723	3 722 778	4 028 268	4 538 050
Euro Zone	624 839	1 219 424	1 893 228	2 043 872	2 451 350	2 913 304	3 120 030	3 480 738
OCEANIA								
MSG	1 611	1 730	2 725	2 236	2 981	3 386	4 124	4 883
INTERREGIONAL								
ACP	95 408	78 702	113 341	112 501	135 547	174 008	217 794	246 421
APEC	627 358	1 331 412	3 111 524	2 956 979	3 338 725	4 058 010	4 684 523	5 464 719
BSEC	29 644	31 886	177 935	193 656	249 082	332 836	414 343	501 379
CIS	..	..	145 717	152 919	194 594	265 481	340 238	420 107

Sources:
- UN, *Yearbook of International Trade Statistics*
- UN, *Monthly Bulletin of Statistics*
- UN, Economic Commission for Europe
- IMF, *International Financial Statistics*
- IMF, *Direction of Trade Statistics*
- World Trade Organization
- Eastern Caribbean Central Bank
- National sources
- UNCTAD secretariat estimates

Imports (c.i.f.) - Importations (c.a.f.) Millions de dollars								Groupements commerciaux
1980	1990	2000	2002	2003	2004	2005	2006	
								AFRIQUE
1 949	2 256	1 396	1 458	2 010	2 447	2 970	3 151	CEPGL
17 549	31 100	34 677	35 659	38 539	47 007	63 033	69 507	COMESA
6 314	7 296	8 522	11 424	14 211	16 277	21 071	24 587	CEEAC
25 607	13 983	20 914	24 691	29 886	32 691	37 005	46 329	CEDEAO
1 231	1 057	1 429	1 109	1 113	1 313	1 489	1 557	UFM
28 959	29 777	48 836	49 500	66 427	84 306	98 016	108 961	SADC
3 018	3 440	4 057	6 175	6 680	7 957	9 697	10 094	CEMAC (UDEAC)
6 371	5 777	7 374	7 997	10 160	12 301	14 296	14 966	UEMOA
25 402	27 771	33 837	38 630	44 755	56 992	62 165	69 530	UMA
								AMÉRIQUE
21 984	18 946	42 190	40 245	39 919	53 596	72 070	90 847	ANCOM
6 001	6 473	20 015	22 129	23 915	27 079	31 192	36 716	MCAC
14 268	7 223	14 089	14 104	15 115	16 927	19 746	22 518	CARICOM
430 925	757 956	1 884 417	1 772 042	1 904 925	2 241 215	2 568 117	2 870 829	ZLEA
94 231	106 276	338 235	300 463	311 802	385 813	448 115	530 870	ALADI
37 801	29 295	89 992	62 342	69 329	95 066	113 996	136 326	MERCOSUR
341 673	683 779	1 686 788	1 604 336	1 726 574	2 012 215	2 285 734	2 533 112	ALENA
423	1 045	1 510	1 406	1 608	1 710	1 935	1 956	OECO
								ASIE
61 826	153 257	452 274	518 263	680 857	906 545	1 084 082	1 298 444	ACAP
65 641	162 292	370 591	355 116	398 759	508 996	593 708	667 883	ANASE
27 528	48 944	93 674	101 250	127 683	176 841	197 581	248 582	ECO
51 991	47 366	85 287	95 496	103 151	150 909	195 155	236 932	CCG
25 272	38 149	79 165	83 776	104 258	141 219	190 545	228 640	SAARC
								EUROPE
54 281	98 592	120 567	120 836	138 722	163 241	180 565	202 521	AELE
920 001	1 591 653	2 495 069	2 564 021	3 088 828	3 708 561	4 075 245	4 646 380	UE 25
710 829	1 245 029	1 870 213	1 896 124	2 312 553	2 765 190	3 030 463	3 413 303	Zone Euro
								OCÉANIE
1 900	2 059	2 186	2 300	2 775	3 375	3 652	4 188	MSG
								INTERRÉGIONAUX
88 589	71 952	114 438	121 096	145 965	175 203	205 692	234 204	ACP
669 769	1 405 143	3 329 166	3 233 727	3 666 712	4 461 296	5 114 681	5 764 461	CEAP
41 951	57 056	171 004	190 974	252 781	333 407	386 574	474 241	CEMN
..	..	81 755	103 958	132 273	172 982	215 843	253 152	CEI

Sources :
- ONU, *Annuaire statistique du commerce international*
- ONU, *Bulletin mensuel de statistique*
- ONU, Commission économique pour l'Europe
- FMI, *International Financial Statistics*
- FMI, *Direction of Trade Statistics*
- Organisation mondiale du commerce
- Banque centrale des Caraïbes orientales
- Sources nationales
- Estimations du secrétariat de la CNUCED

Trade group	Exports (f.o.b) - Exportations (f.a.b.) Percentage										
	1980	1985	1990	1995	2000	2001	2002	2003	2004	2005	2006
AFRICA											
CEPGL	0.12	0.11	0.07	0.03	0.01	0.02	0.02	0.02	0.02	0.02	0.02
COMESA	0.68	0.66	0.53	0.35	0.38	0.37	0.41	0.41	0.44	0.54	0.57
ECCAS	0.44	0.42	0.34	0.22	0.27	0.26	0.28	0.29	0.35	0.48	0.51
ECOWAS	1.64	0.97	0.66	0.43	0.47	0.44	0.46	0.50	0.51	0.56	0.54
MRU	0.06	0.05	0.09	0.03	0.02	0.01	0.01	0.01	0.01	0.01	0.01
SADC	1.69	1.20	1.01	0.77	0.78	0.78	0.80	0.82	0.86	0.93	0.90
CEMAC (UDEAC)	0.23	0.20	0.16	0.12	0.13	0.13	0.13	0.14	0.18	0.23	0.23
UEMOA	0.24	0.22	0.15	0.13	0.10	0.11	0.13	0.13	0.13	0.12	0.11
UMA	2.00	1.49	1.04	0.63	0.74	0.72	0.70	0.74	0.79	0.93	0.89
AMERICA											
ANCOM	1.50	1.24	0.89	0.76	0.90	0.85	0.78	0.74	0.84	1.02	1.08
CACM	0.23	0.19	0.13	0.16	0.18	0.17	0.17	0.16	0.14	0.14	0.14
CARICOM	0.57	0.35	0.14	0.11	0.13	0.12	0.11	0.11	0.12	0.14	0.17
FTAA	19.38	20.90	18.92	19.36	21.93	21.51	19.89	18.24	17.31	17.50	17.65
LAIA	4.35	4.89	3.78	4.01	5.12	5.16	4.94	4.66	4.76	5.04	5.27
MERCOSUR	1.45	1.79	1.33	1.36	1.31	1.42	1.37	1.41	1.48	1.57	1.59
NAFTA	15.32	17.08	16.15	16.57	19.01	18.55	17.09	15.45	14.31	14.18	14.12
OECS	0.01	0.01	0.01	0.01	0.01	0.00	0.00	0.00	0.00	0.00	0.00
ASIA											
APTA	2.27	3.51	4.28	6.04	7.39	7.62	8.49	9.35	10.23	11.13	11.98
ASEAN	3.64	3.68	4.14	6.22	6.66	6.27	6.28	6.01	6.20	6.24	6.33
ECO	0.91	1.29	1.09	1.17	1.28	1.33	1.41	1.55	1.67	1.83	1.84
GCC	7.63	3.20	2.52	2.04	2.73	2.58	2.55	2.68	3.11	3.66	3.52
SAARC	0.65	0.73	0.79	0.90	1.00	1.04	1.11	1.12	1.15	1.27	1.32
EUROPE											
EFTA	2.42	2.45	2.86	2.43	2.23	2.32	2.31	2.27	2.22	2.21	2.23
EU 25	40.42	39.43	44.17	42.09	37.85	39.67	40.42	41.50	40.61	38.58	37.87
Euro Zone	30.75	30.21	35.06	33.34	29.38	31.02	31.58	32.57	31.78	29.88	29.05
OCEANIA											
MSG	0.08	0.07	0.05	0.07	0.04	0.04	0.03	0.04	0.04	0.04	0.04
INTERREGIONAL											
ACP	4.69	3.27	2.26	1.68	1.76	1.72	1.74	1.80	1.90	2.09	2.06
APEC	30.87	37.57	38.27	45.51	48.28	46.40	45.68	44.36	44.27	44.87	45.60
BSEC	1.46	1.93	0.92	2.79	2.76	2.93	2.99	3.31	3.63	3.97	4.18
CIS	..	..	..	2.21	2.26	2.35	2.36	2.59	2.90	3.26	3.51

Sources:
- UN, *Yearbook of International Trade Statistics*
- UN, *Monthly Bulletin of Statistics*
- UN, Economic Commission for Europe
- IMF, *International Financial Statistics*
- IMF, *Direction of Trade Statistics*
- World Trade Organization
- Eastern Caribbean Central Bank
- National sources
- UNCTAD secretariat estimates

Imports (c.i.f.) - Importations (c.a.f.) En pourcentage											Groupements commerciaux
1980	1985	1990	1995	2000	2001	2002	2003	2004	2005	2006	
											AFRIQUE
0.09	0.09	0.06	0.03	0.02	0.02	0.02	0.03	0.03	0.03	0.03	CEPGL
0.85	1.03	0.87	0.55	0.52	0.55	0.54	0.50	0.50	0.59	0.57	COMESA
0.30	0.30	0.20	0.12	0.13	0.16	0.17	0.18	0.17	0.20	0.20	CEEAC
1.23	0.74	0.39	0.37	0.31	0.37	0.37	0.39	0.35	0.35	0.38	CEDEAO
0.06	0.04	0.03	0.03	0.02	0.02	0.02	0.01	0.01	0.01	0.01	UFM
1.40	0.89	0.83	0.80	0.74	0.73	0.75	0.86	0.89	0.91	0.89	SADC
0.15	0.14	0.10	0.06	0.06	0.09	0.09	0.09	0.08	0.09	0.08	CEMAC (UDEAC)
0.31	0.21	0.16	0.14	0.11	0.12	0.12	0.13	0.13	0.13	0.12	UEMOA
1.22	1.02	0.77	0.69	0.51	0.55	0.58	0.58	0.60	0.58	0.57	UMA
											AMÉRIQUE
1.06	0.81	0.53	0.79	0.64	0.71	0.61	0.52	0.57	0.67	0.74	ANCOM
0.29	0.25	0.18	0.25	0.30	0.32	0.33	0.31	0.29	0.29	0.30	MCAC
0.69	0.39	0.20	0.19	0.21	0.22	0.21	0.20	0.18	0.18	0.18	CARICOM
20.78	24.97	21.11	22.65	28.37	27.76	26.69	24.62	23.73	23.97	23.52	ZLEA
4.54	3.25	2.96	4.14	5.09	5.13	4.52	4.03	4.08	4.18	4.35	ALADI
1.82	0.95	0.82	1.54	1.35	1.32	0.94	0.90	1.01	1.06	1.12	MERCOSUR
16.48	22.25	19.05	19.44	25.40	24.74	24.16	22.32	21.30	21.34	20.76	ALENA
0.02	0.03	0.03	0.02	0.02	0.02	0.02	0.02	0.02	0.02	0.02	OECO
											ASIE
2.98	4.62	4.27	6.02	6.81	7.03	7.80	8.80	9.60	10.12	10.64	ACAP
3.17	3.28	4.52	6.81	5.58	5.32	5.35	5.15	5.39	5.54	5.47	ANASE
1.33	1.50	1.36	1.34	1.41	1.34	1.52	1.65	1.87	1.84	2.04	ECO
2.51	2.14	1.32	1.31	1.28	1.41	1.44	1.33	1.60	1.82	1.94	CCG
1.22	1.32	1.06	1.14	1.19	1.20	1.26	1.35	1.49	1.78	1.87	SAARC
											EUROPE
2.62	2.32	2.75	2.20	1.82	1.87	1.82	1.79	1.73	1.69	1.66	AELE
44.37	38.93	44.33	40.40	37.56	38.33	38.61	39.93	39.26	38.04	38.07	UE 25
34.28	29.60	34.68	31.16	28.16	28.62	28.55	29.89	29.27	28.29	27.97	Zone Euro
											OCÉANIE
0.09	0.08	0.06	0.05	0.03	0.03	0.03	0.04	0.04	0.03	0.03	MSG
											INTERRÉGIONAUX
4.27	2.97	2.00	1.80	1.72	1.84	1.82	1.89	1.85	1.92	1.92	ACP
32.30	39.84	39.14	46.54	50.12	48.72	43.70	47.40	47.23	47.75	47.24	OEAP
2.02	2.28	1.59	3.01	2.57	2.62	2.88	3.27	3.53	3.61	3.89	OEMN
..	..	..	1.79	1.23	1.48	1.57	1.71	1.83	2.01	2.07	CEI

Sources :
- ONU, *Annuaire statistique du commerce international*
- ONU, *Bulletin mensuel de statistique*
- ONU, Commission économique pour l'Europe
- FMI, *International Financial Statistics*
- FMI, *Direction of Trade Statistics*
- Organisation mondiale du commerce
- Banque centrale des Caraïbes orientales
- Sources nationales
- Estimations du secrétariat de la CNUCED

Region, country or territory	Exports (f.o.b) - Exportations (f.a.b.) Percentage										
	80-90	80-00	80-05	90-00	90-05	95-05	00-05	02-03	03-04	04-05	05-06
WORLD	**6.0**	**7.1**	**7.1**	**6.8**	**6.9**	**6.5**	**11.3**	**16.3**	**21.8**	**13.9**	**14.8**
DEVELOPED ECONOMIES	7.3	7.3	6.8	5.9	5.8	5.2	9.4	15.3	17.9	9.2	12.6
DEVELOPING ECONOMIES	3.1	7.6	8.2	9.0	9.3	9.1	14.1	17.4	28.2	21.3	17.6
ECONOMIES IN TRANSITION	2.9	0.5	3.0	6.7	9.3	10.2	19.9	27.2	36.0	26.3	22.8
Developed economies: America	**6.0**	**7.5**	**6.7**	**7.5**	**5.6**	**3.8**	**3.9**	**5.5**	**12.6**	**12.8**	**13.9**
Bermuda	6.8	3.9	3.0	-0.7	0.3	-0.1	5.9	9.1	21.7	-32.9	(p)-50.0
Canada	6.8	7.2	6.8	8.3	6.9	5.5	5.5	8.1	11.6	18.0	(p)12.6
Greenland	10.5	2.7	2.4	-3.7	-0.1	2.3	12.7	44.5	26.5	-15.7	-
Saint Pierre and Miquelon	(e)46.2	(e)7.9	(e)5.6	-14.9	(e)-5.0	(e)4.6	(e)13.4	0.0	(e)16.7	(e)57.1	-
United States*	5.7	7.6	6.7	7.2	5.2	3.2	3.3	4.6	12.9	10.8	(p)14.3
Developed economies: Asia	**8.9**	**7.1**	**6.1**	**4.4**	**3.9**	**3.2**	**6.6**	**12.9**	**20.0**	**5.5**	**8.4**
Israel*	8.3	9.8	9.4	11.1	9.3	7.7	7.3	8.3	21.5	10.8	8.6
Japan	8.9	7.0	5.9	4.1	3.6	3.0	6.5	13.2	19.9	5.2	(e)8.3
Developed economies: Europe	**7.5**	**7.3**	**7.0**	**5.6**	**6.2**	**5.9**	**11.8**	**19.1**	**19.2**	**8.5**	**12.8**
Austria*	10.2	8.9	8.8	6.1	7.6	8.2	14.8	23.6	21.8	5.9	12.0
Belgium*	–	–	–	–	–	–	–	18.4	20.0	9.2	10.2
Belgium-Luxembourg*	7.8	8.1	–	6.1	–	–	–	–	–	–	–
Cyprus*(1)	4.7	4.9	3.5	1.1	0.1	-2.0	5.8	8.3	29.7	20.5	(e)-15.7
Czechoslovakia (former) (2)	0.1	–	–	–	–	–	–	–	–	–	–
Czech Republic*	–	–	–	–	–	13.7	23.1	26.6	37.9	16.1	(e)21.4
Denmark*(3)	9.0	7.5	7.0	3.7	4.8	5.1	11.7	15.8	15.9	10.6	8.5
Estonia*(4)	–	–	–	–	–	13.5	14.4	29.7	-1.5	39.2	(e)24.5
Faeroe Islands	10.8	5.9	5.5	1.6	3.5	5.5	5.3	10.5	3.1	-2.5	(p)5.4
Finland	7.4	7.4	7.0	8.0	6.8	4.5	9.0	17.9	15.7	7.5	16.5
France*	7.5	7.4	6.7	5.0	4.9	4.2	8.7	18.3	15.3	2.7	5.5
Germany*	–	–	–	3.9	5.5	6.3	13.5	22.2	21.1	6.9	(e)16.0
Greece*	5.8	6.0	5.4	3.8	3.8	3.4	10.1	28.6	14.4	12.6	21.0
Hungary*	1.6	5.4	7.9	12.7	14.2	16.0	18.5	23.2	29.1	13.3	(p)17.1
Iceland*	7.9	5.4	5.2	3.1	4.3	5.3	10.1	7.1	21.4	1.7	17.3
Ireland*	12.8	13.2	12.5	13.8	11.7	9.6	7.4	5.2	13.0	4.9	2.3
Italy*	8.7	7.7	6.9	4.6	4.9	4.1	10.4	17.8	18.2	5.7	9.8
Latvia*	–	–	–	–	–	12.7	23.3	26.7	37.7	28.3	(e)12.6
Lithuania (4)	–	–	–	–	–	13.9	27.9	33.2	33.5	26.6	(p)19.8
Luxembourg*	–	–	–	–	–	–	–	30.3	22.2	15.9	21.3
Malta	9.2	10.6	9.0	6.3	4.9	3.7	1.5	10.9	6.5	-15.3	(p)13.7
Netherlands*	4.6	6.7	6.9	7.0	7.3	6.6	13.0	21.4	20.7	13.9	13.6
Norway	5.3	6.4	6.9	5.2	7.0	8.0	11.3	13.0	21.1	24.7	19.3
Poland*	1.4	5.2	7.6	9.9	12.7	14.1	24.3	30.5	37.8	21.1	(p)22.1
Portugal*	15.1	11.1	9.5	5.3	5.4	4.6	10.9	22.7	12.7	6.8	13.4
Slovakia*	–	–	–	–	–	14.5	24.6	51.7	25.7	15.9	(p)29.4
Slovenia*	–	–	–	–	–	7.6	16.7	23.3	24.4	12.7	(p)17.3
Spain*	10.8	11.0	10.2	8.4	8.1	6.7	12.5	24.3	16.9	5.7	6.5
Sweden	8.0	6.8	6.3	6.0	5.4	4.0	11.2	25.4	20.7	5.9	12.9
Switzerland*	9.5	7.1	6.4	3.1	4.1	4.5	10.2	14.6	17.7	6.2	(p)12.5
United Kingdom*	5.9	6.6	6.0	5.5	4.7	3.6	6.8	9.2	13.7	10.8	15.7
Developed economies: Oceania	**6.5**	**6.5**	**6.3**	**4.8**	**5.3**	**5.1**	**10.8**	**10.9**	**21.2**	**19.5**	**14.5**
Australia*	6.6	6.7	6.4	5.0	5.5	5.3	10.7	10.0	20.8	22.5	(p)16.9
New Zealand	6.2	5.8	5.6	3.9	4.7	4.3	11.4	14.9	23.1	6.8	(e)2.8
Developing economies: Africa	**-1.4**	**1.9**	**3.6**	**3.3**	**6.4**	**9.1**	**16.3**	**21.8**	**29.7**	**28.8**	**11.7**
Eastern Africa	*1.2*	*3.3*	*3.9*	*4.8*	*5.2*	*4.3*	*11.0*	*7.6*	*19.5*	*10.6*	*15.2*
Burundi*	2.5	-2.1	-3.4	-4.3	-5.3	-5.9	4.4	21.0	27.5	19.0	(e)-5.5
Comoros*	2.8	-3.1	-0.5	-10.9	-0.3	12.6	2.2	38.3	-30.0	-26.2	(e)21.7
Djibouti*	10.9	6.5	6.8	15.1	10.5	8.7	-16.0	-55.1	2.0	4.0	-
Ethiopia (former)	-1.1	–	–	–	–	–	–	–	–	–	–
Eritrea	–	–	–	–	–	(e)-8.2	(e)19.2	(e)-87.2	761.2	-12.3	-
Ethiopia	–	–	–	–	–	4.4	12.8	3.4	36.7	30.2	(e)18.1
Kenya	-1.1	3.8	4.4	6.3	6.0	4.2	13.1	13.9	11.3	22.7	(e)3.0
Madagascar*	-1.2	3.8	4.7	9.0	7.6	6.3	1.5	76.2	21.5	-26.6	(e)0.4
Malawi	2.0	3.4	3.0	0.9	1.4	0.8	5.3	29.0	-8.0	2.8	(e)-0.7
Mauritius	14.4	9.7	7.8	4.3	3.6	2.6	4.4	5.4	5.0	7.6	(e)8.3
Mozambique	-9.6	2.7	8.9	10.3	19.7	28.0	34.1	28.9	44.1	16.1	(e)34.2
Rwanda	-0.9	-5.2	-2.9	-3.9	1.1	4.9	14.5	3.2	69.5	27.8	(e)-7.7
Seychelles	9.3	12.6	13.5	15.5	15.5	15.8	10.6	20.1	6.2	8.3	(e)-40.2
Somalia	-1.1	(e)3.8	(e)5.8	(e)6.5	(e)9.0	(e)9.6	(e)14.0	(e)8.4	(e)8.7	(e)20.0	-

For sources and notes, see end of table.

1.2.1 Taux d'évolution annuels moyens des exportations et importations des pays et des régions géographiques

Imports (c.i.f.) - Importations (c.a.f.) En pourcentage											Régions, pays ou territoires
80-90	80-00	80-05	90-00	90-05	95-05	00-05	02-03	03-04	04-05	05-06	
6.0	**7.0**	**7.1**	**6.7**	**6.9**	**6.7**	**11.2**	**16.5**	**22.1**	**13.4**	**13.9**	**MONDE**
6.9	7.0	6.9	6.2	6.4	6.3	9.9	16.0	18.9	11.5	12.5	ÉCONOMIES DÉVELOPPÉES
4.0	8.1	8.2	8.5	8.3	7.4	13.3	16.8	28.9	16.7	16.6	ÉCONOMIES EN DÉVELOPPEMENT
3.9	0.0	2.2	3.9	7.3	8.1	22.1	28.7	30.2	22.4	17.9	ÉCONOMIES EN TRANSITION
8.1	**7.9**	**7.8**	**9.1**	**8.1**	**7.4**	**7.1**	**8.4**	**16.6**	**14.3**	**10.3**	**Économies développées : Amérique**
4.8	3.3	3.7	2.7	4.1	6.0	7.8	11.7	18.6	-0.3	(ə)11.2	Bermudes
7.9	7.3	6.8	7.5	6.4	5.7	6.5	7.7	14.2	18.5	(p)7.8	Canada
5.9	1.7	1.7	-1.1	1.1	2.8	15.1	18.9	30.7	-0.9	-	Groenland
36.8	13.6	(e)8.9	-1.5	(e)-1.4	(e)-1.2	(e)-0.1	26.3	(e)0.7	(e)-9.5	-	Saint-Pierre-et-Miquelon
8.2	8.1	8.0	9.5	8.4	7.8	7.2	8.6	17.1	13.5	(ɔ)10.8	États-Unis*
5.1	**6.2**	**5.8**	**4.8**	**4.7**	**3.8**	**7.3**	**12.5**	**18.6**	**13.0**	**11.3**	**Économies développées : Asie**
5.9	7.7	7.2	7.7	6.4	4.2	7.8	2.2	18.1	10.0	(p)0.2	Israël*
5.1	6.1	5.7	4.6	4.6	3.7	7.2	13.6	18.7	13.3	(ə)12.3	Japon
6.8	**6.8**	**6.7**	**5.0**	**5.9**	**6.2**	**11.6**	**20.2**	**20.0**	**9.9**	**13.9**	**Économies développées : Europe**
8.7	8.0	7.6	4.5	5.9	6.6	13.7	27.2	20.5	6.4	10.0	Autriche*
							18.6	21.6	11.8	10.8	Belgique*
6.4	7.2	–	5.4	–	–	–	–	–	–	–	Belgique-Luxembourg*
7.6	7.6	6.9	4.3	4.8	4.3	11.0	11.0	32.0	11.0	(ə)11.2	Chypre*(1)
1.7	–	–	–	–			–	–	–	–	Tchécoslovaquie (anc.) (2)
–					11.2	19.3	25.8	33.1	6.6	(ə)21.8	République tchèque*
6.8	6.2	5.9	4.2	4.9	4.7	11.8	14.2	18.7	11.1	13.7	Danemark*(3)
					13.5	20.9	34.7	28.6	21.3	(ə)27.6	Estonie*(4)
8.0	3.0	4.0	5.5	6.9	8.5	8.1	42.8	-9.9	19.7	(p)4.3	Îles Féroé
6.9	5.3	5.5	5.1	6.0	6.0	13.0	24.4	21.0	14.9	16.5	Finlande
6.6	6.3	6.1	3.9	4.8	5.3	9.8	21.2	18.1	7.2	5.8	France*
–	–	–	3.5	4.5	5.0	10.8	23.4	18.4	8.3	(ə)18.4	Allemagne*
6.6	7.5	7.3	5.2	6.2	7.3	14.1	42.2	17.6	2.7	16.8	Grèce*
0.1	6.5	8.6	13.5	14.0	15.1	17.2	26.0	25.3	10.3	(ɔ)14.6	Hongrie*
6.6	5.5	5.6	5.5	6.1	7.3	13.4	22.6	27.4	28.3	31.5	Islande*
7.0	9.4	9.1	10.7	8.9	7.2	6.2	2.9	14.7	11.1	5.8	Irlande*
6.9	5.8	5.8	3.2	4.9	6.2	11.5	20.6	19.4	8.5	13.5	Italie*
–	–	–	–	–	14.4	23.3	29.4	34.5	21.9	(ə)27.9	Lettonie*
–	–	–	–	–	13.2	25.1	28.5	28.1	25.2	(ɔ)24.4	Lituanie (4)
							27.9	24.0	9.4	21.5	Luxembourg*
8.1	8.7	7.4	4.4	3.9	3.2	5.2	19.7	12.5	-0.4	(p)1.9	Malte
4.4	6.4	6.6	6.7	6.8	6.2	12.2	20.8	20.7	14.0	14.2	Pays-Bas*
6.2	5.2	4.9	4.2	4.2	3.6	10.8	13.2	21.8	13.9	17.1	Norvège
-3.2	8.1	9.5	18.3	14.9	11.0	17.0	23.4	29.3	14.8	(ɔ)23.5	Pologne*
10.3	9.8	8.7	5.3	5.5	5.5	9.8	17.6	16.4	11.6	8.7	Portugal*
–	–	–	–	–	13.4	23.2	36.1	28.2	18.7	(ɔ)22.9	Slovaquie*
–	–	–	–	–	7.0	16.0	26.7	26.8	11.7	(ɔ)16.8	Slovénie*
10.6	9.7	9.5	6.0	8.0	9.5	14.9	26.5	23.8	12.0	9.4	Espagne*
6.7	5.5	5.3	4.5	4.8	4.6	11.3	24.9	20.2	11.2	13.2	Suède
8.8	6.1	5.5	2.6	3.6	4.0	8.5	15.3	15.7	8.6	(p)9.2	Suisse*
8.5	7.1	6.8	5.6	5.9	5.9	8.9	9.8	17.8	9.3	17.8	Royaume-Uni*
6.2	**6.5**	**6.5**	**6.2**	**6.5**	**6.2**	**14.3**	**22.7**	**23.2**	**14.3**	**5.7**	**Économies développées : Océanie**
6.4	6.7	6.6	6.4	6.5	6.3	14.1	22.6	22.8	14.5	(p)6.7	Australie*
5.4	5.9	6.0	5.6	6.2	5.6	15.5	23.3	25.0	13.1	(e)0.9	Nouvelle-Zélande
-0.5	**2.3**	**3.5**	**4.4**	**5.7**	**6.3**	**14.3**	**20.2**	**23.0**	**17.4**	**12.8**	**Économies en développement : Afrique**
1.6	*4.0*	*4.5*	*4.5*	*5.3*	*5.2*	*12.7*	*9.3*	*28.2*	*19.7*	*13.1*	*Afrique orientale*
2.2	-1.3	-0.9	-6.9	-2.3	2.3	11.6	21.0	12.5	51.6	(ə)37.0	Burundi*
5.7	3.0	3.1	-1.7	1.5	3.7	17.0	32.4	22.9	4.3	9.8	Comores*
-1.0	-0.1	0.8	0.9	2.3	5.2	0.1	-16.1	9.7	6.1	-	Djibouti*
4.3											Éthiopie (anc.)
–	–	–	–	–	-0.7	1.2	-19.5	10.9	3.1	(ə)13.5	Érythrée
					11.3	25.0	30.6	45.7	33.7	(ə)14.1	Éthiopie
1.7	3.6	4.5	6.0	6.5	5.5	14.1	14.8	22.2	35.1	(ə)16.7	Kenya
-4.3	3.3	4.2	6.3	6.1	6.5	8.5	6.4	133.3	-11.0	(e)5.4	Madagascar*
3.3	4.2	4.4	-0.6	2.7	6.1	17.1	13.1	18.7	24.1	-14.0	Malawi
12.9	9.6	7.9	4.2	3.6	3.0	8.6	9.5	17.2	14.0	(e)9.0	Maurice
0.1	2.1	4.1	1.2	6.4	13.5	17.8	13.6	16.1	18.4	(e)3.8	Mozambique
2.7	-1.1	-0.3	-1.6	1.0	2.6	10.9	4.4	9.7	52.6	(e)18.8	Rwanda
7.2	8.8	8.3	9.6	7.7	5.4	5.9	-2.3	20.5	1.6	(ə)96.4	Seychelles
-19.3	(e)-2.7	(e)2.3	(e)26.6	(e)19.9	(e)7.9	(e)8.9	(e)1.1	(e)1.1	(e)31.5	-	Somalie

Pour les sources et les notes, se reporter à la fin du tableau.

Region, country or territory	Exports (f.o.b) - Exportations (f.a.b.) Percentage										
	80-90	80-00	80-05	90-00	90-05	95-05	00-05	02-03	03-04	04-05	05-06
Uganda	-4.0	2.0	3.2	15.4	10.2	3.3	14.4	26.9	26.2	21.7	12.4
United Republic of Tanzania*	-5.1	3.3	5.4	7.8	9.7	8.8	16.5	24.4	20.3	1.0	(e)16.7
Zambia*	0.9	-0.2	0.9	-2.0	1.7	3.9	19.9	5.5	49.0	26.7	(e)61.0
Zimbabwe	2.5	3.1	(e)2.1	3.2	(e)0.7	(e)-2.4	(e)2.7	-28.2	15.3	(e)-2.5	(e)6.1
Middle Africa	*2.2*	*3.4*	*5.5*	*3.4*	*8.4*	*13.1*	*24.5*	*17.7*	*50.0*	*55.5*	*22.1*
Angola*	6.4	6.6	8.7	6.1	11.4	16.8	25.2	14.2	41.7	78.9	(e)29.2
Cameroon*(5)	1.4	3.7	4.0	-1.2	2.1	5.5	11.8	24.6	10.3	25.3	(e)25.0
Central African Republic*(5)	3.5	3.4	2.2	3.6	0.6	-2.7	-4.8	-17.6	3.4	2.1	-
Chad*	9.4	6.7	10.1	3.2	14.1	23.6	90.6	225.3	264.8	38.4	-
Congo*(5)	2.1	3.7	5.7	7.5	10.2	13.5	16.4	14.9	48.3	22.4	(e)39.5
Dem. Rep. of the Congo*	2.7	-3.5	-2.0	-6.7	-0.9	2.0	24.0	21.4	34.6	18.4	-
Equatorial Guinea	19.8	23.6	(e)29.0	41.2	(e)43.5	(e)47.8	(e)43.3	(e)10.8	(e)119.4	55.3	-
Gabon*(5)	-3.9	1.9	2.7	1.6	3.3	3.9	14.9	17.2	23.8	56.1	(e)24.5
São Tome and Principe*	-8.3	-6.1	-4.7	-6.1	-3.0	-2.2	6.6	33.0	-46.9	-3.7	(e)-2.4
Northern Africa	*-2.3*	*0.9*	*3.1*	*2.3*	*6.5*	*10.5*	*16.6*	*23.8*	*30.2*	*34.2*	*11.6*
Algeria*	-3.1	0.6	3.3	2.2	7.4	13.0	17.5	28.1	34.2	43.9	-
Egypt*	7.3	0.5	2.4	0.7	5.7	10.6	19.4	34.1	19.3	41.7	(e)28.9
Libyan Arab Jamahiriya	-7.5	-2.7	0.4	-2.6	4.3	11.3	18.9	23.6	40.8	43.0	(e)24.6
Morocco*	6.2	7.6	7.2	8.1	6.7	4.1	8.5	11.8	13.0	6.4	(e)14.4
Sudan*	-2.5	2.1	7.4	14.0	19.8	26.1	24.2	30.4	48.6	27.7	(e)5.1
Tunisia	3.5	7.1	7.3	6.0	6.8	6.7	12.8	16.8	20.7	8.4	9.7
Southern Africa	*0.7*	*3.0*	*4.0*	*4.3*	*5.8*	*7.2*	*13.1*	*24.1*	*26.3*	*11.8*	*3.0*
Botswana*	–	–	–	–	(e)9.1	(e)9.1	11.2	30.4	14.6	26.8	(e)-10.8
Lesotho	–	–	–	–	(e)24.1	(e)24.1	28.0	31.6	48.3	-6.8	(e)11.8
Namibia	–	–	–	–	(e)6.6	(e)6.6	11.2	17.6	45.1	13.2	(e)27.6
South Africa	(a)0.7	(a)2.4	(a)3.2	(a)2.5	(a)4.3	(a)5.3	13.0	22.7	26.5	11.9	3.0
Swaziland	–	–	–	–	(e)11.8	(e)11.8	16.9	52.1	23.8	-10.5	(e)4.2
Western Africa	*-4.7*	*1.4*	*3.2*	*3.3*	*6.0*	*8.2*	*15.5*	*23.8*	*24.4*	*26.5*	*10.9*
Benin*	18.8	14.1	11.1	3.3	3.4	2.4	9.9	20.8	5.0	0.1	-
Burkina Faso	7.9	7.2	7.5	12.6	10.1	4.0	15.9	30.8	49.5	-27.5	(e)25.0
Cape Verde*	5.9	6.8	6.6	11.0	8.2	3.4	12.1	20.1	18.7	18.0	(e)15.9
Côte d'Ivoire*	1.7	2.8	3.8	6.0	6.5	5.6	15.5	9.7	19.5	8.2	8.8
Gambia	2.7	-5.3	(e)-5.5	-12.5	(e)-7.8	(e)-0.3	(e)12.4	-7.7	83.3	(e)-2.3	-
Ghana	-2.7	3.1	4.3	9.0	7.9	5.4	13.1	37.8	6.9	2.3	(e)28.4
Guinea	4.0	2.7	2.3	0.6	1.1	1.1	4.0	-14.0	19.1	25.4	-
Guinea-Bissau	4.2	8.9	9.4	13.6	11.6	10.0	9.1	20.9	16.1	30.5	(e)9.4
Liberia*	4.7	0.4	-5.0	-12.6	-16.3	-19.3	-15.0	-38.2	-4.7	27.0	-
Mali*	6.0	8.1	8.8	6.1	8.6	10.1	14.1	6.0	5.3	16.2	(e)19.3
Mauritania*	8.0	2.9	1.7	-2.0	-1.3	-1.5	7.1	-4.0	15.5	54.0	(e)26.7
Niger*	-5.4	-1.4	0.1	0.0	2.5	4.7	16.0	26.0	24.1	31.9	(e)5.9
Nigeria	-8.4	0.7	3.2	3.2	7.0	10.7	16.7	29.5	29.5	35.7	(e)10.2
Senegal*	3.5	3.6	4.1	4.0	4.9	4.7	12.0	17.9	20.1	1.7	(e)7.1
Sierra Leone*	-2.4	-12.8	-6.5	-29.5	-4.9	21.6	66.4	89.5	50.2	14.4	(e)41.9
Togo*	1.1	3.8	4.5	6.7	6.4	4.2	13.1	44.3	-2.4	-2.6	(e)4.2
Developing economies: America	**1.6**	**6.3**	**7.0**	**10.5**	**9.3**	**7.9**	**9.7**	**9.8**	**23.6**	**20.5**	**20.0**
Caribbean	*-6.9*	*-2.0*	*0.1*	*7.0*	*6.5*	*5.8*	*5.9*	*13.2*	*18.9*	*17.9*	*22.5*
Antigua and Barbuda*	-4.8	4.7	(e)4.0	0.4	(e)0.6	(e)1.3	(e)0.9	6.7	-6.3	(e)7.3	-
Aruba (6)	–	(e)35.0	(e)23.9	16.9	12.0	7.7	6.7	37.9	32.7	27.9	-
Bahamas (7)	-18.2	-17.3	-11.7	8.5	7.6	10.5	-4.1	-4.8	-15.8	34.3	(e)6.2
Barbados	-3.0	-0.2	0.5	3.9	2.9	1.4	4.8	3.4	11.4	29.2	(e)-13.4
Cuba*	-0.9	-9.1	(e)-6.5	-1.7	(e)0.8	(e)1.9	(e)7.9	18.0	39.1	(e)-3.5	(e)22.5
Dominica*	15.8	6.1	3.3	0.5	-1.8	-3.0	-4.6	-6.2	0.7	1.7	1.3
Dominican Republic*	-2.1	11.7	11.1	26.6	14.9	3.9	1.3	5.9	8.5	-2.7	-
Grenada*	7.0	3.4	3.1	9.0	4.9	4.3	-17.9	-0.8	-15.6	-14.0	(e)-23.5
Haiti	-1.2	0.4	3.0	12.2	11.4	13.7	9.7	23.6	12.9	20.2	(e)5.1
Jamaica	1.1	3.6	2.9	2.2	1.1	-0.5	3.4	5.9	17.9	7.9	(e)26.2
Montserrat*	-0.2	1.1	-0.7	5.4	-1.0	-6.9	21.5	25.7	138.5	-66.0	(e)28.9
Netherlands Antilles*	(b)-15.7	(b)-5.0	(b)-3.7	0.7	-0.9	-1.8	-14.3	-27.9	17.2	-25.7	-
Saint Kitts and Nevis*	2.7	3.9	5.0	8.9	8.1	8.6	2.2	-10.8	-2.0	8.1	-
Saint Lucia*	11.0	1.5	0.1	-9.7	-5.7	-2.8	9.3	26.4	28.4	-19.6	(e)0.4
Saint Vincent and the Grenadines*	16.2	2.4	0.3	-5.3	-4.6	-2.6	-4.2	-2.8	-12.7	20.0	(e)4.6
Trinidad and Tobago*	-9.4	-0.1	3.5	6.8	10.5	13.8	17.2	33.4	23.1	51.5	(e)49.5
Central America	*4.9*	*10.4*	*10.4*	*15.8*	*12.1*	*8.8*	*5.3*	*3.4*	*13.9*	*13.1*	*16.9*
Belize	2.2	3.6	3.2	4.9	3.0	1.8	2.3	21.5	6.6	0.8	(e)27.8
Costa Rica*	4.6	11.2	10.2	17.0	10.7	5.8	5.1	15.9	3.3	11.5	(e)16.2
El Salvador*	-4.6	2.8	3.4	10.1	6.6	3.0	3.6	1.4	10.1	13.8	(e)21.2
Guatemala*	-2.2	4.5	4.8	10.2	7.1	4.1	5.4	6.4	11.7	18.3	(e)5.3
Honduras*	1.6	3.5	3.5	7.2	4.9	1.6	4.2	0.0	16.4	9.2	(p)14.9

For sources and notes, see end of table.

1.2.1 Taux d'évolution annuels moyens des exportations et importations des pays et des régions géographiques

Imports (c.i.f.) - Importations (c.a.f.) En pourcentage											Régions, pays ou territoires
80-90	80-00	80-05	90-00	90-05	95-05	00-05	02-03	03-04	04-05	05-06	
4.5	8.5	8.1	21.0	12.6	4.3	5.5	12.4	61.9	-6.3	32.1	Ouganda
-0.5	3.0	3.8	0.1	3.4	6.3	13.4	31.9	15.6	8.9	(e)36.4	République-Unie de Tanzanie*
0.0	0.3	2.9	0.3	6.4	12.3	19.7	25.6	28.2	27.6	(e)-7.7	Zambie*
-0.5	4.7	3.3	2.4	0.3	-3.7	7.0	-27.9	23.9	24.8	(e)0.5	Zimbabwe
2.3	**1.6**	**3.8**	**4.2**	**8.1**	**11.1**	**19.7**	**24.9**	**14.6**	**28.8**	**16.4**	**Afrique centrale**
0.7	4.0	6.6	7.8	11.5	16.0	23.0	45.7	6.4	43.2	(e)35.0	Angola*
0.1	-0.2	1.9	2.0	5.7	9.1	13.0	15.8	11.2	20.1	(e)11.3	Cameroun*(5)
7.9	2.0	1.3	0.2	0.1	-0.9	8.5	-2.1	25.8	15.8	6.6	République centrafricaine*(5)
12.6	6.1	8.9	3.9	12.0	15.4	19.6	-52.8	10.6	30.0	8.5	Tchad*
5.3	1.6	3.5	4.8	7.9	8.0	21.1	23.1	31.0	15.8	(e)-8.2	Congo*(5)
3.1	-1.8	-0.2	-0.4	3.1	5.3	22.2	47.5	24.6	14.3	-	Rép. dém. du Congo*
11.9	16.4	19.9	29.3	29.6	27.0	35.3	143.7	26.8	34.6	-3.3	Guinée équatoriale
1.1	1.3	1.8	2.2	2.7	2.6	7.4	10.7	16.6	12.7	(e)14.7	Gabon*(5)
1.6	4.3	4.8	-0.7	3.2	8.3	12.1	30.9	1.6	20.3	(e)33.3	Sao Tomé-et-Principe*
2.7	**2.2**	**2.8**	**2.8**	**4.0**	**4.7**	**12.3**	**9.5**	**24.8**	**18.8**	**9.1**	**Afrique septentrionale**
-2.7	0.2	1.4	-1.3	2.3	4.8	18.1	13.1	40.7	10.3	(p)4.8	Algérie*
12.6	2.4	1.9	4.7	2.8	1.2	4.8	-11.3	15.4	54.4	(e)4.4	Égypte*
-4.4	-1.6	(e)-0.2	-1.6	(e)1.6	(e)3.4	(e)15.4	15.2	20.8	(e)3.3	(e)31.0	Jamahiriya arabe libyenne
3.6	6.3	6.6	5.5	6.7	7.1	13.6	20.1	25.3	14.0	(e)11.2	Maroc*
(e)-8.1	(e)1.0	(e)4.3	9.8	12.2	13.1	24.3	16.3	23.8	47.7	(e)-7.1	Soudan*
2.7	6.3	6.4	5.2	5.7	5.5	9.5	14.5	17.5	2.8	12.8	Tunisie
-1.3	**4.1**	**5.3**	**8.0**	**8.3**	**7.8**	**17.7**	**40.8**	**29.5**	**14.0**	**9.7**	**Afrique australe**
–	–	–	–	(e)5.3	(e)5.3	10.4	29.7	33.6	-2.8	(e)-9.3	Botswana*
–	–	–	–	(e)8.2	(e)8.2	17.2	30.0	29.4	-5.9	10.9	Lesotho
–	–	–	–	(e)6.2	(e)6.2	11.5	51.1	22.2	-3.5	(e)4.7	Namibie
(a)-1.3	(a)3.5	(a)4.5	(a)5.8	(a)6.7	(a)6.2	18.6	40.4	30.1	16.5	11.0	Afrique du Sud
–	–	–	–	(e)10.5	(e)10.5	(e)16.6	71.9	15.7	(e)9.1	(e)4.3	Swaziland
-8.3	**0.1**	**2.0**	**3.8**	**5.4**	**6.5**	**12.2**	**20.9**	**9.8**	**13.6**	**24.7**	**Afrique occidentale**
-4.9	4.0	4.4	9.7	6.7	2.5	9.5	23.0	0.2	0.0	-1.6	Bénin*
4.3	4.0	5.0	3.6	6.3	8.7	18.4	25.1	37.5	0.6	6.0	Burkina Faso
6.9	7.9	7.6	6.2	6.6	5.8	15.3	27.2	10.3	13.4	30.3	Cap-Vert*
-1.5	1.8	2.4	4.3	4.4	3.8	15.4	31.6	32.8	18.7	14.3	Côte d'Ivoire*
2.5	4.3	(e)2.7	0.2	(e)-1.0	(e)-1.8	(e)8.2	(e)-2.6	46.3	3.6	(e)-0.7	Gambie
0.6	6.6	6.7	8.3	7.3	8.5	12.8	19.4	32.9	24.4	(e)19.8	Ghana
9.7	5.0	3.7	-2.6	-0.7	0.5	5.4	-4.0	7.8	18.8	-	Guinée
5.2	2.1	1.5	-4.9	-1.8	-1.5	16.7	11.7	26.8	43.4	4.9	Guinée-Bissau
-7.2	1.8	-0.7	11.1	-0.6	-9.4	-6.9	-4.8	98.5	-3.8	(e)4.9	Libéria*
2.7	5.2	6.0	4.7	6.6	7.4	13.9	34.9	3.1	24.8	(e)-16.6	Mali*
-2.1	3.9	3.7	3.1	3.1	3.0	9.4	8.4	44.0	34.6	-	Mauritanie*
-3.5	-0.2	1.5	0.8	4.1	6.9	17.4	32.8	20.6	6.7	-5.0	Niger*
-15.0	-2.5	0.6	3.1	6.0	8.0	10.7	19.5	-4.8	7.3	(e)48.7	Nigéria
1.4	2.3	4.1	3.9	7.1	9.3	17.8	18.1	18.4	23.2	5.0	Sénégal*
-8.7	-4.4	-0.4	-4.2	4.9	11.9	17.6	14.8	-5.6	20.3	(e)15.3	Sierra Leone*
2.0	2.2	(e)3.3	5.5	(e)6.2	(e)3.9	(e)13.9	(e)31.1	(e)13.5	(e)13.6	(e)1.0	Togo*
-0.2	**7.8**	**7.7**	**11.9**	**8.6**	**5.6**	**5.7**	**3.8**	**21.7**	**16.0**	**17.8**	**Économies en développement : Amérique**
-4.1	**-0.2**	**1.3**	**6.9**	**6.0**	**5.4**	**3.2**	**1.4**	**7.7**	**18.2**	**12.1**	**Caraïbes**
10.9	7.7	6.5	4.3	3.8	3.7	7.9	4.7	7.6	35.3	-	Antigua-et-Barbuda*
–	(e)9.1	(e)7.3	5.6	5.1	5.4	3.4	0.8	3.2	17.8	-	Aruba (6)
-14.3	-8.0	-4.9	7.7	5.5	4.0	1.1	1.9	8.1	17.1	(e)25.3	Bahamas (7)
1.6	3.3	4.0	7.2	6.5	6.0	7.7	11.6	18.2	13.6	(e)-6.1	Barbade
1.5	-4.8	(e)-2.2	2.5	(e)4.8	(e)7.4	(e)7.6	11.6	20.3	(e)35.3	(e)24.3	Cuba*
9.7	6.4	5.1	3.1	2.3	1.8	2.6	10.0	13.5	12.8	1.9	Dominique*
5.4	9.5	8.4	12.0	7.6	4.3	-2.8	-13.7	2.9	9.5	-	République dominicaine*
8.4	7.8	7.3	8.7	7.1	6.9	4.3	27.4	-1.1	14.9	-7.9	Grenade*
-2.9	3.7	5.7	14.4	12.1	8.7	7.4	5.1	10.0	11.3	23.1	Haïti
2.8	5.8	5.7	6.9	5.9	3.9	5.5	3.0	3.7	18.2	(e)22.6	Jamaïque
14.6	3.9	2.5	-6.3	-2.9	-0.6	7.4	11.8	-11.0	17.7	(e)-14.5	Montserrat*
(b)-14.6	(b)-3.5	(b)-1.8	1.8	1.5	1.2	-5.5	14.9	-24.9	18.7	-	Antilles néerlandaises*
10.4	7.1	6.3	3.9	4.1	4.2	1.4	-1.3	0.1	5.4	(e)2.7	Saint-Kitts-et-Nevis*
9.0	6.6	5.5	2.4	2.5	3.0	5.0	30.4	8.5	-4.4	(e)4.2	Sainte-Lucie*
9.7	6.1	5.4	3.9	3.9	4.6	8.6	12.7	12.2	6.6	(e)9.2	Saint-Vincent-et-les Grenadines*
-12.3	0.0	3.0	12.1	11.3	10.3	11.2	6.8	24.8	17.5	(e)14.1	Trinité-et-Tobago*
5.1	**12.2**	**11.7**	**13.9**	**11.1**	**9.8**	**4.8**	**1.9**	**15.4**	**8.4**	**15.6**	**Amérique centrale**
4.0	6.3	(e)6.9	5.9	(e)7.2	(e)9.9	(e)1.8	5.2	(e)-7.3	(e)16.0	(e)10.7	Belize
4.4	10.9	10.5	13.9	10.8	8.1	8.6	6.6	7.9	18.7	(e)19.9	Costa Rica*
2.4	8.3	8.4	11.1	9.3	6.9	7.5	12.1	11.3	10.1	(e)18.6	El Salvador*
0.6	7.6	8.6	11.6	11.0	10.6	11.2	6.6	16.2	12.8	(e)15.6	Guatemala*
0.6	6.2	7.4	13.8	11.6	9.4	10.1	9.9	19.6	17.8	(p)17.4	Honduras*

Pour les sources et les notes, se reporter à la fin du tableau.

Region, country or territory	Exports (f.o.b) - Exportations (f.a.b.) Percentage										
	80-90	80-00	80-05	90-00	90-05	95-05	00-05	02-03	03-04	04-05	05-06
Mexico	5.9	11.0	11.0	16.1	12.5	9.2	5.3	2.9	14.3	13.1	(p)17.0
Nicaragua	-5.8	1.7	3.1	10.3	7.8	4.8	6.7	7.8	25.0	13.5	(p)19.8
Panama*	_	_	_	(e)9.4	(e)6.8	(e)4.6	2.8	2.1	9.2	7.9	(e)27.6
South America	*2.3*	*5.4*	*6.1*	*7.1*	*7.6*	*7.4*	*14.4*	*16.5*	*33.5*	*26.8*	*22.0*
Argentina*	2.1	7.6	7.5	10.1	7.9	4.8	9.1	15.3	16.9	16.0	(e)15.1
Bolivia	-1.9	2.3	3.9	4.3	6.7	8.0	17.4	23.0	34.3	24.5	(p)58.1
Brazil	5.1	5.4	6.1	5.9	7.5	8.5	17.1	21.1	32.0	22.6	16.2
Chile*	8.1	10.0	9.6	9.4	9.1	7.7	17.4	19.2	48.7	25.9	45.4
Colombia	7.7	8.1	7.6	7.4	6.6	5.6	10.0	9.8	24.0	30.3	(p)15.3
Ecuador*	-0.4	4.4	5.2	6.8	7.2	6.4	16.4	23.4	24.6	30.3	(e)22.6
Guyana*	-3.3	4.6	4.2	8.3	4.7	0.6	3.2	3.6	15.5	-6.8	(e)4.6
Paraguay	11.6	7.7	7.1	1.7	4.2	5.0	15.7	30.6	31.0	4.4	12.3
Peru*	-1.5	4.2	5.9	9.0	9.9	9.7	19.6	17.8	38.8	31.5	(p)41.3
Suriname	-0.4	1.2	0.3	3.2	0.5	-0.3	28.0	19.0	317.5	54.9	-
Uruguay	4.5	5.5	4.7	5.2	3.4	1.6	9.6	18.5	32.9	16.2	(p)32.9
Venezuela (Bolivarian Republic of)	-4.4	2.1	3.8	5.5	7.0	8.6	11.5	5.4	47.3	46.0	(p)17.5
Developing economies: Asia	**4.6**	**9.0**	**9.3**	**9.5**	**9.7**	**9.3**	**14.9**	**18.7**	**29.1**	**20.8**	**17.7**
Eastern Asia	*14.9*	*13.1*	*12.3*	*10.0*	*10.2*	*9.9*	*16.4*	*22.1*	*28.0*	*19.7*	*20.1*
China	12.8	14.7	15.5	14.5	16.4	17.5	26.7	34.6	35.4	28.4	(p)27.2
China, Hong Kong SAR	16.8	14.5	12.0	8.3	6.7	4.5	8.5	11.8	15.9	11.6	11.5
China, Macao SAR	11.7	7.2	5.9	3.9	3.2	2.6	1.6	9.5	9.0	-12.0	(e)18.6
China, Taiwan Province of	14.9	10.8	9.2	7.2	6.1	5.0	7.7	10.3	20.9	13.7	(p)13.3
Korea, Dem. People's Rep. of	_	(e)-9.2	(e)-1.9	-9.2	(e)-1.9	(e)4.4	(e)15.6	5.8	29.5	(e)3.0	-
Korea, Republic of (8)	15.0	12.2	11.1	10.1	9.2	7.8	12.9	19.3	31.0	12.0	(p)14.7
Mongolia	5.0	-1.7	0.3	0.7	4.6	7.7	15.8	17.5	41.2	22.4	(p)43.6
Southern Asia	*3.2*	*6.4*	*7.4*	*6.5*	*8.5*	*10.2*	*16.7*	*18.0*	*26.7*	*28.5*	*15.6*
Afghanistan	-10.5	-9.8	-6.9	-2.0	0.9	5.0	31.0	43.8	118.1	8.3	-
Bangladesh	7.8	12.5	11.9	15.7	12.1	8.5	8.6	15.5	15.6	14.1	(e)32.1
Bhutan	19.6	11.5	10.6	7.0	8.2	8.1	23.5	36.3	19.2	66.0	-
India	7.3	9.4	10.0	9.5	10.9	11.4	19.2	17.1	30.0	29.8	(e)21.5
Iran, Islamic Republic of*	-1.2	2.4	4.4	1.2	6.2	11.7	17.9	20.6	30.6	34.4	(p)8.1
Maldives	28.3	13.9	12.0	4.4	6.7	8.3	10.9	14.9	19.1	-10.8	(p)39.4
Nepal	8.1	10.8	9.9	10.7	8.5	8.6	1.1	16.7	14.1	9.8	(e)-1.5
Pakistan	8.1	7.9	7.4	4.3	5.4	5.9	12.7	20.3	12.1	20.0	2.6
Sri Lanka	5.4	9.6	8.5	11.3	7.5	3.9	4.1	9.1	12.3	10.2	(e)6.1
South-Eastern Asia	*6.2*	*11.0*	*10.3*	*11.1*	*9.0*	*6.4*	*10.0*	*11.3*	*25.6*	*14.7*	*16.5*
Brunei Darussalam*	-9.3	(e)-1.7	(e)1.2	(e)2.4	(e)6.2	(e)10.4	(e)10.6	(e)19.4	(e)14.4	(e)23.6	-
Cambodia	18.0	32.7	29.7	28.8	23.2	16.9	6.7	19.0	24.1	12.4	(e)15.9
Indonesia	-1.3	6.1	6.2	8.1	6.7	5.2	7.1	7.8	14.3	19.7	(e)20.2
Lao People's Dem. Rep.*	11.0	16.1	13.2	15.4	9.1	2.5	7.8	27.0	-4.5	40.0	(e)29.5
Malaysia (9)(10)	8.6	12.7	11.4	12.2	9.3	5.9	8.8	6.5	26.5	12.0	(p)13.9
Myanmar	-7.6	7.4	10.6	14.4	16.4	17.8	12.1	-18.5	-4.2	60.2	(e)-3.7
Philippines	3.9	11.4	11.0	18.8	12.6	7.8	1.7	-0.7	9.5	0.5	(e)19.1
Singapore (11)	9.9	12.2	10.8	9.9	8.2	5.5	12.6	15.2	37.8	15.6	(p)17.8
Thailand*	14.0	15.2	13.3	10.5	9.0	6.7	11.1	17.9	19.8	14.5	(p)16.4
Viet Nam	18.9	21.0	20.4	22.7	20.1	17.4	17.7	22.1	27.0	23.4	(e)11.9
Western Asia	*-6.8*	*1.9*	*4.6*	*6.4*	*9.5*	*12.4*	*17.3*	*20.2*	*39.6*	*30.7*	*12.6*
Bahrain	-3.3	2.0	3.6	3.5	6.1	8.5	10.3	14.4	13.4	33.3	(e)19.8
Iraq*	-3.5	-8.6	0.0	31.0	29.9	39.4	2.7	-26.2	90.4	29.9	(e)33.4
Jordan	6.2	6.5	7.5	6.6	9.0	9.7	18.0	11.3	27.3	9.7	20.1
Kuwait*	-7.7	-0.1	3.2	16.5	14.2	10.7	19.4	32.0	41.0	58.0	(e)28.9
Lebanon	-5.2	-0.3	2.9	4.1	8.9	11.9	22.6	45.8	14.6	5.1	(e)25.4
Oman	3.3	6.7	7.7	5.7	8.2	10.6	9.3	4.4	14.3	40.1	(e)17.8
Qatar*	-8.1	1.9	6.2	10.1	14.9	22.3	19.1	24.2	39.6	37.9	-
Saudi Arabia*	-12.7	-0.1	3.0	3.1	7.4	11.3	18.4	28.7	35.1	32.1	
Syrian Arab Republic*	2.4	4.8	(e)5.6	0.9	(e)4.6	(e)7.0	(e)5.0	-12.3	-6.1	(e)22.8	(e)8.1
Turkey*	14.0	10.8	11.0	9.2	11.0	11.8	22.4	34.8	32.4	16.6	(e)14.9
United Arab Emirates	-2.3	5.1	7.1	6.5	9.8	13.2	19.5	14.6	59.5	28.3	(e)18.1
Yemen*	_	_	_	20.6	17.1	11.2	10.0	8.7	18.8	37.2	(e)40.4
Developing economies: Oceania	**4.2**	**4.9**	**4.1**	**2.9**	**2.4**	**1.4**	**10.0**	**32.7**	**12.8**	**16.2**	**13.1**
American Samoa*	8.9	4.3	3.6	1.4	1.8	2.8	4.6	18.4	-3.0	-16.1	(p)15.5
Cook Islands	1.3	-0.1	1.8	-0.9	3.8	8.7	-4.8	21.7	-16.5	-31.9	-
Fiji	1.0	3.1	2.9	2.7	2.2	0.4	7.0	29.7	2.9	1.1	(p)-0.8
French Polynesia*	15.7	14.0	9.7	9.6	2.9	-2.8	-2.3	-9.2	22.4	13.5	(p)12.0
Guam	-1.8	3.8	(e)1.8	-0.5	(e)-2.9	(e)-4.8	(e)-5.9	26.7	-34.2	(e)4.2	-
Kiribati	0.0	2.8	(e)0.4	6.5	(e)-1.4	(e)-9.0	(e)-7.2	-15.6	(e)-30.0	(e)76.0	(e)79.0
Nauru	-2.3	-6.5	(e)-9.2	-6.7	(e)-12.4	(e)-15.0	(e)-21.4	0.0	(e)-12.0	(e)-11.6	-
New Caledonia*	5.5	4.1	4.7	1.7	4.8	7.9	18.3	58.1	24.0	14.0	(e)-11.2

For sources and notes, see end of table.

1.2.1 Taux d'évolution annuels moyens des exportations et importations des pays et des régions géographiques

				Imports (c.i.f.) - Importations (c.a.f.) En pourcentage							Régions, pays ou territoires
80-90	80-00	80-05	90-00	90-05	95-05	00-05	02-03	03-04	04-05	05-06	
6.4	13.4	12.6	14.2	11.3	10.1	4.3	1.1	15.8	7.4	(p)15.5	Mexique
-3.1	3.1	4.5	11.6	9.4	8.1	7.5	7.2	17.7	17.3	(p)15.2	Nicaragua
_	_	_	8.7	5.4	3.0	4.9	3.5	16.5	16.3	(e)10.4	Panama*
-1.7	*7.1*	*6.4*	*11.0*	*6.5*	*1.5*	*7.2*	*7.6*	*34.7*	*26.0*	*21.2*	*Amérique du Sud*
-6.5	10.3	7.5	17.0	5.6	-3.2	4.0	53.9	62.3	27.8	(e)19.5	Argentine*
-0.3	6.8	6.0	9.7	5.8	2.1	4.0	-8.7	14.1	27.0	20.5	Bolivie
-1.9	7.2	6.7	12.7	7.6	1.4	5.2	2.3	30.6	16.9	17.7	Brésil
2.8	9.9	9.0	10.3	7.6	3.9	12.2	13.4	28.5	31.0	(e)16.8	Chili*
0.0	6.9	6.6	9.6	6.9	2.3	11.9	9.3	20.6	26.6	(p)23.4	Colombie
-1.3	5.0	6.6	7.9	9.6	8.4	20.1	4.2	22.7	25.0	(e)17.7	Équateur*
-3.3	5.2	4.7	7.9	4.6	1.6	3.7	0.0	13.1	20.8	(e)9.4	Guyana*
4.2	10.6	8.6	7.0	4.2	-0.9	12.6	46.3	26.6	22.4	55.1	Paraguay
1.3	8.2	7.0	10.8	6.1	0.4	8.3	12.3	20.0	23.8	22.6	Pérou*
-3.1	1.5	(e)2.2	0.9	(e)2.8	(e)4.0	(e)15.7	43.1	13.6	(e)21.9	-	Suriname
-1.2	7.9	5.9	10.1	3.8	-1.6	2.1	11.5	42.2	24.6	(p)23.1	Uruguay
-3.2	2.2	2.5	5.3	3.9	3.7	5.4	-21.5	79.4	54.3	(p)33.8	Venezuela (République bolivarienne du)
6.5	9.4	9.3	8.2	8.6	8.0	15.1	19.7	31.1	16.8	16.7	Économies en développement : Asie
13.3	*12.7*	*11.9*	*9.3*	*9.7*	*9.3*	*15.8*	*23.8*	*28.8*	*14.6*	*16.8*	*Asie orientale*
13.5	13.0	14.3	13.0	16.1	18.5	26.5	39.8	36.0	17.6	(p)19.9	Chine
15.0	14.4	12.0	8.8	6.8	3.8	8.1	11.7	16.9	10.5	12.1	Chine, Hong Kong RAS
10.4	7.5	7.0	2.2	4.5	6.6	12.0	8.8	26.3	12.5	(e)21.2	Chine, Macao RAS
12.4	11.8	10.1	8.5	6.6	4.9	8.3	13.0	32.0	8.6	(p)11.0	Chine, Taiwan Province de
_	(e)-7.0	(e)0.8	-7.0	(e)0.8	(e)8.7	(e)11.3	8.2	24.0	(e)14.3	-	Corée, Rép. populaire dém. de
11.9	11.1	10.2	7.1	7.5	6.3	12.1	17.6	25.5	16.4	(e)18.5	Corée, République de (8)
5.5	-4.2	-1.2	0.5	5.5	10.6	14.8	16.0	27.5	16.0	(p)25.7	Mongolie
2.2	*4.8*	*6.2*	*5.1*	*8.1*	*10.8*	*20.4*	*23.1*	*31.9*	*30.2*	*16.8*	*Asie méridionale*
-0.1	-3.7	1.9	3.6	13.1	24.5	13.4	-14.3	3.6	15.8	-	Afghanistan
3.6	6.9	7.3	10.3	9.1	7.2	12.0	20.2	32.4	10.2	(e)15.3	Bangladesh
5.6	4.8	(e)6.7	7.9	(e)11.0	(e)14.4	(e)24.9	26.7	65.2	(e)21.6	-	Bhoutan
4.2	6.9	8.4	10.1	11.6	12.7	23.1	28.4	37.5	39.7	(e)21.9	Inde
-1.1	0.3	2.7	-4.8	3.5	12.1	22.0	22.3	21.0	12.4	(p)2.4	Iran, Rép. islamique d'*
15.4	15.1	13.5	11.8	10.3	8.7	15.0	20.2	36.3	16.1	(p)24.4	Maldives
6.9	8.6	7.6	9.3	6.5	3.0	5.2	23.6	6.6	-0.5	(e)40.0	Népal
3.0	4.5	4.9	3.1	5.0	5.9	19.0	16.1	37.7	41.3	12.0	Pakistan
2.7	7.8	7.3	8.9	6.7	4.4	7.9	9.3	19.5	10.8	(e)17.2	Sri Lanka
7.2	*10.9*	*9.7*	*7.9*	*6.8*	*4.2*	*11.1*	*12.3*	*27.6*	*16.6*	*12.5*	*Asie du Sud-Est*
3.8	(e)6.9	(e)4.6	(e)1.6	(e)-0.5	(e)-5.0	(e)5.7	(e)-14.7	(e)7.2	(e)4.9	-	Brunéi Darussalam*
-3.1	16.7	16.7	30.8	20.8	11.7	15.3	13.0	22.5	20.1	(e)15.3	Cambodge
2.6	6.6	6.4	2.7	4.4	3.9	17.5	34.5	30.4	26.7	(e)9.8	Indonésie
6.6	10.3	8.2	12.7	6.3	-0.9	6.3	21.3	-3.5	59.8	(e)21.2	Rép. dém. populaire lao*
7.7	12.9	11.2	9.5	7.3	3.7	8.2	2.3	28.5	8.7	(p)14.4	Malaisie (9)(10)
-4.7	12.9	11.8	22.6	12.5	3.4	-5.6	-11.0	5.1	-12.3	(e)-1.1	Myanmar
2.9	10.5	9.6	12.5	8.5	3.6	5.4	6.2	7.2	10.9	(e)12.5	Philippines
8.0	10.6	9.2	7.8	6.1	3.4	9.8	9.9	35.7	15.2	(p)18.8	Singapour (11)
12.7	12.9	11.3	5.0	6.0	4.9	14.2	17.3	24.5	25.2	(p)6.6	Thaïlande*
8.7	13.6	14.7	22.7	19.7	14.8	20.4	30.9	25.0	17.3	(e)-3.0	Viet Nam
-2.6	*3.2*	*4.8*	*6.8*	*8.1*	*9.3*	*17.1*	*14.3*	*49.1*	*18.6*	*23.4*	*Asie occidentale*
-2.3	1.2	2.5	0.3	3.5	6.7	11.7	12.9	16.4	14.5	(e)18.5	Bahreïn
-6.8	-9.7	-1.2	27.4	27.7	33.7	11.6	-16.9	151.7	18.8	(e)3.0	Iraq*
-1.9	2.4	4.1	5.1	7.5	9.1	18.0	13.1	41.5	29.3	9.0	Jordanie
-4.1	0.9	2.4	5.5	6.4	6.3	19.1	22.1	15.0	39.4	(e)-13.2	Koweït*
-5.5	5.5	5.5	8.7	6.1	1.8	8.6	11.2	31.1	-0.4	(e)-2.5	Liban
0.7	5.1	5.8	6.1	6.8	7.0	12.6	9.4	34.9	-0.4	(e)19.9	Oman
-1.4	5.2	6.9	7.4	9.8	9.8	23.0	20.9	22.6	67.6	(e)25.4	Qatar*
-6.1	-0.5	1.1	0.8	3.4	6.0	13.8	5.1	31.9	32.9	(e)6.8	Arabie saoudite*
-8.4	0.4	(e)2.0	3.6	(e)4.8	(e)4.6	(e)16.0	13.9	37.9	(e)14.9	(e)9.2	République arabe syrienne*
9.3	10.7	10.4	10.3	9.9	8.9	18.0	32.2	46.8	2.7	(e)38.9	Turquie*
1.0	8.8	10.0	10.7	11.9	13.6	21.6	5.0	75.3	27.2	37.5	Émirats arabes unis
_	_	_	1.1	4.8	8.7	16.6	25.8	8.5	22.1	(e)-7.3	Yémen*
3.7	3.4	3.5	0.8	2.7	3.8	11.8	26.3	10.5	9.4	6.3	Économies en développement : Océanie
10.7	5.9	4.8	3.0	2.6	2.4	2.0	25.1	-3.2	-16.2	(p)-32.5	Samoa américaines*
9.0	4.9	4.4	-3.8	0.6	5.8	11.1	49.4	5.2	1.8	-	Îles Cook
0.3	3.8	4.4	2.9	4.6	5.2	15.1	33.6	19.5	11.2	(p)14.8	Fidji
6.2	3.9	4.3	1.6	4.0	5.7	10.5	23.7	-5.6	15.0	(p)-2.6	Polynésie française*
2.5	3.5	(e)3.7	-0.8	(e)2.1	(e)3.9	(e)9.8	(e)20.5	(e)27.2	(e)32.1	-	Guam
5.5	6.1	(e)6.4	4.1	(e)6.0	(e)7.3	(e)14.1	3.6	(e)21.4	(e)22.1	(p)-15.8	Kiribati
10.7	2.3	(e)0.4	-11.7	(e)-7.4	(e)-2.4	(e)-12.1	-21.0	(e)-24.0	(e)-6.7	-	Nauru
8.8	6.2	6.0	1.1	4.0	6.3	16.6	51.4	7.1	8.0	(e)7.8	Nouvelle-Calédonie*

Pour les sources et les notes, se reporter à la fin du tableau.

Region, country or territory	Exports (f.o.b) - Exportations (f.a.b.) Percentage										
	80-90	80-00	80-05	90-00	90-05	95-05	00-05	02-03	03-04	04-05	05-06
Papua New Guinea	4.9	6.1	5.0	3.7	2.6	1.0	10.8	34.5	15.9	28.2	(e)22.4
Samoa*	-3.3	-1.6	-0.3	12.0	6.5	1.2	-5.3	9.1	-28.5	11.1	(p)472.5
Solomon Islands*	0.9	4.0	1.4	2.0	-2.4	-7.9	14.7	29.3	31.0	7.7	(e)28.9
Tonga	2.7	3.3	2.8	-3.8	-0.7	1.6	10.1	22.6	-15.0	-33.8	(e)0.9
Tuvalu	(e)14.1	(e)-4.2	(e)-6.7	-38.3	-23.5	-1.3	54.0	-30.4	40.1	-54.0	-
Vanuatu	-6.3	-0.1	0.2	4.8	2.5	0.1	12.4	43.3	38.6	2.0	-
Economies in transition: Asia	–	–	–	–	–	11.9	21.8	29.6	40.2	30.2	30.0
Armenia*	–	–	–	–	–	14.8	27.0	35.7	4.3	32.9	5.6
Azerbaijan*	–	–	–	–	–	24.0	19.0	19.5	39.6	20.2	46.6
Georgia (4)	–	–	–	–	–	16.6	23.4	33.4	40.2	34.0	(p)14.6
Kazakhstan*(4)	–	–	–	–	–	16.6	27.8	33.7	55.4	38.6	(p)37.3
Kyrgyzstan	–	–	–	–	–	3.4	8.5	19.8	23.6	-6.5	(p)18.2
Tajikistan (4)	–	–	–	–	–	2.4	5.8	22.6	14.8	-0.7	(p)53.9
Turkmenistan (4)	–	–	–	–	–	9.1	14.4	27.4	6.6	27.6	(e)7.8
Uzbekistan (4)	–	–	–	–	–	0.2	13.1	26.9	34.2	13.0	-
Economies in transition: Europe	2.9	-0.2	2.4	5.6	8.6	10.0	19.6	26.9	35.5	25.9	21.8
Albania	–	(e)1.8	(e)7.4	8.3	11.7	14.1	22.1	31.9	35.1	8.7	20.4
Bosnia and Herzegovina*(12)	–	–	–	–	–	51.3	20.6	33.1	41.2	24.1	(e)31.8
Belarus	–	–	–	–	–	10.5	18.6	24.0	38.5	16.0	23.5
Bulgaria*	-0.2	-6.7	-3.3	2.2	5.9	7.0	21.2	31.2	31.7	18.2	(p)27.6
Croatia*	–	–	–	–	–	6.6	16.3	26.2	29.7	9.3	18.3
Moldova, Republic of	–	–	–	–	–	2.3	18.8	22.6	24.2	11.3	(p)-3.6
Macedonia, TFYR*	–	–	–	–	–	3.8	10.5	22.5	22.6	21.8	17.6
Romania*	-4.0	-2.7	1.3	8.5	11.9	13.6	23.3	27.0	33.3	18.1	16.6
Russian Federation (4)	–	–	–	–	–	10.0	19.2	26.9	34.8	32.9	(p)24.0
Serbia and Montenegro*	–	–	–	–	–	8.2	23.0	16.5	50.2	14.4	-
Yugoslavia, SFR (former)	3.8	–	–	–	–	–	–	–	–	–	–
USSR (former)	3.7	–	–	–	–	–	–	–	–	–	–
Ukraine (4)	–	–	–	–	–	10.1	20.8	28.5	41.6	4.8	12.1

Sources:
- Growth rates in this table are based on trade figures in table 1.1.1.

Notes:
- Countries which use the Special Trade System as reporting system are marked with an asterisk (*).
(a) Before 1998, data refers to South Africa Customs Union (Botswana, Lesotho, Namibia, South Africa and Swaziland).
(b) Before 1986, includes Aruba.
(1) Excluding military imports.
(2) From 1985 onwards, data are not comparable to those shown for prior periods due to revisions of the koruna-to-US dollar exchange rate.
(3) Prior to 1985, general trade.
(4) Prior to 1994, covers only trade with countries outside the CIS.
(5) Inter-trade between the member countries of CEMAC is excluded.
(6) Prior to 2000, data exclude imports into and exports from the free zone; mineral fuels are also excluded.
(7) From 1990 onwards, trade statistics exclude certain oil and chemical products.
(8) Excluding imports of goods financed through foreign aid.
(9) Inter-trade between the States of Malaysia included.
(10) Excluding military imports and offshore installations of petroleum industry.
(11) Including trans-shipments to and from peninsular Malaysia.
(12) Prior to 1998, data refer to the Federation of Bosnia and Herzegovina only. The other entity of Bosnia and Herzegovina, Republika Srpska, is not included.

Imports (c.i.f.) - Importations (c.a.f.) En pourcentage											Régions, pays ou territoires
80-90	80-00	80-05	90-00	90-05	95-05	00-05	02-03	03-04	04-05	05-06	
0.7	1.2	1.0	-0.8	0.1	0.0	10.5	10.7	22.9	2.9	(e)14.9	Papouasie-Nouvelle-Guinée
3.8	4.3	4.7	0.9	3.8	6.2	13.6	1.0	20.5	20.6	(o)50.7	Samoa*
1.9	3.1	1.8	0.7	-0.5	-2.7	14.9	35.7	30.1	51.6	(e)18.7	Îles Salomon*
4.7	4.0	4.1	1.9	3.5	4.1	10.5	5.0	12.1	4.8	(e)6.6	Tonga
(e)2.0	(e)4.8	(e)4.8	5.2	5.2	6.8	25.8	-8.6	12.7	13.3	-	Tuvalu
2.4	2.5	2.6	0.9	2.1	2.6	9.8	16.8	22.1	2.4	(e)3.8	Vanuatu
–	–	–	–	–	10.4	21.5	27.3	40.1	24.9	28.7	**Économies en transition : Asie**
–	–	–	–	–	7.5	15.5	29.6	5.6	30.9	24.1	Arménie*
–	–	–	–	–	19.0	31.3	57.7	33.9	19.5	25.4	Azerbaïdjan*
–	–	–	–	–	13.4	30.6	43.5	61.9	34.9	(p)47.8	Géorgie (4)
–	–	–	–	–	15.1	27.4	27.7	52.0	35.8	(p)36.4	Kazakhstan*(4)
–	–	–	–	–	3.0	17.9	22.2	31.2	17.7	(p)55.1	Kirghizistan
–	–	–	–	–	5.0	16.1	22.2	35.2	11.7	(p)29.5	Tadjikistan (4)
–	–	–	–	–	18.2	14.1	18.5	32.2	3.7	4.4	Turkménistan (4)
–	–	–	–	–	(e)-1.9	(e)6.6	9.8	27.4	(e)9.4	-	Ouzbekistan (4)
3.9	-0.8	1.5	2.8	6.6	7.9	22.2	28.8	29.1	22.1	16.5	**Économies en transition : Europe**
–	(e)10.2	(e)12.0	9.6	12.2	14.2	19.6	24.0	23.9	13.4	16.8	Albanie
–	–	–	–	–	18.0	15.4	27.1	18.5	14.0	0.1	Bosnie-Herzégovine*(12)
–	–	–	–	–	9.7	17.3	27.1	42.7	1.3	33.6	Bélarus
-0.3	-5.6	-1.6	5.3	9.4	11.8	23.9	36.5	32.7	25.5	(p)26.6	Bulgarie*
–	–	–	–	–	9.2	19.9	32.5	16.8	11.9	15.8	Croatie*
–	–	–	–	–	7.6	24.9	35.1	26.4	29.3	(p)17.5	Moldova, République de
–	–	–	–	–	5.9	12.0	15.6	27.1	10.1	16.6	Macédoine, LERY*
-3.8	-0.7	3.1	6.8	11.5	14.1	26.3	34.4	36.1	23.9	26.3	Roumanie*
–	–	–	–	–	5.1	22.6	24.8	28.0	28.7	9.8	Fédération de Russie (4)
–	–	–	–	–	12.9	25.9	25.8	35.2	2.4	-	Serbie-et-Monténégro*
0.8	–	–	–	–	–	–	–	–	–	–	Yougoslavie, RSF (anc.)
5.7	–	–	–	–	–	–	–	–	–	–	URSS (anc.)
–	–	–	–	–	7.2	21.7	35.6	26.0	24.6	24.6	Ukraine (4)

Sources :
- Les taux d'accroissement donnés dans ce tableau ont été calculés d'après les chiffres du tableau 1.1.1.

Notes :
- Les pays qui utilisent le système du commerce spécial en tant que système d'enregistrement sont marqués par un astérisque (*).
(a) Avant 1998, donnée relative à l'Union Douanière d'Afrique du Sud (Afrique du Sud, Botswana, Lesotho, Namibie et Swaziland).
(b) Avant 1986, y compris Aruba.
(1) Non compris les importations militaires.
(2) A partir de 1985, les chiffres ne sont pas comparables à ceux des années antérieures à cause des révisions du taux de change de la couronne par rapport au dollar des États-Unis.
(3) Avant 1985, commerce général.
(4) Avant 1994, concerne seulement le commerce avec les pays extérieurs à la CEI.
(5) Non-compris le commerce entre les pays membres de CEMAC.
(6) Avant 2000, les données excluent les importations en provenance et les exportations à destination de la zone de libre circulation; les combustibles minéraux sont également exclus.
(7) A partir de 1990, certains produits pétroliers et chimiques ne sont plus inclus dans les statistiques du commerce.
(8) Non-compris les biens d'importation financés par l'aide à l'étranger.
(9) Y compris le commerce entre les États de la Malaisie.
(10) Non-compris les importations militaires et l'installation près des côtes de l'industrie pétrolière
(11) Y compris les transbordements vers et en provenance de la Malaisie péninsulaire.
(12) Avant 1998, les données se réfèrent uniquement à la Fédération de la Bosnie-Herzégovine. L'autre entité de la Bosnie-Herzégovine, Republika Srpska, n'est pas incluse.

Economic grouping	Exports (f.o.b.) - Exportations (f.a.b.) Percentage										
	80-90	80-00	80-05	90-00	90-05	95-05	00-05	02-03	03-04	04-05	05-06
DEVELOPING ECONOMIES	**3.1**	**7.6**	**8.2**	**9.0**	**9.3**	**9.1**	**14.1**	**17.4**	**28.2**	**21.3**	**17.6**
Developing economies excluding China	2.6	7.1	7.5	8.5	8.3	7.7	11.9	14.2	26.6	19.7	15.1
Developing economies excluding LDCs	3.1	7.7	8.2	9.1	9.3	9.0	14.1	17.5	28.1	21.1	17.5
High-income countries	2.8	7.8	7.9	8.7	8.2	7.3	11.3	13.8	27.3	18.8	14.8
Middle-income countries	3.9	6.7	7.1	7.5	7.9	7.8	13.5	17.3	26.5	19.6	13.4
Low-income countries	3.1	8.3	9.8	11.3	12.7	13.5	19.8	23.9	30.8	26.6	24.1
Heavily indebted poor countries	1.0	2.5	3.7	3.9	5.8	6.9	15.3	18.9	28.5	14.9	18.3
Landlocked countries	1.4	9.8	10.5	15.5	13.3	10.2	18.9	24.6	36.6	24.4	24.1
Small island developing states	-5.1	-0.4	1.3	4.4	5.2	5.7	10.7	21.8	14.9	30.7	31.9
Least developed countries	*2.2*	*4.7*	*6.5*	*7.4*	*9.9*	*11.7*	*17.7*	*14.5*	*33.3*	*36.0*	*20.0*
Africa and Haiti	2.6	3.0	5.1	3.8	8.3	12.2	23.0	18.5	44.4	41.2	17.8
Asia	0.3	9.2	10.3	16.4	13.9	10.8	9.0	8.3	14.9	25.8	24.7
Islands	3.1	4.0	3.4	2.9	2.2	0.5	10.5	21.7	15.3	-3.0	44.7
Major petroleum exporters	*-6.4*	*1.6*	*4.0*	*5.0*	*7.9*	*10.9*	*15.1*	*16.6*	*35.3*	*35.0*	*13.8*
Africa	-5.5	0.3	3.0	1.9	6.9	12.0	18.4	24.9	35.0	45.4	14.3
America	-6.5	1.0	3.1	5.3	7.0	8.8	11.2	7.2	42.3	44.6	21.9
Asia	-6.6	2.1	4.3	5.8	8.3	10.9	14.8	15.8	34.7	31.5	12.7
Major exporters of manufactured goods	*11.5*	*12.1*	*11.4*	*10.7*	*10.1*	*9.0*	*14.1*	*17.7*	*27.0*	*18.2*	*18.9*
America	5.5	8.8	9.0	12.5	10.7	8.9	8.7	7.9	19.7	16.3	16.7
Asia	13.0	12.8	11.9	10.4	10.0	9.0	15.0	19.5	28.2	18.4	19.2
Emerging economies	*10.0*	*10.9*	*10.1*	*10.3*	*8.8*	*6.9*	*10.5*	*12.7*	*26.3*	*14.8*	*16.8*
America	4.9	8.5	8.8	11.8	10.2	8.4	9.8	9.6	22.1	17.7	20.2
Asia	12.9	12.2	10.8	9.7	8.2	6.2	10.9	14.2	28.2	13.5	15.2
Newly industrialized economies	*11.5*	*11.9*	*10.6*	*9.5*	*7.9*	*5.8*	*9.7*	*12.6*	*23.8*	*13.0*	*14.9*
First tier	14.4	12.5	10.9	8.8	7.5	5.7	10.4	14.1	25.5	13.0	14.2
Second tier	5.1	10.7	10.0	11.4	8.9	6.2	8.1	8.8	19.6	13.0	16.6
Developing economies: Africa	**-1.4**	**1.9**	**3.6**	**3.3**	**6.4**	**9.1**	**16.3**	**21.8**	**29.7**	**28.8**	**11.7**
Northern Africa excluding Sudan	-2.3	0.9	3.0	2.1	6.2	10.1	16.3	23.5	29.4	34.5	11.9
Sub-Saharan Africa	-0.9	2.5	4.0	4.0	6.5	8.6	16.2	20.9	29.8	25.9	11.5
Sub-Saharan Africa excluding South Africa	-2.0	2.5	4.4	4.8	7.6	10.2	17.6	20.2	31.3	32.0	14.7
Developing economies: America	**1.6**	**6.3**	**7.0**	**10.5**	**9.3**	**7.9**	**9.7**	**9.8**	**23.6**	**20.5**	**20.0**
Central America and Greater Carribean Islands excluding Puerto Rico	3.8	9.0	9.2	15.2	11.7	8.4	5.2	3.6	14.0	12.4	16.6
Central America and Greater Carribean Islands excluding Mexico and Puerto Rico	-0.6	2.6	3.3	10.5	7.1	3.8	4.2	9.1	11.4	7.1	12.9
South America and Central America	3.1	7.3	7.8	10.8	9.5	8.0	9.9	9.7	23.8	20.6	19.8
South America excluding Brazil	0.6	5.5	6.1	7.8	7.6	6.8	12.8	13.7	34.4	29.5	25.6
Developing economies: Asia	**4.6**	**9.0**	**9.3**	**9.5**	**9.7**	**9.3**	**14.9**	**18.7**	**29.1**	**20.8**	**17.7**
Eastern and South-Eastern Asia excluding China	11.2	11.8	10.5	9.5	8.0	6.0	9.9	12.7	23.8	13.3	14.7
Southern Asia excluding India	1.1	4.6	5.7	4.3	6.7	9.2	14.4	18.9	23.5	27.2	9.3

Sources:
- Growth rates in this table are based on trade figures in table 1.1.1.

Imports (c.i.f.) - Importations (c.a.f.) En pourcentage											Groupements économiques
80-90	80-00	80-05	90-00	90-05	95-05	00-05	02-03	03-04	04-05	05-06	
4.0	**8.1**	**8.2**	**8.5**	**8.3**	**7.4**	**13.3**	**16.8**	**28.9**	**16.7**	**16.6**	**ÉCONOMIES EN DÉVELOPPEMENT**
3.4	7.8	7.6	8.1	7.3	5.8	11.0	12.6	27.3	16.5	15.7	Économies en développement sans la Chine
4.1	8.3	8.3	8.6	8.3	7.4	13.3	16.8	29.1	16.7	16.7	Économies en développement sans les PMA
5.2	9.4	8.7	8.7	7.3	5.5	9.3	10.2	26.8	14.8	16.3	Pays à revenu élevé
3.0	6.9	6.8	7.2	6.7	5.1	12.0	14.0	28.1	15.0	15.6	Pays à revenu intermédiaire
2.7	7.0	8.7	9.7	11.9	13.1	21.3	30.2	32.5	20.5	17.5	Pays à revenu faible
-0.1	3.2	4.2	5.9	6.6	6.9	13.3	14.4	23.9	19.1	10.7	Pays pauvres très endettés
2.5	8.9	9.4	13.2	11.3	8.4	16.1	17.2	29.9	19.5	19.1	Pays sans littoral
-4.4	1.0	2.3	5.9	5.5	4.9	8.2	9.0	15.5	14.5	16.2	Petits états insulaires en développement
0.2	*3.9*	*5.2*	*7.1*	*8.1*	*8.5*	*14.2*	*17.4*	*21.3*	*18.4*	*10.7*	*Pays les moins avancés*
0.0	2.8	4.4	5.3	7.5	9.2	16.6	20.6	22.3	22.4	10.2	Afrique et Haïti
0.4	5.7	6.5	10.4	9.2	7.7	10.7	12.7	19.7	12.2	10.8	Asie
5.5	6.8	6.6	5.0	5.6	5.6	14.5	20.3	23.8	17.2	24.1	Îles
-4.2	*1.5*	*3.1*	*3.1*	*5.7*	*7.9*	*16.2*	*12.7*	*38.2*	*24.7*	*17.1*	*Principaux exportateurs de pétrole*
-6.8	-0.8	1.2	0.9	4.2	6.5	15.7	19.4	16.2	12.6	25.1	Afrique
-6.8	0.7	1.8	5.5	4.6	4.5	5.4	-11.0	48.7	43.7	28.1	Amérique
-2.9	2.2	3.8	3.2	6.1	8.5	17.7	13.8	42.1	25.2	14.8	Asie
9.5	*11.7*	*11.0*	*9.8*	*9.2*	*7.8*	*13.2*	*17.5*	*28.4*	*14.7*	*17.4*	*Principaux exportateurs d'articles manufacturés*
2.7	10.9	10.4	13.8	10.3	7.3	4.5	1.3	19.0	9.7	16.1	Amérique
10.9	11.9	11.1	9.1	9.0	7.9	14.8	20.7	29.9	15.5	17.6	Asie
7.6	*11.2*	*10.0*	*9.5*	*7.5*	*5.0*	*8.7*	*9.8*	*27.1*	*14.0*	*15.4*	*Économies émergentes*
1.7	10.6	9.9	13.6	9.5	5.9	5.1	4.3	22.0	12.9	16.6	Amérique
10.6	11.6	10.1	7.7	6.7	4.7	10.4	12.6	29.4	14.4	14.9	Asie
10.4	*11.8*	*10.2*	*7.9*	*6.7*	*4.4*	*9.9*	*12.9*	*25.3*	*14.0*	*13.9*	*Économies nouvellement industrialisées*
11.9	12.1	10.4	8.1	6.8	4.5	9.5	13.1	25.7	12.7	15.1	Premier tier
6.8	11.0	9.8	7.2	6.5	4.1	11.2	12.4	24.1	17.5	10.6	Deuxième tier
-0.5	*2.3*	*3.5*	*4.4*	*5.7*	*6.3*	*14.3*	*20.2*	*23.0*	*17.4*	*12.8*	*Économies en développement : Afrique*
3.1	2.3	2.8	2.6	3.8	4.4	11.8	9.2	24.8	17.3	10.1	Afrique septentrionale sans le Soudan
-2.9	2.4	3.9	5.7	6.9	7.4	15.7	26.4	22.2	17.5	14.0	Afrique subsaharienne
-3.7	1.9	3.6	5.5	7.0	8.2	14.1	19.8	17.3	18.0	15.9	Afrique sub-saharienne sans l'Afrique du Sud
-0.2	*7.8*	*7.7*	*11.9*	*8.6*	*5.6*	*5.7*	*3.3*	*21.7*	*16.0*	*17.8*	*Économies en développement : Amérique*
4.4	10.2	10.1	13.0	10.6	9.4	4.6	1.5	14.9	9.2	15.5	Amérique centrale et Grandes Antilles sans Porto Rico
1.7	4.4	5.2	9.5	8.0	6.9	6.0	3.1	11.3	16.8	15.9	Amérique centrale et Grandes Antilles sans le Mexique et Porto Rico
0.9	9.2	8.8	12.5	8.9	5.6	5.9	4.0	22.9	15.8	18.2	Amérique du Sud et Amérique centrale
-1.6	7.1	6.2	10.2	5.9	1.6	8.5	11.3	37.4	31.5	23.0	Amérique du Sud sans le Brésil
6.5	*9.4*	*9.3*	*8.2*	*8.6*	*8.0*	*15.1*	*19.7*	*31.1*	*16.8*	*16.7*	*Économies en développement : Asie*
10.4	11.8	10.3	8.0	6.8	4.6	10.1	13.2	25.2	14.0	13.4	Asie orientale et Asie du Sud-Est sans la Chine
0.9	3.2	4.4	1.2	5.1	8.7	17.0	17.5	25.3	18.3	9.2	Asie méridionale sans l'Inde

Sources :
- Les taux d'accroissement donnés dans ce tableau ont été calculés d'après les chiffres du tableau 1.1.1.

Trade group	Exports (f.o.b) - Exportations (f.a.b.) Percentage										
	80-90	80-00	80-05	90-00	90-05	95-05	00-05	02-03	03-04	04-05	05-06
AFRICA											
CEPGL	2.6	-3.5	-2.1	-6.5	-1.0	1.8	22.6	20.6	35.8	18.9	-0.5
COMESA	4.1	2.8	4.4	4.1	7.3	10.0	18.5	17.1	28.8	40.4	21.5
ECCAS	2.2	3.2	5.3	3.3	8.3	13.0	24.4	17.7	50.0	55.4	22.0
ECOWAS	-4.9	1.4	3.2	3.4	6.1	8.4	15.6	24.1	24.5	26.3	10.8
MRU	4.3	0.8	-0.5	-7.5	-5.4	-3.9	2.9	-13.2	19.4	24.0	5.5
SADC	1.5	3.1	4.3	4.1	6.2	8.0	15.1	19.7	28.1	22.5	11.4
CEMAC (UDEAC)	-0.3	3.5	5.4	3.6	8.0	12.1	23.9	20.6	59.6	40.8	16.9
UEMOA	2.0	3.4	4.3	5.4	6.1	5.5	14.5	13.8	17.2	6.7	9.3
UMA	-3.5	1.0	3.1	2.2	6.2	9.9	15.9	22.2	30.5	33.8	10.1
AMERICA											
ANCOM	-1.6	3.7	4.9	6.5	7.3	7.8	12.9	10.6	37.5	38.1	22.3
CACM	-0.4	6.2	6.2	12.6	8.3	4.5	5.0	9.7	8.4	13.1	14.2
CARICOM	-8.0	-2.6	0.0	5.3	6.6	8.0	12.4	21.3	24.6	38.1	35.7
FTAA	5.1	7.4	6.9	8.2	6.5	4.9	5.5	6.7	15.6	15.1	15.8
LAIA	3.1	7.0	7.5	10.5	9.5	8.2	10.1	9.7	24.3	20.7	20.1
MERCOSUR	4.5	6.0	6.5	7.0	7.5	7.2	14.6	19.4	27.8	20.6	16.2
NAFTA	6.0	7.8	7.1	8.3	6.3	4.5	4.1	5.1	12.8	12.8	14.3
OECS	9.0	3.3	2.1	-1.7	-1.2	0.0	-2.0	2.0	2.0	-2.7	-1.2
ASIA											
APTA	12.8	12.9	13.1	12.2	13.2	13.4	21.4	28.0	33.3	23.9	23.6
ASEAN	6.2	11.0	10.3	11.1	9.0	6.4	10.0	11.3	25.6	14.7	16.5
ECO	3.9	7.4	8.4	7.5	9.6	11.0	19.8	27.7	31.7	25.0	15.3
GCC	-9.0	1.5	4.2	5.4	8.8	12.2	18.1	22.3	40.9	34.3	10.3
SAARC	7.4	9.4	9.6	9.1	9.8	9.7	16.1	16.9	25.0	26.1	19.1
EUROPE											
EFTA	7.9	6.8	6.6	3.9	5.2	5.8	10.7	13.9	19.1	13.6	15.6
EU 25	7.5	7.3	7.1	5.7	6.2	5.9	11.9	19.4	19.2	8.2	12.7
Euro Zone	8.0	7.4	7.2	5.5	6.1	5.9	11.9	19.9	18.8	7.1	11.6
OCEANIA											
MSG	3.5	5.2	4.2	3.3	2.3	0.5	10.2	33.3	13.6	21.8	18.4
INTERREGIONAL											
ACP	-1.6	1.8	3.3	4.3	6.4	8.0	15.1	20.5	28.4	25.2	13.1
APEC	8.1	9.3	8.6	8.5	7.5	6.2	9.6	12.9	21.5	15.4	16.7
BSEC	3.0	10.4	11.1	17.5	14.6	10.1	19.7	28.6	33.6	24.5	21.0
CIS	_	_	(e)11.3	(e)9.9	(e)11.3	10.2	19.7	27.3	36.4	28.2	23.5

Sources:
- Growth rates in this table are based on trade figures in table 1.1.1.

Imports (c.i.f.) - Importations (c.a.f.) En pourcentage											Groupements commerciaux
80-90	80-00	80-05	90-00	90-05	95-05	00-05	02-03	03-04	04-05	05-06	
											AFRIQUE
3.0	-1.6	-0.2	-1.5	2.1	4.6	19.3	37.8	21.7	21.4	6.1	CEPGL
6.4	3.0	3.5	5.2	5.4	5.3	12.0	8.1	22.0	34.1	10.3	COMESA
2.3	1.4	3.6	3.7	7.6	10.7	19.4	24.4	14.5	29.5	16.7	CEEAC
-8.4	0.1	2.0	3.8	5.5	6.6	12.3	21.0	9.4	13.2	25.2	CEDEAO
-0.7	2.0	1.4	1.6	0.4	-0.9	2.9	0.3	18.0	13.4	4.6	UFM
-0.4	3.9	5.0	6.3	7.3	7.6	17.2	34.2	26.9	16.3	11.2	SADC
2.5	1.5	3.6	3.9	7.6	9.7	17.1	8.2	19.1	21.9	4.1	CEMAC (UDEAC)
-0.2	2.4	3.4	4.2	5.5	5.8	15.5	27.1	21.1	16.2	4.7	UEMOA
-1.0	2.4	3.3	2.0	4.1	5.4	14.1	15.9	27.3	9.1	11.8	UMA
											AMÉRIQUE
-1.5	4.9	5.0	7.9	5.9	3.1	9.5	-0.8	34.3	34.5	26.1	ANCOM
1.4	7.8	8.4	12.5	10.5	8.7	9.2	8.1	13.2	15.2	17.7	MCAC
-7.0	0.0	1.8	7.7	6.9	5.9	6.9	7.2	12.0	16.7	14.0	CARICOM
6.5	8.0	7.8	9.7	8.2	7.0	6.8	7.5	17.7	14.6	11.8	ZLEA
1.0	8.8	8.4	12.3	8.7	5.5	5.7	3.8	23.7	16.1	18.5	ALADI
-2.7	8.1	6.9	13.1	6.7	0.1	4.8	11.2	37.1	19.9	19.6	MERCOSUR
8.0	8.3	8.1	9.6	8.4	7.7	6.8	7.6	16.5	13.6	10.8	ALENA
9.9	6.9	5.9	3.9	3.7	3.9	5.6	14.4	6.4	13.1	1.1	OECC
											ASIE
10.5	11.0	11.6	10.1	12.2	13.2	21.3	31.4	33.1	19.6	19.8	ACAP
7.2	10.9	9.7	7.9	6.8	4.2	11.1	12.3	27.6	16.6	12.5	ANASE
3.4	6.8	7.5	6.0	8.1	9.5	19.2	26.1	38.5	11.7	25.8	ECO
-3.9	2.5	4.1	4.8	7.0	9.2	17.9	8.0	46.3	29.3	21.4	CCG
3.9	6.6	7.6	8.7	9.8	10.3	20.2	24.4	35.5	34.9	20.0	SAARC
											EUROPE
8.0	5.8	5.3	3.1	3.8	4.0	9.3	14.8	17.7	10.6	12.2	AELE
6.7	6.8	6.7	5.2	6.0	6.3	11.7	20.5	20.1	9.9	14.0	UE 25
6.7	6.7	6.6	4.5	5.6	6.1	11.6	22.0	19.6	9.6	12.6	Zone Euro
											OCÉANIE
0.8	2.2	2.2	0.5	1.8	1.9	12.5	20.7	21.6	8.2	14.7	MSG
											INTERRÉGIONAUX
-2.7	1.9	3.4	5.9	6.7	7.0	13.1	20.5	20.0	17.4	13.9	ACP
8.1	9.1	8.7	8.7	8.0	7.0	10.0	13.4	21.7	14.6	12.7	CEAF
3.7	9.3	9.6	12.3	10.9	7.8	20.1	32.4	31.9	15.9	22.7	CEMN
–	–	(e)8.4	(e)6.4	(e)8.4	6.5	21.8	27.2	30.8	24.8	17.3	CEI

Sources :
- Les taux d'accroissement donnés dans ce tableau ont été calculés d'après les chiffres du tableau 1.1.1.

Region, country or territory	Trade balance - Balance commerciale Millions of dollars - Millions de dollars								
	1979-81	1984-86	1989-91	1994-96	1999-01	2001-03	2002-04	2003-05	2004-06
WORLD	**-40 983**	**-65 219**	**-109 616**	**-60 775**	**-181 059**	**-196 315**	**-218 827**	**-253 316**	**-257 134**
DEVELOPED ECONOMIES	-114 992	-90 418	-117 974	-14 665	-322 278	-367 123	-435 130	-570 773	-707 023
DEVELOPING ECONOMIES	74 301	19 098	17 979	-55 750	105 841	139 755	177 569	260 944	366 028
ECONOMIES IN TRANSITION	-292	6 102	-9 622	9 640	35 378	31 053	38 734	56 513	83 860
Developed economies: America	**-31 185**	**-128 392**	**-110 673**	**-166 821**	**-403 624**	**-484 285**	**-572 764**	**-677 911**	**-772 813**
Bermuda	-286	-407	-494	-504	-671	-716	-793	-875	-974
Canada	3 186	9 210	2 935	20 378	27 560	28 393	25 718	26 698	33 253
Greenland	-106	-111	-14	-80	-80	-77	-109	-131	-156
Saint Pierre and Miquelon	-7	-27	-55	-65	-65	-57	-58	-60	-58
United States*	-33 973	-137 057	-113 046	-186 550	-430 368	-511 829	-597 522	-703 544	-804 869
Developed economies: Asia	**-7 533**	**50 709**	**59 551**	**86 952**	**82 837**	**68 590**	**88 206**	**88 956**	**82 725**
Israel*	-4 281	-3 759	-5 188	-9 965	-4 580	-5 686	-4 978	-4 378	-3 132
Japan	-3 253	54 468	64 739	96 918	87 417	74 275	93 184	93 334	85 857
Developed economies: Europe	**-74 697**	**-9 146**	**-63 981**	**71 737**	**6 257**	**57 896**	**67 330**	**41 296**	**4 332**
Austria*	-5 643	-3 986	-8 020	-9 661	-4 611	-1 964	-1 180	-2 020	-1 179
Belgium*			_	_	_	19 229	19 898	19 207	17 466
Belgium-Luxembourg*	-6 059	-1 925	-1 102	10 232	9 471	9 112	_	_	_
Cyprus*(1)	-610	-794	-1 587	-2 368	-2 822	-3 165	-3 709	-4 337	-5 149
Czechoslovakia (former) (2)	1 333	368	-16	_	_	_	_	_	_
Czech Republic*	_	_	_	-4 726	-4 335	-4 762	-4 602	-2 624	-374
Denmark*(3)	-2 594	-1 127	3 127	5 576	5 556	7 543	8 388	9 184	8 277
Estonia*(4)	_	_	_	-577	-367	-539	-1 376	-2 018	-2 830
Faeroe Islands	-47	-86	66	61	-15	-10	-19	-86	-104
Finland	-632	814	-99	9 036	10 801	10 722	10 547	9 254	8 421
France*	-15 280	-8 207	-20 506	5 091	-2 259	-3 191	-7 725	-22 127	-34 757
Germany, Dem. Rep. (former)	-1 081	1 349	_	_	_	_	_	_	_
Germany, Federal Rep. (former)	9 707	32 204	71 529	_	_	_	_	_	_
Germany*	_	_	38 443	56 854	69 906	119 270	155 446	179 279	200 172
Greece*	-5 229	-5 307	-11 062	-14 481	-19 797	-23 588	-30 007	-35 266	-38 900
Hungary*	-586	118	355	-2 945	-3 369	-3 847	-4 363	-4 473	-3 655
Iceland*	-82	-71	-105	-65	-476	-227	-369	-891	-1 603
Ireland*	-2 809	447	3 267	11 584	27 718	35 652	39 210	41 013	41 321
Italy*	-15 163	-8 348	-12 382	31 308	8 324	5 828	2 566	-3 792	-13 331
Latvia*	_	_	_	-550	-1 348	-1 874	-2 395	-2 966	-3 930
Lithuania (4)	_	_	_	-824	-1 775	-2 258	-2 690	-3 169	-3 997
Luxembourg*						-2 650	-3 032	-3 254	-3 568
Malta	-400	-357	-776	-988	-863	-771	-914	-1 237	-1 378
Netherlands*	-1 536	5 111	5 106	15 488	16 505	26 092	31 263	37 212	42 193
Norway	1 341	2 408	6 268	10 146	21 063	26 347	28 824	36 268	46 084
Poland*	-2 225	313	2 389	-7 731	-16 659	-14 251	-14 229	-13 380	-13 738
Portugal*	-4 459	-2 379	-8 402	-9 818	-15 475	-15 017	-16 273	-19 218	-21 835
Slovakia*	_	_	_	-1 123	-2 015	-2 545	-2 547	-2 943	-3 365
Slovenia*	_	_	_	-921	-1 272	-852	-1 118	-1 503	-1 784
Spain*	-10 802	-6 278	-31 291	-13 931	-36 614	-43 265	-55 826	-74 794	-94 298
Sweden	-1 283	3 145	3 697	14 299	14 343	15 176	18 635	20 082	20 895
Switzerland*	-4 400	-3 584	-5 846	1 785	-1 188	2 164	5 124	5 294	6 984
United Kingdom*	-6 158	-12 970	-36 535	-29 017	-62 171	-82 862	-100 198	-115 398	-137 708
Developed economies: Oceania	**-1 576**	**-3 589**	**-2 871**	**-6 533**	**-7 748**	**-9 324**	**-17 902**	**-23 113**	**-21 267**
Australia*	-1 573	-3 210	-3 278	-6 398	-7 079	-8 565	-16 053	-19 984	-17 437
New Zealand	-3	-380	408	-134	-669	-758	-1 849	-3 129	-3 830
Developing economies: Africa	**11 919**	**1 828**	**3 589**	**-6 663**	**2 308**	**4 996**	**10 891**	**26 505**	**42 151**
Eastern Africa	*-3 175*	*-2 507*	*-4 717*	*-6 018*	*-7 317*	*-7 443*	*-8 592*	*-11 136*	*-13 920*
Burundi*	-79	-69	-143	-106	-87	-106	-115	-153	-217
Comoros*	-15	-24	-30	-48	-37	-37	-48	-62	-74
Djibouti*	-197	-187	-186	-164	-185	-193	-208	-221	-231
Ethiopia (former)	-266	-606	-526	_	_	_	_	_	_
Eritrea	_	_	_	-418	-450	-439	-445	-431	-434
Ethiopia	_	_	_	-789	-1 067	-1 373	-1 725	-2 425	-3 107
Kenya	-742	-429	-1 080	-832	-1 235	-1 230	-1 437	-2 013	-2 836
Madagascar*	-275	-36	-119	-112	-120	23	-120	-271	-555
Malawi	-129	-6	-211	-121	-162	-221	-333	-457	-537
Mauritius	-201	-65	-376	-503	-472	-394	-534	-753	-972
Mozambique	-452	-419	-731	-646	-663	-593	-658	-634	-450
Rwanda	-126	-153	-209	-158	-182	-197	-193	-232	-298

For sources and notes, see end of table.

Percentage of imports Part dans les importations en pourcentage									Régions, pays ou territoires
1979-81	1984-86	1989-91	1994-96	1999-01	2001-03	2002-04	2003-05	2004-06	
-2.11	**-3.12**	**-3.16**	**-1.21**	**-2.88**	**-2.84**	**-2.76**	**-2.72**	**-2.38**	**MONDE**
-8.40	-6.05	-4.65	-0.42	-7.32	-7.69	-8.06	-9.18	-9.98	ÉCONOMIES DÉVELOPPÉES
15.71	4.02	2.24	-3.87	5.99	7.03	7.59	9.24	10.82	ÉCONOMIES EN DÉVELOPPEMENT
-0.28	5.03	-7.68	7.95	29.24	18.93	18.95	21.85	26.46	ÉCONOMIES EN TRANSITION
-9.91	**-29.02**	**-17.57**	**-17.98**	**-28.87**	**-33.13**	**-35.91**	**-37.51**	**-37.69**	**Économies développées : Amérique**
-89.77	-90.47	-90.30	-90.65	-93.59	-93.43	-92.68	-93.51	-95.23	Bermudes
5.05	11.33	2.39	12.27	11.94	12.17	10.25	9.35	10.30	Canada
-35.34	-35.59	-3.33	-18.73	-22.36	-20.06	-22.49	-23.67	-26.05	Groenland
-84.90	-84.43	-65.84	-88.60	-92.38	-90.50	-90.23	-88.17	-86.50	Saint-Pierre-et-Miquelon
-13.54	-38.03	-22.34	-24.52	-36.91	-41.70	-44.49	-46.27	-46.64	États-Unis*
-5.35	**35.82**	**24.41**	**24.92**	**21.80**	**17.49**	**20.52**	**18.05**	**14.73**	**Économies développées : Asie**
-44.91	-36.98	-31.25	-34.59	-13.74	-15.90	-13.02	-10.40	-6.85	Israël*
-2.48	41.45	28.47	30.28	25.22	20.84	23.80	20.70	16.64	Japon
-8.43	**-1.04**	**-3.96**	**3.40**	**0.25**	**2.05**	**2.06**	**1.09**	**0.10**	**Économies développées : Europe**
-25.75	-17.73	-17.33	-15.26	-6.33	-2.34	-1.19	-1.75	-0.91	Autriche*
					8.88	8.31	6.86	5.47	Belgique*
-9.31	-3.20	-0.97	6.29	5.11	4.77	–	–	–	Belgique-Luxembourg*
-54.20	-61.36	-63.72	-66.42	-74.34	-78.64	-80.56	-80.17	-81.60	Chypre*(1)
10.92	3.03	-0.13	–	–	–	–	–	–	Tchécoslovaquie (anc.) (2)
			-19.16	-12.80	-10.59	-8.21	-3.90	-0.47	République tchèque*
-14.07	-5.85	9.86	13.09	12.19	14.79	14.32	13.69	10.80	Danemark*(3)
			-24.87	-9.21	-10.38	-21.03	-24.28	-27.09	Estonie*(4)
-22.46	-30.88	20.15	19.79	-2.95	-1.84	-3.10	-12.55	-14.45	Îles Féroé
-4.60	5.95	-0.41	32.20	32.65	29.43	24.70	18.14	14.09	Finlande
-12.38	-7.04	-9.09	1.81	-0.69	-0.91	-1.93	-4.83	-6.91	France*
-5.85	5.48	–	–	–	–	–	–	–	Allemagne, Rép. Dém. d' (anc.)
5.69	19.23	26.52	–	–	–	–	–	–	Allemagne, Rép. Fédérale d' (anc.)
–	–	10.45	13.09	14.38	22.64	25.77	25.67	24.93	Allemagne*
-54.15	-51.49	-57.70	-57.47	-64.23	-67.53	-69.73	-69.74	-68.61	Grèce*
-6.49	1.36	3.70	-18.52	-10.80	-9.69	-9.03	-7.76	-5.46	Hongrie*
-8.62	-7.42	-6.50	-3.68	-19.45	-9.32	-12.86	-24.53	-34.10	Islande*
-26.63	4.28	16.65	37.69	56.02	68.23	70.02	66.76	61.03	Irlande*
-16.67	-9.16	-7.18	16.11	3.59	2.24	0.86	-1.10	-3.40	Italie*
–	–	–	-30.60	-41.98	-43.93	-43.96	-42.61	-44.27	Lettonie*
–	–	–	-23.41	-33.48	-29.13	-27.29	-25.30	-25.41	Lituanie (4)
					-18.41	-18.63	-16.80	-15.60	Luxembourg*
-46.97	-45.38	-41.92	-36.23	-28.85	-25.81	-27.25	-33.65	-35.90	Malte
-1.91	7.04	4.28	8.96	7.82	11.31	11.68	11.77	11.51	Pays-Bas*
8.69	14.52	24.60	31.74	62.25	73.64	70.61	76.43	82.76	Norvège
-14.63	2.73	20.58	-26.49	-34.44	-24.66	-20.23	-15.63	-13.15	Pologne*
-52.16	-28.25	-35.62	-31.07	-38.86	-35.53	-34.33	-35.29	-35.84	Portugal*
–	–	–	-12.25	-14.81	-13.46	-10.66	-9.77	-9.09	Slovaquie*
			-10.54	-12.57	-7.32	-7.92	-8.83	-8.90	Slovénie*
-35.35	-20.07	-37.33	-12.92	-24.61	-24.58	-26.51	-29.68	-32.75	Espagne*
-4.23	10.76	7.24	23.36	21.01	21.32	22.29	20.39	18.53	Suède
-13.69	-10.57	-9.02	2.37	-1.44	2.46	5.27	4.82	5.74	Suisse*
-5.81	-11.41	-17.30	-11.05	-18.34	-22.46	-24.37	-25.01	-25.97	Royaume-Uni*
-5.73	**-11.20**	**-5.55**	**-8.88**	**-9.45**	**-10.26**	**-16.38**	**-17.70**	**-14.36**	**Économies développées : Océanie**
-7.06	-12.36	-7.65	-10.66	-10.38	-11.39	-17.76	-18.52	-14.20	Australie*
-0.06	-6.24	4.59	-0.99	-4.84	-4.85	-9.77	-13.81	-15.14	Nouvelle-Zélande
13.38	**2.45**	**3.86**	**-5.81**	**1.75**	**3.35**	**6.24**	**12.66**	**17.19**	**Économies en développement : Afrique**
-32.24	*-30.96*	*-39.99*	*-38.38*	*-42.20*	*-39.41*	*-39.91*	*-43.33*	*-45.42*	*Afrique orientale*
-49.28	-35.84	-63.80	-54.53	-64.75	-74.83	-74.82	-76.28	-80.40	Burundi*
-50.15	-62.45	-59.90	-83.29	-73.62	-63.73	-68.83	-75.75	-81.91	Comores*
-94.66	-92.26	-89.25	-89.97	-71.65	-74.72	-79.81	-85.23	-85.62	Djibouti*
-39.30	-60.15	-63.00	–	–	–	–	–	–	Éthiopie (anc.)
–	–	–	-83.92	-96.08	-94.45	-92.04	-91.93	-84.71	Érythrée
			-66.12	-69.44	-74.20	-75.77	-77.96	-78.17	Éthiopie
-39.06	-28.48	-51.19	-31.10	-40.58	-36.32	-37.42	-41.86	-47.59	Kenya
-42.55	-10.44	-26.89	-18.68	-13.32	3.18	-13.16	-23.41	-39.32	Madagascar*
-32.26	-2.08	-35.42	-22.75	-27.55	-32.38	-41.34	-47.64	-52.22	Malawi
-34.44	-11.61	-25.05	-24.35	-21.97	-18.15	-21.95	-27.24	-31.10	Maurice
-62.38	-83.32	-84.78	-78.06	-59.16	-40.82	-37.01	-30.71	-19.46	Mozambique
-50.97	-49.73	-67.87	-77.10	-73.42	-74.82	-73.28	-71.28	-72.57	Rwanda

Pour les sources et les notes, se reporter à la fin du tableau.

Region, country or territory	Trade balance - Balance commerciale Millions of dollars - Millions de dollars								
	1979-81	1984-86	1989-91	1994-96	1999-01	2001-03	2002-04	2003-05	2004-06
Seychelles	-72	-74	-128	-191	-233	-198	-180	-178	-400
Somalia	-263	-214	36	-36	-154	-153	-136	-147	-152
Uganda	63	81	-94	-555	-1 012	-831	-890	-1 011	-1 293
United Republic of Tanzania*	-654	-514	-954	-861	-889	-838	-906	-1 104	-1 458
Zambia*	301	15	264	292	-136	-413	-491	-624	-225
Zimbabwe	-68	192	-230	-770	-232	-252	-175	-419	-640
Middle Africa	**2 488**	**1 955**	**4 324**	**5 176**	**6 549**	**6 983**	**10 352**	**17 829**	**27 718**
Angola*	253	646	2 028	2 291	3 428	3 984	5 413	9 143	14 426
Cameroon*(5)	-228	-526	425	452	153	-28	29	123	316
Central African Republic*(5)	9	-41	-6	5	31	22	2	-21	-33
Chad*	-8	-89	-78	-82	-232	-709	-102	1 024	1 624
Congo*(5)	304	411	338	208	1 148	1 145	1 540	2 053	3 221
Dem. Rep. of the Congo*	774	640	475	480	-106	-12	-102	-146	-108
Equatorial Guinea	-6	-11	-14	-41	581	1 019	1 757	2 972	4 028
Gabon*(5)	1 391	930	1 175	1 884	1 574	1 591	1 846	2 721	3 869
São Tome and Principe*	-1	-4	-18	-22	-29	-29	-33	-39	-49
Northern Africa	**6 528**	**-4 085**	**-5 201**	**-10 387**	**-1 969**	**1 428**	**4 920**	**13 891**	**22 161**
Algeria*	2 518	1 521	2 734	-183	8 333	9 260	10 920	17 285	20 333
Egypt*	-3 120	-7 861	-9 394	-8 184	-10 137	-7 100	-6 000	-6 445	-7 159
Libyan Arab Jamahiriya	11 029	5 559	5 624	3 824	6 424	7 044	8 933	13 896	19 781
Morocco*	-1 849	-1 598	-2 467	-2 894	-3 519	-4 460	-5 806	-7 732	-9 428
Sudan*	-835	-514	-415	-772	-328	-501	-236	-213	-44
Tunisia	-1 215	-1 191	-1 644	-2 179	-2 742	-2 815	-2 890	-2 900	-3 056
Southern Africa	**4 322**	**3 794**	**4 425**	**-569**	**-69**	**-1 469**	**-4 549**	**-8 214**	**-11 694**
Botswana*	–	–	–	–	438	519	348	599	749
Lesotho					-504	-489	-596	-660	-700
Namibia	–	–	–	–	-324	-442	-516	-526	-220
South Africa	(a)4322	(a)3794	(a)4425	(a)-569	436	-1 045	-3 822	-7 534	-11 338
Swaziland	–	–	–	–	-115	-11	38	-94	-184
Western Africa	**1 756**	**2 669**	**4 758**	**5 135**	**5 114**	**5 498**	**8 760**	**14 134**	**17 886**
Benin*	-351	-195	41	-162	-266	-292	-318	-334	-326
Burkina Faso	-252	-253	-369	-278	-420	-510	-630	-776	-882
Cape Verde*	-61	-82	-125	-223	-231	-276	-325	-377	-447
Côte d'Ivoire*	106	1 243	751	1 081	1 396	2 301	2 668	2 526	2 449
Gambia	-104	-49	-146	-193	-159	-139	-166	-189	-211
Ghana	77	-171	-335	-435	-1 438	-923	-1 025	-1 591	-2 302
Guinea	104	145	-33	-25	87	47	15	32	63
Guinea-Bissau	-42	-43	-62	-75	5	-1	-4	-9	-15
Liberia*	59	130	881	225	-164	-55	-99	-162	-213
Mali*	-224	-185	-162	-308	-260	-214	-230	-371	-260
Mauritania*	-69	118	161	61	-79	-68	-94	-147	-187
Niger*	-32	-64	-91	-104	-125	-199	-257	-269	-229
Nigeria	3 471	2 495	5 002	6 145	7 731	7 136	10 763	17 745	22 685
Senegal*	-515	-316	-486	-366	-644	-942	-1 145	-1 478	-1 772
Sierra Leone*	-166	-11	-25	-97	-121	-193	-192	-182	-169
Togo*	-245	-95	-244	-111	-200	-173	-201	-284	-364
Developing economies: America	**-9 678**	**21 270**	**10 133**	**-24 295**	**-30 840**	**-6 537**	**12 339**	**31 245**	**50 472**
Caribbean	**-3 422**	**-4 771**	**-7 603**	**-6 023**	**-11 402**	**-11 758**	**-11 178**	**-10 828**	**-10 647**
Antigua and Barbuda*	-53	-151	-219	-306	-355	-355	-377	-446	-484
Aruba (6)	–	-162	-87	897	1 294	1 144	1 233	1 835	2 150
Bahamas (7)	-1 120	-547	-796	-1 047	-1 427	-1 369	-1 389	-1 545	-1 860
Barbados	-317	-278	-490	-506	-846	-861	-970	-1 108	-1 192
Cuba*	-776	-1 813	-2 397	-1 151	-3 216	-3 109	-3 006	-3 868	-5 099
Dominica*	-27	-24	-60	-67	-88	-83	-89	-105	-118
Dominican Republic*	-703	-1 037	-2 320	-1 505	-3 383	-3 111	-2 579	-2 293	-2 362
Grenada*	-30	-46	-83	-110	-165	-176	-198	-231	-241
Haiti	-182	-240	-184	-429	-716	-810	-869	-913	-1 064
Jamaica	-294	-457	-781	-1 328	-1 935	-2 340	-2 420	-2 601	-2 973
Montserrat*	-11	-14	-38	-27	-19	-23	-24	-25	-24
Netherlands Antilles*	(b)-462	(b)-281	-349	-650	-576	-844	-901	-1 118	-954
Saint Kitts and Nevis*	-21	-35	-83	-106	-109	-117	-119	-123	-124
Saint Lucia*	-71	-72	-165	-213	-304	-302	-319	-351	-361
Saint Vincent and the Grenadines*	-36	-21	-60	-86	-133	-144	-165	-185	-204
Trinidad and Tobago*	680	298	509	611	576	741	1 013	2 250	4 462
Central America	**-6 289**	**5 996**	**-7 878**	**-11 953**	**-26 380**	**-29 192**	**-30 682**	**-30 135**	**-30 764**
Belize	-42	-12	-101	-97	-284	-360	-344	-351	-362
Costa Rica*	-401	-79	-374	-698	-593	-1 678	-1 817	-2 104	-2 785
El Salvador*	-1	-241	-721	-1 636	-2 360	-2 812	-3 091	-3 467	-3 911

For sources and notes, see end of table.

40

1979-81	1984-86	1989-91	1994-96	1999-01	2001-03	2002-04	2003-05	2004-06	Régions, pays ou territoires
-78.27	-75.44	-73.25	-70.08	-55.80	-45.29	-40.47	-37.79	-60.15	Seychelles
-66.06	-74.51	51.07	-17.96	-40.91	-33.63	-29.63	-28.77	-28.31	Somalie
22.52	24.78	-31.05	-53.35	-67.91	-63.05	-60.91	-58.71	-60.42	Ouganda
-55.45	-62.99	-73.38	-56.53	-55.61	-45.20	-42.58	-44.31	-48.34	République-Unie de Tanzanie*
31.09	2.42	26.92	41.07	-13.11	-29.96	-30.39	-30.36	-9.70	Zambie*
-5.00	19.27	-12.55	-26.51	-12.10	-12.67	-8.13	-18.69	-24.90	Zimbabwe
47.99	*35.07*	*67.38*	*82.81*	*76.07*	*60.88*	*76.38*	*107.01*	*138.84*	*Afrique centrale*
18.44	51.75	142.70	138.49	110.25	96.23	107.74	139.47	169.99	Angola*
-15.89	-39.75	33.25	40.30	9.91	-1.41	1.37	4.93	11.14	Cameroun*(5)
11.55	-33.77	-4.27	3.11	26.56	18.98	1.94	-14.34	-19.77	République centrafricaine*(5)
-9.03	-47.88	-30.34	-28.03	-53.14	-68.60	-9.30	111.55	152.79	Tchad*
69.80	68.09	45.10	21.93	129.56	97.11	110.10	119.72	170.36	Congo*(5)
73.96	51.78	28.66	46.25	-10.74	-1.04	-6.56	-7.46	-5.09	Rép. dém. du Congo*
-25.99	-37.07	-23.31	-27.21	103.20	119.57	159.30	181.53	211.43	Guinée équatoriale
203.80	114.07	139.90	217.84	169.03	159.84	173.00	224.95	279.16	Gabon*(5)
-5.94	-28.17	-78.11	-80.63	-92.13	-85.80	-86.62	-89.72	-93.50	Sao Tomé-et-Principe*
20.62	*-12.19*	*-12.47*	*-22.26*	*-3.99*	*2.65*	*8.00*	*19.13*	*26.19*	*Afrique septentrionale*
24.96	15.54	27.30	-1.54	88.32	81.04	77.07	101.42	103.01	Algérie*
-53.55	-70.67	-64.62	-70.11	-71.08	-58.44	-49.25	-44.10	-40.20	Égypte*
161.64	115.05	108.00	76.20	151.11	130.51	138.47	191.72	230.56	Jamahiriya arabe libyenne
-44.98	-41.46	-38.38	-31.00	-32.49	-36.01	-39.62	-44.23	-46.51	Maroc*
-59.09	-53.59	-54.99	-57.97	-18.66	-19.52	-7.88	-5.41	-0.96	Soudan*
-35.85	-40.30	-32.69	-29.46	-30.96	-28.18	-26.07	-23.57	-22.44	Tunisie
25.13	*28.00*	*23.82*	*-2.03*	*-0.20*	*-3.80*	*-9.41*	*-13.54*	*-16.55*	*Afrique australe*
–	–	–	–	20.24	24.96	13.43	19.78	23.58	Botswana*
–	–	–	–	-69.54	-57.03	-53.96	-52.12	-50.33	Lesotho
–	–	–	–	-20.68	-27.43	-27.13	-23.40	-9.18	Namibie
(a)25.13	(a)27.00	(a)23.82	(a)-2.03	1.55	-3.18	-9.26	-14.41	-18.39	Afrique du Sud
–	–	–	–	-10.57	-0.92	2.55	-5.08	-9.13	Swaziland
6.97	*19.15*	*32.62*	*28.47*	*22.80*	*20.84*	*29.67*	*41.87*	*45.44*	*Afrique occidentale*
-88.07	-58.18	17.14	-26.50	-40.16	-39.14	-37.98	-37.39	-36.61	Bénin*
-75.81	-76.57	-75.87	-57.55	-64.83	-65.99	-64.41	-67.00	-67.74	Burkina Faso
-94.88	-95.46	-95.26	-96.18	-95.59	-96.16	-96.23	-96.14	-96.18	Cap-Vert*
4.03	70.37	35.70	41.85	50.44	85.18	80.20	60.06	48.32	Côte d'Ivoire*
-72.11	-49.47	-79.42	-88.83	-92.73	-92.24	-91.39	-91.08	-90.34	Gambie
7.46	-20.32	-28.45	-21.32	-45.79	-31.09	-30.04	-37.06	-43.03	Ghana
34.81	42.49	-4.98	-3.48	14.79	7.39	2.32	4.41	8.31	Guinée
-76.78	-76.79	-77.46	-58.64	9.26	-1.90	-5.78	-10.28	-13.47	Guinée-Bissau
11.93	42.95	333.70	48.33	-34.64	-28.39	-43.22	-58.52	-63.74	Libéria*
-56.92	-54.19	-34.57	-43.32	-29.72	-20.24	-19.91	-26.82	-18.37	Mali*
-25.66	53.44	57.23	14.15	-18.18	-16.85	-21.77	-26.08	-28.55	Mauritanie*
-6.14	-18.66	-24.74	-27.07	-30.84	-39.83	-41.94	-37.13	-29.69	Niger*
20.79	33.19	79.82	86.66	80.27	55.03	77.84	120.34	130.97	Nigéria
-50.56	-34.20	-40.35	-28.37	-39.57	-45.94	-47.26	-50.74	-53.13	Sénégal*
-46.40	-7.34	-14.94	-58.63	-88.28	-77.33	-67.28	-58.34	-49.25	Sierra Leone*
-48.88	-32.72	-48.82	-22.48	-35.07	-27.08	-26.83	-32.12	-37.83	Togo*
-8.41	*24.70*	*7.82*	*-9.76*	*-8.40*	*-1.79*	*3.19*	*7.08*	*9.67*	*Économies en développement : Amérique*
-13.98	*-23.56*	*-40.54*	*-32.25*	*-39.46*	*-40.21*	*-37.72*	*-33.42*	*-29.15*	*Caraïbes*
-60.59	-89.35	-88.40	-87.14	-89.37	-88.96	-89.13	-90.45	-91.21	Antigua-et-Barbuda*
–	-84.60	-18.67	159.19	157.90	135.68	144.25	199.88	225.61	Aruba (6)
-18.31	-15.69	-44.74	-85.73	-74.55	-76.05	-77.23	-78.60	-80.55	Bahamas (7)
-62.29	-44.80	-70.66	-68.40	-76.13	-77.49	-79.08	-78.93	-79.02	Barbade
-12.83	-21.54	-38.75	-41.20	-66.61	-66.19	-62.41	-64.96	-67.57	Cuba*
-67.95	-42.29	-53.85	-58.22	-63.39	-66.36	-68.43	-72.26	-74.22	Dominique*
-41.13	-57.20	-75.02	-28.58	-38.59	-36.97	-31.83	-28.59	-28.74	Republique dominicaine*
-61.00	-66.38	-75.62	-83.45	-74.31	-79.69	-84.59	-87.67	-89.96	Grenade*
-49.18	-57.47	-53.98	-82.00	-69.87	-72.94	-71.90	-69.40	-70.20	Haïti
-24.25	-42.41	-41.80	-49.76	-60.72	-66.64	-66.34	-65.72	-65.10	Jamaïque
-88.62	-83.70	-96.08	-90.11	-89.12	-94.66	-90.62	-91.07	-90.64	Montserrat*
(b)-8.71	(b)-12.92	-17.78	-31.88	-22.44	-32.89	-39.54	-48.72	-44.60	Antilles néerlandaises*
-50.09	-63.20	-77.06	-80.95	-69.16	-67.46	-67.77	-68.85	-67.72	Saint-Kitts-et-Nevis*
-60.43	-54.12	-58.82	-69.33	-85.55	-84.78	-83.38	-83.63	-83.86	Sainte-Lucie*
-66.62	-25.70	-44.35	-64.94	-74.35	-78.44	-81.70	-83.29	-84.19	Saint-Vincent-et-les Grenadines*
24.28	18.62	38.18	36.76	17.95	20.00	24.53	46.69	78.37	Trinité-et-Tobago*
-22.39	*24.72*	*-15.09*	*-12.04*	*-13.69*	*-14.39*	*-14.25*	*-12.88*	*-11.63*	*Amérique centrale*
-28.67	-9.81	-44.50	-37.84	-60.37	-67.77	-64.99	-63.52	-61.62	Belize
-28.98	-7.08	-20.12	-17.15	-9.21	-23.50	-23.58	-24.52	-27.99	Costa Rica*
-0.07	-25.14	-56.47	-63.12	-65.54	-69.48	-70.53	-71.19	-70.72	El Salvador*

Pour les sources et les notes, se reporter à la fin du tableau.

Region, country or territory	Trade balance - Balance commerciale Millions of dollars - Millions de dollars								
	1979-81	1984-86	1989-91	1994-96	1999-01	2001-03	2002-04	2003-05	2004-06
Guatemala*	-268	-61	-560	-1 208	-2 556	-3 687	-4 264	-4 765	-5 577
Honduras*	-153	-99	-126	-387	-1 535	-1 744	-1 998	-2 422	-2 934
Mexico	-4 124	8 094	-4 565	-5 395	-15 410	-15 557	-15 524	-12 858	-10 435
Nicaragua	-240	-578	-363	-576	-1 221	-1 218	-1 308	-1 490	-1 718
Panama, excl.Canal-Zone (former)	-985								
Panama*	-1 212	-1 028	-1 068	-1 958	-2 422	-2 137	-2 336	-2 678	-3 042
South America	*33*	*20 045*	*25 614*	*-6 319*	*6 942*	*34 413*	*54 200*	*72 208*	*91 883*
Argentina*	-567	3 411	5 837	-1 620	1 695	12 872	14 841	13 092	11 812
Bolivia	46	44	110	-333	-576	-304	-63	204	678
Brazil	-3 392	9 965	10 688	-3 108	-2 761	10 818	20 979	30 988	38 942
Chile*	-1 783	521	737	-888	907	1 402	3 554	5 837	12 034
Colombia	-1 017	-128	1 333	-3 409	626	-718	-710	-463	-784
Ecuador*	312	835	600	422	652	-851	-781	-380	-130
Guyana*	-38	-16	-50	-59	-114	-79	-67	-118	-192
Paraguay	-275	-265	-290	-1 868	-1 227	-1 039	-1 132	-1 590	-2 512
Peru*	948	567	-122	-3 217	-1 429	202	1 138	2 426	4 902
Suriname	-17	16	-17	-16	-101	-371	-290	-99	109
Uruguay	-489	192	238	-853	-1 097	-363	-90	-214	-303
Venezuela (Bolivarian Republic of)	6 305	4 904	6 551	8 630	10 367	12 844	16 822	22 525	27 285
Developing economies: Asia	**73 251**	**-2 633**	**6 283**	**-23 637**	**135 939**	**143 653**	**157 042**	**206 069**	**276 245**
Eastern Asia	*-8 025*	*2 057*	*10 834*	*-7 130*	*41 457*	*43 970*	*50 236*	*76 059*	*126 543*
China	-1 286	-9 378	3 421	11 434	25 295	26 144	29 328	53 188	103 866
China, Hong Kong SAR	-2 551	104	-336	-15 748	-9 254	-8 956	-9 167	-10 048	-11 698
China, Macao SAR	27	135	62	-37	120	-145	-338	-759	-1 303
China, Taiwan Province of	886	11 511	13 007	9 892	11 206	16 488	13 351	12 520	14 110
Korea, Dem. People's Rep. of	–	–	-936	-353	-846	-963	-1 010	-1 208	-1 321
Korea, Republic of (8)	-4 975	297	-4 524	-12 340	15 020	11 558	18 239	22 518	23 021
Mongolia	-190	-610	-173	21	-85	-156	-168	-152	-77
Southern Asia	*-8 813*	*-12 001*	*-12 297*	*-4 839*	*-7 432*	*-11 853*	*-18 654*	*-28 750*	*-39 353*
Afghanistan	-105	-745	-572	-260	-1 171	-1 979	-2 057	-2 000	-2 022
Bangladesh	-1 666	-1 701	-2 005	-2 441	-2 154	-2 181	-2 909	-3 835	-4 260
Bhutan	-41	-60	-17	-21	-74	-88	-136	-173	-212
India	-5 141	-6 211	-4 336	-3 578	-9 162	-8 924	-14 289	-25 536	-37 320
Iran, Islamic Republic of*	1 592	371	-1 974	6 602	8 815	4 996	6 158	11 405	17 777
Maldives	-20	-26	-64	-184	-291	-287	-346	-454	-582
Nepal	-212	-300	-457	-931	-775	-893	-1 019	-1 079	-1 310
Pakistan	-2 494	-2 812	-2 044	-2 601	-1 524	-1 127	-2 332	-4 994	-8 603
Sri Lanka	-740	-517	-828	-1 425	-1 095	-1 370	-1 723	-2 083	-2 774
South-Eastern Asia	*5 266*	*3 848*	*-14 043*	*-29 388*	*54 750*	*50 741*	*54 606*	*56 688*	*69 244*
Brunei Darussalam*	3 240	2 006	1 237	218	2 171	2 574	2 958	3 829	4 197
Cambodia	-159	-127	-67	-338	-175	-264	-623	-760	-951
Indonesia	11 132	6 807	4 304	6 581	26 236	24 275	21 366	17 809	19 841
Lao People's Dem. Rep.*	-67	-129	-103	-303	-205	-159	-141	-198	-257
Malaysia (9)(10)	1 872	2 793	154	-1 541	16 546	14 985	17 088	21 442	25 490
Myanmar	91	22	-51	-398	-813	198	425	821	1 279
Philippines	-2 473	-819	-4 117	-11 298	1 502	-2 069	-2 205	-4 340	-5 025
Singapore (11)	-4 882	-3 695	-6 723	-6 136	4 210	10 245	16 679	23 634	29 218
Thailand*	-2 498	-1 803	-8 270	-13 385	6 040	3 640	3 267	-547	-1 299
Viet Nam	-990	-1 207	-406	-2 789	-763	-2 685	-4 208	-5 001	-3 436
Western Asia	*84 823*	*3 463*	*21 789*	*17 720*	*47 165*	*60 795*	*70 854*	*102 072*	*119 811*
Bahrain	120	-230	-286	232	1 180	1 024	898	1 465	2 164
Iraq*	7 121	-1 544	2 042	-411	4 804	2 742	1 399	337	2 325
Jordan	-1 940	-1 892	-1 311	-2 121	-2 387	-2 515	-3 058	-4 357	-5 564
Kuwait*	11 948	3 837	1 524	5 358	8 387	8 001	10 546	17 613	28 826
Lebanon	-2 375	-2 046	-2 328	-6 296	-5 817	-5 817	-6 233	-6 940	-7 332
Oman	634	179	2 106	2 073	4 706	5 180	4 913	6 479	8 595
Qatar*	3 577	2 127	1 507	729	6 377	7 201	9 295	12 289	14 191
Saudi Arabia*	62 578	2 926	15 378	24 727	35 590	45 427	60 248	82 503	94 096
Syrian Arab Republic*	-2 257	-1 999	1 127	-1 649	381	1 121	334	-846	-1 619
Turkey*	-4 013	-3 552	-6 988	-13 213	-16 959	-14 742	-22 949	-26 939	-38 854
United Arab Emirates	11 056	6 990	10 207	8 511	9 871	12 554	14 913	19 637	18 146
Yemen Arab Republic (former)	-952	-968	-1 324						
Yemen, Democratic (former)	-673	-545		–	–	–	–	–	–
Yemen*	–	–	-1 122	-220	1 030	620	550	832	2 244
Developing economies: Oceania	**-1 191**	**-1 367**	**-2 025**	**-1 155**	**-1 567**	**-2 357**	**-2 703**	**-2 875**	**-2 840**
American Samoa*	27	-75	-55	-184	-155	-158	-145	-152	-67
Cook Islands	-20	-20	-46	-55	-39	-47	-56	-66	-69
Fiji	-160	-117	-198	-258	-321	-425	-558	-732	-936

For sources and notes, see end of table.

Percentage of imports Part dans les importations en pourcentage									Régions pays ou territoires
1979-81	1984-86	1989-91	1994-96	1999-01	2001-03	2002-04	2003-05	2004-06	
-16.76	-5.35	-32.61	-39.29	-49.99	-59.37	-61.40	-61.24	-62.41	Guatemala*
-16.52	-11.18	-13.17	-25.57	-54.34	-56.87	-58.91	-61.56	-63.10	Honduras*
-19.73	45.49	-10.35	-6.41	-9.11	-8.78	-8.29	-6.36	-4.57	Mexique
-32.11	-65.00	-54.40	-57.70	-67.32	-67.55	-67.13	-66.83	-66.12	Nicaragua
-74.80	–	–	–	–	–	–	–	–	Panama, sans la zone du canal (anc.)
-78.69	-76.24	-75.91	-76.32	-73.71	-70.98	-72.53	-73.98	-73.68	Panama*
0.05	**48.16**	**43.75**	**-4.82**	**4.76**	**25.90**	**38.20**	**41.23**	**41.60**	**Amérique du Sud**
-6.38	77.97	106.77	-7.42	7.15	89.51	98.35	60.45	41.48	Argentine*
5.56	7.14	14.50	-23.38	-32.63	-17.91	-3.59	10.57	29.03	Bolivie
-14.78	66.29	49.06	-6.34	-4.88	20.38	37.69	47.70	49.62	Brésil
-30.08	15.52	9.53	-5.68	5.24	7.80	17.36	22.76	37.73	Chili
-22.94	-3.08	25.71	-25.95	5.36	-5.46	-4.92	-2.68	-3.67	Colombie
15.37	48.21	29.43	10.51	16.15	-13.81	-10.97	-4.52	-1.28	Équateur*
-9.95	-6.91	-17.04	-10.92	-18.46	-13.66	-11.19	-17.61	-25.00	Guyana*
-47.51	-47.65	-24.37	-66.85	-58.60	-49.49	-47.08	-51.09	-59.03	Paraguay
36.44	24.45	-3.51	-37.93	-17.60	2.62	13.12	23.46	38.77	Pérou*
-3.40	4.90	-3.57	-3.10	-20.59	-67.09	-43.55	-12.02	12.32	Suriname
-32.37	24.47	17.08	-28.51	-33.30	-15.08	-3.72	-6.99	-7.72	Uruguay
53.13	60.33	74.77	81.62	64.39	98.39	133.45	130.67	106.52	Venezuela (République bolivarienne du)
27.59	**-0.85**	**1.09**	**-2.21**	**10.76**	**9.80**	**8.86**	**9.52**	**10.59**	**Économies en développement : Asie**
-9.66	**1.66**	**3.93**	**-1.31**	**6.16**	**5.43**	**5.09**	**6.34**	**8.84**	**Asie orientale**
-6.70	-24.99	5.82	8.87	11.96	8.24	6.93	9.77	15.48	Chine
-11.89	0.33	-0.40	-8.54	-4.68	-4.19	-3.87	-3.76	-3.87	Chine, Hong Kong RAS
4.95	16.40	3.85	-1.80	5.38	-5.66	-11.56	-22.44	-32.22	Chine, Macao RAS
4.77	52.04	22.90	10.22	9.39	14.24	9.81	7.86	7.65	Chine, Taiwan Province de
–	–	-32.92	-26.72	-53.91	-49.91	-46.72	-48.38	-48.53	Corée, Rép. populaire dém. de
-21.71	0.95	-6.38	-9.55	10.69	7.35	9.85	10.17	8.68	Corée, République de (8)
-30.36	-46.82	-23.03	5.26	-14.37	-21.98	-20.03	-15.16	-6.26	Mongolie
-23.99	**-29.94**	**-21.94**	**-6.86**	**-7.97**	**-10.39**	**-13.20**	**-15.78**	**-17.29**	**Asie méridionale**
-14.59	-56.07	-72.24	-62.81	-90.42	-95.00	-91.71	-88.26	-86.08	Afghanistan
-69.36	-64.49	-56.32	-41.31	-26.48	-25.38	-29.06	-31.96	-30.07	Bangladesh
-68.98	-71.59	-20.41	-18.60	-40.77	-41.48	-47.54	-44.79	-46.57	Bhoutan
-38.45	-39.96	-20.15	-10.79	-18.46	-14.92	-18.73	-24.58	-27.38	Inde
12.19	2.98	-10.39	49.05	56.47	21.08	20.97	32.94	46.26	Iran, Rép. islamique d'*
-73.98	-52.52	-47.01	-69.63	-73.79	-68.59	-69.06	-73.37	-75.45	Maldives
-65.85	-67.74	-68.86	-71.88	-52.04	-57.68	-60.63	-59.00	-62.05	Népal
-49.75	-49.28	-26.71	-24.02	-14.63	-9.81	-16.57	-26.59	-35.99	Pakistan
-41.49	-27.87	-31.33	-27.81	-18.12	-21.92	-24.91	-26.62	-30.64	Sri Lanka
8.40	**5.55**	**-8.86**	**-8.71**	**16.22**	**13.91**	**12.97**	**11.33**	**11.73**	**Asie du Sud-Est**
622.01	317.26	120.93	10.16	180.54	191.02	206.16	270.94	288.16	Brunéi Darussalam*
-93.73	-86.59	-36.95	-33.76	-8.59	-11.12	-22.51	-23.10	-24.34	Cambodge
106.67	58.58	20.15	17.09	88.91	69.77	49.98	32.10	29.66	Indonésie
-74.26	-71.70	-56.54	-49.29	-38.76	-32.10	-29.03	-32.29	-33.65	Rép. dém. populaire lao*
18.61	22.58	0.52	-2.14	22.44	19.07	19.19	21.32	21.81	Malaisie (9)(10)
26.01	7.91	-13.78	-33.07	-32.09	8.13	19.20	39.63	63.64	Myanmar
-31.73	-14.33	-33.35	-39.82	4.31	-5.56	-5.56	-10.11	-10.61	Philippines
-21.16	-13.78	-11.42	-5.13	3.49	8.53	11.97	14.14	14.34	Singapour (11)
-28.46	-18.77	-25.74	-20.32	10.40	5.40	4.17	-0.57	-1.15	Thaïlande*
-69.11	-62.88	-15.92	-33.30	-5.28	-13.46	-16.84	-16.23	-10.01	Viet Nam
102.21	**4.47**	**25.87**	**14.82**	**29.57**	**34.04**	**31.84**	**36.26**	**33.32**	**Asie occidentale**
3.56	-7.68	-7.83	5.92	28.12	20.58	15.61	22.21	28.15	Bahreïn
58.21	-14.56	36.37	-42.31	41.36	26.92	11.29	1.97	10.32	Iraq*
-77.29	-71.40	-54.37	-55.94	-54.30	-48.09	-48.42	-53.63	-55.49	Jordanie
191.64	61.82	30.41	70.31	111.12	86.17	96.99	128.17	189.95	Koweït*
-72.33	-83.46	-82.14	-91.02	-88.44	-83.45	-81.24	-80.30	-78.88	Liban
36.12	6.48	77.68	48.81	91.03	84.56	68.74	80.11	91.18	Oman
244.47	187.68	95.38	26.68	201.20	170.00	186.47	175.87	148.44	Qatar*
209.32	11.48	62.05	93.66	119.47	139.92	162.89	179.19	168.35	Arabie saoudite*
-53.63	-55.46	46.55	-31.80	9.38	23.76	6.02	-12.53	-20.24	République arabe syrienne*
-54.94	-32.09	-35.45	-38.63	-37.25	-28.22	-32.53	-30.96	-35.02	Turquie*
130.63	105.30	87.60	39.50	28.06	32.04	29.37	28.76	18.79	Émirats arabes unis
-97.06	-79.99	-68.11	–	–	–	–	–	–	Rép. arabe du Yémen (anc.)
-52.20	-53.82		–	–	–	–	–	–	Yémen dém. (anc.)
–	–	-62.42	-10.61	45.45	20.53	15.58	19.92	50.38	Yémen*
-35.78	**-40.58**	**-40.53**	**-20.09**	**-29.25**	**-38.35**	**-38.43**	**-35.74**	**-32.51**	**Économies en développement : Océanie**
22.22	-25.31	-14.77	-39.84	-31.57	-28.90	-25.12	-26.25	-13.82	Samoa américaines*
-82.65	-83.75	-91.25	-93.27	-87.20	-86.40	-88.16	-90.66	-91.98	Îles Cook
-28.86	-26.46	-29.97	-28.57	-36.44	-42.46	-47.02	-51.49	-57.35	Fidji

Pour les sources et les notes, se reporter à la fin du tableau.

Region, country or territory	Trade balance - Balance commerciale Millions of dollars - Millions de dollars								
	1979-81	1984-86	1989-91	1994-96	1999-01	2001-03	2002-04	2003-05	2004-06
French Polynesia*	-494	-571	-768	-742	-796	-1 133	-1 271	-1 401	-1 403
Guam	-251	-219	-321	-298	-322	-329	-364	-483	-557
Kiribati	-4	-10	-22	-27	-35	-44	-52	-61	-64
Nauru	60	42	27	2	5	-12	-11	-8	-7
New Caledonia*	-34	-156	-305	-414	-449	-582	-641	-689	-749
Papua New Guinea	-196	-134	-121	1 029	789	660	708	1 090	1 486
Samoa*	-49	-34	-74	-85	-92	-111	-124	-145	-178
Solomon Islands*	-13	-2	-29	9	-17	-23	-19	-42	-63
Tonga	-29	-34	-47	-61	-62	-72	-80	-89	-99
Tuvalu	-4	-3	-3	-7	-6	-8	-11	-11	-12
Vanuatu	-28	-35	-64	-66	-68	-73	-80	-87	-92
Economies in transition: Asia	–	–	–	**1 136**	**2 902**	**3 455**	**4 818**	**7 040**	**9 963**
Armenia*	–	–	–	-382	-562	-536	-571	-682	-881
Azerbaijan*	–	–	–	-162	450	450	189	70	450
Georgia (4)	–	–	–	-304	-390	-522	-776	-1 168	-1 838
Kazakhstan*(4)	–	–	–	928	2 727	3 266	4 972	7 442	10 794
Kyrgyzstan	–	–	–	-141	-62	-76	-153	-264	-527
Tajikistan (4)	–	–	–	-55	32	-64	-144	-260	-340
Turkmenistan (4)	–	–	–	1 260	660	767	800	1 055	1 258
Uzbekistan (4)	–	–	–	-8	46	170	501	847	1 007
Economies in transition: Europe	**-292**	**6 102**	**-9 622**	**8 504**	**32 477**	**27 598**	**33 916**	**49 473**	**73 897**
Albania	–	–	-202	-567	-885	-1 200	-1 428	-1 693	-1 976
Belarus	–	–	–	-868	-973	-1 173	-1 800	-1 686	-2 010
Bosnia and Herzegovina*(12)	–	–	–	-1 182	-3 056	-3 468	-4 002	-4 562	-4 575
Bulgaria*	322	-416	580	-291	-1 778	-2 582	-3 379	-4 774	-6 327
Croatia*	–	–	–	-2 367	-3 811	-6 107	-7 469	-8 792	-9 822
Moldova, Republic of	–	–	–	-165	-247	-444	-600	-869	-1 212
Macedonia, TFYR*	–	–	–	-464	-631	-785	-1 025	-1 127	-1 268
Romania*	-1 848	237	-1 410	-2 225	-2 915	-4 847	-6 516	-9 432	-13 561
Russian Federation (4)	–	–	–	20 336	48 736	51 793	63 943	87 983	122 840
Serbia and Montenegro*	–	–	–	-1 700	-2 244	-4 094	-5 374	-6 177	-6 615
Yugoslavia, SFR (former)	-5 753	-1 549	-2 239	–	–	–	–	–	–
USSR (former)	6 987	7 830	-6 351	–	–	–	–	–	–
Ukraine	–	–	–	-2 000	281	506	1 565	603	-1 631

Sources:
- Growth rates in this table are based on trade figures in table 1.1.1.

Notes:
- Countries which use the Special Trade System as reporting system are marked with an asterisk (*).
(a) Before 1998, data refers to South Africa Customs Union (Botswana, Lesotho, Namibia, South Africa and Swaziland).
(b) Before 1986, includes Aruba.
(1) Excluding military imports.
(2) From 1985 onwards, data are not comparable to those shown for prior periods due to revisions of the koruna-to-US dollar exchange rate.
(3) Prior to 1985, general trade.
(4) Prior to 1994, covers only trade with countries outside the CIS.
(5) Inter-trade between the member countries of CEMAC is excluded.
(6) Prior to 2000, data exclude imports into and exports from the free zone; mineral fuels are also excluded.
(7) From 1990 onwards, trade statistics exclude certain oil and chemical products.
(8) Excluding imports of goods financed through foreign aid.
(9) Inter-trade between the States of Malaysia included.
(10) Excluding military imports and offshore installations of petroleum industry.
(11) Including trans-shipments to and from peninsular Malaysia.
(12) Prior to 1998, data refer to the Federation of Bosnia and Herzegovina only. The other entity of Bosnia and Herzegovina, Republika Srpska, is not included.

Percentage of imports Part dans les importations en pourcentage									Régions, pays ou territoires
1979-81	1984-86	1989-91	1994-96	1999-01	2001-03	2002-04	2003-05	2004-06	
-94.41	-93.81	-87.55	-76.87	-77.90	-87.13	-88.33	-88.48	-86.96	Polynésie française*
-82.21	-83.78	-81.53	-78.65	-82.07	-83.38	-85.45	-89.06	-91.60	Guam
-29.54	-64.20	-85.69	-82.49	-85.84	-92.37	-94.90	-95.54	-94.10	Kiribati
476.32	222.81	84.93	8.28	26.23	-52.85	-56.62	-50.93	-48.55	Nauru
-8.27	-40.63	-36.39	-44.25	-47.07	-50.24	-45.93	-41.81	-42.18	Nouvelle-Calédonie*
-17.61	-12.39	-8.53	65.54	69.36	53.88	49.61	68.47	82.62	Papouasie-Nouvelle-Guinée
-75.95	-68.99	-88.72	-91.86	-84.57	-88.23	-90.41	-92.01	-85.45	Samoa*
-16.21	-2.24	-27.87	6.22	-17.39	-28.06	-19.72	-31.12	-36.01	Îles Salomon*
-79.84	-83.98	-80.67	-82.25	-87.11	-84.87	-83.65	-86.20	-89.48	Tonga
-97.44	-83.00	-75.83	-92.24	-99.16	-98.99	-98.88	-99.16	-99.20	Tuvalu
-43.04	-52.89	-76.43	-70.35	-73.80	-76.96	-74.27	-71.91	-69.77	Vanuatu
–	–	–	10.13	21.15	20.00	22.43	25.15	27.34	**Économies en transition : Asie**
–	–	–	-59.62	-65.99	-51.18	-47.32	-46.55	-49.76	Arménie*
–	–	–	-20.16	37.11	23.58	7.24	2.04	10.40	Azerbaïdjan*
–	–	–	-64.31	-57.11	-58.18	-61.56	-63.95	-68.74	Géorgie (4)
–	–	–	23.97	54.04	45.70	53.71	57.92	60.18	Kazakhstan*(4)
–	–	–	-25.16	-11.51	-12.85	-20.43	-28.68	-42.00	Kirghizistan
–	–	–	-8.08	4.67	-8.34	-15.43	-22.96	-24.05	Tadjikistan (4)
–	–	–	161.11	35.93	33.42	30.18	34.13	36.45	Turkménistan (4)
–	–	–	-0.23	1.61	6.44	17.73	26.03	28.37	Ouzbékistan (4)
-0.28	5.03	-7.68	7.73	30.28	18.80	18.54	21.45	26.34	**Économies en transition : Europe**
–	–	-46.35	-75.37	-74.34	-76.68	-75.46	-74.80	-74.25	Albanie
–	–	–	-16.73	-12.37	-12.16	-14.54	-11.30	-10.86	Bélarus
–	–	–	-96.75	-75.66	-73.65	-71.98	-68.98	-62.92	Bosnie-Herzégovine*(12)
3.33	-3.00	7.74	-5.21	-27.75	-29.62	-30.39	-32.90	-34.12	Bulgarie*
–	–	–	-34.37	-46.04	-53.76	-53.96	-53.44	-52.02	Croatie*
–	–	–	-18.93	-32.88	-39.98	-42.73	-47.69	-53.79	Moldova, République de
–	–	–	-28.82	-34.01	-39 28	-42.51	-39.95	-38.34	Macédoine, LERY*
-14.18	2.10	-17.09	-23.16	-22.42	-25 32	-26.23	-29.13	-32.75	Roumanie*
–	–	–	33.84	105.82	81.44	81.83	88.35	102.30	Fédération de Russie (4)
–	–	–	-47.97	-56.84	-64.27	-64.42	-62.37	-60.79	Serbie-et-Monténégro*
-39.52	-12.92	-13.86	–	–	–	–	–	–	Yougoslavie, RSF (anc.)
10.52	9.30	-6.84	–	–	–	–	–	–	URSS (anc.)
–	–	–	-13.69	2.03	2.72	6.81	2.05	-4.44	Ukraine

Sources :
- Les taux d'accroissement donnés dans ce tableau ont été calculés d'après es chiffres du tableau 1.1.1.

Notes :
- Les pays qui utilisent le système du commerce spécial en tant que système d'enregistrement sont marqués pa⁻ un astérisque (*).
(a)   Avant 1998, donnée relative à l'Union Douanière d'Afrique du Sud (Afrique du Sud, Botswana, Lesotho, Namibie et Swaziland).
(b)   Avant 1986, y compris Aruba.
(1)   Non compris les importations militaires.
(2)   A partir de 1985, les chiffres ne sont pas comparables à ceux des années antérieures à cause des révisions du taux de change de la couronne par rapport au dollar des États-Unis.
(3)   Avant 1985, commerce général.
(4)   Avant 1994, concerne seulement le commerce avec les pays extérieurs à la CEI.
(5)   Non-compris le commerce entre les pays membres de CEMAC.
(6)   Avant 2000, les données excluent les importations en provenance et les exportations à destination de la zone de libre circulation; les combustibles minéraux sont également exclus.
(7)   A partir de 1990, certains produits pétroliers et chimiques ne sont plus inclus dars les statistiques du commerce.
(8)   Non-compris les biens d'importation financés par l'aide à l'étranger.
(9)   Y compris le commerce entre les États de la Malaisie.
(10)   Non-compris les importations militaires et l'installation près des côtes de l'industrie pétrolière.
(11)   Y compris les transbordements vers et en provenance de la Malaisie péninsulaire.
(12)   Avant 1998, les données se réfèrent uniquement à la Fédération de la Bosnie-Herzégovine. L'autre entité de la Bosnie-Herzégovine, Republika Srpska, n'est pas incluse.

1.3.2 Value of trade balance, and as percentage of imports of economic groupings

Economic grouping	Trade balance - Balance commerciale Millions of dollars - Millions de dollars								
	1979-81	1984-86	1989-91	1994-96	1999-01	2001-03	2002-04	2003-05	2004-06
DEVELOPING ECONOMIES	**74 301**	**19 098**	**17 979**	**-55 750**	**105 841**	**139 755**	**177 569**	**260 944**	**366 028**
Developing economies excluding China	75 616	28 470	14 563	-67 164	80 614	113 698	148 347	207 881	262 311
Developing economies excluding LDCs	82 209	26 244	24 171	-46 446	116 414	151 101	188 953	269 492	368 279
High-income countries	87 425	44 545	41 875	11 595	82 770	119 013	160 186	223 251	277 306
Middle-income countries	-12 712	-4 612	-19 557	-60 171	-16 399	-9 427	-6 384	4 452	6 881
Low-income countries	-412	-20 835	-4 338	-7 174	39 470	30 169	23 767	33 241	81 841
Heavily indebted poor countries	-4 313	-2 999	-2 823	-6 931	-11 707	-11 773	-12 113	-14 087	-15 264
Landlocked countries	-1 577	-3 242	-3 356	-5 859	-5 765	-6 855	-6 095	-4 665	-2 615
Small island developing states	-2 078	-1 933	-3 500	-3 791	-5 885	-6 333	-6 724	-6 392	-5 615
Least developed countries	*-7 871*	*-7 125*	*-6 132*	*-9 218*	*-10 440*	*-11 202*	*-11 219*	*-8 363*	*-2 046*
Africa and Haiti	-3 908	-2 533	-1 240	-3 655	-5 299	-5 570	-4 272	-694	5 055
Asia	-3 771	-4 372	-4 462	-4 911	-4 338	-4 745	-5 911	-6 392	-5 537
Islands	-192	-220	-430	-652	-804	-887	-1 036	-1 277	-1 564
Major petroleum exporters	*134 604*	*36 620*	*59 594*	*75 511*	*148 556*	*158 613*	*189 926*	*259 850*	*330 285*
Africa	18 966	11 562	16 900	14 170	28 639	30 159	39 415	62 842	86 049
America	6 523	4 921	6 711	8 591	10 367	12 740	16 935	23 657	30 673
Asia	109 115	20 137	35 983	52 751	109 550	115 714	133 577	173 351	213 562
Major exporters of manufactured goods	*-32 576*	*7 305*	*-12 588*	*-64 415*	*26 274*	*43 631*	*54 796*	*84 022*	*130 015*
America	-7 515	18 059	6 123	-8 503	-18 171	-4 739	5 455	18 130	28 507
Asia	-25 060	-10 754	-18 711	-55 912	44 445	48 370	49 341	65 892	101 507
Emerging economies	*-18 516*	*31 660*	*6 220*	*-37 737*	*36 024*	*66 654*	*93 610*	*119 052*	*147 794*
America	-8 918	22 558	12 574	-14 227	-16 998	9 738	24 988	39 485	57 255
Asia	-9 597	9 103	-6 355	-23 510	53 023	56 917	68 623	79 567	90 539
Newly industrialized economies	*-3 489*	*15 194*	*-6 504*	*-43 974*	*71 507*	*70 167*	*78 617*	*82 987*	*93 656*
First tier	-11 522	8 216	1 425	-24 331	21 182	29 335	39 101	48 624	54 650
Second tier	8 033	6 978	-7 929	-19 643	50 325	40 832	39 516	34 363	39 006
Developing economies: Africa	**11 919**	**1 828**	**3 589**	**-6 663**	**2 308**	**4 996**	**10 891**	**26 505**	**42 151**
Northern Africa excluding Sudan	7 363	-3 571	-5 148	-9 615	-1 641	1 928	5 156	14 104	22 205
Sub-Saharan Africa	4 557	5 398	8 737	2 952	3 950	3 068	5 735	12 401	19 946
Sub-Saharan Africa excluding South Africa	234	1 604	4 312	3 521	3 514	4 113	9 557	19 935	31 284
Developing economies: America	**-9 678**	**21 270**	**10 133**	**-24 295**	**-30 840**	**-6 537**	**12 339**	**31 245**	**50 472**
Central America and Greater Carribean Islands excluding Puerto Rico	-8 244	2 449	-13 560	-16 367	-35 630	-38 561	-39 556	-39 810	-42 413
Central America and Greater Carribean Islands excluding Mexico and Puerto Rico	-4 120	-5 645	-8 995	-10 972	-20 220	-23 004	-24 033	-26 952	-31 978
South America and Central America	-6 256	26 041	17 736	-18 272	-19 438	5 221	23 517	42 073	61 119
South America excluding Brazil	3 425	10 081	14 926	-3 211	9 703	23 596	33 221	41 220	52 941
Developing economies: Asia	**73 251**	**-2 633**	**6 283**	**-23 637**	**135 939**	**143 653**	**157 042**	**206 069**	**276 245**
Eastern and South-Eastern Asia excluding China	-1 474	15 284	-6 630	-47 952	70 911	68 566	75 513	79 559	91 921
Southern Asia excluding India	-3 672	-5 790	-7 961	-1 261	1 730	-2 929	-4 365	-3 214	-2 033

Sources:
- Data in this table are derived from the trade figures reported in table 1.1.1.

Percentage of imports Part dans les importations en pourcentage									Groupements économiques
1979-81	1984-86	1989-91	1994-96	1999-01	2001-03	2002-04	2003-05	2004-06	
15.71	**4.02**	**2.24**	**-3.87**	**5.99**	**7.03**	**7.59**	**9.24**	**10.82**	**ÉCONOMIES EN DÉVELOPPEMENT**
16.66	6.51	1.96	-5.12	5.18	6.31	7.74	9.12	9.67	Économies en développement sans la Chine
18.22	5.77	3.11	-3.30	6.76	7.81	8.29	9.79	11.16	Économies en développement sans les PMA
40.86	21.24	10.24	1.53	8.99	12.41	14.75	17.53	18.36	Pays à revenu élevé
-9.27	-3.39	-9.05	-16.24	-4.06	-2.12	-1.24	0.73	0.95	Pays à revenu intermédiaire
-0.34	-16.11	-2.45	-2.30	8.92	5.17	3.22	3.55	7.14	Pays à revenu faible
-19.40	-15.80	-12.59	-23.05	-30.85	-27.88	-25.01	-24.37	-22.56	Pays pauvres très endettés
-18.57	-33.86	-29.95	-20.15	-15.58	-15.72	-11.81	-7.40	-3.40	Pays sans littoral
-15.07	-19.35	-31.39	-28.44	-35.44	-35.83	-34.83	-29.24	-22.25	Petits états insulaires en développement
-36.11	**-35.26**	**-25.83**	**-28.36**	**-23.38**	**-21.52**	**-18.70**	**-11.71**	**-2.47**	*Pays les moins avancés*
-25.94	-19.75	-8.05	-19.30	-21.09	-18.48	-12.06	-1.61	9.97	Afrique et Haïti
-59.25	-62.60	-58.08	-38.92	-23.49	-22.85	-25.46	-24.00	-18.28	Asie
-52.34	-54.97	-66.75	-68.29	-75.89	-76.79	-76.72	-78.69	-79.17	Îles
89.74	**29.84**	**43.44**	**44.27**	**74.48**	**69.13**	**69.70**	**75.95**	**77.35**	*Principaux exportateurs de pétrole*
52.54	46.61	68.99	51.54	101.39	83.53	93.99	129.53	149.91	Afrique
32.65	41.33	55.66	60.18	47.40	65.93	89.06	97.15	91.54	Amérique
116.20	23.41	35.75	40.95	73.36	66.49	63.15	64.38	63.54	Asie
-16.59	**3.10**	**-2.46**	**-6.28**	**2.06**	**3.01**	**3.19**	**4.08**	**5.29**	*Principaux exportateurs d'articles manufacturés*
-17.14	55.01	9.30	-6.38	-8.05	-2.06	2.25	6.78	9.30	Amérique
-16.43	-5.30	-4.20	-6.27	4.23	3.97	3.35	3.68	4.72	Asie
-12.80	**21.85**	**1.88**	**-5.70**	**4.58**	**8.23**	**10.23**	**11.13**	**11.70**	*Économies émergentes*
-14.56	52.61	15.23	-7.94	-6.18	3.60	8.70	12.15	15.08	Amérique
-11.51	8.92	-2.56	-4.86	10.35	10.55	10.93	10.68	10.25	Asie
-2.83	**10.09**	**-1.77**	**-5.99**	**9.23**	**8.51**	**8.30**	**7.47**	**7.21**	*Économies nouvellement industrialisées*
-13.39	7.38	0.52	-4.59	3.66	4.83	5.61	5.96	5.72	Premier tier
21.67	17.75	-8.32	-9.60	25.65	18.73	15.82	11.64	11.34	Deuxième tier
13.38	**2.45**	**3.86**	**-5.81**	**1.75**	**3.35**	**6.24**	**12.66**	**17.19**	**Économies en développement : Afrique**
24.35	-10.97	-12.49	-21.21	-3.45	3.76	8.81	20.53	27.75	Afrique septentrionale sans le Soudan
7.74	12.82	16.84	4.26	4.71	3.13	4.95	8.81	12.07	Afrique subsaharienne
0.56	5.61	12.95	8.53	6.31	6.32	12.80	22.54	30.21	Afrique sub-saharienne sans l'Afrique du Sud
-8.41	**24.70**	**7.82**	**-9.76**	**-8.40**	**-1.79**	**3.19**	**7.08**	**9.67**	**Économies en développement : Amérique**
-22.03	6.81	-21.29	-14.81	-16.92	-17.48	-16.97	-15.73	-14.80	Amérique centrale et Grandes Antilles sans Porto Rico
-24.93	-31.05	-45.90	-41.69	-48.90	-52.83	-52.36	-53.04	-54.80	Amérique centrale et Grandes Antilles sans le Mexique et Porto Rico
-6.91	39.53	16.02	-7.94	-5.74	1.56	6.58	10.29	12.59	Amérique du Sud et Amérique centrale
8.66	37.92	40.61	-3.92	10.88	29.57	38.52	37.41	37.18	Amérique du Sud sans le Brésil
27.59	**-0.85**	**1.09**	**-2.21**	**10.76**	**9.80**	**8.86**	**9.52**	**10.59**	**Économies en développement : Asie**
-1.16	9.81	-1.77	-6.38	8.87	8.00	7.67	6.88	6.81	Asie orientale et Asie du Sud-Est sans la Chine
-15.72	-23.59	-23.06	-3.37	3.97	-5.40	-6.71	-4.10	-2.23	Asie méridionale sans l'Inde

Sources :
- Les données de ce tableau ont été calculées d'après les chiffres du commerce du tableau 1.1.1.

Trade group	Value of intra-trade (exports in millions of dollars) Valeur du commerce interne au groupement (exportations en millions de dollars)						Intra-trade of groups regional exports Commerce interne des exportations régionales		
	1980	1990	1995	2000	2004	2005	1980	1990	1995
AFRICA									
CEPGL	2	7	8	10	19	22	3.6	6.2	6.0
COMESA	555	889	1 025	1 328	2 294	2 716	81.3	63.0	46.4
ECCAS	89	163	163	191	238	272	49.3	26.1	36.3
ECOWAS	661	1 532	1 875	2 715	4 366	5 497	73.5	75.5	77.1
MRU	7	0	1	5	6	6	59.3	0.7	1.6
SADC	106	1 070	4 190	4 383	6 589	7 585	50.9	88.6	84.2
CEMAC (UDEAC)	75	139	120	96	174	198	66.6	28.1	40.3
UEMOA	460	621	560	741	1 233	1 390	52.9	49.3	47.2
UMA	109	958	1 109	1 094	1 375	1 926	34.0	69.3	66.9
AMERICA									
ANCOM	1 161	1 312	4 812	5 300	7 261	9 453	5.7	6.5	17.4
CACM	1 174	667	1 594	2 586	3 574	4 064	37.2	23.2	33.0
CARICOM	599	453	875	1 074	1 738	2 082	7.7	14.0	21.1
FTAA	167 719	300 694	525 317	855 646	967 638	1 110 713	96.4	99.2	99.5
LAIA	11 192	13 350	35 986	44 326	56 516	71 326	25.4	21.3	25.8
MERCOSUR	3 424	4 127	14 199	17 829	17 354	21 118	31.8	22.2	43.1
NAFTA	102 218	226 273	394 472	676 142	737 591	824 550	79.0	88.8	87.4
OECS	4	28	38	36	56	63	23.1	22.0	26.8
ASIA									
APTA	783	2 429	21 728	37 895	99 369	127 277	3.6	3.2	12.7
ASEAN	12 413	27 365	79 544	98 060	141 934	165 064	29.0	34.0	42.0
ECO	392	1 243	4 746	4 518	9 978	13 993	17.1	11.1	25.5
GCC	4 632	6 906	6 832	7 958	12 532	16 507	7.2	14.6	12.1
SAARC	613	863	2 024	2 593	5 706	7 062	12.2	10.8	12.5
EUROPE									
EFTA	524	782	925	831	1 119	1 238	1.4	1.1	1.1
EU 25	490 029	1 028 801	1 394 152	1 618 916	2 499 933	2 666 398	85.3	89.1	90.7
Euro Zone	309 700	675 716	869 215	946 891	1 480 221	1 567 451	70.5	71.8	70.7
OCEANIA									
MSG	11	5	18	22	45	51	3.7	1.1	1.5
INTERREGIONAL									
ACP	2 351	4 565	9 596	11 970	19 418	22 952	..	..	..
APEC	357 697	901 730	1 688 929	2 262 085	2 886 463	3 265 077	..	..	..
BSEC	1 190	1 229	25 505	24 737	50 732	65 760	..	..	..
CIS	..	..	31 529	28 753	43 438	59 484	..	..	..

Sources:
- UNCTAD secretariat calculations based on International Monetary Fund (IMF), *Direction of Trade Statistics.*

2

INTERNATIONAL **MERCHANDISE** TRADE BY REGION

COMMERCE INTERNATIONAL DES **MARCHANDISES** PAR RÉGIONS

1
2
3
4
5
6
7
8

Origin / Origine	Year Année	World (millions of dollars) Monde (millions de dollars)	Developed economies / Économies développées — Total	Europe — Total	EU UE	USA États-Unis	Japan Japon	Other Autres	Economies in transition Économies en transition	Developing economies / Économies en développement — Total	Africa Afrique	America Amérique	Eastern, Southern and South-Eastern Asia / Asie orientale, méridionale et du Sud-Est	Western Asia / Asie occidentale	Oceania Océanie
										Percentage / En pourcentage					
Afghanistan	1990	131	79.4	73.8	69.0	3.4	1.5	0.7	0.1	20.5	0.3	0.6	14.7	4.9	..
	2000	(e)142	38.3	35.7	35.4	1.9	0.3	0.4	5.7	56.0	0.6	4.7	48.8	1.3	0.0
	2005	(e)239	40.2	12.7	12.6	25.8	1.1	0.6	3.1	56.7	3.2	1.9	44.7	6.3	0.0
Albania - Albanie	1990	(e)224	68.5	63.5	62.3	1.0	4.0	0.0	16.2	15.2	4.9	0.2	9.9	0.3	..
	2000	260	94.8	93.8	93.6	0.9	0.1	0.0	4.4	0.7	..	..	0.0	0.7	..
	2005	658	89.7	88.7	88.7	1.0	0.0	0.0	7.6	2.5	0.0	0.1	0.6	1.7	..
Algeria - Algérie	1990	11 009	90.8	70.2	70.2	19.2	0.9	0.4	2.3	6.9	2.5	2.1	0.6	1.7	..
	2000	21 871	83.1	63.8	63.4	15.7	0.1	3.6	0.2	16.7	1.4	8.2	0.8	6.3	..
	2005	(e)43 634	85.0	54.4	54.1	22.6	0.1	7.9	0.2	14.8	2.0	6.6	2.3	3.9	0.0
Angola	1990	3 748	90.0	36.4	36.4	50.9	1.3	1.3	5.6	4.4	0.5	3.9	0.0	0.0	..
	2000	(e)7 360	62.4	17.3	17.3	44.6	0.0	0.4	0.0	37.6	0.2	2.4	35.0	0.0	..
	2005	(e)20 194	56.0	14.7	14.7	39.8	0.1	1.4	0.0	44.0	1.5	7.2	35.2	0.0	..
Argentina - Argentine	1990	12 353	51.0	32.3	31.7	13.8	3.2	1.8	5.1	43.8	3.2	27.6	11.2	1.9	0.0
	2000	26 341	33.6	18.4	18.1	12.0	1.4	1.8	0.5	64.2	4.0	48.1	10.1	2.0	0.0
	2005	40 104	31.0	17.2	16.9	11.4	0.7	1.7	2.2	65.3	6.1	40.6	15.7	2.8	0.0
Armenia - Arménie	2000	(e)300	52.5	39.5	36.5	12.6	0.1	0.3	24.3	12.8	0.0	..	10.3	2.5	..
	2005	974	74.2	50.1	46.5	11.2	0.1	12.7	19.3	6.3	0.0	0.6	4.2	1.4	..
Aruba	2000	173	38.2	32.3	32.3	5.8	0.0	0.1	..	61.2	0.1	61.1	0.0	0.0	..
	2005	106	49.3	37.9	37.9	11.3	0.0	0.1	0.0	50.5	..	50.2	0.3	0.1	..
Australia - Australie	1990	38 987	60.0	16.0	13.8	11.0	26.2	6.8	1.2	36.4	1.4	1.0	28.6	2.8	2.6
	2000	63 520	47.9	10.9	10.7	9.8	19.8	7.4	0.3	48.0	2.4	1.3	38.1	4.1	2.1
	2005	105 055	45.9	11.0	10.7	6.7	20.3	7.9	0.4	52.2	2.5	1.6	42.7	3.5	1.8
Austria - Autriche	1990	41 393	86.8	80.6	72.8	3.2	1.6	1.4	5.4	7.8	1.6	0.7	3.9	1.6	0.0
	2000	67 456	88.6	80.9	73.8	5.0	1.3	1.5	4.1	7.3	1.1	1.1	3.8	1.3	0.0
	2005	124 634	83.9	75.2	69.7	5.8	1.2	1.7	7.1	8.7	1.2	1.0	4.8	1.7	0.0
Azerbaijan - Azerbaïdjan	2000	1 745	76.3	68.0	63.1	0.5	0.0	7.8	14.4	8.8	0.6	0.4	1.4	6.4	..
	2005	4 347	52.4	46.9	46.7	1.0	0.0	4.5	30.0	17.7	0.9	0.0	9.6	7.1	..
Bahamas	1990	990	96.4	41.0	29.8	48.3	1.4	5.7	0.0	3.0	0.4	2.1	0.5	..	..
	2000	(e)875	91.0	57.1	51.5	28.9	3.3	1.7	0.4	8.4	0.1	7.7	0.4	0.2	0.0
	2005	(e)2 198	88.5	56.1	54.1	30.0	0.0	2.3	0.1	11.2	0.2	7.7	3.0	0.2	0.0
Bahrain - Bahreïn	1990	3 838	5.4	1.6	1.6	1.8	1.8	0.1	..	10.3	0.1	0.9	3.5	5.8	..
	2000	(e)7 722	12.5	5.2	4.9	4.1	2.8	0.5	0.0	25.4	4.4	0.1	14.7	6.3	0.0
	2005	(e)15 970	9.1	4.1	3.9	2.6	1.8	0.6	0.0	22.7	5.3	0.0	8.4	8.9	0.0
Bangladesh	1990	1 671	75.2	37.3	35.4	30.5	3.9	3.5	4.6	19.7	4.1	0.5	11.9	3.1	0.1
	2000	5 590	75.9	40.8	40.2	31.8	1.2	2.1	0.3	9.2	0.7	0.4	6.0	2.1	0.0
	2005	8 494	75.2	47.2	46.8	23.6	0.8	3.6	0.2	9.6	0.7	0.4	6.7	1.8	0.0
Barbados - Barbade	1990	209	35.8	18.8	18.6	13.5	0.3	3.3	..	25.9	0.0	25.6	0.3	..	..
	2000	273	23.1	16.7	16.4	3.8	0.1	2.5	28.5	31.6	0.1	28.7	0.7	1.6	0.5
	2005	260	38.4	16.9	16.5	18.6	0.0	2.9	0.0	59.5	0.1	58.0	1.2	0.2	0.0
Belarus - Bélarus	2000	7 332	29.8	28.3	28.0	1.4	0.1	0.1	60.8	9.0	1.8	1.4	4.8	1.0	..
	2005	15 976	46.1	44.4	44.1	1.6	0.0	0.1	45.2	8.2	0.6	1.4	5.6	0.6	..
Belgium - Belgique	2005	334 173	87.8	78.0	76.5	6.4	1.0	2.3	1.5	10.2	1.8	1.1	5.2	2.1	0.0
Belgium-Luxembourg - Belgique-Luxembourg	1990	117 475	89.6	81.7	79.1	4.3	1.3	2.3	0.7	8.9	2.5	0.7	4.3	1.3	0.0
	2000	194 843	89.1	79.4	77.5	5.8	1.2	2.7	1.0	9.9	1.8	1.2	5.0	1.9	0.0
Belize	1990	131	77.9	27.8	27.8	45.0	0.7	4.4	..	20.6	0.0	19.3	0.1	1.1	..
	2000	184	93.8	38.0	38.0	52.3	2.0	1.6	..	6.1	..	6.0	0.1	..	..
	2005	(e)305	74.4	38.3	38.3	31.0	2.4	2.7	0.2	25.3	6.6	15.0	3.3	0.4	..
Benin - Bénin	1990	122	47.6	23.9	23.8	23.4	0.1	0.2	0.0	51.9	40.0	5.0	6.9	..	..
	2000	196	20.2	19.5	18.1	0.6	0.1	0.0	0.7	79.2	14.5	10.7	48.1	5.8	..
	2005	300	8.8	8.7	8.1	0.1	..	0.0	0.1	91.1	27.0	0.4	61.3	2.4	..
Bermuda - Bermudes	1990	60	98.7	33.2	33.2	54.8	..	10.7	..	0.4	..	0.4	0.0	..	..
	2000	800	91.3	84.4	78.5	4.5	0.1	2.3	0.1	2.4	0.6	0.9	0.6	0.3	..
	2005	(e)1 755	92.1	86.2	86.2	4.6	0.3	1.1	0.0	1.4	0.3	1.1	0.0	0.0	..

For sources and notes, see end of table.

Pour les sources et les notes, se reporter à la fin du tableau.

Destination / Origin / Origine	Year / Année	World (millions of dollars) / Monde (millions de dollars)	Developed economies / Économies développées — Total	Europe — Total	Europe — EU / UE	USA / États-Unis	Japan / Japon	Other / Autres	Economies in transition / Économies en transition	Developing economies / Économies en développement — Total	Africa / Afrique	America / Amérique	Eastern, Southern and South-Eastern Asia / Asie orientale, méridionale et du Sud-Est	Western Asia / Asie occidentale	Oceania / Océanie
Bolivia - Bolivie	1990	923	52.1	31.2	29.1	20.0	0.3	0.5	2.2	45.4	..	44.8	0.5	0.1	..
	2000	1 475	53.1	28.2	17.1	24.0	0.2	0.7	0.0	45.7	0.1	44.5	1.0	0.1	..
	2005	2 240	23.7	6.9	6.7	12.5	3.3	1.1	0.2	75.6	0.2	72.2	3.1	0.1	..
Bosnia and Herzegovina - Bosnie-Herzégovine	2000	(e)670	79.7	76.6	76.2	2.6	0.1	0.5	16.0	4.3	2.5	0.1	0.6	1.1	..
	2005	(e)2 236	71.8	68.3	67.9	3.0	0.1	0.5	21.9	6.3	1.2	0.0	4.3	0.7	0.0
Brazil - Brésil	1990	31 414	69.5	34.9	33.8	24.6	7.5	2.5	1.3	27.9	3.2	11.7	10.6	2.4	0.0
	2000	59 643	52.7	24.4	22.8	22.4	4.1	1.7	1.1	35.0	2.3	23.3	7.2	2.3	0.0
	2005	118 469	45.8	21.4	20.6	19.2	2.9	2.3	3.4	47.1	5.0	25.4	13.5	3.1	0.0
Brunei Darussalam - Brunéi Darussalam	1990	2 212	63.1	0.2	0.2	3.4	58.1	1.3	..	33.5	..	..	33.5	0.0	..
	2000	3 161	61.6	3.7	3.6	12.0	40.7	5.3	0.0	38.2	0.1	0.0	38.0	0.1	0.0
	2005	(e)5 633	58.1	1.2	1.1	9.5	36.8	10.5	0.0	41.4	0.0	0.0	41.3	0.0	..
Bulgaria - Bulgarie	1990	2 032	58.4	53.6	51.6	2.4	1.6	0.8	17.6	24.0	5.4	0.7	11.9	6.1	0.0
	2000	(e)4 760	55.7	50.0	48.9	4.0	0.4	1.4	18.6	16.6	1.6	0.9	2.4	11.7	0.0
	2005	11 735	62.1	57.8	56.6	3.0	0.1	1.2	14.4	18.3	2.1	1.0	3.3	11.9	0.0
Burkina Faso	1990	152	53.9	52.5	41.8	0.1	1.3	0.0	..	32.9	17.3	..	15.7	..	..
	2000	171	39.3	34.8	34.7	1.7	2.7	0.1	0.5	57.1	15.5	9.7	30.0	1.9	..
	2005	(e)374	12.5	9.7	9.6	0.6	2.2	0.0	0.0	84.3	14.9	0.3	68.5	0.6	..
Burundi	1990	75	55.6	43.2	43.0	11.8	0.5	0.0	..	10.2	8.7	..	0.7	0.9	..
	2000	49	61.7	60.7	35.8	0.7	0.3	0.0	..	17.2	17.0	..	0.0	0.2	..
	2005	(e)94	70.3	64.9	59.0	4.7	0.4	0.3	2.6	10.7	6.6	0.6	3.2	0.3	..
Cambodia - Cambodge	1990	42	15.0	7.1	7.1	..	7.6	0.2	0.7	84.3	0.2	0.8	83.3	0.0	..
	2000	(e)1 123	88.4	21.0	20.6	65.9	1.0	0.6	0.0	10.7	0.0	0.1	10.6	0.0	..
	2005	1 369	71.5	14.6	14.3	48.6	3.5	4.8	0.1	28.3	0.0	0.2	27.9	0.1	0.0
Cameroon - Cameroun	1990	2 026	84.4	69.0	68.2	14.9	0.4	0.2	0.5	15.1	9.3	0.1	5.7	0.1	..
	2000	1 832	66.0	63.7	62.6	1.5	0.1	0.7	0.0	28.3	8.1	0.2	19.3	0.6	..
	2005	(e)3 625	70.9	66.2	66.1	4.3	0.2	0.3	0.1	27.0	10.0	2.8	13.0	1.2	0.0
Canada	1990	126 447	91.4	9.5	8.4	75.4	5.6	0.8	0.8	7.8	0.3	1.7	4.8	0.5	0.0
	2000	275 184	94.9	4.9	4.6	87.4	2.2	0.4	0.1	5.0	0.4	1.5	2.9	0.3	0.0
	2005	359 485	92.9	6.1	5.5	84.2	2.1	0.6	0.2	6.8	0.5	1.9	4.0	0.5	0.0
Cape Verde - Cap-Vert	1990	7	93.1	91.2	90.8	..	..	1.9	0.0	3.6	2.9	0.7	..	..	..
	2000	(e)11	97.5	85.2	85.2	12.3	..	0.0	..	1.9	1.8	0.1	0.0	..	..
	2005	(e)26	92.2	83.0	82.7	9.2	..	0.1	..	7.6	6.6	0.9	0.1	..	..
Central African Republic - République centrafricaine	1990	283	36.1	35.4	35.1	0.7	0.0	0.0	0.0	63.8	59.8	0.0	4.0	0.0	..
	2000	226	89.3	87.4	87.2	1.0	0.3	0.6	0.1	10.6	1.7	0.4	8.3	0.2	..
	2005	(e)115	72.0	65.6	65.6	4.5	1.7	0.2	0.0	27.9	6.9	0.5	14.3	6.3	..
Chad - Tchad	1990	89	88.8	75.0	73.9	1.3	12.5	0.0	0.7	10.5	1.3	0.2	9.0	0.0	..
	2000	(e)86	77.6	70.4	70.4	6.0	1.2	0.0	0.1	22.2	11.4	5.1	5.5	0.3	..
	2005	(e)1 840	82.6	4.5	4.5	78.1	0.0	0.0	0.0	17.4	0.5	0.0	16.9	0.0	..
Chile - Chili	1990	8 678	72.7	38.5	38.3	17.2	16.0	1.1	0.2	24.1	1.3	12.2	9.5	1.1	..
	2000	19 296	56.0	24.4	23.5	16.8	13.2	1.6	0.5	38.5	0.4	21.7	15.0	1.5	0.0
	2005	39 544	53.5	23.2	22.9	15.8	11.5	3.1	0.9	41.6	0.3	16.8	23.4	1.1	0.0
China - Chine	1990	62 760	35.7	11.1	10.7	8.5	14.7	1.5	3.7	59.5	2.0	1.2	54.5	1.7	0.0
	2000	249 208	57.6	16.9	16.4	20.9	16.7	3.1	1.5	40.9	2.0	2.9	33.7	2.3	0.0
	2005	762 337	55.2	19.3	18.9	21.4	11.0	3.4	3.2	41.6	2.4	3.0	33.3	2.8	0.0
China, Hong Kong SAR - Chine, Hong Kong RAS	1990	82 272	53.5	20.0	18.8	24.1	5.7	3.7	0.3	45.5	1.7	1.8	40.6	1.4	0.1
	2000	202 249	48.5	16.4	15.6	23.3	5.5	3.4	0.1	51.2	0.9	2.4	46.8	1.1	0.0
	2005	289 509	39.4	15.1	14.5	16.1	5.3	2.9	0.3	60.3	0.5	1.4	57.2	1.1	0.0
China, Macao SAR - Chine, Macao RAS	1990	1 690	81.0	38.6	37.4	36.2	3.1	3.1	0.1	18.9	0.3	0.3	18.1	0.2	0.0
	2000	2 540	79.5	28.8	28.1	48.3	0.6	1.8	0.0	19.8	0.0	0.4	19.1	0.1	0.0
	2005	2 476	67.9	17.2	17.1	48.7	0.9	1.1	0.0	28.0	0.0	0.5	27.4	0.1	0.0
China, Taiwan Province of - Chine, Taiwan Province de	1990	(e)66 728	68.3	18.3	17.5	32.7	12.6	4.8	0.2	30.8	1.1	1.9	26.0	1.7	0.1
	2000	(e)148 678	53.5	15.8	15.3	23.5	11.3	3.0	0.2	45.3	0.9	2.5	40.5	1.3	0.0
	2005	(e)189 903	37.3	11.9	11.7	15.1	7.7	2.6	0.5	49.4	0.9	2.0	44.7	1.7	0.0
Colombia - Colombie	1990	6 754	79.5	29.6	29.0	44.5	3.8	1.5	0.6	18.2	0.1	17.2	0.7	0.2	0.0
	2000	13 164	67.7	14.1	13.9	50.4	1.8	1.5	0.5	30.9	0.2	29.4	1.2	0.1	0.0
	2005	21 190	59.9	14.1	13.3	41.8	1.6	2.4	0.4	37.9	0.2	34.3	2.6	0.7	0.0

For sources and notes, see end of table.

Pour les sources et les notes, se reporter à la fin du tableau.

53

Destination / Origin	Year / Année	World (millions of dollars) / Monde (millions de dollars)	Developed economies / Économies développées						Economies in transition / Économies en transition	Developing economies / Économies en développement					
			Total	Europe		USA États-Unis	Japan Japon	Other Autres		Total	Africa Afrique	America Amérique	Eastern, Southern and South-Eastern Asia / Asie orientale, méridionale et du Sud-Est	Western Asia / Asie occidentale	Oceania Océanie
				Total	EU UE										
			Percentage / En pourcentage												
Comoros - Comores	1990	23	98.3	76.5	76.5	19.1	2.7	0.0	0.0	1.6	0.3	0.7	0.6	..	..
	2000	(e)16	77.7	53.5	53.2	19.3	3.3	1.5	0.2	20.7	0.6	0.5	19.5	..	0.1
	2005	(e)24	69.4	48.8	48.5	5.6	14.6	0.3	1.0	28.1	2.5	0.1	19.9	5.5	0.1
Congo	1990	1 209	94.1	64.5	54.0	29.5	0.1	0.0	0.1	1.7	1.5	0.0	0.0	0.1	..
	2000	2 154	32.0	10.5	7.2	19.9	0.0	1.5	0.0	68.0	3.3	4.8	59.9	0.0	..
	2005	5 392	35.3	6.6	6.2	28.6	0.0	0.1	0.0	64.5	1.6	1.3	61.2	0.3	..
Costa Rica	1990	1 456	81.2	30.3	29.8	45.7	1.0	4.2	0.1	18.0	0.1	16.4	1.3	0.2	0.0
	2000	5 850	25.1	8.7	8.5	15.5	0.4	0.5	0.1	15.4	0.1	14.8	0.4	0.1	0.0
	2005	7 021	59.0	14.7	14.6	42.6	0.7	1.0	0.3	39.0	0.1	24.8	14.0	0.1	0.0
Côte d'Ivoire	1990	2 813	62.0	54.1	54.0	5.9	1.7	0.2	2.4	35.6	31.9	0.0	3.2	0.4	0.0
	2000	3 850	48.5	39.9	39.5	7.8	0.3	0.6	1.7	37.8	29.6	2.7	5.0	0.6	0.0
	2005	7 251	55.1	40.4	39.8	14.1	0.1	0.5	1.6	40.6	29.8	5.2	5.0	0.6	0.0
Croatia - Croatie	2000	4 071	72.6	69.9	69.0	1.8	0.4	0.5	15.0	7.4	5.5	0.2	0.4	1.3	..
	2005	8 853	66.6	62.4	61.3	3.5	0.3	0.3	19.1	8.2	4.3	0.2	0.5	3.1	..
Cuba	1990	1 357	45.6	32.6	31.8	..	6.4	6.6	4.3	50.1	13.7	12.4	21.9	2.2	..
	2000	(e)1 567	58.4	38.2	37.2	0.0	2.3	17.8	23.2	18.4	2.0	8.9	7.0	0.5	..
	2005	(e)2 167	62.1	39.5	38.4	..	1.3	21.3	4.5	33.4	2.8	16.0	14.4	0.3	0.0
Cyprus - Chypre	1990	945	56.4	53.0	51.9	1.6	0.5	1.4	6.1	27.5	4.8	0.9	1.8	20.0	..
	2000	917	43.6	38.9	38.3	2.4	0.1	2.2	12.7	31.7	4.9	0.1	3.1	23.6	..
	2005	1 452	65.6	61.1	60.5	1.6	1.5	1.3	3.9	13.7	2.9	0.2	3.6	7.0	0.0
Czech Republic - République tchèque	2000	(e)28 922	90.8	87.1	85.3	-	-	3.8	4.3	4.6	0.5	0.6	2.2	1.4	0.0
	2005	78 137	89.7	86.0	84.4	2.6	0.4	0.6	5.3	4.8	0.7	0.6	1.8	1.7	0.0
Czechoslovakia (former) - Tchécoslovaquie (anc.)	1990	11 654	55.9	53.6	50.9	0.8	0.8	0.8	32.4	11.6	2.1	1.5	5.1	2.9	0.0
Dem. Rep. of the Congo - Rép. dém. du Congo	1990	1 353	86.5	65.4	65.2	17.8	2.4	0.9	0.3	13.1	7.7	0.2	4.8	0.4	..
	2000	(e)1 133	97.0	76.3	76.0	19.1	1.5	0.0	0.1	2.7	2.2	0.0	0.4	0.0	..
	2005	(e)1 370	78.2	60.1	60.0	17.8	0.2	0.0	0.1	21.5	4.6	4.5	12.4	0.0	0.0
Denmark - Danemark	1990	34 039	88.7	78.3	69.8	5.0	3.3	2.0	1.5	9.4	2.8	1.0	3.8	1.7	0.0
	2000	50 756	89.7	78.0	70.8	5.9	3.5	2.3	1.7	8.5	1.1	1.5	4.4	1.5	0.0
	2005	84 948	88.1	76.9	69.9	6.4	2.3	2.5	2.3	8.8	0.9	1.2	5.1	1.6	0.0
Djibouti	1990	(e)59	7.8	7.6	7.6	..	0.1	0.0	0.0	92.2	58.2	..	0.7	33.4	..
	2000	(e)151	8.4	8.2	8.2	0.2	0.0	0.0	0.1	91.5	67.4	0.1	1.2	22.8	..
	2005	(e)275	3.3	2.9	2.9	0.3	0.1	0.0	..	96.7	88.1	0.2	1.9	6.4	..
Dominica - Dominique	1990	55	72.5	61.4	61.4	10.9	0.0	0.2	0.2	26.5	..	26.5	..	..	..
	2000	54	39.7	32.1	32.1	7.4	0.0	0.2	..	57.0	0.0	57.0	0.0	..	..
	2005	(e)86	37.7	30.1	29.9	4.0	2.6	0.9	0.0	59.9	0.7	45.0	12.8	1.4	..
Dominican Republic - République dominicaine	1990	744	88.9	19.4	19.4	66.0	2.0	1.6	1.0	8.6	0.5	3.5	4.6	..	..
	2000	5 737	94.5	6.3	6.0	87.3	0.2	0.7	0.0	5.3	0.1	4.1	1.1	0.0	0.0
	2005	(e)5 437	92.2	10.5	10.2	78.9	0.8	2.0	0.1	7.6	0.2	4.8	2.6	0.1	..
Ecuador - Équateur	1990	2 714	62.0	10.8	10.8	48.5	1.9	0.8	0.8	19.8	0.0	17.4	2.4	..	..
	2000	5 788	60.3	15.9	15.5	38.4	4.1	1.9	3.5	35.6	0.2	27.7	7.0	0.7	0.0
	2005	11 176	70.5	17.7	17.2	50.6	1.1	1.1	5.4	23.9	1.0	20.9	1.2	0.8	0.0
Egypt - Égypte	1990	2 585	61.4	43.3	42.4	8.6	2.7	6.8	18.1	18.9	3.7	0.0	6.9	8.2	..
	2000	6 354	63.7	48.0	47.8	12.8	2.0	0.9	0.7	25.9	4.1	0.9	9.7	11.2	0.0
	2005	(e)15 557	52.9	38.2	37.8	13.0	0.7	1.1	1.5	34.9	7.0	1.2	8.1	18.6	0.0
El Salvador	1990	586	64.8	28.6	28.5	33.9	1.1	1.3	..	34.9	0.0	34.7	0.2	0.0	..
	2000	2 941	70.7	4.7	4.7	65.4	0.3	0.2	0.6	28.2	0.3	27.9	0.1	0.0	..
	2005	3 390	66.4	4.4	4.3	61.0	0.5	0.6	0.7	32.2	0.0	31.7	0.4	0.0	..
Equatorial Guinea - Guinée équatoriale	1990	(e)35	93.5	93.5	93.4	..	0.0	0.0	4.8	1.7	1.7	0.0	..	0.0	..
	2000	(e)1 067	74.2	57.1	57.1	13.4	3.6	0.0	0.0	25.8	1.9	1.1	22.7	0.1	..
	2005	(e)6 195	65.9	30.7	30.2	24.6	3.3	7.3	0.0	34.1	0.2	4.9	29.0	0.1	..
Estonia - Estonie	2000	(e)3 831	86.8	84.2	81.0	1.8	0.3	0.4	9.7	3.4	0.7	0.6	1.8	0.3	0.0
	2005	7 669	87.1	82.7	77.7	3.1	0.3	0.9	8.8	3.7	0.6	0.5	1.8	0.9	0.0
Ethiopia - Éthiopie	2000	439	71.4	50.1	43.5	4.0	12.9	4.5	0.3	28.3	13.4	0.1	4.6	10.3	..
	2005	782	61.2	43.5	36.9	5.5	8.5	3.8	0.4	37.8	11.7	0.1	14.7	11.3	..

For sources and notes, see end of table.

Pour les sources et les notes, se reporter à la fin du tableau.

Destination / Origin / Origine	Year / Année	World (millions of dollars) / Monde (millions de dollars)	Developed economies / Économies développées						Economies in transition / Économies en transition	Developing economies / Économies en développement					
			Total	Europe		USA États-Unis	Japan Japon	Other Autres		Total	Africa Afrique	America Amérique	Eastern, Southern and South-Eastern Asia / Asie orientale, méridionale et du Sud-Est	Western Asia / Asie occidentale	Oceania Océanie
				Total	EU UE										
			Percentage / En pourcentage												
Ethiopia (former) - Éthiopie (anc.)	1990	294	67.4	41.2	41.2	10.8	14.9	0.5	4.2	26.0	12.7	2.5	0.7	10.2	..
Faeroe Islands - Îles Féroé	1990	381	98.8	94.8	93.4	4.1	..	0.0	1.1	0.0	0.0	0.0	0.0	..	..
	2000	395	98.6	92.9	87.2	5.6	..	0.0	0.0	0.8	0.6	0.0	0.1	0.0	..
	2005	(e)548	87.5	85.4	77.8	0.8	..	1.3	2.4	9.3	8.9	0.0	0.4	..	0.0
Fiji - Fidji	1990	498	69.2	23.3	23.3	8.4	5.9	31.5	..	5.4	..	..	5.4	..	..
	2000	684	70.8	16.6	16.6	21.1	4.1	29.0	0.0	17.9	0.0	0.0	6.4	0.0	11.5
	2005	(e)866	60.0	13.4	13.4	19.7	5.4	21.4	0.0	20.6	0.0	0.2	3.0	0.1	17.3
Finland - Finlande	1990	26 570	78.1	68.4	63.5	5.8	1.4	2.4	13.1	8.8	1.8	1.4	4.3	1.3	0.0
	2000	45 867	78.2	66.9	62.6	7.4	1.7	2.2	5.1	16.2	1.8	2.7	9.0	2.8	0.0
	2005	65 964	69.9	59.7	56.0	6.2	1.7	2.3	12.7	17.3	2.2	2.2	7.4	5.6	0.0
France	1990	217 097	80.0	70.5	66.0	5.9	1.9	1.7	1.4	15.2	6.5	1.4	4.6	2.4	0.4
	2000	323 482	80.4	68.2	64.1	8.7	1.6	1.9	1.3	16.9	5.7	2.5	5.4	3.0	0.3
	2005	462 661	76.7	66.0	62.6	7.1	1.5	2.0	2.3	19.1	6.3	1.9	6.8	3.7	0.3
Gabon	1990	2 483	82.2	47.4	45.8	29.5	4.1	1.2	0.6	16.9	4.7	9.8	2.4	..	..
	2000	(e)3 793	76.0	22.9	22.8	52.4	0.3	0.3	0.0	18.1	1.6	2.3	13.9	0.3	..
	2005	(e)5 105	68.4	13.5	12.8	52.6	0.2	2.0	1.4	20.4	4.2	4.3	11.5	0.4	0.0
Gambia - Gambie	1990	172	89.4	54.8	52.5	..	34.6	0.0	0.7	9.3	6.8	0.1	2.5	0.0	..
	2000	(e)46	69.0	60.6	60.6	0.6	7.2	0.6	0.8	30.2	18.2	6.2	5.7	0.1	..
	2005	(e)28	29.8	26.4	26.2	1.0	2.3	0.2	0.2	70.0	13.6	0.4	55.3	0.6	..
Georgia - Géorgie	2000	(e)326	30.0	27.5	23.4	2.2	0.1	0.2	40.5	29.2	1.4	0.6	2.9	24.3	..
	2005	851	27.5	19.8	19.4	3.1	0.2	4.3	54.1	18.2	0.2	0.4	2.8	14.9	..
Germany - Allemagne	1990	409 273	83.4	71.9	65.1	7.1	2.6	1.8	4.6	11.8	2.5	1.8	5.3	2.2	0.0
	2000	548 855	83.7	69.3	64.1	10.3	2.2	1.9	2.6	13.4	1.8	2.5	6.4	2.7	0.0
	2005	977 049	80.3	68.1	63.5	8.8	1.7	1.8	4.5	14.9	1.9	2.2	7.6	3.3	0.0
Ghana	1990	1 235	84.6	66.1	64.1	13.1	5.0	0.4	4.7	7.3	2.6	0.5	3.4	0.9	..
	2000	1 486	73.5	55.6	54.2	13.8	3.1	1.0	3.8	14.4	5.7	0.9	5.9	1.9	0.0
	2005	(e)2 364	58.6	47.6	45.9	6.7	3.0	1.3	4.7	24.8	9.0	2.0	9.5	4.3	0.0
Greece - Grèce	1990	8 065	82.5	74.0	72.2	5.6	0.9	2.0	5.4	10.9	3.7	1.0	1.5	4.7	0.0
	2000	10 975	63.1	54.0	51.5	5.3	0.8	2.9	19.4	17.2	3.9	2.0	2.5	8.7	0.0
	2005	17 124	62.1	54.4	53.0	5.3	0.3	2.0	17.5	18.4	4.7	1.0	3.5	9.2	0.0
Greenland - Groenland	1990	391	98.5	97.6	97.5	..	0.9	0.0	..	..	..	..	..	..	..
	2000	332	91.4	57.9	54.7	4.8	26.1	2.6	0.0	7.0	0.1	0.0	6.9	..	..
	2005	(e)513	88.0	72.5	70.0	3.2	12.2	0.1	0.2	9.3	0.2	0.0	9.1	0.0	0.0
Grenada - Grenade	1990	21	68.9	56.2	56.2	7.3	3.2	2.2	..	31.1	..	30.5	..	0.5	..
	2000	(e)77	80.5	30.3	30.3	49.1	..	1.0	..	16.2	..	16.2	..	..	..
	2005	(e)48	44.9	31.9	31.7	11.4	..	1.7	0.1	48.2	0.2	47.2	0.7	0.1	..
Guatemala	1990	1 189	56.8	13.6	13.3	38.9	2.9	1.4	0.6	38.3	1.3	33.5	1.9	1.6	..
	2000	2 699	52.3	11.4	10.9	36.1	2.3	2.5	1.5	45.7	0.3	40.8	1.7	2.4	..
	2005	5 379	58.5	6.3	4.6	50.1	0.7	1.5	0.0	40.4	0.3	37.0	2.1	1.1	0.0
Guinea - Guinée	1990	606	85.6	61.4	57.1	21.2	1.1	1.9	2.3	12.2	8.5	0.6	3.1	0.0	..
	2000	(e)617	80.5	65.2	65.2	11.5	0.0	3.8	11.8	7.7	7.6	..	0.1	0.0	..
	2005	1 328	43.5	35.4	35.3	6.1	0.1	1.8	27.6	15.5	1.9	0.0	13.5	0.0	..
Guinea-Bissau - Guinée-Bissau	1990	34	56.1	55.5	55.5	0.3	0.4	0.0	2.0	41.9	4.4	..	37.5	..	..
	2000	(e)112	4.2	3.8	3.8	0.4	0.0	0.0	0.0	95.8	1.5	46.2	48.0	0.0	..
	2005	(e)113	3.6	3.4	3.4	0.2	0.0	0.0	0.0	96.4	18.0	4.0	74.4	..	..
Guyana	1990	232	83.7	48.7	48.6	20.5	6.3	8.1	2.1	14.0	0.3	13.5	0.2	0.0	..
	2000	(e)597	76.9	29.1	29.1	24.4	0.7	22.7	4.2	18.5	0.3	15.2	3.0	0.0	0.0
	2005	(e)641	71.4	31.1	30.9	18.9	0.6	20.8	0.0	27.9	0.5	21.4	6.0	0.0	0.0
Haiti - Haïti	1990	171	99.3	12.7	12.7	83.0	1.2	2.5	0.0	0.6	..	0.6	0.0	..	..
	2000	324	94.5	5.9	5.4	86.5	0.2	1.9	0.1	5.2	0.6	4.5	0.0	0.1	..
	2005	(e)515	89.2	3.7	3.4	80.9	0.2	4.3	0.0	10.6	0.7	8.5	1.3	0.1	..
Honduras	1990	812	79.6	21.8	21.8	52.8	4.8	0.3	..	3.9	..	3.9	..	..	..
	2000	1 403	68.0	10.0	9.8	53.8	3.8	0.4	0.0	26.9	0.0	25.2	1.6	0.0	..
	2005	4 865	85.9	9.8	9.4	73.3	0.5	2.4	0.4	13.6	0.0	12.2	1.2	0.1	..

For sources and notes, see end of table.

Pour les sources et les notes, se reporter à la fin du tableau.

Destination / Origin / Origine	Year / Année	World (millions of dollars) / Monde (millions de dollars)	Developed economies / Économies développées						Economies in transition / Économies en transition	Developing economies / Économies en développement					
			Total	Europe		USA États-Unis	Japan Japon	Other Autres		Total	Africa Afrique	America Amérique	Eastern, Southern and South-Eastern Asia / Asie orientale, méridionale et du Sud-Est	Western Asia / Asie occidentale	Oceania Océanie
				Total	EU UE										
								Percentage / En pourcentage							
Hungary - Hongrie	1990	9 593	58.9	53.4	51.3	3.5	1.2	0.8	27.2	9.7	1.8	0.8	5.0	2.1	..
	2000	28 087	89.0	82.8	81.4	5.3	0.6	0.4	6.9	4.1	0.4	0.6	2.1	1.1	..
	2005	62 419	82.7	78.5	77.0	3.0	0.6	0.6	10.6	6.7	1.1	0.5	2.0	3.2	0.0
Iceland - Islande	1990	1 591	95.0	78.4	71.2	9.9	6.0	0.7	2.6	2.2	0.7	0.3	1.1	0.2	..
	2000	1 896	96.1	76.4	68.7	12.4	5.3	2.0	0.6	3.3	1.1	0.2	1.9	0.1	..
	2005	2 981	94.4	81.5	76.4	8.1	3.3	1.5	1.6	4.0	1.9	0.2	1.7	0.2	0.0
India - Inde	1990	17 813	57.3	30.5	29.1	15.1	9.3	2.4	16.8	21.5	2.5	0.4	12.6	5.9	0.0
	2000	42 626	54.6	25.5	24.3	21.3	4.1	3.7	2.6	39.4	5.3	2.2	21.4	10.4	0.1
	2005	97 918	45.1	22.9	22.3	16.7	2.4	3.1	1.4	53.2	6.8	2.8	30.1	13.4	0.0
Indonesia - Indonésie	1990	25 683	70.5	12.4	12.3	13.1	42.5	2.4	0.4	29.0	0.7	0.4	25.4	2.5	0.0
	2000	62 118	54.7	14.6	14.3	13.7	23.2	3.3	0.3	45.0	1.8	1.7	38.3	3.1	0.1
	2005	85 623	48.3	12.2	12.0	11.5	21.1	3.5	0.6	51.1	1.9	1.5	44.5	3.0	0.1
Iran, Islamic Republic of - Iran, Rép. islamique d'	1990	19 305	72.3	50.0	42.4	1.5	20.7	0.1	1.9	18.3	..	4.4	10.9	3.1	..
	2000	26 908	45.9	26.8	26.4	0.6	18.1	0.4	1.2	40.4	6.0	0.2	30.0	4.2	0.0
	2005	(e)55 380	40.8	23.5	23.4	0.3	16.9	0.1	1.1	42.8	5.5	0.0	28.4	8.9	0.0
Iraq	1990	10 314	63.2	25.8	25.8	28.6	7.9	0.9	3.8	33.1	2.3	10.2	7.3	13.3	..
	2000	(e)14 916	79.5	33.2	33.2	38.7	4.0	3.6	0.6	19.9	3.1	2.1	10.6	4.2	..
	2005	(e)17 656	80.4	22.9	22.9	49.7	2.3	5.6	0.0	19.5	0.3	3.0	10.9	5.4	..
Ireland - Irlande	1990	23 770	92.7	80.9	78.4	8.2	1.8	1.7	0.8	5.6	1.5	1.0	1.9	1.1	0.0
	2000	76 336	87.1	64.6	61.3	17.0	3.8	1.7	0.5	8.9	1.2	0.9	5.3	1.4	0.0
	2005	110 100	90.8	67.8	63.4	18.7	2.7	1.6	0.6	8.3	0.9	1.1	5.1	1.0	0.0
Israel - Israël	1990	12 005	77.4	39.5	36.8	28.8	7.3	1.8	0.6	13.2	1.3	2.6	8.6	0.7	..
	2000	31 911	71.3	30.2	28.5	36.8	2.6	1.7	1.2	21.0	1.5	2.8	15.2	1.5	0.0
	2005	42 514	71.7	31.2	28.8	36.5	1.9	2.2	2.3	22.5	1.5	3.1	15.5	2.4	0.0
Italy - Italie	1990	170 466	81.7	69.6	64.6	7.6	2.3	2.2	3.6	14.2	4.4	2.0	4.9	2.8	0.1
	2000	236 597	78.3	63.6	59.8	10.4	1.7	2.6	3.8	17.3	3.5	3.8	5.9	4.0	0.0
	2005	372 166	75.7	63.8	59.4	8.0	1.5	2.3	6.1	17.6	3.8	2.6	6.5	4.6	0.0
Jamaica - Jamaïque	1990	1 133	82.1	42.2	31.9	28.4	0.7	10.9	4.4	12.8	4.7	8.0	0.1	0.0	..
	2000	(e)1 301	90.5	40.4	31.6	38.1	2.3	9.7	0.0	9.0	1.6	6.0	1.0	0.5	..
	2005	1 531	83.5	36.7	29.9	25.8	1.0	19.9	1.4	14.3	0.0	5.1	7.5	1.7	..
Japan - Japon	1990	287 839	59.1	22.1	20.7	31.7	..	5.4	1.0	39.7	1.8	3.3	31.6	2.6	0.2
	2000	478 361	51.6	17.6	16.8	30.1	..	3.9	0.2	48.1	1.0	3.8	41.3	1.9	0.1
	2005	594 887	42.3	15.2	14.6	22.9	..	4.2	0.9	56.8	1.4	3.8	48.8	2.7	0.1
Jordan - Jordanie	1990	922	6.9	4.1	4.1	0.6	2.1	0.0	3.6	89.5	8.1	0.1	40.3	40.9	..
	2000	1 284	16.2	4.0	4.0	4.9	1.0	6.3	0.5	81.0	8.7	0.4	32.9	39.0	0.0
	2005	4 301	33.1	3.4	3.3	26.2	0.6	2.9	0.7	57.5	6.4	0.3	12.5	38.2	..
Kazakhstan	2000	(e)9 878	42.1	27.8	23.0	2.1	0.1	12.2	23.7	12.9	0.2	0.7	11.2	0.9	..
	2005	23 610	50.6	44.6	43.7	4.5	1.3	0.2	22.6	20.3	0.1	0.3	17.1	2.8	..
Kenya	1990	1 120	43.8	38.4	37.6	2.5	1.0	1.8	1.4	47.6	38.6	..	8.0	1.0	..
	2000	1 760	36.3	31.4	30.5	2.1	1.1	1.7	0.0	62.4	45.8	0.2	12.6	3.8	..
	2005	3 552	42.1	30.6	29.6	9.4	0.8	1.3	1.0	51.9	39.7	0.3	10.0	1.9	0.0
Korea, Dem. People's Rep. of - Corée, Rép. populaire dém. de	1990	(e)924	43.4	14.0	13.9	..	29.4	0.0	2.9	53.6	10.8	3.6	32.7	6.5	0.0
	2000	(e)925	38.9	13.8	13.6	0.0	24.7	0.4	2.7	58.4	2.8	29.3	22.6	3.5	0.2
	2005	(e)1 331	16.3	6.2	6.1	..	9.0	1.1	1.9	81.8	6.2	10.7	54.5	10.1	0.3
Korea, Republic of - Corée, République de	1990	67 815	67.2	15.7	15.0	28.6	18.6	4.2	..	24.5	1.8	2.9	16.7	2.9	0.1
	2000	172 257	52.3	15.0	14.3	21.9	11.9	3.5	0.9	46.4	1.9	5.3	35.8	3.3	0.1
	2005	284 333	42.1	15.8	15.4	14.6	8.5	3.3	2.2	55.1	2.8	4.9	43.7	3.6	0.1
Kuwait - Koweït	1990	8 351	49.9	23.5	23.4	6.8	18.6	1.0	0.5	38.9	1.8	1.9	29.2	6.0	0.0
	2000	(e)18 761	53.0	13.9	13.8	14.4	24.1	0.6	0.0	47.0	1.0	0.5	42.8	2.7	..
	2005	(e)35 233	42.9	10.5	10.4	11.9	19.7	0.8	0.0	57.1	0.9	0.2	52.7	3.4	..
Kyrgyzstan - Kirghizistan	2000	504	44.8	44.1	37.3	0.6	0.1	0.0	41.4	13.8	0.4	..	11.7	1.7	..
	2005	(e)708	5.9	2.6	2.6	0.7	0.0	2.6	40.1	54.0	0.1	0.0	16.1	37.8	..
Lao People's Dem. Rep. - Rép. dém. populaire lao	1990	64	19.9	11.1	9.9	0.1	7.1	1.6	..	80.1	1.0	0.6	78.4	0.0	..
	2000	(e)391	33.4	27.8	26.2	2.3	2.8	0.5	0.0	45.6	0.2	0.0	45.2	0.2	0.0
	2005	(e)695	23.9	20.5	19.7	0.6	1.1	1.8	0.1	49.1	0.1	0.1	48.7	0.2	0.0

For sources and notes, see end of table.

Pour les sources et les notes, se reporter à la fin du tableau.

Destination / Origin / Origine	Year / Année	World (millions of dollars) / Monde (millions de dollars)	Developed economies / Économies développées						Economies in transition / Économies en transition	Developing economies / Économies en développement					
			Total	Europe Total	Europe EU / UE	USA États-Unis	Japan Japon	Other Autres		Total	Africa Afrique	America Amérique	Eastern, Southern and South-Eastern Asia / Asie orientale, méridionale et du Sud-Est	Western Asia / Asie occidentale	Oceania Océanie
			Percentage / En pourcentage												
Latvia - Lettonie	2000	1 865	87.6	82.2	80.7	3.8	0.4	1.2	8.7	3.3	2.3	0.3	0.4	0.3	0.0
	2005	5 143	84.9	80.7	76.4	2.7	0.9	0.6	12.5	2.3	0.7	0.7	0.7	0.2	0.0
Lebanon - Liban	1990	456	45.9	39.0	27.7	4.9	0.9	1.1	1.4	52.8	9.4	0.1	2.7	40.6	..
	2000	(e)714	39.3	30.1	22.9	6.8	0.8	1.6	0.6	59.1	10.6	0.6	4.8	43.1	0.0
	2005	(e)2 173	24.1	19.4	11.2	3.8	0.1	0.8	0.8	74.2	9.7	0.3	5.6	58.6	0.0
Liberia - Libéria	1990	1 943	86.4	83.7	41.8	2.5	0.0	0.3	0.2	13.4	0.2	1.0	12.2	0.0	0.0
	2000	(e)582	77.2	69.8	61.0	7.1	0.0	0.3	1.6	21.1	2.1	2.6	14.3	2.2	0.0
	2005	(e)989	82.5	72.4	71.8	8.9	0.0	1.1	0.9	16.6	1.5	0.1	14.0	1.1	0.0
Libyan Arab Jamahiriya - Jamahiriya arabe libyenne	1990	13 878	84.8	84.8	84.7	..	0.0	0.0	7.6	7.6	3.3	0.1	0.3	3.9	..
	2000	(e)12 716	88.4	88.3	85.5	..	0.1	0.0	1.5	10.2	3.4	0.3	0.6	5.9	..
	2005	(e)29 019	85.6	79.9	76.5	5.2	0.0	0.5	1.1	13.3	2.3	0.3	3.3	7.5	..
Lithuania - Lituanie	2000	(e)3 810	80.2	74.6	72.1	4.9	0.3	0.4	16.5	3.2	0.1	0.5	0.7	1.8	..
	2005	11 761	76.1	68.3	65.5	4.7	0.1	3.0	18.1	5.7	0.2	0.4	3.7	1.4	0.0
Luxembourg	2005	18 318	89.8	86.8	85.4	2.1	0.2	0.6	0.9	5.2	0.6	0.9	2.1	1.6	0.0
Madagascar	1990	366	87.5	52.4	51.6	29.4	5.5	0.2	0.7	11.7	5.5	0.2	6.1	0.0	0.0
	2000	806	82.5	59.8	59.5	19.2	2.8	0.5	0.0	12.4	3.3	0.1	9.0	0.1	0.0
	2005	(e)1 005	88.0	53.1	52.7	31.0	2.6	1.3	0.2	9.4	2.6	0.1	6.4	0.2	0.1
Malawi	1990	419	76.6	50.6	48.4	11.5	12.8	1.7	..	16.6	15.0	..	1.4	0.2	..
	2000	(e)380	68.4	40.2	38.6	14.1	12.2	1.9	4.3	26.7	18.0	0.8	4.4	3.2	0.4
	2005	(e)629	55.4	31.2	30.4	17.8	4.8	1.6	6.3	37.9	30.6	1.3	2.9	2.6	0.5
Malaysia - Malaisie	1990	29 421	50.8	15.8	15.6	16.9	15.3	2.7	0.8	48.4	0.8	0.7	44.7	2.2	0.1
	2000	98 154	51.4	14.2	14.0	20.5	13.0	3.7	0.1	48.4	0.8	1.5	44.2	1.8	0.1
	2005	140 977	45.3	11.9	11.7	19.7	9.3	4.3	0.5	54.2	1.4	1.1	48.9	2.6	0.1
Maldives	1990	(e)52	61.5	26.5	26.2	24.2	8.5	2.3	..	38.5	..	..	38.5	..	0.0
	2000	76	67.2	18.6	18.6	44.2	4.2	0.2	..	32.8	..	..	32.8	0.0	..
	2005	99	48.2	24.5	24.5	0.8	22.8	0.1	0.0	51.8	..	..	51.7	0.0	..
Mali	1990	252	44.9	37.1	36.2	0.8	1.2	5.7	13.9	40.5	14.4	0.1	26.0	0.0	..
	2000	(e)234	45.1	33.6	33.0	3.8	0.5	7.2	0.3	52.3	9.6	9.9	32.0	0.8	0.0
	2005	(e)247	26.0	21.8	21.6	1.4	0.1	2.7	1.2	67.8	7.1	0.2	59.3	1.2	0.0
Malta - Malte	1990	1 127	82.1	78.0	77.5	3.8	0.1	0.2	3.0	11.6	6.4	0.1	3.5	1.7	..
	2000	2 442	72.9	40.6	34.1	27.4	3.8	1.1	0.1	21.6	2.3	0.2	18.1	1.0	0.0
	2005	2 272	69.4	51.5	50.8	14.4	2.0	1.4	0.7	28.8	7.4	1.3	18.1	2.0	0.0
Mauritania - Mauritanie	1990	469	79.8	60.1	60.0	..	19.7	0.0	13.0	6.8	5.6	0.5	0.7	0.0	..
	2000	(e)529	70.2	56.4	55.8	0.1	13.8	0.0	2.6	25.9	20.8	1.0	3.8	0.3	0.0
	2005	(e)943	72.9	60.3	59.3	0.1	12.2	0.4	5.6	20.0	18.4	0.0	1.0	0.6	0.0
Mauritius - Maurice	1990	1 202	96.2	82.3	81.2	12.7	0.2	1.0	0.1	3.7	2.2	0.1	1.4	0.0	0.0
	2000	1 488	90.4	68.7	67.4	20.2	0.5	1.0	0.0	9.6	7.6	0.3	1.4	0.1	0.1
	2005	2 005	77.9	66.9	65.8	9.7	0.9	0.4	0.2	21.5	9.1	0.2	3.2	9.0	0.0
Mexico - Mexique	1990	27 167	90.8	14.2	13.4	69.3	5.5	1.8	0.1	8.2	0.3	6.6	1.2	0.1	0.0
	2000	166 199	95.1	3.7	3.3	88.7	0.6	2.2	0.0	4.4	0.0	3.7	0.7	0.0	..
	2005	214 233	92.6	4.1	4.0	85.7	0.7	2.2	0.0	6.1	0.1	4.5	1.4	0.1	..
Moldova, Republic of - Moldova, République de	2000	472	30.4	26.5	26.2	3.3	0.0	0.6	67.4	2.2	0.2	0.1	0.7	1.2	..
	2005	1 055	32.0	28.1	27.4	3.6	0.0	0.2	63.6	4.2	0.4	0.4	0.1	3.2	..
Mongolia - Mongolie	1990	(e)91	56.0	36.4	35.9	2.0	17.6	0.0	8.8	35.2	20.7	0.4	13.9	0.1	0.0
	2000	536	36.9	8.6	7.7	24.3	1.5	2.5	9.0	54.0	0.0	0.1	53.7	0.2	..
	2005	1 054	40.6	12.9	12.5	14.2	0.5	12.9	4.6	54.7	0.0	0.1	54.4	0.2	..
Morocco - Maroc	1990	4 586	68.8	62.8	61.8	1.8	3.6	0.6	1.2	19.7	6.2	1.3	7.3	4.9	..
	2000	7 418	81.6	73.2	72.4	3.4	3.8	1.2	1.4	13.9	3.7	1.8	6.3	2.1	0.0
	2005	10 643	75.2	70.0	68.7	2.6	1.1	1.6	1.8	17.8	4.3	3.5	7.1	2.8	0.0
Mozambique	1990	381	34.1	22.3	21.9	6.9	4.0	0.9	0.1	64.5	3.1	0.7	60.3	0.4	..
	2000	364	34.7	25.5	25.5	4.7	4.3	0.1	..	45.0	36.0	0.0	8.9	0.1	..
	2005	1 745	67.2	64.5	64.3	2.2	0.5	0.0	0.0	27.8	22.5	..	4.7	0.5	..
Myanmar	1990	409	17.6	7.6	7.0	2.3	6.9	0.8	2.7	63.6	1.0	0.0	61.6	1.1	..
	2000	(e)1 979	47.3	16.9	16.7	22.4	5.5	2.6	0.0	42.6	0.2	0.2	42.1	0.2	0.0
	2005	(e)3 702	14.1	8.5	8.5	..	5.0	0.6	0.1	78.0	0.4	0.2	76.7	0.8	0.0

For sources and notes, see end of table.

Pour les sources et les notes, se reporter à la fin du tableau.

Destination / Origin / Origine	Year / Année	World (millions of dollars) / Monde (millions de dollars)	Developed economies / Économies développées Total	Europe Total	Europe EU/UE	USA États-Unis	Japan Japon	Other Autres	Economies in transition / Économies en transition	Developing economies / Économies en développement Total	Africa Afrique	America Amérique	Eastern, Southern and South-Eastern Asia / Asie orientale, méridionale et du Sud-Est	Western Asia / Asie occidentale	Oceania Océanie
						Percentage / En pourcentage									
Nepal - Népal	1990	(e)211	85.0	60.0	53.8	23.4	0.8	0.7	0.0	15.0	0.1	0.1	14.8	0.0	..
	2000	(e)676	62.0	24.2	22.5	32.6	3.8	1.4	0.0	36.5	0.0	0.1	36.2	0.3	0.0
	2005	(e)628	38.7	17.7	17.0	17.4	1.5	2.1	0.1	57.7	0.1	0.0	56.9	0.8	0.0
Netherlands - Pays-Bas	1990	130 715	90.4	84.3	81.6	4.0	0.9	1.2	0.9	7.9	2.1	1.1	3.2	1.5	0.0
	2000	229 742	89.9	83.5	81.2	4.4	0.9	1.1	1.3	8.1	1.4	1.1	3.9	1.7	0.0
	2005	405 990	87.7	81.7	79.4	4.3	0.7	1.1	2.5	9.0	1.7	1.1	3.9	2.2	0.0
Netherlands Antilles - Antilles néerlandaises	1990	1 793	45.0	6.6	6.6	33.5	2.7	2.2	..	52.5	3.2	49.1	0.2	..	..
	2000	1 984	29.1	8.7	8.7	16.1	0.1	4.2	0.0	67.3	2.0	61.7	3.5	0.0	0.0
	2005	(e)3 005	34.8	4.9	4.9	29.4	0.2	0.4	0.0	60.9	2.9	55.6	2.4	0.0	0.0
New Caledonia - Nouvelle-Calédonie	1990	405	89.5	55.0	55.0	6.6	25.5	2.4	..	9.0	..	..	8.1	..	0.9
	2000	573	75.8	37.5	37.5	5.2	27.0	6.1	..	24.8	0.0	0.0	23.3	..	1.4
	2005	996	61.6	34.1	34.1	2.5	21.1	3.9	1.5	36.9	4.4	0.0	30.3	..	2.2
New Zealand - Nouvelle-Zélande	1990	9 457	65.5	16.6	16.3	13.1	15.8	19.9	2.0	26.7	1.6	3.1	16.0	2.4	3.7
	2000	12 742	65.4	15.3	15.0	14.8	13.7	21.7	0.2	31.8	1.4	3.3	22.7	2.0	2.5
	2005	21 766	63.6	15.6	15.1	14.1	10.6	23.3	0.7	33.7	2.1	3.4	22.4	2.7	3.2
Nicaragua	1990	331	69.2	34.9	34.8	10.3	5.4	18.6	..	23.5	..	22.6	0.9	..	..
	2000	643	63.9	19.1	18.5	39.7	0.5	4.6	..	30.6	..	30.5	0.1	..	..
	2005	858	52.9	13.8	13.3	34.1	1.2	3.8	..	41.6	..	41.2	0.5	..	..
Niger	1990	283	84.8	64.4	64.4	0.1	20.3	0.0	..	14.2	14.2	..	..	..	..
	2000	196	51.0	34.3	34.2	2.5	13.9	0.3	..	48.9	48.9	..	0.0	0.0	..
	2005	297	71.5	49.5	49.3	20.3	0.5	1.2	0.0	28.5	27.5	0.0	0.9	0.1	..
Nigeria - Nigéria	1990	10 273	92.0	36.6	36.5	54.2	0.0	1.2	0.2	7.6	6.5	0.7	0.3	0.0	..
	2000	(e)27 042	68.2	23.0	23.0	42.5	0.4	2.3	..	31.6	7.0	5.0	19.5	0.0	..
	2005	(e)43 478	77.8	22.7	21.7	52.5	2.1	0.5	0.0	21.2	8.8	7.5	4.3	0.6	0.0
Norway - Norvège	1990	33 907	93.3	81.9	80.7	6.5	1.7	3.1	0.7	5.8	1.2	1.2	2.1	1.4	0.0
	2000	57 592	95.0	79.1	78.2	8.0	1.7	6.3	0.7	4.4	0.5	0.8	2.6	0.5	..
	2005	103 260	93.2	81.4	80.7	6.7	1.0	4.2	1.2	5.5	0.6	1.1	3.2	0.6	..
Oman	1990	4 584	18.8	13.0	12.4	3.7	2.1	0.1	0.0	81.1	4.4	0.0	15.6	61.2	0.0
	2000	10 667	21.8	1.3	1.3	1.2	18.2	1.1	0.1	78.1	1.7	0.0	64.4	12.0	0.0
	2005	(e)17 404	20.9	3.0	3.0	3.1	14.2	0.6	0.1	79.1	1.9	0.0	67.0	10.2	..
Pakistan	1990	5 587	62.0	38.3	37.1	12.4	8.2	3.1	2.7	31.0	2.2	0.3	19.0	9.5	0.0
	2000	8 876	60.1	28.6	27.9	25.2	2.6	3.7	0.5	38.9	4.0	2.0	20.3	12.7	0.0
	2005	16 046	55.1	27.1	26.5	24.8	0.9	2.3	0.8	43.7	5.7	1.7	22.2	14.0	0.0
Panama	1990	321	78.3	31.6	31.6	45.2	0.6	0.9	0.1	19.8	0.0	19.6	0.2	0.0	..
	2000	779	65.1	17.7	17.7	45.4	1.5	0.4	0.0	27.9	0.1	24.5	3.4	0.0	..
	2005	964	71.1	25.6	25.6	44.9	0.4	0.2	0.0	24.8	0.0	19.1	5.6	0.0	..
Papua New Guinea - Papouasie-Nouvelle-Guinée	1990	1 266	82.0	24.7	24.1	2.4	27.8	27.2	..	17.6	0.2	0.0	17.1	0.0	0.3
	2000	2 814	53.4	10.2	10.2	1.3	11.3	30.7	0.0	14.2	0.0	0.0	13.9	0.0	0.3
	2005	(e)5 236	48.3	8.7	8.7	1.1	8.6	29.9	0.1	13.6	0.0	0.0	13.2	0.0	0.3
Paraguay	1990	1 063	39.1	33.4	28.6	3.9	0.2	1.6	0.1	51.1	0.3	47.2	3.3	0.2	..
	2000	869	18.3	13.8	13.6	3.9	0.3	0.2	0.0	78.8	0.1	74.5	4.1	0.2	..
	2005	1 688	12.5	7.1	6.1	3.3	1.1	1.1	6.2	71.0	1.1	62.2	6.3	1.4	0.0
Peru - Pérou	1990	3 276	70.7	33.8	33.0	22.3	13.4	1.1	3.8	24.9	0.7	15.7	7.8	0.6	0.0
	2000	6 872	64.1	28.8	20.1	28.1	4.7	2.5	0.7	33.6	0.6	18.6	13.7	0.7	0.0
	2005	17 269	61.4	20.5	15.9	31.1	3.5	6.3	0.8	36.5	0.4	20.5	15.3	0.3	0.0
Philippines	1990	8 195	79.3	18.8	18.5	37.9	19.8	2.8	0.0	20.0	0.3	0.9	17.5	1.1	0.3
	2000	38 216	64.7	18.3	18.1	29.8	14.7	1.9	0.0	34.9	0.1	1.1	33.2	0.4	0.1
	2005	41 215	54.5	17.1	17.0	18.0	17.5	1.9	0.1	45.3	0.2	0.7	43.8	0.6	0.1
Poland - Pologne	1990	13 627	70.3	65.8	60.1	2.8	0.8	0.9	18.6	9.9	2.6	1.5	3.8	2.1	..
	2000	31 645	86.9	82.5	80.6	3.2	0.2	1.1	7.9	5.0	1.2	1.2	1.9	0.8	0.0
	2005	89 167	83.6	80.3	77.3	2.1	0.2	1.0	10.7	5.5	0.9	0.9	1.9	1.9	0.0
Portugal	1990	16 402	91.6	84.4	81.0	4.8	1.0	1.4	0.5	6.9	4.6	0.6	1.2	0.4	0.0
	2000	23 297	91.1	83.2	80.7	6.0	0.5	1.4	0.2	8.0	4.0	1.7	1.4	0.9	0.0
	2005	38 140	84.5	77.9	76.7	5.4	0.3	1.0	0.6	10.6	5.0	1.3	2.9	1.5	0.0

For sources and notes, see end of table.

Pour les sources et les notes, se reporter à la fin du tableau.

Destination / Origin	Year / Année	World (millions of dollars) / Monde (millions de dollars)	Developed economies / Économies développées — Total	Europe — Total	Europe — EU / UE	USA / États-Unis	Japan / Japon	Other / Autres	Economies in transition / Économies en transition	Developing economies / Économies en développement — Total	Africa / Afrique	America / Amérique	Eastern, Southern and South-Eastern Asia / Asie orientale, méridionale et du Sud-Est	Western Asia / Asie occidentale	Oceania / Océanie
								Percentage / En pourcentage							
Qatar	1990	3 293	63.9	2.3	2.3	1.6	59.5	0.5	0.0	33.4	0.7	8.9	18.1	5.7	0.0
	2000	(e)11 593	50.8	1.1	1.0	3.1	45.0	1.6	0.0	39.5	0.9	0.1	32.3	6.1	..
	2005	26 183	46.0	5.9	5.7	1.7	36.9	1.5	0.0	46.8	1.3	0.0	40.8	4.7	..
Romania - Roumanie	1990	5 871	50.8	42.4	40.8	5.8	1.6	1.0	29.7	18.6	3.7	1.9	6.6	6.4	..
	2000	10 367	76.0	71.0	69.9	3.7	0.2	1.1	8.4	15.2	3.6	0.8	2.4	8.3	0.0
	2005	27 729	74.4	69.2	67.8	4.1	0.3	0.9	8.9	16.6	2.2	0.6	3.2	10.7	0.0
Russian Federation - Fédération de Russie	2000	102 999	69.2	57.6	52.9	7.7	2.7	1.2	15.2	15.4	1.1	0.9	9.7	3.7	0.0
	2005	239 277	66.2	60.7	55.9	3.1	1.6	0.7	15.3	17.7	1.1	0.9	10.4	5.4	0.0
Rwanda	1990	100	72.7	64.4	64.3	6.1	1.9	0.3	..	10.4	2.0	..	8.4	..	..
	2000	(e)99	41.2	35.7	35.3	5.1	0.4	0.0	2.5	22.3	7.3	0.0	14.5	0.5	..
	2005	(e)162	28.2	24.1	24.0	3.8	0.0	0.3	2.5	22.1	3.8	0.4	17.6	0.4	..
Saint Kitts and Nevis - Saint-Kitts-et-Nevis	1990	(e)24	96.0	34.4	34.2	61.3	0.2	0.1	..	4.0	0.0	3.7	0.2	..	..
	2000	(e)33	88.2	21.8	21.8	65.9	0.3	0.2	..	8.3	0.0	7.8	0.5	..	..
	2005	(e)83	87.2	17.6	17.6	61.3	0.1	8.1	1.3	7.4	3.3	4.0	0.0	..	..
Saint Lucia - Sainte-Lucie	1990	(e)146	91.3	68.9	68.9	16.7	0.1	5.7	..	8.7	0.0	8.7	0.0	..	..
	2000	45	73.3	54.2	54.1	17.8	0.7	0.7	0.0	26.0	0.0	25.6	0.3	0.0	..
	2005	(e)164	65.0	46.0	46.0	18.7	0.0	0.3	0.0	34.7	0.0	15.4	19.3	0.0	..
Saint Vincent and the Grenadines - Saint-Vincent-et-les Grenadines	1990	83	65.4	54.7	54.7	10.6	0.0	0.1	..	34.1	..	34.1	0.0	..	0.0
	2000	51	49.5	46.3	46.3	2.6	0.0	0.5	1.3	46.9	..	45.9	0.1	1.0	..
	2005	40	36.7	27.2	27.2	9.2	0.0	0.3	0.0	62.4	0.0	62.2	0.2	..	..
Samoa	1990	12	71.9	19.2	19.1	6.5	0.9	45.4	..	14.9	0.1	..	4.5	..	10.3
	2000	69	73.0	3.0	3.0	10.6	0.3	59.1	..	20.6	0.1	0.1	17.7	0.0	2.8
	2005	(e)233	84.9	0.2	0.2	6.5	0.4	77.9	..	14.9	..	..	0.2	0.0	14.6
São Tome and Principe - Sao Tomé-et-Principe	1990	29	73.8	73.8	73.5	..	..	0.0	..	26.2	0.0	0.3	25.8	..	..
	2000	(e)18	85.4	75.4	70.2	2.6	2.7	4.7	0.2	14.4	0.3	0.4	4.5	9.2	..
	2005	(e)18	84.0	81.8	81.5	1.0	0.6	0.6	..	16.0	2.9	2.8	4.6	5.8	..
Saudi Arabia - Arabie saoudite	1990	44 417	63.3	18.4	18.3	24.0	19.0	1.9	0.7	35.9	4.0	3.3	19.1	9.4	0.0
	2000	74 729	54.9	17.9	17.7	17.4	17.3	2.3	0.0	45.1	5.5	1.5	31.8	6.3	0.0
	2005	(e)157 087	51.2	16.2	16.1	16.8	16.5	1.7	0.1	48.7	3.3	1.1	35.4	8.8	0.0
Senegal - Sénégal	1990	861	49.8	47.7	47.7	0.0	1.9	0.1	0.0	32.8	19.0	0.0	13.7	0.1	..
	2000	693	48.3	46.3	45.3	0.5	1.2	0.2	0.0	43.7	28.2	0.5	14.5	0.4	..
	2005	1 443	28.1	26.2	25.9	1.1	0.8	0.1	0.0	59.3	43.1	0.3	15.3	0.5	0.2
Serbia and Montenegro - Serbie-et-Monténégro	2000	(e)1 036	80.4	79.2	77.7	0.3	0.3	0.6	8.7	10.9	4.3	0.2	2.0	4.5	0.0
	2005	(e)1 908	76.7	72.3	71.3	2.8	0.1	1.4	11.3	11.9	3.9	0.1	1.7	6.2	0.0
Seychelles	1990	14	92.4	92.0	92.0	0.1	0.1	0.1	..	7.6	1.2	..	6.3	..	..
	2000	124	93.0	91.7	91.7	0.1	1.0	0.2	..	4.5	4.0	..	0.5	..	..
	2005	(e)422	87.6	75.4	75.3	1.3	9.8	1.1	0.4	10.1	5.9	0.0	3.8	0.4	0.0
Sierra Leone	1990	137	92.0	66.2	66.1	25.8	..	0.0	..	..	..	..	..	..	..
	2000	126	91.1	86.3	86.2	2.9	0.4	1.6	0.2	6.5	4.0	0.4	2.1	0.0	..
	2005	(e)196	88.9	82.9	82.9	4.6	0.1	1.3	1.0	7.1	3.6	0.1	3.4	0.0	..
Singapore - Singapour	1990	52 804	50.3	16.5	15.6	21.2	8.7	3.9	0.9	46.6	1.5	1.2	40.7	2.2	1.0
	2000	138 046	42.5	14.5	14.0	17.3	7.5	3.2	0.1	57.2	1.2	1.9	52.3	1.3	0.4
	2005	207 338	36.4	13.8	13.3	11.5	6.0	5.1	0.2	63.0	1.2	2.2	56.4	2.4	0.8
Slovakia - Slovaquie	2000	11 874	92.5	90.7	88.6	1.4	0.1	0.3	4.5	2.8	0.5	0.5	1.2	0.6	0.0
	2005	31 879	90.4	86.6	85.6	3.1	0.3	0.4	5.9	3.7	0.6	0.4	1.2	1.5	0.0
Slovenia - Slovénie	2000	8 729	76.6	72.8	71.3	3.1	0.1	0.6	19.3	3.9	0.7	0.5	1.4	1.3	0.0
	2005	18 726	72.5	69.9	68.4	2.0	0.1	0.5	22.5	4.9	1.2	0.4	1.4	1.9	0.0
Yugoslavia, SFR (former) - Yougoslavie, RSF (anc.)	1990	14 356	65.8	59.7	58.1	4.8	0.3	1.0	21.1	13.1	5.0	0.8	3.1	4.2	0.0
Solomon Islands - Îles Salomon	1990	75	72.6	21.8	21.8	3.7	41.5	5.6	..	19.6	0.0	..	17.5	0.0	2.1
	2000	(e)101	35.4	10.6	10.6	0.7	20.8	3.3	..	54.5	..	0.0	52.1	0.0	2.3
	2005	(e)210	17.5	8.5	8.5	0.9	6.4	1.7	..	73.6	0.1	0.0	71.1	0.0	2.5
Somalia - Somalie	1990	150	40.4	40.1	37.6	..	0.3	0.0	0.2	59.4	1.3	0.0	1.6	56.5	..
	2000	(e)62	3.4	2.2	2.0	0.7	0.4	0.1	0.0	96.5	11.2	0.1	4.4	80.9	..
	2005	(e)250	1.0	0.6	0.6	0.1	0.2	0.1	0.0	99.0	5.0	0.0	10.8	83.2	..

For sources and notes, see end of table.

Pour les sources et les notes, se reporter à la fin du tableau.

Destination / Origin / Origine	Year / Année	World (millions of dollars) / Monde (millions de dollars)	Developed economies / Économies développées Total	Europe Total	Europe EU UE	USA États-Unis	Japan Japon	Other Autres	Economies in transition / Économies en transition	Developing economies / Économies en développement Total	Africa Afrique	America Amérique	Eastern, Southern and South-Eastern Asia / Asie orientale, méridionale et du Sud-Est	Western Asia / Asie occidentale	Oceania / Océanie
South Africa - Afrique du Sud	1990	24 704	43.9	27.9	25.3	7.4	6.7	1.9	..	5.0	1.7	0.7	2.2	0.4	0.0
	2000	30 429	46.3	29.8	28.6	7.9	4.5	4.1	0.2	26.6	13.2	1.8	10.1	1.5	0.0
	2005	51 562	60.5	35.4	32.9	9.5	9.9	5.7	0.3	29.5	13.9	1.4	12.5	1.6	0.0
Spain - Espagne	1990	55 688	82.5	74.2	71.9	5.8	1.1	1.3	0.9	13.2	4.5	3.7	3.1	1.8	0.0
	2000	108 186	81.1	73.5	71.6	5.0	1.0	1.6	0.9	15.5	3.4	6.0	3.0	3.0	0.0
	2005	191 908	80.0	73.9	71.0	4.1	0.7	1.3	1.6	15.3	4.2	4.9	3.2	2.9	0.0
Sri Lanka	1990	1 895	62.4	27.8	26.9	25.9	5.4	3.4	3.1	30.5	5.5	2.0	13.1	9.8	0.1
	2000	5 459	74.0	26.2	25.4	40.2	4.2	3.5	2.0	17.9	1.7	1.4	9.3	5.5	0.0
	2005	6 384	63.3	26.7	26.0	31.1	2.3	3.2	2.5	26.9	1.3	3.1	16.0	6.5	0.0
Sudan - Soudan	1990	515	47.9	39.0	38.8	2.8	6.0	0.1	9.1	43.0	7.1	0.0	24.9	10.5	0.4
	2000	(e)1 621	27.8	10.5	10.5	0.1	17.2	0.0	0.2	71.9	2.8	0.7	58.4	9.5	0.5
	2005	4 822	16.3	2.7	2.7	0.3	12.0	1.3	0.0	83.5	3.0	0.3	73.8	6.3	..
Suriname	1990	456	93.6	75.6	38.7	11.8	6.2	0.0	..	6.4	..	6.4	0.0	..	..
	2000	499	88.1	51.7	29.0	24.9	4.1	7.5	0.0	11.9	1.7	9.5	0.7	0.0	..
	2005	(e)929	83.3	49.0	22.1	16.8	1.2	16.4	0.0	16.7	1.8	5.7	1.7	7.5	..
Sweden - Suède	1990	53 069	87.9	72.6	60.8	9.6	2.2	3.4	1.4	10.8	1.6	2.0	5.3	1.8	0.0
	2000	87 867	84.1	68.4	59.6	10.2	2.8	2.7	1.4	14.5	1.7	3.1	7.1	2.6	0.0
	2005	130 194	81.5	66.6	56.6	10.6	1.5	2.7	2.9	13.6	2.3	2.1	6.8	2.3	0.0
Switzerland - Suisse	1990	63 806	81.9	66.0	65.4	8.0	4.8	3.2	2.0	16.0	2.0	2.4	8.7	2.9	0.0
	2000	80 535	82.0	61.8	61.4	13.1	4.2	2.9	1.2	16.8	1.5	2.9	9.4	3.0	0.0
	2005	130 884	80.2	62.8	62.4	10.9	3.6	2.9	2.1	17.6	1.4	2.3	10.2	3.7	0.0
Syrian Arab Republic - République arabe syrienne	1990	4 210	43.4	42.4	42.0	0.9	0.1	0.0	33.8	21.9	2.8	0.0	0.5	18.6	..
	2000	4 759	66.7	62.7	62.7	3.0	0.3	0.7	1.7	28.7	2.7	0.1	1.7	24.2	0.0
	2005	10 315	35.5	32.1	32.0	3.1	0.1	0.2	1.3	63.2	10.1	0.6	0.9	51.5	0.0
Tajikistan - Tadjikistan	2000	(e)770	39.5	39.4	30.1	0.1	..	0.0	48.6	11.8	0.1	..	4.1	7.6	..
	2005	909	57.7	57.7	54.7	0.0	0.0	0.0	19.9	22.4	0.0	..	6.6	15.8	..
Thailand - Thaïlande	1990	23 072	68.1	24.8	23.4	22.7	17.2	3.4	0.6	30.8	2.4	1.4	22.6	4.3	0.1
	2000	68 963	57.6	17.2	16.3	21.3	14.7	4.4	0.2	41.7	1.8	1.5	36.1	2.2	0.1
	2005	110 174	48.0	14.2	13.5	15.4	13.6	4.8	0.4	51.2	2.6	1.8	43.3	3.4	0.2
Macedonia, TFYR - Macédoine, LERY	2000	1 319	63.3	49.8	46.8	12.6	0.2	0.8	34.6	1.9	0.5	0.1	0.3	1.0	..
	2005	2 041	56.2	53.5	53.1	2.2	0.4	0.2	35.5	4.1	0.2	0.2	1.3	2.4	0.0
Togo	1990	267	58.6	44.4	43.1	1.1	0.1	13.0	5.1	33.7	17.0	2.2	14.3	0.1	..
	2000	(e)192	21.6	21.2	20.3	0.3	0.0	0.2	0.8	74.7	41.9	6.5	25.4	0.9	0.0
	2005	364	12.2	9.3	9.2	1.1	0.0	1.8	0.6	85.4	71.9	1.9	11.5	0.1	..
Tonga	1990	13	92.4	1.6	1.6	25.9	30.0	34.8	..	5.5	..	..	0.0	..	5.5
	2000	18	92.4	6.6	6.6	30.4	49.2	6.3	..	7.4	0.0	..	3.7	0.1	3.6
	2005	(e)19	87.4	3.0	3.0	33.4	41.8	9.1	..	12.3	..	0.3	3.0	0.1	8.9
Trinidad and Tobago - Trinité-et-Tobago	1990	1 986	71.8	15.1	13.8	53.9	0.8	1.9	..	22.5	0.6	21.1	0.6	0.2	0.0
	2000	3 041	61.8	13.4	13.4	46.8	0.1	1.5	0.0	36.9	0.6	35.9	0.4	0.0	0.0
	2005	(e)11 062	75.9	5.3	5.2	68.6	0.0	2.0	0.0	23.3	0.1	22.6	0.3	0.3	..
Tunisia - Tunisie	1990	3 556	78.9	77.7	77.3	0.9	0.3	0.1	3.0	18.0	9.5	0.9	4.1	3.5	0.0
	2000	5 996	80.5	79.4	78.5	0.7	0.2	0.1	0.3	15.4	8.3	1.1	3.4	2.5	0.0
	2005	10 488	81.8	80.5	80.0	0.9	0.2	0.1	0.2	14.3	9.0	0.7	2.5	2.1	0.0
Turkey - Turquie	1990	13 385	69.1	59.0	56.5	7.2	1.8	1.0	5.8	22.4	5.6	0.3	7.7	8.7	0.0
	2000	27 769	70.8	55.5	54.3	11.3	0.5	3.5	9.2	14.4	4.9	1.0	3.7	4.8	0.0
	2005	73 451	63.4	53.4	52.3	6.7	0.3	2.9	12.2	19.1	4.9	0.9	3.8	9.5	0.0
Turkmenistan - Turkménistan	2000	(e)2 505	26.1	24.7	21.1	0.5	..	0.8	52.9	19.5	0.2	..	11.6	7.7	..
	2005	(e)5 694	19.4	15.9	15.8	2.3	0.0	1.2	56.0	23.1	0.0	0.1	17.6	5.3	0.0
Uganda - Ouganda	1990	181	90.5	76.1	75.5	7.9	3.5	2.9	0.7	8.8	6.9	0.0	1.2	0.7	0.0
	2000	(e)400	56.6	50.5	25.3	2.1	2.0	2.0	0.2	40.7	31.6	0.2	7.8	1.1	..
	2005	(e)675	57.4	51.5	50.8	3.9	1.0	1.0	1.8	33.4	19.7	0.1	8.6	4.9	0.0
Ukraine	2000	(e)14 579	35.4	28.7	27.6	5.0	0.5	1.2	35.0	28.5	5.0	2.3	12.1	9.0	0.0
	2005	33 959	32.6	28.4	27.1	2.8	0.2	1.2	35.1	31.5	7.0	1.5	11.4	11.5	0.0
USSR (former) - URSS (anc.)	1990	45 924	75.5	66.1	64.6	2.3	6.7	0.4	9.7	14.8	1.7	0.5	9.4	3.2	0.0

For sources and notes, see end of table.

Pour les sources et les notes, se reporter à la fin du tableau.

Destination / Origin / Origine	Year / Année	World (millions of dollars) / Monde (millions de dollars)	Developed economies / Économies développées					Economies in transition / Économies en transition	Developing economies / Économies en développement					
			Total	Europe		USA États-Unis	Japan Japon	Other Autres		Total	Africa Afrique	America Amérique	Eastern, Southern and South-Eastern Asia / Asie orientale, méridionale et du Sud-Est	Western Asia / Asie occidentale	Oceania Océanie
				Total	EU UE										
								Percentage / En pourcentage							
United Arab Emirates - Émirats arabes unis	1990	21 917	53.4	9.5	9.3	4.0	37.7	2.3	0.4	33.4	2.7	0.5	25.2	5.0	0.0
	2000	(e)40 858	42.3	5.2	5.0	2.2	33.0	1.9	0.7	43.6	3.8	0.2	32.7	7.0	0.0
	2005	(e)93 248	38.4	11.7	11.2	1.5	24.5	0.7	0.6	46.3	3.5	0.1	35.4	7.2	0.0
United Kingdom - Royaume-Uni	1990	185 127	81.6	62.0	58.4	12.6	2.5	4.4	1.0	16.6	3.5	1.6	7.2	4.2	0.0
	2000	282 838	84.2	62.0	59.0	15.8	2.0	4.5	0.9	14.6	2.4	1.6	7.2	3.4	0.0
	2005	370 275	78.0	57.3	53.6	15.1	1.9	3.7	1.8	18.0	2.8	1.5	8.4	5.3	0.0
United Republic of Tanzania - République-Unie de Tanzanie	1990	416	54.0	42.9	41.1	6.8	3.9	0.5	0.8	42.2	8.2	0.0	32.3	1.7	..
	2000	(e)735	59.1	51.6	50.4	2.1	4.8	0.6	0.7	40.0	19.1	0.2	19.0	1.8	0.0
	2005	(e)1 480	43.7	27.4	24.6	2.2	4.6	9.6	1.6	47.7	18.5	0.1	24.5	4.6	0.0
United States - États-Unis	1990	393 106	65.1	28.3	26.6	..	12.4	24.5	1.0	33.6	2.0	13.5	15.4	2.5	0.1
	2000	772 124	57.1	23.2	21.7	..	8.4	25.5	0.5	42.3	1.4	21.6	17.2	2.0	0.0
	2005	904 257	54.8	22.1	20.6	..	6.1	26.5	0.8	44.3	1.7	21.1	18.5	2.9	0.0
Uruguay	1990	1 730	41.7	27.9	27.5	9.5	1.2	3.2	5.3	51.6	1.6	39.8	8.0	2.2	..
	2000	2 295	32.6	17.2	16.3	8.4	1.5	5.6	0.3	66.1	1.8	54.3	9.6	0.4	0.0
	2005	3 403	46.1	18.6	17.1	23.2	0.9	3.4	1.3	49.1	3.8	34.7	9.5	1.0	0.1
Uzbekistan - Ouzbékistan	2000	(e)2 181	31.8	26.4	26.3	1.5	3.3	0.6	52.5	15.7	0.1	1.2	10.8	3.6	..
	2005	(e)3 443	24.2	17.5	17.3	2.6	3.3	0.9	47.0	28.8	0.1	0.0	21.8	6.9	..
Vanuatu	1990	25	89.9	57.9	54.3	3.7	20.6	7.7	0.3	9.5	0.2	0.3	2.2	0.3	6.5
	2000	(e)86	35.6	5.8	5.7	9.8	18.9	1.1	0.0	64.1	0.1	0.0	60.5	..	3.5
	2005	(e)233	25.7	14.5	14.5	1.1	6.9	3.2	0.0	74.1	0.7	1.0	62.0	7.7	2.6
Venezuela (Bolivarian Republic of) - (République bolivarienne du)	1990	18 044	71.3	14.2	14.0	51.5	2.8	2.7	0.1	16.2	0.1	14.5	1.6	0.0	..
	2000	33 358	58.9	5.1	5.0	51.9	0.7	1.2	0.1	35.4	0.0	34.6	0.6	0.2	..
	2005	(e)63 035	60.5	6.8	6.7	50.9	0.4	2.4	0.1	20.0	0.2	17.4	2.3	0.1	0.0
Viet Nam	1990	2 525	23.9	10.0	9.8	0.0	13.5	0.4	38.2	28.4	0.2	0.5	27.6	0.2	..
	2000	14 483	54.4	21.8	20.5	5.1	17.8	9.7	1.2	43.8	1.0	0.9	39.2	2.7	0.0
	2005	32 442	58.4	17.3	16.9	18.3	13.6	9.2	0.9	33.5	0.3	0.2	32.0	1.0	..
Yemen - Yémen	1990	(e)1 561	87.5	56.7	56.6	23.3	5.2	2.3	0.4	11.6	1.4	0.0	8.4	1.8	..
	2000	(e)4 076	12.3	2.3	1.2	6.2	2.1	1.7	1.1	83.9	2.0	1.6	76.3	4.0	..
	2005	5 606	17.8	6.4	0.9	3.3	6.3	1.8	0.0	81.7	1.7	0.0	71.1	9.0	0.0
Zambia - Zambie	1990	544	64.1	31.5	30.6	1.6	31.0	0.0	..	35.9	7.8	0.0	22.7	5.4	..
	2000	757	54.4	45.9	36.4	1.6	0.0	6.8	0.0	45.6	41.8	0.1	3.6	0.1	..
	2005	1 839	55.4	52.8	24.1	0.8	1.6	0.2	0.0	44.6	40.6	0.0	3.9	0.0	0.0
Zimbabwe	1990	1 491	59.3	44.1	42.1	7.6	5.5	2.1	1.0	39.4	32.1	0.7	6.2	0.4	0.0
	2000	3 281	27.4	19.5	17.2	3.2	4.0	0.7	0.9	27.4	17.9	0.8	7.7	0.9	0.0
	2005	1 810	36.6	24.8	24.0	4.9	6.7	0.3	1.8	61.5	42.7	1.3	14.6	2.9	0.0

Sources:
- International Monetary Fund, *Direction of Trade Statistics*

Sources :
- Fonds monétaire international, *Direction of Trade Statistics*

Origin / Origine (Destination)	Year Année	World (millions of dollars) Monde (millions de dollars)	Developed economies / Économies développées — Total	Europe Total	Europe EU UE	USA États-Unis	Japan Japon	Other Autres	Economies in transition Économies en transition	Developing economies / Économies en développement — Total	Africa Afrique	America Amérique	Eastern, Southern and South-Eastern Asia / Asie orientale, méridionale et du Sud-Est	Western Asia / Asie occidentale	Oceania Océanie
Afghanistan	1990	479	45.9	16.9	16.3	1.0	27.8	0.2	0.2	53.9	0.0	0.5	52.6	0.7	..
	2000	(e)621	19.8	8.7	8.5	2.0	9.2	0.0	22.8	57.4	5.6	0.1	49.6	2.1	..
	2005	(e)3 002	28.0	14.9	14.7	9.6	2.8	0.7	13.4	58.6	1.9	0.1	51.2	5.4	..
Albania - Albanie	1990	423	61.8	58.7	56.6	2.7	0.3	0.1	14.7	23.5	13.7	0.2	8.1	1.5	..
	2000	(e)1 084	82.0	79.9	78.2	1.5	0.4	0.2	9.2	8.4	0.2	0.4	1.9	5.9	..
	2005	2 622	67.1	64.9	63.9	1.4	0.4	0.4	14.7	17.8	0.6	1.4	8.1	7.7	..
Algeria - Algérie	1990	9 679	88.3	67.6	66.3	11.6	4.6	4.4	2.7	8.3	1.8	2.6	1.4	2.5	..
	2000	9 027	78.9	59.8	59.6	11.6	3.0	4.6	5.4	15.7	2.1	2.9	6.3	4.5	0.0
	2005	(e)23 476	70.9	61.4	60.8	5.4	2.5	1.6	4.7	24.4	2.2	4.8	11.2	6.3	..
Angola	1990	1 723	85.0	72.9	70.3	9.6	1.9	0.7	0.2	14.8	2.3	7.3	5.2	..	..
	2000	(e)2 203	63.0	50.4	46.7	10.9	1.3	0.4	2.0	34.9	20.2	6.0	8.3	0.5	..
	2005	(e)8 136	51.2	36.1	33.7	12.5	1.6	1.0	0.5	48.1	8.5	9.1	30.0	0.5	..
Argentina - Argentine	1990	4 078	59.6	31.9	29.4	21.5	3.3	2.9	0.6	39.8	0.5	34.8	4.2	0.3	..
	2000	25 281	49.6	24.6	23.6	19.1	4.0	2.0	0.6	47.5	1.8	34.3	11.1	0.3	0.0
	2005	28 661	36.1	17.8	16.9	14.1	2.8	1.4	1.0	59.8	0.6	45.0	14.0	0.2	0.0
Armenia - Arménie	2000	(e)885	51.2	38.5	35.9	11.6	0.4	0.6	20.5	23.0	0.0	2.4	10.7	10.0	..
	2005	1 801	45.1	30.7	28.1	6.2	1.3	6.9	34.7	20.0	0.2	2.3	12.4	5.1	..
Aruba	2000	794	77.3	21.6	21.2	51.4	2.8	1.5	0.1	22.4	1.5	18.8	1.9	0.2	..
	2005	1 030	79.8	21.3	20.4	55.9	2.0	0.6	0.0	20.1	0.0	16.9	3.2	0.0	..
Australia - Australie	1990	43 052	76.8	27.3	25.7	24.1	18.7	6.7	0.2	22.8	0.4	1.2	17.2	3.0	1.1
	2000	74 275	61.6	22.6	21.4	20.1	13.2	5.8	0.1	37.1	0.9	1.2	30.8	2.6	1.6
	2005	130 949	54.2	24.3	23.2	13.9	11.0	5.0	0.1	45.1	1.2	1.4	39.3	1.8	1.5
Austria - Autriche	1990	49 288	88.3	79.4	74.5	3.6	4.5	0.8	3.2	8.5	2.5	1.0	4.2	0.8	0.0
	2000	72 117	90.8	84.4	79.6	4.1	1.5	0.8	3.5	5.7	1.1	0.4	2.9	1.2	0.0
	2005	127 044	87.3	83.6	79.0	2.2	1.0	0.5	5.5	7.1	0.9	0.5	4.2	1.5	0.0
Azerbaijan - Azerbaïdjan	2000	1 172	40.5	27.6	22.3	10.0	1.4	1.5	33.4	25.9	2.1	0.6	10.3	12.9	0.0
	2005	4 210	36.9	31.0	29.6	3.4	1.7	0.8	34.7	28.4	1.2	0.4	18.5	8.4	..
Bahamas	1990	2 312	83.9	23.2	19.0	38.1	20.4	2.2	0.2	15.3	1.6	7.7	5.1	1.0	..
	2000	(e)3 931	67.0	27.1	24.5	29.5	9.8	0.6	2.5	28.9	1.3	8.4	18.6	0.6	0.0
	2005	(e)9 186	46.1	21.7	18.2	21.2	2.6	0.5	3.3	49.1	0.1	22.9	25.2	1.0	0.0
Bahrain - Bahreïn	1990	3 711	34.5	16.9	16.4	7.1	5.0	5.5	..	59.2	0.1	1.0	4.8	53.3	..
	2000	(e)3 541	46.4	27.7	25.8	12.8	4.0	1.9	0.1	53.0	0.6	2.7	14.0	35.6	0.0
	2005	(e)7 103	38.5	24.6	22.8	5.4	6.6	1.9	0.2	60.7	0.7	2.3	13.8	43.9	0.0
Bangladesh	1990	3 656	44.0	20.7	18.5	5.1	13.2	5.0	1.3	41.3	0.3	1.5	34.6	5.0	..
	2000	9 001	26.3	11.3	9.7	2.4	9.4	3.1	0.9	56.0	1.0	1.4	48.3	5.1	0.1
	2005	13 851	19.4	10.4	8.8	2.4	4.1	2.5	3.0	68.5	0.5	1.5	52.7	13.8	..
Barbados - Barbade	1990	700	68.7	22.1	21.0	33.7	5.3	7.6	0.0	30.3	0.0	27.1	3.2	0.0	..
	2000	1 156	69.0	16.4	15.5	41.5	5.2	5.9	0.1	30.9	0.1	25.2	4.6	0.9	0.0
	2005	1 600	61.6	14.5	12.6	37.2	5.2	4.8	0.0	38.3	0.1	32.1	6.0	0.1	..
Belarus - Bélarus	2000	8 646	24.2	21.9	21.2	1.6	0.5	0.2	70.5	4.1	0.3	1.5	2.1	0.2	0.0
	2005	16 708	24.8	22.7	21.4	1.4	0.3	0.4	67.0	5.1	0.2	1.2	3.2	0.5	0.0
Belgium - Belgique	2005	318 549	84.0	74.1	71.7	5.4	2.7	1.9	2.3	13.6	2.7	1.9	7.4	1.6	0.0
Belgium-Luxembourg - Belgique-Luxembourg	1990	119 414	88.4	80.2	77.5	4.4	2.1	1.8	1.4	10.1	4.0	1.6	3.7	0.9	0.0
	2000	186 511	85.8	73.2	71.3	7.3	2.9	2.4	1.4	12.7	3.0	1.9	7.0	0.8	0.0
Belize	1990	211	77.3	15.8	15.6	57.9	1.2	2.3	0.0	22.6	0.0	18.7	3.8	0.1	0.0
	2000	443	66.7	11.6	11.5	50.3	2.5	2.2	0.0	33.3	..	31.2	1.9	0.1	..
	2005	(e)769	50.7	17.2	17.0	31.0	1.5	1.0	8.9	40.4	0.5	32.6	7.3	0.1	..
Benin - Bénin	1990	265	49.4	37.4	35.5	8.7	3.1	0.1	0.8	49.6	27.8	1.8	19.6	0.4	..
	2000	563	57.7	49.8	49.5	4.1	3.4	0.5	0.9	40.9	24.1	0.5	14.0	2.2	0.0
	2005	893	50.4	46.3	43.1	2.0	1.5	0.5	0.1	49.5	30.3	1.1	15.6	2.5	..
Bermuda - Bermudes	1990	595	86.5	16.9	15.7	59.5	5.2	5.0	0.0	12.1	0.0	9.6	2.4	0.0	0.0
	2000	4 156	59.9	43.1	42.8	11.2	5.0	0.7	34.9	5.2	0.0	3.8	1.2	0.2	0.0
	2005	(e)3 477	70.5	52.1	50.0	15.5	0.8	2.2	2.0	27.4	0.0	1.5	25.8	0.0	0.0

For sources and notes, see end of table.

Pour les sources et les notes, se reporter à la fin du tableau.

2.1 Country trade structure by partner: Imports by main region of origin
2.1 Structure du commerce des pays partenaires : Importations par principales régions d'origine

Origin / Origine — Destination	Year Année	World (millions of dollars) Monde (millions de dollars)	Developed economies — Économies développées						Economies in transition Économies en transition	Developing economies — Économies en développement					
			Total	Europe Total (Tota)	Europe EU UE	USA États-Unis	Japan Japon	Other Autres		Total	Africa Afrique	America Amérique	Eastern, Southern and South-Eastern Asia (Asie orientale, méridionale et du Sud-Est)	Western Asia (Asie occidentale)	Oceania Océanie
			Percentage / En pourcentage												
Bolivia - Bolivie	1990	700	50.0	16.8	16.3	22.3	9.9	1.0	0.5	49.2	0.1	47.2	1.8	0.0	0.0
	2000	2 023	40.8	11.9	11.4	22.5	5.2	1.1	0.1	58.9	0.1	51.3	7.5	0.1	0.0
	2005	2 343	30.7	9.9	9.5	13.8	6.1	0.9	0.2	68.9	0.2	60.4	8.3	0.0	0.0
Bosnia and Herzegovina - Bosnie-Herzégovine	2000	(e)2 644	74.6	72.3	71.4	1.8	0.2	0.4	23.9	1.5	0.0	0.1	0.3	1.1	..
	2005	(e)5 805	65.1	64.7	63.9	0.3	0.1	0.1	31.4	3.5	0.0	0.4	0.6	2.5	..
Brazil - Brésil	1990	24 977	56.5	26.4	24.2	19.8	7.1	3.1	0.7	42.8	2.9	17.6	7.7	14.7	..
	2000	61 875	59.7	28.1	25.9	23.1	5.3	3.1	1.4	38.7	5.2	21.0	10.3	2.2	0.0
	2005	80 928	50.7	25.7	23.6	17.5	4.6	2.9	1.6	46.5	9.1	16.2	18.3	2.9	0.0
Brunei Darussalam - Brunéi Darussalam	1990	1 000	51.1	18.5	18.1	15.3	14.6	2.7	0.0	47.2	..	0.2	46.9	0.0	..
	2000	1 427	33.7	16.0	15.8	10.8	4.7	2.2	0.0	66.2	0.1	0.1	65.8	0.2	0.0
	2005	(e)1 668	22.0	10.0	9.8	3.3	6.9	1.8	0.0	77.8	0.3	0.1	76.9	0.5	0.0
Bulgaria - Bulgarie	1990	3 462	70.3	64.7	61.6	2.7	1.7	1.2	7.0	22.7	9.0	2.6	9.6	1.5	0.0
	2000	6 362	54.8	50.4	49.0	3.0	1.0	0.5	32.8	10.5	0.7	2.9	3.2	3.6	0.0
	2005	18 195	55.4	50.7	49.6	2.6	1.2	1.0	26.0	17.6	0.4	4.0	6.8	6.3	0.0
Burkina Faso	1990	536	58.7	46.8	46.1	6.3	4.2	1.4	0.1	30.8	26.6	0.5	3.7	..	..
	2000	498	51.5	45.8	45.7	3.5	1.8	0.5	0.5	41.8	37.3	0.3	3.9	0.4	0.0
	2005	(e)1 097	42.3	38.0	37.8	2.5	0.4	1.4	2.3	49.0	41.0	2.0	5.4	0.5	0.0
Burundi	1990	235	55.7	47.2	46.1	1.0	7.3	0.2	0.0	29.3	10.7	..	18.6	..	..
	2000	147	33.4	24.7	24.0	2.6	5.2	0.9	0.4	44.3	23.7	..	8.6	12.1	..
	2005	(e)276	45.1	37.6	34.1	3.0	3.2	1.3	0.0	49.6	35.9	0.2	11.7	1.8	..
Cambodia - Cambodge	1990	56	40.0	28.5	28.2	..	9.0	2.5	0.0	59.9	0.1	0.5	55.8	3.5	..
	2000	(e)1 424	15.5	8.1	6.6	2.3	4.1	1.0	0.0	83.6	0.0	0.1	83.4	0.1	0.0
	2005	1 268	20.8	14.5	14.2	1.3	4.1	0.8	0.1	79.0	0.1	0.1	78.8	0.0	0.0
Cameroon - Cameroun	1990	1 555	81.9	69.4	67.9	4.7	5.7	2.1	0.9	17.0	8.2	1.9	6.6	0.2	..
	2000	1 490	51.9	40.4	39.8	4.8	4.9	1.8	1.2	37.7	29.3	0.9	6.1	1.5	..
	2005	(e)2 547	54.6	47.5	46.9	5.1	0.8	1.3	1.3	43.6	19.1	5.2	17.8	1.5	..
Canada	1990	131 642	84.6	14.1	12.5	62.9	6.8	0.8	0.3	11.2	0.8	3.3	6.5	0.7	0.0
	2000	262 776	82.1	12.3	10.6	64.3	4.7	0.8	0.3	15.7	0.8	5.0	9.3	0.6	0.0
	2005	344 379	75.4	14.1	12.0	56.7	3.8	0.8	0.7	23.1	1.8	7.0	13.2	1.0	0.0
Cape Verde - Cap-Vert	1990	145	83.8	79.2	78.9	4.5	..	0.1	3.4	9.4	4.1	4.4	0.9	..	..
	2000	(e)237	85.3	75.1	74.9	4.5	5.3	0.4	1.2	12.0	2.0	2.9	5.1	2.0	0.0
	2005	(e)498	77.6	75.2	75.1	2.1	..	0.2	0.2	17.8	8.6	6.5	2.0	0.7	0.0
Central African Republic - République centrafricaine	1990	184	69.5	64.4	63.6	0.8	4.3	0.0	0.2	30.1	24.4	0.8	4.7	0.2	..
	2000	121	56.3	50.1	50.0	2.1	3.6	0.4	2.0	17.9	12.7	0.2	3.9	1.2	..
	2005	(e)223	44.4	36.3	36.0	7.3	0.6	0.2	0.1	26.5	16.5	1.2	7.0	1.7	..
Chad - Tchad	1990	167	75.0	65.9	65.4	5.3	3.8	0.1	0.1	24.9	21.3	0.2	3.1	0.2	..
	2000	(e)139	73.9	64.9	64.3	7.4	1.4	0.2	0.7	25.4	14.0	..	4.8	6.5	..
	2005	(e)488	64.2	50.5	50.0	12.1	0.1	1.5	1.5	34.3	22.6	0.2	4.8	6.6	..
Chile - Chili	1990	7 227	58.5	27.7	26.1	19.0	7.9	3.9	..	36.5	7.8	24.1	4.5	..	..
	2000	18 535	42.0	16.5	15.7	17.8	3.8	3.9	0.6	46.9	2.8	32.2	11.7	0.3	0.0
	2005	32 321	36.1	16.2	15.6	14.6	3.2	2.1	0.4	60.7	4.9	35.3	15.9	4.5	0.0
China - Chine	1990	53 810	51.3	19.3	18.2	12.2	14.2	5.5	4.8	42.9	0.7	2.8	38.6	0.9	0.0
	2000	225 175	47.3	14.6	13.6	9.9	18.4	4.4	3.4	46.0	2.5	2.4	37.4	3.5	0.1
	2005	660 218	38.5	11.9	11.1	7.4	15.2	4.0	3.2	49.9	3.2	4.0	39.0	3.6	0.1
China, Hong Kong SAR - Chine, Hong Kong RAS	1990	82 490	38.6	12.3	10.4	8.1	16.1	2.1	0.1	61.2	0.6	0.7	59.6	0.3	0.0
	2000	213 328	30.8	10.0	8.8	6.8	12.0	2.0	0.2	68.9	0.3	0.6	67.5	0.5	0.0
	2005	299 967	26.6	8.9	7.6	5.1	11.0	1.6	0.2	73.2	0.4	0.7	71.4	0.7	0.0
China, Macao SAR - Chine, Macao RAS	1990	1 532	27.6	9.5	9.3	5.1	11.5	1.4	0.4	72.0	0.2	0.2	71.3	0.2	..
	2000	2 255	23.3	9.9	9.6	4.5	6.3	2.6	0.0	76.7	0.2	0.3	75.6	0.6	0.0
	2005	3 913	30.4	14.0	13.1	4.1	10.9	1.5	0.3	69.4	0.5	0.4	68.0	0.4	0.0
China, Taiwan Province of - Chine, Taiwan Province de	1990	(e)55 244	76.0	18.0	15.6	23.1	29.7	5.2	0.2	22.8	0.5	2.4	14.3	5.6	0.0
	2000	(e)141 592	61.8	12.5	11.6	17.8	27.3	4.2	1.3	35.7	2.3	1.5	28.1	3.7	0.1
	2005	(e)184 845	51.7	11.1	10.1	11.5	25.0	4.1	1.3	39.9	1.9	1.9	27.2	8.7	0.1
Colombia - Colombie	1990	5 589	75.7	26.1	23.1	35.4	8.9	5.3	0.6	23.0	0.1	21.6	1.3	0.0	0.0
	2000	11 320	62.0	18.5	17.4	35.4	5.5	2.5	0.4	36.3	0.5	28.7	7.1	0.1	0.0
	2005	21 202	49.1	14.9	13.8	28.5	3.3	2.4	1.0	46.3	0.4	31.1	14.6	0.1	0.0

For sources and notes, see end of table.

Pour les sources et les notes, se reporter à la fin du tableau.

Origin / Origine (Destination)	Year / Année	World (millions of dollars) / Monde (millions de dollars)	Developed economies / Économies développées						Economies in transition / Économies en transition	Developing economies / Économies en développement					
			Total	Europe Total	EU UE	USA États-Unis	Japan Japon	Other Autres		Total	Africa Afrique	America Amérique	Eastern, Southern and South-Eastern Asia / Asie orientale, méridionale et du Sud-Est	Western Asia / Asie occidentale	Oceania Océanie
									Percentage / En pourcentage						
Comoros - Comores	1990	86	89.8	84.1	84.0	..	5.5	0.2	..	10.2	5.1	0.1	4.9	0.1	..
	2000	(e)70	42.9	36.3	36.3	1.3	0.4	5.0	0.0	55.8	33.6	0.3	14.5	7.5	..
	2005	(e)114	41.1	39.8	39.7	0.3	0.3	0.7	1.1	56.1	21.5	1.9	19.7	13.0	..
Congo	1990	598	76.4	66.0	65.0	5.9	4.2	0.3	0.7	9.6	3.9	1.0	3.4	1.4	..
	2000	492	66.1	48.1	47.3	13.6	4.3	0.2	4.3	22.5	13.7	0.4	7.3	1.1	..
	2005	1 574	56.8	48.2	47.7	7.3	0.5	0.9	0.4	40.2	9.3	5.6	24.0	1.4	..
Costa Rica	1990	2 026	65.6	14.9	13.9	40.6	8.4	1.7	0.2	33.6	0.0	28.1	5.4	0.0	0.0
	2000	6 389	37.8	9.7	9.2	23.6	3.1	1.4	0.4	26.8	0.0	22.8	3.8	0.1	0.1
	2005	9 807	61.7	13.5	12.7	41.3	5.6	1.3	0.8	36.6	0.0	26.8	9.7	0.1	0.0
Côte d'Ivoire	1990	2 098	59.5	51.6	50.7	4.8	2.4	0.7	0.8	36.0	29.9	2.2	3.6	0.2	..
	2000	2 734	42.1	35.6	34.8	3.2	2.7	0.6	2.6	42.6	28.6	2.8	8.2	3.0	..
	2005	5 873	44.8	41.0	39.8	2.0	1.4	0.4	1.2	51.7	30.3	3.4	16.7	1.4	..
Croatia - Croatie	2000	7 688	77.0	71.6	69.3	2.9	1.7	0.7	10.6	9.5	2.4	1.2	3.6	2.3	..
	2005	18 356	70.3	66.3	64.6	2.2	1.5	0.3	15.3	11.7	0.9	1.5	7.6	1.7	..
Cuba	1990	2 956	49.1	40.6	39.4	0.1	2.7	5.8	2.7	48.1	0.7	36.1	11.4	0.0	..
	2000	(e)3 810	44.8	37.6	37.5	0.1	0.8	6.3	3.3	52.0	1.2	41.5	9.2	0.0	..
	2005	(e)4 811	59.0	37.2	36.8	8.3	4.0	9.5	3.8	37.2	1.5	20.2	15.5	0.1	..
Cyprus - Chypre	1990	2 565	81.5	61.0	59.2	7.1	11.5	1.9	4.3	14.1	1.9	0.8	7.9	3.5	0.0
	2000	3 710	75.3	53.9	52.6	10.8	6.0	4.5	6.0	18.7	1.7	1.1	11.6	4.3	..
	2005	6 285	79.9	67.9	67.0	1.6	2.8	7.6	3.9	14.6	1.4	2.3	8.1	2.9	0.0
Czech Republic - République tchèque	2000	34 808	84.8	77.9	75.3	4.3	1.9	0.7	8.3	6.7	0.7	0.9	4.7	0.4	0.0
	2005	76 507	79.6	73.3	70.9	2.6	3.1	0.6	8.5	11.7	0.6	0.9	9.4	0.8	0.0
Czechoslovakia (former) - Tchécoslovaquie (anc.)	1990	15 070	64.1	62.2	57.7	0.6	0.5	0.8	26.0	9.9	0.7	2.2	6.5	0.5	..
Dem. Rep. of the Congo - Rép. dém. du Congo	1990	1 304	70.8	58.9	57.4	7.0	4.1	0.8	0.6	28.5	11.7	0.9	15.9	0.0	0.0
	2000	(e)669	46.7	42.7	41.5	1.7	1.5	0.8	0.1	52.6	43.5	0.2	8.6	0.2	0.0
	2005	(e)1 649	47.5	40.8	39.9	4.3	1.1	1.2	0.2	52.0	43.4	2.1	6.3	0.3	0.0
Denmark - Danemark	1990	31 372	89.4	77.1	69.6	6.2	4.1	2.0	1.1	9.5	0.9	2.1	5.3	1.2	0.0
	2000	45 530	88.1	80.9	72.2	4.3	1.5	1.4	1.1	10.6	0.4	1.5	7.9	0.8	0.0
	2005	75 430	84.4	79.2	70.9	2.7	1.1	1.3	1.7	13.8	0.4	1.6	9.7	2.1	0.0
Djibouti	1990	(e)215	58.0	49.0	47.6	3.3	5.4	0.3	0.6	36.9	12.2	0.2	14.2	10.4	..
	2000	(e)614	37.1	30.3	30.1	3.0	3.6	0.2	0.1	58.7	11.3	0.3	26.1	21.0	..
	2005	(e)1 207	21.3	12.4	12.3	4.4	4.2	0.3	1.0	73.7	6.2	0.6	39.9	27.1	..
Dominica - Dominique	1990	118	70.0	28.0	27.0	33.1	6.2	2.6	0.0	29.8	0.1	25.9	3.9	0.0	..
	2000	147	62.9	14.8	14.3	37.5	6.3	4.4	0.0	36.2	0.0	33.9	2.2	0.2	..
	2005	(e)265	42.9	10.8	9.6	25.5	4.7	1.9	0.1	56.3	0.1	25.4	30.7	0.1	..
Dominican Republic - République dominicaine	1990	2 194	66.0	12.1	11.5	41.4	10.1	2.4	0.0	33.9	0.2	30.9	2.8	0.0	..
	2000	(e)10 426	72.3	8.3	8.0	60.5	3.0	0.6	0.2	27.3	0.3	21.4	5.2	0.3	0.1
	2005	(e)10 362	65.9	11.0	10.5	50.0	3.3	1.6	0.4	33.6	0.5	26.5	6.6	0.1	0.0
Ecuador - Équateur	1990	1 862	69.6	26.7	23.9	31.3	9.2	2.4	0.4	27.9	0.6	25.3	2.1	..	..
	2000	3 930	51.1	14.6	13.8	28.4	5.8	2.4	1.4	46.6	1.4	36.8	7.8	0.5	0.0
	2005	9 849	40.6	12.8	12.2	22.1	3.8	1.9	0.8	58.5	0.1	44.5	13.5	0.4	0.0
Egypt - Égypte	1990	9 280	71.8	48.7	45.9	14.0	3.7	5.4	6.3	15.9	1.4	2.9	8.6	2.9	..
	2000	22 041	62.5	39.3	37.6	16.9	3.7	2.6	4.7	26.2	1.6	3.1	14.6	6.9	..
	2005	(e)32 972	51.0	35.6	34.4	10.6	2.6	2.2	7.5	34.8	2.7	5.1	16.5	10.6	0.0
El Salvador	1990	1 277	61.4	14.0	12.8	42.4	3.5	1.5	0.0	35.0	0.0	33.2	1.8	0.0	..
	2000	4 948	60.6	6.9	6.6	50.0	2.5	1.1	0.8	35.6	0.1	33.0	2.4	0.1	..
	2005	6 766	53.0	6.6	5.9	43.4	1.8	1.2	0.7	44.2	0.1	39.1	5.1	0.0	..
Equatorial Guinea - Guinée équatoriale	1990	102	52.9	52.6	52.0	..	0.2	0.1	2.2	45.0	43.1	0.2	1.6	..	..
	2000	(e)314	82.2	45.6	43.9	32.4	4.1	0.1	0.7	17.1	13.0	1.7	2.3	0.2	..
	2005	(e)1 118	83.6	57.1	56.0	24.5	0.6	1.4	0.2	16.3	11.8	0.9	3.1	0.5	..
Estonia - Estonie	2000	(e)5 334	69.8	61.9	60.0	2.3	5.3	0.3	17.0	13.3	1.3	0.4	5.9	5.6	0.0
	2005	10 179	81.1	77.3	76.1	1.5	2.0	0.2	11.8	7.1	0.1	0.4	6.2	0.5	0.0
Ethiopia - Éthiopie	2000	1 226	43.0	31.2	30.2	4.6	6.1	1.1	1.4	45.9	4.9	0.2	17.5	23.3	..
	2005	4 082	40.7	22.9	22.1	12.4	3.3	2.1	0.6	46.6	4.6	0.7	23.5	17.7	..

For sources and notes, see end of table.   Pour les sources et les notes, se reporter à la fin du tableau.

Origin / Origine Destination	Year Année	World (millions of dollars) Monde (millions de dollars)	Developed economies / Économies développées						Economies in transition Économies en transition	Developing economies / Économies en développement					
			Total	Europe		USA États-Unis	Japan Japon	Other Autres		Total	Africa Afrique	America Amérique	Eastern, Southern and South-Eastern Asia Asie orientale, méridionale et du Sud-Est	Western Asia Asie occidentale	Oceania Océanie
				Total	EU UE										
						Percentage / En pourcentage									
Ethiopia (former) - Éthiopie (anc.)	1990	1 078	65.5	52.3	49.9	5.4	6.5	1.2	14.5	12.2	3.3	0.2	5.6	3.1	..
Faeroe Islands - Îles Féroé	1990	334	97.0	93.2	67.2	1.4	2.0	0.5	1.3	1.3	..	0.2	1.0	0.1	..
	2000	455	97.6	96.6	60.0	0.8	..	0.2	0.1	1.6	..	0.5	1.1	0.1	..
	2005	(e)715	98.2	97.2	72.2	0.4	..	0.6	0.0	0.9	0.0	0.6	0.2	0.1	..
Fiji - Fidji	1990	755	74.1	5.6	5.6	13.1	11.0	44.4	..	19.7	..	..	19.7	..	..
	2000	762	73.1	3.7	3.6	3.4	4.0	62.1	0.0	25.9	0.1	0.3	25.1	0.0	0.3
	2005	(e)1 451	53.7	4.7	4.6	2.1	3.5	43.3	0.0	45.1	0.3	0.2	44.2	0.0	0.4
Finland - Finlande	1990	26 944	82.5	68.0	62.7	6.8	6.4	1.3	10.2	7.2	0.4	1.8	4.0	1.0	0.1
	2000	34 306	79.7	69.7	64.6	4.8	3.7	1.4	9.7	8.4	0.6	1.4	6.1	0.2	0.1
	2005	58 945	75.7	68.7	65.8	3.5	2.2	1.4	14.6	9.8	0.4	1.7	7.1	0.5	0.0
France	1990	240 690	81.0	67.7	63.8	7.9	3.9	1.4	2.0	14.4	5.0	2.1	5.0	2.3	0.1
	2000	331 839	82.2	71.2	66.4	7.4	2.3	1.3	1.9	15.0	3.9	1.8	6.7	2.6	0.0
	2005	503 707	78.8	70.9	66.9	5.1	1.6	1.2	3.2	17.0	5.0	1.6	7.7	2.6	0.1
Gabon	1990	847	83.4	71.5	70.3	6.4	4.9	0.7	0.1	12.4	6.9	1.0	4.6	0.0	..
	2000	(e)1 395	88.8	80.9	80.6	5.1	2.3	0.5	0.0	10.1	5.6	0.7	3.4	0.3	0.0
	2005	(e)1 698	75.2	65.5	64.2	6.4	2.6	0.7	0.1	22.8	12.4	3.3	6.5	0.6	0.0
Gambia - Gambie	1990	231	53.7	49.8	49.1	.	3.8	0.1	3.5	38.9	9.6	0.3	28.9	0.1	..
	2000	(e)334	35.4	30.5	30.1	2.5	2.0	0.5	0.1	64.5	17.1	5.4	38.7	3.4	..
	2005	(e)638	29.2	22.3	22.1	5.3	0.6	1.0	1.0	69.8	24.0	6.1	34.2	5.4	..
Georgia - Géorgie	2000	(e)722	41.0	29.4	26.1	9.6	1.0	1.0	37.3	20.8	0.1	1.0	2.4	17.4	..
	2005	2 491	34.9	27.8	27.0	6.0	0.3	0.9	44.9	20.2	0.2	1.7	3.8	14.4	0.0
Germany - Allemagne	1990	346 466	81.6	67.5	61.8	6.6	5.9	1.6	3.7	14.6	3.0	2.7	7.1	1.8	0.1
	2000	500 279	80.0	65.2	59.7	8.6	4.9	1.3	3.9	16.0	2.2	1.9	10.1	1.7	0.0
	2005	776 934	76.2	65.2	59.0	6.6	3.4	0.9	5.2	18.6	2.1	2.1	12.5	1.8	0.0
Ghana	1990	1 614	64.1	46.8	45.3	9.4	4.8	3.1	0.7	35.1	23.1	4.8	7.1	0.1	..
	2000	2 871	57.1	45.4	44.7	7.1	1.6	3.0	0.8	41.2	22.7	3.4	14.2	0.8	0.0
	2005	(e)5 903	41.1	29.7	28.8	6.3	1.8	3.3	1.1	56.8	26.2	5.4	24.2	1.0	0.0
Greece - Grèce	1990	19 764	82.5	71.8	69.5	3.7	5.9	1.1	4.2	13.2	3.5	1.7	5.2	2.7	0.0
	2000	28 324	69.9	62.4	60.6	3.2	3.0	1.3	8.0	22.1	3.4	1.1	11.6	6.0	0.0
	2005	53 986	63.9	57.4	55.7	3.5	2.1	0.8	12.4	23.5	2.6	1.5	12.8	6.6	0.0
Greenland - Groenland	1990	435	98.0	88.8	79.1	4.6	3.9	0.7	0.1	1.8	0.1	0.3	1.4	0.0	..
	2000	413	98.8	97.4	86.2	0.4	0.1	1.0	0.0	0.5	0.0	0.1	0.3	0.0	..
	2005	(e)725	98.8	95.4	92.1	0.8	0.0	2.5	0.0	0.4	0.0	0.0	0.3	0.0	..
Grenada - Grenade	1990	109	66.7	22.2	21.6	30.6	7.1	6.8	0.1	33.1	0.0	28.6	4.4	0.0	..
	2000	(e)246	66.5	14.2	14.2	44.8	4.3	3.3	..	26.7	..	25.2	1.4	..	..
	2005	(e)339	48.5	15.2	14.8	26.8	3.7	2.8	0.0	42.5	0.1	39.1	3.3	0.0	..
Guatemala	1990	1 698	63.1	16.6	14.9	39.1	5.8	1.6	0.0	35.9	0.5	31.5	3.9	0.0	..
	2000	5 171	54.8	8.5	8.0	40.2	3.2	3.0	1.0	43.2	0.1	38.7	4.4	0.1	0.0
	2005	10 500	52.8	10.1	7.3	38.1	2.6	2.0	0.1	44.9	0.0	32.8	12.0	0.1	..
Guinea - Guinée	1990	583	75.3	62.4	61.3	8.1	3.6	1.1	0.1	24.7	14.4	2.8	7.4	0.0	..
	2000	(e)533	58.2	45.5	44.5	5.6	5.2	2.0	0.9	40.6	25.0	0.8	13.4	1.4	0.0
	2005	1 873	36.6	27.6	27.1	7.3	0.8	0.8	1.6	32.4	12.2	1.5	17.0	1.7	0.0
Guinea-Bissau - Guinée-Bissau	1990	124	73.3	61.3	61.2	1.1	10.9	0.0	3.2	21.5	12.8	0.8	8.0	0.0	..
	2000	(e)106	47.2	44.8	43.7	0.6	1.6	0.1	0.2	44.6	14.2	2.7	27.6	0.1	..
	2005	(e)213	55.4	54.1	53.4	1.1	0.2	0.0	..	35.6	23.8	3.6	8.1	0.1	..
Guyana	1990	279	63.5	24.7	23.6	29.9	5.1	3.8	0.7	35.8	0.0	31.5	2.9	1.4	..
	2000	(e)651	42.0	11.3	11.3	26.9	2.0	1.8	0.0	58.0	0.1	52.7	5.1	0.2	..
	2005	(e)722	44.6	11.6	11.4	26.7	3.4	3.0	0.1	55.2	0.3	44.2	10.4	0.3	..
Haiti - Haïti	1990	525	77.8	12.6	11.7	58.0	3.8	3.4	0.0	22.0	0.1	15.9	6.0	0.0	..
	2000	(e)737	55.1	9.6	9.0	37.3	4.1	4.0	0.1	43.4	0.4	36.5	5.4	1.1	0.0
	2005	1 555	62.7	9.9	9.7	48.7	1.8	2.4	0.1	37.0	0.3	27.9	8.2	0.6	0.0
Honduras	1990	880	64.6	15.5	15.5	39.5	8.6	0.9	..	24.3	..	24.3	..	..	..
	2000	2 853	57.7	4.8	4.3	47.5	4.1	1.2	0.1	40.5	0.0	35.7	4.7	0.0	0.0
	2005	6 787	62.2	7.4	7.2	52.6	1.5	0.7	0.4	37.0	0.2	29.6	7.1	0.1	0.0

For sources and notes, see end of table.

Pour les sources et les notes, se reporter à la fin du tableau.

Origin / Origine	Year Année	World (millions of dollars) Monde (millions de dollars)	Developed economies / Économies développées — Total	Europe Total	EU UE	USA États-Unis	Japan Japon	Other Autres	Economies in transition Économies en transition	Developing economies / Économies en développement — Total	Africa Afrique	America Amérique	Eastern, Southern and South-Eastern Asia / Asie orientale, méridionale et du Sud-Est	Western Asia / Asie occidentale	Oceania Océanie
Hungary - Hongrie	1990	8 621	64.5	59.2	56.0	2.6	2.1	0.5	23.1	10.2	3.4	2.5	3.6	0.6	..
	2000	32 187	75.9	66.3	64.8	3.8	5.3	0.5	10.6	13.1	0.4	1.3	11.1	0.4	..
	2005	66 326	74.0	68.8	67.8	1.7	3.1	0.4	11.8	14.2	0.1	0.5	12.9	0.7	0.0
Iceland - Islande	1990	1 678	91.3	68.2	61.9	14.2	5.6	3.3	5.0	3.7	0.3	0.6	2.7	0.1	..
	2000	2 586	89.9	70.0	60.5	11.0	4.9	4.0	1.9	8.2	0.3	2.2	5.3	0.4	0.0
	2005	4 848	87.0	71.2	61.9	9.1	4.7	2.1	1.1	11.9	0.4	1.8	8.8	0.9	0.0
India - Inde	1990	23 991	58.6	35.0	34.0	11.0	7.5	5.1	6.3	34.6	3.1	2.2	13.2	16.0	0.0
	2000	50 336	41.6	27.3	21.2	6.3	4.0	4.0	1.5	33.4	6.4	1.5	18.1	7.3	0.1
	2005	134 690	34.4	21.2	16.3	5.6	2.6	5.0	2.2	33.2	3.3	1.7	21.9	6.1	0.1
Indonesia - Indonésie	1990	22 005	66.2	22.0	20.8	11.4	24.8	7.9	0.4	33.0	0.7	2.3	27.1	2.8	0.0
	2000	33 515	47.1	13.2	12.5	10.1	16.1	7.6	0.7	51.2	2.5	1.8	38.7	8.2	0.1
	2005	57 700	35.6	10.7	10.1	6.7	12.0	6.1	1.5	62.4	2.8	2.0	49.6	7.9	0.1
Iran, Islamic Republic of - Iran, Rép. islamique d'	1990	18 722	65.9	53.1	49.9	0.3	10.3	2.2	3.3	21.4	..	3.7	8.0	9.7	..
	2000	14 347	52.3	40.4	38.1	0.7	4.8	6.4	11.1	35.9	1.5	6.7	17.2	10.5	..
	2005	(e)43 589	47.0	42.3	40.7	0.2	3.4	1.1	12.0	40.7	0.6	3.3	22.3	14.5	..
Iraq	1990	6 526	71.3	50.0	48.3	10.8	4.6	5.9	2.7	26.0	2.1	2.3	5.9	15.7	..
	2000	(e)3 414	49.9	35.5	33.3	0.4	1.4	12.7	5.7	44.4	4.6	3.2	30.4	6.2	..
	2005	(e)12 937	32.4	17.3	16.9	11.7	1.1	2.4	2.3	65.3	2.3	0.6	8.6	53.7	..
Ireland - Irlande	1990	20 830	92.9	71.8	70.3	14.4	5.5	1.1	0.5	6.0	1.3	1.0	3.5	0.3	0.0
	2000	50 642	81.5	59.6	57.1	16.2	4.0	1.6	0.2	12.4	0.6	0.6	10.8	0.3	0.0
	2005	68 549	85.1	67.7	64.7	13.8	2.7	1.0	0.2	12.5	0.6	0.8	10.6	0.5	0.0
Israel - Israël	1990	15 338	83.9	61.3	51.9	17.8	3.6	1.2	0.4	6.4	1.8	1.1	3.3	0.2	..
	2000	36 802	70.7	48.0	42.6	18.1	3.2	1.3	1.8	14.4	1.0	0.9	10.8	1.7	..
	2005	44 942	61.5	44.3	38.6	13.4	2.8	1.0	3.3	20.8	0.7	2.2	15.1	2.9	..
Italy - Italie	1990	181 773	77.2	68.1	63.1	5.1	2.3	1.7	4.3	18.3	8.4	2.5	4.8	2.6	0.0
	2000	235 280	72.6	63.0	59.4	5.3	2.5	1.8	6.2	21.2	7.8	2.5	7.9	3.0	0.0
	2005	384 169	67.8	61.5	57.8	3.5	1.6	1.2	8.0	24.0	8.0	2.4	9.8	3.8	0.0
Jamaica - Jamaïque	1990	1 867	73.1	12.7	11.4	48.5	4.9	7.0	0.3	24.6	0.0	21.8	2.7	0.0	0.0
	2000	(e)3 307	66.2	9.0	8.2	47.2	5.8	4.2	0.1	30.8	0.1	26.0	4.0	0.8	..
	2005	4 736	57.9	8.3	7.4	41.4	4.6	3.6	0.1	40.4	0.6	33.7	5.8	0.3	0.0
Japan - Japon	1990	235 334	50.8	18.3	16.3	22.5	..	10.1	1.5	47.6	1.6	4.0	30.2	11.5	0.3
	2000	379 577	39.9	13.8	12.6	19.1	..	7.0	1.3	58.8	1.3	2.8	43.1	11.4	0.2
	2005	515 194	32.5	12.6	11.4	12.7	..	7.1	1.4	66.2	1.9	2.8	46.4	14.8	0.2
Jordan - Jordanie	1990	2 581	57.2	34.5	33.2	17.5	3.2	2.0	3.3	39.5	3.0	0.5	9.1	26.9	0.0
	2000	4 597	50.6	32.8	31.6	9.9	3.9	4.0	3.5	43.0	1.9	2.7	14.5	23.9	..
	2005	10 497	36.4	25.5	24.2	5.6	2.8	2.5	4.7	58.7	4.6	1.8	20.2	32.1	..
Kazakhstan	2000	(e)5 048	33.1	24.6	23.5	5.5	2.1	0.9	54.4	12.2	0.5	2.0	6.4	3.3	0.0
	2005	20 139	29.2	24.5	24.0	2.9	1.0	0.8	43.2	27.5	0.2	0.6	24.0	2.7	0.0
Kenya	1990	2 048	67.0	45.4	44.2	8.4	11.9	1.3	0.3	21.3	2.3	0.7	7.7	10.6	..
	2000	3 253	43.4	31.9	30.7	4.1	5.1	2.4	1.9	54.4	9.1	1.5	15.4	28.4	..
	2005	6 812	36.5	20.3	19.5	10.2	4.1	1.9	1.5	61.0	11.2	1.7	24.0	24.1	0.0
Korea, Dem. People's Rep. of - Corée, Rép. populaire dém. de	1990	(e)1 326	39.5	17.4	16.9	..	14.6	7.5	0.4	60.1	1.4	0.9	57.1	0.8	..
	2000	(e)2 103	21.3	9.5	9.2	0.1	10.7	0.9	2.6	76.1	14.4	7.9	49.3	4.6	0.0
	2005	(e)2 979	11.0	7.6	7.5	0.2	2.3	0.9	9.2	79.8	12.7	6.8	56.6	3.7	0.0
Korea, Republic of - Corée, République de	1990	74 405	66.9	13.1	12.2	22.8	25.0	6.1	..	20.6	0.8	2.3	10.3	7.0	0.2
	2000	160 481	54.8	10.9	10.1	18.2	19.8	5.7	1.6	43.5	2.0	2.0	25.3	14.0	0.1
	2005	261 209	46.8	11.1	10.5	11.8	18.5	5.3	1.8	51.4	1.3	2.6	31.0	16.4	0.1
Kuwait - Koweït	1990	4 049	62.0	37.9	36.4	10.9	11.4	1.9	3.2	17.6	0.1	1.0	14.1	2.5	..
	2000	7 359	58.4	34.2	32.8	12.1	8.7	3.4	0.2	41.3	1.4	1.5	20.3	18.1	0.0
	2005	(e)15 366	62.2	36.1	34.3	14.1	8.4	3.5	0.6	37.2	0.7	1.8	18.0	16.7	0.0
Kyrgyzstan - Kirghizistan	2000	555	28.2	14.6	13.7	9.7	1.8	2.1	54.1	17.7	..	0.1	11.4	6.1	0.1
	2005	(e)2 216	8.8	7.0	6.8	1.5	0.1	0.2	36.9	54.3	0.0	0.2	48.9	5.0	..
Lao People's Dem. Rep. - Rép. dém. populaire lao	1990	149	25.9	9.7	9.0	0.7	14.5	0.9	0.0	73.7	0.1	0.2	73.3	0.1	..
	2000	(e)690	11.6	6.6	6.5	0.7	3.4	0.9	0.2	86.6	0.0	0.0	86.5	0.0	..
	2005	(e)1 267	8.5	4.3	4.1	0.9	1.7	1.6	0.9	88.7	0.2	0.0	88.4	0.0	..

For sources and notes, see end of table.

Pour les sources et les notes, se reporter à la fin du tableau.

Origin / Origine Destination	Year Année	World (millions of dollars) Monde (millions de dollars)	Developed economies / Économies développées						Economies in transition Économies en transition	Developing economies / Économies en développement					
			Total	Europe		USA États-Unis	Japan Japon	Other Autres		Total	Africa Afrique	America Amérique	Eastern, Southern and South-Eastern Asia Asie orientale, méridionale et du Sud-Est	Western Asia Asie occidentale	Oceania Océanie
				Total	EU UE										
			Percentage / En pourcentage												
Latvia - Lettonie	2000	3 184	79.9	77.0	74.0	2.0	0.1	0.8	17.3	2.4	0.1	0.2	1.6	0.5	0.0
	2005	8 659	79.2	77.4	75.1	1.1	0.3	0.4	17.0	3.9	0.1	0.2	2.9	0.7	..
Lebanon - Liban	1990	2 515	62.9	54.4	50.5	4.3	3.9	0.3	4.3	32.8	1.4	1.5	12.2	17.8	..
	2000	(e)6 228	64.4	52.7	45.7	7.3	3.4	1.0	6.3	27.9	2.8	1.9	11.2	12.1	0.0
	2005	(e)9 652	53.3	45.4	42.6	5.3	1.8	0.7	6.8	37.8	2.9	2.0	11.7	21.2	0.0
Liberia - Libéria	1990	4 259	68.1	38.9	33.5	1.1	28.0	0.1	5.7	26.2	0.7	1.0	24.6	0.0	..
	2000	(e)5 494	57.5	41.9	40.6	0.9	14.7	0.0	4.2	38.3	2.9	1.0	34.1	0.2	..
	2005	(e)5 732	33.2	10.4	9.2	1.4	21.2	0.2	6.1	60.8	2.5	1.0	56.2	1.1	..
Libyan Arab Jamahiriya - Jamahiriya arabe libyenne	1990	5 663	77.5	70.8	66.8	1.2	4.3	1.2	1.5	19.9	5.3	2.7	6.0	5.9	..
	2000	(e)4 018	70.8	66.9	65.1	0.5	2.6	0.9	1.8	27.2	10.4	2.8	7.8	6.1	..
	2005	(e)8 770	61.2	57.4	55.4	1.1	1.7	1.0	4.2	34.4	7.6	3.5	13.3	9.9	..
Lithuania - Lituanie	2000	(e)5 457	60.5	55.8	54.0	2.4	1.9	0.5	32.0	6.0	0.3	0.9	4.2	0.6	0.0
	2005	15 483	63.0	60.4	59.3	2.0	0.3	0.2	31.4	5.6	0.2	0.5	4.1	0.7	..
Luxembourg	2005	21 639	79.3	75.0	72.8	3.1	0.8	0.4	0.4	19.1	0.2	0.3	16.8	1.9	0.0
Madagascar	1990	608	57.4	49.0	47.4	2.2	6.0	0.3	0.7	14.8	2.0	0.9	11.6	0.3	..
	2000	734	34.2	24.2	23.9	5.9	2.9	1.2	0.1	57.5	6.4	3.3	32.4	15.5	0.0
	2005	(e)1 889	29.6	26.6	26.1	1.6	1.0	0.3	0.0	58.8	14.0	1.6	37.9	5.2	0.0
Malawi	1990	627	48.9	38.9	37.6	2.0	7.0	1.0	0.0	45.1	42.1	..	3.0	..	..
	2000	(e)562	16.5	10.8	10.5	2.6	2.3	0.8	0.2	82.0	71.8	1.2	9.1	0.0	..
	2005	(e)773	18.7	13.3	13.0	4.0	0.8	0.6	0.0	80.6	67.2	0.5	12.3	0.6	..
Malaysia - Malaisie	1990	29 173	63.8	17.5	16.1	16.9	24.2	5.1	0.4	35.6	0.5	1.8	32.1	1.1	0.1
	2000	82 204	52.7	12.3	11.0	16.6	21.1	2.8	0.3	45.1	0.5	0.8	41.9	1.9	0.0
	2005	113 609	43.2	12.9	11.7	13.0	14.6	2.7	0.5	56.1	0.6	1.6	50.9	3.0	0.0
Maldives	1990	(e)138	17.4	13.3	13.0	0.5	3.3	0.3	0.0	82.6	..	0.0	82.0	0.5	..
	2000	389	20.5	10.5	9.6	2.2	3.4	4.4	0.0	79.1	0.4	0.1	69.8	8.8	..
	2005	745	21.7	15.1	14.2	1.1	1.8	3.7	0.0	78.1	0.4	0.3	58.8	18.6	..
Mali	1990	714	45.2	41.7	41.0	1.4	1.4	0.8	0.7	35.3	28.7	0.2	4.0	2.4	..
	2000	(e)1 286	30.5	26.6	26.4	3.0	0.5	0.5	0.2	35.3	26.8	0.4	7.8	0.3	0.0
	2005	(e)2 068	28.7	25.9	25.7	1.7	0.3	0.9	1.3	36.8	29.3	0.9	6.0	0.7	0.0
Malta - Malte	1990	1 951	87.1	79.5	78.5	3.3	3.7	0.5	2.1	10.7	3.6	1.2	5.1	0.8	..
	2000	3 400	75.8	62.3	60.5	10.6	2.0	0.9	0.5	23.7	1.6	0.5	20.2	1.3	..
	2005	3 587	84.6	76.7	75.0	5.5	1.7	0.6	0.4	15.0	0.9	0.8	11.7	1.5	0.0
Mauritania - Mauritanie	1990	388	78.0	69.1	68.3	6.2	2.3	0.4	0.6	17.0	6.7	1.0	8.9	0.4	..
	2000	(e)651	64.1	58.6	58.4	2.6	2.5	0.4	2.7	24.5	9.0	0.6	13.4	1.5	..
	2005	(e)1 368	60.2	50.0	48.0	6.9	2.3	1.0	2.0	28.3	9.4	3.9	12.4	2.7	..
Mauritius - Maurice	1990	1 620	54.1	39.0	37.2	4.8	5.9	4.4	0.1	45.8	12.9	1.1	26.1	5.7	0.0
	2000	2 088	40.6	28.9	27.3	2.9	4.1	4.7	0.3	59.1	18.6	1.4	33.7	5.4	0.0
	2005	3 165	41.9	32.0	30.7	2.2	3.6	4.1	0.1	57.9	12.0	1.8	30.8	13.4	0.0
Mexico - Mexique	1990	33 022	91.7	19.2	17.8	66.1	4.3	2.1	0.1	7.5	0.3	4.4	2.8	0.0	0.0
	2000	194 749	87.0	8.7	8.2	72.0	3.7	2.7	0.3	10.6	0.2	2.6	7.7	0.2	..
	2005	244 001	74.3	11.5	10.9	53.4	5.9	3.5	0.4	24.0	0.1	5.8	17.8	0.3	..
Moldova, Republic of - Moldova, République de	2000	776	44.1	37.1	36.1	6.2	0.3	0.5	51.0	4.9	0.1	0.2	2.2	2.4	0.0
	2005	2 293	36.9	33.7	32.8	1.8	0.9	0.6	52.3	10.6	0.4	0.8	5.3	4.1	..
Mongolia - Mongolie	1990	(e)144	67.8	57.1	54.3	..	10.7	0.1	8.9	23.2	0.7	0.1	22.5	0.0	..
	2000	614	29.9	12.7	12.1	4.6	11.9	0.7	36.4	33.7	0.0	0.0	33.5	0.2	..
	2005	1 160	23.5	9.9	9.8	3.1	7.1	3.4	40.2	36.3	0.0	0.5	35.6	0.2	0.0
Morocco - Maroc	1990	7 919	61.9	52.8	51.3	5.5	1.6	2.1	3.0	22.5	6.6	2.3	3.2	10.4	..
	2000	11 531	68.0	58.4	57.1	5.6	1.7	2.3	3.6	26.9	4.6	3.2	8.7	10.4	..
	2005	20 336	58.2	51.7	50.4	3.4	1.8	1.3	8.3	31.4	5.4	4.3	11.5	10.1	..
Mozambique	1990	913	57.7	43.8	42.5	6.1	4.8	3.1	0.0	42.2	11.1	1.6	17.9	11.6	..
	2000	1 046	26.5	16.9	16.7	3.5	4.6	1.5	..	61.2	51.8	0.6	8.2	0.6	..
	2005	2 467	26.8	22.5	21.6	2.6	0.8	0.9	..	64.4	47.2	2.2	13.1	1.9	..
Myanmar	1990	668	42.9	19.6	16.4	2.9	16.6	3.9	3.8	53.2	0.5	0.1	52.6	0.0	..
	2000	(e)3 039	12.4	4.0	4.0	0.6	7.1	0.7	0.6	86.9	0.1	0.0	86.6	0.2	..
	2005	(e)3 569	7.4	3.3	3.2	0.2	2.8	1.1	0.5	91.9	0.2	0.1	91.4	0.2	..

For sources and notes, see end of table.   Pour les sources et les notes, se reporter à la fin du tableau.

Origin / Origine Destination	Year Année	World (millions of dollars) Monde (millions de dollars)	Developed economies Économies développées Total	Europe Total	Europe EU UE	USA États-Unis	Japan Japon	Other Autres	Economies in transition Économies en transition	Developing economies Économies en développement Total	Africa Afrique	America Amérique	Eastern, Southern and South-Eastern Asia Asie orientale, méridionale et du Sud-Est	Western Asia Asie occidentale	Oceania Océanie
Nepal - Népal	1990	(e)587	46.6	19.3	18.2	2.4	18.7	6.2	0.8	52.6	0.2	0.5	51.9	0.0	..
	2000	(e)1 058	17.6	9.0	8.6	2.8	3.2	2.6	0.5	79.4	0.0	0.0	64.2	15.1	..
	2005	(e)1 917	9.8	6.1	5.9	1.4	1.1	1.1	0.4	86.8	0.1	0.1	65.7	20.9	..
Netherlands - Pays-Bas	1990	123 383	83.6	71.0	68.1	7.8	3.2	1.5	1.6	14.8	2.8	2.8	5.9	3.3	0.0
	2000	215 716	71.7	55.3	52.9	10.2	4.7	1.5	2.1	24.0	2.1	3.2	15.7	2.9	0.0
	2005	363 218	64.6	52.3	49.2	7.6	3.2	1.4	5.0	30.2	2.7	4.2	19.4	3.9	0.0
Netherlands Antilles - Antilles néerlandaises	1990	2 136	25.0	9.1	8.9	12.8	2.2	0.9	0.0	73.4	..	71.0	1.8	0.6	..
	2000	2 853	23.8	8.8	8.7	13.0	1.1	0.9	0.0	75.4	0.9	70.3	0.7	3.4	..
	2005	(e)6 017	36.7	14.6	14.0	20.7	0.9	0.5	0.0	61.2	0.2	56.3	4.5	0.2	0.0
New Caledonia - Nouvelle-Calédonie	1990	749	88.4	65.5	65.1	6.0	4.9	12.1	0.1	9.3	0.8	0.1	7.2	..	1.2
	2000	924	83.7	54.7	54.0	3.5	3.3	22.2	0.0	15.5	0.3	0.5	14.1	0.1	0.5
	2005	1 790	74.0	50.4	50.0	2.4	2.2	19.1	0.2	24.6	0.1	0.5	23.5	0.1	0.5
New Zealand - Nouvelle-Zélande	1990	9 566	80.5	24.9	23.1	17.8	15.4	22.4	0.1	18.7	0.3	1.2	11.0	5.2	1.1
	2000	13 953	71.0	18.5	17.6	17.4	11.3	23.9	0.1	28.4	1.2	1.8	19.3	5.6	0.5
	2005	26 133	64.2	19.7	18.9	11.0	11.0	22.4	0.2	35.7	1.7	1.2	28.3	4.2	0.4
Nicaragua	1990	667	41.8	20.3	19.1	11.8	6.7	3.0	..	38.5	..	36.5	2.0	..	..
	2000	1 805	41.1	7.3	6.8	25.0	7.4	1.5	..	47.3	..	45.8	1.5	..	..
	2005	2 595	31.8	6.2	5.9	20.1	4.5	0.8	..	51.6	..	51.0	0.6	..	..
Niger	1990	389	57.7	44.5	44.1	5.8	5.9	1.5	0.0	35.4	27.8	0.1	7.0	0.5	..
	2000	774	16.0	11.7	11.6	1.8	2.1	0.4	0.3	83.2	13.7	0.2	4.9	64.4	..
	2005	837	51.9	39.1	37.2	10.6	0.5	1.7	0.2	47.8	23.5	1.2	13.2	2.5	7.5
Nigeria - Nigéria	1990	4 317	80.1	64.1	60.8	8.7	6.0	1.4	1.4	16.9	0.7	4.3	11.7	0.2	0.0
	2000	(e)5 824	67.9	50.6	48.3	11.3	4.9	1.1	4.3	27.4	4.3	4.2	17.3	1.6	0.0
	2005	(e)24 475	44.5	34.0	32.9	7.3	2.3	0.9	2.5	37.8	6.2	5.3	23.2	3.1	0.0
Norway - Norvège	1990	26 748	84.6	69.6	68.0	7.9	4.4	2.7	1.9	13.4	4.5	4.6	4.0	0.3	0.0
	2000	31 644	85.1	71.3	69.8	6.9	3.7	3.2	3.0	12.0	0.9	2.7	8.0	0.5	..
	2005	54 907	81.5	70.4	69.2	5.0	3.2	2.9	3.2	15.3	1.3	2.7	10.3	0.9	0.0
Oman	1990	2 726	60.2	31.4	29.1	9.2	16.7	2.9	0.5	37.7	0.5	0.4	9.8	27.0	..
	2000	5 039	47.1	20.2	19.3	5.4	18.1	3.4	1.0	51.9	0.6	1.3	15.8	34.2	..
	2005	(e)9 669	50.6	25.6	24.8	6.7	15.8	2.5	1.1	48.3	1.0	1.3	15.7	30.3	..
Pakistan	1990	7 383	56.1	27.8	24.9	12.8	11.9	3.6	1.5	40.8	2.3	1.0	20.3	17.2	0.0
	2000	10 722	33.5	18.1	15.4	6.1	5.7	3.6	1.0	65.3	3.0	1.2	25.3	35.7	0.1
	2005	25 410	34.3	19.1	17.1	6.0	6.4	2.7	3.0	60.6	3.2	1.7	26.7	29.0	0.0
Panama	1990	1 510	48.9	8.3	7.7	34.4	4.9	1.2	0.2	30.8	0.1	26.3	4.4	0.0	..
	2000	3 405	49.1	8.9	8.5	32.9	5.5	1.8	0.1	38.0	0.1	32.6	5.1	0.2	..
	2005	4 155	40.0	6.6	6.4	27.5	4.5	1.3	0.2	42.2	0.0	35.5	6.6	0.1	..
Papua New Guinea - Papouasie-Nouvelle-Guinée	1990	1 315	82.0	6.9	6.7	9.6	13.3	52.1	0.1	17.7	0.3	0.5	16.8	0.0	0.1
	2000	(e)1 228	62.7	3.0	2.8	2.1	4.0	53.5	0.1	36.0	0.9	0.2	34.5	0.0	0.4
	2005	(e)2 018	68.6	2.3	2.0	3.0	4.3	58.9	0.1	29.8	0.3	0.1	28.8	0.1	0.5
Paraguay	1990	1 341	44.1	16.0	15.3	12.4	15.4	0.3	0.0	53.7	4.8	34.9	14.0	0.0	..
	2000	2 255	25.3	13.1	11.4	7.2	4.5	0.5	0.0	74.7	0.2	58.0	16.4	0.1	..
	2005	3 577	19.3	10.5	6.3	5.3	2.9	0.6	0.1	78.0	0.3	51.1	26.6	0.0	..
Peru - Pérou	1990	3 172	56.1	22.8	17.4	27.8	2.3	3.4	0.3	29.9	0.3	27.6	2.0	0.0	..
	2000	8 040	48.6	14.0	13.0	24.7	6.0	3.9	0.7	50.0	1.3	38.1	10.4	0.1	0.0
	2005	13 222	36.5	12.3	11.4	18.2	3.5	2.5	1.2	61.7	3.3	41.8	16.2	0.4	0.0
Philippines	1990	12 994	56.5	12.8	12.1	19.5	18.4	5.7	0.4	43.0	0.7	2.6	28.9	10.4	0.4
	2000	34 491	52.2	9.8	9.2	18.6	18.9	4.9	0.3	46.8	0.2	0.8	38.8	6.8	0.1
	2005	47 414	47.3	8.5	7.9	19.2	17.0	2.6	0.9	51.8	0.2	1.3	44.3	5.7	0.3
Poland - Pologne	1990	8 976	68.4	63.8	55.9	1.6	2.3	0.6	22.8	8.2	0.5	0.9	5.2	1.5	..
	2000	48 940	78.3	70.9	68.7	4.4	2.2	0.8	11.5	10.2	0.6	1.3	7.7	0.5	0.0
	2005	101 389	79.5	77.0	74.8	1.2	0.9	0.4	11.8	8.5	0.4	1.2	5.8	1.1	0.0
Portugal	1990	25 105	83.0	75.3	72.0	3.9	2.6	1.2	0.2	16.6	7.4	3.6	3.2	2.4	0.0
	2000	38 224	84.6	78.4	75.4	3.1	2.6	0.5	1.0	14.5	4.6	2.8	4.8	2.1	0.0
	2005	61 154	79.0	75.2	73.4	2.2	1.2	0.4	1.6	16.3	6.9	3.6	3.5	2.3	0.0

For sources and notes, see end of table.

Pour les sources et les notes, se reporter à la fin du tableau.

Origin / Origine (Destination)	Year Année	World (millions of dollars) Monde (millions de dollars)	Developed economies Économies développées						Economies in transition Économies en transition	Developing economies Économies en développement					
			Total	Europe		USA États-Unis	Japan Japon	Other Autres		Total	Africa Afrique	America Amérique	Eastern, Southern and South-Eastern Asia Asie orientale, méridionale et du Sud-Est	Western Asia Asie occidentale	Oceania Océanie
				Total	EU UE										
									Percentage / En pourcentage						
Qatar	1990	1 695	71.8	44.8	43.3	9.5	14.6	2.9	0.6	25.6	0.4	2.1	11.4	11.8	..
	2000	3 252	61.5	37.3	35.4	10.3	11.0	2.9	0.1	37.0	0.4	1.5	18.4	16.8	..
	2005	10 499	65.3	42.8	40.6	10.3	10.4	1.8	0.2	34.4	0.6	2.0	16.0	15.8	..
Romania - Roumanie	1990	10 293	40.5	33.5	31.4	4.6	0.8	1.6	28.3	30.6	6.6	2.1	9.5	12.4	
	2000	13 054	72.5	66.4	65.1	3.0	1.3	1.8	14.3	9.5	0.6	2.3	4.4	2.3	..
	2005	40 321	69.0	63.7	62.4	2.8	1.4	1.0	15.5	15.3	0.5	1.8	7.9	5.0	0.0
Russian Federation - Fédération de Russie	2000	33 853	51.5	40.3	39.0	8.0	1.7	1.5	35.2	13.1	1.1	3.5	7.2	1.1	0.0
	2005	97 405	58.2	46.3	44.6	4.7	6.0	1.2	18.9	22.5	1.0	4.2	15.4	1.9	0.0
Rwanda	1990	288	61.0	52.2	50.7	0.7	6.9	1.2	0.2	33.2	21.1	0.3	10.6	1.2	..
	2000	251	34.5	22.4	22.3	7.9	3.8	0.4	1.6	40.8	33.9	0.0	4.2	2.7	..
	2005	(e)520	30.7	21.0	20.9	2.2	2.8	4.7	1.3	42.7	33.4	0.1	5.8	3.5	..
Saint Kitts and Nevis - Saint-Kitts-et-Nevis	1990	(e)108	87.6	26.2	25.4	52.8	3.8	4.9	..	12.4	..	11.7	0.8	..	..
	2000	(e)196	77.4	9.0	8.8	56.9	3.7	7.8	0.0	21.9	0.1	21.0	0.9	0.0	0.0
	2005	(e)296	72.1	18.5	18.1	46.9	4.2	2.5	1.6	25.5	0.1	24.2	1.1	0.2	0.0
Saint Lucia - Sainte-Lucie	1990	(e)200	84.4	27.3	26.7	45.4	7.6	4.2	0.0	15.6	..	12.5	3.1	..	..
	2000	350	68.4	17.9	17.7	40.9	4.5	5.1	0.0	31.5	0.1	26.3	4.9	0.1	0.0
	2005	(e)657	61.0	33.8	33.4	22.5	2.7	1.9	0.0	38.9	0.1	36.8	1.9	0.2	0.0
Saint Vincent and the Grenadines - Saint-Vincent-et-les Grenadines	1990	136	70.9	27.2	26.8	36.5	3.3	3.9	0.0	28.9	0.0	25.1	3.8	0.0	..
	2000	162	62.1	16.1	15.8	38.2	3.7	4.0	0.0	37.8	0.0	35.9	1.8	0.0	..
	2005	241	57.7	15.4	15.0	33.3	4.2	4.9	0.0	42.2	0.1	35.9	6.1	0.1	..
Samoa	1990	100	58.0	7.5	7.5	8.0	7.3	35.2	0.0	5.8	..	0.0	4.2	..	1.6
	2000	271	77.2	1.1	1.1	26.1	8.8	41.3	..	22.1	0.0	1.1	8.6	0.1	12.3
	2005	(e)641	76.1	1.4	1.4	13.5	7.5	53.7	0.0	23.9	0.1	0.8	16.6	0.0	6.5
São Tome and Principe - Sao Tomé-et-Principe	1990	51	99.2	65.4	59.7	28.2	4.1	1.5	..	0.8	0.2	0.2	0.3	..	..
	2000	(e)40	87.7	82.1	81.5	2.5	3.0	0.1	2.3	10.0	6.5	1.3	2.2	0.1	..
	2005	(e)64	81.9	63.3	63.2	17.3	1.1	0.2	0.9	17.2	5.6	1.8	8.9	0.9	..
Saudi Arabia - Arabie saoudite	1990	24 081	77.8	43.5	36.9	16.7	15.3	2.3	0.6	21.3	2.0	1.6	13.1	4.6	0.0
	2000	30 299	66.8	33.3	30.0	19.2	10.4	3.8	..	20.5	1.4	2.4	11.7	5.0	..
	2005	59 509	61.7	33.7	31.4	14.8	9.0	4.2	2.0	35.4	3.1	3.7	20.9	7.8	0.0
Senegal - Sénégal	1990	1 387	65.8	55.6	54.9	6.2	2.9	1.2	0.5	32.3	21.1	1.9	8.8	0.6	0.0
	2000	1 463	57.0	48.7	48.1	3.9	2.7	1.7	0.0	38.3	20.9	1.7	14.5	1.2	..
	2005	3 215	49.6	42.5	42.0	4.2	1.8	1.2	1.9	44.5	21.2	6.7	14.0	2.6	..
Serbia and Montenegro - Serbie-et-Monténégro	2000	(e)3 348	71.9	69.7	67.0	1.1	1.0	0.1	17.4	10.6	4.7	0.1	2.6	3.3	..
	2005	(e)5 758	69.2	66.0	63.0	2.5	0.2	0.5	14.1	16.8	6.5	0.5	4.8	5.0	..
Seychelles	1990	186	47.6	38.0	37.7	1.8	6.1	1.6	0.1	52.1	17.9	0.2	17.0	17.0	..
	2000	338	44.0	39.4	38.9	1.8	1.1	1.8	..	55.8	15.1	0.1	17.5	23.0	..
	2005	(e)763	43.3	38.6	38.2	3.0	0.8	0.8	1.5	46.2	16.6	0.1	12.0	17.5	..
Sierra Leone	1990	197	65.4	50.5	49.4	8.6	5.2	1.2	0.5	32.4	24.5	0.5	7.3	0.0	..
	2000	(e)316	76.4	67.8	67.5	6.4	2.0	0.3	0.1	20.0	6.6	0.6	11.9	0.8	..
	2005	(e)611	53.3	43.6	43.4	6.8	1.3	1.6	0.7	42.0	20.1	2.2	17.8	1.9	..
Singapore - Singapour	1990	60 959	54.6	15.5	14.0	16.1	20.1	2.9	0.3	44.3	0.6	1.2	32.5	10.0	0.0
	2000	134 633	48.5	13.8	11.9	15.1	17.2	2.5	0.3	50.7	0.5	0.7	42.6	6.9	0.0
	2005	189 745	38.5	13.6	12.2	12.4	10.1	2.4	0.6	60.0	0.6	1.0	48.7	9.5	0.0
Slovakia - Slovaquie	2000	14 054	75.0	70.9	69.5	2.1	1.7	0.3	19.4	4.8	0.3	0.5	3.7	0.3	0.0
	2005	35 261	80.4	78.6	77.9	0.7	1.1	0.1	13.3	6.2	0.1	0.2	5.4	0.4	0.0
Slovenia - Slovénie	2000	10 090	84.0	78.0	76.0	3.0	1.6	1.3	9.4	6.6	1.0	0.8	4.1	0.6	0.0
	2005	20 139	82.7	80.2	78.9	0.9	0.8	0.8	10.3	7.0	0.9	1.0	2.9	2.1	..
Yugoslavia, SFR (former) - Yougoslavie, RSF (anc.)	1990	19 227	70.9	63.1	60.7	4.4	2.2	1.1	14.3	14.7	3.9	2.5	5.9	2.4	0.0
Solomon Islands - Îles Salomon	1990	99	74.8	5.8	5.8	6.1	21.0	41.9	..	20.3	0.1	0.0	17.2	..	3.0
	2000	(e)124	45.9	2.5	2.3	5.1	5.3	32.9	..	40.6	0.5	0.1	33.8	..	6.1
	2005	(e)208	39.5	3.6	3.5	1.2	3.8	30.9	0.0	47.6	0.6	0.1	38.5	0.0	8.4
Somalia - Somalie	1990	394	68.8	62.6	53.6	3.2	2.3	0.7	0.3	28.2	11.3	0.3	10.2	6.3	..
	2000	(e)329	14.8	12.8	12.7	1.6	0.2	0.3	0.2	74.1	40.1	6.3	15.0	12.7	..
	2005	(e)626	4.4	2.6	2.6	1.6	0.0	0.2	0.6	81.9	40.4	7.9	15.4	18.1	..

For sources and notes, see end of table.

Pour les sources et les notes, se reporter à la fin du tableau.

Origin / Origine (Destination)	Year Année	World (millions of dollars) Monde (millions de dollars)	Developed economies Économies développées					Economies in transition Économies en transition	Developing economies Économies en développement					
			Total	Europe Total	EU UE	USA États-Unis	Japan Japon	Other Autres		Total	Africa Afrique	America Amérique	Eastern, Southern and South-Eastern Asia Asie orientale, méridionale et du Sud-Est	Western Asia Asie occiden-tale	Oceania Océanie
										Percentage / En pourcentage					
South Africa - Afrique du Sud	1990	19 136	71.8	47.1	44.4	12.5	9.7	2.5	0.0	4.9	0.4	1.9	2.5	0.1	0.0
	2000	29 355	67.4	43.2	40.6	11.9	8.0	4.4	0.4	31.8	2.1	2.4	18.4	8.9	..
	2005	59 653	63.9	40.1	38.6	7.9	6.8	9.1	0.3	35.3	3.8	4.0	25.2	2.2	0.1
Spain - Espagne	1990	87 814	78.9	65.2	63.2	8.3	4.4	1.0	1.8	18.6	6.6	4.6	5.5	1.9	0.0
	2000	144 679	75.6	67.6	65.9	4.6	2.3	1.1	2.0	22.4	7.6	4.1	7.8	2.8	0.0
	2005	288 932	71.9	66.1	63.8	2.6	2.0	1.1	3.2	24.4	7.5	4.6	9.0	3.3	0.0
Sri Lanka	1990	2 636	41.0	17.1	16.3	7.9	12.3	3.7	1.0	57.9	4.4	1.1	48.9	3.5	0.0
	2000	6 688	32.0	13.8	12.0	3.8	9.7	4.7	0.1	59.4	0.6	0.5	52.9	5.4	..
	2005	8 863	23.4	13.2	11.9	2.3	4.3	3.6	0.1	73.6	0.8	1.2	65.6	6.1	0.0
Sudan - Soudan	1990	1 305	51.1	42.8	41.3	3.6	3.9	0.8	3.5	45.4	16.2	0.1	9.5	19.5	..
	2000	(e)1 453	42.0	33.2	31.8	1.3	2.3	5.2	1.6	56.4	5.6	1.5	31.1	18.2	..
	2005	6 670	29.6	17.9	17.1	1.9	5.1	4.7	2.5	66.9	8.1	2.8	33.2	22.8	..
Suriname	1990	484	73.6	30.7	30.4	40.1	2.8	0.1	..	24.6	..	22.0	2.7	..	..
	2000	480	65.5	26.7	26.3	30.1	7.4	1.3	0.0	34.5	4.2	23.1	7.1	0.1	..
	2005	(e)915	65.1	29.4	29.1	29.3	5.2	1.3	0.0	34.9	0.1	22.3	12.2	0.4	..
Sweden - Suède	1990	49 355	88.7	72.5	62.0	9.4	5.6	1.2	2.2	9.1	0.6	2.0	5.8	0.7	0.0
	2000	72 954	90.1	79.7	70.2	6.7	2.9	0.8	1.1	8.8	0.5	1.2	6.5	0.6	0.0
	2005	111 302	83.4	76.7	67.8	3.6	2.3	0.9	3.9	10.2	0.5	1.4	7.2	1.1	0.0
Switzerland - Suisse	1990	69 705	91.7	79.5	78.8	6.1	4.4	1.8	0.7	7.6	1.7	1.1	3.7	1.0	0.0
	2000	82 543	88.0	76.3	76.0	7.8	2.8	1.0	3.0	9.0	1.7	1.2	5.4	0.7	0.0
	2005	126 523	88.6	80.2	80.0	5.6	1.9	0.9	1.1	10.2	2.3	0.9	5.7	1.2	0.0
Syrian Arab Republic - République arabe syrienne	1990	2 392	63.3	48.8	48.0	10.8	3.3	0.3	7.0	21.7	2.7	2.9	4.3	11.9	..
	2000	5 402	43.7	36.6	35.6	4.3	2.4	0.4	7.7	30.3	2.1	2.2	17.4	8.5	..
	2005	15 951	27.9	24.6	23.7	1.1	1.7	0.6	9.1	63.0	8.3	3.0	19.3	32.4	..
Tajikistan - Tadjikistan	2000	(e)671	6.0	5.7	5.7	..	0.0	0.2	89.6	4.4	0.1	..	3.3	1.0	..
	2005	1 330	12.9	11.4	10.8	0.9	0.4	0.1	70.8	16.3	0.0	2.3	10.5	3.5	..
Thailand - Thaïlande	1990	33 414	63.6	19.0	16.9	10.8	30.4	3.5	0.7	34.8	0.9	2.0	28.4	3.5	0.0
	2000	61 924	51.5	11.7	10.4	11.8	24.7	3.3	1.0	45.4	1.3	1.3	33.6	9.2	0.1
	2005	118 158	43.6	10.3	9.1	7.4	22.0	3.9	1.6	53.2	1.4	1.7	37.5	12.4	0.2
Macedonia, TFYR - Macédoine, LERY	2000	2 085	55.5	50.0	48.6	4.0	1.0	0.5	36.7	7.7	0.6	1.8	2.5	2.7	0.0
	2005	3 225	50.7	47.5	45.5	1.4	0.7	1.1	36.9	12.4	0.3	1.8	6.7	3.6	0.0
Togo	1990	581	69.8	59.0	57.2	5.3	4.3	1.1	0.2	26.1	17.0	0.8	8.1	0.2	..
	2000	(e)324	58.4	50.3	49.9	1.6	3.2	3.4	3.5	34.8	22.7	0.4	9.8	1.8	0.1
	2005	590	47.8	43.1	42.6	1.2	1.8	1.7	2.7	46.2	17.7	2.9	22.1	3.4	0.0
Tonga	1990	67	68.1	1.8	1.7	10.3	6.0	50.0	0.0	24.3	..	0.1	11.7	..	12.5
	2000	83	64.4	4.6	4.6	10.2	15.1	34.3	..	35.6	..	0.2	17.0	..	18.4
	2005	(e)128	60.2	5.4	5.4	8.4	2.4	44.0	0.0	39.8	0.1	0.9	10.4	0.0	28.3
Trinidad and Tobago - Trinité-et-Tobago	1990	1 230	69.5	17.5	16.9	40.9	3.6	7.6	0.0	29.1	3.4	21.4	4.2	0.2	0.0
	2000	2 353	53.3	11.5	11.0	34.3	3.5	4.0	0.3	46.1	3.9	37.3	4.9	0.1	0.0
	2005	(e)5 813	50.5	12.9	12.7	27.2	5.4	4.9	0.4	49.0	6.9	35.6	6.3	0.1	0.0
Tunisia - Tunisie	1990	6 128	76.1	68.0	66.8	4.9	1.6	1.6	2.5	16.2	5.4	2.5	4.4	3.8	0.0
	2000	8 601	79.4	72.4	71.4	4.6	2.0	0.4	2.7	16.4	6.5	1.6	4.7	3.6	0.0
	2005	13 173	74.6	70.2	69.1	2.5	1.6	0.3	5.3	19.2	6.4	2.4	6.3	4.1	0.0
Turkey - Turquie	1990	23 147	63.9	47.5	44.9	9.9	4.8	1.7	7.5	26.2	5.8	2.4	7.9	10.1	0.0
	2000	54 503	64.5	52.4	50.2	7.2	3.0	2.0	12.7	19.7	5.0	1.2	10.2	3.3	0.0
	2005	116 562	54.6	46.0	42.2	4.6	2.7	1.3	18.0	26.6	5.2	1.7	17.0	2.7	0.0
Turkmenistan - Turkménistan	2000	(e)1 788	25.7	14.1	13.7	3.5	8.1	0.1	38.2	29.8	..	0.1	7.3	22.5	..
	2005	(e)2 709	29.7	18.2	16.5	9.6	0.6	1.2	37.0	33.0	..	0.1	11.4	21.5	..
Uganda - Ouganda	1990	582	50.0	39.9	39.1	4.9	4.6	0.6	0.4	49.6	38.8	0.2	8.7	1.8	..
	2000	(e)955	35.2	22.0	20.1	3.2	7.1	2.9	0.4	64.7	40.7	1.4	16.5	6.1	..
	2005	(e)1 697	30.9	22.3	22.0	4.1	4.0	0.7	0.7	67.6	43.3	0.5	13.4	10.4	0.0
Ukraine	2000	(e)13 955	34.4	30.1	28.2	2.6	0.7	1.0	58.5	6.8	1.0	1.3	3.4	1.2	..
	2005	36 153	38.1	33.9	32.8	2.0	1.5	0.7	48.1	13.7	1.2	1.3	9.3	1.8	0.0
USSR (former) - URSS (anc.)	1990	58 559	73.2	59.9	58.1	5.8	4.8	2.7	7.9	18.9	2.1	1.9	11.4	3.6	..

For sources and notes, see end of table.   Pour les sources et les notes, se reporter à la fin du tableau.

Origin / Origine	Year Année	World (millions of dollars) Monde (millions de dollars)	Developed economies Économies développées					Economies in transition Économies en transition	Developing economies Économies en développement					
			Total	Europe		USA États-Unis	Japan Japon	Other Autres		Total	Africa Afrique	America Amérique	Eastern, Southern and South-Eastern Asia Asie orientale, méridionale et du Sud-Est	Western Asia Asie occiden-tale	Oceania Océanie
Destination				Total	EU UE										
			Percentage / En pourcentage												
United Arab Emirates - Émirats arabes unis	1990	11 472	60.7	34.9	33.0	9.1	14.2	2.4	0.7	35.0	0.5	1.0	24.8	8.6	..
	2000	25 464	59.5	38.8	37.2	7.9	9.6	3.3	0.6	39.4	1.0	0.7	30.9	6.9	..
	2005	(e)99 268	51.6	35.1	33.7	9.4	5.4	1.7	1.9	45.5	1.6	1.3	36.1	6.6	..
United Kingdom - Royaume-Uni	1990	223 048	85.1	65.2	58.3	11.2	5.4	3.4	1.0	13.2	2.4	1.8	7.4	1.5	0.1
	2000	334 971	78.5	57.0	51.5	13.4	4.7	3.3	1.0	20.2	2.6	1.9	13.9	1.7	0.1
	2005	482 615	71.8	56.8	50.4	8.7	3.3	3.0	2.6	23.0	3.3	1.9	14.9	2.8	0.0
United Republic of Tanzania - République-Unie de Tanzanie	1990	1 022	73.1	61.0	58.7	1.6	7.7	2.7	0.8	22.9	3.6	0.9	10.5	7.7	..
	2000	(e)1 521	45.3	23.5	22.4	3.9	9.3	8.6	0.7	53.9	20.6	2.0	20.3	11.0	0.0
	2005	(e)3 617	28.5	20.6	20.1	2.9	2.9	2.1	1.9	65.0	25.7	1.4	23.8	14.2	0.0
United States - États-Unis	1990	517 020	59.7	21.7	20.2	..	18.0	20.0	0.4	39.8	3.3	13.0	20.1	3.4	0.0
	2000	1 238 240	52.3	19.9	18.6	..	12.1	20.3	0.9	46.8	2.3	17.0	25.2	2.4	0.0
	2005	1 732 510	46.2	19.6	18.3	..	8.2	18.5	1.3	52.5	3.9	17.4	28.0	3.1	0.0
Uruguay	1990	1 317	35.7	20.5	19.7	10.5	3.3	1.5	3.4	59.2	1.0	50.1	7.0	1.1	..
	2000	3 466	32.5	19.6	18.8	9.8	1.7	1.4	3.3	63.8	3.8	51.7	7.5	0.7	..
	2005	3 879	19.7	10.9	10.4	6.7	1.1	1.0	8.1	71.8	8.7	51.9	11.1	0.1	..
Uzbekistan - Ouzbékistan	2000	(e)2 072	40.7	30.0	29.3	8.8	1.3	0.6	38.9	20.3	0.0	0.1	15.8	4.4	..
	2005	(e)3 559	26.6	22.8	21.9	2.3	1.1	0.4	44.1	29.3	0.1	0.2	24.2	4.7	..
Vanuatu	1990	286	96.6	21.9	21.8	2.3	60.9	11.5	0.0	3.2	..	0.3	1.9	0.0	0.9
	2000	(e)124	59.1	6.7	6.4	1.2	19.1	32.0	..	39.1	0.2	0.4	28.1	..	10.4
	2005	(e)268	58.6	12.3	12.2	3.7	16.6	26.0	0.0	39.4	1.3	0.2	25.4	0.1	12.4
Venezuela (Bolivarian Republic of) - (République bolivarienne du)	1990	6 682	83.4	28.7	27.1	46.7	3.9	4.2	0.1	15.4	0.0	13.2	2.1	0.1	..
	2000	17 246	54.7	16.2	15.6	33.5	2.7	2.3	0.2	25.6	0.6	21.4	3.6	0.1	..
	2005	24 029	51.7	14.8	13.7	31.6	3.3	2.1	0.2	46.1	0.2	39.2	6.4	0.2	0.0
Viet Nam	1990	2 842	20.0	13.5	13.1	0.0	5.9	0.5	7.7	29.9	0.1	0.2	29.6	..	..
	2000	15 637	29.2	9.6	8.7	2.3	14.7	2.6	2.4	67.7	0.3	0.4	66.0	0.9	0.0
	2005	36 978	25.0	9.4	7.0	2.3	11.1	2.1	2.6	70.4	0.3	0.9	67.6	1.6	..
Yemen - Yémen	1990	(e)2 385	47.1	31.1	30.6	5.1	4.2	6.7	10.3	42.5	5.4	0.8	16.6	19.7	..
	2000	(e)2 323	33.8	23.3	18.6	4.4	3.2	3.0	0.3	63.3	5.7	3.6	19.0	35.0	..
	2005	4 800	31.2	23.4	14.8	4.5	2.0	1.3	1.5	66.3	5.4	5.1	15.5	40.3	0.0
Zambia - Zambie	1990	1 218	57.8	40.1	38.9	10.1	6.7	1.0	0.2	42.0	31.5	0.2	7.1	3.1	0.0
	2000	1 101	23.8	14.3	13.4	5.0	3.2	1.3	0.0	75.5	69.1	0.3	4.5	1.6	0.0
	2005	2 561	28.2	23.2	22.4	1.6	1.6	1.8	0.0	71.7	59.0	0.4	8.5	3.9	0.0
Zimbabwe	1990	1 849	48.8	32.7	30.6	6.9	4.5	4.7	0.5	39.3	32.9	1.4	4.9	0.1	0.0
	2000	1 842	28.9	17.6	16.4	5.9	4.0	1.4	0.2	59.9	49.8	1.1	7.9	1.1	0.1
	2005	2 440	10.9	7.5	7.1	2.0	0.8	0.6	0.0	79.1	64.3	0.1	10.1	4.6	..

Sources:
- International Monetary Fund, *Direction of Trade Statistics*

Sources :
- Fonds monétaire international, *Direction of Trade Statistics*

Destination / Product group	Year / Année	World / Monde	Developed economies / Économies développées							Economies in transition / Économies en transition
			Total	Europe		Canada	USA / États-Unis	Japan / Japon	Other developed countries / Autres économies développées	
				Total	EU / UE					
Millions of dollars										
All products	1995	5 050 560	3 406 575	2 115 229	1 993 742	164 406	743 402	293 060	90 478	111 427
	2000	6 291 022	4 233 117	2 387 189	2 253 723	231 450	1 173 878	329 497	111 103	110 852
	2005	10 250 631	6 635 134	4 090 839	3 863 192	303 061	1 592 158	472 135	176 941	310 990
Share by destination (percentage)										
All products	1995	100.0	67.4	41.9	39.5	3.3	14.7	5.8	1.8	2.2
	2000	100.0	67.3	37.9	35.8	3.7	18.7	5.2	1.8	1.8
	2005	100.0	64.7	39.9	37.7	3.0	15.5	4.6	1.7	3.0
All food items	1995	100.0	68.4	48.1	46.5	2.0	7.5	9.6	1.1	4.9
(SITC 0 + 1 + 22 + 4)	2000	100.0	66.1	41.9	40.4	2.8	10.8	9.2	1.3	3.4
	2005	100.0	67.9	47.3	45.8	2.6	10.1	6.5	1.4	5.0
Agricultural raw materials	1995	100.0	68.3	41.3	39.5	2.1	11.7	12.2	1.0	1.2
(SITC 2 - 22 - 27 - 28)	2000	100.0	66.2	38.9	37.5	2.8	14.6	8.9	1.0	1.6
	2005	100.0	60.9	38.1	36.6	2.3	13.2	6.4	0.9	2.2
Ores and metals	1995	100.0	69.8	44.9	42.1	3.1	10.4	10.5	0.9	1.9
(SITC 27 + 28 + 68)	2000	100.0	65.7	40.7	38.1	3.2	12.3	8.6	0.9	1.9
	2005	100.0	59.5	38.6	35.5	2.6	9.9	7.7	0.7	2.2
Fuels (SITC 3)	1995	100.0	64.3	34.2	32.2	1.3	16.4	11.4	1.0	3.2
	2000	100.0	65.6	32.8	30.5	1.4	21.0	9.2	1.1	1.9
	2005	100.0	66.1	34.6	31.7	1.7	19.3	9.2	1.3	1.8
Manufactured goods	1995	100.0	67.9	42.1	39.6	3.6	15.8	4.4	2.0	1.8
(SITC 5 to 8 less 68)	2000	100.0	67.9	38.1	36.1	4.1	19.4	4.2	1.9	1.5
	2005	100.0	65.1	40.5	38.4	3.3	15.9	3.5	1.9	3.1
Share by major product group (percentage)										
All products	1995	100.0	100.0	100.0	100.0	100.0	100.0	100.0	100.0	100.0
	2000	100.0	100.0	100.0	100.0	100.0	100.0	100.0	100.0	100.0
	2005	100.0	100.0	100.0	100.0	100.0	100.0	100.0	100.0	100.0
All food items	1995	9.0	9.1	10.3	10.6	5.6	4.6	14.9	5.6	20.0
(SITC 0 + 1 + 22 + 4)	2000	6.7	6.6	7.4	7.5	5.1	3.9	11.8	5.1	12.8
	2005	6.4	6.8	7.6	7.8	5.7	4.2	9.2	5.1	10.6
Agricultural raw materials	1995	2.7	2.7	2.6	2.7	1.7	2.1	5.6	1.5	1.5
(SITC 2 - 22 - 27 - 28)	2000	1.8	1.8	1.9	1.9	1.4	1.4	3.1	1.1	1.6
	2005	1.6	1.5	1.5	1.5	1.2	1.3	2.2	0.8	1.1
Ores and metals	1995	3.3	3.4	3.5	3.5	3.1	2.3	5.9	1.6	2.8
(SITC 27 + 28 + 68)	2000	2.8	2.8	3.0	3.0	2.4	1.9	4.6	1.5	3.1
	2005	3.3	3.0	3.2	3.1	2.9	2.1	5.5	1.4	2.5
Fuels (SITC 3)	1995	7.5	7.1	6.1	6.1	3.0	8.3	14.6	4.1	10.8
	2000	10.6	10.3	9.2	9.0	4.1	12.0	18.6	6.8	11.5
	2005	13.3	13.5	11.5	11.1	7.5	16.5	26.5	9.6	7.6
Manufactured goods	1995	74.7	75.3	75.1	74.9	83.6	80.0	57.1	84.3	61.4
(SITC 5 to 8 less 68)	2000	75.3	76.0	75.7	75.9	84.7	78.5	60.9	82.4	65.1
	2005	71.7	72.2	72.8	73.2	79.3	73.6	54.8	79.6	73.7

Sources:
- UNCTAD secretariat calculations based on UN DESA Statistics Division's data

2.2.A Structure des exportations par partenaires et groupes de produits
Monde

			Developing economies — Économies en développement								Destination
				Asia — Asie							
Total	Africa Afrique	America Amérique	Total	Eastern, Southern and South-Eastern Asia Asie orientale, méridionale et du Sud-Est	China Chine	Western Asia Asie occidentale	Oceania Océanie	Major petroleum exporters Principaux exportateurs de pétrole	Major exporters of manufactures Principaux exportateurs d'articles manufacturés	Year Année	Groupes de produits
Millions de dollars											
1 406 221	115 068	242 694	1 042 845	924 806	145 672	118 039	5 615	165 334	974 805	1995	Total tous produits
1 763 114	127 705	359 831	1 268 841	1 118 697	207 436	150 143	6 738	181 032	1 274 974	2000	
3 111 472	240 623	488 785	2 368 993	2 052 445	574 616	316 548	13 070	409 946	2 179 995	2005	
Parts par destinations (en pourcentage)											
27.8	2.3	4.8	20.6	18.3	2.9	2.3	0.1	3.3	19.3	1995	Total tous produits
28.0	2.0	5.7	20.2	17.8	3.3	2.4	0.1	2.9	20.3	2000	
30.4	2.3	4.8	23.1	20.0	5.6	3.1	0.1	4.0	21.3	2005	
25.4	3.8	4.8	16.5	13.1	2.3	3.4	0.2	5.2	13.0	1995	Produits alimentaires
26.8	4.0	6.0	16.6	12.7	2.2	3.9	0.2	5.8	13.4	2000	(CTCI 0 + 1 + 22 + 4)
26.3	4.4	5.1	16.6	12.6	2.8	4.0	0.2	6.0	12.7	2005	
30.1	2.3	3.7	24.0	22.1	5.4	1.9	0.0	3.0	22.6	1995	Matières premières
31.5	2.2	4.4	24.9	22.6	7.7	2.3	0.0	3.1	23.8	2000	d'origine agricole
36.2	2.5	4.0	29.7	27.0	13.4	2.6	0.1	3.0	27.6	2005	(CTCI 2 - 22 - 27 - 28)
25.8	1.2	3.0	21.6	19.5	3.3	2.2	0.0	2.4	20.7	1995	Minerais et métaux
27.3	1.2	3.7	22.4	20.4	5.4	2.0	0.0	2.0	22.6	2000	(CTCI 27 + 28 + 68)
35.9	1.4	3.4	31.0	28.3	12.6	2.7	0.1	2.6	30.3	2005	
19.1	1.6	4.6	12.7	11.5	1.5	1.2	0.2	1.3	12.7	1995	Combustibles (CTCI 3)
26.8	2.1	5.2	19.2	17.6	2.3	1.6	0.3	1.5	19.2	2000	
26.9	1.8	4.5	20.4	18.6	3.7	1.8	0.2	2.4	18.7	2005	
29.3	2.2	5.0	22.0	19.6	3.0	2.4	0.1	3.4	20.7	1995	Articles manufacturés
28.5	1.9	5.9	20.6	18.2	3.4	2.4	0.1	2.9	21.0	2000	(CTCI 5 à 8 moins 68)
31.4	2.3	4.9	24.0	20.7	5.9	3.3	0.1	4.2	22.3	2005	
Parts par principaux groupes de produits (en pourcentage)											
100.0	100.0	100.0	100.0	100.0	100.0	100.0	100.0	100.0	100.0	1995	Total tous produits
100.0	100.0	100.0	100.0	100.0	100.0	100.0	100.0	100.0	100.0	2000	
100.0	100.0	100.0	100.0	100.0	100.0	100.0	100.0	100.0	100.0	2005	
8.2	15.1	9.0	7.2	6.4	7.2	13.0	14.4	14.1	6.0	1995	Produits alimentaires
6.4	13.3	7.0	5.5	4.8	4.4	11.0	10.8	13.4	4.4	2000	(CTCI 0 + 1 + 22 + 4)
5.6	12.0	7.0	4.6	4.1	3.2	8.3	9.1	9.7	3.8	2005	
2.9	2.7	2.1	3.1	3.2	5.0	2.2	0.9	2.4	3.1	1995	Matières premières
2.0	2.0	1.4	2.2	2.3	4.3	1.7	0.8	1.9	2.1	2000	d'origine agricole
1.9	1.7	1.3	2.0	2.1	3.7	1.3	1.1	1.2	2.0	2005	(CTCI 2 - 22 - 27 - 28)
3.0	1.7	2.0	3.4	3.5	3.8	3.1	0.5	2.4	3.5	1995	Minerais et métaux
2.8	1.7	1.8	3.1	3.3	4.7	2.3	0.5	2.0	3.2	2000	(CTCI 27 + 28 + 68)
3.9	2.0	2.4	4.4	4.7	7.5	2.9	1.3	2.1	4.7	2005	
5.1	5.2	7.2	4.6	4.7	3.8	3.8	11.2	2.9	4.9	1995	Combustibles (CTCI 3)
10.1	10.8	9.7	10.1	10.5	7.5	7.1	25.7	5.5	10.0	2000	
11.8	10.0	12.5	11.7	12.3	8.7	7.9	18.5	7.8	11.7	2005	
78.6	73.6	77.5	79.5	79.9	78.6	76.3	70.6	76.7	80.1	1995	Articles manufacturés
76.7	70.7	77.6	77.1	77.3	77.8	76.0	58.8	75.5	78.2	2000	(CTCI 5 à 8 moins 68)
74.2	71.4	74.0	74.5	74.3	75.0	76.3	64.0	76.0	75.2	2005	

Sources :
- Calculs du secrétariat de la CNUCED sur la base des données de ONU DAES Division de statistique

Origin / Product group	Year Année	World Monde	Developed economies — Économies développées — Total	Europe Total	Europe EU UE	Canada	USA États-Unis	Japan Japon	Other developed countries Autres économies développées	Economies in transition Économies en transition
Millions of dollars										
All products	1995	5 072 820	3 493 676	2 109 173	1 973 446	197 170	627 086	472 431	87 816	129 026
	2000	6 454 799	3 956 888	2 232 560	2 081 092	285 146	813 598	512 264	113 320	167 449
	2005	10 481 371	6 053 649	3 934 563	3 662 759	360 983	919 645	659 872	178 587	384 087
Share by origin (percentage)										
All products	1995	100.0	68.9	41.6	38.9	3.9	12.4	9.3	1.7	2.5
	2000	100.0	61.3	34.6	32.2	4.4	12.6	7.9	1.8	2.6
	2005	100.0	57.8	37.5	34.9	3.4	8.8	6.3	1.7	3.7
All food items	1995	100.0	66.2	44.1	42.3	3.6	13.9	0.5	4.1	2.1
(SITC 0 + 1 + 22 + 4)	2000	100.0	61.6	38.2	36.4	4.5	13.3	0.5	5.0	2.1
	2005	100.0	62.3	43.4	41.5	3.7	10.1	0.5	4.7	2.6
Agricultural raw materials	1995	100.0	66.0	30.0	28.9	12.3	16.6	1.6	5.4	5.6
(SITC 2 - 22 - 27 - 28)	2000	100.0	63.4	27.7	26.7	14.1	14.4	1.8	5.4	5.5
	2005	100.0	61.5	32.3	31.5	10.3	12.6	1.8	4.4	6.9
Ores and metals	1995	100.0	60.2	33.9	30.5	7.5	9.2	2.8	6.9	9.7
(SITC 27 + 28 + 68)	2000	100.0	53.6	28.5	24.8	6.5	7.8	3.2	7.7	13.0
	2005	100.0	51.2	27.8	25.0	5.6	6.3	3.0	8.6	9.9
Fuels (SITC 3)	1995	100.0	29.6	18.8	13.5	4.3	3.2	0.5	2.8	9.2
	2000	100.0	26.7	17.0	11.7	5.0	2.1	0.3	2.4	8.5
	2005	100.0	27.6	18.0	13.4	4.9	2.2	0.3	2.2	11.8
Manufactured goods	1995	100.0	73.5	44.3	41.9	3.2	13.1	12.1	0.9	1.4
(SITC 5 to 8 less 68)	2000	100.0	66.2	36.7	34.8	3.8	14.4	10.2	1.0	1.2
	2005	100.0	63.0	40.8	38.9	2.8	10.1	8.4	0.9	1.8
Share by major product group (percentage)										
All products	1995	100.0	100.0	100.0	100.0	100.0	100.0	100.0	100.0	100.0
	2000	100.0	100.0	100.0	100.0	100.0	100.0	100.0	100.0	100.0
	2005	100.0	100.0	100.0	100.0	100.0	100.0	100.0	100.0	100.0
All food items	1995	9.1	8.8	9.7	9.9	8.5	10.3	0.5	21.5	7.6
(SITC 0 + 1 + 22 + 4)	2000	6.9	7.0	7.7	7.8	7.1	7.4	0.5	19.6	5.6
	2005	6.6	7.2	7.7	7.9	7.1	7.7	0.5	18.3	4.8
Agricultural raw materials	1995	2.9	2.8	2.1	2.2	9.3	4.0	0.5	9.3	6.5
(SITC 2 - 22 - 27 - 28)	2000	2.0	2.1	1.6	1.7	6.5	2.3	0.5	6.3	4.3
	2005	1.7	1.8	1.4	1.5	5.0	2.4	0.5	4.3	3.1
Ores and metals	1995	3.7	3.2	3.0	2.9	7.1	2.7	1.1	14.7	14.1
(SITC 27 + 28 + 68)	2000	3.2	2.8	2.6	2.4	4.6	2.0	1.3	14.0	15.9
	2005	3.6	3.2	2.6	2.5	5.8	2.5	1.7	17.8	9.6
Fuels (SITC 3)	1995	7.5	3.2	3.4	2.6	8.4	1.9	0.4	12.2	27.1
	2000	10.4	4.5	5.1	3.8	11.8	1.7	0.3	14.1	34.0
	2005	13.6	6.5	6.5	5.2	19.4	3.4	0.6	17.9	44.1
Manufactured goods	1995	74.0	79.0	78.8	79.6	61.5	78.5	95.8	37.6	41.0
(SITC 5 to 8 less 68)	2000	74.4	80.3	78.9	80.3	63.7	85.2	96.0	42.2	35.4
	2005	71.3	77.8	77.6	79.5	57.7	82.0	95.3	37.9	34.2

Sources:
- UNCTAD secretariat calculations based on UN DESA Statistics Division's data

| | | | Developing economies / Économies en développement | | | | | | | | Origine |
Total	Africa Afrique	America Amérique	Asia Asie — Total	Eastern, Southern and South-Eastern Asia / Asie orientale, méridionale et du Sud-Est	China Chine	Western Asia / Asie occidentale	Oceania Océanie	Major petroleum exporters / Principaux exportateurs de pétrole	Major exporters of manufactures / Principaux exportateurs d'articles manufacturés	Year Année	Groupes de produits
Millions de dollars											
1 394 617	110 396	242 352	1 036 920	906 735	230 441	130 185	4 950	240 018	959 776	1995	**Total tous produits**
2 100 706	157 539	379 517	1 559 346	1 340 726	412 472	218 619	4 304	394 949	1 451 013	2000	
3 906 929	311 792	613 479	2 973 939	2 531 416	1 049 359	442 523	7 718	747 966	2 702 038	2005	
Parts par origines (en pourcentage)											
27.5	2.2	4.8	20.4	17.9	4.5	2.6	0.1	4.7	18.9	1995	**Total tous produits**
32.5	2.4	5.9	24.2	20.8	6.4	3.4	0.1	6.1	22.5	2000	
37.3	3.0	5.9	28.4	24.2	10.0	4.2	0.1	7.1	25.8	2005	
31.4	3.8	12.5	14.8	13.4	2.7	1.4	0.3	2.2	15.9	1995	Produits alimentaires
33.5	3.9	13.9	15.4	13.9	3.6	1.5	0.2	2.7	16.6	2000	(CTCI 0 + 1 + 22 + 4)
34.9	4.0	15.3	15.4	13.6	3.7	1.8	0.2	2.9	17.4	2005	
28.1	4.3	6.5	16.9	16.3	2.3	0.6	0.5	3.8	15.1	1995	Matières premières
28.6	4.5	7.0	16.8	16.2	3.0	0.7	0.3	4.2	15.3	2000	d'origine agricole
31.4	4.7	7.9	18.5	17.7	3.1	0.8	0.3	4.8	16.9	2005	(CTCI 2 - 22 - 27 - 28)
29.5	5.1	12.5	11.3	9.2	2.4	2.1	0.5	4.1	12.9	1995	Minerais et métaux
30.9	6.1	12.1	12.5	10.5	2.9	2.0	0.3	4.1	13.6	2000	(CTCI 27 + 28 + 68)
38.5	6.2	15.4	16.7	14.5	4.1	2.2	0.3	5.1	17.6	2005	
57.5	11.6	8.2	37.5	14.6	1.6	22.8	0.2	44.0	9.0	1995	Combustibles (CTCI 3)
59.2	11.7	9.8	37.6	13.1	1.3	24.5	0.1	45.2	8.8	2000	
54.9	12.2	8.5	34.1	12.7	1.2	21.3	0.1	40.3	9.4	2005	
24.3	0.8	3.1	20.4	19.6	5.4	0.8	0.0	1.2	21.1	1995	Articles manufacturés
29.6	0.8	4.3	24.4	23.6	7.8	0.9	0.0	1.3	26.0	2000	(CTCI 5 à 8 moins 68)
35.1	0.9	4.0	30.1	28.6	13.1	1.5	0.0	1.6	30.9	2005	
Parts par principaux groupes de produits (en pourcentage)											
100.0	100.0	100.0	100.0	100.0	100.0	100.0	100.0	100.0	100.0	1995	**Total tous produits**
100.0	100.0	100.0	100.0	100.0	100.0	100.0	100.0	100.0	100.0	2000	
100.0	100.0	100.0	100.0	100.0	100.0	100.0	100.0	100.0	100.0	2005	
10.4	15.7	23.9	6.6	6.8	5.5	5.0	26.1	4.3	7.7	1995	Produits alimentaires
7.1	11.1	16.4	4.4	4.7	3.9	3.1	23.7	3.0	5.1	2000	(CTCI 0 + 1 + 22 + 4)
6.2	8.9	17.4	3.6	3.7	2.4	2.9	21.6	2.7	4.5	2005	
3.0	5.8	4.0	2.4	2.7	1.5	0.7	14.7	2.4	2.4	1995	Matières premières
1.8	3.8	2.4	1.4	1.6	0.9	0.4	9.1	1.4	1.4	2000	d'origine agricole
1.4	2.6	2.2	1.1	1.2	0.5	0.3	7.7	1.1	1.1	2005	(CTCI 2 - 22 - 27 - 28)
4.0	8.7	9.7	2.0	1.9	1.9	3.0	19.6	3.2	2.5	1995	Minerais et métaux
3.0	7.9	6.5	1.6	1.6	1.4	1.9	13.8	2.1	1.9	2000	(CTCI 27 + 28 + 68)
3.7	7.4	9.3	2.1	2.1	1.5	1.8	12.5	2.5	2.4	2005	
15.7	40.1	13.0	13.8	6.2	2.6	66.9	13.4	69.9	3.6	1995	Combustibles (CTCI 3)
18.9	49.8	17.2	16.1	6.6	2.0	74.9	17.6	76.6	4.1	2000	
20.1	56.0	19.9	16.4	7.2	1.6	68.9	14.0	77.0	5.0	2005	
65.4	25.6	47.4	74.0	81.2	87.9	23.6	18.0	19.1	82.4	1995	Articles manufacturés
67.7	24.8	54.8	75.3	84.4	91.2	19.3	27.2	16.3	85.9	2000	(CTCI 5 à 8 moins 68)
67.1	22.7	48.5	75.6	84.5	93.4	24.9	32.5	15.6	85.6	2005	

Sources :
- Calculs du secrétariat de la CNUCED sur la base des données de ONU DAES Division de statistique

2.2.B Export structure by partner and product group
Developed economies

Destination / Product group	Year Année	World Monde	Developed economies — Économies développées: Total	Europe: Total	Europe: EU UE	Canada	USA États-Unis	Japan Japon	Other developed countries Autres économies développées	Economies in transition Économies en transition
Millions of dollars										
All products	1995	3 515 731	2 565 735	1 790 224	1 684 603	148 139	425 792	133 578	68 003	58 944
	2000	4 101 401	3 055 731	2 011 515	1 903 589	207 664	631 806	129 215	75 531	60 187
	2005	6 155 118	4 520 333	3 215 111	3 039 712	257 037	793 784	146 493	107 907	177 782
Share by destination (percentage)										
All products	1995	100.0	73.0	50.9	47.9	4.2	12.1	3.8	1.9	1.7
	2000	100.0	74.5	49.0	46.4	5.1	15.4	3.2	1.8	1.5
	2005	100.0	73.4	52.2	49.4	4.2	12.9	2.4	1.8	2.9
All food items	1995	100.0	75.2	58.5	56.6	2.6	5.2	7.7	1.1	4.1
(SITC 0 + 1 + 22 + 4)	2000	100.0	75.7	54.6	52.8	3.7	8.2	7.8	1.3	2.7
	2005	100.0	78.0	60.1	58.0	3.5	7.9	5.2	1.3	3.5
Agricultural raw materials	1995	100.0	75.6	48.0	45.8	2.9	12.2	11.5	1.1	0.7
(SITC 2 - 22 - 27 - 28)	2000	100.0	73.4	44.2	42.7	4.0	16.1	7.9	1.1	1.0
	2005	100.0	68.8	45.6	43.6	3.2	14.0	5.0	0.9	1.8
Ores and metals	1995	100.0	75.8	53.6	50.8	4.2	10.5	6.4	1.0	0.7
(SITC 27 + 28 + 68)	2000	100.0	73.9	49.5	46.9	4.4	13.2	6.1	0.8	0.9
	2005	100.0	68.1	48.5	45.9	3.4	10.5	5.1	0.7	1.2
Fuels (SITC 3)	1995	100.0	81.7	55.1	51.6	2.8	18.5	4.6	0.7	1.6
	2000	100.0	85.1	52.9	50.2	3.3	25.5	2.6	0.7	0.6
	2005	100.0	84.7	54.5	51.6	3.4	23.8	2.4	0.6	0.6
Manufactured goods	1995	100.0	72.8	50.4	47.3	4.5	12.7	3.0	2.2	1.5
(SITC 5 to 8 less 68)	2000	100.0	74.0	48.6	46.0	5.4	15.4	2.6	2.0	1.5
	2005	100.0	72.6	51.7	48.8	4.4	12.5	1.9	1.9	3.2
Share by major product group (percentage)										
All products	1995	100.0	100.0	100.0	100.0	100.0	100.0	100.0	100.0	100.0
	2000	100.0	100.0	100.0	100.0	100.0	100.0	100.0	100.0	100.0
	2005	100.0	100.0	100.0	100.0	100.0	100.0	100.0	100.0	100.0
All food items	1995	8.7	9.0	10.0	10.3	5.4	3.7	17.7	5.0	21.1
(SITC 0 + 1 + 22 + 4)	2000	6.8	6.9	7.6	7.8	4.9	3.6	16.8	5.0	12.4
	2005	6.9	7.3	7.9	8.1	5.7	4.2	15.1	5.2	8.4
Agricultural raw materials	1995	2.6	2.7	2.4	2.5	1.8	2.6	7.8	1.4	1.1
(SITC 2 - 22 - 27 - 28)	2000	1.9	1.8	1.7	1.7	1.5	2.0	4.7	1.1	1.3
	2005	1.6	1.5	1.4	1.4	1.3	1.8	3.5	0.9	1.0
Ores and metals	1995	3.0	3.1	3.1	3.1	2.9	2.6	5.0	1.6	1.2
(SITC 27 + 28 + 68)	2000	2.6	2.6	2.7	2.7	2.3	2.3	5.1	1.2	1.5
	2005	3.0	2.8	2.8	2.8	2.4	2.4	6.4	1.1	1.2
Fuels (SITC 3)	1995	3.3	3.7	3.6	3.6	2.2	5.1	4.0	1.2	3.1
	2000	4.7	5.4	5.1	5.1	3.1	7.8	4.0	1.9	2.0
	2005	6.5	7.5	6.8	6.8	5.3	12.0	6.7	2.1	1.4
Manufactured goods	1995	79.1	78.9	78.3	78.1	84.5	82.7	63.3	87.9	72.2
(SITC 5 to 8 less 68)	2000	80.7	80.2	80.0	80.0	85.8	80.5	67.7	87.8	81.6
	2005	77.8	76.9	77.0	76.9	81.9	75.6	63.6	86.4	86.2

Sources:
- UNCTAD secretariat calculations based on UN DESA Statistics Division's data

			Developing economies Économies en développement							Destination	
Total	Africa Afrique	America Amérique	Asia Asie Total	Eastern, Southern and South-Eastern Asia Asie orientale, méridionale et du Sud-Est	China Chine	Western Asia Asie occidentale	Oceania Océanie	Major petroleum exporters Principaux exportateurs de pétrole	Major exporters of manufactures Principaux exportateurs d'articles manufacturés	Year Année	Groupes de produits
Millions de dollars											
817 017	79 034	166 844	566 852	490 910	58 362	75 941	4 287	106 255	556 904	1995	Total tous produits
931 677	78 450	251 890	597 598	506 400	76 590	91 198	3 739	104 169	670 938	2000	
1 399 859	133 285	303 168	955 997	777 658	208 129	178 339	7 409	201 376	966 311	2005	
Parts par destinations (en pourcentage)											
23.2	2.2	4.7	16.1	14.0	1.7	2.2	0.1	3.0	15.8	1995	Total tous produits
22.7	1.9	6.1	14.6	12.3	1.9	2.2	0.1	2.5	16.4	2000	
22.7	2.2	4.9	15.5	12.6	3.4	2.9	0.1	3.3	15.7	2005	
19.1	3.6	4.1	11.2	8.6	1.3	2.6	0.2	4.0	9.8	1995	Produits alimentaires
20.2	3.5	5.3	11.2	8.3	1.2	2.9	0.2	4.5	10.4	2000	(CTCI 0 + 1 + 22 + 4)
17.5	2.9	4.6	9.7	7.3	1.6	2.4	0.2	3.7	9.3	2005	
23.1	2.0	3.4	17.7	16.2	3.7	1.5	0.0	2.7	17.1	1995	Matières premières
24.8	1.7	4.6	18.4	16.5	4.6	1.9	0.1	2.7	18.8	2000	d'origine agricole
28.6	2.0	4.2	22.2	19.9	9.8	2.3	0.1	2.6	22.2	2005	(CTCI 2 - 22 - 27 - 28)
19.8	1.0	2.2	16.5	14.5	1.7	2.0	0.0	1.9	16.2	1995	Minerais et métaux
20.6	1.0	3.0	16.5	15.4	3.6	1.1	0.0	1.3	17.7	2000	(CTCI 27 + 28 + 68)
27.5	1.0	2.6	23.8	22.0	10.2	1.8	0.1	1.6	24.3	2005	
12.7	1.5	3.7	7.2	6.4	0.4	0.8	0.3	1.3	8.4	1995	Combustibles (CTCI 3)
10.5	1.4	3.8	5.1	4.3	0.5	0.9	0.2	0.9	7.3	2000	
10.9	1.7	3.7	5.4	4.3	0.6	1.1	0.1	1.4	6.5	2005	
24.5	2.2	5.0	17.1	14.9	1.7	2.2	0.1	3.1	16.9	1995	Articles manufacturés
23.8	1.9	6.5	15.3	13.0	1.9	2.3	0.1	2.6	17.3	2000	(CTCI 5 à 8 moins 68)
23.8	2.2	5.2	16.3	13.1	3.4	3.2	0.1	3.5	16.5	2005	
Parts par principaux groupes de produits (en pourcentage)											
100.0	100.0	100.0	100.0	100.0	100.0	100.0	100.0	100.0	100.0	1995	Total tous produits
100.0	100.0	100.0	100.0	100.0	100.0	100.0	100.0	100.0	100.0	2000	
100.0	100.0	100.0	100.0	100.0	100.0	100.0	100.0	100.0	100.0	2005	
7.1	13.9	7.5	6.0	5.3	6.6	10.5	16.3	11.5	5.4	1995	Produits alimentaires
6.1	12.6	5.8	5.3	4.6	4.3	8.9	15.5	12.0	4.3	2000	(CTCI 0 + 1 + 22 + 4)
5.3	9.3	6.4	4.3	4.0	3.3	5.7	12.1	7.8	4.1	2005	
2.6	2.2	1.9	2.8	3.0	5.7	1.8	1.0	2.3	2.8	1995	Matières premières
2.0	1.7	1.4	2.4	2.5	4.6	1.6	1.2	2.0	2.1	2000	d'origine agricole
2.1	1.5	1.4	2.3	2.6	4.8	1.3	1.8	1.3	2.3	2005	(CTCI 2 - 22 - 27 - 28)
2.5	1.4	1.4	3.0	3.1	3.0	2.8	0.5	1.9	3.0	1995	Minerais et métaux
2.4	1.4	1.3	3.0	3.3	5.0	1.3	0.6	1.3	2.8	2000	(CTCI 27 + 28 + 68)
3.6	1.4	1.6	4.6	5.2	9.0	1.8	2.1	1.5	4.6	2005	
1.8	2.2	2.6	1.5	1.5	0.8	1.3	6.9	1.4	1.8	1995	Combustibles (CTCI 3)
2.2	3.4	2.9	1.7	1.6	1.2	1.8	11.4	1.6	2.1	2000	
3.1	5.1	4.9	2.3	2.2	1.1	2.4	6.5	2.8	2.7	2005	
83.3	78.3	83.8	83.9	84.2	81.1	81.7	73.0	81.1	84.2	1995	Articles manufacturés
84.4	79.4	85.2	84.9	84.9	82.8	84.7	65.3	81.2	85.4	2000	(CTCI 5 à 8 moins 68)
81.4	79.2	82.0	81.6	80.8	77.2	85.2	71.0	82.3	81.7	2005	

Sources :
- Calculs du secrétariat de la CNUCED sur la base des données de ONU DAES Division de statistique

Origin / Product group	Year / Année	World / Monde	Developed economies / Économies développées							Economies in transition / Économies en transition
			Total	Europe		Canada	USA / États-Unis	Japan / Japon	Other developed countries / Autres économies développées	
				Total	EU / UE					
Millions of dollars										
All products	**1995**	**3 508 985**	**2 564 724**	**1 748 533**	**1 637 594**	**177 045**	**356 063**	**230 110**	**52 973**	**65 474**
	2000	**4 496 517**	**3 043 483**	**1 989 528**	**1 864 619**	**262 168**	**454 289**	**268 160**	**69 338**	**95 596**
	2005	**6 888 884**	**4 433 873**	**3 229 912**	**3 010 090**	**328 854**	**494 598**	**281 147**	**99 361**	**221 605**
Share by origin (percentage)										
All products	**1995**	**100.0**	**73.1**	**49.8**	**46.7**	**5.0**	**10.1**	**6.6**	**1.5**	**1.9**
	2000	**100.0**	**67.7**	**44.2**	**41.5**	**5.8**	**10.1**	**6.0**	**1.5**	**2.1**
	2005	**100.0**	**64.4**	**46.9**	**43.7**	**4.8**	**7.2**	**4.1**	**1.4**	**3.2**
All food items	1995	100.0	70.7	52.9	50.8	3.7	10.7	0.2	3.3	1.2
(SITC 0 + 1 + 22 + 4)	2000	100.0	69.2	49.9	47.8	4.9	10.2	0.2	3.9	1.4
	2005	100.0	70.3	54.7	52.6	4.2	7.2	0.2	4.0	1.4
Agricultural raw materials	1995	100.0	72.1	37.9	36.4	16.0	13.3	0.5	4.5	4.9
(SITC 2 - 22 - 27 - 28)	2000	100.0	71.8	37.5	36.4	18.3	11.2	0.7	4.1	4.4
	2005	100.0	68.4	42.8	41.8	13.9	7.9	0.6	3.1	5.2
Ores and metals	1995	100.0	64.7	41.5	37.1	9.4	7.8	0.6	5.5	10.0
(SITC 27 + 28 + 68)	2000	100.0	60.4	38.3	33.7	8.5	6.9	0.9	5.8	13.5
	2005	100.0	59.8	40.3	36.3	8.1	5.5	0.7	5.2	9.7
Fuels (SITC 3)	1995	100.0	36.5	25.4	17.8	6.1	2.3	0.1	2.6	7.0
	2000	100.0	35.5	24.7	17.2	7.3	1.3	0.1	2.1	8.2
	2005	100.0	35.9	25.4	18.8	7.1	1.5	0.1	1.8	12.4
Manufactured goods	1995	100.0	77.6	52.7	49.9	4.3	11.0	8.7	0.8	0.9
(SITC 5 to 8 less 68)	2000	100.0	72.0	46.5	44.3	5.0	11.7	7.8	1.0	0.9
	2005	100.0	69.1	50.3	48.0	3.9	8.5	5.6	0.9	1.3
Share by major product group (percentage)										
All products	**1995**	**100.0**	**100.0**	**100.0**	**100.0**	**100.0**	**100.0**	**100.0**	**100.0**	**100.0**
	2000	**100.0**	**100.0**	**100.0**	**100.0**	**100.0**	**100.0**	**100.0**	**100.0**	**100.0**
	2005	**100.0**	**100.0**	**100.0**	**100.0**	**100.0**	**100.0**	**100.0**	**100.0**	**100.0**
All food items	1995	9.3	9.0	9.9	10.2	6.8	9.9	0.3	20.2	6.2
(SITC 0 + 1 + 22 + 4)	2000	6.9	7.1	7.8	8.0	5.8	7.0	0.3	17.6	4.4
	2005	6.9	7.5	8.1	8.3	6.1	6.9	0.3	19.3	3.0
Agricultural raw materials	1995	2.9	2.9	2.2	2.3	9.3	3.8	0.2	8.7	7.7
(SITC 2 - 22 - 27 - 28)	2000	1.9	2.1	1.6	1.7	6.1	2.2	0.2	5.1	4.0
	2005	1.5	1.6	1.4	1.5	4.5	1.7	0.2	3.3	2.5
Ores and metals	1995	3.8	3.3	3.1	3.0	7.0	2.9	0.3	13.7	20.3
(SITC 27 + 28 + 68)	2000	3.1	2.8	2.7	2.5	4.6	2.1	0.5	11.7	19.9
	2005	3.1	2.9	2.7	2.6	5.4	2.4	0.5	11.3	9.5
Fuels (SITC 3)	1995	7.4	3.7	3.8	2.8	8.9	1.7	0.2	12.7	27.7
	2000	10.1	5.3	5.6	4.2	12.6	1.3	0.2	13.4	38.7
	2005	13.9	7.8	7.5	6.0	20.8	2.9	0.5	17.6	53.7
Manufactured goods	1995	73.6	78.1	77.9	78.8	62.7	79.8	98.0	41.2	34.8
(SITC 5 to 8 less 68)	2000	74.4	79.2	78.3	79.6	64.2	85.9	97.2	49.5	30.9
	2005	70.8	76.1	75.9	77.9	57.8	83.4	96.7	45.9	28.7

Sources:
- UNCTAD secretariat calculations based on UN DESA Statistics Division's data

Total	Developing economies — Économies en développement							Major petroleum exporters — Principaux exportateurs de pétrole	Major exporters of manufactures — Principaux exportateurs d'articles manufacturés	Year — Année	Origine — Groupes de produits
	Africa — Afrique	America — Amérique	Asia — Asie Total	Eastern, Southern and South-Eastern Asia — Asie orientale, méridionale et du Sud-Est	China — Chine	Western Asia — Asie occidentale	Oceania — Océanie				
Millions de dollars											
833 238	82 079	172 350	574 776	502 399	126 038	72 377	4 033	151 427	557 352	1 995	**Total tous produits**
1 295 149	111 637	289 684	890 609	766 597	250 095	124 012	3 219	240 834	891 535	2000	
2 170 675	215 828	433 624	1 515 705	1 284 948	630 809	230 757	5 517	424 946	1 469 621	2005	
Parts par origines (en pourcentage)											
23.7	2.3	4.9	16.4	14.3	3.6	2.1	0.1	4.3	15.9	1995	**Total tous produits**
28.8	2.5	6.4	19.8	17.0	5.6	2.8	0.1	5.4	19.8	2000	
31.5	3.1	6.3	22.0	18.7	9.2	3.3	0.1	6.2	21.3	2005	
27.9	4.2	12.1	11.3	10.5	2.1	0.9	0.3	1.7	13.7	1995	Produits alimentaires
29.3	3.8	13.3	12.0	11.1	3.0	0.8	0.2	1.7	14.9	2000	(CTCI 0 + 1 + 22 + 4)
28.3	3.8	13.3	11.0	9.9	3.2	1.1	0.2	1.5	14.5	2005	
22.7	3.9	6.1	12.3	11.8	1.9	0.5	0.4	3.5	11.8	1995	Matières premières
23.5	3.9	7.5	11.9	11.4	2.8	0.5	0.2	2.9	12.7	2000	d'origine agricole
26.3	4.2	8.5	13.5	13.0	3.5	0.5	0.1	3.6	14.2	2005	(CTCI 2 - 22 - 27 - 28)
24.7	5.2	12.1	6.8	5.8	1.6	1.0	0.6	3.1	10.0	1995	Minerais et métaux
25.6	6.5	11.6	7.1	6.0	1.9	1.1	0.3	3.2	9.5	2000	(CTCI 27 + 28 + 68)
29.8	6.7	14.5	8.2	7.1	2.9	1.2	0.3	3.3	11.2	2005	
52.9	13.6	9.0	30.2	10.6	1.2	19.6	0.2	42.7	6.3	1995	Combustibles (CTCI 3)
53.3	12.9	10.7	29.6	8.8	0.8	20.8	0.1	42.3	6.9	2000	
48.5	13.7	10.3	24.4	7.5	0.6	16.9	0.1	37.1	6.8	2005	
20.7	0.8	3.2	16.7	16.1	4.3	0.6	0.0	1.0	17.9	1995	Articles manufacturés
26.4	0.8	5.0	20.6	19.8	6.9	0.7	0.0	1.1	23.1	2000	(CTCI 5 à 8 moins 68)
29.5	0.9	4.4	24.1	22.9	12.2	1.2	0.0	1.0	26.0	2005	
Parts par principaux groupes de produits (en pourcentage)											
100.0	100.0	100.0	100.0	100.0	100.0	100.0	100.0	100.0	100.0	1995	**Total tous produits**
100.0	100.0	100.0	100.0	100.0	100.0	100.0	100.0	100.0	100.0	2000	
100.0	100.0	100.0	100.0	100.0	100.0	100.0	100.0	100.0	100.0	2005	
11.0	16.6	22.9	6.5	6.8	5.6	4.0	26.1	3.7	8.1	1995	Produits alimentaires
7.0	10.6	14.2	4.2	4.5	3.7	2.0	23.9	2.2	5.2	2000	(CTCI 0 + 1 + 22 + 4)
6.2	8.3	14.6	3.5	3.7	2.4	2.3	20.5	1.7	4.7	2005	
2.8	4.9	3.6	2.2	2.4	1.5	0.7	10.9	2.4	2.2	1995	Matières premières
1.6	3.1	2.3	1.2	1.3	1.0	0.4	5.1	1.1	1.2	2000	d'origine agricole
1.3	2.1	2.1	0.9	1.1	0.6	0.2	2.3	0.9	1.0	2005	(CTCI 2 - 22 - 27 - 28)
3.9	8.3	9.3	1.6	1.5	1.7	1.8	20.0	2.7	2.4	1995	Minerais et métaux
2.8	8.2	5.6	1.1	1.1	1.1	1.3	14.8	1.9	1.5	2000	(CTCI 27 + 28 + 68)
3.0	6.7	7.3	1.2	1.2	1.0	1.1	13.5	1.7	1.7	2005	
16.6	43.1	13.6	13.7	5.5	2.5	70.6	14.5	73.5	2.9	1995	Combustibles (CTCI 3)
18.7	52.3	16.8	15.0	5.2	1.4	75.8	18.8	79.6	3.5	2000	
21.4	60.9	22.8	15.4	5.6	0.9	70.2	16.8	83.7	4.4	2005	
64.2	23.8	47.9	75.1	82.8	88.3	22.1	18.7	16.3	83.0	1995	Articles manufacturés
68.2	24.0	57.8	77.3	86.6	92.2	20.1	25.9	14.9	86.6	2000	(CTCI 5 à 8 moins 68)
66.3	20.8	49.9	77.6	87.0	94.3	25.3	30.6	11.4	86.4	2005	

Sources :
- Calculs du secrétariat de la CNUCED sur la base des données de ONU DAES Division de statistique

2.2.C Export structure by partner and product group
Economies in transition

Product group	Year / Année	World / Monde	Developed economies / Économies développées — Total	Europe Total	Europe EU / UE	Canada	USA / États-Unis	Japan / Japon	Other developed countries / Autres économies développées	Economies in transition / Économies en transition
Millions of dollars										
All products	1995	118 340	62 693	54 940	50 594	178	4 472	2 579	523	36 874
	2000	167 524	100 398	87 652	81 500	279	6 684	3 009	2 774	36 424
	2005	392 944	209 128	192 047	176 165	1 118	9 323	4 026	2 615	76 902
Share by destination (percentage)										
All products	1995	100.0	51.9	45.5	41.9	0.1	3.7	2.1	0.4	30.6
	2000	100.0	59.9	52.3	48.6	0.2	4.0	1.8	1.7	21.7
	2005	100.0	53.2	48.9	44.8	0.3	2.4	1.0	0.7	19.6
All food items	1995	100.0	29.5	25.1	24.1	0.1	1.6	1.7	0.9	61.7
(SITC 0 + 1 + 22 + 4)	2000	100.0	32.5	26.9	25.1	0.2	1.5	2.7	1.3	53.5
	2005	100.0	28.9	25.2	24.5	0.1	1.1	1.1	1.3	49.8
Agricultural raw materials	1995	100.0	62.2	53.0	51.2	0.0	0.9	8.0	0.2	13.5
(SITC 2 - 22 - 27 - 28)	2000	100.0	58.4	48.9	46.3	0.0	0.6	8.4	0.4	14.1
	2005	100.0	49.8	42.8	42.5	0.1	0.7	5.9	0.3	11.8
Ores and metals	1995	100.0	77.9	57.3	49.7	0.2	10.3	9.9	0.2	13.5
(SITC 27 + 28 + 68)	2000	100.0	72.8	57.4	53.5	0.2	7.9	7.2	0.2	12.1
	2005	100.0	66.0	55.3	44.6	0.1	5.5	4.9	0.2	13.6
Fuels (SITC 3)	1995	100.0	62.9	61.0	55.1	0.0	0.8	0.6	0.5	24.1
	2000	100.0	70.7	67.1	63.0	0.0	0.4	0.5	2.8	16.5
	2005	100.0	75.3	71.8	64.8	0.4	1.4	0.8	0.9	12.8
Manufactured goods	1995	100.0	41.5	34.9	33.2	0.3	5.3	0.7	0.4	32.2
(SITC 5 to 8 less 68)	2000	100.0	50.4	43.6	42.3	0.4	5.6	0.4	0.4	23.3
	2005	100.0	47.3	41.8	40.8	0.3	4.1	0.3	0.7	26.0
Share by major product group (percentage)										
All products	1995	100.0	100.0	100.0	100.0	100.0	100.0	100.0	100.0	100.0
	2000	100.0	100.0	100.0	100.0	100.0	100.0	100.0	100.0	100.0
	2005	100.0	100.0	100.0	100.0	100.0	100.0	100.0	100.0	100.0
All food items	1995	7.2	4.1	3.9	4.1	5.8	3.1	5.8	15.2	14.4
(SITC 0 + 1 + 22 + 4)	2000	3.8	2.0	1.9	1.9	4.3	1.4	5.6	2.9	9.3
	2005	4.2	2.3	2.1	2.3	1.9	1.9	4.7	8.1	10.6
Agricultural raw materials	1995	5.4	6.4	6.2	6.5	0.6	1.3	20.1	2.6	2.4
(SITC 2 - 22 - 27 - 28)	2000	4.0	3.9	3.8	3.8	1.0	0.6	18.9	0.9	2.6
	2005	2.8	2.6	2.5	2.7	1.1	0.8	16.2	1.2	1.7
Ores and metals	1995	10.0	15.0	12.6	11.8	10.3	27.8	46.3	5.2	4.4
(SITC 27 + 28 + 68)	2000	9.7	11.8	10.6	10.7	9.9	19.3	39.0	0.9	5.4
	2005	7.1	8.8	8.1	7.1	2.3	16.6	33.9	2.3	5.0
Fuels (SITC 3)	1995	33.0	40.0	44.3	43.4	9.5	6.9	9.4	37.8	26.1
	2000	39.4	46.4	50.5	51.0	0.2	3.5	10.0	65.5	29.8
	2005	40.7	57.6	59.8	58.8	53.8	24.7	32.6	52.5	26.7
Manufactured goods	1995	42.2	33.7	32.3	33.4	73.4	60.8	12.9	39.0	44.5
(SITC 5 to 8 less 68)	2000	34.6	29.1	28.9	30.1	82.3	48.7	6.9	8.1	37.2
	2005	31.9	28.3	27.3	29.0	37.6	55.0	10.5	34.6	42.4

Sources:
- UNCTAD secretariat calculations based on UN DESA Statistics Division's data

Developing economies / Économies en développement								Major petroleum exporters / Principaux exportateurs de pétrole	Major exporters of manufactures / Principaux exportateurs d'articles manufacturés	Year / Année	Destination / Groupes de produits
Total	Africa / Afrique	America / Amérique	Asia / Asie Total	Eastern, Southern and South-Eastern Asia / Asie orientale, méridionale et du Sud-Est	China / Chine	Western Asia / Asie occidentale	Oceania / Océanie				
Millions de dollars											
21 123	1 867	3 271	15 982	11 650	5 026	4 332	3	2 509	13 051	1995	**Total tous produits**
30 596	2 729	6 193	21 668	14 298	6 836	7 370	6	3 542	18 232	2000	
65 902	6 262	6 966	52 631	33 448	15 766	19 183	42	10 198	41 692	2005	
Parts par destinations (en pourcentage)											
17.5	1.5	2.7	13.2	9.7	4.2	3.6	0.0	2.1	10.8	1995	**Total tous produits**
18.3	1.6	3.7	12.9	8.5	4.1	4.4	0.0	2.1	10.9	2000	
16.8	1.6	1.8	13.4	8.5	4.0	4.9	0.0	2.6	10.6	2005	
8.7	1.9	0.2	6.7	1.6	0.4	5.1	0.0	1.8	4.4	1995	Produits alimentaires
13.7	2.8	0.3	10.6	5.5	1.2	5.2	0.0	3.5	5.9	2000	(CTCI 0 + 1 + 22 + 4)
20.8	7.2	0.2	13.4	5.5	0.9	7.9	0.0	7.4	5.2	2005	
24.2	2.0	1.2	21.0	14.0	6.2	7.0	0.0	1.8	18.9	1995	Matières premières
27.5	3.5	0.7	23.3	16.5	10.1	6.8	0.0	3.1	19.9	2000	d'origine agricole
38.3	3.1	0.1	35.1	28.8	22.8	6.3	0.0	3.2	29.6	2005	(CTCI 2 - 22 - 27 - 28)
8.6	0.3	0.1	8.2	5.5	1.1	2.7	0.0	0.8	7.4	1995	Minerais et métaux
15.1	0.7	0.7	13.7	8.9	5.5	4.7	0.0	0.5	13.2	2000	(CTCI 27 + 28 + 68)
20.4	0.7	0.4	19.4	11.5	6.9	7.9	0.0	0.8	18.5	2005	
11.2	0.2	5.4	5.6	3.3	0.1	2.3	0.0	1.5	3.8	1995	Combustibles (CTCI 3)
12.9	0.2	7.0	5.6	2.2	0.7	3.4	0.0	0.5	4.7	2000	
11.8	0.4	2.6	8.9	5.1	3.1	3.8	0.0	1.0	7.3	2005	
26.1	2.8	2.0	21.2	16.9	8.7	4.3	0.0	3.0	17.8	1995	Articles manufacturés
26.3	3.1	2.3	20.8	15.1	6.8	5.7	0.0	4.1	17.4	2000	(CTCI 5 à 8 moins 68)
26.5	3.1	2.1	21.2	14.2	4.8	7.0	0.0	5.3	16.4	2005	
Parts par principaux groupes de produits (en pourcentage)											
100.0	100.0	100.0	100.0	100.0	100.0	100.0	100.0	100.0	100.0	1995	**Total tous produits**
100.0	100.0	100.0	100.0	100.0	100.0	100.0	100.0	100.0	100.0	2000	
100.0	100.0	100.0	100.0	100.0	100.0	100.0	100.0	100.0	100.0	2005	
3.6	8.6	0.5	3.6	1.2	0.7	10.1	7.4	6.4	2.9	1995	Produits alimentaires
2.8	6.4	0.3	3.1	2.4	1.1	4.4	9.5	6.1	2.0	2000	(CTCI 0 + 1 + 22 + 4)
5.2	18.7	0.5	4.2	2.7	1.0	6.7	0.3	11.9	2.0	2005	
7.4	6.8	2.3	8.5	7.8	7.9	10.5	6.4	4.6	9.3	1995	Matières premières
6.1	8.7	0.7	7.3	7.8	10.0	6.3	3.5	5.9	7.3	2000	d'origine agricole
6.4	5.5	0.1	7.4	9.5	15.9	3.6	0.0	3.5	7.8	2005	(CTCI 2 - 22 - 27 - 28)
4.9	1.9	0.4	6.2	5.7	2.6	7.6	0.3	3.6	6.8	1995	Minerais et métaux
8.0	4.3	1.8	10.3	10.2	13.0	10.5	4.7	2.1	11.8	2000	(CTCI 27 + 28 + 68)
8.7	3.0	1.4	10.3	9.6	12.3	11.5	0.0	2.3	12.4	2005	
21.1	3.7	66.1	13.9	11.2	0.7	21.2	50.4	23.8	11.5	1995	Combustibles (CTCI 3)
27.7	5.2	75.0	17.0	10.0	6.7	30.7	22.0	9.7	17.0	2000	
28.7	10.2	59.3	26.9	24.4	31.9	31.3	0.6	15.4	28.1	2005	
62.9	77.8	30.5	67.8	74.1	88.1	50.6	35.4	61.1	69.4	1995	Articles manufacturés
49.8	65.9	21.9	55.8	61.4	57.8	44.8	49.6	67.1	55.4	2000	(CTCI 5 à 8 moins 68)
50.3	61.5	38.5	50.5	53.2	38.1	45.7	99.1	64.5	49.2	2005	

Sources :
- Calculs du secrétariat de la CNUCED sur la base des données de ONU DAES Division de statistique

Origin Product group	Year Année	World Monde	Developed economies Économies développées							Economies in transition Économies en transition
			Total	Europe		Canada	USA États-Unis	Japan Japon	Other developed countries Autres économies développées	
				Total	EU UE					
			Millions of dollars							
All products	1995	93 090	46 695	40 305	38 773	403	4 068	1 236	682	37 782
	2000	108 128	54 714	46 926	45 388	386	5 175	1 485	741	40 959
	2005	289 235	152 741	130 935	126 781	1 159	10 496	8 587	1 564	82 660
			Share by origin (percentage)							
All products	**1995**	**100.0**	**49.0**	**42.3**	**40.7**	**0.4**	**4.3**	**1.3**	**0.7**	**39.7**
	2000	**100.0**	**50.6**	**43.4**	**42.0**	**0.4**	**4.8**	**1.4**	**0.7**	**37.9**
	2005	**100.0**	**52.8**	**45.3**	**43.8**	**0.4**	**3.6**	**3.0**	**0.5**	**28.6**
All food items	1995	100.0	49.0	38.5	36.7	0.5	8.4	0.0	1.5	27.9
(SITC 0 + 1 + 22 + 4)	2000	100.0	47.3	38.9	37.1	0.3	7.5	0.0	0.6	25.7
	2005	100.0	44.2	37.8	34.8	0.7	4.9	0.0	0.7	22.7
Agricultural raw materials	1995	100.0	38.8	32.2	31.1	0.3	4.6	0.2	1.4	52.7
(SITC 2 - 22 - 27 - 28)	2000	100.0	41.1	34.3	32.9	0.5	4.6	0.5	1.2	49.8
	2005	100.0	49.0	42.9	42.4	0.3	3.4	0.3	2.1	37.0
Ores and metals	1995	100.0	24.6	19.8	18.6	0.4	1.4	0.0	3.1	50.5
(SITC 27 + 28 + 68)	2000	100.0	25.6	18.4	17.8	0.2	0.9	0.3	5.8	52.5
	2005	100.0	24.8	20.3	18.7	0.4	1.1	0.1	2.8	48.7
Fuels (SITC 3)	1995	100.0	11.0	9.4	8.8	0.0	1.1	0.2	0.3	81.1
	2000	100.0	7.8	6.8	6.4	0.1	0.8	0.1	0.1	89.1
	2005	100.0	7.8	6.6	6.2	0.1	0.9	0.1	0.2	89.5
Manufactured goods	1995	100.0	65.1	57.4	55.4	0.6	4.5	2.2	0.5	25.7
(SITC 5 to 8 less 68)	2000	100.0	67.9	59.4	57.6	0.5	5.3	2.3	0.5	21.7
	2005	100.0	66.0	56.7	55.3	0.4	4.2	4.3	0.5	16.0
			Share by major commodity group (percentage)							
All products	**1995**	**100.0**	**100.0**	**100.0**	**100.0**	**100.0**	**100.0**	**100.0**	**100.0**	**100.0**
	2000	**100.0**	**100.0**	**100.0**	**100.0**	**100.0**	**100.0**	**100.0**	**100.0**	**100.0**
	2005	**100.0**	**100.0**	**100.0**	**100.0**	**100.0**	**100.0**	**100.0**	**100.0**	**100.0**
All food items	1995	16.2	16.2	14.7	14.6	20.2	31.9	0.5	34.6	11.4
(SITC 0 + 1 + 22 + 4)	2000	12.9	12.1	11.6	11.4	11.4	20.3	0.1	11.7	8.7
	2005	10.8	9.0	9.0	8.6	18.7	14.5	0.1	14.4	8.6
Agricultural raw materials	1995	1.9	1.5	1.4	1.4	1.5	2.0	0.3	3.6	2.5
(SITC 2 - 22 - 27 - 28)	2000	1.7	1.4	1.4	1.4	2.5	1.7	0.6	3.0	2.3
	2005	1.2	1.1	1.1	1.2	0.9	1.1	0.1	4.6	1.5
Ores and metals	1995	3.9	2.0	1.8	1.8	3.7	1.3	0.0	16.6	5.0
(SITC 27 + 28 + 68)	2000	4.5	2.3	1.9	1.9	2.8	0.8	0.9	38.0	6.2
	2005	3.3	1.5	1.5	1.4	3.1	1.0	0.1	16.9	5.6
Fuels (SITC 3)	1995	18.8	4.2	4.2	4.1	0.9	4.9	2.4	6.9	38.5
	2000	16.4	2.5	2.6	2.5	3.5	2.6	0.8	2.3	38.5
	2005	12.1	1.8	1.8	1.7	2.4	3.0	0.2	3.7	37.8
Manufactured goods	1995	56.2	74.6	76.2	76.4	73.4	59.1	96.5	38.0	36.5
(SITC 5 to 8 less 68)	2000	59.1	79.3	80.8	81.0	78.5	65.7	97.1	43.6	33.8
	2005	68.8	86.0	86.2	86.8	72.3	78.9	99.2	57.3	38.6

Sources:
- UNCTAD secretariat calculations based on UN DESA Statistics Division's data

Total	Africa / Afrique	America / Amérique	Asia / Asie — Total	Eastern, Southern and South-Eastern Asia / Asie orientale, méridionale et du Sud-Est	China / Chine	Western Asia / Asie occidentale	Oceania / Océanie	Major petroleum exporters / Principaux exportateurs de pétrole	Major exporters of manufactures / Principaux exportateurs d'articles manufacturés	Year / Année	Origine / Groupes de produits
colspan across Developing economies / Économies en développement											
Millions de dollars											
10 757	1 286	2 006	7 455	5 433	1 201	2 021	10	1 616	6 280	1995	Total tous produits
11 947	970	2 443	8 523	5 835	1 867	2 688	11	1 473	7 960	2000	
49 595	2 239	7 517	39 783	30 934	15 729	8 849	56	2 739	41 006	2005	
Parts par origines (en pourcentage)											
11.3	1.3	2.1	7.8	5.7	1.3	2.1	0.0	1.7	6.6	1995	Total tous produits
11.0	0.9	2.3	7.9	5.4	1.7	2.5	0.0	1.4	7.4	2000	
17.1	0.8	2.6	13.8	10.7	5.4	3.1	0.0	0.9	14.2	2005	
22.8	1.7	9.8	11.3	7.7	2.5	3.6	0.0	2.3	10.8	1995	Produits alimentaires
26.9	2.7	12.7	11.5	8.4	1.6	3.0	0.0	2.0	13.8	2000	(CTCI 0 + 1 + 22 + 4)
32.9	3.0	17.7	12.2	9.1	2.6	3.1	0.1	2.1	19.8	2005	
8.1	1.6	1.4	5.0	4.6	0.7	0.5	0.0	2.3	3.2	1995	Matières premières
9.0	0.9	1.6	6.5	5.5	0.9	1.0	0.0	1.7	4.8	2000	d'origine agricole
13.9	1.3	3.5	9.1	7.4	2.1	1.7	0.0	1.2	7.7	2005	(CTCI 2 - 22 - 27 - 28)
24.3	6.3	8.3	9.8	7.3	1.3	2.4	0.0	2.2	8.0	1995	Minerais et métaux
21.8	5.6	8.9	7.2	4.4	1.4	2.9	0.0	2.5	8.5	2000	(CTCI 27 + 28 + 68)
26.5	7.4	9.5	9.4	5.9	2.6	3.5	0.2	2.9	11.8	2005	
7.2	3.6	0.2	3.4	2.9	0.3	0.5	0.0	4.1	0.8	1995	Combustibles (CTCI 3)
3.1	0.9	0.4	1.9	0.7	0.4	1.2	0.0	2.0	0.6	2000	
2.6	0.6	0.3	1.8	1.1	0.5	0.7	0.0	1.3	0.9	2005	
9.0	0.2	0.2	8.6	6.2	1.3	2.4	0.0	0.6	7.7	1995	Articles manufacturés
9.8	0.2	0.2	9.4	6.5	2.3	2.9	0.0	1.0	8.4	2000	(CTCI 5 à 8 moins 68)
17.7	0.2	0.4	17.1	13.5	7.2	3.6	0.0	0.7	16.6	2005	
Parts par principaux groupes de produits (en pourcentage)											
100.0	100.0	100.0	100.0	100.0	100.0	100.0	100.0	100.0	100.0	1995	Total tous produits
100.0	100.0	100.0	100.0	100.0	100.0	100.0	100.0	100.0	100.0	2000	
100.0	100.0	100.0	100.0	100.0	100.0	100.0	100.0	100.0	100.0	2005	
32.7	19.9	75.6	23.3	21.8	31.5	27.5	20.9	22.3	26.6	1995	Produits alimentaires
31.4	38.5	72.9	18.8	20.1	11.8	15.8	19.0	19.1	24.2	2000	(CTCI 0 + 1 + 22 + 4)
20.8	41.8	73.6	9.6	9.2	5.2	10.9	28.8	23.5	15.1	2005	
1.3	2.3	1.3	1.2	1.5	1.0	0.4	0.0	2.6	0.9	1995	Matières premières
1.4	1.8	1.2	1.4	1.8	0.9	0.7	1.2	2.2	1.1	2000	d'origine agricole
1.0	2.0	1.6	0.8	0.8	0.5	0.7	0.2	1.5	0.6	2005	(CTCI 2 - 22 - 27 - 28)
8.4	18.1	15.3	4.9	5.0	4.0	4.5	1.4	5.0	4.7	1995	Minerais et métaux
8.9	28.2	17.7	4.1	3.6	3.7	5.2	10.8	8.3	5.2	2000	(CTCI 27 + 28 + 68)
5.1	31.5	11.9	2.2	1.8	1.6	3.8	34.4	9.9	2.7	2005	
12.0	50.7	1.5	8.2	9.6	4.2	4.4	0.0	45.0	2.2	1995	Combustibles (CTCI 3)
4.6	16.1	2.5	3.9	2.2	4.2	7.7	0.3	24.6	1.4	2000	
1.9	9.0	1.5	1.5	1.2	1.0	2.7	0.0	17.2	0.7	2005	
44.8	7.6	5.9	61.6	61.2	59.2	62.9	77.2	21.4	65.3	1995	Articles manufacturés
52.3	11.0	4.8	70.7	71.3	79.0	69.2	66.0	43.3	67.3	2000	(CTCI 5 à 8 moins 68)
71.1	15.3	11.2	85.6	86.8	91.7	81.2	36.4	47.5	80.6	2005	

Sources :
- Calculs du secrétariat de la CNUCED sur la base des données de ONU DAES Division de statistique

2.2.D Export structure by partner and product group
Developing economies

Destination / Product group	Year / Année	World / Monde	Developed economies / Économies développées Total	Europe Total	EU / UE	Canada	USA / États-Unis	Japan / Japon	Other developed countries / Autres économies développées	Economies in transition / Économies en transition
Millions of dollars										
All products	1995	1 416 488	778 147	270 065	258 545	16 089	313 138	156 903	21 952	15 609
	2000	2 022 097	1 156 239	367 273	347 885	23 506	535 388	197 273	32 799	14 241
	2005	3 702 570	1 905 672	683 680	647 316	44 907	789 051	321 616	66 419	56 306
Share by destination (percentage)										
All products	1995	100.0	54.9	19.1	18.3	1.1	22.1	11.1	1.5	1.1
	2000	100.0	57.2	18.2	17.2	1.2	26.5	9.8	1.6	0.7
	2005	100.0	51.5	18.5	17.5	1.2	21.3	8.7	1.8	1.5
All food items	1995	100.0	55.9	26.6	25.6	0.8	13.0	14.4	1.2	3.3
(SITC 0 + 1 + 22 + 4)	2000	100.0	54.1	22.5	21.7	1.2	16.6	12.5	1.3	2.5
	2005	100.0	51.3	24.3	23.8	1.1	14.9	9.5	1.4	4.5
Agricultural raw materials	1995	100.0	51.7	23.3	22.7	0.6	12.3	14.5	1.0	0.4
(SITC 2 - 22 - 27 - 28)	2000	100.0	50.5	23.8	23.0	0.6	13.7	11.5	1.0	0.4
	2005	100.0	47.0	21.3	20.7	1.0	14.4	9.3	0.9	0.8
Ores and metals	1995	100.0	55.0	23.1	21.8	1.4	10.3	19.4	0.8	1.6
(SITC 27 + 28 + 68)	2000	100.0	51.8	23.0	20.9	1.7	11.9	13.9	1.3	1.0
	2005	100.0	45.4	20.4	18.3	2.0	9.9	12.1	0.9	1.3
Fuels (SITC 3)	1995	100.0	55.3	18.2	17.8	0.8	18.2	16.9	1.2	0.2
	2000	100.0	57.4	19.6	17.9	0.7	22.3	13.7	1.1	0.2
	2005	100.0	54.8	17.2	15.0	1.1	20.6	14.3	1.7	0.1
Manufactured goods	1995	100.0	55.0	17.8	17.0	1.3	25.5	8.7	1.7	1.0
(SITC 5 to 8 less 68)	2000	100.0	58.1	16.9	16.4	1.3	29.9	8.2	1.8	0.7
	2005	100.0	51.5	18.4	17.9	1.2	23.2	6.8	1.9	1.8
Share by major product group (percentage)										
All products	1995	100.0	100.0	100.0	100.0	100.0	100.0	100.0	100.0	100.0
	2000	100.0	100.0	100.0	100.0	100.0	100.0	100.0	100.0	100.0
	2005	100.0	100.0	100.0	100.0	100.0	100.0	100.0	100.0	100.0
All food items	1995	9.8	9.9	13.6	13.7	7.2	5.7	12.7	7.4	29.4
(SITC 0 + 1 + 22 + 4)	2000	6.7	6.3	8.3	8.4	6.6	4.2	8.6	5.4	23.4
	2005	6.0	5.9	7.8	8.1	5.6	4.2	6.5	4.8	17.5
Agricultural raw materials	1995	2.7	2.5	3.3	3.3	1.5	1.5	3.5	1.7	1.0
(SITC 2 - 22 - 27 - 28)	2000	1.5	1.4	2.0	2.1	0.8	0.8	1.8	0.9	0.8
	2005	1.3	1.2	1.5	1.5	1.1	0.9	1.4	0.7	0.7
Ores and metals	1995	3.4	3.4	4.2	4.1	4.4	1.6	6.0	1.8	5.0
(SITC 27 + 28 + 68)	2000	2.7	2.4	3.4	3.2	3.9	1.2	3.8	2.1	4.0
	2005	3.4	3.0	3.8	3.6	5.7	1.6	4.7	1.8	2.9
Fuels (SITC 3)	1995	15.6	15.7	14.9	15.2	10.4	12.8	23.8	12.4	3.4
	2000	20.1	20.2	21.8	20.9	12.8	16.9	28.3	13.3	4.6
	2005	21.6	23.0	20.0	18.5	19.0	20.9	35.5	20.1	1.4
Manufactured goods	1995	66.5	66.6	62.1	62.1	75.2	76.6	52.5	74.3	60.7
(SITC 5 to 8 less 68)	2000	67.8	69.0	63.2	64.5	74.9	76.5	57.2	76.3	66.8
	2005	65.9	65.9	65.5	67.5	65.4	71.7	51.4	70.4	77.2

Sources:
- UNCTAD secretariat calculations based on UN DESA Statistics Division's data

2.2.D Structure des exportations par partenaires et groupes de produits
Économies en développement

			Developing economies / Économies en développement							Year Année	Destination
				Asia / Asie				Major petroleum exporters / Principaux exportateurs de pétrole	Major exporters of manufactures / Principaux exportateurs d'articles manufacturés		
Total	Africa Afrique	America Amérique	Total	Eastern, Southern and South-Eastern Asia / Asie orientale, méridionale et du Sud-Est	China Chine	Western Asia / Asie occidentale	Oceania Océanie				Groupes de produits
Millions de dollars											
568 082	34 167	72 578	460 011	422 245	82 284	37 766	1 325	56 570	404 849	1995	**Total tous produits**
800 841	46 526	101 748	649 575	597 999	124 011	51 576	2 993	73 320	585 804	2000	
1 645 711	101 076	178 651	1 360 365	1 241 339	350 721	119 026	5 619	198 372	1 171 992	2005	
Parts par destinations (en pourcentage)											
40.1	2.4	5.1	32.5	29.8	5.8	2.7	0.1	4.0	28.6	1995	**Total tous produits**
39.6	2.3	5.0	32.1	29.6	6.1	2.6	0.1	3.6	29.0	2000	
44.4	2.7	4.8	36.7	33.5	9.5	3.2	0.2	5.4	31.7	2005	
40.3	4.5	6.8	28.9	23.9	4.8	5.0	0.1	7.9	20.7	1995	Produits alimentaires
41.1	5.1	7.8	28.1	22.1	4.3	6.0	0.1	8.5	19.9	2000	(CTCI 0 + 1 + 22 + 4)
43.8	6.9	6.6	30.2	23.4	5.2	6.8	0.1	10.3	19.7	2005	
47.6	3.2	4.9	39.6	37.6	9.5	2.0	0.0	3.8	36.3	1995	Matières premières
48.8	3.1	4.6	41.1	38.8	15.0	2.3	0.0	3.9	37.0	2000	d'origine agricole
51.8	3.3	4.4	44.1	41.6	18.7	2.5	0.0	3.8	38.5	2005	(CTCI 2 - 22 - 27 - 28)
42.8	1.6	5.3	35.9	33.5	7.4	2.4	0.0	3.9	33.7	1995	Minerais et métaux
44.5	1.8	5.9	36.8	33.9	9.1	2.9	0.0	3.9	35.3	2000	(CTCI 27 + 28 + 68)
51.5	2.1	5.2	44.1	41.1	17.4	3.0	0.0	4.3	41.8	2005	
23.8	1.9	5.0	16.9	15.7	2.3	1.2	0.1	1.2	16.7	1995	Combustibles (CTCI 3)
36.8	2.7	5.7	28.1	26.4	3.5	1.7	0.3	1.9	27.2	2000	
38.0	2.1	5.3	30.3	28.5	5.3	1.8	0.2	3.1	27.1	2005	
43.7	2.3	5.0	36.4	33.6	6.7	2.7	0.1	4.2	32.1	1995	Articles manufacturés
40.1	1.9	4.6	33.5	31.0	6.9	2.4	0.1	3.6	30.2	2000	(CTCI 5 à 8 moins 68)
46.5	2.6	4.5	39.3	36.0	10.8	3.3	0.1	5.7	34.0	2005	
Parts par principaux groupes de produits (en pourcentage)											
100.0	100.0	100.0	100.0	100.0	100.0	100.0	100.0	100.0	100.0	1995	**Total tous produits**
100.0	100.0	100.0	100.0	100.0	100.0	100.0	100.0	100.0	100.0	2000	
100.0	100.0	100.0	100.0	100.0	100.0	100.0	100.0	100.0	100.0	2005	
9.8	18.4	12.9	8.7	7.8	8.1	18.5	8.1	19.4	7.1	1995	Produits alimentaires
6.9	14.9	10.4	5.8	5.0	4.6	15.7	4.9	15.7	4.6	2000	(CTCI 0 + 1 + 22 + 4)
5.9	15.0	8.1	4.9	4.1	3.2	12.5	5.3	11.4	3.7	2005	
3.2	3.5	2.6	3.3	3.4	4.4	2.0	0.4	2.6	3.4	1995	Matières premières
1.9	2.1	1.4	2.0	2.0	3.8	1.4	0.2	1.7	2.0	2000	d'origine agricole
1.5	1.6	1.2	1.6	1.6	2.6	1.0	0.2	0.9	1.6	2005	(CTCI 2 - 22 - 27 - 28)
3.7	2.3	3.6	3.8	3.9	4.4	3.1	0.4	3.3	4.1	1995	Minerais et métaux
3.0	2.1	3.1	3.1	3.1	4.0	3.0	0.3	2.9	3.2	2000	(CTCI 27 + 28 + 68)
4.0	2.7	3.7	4.1	4.2	6.3	3.2	0.2	2.7	4.5	2005	
9.3	12.1	15.0	8.1	8.2	6.2	7.0	24.9	4.7	9.1	1995	Combustibles (CTCI 3)
18.7	23.5	22.6	17.6	18.0	11.5	13.2	43.5	10.8	18.9	2000	
18.4	16.6	23.6	17.8	18.3	12.1	12.3	34.5	12.5	18.4	2005	
72.6	62.6	65.1	74.5	75.0	76.2	68.4	63.1	69.2	74.7	1995	Articles manufacturés
68.7	56.4	62.3	70.7	71.2	75.9	65.1	50.8	67.7	70.6	2000	(CTCI 5 à 8 moins 68)
68.9	61.7	61.9	70.5	70.7	75.4	67.9	54.4	70.1	70.8	2005	

Sources :
- Calculs du secrétariat de la CNUCED sur la base des données de ONU DAES Division de statistique

Product group	Year / Année	World Monde	Developed economies / Économies développées Total	Europe Total	Europe EU / UE	Canada	USA États-Unis	Japan Japon	Other developed countries / Autres économies développées	Economies in transition / Économies en transition
Millions of dollars										
All products	1995	1 470 744	882 258	320 334	297 079	19 722	266 954	241 086	34 161	25 769
	2000	1 850 154	978 401	315 816	290 794	22 592	354 134	242 619	43 240	30 895
	2005	3 303 253	1 467 035	573 716	525 887	30 969	414 551	370 137	77 661	79 822
Share by origin (percentage)										
All products	1995	100.0	60.0	21.8	20.2	1.3	18.2	16.4	2.3	1.8
	2000	100.0	52.9	17.1	15.7	1.2	19.1	13.1	2.3	1.7
	2005	100.0	44.4	17.4	15.9	0.9	12.5	11.2	2.4	2.4
All food items	1995	100.0	56.2	20.4	19.6	3.9	23.5	1.6	6.7	1.2
(SITC 0 + 1 + 22 + 4)	2000	100.0	52.9	17.4	16.6	4.1	21.9	1.4	8.0	1.2
	2005	100.0	45.2	15.8	14.7	2.9	18.4	1.2	7.0	2.4
Agricultural raw materials	1995	100.0	53.1	11.9	11.6	4.5	24.6	4.2	7.8	5.3
(SITC 2 - 22 - 27 - 28)	2000	100.0	52.6	12.7	12.3	6.0	21.5	4.2	8.2	5.9
	2005	100.0	50.6	14.3	13.9	4.9	20.9	3.9	6.6	8.3
Ores and metals	1995	100.0	51.3	15.4	14.3	3.1	13.5	8.6	10.8	6.0
(SITC 27 + 28 + 68)	2000	100.0	46.1	12.2	10.5	2.1	10.5	8.7	12.6	8.6
	2005	100.0	40.1	9.6	8.7	2.2	7.7	6.7	13.9	7.6
Fuels (SITC 3)	1995	100.0	15.4	3.6	3.5	0.7	5.7	1.6	3.9	2.2
	2000	100.0	11.2	3.1	2.5	0.3	3.9	0.6	3.4	2.1
	2005	100.0	10.8	2.6	2.1	0.3	3.9	0.6	3.3	4.4
Manufactured goods	1995	100.0	64.6	24.1	22.5	0.9	18.4	20.2	1.0	1.5
(SITC 5 to 8 less 68)	2000	100.0	59.0	19.0	17.8	0.9	21.5	16.5	0.9	1.1
	2005	100.0	50.4	20.3	19.1	0.7	13.9	14.5	0.9	1.5
Share by major product group (percentage)										
All products	1995	100.0	100.0	100.0	100.0	100.0	100.0	100.0	100.0	100.0
	2000	100.0	100.0	100.0	100.0	100.0	100.0	100.0	100.0	100.0
	2005	100.0	100.0	100.0	100.0	100.0	100.0	100.0	100.0	100.0
All food items	1995	8.1	7.5	7.6	7.8	23.6	10.4	0.8	23.2	5.4
(SITC 0 + 1 + 22 + 4)	2000	6.7	6.7	6.8	7.1	22.4	7.6	0.7	23.0	4.9
	2005	5.7	5.8	5.2	5.3	17.4	8.4	0.6	17.0	5.6
Agricultural raw materials	1995	3.1	2.7	1.7	1.8	10.3	4.2	0.8	10.3	9.3
(SITC 2 - 22 - 27 - 28)	2000	2.3	2.3	1.7	1.8	11.2	2.6	0.7	8.1	8.1
	2005	1.9	2.2	1.6	1.7	10.1	3.2	0.7	5.4	6.6
Ores and metals	1995	3.5	3.0	2.5	2.5	8.0	2.6	1.8	16.1	12.0
(SITC 27 + 28 + 68)	2000	3.2	2.8	2.3	2.1	5.5	1.7	2.1	17.2	16.5
	2005	4.4	4.0	2.4	2.4	10.3	2.7	2.7	26.2	13.9
Fuels (SITC 3)	1995	7.0	1.8	1.2	1.2	3.6	2.2	0.7	11.6	8.9
	2000	10.7	2.3	1.9	1.7	2.4	2.2	0.5	15.5	13.3
	2005	13.2	3.2	2.0	1.8	4.4	4.1	0.7	18.6	23.8
Manufactured goods	1995	76.0	81.8	84.0	84.8	50.6	77.1	93.7	32.0	63.4
(SITC 5 to 8 less 68)	2000	75.2	83.9	83.8	85.4	57.8	84.6	94.8	30.4	51.6
	2005	72.5	82.3	84.8	86.9	57.1	80.4	94.2	27.2	44.7

Sources:
- UNCTAD secretariat calculations based on UN DESA Statistics Division's data

Developing economies / Économies en développement										Origine	
Total	Africa / Afrique	America / Amérique	Asia / Asie — Total	Eastern, Southern and South-Eastern Asia / Asie orientale, méridionale et du Sud-Est	China / Chine	Western Asia / Asie occidentale	Oceania / Océanie	Major petroleum exporters / Principaux exportateurs de pétrole	Major exporters of manufactures / Principaux exportateurs d'articles manufacturés	Year / Année	Groupes de produits
Millions de dollars											
550 622	27 031	67 995	454 689	398 903	103 201	55 786	906	86 975	396 143	1995	Total tous produits
793 610	44 932	87 390	660 214	568 295	160 510	91 919	1 074	152 642	551 517	2000	
1 686 659	93 725	172 338	1 418 451	1 215 534	402 821	202 917	2 145	320 282	1 191 411	2005	
Parts par origines (en pourcentage)											
37.4	1.8	4.6	30.9	27.1	7.0	3.8	0.1	5.9	26.9	1995	Total tous produits
42.9	2.4	4.7	35.7	30.7	8.7	5.0	0.1	8.3	29.8	2000	
51.1	2.8	5.2	42.9	36.8	12.2	6.1	0.1	9.7	36.1	2005	
42.1	2.9	14.2	24.8	22.2	4.4	2.7	0.2	3.6	22.7	1995	Produits alimentaires
44.7	4.2	15.6	24.7	21.6	5.5	3.0	0.2	5.2	21.2	2000	(CTCI 0 + 1 + 22 + 4)
52.1	4.7	20.1	26.9	23.5	5.0	3.5	0.3	6.5	24.5	2005	
41.2	5.2	7.5	27.9	26.9	3.4	1.0	0.6	4.6	23.1	1995	Matières premières
40.1	5.8	6.2	27.5	26.5	3.5	1.0	0.5	7.1	21.0	2000	d'origine agricole
41.0	5.8	7.1	27.3	26.2	2.6	1.1	0.7	7.0	21.8	2005	(CTCI 2 - 22 - 27 - 28)
42.2	4.9	13.9	23.2	18.3	4.5	4.9	0.3	6.9	20.7	1995	Minerais et métaux
44.5	5.0	13.4	25.9	22.0	5.2	3.9	0.2	6.4	23.6	2000	(CTCI 27 + 28 + 68)
52.2	5.4	17.0	29.7	26.1	6.1	3.6	0.1	7.9	27.4	2005	
77.8	8.1	7.8	61.9	27.0	2.8	34.9	0.1	54.2	17.2	1995	Combustibles (CTCI 3)
77.6	10.0	8.4	59.1	24.1	2.4	35.0	0.1	55.7	14.0	2000	
73.1	9.8	5.3	57.9	25.2	2.5	32.7	0.0	50.4	15.9	2005	
33.3	0.8	2.9	29.6	28.4	8.1	1.2	0.0	1.9	29.1	1995	Articles manufacturés
38.3	0.9	2.9	34.5	33.4	10.4	1.1	0.0	2.0	33.7	2000	(CTCI 5 à 8 moins 68)
47.8	1.1	3.4	43.4	41.5	15.5	1.9	0.0	2.8	42.2	2005	
Parts par principaux groupes de produits (en pourcentage)											
100.0	100.0	100.0	100.0	100.0	100.0	100.0	100.0	100.0	100.0	1995	Total tous produits
100.0	100.0	100.0	100.0	100.0	100.0	100.0	100.0	100.0	100.0	2000	
100.0	100.0	100.0	100.0	100.0	100.0	100.0	100.0	100.0	100.0	2005	
9.1	12.6	24.7	6.5	6.6	5.1	5.6	26.5	5.0	6.8	1995	Produits alimentaires
7.0	11.6	22.1	4.6	4.7	4.2	4.1	23.0	4.2	4.7	2000	(CTCI 0 + 1 + 22 + 4)
5.8	9.5	22.1	3.6	3.6	2.3	3.2	24.1	3.8	3.9	2005	
3.4	8.7	5.0	2.8	3.0	1.5	0.8	31.6	2.4	2.6	1995	Matières premières
2.1	5.5	3.0	1.8	2.0	0.9	0.5	21.3	2.0	1.6	2000	d'origine agricole
1.6	3.9	2.7	1.2	1.4	0.4	0.4	22.0	1.4	1.2	2005	(CTCI 2 - 22 - 27 - 28)
3.9	9.2	10.4	2.6	2.3	2.2	4.5	18.0	4.1	2.7	1995	Minerais et métaux
3.3	6.6	9.1	2.3	2.3	1.9	2.5	10.8	2.5	2.5	2000	(CTCI 27 + 28 + 68)
4.5	8.4	14.4	3.1	3.1	2.2	2.6	9.4	3.6	3.4	2005	
14.5	30.7	11.8	14.0	7.0	2.8	64.4	8.6	64.2	4.5	1995	Combustibles (CTCI 3)
19.4	44.3	19.1	17.8	8.4	3.0	75.6	14.2	72.3	5.0	2000	
18.9	45.7	13.4	17.8	9.1	2.7	70.3	7.0	68.6	5.8	2005	
67.6	31.9	47.6	72.8	79.6	87.8	24.1	14.5	23.9	82.0	1995	Articles manufacturés
67.1	27.0	46.2	72.6	81.7	89.7	16.8	30.5	18.2	85.1	2000	(CTCI 5 à 8 moins 68)
68.0	27.2	46.6	73.3	81.9	92.0	22.0	37.2	20.8	84.8	2005	

Sources :
- Calculs du secrétariat de la CNUCED sur la base des données de ONU DAES Division de statistique

2.2.E Export structure by partner and product group
Developing economies: Africa

Destination / Product group	Year / Année	World / Monde	Developed economies / Économies développées							Economies in transition / Économies en transition
			Total	Europe		Canada	USA / États-Unis	Japan / Japon	Other developed countries / Autres économies développées	
				Total	EU / UE					
Millions of dollars										
All products	1995	103 430	70 315	49 553	46 400	1 009	15 363	3 347	1 043	965
	2000	148 712	95 300	63 760	61 540	1 800	25 778	2 462	1 500	666
	2005	271 001	180 714	114 247	109 652	5 143	50 275	8 285	2 764	1 179
Share by destination (percentage)										
All products	1995	100.0	68.0	47.9	44.9	1.0	14.9	3.2	1.0	0.9
	2000	100.0	64.1	42.9	41.4	1.2	17.3	1.7	1.0	0.4
	2005	100.0	66.7	42.2	40.5	1.9	18.6	3.1	1.0	0.4
All food items	1995	100.0	72.6	61.2	58.6	0.6	3.5	6.5	0.8	2.1
(SITC 0 + 1 + 22 + 4)	2000	100.0	60.8	49.0	47.3	0.7	4.5	5.6	1.0	1.5
	2005	100.0	61.6	51.0	49.6	0.8	5.4	3.5	0.9	2.9
Agricultural raw materials	1995	100.0	59.6	48.4	47.3	0.2	3.9	6.4	0.7	0.5
(SITC 2 - 22 - 27 - 28)	2000	100.0	54.6	45.2	42.9	0.2	3.3	5.4	0.5	0.2
	2005	100.0	48.3	38.8	37.0	0.1	3.1	6.1	0.2	0.4
Ores and metals	1995	100.0	65.8	44.6	41.5	1.7	7.7	10.6	1.2	1.7
(SITC 27 + 28 + 68)	2000	100.0	66.5	46.0	42.4	1.2	8.7	9.0	1.5	1.4
	2005	100.0	67.6	38.3	29.1	0.8	12.6	14.7	1.2	0.9
Fuels (SITC 3)	1995	100.0	78.3	47.9	46.0	1.6	27.1	1.0	0.7	0.8
	2000	100.0	70.1	40.7	40.2	1.8	26.7	0.4	0.5	0.3
	2005	100.0	68.6	37.8	37.1	2.7	26.3	1.4	0.2	0.1
Manufactured goods	1995	100.0	64.1	52.2	48.3	0.6	7.1	2.4	1.9	0.7
(SITC 5 to 8 less 68)	2000	100.0	65.8	52.3	50.0	0.5	8.8	1.7	2.4	0.3
	2005	100.0	66.6	51.8	50.8	0.6	7.7	3.3	3.2	0.4
Share by major product group (percentage)										
All products	1995	100.0	100.0	100.0	100.0	100.0	100.0	100.0	100.0	100.0
	2000	100.0	100.0	100.0	100.0	100.0	100.0	100.0	100.0	100.0
	2005	100.0	100.0	100.0	100.0	100.0	100.0	100.0	100.0	100.0
All food items	1995	13.8	14.7	17.6	18.0	7.8	3.3	27.5	11.5	30.7
(SITC 0 + 1 + 22 + 4)	2000	9.1	8.6	10.4	10.4	5.5	2.4	30.7	9.0	31.1
	2005	7.9	7.3	9.5	9.7	3.4	2.3	9.1	6.7	51.9
Agricultural raw materials	1995	5.2	4.5	5.2	5.4	1.0	1.4	10.2	3.3	3.0
(SITC 2 - 22 - 27 - 28)	2000	2.9	2.5	3.1	3.1	0.5	0.6	9.7	1.6	1.1
	2005	2.6	1.9	2.4	2.4	0.2	0.4	5.2	0.6	2.2
Ores and metals	1995	5.9	5.7	5.5	5.5	10.5	3.0	19.3	6.9	10.8
(SITC 27 + 28 + 68)	2000	4.1	4.2	4.4	4.2	3.9	2.1	22.2	6.2	12.8
	2005	6.9	7.0	6.3	5.0	2.9	4.7	33.5	7.9	13.6
Fuels (SITC 3)	1995	41.0	47.2	41.0	42.1	65.3	74.8	12.5	29.0	36.5
	2000	53.6	58.6	50.9	52.1	79.6	82.6	11.7	26.3	37.8
	2005	58.5	60.2	52.5	53.7	84.3	82.9	27.8	13.8	13.6
Manufactured goods	1995	25.7	24.2	27.9	27.6	14.6	12.2	18.8	48.5	19.0
(SITC 5 to 8 less 68)	2000	24.2	24.8	29.5	29.2	10.4	12.3	25.5	56.8	15.8
	2005	22.8	22.8	28.0	28.6	7.5	9.5	24.5	70.9	18.7

Sources:
- UNCTAD secretariat calculations based on UN DESA Statistics Division's data

2.2.E Structure des exportations par partenaires et groupes de produits
Économies en développement : Afrique

Total	Africa Afrique	America Amérique	Total (Asia/Asie)	Eastern, Southern and South-Eastern Asia / Asie orientale, méridionale et du Sud-Est	China Chine	Western Asia / Asie occidentale	Oceania Océanie	Major petroleum exporters / Principaux exportateurs de pétrole	Major exporters of manufactures / Principaux exportateurs d'articles manufacturés	Year Année	Destination / Groupes de produits
Millions de dollars											
24 317	10 775	2 367	11 166	8 678	913	2 489	9	3 119	10 228	1995	Total tous produits
40 828	14 588	4 709	20 939	16 744	4 203	4 195	591	4 536	20 565	2000	
83 407	27 972	9 004	46 070	37 576	19 553	8 494	361	10 210	44 308	2005	
Parts par destinations (en pourcentage)											
23.5	10.4	2.3	10.8	8.4	0.9	2.4	0.0	3.0	9.9	1995	Total tous produits
27.5	9.8	3.2	14.1	11.3	2.8	2.8	0.4	3.1	13.8	2000	
30.8	10.3	3.3	17.0	13.9	7.2	3.1	0.1	3.8	16.3	2005	
23.4	14.3	0.5	8.6	4.8	0.5	3.8	0.0	5.7	4.0	1995	Produits alimentaires
34.3	20.3	0.7	13.2	6.9	0.8	6.2	0.1	10.1	5.6	2000	(CTCI 0 + 1 + 22 + 4)
33.7	20.5	0.4	12.7	6.9	1.1	5.9	0.1	8.4	5.9	2005	
39.4	12.9	1.5	24.9	22.2	3.9	2.6	0.0	4.6	21.1	1995	Matières premières
44.6	15.2	1.6	27.8	25.1	5.9	2.7	0.0	4.4	23.9	2000	d'origine agricole
50.2	14.4	0.6	35.2	32.2	12.3	3.0	0.0	4.4	27.0	2005	(CTCI 2 - 22 - 27 - 28)
32.5	7.7	1.3	23.5	20.4	2.4	3.0	0.0	4.4	19.6	1995	Minerais et métaux
31.0	8.1	3.3	19.6	17.9	3.7	1.7	0.0	2.5	19.8	2000	(CTCI 27 + 28 + 68)
25.8	7.1	1.0	17.6	16.2	7.7	1.4	0.0	1.7	16.8	2005	
18.0	5.3	3.5	9.2	6.8	0.7	2.4	0.0	1.1	10.6	1995	Combustibles (CTCI 3)
27.4	5.3	4.7	16.7	14.0	4.2	2.7	0.7	1.5	18.6	2000	
29.5	5.8	4.7	18.9	16.1	10.3	2.7	0.2	2.3	20.5	2005	
34.1	20.1	2.4	11.6	9.4	0.7	2.3	0.0	4.9	10.0	1995	Articles manufacturés
28.1	16.9	1.7	9.5	6.9	0.6	2.6	0.0	4.4	7.5	2000	(CTCI 5 à 8 moins 68)
32.0	18.1	2.1	11.7	8.1	1.2	3.6	0.1	6.5	8.6	2005	
Parts par principaux groupes de produits (en pourcentage)											
100.0	100.0	100.0	100.0	100.0	100.0	100.0	100.0	100.0	100.0	1995	Total tous produits
100.0	100.0	100.0	100.0	100.0	100.0	100.0	100.0	100.0	100.0	2000	
100.0	100.0	100.0	100.0	100.0	100.0	100.0	100.0	100.0	100.0	2005	
13.7	18.9	2.9	11.0	8.0	8.3	21.5	17.0	26.0	5.6	1995	Produits alimentaires
11.3	18.8	2.0	8.5	5.6	2.7	20.1	2.2	29.9	3.7	2000	(CTCI 0 + 1 + 22 + 4)
8.7	15.7	0.9	5.9	3.9	1.2	14.8	8.6	17.6	2.9	2005	
8.6	6.4	3.5	11.9	13.7	22.8	5.7	8.4	7.9	11.0	1995	Matières premières
4.8	4.6	1.5	5.8	6.6	6.1	2.9	0.1	4.2	5.1	2000	d'origine agricole
4.3	3.6	0.5	5.4	6.1	4.5	2.5	0.4	3.0	4.3	2005	(CTCI 2 - 22 - 27 - 28)
8.2	4.4	3.3	12.8	14.4	16.3	7.5	16.8	8.6	11.7	1995	Minerais et métaux
4.6	3.4	4.2	5.7	6.5	5.3	2.5	0.0	3.3	5.8	2000	(CTCI 27 + 28 + 68)
5.8	4.8	2.2	7.2	8.1	7.5	3.1	0.1	3.1	7.1	2005	
31.4	20.7	63.3	34.9	33.4	31.2	40.1	18.3	15.2	43.9	1995	Combustibles (CTCI 3)
53.6	29.2	79.4	63.5	66.4	80.4	51.9	95.9	26.4	72.2	2000	
56.1	33.1	82.1	65.0	68.1	83.2	51.0	66.6	35.4	73.2	2005	
37.2	49.4	26.8	27.7	28.6	21.3	24.5	39.5	42.0	25.9	1995	Articles manufacturés
24.8	41.6	12.9	16.3	14.8	5.3	22.2	1.8	35.1	13.1	2000	(CTCI 5 à 8 moins 68)
23.7	39.9	14.3	15.7	13.3	3.7	26.2	24.2	39.3	12.0	2005	

Sources :
- Calculs du secrétariat de la CNUCED sur la base des données de ONU DAES Division de statistique

Origin Product group	Year Année	World Monde	Developed economies Économies développées							Economies in transition Économies en transition
			Total	Europe		Canada	USA États-Unis	Japan Japon	Other developed countries Autres économies développées	
				Total	EU UE					
Millions of dollars										
All products	1995	107 614	74 657	55 249	53 109	1 439	10 408	6 242	1 320	2 128
	2000	120 640	70 289	51 593	49 632	1 327	10 017	5 115	2 238	2 734
	2005	233 031	123 503	93 422	90 358	1 850	15 476	9 516	3 239	6 410
Share by origin (percentage)										
All products	1995	100.0	69.4	51.3	49.4	1.3	9.7	5.8	1.2	2.0
	2000	100.0	58.3	42.8	41.1	1.1	8.3	4.2	1.9	2.3
	2005	100.0	53.0	40.1	38.8	0.8	6.6	4.1	1.4	2.8
All food items	1995	100.0	64.9	40.5	38.7	4.3	17.5	0.2	2.4	1.3
(SITC 0 + 1 + 22 + 4)	2000	100.0	57.8	34.9	33.6	4.1	13.9	0.1	4.8	1.6
	2005	100.0	47.3	29.9	28.8	2.3	11.9	0.1	3.1	3.3
Agricultural raw materials	1995	100.0	60.6	46.9	46.3	1.8	8.5	0.9	2.5	9.1
(SITC 2 - 22 - 27 - 28)	2000	100.0	57.9	43.7	43.0	3.1	7.7	1.2	2.3	12.1
	2005	100.0	54.2	43.3	42.7	2.6	5.4	1.1	1.7	12.8
Ores and metals	1995	100.0	64.9	44.8	42.6	5.1	4.3	0.6	10.2	5.0
(SITC 27 + 28 + 68)	2000	100.0	56.5	31.4	29.7	1.8	2.2	0.9	20.1	8.1
	2005	100.0	44.1	26.3	25.6	0.8	2.6	0.4	13.9	6.6
Fuels (SITC 3)	1995	100.0	19.3	14.1	14.0	0.3	4.4	0.0	0.5	1.9
	2000	100.0	12.8	10.9	10.8	0.1	1.3	0.0	0.5	1.3
	2005	100.0	15.0	12.5	11.8	0.3	1.4	0.1	0.7	4.6
Manufactured goods	1995	100.0	75.8	58.2	55.9	0.6	8.6	7.8	0.7	1.7
(SITC 5 to 8 less 68)	2000	100.0	66.8	51.5	49.4	0.5	8.8	5.1	0.9	2.1
	2005	100.0	61.5	48.1	46.5	0.6	6.8	5.2	0.8	2.1
Share by major product group (percentage)										
All products	1995	100.0	100.0	100.0	100.0	100.0	100.0	100.0	100.0	100.0
	2000	100.0	100.0	100.0	100.0	100.0	100.0	100.0	100.0	100.0
	2005	100.0	100.0	100.0	100.0	100.0	100.0	100.0	100.0	100.0
All food items	1995	17.1	16.0	13.5	13.4	55.1	30.9	0.5	32.9	11.6
(SITC 0 + 1 + 22 + 4)	2000	15.6	15.5	12.7	12.8	57.7	26.2	0.4	40.2	11.2
	2005	13.8	12.3	10.3	10.3	40.3	24.8	0.3	31.1	16.5
Agricultural raw materials	1995	3.1	2.7	2.8	2.9	4.3	2.7	0.5	6.3	14.3
(SITC 2 - 22 - 27 - 28)	2000	2.2	2.2	2.3	2.3	6.2	2.1	0.6	2.8	12.0
	2005	1.8	1.8	2.0	2.0	6.0	1.5	0.5	2.3	8.4
Ores and metals	1995	2.1	2.0	1.9	1.9	8.2	1.0	0.2	17.8	5.4
(SITC 27 + 28 + 68)	2000	2.0	2.0	1.5	1.5	3.4	0.5	0.4	21.9	7.2
	2005	2.1	1.8	1.4	1.4	2.2	0.8	0.2	21.4	5.1
Fuels (SITC 3)	1995	7.3	2.0	2.0	2.1	1.4	3.3	0.1	3.2	7.0
	2000	12.6	2.8	3.2	3.3	1.4	2.0	0.0	3.1	7.0
	2005	12.3	3.5	3.9	3.8	4.1	2.6	0.4	6.1	20.4
Manufactured goods	1995	69.6	76.1	78.8	78.9	30.9	61.6	93.8	39.3	61.3
(SITC 5 to 8 less 68)	2000	64.7	74.2	77.8	77.7	31.2	68.4	78.5	31.4	61.2
	2005	66.4	77.0	79.6	79.6	47.3	68.2	84.6	38.5	49.6

Sources:
- UNCTAD secretariat calculations based on UN DESA Statistics Division's data

| Developing economies / Économies en développement | | | | | | | | | | Year / Année | Origine |
Total	Africa / Afrique	America / Amérique	Asia / Asie — Total	Eastern, Southern and South-Eastern Asia / Asie orientale, méridionale et du Sud-Est	China / Chine	Western Asia / Asie occidentale	Oceania / Océanie	Major petroleum exporters / Principaux exportateurs de pétrole	Major exporters of manufactures / Principaux exportateurs d'articles manufacturés		Groupes de produits
Millions de dollars											
28 765	9 003	2 923	16 821	13 002	2 201	3 820	18	6 455	12 915	1995	**Total tous produits**
42 909	16 206	2 908	23 745	15 225	3 877	8 520	50	12 686	14 494	2000	
96 304	30 348	8 888	56 894	40 736	14 897	16 158	173	23 766	42 441	2005	
Parts par origines (en pourcentage)											
26.7	8.4	2.7	15.6	12.1	2.0	3.5	0.0	6.0	12.0	1995	**Total tous produits**
35.6	13.4	2.4	19.7	12.6	3.2	7.1	0.0	10.5	12.0	2000	
41.3	13.0	3.8	24.4	17.5	6.4	6.9	0.1	10.2	18.2	2005	
32.8	8.4	9.8	14.6	12.5	2.0	2.0	0.0	2.3	15.3	1995	Produits alimentaires
37.6	14.5	8.9	13.9	11.7	2.8	2.2	0.2	2.2	13.2	2000	(CTCI 0 + 1 + 22 + 4)
49.0	15.4	16.3	17.0	14.4	1.9	2.5	0.3	3.5	18.8	2005	
29.2	13.3	3.8	12.1	9.3	0.3	2.8	0.0	4.8	10.0	1995	Matières premières
27.4	14.7	3.1	9.6	7.1	0.5	2.5	0.0	4.2	7.6	2000	d'origine agricole
31.8	15.2	2.6	14.0	11.4	1.6	2.6	0.0	4.5	11.4	2005	(CTCI 2 - 22 - 27 - 28)
29.7	14.4	3.0	12.3	3.8	1.5	8.5	0.0	7.4	6.9	1995	Minerais et métaux
32.2	16.9	3.5	11.7	4.9	1.6	6.8	0.1	6.7	7.4	2000	(CTCI 27 + 28 + 68)
48.8	28.7	4.5	15.5	7.4	3.0	8.1	0.0	8.8	10.8	2005	
69.9	28.3	1.6	39.9	19.7	0.2	20.1	0.1	55.1	1.4	1995	Combustibles (CTCI 3)
81.8	33.9	0.4	47.5	11.7	0.5	35.7	0.0	62.8	1.0	2000	
71.6	30.7	1.0	39.9	11.7	0.3	28.1	0.0	56.8	2.3	2005	
20.7	5.9	1.1	13.8	11.7	2.4	2.1	0.0	1.8	12.6	1995	Articles manufacturés
27.7	9.5	1.2	17.0	13.8	4.1	3.1	0.0	3.1	14.4	2000	(CTCI 5 à 8 moins 68)
35.6	9.3	1.7	24.6	20.3	9.0	4.3	0.0	3.6	21.9	2005	
Parts par principaux groupes de produits (en pourcentage)											
100.0	100.0	100.0	100.0	100.0	100.0	100.0	100.0	100.0	100.0	1995	**Total tous produits**
100.0	100.0	100.0	100.0	100.0	100.0	100.0	100.0	100.0	100.0	2000	
100.0	100.0	100.0	100.0	100.0	100.0	100.0	100.0	100.0	100.0	2005	
20.9	17.2	61.5	15.9	17.7	16.3	9.9	12.3	6.5	21.8	1995	Produits alimentaires
16.5	16.9	57.9	11.1	14.5	13.5	4.9	75.3	3.3	17.2	2000	(CTCI 0 + 1 + 22 + 4)
16.4	16.4	59.2	9.6	11.4	4.0	5.0	61.3	4.7	14.3	2005	
3.4	4.9	4.3	2.4	2.4	0.4	2.5	0.3	2.5	2.6	1995	Matières premières
1.7	2.4	2.9	1.1	1.3	0.4	0.8	0.2	0.9	1.4	2000	d'origine agricole
1.4	2.1	1.2	1.0	1.2	0.5	0.7	0.2	0.8	1.1	2005	(CTCI 2 - 22 - 27 - 28)
2.4	3.7	2.4	1.7	0.7	1.5	5.1	0.7	2.7	1.2	1995	Minerais et métaux
1.8	2.5	2.9	1.2	0.8	1.0	2.0	3.8	1.3	1.2	2000	(CTCI 27 + 28 + 68)
2.5	4.7	2.5	1.4	0.9	1.0	2.5	1.1	1.8	1.3	2005	
19.1	24.7	4.4	18.6	11.9	0.7	41.4	33.1	67.0	0.9	1995	Combustibles (CTCI 3)
28.9	31.7	2.2	30.3	11.7	1.9	63.7	0.0	75.2	1.1	2000	
21.4	29.1	3.3	20.2	8.3	0.6	50.1	1.6	68.7	1.6	2005	
53.9	48.9	27.0	61.3	67.2	80.8	41.1	53.2	21.3	73.3	1995	Articles manufacturés
50.3	45.8	31.8	55.7	71.0	82.9	28.4	20.5	19.2	77.8	2000	(CTCI 5 à 8 moins 68)
57.2	47.3	29.3	66.9	76.9	93.7	41.5	35.8	23.7	79.7	2005	

Sources :
- Calculs du secrétariat de la CNUCED sur la base des données de ONU DAES Division de statistique

2.2.F Export structure by partner and product group
Developing economies: America

Destination / Product group	Year Année	World Monde	Developed economies / Économies développées — Total	Europe Total	Europe EU UE	Canada	USA États-Unis	Japan Japon	Other developed countries Autres économies développées	Economies in transition Économies en transition
Millions of dollars										
All products	1995	225 642	157 165	39 836	37 587	3 895	103 466	8 971	998	1 904
	2000	352 717	265 201	42 066	39 339	6 047	207 881	7 569	1 639	1 569
	2005	561 955	378 181	72 250	68 072	11 213	281 113	11 384	2 221	6 387
Share by destination (percentage)										
All products	1995	100.0	69.7	17.7	16.7	1.7	45.9	4.0	0.4	0.8
	2000	100.0	75.2	11.9	11.2	1.7	58.9	2.1	0.5	0.4
	2005	100.0	67.3	12.9	12.1	2.0	50.0	2.0	0.4	1.1
All food items	1995	100.0	64.0	33.3	32.4	0.9	23.7	5.3	0.8	3.2
(SITC 0 + 1 + 22 + 4)	2000	100.0	61.2	27.1	26.1	1.4	27.4	4.4	0.9	2.4
	2005	100.0	56.2	27.6	27.0	1.2	22.5	4.0	0.8	5.6
Agricultural raw materials	1995	100.0	66.2	30.3	28.8	0.4	25.2	10.1	0.2	0.1
(SITC 2 - 22 - 27 - 28)	2000	100.0	71.8	30.2	29.0	0.6	32.4	8.3	0.3	0.2
	2005	100.0	66.0	26.2	25.0	0.8	32.6	5.7	0.6	0.9
Ores and metals	1995	100.0	70.8	31.4	29.5	2.6	18.9	17.8	0.3	0.9
(SITC 27 + 28 + 68)	2000	100.0	67.8	30.5	27.1	3.3	20.6	13.2	0.2	0.9
	2005	100.0	57.1	26.0	24.3	4.2	15.7	11.1	0.1	1.4
Fuels (SITC 3)	1995	100.0	70.2	8.5	8.4	1.2	58.8	1.5	0.3	0.0
	2000	100.0	71.2	6.3	6.2	1.3	62.7	0.6	0.2	0.0
	2005	100.0	63.5	6.9	6.2	1.2	55.1	0.0	0.3	0.0
Manufactured goods	1995	100.0	71.8	8.9	8.1	2.1	59.2	1.2	0.4	0.1
(SITC 5 to 8 less 68)	2000	100.0	81.5	6.3	6.0	1.7	72.3	0.6	0.5	0.0
	2005	100.0	74.1	7.5	7.4	1.9	63.8	0.5	0.4	0.2
Share by major product group (percentage)										
All products	1995	100.0	100.0	100.0	100.0	100.0	100.0	100.0	100.0	100.0
	2000	100.0	100.0	100.0	100.0	100.0	100.0	100.0	100.0	100.0
	2005	100.0	100.0	100.0	100.0	100.0	100.0	100.0	100.0	100.0
All food items	1995	22.5	20.6	42.3	43.7	12.3	11.6	29.8	39.3	85.5
(SITC 0 + 1 + 22 + 4)	2000	15.1	12.3	34.3	35.4	12.0	7.0	31.2	30.7	81.6
	2005	16.1	13.5	34.7	35.9	9.9	7.3	32.0	32.9	80.2
Agricultural raw materials	1995	3.8	3.6	6.4	6.5	0.9	2.1	9.5	1.7	0.4
(SITC 2 - 22 - 27 - 28)	2000	2.2	2.1	5.6	5.8	0.8	1.2	8.6	1.5	1.1
	2005	2.1	2.0	4.2	4.3	0.9	1.3	5.8	2.9	1.6
Ores and metals	1995	9.1	9.2	16.1	16.0	13.6	3.7	40.5	5.1	9.2
(SITC 27 + 28 + 68)	2000	6.4	5.8	16.4	15.5	12.1	2.2	39.3	3.0	13.6
	2005	9.0	7.6	18.2	18.0	19.0	2.8	49.3	2.8	10.9
Fuels (SITC 3)	1995	14.6	14.8	7.0	7.4	10.1	18.8	5.4	9.5	0.5
	2000	18.0	17.1	9.5	10.1	14.0	19.2	4.7	8.6	0.4
	2005	22.3	21.1	12.0	11.5	13.6	24.6	0.0	14.8	0.2
Manufactured goods	1995	48.7	50.2	24.4	23.7	60.7	62.9	14.7	44.2	4.5
(SITC 5 to 8 less 68)	2000	57.0	61.7	30.3	30.7	58.1	69.9	15.9	56.0	3.2
	2005	49.1	54.1	28.8	29.9	46.9	62.6	12.8	45.8	7.1

Sources:
- UNCTAD secretariat calculations based on UN DESA Statistics Division's data

Total	Africa / Afrique	America / Amérique	Total	Eastern, Southern and South-Eastern Asia / Asie orientale, méridionale et du Sud-Est	China / Chine	Western Asia / Asie occidentale	Oceania / Océanie	Major petroleum exporters / Principaux exportateurs de pétrole	Major exporters of manufactures / Principaux exportateurs d'articles manufacturés	Year / Année	Destination / Groupes de produits
				Asia / Asie							

Millions de dollars

Total	Africa / Afrique	America / Amérique	Total	Eastern, Southern and South-Eastern Asia	China / Chine	Western Asia	Oceania / Océanie	Major petroleum exporters	Major exporters of manufactures	Year	Groupes de produits
65 173	2 966	46 523	15 655	13 825	2 621	1 830	29	7 658	24 161	1995	Total tous produits
79 834	2 866	61 107	15 846	13 522	3 775	2 324	15	11 196	27 633	2000	
165 246	9 425	106 774	49 012	43 179	18 617	5 834	34	19 695	61 856	2005	

Parts par destinations (en pourcentage)

Total	Afrique	Amérique	Total	Eastern...	Chine	Western	Océanie	pétrole	manufacturés	Year	Groupes de produits
28.9	1.3	20.6	6.9	6.1	1.2	0.8	0.0	3.4	10.7	1995	Total tous produits
22.6	0.8	17.3	4.5	3.8	1.1	0.7	0.0	3.2	7.8	2000	
29.4	1.7	19.0	8.7	7.7	3.3	1.0	0.0	3.5	11.0	2005	
32.5	3.6	17.4	11.6	9.6	2.9	1.9	0.0	5.5	13.5	1995	Produits alimentaires
33.2	2.9	18.5	11.7	9.3	3.1	2.4	0.0	5.5	13.4	2000	(CTCI 0 + 1 + 22 + 4)
37.9	5.5	14.6	17.8	14.2	6.4	3.6	0.0	8.0	15.7	2005	
33.4	1.1	15.3	17.1	16.0	3.3	1.1	0.0	4.3	18.7	1995	Matières premières
27.8	0.8	13.5	13.5	12.5	4.5	1.0	0.0	3.5	15.9	2000	d'origine agricole
33.0	0.7	12.0	20.3	18.9	10.7	1.4	0.0	2.9	21.3	2005	(CTCI 2 - 22 - 27 - 28)
27.4	0.8	12.0	14.7	13.7	2.3	0.9	0.0	2.8	18.5	1995	Minerais et métaux
30.1	1.1	12.6	16.4	14.5	4.9	1.9	0.0	3.1	20.4	2000	(CTCI 27 + 28 + 68)
41.4	1.2	12.2	28.0	26.6	15.1	1.4	0.0	2.9	32.2	2005	
28.4	0.3	26.8	1.3	1.3	0.0	0.0	0.0	3.8	9.2	1995	Combustibles (CTCI 3)
26.1	0.1	24.6	1.3	1.2	0.1	0.1	0.0	6.1	6.1	2000	
28.1	0.4	23.7	3.9	3.8	0.6	0.1	0.0	1.3	6.1	2005	
28.0	0.7	22.7	4.5	4.0	0.4	0.5	0.0	2.4	8.1	1995	Articles manufacturés
18.1	0.4	15.7	2.0	1.8	0.3	0.2	0.0	1.7	5.4	2000	(CTCI 5 à 8 moins 68)
25.6	1.1	20.3	4.1	3.6	1.1	0.5	0.0	3.3	7.7	2005	

Parts par principaux groupes de produits (en pourcentage)

Total	Afrique	Amérique	Total	Eastern...	Chine	Western	Océanie	pétrole	manufacturés	Year	Groupes de produits
100.0	100.0	100.0	100.0	100.0	100.0	100.0	100.0	100.0	100.0	1995	Total tous produits
100.0	100.0	100.0	100.0	100.0	100.0	100.0	100.0	100.0	100.0	2000	
100.0	100.0	100.0	100.0	100.0	100.0	100.0	100.0	100.0	100.0	2005	
25.3	60.7	19.0	37.4	35.3	55.6	53.3	30.0	36.3	28.2	1995	Produits alimentaires
22.2	54.9	16.2	39.3	36.5	43.1	55.6	73.7	26.2	25.8	2000	(CTCI 0 + 1 + 22 + 4)
20.8	52.7	12.4	33.0	29.8	31.3	56.3	60.5	37.0	23.1	2005	
4.3	3.0	2.8	9.2	9.8	10.6	5.1	0.3	4.7	6.6	1995	Matières premières
2.7	2.1	1.7	6.7	7.3	9.5	3.5	0.3	2.4	4.5	2000	d'origine agricole
2.3	0.9	1.3	4.8	5.1	6.7	2.7	0.6	1.7	4.0	2005	(CTCI 2 - 22 - 27 - 28)
8.6	5.2	5.3	19.1	20.3	17.6	10.1	0.1	7.5	15.6	1995	Minerais et métaux
8.5	8.5	4.7	23.4	24.2	29.1	18.7	0.0	6.2	16.6	2000	(CTCI 27 + 28 + 68)
12.7	6.6	5.8	28.9	31.1	41.0	12.3	0.2	7.4	26.3	2005	
14.4	3.5	19.0	2.7	3.0	0.1	0.8	3.1	16.5	12.6	1995	Combustibles (CTCI 3)
20.8	3.2	25.6	5.2	5.8	1.3	1.8	0.6	34.4	14.0	2000	
21.3	6.0	27.9	10.1	11.1	4.3	2.6	1.4	8.0	12.4	2005	
47.2	27.4	53.8	31.3	31.4	16.0	30.6	66.5	35.0	36.9	1995	Articles manufacturés
45.6	30.1	51.6	25.2	26.2	16.9	19.6	25.3	30.5	39.0	2000	(CTCI 5 à 8 moins 68)
42.7	33.4	52.5	23.2	22.9	16.7	25.9	37.2	45.8	34.2	2005	

Sources :
- Calculs du secrétariat de la CNUCED sur la base des données de ONU DAES Division de statistique

Product group	Year / Année	World / Monde	Developed economies / Économies développées — Total	Europe Total	Europe EU / UE	Canada	USA / États-Unis	Japan / Japon	Other developed countries / Autres économies développées	Economies in transition / Économies en transition
Millions of dollars										
All products	1995	237 890	169 118	47 049	44 079	5 245	102 469	12 737	1 618	1 534
	2000	369 090	261 473	53 529	50 511	8 106	182 403	14 932	2 504	2 100
	2005	504 192	300 168	77 439	72 587	10 334	184 184	23 861	4 349	4 145
Share by origin (percentage)										
All products	1995	100.0	71.1	19.8	18.5	2.2	43.1	5.4	0.7	0.6
	2000	100.0	70.8	14.5	13.7	2.2	49.4	4.0	0.7	0.6
	2005	100.0	59.5	15.4	14.4	2.0	36.5	4.7	0.9	0.8
All food items	1995	100.0	58.0	15.1	13.9	5.2	35.6	0.1	2.0	0.1
(SITC 0 + 1 + 22 + 4)	2000	100.0	58.6	11.1	10.3	5.8	39.8	0.0	2.0	0.1
	2005	100.0	57.9	9.1	8.5	5.0	41.5	0.0	2.2	0.1
Agricultural raw materials	1995	100.0	60.6	7.6	7.4	3.5	46.9	0.5	2.1	1.7
(SITC 2 - 22 - 27 - 28)	2000	100.0	67.4	7.8	7.5	2.4	55.1	0.7	1.4	0.8
	2005	100.0	62.7	8.6	8.4	2.7	49.8	0.6	1.0	0.5
Ores and metals	1995	100.0	52.6	11.3	10.1	5.8	33.1	0.8	1.7	0.4
(SITC 27 + 28 + 68)	2000	100.0	51.6	9.5	9.1	3.2	37.1	0.7	1.2	2.6
	2005	100.0	42.7	7.8	7.6	3.2	30.4	0.5	0.8	1.2
Fuels (SITC 3)	1995	100.0	29.7	6.2	6.0	1.4	20.0	0.3	1.8	3.0
	2000	100.0	25.5	3.9	3.4	0.5	19.6	0.2	1.2	1.0
	2005	100.0	34.4	5.1	4.0	0.8	25.6	0.3	2.5	1.2
Manufactured goods	1995	100.0	76.6	22.6	21.1	1.7	45.7	6.2	0.4	0.5
(SITC 5 to 8 less 68)	2000	100.0	77.3	16.3	15.4	2.0	53.7	4.9	0.5	0.5
	2005	100.0	63.6	17.7	16.7	1.9	37.6	6.0	0.5	0.8
Share by major product group (percentage)										
All products	1995	100.0	100.0	100.0	100.0	100.0	100.0	100.0	100.0	100.0
	2000	100.0	100.0	100.0	100.0	100.0	100.0	100.0	100.0	100.0
	2005	100.0	100.0	100.0	100.0	100.0	100.0	100.0	100.0	100.0
All food items	1995	9.5	7.7	7.2	7.1	22.5	7.8	0.1	27.9	1.2
(SITC 0 + 1 + 22 + 4)	2000	7.4	6.1	5.6	5.6	19.4	5.9	0.1	21.5	1.5
	2005	7.2	7.0	4.3	4.3	17.6	8.2	0.1	18.5	0.6
Agricultural raw materials	1995	2.3	2.0	0.9	0.9	3.7	2.5	0.2	7.2	6.1
(SITC 2 - 22 - 27 - 28)	2000	1.6	1.5	0.9	0.9	1.8	1.8	0.3	3.2	2.2
	2005	1.4	1.5	0.8	0.8	1.8	1.9	0.2	1.6	0.9
Ores and metals	1995	2.4	1.8	1.4	1.3	6.3	1.9	0.4	5.9	1.6
(SITC 27 + 28 + 68)	2000	2.0	1.5	1.3	1.3	2.9	1.5	0.4	3.5	9.0
	2005	2.5	1.8	1.3	1.3	3.9	2.1	0.3	2.4	3.8
Fuels (SITC 3)	1995	7.0	2.9	2.2	2.3	4.5	3.2	0.4	18.5	32.4
	2000	8.1	2.9	2.2	2.0	2.0	3.2	0.5	14.7	14.5
	2005	10.6	6.1	3.6	3.0	4.3	7.4	0.7	30.5	15.2
Manufactured goods	1995	76.3	82.1	87.0	87.0	59.2	80.9	88.6	40.5	58.7
(SITC 5 to 8 less 68)	2000	79.4	86.7	89.1	89.2	72.6	86.3	95.6	56.8	72.3
	2005	77.5	82.8	89.3	89.8	72.1	79.7	97.5	46.6	77.2

Sources:
- UNCTAD secretariat calculations based on UN DESA Statistics Division's data

2.2.F Structure des importations par partenaires et groupes de produits
Économies en développement : Amérique

Total	Africa / Afrique	America / Amérique	Asia / Asie — Total	Eastern, Southern and South-Eastern Asia / Asie orientale, méridionale et du Sud-Est	China / Chine	Western Asia / Asie occidentale	Oceania / Océanie	Major petroleum exporters / Principaux exportateurs de pétrole	Major exporters of manufactures / Principaux exportateurs d'articles manufacturés	Year / Année	Origine / Groupes de produits
Developing economies — Économies en développement											
Millions de dollars											
65 890	2 525	45 110	18 230	16 253	2 691	1 977	24	10 692	29 514	1995	Total tous produits
100 926	5 155	63 534	32 228	30 233	8 475	1 995	8	17 695	48 099	2000	
198 372	11 110	104 756	82 491	79 200	36 182	3 291	16	25 071	116 720	2005	
Parts par origines (en pourcentage)											
27.7	1.1	19.0	7.7	6.8	1.1	0.8	0.0	4.5	12.4	1995	Total tous produits
27.3	1.4	17.2	8.7	8.2	2.3	0.5	0.0	4.8	13.0	2000	
39.3	2.2	20.8	16.4	15.7	7.2	0.7	0.0	5.0	23.1	2005	
41.5	0.4	38.8	2.3	2.1	0.4	0.2	0.0	2.1	6.5	1995	Produits alimentaires
40.3	0.4	37.5	2.4	2.2	0.7	0.2	0.0	1.9	6.9	2000	(CTCI 0 + 1 + 22 + 4)
41.8	0.2	38.1	3.5	3.2	1.1	0.3	0.0	1.5	7.5	2005	
37.2	2.5	25.6	9.2	9.1	0.4	0.1	0.0	3.3	11.9	1995	Matières premières
31.0	3.4	20.5	7.1	7.1	1.2	0.1	0.0	2.2	10.7	2000	d'origine agricole
36.7	0.6	24.2	11.8	11.6	1.4	0.2	0.0	3.8	16.3	2005	(CTCI 2 - 22 - 27 - 28)
46.8	3.0	42.1	1.6	1.5	0.4	0.1	0.0	5.5	10.8	1995	Minerais et métaux
44.8	3.0	39.3	2.4	2.2	0.9	0.2	0.0	4.5	12.6	2000	(CTCI 27 + 28 + 68)
56.0	2.3	50.8	2.8	2.5	1.7	0.3	0.0	4.5	14.9	2005	
66.9	8.8	44.5	13.6	3.0	0.9	10.6	0.0	41.7	5.0	1995	Combustibles (CTCI 3)
73.0	13.1	52.5	7.4	2.0	0.8	5.3	0.0	45.1	3.7	2000	
64.0	17.8	37.9	8.3	3.5	0.9	4.7	0.0	34.6	7.7	2005	
22.3	0.4	13.8	8.1	8.0	1.3	0.1	0.0	1.5	14.2	1995	Articles manufacturés
20.8	0.2	11.3	9.2	9.1	2.7	0.1	0.0	1.1	14.2	2000	(CTCI 5 à 8 moins 68)
35.2	0.3	15.8	19.1	19.0	8.8	0.2	0.0	1.3	27.0	2005	
Parts par principaux groupes de produits (en pourcentage)											
100.0	100.0	100.0	100.0	100.0	100.0	100.0	100.0	100.0	100.0	1995	Total tous produits
100.0	100.0	100.0	100.0	100.0	100.0	100.0	100.0	100.0	100.0	2000	
100.0	100.0	100.0	100.0	100.0	100.0	100.0	100.0	100.0	100.0	2005	
14.2	3.3	19.4	2.9	2.9	3.2	2.4	4.1	4.4	5.0	1995	Produits alimentaires
10.9	2.3	16.0	2.0	2.0	2.2	3.3	13.4	2.9	3.9	2000	(CTCI 0 + 1 + 22 + 4)
7.7	0.7	13.3	1.6	1.5	1.1	2.9	8.8	2.3	2.3	2005	
3.1	5.4	3.1	2.8	3.1	0.8	0.2	0.3	1.7	2.2	1995	Matières premières
1.8	3.9	1.9	1.3	1.4	0.8	0.2	1.2	0.7	1.3	2000	d'origine agricole
1.3	0.4	1.6	1.0	1.0	0.3	0.5	2.4	1.0	1.0	2005	(CTCI 2 - 22 - 27 - 28)
4.1	6.8	5.4	0.5	0.5	0.9	0.3	0.1	2.9	2.1	1995	Minerais et métaux
3.3	4.3	4.6	0.6	0.6	0.8	0.6	0.0	1.9	1.9	2000	(CTCI 27 + 28 + 68)
3.6	2.6	6.2	0.4	0.4	0.6	1.1	8.2	2.3	1.6	2005	
16.8	57.9	16.3	12.3	3.0	5.5	88.6	0.0	64.6	2.8	1995	Combustibles (CTCI 3)
21.7	76.3	24.9	6.9	2.0	2.8	80.6	0.0	76.7	2.3	2000	
17.3	85.7	19.4	5.4	2.4	1.3	76.9	0.0	73.9	3.5	2005	
61.3	26.5	55.4	80.7	89.5	89.3	8.4	95.4	25.8	87.2	1995	Articles manufacturés
60.3	13.2	52.3	83.6	88.2	91.9	15.3	85.3	17.7	86.7	2000	(CTCI 5 à 8 moins 68)
69.3	10.5	58.9	90.5	93.5	95.4	18.2	73.5	20.0	90.3	2005	

Sources :
- Calculs du secrétariat de la CNUCED sur la base des données de ONU DAES Division de statistique

Destination / Product group	Year / Année	World / Monde	Developed economies / Économies développées							Economies in transition / Économies en transition
			Total	Europe		Canada	USA / États-Unis	Japan / Japon	Other developed countries / Autres économies développées	
				Total	EU / UE					
Millions of dollars										
All products	1995	1 082 579	546 192	179 534	173 419	11 156	194 076	142 672	18 754	12 736
	2000	1 516 384	803 323	270 084	255 649	15 656	301 501	186 719	29 362	12 000
	2005	2 863 589	1 343 993	496 094	468 516	28 542	457 382	301 399	60 576	48 704
Share by destination (percentage)										
All products	1995	100.0	50.5	16.6	16.0	1.0	17.9	13.2	1.7	1.2
	2000	100.0	53.0	17.8	16.9	1.0	19.9	12.3	1.9	0.8
	2005	100.0	46.9	17.3	16.4	1.0	16.0	10.5	2.1	1.7
All food items	1995	100.0	46.6	14.6	13.9	0.8	7.5	22.3	1.4	3.7
(SITC 0 + 1 + 22 + 4)	2000	100.0	47.7	14.1	13.6	1.1	10.6	20.3	1.6	2.7
	2005	100.0	44.9	16.1	15.7	1.2	10.3	15.3	2.0	3.8
Agricultural raw materials	1995	100.0	44.5	15.7	15.5	0.9	9.9	16.8	1.3	0.5
(SITC 2 - 22 - 27 - 28)	2000	100.0	40.7	16.3	16.1	0.8	8.4	14.1	1.3	0.5
	2005	100.0	39.2	15.3	15.2	1.3	9.9	11.4	1.2	0.9
Ores and metals	1995	100.0	35.4	8.9	8.7	0.3	3.2	22.1	1.0	2.4
(SITC 27 + 28 + 68)	2000	100.0	35.2	11.3	10.8	0.5	5.2	16.1	2.2	1.1
	2005	100.0	27.6	9.6	9.3	0.5	4.1	12.1	1.3	1.3
Fuels (SITC 3)	1995	100.0	45.0	11.8	11.8	0.4	6.4	25.2	1.3	0.1
	2000	100.0	50.5	16.6	14.0	0.3	11.2	21.0	1.5	0.2
	2005	100.0	48.6	13.3	10.4	0.5	10.5	21.8	2.5	0.1
Manufactured goods	1995	100.0	52.3	17.9	17.2	1.2	21.5	9.9	1.9	1.1
(SITC 5 to 8 less 68)	2000	100.0	54.5	18.4	17.9	1.2	23.0	9.8	2.0	0.8
	2005	100.0	48.1	18.8	18.3	1.1	18.4	7.7	2.1	2.0
Share by major product group (percentage)										
All products	1995	100.0	100.0	100.0	100.0	100.0	100.0	100.0	100.0	100.0
	2000	100.0	100.0	100.0	100.0	100.0	100.0	100.0	100.0	100.0
	2005	100.0	100.0	100.0	100.0	100.0	100.0	100.0	100.0	100.0
All food items	1995	6.7	6.2	5.9	5.8	5.2	2.8	11.3	5.5	20.9
(SITC 0 + 1 + 22 + 4)	2000	4.4	4.0	3.5	3.6	4.7	2.4	7.3	3.7	15.3
	2005	3.7	3.6	3.5	3.6	4.3	2.4	5.4	3.5	8.4
Agricultural raw materials	1995	2.2	1.9	2.1	2.1	1.8	1.2	2.8	1.6	0.9
(SITC 2 - 22 - 27 - 28)	2000	1.2	1.0	1.1	1.2	0.9	0.5	1.4	0.8	0.8
	2005	1.0	0.9	0.9	1.0	1.4	0.6	1.1	0.6	0.6
Ores and metals	1995	2.0	1.4	1.1	1.1	0.6	0.3	3.3	1.1	4.0
(SITC 27 + 28 + 68)	2000	1.6	1.0	1.0	1.0	0.8	0.4	2.0	1.7	2.2
	2005	1.9	1.1	1.1	1.1	1.1	0.5	2.2	1.2	1.5
Fuels (SITC 3)	1995	13.3	11.9	9.5	9.8	5.5	4.7	25.5	9.7	1.4
	2000	17.3	16.5	16.2	14.4	4.6	9.7	29.5	13.1	3.3
	2005	17.9	18.5	13.8	11.4	9.3	11.8	37.1	20.8	1.2
Manufactured goods	1995	74.4	77.2	80.1	79.9	85.9	89.0	56.1	81.1	72.3
(SITC 5 to 8 less 68)	2000	74.7	76.9	77.3	79.2	88.7	86.6	59.3	78.6	77.9
	2005	73.3	75.1	79.6	82.1	83.1	84.2	53.6	71.8	87.9

Sources:
- UNCTAD secretariat calculations based on UN DESA Statistics Division's data

			Developing economies								
			Économies en développement								Destination
Total	Africa Afrique	America Amérique	Asia Asie Total	Eastern, Southern and South-Eastern Asia Asie orientale, méridionale et du Sud-Est	China Chine	Western Asia Asie occidentale	Oceania Océanie	Major petroleum exporters Principaux exportateurs de pétrole	Major exporters of manufactures Principaux exportateurs d'articles manufacturés	Year Année	Groupes de produits
Millions de dollars											
477 747	20 420	23 680	432 380	398 939	78 662	33 441	1 267	45 788	369 655	1995	**Total tous produits**
679 392	29 060	35 803	612 212	567 156	116 009	45 055	2 318	57 578	536 922	2000	
1 395 654	63 580	62 783	1 264 215	1 159 517	312 412	104 698	5 076	168 406	1 064 740	2005	
Parts par destinations (en pourcentage)											
44.1	1.9	2.2	39.9	36.9	7.3	3.1	0.1	4.2	34.1	1995	**Total tous produits**
44.8	1.9	2.4	40.4	37.4	7.7	3.0	0.2	3.8	35.4	2000	
48.7	2.2	2.2	44.1	40.5	10.9	3.7	0.2	5.9	37.2	2005	
49.4	3.4	0.6	45.2	37.7	7.0	7.6	0.1	10.2	29.1	1995	Produits alimentaires
49.0	3.8	0.8	44.2	35.4	5.9	8.8	0.1	10.7	28.1	2000	(CTCI 0 + 1 + 22 + 4)
51.0	5.4	1.1	44.3	34.6	4.9	9.7	0.2	12.6	25.9	2005	
54.9	1.8	2.0	51.0	48.8	13.2	2.3	0.0	3.6	46.0	1995	Matières premières
58.5	1.3	1.6	55.6	52.9	21.4	2.7	0.0	4.1	48.7	2000	d'origine agricole
59.6	1.7	2.3	55.6	52.8	23.4	2.8	0.0	4.0	48.0	2005	(CTCI 2 - 22 - 27 - 28)
61.8	0.8	0.3	60.7	56.9	14.0	3.8	0.0	4.9	53.1	1995	Minerais et métaux
63.5	1.0	0.6	61.9	57.7	15.1	4.2	0.0	5.3	54.6	2000	(CTCI 27 + 28 + 68)
70.8	1.3	0.5	69.0	64.0	23.4	5.0	0.0	6.6	60.4	2005	
24.6	1.2	0.4	22.7	21.6	3.3	1.1	0.2	0.6	20.2	1995	Combustibles (CTCI 3)
42.3	2.5	1.4	38.1	36.4	4.1	1.7	0.3	1.1	34.9	2000	
43.0	1.4	1.0	40.4	38.4	5.0	2.0	0.3	3.8	34.3	2005	
46.2	1.9	2.7	41.6	38.5	7.7	3.1	0.1	4.4	36.1	1995	Articles manufacturés
44.4	1.7	2.7	39.9	37.0	8.2	2.8	0.1	3.9	35.3	2000	(CTCI 5 à 8 moins 68)
49.7	2.3	2.5	44.8	41.1	12.4	3.7	0.1	6.0	38.3	2005	
Parts par principaux groupes de produits (en pourcentage)											
100.0	100.0	100.0	100.0	100.0	100.0	100.0	100.0	100.0	100.0	1995	**Total tous produits**
100.0	100.0	100.0	100.0	100.0	100.0	100.0	100.0	100.0	100.0	2000	
100.0	100.0	100.0	100.0	100.0	100.0	100.0	100.0	100.0	100.0	2005	
7.5	12.0	2.0	7.6	6.8	6.5	16.4	7.4	16.1	5.7	1995	Produits alimentaires
4.9	8.9	1.6	4.9	4.2	3.5	13.2	4.3	12.6	3.5	2000	(CTCI 0 + 1 + 22 + 4)
3.9	9.1	1.9	3.7	3.2	1.7	9.9	3.8	8.0	2.6	2005	
2.7	2.1	2.0	2.8	2.9	3.9	1.6	0.3	1.9	2.9	1995	Matières premières
1.6	0.8	0.8	1.7	1.8	3.5	1.1	0.2	1.3	1.7	2000	d'origine agricole
1.3	0.8	1.1	1.3	1.3	2.2	0.8	0.1	0.7	1.3	2005	(CTCI 2 - 22 - 27 - 28)
2.8	0.8	0.3	3.0	3.0	3.8	2.4	0.3	2.3	3.1	1995	Minerais et métaux
2.2	0.8	0.4	2.4	2.4	3.1	2.2	0.3	2.2	2.4	2000	(CTCI 27 + 28 + 68)
2.8	1.1	0.4	3.0	3.1	4.2	2.7	0.2	2.2	3.1	2005	
7.4	8.8	2.4	7.6	7.8	6.0	4.9	25.6	2.0	7.9	1995	Combustibles (CTCI 3)
16.4	22.7	10.1	16.4	16.9	9.3	10.2	31.6	5.0	17.1	2000	
15.8	10.9	8.0	16.4	17.0	8.2	9.7	32.9	11.6	16.5	2005	
77.9	74.7	91.3	77.4	77.7	79.0	73.7	63.3	76.8	78.7	1995	Articles manufacturés
74.1	66.4	86.9	73.8	74.0	80.3	71.5	63.2	77.5	74.5	2000	(CTCI 5 à 8 moins 68)
74.8	75.5	84.6	74.3	74.4	83.4	73.6	57.1	74.9	75.4	2005	

Sources :
- Calculs du secrétariat de la CNUCED sur la base des données de ONU DAES Division de statistique

2.2.G Import structure by partner and product group
Developing economies: Asia

Origin / Product group	Year Année	World Monde	Developed economies / Économies développées Total	Europe Total	Europe EU UE	Canada	USA États-Unis	Japan Japon	Other developed countries Autres économies développées	Economies in transition Économies en transition
Millions of dollars										
All products	1995	1 119 607	633 909	216 599	198 465	13 025	153 713	221 302	29 270	22 106
	2000	1 355 315	655 770	222 151	202 123	13 144	161 338	222 179	36 958	26 047
	2005	2 557 239	1 037 698	400 952	361 072	18 760	214 308	336 276	67 402	69 252
Share by origin (percentage)										
All products	1995	100.0	56.6	19.3	17.7	1.2	13.7	19.8	2.6	2.0
	2000	100.0	48.4	16.4	14.9	1.0	11.9	16.4	2.7	1.9
	2005	100.0	40.6	15.7	14.1	0.7	8.4	13.1	2.6	2.7
All food items	1995	100.0	53.1	17.2	16.6	3.5	21.5	2.3	8.6	1.5
(SITC 0 + 1 + 22 + 4)	2000	100.0	50.0	16.1	15.3	3.6	17.6	2.2	10.5	1.5
	2005	100.0	40.3	13.9	12.8	2.4	13.1	1.9	9.1	2.9
Agricultural raw materials	1995	100.0	51.2	9.3	9.0	4.9	22.7	5.1	9.1	5.5
(SITC 2 - 22 - 27 - 28)	2000	100.0	50.9	12.5	12.1	6.8	16.7	5.0	9.9	6.3
	2005	100.0	48.7	12.8	12.3	5.4	18.3	4.6	7.6	8.9
Ores and metals	1995	100.0	50.3	14.3	13.3	2.6	11.4	10.0	12.0	6.8
(SITC 27 + 28 + 68)	2000	100.0	45.3	12.2	10.2	1.9	6.8	10.3	13.9	9.6
	2005	100.0	39.7	9.1	8.2	2.1	5.7	7.6	15.2	8.2
Fuels (SITC 3)	1995	100.0	11.6	2.0	2.0	0.6	2.8	2.0	4.2	2.1
	2000	100.0	8.0	2.2	1.5	0.2	1.0	0.7	3.8	2.4
	2005	100.0	6.9	1.5	1.0	0.2	0.9	0.7	3.6	4.8
Manufactured goods	1995	100.0	61.0	21.4	19.9	0.7	13.6	24.3	1.0	1.6
(SITC 5 to 8 less 68)	2000	100.0	54.2	18.4	17.2	0.7	13.3	20.8	1.0	1.3
	2005	100.0	46.6	18.5	17.3	0.5	9.5	17.2	0.9	1.6
Share by major product group (percentage)										
All products	1995	100.0	100.0	100.0	100.0	100.0	100.0	100.0	100.0	100.0
	2000	100.0	100.0	100.0	100.0	100.0	100.0	100.0	100.0	100.0
	2005	100.0	100.0	100.0	100.0	100.0	100.0	100.0	100.0	100.0
All food items	1995	6.8	6.4	6.1	6.4	20.6	10.7	0.8	22.6	5.1
(SITC 0 + 1 + 22 + 4)	2000	5.7	5.8	5.6	5.8	20.7	8.4	0.8	21.9	4.5
	2005	4.6	4.6	4.1	4.2	15.1	7.2	0.7	15.9	4.9
Agricultural raw materials	1995	3.2	2.9	1.6	1.6	13.7	5.4	0.8	11.2	9.0
(SITC 2 - 22 - 27 - 28)	2000	2.5	2.6	1.9	2.0	17.5	3.5	0.8	9.1	8.2
	2005	2.1	2.5	1.7	1.8	15.0	4.5	0.7	6.0	6.8
Ores and metals	1995	3.9	3.4	2.9	2.9	8.7	3.2	2.0	17.6	13.3
(SITC 27 + 28 + 68)	2000	3.6	3.4	2.7	2.5	7.3	2.1	2.3	18.5	18.0
	2005	5.0	4.9	2.9	2.9	14.6	3.4	2.9	29.0	15.3
Fuels (SITC 3)	1995	7.0	1.4	0.7	0.8	3.4	1.4	0.7	11.2	7.5
	2000	11.2	1.9	1.5	1.2	2.7	1.0	0.5	15.8	13.8
	2005	13.8	2.3	1.3	1.0	4.5	1.4	0.7	18.8	24.7
Manufactured goods	1995	76.5	82.5	84.7	85.9	49.3	75.6	94.0	29.7	63.9
(SITC 5 to 8 less 68)	2000	75.0	84.0	84.2	86.6	51.3	83.9	95.1	28.1	49.0
	2005	72.2	82.8	85.1	88.2	49.9	81.9	94.2	24.1	42.3

Sources:
- UNCTAD secretariat calculations based on UN DESA Statistics Division's data

Total	Africa / Afrique	America / Amérique	Total	Eastern, Southern and South-Eastern Asia / Asie orientale, méridionale et du Sud-Est	China / Chine	Western Asia / Asie occidentale	Oceania / Océanie	Major petroleum exporters / Principaux exportateurs de pétrole	Major exporters of manufactures / Principaux exportateurs d'articles manufacturés	Year / Année	Origine / Groupes de produits
											Developing economies / Économies en développement — Asia / Asie
Millions de dollars											
454 777	15 494	19 929	418 508	368 520	98 238	49 988	845	69 791	352 627	1995	Total tous produits
648 271	23 541	20 651	603 137	521 736	148 059	81 401	941	122 165	487 906	2000	
1 388 800	52 228	58 649	1 276 082	1 092 629	351 388	183 453	1 842	271 335	1 029 390	2005	
Parts par origines (en pourcentage)											
40.6	1.4	1.8	37.4	32.9	8.8	4.5	0.1	6.2	31.5	1995	Total tous produits
47.8	1.7	1.5	44.5	38.5	10.9	6.0	0.1	9.0	36.0	2000	
54.3	2.0	2.3	49.9	42.7	13.7	7.2	0.1	10.6	40.3	2005	
44.9	2.3	8.2	34.1	30.6	6.3	3.6	0.3	4.5	29.4	1995	Produits alimentaires
48.4	3.1	9.7	35.4	31.1	7.9	4.3	0.2	7.1	28.3	2000	(CTCI 0 + 1 + 22 + 4)
56.4	3.3	15.8	37.0	32.3	7.1	4.8	0.3	8.9	31.5	2005	
43.0	4.9	5.1	32.2	31.3	4.1	0.9	0.8	4.8	26.1	1995	Matières premières
42.7	5.6	4.0	32.5	31.4	4.1	1.1	0.7	8.1	23.9	2000	d'origine agricole
42.3	5.7	5.3	30.5	29.3	2.9	1.2	0.9	7.7	23.4	2005	(CTCI 2 - 22 - 27 - 28)
42.3	4.6	10.7	26.6	21.3	5.2	5.4	0.4	7.1	22.8	1995	Minerais et métaux
45.1	4.7	10.0	30.1	25.8	6.0	4.3	0.2	6.6	26.0	2000	(CTCI 27 + 28 + 68)
52.0	4.8	14.1	32.9	29.1	6.6	3.8	0.2	8.2	29.3	2005	
81.2	5.9	0.6	74.5	32.7	3.5	41.8	0.1	57.2	21.2	1995	Combustibles (CTCI 3)
78.3	7.1	0.5	70.6	29.6	2.9	41.0	0.1	57.3	17.3	2000	
74.5	6.9	0.7	66.9	29.4	2.9	37.4	0.0	52.4	18.0	2005	
36.8	0.4	0.8	35.6	34.3	10.1	1.4	0.0	1.9	33.7	1995	Articles manufacturés
44.2	0.4	0.6	43.1	41.9	13.1	1.2	0.0	2.2	40.9	2000	(CTCI 5 à 8 moins 68)
51.6	0.5	0.9	50.1	48.1	17.4	2.0	0.0	3.0	47.1	2005	
Parts par principaux groupes de produits (en pourcentage)											
100.0	100.0	100.0	100.0	100.0	100.0	100.0	100.0	100.0	100.0	1995	Total tous produits
100.0	100.0	100.0	100.0	100.0	100.0	100.0	100.0	100.0	100.0	2000	
100.0	100.0	100.0	100.0	100.0	100.0	100.0	100.0	100.0	100.0	2005	
7.6	11.5	31.3	6.2	6.3	4.9	5.5	27.8	4.9	6.4	1995	Produits alimentaires
5.7	10.0	36.0	4.5	4.6	4.1	4.0	19.9	4.4	4.5	2000	(CTCI 0 + 1 + 22 + 4)
4.8	7.4	32.1	3.4	3.5	2.4	3.1	19.9	3.9	3.6	2005	
3.4	11.3	9.3	2.8	3.1	1.5	0.7	33.7	2.5	2.7	1995	Matières premières
2.2	8.0	6.5	1.8	2.0	0.9	0.4	23.7	2.3	1.7	2000	d'origine agricole
1.6	5.7	4.7	1.3	1.4	0.4	0.3	25.3	1.5	1.2	2005	(CTCI 2 - 22 - 27 - 28)
4.0	12.8	23.1	2.7	2.5	2.3	4.6	19.3	4.4	2.8	1995	Minerais et métaux
3.4	9.8	23.8	2.5	2.4	2.0	2.6	12.0	2.7	2.6	2000	(CTCI 27 + 28 + 68)
4.8	11.8	31.0	3.3	3.4	2.4	2.6	10.8	3.9	3.7	2005	
13.9	29.8	2.5	13.9	6.9	2.8	65.2	8.2	63.9	4.7	1995	Combustibles (CTCI 3)
18.4	45.8	3.6	17.8	8.7	3.0	76.7	14.6	71.4	5.4	2000	
18.9	46.8	4.3	18.5	9.5	2.9	71.9	6.8	68.1	6.2	2005	
69.4	22.9	32.8	72.9	79.7	87.9	23.4	10.4	23.8	81.9	1995	Articles manufacturés
69.3	17.2	29.2	72.7	81.6	89.8	15.6	29.6	18.1	85.2	2000	(CTCI 5 à 8 moins 68)
68.5	19.1	27.4	72.5	81.3	91.6	20.3	37.1	20.6	84.5	2005	

Sources :
- Calculs du secrétariat de la CNUCED sur la base des données de ONU DAES Division de statistique

Destination / Product group	Year / Année	World / Monde	Developed economies / Économies développées							Economies in transition / Économies en transition
			Total	Europe Total	Europe EU/UE	Canada	USA / États-Unis	Japan / Japon	Other developed countries / Autres économies développées	
Millions of dollars										
All products	1995	949 608	487 920	154 985	149 216	10 630	183 436	121 284	17 586	9 517
	2000	1 297 082	694 322	225 848	211 916	14 734	270 341	155 377	28 022	8 633
	2005	2 381 627	1 126 378	411 442	386 471	25 494	401 472	231 175	56 796	37 557
Share by destination (percentage)										
All products	1995	100.0	51.4	16.3	15.7	1.1	19.3	12.8	1.9	1.0
	2000	100.0	53.5	17.4	16.3	1.1	20.8	12.0	2.2	0.7
	2005	100.0	47.3	17.3	16.2	1.1	16.9	9.7	2.4	1.6
All food items	1995	100.0	47.6	12.9	12.2	0.9	7.8	24.6	1.5	2.8
(SITC 0 + 1 + 22 + 4)	2000	100.0	49.1	12.7	12.2	1.2	11.3	22.3	1.6	2.1
	2005	100.0	45.8	13.8	13.6	1.3	11.3	17.3	2.1	3.2
Agricultural raw materials	1995	100.0	44.3	14.7	14.5	0.9	10.1	17.3	1.3	0.5
(SITC 2 - 22 - 27 - 28)	2000	100.0	40.6	15.4	15.3	0.8	8.6	14.5	1.3	0.4
	2005	100.0	39.4	14.7	14.6	1.4	10.3	11.8	1.2	0.9
Ores and metals	1995	100.0	35.7	7.0	6.9	0.4	3.3	24.0	1.0	2.5
(SITC 27 + 28 + 68)	2000	100.0	34.6	9.6	9.2	0.5	5.1	17.2	2.2	0.7
	2005	100.0	27.6	8.3	8.1	0.6	4.2	13.2	1.3	0.8
Fuels (SITC 3)	1995	100.0	46.8	12.9	12.8	0.4	2.5	29.0	2.1	0.2
	2000	100.0	49.6	17.9	11.0	0.1	3.2	24.8	3.6	0.1
	2005	100.0	47.1	16.2	8.8	0.1	3.2	21.9	5.7	0.2
Manufactured goods	1995	100.0	52.6	17.1	16.5	1.2	22.1	10.3	1.9	0.9
(SITC 5 to 8 less 68)	2000	100.0	54.6	17.7	17.2	1.2	23.5	10.1	2.0	0.6
	2005	100.0	48.1	17.8	17.3	1.2	19.0	8.1	2.1	1.7
Share by major product group (percentage)										
All products	1995	100.0	100.0	100.0	100.0	100.0	100.0	100.0	100.0	100.0
	2000	100.0	100.0	100.0	100.0	100.0	100.0	100.0	100.0	100.0
	2005	100.0	100.0	100.0	100.0	100.0	100.0	100.0	100.0	100.0
All food items	1995	6.9	6.4	5.4	5.3	5.2	2.8	13.2	5.5	19.3
(SITC 0 + 1 + 22 + 4)	2000	4.7	4.3	3.4	3.5	4.8	2.5	8.8	3.6	14.9
	2005	3.9	3.8	3.1	3.3	4.6	2.6	7.0	3.4	8.0
Agricultural raw materials	1995	2.4	2.1	2.2	2.2	1.9	1.3	3.2	1.6	1.2
(SITC 2 - 22 - 27 - 28)	2000	1.4	1.1	1.2	1.3	1.0	0.6	1.7	0.8	0.9
	2005	1.2	1.0	1.0	1.1	1.5	0.7	1.5	0.6	0.7
Ores and metals	1995	1.9	1.3	0.8	0.8	0.6	0.3	3.5	1.0	4.6
(SITC 27 + 28 + 68)	2000	1.6	1.0	0.9	0.9	0.7	0.4	2.3	1.6	1.8
	2005	2.0	1.2	1.0	1.0	1.2	0.5	2.8	1.1	1.0
Fuels (SITC 3)	1995	5.8	5.3	4.6	4.7	1.9	0.8	13.2	6.6	1.3
	2000	7.5	7.0	7.8	5.1	0.6	1.2	15.6	12.7	1.7
	2005	8.2	8.2	7.7	4.5	0.5	1.6	18.5	19.7	0.9
Manufactured goods	1995	81.4	83.4	85.4	85.3	89.4	93.0	65.6	84.2	72.9
(SITC 5 to 8 less 68)	2000	84.1	86.0	85.8	88.6	92.6	94.9	71.3	79.1	80.5
	2005	83.6	85.1	86.1	89.3	91.3	94.2	69.6	73.4	89.3

Sources:
- UNCTAD secretariat calculations based on UN DESA Statistics Division's data

Total	Africa Afrique	America Amérique	Asia Asie Total	Eastern, Southern and South-Eastern Asia Asie orientale, méridionale et du Sud-Est	China Chine	Western Asia Asie occidentale	Oceania Océanie	Major petroleum exporters Principaux exportateurs de pétrole	Major exporters of manufactures Principaux exportateurs d'articles manufacturés	Year Année	Destination Groupes de produits
Millions de dollars											
445 213	17 322	23 294	403 330	380 721	77 068	22 609	1 267	34 629	353 611	1995	**Total tous produits**
596 024	21 617	33 932	538 172	507 289	110 795	30 883	2 303	46 818	478 789	2000	
1 212 028	47 667	59 512	1 099 899	1 026 116	294 878	73 782	4 951	130 782	944 584	2005	
Parts par destinations (en pourcentage)											
46.9	1.8	2.5	42.5	40.1	8.1	2.4	0.1	3.6	37.2	1995	**Total tous produits**
45.9	1.7	2.6	41.4	39.1	8.5	2.4	0.2	3.6	36.9	2000	
50.9	2.0	2.5	46.2	43.1	12.4	3.1	0.2	5.5	39.7	2005	
49.3	3.2	0.6	45.4	41.0	7.8	4.4	0.1	7.1	32.0	1995	Produits alimentaires
48.6	3.6	0.9	44.0	38.0	6.5	5.9	0.2	8.5	30.6	2000	(CTCI 0 + 1 + 22 + 4)
50.9	5.1	1.2	44.4	38.0	5.6	6.4	0.2	9.3	29.1	2005	
55.1	1.5	2.1	51.6	49.7	13.5	1.8	0.0	3.2	46.9	1995	Matières premières
58.9	1.1	1.6	56.2	54.2	22.2	2.0	0.0	3.7	49.8	2000	d'origine agricole
59.7	1.4	2.4	55.9	53.5	24.1	2.3	0.0	3.6	48.9	2005	(CTCI 2 - 22 - 27 - 28)
61.8	0.4	0.3	61.1	59.8	16.4	1.2	0.0	2.4	56.2	1995	Minerais et métaux
64.6	0.6	0.6	63.4	61.5	17.2	1.9	0.0	3.1	58.6	2000	(CTCI 27 + 28 + 68)
71.6	0.7	0.5	70.4	67.2	25.6	3.2	0.0	5.0	63.4	2005	
42.7	2.3	0.7	39.1	38.6	6.6	0.5	0.6	0.8	35.2	1995	Combustibles (CTCI 3)
50.2	2.5	2.1	44.9	44.1	6.0	0.8	0.7	2.1	39.5	2000	
51.7	0.7	1.3	48.8	47.1	6.5	1.7	0.9	6.5	38.6	2005	
46.3	1.7	2.8	41.7	39.3	8.0	2.4	0.1	3.6	37.0	1995	Articles manufacturés
44.7	1.5	2.8	40.2	37.9	8.5	2.3	0.1	3.4	36.3	2000	(CTCI 5 à 8 moins 68)
50.2	2.0	2.6	45.4	42.3	12.9	3.1	0.1	5.2	39.7	2005	
Parts par principaux groupes de produits (en pourcentage)											
100.0	100.0	100.0	100.0	100.0	100.0	100.0	100.0	100.0	100.0	1995	**Total tous produits**
100.0	100.0	100.0	100.0	100.0	100.0	100.0	100.0	100.0	100.0	2000	
100.0	100.0	100.0	100.0	100.0	100.0	100.0	100.0	100.0	100.0	2005	
7.2	11.9	1.8	7.3	7.0	6.6	12.6	7.4	13.3	5.9	1995	Produits alimentaires
5.0	10.1	1.5	5.0	4.6	3.6	11.7	4.3	11.0	3.9	2000	(CTCI 0 + 1 + 22 + 4)
3.9	9.9	1.9	3.8	3.5	1.8	8.1	3.8	6.6	2.9	2005	
2.8	1.9	2.0	2.9	3.0	4.0	1.8	0.3	2.1	3.0	1995	Matières premières
1.8	0.9	0.9	1.9	1.9	3.6	1.2	0.2	1.4	1.9	2000	d'origine agricole
1.4	0.9	1.1	1.4	1.5	2.3	0.9	0.1	0.8	1.5	2005	(CTCI 2 - 22 - 27 - 28)
2.5	0.4	0.3	2.7	2.8	3.8	1.0	0.3	1.2	2.8	1995	Minerais et métaux
2.2	0.6	0.4	2.4	2.5	3.2	1.3	0.3	1.3	2.5	2000	(CTCI 27 + 28 + 68)
2.9	0.7	0.4	3.1	3.2	4.2	2.1	0.2	1.9	3.3	2005	
5.3	7.2	1.6	5.4	5.6	4.7	1.3	25.6	1.2	5.5	1995	Combustibles (CTCI 3)
8.3	11.1	6.1	8.2	8.5	5.3	2.4	31.8	4.3	8.1	2000	
8.3	2.8	4.3	8.7	9.0	4.3	4.5	33.8	9.7	8.0	2005	
80.4	76.7	92.2	80.0	79.8	80.1	82.5	63.3	81.4	81.0	1995	Articles manufacturés
81.9	76.9	91.0	81.6	81.6	84.0	81.3	63.0	80.3	82.8	2000	(CTCI 5 à 8 moins 68)
82.4	83.0	88.1	82.2	82.1	87.1	83.2	56.1	79.7	83.7	2005	

Sources :
- Calculs du secrétariat de la CNUCED sur la base des données de ONU DAES Division de statistique

2.2.H Import structure by partner and product group
Developing Asia: Eastern, Southern and South-Eastern Asia

Origin / Product group	Year / Année	World / Monde	Developed economies / Économies développées — Total	Europe — Total	Europe — EU / UE	Canada	USA / États-Unis	Japan / Japon	Other developed countries / Autres économies développées	Economies in transition / Économies en transition
Millions of dollars										
All products	1995	999 843	557 624	165 972	151 333	12 058	138 839	213 038	27 717	16 398
	2000	1 204 600	563 980	159 345	142 886	11 985	146 774	212 171	33 705	17 475
	2005	2 221 850	862 930	279 071	250 729	17 142	188 577	316 729	61 410	42 398
Share by origin (percentage)										
All products	1995	100.0	55.8	16.6	15.1	1.2	13.9	21.3	2.8	1.6
	2000	100.0	46.8	13.2	11.9	1.0	12.2	17.6	2.8	1.5
	2005	100.0	38.8	12.6	11.3	0.8	8.5	14.3	2.8	1.9
All food items	1995	100.0	53.9	13.7	13.2	4.2	23.5	2.8	9.7	0.7
(SITC 0 + 1 + 22 + 4)	2000	100.0	50.5	12.4	11.6	4.2	19.1	2.9	12.0	1.3
	2005	100.0	40.3	10.7	9.7	2.9	14.3	2.5	10.0	2.2
Agricultural raw materials	1995	100.0	51.2	7.4	7.1	5.1	23.8	5.5	9.3	4.1
(SITC 2 - 22 - 27 - 28)	2000	100.0	50.6	10.6	10.2	7.3	16.9	5.4	10.4	5.1
	2005	100.0	48.2	10.9	10.4	5.7	18.4	5.0	8.2	8.2
Ores and metals	1995	100.0	49.5	11.6	10.5	2.7	11.4	11.1	12.7	6.5
(SITC 27 + 28 + 68)	2000	100.0	46.2	10.9	8.8	2.1	7.3	11.2	14.6	7.8
	2005	100.0	40.8	7.7	6.7	2.3	5.9	8.4	16.4	5.9
Fuels (SITC 3)	1995	100.0	11.5	1.4	1.4	0.6	2.7	2.2	4.5	1.0
	2000	100.0	7.3	1.3	0.8	0.2	0.9	0.8	4.0	1.3
	2005	100.0	6.4	0.9	0.6	0.2	0.8	0.8	3.8	3.1
Manufactured goods	1995	100.0	59.9	18.5	17.1	0.8	13.6	26.0	1.1	1.4
(SITC 5 to 8 less 68)	2000	100.0	52.3	14.8	13.7	0.7	13.7	22.2	1.0	1.0
	2005	100.0	44.3	14.9	13.8	0.5	9.6	18.5	0.8	1.2
Share by major product group (percentage)										
All products	1995	100.0	100.0	100.0	100.0	100.0	100.0	100.0	100.0	100.0
	2000	100.0	100.0	100.0	100.0	100.0	100.0	100.0	100.0	100.0
	2005	100.0	100.0	100.0	100.0	100.0	100.0	100.0	100.0	100.0
All food items	1995	6.1	5.9	5.1	5.3	21.4	10.3	0.8	21.4	2.8
(SITC 0 + 1 + 22 + 4)	2000	4.9	5.2	4.5	4.8	20.6	7.6	0.8	20.8	4.4
	2005	4.1	4.2	3.4	3.5	15.3	6.8	0.7	14.7	4.7
Agricultural raw materials	1995	3.3	3.0	1.5	1.6	14.1	5.7	0.9	11.1	8.4
(SITC 2 - 22 - 27 - 28)	2000	2.6	2.8	2.1	2.2	18.8	3.6	0.8	9.5	9.0
	2005	2.1	2.7	1.9	2.0	15.9	4.6	0.8	6.4	9.2
Ores and metals	1995	3.9	3.4	2.7	2.7	8.8	3.2	2.0	17.8	15.3
(SITC 27 + 28 + 68)	2000	3.7	3.6	3.1	2.8	7.8	2.2	2.4	19.3	19.8
	2005	5.1	5.4	3.2	3.1	15.5	3.6	3.0	30.5	15.9
Fuels (SITC 3)	1995	7.0	1.5	0.6	0.6	3.6	1.4	0.7	11.5	4.4
	2000	11.7	1.8	1.2	0.8	2.6	0.9	0.5	16.8	10.8
	2005	14.6	2.4	1.0	0.8	4.4	1.4	0.8	20.1	23.6
Manufactured goods	1995	76.9	82.7	85.8	87.0	48.0	75.4	93.8	30.2	67.6
(SITC 5 to 8 less 68)	2000	75.4	84.2	84.4	87.2	49.7	84.5	94.9	26.4	53.9
	2005	72.6	82.8	86.0	88.6	48.2	82.2	93.9	21.9	46.2

Sources:
- UNCTAD secretariat calculations based on UN DESA Statistics Division's data

Total	Africa Afrique	America Amérique	Total (Asia Asie)	Eastern, Southern and South-Eastern Asia — Asie orientale, méridionale et du Sud-Est	China Chine	Western Asia — Asie occidentale	Oceania Océanie	Major petroleum exporters — Principaux exportateurs de pétrole	Major exporters of manufactures — Principaux exportateurs d'articles manufacturés	Year Année	Origine — Groupes de produits
											Developing economies — Économies en développement

Millions de dollars

Total	Africa Afrique	America Amérique	Total	Eastern, Southern and South-Eastern Asia	China Chine	Western Asia	Oceania Océanie	Major petroleum exporters	Major exporters of manufactures	Year Année	Origine
417 371	12 495	17 659	386 377	348 614	95 169	37 763	840	56 435	333 515	1995	**Total tous produits**
600 180	18 797	17 716	562 731	495 317	141 824	67 414	936	104 479	463 529	2000	
1 268 232	40 859	51 508	1 174 047	1 020 080	328 917	153 968	1 818	235 928	958 630	2005	

Parts par origines (en pourcentage)

Total	Africa	America	Total	Eastern...	China	Western Asia	Oceania	Maj. petrol.	Maj. manuf.	Year	Origine
41.7	1.2	1.8	38.6	34.9	9.5	3.8	0.1	5.6	33.4	1995	**Total tous produits**
49.8	1.6	1.5	46.7	41.1	11.8	5.6	0.1	8.7	38.5	2000	
57.1	1.8	2.3	52.8	45.9	14.8	6.9	0.1	10.6	43.1	2005	
44.7	1.7	8.4	34.3	33.7	7.6	0.7	0.4	2.6	31.8	1995	Produits alimentaires
48.1	2.3	10.3	35.2	34.1	9.9	1.1	0.3	4.5	31.5	2000	(CTCI 0 + 1 + 22 + 4)
57.2	2.1	16.9	37.8	36.3	8.8	1.4	0.4	7.2	34.3	2005	
44.3	4.8	5.3	33.4	32.8	4.4	0.6	0.9	4.5	27.4	1995	Matières premières
44.2	5.6	4.1	33.9	33.2	4.4	0.7	0.7	8.2	25.1	2000	d'origine agricole
43.5	5.8	5.3	31.4	30.6	2.9	0.8	1.0	7.7	24.4	2005	(CTCI 2 - 22 - 27 - 28)
43.6	4.5	11.4	27.4	22.9	5.7	4.5	0.4	6.2	24.4	1995	Minerais et métaux
46.0	4.7	10.1	31.0	27.6	6.5	3.4	0.3	5.8	27.5	2000	(CTCI 27 + 28 + 68)
53.2	4.9	15.1	33.0	30.1	7.2	2.9	0.2	7.0	30.7	2005	
81.8	5.1	0.7	76.0	35.1	3.9	40.9	0.1	55.8	23.3	1995	Combustibles (CTCI 3)
80.0	6.6	0.5	72.8	31.5	3.2	41.3	0.1	57.4	18.6	2000	
76.9	6.5	0.7	69.6	31.1	3.1	38.5	0.0	53.3	19.3	2005	
38.1	0.4	0.7	37.0	36.1	10.9	0.8	0.0	1.5	35.6	1995	Articles manufacturés
46.3	0.3	0.6	45.4	44.6	14.0	0.7	0.0	1.7	43.6	2000	(CTCI 5 à 8 moins 68)
54.3	0.5	0.9	52.9	51.6	18.6	1.3	0.0	2.6	50.4	2005	

Parts par principaux groupes de produits (en pourcentage)

Total	Africa	America	Total	Eastern...	China	Western Asia	Oceania	Maj. petrol.	Maj. manuf.	Year	Origine
100.0	100.0	100.0	100.0	100.0	100.0	100.0	100.0	100.0	100.0	1995	**Total tous produits**
100.0	100.0	100.0	100.0	100.0	100.0	100.0	100.0	100.0	100.0	2000	
100.0	100.0	100.0	100.0	100.0	100.0	100.0	100.0	100.0	100.0	2005	
6.6	8.1	28.9	5.4	5.9	4.9	1.1	27.5	2.8	5.8	1995	Produits alimentaires
4.7	7.1	34.1	3.7	4.0	4.1	0.9	20.0	2.5	4.0	2000	(CTCI 0 + 1 + 22 + 4)
4.1	4.7	29.7	2.9	3.2	2.4	0.8	20.2	2.8	3.2	2005	
3.5	12.7	9.9	2.9	3.1	1.5	0.6	33.9	2.6	2.7	1995	Matières premières
2.3	9.2	7.1	1.9	2.1	1.0	0.3	23.8	2.4	1.7	2000	d'origine agricole
1.6	6.8	4.9	1.3	1.4	0.4	0.2	25.7	1.6	1.2	2005	(CTCI 2 - 22 - 27 - 28)
4.1	13.9	25.1	2.7	2.5	2.3	4.6	19.4	4.2	2.8	1995	Minerais et métaux
3.4	11.1	25.4	2.4	2.5	2.1	2.2	12.0	2.5	2.6	2000	(CTCI 27 + 28 + 68)
4.8	13.7	33.5	3.2	3.4	2.5	2.2	10.9	3.4	3.7	2005	
13.8	28.5	2.8	13.8	7.1	2.9	76.2	8.3	69.5	4.9	1995	Combustibles (CTCI 3)
18.7	49.1	4.0	18.2	8.9	3.1	86.2	14.7	77.3	5.6	2000	
19.7	51.7	4.4	19.2	9.9	3.1	81.3	6.9	73.3	6.5	2005	
70.3	22.5	32.6	73.6	79.8	87.8	17.2	10.4	20.4	82.1	1995	Articles manufacturés
70.1	16.7	29.3	73.2	81.8	89.6	9.8	29.3	14.8	85.4	2000	(CTCI 5 à 8 moins 68)
69.0	17.8	27.2	72.7	81.5	91.3	14.1	36.3	17.8	84.8	2005	

Sources :
- Calculs du secrétariat de la CNUCED sur la base des données de ONU DAES Division de statistique

Destination / Product group	Year Année	World Monde	Developed economies / Économies développées							Economies in transition / Économies en transition
			Total	Europe		Canada	USA États-Unis	Japan Japon	Other developed countries Autres économies développées	
				Total	EU UE					
			Millions of dollars							
All products	**1995**	**132 971**	**58 272**	**24 549**	**24 203**	**526**	**10 640**	**21 388**	**1 169**	**3 218**
	2000	**219 302**	**109 001**	**44 236**	**43 733**	**922**	**31 160**	**31 342**	**1 341**	**3 367**
	2005	**481 962**	**217 615**	**84 653**	**82 045**	**3 048**	**55 910**	**70 223**	**3 781**	**11 147**
		Share by destination (percentage)								
All products	**1995**	**100.0**	**43.8**	**18.5**	**18.2**	**0.4**	**8.0**	**16.1**	**0.9**	**2.4**
	2000	**100.0**	**49.7**	**20.2**	**19.9**	**0.4**	**14.2**	**14.3**	**0.6**	**1.5**
	2005	**100.0**	**45.2**	**17.6**	**17.0**	**0.6**	**11.6**	**14.6**	**0.8**	**2.3**
All food items	1995	100.0	37.5	30.5	29.4	0.4	4.7	1.0	0.9	11.6
(SITC 0 + 1 + 22 + 4)	2000	100.0	34.6	27.4	26.2	0.4	4.0	1.3	1.5	8.6
	2005	100.0	38.4	32.0	30.7	0.4	3.4	1.2	1.4	8.4
Agricultural raw materials	1995	100.0	49.7	44.3	43.4	0.1	2.0	1.5	1.8	0.9
(SITC 2 - 22 - 27 - 28)	2000	100.0	42.8	38.0	37.1	0.2	1.7	2.1	0.8	2.1
	2005	100.0	34.8	32.0	31.5	0.2	1.1	0.8	0.7	2.9
Ores and metals	1995	100.0	33.9	17.9	17.6	0.1	2.4	12.9	0.7	1.8
(SITC 27 + 28 + 68)	2000	100.0	38.5	22.0	21.1	0.3	5.7	8.8	1.8	3.4
	2005	100.0	28.2	19.4	18.8	0.1	3.1	4.2	1.3	5.2
Fuels (SITC 3)	1995	..	..	..	..	..	..	..	..	..
	2000	100.0	50.2	15.6	15.6	0.4	15.7	18.4	0.2	0.2
	2005	100.0	49.5	11.5	11.4	0.8	15.0	21.7	0.5	0.1
Manufactured goods	1995	100.0	45.7	35.7	35.0	0.3	7.1	1.4	1.2	7.1
(SITC 5 to 8 less 68)	2000	100.0	50.9	37.0	36.3	0.6	10.9	0.2	2.2	5.9
	2005	100.0	46.8	37.7	36.9	0.4	6.5	0.5	1.7	8.6
		Share by major product group (percentage)								
All products	**1995**	**100.0**	**100.0**	**100.0**	**100.0**	**100.0**	**100.0**	**100.0**	**100.0**	**100.0**
	2000	**100.0**	**100.0**	**100.0**	**100.0**	**100.0**	**100.0**	**100.0**	**100.0**	**100.0**
	2005	**100.0**	**100.0**	**100.0**	**100.0**	**100.0**	**100.0**	**100.0**	**100.0**	**100.0**
All food items	1995	5.4	4.6	8.9	8.6	5.2	3.1	0.3	5.7	25.7
(SITC 0 + 1 + 22 + 4)	2000	3.0	2.1	4.0	3.9	2.6	0.8	0.3	7.4	16.6
	2005	2.8	2.4	5.0	5.0	1.8	0.8	0.2	5.0	10.0
Agricultural raw materials	1995	0.6	0.7	1.4	1.4	0.2	0.1	0.1	1.2	0.2
(SITC 2 - 22 - 27 - 28)	2000	0.3	0.3	0.6	0.6	0.1	0.0	0.0	0.4	0.4
	2005	0.2	0.2	0.4	0.4	0.1	0.0	0.0	0.2	0.3
Ores and metals	1995	2.7	2.1	2.6	2.6	0.5	0.8	2.2	2.2	2.0
(SITC 27 + 28 + 68)	2000	1.5	1.2	1.6	1.6	1.0	0.6	0.9	4.3	3.3
	2005	1.4	0.9	1.5	1.5	0.2	0.4	0.4	2.4	3.1
Fuels (SITC 3)	1995	67.0	67.2	40.4	40.9	77.8	73.3	95.3	57.0	1.6
	2000	76.3	77.1	59.1	59.6	69.3	84.1	98.4	20.6	7.6
	2005	65.9	72.3	43.2	44.1	83.2	85.3	98.3	38.3	2.4
Manufactured goods	1995	24.1	25.1	46.5	46.2	16.2	21.3	2.1	33.9	70.5
(SITC 5 to 8 less 68)	2000	18.6	19.0	34.0	33.8	26.4	14.3	0.3	66.9	71.1
	2005	22.3	23.1	47.8	48.2	14.0	12.5	0.7	48.9	83.2

Sources:
- UNCTAD secretariat calculations based on UN DESA Statistics Division's data

Total	Africa / Afrique	America / Amérique	Asia / Asie — Total	Eastern, Southern and South-Eastern Asia / Asie orientale, méridionale et du Sud-Est	China / Chine	Western Asia / Asie occidentale	Oceania / Océanie	Major petroleum exporters / Principaux exportateurs de pétrole	Major exporters of manufactures / Principaux exportateurs d'articles manufacturés	Year / Année	Destination / Groupes de produits
Millions de dollars											
32 535	3 098	386	29 050	18 218	1 594	10 832	1	11 159	16 044	1995	Total tous produits
83 368	7 443	1 871	74 039	59 867	5 213	14 172	15	10 760	58 133	2000	
183 626	15 913	3 271	164 316	133 401	17 535	30 915	126	37 624	120 157	2005	
Parts par destinations (en pourcentage)											
24.5	2.3	0.3	21.8	13.7	1.2	8.1	0.0	8.4	12.1	1995	Total tous produits
38.0	3.4	0.9	33.8	27.3	2.4	6.5	0.0	4.9	26.5	2000	
38.1	3.3	0.7	34.1	27.7	3.6	6.4	0.0	7.8	24.9	2005	
49.7	5.3	0.6	43.8	7.1	0.1	36.7	0.0	38.9	2.7	1995	Produits alimentaires
53.2	6.1	0.8	46.3	10.1	0.3	36.2	0.0	32.2	4.1	2000	(CTCI 0 + 1 + 22 + 4)
52.0	8.1	0.6	43.3	10.3	0.4	33.0	0.0	36.2	3.2	2005	
48.1	12.0	0.3	35.8	21.2	2.8	14.5	0.0	15.4	19.3	1995	Matières premières
47.6	6.8	0.4	40.4	19.5	1.3	20.9	0.0	12.7	20.5	2000	d'origine agricole
57.0	8.2	0.1	48.7	33.1	4.1	15.6	0.0	14.4	23.7	2005	(CTCI 2 - 22 - 27 - 28)
61.7	2.7	0.2	58.7	42.5	2.1	16.2	0.0	17.2	38.0	1995	Minerais et métaux
56.4	3.3	0.2	52.8	34.1	2.0	18.7	0.0	18.9	30.0	2000	(CTCI 27 + 28 + 68)
65.0	5.4	0.4	59.2	40.5	7.4	18.7	0.0	18.5	37.9	2005	
..	..	..	..	..	..	..	..	..	..	1995	Combustibles (CTCI 3)
37.1	2.5	0.9	33.6	31.3	2.9	2.3	0.0	0.5	31.7	2000	
37.7	1.8	0.8	35.2	33.0	4.0	2.1	0.0	2.2	31.6	2005	
44.3	6.2	0.4	37.7	19.0	1.3	18.8	0.0	21.8	14.3	1995	Articles manufacturés
37.9	6.5	0.7	30.7	13.2	0.5	17.4	0.0	17.2	8.8	2000	(CTCI 5 à 8 moins 68)
41.5	7.9	0.6	32.9	18.3	3.6	14.6	0.1	20.3	11.8	2005	
Parts par principaux groupes de produits (en pourcentage)											
100.0	100.0	100.0	100.0	100.0	100.0	100.0	100.0	100.0	100.0	1995	Total tous produits
100.0	100.0	100.0	100.0	100.0	100.0	100.0	100.0	100.0	100.0	2000	
100.0	100.0	100.0	100.0	100.0	100.0	100.0	100.0	100.0	100.0	2005	
10.9	12.3	11.9	10.7	2.8	0.5	24.1	10.0	24.9	1.2	1995	Produits alimentaires
4.1	5.3	2.7	4.0	1.1	0.4	16.5	0.2	19.3	0.5	2000	(CTCI 0 + 1 + 22 + 4)
3.8	6.8	2.5	3.5	1.0	0.3	14.3	1.0	12.8	0.4	2005	
1.2	3.1	0.6	1.0	0.9	1.4	1.1	4.2	1.1	1.0	1995	Matières premières
0.4	0.6	0.1	0.4	0.2	0.2	1.0	0.0	0.8	0.2	2000	d'origine agricole
0.3	0.5	0.0	0.3	0.3	0.2	0.5	0.0	0.4	0.2	2005	(CTCI 2 - 22 - 27 - 28)
6.8	3.2	2.3	7.3	8.4	4.7	5.4	7.1	5.6	8.5	1995	Minerais et métaux
2.2	1.4	0.4	2.3	1.9	1.2	4.3	0.0	5.7	1.7	2000	(CTCI 27 + 28 + 68)
2.3	2.2	0.8	2.4	2.0	2.8	4.0	0.0	3.2	2.1	2005	
36.6	17.7	49.6	38.4	54.0	68.2	12.4	0.0	4.6	60.4	1995	Combustibles (CTCI 3)
74.4	56.3	82.4	76.0	87.6	94.5	27.0	0.0	7.6	91.3	2000	
65.3	35.2	74.9	68.0	78.7	73.2	22.1	0.1	18.3	83.6	2005	
43.6	63.5	35.6	41.5	33.3	25.2	55.4	78.6	62.4	28.5	1995	Articles manufacturés
18.5	35.9	14.3	16.9	9.0	3.7	50.1	99.8	65.2	6.2	2000	(CTCI 5 à 8 moins 68)
24.2	53.2	20.3	21.5	14.7	21.8	50.5	97.5	57.9	10.5	2005	

Sources :
- Calculs du secrétariat de la CNUCED sur la base des données de ONU DAES Division de statistique

Origin / Product group	Year Année	World Monde	Developed economies Économies développées							Economies in transition Économies en transition
			Total	Europe Total	EU UE	Canada	USA États-Unis	Japan Japon	Other developed countries Autres économies développées	

Millions of dollars

Product group	Year	World	Total	Europe Total	EU	Canada	USA	Japan	Other dev.	Econ. in transition
All products	1995	119 765	76 285	50 627	47 132	967	14 873	8 264	1 554	5 708
	2000	150 715	91 789	62 805	59 237	1 159	14 564	10 008	3 253	8 572
	2005	335 390	174 768	121 881	110 343	1 618	25 731	19 547	5 992	26 853

Share by origin (percentage)

Product group	Year	World	Total	Europe Total	EU	Canada	USA	Japan	Other dev.	Econ. in transition
All products	1995	100.0	63.7	42.3	39.4	0.8	12.4	6.9	1.3	4.8
	2000	100.0	60.9	41.7	39.3	0.8	9.7	6.6	2.2	5.7
	2005	100.0	52.1	36.3	32.9	0.5	7.7	5.8	1.8	8.0
All food items	1995	100.0	50.0	30.8	30.0	0.6	13.9	0.2	4.5	4.4
(SITC 0 + 1 + 22 + 4)	2000	100.0	48.0	28.0	27.0	1.4	12.7	0.1	5.8	2.2
	2005	100.0	40.6	24.4	22.7	0.7	9.2	0.1	6.1	4.9
Agricultural raw materials	1995	100.0	51.1	29.8	29.0	2.7	10.8	0.9	6.9	20.3
(SITC 2 - 22 - 27 - 28)	2000	100.0	54.2	32.3	31.8	1.7	14.9	0.6	4.5	18.7
	2005	100.0	52.9	31.0	30.3	1.9	17.6	0.6	1.9	15.8
Ores and metals	1995	100.0	57.9	39.4	38.4	1.8	11.4	0.4	4.9	10.3
(SITC 27 + 28 + 68)	2000	100.0	36.6	24.6	23.6	0.5	2.9	1.3	7.3	26.8
	2005	100.0	31.2	20.0	19.2	0.5	4.2	0.9	5.5	26.4
Fuels (SITC 3)	1995	100.0	12.4	7.8	7.8	0.2	3.1	0.0	1.3	12.3
	2000	100.0	16.4	12.6	10.6	0.4	2.0	0.1	1.4	14.7
	2005	100.0	11.6	8.5	6.4	0.3	1.5	0.1	1.2	25.4
Manufactured goods	1995	100.0	70.7	47.0	44.3	0.7	13.3	9.3	0.4	3.5
(SITC 5 to 8 less 68)	2000	100.0	69.9	48.3	46.3	0.7	10.4	9.1	1.4	3.1
	2005	100.0	62.4	43.6	41.4	0.5	8.8	8.3	1.2	4.2

Share by major product group (percentage)

Product group	Year	World	Total	Europe Total	EU	Canada	USA	Japan	Other dev.	Econ. in transition
All products	1995	100.0	100.0	100.0	100.0	100.0	100.0	100.0	100.0	100.0
	2000	100.0	100.0	100.0	100.0	100.0	100.0	100.0	100.0	100.0
	2005	100.0	100.0	100.0	100.0	100.0	100.0	100.0	100.0	100.0
All food items	1995	12.9	10.1	9.4	9.8	9.9	14.3	0.3	44.5	11.8
(SITC 0 + 1 + 22 + 4)	2000	12.1	9.5	8.1	8.3	21.6	15.9	0.2	32.6	4.8
	2005	8.4	6.6	5.7	5.8	12.5	10.1	0.2	29.0	5.2
Agricultural raw materials	1995	2.6	2.1	1.8	1.9	8.7	2.2	0.3	13.7	10.9
(SITC 2 - 22 - 27 - 28)	2000	2.0	1.8	1.6	1.6	4.5	3.1	0.2	4.2	6.6
	2005	1.5	1.5	1.3	1.4	5.9	3.4	0.1	1.5	2.9
Ores and metals	1995	3.6	3.3	3.3	3.5	7.9	3.3	0.2	13.5	7.7
(SITC 27 + 28 + 68)	2000	3.1	1.8	1.8	1.8	2.2	0.9	0.6	10.4	14.5
	2005	4.3	2.6	2.4	2.5	4.7	2.3	0.7	13.3	14.2
Fuels (SITC 3)	1995	6.3	1.2	1.2	1.3	1.2	1.6	0.0	6.5	16.4
	2000	7.7	2.1	2.3	2.1	3.6	1.6	0.1	5.1	20.0
	2005	8.3	1.8	1.9	1.6	5.6	1.6	0.1	5.4	26.4
Manufactured goods	1995	73.0	81.0	81.1	82.2	65.1	78.1	98.8	20.7	53.1
(SITC 5 to 8 less 68)	2000	72.1	82.8	83.6	85.1	67.6	77.8	98.7	45.5	39.0
	2005	69.4	83.0	83.2	87.3	67.5	79.5	98.6	46.9	36.2

Sources:
- UNCTAD secretariat calculations based on UN DESA Statistics Division's data

Total	Africa / Afrique	America / Amérique	Asia / Asie Total	Eastern, Southern and South-Eastern Asia / Asie orientale, méridionale et du Sud-Est	China / Chine	Western Asia / Asie occidentale	Oceania / Océanie	Major petroleum exporters / Principaux exportateurs de pétrole	Major exporters of manufactures / Principaux exportateurs d'articles manufacturés	Year / Année	Origine / Groupes de produits
											Developing economies / Économies en développement
Millions de dollars											
37 406	2 999	2 270	32 132	19 907	3 069	12 225	5	13 356	19 112	1995	Total tous produits
48 091	4 745	2 935	40 406	26 419	6 235	13 987	5	17 686	24 378	2000	
120 568	11 369	7 141	102 034	72 549	22 471	29 485	24	35 407	70 760	2005	
Parts par origines (en pourcentage)											
31.2	2.5	1.9	26.8	16.6	2.6	10.2	0.0	11.2	16.0	1995	Total tous produits
31.9	3.1	1.9	26.8	17.5	4.1	9.3	0.0	11.7	16.2	2000	
35.9	3.4	2.1	30.4	21.6	6.7	8.8	0.0	10.6	21.1	2005	
45.5	4.9	7.3	33.2	18.1	1.1	15.1	0.0	12.0	20.2	1995	Produits alimentaires
49.2	5.7	7.7	35.9	21.3	1.5	14.6	0.0	15.3	17.9	2000	(CTCI 0 + 1 + 22 + 4)
54.0	6.8	12.4	34.7	19.4	1.5	15.4	0.0	14.2	22.4	2005	
28.5	5.7	3.5	19.4	15.2	0.5	4.2	0.0	7.8	12.1	1995	Matières premières
26.6	5.3	3.0	18.2	13.3	0.8	4.9	0.0	7.3	11.2	2000	d'origine agricole
31.0	4.3	5.2	21.5	16.5	2.6	5.0	0.0	7.7	14.2	2005	(CTCI 2 - 22 - 27 - 28)
30.6	6.0	4.3	20.3	6.5	0.5	13.8	0.0	15.5	8.1	1995	Minerais et métaux
35.8	4.7	9.3	21.8	8.2	1.3	13.6	0.0	14.5	11.6	2000	(CTCI 27 + 28 + 68)
42.0	3.8	6.3	31.9	21.4	2.0	10.5	0.0	17.6	18.0	2005	
75.1	13.9	0.1	61.0	10.9	0.3	50.1	0.0	70.4	1.5	1995	Combustibles (CTCI 3)
58.2	13.4	0.3	44.5	7.5	0.3	37.0	0.0	55.6	1.0	2000	
47.7	11.8	0.8	35.0	10.6	0.7	24.5	0.0	42.4	3.0	2005	
25.4	0.8	0.9	23.7	17.7	3.2	6.0	0.0	5.8	17.2	1995	Articles manufacturés
26.2	0.8	0.8	24.6	19.1	5.4	5.6	0.0	6.1	18.3	2000	(CTCI 5 à 8 moins 68)
32.9	1.2	0.9	30.9	24.2	9.2	6.7	0.0	5.9	24.6	2005	
Parts par principaux groupes de produits (en pourcentage)											
100.0	100.0	100.0	100.0	100.0	100.0	100.0	100.0	100.0	100.0	1995	Total tous produits
100.0	100.0	100.0	100.0	100.0	100.0	100.0	100.0	100.0	100.0	2000	
100.0	100.0	100.0	100.0	100.0	100.0	100.0	100.0	100.0	100.0	2005	
18.7	25.4	49.8	15.9	14.0	5.4	19.0	78.9	13.8	16.3	1995	Produits alimentaires
18.6	21.7	47.7	16.2	14.7	4.3	19.0	2.2	15.8	13.4	2000	(CTCI 0 + 1 + 22 + 4)
12.7	17.0	49.1	9.6	7.5	1.9	14.8	2.2	11.4	9.0	2005	
2.3	5.8	4.7	1.8	2.3	0.5	1.0	0.0	1.8	1.9	1995	Matières premières
1.7	3.4	3.1	1.4	1.5	0.4	1.1	5.0	1.2	1.4	2000	d'origine agricole
1.3	1.9	3.6	1.0	1.1	0.6	0.8	1.0	1.1	1.0	2005	(CTCI 2 - 22 - 27 - 28)
3.5	8.5	8.2	2.7	1.4	0.7	4.8	6.7	5.0	1.8	1995	Minerais et métaux
3.5	4.6	14.7	2.5	1.4	0.9	4.5	6.4	3.8	2.2	2000	(CTCI 27 + 28 + 68)
5.0	4.8	12.8	4.5	4.3	1.3	5.1	0.5	7.2	3.7	2005	
15.3	35.3	0.4	14.4	4.2	0.8	31.2	0.0	40.1	0.6	1995	Combustibles (CTCI 3)
14.1	33.0	1.3	12.8	3.3	0.5	30.8	0.0	36.7	0.5	2000	
11.0	29.0	3.3	9.6	4.1	0.9	23.1	0.0	33.4	1.2	2005	
59.4	24.4	34.1	64.4	77.7	92.3	42.8	14.3	38.2	78.7	1995	Articles manufacturés
59.3	18.9	28.3	66.3	78.6	93.4	43.2	86.4	37.5	81.5	2000	(CTCI 5 à 8 moins 68)
63.6	23.7	28.5	70.5	77.7	95.1	52.8	96.4	38.6	80.9	2005	

Sources :
- Calculs du secrétariat de la CNUCED sur la base des données de ONU DAES Division de statistique

Destination / Product group	Year / Année	World / Monde	Developed economies / Économies développées							Economies in transition / Économies en transition
			Total	Europe		Canada	USA / États-Unis	Japan / Japon	Other developed countries / Autres économies développées	
				Total	EU / UE					
Millions of dollars										
All products	1 995	4 837	4 475	1 142	1 140	28	234	1 914	1 156	4
	2 000	4 284	1 603	551	545	4	228	522	298	6
	2005	6 026	2 784	1 089	1 076	8	281	548	858	35
Share by destination (percentage)										
All products	1995	100.0	84.1	21.5	21.4	0.5	4.4	36.0	21.7	0.1
	2000	..	..	..	..	..	..	..	..	..
	2005	100.0	46.2	18.1	17.9	0.1	4.7	9.1	14.2	0.6
All food items	1995	100.0	81.1	52.5	52.5	2.2	5.1	13.5	7.8	0.2
(SITC 0 + 1 + 22 + 4)	2000	100.0	51.6	26.4	26.2	0.1	10.6	8.4	6.1	0.1
	2005	100.0	76.2	41.1	41.0	0.3	16.4	9.9	8.5	0.2
Agricultural raw materials	1995	100.0	61.8	1.8	1.8	0.0	0.3	58.1	1.6	0.0
(SITC 2 - 22 - 27 - 28)	2000	100.0	45.6	5.8	5.8	0.0	2.2	29.8	7.8	0.0
	2005	100.0	42.3	4.6	4.2	0.0	5.7	21.3	10.7	0.4
Ores and metals	1995	100.0	83.9	23.6	23.6	0.0	2.2	51.8	6.3	0.0
(SITC 27 + 28 + 68)	2000	..	..	..	..	..	..	..	..	..
	2005	..	..	..	..	..	..	..	..	..
Fuels (SITC 3)	1995	100.0	88.8	0.0	0.0	0.0	3.5	1.9	83.4	0.0
	2000	..	..	..	..	..	..	..	..	..
	2005	..	..	..	..	..	..	..	..	..
Manufactured goods	1995	100.0	86.3	27.6	27.4	0.4	10.5	35.1	12.7	0.2
(SITC 5 to 8 less 68)	2000	100.0	67.0	19.2	18.8	0.2	11.4	22.7	13.5	0.2
	2005	100.0	58.1	23.6	23.5	0.3	4.7	13.6	16.0	0.1
Share by major product group (percentage)										
All products	1995	100.0	100.0	100.0	100.0	100.0	100.0	100.0	100.0	100.0
	2000	100.0	100.0	100.0	100.0	100.0	100.0	100.0	100.0	100.0
	2005	100.0	100.0	100.0	100.0	100.0	100.0	100.0	100.0	100.0
All food items	1995	20.4	19.7	49.9	50.0	84.3	23.8	7.7	7.4	41.2
(SITC 0 + 1 + 22 + 4)	2000	15.5	21.3	31.7	31.9	26.1	30.8	10.7	13.6	8.4
	2005	18.8	31.1	42.9	43.2	37.1	66.1	20.5	11.3	8.0
Agricultural raw materials	1995	12.5	9.2	1.0	1.0	0.2	0.8	20.2	0.9	0.0
(SITC 2 - 22 - 27 - 28)	2000	3.0	3.6	1.3	1.4	0.6	1.2	7.3	3.3	0.8
	2005	3.1	2.9	0.8	0.7	0.3	3.8	7.3	2.3	2.1
Ores and metals	1995	17.6	17.6	19.4	19.4	0.0	9.0	25.4	5.1	0.0
(SITC 27 + 28 + 68)	2000	34.5	20.2	23.2	23.5	6.1	1.6	27.9	15.5	45.3
	2005	30.5	19.9	18.0	17.4	0.1	0.1	28.6	23.4	84.4
Fuels (SITC 3)	1995	11.6	12.2	0.0	0.0	0.0	9.3	0.6	44.5	0.0
	2000	16.3	0.2	0.0	0.0	0.0	0.0	0.0	1.2	0.0
	2005	14.3	0.4	0.2	0.3	0.0	0.0	0.0	1.0	0.0
Manufactured goods	1995	22.3	22.9	28.7	28.6	15.2	53.3	21.8	13.0	58.8
(SITC 5 to 8 less 68)	2000	29.1	52.1	43.4	43.0	61.2	62.3	54.1	56.6	45.4
	2005	29.0	36.5	38.0	38.2	60.6	29.1	43.4	32.5	5.3

Sources:
- UNCTAD secretariat calculations based on UN DESA Statistics Division's data

Total	Africa / Afrique	America / Amérique	Asia / Asie				Oceania / Océanie	Major petroleum exporters / Principaux exportateurs de pétrole	Major exporters of manufactures / Principaux exportateurs d'articles manufacturés	Year / Année	Destination / Groupes de produits
			Total	Eastern, Southern and South-Eastern Asia / Asie orientale, méridionale et du Sud-Est	China / Chine	Western Asia / Asie occidentale					
Millions de dollars											
844	6	9	810	804	87	6	19	5	805	1 995	Total tous produits
787	12	129	577	576	24	1	69	10	685	2000	
1 404	99	90	1 067	1 067	139	1	148	61	1 087	2005	
Parts par destinations (en pourcentage)											
15.9	0.1	0.2	15.2	15.1	1.6	0.1	0.4	0.1	15.1	1995	Total tous produits
..	..	..	..	..	..	..	..	..	..	2000	
23.3	1.6	1.5	17.7	17.7	2.3	0.0	2.5	1.0	18.0	2005	
18.7	0.1	0.1	18.3	18.0	1.1	0.3	0.3	0.3	17.6	1995	Produits alimentaires
14.0	0.3	0.0	10.0	9.9	0.1	0.1	3.7	0.5	7.9	2000	(CTCI 0 + 1 + 22 + 4)
22.4	2.6	0.2	14.7	14.7	0.1	0.0	4.9	4.8	11.8	2005	
38.2	0.0	0.0	38.1	38.1	4.3	0.0	0.2	0.0	38.0	1995	Matières premières
53.4	0.1	0.1	51.7	51.7	16.7	0.0	1.5	0.2	50.1	2000	d'origine agricole
57.2	0.5	0.8	54.2	54.2	30.3	0.0	1.8	0.4	51.4	2005	(CTCI 2 - 22 - 27 - 28)
16.1	0.0	0.0	16.1	16.1	0.0	0.0	0.0	0.0	16.1	1995	Minerais et métaux
..	..	..	..	..	..	..	..	..	..	2000	(CTCI 27 + 28 + 68)
..	..	..	..	..	..	..	..	..	..	2005	
11.2	0.0	0.0	10.7	10.7	7.5	0.0	0.4	0.0	10.7	1995	Combustibles (CTCI 3)
..	..	..	..	..	..	..	..	..	..	2000	
..	..	..	..	..	..	..	..	..	..	2005	
13.5	0.5	0.7	11.4	11.2	0.0	0.2	0.9	0.1	11.7	1995	Articles manufacturés
31.8	0.3	10.4	17.9	17.8	0.2	0.0	3.2	0.5	27.9	2000	(CTCI 5 à 8 moins 68)
41.5	2.1	4.9	31.0	31.0	3.8	0.0	3.4	0.3	35.3	2005	
Parts par principaux groupes de produits (en pourcentage)											
100.0	100.0	100.0	100.0	100.0	100.0	100.0	100.0	100.0	100.0	1995	Total tous produits
100.0	100.0	100.0	100.0	100.0	100.0	100.0	100.0	100.0	100.0	2000	
100.0	100.0	100.0	100.0	100.0	100.0	100.0	100.0	100.0	100.0	2005	
24.1	11.5	9.6	24.6	24.3	14.1	62.2	14.3	62.6	23.7	1995	Produits alimentaires
11.8	17.0	0.1	11.5	11.4	1.4	55.9	35.3	33.7	7.6	2000	(CTCI 0 + 1 + 22 + 4)
18.1	30.3	2.9	15.6	15.6	0.9	13.6	37.3	89.8	12.3	2005	
30.1	0.1	0.5	31.3	31.5	32.7	0.0	5.8	4.5	31.4	1995	Matières premières
8.7	1.2	0.1	11.4	11.4	90.1	0.0	2.8	2.2	9.3	2000	d'origine agricole
7.7	0.9	1.7	9.5	9.5	41.1	4.2	2.2	1.1	8.9	2005	(CTCI 2 - 22 - 27 - 28)
17.9	0.3	0.0	18.7	18.8	0.0	0.4	0.3	0.1	18.7	1995	Minerais et métaux
28.8	49.4	0.0	38.0	38.1	0.0	0.0	1.6	6.1	32.0	2000	(CTCI 27 + 28 + 68)
9.9	20.4	0.0	11.0	11.0	10.3	0.0	1.2	0.0	9.1	2005	
8.1	0.0	0.0	8.2	8.2	53.0	0.0	14.3	0.0	8.2	1995	Combustibles (CTCI 3)
0.3	0.0	0.0	0.3	0.3	0.0	0.0	1.0	0.0	0.3	2000	
12.5	10.4	0.0	13.0	13.0	0.0	0.0	18.0	0.2	12.7	2005	
18.9	87.6	89.8	16.7	16.6	0.1	37.4	56.4	32.7	17.3	1995	Articles manufacturés
50.3	31.2	99.8	38.6	38.6	8.3	44.1	58.4	57.3	50.7	2000	(CTCI 5 à 8 moins 68)
51.7	37.7	95.3	50.8	50.8	47.6	69.0	40.8	8.6	56.8	2005	

Sources :
- Calculs du secrétariat de la CNUCED sur la base des données de ONU DAES Division de statistique

2.2.J   Import structure by partner and product group
Developing economies: Oceania

Product group	Year / Année	World / Monde	Developed economies / Économies développées							Economies in transition / Économies en transition
			Total	Europe		Canada	USA / États-Unis	Japan / Japon	Other developed countries / Autres économies développées	
				Total	EU / UE					
Millions of dollars										
All products	1995	5 634	4 573	1 437	1 426	13	365	805	1 953	1
	2000	5 109	3 549	1 224	1 208	16	376	393	1 540	14
	2005	8 790	5 666	1 903	1 871	26	582	485	2 671	15
Share by origin (percentage)										
All products	1995	100.0	79.3	24.9	24.7	0.2	6.3	14.0	33.9	0.0
	2000	100.0	69.5	24.0	23.6	0.3	7.4	7.7	30.1	0.3
	2005	100.0	63.9	21.5	21.1	0.3	6.6	5.5	30.1	0.2
All food items	1995	100.0	86.5	23.8	23.7	0.2	10.5	5.2	46.9	0.0
(SITC 0 + 1 + 22 + 4)	2000	100.0	85.3	21.2	21.0	0.4	14.1	1.5	48.0	0.1
	2005	100.0	80.1	20.3	20.1	0.3	10.9	1.1	47.5	0.0
Agricultural raw materials	1995	100.0	89.4	6.4	6.4	0.0	27.9	3.0	52.1	0.1
(SITC 2 - 22 - 27 - 28)	2000	100.0	82.1	8.2	8.2	1.2	33.8	0.9	38.0	0.1
	2005	100.0	84.4	5.9	5.8	5.0	14.7	0.7	58.0	0.0
Ores and metals	1995	100.0	86.8	29.5	29.5	0.0	4.0	2.0	51.3	0.0
(SITC 27 + 28 + 68)	2000	100.0	74.5	29.8	29.7	0.0	7.9	2.3	34.5	0.1
	2005	100.0	82.7	29.7	29.7	1.2	5.2	2.7	43.9	0.0
Fuels (SITC 3)	1995	100.0	61.7	0.9	0.9	0.0	1.5	0.0	59.3	0.0
	2000	100.0	56.1	0.6	0.6	0.0	0.7	0.0	54.8	1.6
	2005	100.0	21.3	0.4	0.4	0.0	0.5	0.0	20.4	0.3
Manufactured goods	1995	100.0	80.1	29.5	29.2	0.3	5.3	18.3	26.7	0.0
(SITC 5 to 8 less 68)	2000	100.0	68.6	30.5	30.0	0.4	6.5	11.2	20.0	0.0
	2005	100.0	69.0	26.9	26.4	0.3	6.7	7.9	27.3	0.2
Share by major product group (percentage)										
All products	1995	100.0	100.0	100.0	100.0	100.0	100.0	100.0	100.0	100.0
	2000	100.0	100.0	100.0	100.0	100.0	100.0	100.0	100.0	100.0
	2005	100.0	100.0	100.0	100.0	100.0	100.0	100.0	100.0	100.0
All food items	1995	16.1	17.5	15.3	15.4	12.3	26.5	6.0	22.2	18.8
(SITC 0 + 1 + 22 + 4)	2000	16.5	20.2	14.6	14.7	20.2	31.6	3.3	26.2	4.9
	2005	15.1	18.9	14.3	14.4	18.2	25.0	2.9	23.8	2.2
Agricultural raw materials	1995	1.0	1.1	0.3	0.3	0.1	4.3	0.2	1.5	2.8
(SITC 2 - 22 - 27 - 28)	2000	1.1	1.3	0.4	0.4	4.0	4.9	0.1	1.3	0.2
	2005	0.9	1.2	0.2	0.2	15.3	2.0	0.1	1.7	0.2
Ores and metals	1995	0.6	0.7	0.7	0.7	0.0	0.4	0.1	0.9	1.3
(SITC 27 + 28 + 68)	2000	0.7	0.8	0.9	0.9	0.0	0.8	0.2	0.8	0.2
	2005	0.7	0.9	1.0	1.0	2.9	0.5	0.3	1.0	0.0
Fuels (SITC 3)	1995	10.1	7.9	0.3	0.4	0.2	2.4	0.0	17.7	5.2
	2000	14.8	12.0	0.4	0.4	0.0	1.3	0.1	26.9	84.0
	2005	15.5	5.2	0.3	0.3	0.0	1.1	0.1	10.5	26.4
Manufactured goods	1995	69.9	70.6	82.6	82.6	85.7	58.2	91.9	55.1	71.9
(SITC 5 to 8 less 68)	2000	65.6	64.8	83.5	83.4	75.4	57.8	96.0	43.5	10.5
	2005	66.7	72.0	83.5	83.4	63.3	67.7	96.1	60.5	71.1

Sources:
- UNCTAD secretariat calculations based on UN DESA Statistics Division's data

Total	Africa / Afrique	America / Amérique	Asia / Asie — Total	Eastern, Southern and South-Eastern Asia / Asie orientale, méridionale et du Sud-Est	China / Chine	Western Asia / Asie occidentale	Oceania / Océanie	Major petroleum exporters / Principaux exportateurs de pétrole	Major exporters of manufactures / Principaux exportateurs d'articles manufacturés	Year / Année	Origine / Groupes de produits
Millions de dollars											
1 191	9	33	1 130	1 128	71	1	19	36	1 087	1995	Total tous produits
1 504	29	297	1 104	1 101	99	3	74	95	1 018	2000	
3 184	40	46	2 984	2 970	354	15	114	110	2 860	2005	
Parts par origines (en pourcentage)											
20.7	0.2	0.6	19.6	19.6	1.2	0.0	0.3	0.6	18.9	1995	Total tous produits
29.4	0.6	5.8	21.6	21.6	1.9	0.1	1.5	1.9	19.9	2000	
35.9	0.4	0.5	33.7	33.5	4.0	0.2	1.3	1.2	32.3	2005	
13.5	0.4	1.4	11.4	11.4	0 8	0.0	0.3	0.2	10.3	1995	Produits alimentaires
14.1	0.7	3.6	7.3	7.3	0 8	0.1	2.5	0.9	6.0	2000	(CTCI 0 + 1 + 22 + 4)
18.2	0.6	2.0	12.4	12.3	4 1	0.1	3.2	0.8	11.4	2005	
10.5	1.0	0.2	7.4	7.2	0 0	0.2	1.9	0.2	6.8	1995	Matières premières
17.7	0.2	2.1	5.0	5.0	0 2	0.0	10.4	1.4	3.9	2000	d'origine agricole
15.6	0.6	0.5	8.1	8.1	1.2	0.0	6.3	1.3	6.7	2005	(CTCI 2 - 22 - 27 - 28)
13.1	1.1	0.1	11.7	11.5	0 1	0.2	0.2	0.2	11.5	1995	Minerais et métaux
25.2	0.1	4.9	17.8	17.8	0 3	0.1	2.4	2.6	15.1	2000	(CTCI 27 + 28 + 68)
17.3	0.3	0.4	15.6	15.3	2.1	0.3	0.9	1.8	14.1	2005	
38.2	0.2	0.1	37.4	37.4	0.0	0.0	0.4	0.2	37.2	1995	Combustibles (CTCI 3)
42.1	2.3	6.0	31.7	31.7	0.0	0.0	2.0	2.5	31.3	2000	
78.2	0.4	0.0	76.3	76.3	0.1	0.0	1.6	0.0	75.6	2005	
19.9	0.1	0.5	19.1	19.0	1.6	0.0	0.3	0.8	18.3	1995	Articles manufacturés
31.1	0.2	6.5	23.6	23.5	2.7	0.1	0.9	2.0	21.5	2000	(CTCI 5 à 8 moins 68)
30.7	0.4	0.3	29.2	29.0	5.0	0.2	0.7	1.6	27.6	2005	
Parts par principaux groupes de produits (en pourcentage)											
100.0	100.0	100.0	100.0	100.0	100.0	100.0	100.0	100.0	100.0	1995	Total tous produits
100.0	100.0	100.0	100.0	100.0	100.0	100.0	100.0	100.0	100.0	2000	
100.0	100.0	100.0	100.0	100.0	100.0	100.0	100.0	100.0	100.0	2005	
10.5	39.6	39.6	9.3	9.3	10.1	11.1	13.4	5.7	8.8	1995	Produits alimentaires
7.9	20.5	10.2	5.6	5.5	6.4	14.1	27.8	8.2	5.0	2000	(CTCI 0 + 1 + 22 + 4)
7.6	18.8	57.2	5.6	5.5	15.7	12.8	38.0	10.2	5.4	2005	
0.5	6.4	0.3	0.4	0.4	0.0	7.2	5.6	0.3	0.4	1995	Matières premières
0.6	0.4	0.4	0.2	0.2	0.1	0.0	7.6	0.8	0.2	2000	d'origine agricole
0.4	1.3	0.8	0.2	0.2	0.3	0.0	4.3	0.9	0.2	2005	(CTCI 2 - 22 - 27 - 28)
0.4	4.0	0.1	0.4	0.4	0.0	4.1	0.3	0.2	0.4	1995	Minerais et métaux
0.6	0.1	0.6	0.6	0.6	0.1	0.6	1.2	1.1	0.6	2000	(CTCI 27 + 28 + 68)
0.3	0.5	0.6	0.3	0.3	0.4	1.3	0.5	1.0	0.3	2005	
18.7	13.9	2.2	19.3	19.3	0.0	0.0	13.6	3.5	19.9	1995	Combustibles (CTCI 3)
21.2	60.7	15.4	21.7	21.8	0.1	0.0	20.4	19.5	23.3	2000	
33.8	12.7	0.1	35.2	35.3	0.3	1.3	19.0	0.3	36.3	2005	
67.3	36.2	57.7	68.0	68.0	89.8	77.6	57.0	90.2	67.8	1995	Articles manufacturés
69.4	18.1	73.0	71.6	71.6	92.7	84.6	41.7	70.3	70.8	2000	(CTCI 5 à 8 moins 68)
57.1	66.1	41.2	57.9	57.8	83.3	83.5	37.1	87.4	57.0	2005	

Sources :
- Calculs du secrétariat de la CNUCED sur la base des données de ONU DAES Division de statistique

2.2.K Export structure by partner and product group
Major petroleum exporters

Destination / Product group	Year Année	World Monde	Developed economies Économies développées							Economies in transition Économies en transition
			Total	Europe		Canada	USA États-Unis	Japan Japon	Other developed countries Autres économies développées	
				Total	EU UE					
Millions of dollars										
All products	1995	237 409	128 259	48 412	47 364	2 009	37 591	38 214	2 034	1 882
	2000	393 249	222 207	85 430	78 113	3 194	78 431	52 754	2 398	1 957
	2005	760 880	394 143	140 555	122 170	8 170	130 679	109 480	5 259	4 113
Share by destination (percentage)										
All products	1995	100.0	54.0	20.4	20.0	0.8	15.8	16.1	0.9	0.8
	2000	100.0	56.5	21.7	19.9	0.8	19.9	13.4	0.6	0.5
	2005	100.0	51.8	18.5	16.1	1.1	17.2	14.4	0.7	0.5
All food items	1995	100.0	44.5	22.8	22.4	0.6	6.7	14.0	0.5	5.0
(SITC 0 + 1 + 22 + 4)	2000	100.0	37.2	16.3	16.1	0.4	10.0	9.8	0.6	3.2
	2005	100.0	28.3	15.1	15.0	0.4	7.7	4.5	0.6	3.3
Agricultural raw materials	1995	100.0	57.2	24.3	24.0	1.8	22.7	7.0	1.3	1.5
(SITC 2 - 22 - 27 - 28)	2000	100.0	46.5	23.9	23.2	1.3	12.3	7.3	1.7	0.6
	2005	100.0	44.7	18.9	18.8	1.6	15.0	8.1	1.0	0.8
Ores and metals	1995	100.0	48.5	12.3	12.0	0.4	5.3	30.2	0.4	0.8
(SITC 27 + 28 + 68)	2000	100.0	50.2	17.3	16.4	0.4	6.4	25.6	0.5	1.5
	2005	100.0	36.1	11.0	10.2	0.6	4.6	19.6	0.3	1.3
Fuels (SITC 3)	1995	100.0	57.1	20.8	20.3	0.9	16.9	17.9	0.7	0.2
	2000	100.0	60.1	23.2	21.0	0.8	21.3	14.4	0.4	0.2
	2005	100.0	58.3	20.0	17.2	1.2	19.4	17.0	0.6	0.1
Manufactured goods	1995	100.0	44.6	19.2	18.6	0.8	14.4	8.7	1.6	2.0
(SITC 5 to 8 less 68)	2000	100.0	42.9	15.5	15.1	0.9	17.0	7.8	1.8	1.7
	2005	100.0	37.3	16.4	16.0	0.7	13.3	5.4	1.5	2.9
Share by major product group (percentage)										
All products	1995	100.0	100.0	100.0	100.0	100.0	100.0	100.0	100.0	100.0
	2000	100.0	100.0	100.0	100.0	100.0	100.0	100.0	100.0	100.0
	2005	100.0	100.0	100.0	100.0	100.0	100.0	100.0	100.0	100.0
All food items	1995	4.1	3.4	4.6	4.6	2.7	1.7	3.5	2.2	25.8
(SITC 0 + 1 + 22 + 4)	2000	2.5	1.7	1.9	2.1	1.4	1.3	1.9	2.7	16.5
	2005	2.3	1.3	1.9	2.2	0.8	1.0	0.7	2.0	14.3
Agricultural raw materials	1995	1.9	2.0	2.2	2.2	4.1	2.7	0.8	2.9	3.5
(SITC 2 - 22 - 27 - 28)	2000	0.8	0.7	0.9	1.0	1.4	0.5	0.5	2.4	0.9
	2005	0.8	0.7	0.8	0.9	1.2	0.7	0.5	1.2	1.2
Ores and metals	1995	2.8	2.6	1.7	1.7	1.2	0.9	5.3	1.4	2.8
(SITC 27 + 28 + 68)	2000	1.8	1.6	1.4	1.5	0.9	0.6	3.4	1.5	5.2
	2005	1.9	1.3	1.1	1.2	1.0	0.5	2.5	0.9	4.4
Fuels (SITC 3)	1995	72.2	76.3	73.6	73.6	74.6	77.0	80.2	59.4	19.9
	2000	79.3	84.3	84.7	83.7	79.7	84.5	85.4	47.2	24.1
	2005	77.0	86.7	83.6	82.4	88.9	87.2	91.1	62.9	9.0
Manufactured goods	1995	18.8	15.5	17.6	17.5	17.4	17.1	10.1	34.1	47.9
(SITC 5 to 8 less 68)	2000	15.4	11.7	11.0	11.7	16.5	13.1	8.9	45.7	51.9
	2005	13.1	9.4	11.6	13.0	8.0	10.1	4.9	28.3	69.8

Sources:
- UNCTAD secretariat calculations based on UN DESA Statistics Division's data

2.2.K Structure des exportations par partenaires et groupes de produits
Principaux exportateurs de pétrole

Total	Africa / Afrique	America / Amérique	Asia / Asie — Total	Eastern, Southern and South-Eastern Asia / Asie orientale, méridionale et du Sud-Est	China / Chine	Western Asia / Asie occidentale	Oceania / Océanie	Major petroleum exporters / Principaux exportateurs de pétrole	Major exporters of manufactures / Principaux exportateurs d'articles manufacturés	Year / Année	Destination / Groupes de produits
Millions de dollars											
63 083	5 270	10 554	47 235	35 983	3 679	11 251	24	11 434	37 374	1995	Total tous produits
148 714	12 310	17 395	118 878	101 496	10 752	17 382	132	14 716	104 709	2000	
283 191	19 957	28 468	234 620	203 383	37 495	31 237	146	35 916	197 050	2005	
Parts par destinations (en pourcentage)											
26.6	2.2	4.4	19.9	15.2	1.5	4.7	0.0	4.8	15.7	1995	Total tous produits
37.8	3.1	4.4	30.2	25.8	2.7	4.4	0.0	3.7	26.6	2000	
37.2	2.6	3.7	30.8	26.7	4.9	4.1	0.0	4.7	25.9	2005	
49.7	3.4	6.3	40.0	19.6	2.1	20.5	0.0	20.3	16.5	1995	Produits alimentaires
58.7	3.8	4.7	50.1	27.9	2.4	22.3	0.1	19.5	24.0	2000	(CTCI 0 + 1 + 22 + 4)
68.2	6.6	2.7	58.8	35.9	5.0	22.9	0.1	23.1	27.5	2005	
40.8	3.3	3.6	33.9	29.8	5.2	4.1	0.0	3.7	31.0	1995	Matières premières
52.6	2.4	3.2	47.1	40.9	18.4	6.1	0.1	2.9	43.2	2000	d'origine agricole
54.4	3.3	3.9	47.2	42.8	20.4	4.4	0.0	3.5	42.4	2005	(CTCI 2 - 22 - 27 - 28)
47.8	1.1	4.3	42.4	33.4	1.4	9.0	0.0	8.9	34.0	1995	Minerais et métaux
47.6	1.4	3.9	42.3	33.0	2.3	9.4	0.0	8.9	33.5	2000	(CTCI 27 + 28 + 68)
62.5	2.4	3.9	56.2	46.6	7.8	9.6	0.0	9.5	47.3	2005	
17.2	1.7	4.0	11.5	10.1	1.2	1.4	0.0	1.1	11.8	1995	Combustibles (CTCI 3)
34.0	2.8	4.4	26.7	24.7	2.7	2.0	0.0	1.4	26.4	2000	
32.8	1.9	3.9	27.0	25.3	4.8	1.7	0.0	1.6	25.7	2005	
52.6	4.1	6.0	42.4	29.3	2.3	13.1	0.0	14.8	26.2	1995	Articles manufacturés
51.7	4.8	4.5	42.3	29.2	2.0	13.1	0.1	12.5	26.2	2000	(CTCI 5 à 8 moins 68)
59.5	6.9	4.1	48.5	35.4	5.9	13.1	0.1	18.1	28.8	2005	
Parts par principaux groupes de produits (en pourcentage)											
100.0	100.0	100.0	100.0	100.0	100.0	100.0	100.0	100.0	100.0	1995	Total tous produits
100.0	100.0	100.0	100.0	100.0	100.0	100.0	100.0	100.0	100.0	2000	
100.0	100.0	100.0	100.0	100.0	100.0	100.0	100.0	100.0	100.0	2005	
7.6	6.2	5.8	8.2	5.3	5.4	17.6	5.9	17.2	4.3	1995	Produits alimentaires
3.9	3.1	2.7	4.2	2.7	2.2	12.8	8.6	13.2	2.3	2000	(CTCI 0 + 1 + 22 + 4)
4.3	5.9	1.7	4.4	3.1	2.3	13.0	11.5	11.4	2.5	2005	
2.9	2.7	1.5	3.2	3.7	6.3	1.6	0.1	1.4	3.7	1995	Matières premières
1.2	0.6	0.6	1.3	1.3	5.6	1.1	1.6	0.7	1.3	2000	d'origine agricole
1.2	1.0	0.8	1.2	1.3	3.3	0.9	1.2	0.6	1.3	2005	(CTCI 2 - 22 - 27 - 28)
5.1	1.4	2.7	6.1	6.3	2.6	5.4	0.2	5.2	6.1	1995	Minerais et métaux
2.2	0.8	1.6	2.5	2.3	1.5	3.7	1.3	4.2	2.2	2000	(CTCI 27 + 28 + 68)
3.1	1.7	1.9	3.4	3.2	2.9	4.3	1.0	3.8	3.4	2005	
46.7	54.9	64.4	41.8	48.0	57.9	22.0	4.3	16.8	54.3	1995	Combustibles (CTCI 3)
71.3	71.9	79.6	70.0	75.8	79.2	36.2	24.3	29.9	78.6	2000	
68.0	55.9	81.3	67.4	72.9	75.3	31.8	8.3	26.8	76.3	2005	
37.2	34.7	25.5	40.0	36.3	27.7	51.9	89.5	57.9	31.2	1995	Articles manufacturés
21.1	23.4	15.6	21.6	17.4	11.5	45.5	64.2	51.4	15.2	2000	(CTCI 5 à 8 moins 68)
20.9	34.3	14.2	20.6	17.3	15.6	41.8	77.9	50.1	14.6	2005	

Sources :
- Calculs du secrétariat de la CNUCED sur la base des données de ONU DAES Division de statistique

2.2.K Import structure by partner and product group
Major petroleum exporters

Origin / Product group	Year / Année	World / Monde	Developed economies / Économies développées							Economies in transition / Économies en transition
			Total	Europe		Canada	USA / États-Unis	Japan / Japon	Other developed countries / Autres économies développées	
				Total	EU / UE					
Millions of dollars										
All products	**1995**	**169 419**	**109 245**	**59 931**	**56 065**	**3 222**	**23 556**	**18 433**	**4 103**	**3 235**
	2000	**177 743**	**100 172**	**53 766**	**50 654**	**3 102**	**22 690**	**15 601**	**5 013**	**3 679**
	2005	**375 047**	**187 508**	**112 589**	**103 500**	**3 099**	**36 880**	**27 003**	**7 936**	**9 233**
Share by origin (percentage)										
All products	**1995**	**100.0**	**64.5**	**35.4**	**33.1**	**1.9**	**13.9**	**10.9**	**2.4**	**1.9**
	2000	**100.0**	**56.4**	**30.2**	**28.5**	**1.7**	**12.8**	**8.8**	**2.8**	**2.1**
	2005	**100.0**	**50.0**	**30.0**	**27.6**	**0.8**	**9.8**	**7.2**	**2.1**	**2.5**
All food items	1995	100.0	54.1	27.6	26.8	5.7	13.1	0.2	7.5	1.3
(SITC 0 + 1 + 22 + 4)	2000	100.0	51.0	26.4	25.7	5.1	11.3	0.2	7.9	1.1
	2005	100.0	44.4	25.4	23.5	1.8	10.0	0.2	7.0	2.8
Agricultural raw materials	1995	100.0	59.3	18.4	18.2	5.3	23.5	4.9	7.2	5.9
(SITC 2 - 22 - 27 - 28)	2000	100.0	59.2	19.8	18.9	7.8	17.0	4.2	10.3	4.5
	2005	100.0	51.8	26.6	25.3	4.7	13.0	2.6	4.8	9.0
Ores and metals	1995	100.0	47.7	23.4	22.5	1.8	9.0	2.0	11.4	3.7
(SITC 27 + 28 + 68)	2000	100.0	43.6	19.5	18.3	0.9	5.8	3.0	14.5	4.4
	2005	100.0	33.9	16.1	15.4	1.5	3.5	2.1	10.7	4.4
Fuels (SITC 3)	1995	100.0	18.8	8.8	8.8	0.1	4.9	0.5	4.5	3.3
	2000	100.0	7.9	4.5	3.7	0.1	2.2	0.4	0.8	0.4
	2005	100.0	7.3	4.4	3.2	0.0	1.5	0.1	1.2	1.7
Manufactured goods	1995	100.0	69.5	38.8	36.7	1.1	14.5	14.3	0.7	1.8
(SITC 5 to 8 less 68)	2000	100.0	62.5	34.0	32.3	1.0	14.4	12.0	1.2	2.3
	2005	100.0	58.2	34.7	32.6	0.7	11.7	10.0	1.1	2.3
Share by major product group (percentage)										
All products	**1995**	**100.0**	**100.0**	**100.0**	**100.0**	**100.0**	**100.0**	**100.0**	**100.0**	**100.0**
	2000	**100.0**	**100.0**	**100.0**	**100.0**	**100.0**	**100.0**	**100.0**	**100.0**	**100.0**
	2005	**100.0**	**100.0**	**100.0**	**100.0**	**100.0**	**100.0**	**100.0**	**100.0**	**100.0**
All food items	1995	15.0	12.6	11.7	12.1	44.7	14.1	0.3	46.7	9.9
(SITC 0 + 1 + 22 + 4)	2000	15.9	14.4	13.9	14.4	47.0	14.2	0.4	44.8	8.2
	2005	11.3	10.0	9.6	9.6	25.1	11.5	0.3	37.4	13.0
Agricultural raw materials	1995	2.8	2.6	1.4	1.5	7.7	4.7	1.3	8.3	8.6
(SITC 2 - 22 - 27 - 28)	2000	2.4	2.5	1.6	1.6	10.8	3.2	1.1	8.8	5.3
	2005	1.4	1.4	1.2	1.3	7.7	1.8	0.5	3.1	5.0
Ores and metals	1995	3.0	2.2	2.0	2.1	2.9	2.0	0.6	14.3	5.9
(SITC 27 + 28 + 68)	2000	2.6	2.0	1.7	1.7	1.3	1.2	0.9	13.2	5.4
	2005	3.0	2.0	1.6	1.7	5.4	1.1	0.9	15.1	5.3
Fuels (SITC 3)	1995	4.1	1.2	1.0	1.1	0.3	1.4	0.2	7.5	6.9
	2000	7.0	1.0	1.0	0.9	0.2	1.2	0.3	2.0	1.5
	2005	9.1	1.3	1.4	1.1	0.1	1.4	0.2	5.3	6.5
Manufactured goods	1995	74.0	79.8	81.2	82.1	42.1	77.3	97.5	22.8	68.6
(SITC 5 to 8 less 68)	2000	71.0	78.8	79.7	80.4	40.6	80.0	97.1	29.8	78.4
	2005	69.9	81.4	80.8	82.5	59.8	82.9	97.0	37.5	66.2

Sources:
- UNCTAD secretariat calculations based on UN DESA Statistics Division's data

2.2.K Structure des importations par partenaires et groupes de produits
Principaux exportateurs de pétrole

			Developing economies / Économies en développement					Major petroleum exporters / Principaux exportateurs de pétrole	Major exporters of manufactures / Principaux exportateurs d'articles manufacturés	Year / Année	Origine / Groupes de produits
Total	Africa / Afrique	America / Amérique	Total (Asia / Asie)	Eastern, Southern and South-Eastern Asia / Asie orientale, méridionale et du Sud-Est	China / Chine	Western Asia / Asie occidentale	Oceania / Océanie				
Millions de dollars											
56 310	**3 558**	**8 206**	**44 538**	**32 506**	**4 736**	**12 032**	**8**	**12 448**	**34 111**	**1995**	**Total tous produits**
70 371	**4 563**	**10 647**	**55 077**	**39 264**	**7 978**	**15 813**	**84**	**18 935**	**40 358**	**2000**	
163 219	**9 735**	**19 881**	**133 413**	**96 671**	**26 010**	**36 743**	**189**	**37 678**	**103 893**	**2005**	
Parts par origines (en pourcentage)											
33.2	**2.1**	**4.8**	**26.3**	**19.2**	**2.8**	**7.1**	**0.0**	**7.3**	**20.1**	**1995**	**Total tous produits**
39.6	**2.6**	**6.0**	**31.0**	**22.1**	**4.5**	**8.9**	**0.0**	**10.7**	**22.7**	**2000**	
43.5	**2.6**	**5.3**	**35.6**	**25.8**	**6.9**	**9.8**	**0.1**	**10.0**	**27.7**	**2005**	
44.4	4.2	13.1	27.2	17.9	2.0	9.3	0.0	7.3	19.6	1995	Produits alimentaires
46.2	5.3	11.2	29.5	19.7	2.6	9.8	0.2	10.1	19.6	2000	(CTCI 0 + 1 + 22 + 4)
52.3	5.5	17.1	29.4	18.3	2.1	11.1	0.3	9.7	23.9	2005	
34.7	6.0	8.2	20.5	17.7	0.9	2.8	0.0	3.5	18.8	1995	Matières premières
34.2	6.1	6.8	21.3	18.3	3.3	3.0	0.1	3.2	20.0	2000	d'origine agricole
39.2	6.2	7.8	25.2	20.0	2.1	5.2	0.1	5.8	21.1	2005	(CTCI 2 - 22 - 27 - 28)
48.3	7.2	13.9	27.2	14.2	2.3	13.0	0.0	14.2	19.3	1995	Minerais et métaux
50.3	6.4	14.6	29.3	15.9	2.7	13.5	0.0	14.4	23.5	2000	(CTCI 27 + 28 + 68)
61.6	5.3	9.9	46.3	33.1	4.1	13.2	0.0	22.1	30.9	2005	
75.6	6.1	11.6	57.9	21.9	1.2	36.0	0.0	54.5	18.7	1995	Combustibles (CTCI 3)
90.6	6.5	17.6	66.5	27.9	3.3	38.7	0.0	59.0	25.3	2000	
72.0	5.9	4.0	62.0	37.8	4.2	24.2	0.1	33.3	35.5	2005	
28.2	1.1	2.3	24.8	19.8	3.2	5.0	0.0	4.6	20.6	1995	Articles manufacturés
32.9	1.2	3.3	28.4	22.6	5.2	5.8	0.0	6.1	23.3	2000	(CTCI 5 à 8 moins 68)
39.1	1.4	3.6	34.0	26.0	8.8	8.0	0.0	7.0	28.2	2005	
Parts par principaux groupes de produits (en pourcentage)											
100.0	**100.0**	**100.0**	**100.0**	**100.0**	**100.0**	**100.0**	**100.0**	**100.0**	**100.0**	**1995**	**Total tous produits**
100.0	**100.0**	**100.0**	**100.0**	**100.0**	**100.0**	**100.0**	**100.0**	**100.0**	**100.0**	**2000**	
100.0	**100.0**	**100.0**	**100.0**	**100.0**	**100.0**	**100.0**	**100.0**	**100.0**	**100.0**	**2005**	
20.0	29.7	40.4	15.5	14.0	10.9	19.6	49.9	15.0	14.6	1995	Produits alimentaires
18.6	33.2	29.9	15.2	14.2	9.2	17.5	54.6	15.1	13.8	2000	(CTCI 0 + 1 + 22 + 4)
13.6	24.1	36.4	9.3	8.0	3.4	12.7	64.5	10.9	9.7	2005	
2.9	7.9	4.7	2.2	2.6	0.9	1.1	2.7	1.3	2.6	1995	Matières premières
2.1	5.6	2.7	1.6	2.0	1.8	0.8	6.4	0.7	2.1	2000	d'origine agricole
1.2	3.2	2.0	1.0	1.1	0.4	0.7	2.1	0.8	1.0	2005	(CTCI 2 - 22 - 27 - 28)
4.4	10.4	8.7	3.1	2.2	2.5	5.6	0.4	5.9	2.9	1995	Minerais et métaux
3.3	6.4	6.3	2.4	1.9	1.6	3.9	0.8	3.5	2.7	2000	(CTCI 27 + 28 + 68)
4.2	6.1	5.6	3.9	3.8	1.8	4.0	0.2	6.6	3.3	2005	
9.3	11.8	9.8	9.0	4.6	1.7	20.7	0.0	30.2	3.8	1995	Combustibles (CTCI 3)
16.1	17.8	20.7	15.1	8.9	5.1	30.6	0.0	39.0	7.8	2000	
15.1	20.8	7.0	15.9	13.4	5.5	22.6	19.5	30.3	11.7	2005	
62.8	39.7	35.5	69.7	76.3	83.9	51.9	47.0	46.4	75.6	1995	Articles manufacturés
59.0	33.1	39.0	65.1	72.7	82.0	46.0	38.1	40.8	72.9	2000	(CTCI 5 à 8 moins 68)
62.7	38.7	47.9	66.8	70.5	88.6	57.1	13.6	48.5	71.1	2005	

Sources :
- Calculs du secrétariat de la CNUCED sur la base des données de ONU DAES Division de statistique

| Product group | Year / Année | World / Monde | Developed economies / Économies développées | | | | | | | Economies in transition / Économies en transition |
| | | | Total | Europe | | Canada | USA / États-Unis | Japan / Japon | Other developed countries / Autres économies développées | |
				Total	EU / UE					
Millions of dollars										
All products	**1 995**	**1 004 321**	**547 007**	**162 631**	**155 968**	**12 216**	**248 698**	**106 502**	**16 960**	**11 474**
	2 000	**1 409 579**	**820 477**	**226 690**	**218 327**	**17 745**	**415 292**	**134 348**	**26 401**	**10 457**
	2005	**2 557 047**	**1 291 106**	**428 749**	**416 861**	**30 281**	**584 729**	**193 414**	**53 933**	**48 158**
Share by destination (percentage)										
All products	**1995**	**100.0**	**54.5**	**16.2**	**15.5**	**1.2**	**24.8**	**10.6**	**1.7**	**1.1**
	2000	**100.0**	**58.2**	**16.1**	**15.5**	**1.3**	**29.5**	**9.5**	**1.9**	**0.7**
	2005	**100.0**	**50.5**	**16.8**	**16.3**	**1.2**	**22.9**	**7.6**	**2.1**	**1.9**
All food items	1995	100.0	53.5	18.4	17.7	0.8	13.9	19.0	1.3	3.6
(SITC 0 + 1 + 22 + 4)	2000	100.0	58.1	18.9	18.2	1.1	18.9	17.5	1.6	2.5
	2005	100.0	53.0	20.3	19.7	1.2	16.5	13.3	1.7	5.5
Agricultural raw materials	1995	100.0	49.5	17.7	17.3	0.6	12.2	17.8	1.2	0.2
(SITC 2 - 22 - 27 - 28)	2000	100.0	49.4	19.4	19.0	0.6	13.9	14.4	1.1	0.2
	2005	100.0	45.7	18.9	18.4	1.2	13.8	10.8	1.1	0.8
Ores and metals	1995	100.0	47.3	14.3	14.0	0.6	12.5	19.2	0.8	1.2
(SITC 27 + 28 + 68)	2000	100.0	45.3	16.7	15.4	0.7	13.2	12.8	1.9	0.9
	2005	100.0	36.3	13.9	13.1	1.1	9.8	10.2	1.2	1.5
Fuels (SITC 3)	1995	100.0	46.4	4.7	4.5	0.2	21.4	18.4	1.8	0.3
	2000	100.0	47.6	5.2	5.0	0.6	23.7	15.4	2.6	0.3
	2005	100.0	43.1	6.6	6.6	0.5	21.9	8.9	5.2	0.2
Manufactured goods	1995	100.0	55.3	16.4	15.8	1.3	26.6	9.1	1.8	1.0
(SITC 5 to 8 less 68)	2000	100.0	59.3	16.4	15.8	1.3	31.1	8.6	1.8	0.7
	2005	100.0	51.4	17.3	16.8	1.2	23.9	7.1	1.9	1.8
Share by major product group (percentage)										
All products	**1995**	**100.0**	**100.0**	**100.0**	**100.0**	**100.0**	**100.0**	**100.0**	**100.0**	**100.0**
	2000	**100.0**	**100.0**	**100.0**	**100.0**	**100.0**	**100.0**	**100.0**	**100.0**	**100.0**
	2005	**100.0**	**100.0**	**100.0**	**100.0**	**100.0**	**100.0**	**100.0**	**100.0**	**100.0**
All food items	1995	7.8	7.7	8.9	8.9	5.3	4.4	14.0	6.2	24.7
(SITC 0 + 1 + 22 + 4)	2000	5.1	5.1	6.0	6.0	4.7	3.3	9.4	4.5	17.1
	2005	4.7	4.9	5.7	5.7	4.9	3.4	8.2	3.8	13.8
Agricultural raw materials	1995	2.2	2.0	2.4	2.4	1.1	1.1	3.6	1.5	0.5
(SITC 2 - 22 - 27 - 28)	2000	1.3	1.1	1.6	1.6	0.6	0.6	2.0	0.8	0.4
	2005	1.1	1.0	1.2	1.2	1.0	0.6	1.5	0.5	0.5
Ores and metals	1995	2.2	1.9	1.9	2.0	1.1	1.1	4.0	1.1	2.3
(SITC 27 + 28 + 68)	2000	1.8	1.4	1.9	1.8	1.0	0.8	2.4	1.8	2.2
	2005	2.2	1.6	1.9	1.8	2.1	1.0	3.0	1.3	1.8
Fuels (SITC 3)	1995	3.3	2.8	1.0	1.0	0.6	2.9	5.8	3.5	0.9
	2000	4.6	3.7	1.5	1.5	2.2	3.7	7.4	6.3	1.5
	2005	5.8	5.0	2.3	2.3	2.5	5.6	6.8	14.5	0.7
Manufactured goods	1995	82.8	84.1	84.1	84.2	91.1	89.0	71.3	86.6	71.0
(SITC 5 to 8 less 68)	2000	86.5	88.1	88.1	88.5	91.1	91.2	78.4	84.5	78.6
	2005	85.3	86.8	87.9	88.1	89.1	89.0	79.6	78.1	82.9

Sources:
- UNCTAD secretariat calculations based on UN DESA Statistics Division's data

Total	Africa / Afrique	America / Amérique	Developing economies — Économies en développement — Asia / Asie Total	Eastern, Southern and South-Eastern Asia / Asie orientale, méridionale et du Sud-Est	China / Chine	Western Asia / Asie occidentale	Oceania / Océanie	Major petroleum exporters / Principaux exportateurs de pétrole	Major exporters of manufactures / Principaux exportateurs d'articles manufacturés	Year / Année	Destination / Groupes de produits
Millions de dollars											
442 404	17 472	37 445	386 237	364 149	75 602	22 088	1 250	36 354	338 034	1 995	**Total tous produits**
572 651	20 432	51 990	498 026	469 763	106 636	28 263	2 204	47 607	444 331	2000	
1 211 351	54 249	99 035	1 053 147	977 963	290 792	75 184	4 919	140 987	902 687	2005	
Parts par destinations (en pourcentage)											
44.1	1.7	3.7	38.5	36.3	7.5	2.2	0.1	3.6	33.7	1995	**Total tous produits**
40.6	1.4	3.7	35.3	33.3	7.6	2.0	0.2	3.4	31.5	2000	
47.4	2.1	3.9	41.2	38.2	11.4	2.9	0.2	5.5	35.3	2005	
42.7	3.5	2.1	36.9	32.8	6.9	4.1	0.1	6.9	25.4	1995	Produits alimentaires
38.9	3.5	2.7	32.7	28.2	5.1	4.5	0.1	7.2	22.1	2000	(CTCI 0 + 1 + 22 + 4)
41.3	5.4	2.5	33.2	27.5	5.3	5.7	0.1	9.7	20.7	2005	
50.1	1.5	2.9	45.7	44.1	12.6	1.6	0.0	3.5	41.1	1995	Matières premières
50.1	1.1	2.8	46.2	44.6	18.3	1.6	0.0	3.9	40.7	2000	d'origine agricole
53.2	1.3	3.2	48.7	46.7	22.3	2.0	0.0	3.7	42.0	2005	(CTCI 2 - 22 - 27 - 28)
51.1	0.8	2.5	47.8	46.2	13.5	1.6	0.0	3.3	43.3	1995	Minerais et métaux
53.6	1.2	3.2	49.1	47.0	14.1	2.2	0.0	3.8	44.4	2000	(CTCI 27 + 28 + 68)
62.1	1.6	2.8	57.7	54.6	24.0	3.1	0.0	5.6	51.6	2005	
50.0	0.3	2.5	46.2	46.0	8.2	0.2	1.0	1.5	40.7	1995	Combustibles (CTCI 3)
47.6	0.7	4.8	40.9	40.6	6.0	0.4	1.1	4.0	34.0	2000	
55.2	1.3	5.4	47.4	45.2	5.3	2.2	1.1	8.7	34.7	2005	
43.5	1.7	4.0	37.8	35.6	7.3	2.2	0.1	3.5	33.6	1995	Articles manufacturés
39.9	1.4	3.7	34.7	32.8	7.5	1.9	0.1	3.1	31.5	2000	(CTCI 5 à 8 moins 68)
46.6	2.0	3.8	40.7	37.9	11.7	2.8	0.1	5.1	35.7	2005	
Parts par principaux groupes de produits (en pourcentage)											
100.0	100.0	100.0	100.0	100.0	100.0	100.0	100.0	100.0	100.0	1995	**Total tous produits**
100.0	100.0	100.0	100.0	100.0	100.0	100.0	100.0	100.0	100.0	2000	
100.0	100.0	100.0	100.0	100.0	100.0	100.0	100.0	100.0	100.0	2005	
7.6	15.9	4.5	7.5	7.1	7.1	14.7	7.3	14.8	5.9	1995	Produits alimentaires
4.9	12.3	3.7	4.7	4.3	3.5	11.5	3.8	11.0	3.6	2000	(CTCI 0 + 1 + 22 + 4)
4.1	12.1	3.1	3.8	3.4	2.2	9.1	3.6	8.3	2.8	2005	
2.5	1.9	1.7	2.6	2.6	3.6	1.6	0.3	2.1	2.6	1995	Matières premières
1.6	1.0	1.0	1.7	1.7	3.2	1.1	0.1	1.5	1.7	2000	d'origine agricole
1.2	0.7	0.9	1.3	1.3	2.1	0.7	0.1	0.7	1.3	2005	(CTCI 2 - 22 - 27 - 28)
2.6	1.0	1.5	2.7	2.8	3.9	1.6	0.3	2.0	2.8	1995	Minerais et métaux
2.4	1.5	1.6	2.5	2.5	3.3	2.0	0.2	2.0	2.5	2000	(CTCI 27 + 28 + 68)
2.9	1.7	1.6	3.1	3.2	4.7	2.3	0.2	2.3	3.3	2005	
3.8	0.5	2.3	4.0	4.2	3.6	0.3	25.9	1.3	4.0	1995	Combustibles (CTCI 3)
5.3	2.1	5.9	5.3	5.5	3.6	0.8	33.0	5.4	4.9	2000	
6.8	3.5	8.2	6.7	6.9	2.7	4.4	33.7	9.1	5.7	2005	
81.9	79.0	88.6	81.4	81.4	80.8	81.1	63.1	79.2	82.7	1995	Articles manufacturés
85.0	82.6	87.6	84.9	85.1	86.1	82.3	62.4	78.6	86.5	2000	(CTCI 5 à 8 moins 68)
83.9	79.6	83.8	84.3	84.5	87.9	82.1	56.4	78.3	86.3	2005	

Sources :
- Calculs du secrétariat de la CNUCED sur la base des données de ONU DAES Division de statistique

Product group	Year Année	World Monde	Developed economies / Économies développées							Economies in transition Économies en transition
			Total	Europe		Canada	USA États-Unis	Japan Japon	Other developed countries Autres économies développées	
				Total	EU UE					
Millions of dollars										
All products	1995	1 066 078	632 684	185 223	169 592	13 271	202 204	206 557	25 428	18 540
	2000	1 392 770	750 753	203 393	185 215	15 825	286 602	212 665	32 267	22 782
	2005	2 447 471	1 067 635	343 691	310 766	23 469	318 487	321 566	60 421	59 558
Share by origin (percentage)										
All products	1995	100.0	53.9	14.6	13.3	1.1	20.6	15.3	2.3	1.6
	2000	100.0	43.6	14.0	12.7	1.0	13.0	13.1	2.5	2.4
	2005	100.0	58.1	15.4	14.6	3.8	28.4	2.7	7.7	1.3
All food items	1995	100.0	56.4	12.5	11.5	3.9	28.4	2.7	8.9	1.5
(SITC 0 + 1 + 22 + 4)	2000	100.0	48.1	10.5	9.8	3.4	23.9	2.3	8.0	2.3
	2005	100.0	52.6	8.3	8.0	5.0	25.9	4.7	8.8	5.0
Agricultural raw materials	1995	100.0	53.7	11.4	11.2	6.3	22.5	4.6	8.8	5.6
(SITC 2 - 22 - 27 - 28)	2000	100.0	51.7	11.5	11.3	5.5	22.6	4.5	7.6	8.2
	2005	100.0	51.9	13.0	12.0	3.0	14.5	10.3	11.0	6.7
Ores and metals	1995	100.0	47.4	11.4	9.4	2.2	11.4	9.9	12.5	9.4
(SITC 27 + 28 + 68)	2000	100.0	41.5	8.4	7.5	2.3	8.4	7.6	14.7	8.2
	2005	100.0	14.3	1.9	1.8	0.8	5.4	2.0	4.2	1.8
Fuels (SITC 3)	1995	100.0	11.2	2.1	1.5	0.3	4.0	0.7	4.1	2.3
	2000	100.0	10.3	1.5	1.1	0.3	3.7	0.8	4.0	4.7
	2005	100.0	63.6	19.3	17.9	0.8	19.1	23.5	1.0	1.4
Manufactured goods	1995	100.0	59.9	16.3	15.3	0.9	22.9	18.8	0.9	1.0
(SITC 5 to 8 less 68)	2000	100.0	49.2	16.6	15.5	0.7	14.3	16.7	0.8	1.3
	2005	100.0	100.0	100.0	100.0	100.0	100.0	100.0	100.0	100.0
Share by major product group (percentage)										
All products	1995	100.0	100.0	100.0	100.0	100.0	100.0	100.0	100.0	100.0
	2000	100.0	100.0	100.0	100.0	100.0	100.0	100.0	100.0	100.0
	2005	100.0	100.0	100.0	100.0	100.0	100.0	100.0	100.0	100.0
All food items	1995	5.8	5.7	5.1	5.3	17.7	8.7	0.8	18.6	4.4
(SITC 0 + 1 + 22 + 4)	2000	4.4	4.6	3.7	3.8	15.0	6.0	0.8	16.8	4.0
	2005	3.8	4.2	2.9	2.9	13.6	7.0	0.7	12.3	3.5
Agricultural raw materials	1995	3.2	2.8	1.5	1.6	12.8	4.4	0.8	11.7	9.1
(SITC 2 - 22 - 27 - 28)	2000	2.3	2.3	1.8	1.9	12.9	2.5	0.7	8.8	8.0
	2005	2.0	2.4	1.6	1.8	11.5	3.5	0.7	6.2	6.8
Ores and metals	1995	3.9	3.4	2.9	2.9	9.4	3.0	2.0	17.9	14.9
(SITC 27 + 28 + 68)	2000	3.5	3.1	2.8	2.5	7.0	2.0	2.3	19.1	20.4
	2005	5.1	4.8	3.0	3.0	12.3	3.3	2.9	30.2	17.0
Fuels (SITC 3)	1995	7.1	1.7	0.8	0.8	4.5	2.0	0.7	12.4	7.5
	2000	10.6	2.2	1.5	1.2	2.9	2.1	0.5	18.6	14.6
	2005	13.6	3.2	1.5	1.2	4.9	3.8	0.8	21.9	26.0
Manufactured goods	1995	77.2	82.8	85.8	86.7	50.7	77.6	93.6	30.8	62.8
(SITC 5 to 8 less 68)	2000	77.2	85.7	86.4	88.6	61.3	86.0	95.0	29.4	45.8
	2005	73.9	83.3	87.2	90.1	57.2	81.4	94.1	22.9	40.1

Sources:
- UNCTAD secretariat calculations based on UN DESA Statistics Division's data

Total	Africa / Afrique	America / Amérique	Asia / Asie Total	Eastern, Southern and South-Eastern Asia / Asie orientale, méridionale et du Sud-Est	China / Chine	Western Asia / Asie occidentale	Oceania / Océanie	Major petroleum exporters / Principaux exportateurs de pétrole	Major exporters of manufactures / Principaux exportateurs d'articles manufacturés	Year / Année	Origine / Groupes de produits
Millions de dollars											
406 035	14 124	28 419	362 638	326 181	91 035	36 457	854	58 764	311 595	1995	Total tous produits
594 074	23 371	33 222	536 595	474 954	139 622	61 641	885	104 885	445 989	2000	
1 271 198	51 340	75 784	1 142 323	1 003 848	337 921	138 475	1 750	232 245	946 717	2005	
Parts par origines (en pourcentage)											
42.7	1.7	2.4	38.5	34.1	10.0	4.4	0.1	7.5	32.0	1995	Total tous produits
51.9	2.1	3.1	46.7	41.0	13.8	5.7	0.1	9.5	38.7	2000	
40.4	1.3	12.1	26.7	26.3	6.5	0.4	0.4	2.2	25.0	2005	
42.0	1.9	13.4	26.4	26.0	8.2	0.4	0.3	3.7	23.6	1995	Produits alimentaires
49.3	2.0	18.7	28.2	27.8	7.5	0.4	0.4	5.7	25.7	2000	(CTCI 0 + 1 + 22 + 4)
42.3	4.7	6.0	30.8	30.3	4.2	0.5	0.8	4.6	24.8	2005	
40.6	5.3	4.9	29.7	29.1	3.8	0.7	0.7	8.1	21.7	1995	Matières premières
40.0	4.9	6.1	28.1	27.5	2.8	0.6	0.9	7.5	21.5	2000	d'origine agricole
41.0	4.3	12.8	23.4	19.8	5.0	3.7	0.4	5.7	21.1	2005	(CTCI 2 - 22 - 27 - 28)
43.1	4.5	12.2	26.2	23.4	5.7	2.8	0.2	5.3	23.4	1995	Minerais et métaux
50.3	4.7	16.7	28.7	26.4	6.4	2.4	0.2	6.4	27.3	2000	(CTCI 27 + 28 + 68)
78.8	7.0	3.2	68.6	29.5	2.9	39.1	0.1	56.7	18.0	2005	
74.9	8.7	3.1	63.0	25.8	2.7	37.2	0.1	55.9	13.7	1995	Combustibles (CTCI 3)
71.7	8.8	1.8	61.1	25.6	2.4	35.6	0.0	52.5	14.2	2000	
34.5	0.4	1.4	32.7	32.1	9.8	0.6	0.0	1.3	31.7	2005	
38.8	0.3	1.2	37.2	36.8	11.8	0.4	0.0	1.3	36.1	1995	Articles manufacturés
49.3	0.4	1.6	47.3	46.4	17.3	0.8	0.0	2.0	45.6	2000	(CTCI 5 à 8 moins 68)
100.0	100.0	100.0	100.0	100.0	100.0	100.0	100.0	100.0	100.0	2005	
Parts par principaux groupes de produits (en pourcentage)											
100.0	100.0	100.0	100.0	100.0	100.0	100.0	100.0	100.0	100.0	1995	Total tous produits
100.0	100.0	100.0	100.0	100.0	100.0	100.0	100.0	100.0	100.0	2000	
100.0	100.0	100.0	100.0	100.0	100.0	100.0	100.0	100.0	100.0	2005	
6.1	5.7	26.2	4.5	5.0	4.4	0.6	27.1	2.3	4.9	1995	Produits alimentaires
4.3	5.0	24.6	3.0	3.3	3.6	0.4	18.7	2.1	3.2	2000	(CTCI 0 + 1 + 22 + 4)
3.6	3.7	22.9	2.3	2.6	2.1	0.3	19.5	2.3	2.5	2005	
3.5	11.3	7.1	2.9	3.2	1.6	0.5	33.4	2.7	2.7	1995	Matières premières
2.2	7.4	4.7	1.8	2.0	0.9	0.3	24.3	2.5	1.6	2000	d'origine agricole
1.5	4.7	4.0	1.2	1.3	0.4	0.2	26.4	1.6	1.1	2005	(CTCI 2 - 22 - 27 - 28)
4.1	12.5	18.6	2.7	2.5	2.3	4.1	19.1	4.0	2.8	1995	Minerais et métaux
3.6	9.5	18.1	2.4	2.4	2.0	2.2	12.7	2.5	2.6	2000	(CTCI 27 + 28 + 68)
4.9	11.4	27.3	3.1	3.3	2.4	2.1	10.7	3.4	3.6	2005	
14.6	37.1	8.4	14.3	6.8	2.4	80.8	8.1	72.8	4.3	1995	Combustibles (CTCI 3)
18.6	55.2	13.6	17.3	8.0	2.8	89.0	15.6	78.6	4.5	2000	
18.8	56.9	7.9	17.8	8.5	2.4	85.4	5.2	75.1	5.0	2005	
69.8	20.8	39.1	74.3	81.0	88.8	13.7	11.8	18.0	85.7	1995	Articles manufacturés
70.1	14.6	38.5	74.6	83.3	90.5	7.7	28.6	13.2	87.1	2000	(CTCI 5 à 8 moins 68)
70.1	15.3	37.1	74.8	83.6	92.4	10.8	38.0	15.8	87.2	2005	

Sources :
- Calculs du secrétariat de la CNUCED sur la base des données de ONU DAES Division de statistique

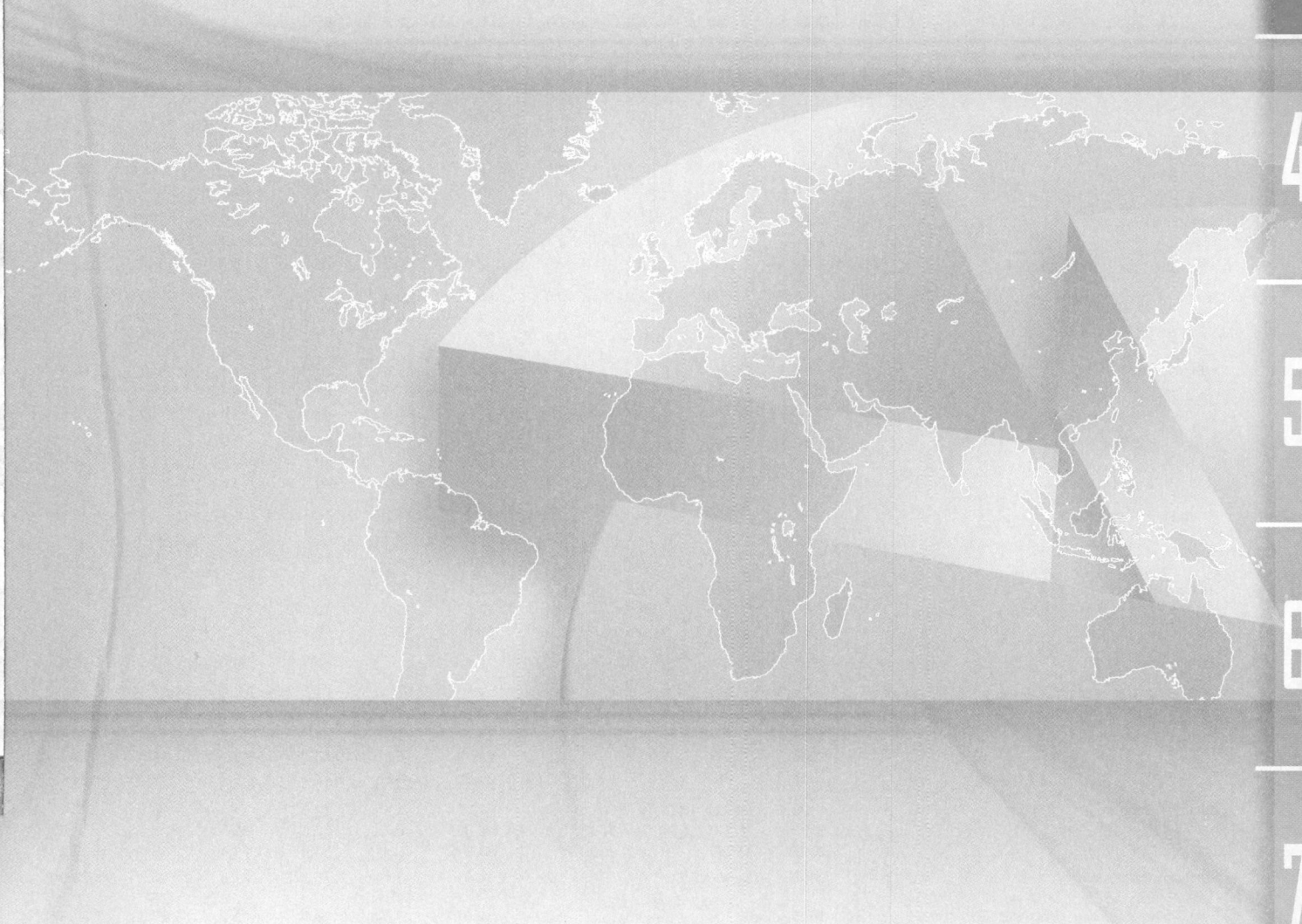

3

INTERNATIONAL **MERCHANDISE** TRADE BY PRODUCT

COMMERCE INTERNATIONAL DES **MARCHANDISES** PAR PRODUITS

1
2
3
4
5
6
7
8

Country or territory / Pays ou territoires	Year / Année	Total value (millions of dollars) / Valeur totale (millions de dollars)	By main SITC Rev.3 product group (percentage) / Par principaux groupes de produits de la CTCI Rév.3 (en pourcentage)					Of which: / dont :		
			All food items / Produits alimentaires	Agricultural raw materials / Matières premières agricoles	Fuels / Combustibles	Ores and metals / Minérais et métaux	Manufactured products / Produits manufacturés	Chemical products / Produits chimiques	Machinery and transport equipment / Machines et matériel de transport	Other manufactured products / Produits manufacturés divers
			0+1+22+4	2 - (22+27+28)	3	27+28+68	5+6+7+8 - 68	5	7	(6+8) - 68
Albania - Albanie	1995	202	11.1	9.0	3.0	11.6	65.3	1.4	1.7	62.2
	2000	261	6.6	6.0	1.9	3.7	81.8	0.7	1.9	79.2
	2005	662	5.8	4.4	2.6	7.4	79.8	0.5	4.1	75.2
Algeria - Algérie	1995	9 357	1.2	0.1	95.2	0.5	3.0	1.2	0.4	1.4
	2000	22 031	0.2	0.0	98.1	0.3	1.4	0.7	0.2	0.5
	2005	46 165	0.2	0.0	98.2	0.4	1.2	0.6	0.1	0.5
Andorra - Andorre	1995	48	6.5	1.6	0.2	2.3	89.4	3.6	33.8	52.0
	2000	45	8.2	1.3	0.1	2.2	85.6	8.2	25.4	52.1
	2005	123	11.7	0.6	0.0	2.6	83.4	6.2	49.6	27.6
Angola	1995	3 717	1.0	0.0	94.0	0.2	4.8	0.0	0.2	4.6
	2000	7 696	0.6	0.0	91.1	0.1	8.2	0.0	0.1	8.1
	2005	23 194	0.2	0.0	98.2	0.2	1.5	0.0	0.1	1.3
Argentina - Argentine	1995	20 963	49.8	4.3	10.3	1.6	33.9	6.4	10.9	16.6
	2000	26 410	43.4	1.8	17.7	3.3	32.2	7.2	12.7	12.3
	2005	40 106	46.5	1.4	16.4	3.2	30.6	8.5	10.7	11.4
Armenia - Arménie	1995	263	11.1	4.7	0.8	26.9	55.6	1.9	13.4	40.2
	2000	294	9.4	3.4	7.0	17.9	59.2	1.2	10.5	47.5
	2005	937	12.0	0.9	2.0	10.9	70.3	0.4	3.2	66.7
Aruba	1995	666	3.0	0.0	95.4	0.3	1.2	0.7	0.3	0.2
	2000	1 788	2.6	0.0	94.7	0.2	2.2	0.2	0.6	1.3
	2005	3 878	0.5	0.0	97.8	0.2	1.0	0.1	0.8	0.1
Australia - Australie	1995	53 001	19.6	8.1	16.7	19.3	26.9	4.1	12.8	10.1
	2000	61 881	20.3	6.2	21.5	21.1	24.5	4.4	11.7	8.4
	2005	105 751	16.1	3.9	25.6	22.8	20.5	4.6	9.5	6.4
Austria - Autriche	1995	57 583	3.8	3.3	1.0	3.3	88.0	9.2	39.1	39.7
	2000	58 603	5.2	3.0	1.4	2.6	86.9	9.2	43.0	34.7
	2005	113 532	6.4	1.9	4.7	2.7	80.3	8.1	41.2	31.1
Azerbaijan - Azerbaïdjan	1995	637	4.4	8.3	66.4	1.2	19.7	6.5	7.6	5.6
	2000	1 745	3.2	2.4	85.1	2.9	6.4	2.0	3.6	0.9
	2005	4 347	7.5	1.0	76.8	3.7	11.0	2.3	6.8	1.9
Bahrain - Bahreïn	1995	3 475	2.8	0.0	52.3	25.9	18.9	6.4	1.7	10.9
	2000	6 195	0.9	0.1	72.5	16.0	10.6	2.4	1.0	7.1
	2005	9 733	0.5	0.0	80.0	12.8	6.7	2.7	1.5	2.5
Bangladesh	1995	3 407	10.4	2.7	0.4	..	85.2	3.0	1.6	80.5
	2000	5 035	7.0	1.5	0.2	0.0	91.1	1.2	1.4	88.5
	2005	6 612	7.9	1.9	0.4	0.1	89.6	0.3	0.4	88.9
Barbados - Barbade	1995	238	29.0	0.9	14.4	1.5	54.1	13.9	19.8	20.5
	2000	273	27.8	0.1	22.1	0.2	48.7	13.7	14.0	21.0
	2005	361	23.7	0.1	31.6	0.6	43.1	11.7	11.0	20.4
Belarus - Bélarus	1995	4 721	8.7	3.1	7.9	1.1	79.2	14.3	28.8	36.2
	2000	7 331	6.8	3.6	19.8	0.8	66.5	12.9	23.9	29.6
	2005	15 977	8.3	2.5	34.8	0.5	51.9	11.1	18.7	22.2
Belgium - Belgique	2005	334 106	8.1	1.2	6.9	2.6	78.8	27.6	25.2	25.9
Belgium-Luxembourg - Belgique-Luxembourg	1995	168 154	10.3	1.2	2.6	3.6	76.4	16.2	27.3	32.9
	2000	187 632	8.9	1.5	3.9	3.0	81.6	20.2	29.5	31.8
Belize	1995	162	79.7	1.3	3.2	0.2	15.7	1.2	3.0	11.6
	2000	200	81.7	1.3	2.0	0.0	14.6	0.3	1.3	12.9
	2005	208	85.1	0.7	0.4	0.0	13.5	2.7	0.7	10.0
Benin - Bénin	1995	333	11.8	38.9	2.8	38.9	6.6	0.2	1.5	4.9
	2000	188	20.1	69.7	..	0.1	7.1	0.7	1.3	5.1
	2005	288	24.2	59.5	0.7	0.5	12.5	0.9	3.2	8.3

For sources and notes, see end of table.

Pour les sources et les notes, se reporter à la fin du tableau.

Country or territory / Pays ou territoires	Year / Année	Total value (millions of dollars) / Valeur totale (millions de dollars)	By main SITC Rev.3 product group (percentage) Par principaux groupes de produits de la CTCI Rév.3 (en pourcentage)					Of which: / dont :		
			All food items / Produits alimentaires	Agricultural raw materials / Matières premières agricoles	Fuels / Combus-tibles	Ores and metals / Minérais et métaux	Manu-factured products / Produits manu-facturés	Chemical products / Produits chimiques	Machinery and transport equipment / Machines et matériel de transport	Other manu-factured products / Produits manu-facturés divers
			0+1+22+4	2 - (22+27+28)	3	27+28+63	5+6+7+8 - 68	5	7	(6+8) - 68
Bolivia - Bolivie	1995	1 181	19.1	8.7	12.9	31.5	16.5	1.1	3.2	12.2
	2000	1 457	28.4	3.0	12.2	23.1	27.1	0.8	13.3	13.0
	2005	2 797	20.2	1.7	47.8	16.4	10.9	1.3	1.6	8.0
Bosnia and Herzegovina - Bosnie-Herzégovine	1995	85	17.2	21.4	4.0	6.0	51.3	2.8	14.9	33.6
	2000	1 057	3.7	20.1	6.0	23.4	46.8	3.9	6.4	36.5
	2005	2 388	5.8	9.8	8.9	22.5	52.9	3.4	16.7	32.8
Botswana	2000	2 763	2.8	0.3	0.1	7.0	89.5	1.0	3.6	85.0
	2005	3 968	1.8	0.1	0.1	10.5	87.5	0.3	0.8	86.5
Brazil - Brésil	1995	46 505	28.5	5.2	0.9	10.3	53.0	6.6	19.0	27.4
	2000	55 282	23.2	4.8	1.6	10.1	57.6	6.5	28.1	23.1
	2005	116 129	26.2	4.0	6.1	10.2	53.1	6.3	26.2	20.6
Brunei Darussalam - Brunéi Darussalam	1995	2 366	0.1	0.0	91.6	0.0	8.3	0.1	4.5	3.6
	2000	3 872	0.0	0.0	89.5	0.0	10.5	0.1	4.0	6.4
	2005	5 683	0.0	0.0	87.8	0.1	12.1	0.1	5.4	6.7
Bulgaria - Bulgarie	1995	5 214	18.6	3.1	6.7	9.9	61.7	18.8	12.8	30.1
	2000	4 822	9.8	2.7	11.7	12.7	56.7	10.1	9.6	37.1
	2005	11 725	10.5	1.8	10.4	14.2	59.3	7.6	14.2	37.5
Burkina Faso	1995	171	22.1	59.1	1.6	0.3	8.6	0.4	3.1	5.0
	2000	184	18.8	58.0	3.2	0.0	18.1	1.7	4.6	11.8
	2005	285	16.3	71.9	2.8	0.6	7.9	0.5	3.7	3.7
Burundi	1995	179	59.8	2.7	..	0.7	2.2	0.5	0.1	1.6
	2000	43	85.8	7.1	..	0.7	0.5	0.0	0.3	0.2
	2005	117	45.1	2.2	0.0	1.3	3.2	0.1	2.3	0.8
Cambodia - Cambodge	1995	332	3.5	72.5	0.0	0.3	23.7	0.3	0.7	22.6
	2000	1 389	1.0	2.9	0.0	0.0	95.6	0.0	0.7	94.9
	2005	3 144	1.1	1.8	0.0	0.0	97.1	0.1	0.5	96.5
Cameroon - Cameroun	1995	1 539	27.0	27.5	29.2	8.4	7.9	1.0	1.1	5.8
	2000	1 833	14.9	21.0	54.2	5.6	4.3	0.4	0.5	3.4
	2005	2 447	17.1	13.0	49.6	5.6	3.3	0.6	0.7	2.0
Canada	1995	191 118	7.6	9.2	9.1	6.7	62.1	5.9	38.5	17.7
	2000	277 113	6.4	6.2	13.1	4.3	63.4	5.3	40.2	17.9
	2005	360 136	6.7	4.7	20.2	5.5	57.3	7.2	32.9	17.2
Cape Verde - Cap-Vert	1995	32	6.1	0.3	34.1	0.1	59.4	0.8	38.3	20.2
	2000	49	4.0	0.1	48.5	0.0	47.4	0.5	25.1	21.9
	2005	89	13.9	0.0	46.8	0.1	39.2	0.4	22.1	16.7
Central African Republic - République centrafricaine	1995	120	4.2	19.8	0.8	30.1	44.5	0.4	8.8	35.3
	2000	79	10.6	13.1	0.5	7.6	68.2	0.1	2.5	65.6
	2005	116	0.8	41.1	0.4	16.9	36.0	0.1	1.3	34.7
Chile - Chili	1995	15 901	23.7	13.6	0.2	47.1	11.7	3.5	1.8	6.5
	2000	18 214	24.3	10.8	1.1	44.5	15.4	5.6	2.7	7.0
	2005	38 596	19.3	6.9	2.1	55.3	13.3	5.4	1.7	6.2
China - Chine	1995	148 779	8.3	1.8	3.6	2.1	84.0	6.1	21.1	56.8
	2000	249 203	5.4	1.1	3.2	1.8	88.2	4.9	33.1	50.2
	2005	761 953	3.2	0.5	2.3	1.8	91.9	4.7	46.2	41.0
China, Hong Kong SAR - Chine, Hong Kong RAS	1995	173 871	3.0	1.3	1.0	1.7	92.5	6.2	32.4	53.9
	2000	202 683	1.8	1.0	0.3	1.4	95.0	5.1	38.3	51.5
	2005	292 119	0.9	0.6	0.3	1.4	95.8	4.8	52.3	38.7
China, Macao SAR - Chine, Macao RAS	1995	2 025	1.7	2.4	0.0	0.0	95.9	1.1	4.4	90.5
	2000	2 547	1.0	0.8	0.7	0.1	97.5	0.9	5.7	91.0
	2005	2 476	1.2	0.4	2.5	0.9	95.1	0.9	6.2	88.0

For sources and notes, see end of table.

Pour les sources et les notes, se reporter à la fin du tableau.

3

Country or territory / Pays ou territoires	Year / Année	Total value (millions of dollars) / Valeur totale (millions de dollars)	By main SITC Rev.3 product group (percentage) / Par principaux groupes de produits de la CTCI Rév.3 (en pourcentage)					Of which: / dont :		
			All food items / Produits alimentaires	Agricultural raw materials / Matières premières agricoles	Fuels / Combustibles	Ores and metals / Minérais et métaux	Manu-factured products / Produits manu-facturés	Chemical products / Produits chimiques	Machinery and transport equipment / Machines et matériel de transport	Other manu-factured products / Produits manu-facturés divers
			0+1+22+4	2 - (22+27+28)	3	27+28+68	5+6+7+8 - 68	5	7	(6+8) - 68
China, Taiwan Province of - Chine, Taiwan Province de	1995	111 343	3.4	1.6	0.7	1.4	92.8	6.8	48.1	37.9
	2000	148 316	1.2	1.1	1.1	1.2	95.1	6.2	58.4	30.5
	2005	189 393	1.2	1.2	4.7	1.7	90.7	10.5	49.8	30.4
Colombia - Colombie	1995	10 201	30.8	5.4	27.2	0.6	34.2	7.9	2.6	23.7
	2000	13 158	19.0	4.7	43.1	0.7	32.5	10.2	4.3	18.0
	2005	21 190	17.2	4.5	39.2	1.3	34.7	8.4	6.0	20.3
Congo	1995	1 090	1.0	8.3	87.6	0.3	2.7	0.3	0.4	2.1
	2000	2 468	1.6	5.2	83.0	4.0	6.2	0.1	0.3	5.8
	2005	5 002	1.4	9.0	82.0	5.4	2.1	0.2	0.2	1.7
Costa Rica	1995	2 702	63.4	5.0	0.8	1.1	25.1	6.5	3.2	15.4
	2000	5 487	30.0	3.0	0.6	0.8	65.5	5.4	39.4	20.7
	2005	7 151	29.7	3.0	0.5	1.2	65.3	7.7	30.1	27.6
Côte d'Ivoire	1995	3 737	58.7	16.0	9.8	0.2	14.3	4.2	1.4	8.6
	2000	3 628	49.8	13.8	20.3	0.2	14.4	4.2	1.0	9.2
	2005	7 248	38.2	8.2	27.7	0.2	24.9	3.6	9.8	11.4
Croatia - Croatie	1995	4 633	10.8	4.6	8.4	2.3	73.8	17.6	16.8	39.5
	2000	4 432	8.9	4.5	11.0	3.0	72.6	12.5	27.0	33.1
	2005	8 773	10.5	3.4	13.9	3.8	68.5	9.9	28.9	29.6
Cuba	1995	1 623	78.8	0.2	0.3	13.8	6.6	3.8	0.5	2.3
	2000	1 676	50.0	0.2	3.1	37.3	9.4	2.5	0.7	6.2
	2005	2 251	30.2	0.1	0.5	47.7	21.5	7.6	2.3	11.7
Cyprus - Chypre	1995	1 231	50.5	0.4	3.7	1.2	44.1	6.4	12.2	25.6
	2000	954	43.5	0.6	10.7	3.1	42.1	7.4	16.0	18.7
	2005	1 546	18.0	0.5	15.0	2.8	62.8	10.5	41.0	11.2
Czech Republic - République tchèque	1995	21 686	6.0	3.7	4.3	2.8	81.6	9.2	29.3	43.1
	2000	29 053	4.1	2.4	3.1	1.9	88.4	7.1	44.5	36.9
	2005	78 209	4.0	1.4	3.0	1.6	88.2	6.1	50.2	31.8
Dem. Rep. of the Congo - Rép. dém. du Congo	1995	1 563	14.0	6.7	9.4	18.4	51.2	0.2	0.3	50.6
	2000	807	3.2	1.9	22.8	11.5	60.1	1.8	0.4	57.9
	2005	2 137	2.0	5.0	9.1	38.1	45.8	0.2	1.0	44.6
Denmark - Danemark	1995	48 789	24.0	2.9	2.6	1.2	59.8	9.7	25.1	25.0
	2000	49 210	19.7	2.5	7.0	1.0	64.2	10.9	26.5	26.8
	2005	82 415	17.6	2.5	9.4	1.3	65.3	13.2	28.1	24.1
Dominican Republic - République dominicaine	1995	2 546	14.9	0.3	0.0	1.3	82.7	1.7	6.1	74.9
	2000	875	12.1	0.4	0.0	0.5	86.5	1.2	8.9	76.3
	2005	1 204	15.2	0.3	0.0	1.1	81.6	2.1	10.1	69.4
Ecuador - Équateur	1995	4 361	51.8	3.0	35.1	0.3	7.6	1.2	2.0	4.4
	2000	4 822	36.5	3.9	50.7	0.2	8.6	1.6	1.9	5.1
	2005	9 869	28.2	4.4	59.5	0.4	7.3	1.2	2.2	3.9
Egypt - Égypte	1995	3 444	9.9	6.1	37.3	6.4	40.3	5.8	0.6	33.8
	2000	4 713	8.0	5.0	41.9	3.9	38.4	6.6	1.0	30.8
	2005	11 215	9.8	7.0	43.2	3.6	30.5	5.6	1.4	23.5
El Salvador	1995	985	57.1	1.2	0.1	2.9	38.8	11.5	2.8	24.6
	2000	1 341	42.4	0.6	4.9	2.4	48.4	13.0	3.9	31.5
	2005	1 498	31.9	0.8	4.2	3.0	60.0	13.0	5.3	41.6
Equatorial Guinea - Guinée équatoriale	1995	86	7.6	52.2	33.1	0.0	7.0	0.0	0.6	6.4
	2000	1 096	3.3	8.1	87.9	0.0	0.7	0.0	0.1	0.6
	2005	2 920	0.2	2.6	92.5	0.0	4.7	3.8	0.2	0.7
Estonia - Estonie	1995	1 840	16.1	9.6	7.1	3.1	64.1	8.3	19.9	35.9
	2000	3 830	8.0	9.6	4.5	5.5	72.3	5.6	36.0	30.7
	2005	7 710	6.5	6.7	7.1	2.2	68.3	4.5	32.9	30.8

For sources and notes, see end of table.

Pour les sources et les notes, se reporter à la fin du tableau.

Country or territory / Pays ou territoires	Year / Année	Total value (millions of dollars) / Valeur totale (millions de dollars)	By main SITC Rev.3 product group (percentage) / Par principaux groupes de produits de la CTCI Rév.3 (en pourcentage)							
			All food items / Produits alimentaires	Agricultural raw materials / Matières premières agricoles	Fuels / Combustibles	Ores and metals / Minérais et métaux	Manufactured products / Produits manufacturés	Of which: / dont :		
								Chemical products / Produits chimiques	Machinery and transport equipment / Machines et matériel de transport	Other manufactured products / Produits manufacturés divers
			0+1+22+4	2 - (22+27+28)	3	27+28+68	5+6+7+8 - 68	5	7	(6+8) - 68
Ethiopia - Éthiopie	1995	422	72.5	13.4	2.9	0.1	11.2	0.3	0.0	10.8
	2000	482	66.5	17.6	..	0.9	9.2	0.0	0.1	9.1
	2005	849	62.0	25.9	..	0.7	11.4	0.1	0.0	11.3
Faeroe Islands - Îles Féroé	1995	362	91.1	2.2	-	-	6.7	0.1	4.8	1.8
	2000	472	93.4	1.3	0.0	-	5.3	0.1	3.8	1.4
	2005	598	92.1	2.1	-	-	5.7	0.0	5.3	0.5
Fiji - Fidji	1995	617	51.6	7.1	0.4	0.2	33.2	0.3	1.0	31.9
	2000	469	34.9	4.6	..	0.2	46.1	0.8	0.2	45.1
	2005	702	43.7	4.4	23.5	0.6	21.7	1.6	2.7	17.4
Finland - Finlande	1995	40 409	2.4	8.4	1.9	3.1	83.3	6.0	35.4	42.0
	2000	45 475	1.7	6.3	3.4	3.1	84.8	6.0	45.3	33.6
	2005	65 238	1.9	5.2	4.4	3.5	84.3	7.6	44.1	32.6
France	1995	277 845	14.4	1.5	2.4	2.6	79.0	14.9	39.4	24.7
	2000	295 344	11.1	1.1	2.8	2.0	82.8	15.3	45.0	22.5
	2005	434 425	10.7	0.9	4.1	2.1	80.1	15.9	41.6	22.6
French Polynesia - Polynésie française	1995	185	2.9	1.1	0.0	0.1	95.9	0.8	22.1	73.1
	2000	244	5.9	0.8	0.0	0.2	92.6	0.6	14.1	77.9
	2005	210	12.9	2.2	0.0	0.1	84.8	1.3	13.6	69.9
Gabon	1995	2 718	0.2	13.1	82.7	2.0	1.9	0.4	0.4	1.1
	2000	2 602	0.8	11.8	83.3	1.7	2.3	0.1	0.4	1.9
	2005	4 340	1.2	9.8	76.2	5.5	7.0	0.1	1.7	5.1
Gambia - Gambie	1995	19	58.8	0.5	0.2	1.0	36.8	2.4	7.0	27.5
	2000	16	80.8	1.2	0.1	0.2	17.0	9.6	4.7	2.6
	2005	5	78.4	4.3	..	0.3	16.9	0.5	11.3	5.2
Georgia - Géorgie	1995	158	29.3	3.3	18.8	8.0	40.6	11.1	5.7	23.8
	2000	330	27.4	3.0	8.4	28.4	32.8	10.4	12.7	9.7
	2005	866	34.9	2.1	3.2	17.1	38.7	6.7	17.0	15.0
Germany - Allemagne	1995	523 697	5.1	1.1	1.0	2.6	84.6	13.2	46.9	24.4
	2000	549 637	4.2	0.9	1.4	2.5	84.0	12.7	49.9	21.4
	2005	977 028	4.2	0.8	2.1	2.4	83.3	13.6	48.8	20.9
Ghana	1995	1 754	40.9	10.3	3.4	6.1	9.3	0.1	0.5	8.7
	2000	1 671	30.7	6.5	4.9	11.9	9.3	0.6	1.2	7.5
	2005	1 820	71.6	4.6	3.1	2.1	11.5	1.9	2.2	7.4
Gibraltar	1995	116	15.2	0.4	0.9	2.8	80.0	4.1	22.6	53.3
	2000	124	2.4	0.5	7.8	7.2	82.1	7.1	20.3	54.8
	2005	143	0.8	0.1	3.1	0.7	95.2	2.3	68.6	24.3
Greece - Grèce	1995	10 955	29.5	4.4	6.5	7.9	49.8	4.9	8.0	36.9
	2000	10 964	21.8	3.3	14.7	7.7	49.7	8.0	12.0	29.6
	2005	17 434	22.0	2.4	9.4	8.3	55.3	14.6	12.7	28.0
Greenland - Groenland	1995	364	95.1	0.6	0.8	0.0	1.5	0.0	0.3	1.2
	2000	263	95.4	0.4	0.0	0.0	1.6	0.0	1.0	0.6
	2005	389	94.0	0.5	0.0	0.0	5.5	0.0	4.2	1.3
Grenada - Grenade	1995	22	79.5	0.1	0.0	0.2	20.3	2.6	3.8	13.8
	2000	76	33.1	0.0	0.0	0.1	66.8	1.4	58.6	6.9
	2005	27	63.5	0.0	0.0	0.2	36.3	4.7	13.6	18.1
Guatemala	1995	1 936	65.2	4.1	2.0	0.5	28.2	10.9	1.8	15.5
	2000	2 699	56.2	3.8	6.0	1.9	32.1	11.7	2.4	18.0
	2005	5 381	33.8	3.3	5.7	0.5	56.7	11.0	2.6	43.1
Guinea - Guinée	1995	702	7.4	1.1	0.5	63.7	24.9	18.2	2.1	4.6
	2000	522	2.5	2.4	0.0	51.7	24.7	10.9	0.9	12.9
	2005	986	1.5	0.6	0.1	54.0	19.1	17.2	0.1	1.8

For sources and notes, see end of table.

Pour les sources et les notes, se reporter à la fin du tableau.

Country or territory / Pays ou territoires	Year / Année	Total value (millions of dollars) / Valeur totale (millions de dollars)	By main SITC Rev.3 product group (percentage) / Par principaux groupes de produits de la CTCI Rév.3 (en pourcentage)					Of which: / dont :		
			All food items / Produits alimentaires	Agricultural raw materials / Matières premières agricoles	Fuels / Combustibles	Ores and metals / Minérais et métaux	Manufactured products / Produits manu-facturés	Chemical products / Produits chimiques	Machinery and transport equipment / Machines et matériel de transport	Other manu-factured products / Produits manu-facturés divers
			0+1+22+4	2 - (22+27+28)	3	27+28+68	5+6+7+8 - 68	5	7	(6+8) - 68
Guyana	1995	455	44.9	2.2	0.0	15.6	11.3	0.7	1.1	9.4
	2000	520	43.4	2.9	0.0	15.2	11.9	0.8	1.8	9.4
	2005	539	53.3	6.4	0.0	6.9	17.0	0.8	2.1	14.0
Haiti - Haïti	1995	35	37.5	0.3	..	0.0	62.2	7.1	1.4	53.6
	2000	310	10.0	0.5	0.4	0.2	88.8	1.5	0.8	86.5
	2005	469	5.7	0.4	0.0	0.8	93.0	2.4	3.2	87.4
Honduras	1995	656	86.9	3.3	0.0	0.5	9.1	1.7	0.7	6.7
	2000	1 076	67.8	4.9	2.3	5.8	19.2	6.5	0.6	12.1
	2005	1 883	54.4	2.6	0.5	5.1	35.7	5.4	15.9	14.5
Hungary - Hongrie	1995	12 452	21.4	2.3	3.1	5.0	68.1	11.5	26.1	30.5
	2000	28 092	7.3	1.0	1.6	2.2	86.1	6.1	59.7	20.4
	2005	63 241	6.2	0.6	2.6	1.9	83.9	7.6	58.8	17.6
Iceland - Islande	1995	1 803	75.5	0.5	0.0	12.0	11.6	0.7	5.1	5.8
	2000	1 901	65.2	0.9	0.4	19.3	13.3	1.4	5.5	6.4
	2005	3 091	58.5	0.8	1.4	19.0	19.3	3.5	9.3	6.5
India - Inde	1995	31 699	18.7	1.3	1.7	3.6	73.2	8.1	7.5	57.5
	2000	45 250	12.9	1.2	4.3	2.9	76.5	10.5	7.9	58.1
	2005	103 404	8.9	1.5	11.5	7.2	69.8	11.6	10.9	47.3
Indonesia - Indonésie	1995	45 418	11.4	6.7	25.3	6.0	50.5	3.4	8.4	38.8
	2000	62 124	8.9	3.6	25.2	4.9	56.7	5.1	17.3	34.3
	2005	85 660	11.7	5.1	27.7	8.4	46.9	5.2	15.9	25.8
Iran, Islamic Republic of - Iran, Rép. islamique d'	1995	18 360	3.6	1.0	85.8	0.6	9.1	1.9	0.3	6.9
	2000	28 345	2.9	0.4	88.9	0.8	7.1	1.2	0.5	5.4
	2005	60 012	3.5	0.3	83.1	1.2	8.3	2.7	0.8	4.9
Ireland - Irlande	1995	43 789	19.4	1.1	0.4	1.1	71.1	18.4	34.5	18.1
	2000	76 288	8.3	0.5	0.3	0.8	85.9	32.8	40.2	12.8
	2005	109 994	8.4	0.4	0.7	0.8	85.7	45.6	26.5	13.6
Israel - Israël	1995	19 047	5.4	1.8	0.0	1.4	89.1	14.7	26.8	47.5
	2000	31 407	2.6	1.1	0.7	1.2	94.1	12.9	35.6	45.6
	2005	42 771	2.5	0.7	0.1	1.1	82.7	14.8	18.2	49.7
Italy - Italie	1995	230 441	6.6	0.7	1.2	1.4	89.2	8.0	37.7	43.6
	2000	240 516	6.1	0.7	2.0	1.4	88.5	9.4	38.3	40.7
	2005	367 866	6.4	0.6	3.5	1.5	85.4	10.7	37.0	37.7
Jamaica - Jamaïque	1995	1 424	21.7	0.3	0.5	49.4	28.1	2.7	3.1	22.4
	2000	1 308	22.0	0.2	0.3	56.9	20.6	5.4	2.1	13.2
	2005	1 523	22.0	0.1	2.4	65.8	9.7	5.5	1.7	2.5
Japan - Japon	1995	442 937	0.5	0.6	0.6	1.0	95.2	6.8	70.3	18.1
	2000	479 248	0.5	0.5	0.3	1.2	93.9	7.3	68.8	17.8
	2005	594 941	0.5	0.5	0.7	1.7	91.9	8.8	64.1	18.9
Jordan - Jordanie	1995	1 769	22.3	1.8	0.0	19.8	54.9	27.0	13.1	14.9
	2000	1 293	14.0	0.6	0.0	11.1	73.8	22.2	19.1	32.5
	2005	4 279	15.0	0.3	0.2	12.3	71.9	20.9	12.3	38.7
Kazakhstan	1995	5 227	9.9	2.8	25.0	24.1	38.1	10.3	6.0	21.9
	2000	8 789	6.8	1.4	52.0	19.9	17.9	2.5	2.1	13.3
	2005	27 849	2.4	0.7	70.1	14.0	12.0	1.9	1.2	8.9
Kenya	1995	1 826	56.1	7.4	6.1	2.8	27.6	6.6	1.6	19.3
	2000	1 571	59.0	8.6	8.1	3.2	20.7	5.6	0.5	14.6
	2005	3 292	39.6	12.0	22.9	4.2	21.0	4.2	1.6	15.2
Korea, Republic of - Corée, République de	1995	125 056	2.3	1.3	2.0	1.0	91.5	7.2	52.5	31.9
	2000	172 267	1.5	0.9	5.4	1.2	89.9	8.0	58.2	23.7
	2005	284 418	1.1	0.8	5.5	1.7	90.8	9.8	61.0	20.1

For sources and notes, see end of table.

Pour les sources et les notes, se reporter à la fin du tableau.

Country or territory / Pays ou territoires	Year / Année	Total value (millions of dollars) / Valeur totale (millions de dollars)	All food items / Produits alimentaires	Agricultural raw materials / Matières premières agricoles	Fuels / Combustibles	Ores and metals / Minérais et métaux	Manufactured products / Produits manufacturés	Chemical products / Produits chimiques	Machinery and transport equipment / Machines et matériel de transport	Other manufactured products / Produits manufacturés divers
			0+1+22+4	2 - (22+27+28)	3	27+28+68	5+6+7+8 - 68	5	7	(6+8) - 68
Kuwait - Koweït	1995	12 944	0.3	0.0	94.7	0.3	4.7	2.0	1.4	1.3
	2000	19 401	0.3	0.1	93.5	0.2	5.9	4.3	0.8	0.8
	2005	45 057	0.2	0.1	92.6	0.7	6.5	4.9	0.6	1.0
Kyrgyzstan - Kirghizistan	1995	412	22.8	12.7	11.1	11.7	41.1	11.8	9.3	19.9
	2000	504	10.4	8.7	16.4	6.9	19.0	2.9	9.7	6.3
	2005	672	11.3	8.2	11.7	3.8	27.5	1.0	7.6	18.9
Lao People's Dem. Rep. - Rép. dém. populaire lao	1995	310	9.8	28.9	0.2	5.8	55.2	1.5	9.6	44.2
	2000	324	8.0	32.7	0.4	1.4	57.5	0.2	18.4	38.9
	2005	500	7.1	38.1	0.7	1.0	53.1	0.6	2.2	50.4
Latvia - Lettonie	1995	1 305	14.4	23.0	1.7	0.9	58.1	6.9	16.3	34.9
	2000	1 869	5.7	30.0	2.5	6.0	55.5	6.4	7.1	42.0
	2005	5 303	11.3	17.1	8.9	3.5	55.4	6.0	12.4	37.0
Lebanon - Liban	1995	656	19.5	1.5	0.1	8.1	68.7	12.5	14.4	41.9
	2000	714	18.4	1.8	0.2	6.9	66.0	13.5	12.3	40.2
	2005	1 835	14.3	1.2	0.3	10.4	62.7	10.3	16.7	35.7
Lesotho	2000	336	5.0	0.1	..	0.0	94.9	0.3	7.7	86.9
	2005	611	7.2	5.1	0.0	0.1	87.7	0.6	5.1	81.9
Libyan Arab Jamahiriya - Jamahiriya arabe libyenne	1995	9 364	0.3	0.1	94.8	0.0	4.9	3.3	0.0	1.6
	2000	10 415	0.5	0.2	92.6	0.0	6.7	4.2	0.1	2.3
	2005	19 419	0.1	0.1	95.3	0.2	4.3	2.6	0.1	1.6
Lithuania - Lituanie	1995	2 706	18.1	7.8	11.4	5.0	57.7	14.3	15.7	27.7
	2000	3 809	11.6	5.2	20.9	2.1	60.0	9.5	17.3	33.2
	2005	12 070	12.4	3.3	26.6	1.5	55.5	8.4	21.5	25.5
Luxembourg	2005	12 715	6.9	0.7	0.5	5.7	81.6	6.4	24.7	50.4
Madagascar	1995	360	67.6	5.8	4.0	6.8	14.1	2.1	0.9	11.1
	2000	817	33.1	3.4	3.3	1.8	58.2	1.0	0.8	56.4
	2005	313	60.8	6.2	4.4	5.1	22.5	1.7	1.1	19.6
Malawi	1995	433	88.0	2.1	0.1	0.1	9.7	0.4	2.0	7.3
	2000	379	87.3	2.9	0.2	0.2	9.4	0.7	2.8	6.0
	2005	495	79.5	3.8	0.0	0.2	16.4	0.4	3.3	12.7
Malaysia - Malaisie	1995	73 778	9.5	6.2	7.0	1.3	74.7	3.0	55.1	16.5
	2000	98 230	5.5	2.6	9.6	1.0	80.4	3.8	62.5	14.0
	2005	140 963	7.0	2.5	13.3	1.1	74.4	5.4	54.3	14.7
Maldives	1995	50	73.8	0.7	..	0.2	25.3	0.0	..	25.3
	2000	76	53.7	0.0	..	0.1	46.2	0.0	..	46.1
	2005	154	66.7	0.0	24.2	0.7	8.4	0.1	3.4	5.0
Mali	1995	442	18.2	58.3	1.0	0.0	5.3	0.3	1.1	3.9
	2000	473	1.7	34.4	1.0	0.2	4.8	0.5	2.8	1.5
	2005	1 148	6.8	35.9	0.4	0.1	5.1	0.3	2.9	1.9
Malta - Malte	1995	1 913	2.1	0.1	1.5	0.5	95.6	2.2	66.3	27.1
	2000	2 438	2.6	0.1	4.4	0.3	92.5	1.6	70.9	20.0
	2005	2 275	3.5	0.1	0.1	0.3	95.0	3.5	64.7	26.9
Mauritania - Mauritanie	1995	508	53.0	0.1	3.9	38.5	1.9	0.0	1.3	0.5
	2000	343	20.8	0.0	..	45.7	0.0	..	..	0.0
	2005	687	47.1	0.3	0.0	50.1	2.4	0.1	0.9	1.5
Mauritius - Maurice	1995	1 538	28.9	0.7	0.0	0.2	70.2	0.8	2.3	67.1
	2000	1 490	18.5	0.5	0.0	0.2	80.8	0.9	1.3	78.6
	2005	2 004	29.0	0.5	0.1	0.5	69.8	1.5	16.2	52.2
Mexico - Mexique	1995	79 541	7.7	1.3	10.3	2.9	77.5	5.0	52.3	20.2
	2000	166 192	4.9	0.6	9.7	1.3	83.4	3.2	59.2	21.0
	2005	214 207	5.4	0.5	14.9	1.8	77.0	3.7	53.2	20.1

For sources and notes, see end of table.

Pour les sources et les notes, se reporter à la fin du tableau.

Country or territory / Pays ou territoires	Year / Année	Total value (millions of dollars) / Valeur totale (millions de dollars)	By main SITC Rev.3 product group (percentage) / Par principaux groupes de produits de la CTCI Rév.3 (en pourcentage)					Of which: / dont :		
			All food items / Produits alimentaires	Agricultural raw materials / Matières premières agricoles	Fuels / Combustibles	Ores and metals / Minérais et métaux	Manufactured products / Produits manufacturés	Chemical products / Produits chimiques	Machinery and transport equipment / Machines et matériel de transport	Other manufactured products / Produits manufacturés divers
			0+1+22+4	2 - (22+27+28)	3	27+28+68	5+6+7+8 - 68	5	7	(6+8) - 68
Moldova, Republic of - Moldova, République de	1995	746	71.7	1.8	0.9	3.0	22.7	1.4	7.9	13.4
	2000	472	59.8	3.1	0.1	1.8	34.9	1.8	6.2	26.9
	2005	1 091	53.2	5.6	0.2	2.3	38.8	1.7	5.6	31.4
Mongolia - Mongolie	1995	473	2.2	27.7	0.0	59.9	10.2	0.6	1.7	7.8
	2000	466	3.8	27.9	0.5	40.9	25.6	0.3	0.4	24.9
	2005	1 064	1.2	9.4	3.8	39.8	14.6	0.1	0.7	13.7
Morocco - Maroc	1995	4 719	31.4	3.4	2.2	11.5	51.4	20.8	3.2	27.4
	2000	7 432	21.5	2.0	3.7	8.7	64.1	12.0	11.0	41.0
	2005	10 632	21.5	1.9	5.2	9.0	62.3	13.4	13.7	35.3
Mozambique	1995	174	65.5	15.8	2.0	2.3	13.1	0.4	4.8	7.9
	2000	364	42.9	11.3	21.0	17.3	6.8	0.2	3.0	3.6
	2005	1 783	11.7	3.8	15.0	58.1	7.0	0.1	3.4	3.6
Myanmar	1995	859	41.9	38.6	0.2	2.3	17.1	1.0	0.9	15.1
	2000	1 641	20.1	22.3	6.1	3.3	48.2	0.5	1.3	46.4
	2005	4 115	17.8	21.9	31.7	2.4	26.2	0.1	0.5	25.6
Namibia - Namibie	2000	1 327	28.8	1.0	2.1	10.9	54.7	0.7	3.1	50.9
	2005	2 764	28.0	0.7	0.5	20.2	48.6	3.1	5.5	40.0
Nepal - Népal	1995	333	8.4	1.2	..	0.1	90.2	1.3	0.2	88.8
	2000	709	10.0	0.5	..	0.2	66.8	8.5	0.5	57.7
	2005	830	20.6	1.1	0.0	4.3	74.0	6.8	0.4	66.8
Netherlands - Pays-Bas	1995	177 626	19.8	3.9	7.1	2.7	62.5	16.4	26.6	19.5
	2000	180 072	15.0	3.2	9.9	2.2	69.4	13.9	36.7	18.8
	2005	320 065	13.9	3.1	11.8	2.8	68.0	17.2	32.9	17.9
Netherlands Antilles - Antilles néerlandaises	1995	1 460	12.4	0.1	64.2	2.7	20.5	1.7	6.5	12.3
	2000	1 586	4.1	0.4	85.0	3.9	6.6	0.8	2.4	3.4
	2005	1 658	4.4	0.1	76.2	3.2	15.8	3.1	7.7	4.9
New Caledonia - Nouvelle-Calédonie	1995	568	2.7	0.4	..	39.9	57.0	0.1	0.6	56.3
	2000	635	4.0	0.1	0.9	34.4	60.6	0.2	1.8	58.6
	2005	1 114	3.0	0.1	1.4	27.6	67.8	0.2	1.9	65.7
New Zealand - Nouvelle-Zélande	1995	13 745	42.4	18.0	1.6	4.8	30.6	7.6	8.6	14.4
	2000	13 272	43.9	13.7	2.6	4.7	30.0	6.9	10.4	12.8
	2005	21 730	49.6	10.2	1.5	4.1	30.4	5.4	11.5	13.5
Nicaragua	1995	509	73.5	2.9	0.6	0.8	20.3	1.2	6.1	13.0
	2000	629	84.9	2.0	1.7	0.4	7.3	1.9	0.7	4.8
	2005	866	80.5	2.1	1.4	1.0	9.8	3.8	1.1	4.9
Niger	1995	273	27.1	2.4	0.6	55.4	14.4	0.6	5.9	7.9
	2000	330	38.7	2.8	1.1	27.7	29.7	1.1	12.8	15.9
	2005	348	19.3	3.0	1.5	43.3	11.6	0.2	7.8	3.6
Nigeria - Nigéria	1995	13 052	2.8	2.4	92.6	0.2	2.1	0.4	0.2	1.5
	2000	27 079	0.1	0.0	99.6	0.0	0.2	0.0	0.1	0.1
	2005	42 277	0.0	0.0	97.9	0.0	2.1	0.1	1.8	0.2
Norway - Norvège	1995	41 740	8.3	1.5	47.3	8.7	26.8	3.1	13.3	10.4
	2000	59 899	6.4	0.7	63.9	6.1	18.5	2.6	9.2	6.7
	2005	103 759	5.2	0.5	67.7	6.0	17.1	2.7	8.2	6.2
Oman	1995	5 917	5.1	0.0	78.6	1.8	13.9	0.4	9.6	3.9
	2000	10 852	3.7	0.0	82.5	0.9	12.4	0.9	8.3	3.2
	2005	20 370	2.5	0.0	85.7	0.8	5.6	1.5	1.7	2.5
Pakistan	1995	8 158	11.8	3.8	1.0	0.2	83.0	0.7	0.5	81.8
	2000	9 201	10.5	2.9	1.4	0.2	84.8	1.6	1.0	82.2
	2005	16 050	12.0	1.5	4.2	0.4	81.8	3.0	1.8	77.0

For sources and notes, see end of table.

Pour les sources et les notes, se reporter à la fin du tableau.

Country or territory / Pays ou territoires	Year / Année	Total value (millions of dollars) / Valeur totale (millions de dollars)	By main SITC Rev.3 product group (percentage) / Par principaux groupes de produits de la CTCI Rév.3 (en pourcentage)					Of which: / dont :		
			All food items / Produits alimentaires	Agricultural raw materials / Matières premières agricoles	Fuels / Combustibles	Ores and metals / Minérais et métaux	Manufactured products / Produits manufacturés	Chemical products / Produits chimiques	Machinery and transport equipment / Machines et matériel de transport	Other manufactured products / Produits manufacturés divers
			0+1+22+4	2 - (22+27+28)	3	27+28+68	5+6+7+8 - 68	5	7	(6+8) - 68
Palau, Pacific Islands (former) - Palaos, Îles du Pacifique (anc.)	1995	14	74.9	1.8	0.0	0.1	23.2	0.1	4.4	18.8
	2000	11	55.9	0.2	0.0	0.5	43.5	0.1	0.6	42.8
	2005	13	80.0	0.2	..	15.9	3.8	0.0	0.9	2.9
Panama	1995	577	74.3	0.5	3.1	1.1	20.2	5.1	0.2	14.9
	2000	772	73.7	1.5	6.7	2.1	15.9	5.0	0.1	10.8
	2005	964	85.0	0.8	0.7	4.0	9.1	2.6	0.1	6.4
Papua New Guinea - Papouasie-Nouvelle-Guinée	1995	2 652	20.8	19.3	23.1	24.9	0.8	0.1	0.6	0.2
	2000	2 407	15.3	2.3	28.8	51.3	2.2	0.0	2.0	0.2
	2005	3 275	19.3	2.6	20.4	46.3	5.0	0.1	3.0	1.9
Paraguay	1995	919	43.9	36.4	0.2	0.3	19.3	2.6	0.8	15.9
	2000	871	64.8	15.5	0.1	0.4	19.3	2.6	0.5	16.2
	2005	1 688	75.7	9.2	0.0	1.3	13.8	2.7	0.9	10.2
Peru - Pérou	1995	5 440	28.8	2.5	4.9	41.7	13.6	2.2	0.6	10.8
	2000	6 866	25.3	2.5	5.9	32.7	16.9	2.4	1.1	13.4
	2005	17 114	17.0	1.5	9.3	40.0	14.3	2.4	0.8	11.0
Philippines	1995	17 447	12.8	1.2	1.5	4.3	40.8	2.0	22.2	16.7
	2000	38 078	4.8	0.6	1.3	1.6	91.3	0.9	76.1	14.3
	2005	41 221	6.1	0.5	1.9	2.3	89.1	1.3	74.6	13.1
Poland - Pologne	1995	22 862	10.4	2.8	8.2	7.3	71.1	7.7	21.1	42.4
	2000	31 613	7.9	1.8	5.1	4.9	80.2	6.8	34.2	39.2
	2005	89 378	9.4	1.2	5.1	4.0	78.2	6.7	38.6	32.9
Portugal	1995	23 370	7.2	4.6	3.2	1.8	83.1	4.9	26.8	51.4
	2000	24 365	6.8	3.5	2.6	1.9	85.1	5.7	34.4	45.0
	2005	38 086	7.9	1.8	4.3	2.7	74.6	6.5	31.0	37.1
Qatar	1995	3 557	0.4	0.0	80.2	0.2	19.1	11.2	1.3	6.6
	2000	8 847	0.1	0.0	89.5	0.1	10.2	5.3	1.2	3.7
	2005	25 762	0.1	0.0	83.7	0.2	7.0	5.2	1.1	0.7
Romania - Roumanie	1995	7 910	6.6	3.3	7.9	3.5	78.3	10.7	13.1	54.4
	2000	10 367	3.1	4.9	7.2	7.5	76.7	5.8	18.8	52.1
	2005	27 730	3.0	2.3	10.7	4.2	79.2	5.7	25.4	48.1
Russian Federation - Fédération de Russie	1995	65 857	2.1	3.9	51.2	11.8	31.0	7.0	8.3	15.6
	2000	103 093	1.2	3.1	51.3	9.1	23.0	4.9	5.9	12.3
	2005	241 244	1.6	2.8	49.0	6.6	19.0	4.2	4.1	10.8
Rwanda	1995	52	57.0	15.9	0.2	12.4	14.1	0.6	6.8	6.6
	2000	52	57.0	3.2	0.0	37.7	2.1	0.5	0.0	1.6
	2005	125	52.3	7.3	6.8	23.3	10.4	0.5	6.7	3.2
Saint Kitts and Nevis - Saint-Kitts-et-Nevis	1995	19	54.3	0.3	0.2	0.1	45.1	0.8	36.6	7.7
	2000	33	24.6	0.0	0.0	0.0	75.4	0.2	66.3	8.9
	2005	34	4.1	0.1	0.0	0.0	95.8	0.1	90.6	5.1
Saint Lucia - Sainte-Lucie	1995	109	58.5	0.4	0.0	0.0	41.0	0.8	11.2	28.9
	2000	43	72.3	0.4	0.0	0.0	27.3	1.3	11.4	14.6
	2005	64	46.0	0.2	15.5	1.1	36.0	2.4	17.9	15.7
Saint Vincent and the Grenadines - Saint-Vincent-et-les Grenadines	1995	59	81.0	0.2	0.0	0.1	18.8	1.0	4.0	13.8
	2000	51	74.6	0.2	0.0	0.1	25.2	1.9	13.7	9.6
	2005	40	74.8	0.2	0.1	0.2	24.9	0.8	9.4	14.7
Samoa	1995	9	12.8	1.1	..	2.1	83.9	0.1	73.0	10.7
	2000	14	32.1	0.5	0.2	0.1	67.2	0.2	63.1	3.9
	2005	95	22.5	0.4	0.3	0.1	76.6	0.3	71.9	4.4
Saudi Arabia - Arabie saoudite	1995	49 030	0.9	0.1	86.8	0.6	11.6	8.4	1.0	2.2
	2000	77 480	0.6	0.1	91.5	0.1	7.7	5.4	0.8	1.5
	2005	160 126	0.3	0.1	89.6	0.4	9.6	8.1	0.5	0.9

For sources and notes, see end of table.

Pour les sources et les notes, se reporter à la fin du tableau.

3

Country or territory / Pays ou territoires	Year / Année	Total value (millions of dollars) / Valeur totale (millions de dollars)	By main SITC Rev.3 product group (percentage) / Par principaux groupes de produits de la CTCI Rév.3 (en pourcentage)					Of which: / dont :		
			All food items / Produits alimentaires	Agricultural raw materials / Matières premières agricoles	Fuels / Combustibles	Ores and metals / Minérais et métaux	Manufactured products / Produits manufacturés	Chemical products / Produits chimiques	Machinery and transport equipment / Machines et matériel de transport	Other manufactured products / Produits manufacturés divers
			0+1+22+4	2 - (22+27+28)	3	27+28+68	5+6+7+8 - 68	5	7	(6+8) - 68
Senegal - Sénégal	1995	531	15.4	8.5	15.1	10.6	49.7	39.5	2.5	7.7
	2000	693	52.4	1.7	14.0	4.8	27.1	17.4	3.5	6.2
	2005	1 471	28.8	2.1	21.1	2.8	44.9	21.7	11.6	11.6
Serbia and Montenegro - Serbie-et-Monténégro	1995	1 503	28.7	4.0	2.2	15.1	50.0	9.2	12.4	28.4
	2000	1 711	17.0	5.7	0.3	15.6	61.4	8.5	12.6	40.4
	2005	4 350	20.6	4.0	2.4	10.9	61.7	10.3	11.1	40.3
Seychelles	1995	53	45.9	0.0	46.7	0.1	7.3	0.5	3.0	3.9
	2000	194	75.7	0.1	21.9	0.0	2.3	0.4	1.2	0.7
	2005	340	57.0	0.0	36.4	0.0	6.5	3.6	0.2	2.7
Singapore - Singapour	1995	118 263	3.9	1.1	6.8	2.0	83.7	6.0	65.6	12.1
	2000	137 806	2.2	0.5	9.7	1.1	85.4	7.0	67.4	11.0
	2005	229 652	1.7	0.3	12.2	1.1	80.6	11.4	58.7	10.5
Slovakia - Slovaquie	1995	8 374	6.2	3.6	4.2	3.6	82.3	12.6	19.0	50.8
	2000	11 885	3.2	2.2	7.0	3.4	84.1	7.9	39.5	36.7
	2005	31 997	4.3	1.6	7.2	2.7	84.0	5.8	44.6	33.6
Slovenia - Slovénie	1995	8 316	3.9	1.8	1.2	3.4	89.5	10.5	31.4	47.6
	2000	8 732	3.7	1.6	0.7	4.2	89.7	11.0	36.0	42.8
	2005	19 285	3.3	1.8	2.1	4.7	88.1	12.4	38.9	36.8
South Africa - Afrique du Sud	1995	28 226	7.9	4.4	8.9	8.0	42.8	7.0	8.8	27.1
	2000	30 209	7.4	3.3	8.8	9.3	46.3	6.8	15.1	24.4
	2005	46 995	8.5	2.7	10.4	22.3	55.5	8.4	20.4	26.7
Spain - Espagne	1995	89 616	15.4	1.6	1.7	2.4	77.9	8.5	42.4	27.1
	2000	113 343	13.5	1.3	3.7	2.3	77.5	9.4	42.5	25.6
	2005	192 798	14.1	1.2	4.3	2.5	76.3	12.0	40.2	24.2
Sri Lanka	1995	3 773	18.8	4.3	0.4	0.7	75.7	0.9	3.6	71.2
	2000	5 433	21.1	1.6	0.4	0.3	76.6	0.7	6.2	69.8
	2005	6 160	22.2	2.1	0.0	3.6	70.2	1.3	4.5	64.4
Sudan - Soudan	1995	685	44.4	46.1	0.3	0.4	6.2	0.0	0.0	6.1
	2000	1 631	16.7	4.7	66.7	0.5	7.6	0.1	5.4	2.1
	2005	4 355	6.8	4.8	86.0	0.4	0.1	0.0	0.0	0.0
Suriname	1995	483	18.3	0.3	2.2	74.0	2.0	0.0	1.1	0.9
	2000	514	14.4	0.7	6.7	62.1	4.5	0.9	2.6	1.0
	2005	1 113	10.7	0.5	1.0	62.1	2.5	1.2	0.3	1.0
Swaziland	2000	891	33.6	10.7	0.7	0.4	54.3	20.1	9.7	24.5
	2005	1 604	14.6	7.9	0.7	0.2	76.5	47.9	3.6	25.0
Sweden - Suède	1995	77 436	2.2	6.5	1.9	2.9	78.7	6.6	42.1	29.9
	2000	77 262	2.5	1.0	3.1	2.7	84.9	10.0	46.5	28.4
	2005	130 264	3.5	4.0	5.0	3.1	78.4	10.6	41.8	26.1
Switzerland - Suisse	1995	81 641	3.0	0.7	0.1	2.5	93.3	26.0	31.4	35.8
	2000	81 534	2.5	0.6	0.4	5.6	90.7	27.3	30.6	32.8
	2005	125 927	2.7	0.4	0.4	2.8	93.6	35.9	25.7	32.0
Syrian Arab Republic - République arabe syrienne	1995	3 970	12.3	7.0	62.5	0.8	17.4	0.6	0.8	16.0
	2000	4 633	8.8	4.6	76.4	0.7	7.8	0.3	0.1	7.4
	2005	6 609	14.7	3.6	67.6	1.1	11.3	1.5	0.9	9.0
Tajikistan - Tadjikistan	1995	749	11.4	44.9	1.3	26.2	16.2	2.5	2.4	11.3
	2000	692	4.2	12.2	13.3	53.9	12.8	1.4	7.8	3.6
	2005	892	7.3	27.9	0.3	49.8	14.2	1.0	2.5	10.8
Thailand - Thaïlande	1995	56 439	19.3	5.4	0.7	0.6	73.1	4.4	33.7	35.0
	2000	68 787	14.5	3.3	3.2	1.3	75.3	5.9	43.7	25.7
	2005	110 110	11.6	4.5	4.3	1.2	76.6	8.1	44.7	23.8

For sources and notes, see end of table.

Pour les sources et les notes, se reporter à la fin du tableau.

Country or territory Pays ou territoires	Year Année	Total value (millions of dollars) Valeur totale (millions de dollars)	By main SITC Rev.3 product group (percentage) Par principaux groupes de produits de la CTCI Rév.3 (en pourcentage)					Of which: / dont :		
			All food items Produits alimentaires	Agricultural raw materials Matières premières agricoles	Fuels Combus-tibles	Ores and metals Minérais et métaux	Manu-factured products Produits manu-facturés	Chemical products Produits chimiques	Machinery and transport equipment Machines et matériel de transport	Other manu-factured products Produits manu-facturés divers
			0+1+22+4	2 - (22+27+28)	3	27+28+68	5+6+7+8 - 68	5	7	(6+8) - 68
Macedonia, TFYR - Macédoine, LERY	1995	1 204	18.3	5.2	0.4	17.7	58.2	5.5	12.9	39.7
	2000	1 323	15.0	1.7	4.8	8.8	69.4	4.5	6.3	58.6
	2005	2 041	16.4	0.8	8.0	3.0	71.6	4.4	5.4	61.8
Togo	1995	383	14.1	24.7	18.7	17.7	15.2	1.2	5.1	8.9
	2000	192	19.6	23.4	0.6	25.5	30.8	0.7	3.9	26.3
	2005	360	21.5	8.9	1.2	10.3	58.1	5.2	1.9	51.0
Trinidad and Tobago - Trinité-et-Tobago	1995	2 467	8.4	0.2	47.9	0.2	43.4	25.0	2.3	16.1
	2000	4 273	5.7	0.1	65.3	0.1	28.8	17.3	1.2	10.3
	2005	9 611	3.1	0.0	70.2	0.4	26.2	19.0	1.4	5.7
Tunisia - Tunisie	1995	5 475	9.8	0.6	8.5	1.7	79.4	11.9	9.4	58.1
	2000	5 850	8.7	0.7	12.1	1.5	77.0	10.6	14.0	52.4
	2005	10 494	10.4	0.6	12.9	1.2	74.9	9.4	19.2	46.3
Turkey - Turquie	1995	21 599	19.6	1.5	1.3	3.3	74.3	4.1	11.1	59.1
	2000	27 485	12.8	1.1	1.1	2.6	81.3	3.9	20.6	56.8
	2005	73 476	10.5	0.5	3.6	2.5	81.4	3.8	29.3	48.3
Turkmenistan - Turkménistan	1995	1 939	0.8	13.0	76.5	1.3	8.4	0.6	0.1	7.7
	2000	2 506	0.3	9.9	81.0	0.4	6.9	0.4	0.6	5.8
	2005	3 792	0.1	2.5	91.1	0.4	6.0	1.2	0.3	4.5
Turks and Caicos Islands - Îles Turques et Caïques	1995	5	57.7	0.2	14.1	0.1	27.8	3.0	0.7	24.2
	2000	9	46.8	1.3	0.3	0.1	49.7	0.2	33.2	16.3
	2005	12	43.3	0.8	0.0	0.0	55.1	0.3	16.7	38.2
Uganda - Ouganda	1995	575	86.0	4.4	0.1	0.6	4.2	1.0	1.2	2.0
	2000	402	60.1	12.5	7.1	4.1	5.3	1.1	2.5	1.8
	2005	813	58.2	10.6	4.7	2.1	15.5	2.4	5.2	7.8
Ukraine	1995	13 162	19.2	1.0	4.4	8.3	67.1	13.0	14.3	39.9
	2000	14 573	9.2	1.7	5.5	14.1	67.1	9.0	12.3	45.7
	2005	34 228	12.4	1.5	9.8	7.0	68.5	9.1	13.1	46.4
United Arab Emirates - Émirats arabes unis	1995	27 582	3.5	0.3	72.2	4.0	19.1	2.9	6.9	9.3
	2000	37 720	3.0	0.2	76.2	2.8	17.4	1.2	6.6	9.6
	2005	106 169	2.0	0.2	48.1	1.2	19.2	1.0	8.5	9.7
United Kingdom - Royaume-Uni	1995	234 372	7.6	0.7	6.2	2.7	81.9	12.4	43.8	25.8
	2000	282 853	5.4	0.6	8.5	2.3	82.6	13.4	47.2	22.1
	2005	384 365	5.2	0.6	9.5	2.8	77.0	14.9	39.6	22.5
United Republic of Tanzania - République-Unie de Tanzanie	1995	683	65.4	23.2	0.3	0.3	10.4	0.7	1.3	8.3
	2000	656	54.8	11.1	0.1	0.4	16.2	0.8	1.0	14.4
	2005	1 415	37.2	11.0	0.1	7.7	9.5	1.3	0.5	7.6
United States - États-Unis	1995	582 965	10.1	3.7	1.8	2.5	78.0	10.6	48.3	19.1
	2000	780 332	7.0	2.2	1.7	1.8	83.5	10.6	52.8	20.1
	2005	904 339	6.8	2.3	2.9	2.7	81.3	13.3	48.0	20.1
Uruguay	1995	2 106	44.2	14.9	1.0	0.7	38.7	5.6	6.0	27.2
	2000	2 299	46.3	9.3	1.5	0.5	41.5	6.2	8.5	26.8
	2005	3 405	54.5	9.2	4.8	0.5	29.7	5.8	2.9	21.0
Uzbekistan - Ouzbékistan	1995	3 720	7.9	52.0	12.9	4.2	15.4	3.5	2.9	9.0
	2000	3 224	9.2	39.3	19.5	5.9	19.1	3.2	5.1	10.8
	2005	3 379	12.5	30.2	12.4	11.5	28.4	6.2	8.9	13.3
Venezuela (Bolivarian Republic of) - Venezuela (République bolivarienne du)	1995	19 093	2.8	0.1	76.3	6.6	13.7	4.1	2.8	6.8
	2000	30 948	1.5	0.2	86.1	3.3	8.8	2.8	1.1	4.9
	2005	55 487	0.5	0.0	88.7	2.2	8.4	1.8	1.3	5.3
Viet Nam	1995	5 217	31.6	3.3	18.8	0.5	45.9	1.1	7.3	37.5
	2000	14 483	25.3	2.0	26.4	0.4	42.6	1.0	8.7	33.0
	2005	34 863	16.8	1.8	21.4	0.9	59.1	1.2	9.4	48.5

For sources and notes, see end of table.

Pour les sources et les notes, se reporter à la fin du tableau.

Country or territory / Pays ou territoires	Year / Année	Total value (millions of dollars) / Valeur totale (millions de dollars)	By main SITC Rev.3 product group (percentage) / Par principaux groupes de produits de la CTCI Rév.3 (en pourcentage)					Of which: / dont :		
			All food items / Produits alimentaires	Agricultural raw materials / Matières premières agricoles	Fuels / Combustibles	Ores and metals / Minérais et métaux	Manufactured products / Produits manufacturés	Chemical products / Produits chimiques	Machinery and transport equipment / Machines et matériel de transport	Other manufactured products / Produits manufacturés divers
			0+1+22+4	2 - (22+27+28)	3	27+28+68	5+6+7+8 - 68	5	7	(6+8) - 68
Yemen - Yémen	1995	1 917	2.7	0.6	94.3	0.5	1.9	0.1	0.9	0.8
	2000	4 078	2.1	0.4	96.5	0.1	0.9	0.3	0.3	0.3
	2005	5 609	4.4	0.2	92.1	0.1	2.7	0.3	1.8	0.5
Zambia - Zambie	1995	1 055	2.7	0.6	3.3	86.5	6.9	0.2	1.6	5.2
	2000	666	10.2	3.6	1.5	55.5	27.7	0.6	3.4	23.7
	2005	1 852	13.1	5.4	0.7	63.2	17.5	0.8	1.3	15.3
Zimbabwe	1995	1 846	43.4	6.8	1.3	11.6	36.9	2.6	2.7	31.6
	2000	1 925	47.1	12.5	1.1	10.9	28.0	2.8	2.4	22.9
	2005	1 877	30.4	15.5	1.6	22.7	28.2	1.4	2.3	24.5

Sources:
- UNCTAD secretariat calculations based on UN DESA Statistics Division's data

Sources :
- Calculs du secrétariat de la CNUCED sur la base des données de ONU DAES Division de statistique

Country or territory Pays ou territoires	Year Année	Total value (millions of dollars) Valeur totale (millions de dollars)	By main SITC Rev.3 product group (percentage) Par principaux groupes de produits de la CTCI Rév.3 (en pourcentage)							
			All food items Produits alimentaires	Agricultural raw materials Matières premières agricoles	Fuels Combus-tibles	Ores and metals Minérais et métaux	Manu-factured products Produits manu-facturés	Of which: / dont :		
								Chemical products Produits chimiques	Machinery and transport equipment Machines et matériel de transport	Other manu-factured products Produits manu-facturés divers
			0+1+22+4	2 - (22+27+28)	3	27+28+68	5+6+7+8 - 68	5	7	(6+8) - 68
Albania - Albanie	1995	715	34.3	0.9	2.6	1.0	61.2	5.9	22.8	32.5
	2000	1 089	21.8	0.9	9.0	1.5	66.6	7.0	21.6	38.1
	2005	2 635	17.4	1.1	8.6	2.3	70.6	8.5	23.6	38.6
Algeria - Algérie	1995	10 782	29.5	3.2	1.1	1.6	64.7	11.3	30.5	22.9
	2000	9 152	28.2	2.6	1.4	1.2	66.6	11.6	34.5	20.6
	2005	20 197	21.9	1.9	0.9	1.3	73.9	12.0	40.9	21.0
Andorra - Andorre	1995	1 025	29.7	0.7	3.6	0.7	65.2	9.2	20.0	36.0
	2000	1 011	19.9	0.5	4.4	0.8	74.0	10.3	23.1	40.6
	2005	1 765	18.2	0.4	4.3	0.6	76.2	10.1	29.8	36.3
Angola	1995	1 450	25.8	0.9	0.7	0.4	72.2	6.1	43.9	22.3
	2000	2 962	27.9	0.9	4.6	0.5	66.2	6.2	36.5	23.4
	2005	5 089	19.0	0.5	0.8	0.6	79.0	4.3	57.1	17.6
Argentina - Argentine	1995	20 122	5.5	2.0	4.2	2.7	85.5	17.8	44.5	23.1
	2000	23 851	4.9	1.5	3.6	2.4	87.2	18.4	45.1	23.6
	2005	28 689	2.8	1.5	5.0	3.5	86.4	19.8	46.6	19.9
Armenia - Arménie	1995	662	31.7	0.5	27.8	0.5	39.3	10.2	11.6	17.5
	2000	840	25.0	0.9	20.8	0.9	51.0	10.8	14.7	25.5
	2005	1 692	17.7	0.8	15.5	2.6	59.0	7.8	18.4	32.8
Aruba	1995	571	23.0	3.4	..	1.4	72.3	10.3	26.5	35.5
	2000	835	31.2	0.3	..	2.0	66.5	11.7	20.9	33.8
	2005	1 030	6.9	0.4	..	2.5	26.9	4.8	4.6	17.6
Australia - Australie	1995	57 423	5.0	1.7	5.0	1.3	86.0	11.1	47.0	27.9
	2000	71 178	4.6	1.4	8.3	1.1	83.2	11.5	46.2	25.6
	2005	118 922	4.6	0.9	11.1	1.0	80.2	11.4	44.3	24.6
Austria - Autriche	1995	66 406	5.7	3.2	4.4	3.9	81.7	10.7	36.8	34.3
	2000	64 039	5.8	2.8	5.8	2.9	82.5	10.3	41.1	31.0
	2005	115 406	6.2	2.2	12.5	3.5	74.4	10.3	36.8	27.3
Azerbaijan - Azerbaïdjan	1995	668	39.1	1.0	4.5	2.3	53.1	7.5	23.6	22.0
	2000	1 172	18.6	1.7	4.9	3.6	71.2	7.9	40.0	23.3
	2005	4 211	10.5	1.0	11.9	2.2	74.2	5.5	43.5	25.2
Bahrain - Bahreïn	1995	3 679	12.3	1.0	36.7	4.7	45.0	5.7	16.8	22.4
	2000	4 633	9.7	0.8	45.5	6.8	37.2	4.7	16.1	16.4
	2005	7 540	5.9	0.4	56.7	5.5	31.5	3.7	15.8	12.0
Bangladesh	1995	5 438	17.3	3.4	7.7	2.3	69.2	10.2	14.7	44.3
	2000	7 572	19.7	5.7	7.7	2.2	64.6	11.2	17.1	36.3
	2005	9 411	18.9	8.8	7.8	2.5	62.0	11.2	21.0	29.7
Barbados - Barbade	1995	766	18.3	2.4	8.5	1.1	69.5	12.2	26.8	30.5
	2000	1 156	15.4	2.3	11.5	1.0	69.5	9.7	27.8	32.0
	2005	1 672	15.1	1.9	17.1	1.0	64.4	9.2	27.8	27.4
Belarus - Bélarus	1995	5 472	11.3	2.5	24.2	3.1	58.9	12.0	23.0	23.8
	2000	8 492	12.1	2.3	30.4	3.6	50.0	11.9	16.8	21.2
	2005	16 699	9.4	1.7	33.0	3.2	46.3	9.5	18.2	18.6
Belgium - Belgique	2005	320 130	7.6	1.2	12.4	3.6	74.5	25.0	25.7	23.7
Belgium-Luxembourg - Belgique-Luxembourg	1995	153 388	11.2	2.1	6.1	4.8	70.6	13.7	26.3	30.6
	2000	176 875	8.6	1.9	8.5	3.8	77.0	16.6	30.7	29.7
Belize	1995	259	19.1	0.3	11.5	0.7	68.4	10.7	25.8	31.9
	2000	447	14.0	0.6	17.0	0.5	67.5	10.3	28.7	28.4
	2005	439	16.1	0.8	22.3	0.5	60.0	10.1	22.8	27.1
Benin - Bénin	1995	717	27.4	2.7	9.4	1.0	59.5	13.7	18.0	27.7
	2000	547	21.9	5.3	19.2	1.0	52.6	10.3	15.1	27.3
	2005	899	29.8	4.2	20.4	0.9	43.9	6.7	12.1	25.1

For sources and notes, see end of table.

Pour les sources et les notes, se reporter à la fin du tableau.

3.1   Country trade structure
by product group
Imports

3.1   Structure du commerce des pays
par groupes de produits
Importations

Country or territory / Pays ou territcires	Year / Année	Total value (millions of dollars) / Valeur totale (millions de dollars)	By main SITC Rev.3 product group (percentage) / Par principaux groupes de produits de la CTCI Rév.3 (en pourcentage)					Of which: / dont :		
			All food items / Produits alimentaires	Agricultural raw materials / Matières premières agricoles	Fuels / Combus-tibles	Ores and metals / Minérais et métaux	Manu-factured products / Produits manu-facturés	Chemical products / Produits chimiques	Machinery and transport equipment / Machines et matériel de transport	Other manu-factured products / Produits manu-facturés divers
			0+1+22+4	2 - (22+27+28)	3	27+28+68	5+6+7+8 - 68	5	7	(6+8) - 68
Bolivia - Bolivie	1995	1 396	9.5	1.7	4.5	2.6	81.1	13.7	46.3	21.1
	2000	1 849	13.5	1.6	4.8	0.6	78.8	14.3	36.9	27.6
	2005	2 343	10.2	1.4	10.3	0.7	76.5	19.2	30.5	26.9
Bosnia and Herzegovina - Bosnie-Herzégovine	1995	100	42.8	0.9	7.4	1.0	47.9	10.0	12.8	25.1
	2000	3 049	21.4	1.0	7.8	1.9	67.9	11.1	22.9	33.9
	2005	7 054	17.4	1.2	13.0	3.0	65.3	10.8	25.5	29.0
Botswana	2000	2 072	14.0	0.8	4.9	2.2	73.3	6.8	34.6	31.9
	2005	2 340	5.0	1.3	2.5	0.8	90.3	6.8	45.5	38.0
Brazil - Brésil	1995	53 734	10.7	2.7	12.1	3.4	71.1	15.2	39.2	16.7
	2000	58 931	6.8	2.0	15.1	3.1	73.1	17.9	41.2	14.0
	2005	76 436	4.6	1.5	18.8	3.9	71.2	19.9	36.9	14.3
Brunei Darussalam - Brunéi Darussalam	1995	2 068	13.6	0.6	0.2	3.3	82.2	6.4	39.2	36.7
	2000	1 096	17.9	0.3	0.2	1.2	80.4	7.7	30.9	41.8
	2005	1 355	17.7	0.3	0.9	1.0	80.1	7.6	35.4	37.0
Bulgaria - Bulgarie	1995	5 442	7.9	2.7	35.0	4.6	49.7	11.5	16.6	21.6
	2000	6 505	5.2	1.3	25.8	5.7	59.0	9.4	24.9	24.7
	2005	18 180	4.7	1.4	5.4	6.5	65.4	9.5	30.1	25.8
Burkina Faso	1995	484	21.2	1.5	14.0	1.2	62.1	14.7	19.7	27.7
	2000	724	12.6	0.6	25.2	0.9	60.7	8.4	37.1	15.2
	2005	1 271	12.0	0.6	24.5	0.6	62.3	11.6	33.7	17.0
Burundi	1995	270	20.9	1.9	11.3	1.2	64.1	14.1	29.3	20.7
	2000	150	22.9	2.4	11.8	2.2	60.0	13.3	22.9	23.8
	2005	257	6.5	1.4	8.4	0.8	82.4	12.4	34.5	35.4
Cambodia - Cambodge	1995	215	25.3	1.6	7.9	7.7	57.5	6.2	34.7	16.6
	2000	1 439	9.5	3.3	12.7	0.4	71.0	6.7	16.2	48.1
	2005	2 478	7.8	2.4	9.8	0.3	78.7	6.0	13.9	58.8
Cameroon - Cameroun	1995	1 079	17.4	2.5	2.4	5.6	72.0	16.5	30.5	24.9
	2000	1 489	18.2	1.6	23.2	3.6	53.6	11.9	23.0	18.7
	2005	2 737	18.0	1.8	26.3	3.5	50.4	11.0	20.1	19.3
Canada	1995	164 371	5.7	1.7	3.6	3.3	82.8	8.1	51.6	23.1
	2000	240 091	5.0	1.4	5.2	2.5	83.7	8.4	52.0	23.4
	2005	314 436	5.6	1.2	9.2	2.8	79.0	10.1	45.5	23.4
Cape Verde - Cap-Vert	1995	327	31.1	2.6	14.3	0.2	51.6	5.4	22.8	23.4
	2000	237	31.0	2.2	6.1	0.3	60.5	6.6	28.5	25.4
	2005	438	30.5	1.8	8.9	0.5	58.3	7.4	24.3	26.6
Central African Republic - République centrafricaine	1995	265	15.6	9.8	8.7	1.6	64.2	8.0	42.2	14.0
	2000	70	29.3	4.3	7.5	4.5	54.3	12.8	23.2	18.2
	2005	186	17.1	27.2	16.9	1.5	36.7	6.9	16.9	12.9
Chile - Chili	1995	14 903	6.7	1.7	9.0	2.2	79.2	12.2	42.3	24.7
	2000	16 620	7.4	1.2	18.1	1.1	71.4	12.7	35.0	23.7
	2005	29 857	6.2	1.0	21.7	3.5	67.2	11.5	35.9	19.8
China - Chine	1995	132 083	7.0	5.2	3.9	4.4	78.8	13.1	39.9	25.9
	2000	225 094	4.0	4.7	9.2	5.9	75.5	13.4	40.8	21.2
	2005	659 953	3.3	3.6	9.7	8.4	74.7	11.8	44.0	18.9
China, Hong Kong SAR - Chine, Hong Kong RAS	1995	196 072	5.4	1.6	1.9	2.1	87.0	7.4	36.5	43.1
	2000	214 042	4.3	1.2	2.1	1.7	90.0	6.3	42.4	41.3
	2005	300 160	2.9	0.8	2.7	1.7	91.6	6.2	52.1	33.3
China, Macao SAR - Chine, Macao RAS	1995	2 025	14.0	2.7	5.1	0.6	77.3	4.5	18.9	53.9
	2000	2 261	11.5	1.4	7.7	0.4	78.9	3.8	15.8	59.3
	2005	3 913	12.2	0.5	7.7	0.5	79.0	4.4	24.1	50.5

For sources and notes, see end of table.

Pour les sources et les notes, se reporter à la fin du tableau.

3.1   Country trade structure
      by product group
      Imports

3.1   Structure du commerce des pays
      par groupes de produits
      Importations

Country or territory / Pays ou territoires	Year / Année	Total value (millions of dollars) / Valeur totale (millions de dollars)	By main SITC Rev.3 product group (percentage) / Par principaux groupes de produits de la CTCI Rév.3 (en pourcentage)							
			All food items / Produits alimentaires	Agricultural raw materials / Matières premières agricoles	Fuels / Combustibles	Ores and metals / Minérais et métaux	Manufactured products / Produits manufacturés	Of which: / dont :		
								Chemical products / Produits chimiques	Machinery and transport equipment / Machines et matériel de transport	Other manufactured products / Produits manufacturés divers
			0+1+22+4	2 - (22+27+28)	3	27+28+68	5+6−7+8 − 68	5	7	(6+8) − 68
China, Taiwan Province of - Chine, Taiwan Province de	1995	103 506	5.4	4.2	6.9	6.0	74.3	13.3	40.2	20.8
	2000	139 991	3.6	2.1	9.3	4.5	78.9	11.1	50.2	17.6
	2005	181 592	3.6	1.6	15.5	5.7	72.1	12.6	41.0	18.5
Colombia - Colombie	1995	13 883	9.4	2.5	2.8	2.5	78.0	18.1	37.3	22.6
	2000	11 757	11.9	2.8	2.1	2.4	80.6	23.2	32.9	24.5
	2005	21 204	8.7	1.6	2.6	2.6	83.7	20.8	40.4	22.5
Congo	1995	556	20.8	0.9	19.5	0.8	58.0	14.0	20.3	23.8
	2000	657	24.8	2.7	2.0	1.1	69.4	13.3	29.8	26.4
	2005	875	24.7	2.3	1.5	1.3	69.8	12.8	28.3	23.8
Costa Rica	1995	3 205	10.2	1.2	8.5	2.0	77.4	19.8	26.6	31.0
	2000	6 029	7.4	0.8	8.1	1.8	81.6	14.7	37.9	29.0
	2005	9 173	6.4	1.1	10.8	1.3	80.1	15.0	39.7	25.4
Côte d'Ivoire	1995	2 472	20.9	0.9	19.2	1.5	56.6	13.0	24.5	19.2
	2000	2 482	17.2	1.1	33.7	1.4	46.2	14.3	16.4	15.4
	2005	5 865	14.6	0.5	28.0	1.0	54.8	9.4	24.2	21.2
Croatia - Croatie	1995	7 509	11.8	1.8	11.6	2.5	66.6	10.8	26.7	29.0
	2000	7 887	8.3	1.6	14.5	2.3	73.3	12.7	32.6	28.0
	2005	18 560	8.3	1.3	15.1	2.3	72.9	11.1	32.9	28.9
Cuba	1995	2 784	21.2	1.6	22.9	1.6	52.7	12.3	20.1	20.3
	2000	4 843	15.8	1.3	23.9	1.2	57.8	8.8	25.1	23.8
	2005	7 592	21.6	0.9	23.4	1.3	52.9	9.6	21.6	21.6
Cyprus - Chypre	1995	3 694	20.4	1.3	7.7	1.2	68.5	8.8	27.6	32.1
	2000	3 846	18.6	1.0	12.8	1.2	66.2	8.6	28.0	29.5
	2005	6 382	12.4	1.1	16.1	1.1	67.6	8.9	30.9	27.8
Czech Republic - République tchèque	1995	25 303	6.7	2.7	7.8	4.2	77.4	11.8	36.1	29.4
	2000	32 243	4.9	2.1	9.6	3.6	79.7	11.2	40.1	28.4
	2005	76 527	5.3	1.5	6.6	3.6	78.8	10.8	39.5	28.4
Dem. Rep. of the Congo - Rép. dém. du Congo	1995	862	23.5	3.1	10.5	1.0	62.0	9.5	21.0	31.5
	2000	694	27.7	2.3	14.2	1.8	54.0	11.7	21.8	20.6
	2005	2 253	25.6	2.1	9.4	1.7	61.3	12.1	25.4	23.8
Denmark - Danemark	1995	43 142	12.0	3.0	3.3	2.0	72.8	11.2	32.0	29.5
	2000	44 587	11.4	2.7	5.7	1.7	75.9	9.8	35.9	30.2
	2005	74 265	11.3	2.2	6.7	1.7	76.4	10.9	36.3	29.2
Dominican Republic - République dominicaine	1995	3 092	13.5	1.7	9.2	0.6	74.9	8.0	21.5	45.4
	2000	6 165	10.4	1.3	16.6	0.5	71.1	5.9	26.9	38.3
	2005	5 337	12.0	1.5	13.4	0.9	71.9	8.3	21.0	42.5
Ecuador - Équateur	1995	4 195	7.6	2.8	5.9	1.9	81.8	17.6	40.1	24.1
	2000	3 446	9.0	3.3	8.1	1.8	76.5	23.9	26.6	26.0
	2005	9 609	8.0	1.3	12.0	1.2	77.4	16.8	36.8	23.9
Egypt - Égypte	1995	11 739	28.4	7.1	1.2	2.7	60.6	13.2	25.3	22.1
	2000	14 010	25.2	4.8	7.6	2.4	55.4	11.6	25.3	18.5
	2005	20 582	22.3	5.1	8.3	3.9	49.5	12.0	19.0	18.5
El Salvador	1995	2 628	14.8	2.0	9.2	1.6	72.4	17.2	30.1	25.2
	2000	3 795	16.2	2.1	15.7	1.2	64.8	14.9	26.5	23.4
	2005	5 385	17.7	1.9	14.3	1.1	64.7	16.1	23.7	25.0
Equatorial Guinea - Guinée équatoriale	1995	50	24.3	2.5	3.2	0.6	69.3	10.1	26.5	32.7
	2000	428	10.3	0.6	9.9	0.3	78.9	5.6	52.5	20.7
	2005	1 109	15.0	0.8	1.9	1.0	81.3	3.5	50.2	27.6
Estonia - Estonie	1995	2 546	13.8	2.9	10.9	1.4	70.9	9.6	29.8	31.4
	2000	5 052	9.9	3.3	7.2	3.5	76.1	9.2	41.3	25.6
	2005	10 165	7.6	3.2	8.9	1.4	71.4	8.5	38.7	24.2

For sources and notes, see end of table.

Pour les sources et les notes, se reporter à la fin du tableau.

Country or territory / Pays ou territoires	Year / Année	Total value (millions of dollars) / Valeur totale (millions de dollars)	By main SITC Rev.3 product group (percentage) / Par principaux groupes de produits de la CTCI Rév.3 (en pourcentage)					Of which: / dont :		
			All food items / Produits alimentaires	Agricultural raw materials / Matières premières agricoles	Fuels / Combustibles	Ores and metals / Minérais et métaux	Manufactured products / Produits manufacturés	Chemical products / Produits chimiques	Machinery and transport equipment / Machines et matériel de transport	Other manufactured products / Produits manufacturés divers
			0+1+22+4	2 - (22+27+28)	3	27+28+68	5+6+7+8 - 68	5	7	(6+8) - 68
Ethiopia - Éthiopie	1995	1 141	13.8	1.9	11.1	0.8	72.4	14.1	35.5	22.7
	2000	1 260	7.0	1.2	20.1	0.7	71.0	11.5	31.9	27.6
	2005	4 127	21.5	0.7	11.9	1.5	64.4	8.9	30.6	24.8
Faeroe Islands - Îles Féroé	1995	303	23.1	3.6	12.1	1.2	60.0	7.6	28.5	23.9
	2000	520	20.8	2.5	8.3	0.9	67.6	7.1	37.4	23.0
	2005	748	18.1	3.2	14.2	1.4	61.0	8.0	26.5	26.6
Fiji - Fidji	1995	872	14.4	0.6	13.6	0.8	70.4	7.1	24.2	39.2
	2000	776	13.7	0.6	6.8	0.8	71.0	7.0	20.4	43.5
	2005	1 607	14.7	0.4	28.8	0.9	54.9	7.7	21.7	25.5
Finland - Finlande	1995	29 520	6.0	3.6	8.8	5.7	74.3	12.2	38.7	23.4
	2000	33 886	5.2	2.4	11.9	5.6	72.6	10.5	42.1	20.0
	2005	58 473	5.2	2.9	13.7	6.4	70.0	11.3	39.2	19.5
France	1995	275 510	10.7	2.5	6.9	3.5	76.1	12.5	35.4	28.2
	2000	303 797	7.9	1.9	9.9	2.9	77.3	12.2	39.2	25.9
	2005	475 999	7.8	1.5	13.4	2.6	74.7	13.3	35.7	25.7
French Polynesia - Polynésie française	1995	1 019	21.6	1.5	5.5	0.7	70.5	8.5	34.7	27.4
	2000	1 072	20.0	1.9	7.2	0.8	70.0	8.6	33.3	28.1
	2005	1 702	19.0	1.3	9.6	0.8	69.2	8.4	35.8	25.0
Gabon	1995	884	19.1	0.7	3.4	1.1	75.6	10.7	39.3	25.7
	2000	952	18.2	0.5	4.1	1.0	76.1	8.6	48.0	19.5
	2005	1 087	24.2	0.6	3.2	1.2	70.2	10.6	35.3	24.3
Gambia - Gambie	1995	215	36.4	0.7	14.1	0.3	45.8	5.9	22.0	17.9
	2000	189	34.5	0.7	11.9	0.8	51.2	5.6	21.9	23.7
	2005	260	37.7	1.4	16.0	1.0	43.6	4.1	21.5	18.0
Georgia - Géorgie	1995	412	36.1	0.2	38.8	0.5	24.5	4.8	9.7	9.9
	2000	651	22.6	0.6	21.2	0.7	54.9	10.1	26.7	18.1
	2005	2 491	17.4	0.4	19.9	0.6	61.7	9.6	29.4	22.8
Germany - Allemagne	1995	464 145	9.8	2.6	6.2	4.0	70.0	9.1	31.8	29.0
	2000	500 814	6.6	1.7	8.7	3.5	67.4	8.9	35.8	22.6
	2005	776 843	6.5	1.4	11.1	3.7	67.8	11.3	35.3	21.2
Ghana	1995	1 750	8.6	1.1	6.3	2.8	81.2	10.1	47.3	23.8
	2000	2 933	12.8	2.4	21.4	2.9	59.5	9.8	30.4	19.3
	2005	5 068	20.8	1.3	1.6	2.1	74.2	13.5	39.3	21.5
Gibraltar	1995	406	11.4	0.5	60.1	0.2	26.9	2.4	12.6	11.9
	2000	447	8.4	0.2	9.0	1.7	80.5	4.7	61.4	14.5
	2005	469	10.2	0.3	17.2	1.5	70.7	7.3	45.2	18.1
Greece - Grèce	1995	25 927	16.0	2.5	7.2	3.0	71.1	13.2	27.4	30.5
	2000	29 816	11.3	1.5	13.4	2.7	71.0	11.6	34.6	24.8
	2005	54 894	11.2	1.2	17.9	3.0	66.4	14.4	28.9	23.1
Greenland - Groenland	1995	421	14.2	1.2	5.8	0.4	59.3	4.3	24.6	30.4
	2000	347	15.3	0.8	18.9	0.4	52.3	3.5	26.8	22.0
	2005	497	19.2	1.6	9.9	0.5	68.7	4.9	26.8	37.0
Grenada - Grenade	1995	129	27.5	2.5	7.8	0.4	61.8	8.8	21.3	31.7
	2000	239	18.4	2.2	8.8	0.8	69.9	6.6	32.9	30.4
	2005	288	23.6	2.6	6.1	0.5	67.2	6.1	25.5	35.5
Guatemala	1995	3 292	11.9	1.5	12.4	1.2	73.0	17.2	31.5	24.3
	2000	4 882	12.1	1.7	12.7	1.3	72.2	16.4	32.6	23.3
	2005	10 500	10.9	1.2	15.5	1.0	71.3	15.8	23.1	32.4
Guinea - Guinée	1995	819	31.0	1.0	19.1	0.8	47.4	6.6	20.9	19.9
	2000	612	24.2	1.2	24.9	0.7	48.7	8.7	19.0	21.0
	2005	733	23.2	1.2	21.7	0.8	53.1	12.9	19.2	21.1

For sources and notes, see end of table.   Pour les sources et les notes, se reporter à la fin du tableau.

3.1 Country trade structure
by product group
Imports

3.1 Structure du commerce des pays
par groupes de produits
Importations

Country or territory / Pays ou territoires	Year / Année	Total value (millions of dollars) / Valeur totale (millions de dollars)	By main SITC Rev.3 product group (percentage) / Par principaux groupes de produits de la CTCI Rév.3 (en pourcentage)					Of which: / dont :		
			All food items / Produits alimentaires	Agricultural raw materials / Matières premières agricoles	Fuels / Combustibles	Ores and metals / Minérais et métaux	Manufactured products / Produits manufacturés	Chemical products / Produits chimiques	Machinery and transport equipment / Machines et matériel de transport	Other manufactured products / Produits manufacturés divers
			0+1+22+4	2 - (22+27+28)	3	27+28+68	5+6+7+8 - 68	5	7	(6+8) - 68
Guyana	1995	472	15.8	0.5	6.3	0.6	76.9	12.5	39.0	25.5
	2000	573	13.9	0.5	22.3	0.4	62.7	11.4	27.0	24.2
	2005	778	15.1	0.5	29.4	0.7	53.4	10.6	22.0	20.8
Haiti - Haïti	1995	608	41.5	2.0	4.1	0.6	51.7	6.0	23.4	22.3
	2000	982	35.6	1.6	6.6	0.8	55.3	6.0	14.8	34.5
	2005	1 320	39.5	1.3	2.0	0.4	56.6	6.1	17.4	33.2
Honduras	1995	1 728	12.6	1.1	11.5	1.2	73.6	17.3	29.1	27.2
	2000	2 482	22.2	2.4	18.3	1.0	50.1	20.7	6.3	23.0
	2005	4 565	15.8	0.8	19.8	0.9	62.7	16.6	22.4	23.7
Hungary - Hongrie	1995	15 186	5.7	3.0	11.9	4.3	75.2	14.5	30.1	30.6
	2000	32 079	2.9	1.5	4.7	2.7	84.0	8.9	51.0	24.1
	2005	66 741	3.8	1.1	6.5	2.0	76.9	8.8	48.9	19.3
Iceland - Islande	1995	1 751	11.8	1.6	7.2	4.6	74.7	9.3	32.4	32.9
	2000	2 380	9.1	1.2	9.4	4.8	75.5	7.9	39.7	27.8
	2005	4 979	7.8	1.3	9.4	4.1	77.3	7.8	41.9	27.7
India - Inde	1995	36 592	4.2	4.0	23.7	6.8	52.8	15.4	20.2	17.3
	2000	51 377	4.4	3.2	34.7	4.7	42.9	9.0	15.1	18.8
	2005	149 750	3.1	1.9	33.7	4.7	48.4	9.3	22.8	16.4
Indonesia - Indonésie	1995	40 629	8.8	6.2	7.4	4.6	72.9	15.4	40.1	17.4
	2000	33 515	10.0	7.1	18.1	3.6	61.2	17.6	27.5	16.1
	2005	57 701	8.1	3.5	30.3	3.3	54.8	14.0	26.5	14.3
Iran, Islamic Republic of - Iran, Rép. islamique d'	1995	13 882	20.9	2.4	1.8	3.2	69.8	13.3	35.6	20.9
	2000	13 626	19.0	2.6	2.3	2.5	73.7	14.5	35.3	23.9
	2005	38 675	7.9	1.9	9.7	2.1	69.4	10.8	37.0	21.6
Ireland - Irlande	1995	32 321	8.5	1.2	3.3	2.1	75.7	12.8	42.3	20.7
	2000	50 689	6.3	1.0	4.1	1.2	81.8	11.0	53.1	17.7
	2005	70 292	7.9	1.0	6.9	1.4	76.9	12.9	43.9	20.1
Israel - Israël	1995	28 344	6.6	1.6	5.9	2.2	81.7	9.3	34.0	38.4
	2000	35 742	5.4	1.0	10.0	1.8	81.3	8.9	34.8	37.5
	2005	45 032	5.5	1.0	15.0	1.9	75.9	10.2	27.6	38.1
Italy - Italie	1995	200 320	11.5	5.6	7.3	5.0	66.9	13.1	29.8	24.0
	2000	238 257	8.5	4.0	9.7	4.4	68.0	12.2	33.3	22.6
	2005	380 561	8.5	2.6	11.9	4.1	65.9	13.0	30.1	22.9
Jamaica - Jamaïque	1995	2 773	14.3	1.6	12.7	0.9	67.6	9.9	27.5	30.3
	2000	3 192	15.5	1.5	18.4	0.6	61.3	10.7	23.3	27.3
	2005	4 514	15.6	1.6	23.4	0.5	57.1	10.5	22.3	24.3
Japan - Japon	1995	336 094	16.1	6.2	16.0	6.5	53.0	7.1	22.6	23.3
	2000	379 663	12.8	3.6	20.4	5.5	56.1	6.9	27.9	21.3
	2005	515 866	10.4	2.4	25.8	6.0	53.6	7.3	25.7	20.6
Jordan - Jordanie	1995	3 696	20.6	2.1	12.9	2.5	60.5	12.3	24.5	23.7
	2000	4 013	21.2	2.3	4.8	2.5	65.9	12.0	32.3	21.6
	2005	10 455	13.6	1.2	23.1	1.9	57.7	8.8	25.1	23.8
Kazakhstan	1995	3 805	9.8	2.1	25.0	4.6	58.4	9.4	27.8	21.3
	2000	5 033	9.1	0.9	11.2	3.1	75.3	11.9	38.8	24.6
	2005	17 352	7.3	0.9	11.9	1.6	78.3	9.3	41.4	27.5
Kenya	1995	2 818	10.1	1.9	14.7	2.0	71.3	17.6	33.5	20.2
	2000	2 891	14.0	2.5	22.2	1.5	59.9	14.7	27.8	17.4
	2005	6 163	10.4	2.1	24.3	1.6	61.6	15.7	24.3	21.6
Korea, Republic of - Corée, République de	1995	135 113	5.4	5.5	14.1	6.3	66.7	9.7	36.6	20.3
	2000	160 479	4.8	3.2	23.7	5.5	61.4	8.4	36.8	16.1
	2005	261 236	4.4	2.0	25.8	6.7	60.7	9.4	31.6	19.7

For sources and notes, see end of table.

Pour les sources et les notes, se reporter à la fin du tableau.

Country or territory / Pays ou territoires	Year / Année	Total value (millions of dollars) / Valeur totale (millions de dollars)	By main SITC Rev.3 product group (percentage) / Par principaux groupes de produits de la CTCI Rév.3 (en pourcentage)					Of which: / dont :		
			All food items / Produits alimentaires	Agricultural raw materials / Matières premières agricoles	Fuels / Combustibles	Ores and metals / Minérais et métaux	Manufactured products / Produits manufacturés	Chemical products / Produits chimiques	Machinery and transport equipment / Machines et matériel de transport	Other manufactured products / Produits manufacturés divers
			0+1+22+4	2 - (22+27+28)	3	27+28+68	5+6+7+8 - 68	5	7	(6+8) - 68
Kuwait - Koweït	1995	7 790	15.5	1.1	0.5	1.7	80.8	7.3	41.2	32.3
	2000	7 157	17.5	0.9	0.6	2.2	77.6	8.5	37.4	31.8
	2005	16 143	10.5	0.5	1.5	1.2	86.2	6.4	51.1	28.7
Kyrgyzstan - Kirghizistan	1995	522	18.3	2.7	35.9	2.5	40.5	6.3	18.4	15.9
	2000	554	14.6	1.8	23.2	1.3	59.1	12.0	25.6	21.4
	2005	1 108	15.0	1.7	28.9	2.1	52.1	14.2	18.0	19.8
Lao People's Dem. Rep. - Rép. dém. populaire lao	1995	580	18.4	0.3	8.5	0.8	69.0	6.8	35.0	27.2
	2000	529	14.1	0.6	21.4	0.9	62.5	6.7	31.8	24.0
	2005	783	15.5	0.6	15.2	0.8	66.9	7.3	31.3	28.2
Latvia - Lettonie	1995	1 818	10.5	1.7	21.2	1.0	65.6	12.7	25.4	27.5
	2000	3 191	12.3	2.0	12.3	2.0	71.4	12.5	28.2	30.7
	2005	8 770	10.8	2.7	15.1	1.5	66.5	10.2	28.7	27.7
Lebanon - Liban	1995	5 480	19.4	1.8	8.2	2.2	62.7	8.9	25.7	28.1
	2000	6 227	17.8	1.7	16.5	2.1	56.0	10.2	21.8	24.0
	2005	9 356	15.5	1.3	21.1	2.2	56.2	11.0	20.8	24.5
Lesotho	2000	613	17.6	0.9	18.9	2.3	48.4	5.9	7.7	34.8
	2005	1 278	24.4	0.9	8.1	0.9	65.8	13.1	13.0	39.7
Libyan Arab Jamahiriya - Jamahiriya arabe libyenne	1995	5 033	22.8	0.9	0.2	0.7	74.8	7.5	36.0	31.4
	2000	3 731	27.4	0.9	0.3	1.3	69.8	7.4	33.3	29.2
	2005	6 529	16.8	0.6	0.7	0.9	81.1	4.1	48.0	29.0
Lithuania - Lituanie	1995	3 649	13.1	3.9	19.4	3.9	57.8	12.5	21.7	23.6
	2000	5 456	9.7	3.0	21.7	2.2	60.7	12.3	24.3	24.1
	2005	15 704	8.0	2.3	24.2	1.5	62.5	11.0	29.7	21.8
Luxembourg	2005	17 586	10.2	1.1	9.2	6.4	68.3	9.5	31.3	27.5
Madagascar	1995	550	16.3	1.8	14.0	0.6	65.1	13.0	25.7	26.4
	2000	943	13.8	0.4	23.4	0.3	61.7	8.1	16.5	37.0
	2005	1 072	13.5	0.4	23.3	0.4	61.8	8.6	30.7	22.6
Malawi	1995	500	13.9	0.6	11.1	0.9	73.4	22.6	27.6	23.2
	2000	532	9.8	1.5	15.7	0.7	72.1	12.7	33.1	26.4
	2005	1 165	18.2	1.0	10.5	0.8	69.4	21.4	22.0	25.9
Malaysia - Malaisie	1995	77 046	4.8	1.2	2.3	3.2	83.6	7.1	60.0	16.6
	2000	81 290	4.3	1.3	4.8	3.0	83.8	7.2	62.6	13.9
	2005	114 584	5.1	1.2	8.1	3.6	79.0	7.9	57.4	13.8
Maldives	1995	268	24.0	2.1	11.4	1.9	60.7	5.9	26.5	28.4
	2000	389	23.6	1.8	11.7	1.9	61.0	5.4	25.1	30.6
	2005	745	15.6	3.6	15.5	2.3	63.0	5.3	30.8	27.0
Mali	1995	773	20.0	0.8	15.6	1.1	62.6	14.9	21.7	26.0
	2000	806	15.1	0.9	23.6	0.7	59.5	13.8	25.2	20.6
	2005	1 703	13.7	0.6	21.1	0.6	63.7	17.4	22.4	23.9
Malta - Malte	1995	2 942	10.1	0.8	3.9	1.0	83.3	6.9	51.9	24.5
	2000	3 399	8.4	0.5	7.1	0.7	82.5	6.2	57.1	19.2
	2005	3 660	11.8	0.8	7.4	0.7	78.4	9.1	45.4	23.9
Mauritania - Mauritanie	1995	455	23.6	0.6	22.0	0.3	53.4	4.3	33.3	15.8
	2000	354	18.7	0.4	22.9	0.3	40.9	3.1	25.3	12.6
	2005	1 342	10.2	0.2	10.0	0.2	79.3	2.4	67.3	9.7
Mauritius - Maurice	1995	2 000	16.6	3.1	6.9	0.8	71.8	7.7	19.2	44.9
	2000	2 081	14.2	2.4	11.7	1.1	70.4	7.7	22.6	40.1
	2005	3 160	16.7	1.9	16.4	1.0	63.8	7.9	28.1	27.7
Mexico - Mexique	1995	72 453	6.3	2.3	2.1	2.2	80.1	9.8	43.2	27.1
	2000	174 412	4.9	1.4	3.0	2.0	85.9	8.7	51.2	26.0
	2005	221 819	6.0	1.4	5.5	2.5	83.5	11.0	48.1	24.3

For sources and notes, see end of table.

Pour les sources et les notes, se reporter à la fin du tableau.

Country or territory / Pays ou territoires	Year / Année	Total value (millions of dollars) / Valeur totale (millions de dollars)	By main SITC Rev.3 product group (percentage) / Par principaux groupes de produits de la CTCI Rév.3 (en pourcentage)					Of which: / dont :		
			All food items / Produits alimentaires	Agricultural raw materials / Matières premières agricoles	Fuels / Combustibles	Ores and metals / Minérais et métaux	Manufactured products / Produits manufacturés	Chemical products / Produits chimiques	Machinery and transport equipment / Machines et matériel de transport	Other manufactured products / Produits manufacturés divers
			0+1+22+4	2 - (22+27+28)	3	27+28+68	5+6+7+8 - 68	5	7	(6+8) - 68
Moldova, Republic of - Moldova, République de	1995	841	8.1	2.6	45.9	1.5	41.7	9.2	15.2	17.3
	2000	777	13.1	2.4	32.4	1.1	51.0	11.3	14.3	25.4
	2005	2 293	11.5	4.0	21.2	0.9	62.4	13.3	18.8	30.4
Mongolia - Mongolie	1995	415	14.3	0.7	19.3	0.7	65.1	5.0	39.7	20.3
	2000	615	16.6	0.6	19.1	0.4	63.4	4.9	33.7	24.8
	2005	1 183	13.0	0.4	26.6	0.5	59.5	5.0	31.2	23.2
Morocco - Maroc	1995	8 540	19.5	6.3	13.7	4.0	56.4	11.9	23.3	21.2
	2000	11 533	13.7	3.1	17.7	2.5	62.9	8.7	27.5	26.7
	2005	20 342	10.7	2.8	21.8	2.8	61.7	9.3	26.2	26.2
Mozambique	1995	727	22.3	3.3	9.9	0.6	62.3	10.7	35.8	15.7
	2000	1 162	14.0	0.4	13.3	0.8	69.2	6.5	38.9	23.7
	2005	2 408	14.4	1.0	1.6	0.4	49.4	6.2	25.8	17.4
Myanmar	1995	1 337	21.9	0.7	4.0	0.5	71.7	9.6	33.1	29.0
	2000	2 384	11.7	0.4	15.1	0.7	72.1	11.7	27.3	33.1
	2005	1 931	12.6	0.6	12.8	0.9	73.0	12.7	29.8	30.5
Namibia - Namibie	2000	1 435	16.9	0.7	3.1	0.9	78.2	8.6	37.7	32.0
	2005	2 516	17.7	0.7	2.0	1.0	78.0	10.7	37.5	29.7
Nepal - Népal	1995	1 047	12.1	2.9	11.7	3.3	45.7	10.6	18.5	16.6
	2000	1 558	11.9	3.5	15.2	2.8	45.6	10.7	17.2	17.7
	2005	1 860	17.3	4.6	15.6	3.9	58.6	10.2	16.0	32.4
Netherlands - Pays-Bas	1995	157 929	13.9	2.4	7.7	3.5	71.9	13.1	32.9	25.9
	2000	174 671	9.8	2.0	11.5	2.9	73.8	10.6	41.4	21.8
	2005	283 172	9.7	1.6	16.2	3.5	68.9	12.7	36.2	19.9
Netherlands Antilles - Antilles néerlandaises	1995	1 807	9.8	0.5	51.1	0.4	38.1	3.0	17.0	18.1
	2000	2 018	9.1	0.7	58.5	6.1	25.6	4.3	10.3	10.9
	2005	1 990	13.0	0.5	20.3	2.8	63.4	6.6	19.4	37.4
New Caledonia - Nouvelle-Calédonie	1995	951	15.7	1.0	11.4	0.7	71.2	9.1	34.3	27.8
	2000	1 017	15.1	1.0	14.7	0.8	68.3	9.1	33.2	26.0
	2005	1 774	13.2	0.8	15.8	0.9	69.0	9.2	35.0	24.8
New Zealand - Nouvelle-Zélande	1995	13 958	7.4	1.2	5.3	3.5	82.5	13.1	42.2	27.2
	2000	13 904	7.7	0.9	10.4	3.1	77.8	12.3	39.4	26.1
	2005	26 219	7.6	0.8	12.1	2.3	76.7	11.2	40.7	24.8
Nicaragua	1995	1 009	17.9	0.9	17.9	0.6	62.6	17.5	23.1	22.0
	2000	1 721	15.9	0.6	17.8	0.8	64.9	14.7	24.8	25.3
	2005	2 520	13.2	0.5	18.3	0.4	64.8	17.1	23.1	24.6
Niger	1995	345	32.4	0.7	12.9	3.1	51.0	11.4	17.3	22.3
	2000	385	35.1	3.6	21.4	1.7	38.2	9.8	13.0	15.4
	2005	736	34.2	4.0	14.6	1.4	45.7	7.4	19.2	19.1
Nigeria - Nigéria	1995	4 932	11.3	0.9	5.1	1.0	81.7	17.8	36.1	27.8
	2000	5 817	19.9	0.9	1.7	2.4	75.0	20.2	33.6	21.2
	2005	15 200	15.5	0.6	16.0	1.6	66.3	10.3	38.0	18.0
Norway - Norvège	1995	32 706	6.8	2.7	2.9	6.7	80.0	9.6	37.7	32.7
	2000	34 358	6.5	2.1	3.5	6.7	80.3	8.7	44.6	27.0
	2005	55 488	6.8	1.9	4.2	7.7	78.9	9.4	39.5	30.1
Oman	1995	4 249	19.8	0.8	1.5	2.4	68.2	6.8	39.4	22.0
	2000	5 039	22.3	0.7	1.6	3.0	68.7	6.4	43.3	19.1
	2005	8 827	12.0	0.5	4.2	4.0	77.0	8.2	48.2	20.6
Pakistan	1995	11 704	17.5	5.5	16.1	2.6	56.7	17.0	28.9	10.8
	2000	11 070	13.8	3.2	32.5	2.1	46.0	18.1	18.5	9.3
	2005	25 097	10.4	4.2	21.1	3.3	59.0	16.3	29.4	13.3

For sources and notes, see end of table.

Pour les sources et les notes, se reporter à la fin du tableau.

Country or territory / Pays ou territoires	Year / Année	Total value (millions of dollars) / Valeur totale (millions de dollars)	All food items / Produits alimentaires	Agricultural raw materials / Matières premières agricoles	Fuels / Combustibles	Ores and metals / Minérais et métaux	Manufactured products / Produits manufacturés	Chemical products / Produits chimiques	Machinery and transport equipment / Machines et matériel de transport	Other manufactured products / Produits manufacturés divers
			0+1+22+4	2 - (22+27+28)	3	27+28+68	5+6+7+8 - 68	5	7	(6+8) - 68
Palau, Pacific Islands (former) - Palaos, Îles du Pacifique (anc.)	1995	56	28.0	3.6	4.5	0.3	63.6	4.0	28.6	30.9
	2000	114	26.3	2.3	14.7	1.1	55.6	2.6	30.0	23.1
	2005	137	22.8	2.8	0.1	2.3	72.1	5.5	30.9	35.7
Panama	1995	2 511	10.7	0.8	13.6	1.4	73.1	13.5	29.0	30.6
	2000	3 378	11.7	0.5	18.6	0.9	68.4	11.6	29.6	27.2
	2005	4 155	12.5	0.5	17.9	1.0	68.0	12.8	29.0	26.3
Papua New Guinea - Papouasie-Nouvelle-Guinée	1995	1 398	14.8	0.9	11.2	0.6	72.5	6.6	40.9	24.9
	2000	1 035	18.3	0.7	22.1	0.9	57.6	7.1	29.5	21.0
	2005	1 724	16.5	0.7	13.3	0.5	68.9	8.4	35.0	25.5
Paraguay	1995	3 136	18.5	0.2	6.5	0.7	74.0	9.0	42.3	22.7
	2000	2 193	17.2	0.5	13.5	0.7	67.9	14.2	29.1	24.6
	2005	3 715	8.2	1.2	14.5	0.9	75.1	15.2	36.1	23.8
Peru - Pérou	1995	7 584	13.5	1.9	8.8	0.8	75.0	13.2	39.2	22.6
	2000	7 415	11.6	1.8	15.6	0.6	70.3	15.5	32.8	22.1
	2005	12 502	11.4	1.8	19.8	1.0	66.0	16.1	28.3	21.6
Philippines	1995	28 487	8.3	2.2	9.2	3.2	57.8	9.2	32.5	16.2
	2000	37 007	7.0	1.4	11.1	2.5	69.3	8.0	48.0	13.3
	2005	46 954	7.3	0.9	13.9	2.4	75.3	7.6	55.9	11.7
Poland - Pologne	1995	29 019	9.6	3.2	9.1	3.3	74.4	14.9	29.9	29.5
	2000	48 834	6.1	2.0	10.8	2.9	78.2	14.1	37.1	27.0
	2005	101 539	6.1	1.8	11.4	2.9	75.5	14.0	35.1	26.4
Portugal	1995	33 565	13.6	3.6	8.1	2.1	72.0	10.4	33.8	27.9
	2000	39 947	11.2	2.6	10.3	2.4	73.1	9.4	37.3	26.3
	2005	61 167	11.0	1.5	14.7	2.5	65.2	10.6	30.7	23.9
Qatar	1995	3 398	9.4	0.6	0.4	2.3	87.0	5.0	48.3	33.7
	2000	3 252	11.7	0.6	0.4	2.6	84.4	6.4	44.8	33.2
	2005	10 061	6.6	0.7	0.2	2.2	89.3	6.6	49.1	33.6
Romania - Roumanie	1995	10 278	8.5	2.3	21.4	3.6	63.3	10.6	24.8	28.0
	2000	13 054	7.0	1.4	12.1	3.8	75.2	10.0	29.2	36.1
	2005	40 463	6.0	1.0	13.9	2.7	76.0	10.2	33.2	32.6
Russian Federation - Fédération de Russie	1995	31 944	26.1	1.2	4.0	4.9	63.8	10.5	28.8	24.5
	2000	33 921	20.2	2.1	4.4	6.4	53.9	11.4	22.8	19.7
	2005	98 577	16.1	1.0	1.5	3.2	71.9	12.7	39.9	19.4
Rwanda	1995	241	18.9	2.5	11.5	2.8	64.3	9.3	31.8	23.2
	2000	211	20.8	2.9	14.4	1.9	60.0	8.9	21.7	29.3
	2005	433	11.7	4.0	15.6	2.0	66.7	12.1	28.7	25.8
Saint Kitts and Nevis - Saint-Kitts-et-Nevis	1995	132	21.1	2.5	4.3	0.9	71.2	8.3	27.8	35.1
	2000	196	19.0	2.5	7.6	0.7	70.1	7.5	28.1	34.6
	2005	210	18.5	1.5	8.8	0.8	70.4	6.9	31.2	32.3
Saint Lucia - Sainte-Lucie	1995	306	26.7	2.4	7.6	1.0	62.2	9.4	19.1	33.7
	2000	355	23.6	2.4	9.3	0.9	63.8	8.2	24.6	31.0
	2005	475	22.1	2.2	14.0	0.9	60.8	7.4	21.7	31.7
Saint Vincent and the Grenadines - Saint-Vincent-et-les Grenadines	1995	134	22.5	2.6	6.0	0.5	68.3	12.9	17.7	37.7
	2000	162	26.7	2.4	9.6	0.7	60.6	10.1	19.0	31.6
	2005	240	21.5	2.4	13.9	0.6	61.7	9.2	22.1	30.4
Samoa	1995	94	16.8	0.9	7.2	0.4	74.8	5.1	47.3	22.4
	2000	106	24.4	1.4	12.5	0.5	61.2	7.7	26.8	26.7
	2005	253	23.4	2.0	14.3	0.9	59.4	6.2	18.9	34.3
Saudi Arabia - Arabie saoudite	1995	28 085	16.1	1.2	0.2	3.5	75.0	9.6	35.6	29.7
	2000	30 237	17.8	1.0	0.2	3.0	74.2	9.6	39.2	25.4
	2005	59 511	14.6	0.7	0.2	4.1	79.0	9.7	45.2	24.0

For sources and notes, see end of table.   Pour les sources et les notes, se reporter à la fin du tableau.

Country or territory / Pays ou territoires	Year / Année	Total value (millions of dollars) / Valeur totale (millions de dollars)	By main SITC Rev.3 product group (percentage) / Par principaux groupes de produits de la CTCI Rév.3 (en pourcentage)					Of which: / dont :		
			All food items / Produits alimentaires	Agricultural raw materials / Matières premières agricoles	Fuels / Combustibles	Ores and metals / Minérais et métaux	Manufactured products / Produits manufacturés	Chemical products / Produits chimiques	Machinery and transport equipment / Machines et matériel de transport	Other manufactured products / Produits manufacturés divers
			0+1+22+4	2 - (22+27+28)	3	27+28+68	5+6+7+8 - 68	5	7	(6+8) - 68
Senegal - Sénégal	1995	1 224	32.5	2.2	10.0	1.6	53.7	13.9	18.1	21.7
	2000	1 553	23.3	2.1	22.5	1.3	50.8	10.6	22.8	17.3
	2005	3 498	28.1	1.6	22.9	2.2	45.1	9.2	20.1	15.8
Serbia and Montenegro - Serbie-et-Monténégro	1995	2 643	14.4	4.1	14.0	7.1	60.3	14.4	19.6	26.4
	2000	3 711	9.3	3.6	20.1	3.7	63.3	15.0	22.1	26.3
	2005	11 637	8.2	1.5	15.0	4.2	70.8	12.9	31.4	26.4
Seychelles	1995	255	21.2	1.4	17.4	0.7	59.1	6.5	27.0	25.5
	2000	342	22.2	1.1	10.0	0.7	66.1	5.6	28.9	31.6
	2005	675	21.5	1.0	23.5	0.3	48.3	4.3	24.6	19.3
Singapore - Singapour	1995	124 503	4.6	0.9	8.1	2.3	83.0	6.5	57.9	18.7
	2000	134 546	3.2	0.4	12.1	1.6	81.6	5.7	60.7	15.1
	2005	200 050	2.8	0.4	17.7	1.6	76.1	6.2	55.8	14.1
Slovakia - Slovaquie	1995	8 162	8.9	2.8	12.7	5.9	69.6	14.5	30.2	24.9
	2000	12 774	5.6	1.8	17.5	3.7	71.3	11.0	35.7	24.7
	2005	34 446	5.8	1.3	13.8	3.5	74.9	9.6	37.7	27.6
Slovenia - Slovénie	1995	9 492	7.8	4.6	6.6	4.3	73.8	12.1	33.8	28.0
	2000	10 115	6.0	3.6	9.1	5.2	75.9	12.4	34.2	29.3
	2005	20 353	6.4	2.6	10.2	5.9	74.8	12.4	32.9	29.5
South Africa - Afrique du Sud	1995	26 745	6.7	2.3	8.3	2.4	77.8	12.4	44.9	20.5
	2000	26 785	4.7	1.5	14.3	2.6	67.7	11.6	36.4	19.7
	2005	55 033	4.5	1.1	14.3	2.6	68.9	10.0	39.4	19.5
Spain - Espagne	1995	113 399	13.6	3.0	8.3	3.9	70.9	12.1	35.6	23.2
	2000	152 898	9.1	2.0	12.1	3.2	72.9	10.7	40.7	21.5
	2005	289 611	9.2	1.4	14.0	3.3	71.5	11.6	37.9	22.0
Sri Lanka	1995	5 037	15.3	1.7	2.3	1.5	79.1	9.5	25.7	43.9
	2000	6 281	14.2	1.3	9.4	1.1	72.7	9.1	18.5	45.1
	2005	8 307	12.4	1.2	13.4	3.5	68.9	10.0	20.2	38.7
Sudan - Soudan	1995	1 185	24.4	1.8	13.9	0.5	59.4	10.8	27.8	20.8
	2000	1 657	21.7	1.0	7.4	0.9	69.1	12.1	33.9	23.1
	2005	6 976	13.0	0.7	1.2	1.0	83.5	9.2	46.2	28.2
Suriname	1995	583	14.0	0.1	11.8	1.2	73.0	16.0	35.7	21.3
	2000	526	18.1	0.4	6.7	0.9	73.3	10.6	36.3	26.4
	2005	905	13.9	0.1	13.9	0.8	69.6	8.9	37.9	22.9
Swaziland	2000	1 099	18.7	2.3	12.6	0.8	64.2	11.2	27.3	25.7
	2005	2 223	18.6	2.2	12.8	1.0	65.4	11.8	23.0	30.5
Sweden - Suède	1995	61 647	6.7	2.2	5.8	3.8	80.0	10.7	41.8	27.5
	2000	67 741	6.3	1.1	8.9	3.3	75.2	9.6	41.4	24.2
	2005	111 351	7.4	1.6	11.7	3.3	73.3	10.3	38.6	24.3
Switzerland - Suisse	1995	80 152	6.4	2.0	2.9	3.0	85.4	14.6	33.4	37.3
	2000	83 584	5.5	1.4	4.6	5.7	82.7	16.4	33.2	33.0
	2005	121 216	5.6	1.1	6.0	3.6	83.1	22.6	28.8	31.6
Syrian Arab Republic - République arabe syrienne	1995	4 709	16.7	3.3	1.1	1.3	75.6	10.2	31.6	33.9
	2000	3 815	19.0	3.3	3.7	1.8	64.7	13.0	20.9	30.8
	2005	8 101	16.7	3.9	7.3	2.7	64.0	13.8	23.9	26.2
Tajikistan - Tadjikistan	1995	804	29.9	0.8	18.7	11.3	39.3	6.6	19.9	12.8
	2000	644	10.2	0.7	37.5	0.1	51.3	36.4	9.6	5.3
	2005	1 578	13.3	2.6	12.2	20.0	51.8	8.7	16.9	26.2
Thailand - Thaïlande	1995	70 781	3.8	4.1	6.7	3.2	80.3	10.5	47.5	22.3
	2000	61 451	4.3	2.9	12.3	3.1	75.8	11.1	44.6	20.1
	2005	118 164	4.0	2.0	17.7	3.9	69.5	10.2	38.0	21.3

For sources and notes, see end of table.

Pour les sources et les notes, se reporter à la fin du tableau.

Country or territory / Pays ou territoires	Year / Année	Total value (millions of dollars) / Valeur totale (millions de dollars)	By main SITC Rev.3 product group (percentage) / Par principaux groupes de produits de la CTCI Rév.3 (en pourcentage)						Of which: / dont :		
			All food items / Produits alimentaires	Agricultural raw materials / Matières premières agricoles	Fuels / Combustibles	Ores and metals / Minérais et métaux	Manufactured products / Produits manufacturés	Chemical products / Produits chimiques	Machinery and transport equipment / Machines et matériel de transport	Other manufactured products / Produits manufacturés divers
			0+1+22+4	2 - (22+27+28)	3	27+28+68	5+6+7+8 - 68	5	7	(6+8) - 68
Macedonia, TFYR - Macédoine, LERY	1995	1 719	17.4	3.3	11.6	3.0	54.2	11.9	19.5	22.8
	2000	2 094	12.1	1.8	13.8	1.9	45.1	9.0	19.6	16.5
	2005	3 228	12.7	1.3	19.2	3.2	63.6	10.3	17.4	35.8
Togo	1995	556	18.4	1.9	29.9	1.3	48.5	8.5	17.2	22.8
	2000	324	18.4	1.7	18.8	1.6	59.5	10.7	18.6	30.3
	2005	593	15.5	0.8	29.0	2.1	52.6	8.1	16.0	28.5
Trinidad and Tobago - Trinité-et-Tobago	1995	1 724	15.7	0.7	0.5	5.7	77.0	13.1	36.7	27.2
	2000	3 308	8.3	1.0	32.3	2.0	56.1	7.9	30.6	17.6
	2005	5 694	9.0	0.6	34.8	4.3	51.2	7.3	26.4	17.4
Tunisia - Tunisie	1995	7 903	12.5	4.2	7.2	3.0	72.8	9.1	25.9	37.8
	2000	8 566	8.2	3.1	10.5	2.5	75.5	8.9	32.5	34.0
	2005	13 174	8.5	2.6	13.7	3.0	72.0	10.5	28.8	32.7
Turkey - Turquie	1995	35 707	7.0	5.6	12.9	5.8	68.6	15.0	32.2	21.5
	2000	54 150	3.9	3.7	13.9	4.0	70.7	13.6	37.6	19.6
	2005	116 774	2.8	2.7	13.5	5.9	66.4	13.8	32.4	20.2
Turkmenistan - Turkménistan	1995	775	24.5	0.4	2.7	1.7	70.7	11.3	36.7	22.7
	2000	1 786	11.7	0.4	1.2	1.0	79.8	8.9	43.8	27.1
	2005	2 230	5.9	0.8	0.5	0.5	92.3	9.2	58.0	25.2
Turks and Caicos Islands - Îles Turques et Caïques	1995	38	15.8	2.3	1.3	0.4	80.2	27.9	22.7	29.6
	2000	149	21.4	2.2	10.4	0.9	65.0	6.0	29.4	29.6
	2005	221	18.4	2.7	7.7	1.2	70.0	5.9	28.3	35.8
Uganda - Ouganda	1995	1 038	15.8	2.6	1.8	2.0	77.8	10.7	34.8	32.4
	2000	936	14.1	2.2	17.5	1.5	64.7	11.4	27.1	26.1
	2005	2 054	15.0	1.5	17.0	1.2	65.3	13.1	26.2	26.1
Ukraine	1995	15 905	7.9	2.4	48.2	3.2	38.3	6.8	17.2	14.3
	2000	13 956	6.3	1.5	43.0	5.4	41.1	8.8	17.5	14.8
	2005	36 122	7.2	1.3	29.5	3.9	57.1	11.8	26.4	18.8
United Arab Emirates - Émirats arabes unis	1995	20 707	10.1	0.9	1.6	2.2	85.1	6.4	37.4	41.3
	2000	27 192	11.1	0.8	0.8	2.0	84.9	7.9	39.8	37.1
	2005	78 315	7.5	0.6	0.7	4.2	68.0	5.8	31.3	31.0
United Kingdom - Royaume-Uni	1995	261 456	10.1	2.4	3.5	3.4	79.9	10.3	41.3	28.3
	2000	339 445	7.8	1.7	4.3	2.8	81.5	9.5	45.3	26.7
	2005	515 782	8.5	1.3	8.3	2.3	72.2	10.4	35.8	26.0
United Republic of Tanzania - République-Unie de Tanzanie	1995	1 653	10.0	1.2	0.5	3.8	84.4	19.6	38.4	26.4
	2000	1 586	14.6	2.5	18.5	1.2	63.1	10.2	32.7	20.2
	2005	2 757	11.9	1.3	9.9	1.1	75.8	17.6	34.9	23.3
United States - États-Unis	1995	770 821	4.8	2.1	8.2	2.7	78.9	5.5	46.4	27.0
	2000	1 258 080	4.1	1.4	11.1	2.2	77.0	6.0	44.8	26.2
	2005	1 732 321	4.2	1.3	17.2	2.2	71.6	7.6	38.3	25.7
Uruguay	1995	2 866	10.4	4.0	10.1	1.2	74.4	15.3	34.5	24.5
	2000	3 466	11.5	2.6	15.3	1.1	69.5	16.9	28.0	24.5
	2005	3 879	8.1	3.1	24.3	1.6	62.9	19.4	23.2	20.3
Uzbekistan - Ouzbékistan	1995	2 874	16.1	1.8	1.5	3.0	77.6	9.6	37.5	30.4
	2000	2 913	11.2	1.0	8.7	3.2	75.9	11.1	40.7	24.2
	2005	3 126	5.3	2.3	0.6	1.1	90.7	11.6	50.1	29.0
Venezuela (Bolivarian Republic of) / Venezuela (République bolivarienne du)	1995	10 791	14.3	4.5	1.1	3.7	76.5	16.4	37.0	23.1
	2000	14 584	11.7	1.8	3.6	1.8	81.1	14.1	41.7	25.3
	2005	21 848	9.9	1.1	0.8	1.5	86.7	13.5	48.8	24.5
Viet Nam	1995	7 823	5.2	2.5	10.7	2.1	79.3	17.4	29.5	32.4
	2000	15 637	5.2	2.9	13.5	2.3	72.8	15.3	30.0	27.5
	2005	33 842	6.2	3.0	11.7	2.6	76.2	14.2	30.5	31.5

For sources and notes, see end of table.

Pour les sources et les notes, se reporter à la fin du tableau.

3.1   Country trade structure
       by product group
       Imports

3.1   Structure du commerce des pays
       par groupes de produits
       Importations

Country or territory Pays ou territoires	Year Année	Total value (millions of dollars) Valeur totale (millions de dollars)	By main SITC Rev.3 product group (percentage) Par principaux groupes de produits de la CTCI Rév.3 (en pourcentage)					Of which: / dont :		
			All food items Produits alimentaires	Agricultural raw materials Matières premières agricoles	Fuels Combus-tibles	Ores and metals Minérais et métaux	Manu-factured products Produits manu-facturés	Chemical products Produits chimiques	Machinery and transport equipment Machines et matériel de transport	Other manu-factured products Produits manu-facturés divers
			0+1+22+4	2 - (22+27+28)	3	27+28+68	5+6+7+8 - 68	5	7	(6+8) - 68
Yemen - Yémen	1995	1 816	29.0	2.4	7.9	1.4	59.4	8.2	23.1	28.1
	2000	2 308	35.9	1.5	12.1	1.2	49.3	9.8	21.0	18.6
	2005	4 863	23.7	1.0	21.4	1.1	52.8	8.1	22.5	22.2
Zambia - Zambie	1995	708	9.9	2.3	13.2	2.1	72.3	13.5	38.0	20.9
	2000	993	7.3	2.4	17.9	2.5	69.2	13.6	30.4	25.1
	2005	2 575	6.3	1.3	11.6	2.7	77.9	17.7	31.1	29.1
Zimbabwe	1995	2 659	6.0	1.9	9.0	2.1	78.2	13.8	42.4	22.1
	2000	1 867	3.9	1.5	43.0	2.6	49.0	15.1	20.0	13.9
	2005	2 751	18.8	1.8	13.7	7.4	56.6	12.3	26.4	17.9

Sources:
- UNCTAD secretariat calculations based on UN DESA Statistics Division's data

Sources :
- Calculs du secrétariat de la CNUCED sur la base des données de ONU DAES Division de statistique

3

Products ranked by average 2004-2005 values SITC Revision 3 (3-digit level) / Produits classés d'après la moyenne des valeurs de 2004-2005 CTCI révision 3 (positions à 3 chiffres)	1995			2005			Growth rates (percentage) Taux d'accroissement (en pourcentage) 1995-2005	
	Value (millions of dollars) / Valeur (millions de dollars)	% of the country grouping exports / En % des exportations du groupe de pays	% of world product exports / En % des exportations mondiales des produits	Value (millions of dollars) / Valeur (millions de dollars)	% of the country grouping exports / En % des exportations du groupe de pays	% of world product exports / En % des exportations mondiales des produits	Value / Valeur	Difference from world / Différence par rapport au monde
All commodity groups	**5 050 560**	**100.00**	**100.00**	**10 250 631**	**100.00**	**100.00**	**6.57**	**0.00**
333 Crude petroleum & bituminous oil	205 936	4.08	100.00	739 769	7.22	100.00	12.52	0.00
781 Passenger cars and race cars	232 452	4.60	100.00	485 053	4.73	100.00	7.35	0.00
776 Valves tubes; diodes, transistors	189 016	3.74	100.00	364 918	3.56	100.00	6.49	0.00
764 Telecommunicate equipment part nes	121 662	2.41	100.00	351 538	3.43	100.00	10.36	0.00
334 Heavy petroleum & bituminous oil	92 143	1.82	100.00	367 380	3.58	100.00	12.69	0.00
931 Transaction commodity unclassified	125 466	2.48	100.00	342 494	3.34	100.00	8.35	0.00
752 Computer equipment nes	131 912	2.61	100.00	270 005	2.63	100.00	5.97	0.00
784 Motor vehicle parts and accessories	112 746	2.23	100.00	232 528	2.27	100.00	7.05	0.00
542 Medicines including veterinary	45 340	0.90	100.00	204 917	2.00	100.00	17.06	0.00
759 Office equipment part & accessories	98 970	1.96	100.00	199 954	1.95	100.00	6.79	0.00
778 Electrical machinery apparatus nes	80 368	1.59	100.00	147 296	1.44	100.00	5.88	0.00
772 Electrical circuit equipment	66 460	1.32	100.00	141 877	1.38	100.00	7.14	0.00
792 Aircraft, spacecraft & equipment	68 231	1.35	100.00	127 876	1.25	100.00	4.85	0.00
343 Natural gas, liquefied or not	34 754	0.69	100.00	124 630	1.22	100.00	12.66	0.00
874 Measure analyze control device nes	52 692	1.04	100.00	110 458	1.08	100.00	7.23	0.00
713 Internal combustion engine part nes	55 416	1.10	100.00	112 926	1.10	100.00	6.69	0.00
728 Special industrial machine part nes	60 136	1.19	100.00	97 015	0.95	100.00	4.22	0.00
641 Paper and paperboard	72 227	1.43	100.00	95 408	0.93	100.00	3.35	0.00
821 Furniture part; bedding furnishing	45 209	0.90	100.00	97 185	0.95	100.00	7.52	0.00
845 Articles of apparel nes	45 134	0.89	100.00	91 539	0.89	100.00	6.71	0.00
782 Goods and service vehicles	45 235	0.90	100.00	89 074	0.87	100.00	5.85	0.00
699 Base metal manufactures nes	41 845	0.83	100.00	89 534	0.87	100.00	6.95	0.00
667 Pearls, precious semiprecious stone	39 711	0.79	100.00	90 140	0.88	100.00	8.13	0.00
893 Articles of plastic nes	42 194	0.84	100.00	84 301	0.82	100.00	6.87	0.00
515 Organo-inorganic compound acid salt	26 785	0.53	100.00	79 424	0.77	100.00	11.22	0.00
684 Aluminium	45 506	0.90	100.00	74 943	0.73	100.00	5.03	0.00
743 Gas pump, compressor, fan, filter	34 719	0.69	100.00	69 280	0.68	100.00	6.84	0.00
793 Ships boats floating structures	36 670	0.73	100.00	68 345	0.67	100.00	6.21	0.00
741 Heating cooling equipment parts nes	38 307	0.76	100.00	67 987	0.66	100.00	5.08	0.00
714 Non-electric engines excluding 712 713 718	26 243	0.52	100.00	68 174	0.67	100.00	9.34	0.00
851 Footwear	46 970	0.93	100.00	67 956	0.66	100.00	2.86	0.00
541 Pharmaceuticals excluding medicines	26 368	0.52	100.00	66 327	0.65	100.00	9.84	0.00
723 Civil engineering plant & equipment	29 635	0.59	100.00	68 992	0.67	100.00	7.16	0.00
842 Female clothing, woven	37 016	0.73	100.00	63 918	0.62	100.00	5.13	0.00
775 Household equipment nes	31 703	0.63	100.00	63 413	0.62	100.00	6.72	0.00
598 Miscellaneous chemical products nes	29 574	0.59	100.00	63 291	0.62	100.00	7.35	0.00
575 Other plastics, in primary forms	29 752	0.59	100.00	65 180	0.64	100.00	7.48	0.00
673 Flat iron non-alloy steel products	35 757	0.71	100.00	65 322	0.64	100.00	5.22	0.00
894 Baby carriage toy game sport good	41 064	0.81	100.00	64 046	0.62	100.00	3.58	0.00
763 Sound TV recorder or reproducer	21 475	0.43	100.00	62 160	0.61	100.00	12.21	0.00
773 Electrical distribute equipment nes	29 832	0.59	100.00	60 591	0.59	100.00	6.04	0.00
682 Copper	35 260	0.70	100.00	62 655	0.61	100.00	4.39	0.00
582 Plastic sheet film foil & strips	29 389	0.58	100.00	56 836	0.55	100.00	6.45	0.00
761 Television video receive project	24 016	0.48	100.00	57 225	0.56	100.00	8.82	0.00
872 Medical instruments appliances nes	19 085	0.38	100.00	52 431	0.51	100.00	10.17	0.00
676 Iron steel bar rod section piling	27 524	0.54	100.00	51 568	0.50	100.00	5.59	0.00
841 Male clothing, woven	36 937	0.73	100.00	51 262	0.50	100.00	2.45	0.00
744 Mechanical handling equipment nes	28 086	0.56	100.00	51 670	0.50	100.00	4.82	0.00
716 Rotating electric plant parts nes	25 673	0.51	100.00	50 950	0.50	100.00	6.59	0.00
679 Iron steel pipe tube fittings etc	24 260	0.48	100.00	53 700	0.52	100.00	5.98	0.00
898 Music instrument device recording	30 073	0.60	100.00	50 105	0.49	100.00	4.11	0.00
511 Hydrocarbons nes; derivatives	20 884	0.41	100.00	48 718	0.48	100.00	9.24	0.00
112 Alcoholic beverages	27 688	0.55	100.00	45 622	0.45	100.00	4.87	0.00
771 Electric power machine part excluding 716	23 648	0.47	100.00	45 469	0.44	100.00	5.45	0.00
057 Fruit nut (exc oil), fresh or dried	26 544	0.53	100.00	45 983	0.45	100.00	4.43	0.00
899 Manufactured articles nes	19 854	0.39	100.00	44 254	0.43	100.00	8.20	0.00
675 Flat rolled products of alloy steel	20 377	0.40	100.00	44 226	0.43	100.00	8.04	0.00
553 Perfume toilet cosmetics, excluding soap	18 758	0.37	100.00	43 489	0.42	100.00	8.50	0.00
625 Rubber for wheels, incl inner tube	23 209	0.46	100.00	43 226	0.42	100.00	5.07	0.00
651 Textile yarn	33 198	0.66	100.00	40 748	0.40	100.00	1.73	0.00

For sources and notes, see end of table.

Pour les sources et les notes, se reporter à la fin du tableau

Products ranked by average 2004-2005 values SITC Revision 3 (3-digit level) Produits classés d'après la moyenne des valeurs de 2004-2005 CTCI révision 3 (positions à 3 chiffres)	1995			2005			Growth rates (percentage) Taux d'accroissement (en pourcentage) 1995-2005	
	Value (millions of dollars) Valeur (millions de dollars)	% of the country grouping exports En % des exportations du groupe de pays	% of world product exports En % des exportations mondiales des produits	Value (millions of dollars) Valeur (millions de dollars)	% of the country grouping exports En % des exportations du groupe de pays	% of world product exports En % des exportations mondiales des produits	Value Valeur	Difference from world Différence par rapport au monde
747 Pipe, boiler, tank & vat appliances	19 496	0.39	100.00	40 732	0.40	100.00	6.82	0.00
321 Coal excluding non-agglomomerated	18 735	0.37	100.00	45 879	0.45	100.00	6.52	0.00
871 Optical instruments apparatus nes	5 592	0.11	100.00	44 704	0.44	100.00	20.34	0.00
745 Non-electrical machinery tool nes	21 829	0.43	100.00	39 235	0.38	100.00	5.25	0.00
892 Printed matter	25 458	0.50	100.00	39 180	0.38	100.00	4.10	0.00
897 Jewellery nes (667)	19 408	0.38	100.00	39 950	0.39	100.00	6.81	0.00
533 Pigment, paint, varnish & related	20 038	0.40	100.00	38 688	0.38	100.00	6.49	0.00
971 Gold non-monetary excluding ores	21 659	0.43	100.00	36 792	0.36	100.00	3.62	0.00
012 Meat nes, fresh chilled frozen	24 149	0.48	100.00	38 863	0.38	100.00	3.73	0.00
571 Primary form ethylene polymers	16 323	0.32	100.00	38 964	0.38	100.00	7.96	0.00
642 Cut paper and paperboard articles	25 484	0.50	100.00	35 755	0.35	100.00	3.09	0.00
248 Wood simply worked, railway sleeper	26 206	0.52	100.00	34 992	0.34	100.00	2.29	0.00
574 Polyacetals and polyesters, etc	15 887	0.31	100.00	35 821	0.35	100.00	7.98	0.00
742 Liquid pump; liquid elevator parts	17 756	0.35	100.00	33 644	0.33	100.00	6.06	0.00
514 Nitrogen function compounds	18 856	0.37	100.00	33 814	0.33	100.00	5.43	0.00
674 Flat plated iron non-alloy steel	18 215	0.36	100.00	34 182	0.33	100.00	5.92	0.00
653 Man-made woven fabrics	35 671	0.71	100.00	32 232	0.31	100.00	-1.51	0.00
034 Fish, fresh live chilled frozen	18 998	0.38	100.00	33 574	0.33	100.00	5.44	0.00
054 Vegetable & vegetable products nes	20 913	0.41	100.00	32 163	0.31	100.00	4.54	0.00
785 Motorcycles, mopeds and cycles	18 419	0.36	100.00	32 377	0.32	100.00	5.48	0.00
098 Edible products & preparations nes	17 455	0.35	100.00	32 249	0.31	100.00	6.10	0.00
513 Carboxylic acid and compounds	16 903	0.33	100.00	32 487	0.32	100.00	6.81	0.00
081 Animal feed excluding unmilled cereal	20 511	0.41	100.00	30 364	0.30	100.00	3.02	0.00
658 Made-up textile articles nes	13 302	0.26	100.00	31 322	0.31	100.00	8.38	0.00
695 Tools for use in hand or in machine	17 411	0.34	100.00	30 112	0.29	100.00	5.10	0.00
512 Alcohols, phenols; derivatives	13 624	0.27	100.00	31 230	0.30	100.00	7.90	0.00
783 Road motor vehicles nes	16 807	0.33	100.00	29 983	0.29	100.00	5.15	0.00
657 Special yarn and textile fabric etc	21 104	0.42	100.00	29 493	0.29	100.00	2.91	0.00
634 Veneer, plywood & other wood nes	17 162	0.34	100.00	29 363	0.29	100.00	4.90	0.00
652 Woven cotton fabrics	22 203	0.44	100.00	28 785	0.28	100.00	2.68	0.00
884 Optical goods fibres nes	10 140	0.20	100.00	30 496	0.30	100.00	10.72	0.00
748 Mechanical transmission equipment	14 744	0.29	100.00	29 390	0.29	100.00	6.41	0.00
672 Ingots, iron steel primary products	12 721	0.25	100.00	28 481	0.28	100.00	7.78	0.00
522 Inorganic chemical elem oxide salt	16 268	0.32	100.00	28 836	0.28	100.00	4.68	0.00
844 Female clothing, knitted crocheted	13 456	0.27	100.00	25 878	0.25	100.00	5.73	0.00
731 Machine tools for material removal	16 297	0.32	100.00	26 988	0.26	100.00	3.30	0.00
251 Pulp and waste paper	27 461	0.54	100.00	25 781	0.25	100.00	1.77	0.00
724 Textile leather machinery parts nes	25 255	0.50	100.00	25 213	0.25	100.00	-0.01	0.00
691 Iron steel aluminium structures nes	13 725	0.27	100.00	26 637	0.26	100.00	6.04	0.00
774 Electrodiagnostic equipment	12 420	0.25	100.00	25 811	0.25	100.00	7.29	0.00
885 Watches and clocks	22 900	0.45	100.00	25 088	0.24	100.00	0.56	0.00
664 Glass	14 032	0.28	100.00	24 876	0.24	100.00	6.15	0.00
048 Cereal & preparation flour starch	12 655	0.25	100.00	24 587	0.24	100.00	6.20	0.00
282 Ferrous iron & steel, waste & scrap	7 872	0.16	100.00	23 752	0.23	100.00	12.29	0.00
342 Liquefied propane and butane	5 795	0.11	100.00	25 061	0.24	100.00	15.35	0.00
671 Pig & sponge iron, ferro alloys etc	10 480	0.21	100.00	25 506	0.25	100.00	8.13	0.00
562 Manufactured fertilizer excluding crude	17 671	0.35	100.00	23 666	0.23	100.00	2.37	0.00
831 Case bag: storage travel shopping	14 993	0.30	100.00	23 897	0.23	100.00	3.97	0.00
281 Iron ore and concentrates	8 584	0.17	100.00	27 688	0.27	100.00	8.65	0.00
516 Other organic chemicals	11 118	0.22	100.00	24 207	0.24	100.00	7.20	0.00
292 Crude vegetable materials nes	15 020	0.30	100.00	22 417	0.22	100.00	4.12	0.00
554 Soaps cleansers polishes	11 432	0.23	100.00	22 075	0.22	100.00	6.68	0.00
786 Trailer caravan transport container	9 847	0.19	100.00	22 773	0.22	100.00	8.09	0.00
222 Oil seed etc for soft oil	12 242	0.24	100.00	21 301	0.21	100.00	4.88	0.00
749 Non-electric machinery part nes	12 852	0.25	100.00	21 574	0.21	100.00	4.89	0.00
022 Milk products, excluding butter & cheese	15 436	0.31	100.00	21 571	0.21	100.00	3.31	0.00
611 Leather	15 886	0.31	100.00	20 354	0.20	100.00	2.89	0.00
635 Wood manufactures nes	11 268	0.22	100.00	20 830	0.20	100.00	5.99	0.00
882 Photo cinematographic supply excluding 883	17 652	0.35	100.00	20 042	0.20	100.00	0.92	0.00
663 Mineral manufactures nes	13 084	0.26	100.00	21 220	0.21	100.00	4.00	0.00
011 Beef, fresh chilled frozen	15 849	0.31	100.00	21 339	0.21	100.00	3.24	0.00

For sources and notes, see end of table.

Pour les sources et les notes, se reporter à la fin du tableau

Products ranked by average 2004-2005 values SITC Revision 3 (3-digit level) / Produits classés d'après la moyenne des valeurs de 2004-2005 CTCI révision 3 (positions à 3 chiffres)	1995			2005			Growth rates (percentage) Taux d'accroissement (en pourcentage) 1995-2005	
	Value (millions of dollars) / Valeur (millions de dollars)	% of the country grouping exports / En % des exportations du groupe de pays	% of world product exports / En % des exportations mondiales des produits	Value (millions of dollars) / Valeur (millions de dollars)	% of the country grouping exports / En % des exportations du groupe de pays	% of world product exports / En % des exportations mondiales des produits	Value / Valeur	Difference from world / Différence par rapport au monde
694 Nails screws nuts bolts rivets	10 824	0.21	100.00	20 990	0.20	100.00	6.19	0.00
848 Headgear, non-textile clothing	12 721	0.25	100.00	20 980	0.20	100.00	4.91	0.00
655 Knitted or crocheted fabrics nes	12 054	0.24	100.00	19 864	0.19	100.00	4.65	0.00
351 Electric current	7 772	0.15	100.00	21 674	0.21	100.00	10.01	0.00
681 Silver, platinum, platinum metals	6 211	0.12	100.00	20 777	0.20	100.00	11.52	0.00
721 Agricultural machine nes excluding tractor	10 479	0.21	100.00	20 368	0.20	100.00	5.33	0.00
036 Crustacean mollusc aquat invertebra	16 422	0.33	100.00	19 532	0.19	100.00	1.86	0.00
746 Ball or roller bearings	12 165	0.24	100.00	19 590	0.19	100.00	4.20	0.00
041 Wheat meslin, incl spelt, unmilled	17 321	0.34	100.00	17 774	0.17	100.00	-0.46	0.00
762 Radio broadcast receivers	22 482	0.45	100.00	18 548	0.18	100.00	-1.75	0.00
813 Lighting fixtures and fittings nes	9 838	0.19	100.00	18 953	0.18	100.00	6.20	0.00
572 Primary form styrene polymers	11 045	0.22	100.00	18 983	0.19	100.00	5.77	0.00
697 Base metal household equipment nes	9 976	0.20	100.00	18 580	0.18	100.00	6.11	0.00
629 Articles of rubber nes	9 191	0.18	100.00	18 183	0.18	100.00	6.72	0.00
726 Printing bookbinding machines parts	13 977	0.28	100.00	18 495	0.18	100.00	1.62	0.00
881 Photographic device nes	12 793	0.25	100.00	16 834	0.16	100.00	2.68	0.00
661 Lime cement construction material	11 026	0.22	100.00	18 822	0.18	100.00	3.93	0.00
122 Manufactured tabacco	18 937	0.37	100.00	17 722	0.17	100.00	-1.87	0.00
846 Clothing accessory excluding 831 848 851	10 574	0.21	100.00	17 359	0.17	100.00	3.93	0.00
665 Glassware	10 128	0.20	100.00	17 247	0.17	100.00	5.17	0.00
662 Clay and refractory materials	10 860	0.22	100.00	17 099	0.17	100.00	4.31	0.00
024 Cheese and curd	11 065	0.22	100.00	16 945	0.17	100.00	3.90	0.00
335 Residual petroleum products nes	6 039	0.12	100.00	17 641	0.17	100.00	9.86	0.00
061 Sugar, mollasses and honey	15 717	0.31	100.00	17 198	0.17	100.00	-0.08	0.00
421 Fixed veg fat and oil, "soft"	12 157	0.24	100.00	16 455	0.16	100.00	2.09	0.00
791 Railway vehicles and equipment	7 070	0.14	100.00	16 023	0.16	100.00	7.99	0.00
288 Non ferrous base metal waste nes	9 198	0.18	100.00	17 928	0.17	100.00	5.41	0.00
591 Household and garden chemicals	10 684	0.21	100.00	16 075	0.16	100.00	3.26	0.00
056 Vegetables roots tubers nes	10 759	0.21	100.00	15 852	0.15	100.00	4.09	0.00
551 Essential oils, perfumes & flavours	5 657	0.11	100.00	15 850	0.15	100.00	10.48	0.00
737 Metalwork machinery nes excluding tools	10 068	0.20	100.00	15 856	0.15	100.00	2.91	0.00
283 Copper ores and concentrates	6 853	0.14	100.00	17 216	0.17	100.00	8.56	0.00
287 Base metal ores & concentrates nes	5 842	0.12	100.00	18 048	0.18	100.00	7.50	0.00
843 Male clothing, knitted crocheted	7 991	0.16	100.00	14 789	0.14	100.00	4.82	0.00
037 Fish shellfish, prepared preserved	8 773	0.17	100.00	14 767	0.14	100.00	4.50	0.00
071 Coffee and coffee substitutes	15 551	0.31	100.00	15 828	0.15	100.00	-3.42	0.00
751 Office machines	15 990	0.32	100.00	15 046	0.15	100.00	-2.23	0.00
592 Starches, glutenes, glues, etc	7 664	0.15	100.00	13 940	0.14	100.00	5.71	0.00
896 Work of art & collections; antiques	6 483	0.13	100.00	14 543	0.14	100.00	7.97	0.00
722 Tractors	8 569	0.17	100.00	14 141	0.14	100.00	3.20	0.00
422 Fixed veg fat and oil, excluding "soft"	7 747	0.15	100.00	13 344	0.13	100.00	4.67	0.00
683 Nickel	5 144	0.10	100.00	13 546	0.13	100.00	9.65	0.00
621 Rubber material e.g. paste tube rod	6 585	0.13	100.00	12 968	0.13	100.00	6.48	0.00
073 Chocolate & cocoa preparations nes	7 987	0.16	100.00	12 290	0.12	100.00	4.10	0.00
001 Live animal excluding fish & crustacean	10 399	0.21	100.00	12 693	0.12	100.00	1.71	0.00
573 Vinyl chloride etc polymers	7 677	0.15	100.00	12 215	0.12	100.00	4.76	0.00
044 Maize unmilled, excluding sweet corn	10 914	0.22	100.00	11 193	0.11	100.00	0.16	0.00
523 Inorganic acid metal salt peroxy	7 550	0.15	100.00	12 211	0.12	100.00	3.88	0.00
263 Cotton	10 970	0.22	100.00	11 398	0.11	100.00	-0.69	0.00
659 Floor coverings etc	9 519	0.19	100.00	11 557	0.11	100.00	0.61	0.00
735 Machine part accessory for 731 733	6 521	0.13	100.00	11 624	0.11	100.00	4.54	0.00
581 Plastic tube pipe hose & fittings	5 467	0.11	100.00	11 688	0.11	100.00	7.22	0.00
654 Other woven textile fabrics nes	10 969	0.22	100.00	11 042	0.11	100.00	-0.27	0.00
812 Sanitary plumb heat fixtures nes	5 425	0.11	100.00	11 240	0.11	100.00	6.80	0.00
232 Synthetic & reclaimed rubber; waste	5 877	0.12	100.00	11 916	0.12	100.00	6.12	0.00
718 Power generating machinery part nes	5 204	0.10	100.00	11 368	0.11	100.00	7.68	0.00
597 Additive e.g. lubricate, antifreeze	7 284	0.14	100.00	11 163	0.11	100.00	3.29	0.00
692 Metal storage transport container	6 985	0.14	100.00	11 089	0.11	100.00	3.49	0.00
531 Synthetic organic colour agents	9 849	0.20	100.00	10 349	0.10	100.00	-0.05	0.00
895 Office and stationery supplies nes	6 985	0.14	100.00	10 459	0.10	100.00	3.58	0.00
111 Non alcoholic beverage nes	4 500	0.09	100.00	10 511	0.10	100.00	9.51	0.00

For sources and notes, see end of table.   Pour les sources et les notes, se reporter à la fin du tableau

Products ranked by average 2004-2005 values SITC Revision 3 (3-digit level) Produits classés d'après la moyenne des valeurs de 2004-2005 CTCI révision 3 (positions à 3 chiffres)	1995			2005			Growth rates (percentage) Taux d'accroissement (en pourcentage) 1995-2005	
	Value (millions of dollars) Valeur (millions de dollars)	% of the country grouping exports En % des exportations du groupe de pays	% of world product exports En % des exportations mondiales des produits	Value (millions of dollars) Valeur (millions de dollars)	% of the country grouping exports En % des exportations du groupe de pays	% of world product exports En % des exportations mondiales des produits	Value Valeur	Difference from world Différence par rapport au monde
278 Other crude minerals	7 434	0.15	100.00	10 460	0.10	100.00	2.95	0.00
247 Wood in rough or roughly squared	9 244	0.18	100.00	10 649	0.10	100.00	1.10	0.00
017 Meat offal preserved nes	5 871	0.12	100.00	10 424	0.10	100.00	4.75	0.00
058 Fruit preserve preparation excluding juice	6 058	0.12	100.00	10 022	0.10	100.00	4.43	0.00
344 Petroleum and hydrocarbon gas nes	2 680	0.05	100.00	9 801	0.10	100.00	12.64	0.00
285 Aluminium ore concentrate alumina	5 228	0.10	100.00	10 596	0.10	100.00	5.65	0.00
042 Rice	7 468	0.15	100.00	9 195	0.09	100.00	0.60	0.00
725 Paper & pulp mill, cut manufacture	8 076	0.16	100.00	9 147	0.09	100.00	0.09	0.00
727 Food processing machine excluding domestic	6 461	0.13	100.00	9 179	0.09	100.00	2.43	0.00
231 Natural rubber, latex, gum, etc	7 758	0.15	100.00	9 373	0.09	100.00	1.70	0.00
059 Fruit & vegetable juice unferment	5 890	0.12	100.00	8 814	0.09	100.00	3.25	0.00
693 Wire products and fencing grills	4 799	0.10	100.00	8 881	0.09	100.00	5.39	0.00
733 Metal work tool no material removal	6 984	0.14	100.00	8 913	0.09	100.00	0.74	0.00
072 Cocoa	5 215	0.10	100.00	8 442	0.08	100.00	4.93	0.00
656 Tulle lace embroidery trim etc	4 538	0.09	100.00	8 181	0.08	100.00	5.62	0.00
891 Arms and ammunition	7 808	0.15	100.00	7 371	0.07	100.00	-1.65	0.00
325 Coke, semi coke, retort carbon	2 320	0.05	100.00	6 303	0.06	100.00	12.29	0.00
696 Cutlery	4 169	0.08	100.00	7 207	0.07	100.00	5.65	0.00
121 Unmanufactured tabacco and refuse	5 228	0.10	100.00	7 081	0.07	100.00	0.57	0.00
678 Wire of iron or steel	4 278	0.08	100.00	7 074	0.07	100.00	4.79	0.00
689 Misc non-ferrous base metals	3 279	0.06	100.00	7 339	0.07	100.00	5.79	0.00
525 Radio active & associated materials	4 574	0.09	100.00	7 232	0.07	100.00	3.87	0.00
062 Sugar confectionery	4 479	0.09	100.00	6 593	0.06	100.00	3.49	0.00
666 Pottery	5 799	0.11	100.00	6 511	0.06	100.00	0.49	0.00
873 Meters and counters nes	3 579	0.07	100.00	6 538	0.06	100.00	6.19	0.00
686 Zinc	4 126	0.08	100.00	6 770	0.07	100.00	2.77	0.00
524 Other inorganic chemicals	3 127	0.06	100.00	6 618	0.06	100.00	6.37	0.00
284 Nickel ores, concentrates, etc	2 041	0.04	100.00	6 164	0.06	100.00	9.92	0.00
273 Stone, sand and gravel	3 687	0.07	100.00	5 966	0.06	100.00	4.43	0.00
266 Synthetic fibres for spinning	5 912	0.12	100.00	5 877	0.06	100.00	-0.29	0.00
211 Raw hides & skins, excluding furskins	5 956	0.12	100.00	5 633	0.05	100.00	0.23	0.00
431 Processed animal & veg fats & oils	4 701	0.09	100.00	5 546	0.05	100.00	3.27	0.00
811 Prefabricated buildings	2 706	0.05	100.00	5 294	0.05	100.00	5.50	0.00
268 Wool & animal hair, incl wool tops	7 206	0.14	100.00	4 900	0.05	100.00	-3.83	0.00
291 Crude animal materials nes	3 669	0.07	100.00	5 061	0.05	100.00	2.37	0.00
289 Prec metal ore concentrate excluding gold	1 224	0.02	100.00	4 630	0.05	100.00	9.23	0.00
023 Butter fats oils derived from milk	4 006	0.08	100.00	4 190	0.04	100.00	-0.17	0.00
074 Tea and maté	2 503	0.05	100.00	4 117	0.04	100.00	3.56	0.00
712 Steam vapour turbines & parts nes	2 709	0.05	100.00	4 125	0.04	100.00	2.44	0.00
583 Plastic rod stick & profile shapes	1 474	0.03	100.00	3 599	0.04	100.00	9.25	0.00
035 Fish, dried salted smoked	2 769	0.05	100.00	3 649	0.04	100.00	2.40	0.00
711 Steam generating boilers & parts	3 094	0.06	100.00	3 875	0.04	100.00	-0.64	0.00
043 Barley grain unmilled	2 788	0.06	100.00	3 662	0.04	100.00	0.85	0.00
267 Man made fibre for spinning; waste	2 971	0.06	100.00	3 251	0.03	100.00	1.09	0.00
579 Plastic waste, parings and scrap	1 250	0.02	100.00	3 532	0.03	100.00	11.64	0.00
075 Spices	1 883	0.04	100.00	3 069	0.03	100.00	4.42	0.00
612 Leather manufactures nes	1 030	0.02	100.00	3 146	0.03	100.00	12.13	0.00
687 Tin	1 583	0.03	100.00	3 172	0.03	100.00	4.03	0.00
246 Wood chips, particles and waste	2 099	0.04	100.00	2 885	0.03	100.00	2.41	0.00
016 Meat offal preserved	1 641	0.03	100.00	2 528	0.02	100.00	4.41	0.00
091 Margarine and shortening	1 657	0.03	100.00	2 717	0.03	100.00	3.24	0.00
685 Lead	1 446	0.03	100.00	2 813	0.03	100.00	3.48	0.00
411 Animals oils and fats	2 260	0.04	100.00	2 465	0.02	100.00	1.10	0.00
046 Wheat meal & flour, meslin flour	2 807	0.06	100.00	2 478	0.02	100.00	-3.07	0.00
212 Raw furskins and furskin pieces	1 260	0.02	100.00	2 274	0.02	100.00	4.79	0.00
025 Eggs, yolks and albumin	1 438	0.03	100.00	2 166	0.02	100.00	3.08	0.00
677 Iron steel rail railway materials	1 251	0.02	100.00	2 219	0.02	100.00	4.71	0.00
269 Worn clothing, textile article; rag	1 501	0.03	100.00	2 013	0.02	100.00	1.49	0.00
593 Explosives and pyrotechnic products	1 154	0.02	100.00	1 917	0.02	100.00	4.72	0.00
272 Crude fertilizer, excluding manufactured	1 296	0.03	100.00	1 842	0.02	100.00	1.25	0.00
613 Furskin tanned dressed etc	1 323	0.03	100.00	1 719	0.02	100.00	-0.01	0.00

Sources:
- UNCTAD secretariat calculations based on UN DESA Statistics Division's data

Sources :
- Calculs du secrétariat de la CNUCED sur la base des données de ONU DAES Division de statistique

Products ranked by average 2004-2005 values SITC Revision 3 (3-digit level) Produits classés d'après la moyenne des valeurs de 2004-2005 CTCI révision 3 (positions à 3 chiffres)	1995			2005			Growth rates (percentage) Taux d'accroissement (en pourcentage) 1995-2005	
	Value (millions of dollars) Valeur (millions de dollars)	% of the country grouping exports En % des exportations du groupe de pays	% of world product exports En % des exportations mondiales des produits	Value (millions of dollars) Valeur (millions de dollars)	% of the country grouping exports En % des exportations du groupe de pays	% of world product exports En % des exportations mondiales des produits	Value Valeur	Difference from world Différence par rapport au monde
All commodity groups	**3 515 731**	**100.00**	**69.61**	**6 155 118**	**100.00**	**60.05**	**5.18**	**-1.39**
781 Passenger cars and race cars	213 579	6.07	91.88	421 747	6.85	86.95	6.89	-0.46
931 Transaction commodity unclassified	103 930	2.96	82.84	237 762	3.86	69.42	7.10	-1.25
542 Medicines including veterinary	41 968	1.19	92.56	194 583	3.16	94.96	17.49	0.43
784 Motor vehicle parts and accessories	102 656	2.92	91.05	187 916	3.05	80.81	6.01	-1.04
764 Telecommunicate equipment part nes	82 986	2.36	68.21	172 604	2.80	49.10	6.24	-4.12
776 Valves tubes; diodes, transistors	113 787	3.24	60.20	151 642	2.46	41.56	3.09	-3.40
334 Heavy petroleum & bituminous oil	39 207	1.12	42.55	149 425	2.43	40.67	12.31	-0.38
752 Computer equipment nes	88 513	2.52	67.10	116 129	1.89	43.01	1.47	-4.49
792 Aircraft, spacecraft & equipment	63 959	1.82	93.74	116 546	1.89	91.14	4.44	-0.40
333 Crude petroleum & bituminous oil	34 903	0.99	16.95	105 306	1.71	14.23	10.93	-1.59
713 Internal combustion engine part nes	48 750	1.39	87.97	95 951	1.56	84.97	6.43	-0.26
874 Measure analyze control device nes	48 537	1.38	92.12	93 092	1.51	84.28	6.19	-1.04
778 Electrical machinery apparatus nes	58 027	1.65	72.20	85 589	1.39	58.11	3.55	-2.33
772 Electrical circuit equipment	50 987	1.45	76.72	85 925	1.40	60.56	4.79	-2.36
759 Office equipment part & accessories	64 498	1.83	65.17	87 706	1.42	43.86	2.37	-4.42
641 Paper and paperboard	64 652	1.84	89.51	81 607	1.33	85.53	2.95	-0.40
728 Special industrial machine part nes	53 671	1.53	89.25	80 744	1.31	83.23	3.55	-0.68
515 Organo-inorganic compound acid salt	24 024	0.68	89.69	69 170	1.12	87.09	10.73	-0.49
782 Goods and service vehicles	39 843	1.13	88.08	67 506	1.10	75.79	4.49	-1.35
343 Natural gas, liquefied or not	11 717	0.33	33.71	72 032	1.17	57.80	17.91	5.24
714 Non-electric engines excluding 712 713 718	24 503	0.70	93.37	62 524	1.02	91.71	8.94	-0.40
821 Furniture part; bedding furnishing	34 564	0.98	76.45	60 130	0.98	61.87	5.28	-2.24
699 Base metal manufactures nes	32 091	0.91	76.69	62 214	1.01	69.49	6.02	-0.93
541 Pharmaceuticals excluding medicines	22 959	0.65	87.07	59 478	0.97	89.67	10.25	0.41
893 Articles of plastic nes	28 705	0.82	68.03	56 055	0.91	66.49	6.65	-0.22
667 Pearls, precious semiprecious stone	26 843	0.76	67.60	55 252	0.90	61.30	6.82	-1.31
743 Gas pump, compressor, fan, filter	28 338	0.81	81.62	52 577	0.85	75.89	6.03	-0.81
598 Miscellaneous chemical products nes	25 785	0.73	87.19	53 216	0.86	84.08	7.08	-0.27
723 Civil engineering plant & equipment	25 967	0.74	87.62	54 947	0.89	79.64	6.22	-0.95
575 Other plastics, in primary forms	25 710	0.73	86.42	51 156	0.83	78.48	6.34	-1.14
684 Aluminium	32 684	0.93	71.82	49 737	0.81	66.37	4.16	-0.87
741 Heating cooling equipment parts nes	31 320	0.89	81.76	47 969	0.78	70.56	3.31	-1.76
582 Plastic sheet film foil & strips	24 559	0.70	83.57	44 615	0.72	78.50	5.96	-0.49
744 Mechanical handling equipment nes	24 939	0.71	88.80	43 876	0.71	84.92	4.49	-0.33
872 Medical instruments appliances nes	16 686	0.47	87.43	43 057	0.70	82.12	9.33	-0.83
112 Alcoholic beverages	23 991	0.68	86.65	37 719	0.61	82.68	4.41	-0.46
793 Ships boats floating structures	26 365	0.75	71.90	36 231	0.59	53.01	3.88	-2.32
553 Perfume toilet cosmetics, excluding soap	16 665	0.47	88.84	36 300	0.59	83.47	7.79	-0.71
775 Household equipment nes	22 642	0.64	71.42	34 857	0.57	54.97	3.81	-2.91
773 Electrical distribute equipment nes	20 081	0.57	67.31	34 297	0.56	56.60	4.44	-1.60
745 Non-electrical machinery tool nes	20 109	0.57	92.12	33 137	0.54	84.46	4.37	-0.88
898 Music instrument device recording	23 694	0.67	78.79	34 144	0.55	68.14	2.32	-1.78
673 Flat iron non-alloy steel products	23 318	0.66	65.21	34 923	0.57	53.46	3.62	-1.60
679 Iron steel pipe tube fittings etc	19 162	0.55	78.99	35 650	0.58	66.39	4.33	-1.64
716 Rotating electric plant parts nes	18 851	0.54	73.43	33 961	0.55	66.65	5.60	-0.98
533 Pigment, paint, varnish & related	16 791	0.48	83.80	31 897	0.52	82.45	6.23	-0.26
676 Iron steel bar rod section piling	19 799	0.56	71.93	32 155	0.52	62.35	4.39	-1.20
675 Flat rolled products of alloy steel	17 585	0.50	86.30	32 598	0.53	73.71	6.63	-1.41
511 Hydrocarbons nes; derivatives	16 656	0.47	79.75	31 911	0.52	65.50	7.17	-2.07
747 Pipe, boiler, tank & vat appliances	17 453	0.50	89.52	31 553	0.51	77.46	5.18	-1.65
892 Printed matter	21 858	0.62	85.86	30 755	0.50	78.50	3.25	-0.89
012 Meat nes, fresh chilled frozen	19 124	0.54	79.19	31 411	0.51	80.82	3.90	0.17
845 Articles of apparel nes	19 029	0.54	42.16	29 210	0.47	31.91	3.84	-2.87
899 Manufactured articles nes	10 648	0.30	53.63	30 587	0.50	69.12	11.27	3.07
742 Liquid pump; liquid elevator parts	16 323	0.46	91.93	28 778	0.47	85.54	5.33	-0.73
625 Rubber for wheels, incl inner tube	17 692	0.50	76.23	28 397	0.46	65.69	3.80	-1.27
642 Cut paper and paperboard articles	20 846	0.59	81.80	27 332	0.44	76.44	2.41	-0.68
682 Copper	19 921	0.57	56.50	27 465	0.45	43.83	2.25	-2.14
851 Footwear	19 651	0.56	41.84	25 747	0.42	37.89	2.03	-0.83
514 Nitrogen function compounds	16 057	0.46	85.16	25 414	0.41	75.16	4.52	-0.91

For sources and notes, see end of table.

Pour les sources et les notes, se reporter à la fin du tableau

Products ranked by average 2004-2005 values SITC Revision 3 (3-digit level) / Produits classés d'après la moyenne des valeurs de 2004-2005 CTCI révision 3 (positions à 3 chiffres)		1995			2005			Growth rates (percentage) Taux d'accroissement (en pourcentage) 1995-2005	
		Value (millions of dollars) / Valeur (millions de dollars)	% of the country grouping exports / En % des exportations du groupe de pays	% of world product exports / En % des exportations mondiales des produits	Value (millions of dollars) / Valeur (millions de dollars)	% of the country grouping exports / En % des exportations du groupe de pays	% of world product exports / En % des exportations mondiales des produits	Value / Valeur	Difference from world / Différence par rapport au monde
763	Sound TV recorder or reproducer	9 805	0.28	45.66	25 265	0.41	40.65	10.42	-1.79
248	Wood simply worked, railway sleeper	20 204	0.57	77.10	24 711	0.40	70.62	1.20	-1.09
057	Fruit nut (exc oil), fresh or dried	15 418	0.44	58.08	25 786	0.42	56.08	4.31	-0.12
098	Edible products & preparations nes	14 469	0.41	82.89	25 073	0.41	77.75	5.60	-0.49
894	Baby carriage toy game sport good	16 347	0.46	39.81	25 372	0.41	39.61	3.65	0.07
783	Road motor vehicles nes	15 572	0.44	92.65	24 794	0.40	82.69	4.15	-1.00
748	Mechanical transmission equipment	13 348	0.38	90.53	24 864	0.40	84.60	5.66	-0.75
774	Electrodiagnostic equipment	11 990	0.34	96.54	23 494	0.38	91.02	6.72	-0.57
761	Television video receive project	9 438	0.27	39.30	23 687	0.38	41.39	8.85	0.03
674	Flat plated iron non-alloy steel	14 712	0.42	80.77	22 958	0.37	67.16	4.05	-1.86
571	Primary form ethylene polymers	11 926	0.34	73.07	24 205	0.39	62.12	6.24	-1.72
321	Coal excluding non-agglomomerated	12 933	0.37	69.03	25 913	0.42	56.48	3.29	-3.23
771	Electric power machine part excluding 716	13 586	0.39	57.45	21 602	0.35	47.51	3.40	-2.06
695	Tools for use in hand or in machine	13 871	0.39	79.67	21 446	0.35	71.22	3.97	-1.13
574	Polyacetals and polyesters, etc	11 829	0.34	74.46	22 267	0.36	62.16	5.80	-2.18
731	Machine tools for material removal	14 246	0.41	87.42	22 113	0.36	81.94	2.62	-0.69
054	Vegetable & vegetable products nes	14 006	0.40	66.97	20 700	0.34	64.36	4.45	-0.09
048	Cereal & preparation flour starch	10 782	0.31	85.20	20 577	0.33	83.69	6.11	-0.08
884	Optical goods fibres nes	7 883	0.22	77.74	20 767	0.34	68.10	9.38	-1.34
897	Jewellery nes (667)	12 427	0.35	64.03	20 589	0.33	51.54	4.72	-2.08
251	Pulp and waste paper	22 543	0.64	82.09	19 565	0.32	75.89	1.10	-0.67
657	Special yarn and textile fabric etc	13 981	0.40	66.25	19 579	0.32	66.39	3.32	0.41
785	Motorcycles, mopeds and cycles	11 385	0.32	61.81	19 601	0.32	60.54	5.16	-0.32
842	Female clothing, woven	14 154	0.40	38.24	19 311	0.31	30.21	2.33	-2.80
513	Carboxylic acid and compounds	12 861	0.37	76.09	19 729	0.32	60.73	4.16	-2.65
034	Fish, fresh live chilled frozen	11 654	0.33	61.34	19 710	0.32	58.71	4.74	-0.70
724	Textile leather machinery parts nes	21 199	0.60	83.94	18 090	0.29	71.75	-1.40	-1.40
634	Veneer, plywood & other wood nes	8 989	0.26	52.38	18 575	0.30	63.26	7.49	2.59
664	Glass	11 483	0.33	81.84	18 392	0.30	73.94	5.10	-1.05
022	Milk products, excluding butter & cheese	14 269	0.41	92.44	18 490	0.30	85.72	2.57	-0.74
282	Ferrous iron & steel, waste & scrap	6 639	0.19	84.34	17 809	0.29	74.98	11.49	-0.80
691	Iron steel aluminium structures nes	10 618	0.30	77.36	18 748	0.30	70.38	4.88	-1.15
651	Textile yarn	16 241	0.46	48.92	17 146	0.28	42.08	0.22	-1.51
081	Animal feed excluding unmilled cereal	13 201	0.38	64.36	17 654	0.29	58.14	2.20	-0.82
721	Agricultural machine nes excluding tractor	9 826	0.28	93.76	18 262	0.30	89.66	4.88	-0.45
554	Soaps cleansers polishes	9 351	0.27	81.80	17 489	0.28	79.23	6.45	-0.23
971	Gold non-monetary excluding ores	14 544	0.41	67.15	18 286	0.30	49.70	0.10	-3.52
882	Photo cinematographic supply excluding 883	15 761	0.45	89.29	16 399	0.27	81.82	0.02	-0.91
663	Mineral manufactures nes	11 332	0.32	86.61	17 267	0.28	81.37	3.34	-0.67
351	Electric current	6 415	0.18	82.55	18 246	0.30	84.18	10.38	0.37
292	Crude vegetable materials nes	10 871	0.31	72.38	16 459	0.27	73.42	4.48	0.36
749	Non-electric machinery part nes	10 722	0.30	83.43	15 889	0.26	73.65	3.71	-1.19
726	Printing bookbinding machines parts	13 366	0.38	95.63	16 733	0.27	90.47	0.99	-0.63
841	Male clothing, woven	12 888	0.37	34.89	15 884	0.26	30.99	1.07	-1.38
024	Cheese and curd	10 825	0.31	97.83	15 771	0.26	93.08	3.49	-0.41
516	Other organic chemicals	8 990	0.26	80.86	16 123	0.26	66.60	5.35	-1.85
512	Alcohols, phenols; derivatives	9 500	0.27	69.73	15 723	0.26	50.35	4.55	-3.34
885	Watches and clocks	11 975	0.34	52.29	15 247	0.25	60.77	2.42	1.86
011	Beef, fresh chilled frozen	13 895	0.40	87.67	15 277	0.25	71.59	1.65	-1.58
522	Inorganic chemical elem oxide salt	9 723	0.28	59.77	15 704	0.26	54.46	3.90	-0.77
041	Wheat meslin, incl spelt, unmilled	15 262	0.43	88.11	13 613	0.22	76.59	-2.06	-1.60
746	Ball or roller bearings	9 972	0.28	81.97	14 829	0.24	75.70	3.37	-0.83
629	Articles of rubber nes	7 782	0.22	84.67	14 179	0.23	77.98	6.03	-0.69
786	Trailer caravan transport container	6 284	0.18	63.82	13 918	0.23	61.12	7.32	-0.77
694	Nails screws nuts bolts rivets	7 912	0.23	73.10	13 721	0.22	65.37	5.04	-1.14
635	Wood manufactures nes	7 282	0.21	64.63	13 373	0.22	64.20	5.77	-0.23
551	Essential oils, perfumes & flavours	4 764	0.14	84.22	13 339	0.22	84.16	10.43	-0.05
122	Manufactured tabacco	13 564	0.39	71.63	13 372	0.22	75.45	-1.33	0.54
881	Photographic device nes	8 744	0.25	68.35	12 306	0.20	73.10	3.10	0.42
653	Man-made woven fabrics	15 593	0.44	43.71	12 161	0.20	37.73	-2.48	-0.97
896	Work of art & collections; antiques	6 151	0.17	94.88	13 385	0.22	92.04	7.67	-0.31

For sources and notes, see end of table.

Pour les sources et les notes, se reporter à la fin du tableau

Products ranked by average 2004-2005 values SITC Revision 3 (3-digit level) / Produits classés d'après la moyenne des valeurs de 2004-2005 CTCI révision 3 (positions à 3 chiffres)	1995			2005			Growth rates (percentage) Taux d'accroissement (en pourcentage) 1995-2005	
	Value (millions of dollars) Valeur (millions de dollars)	% of the country grouping exports En % des exportations du groupe de pays	% of world product exports En % des exportations mondiales des produits	Value (millions of dollars) Valeur (millions de dollars)	% of the country grouping exports En % des exportations du groupe de pays	% of world product exports En % des exportations mondiales des produits	Value Valeur	Difference from world Différence par rapport au monde
791 Railway vehicles and equipment	6 304	0.18	89.16	12 689	0.21	79.19	6.96	-1.03
662 Clay and refractory materials	9 509	0.27	87.56	12 040	0.20	70.41	2.33	-1.98
665 Glassware	8 026	0.23	79.24	12 110	0.20	70.21	3.94	-1.23
591 Household and garden chemicals	9 189	0.26	86.01	12 114	0.20	75.36	2.03	-1.23
737 Metalwork machinery nes excluding tools	9 022	0.26	89.61	12 555	0.20	79.18	1.44	-1.47
288 Non ferrous base metal waste nes	6 750	0.19	73.38	13 114	0.21	73.15	6.50	1.10
722 Tractors	8 001	0.23	93.37	12 043	0.20	85.16	2.30	-0.90
562 Manufactured fertilizer excluding crude	10 391	0.30	58.80	10 732	0.17	45.35	0.46	-1.92
652 Woven cotton fabrics	9 862	0.28	44.42	10 758	0.17	37.37	1.44	-1.24
681 Silver, platinum, platinum metals	4 997	0.14	80.44	11 796	0.19	56.78	8.33	-3.19
222 Oil seed etc for soft oil	8 689	0.25	70.98	10 590	0.17	49.72	1.37	-3.51
056 Vegetables roots tubers nes	7 470	0.21	69.43	10 950	0.18	69.08	4.19	0.10
592 Starches, glutenes, glues, etc	6 322	0.18	82.48	10 883	0.18	78.07	5.22	-0.49
335 Residual petroleum products nes	4 572	0.13	75.70	11 243	0.18	63.73	9.06	-0.80
871 Optical instruments apparatus nes	3 948	0.11	70.59	10 648	0.17	23.82	10.40	-9.94
621 Rubber material e.g. paste tube rod	5 778	0.16	87.74	10 581	0.17	81.59	5.80	-0.67
073 Chocolate & cocoa preparations nes	7 379	0.21	92.39	10 387	0.17	84.51	3.25	-0.85
672 Ingots, Iron steel primary products	5 751	0.16	45.21	10 798	0.18	37.91	5.85	-1.93
813 Lighting fixtures and fittings nes	6 177	0.18	62.79	10 154	0.16	53.57	4.23	-1.97
735 Machine part accessory for 731 733	6 051	0.17	92.80	9 684	0.16	83.32	3.54	-1.00
001 Live animal excluding fish & crustacean	8 103	0.23	77.92	10 105	0.16	79.61	1.51	-0.20
581 Plastic tube pipe hose & fittings	4 639	0.13	84.86	9 561	0.16	81.80	6.61	-0.61
597 Additive e.g. lubricate, antifreeze	6 628	0.19	90.99	9 652	0.16	86.46	2.64	-0.65
281 Iron ore and concentrates	3 681	0.10	42.88	11 607	0.19	41.92	7.61	-1.04
611 Leather	7 587	0.22	47.76	8 453	0.14	41.53	1.59	-1.30
831 Case bag: storage travel shopping	4 742	0.13	31.63	9 178	0.15	38.41	6.36	2.39
658 Made-up textile articles nes	5 532	0.16	41.59	8 758	0.14	27.96	4.30	-4.07
718 Power generating machinery part nes	4 637	0.13	89.10	9 377	0.15	82.48	6.79	-0.89
573 Vinyl chloride etc polymers	5 751	0.16	74.92	8 887	0.14	72.76	4.51	-0.24
421 Fixed veg fat and oil, "soft"	7 150	0.20	58.82	9 032	0.15	54.89	0.91	-1.18
697 Base metal household equipment nes	5 721	0.16	57.35	8 627	0.14	46.43	3.58	-2.53
661 Lime cement construction material	7 277	0.21	66.00	8 689	0.14	46.16	0.83	-3.10
812 Sanitary plumb heat fixtures nes	4 722	0.13	87.04	8 683	0.14	77.25	5.42	-1.38
572 Primary form styrene polymers	6 280	0.18	56.85	8 534	0.14	44.96	3.21	-2.56
683 Nickel	3 548	0.10	68.98	8 602	0.14	63.50	8.32	-1.33
727 Food processing machine excluding domestic	5 923	0.17	91.68	8 270	0.13	90.09	2.38	-0.06
725 Paper & pulp mill, cut manufacture	7 545	0.21	93.43	8 153	0.13	89.13	-0.31	-0.40
692 Metal storage transport container	5 740	0.16	82.18	8 346	0.14	75.26	2.68	-0.81
111 Non alcoholic beverage nes	3 448	0.10	76.62	8 219	0.13	78.20	10.03	0.53
044 Maize unmilled, excluding sweet corn	9 656	0.27	88.47	7 474	0.12	66.77	-2.10	-2.27
751 Office machines	11 358	0.32	71.03	7 836	0.13	52.08	-4.95	-2.71
342 Liquefied propane and butane	2 799	0.08	48.30	8 494	0.14	33.89	10.42	-4.93
846 Clothing accessory excluding 831 848 851	6 150	0.17	58.16	7 592	0.12	43.74	0.76	-3.17
036 Crustacean mollusc aquat invertebra	5 066	0.14	30.85	7 491	0.12	38.35	4.39	2.53
523 Inorganic acid metal salt peroxy	5 400	0.15	71.53	7 546	0.12	61.79	2.50	-1.37
232 Synthetic & reclaimed rubber; waste	4 382	0.12	74.55	7 843	0.13	65.82	4.82	-1.29
659 Floor coverings etc	6 498	0.18	68.26	7 157	0.12	61.93	-0.14	-0.75
531 Synthetic organic colour agents	7 750	0.22	78.69	6 843	0.11	66.12	-1.68	-1.63
655 Knitted or crocheted fabrics nes	4 720	0.13	39.16	6 901	0.11	34.74	3.49	-1.15
061 Sugar, mollasses and honey	7 104	0.20	45.20	7 062	0.11	41.06	-0.63	-0.55
344 Petroleum and hydrocarbon gas nes	1 964	0.06	73.28	6 738	0.11	68.75	12.02	-0.63
654 Other woven textile fabrics nes	7 594	0.22	69.23	6 637	0.11	60.10	-1.75	-1.48
733 Metal work tool no material removal	6 022	0.17	86.23	6 959	0.11	78.07	-0.21	-0.95
895 Office and stationery supplies nes	4 984	0.14	71.34	6 582	0.11	62.93	2.21	-1.37
017 Meat offal preserved nes	4 351	0.12	74.11	6 671	0.11	63.99	3.13	-1.62
278 Other crude minerals	4 990	0.14	67.13	6 479	0.11	61.94	2.12	-0.83
891 Arms and ammunition	7 447	0.21	95.37	6 347	0.10	86.12	-2.59	-0.94
762 Radio broadcast receivers	6 552	0.19	29.14	6 412	0.10	34.57	0.12	1.87
844 Female clothing, knitted crocheted	4 835	0.14	35.93	6 213	0.10	24.01	0.96	-4.77
287 Base metal ores & concentrates nes	2 991	0.09	51.19	7 391	0.12	40.95	4.49	-3.01
525 Radio active & associated materials	3 879	0.11	84.81	6 314	0.10	87.30	4.42	0.55

For sources and notes, see end of table.

Products ranked by average 2004-2005 values SITC Revision 3 (3-digit level) Produits classés d'après la moyenne des valeurs de 2004-2005 CTCI révision 3 (positions à 3 chiffres)	1995			2005			Growth rates (percentage) Taux d'accroissement (en pourcentage) 1995-2005	
	Value (millions of dollars) Valeur (millions de dollars)	% of the country grouping exports En % des exportations du groupe de pays	% of world product exports En % des exportations mondiales des produits	Value (millions of dollars) Valeur (millions de dollars)	% of the country grouping exports En % des exportations du groupe de pays	% of world product exports En % des exportations mondiales des produits	Value Valeur	Difference from world Différence par rapport au monde
671 Pig & sponge iron, ferro alloys etc	2 908	0.08	27.75	6 615	0.11	25.94	4.91	-3.22
848 Headgear, non-textile clothing	3 693	0.11	29.03	5 857	0.10	27.92	4.10	-0.81
263 Cotton	5 129	0.15	46.75	5 442	0.09	47.75	1.34	2.03
285 Aluminium ore concentrate alumina	3 052	0.09	58.37	5 995	0.10	56.57	5.21	-0.45
693 Wire products and fencing grills	3 509	0.10	73.13	5 481	0.09	61.71	3.99	-1.40
037 Fish shellfish, prepared preserved	3 852	0.11	43.90	5 300	0.09	35.89	2.90	-1.60
059 Fruit & vegetable juice unferment	3 514	0.10	59.66	5 211	0.08	59.13	3.72	0.47
071 Coffee and coffee substitutes	3 390	0.10	21.80	5 563	0.09	35.15	2.94	6.36
058 Fruit preserve preparation excluding juice	3 710	0.11	61.25	5 172	0.08	51.61	2.94	-1.49
873 Meters and counters nes	3 228	0.09	90.20	4 818	0.08	73.70	4.54	-1.65
247 Wood in rough or roughly squared	5 154	0.15	55.75	4 839	0.08	45.44	-0.45	-1.54
211 Raw hides & skins, excluding furskins	4 800	0.14	80.58	4 471	0.07	79.36	0.14	-0.09
678 Wire of iron or steel	3 111	0.09	72.71	4 476	0.07	63.27	3.29	-1.49
811 Prefabricated buildings	2 504	0.07	92.53	4 371	0.07	82.56	4.50	-1.00
062 Sugar confectionery	3 067	0.09	68.47	4 188	0.07	63.52	2.94	-0.55
023 Butter fats oils derived from milk	3 805	0.11	94.98	3 921	0.06	93.58	-0.26	-0.08
524 Other inorganic chemicals	2 255	0.06	72.13	3 889	0.06	58.76	5.30	-1.07
689 Misc non-ferrous base metals	1 951	0.06	59.50	4 136	0.07	56.36	5.17	-0.62
686 Zinc	2 628	0.07	63.70	4 011	0.07	59.24	1.86	-0.91
273 Stone, sand and gravel	2 661	0.08	72.18	3 719	0.06	62.34	3.03	-1.40
696 Cutlery	2 377	0.07	57.02	3 626	0.06	50.32	4.82	-0.83
656 Tulle lace embroidery trim etc	2 604	0.07	57.39	3 486	0.06	42.62	3.17	-2.45
268 Wool & animal hair, incl wool tops	5 319	0.15	73.80	3 358	0.05	68.54	-4.29	-0.46
583 Plastic rod stick & profile shapes	1 409	0.04	95.56	3 254	0.05	90.42	8.74	-0.51
712 Steam vapour turbines & parts nes	2 509	0.07	92.63	3 496	0.06	84.75	1.46	-0.99
072 Cocoa	1 672	0.05	32.06	3 009	0.05	35.64	6.19	1.26
284 Nickel ores, concentrates, etc	1 139	0.03	55.81	3 076	0.05	49.90	9.65	-0.27
291 Crude animal materials nes	2 082	0.06	56.75	3 064	0.05	60.54	2.97	0.60
666 Pottery	3 347	0.10	57.73	2 803	0.05	43.05	-1.95	-2.44
843 Male clothing, knitted crocheted	2 305	0.07	28.85	2 805	0.05	18.97	-0.48	-5.30
325 Coke, semi coke, retort carbon	1 423	0.04	61.31	2 738	0.04	43.44	7.03	-5.26
283 Copper ores and concentrates	1 811	0.05	26.43	3 525	0.06	20.48	3.71	-4.85
043 Barley grain unmilled	2 471	0.07	88.63	2 757	0.04	75.30	-1.11	-1.96
431 Processed animal & veg fats & oils	2 261	0.06	48.10	2 550	0.04	45.98	3.69	0.42
035 Fish, dried salted smoked	2 084	0.06	75.28	2 703	0.04	74.08	2.00	-0.40
121 Unmanufactured tabacco and refuse	2 414	0.07	46.16	2 506	0.04	35.39	-0.36	-0.93
267 Man made fibre for spinning; waste	2 541	0.07	85.54	2 570	0.04	79.03	0.63	-0.46
016 Meat offal preserved	1 598	0.05	97.40	2 478	0.04	98.03	4.48	0.07
711 Steam generating boilers & parts	2 703	0.08	87.36	2 810	0.05	72.52	-2.94	-2.30
289 Prec metal ore concentrate excluding gold	866	0.02	70.73	2 490	0.04	53.77	12.00	2.77
266 Synthetic fibres for spinning	2 734	0.08	46.25	2 400	0.04	40.84	-1.90	-1.61
042 Rice	2 238	0.06	29.96	2 262	0.04	24.61	-1.11	-1.70
411 Animals oils and fats	2 017	0.06	89.27	2 095	0.03	84.98	0.69	-0.41
677 Iron steel rail railway materials	1 011	0.03	80.79	1 890	0.03	85.16	5.51	0.80
579 Plastic waste, parings and scrap	620	0.02	49.64	2 019	0.03	57.16	13.59	1.95
025 Eggs, yolks and albumin	1 199	0.03	83.38	1 745	0.03	80.54	3.05	-0.03
246 Wood chips, particles and waste	1 449	0.04	69.03	1 819	0.03	63.05	1.26	-1.15
422 Fixed veg fat and oil, excluding "soft"	782	0.02	10.09	1 778	0.03	13.32	7.00	2.33
091 Margarine and shortening	1 220	0.03	73.63	1 815	0.03	66.82	2.10	-1.15
212 Raw furskins and furskin pieces	1 039	0.03	82.47	1 695	0.03	74.56	3.10	-1.69
612 Leather manufactures nes	506	0.01	49.18	1 525	0.02	48.47	11.89	-0.24
685 Lead	920	0.03	63.64	1 612	0.03	57.30	1.90	-1.58
269 Worn clothing, textile article; rag	1 187	0.03	79.12	1 520	0.02	75.42	1.27	-0.22
633 Cork manufactures	950	0.03	96.85	1 379	0.02	93.11	4.27	-0.40
045 Grain, excluding wheat rice barley maize	1 536	0.04	88.64	1 363	0.02	86.98	-1.65	-0.09
046 Wheat meal & flour, meslin flour	1 962	0.06	69.87	1 233	0.02	49.77	-4.66	-1.59
593 Explosives and pyrotechnic products	664	0.02	57.53	1 188	0.02	61.95	5.60	0.88
074 Tea and maté	576	0.02	23.02	1 001	0.02	24.30	5.25	1.69
223 Oil seed for non soft oil	412	0.01	57.35	1 007	0.02	70.93	6.82	1.82
322 Briquettes, lignite and peat	830	0.02	92.33	909	0.01	92.19	0.44	-0.12
532 Dyeing and tanning extracts	545	0.02	64.02	855	0.01	60.80	3.45	-0.48

Sources:
- UNCTAD secretariat calculations based on UN DESA Statistics Division's data

Sources :
- Calculs du secrétariat de la CNUCED sur la base des données de ONU DAES Division de statistique

Products ranked by average 2004-2005 values SITC Revision 3 (3-digit level) / Produits classés d'après la moyenne des valeurs de 2004-2005 CTCI révision 3 (positions à 3 chiffres)	1995			2005			Growth rates (percentage) Taux d'accroissement (en pourcentage) 1995-2005	
	Value (millions of dollars) Valeur (millions de dollars)	% of the country grouping exports En % des exportations du groupe de pays	% of world product exports En % des exportations mondiales des produits	Value (millions of dollars) Valeur (millions de dollars)	% of the country grouping exports En % des exportations du groupe de pays	% of world product exports En % des exportations mondiales des produits	Value Valeur	Difference from world Différence par rapport au monde
All commodity groups	1 416 488	100.00	28.05	3 702 570	100.00	36.12	9.13	2.56
333 Crude petroleum & bituminous oil	156 874	11.07	76.18	535 051	14.45	72.33	11.76	-0.76
776 Valves tubes; diodes, transistors	75 105	5.30	39.73	212 948	5.75	58.36	10.19	3.70
764 Telecommunicate equipment part nes	38 243	2.70	31.43	177 949	4.81	50.62	17.09	6.73
752 Computer equipment nes	43 321	3.06	32.84	153 657	4.15	56.91	11.75	5.78
334 Heavy petroleum & bituminous oil	43 341	3.06	47.04	170 068	4.59	46.29	12.30	-0.39
759 Office equipment part & accessories	34 423	2.43	34.78	112 062	3.03	56.04	12.22	5.43
781 Passenger cars and race cars	18 158	1.28	7.81	62 001	1.67	12.78	11.61	4.25
845 Articles of apparel nes	25 554	1.80	56.62	60 379	1.63	65.96	8.30	1.59
778 Electrical machinery apparatus nes	21 856	1.54	27.20	60 634	1.64	41.16	10.92	5.03
772 Electrical circuit equipment	15 168	1.07	22.82	54 863	1.48	38.67	12.72	5.57
931 Transaction commodity unclassified	21 499	1.52	17.14	53 028	1.43	15.48	8.51	0.17
343 Natural gas, liquefied or not	9 652	0.68	27.77	48 162	1.30	38.64	15.34	2.68
842 Female clothing, woven	21 611	1.53	58.38	41 338	1.12	64.67	6.36	1.22
784 Motor vehicle parts and accessories	9 529	0.67	8.45	42 703	1.15	18.36	14.48	7.43
851 Footwear	26 177	1.85	55.73	39 600	1.07	58.27	3.12	0.26
894 Baby carriage toy game sport good	24 604	1.74	59.92	38 328	1.04	59.85	3.47	-0.11
763 Sound TV recorder or reproducer	11 641	0.82	54.21	36 874	1.00	59.32	13.93	1.72
821 Furniture part; bedding furnishing	9 627	0.68	21.30	34 598	0.93	35.60	13.34	5.82
667 Pearls, precious semiprecious stone	12 809	0.90	32.25	32 924	0.89	36.53	10.62	2.49
841 Male clothing, woven	22 912	1.62	62.03	32 649	0.88	63.69	2.77	0.32
761 Television video receive project	14 470	1.02	60.25	33 304	0.90	58.20	8.87	0.05
871 Optical instruments apparatus nes	1 599	0.11	28.60	33 929	0.92	75.90	30.79	10.45
793 Ships boats floating structures	8 682	0.61	23.68	29 345	0.79	42.94	11.00	4.80
682 Copper	12 939	0.91	36.70	29 556	0.80	47.17	6.68	2.28
775 Household equipment nes	8 787	0.62	27.72	27 508	0.74	43.38	11.91	5.19
893 Articles of plastic nes	13 356	0.94	31.65	27 571	0.74	32.71	7.18	0.31
699 Base metal manufactures nes	9 235	0.65	22.07	25 766	0.70	28.78	9.51	2.56
773 Electrical distribute equipment nes	9 273	0.65	31.08	23 989	0.65	39.59	8.15	2.11
651 Textile yarn	16 330	1.15	49.19	22 638	0.61	55.56	2.99	1.26
771 Electric power machine part excluding 716	9 840	0.69	41.61	23 217	0.63	51.06	7.83	2.38
658 Made-up textile articles nes	7 582	0.54	57.00	22 033	0.60	70.34	10.71	2.34
971 Gold non-monetary excluding ores	6 825	0.48	31.51	17 818	0.48	48.43	7.95	4.33
653 Man-made woven fabrics	19 919	1.41	55.84	19 903	0.54	61.75	-0.81	0.69
844 Female clothing, knitted crocheted	8 456	0.60	62.84	18 933	0.51	73.16	7.63	1.90
741 Heating cooling equipment parts nes	6 795	0.48	17.74	19 398	0.52	28.53	11.30	6.22
782 Goods and service vehicles	4 720	0.33	10.44	20 081	0.54	22.54	12.90	7.05
057 Fruit nut (exc oil), fresh or dried	10 855	0.77	40.90	19 443	0.53	42.28	4.51	0.08
897 Jewellery nes (667)	6 964	0.49	35.88	18 870	0.51	47.23	9.51	2.70
684 Aluminium	8 321	0.59	18.29	17 466	0.47	23.31	8.59	3.56
652 Woven cotton fabrics	11 978	0.85	53.95	17 626	0.48	61.23	3.66	0.98
673 Flat iron non-alloy steel products	8 159	0.58	22.82	18 641	0.50	28.54	7.10	1.87
342 Liquefied propane and butane	2 926	0.21	50.49	15 766	0.43	62.91	18.89	3.54
716 Rotating electric plant parts nes	6 514	0.46	25.37	16 347	0.44	32.08	8.93	2.34
874 Measure analyze control device nes	3 905	0.28	7.41	16 426	0.44	14.87	15.66	8.43
713 Internal combustion engine part nes	6 281	0.44	11.33	16 193	0.44	14.34	8.65	1.96
743 Gas pump, compressor, fan filter	6 210	0.44	17.89	15 960	0.43	23.04	9.78	2.93
728 Special industrial machine part nes	6 181	0.44	10.28	15 640	0.42	16.12	8.89	4.66
898 Music instrument device recording	6 274	0.44	20.86	15 809	0.43	31.55	9.58	5.48
511 Hydrocarbons nes; derivatives	3 748	0.26	17.94	15 506	0.42	31.83	15.76	6.52
848 Headgear, non-textile clothing	8 956	0.63	70.40	14 963	0.40	71.32	5.23	0.32
831 Case bag: storage travel shopping	10 205	0.72	68.06	14 534	0.39	60.82	2.60	-1.37
321 Coal excluding non-agglomerated	4 483	0.32	23.93	15 504	0.42	33.79	11.90	5.38
676 Iron steel bar rod section piling	5 009	0.35	18.20	14 337	0.39	27.80	9.48	3.89
512 Alcohols, phenols; derivatives	3 380	0.24	24.81	14 562	0.39	46.63	14.90	7.00
899 Manufactured articles nes	9 109	0.64	45.88	13 520	0.37	30.55	3.40	-4.81
571 Primary form ethylene polymers	3 937	0.28	24.12	13 991	0.38	35.91	12.22	4.26
655 Knitted or crocheted fabrics nes	7 292	0.51	60.50	12 890	0.35	64.89	5.33	0.68
034 Fish, fresh live chilled frozen	7 114	0.50	37.44	13 348	0.36	39.76	6.49	1.05
671 Pig & sponge iron, ferro alloys etc	5 865	0.41	55.96	13 424	0.36	52.63	8.79	0.66
679 Iron steel pipe tube fittings etc	3 824	0.27	15.76	14 564	0.39	27.12	11.25	5.27

For sources and notes, see end of table.

Pour les sources et les notes, se reporter à la fin du tableau

Products ranked by average 2004-2005 values SITC Revision 3 (3-digit level) / Produits classés d'après la moyenne des valeurs de 2004-2005 CTCI révision 3 (positions à 3 chiffres)	1995			2005			Growth rates (percentage) Taux d'accroissement (en pourcentage) 1995-2005	
	Value (millions of dollars) / Valeur (millions de dollars)	% of the country grouping exports / En % des exportations du groupe de pays	% of world product exports / En % des exportations mondiales des produits	Value (millions of dollars) / Valeur (millions de dollars)	% of the country grouping exports / En % des exportations du groupe de pays	% of world product exports / En % des exportations mondiales des produits	Value / Valeur	Difference from world / Différence par rapport au monde
575 Other plastics, in primary forms	3 830	0.27	12.87	13 546	0.37	20.78	13.59	6.11
081 Animal feed excluding unmilled cereal	7 158	0.51	34.90	12 313	0.33	40.55	4.23	1.21
625 Rubber for wheels, incl inner tube	4 790	0.34	20.64	13 503	0.36	31.24	9.05	3.98
785 Motorcycles, mopeds and cycles	6 991	0.49	37.96	12 663	0.34	39.11	6.00	0.51
574 Polyacetals and polyesters, etc	4 002	0.28	25.19	13 334	0.36	37.22	13.48	5.50
283 Copper ores and concentrates	4 955	0.35	72.29	13 386	0.36	77.75	9.78	1.22
762 Radio broadcast receivers	15 924	1.12	70.83	12 126	0.33	65.37	-2.62	-0.87
723 Civil engineering plant & equipment	3 389	0.24	11.44	13 240	0.36	19.19	12.47	5.31
036 Crustacean mollusc aquat invertebra	11 282	0.80	68.70	11 975	0.32	61.31	0.58	-1.28
281 Iron ore and concentrates	4 206	0.30	49.00	13 568	0.37	49.01	9.57	0.92
422 Fixed veg fat and oil, excluding "soft"	6 964	0.49	89.89	11 550	0.31	86.55	4.36	-0.31
843 Male clothing, knitted crocheted	5 592	0.39	69.98	11 722	0.32	79.26	6.58	1.76
513 Carboxylic acid and compounds	3 858	0.27	22.82	12 257	0.33	37.73	13.67	6.85
641 Paper and paperboard	6 670	0.47	9.23	11 781	0.32	12.35	5.95	2.60
611 Leather	8 143	0.57	51.26	11 184	0.30	54.95	3.57	0.68
582 Plastic sheet film foil & strips	4 724	0.33	16.07	11 917	0.32	20.97	8.57	2.12
054 Vegetable & vegetable products nes	6 564	0.46	31.39	10 969	0.30	34.10	4.81	0.27
522 Inorganic chemical elem oxide salt	5 174	0.37	31.80	11 009	0.30	38.18	6.45	1.78
675 Flat rolled products of alloy steel	2 486	0.18	12.20	10 180	0.27	23.02	13.36	5.33
222 Oil seed etc for soft oil	2 939	0.21	24.01	10 193	0.28	47.85	12.46	7.58
885 Watches and clocks	10 896	0.77	47.58	9 818	0.27	39.13	-1.70	-2.25
515 Organo-inorganic compound acid salt	2 471	0.17	9.22	9 615	0.26	12.11	15.76	4.54
792 Aircraft, spacecraft & equipment	3 922	0.28	5.75	10 219	0.28	7.99	8.91	4.06
572 Primary form styrene polymers	4 572	0.32	41.40	10 313	0.28	54.33	8.76	2.99
674 Flat plated iron non-alloy steel	3 212	0.23	17.63	10 094	0.27	29.53	11.36	5.45
657 Special yarn and textile fabric etc	6 895	0.49	32.67	9 617	0.26	32.61	2.10	-0.81
697 Base metal household equipment nes	4 150	0.29	41.60	9 539	0.26	51.34	8.81	2.69
634 Veneer, plywood & other wood nes	7 767	0.55	45.26	9 447	0.26	32.17	0.50	-4.40
598 Miscellaneous chemical products nes	3 631	0.26	12.28	9 704	0.26	15.33	9.03	1.68
846 Clothing accessory excluding 831 848 851	4 310	0.30	40.76	9 449	0.26	54.43	7.41	3.48
071 Coffee and coffee substitutes	12 129	0.86	77.99	10 221	0.28	64.57	-5.96	-2.54
884 Optical goods fibres nes	2 233	0.16	22.02	9 668	0.26	31.70	14.68	3.96
672 Ingots, iron steel primary products	4 286	0.30	33.70	9 143	0.25	32.10	7.33	-0.45
037 Fish shellfish, prepared preserved	4 819	0.34	54.93	9 270	0.25	62.78	5.61	1.11
231 Natural rubber, latex, gum, etc	7 565	0.53	97.51	9 145	0.25	97.57	1.69	0.00
872 Medical instruments appliances nes	2 334	0.16	12.23	9 224	0.25	17.59	15.21	5.05
542 Medicines including veterinary	2 962	0.21	6.53	9 644	0.26	4.71	11.05	-6.01
061 Sugar, mollasses and honey	7 681	0.54	48.87	9 337	0.25	54.29	0.48	0.56
661 Lime cement construction material	3 401	0.24	30.85	9 406	0.25	49.97	8.47	4.54
681 Silver, platinum, platinum metals	1 188	0.08	19.13	8 745	0.24	42.09	20.74	9.22
287 Base metal ores & concentrates nes	2 634	0.19	45.08	10 187	0.28	56.45	10.53	3.02
813 Lighting fixtures and fittings nes	3 596	0.25	36.55	8 665	0.23	45.72	9.08	2.88
747 Pipe, boiler, tank & vat appliances	1 876	0.13	9.62	8 695	0.23	21.35	16.25	9.43
786 Trailer caravan transport container	3 450	0.24	35.03	8 619	0.23	37.85	9.65	1.56
642 Cut paper and paperboard articles	4 451	0.31	17.46	8 057	0.22	22.53	5.65	2.56
695 Tools for use in hand or in machine	3 408	0.24	19.58	8 383	0.23	27.84	8.69	3.59
892 Printed matter	3 157	0.22	12.40	7 850	0.21	20.04	9.18	5.08
514 Nitrogen function compounds	2 660	0.19	14.11	8 089	0.22	23.92	9.45	4.02
516 Other organic chemicals	2 050	0.14	18.44	7 707	0.21	31.84	12.66	5.46
042 Rice	5 201	0.37	69.64	6 912	0.19	75.17	1.26	0.67
635 Wood manufactures nes	3 872	0.27	34.37	6 871	0.19	32.99	6.03	0.04
248 Wood simply worked, railway sleeper	4 980	0.35	19.00	6 917	0.19	19.77	3.68	1.39
694 Nails screws nuts bolts rivets	2 798	0.20	25.85	7 036	0.19	33.52	9.02	2.83
012 Meat nes, fresh chilled frozen	4 784	0.34	19.81	7 195	0.19	18.52	3.30	-0.43
724 Textile leather machinery parts nes	3 977	0.28	15.75	7 026	0.19	27.87	5.50	5.50
421 Fixed veg fat and oil, "soft"	4 684	0.33	38.53	6 397	0.17	38.88	2.81	0.72
744 Mechanical handling equipment nes	2 852	0.20	10.15	7 214	0.19	13.96	7.32	2.50
553 Perfume toilet cosmetics, excluding soap	1 947	0.14	10.38	6 807	0.18	15.65	13.26	4.76
112 Alcoholic beverages	2 819	0.20	10.18	6 560	0.18	14.38	8.61	3.74
691 Iron steel aluminium structures nes	2 960	0.21	21.56	7 151	0.19	26.85	9.37	3.34
098 Edible products & preparations nes	2 754	0.19	15.78	6 628	0.18	20.55	8.07	1.98

For sources and notes, see end of table.

Pour les sources et les notes, se reporter à la fin du tableau

Products ranked by average 2004-2005 values SITC Revision 3 (3-digit level) Produits classés d'après la moyenne des valeurs de 2004-2005 CTCI révision 3 (positions à 3 chiffres)	1995			2005			Growth rates (percentage) Taux d'accroissement (en pourcentage) 1995-2005	
	Value (millions of dollars) Valeur (millions de dollars)	% of the country grouping exports En % des exportations du groupe de pays	% of world product exports En % des exportations mondiales des produits	Value (millions of dollars) Valeur (millions de dollars)	% of the country grouping exports En % des exportations du groupe de pays	% of world product exports En % des exportations mondiales des produits	Value Valeur	Difference from world Différence par rapport au monde
541 Pharmaceuticals excluding medicines	3 179	0.22	12.06	6 601	0.18	9.95	7.13	-2.71
751 Office machines	4 601	0.32	28.78	7 181	0.19	47.73	2.50	4.73
533 Pigment, paint, varnish & related	3 007	0.21	15.01	6 345	0.17	16.40	8.10	1.61
562 Manufactured fertilizer excluding crude	3 820	0.27	21.62	6 194	0.17	26.17	4.55	2.17
664 Glass	2 404	0.17	17.13	6 209	0.17	24.96	10.27	4.12
292 Crude vegetable materials nes	4 032	0.28	26.84	5 841	0.16	26.06	3.14	-0.98
745 Non-electrical machinery tool nes	1 651	0.12	7.56	5 913	0.16	15.07	12.81	7.56
335 Residual petroleum products nes	1 243	0.09	20.59	5 895	0.16	33.42	12.70	2.84
072 Cocoa	3 539	0.25	67.85	5 412	0.15	64.11	4.27	-0.65
749 Non-electric machinery part nes	2 082	0.15	16.20	5 544	0.15	25.70	9.52	4.62
011 Beef, fresh chilled frozen	1 591	0.11	10.04	5 782	0.16	27.10	11.90	8.67
251 Pulp and waste paper	4 482	0.32	16.32	5 394	0.15	20.92	3.93	2.15
881 Photographic device nes	4 032	0.28	31.52	4 509	0.12	26.79	1.53	-1.15
714 Non-electric engines excluding 712 713 718	1 330	0.09	5.07	4 566	0.12	6.70	17.76	8.42
665 Glassware	1 870	0.13	18.46	4 755	0.13	27.57	9.30	4.13
056 Vegetables roots tubers nes	3 104	0.22	28.85	4 654	0.13	29.36	3.96	-0.13
731 Machine tools for material removal	1 889	0.13	11.59	4 665	0.13	17.29	7.65	4.35
783 Road motor vehicles nes	1 098	0.08	6.54	4 710	0.13	15.71	12.71	7.56
656 Tulle lace embroidery trim etc	1 924	0.14	42.40	4 637	0.13	56.68	8.11	2.48
662 Clay and refractory materials	1 164	0.08	10.72	4 667	0.13	27.30	13.69	9.38
058 Fruit preserve preparation excluding juice	2 189	0.15	36.13	4 477	0.12	44.68	6.26	1.83
263 Cotton	3 300	0.23	30.08	4 383	0.12	38.46	0.72	1.40
121 Unmanufactured tabacco and refuse	2 613	0.18	49.98	4 306	0.12	60.80	1.24	0.67
654 Other woven textile fabrics nes	3 218	0.23	29.34	4 143	0.11	37.52	2.48	2.75
554 Soaps cleansers polishes	1 988	0.14	17.39	4 131	0.11	18.72	7.01	0.33
742 Liquid pump; liquid elevator parts	1 112	0.08	6.26	4 462	0.12	13.26	13.83	7.77
659 Floor coverings etc	2 935	0.21	30.83	4 277	0.12	37.01	2.07	1.46
746 Ball or roller bearings	1 837	0.13	15.10	4 194	0.11	21.41	8.05	3.85
748 Mechanical transmission equipment	1 297	0.09	8.80	4 194	0.11	14.27	12.10	5.70
895 Office and stationery supplies nes	1 984	0.14	28.40	3 855	0.10	36.86	6.50	2.93
122 Manufactured tabacco	4 968	0.35	26.24	3 802	0.10	21.45	-3.74	-1.87
591 Household and garden chemicals	1 439	0.10	13.47	3 904	0.11	24.28	8.96	5.70
288 Non ferrous base metal waste nes	1 928	0.14	20.97	4 485	0.12	25.02	6.30	0.89
523 Inorganic acid metal salt peroxy	1 747	0.12	23.13	4 107	0.11	33.63	8.04	4.16
882 Photo cinematographic supply excluding 883	1 872	0.13	10.61	3 589	0.10	17.91	6.55	5.63
629 Articles of rubber nes	1 267	0.09	13.78	3 801	0.10	20.91	10.45	3.73
325 Coke, semi coke, retort carbon	763	0.05	32.90	2 762	0.07	43.82	16.39	4.11
666 Pottery	2 376	0.17	40.97	3 595	0.10	55.21	3.12	2.63
531 Synthetic organic colour agents	2 074	0.15	21.06	3 492	0.09	33.74	4.47	4.52
696 Cutlery	1 777	0.13	42.62	3 525	0.10	48.91	6.61	0.95
663 Mineral manufactures nes	1 543	0.11	11.79	3 611	0.10	17.02	8.30	4.30
048 Cereal & preparation flour starch	1 755	0.12	13.87	3 526	0.10	14.34	5.91	-0.29
266 Synthetic fibres for spinning	3 013	0.21	50.96	3 298	0.09	56.11	0.95	1.25
285 Aluminium ore concentrate alumina	1 936	0.14	37.04	3 655	0.10	34.49	5.57	-0.08
278 Other crude minerals	2 171	0.15	29.21	3 413	0.09	32.63	4.39	1.44
059 Fruit & vegetable juice unferment	2 214	0.16	37.59	3 376	0.09	38.30	2.66	-0.59
017 Meat offal preserved nes	1 368	0.10	23.31	3 507	0.09	33.64	9.80	5.05
044 Maize unmilled, excluding sweet corn	1 138	0.08	10.42	3 256	0.09	29.09	8.03	7.87
284 Nickel ores, concentrates, etc	898	0.06	44.01	3 088	0.08	50.10	10.18	0.26
074 Tea and maté	1 895	0.13	75.71	3 046	0.08	73.99	3.06	-0.50
737 Metalwork machinery nes excluding tools	904	0.06	8.98	3 032	0.08	19.12	12.50	9.59
431 Processed animal & veg fats & oils	2 414	0.17	51.35	2 936	0.08	52.94	2.68	-0.59
573 Vinyl chloride etc polymers	1 663	0.12	21.66	3 026	0.08	24.77	5.85	1.09
693 Wire products and fencing grills	1 126	0.08	23.47	3 066	0.08	34.52	8.90	3.50
592 Starches, glutenes, glues, etc	1 172	0.08	15.29	2 823	0.08	20.25	8.65	2.93
232 Synthetic & reclaimed rubber; waste	1 018	0.07	17.31	3 025	0.08	25.39	10.51	4.40
687 Tin	1 255	0.09	79.33	2 735	0.07	86.22	4.65	0.62
689 Misc non-ferrous base metals	889	0.06	27.09	2 647	0.07	36.06	9.84	4.05
344 Petroleum and hydrocarbon gas nes	510	0.04	19.02	2 798	0.08	28.55	16.81	4.17
551 Essential oils, perfumes & flavours	870	0.06	15.38	2 471	0.07	15.59	11.02	0.54
247 Wood in rough or roughly squared	3 181	0.22	34.41	2 663	0.07	25.01	-3.13	-4.22

For sources and notes, see end of table.

Pour les sources et les notes, se reporter à la fin du tableau

Products ranked by average 2004-2005 values SITC Revision 3 (3-digit level) / Produits classés d'après la moyenne des valeurs de 2004-2005 CTCI révision 3 (positions à 3 chiffres)	1995			2005			Growth rates (percentage) Taux d'accroissement (en pourcentage) 1995-2005	
	Value (millions of dollars) / Valeur (millions de dollars)	% of the country grouping exports / En % des exportations du groupe de pays	% of world product exports / En % des exportations mondiales des produits	Value (millions of dollars) / Valeur (millions de dollars)	% of the country grouping exports / En % des exportations du groupe de pays	% of world product exports / En % des exportations mondiales des produits	Value / Valeur	Difference from world / Différence par rapport au monde
001 Live animal excluding fish & crustacean	2 119	0.15	20.38	2 374	0.06	18.71	2.34	0.63
282 Ferrous iron & steel, waste & scrap	766	0.05	9.73	2 381	0.06	10.02	12.29	0.00
692 Metal storage transport container	1 171	0.08	16.77	2 512	0.07	22.65	6.34	2.85
022 Milk products, excluding butter & cheese	969	0.07	6.28	2 435	0.07	11.29	9.15	5 84
075 Spices	1 450	0.10	77.03	2 290	0.06	74.61	3.82	-0.59
041 Wheat meslin, incl spelt, unmilled	1 367	0.10	7.89	1 905	0.05	10.72	4.91	5.38
812 Sanitary plumb heat fixtures nes	609	0.04	11.22	2 304	0.06	20.50	14.21	7.40
686 Zinc	1 072	0.08	25.98	2 182	0.06	32.23	5.80	3.02
062 Sugar confectionery	1 322	0.09	29.51	2 238	0.06	33.95	4.60	1.11
678 Wire of iron or steel	977	0.07	22.83	2 181	0.06	30.83	8.27	3.48
774 Electrodiagnostic equipment	414	0.03	3.33	2 269	0.06	8.79	16.79	9.50
621 Rubber material e.g. paste tube rod	738	0.05	11.21	2 224	0.06	17.15	10.63	4.16
111 Non alcoholic beverage nes	994	0.07	22.08	2 061	0.06	19.61	7.58	-1.92
273 Stone, sand and gravel	945	0.07	25.62	2 029	0.05	34.00	7.40	2.96
291 Crude animal materials nes	1 551	0.11	42.27	1 938	0.05	38.29	1.37	-1.00
524 Other inorganic chemicals	759	0.05	24.27	2 316	0.06	34.99	7.58	1.22
289 Prec metal ore concentrate excluding gold	341	0.02	27.82	2 012	0.05	43.44	6.92	-2.31
351 Electric current	622	0.04	8.00	2 157	0.06	9.95	13.79	3.78
581 Plastic tube pipe hose & fittings	806	0.06	14.75	1 925	0.05	16.47	10.46	3.24
733 Metal work tool no material removal	917	0.06	13.13	1 839	0.05	20.63	5.49	4.75
721 Agricultural machine nes excluding tractor	487	0.03	4.65	1 720	0.05	8.44	11.33	6.00
726 Printing bookbinding machines parts	601	0.04	4.30	1 734	0.05	9.38	10.69	9.07
683 Nickel	333	0.02	6.48	1 317	0.04	9.72	17.46	7.81
735 Machine part accessory for 731 733	408	0.03	6.25	1 730	0.05	14.88	13.49	8.96
612 Leather manufactures nes	519	0.04	50.44	1 540	0.04	48.95	11.83	-0.30
873 Meters and counters nes	331	0.02	9.24	1 657	0.04	25.34	14.63	8.44
268 Wool & animal hair, incl wool tops	1 737	0.12	24.10	1 460	0.04	29.81	-2.41	1.42
722 Tractors	319	0.02	3.72	1 533	0.04	10.84	15.58	12.38
791 Railway vehicles and equipment	319	0.02	4.52	1 569	0.04	9.79	11.32	3.33
597 Additive e.g. lubricate, antifreeze	575	0.04	7.89	1 430	0.04	12.81	9.30	6.02
579 Plastic waste, parings and scrap	624	0.04	49.93	1 491	0.04	42.22	9.51	-2.13
272 Crude fertilizer, excluding manufactured	929	0.07	71 72	1 345	0.04	72.99	1.41	0.16
073 Chocolate & cocoa preparations nes	491	0.03	6 15	1 318	0.04	10.72	9.17	5.07
896 Work of art & collections; antiques	293	0.02	4.51	1 132	0.03	7.79	13.07	5.09
246 Wood chips, particles and waste	632	0.04	30.13	995	0.03	34.51	4.49	2.08
891 Arms and ammunition	244	0.02	3.12	906	0.02	12.29	13.72	15.37
685 Lead	402	0.03	27.79	991	0.03	35.24	6.95	3.47
211 Raw hides & skins, excluding furskins	757	0.05	12.71	896	0.02	15.91	3.68	3.44
035 Fish, dried salted smoked	674	0.05	24.34	906	0.02	24.84	3.42	1.02
046 Wheat meal & flour, meslin flour	590	0.04	21.01	1 042	0.03	42.03	0.92	3.98
725 Paper & pulp mill, cut manufacture	511	0.04	6.33	938	0.03	10.25	4.60	4.50
613 Furskin tanned dressed etc	345	0 02	26.08	916	0.02	53.28	7.59	7.60
711 Steam generating boilers & parts	275	0 02	8.90	900	0.02	23.23	11.94	12.58
091 Margarine and shortening	417	0 03	25.13	811	0.02	29.84	5.60	2.35
727 Food processing machine excluding domestic	478	0.03	7.39	840	0.02	9.15	3.42	0.99
718 Power generating machinery part nes	235	0.02	4.52	918	0.02	8.07	11.84	4.17
277 Natural abrasives nes	381	0.03	38.07	724	0.02	62.23	10.21	7.78
811 Prefabricated buildings	146	0.01	5.39	762	0.02	14.40	15.20	9.71
593 Explosives and pyrotechnic products	397	0.03	34.37	682	0.02	35.59	5.22	0.50
267 Man made fibre for spinning; waste	380	0.03	12.78	622	0.02	19.12	3.53	2.44
212 Raw furskins and furskin pieces	150	0.01	11.91	488	0.01	21.48	13.69	8.89
274 Sulphur and unroasted iron pyrites	142	0.01	16.80	523	0.01	37.79	14.89	10.30
024 Cheese and curd	154	0.01	1.39	594	0.02	3.51	11.14	7.23
532 Dyeing and tanning extracts	305	0.02	35.79	548	0.01	38.94	4.73	0.80
525 Radio active & associated materials	321	0.02	7.03	447	0.01	6.18	1.55	-2.32
269 Worn clothing, textile article; rag	310	0.02	20.69	474	0.01	23.50	1.83	0.33
712 Steam vapour turbines & parts nes	127	0.01	4.67	453	0.01	10.99	12.02	9.58
411 Animals oils and fats	232	0.02	10.27	359	0.01	14.58	4.70	3.60
025 Eggs, yolks and albumin	175	0.01	12.17	381	0.01	17.59	5.31	2.23
223 Oil seed for non soft oil	266	0.02	37.01	377	0.01	26.60	2.60	-2.40
261 Silk	520	0.04	86.38	295	0.01	83.91	-6.60	-0.47

Sources:
- UNCTAD secretariat calculations based on UN DESA Statistics Division's data

Sources :
- Calculs du secrétariat de la CNUCED sur la base des données de ONU DAES Division de statistique

Leading products exported based on average 2004-2005 values SITC Revision 3 (3-digit level) / Principaux produits exportés d'après la moyenne des valeurs de 2004-2005 CTCI révision 3 (positions à 3 chiffres)	2004-2005			
	Value (f.o.b., thousands of dollars) / Valeur (f.a.b., milliers de dollars)	As percentage En pourcentage		
		of country total / du total du pays	of ** (1) / des ** (1)	of world / du monde
Albania - Albanie (**=Transition)				
All commodity groups	628 892	100.00	0.18	0.01
851 Footwear	173 269	27.55	6.73	0.27
841 Male clothing, woven	83 967	13.35	3.12	0.17
845 Articles of apparel nes	43 855	6.97	2.21	0.05
844 Female clothing, knitted crocheted	28 142	4.47	3.76	0.11
699 Base metal manufactures nes	24 830	3.95	1.63	0.03
671 Pig & sponge iron, ferro alloys etc	24 191	3.85	0.48	0.10
842 Female clothing, woven	19 800	3.15	0.60	0.03
37 Fish shellfish, prepared preserved	16 129	2.56	9.54	0.11
288 Non ferrous base metal waste nes	15 306	2.43	5.40	0.10
292 Crude vegetable materials nes	14 872	2.36	12.45	0.07
Remainder	184 531	29.34		
Algeria - Algérie (**=Developing)				
All commodity groups	39 123 936	100.00	1.16	0.41
333 Crude petroleum & bituminous oil	21 426 804	54.77	4.67	3.36
343 Natural gas, liquefied or not	9 986 296	25.52	25.52	9.01
342 Liquefied propane and butane	3 421 610	8.75	22.28	14.51
334 Heavy petroleum & bituminous oil	3 258 075	8.33	2.26	1.04
335 Residual petroleum products nes	304 942	0.78	5.69	1.85
522 Inorganic chemical elem oxide salt	158 920	0.41	1.57	0.59
282 Ferrous iron & steel, waste & scrap	77 752	0.20	3.35	0.33
673 Flat iron non-alloy steel products	61 033	0.16	0.36	0.10
562 Manufactured fertilizer excl. crude	54 419	0.14	0.92	0.24
686 Zinc	31 093	0.08	1.48	0.49
Remainder	342 992	0.88		
Andorra - Andorre (**=Developed)				
All commodity groups	122 826	100.00	0.00	0.00
781 Passenger cars and race cars	26 187	21.32	0.01	0.01
763 Sound TV recorder or reproducer	25 879	21.07	0.10	0.04
61 Sugar, mollasses and honey	9 880	8.04	0.14	0.06
553 Perfume toilet cosmetics, excl. soap	5 778	4.70	0.02	0.01
899 Manufactured articles nes	4 781	3.89	0.02	0.01
898 Music instrument device recording	4 083	3.32	0.01	0.01
611 Leather	3 591	2.92	0.04	0.02
98 Edible products & preparations nes	2 864	2.33	0.01	0.01
872 Medical instruments appliances nes	2 851	2.32	0.01	0.01
892 Printed matter	2 764	2.25	0.01	0.01
Remainder	34 167	27.82		
Angola (**=Developing)				
All commodity groups	18 078 713	100.00	0.54	0.19
333 Crude petroleum & bituminous oil	17 433 148	96.43	3.80	2.73
334 Heavy petroleum & bituminous oil	297 886	1.65	0.21	0.10
667 Pearls, precious semiprecious stone	228 092	1.26	0.73	0.27
273 Stone, sand and gravel	17 911	0.10	0.95	0.31
36 Crustacean mollusc aquat invertebra	11 148	0.06	0.10	0.06
342 Liquefied propane and butane	10 243	0.06	0.07	0.04
344 Petroleum and hydrocarbon gas nes	5 668	0.03	0.23	0.06
288 Non ferrous base metal waste nes	4 898	0.03	0.13	0.03
283 Copper ores and concentrates	4 481	0.02	0.04	0.03
874 Measure analyze control device nes	4 213	0.02	0.03	0.00
Remainder	61 025	0.34		
Argentina - Argentine (**=Developing)				
All commodity groups	37 210 388	100.00	1.10	0.39
81 Animal feed excluding unmilled cereal	3 933 756	10.57	32.59	13.08
421 Fixed veg fat and oil, "soft"	3 047 441	8.19	47.73	19.08
333 Crude petroleum & bituminous oil	2 382 420	6.40	0.52	0.37
334 Heavy petroleum & bituminous oil	2 263 545	6.08	1.57	0.73
222 Oil seed etc for soft oil	2 123 327	5.71	21.57	9.96
41 Wheat meslin, incl spelt, unmilled	1 323 033	3.56	61.22	7.12
44 Maize unmilled, excluding sweet corn	1 280 610	3.44	41.97	11.21
11 Beef, fresh chilled frozen	996 974	2.68	19.59	4.97
283 Copper ores and concentrates	833 128	2.24	7.06	5.62
782 Goods and service vehicles	813 598	2.19	4.50	0.96
Remainder	18 212 556	48.94		

Leading products exported based on average 2004-2005 values SITC Revision 3 (3-digit level) / Principaux produits exportés d'après la moyenne des valeurs de 2004-2005 CTCI révision 3 (positions à 3 chiffres)	2004-2005			
	Value (f.o.b., thousands of dollars) / Valeur (f.a.b., milliers de dollars)	As percentage En pourcentage		
		of country total / du total du pays	of ** (1) / des ** (1)	of world / du monde
Armenia - Arménie (**=Transition)				
All commodity groups	824 609	100.00	0.23	0.01
667 Pearls, precious semiprecious stone	242 566	29.42	22.20	0.29
671 Pig & sponge iron, ferro alloys etc	150 031	18.19	2.97	0.64
112 Alcoholic beverages	68 427	8.30	5.77	0.15
971 Gold non-monetary excluding ores	40 014	4.85	5.79	0.11
682 Copper	39 392	4.78	0.78	0.07
287 Base metal ores & concentrates nes	36 314	4.40	8.52	0.25
897 Jewellery nes (667)	34 281	4.16	7.77	0.09
845 Articles of apparel nes	24 234	2.94	1.22	0.03
283 Copper ores and concentrates	22 771	2.76	7.63	0.15
351 Electric current	18 460	2.24	1.65	0.09
Remainder	148 117	17.96		
Aruba (**=Developing)				
All commodity groups	3 186 369	100.00	0.09	0.03
334 Heavy petroleum & bituminous oil	3 046 237	95.60	2.12	0.98
335 Residual petroleum products nes	37 866	1.19	0.71	0.23
333 Crude petroleum & bituminous oil	27 285	0.86	0.01	0.00
971 Gold non-monetary excluding ores	24 905	0.78	0.13	0.07
61 Sugar, mollasses and honey	9 581	0.30	0.11	0.06
792 Aircraft, spacecraft & equipment	8 347	0.26	0.09	0.01
744 Mechanical handling equipment nes	5 121	0.16	0.08	0.01
764 Telecommunicate equipment part nes	4 650	0.15	0.00	0.00
73 Chocolate & cocoa preparations nes	4 583	0.14	0.37	0.04
274 Sulphur and unroasted iron pyrites	3 864	0.12	0.73	0.29
Remainder	13 930	0.44		
Australia - Australie (**=Developed)				
All commodity groups	101 491 957	100.00	1.72	1.05
321 Coal excluding non-agglomomerated	13 235 679	13.04	62.24	34.20
931 Transaction commodity unclassified	11 746 382	11.57	5.90	4.14
281 Iron ore and concentrates	6 429 059	6.33	71.68	28.58
971 Gold non-monetary excluding ores	4 294 059	4.23	25.40	11.50
333 Crude petroleum & bituminous oil	4 247 842	4.19	4.50	0.67
11 Beef, fresh chilled frozen	3 474 900	3.42	23.63	17.31
285 Aluminium ore concentrate alumina	3 271 644	3.22	60.25	34.93
684 Aluminium	3 163 373	3.12	6.69	4.40
41 Wheat meslin, incl spelt, unmilled	2 677 513	2.64	18.35	14.41
343 Natural gas, liquefied or not	2 355 743	2.32	3.84	2.13
Remainder	46 595 763	45.91		
Austria - Autriche (**=Developed)				
All commodity groups	108 636 915	100.00	1.84	1.13
781 Passenger cars and race cars	7 710 563	7.10	1.87	1.64
713 Internal combustion engine part nes	4 041 018	3.72	4.41	3.77
641 Paper and paperboard	3 251 614	2.99	4.00	3.45
351 Electric current	3 166 000	2.91	19.02	16.23
784 Motor vehicle parts and accessories	3 061 979	2.82	1.66	1.37
728 Special industrial machine part nes	2 719 253	2.50	3.38	2.84
931 Transaction commodity unclassified	2 424 351	2.23	1.22	0.86
699 Base metal manufactures nes	2 311 957	2.13	3.88	2.73
542 Medicines including veterinary	1 941 266	1.79	1.04	0.99
772 Electrical circuit equipment	1 869 982	1.72	2.22	1.39
Remainder	76 138 931	70.09		
Azerbaijan - Azerbaïdjan (**=Transition)				
All commodity groups	3 981 300	100.00	1.13	0.04
333 Crude petroleum & bituminous oil	2 241 624	56.30	2.66	0.35
334 Heavy petroleum & bituminous oil	893 813	22.45	2.34	0.29
793 Ships boats floating structures	201 821	5.07	7.78	0.31
57 Fruit nut (exc oil), fresh or dried	90 111	2.26	13.63	0.21
285 Aluminium ore concentrate alumina	74 347	1.87	10.88	0.79
684 Aluminium	50 779	1.28	0.70	0.07
571 Primary form ethylene polymers	43 116	1.08	5.68	0.12
263 Cotton	38 071	0.96	2.53	0.34
676 Iron steel bar rod section piling	26 230	0.66	0.55	0.05
54 Vegetable & vegetable products nes	22 774	0.57	4.76	0.07
Remainder	298 615	7.50		

For sources and notes, see end of table.

Pour les sources et les notes, se reporter à la fin du tableau.

156

Bahrain - Bahreïn (**=Developing)

Leading products exported based on average 2004-2005 values SITC Revision 3 (3-digit level) / Principaux produits exportés d'après la moyenne des valeurs de 2004-2005 CTCI révision 3 (positions à 3 chiffres)	Value (f.o.b., thousands of dollars) / Valeur (f.a.b., milliers de dollars)	of country total / du total du pays	of ** (1) / des ** (1)	of world / du monde
All commodity groups	8 624 456	100.00	0.26	0.09
334 Heavy petroleum & bituminous oil	6 669 220	77.33	4.63	2.14
684 Aluminium	981 137	11.38	5.65	1.37
281 Iron ore and concentrates	181 313	2.10	1.58	0.81
562 Manufactured fertilizer excl. crude	114 337	1.33	1.94	0.50
842 Female clothing, woven	101 940	1.18	0.26	0.17
512 Alcohols, phenols; derivatives	69 741	0.81	0.53	0.24
781 Passenger cars and race cars	57 617	0.67	0.10	0.01
652 Woven cotton fabrics	45 329	0.53	0.27	0.16
741 Heating cooling equipment parts nes	34 413	0.40	0.19	0.05
641 Paper and paperboard	21 741	0.25	0.20	0.02
Remainder	347 668	4.03		

Bangladesh (**=Developing)

Product	Value	of country total	of ** (1)	of world
All commodity groups	6 204 658	100.00	0.18	0.06
845 Articles of apparel nes	1 989 948	32.07	3.53	2.27
841 Male clothing, woven	1 347 213	21.71	4.39	2.74
843 Male clothing, knitted crocheted	561 892	9.06	4.99	3.91
842 Female clothing, woven	504 931	8.14	1.31	0.83
36 Crustacean mollusc aquat invertebra	379 767	6.12	3.26	1.99
844 Female clothing, knitted crocheted	264 854	4.27	1.43	1.04
611 Leather	224 653	3.62	2.05	1.10
658 Made-up textile articles nes	167 494	2.70	0.84	0.58
651 Textile yarn	96 374	1.55	0.44	0.24
264 Jute & bast fibre nes, raw & retted	81 531	1.31	90.31	84.21
Remainder	586 000	9.44		

Barbados - Barbade (**=Developing)

Product	Value	of country total	of ** (1)	of world
All commodity groups	278 139	100.00	0.01	0.00
334 Heavy petroleum & bituminous oil	48 685	17.50	0.03	0.02
112 Alcoholic beverages	28 274	10.17	0.46	0.06
61 Sugar, molasses and honey	22 617	8.13	0.27	0.14
333 Crude petroleum & bituminous oil	15 986	5.75	0.00	0.00
661 Lime cement construction material	15 608	5.61	0.19	0.09
772 Electrical circuit equipment	14 211	5.11	0.03	0.01
542 Medicines including veterinary	14 001	5.03	0.16	0.01
591 Household and garden chemicals	11 384	4.09	0.31	0.07
764 Telecommunicate equipment part nes	8 915	3.21	0.01	0.00
892 Printed matter	6 887	2.48	0.09	0.02
Remainder	91 571	32.92		

Belarus - Bélarus (**=Transition)

Product	Value	of country total	of ** (1)	of world
All commodity groups	14 864 456	100.00	4.23	0.15
334 Heavy petroleum & bituminous oil	4 073 392	27.40	10.65	1.31
562 Manufactured fertilizer excl. crude	990 657	6.66	16.83	4.29
782 Goods and service vehicles	597 824	4.02	44.13	0.71
722 Tractors	385 921	2.60	76.41	2.87
676 Iron steel bar rod section piling	372 295	2.50	7.74	0.76
333 Crude petroleum & bituminous oil	360 666	2.43	0.43	0.06
775 Household equipment nes	317 561	2.14	32.61	0.52
821 Furniture part; bedding furnishing	271 972	1.83	11.67	0.29
783 Road motor vehicles nes	229 738	1.55	51.34	0.80
784 Motor vehicle parts and accessories	217 802	1.47	12.84	0.10
Remainder	7 046 628	47.41		

Belgium - Belgique (**=Developed)

Product	Value	of country total	of ** (1)	of world
All commodity groups	320 272 284	100.00	5.42	3.32
781 Passenger cars and race cars	28 845 871	9.01	7.00	6.13
542 Medicines including veterinary	27 913 563	8.72	14.99	14.29
667 Pearls, precious semiprecious stone	15 291 467	4.77	29.38	18.13
515 Organo-inorganic compound acid salt	12 084 498	3.77	18.48	15.97
334 Heavy petroleum & bituminous oil	11 495 954	3.59	8.85	3.68
784 Motor vehicle parts and accessories	6 657 475	2.08	3.62	2.98
575 Other plastics, in primary forms	6 408 703	2.00	13.42	10.58
343 Natural gas, liquefied or not	5 236 391	1.63	8.54	4.73
931 Transaction commodity unclassified	4 985 701	1.56	2.50	1.76
541 Pharmaceuticals excluding medicines	4 874 841	1.52	8.57	7.71
Remainder	196 477 819	61.35		

Belize (**=Developing)

Product	Value	of country total	of ** (1)	of world
All commodity groups	209 246	100.00	0.01	0.00
59 Fruit & vegetable juice unferment	48 180	23.03	1.52	0.57
36 Crustacean mollusc aquat invertebra	47 699	22.80	0.41	0.25
61 Sugar, mollasses and honey	38 711	18.50	0.46	0.24
57 Fruit nut (exc oil), fresh or dried	38 058	18.19	0.21	0.09
843 Male clothing, knitted crocheted	17 608	8.41	0.16	0.12
54 Vegetable & vegetable products nes	3 474	1.66	0.03	0.01
551 Essential oils, perfumes & flavours	3 099	1.48	0.13	0.02
248 Wood simply worked, railway sleeper	1 243	0.59	0.02	0.00
642 Cut paper and paperboard articles	1 134	0.54	0.01	0.00
634 Veneer, plywood & other wood nes	1 037	0.50	0.01	0.00
Remainder	9 003	4.30		

Benin - Bénin (**=Developing)

Product	Value	of country total	of ** (1)	of world
All commodity groups	293 254	100.00	0.01	0.00
263 Cotton	185 281	63.18	4.57	1.65
122 Manufactured tabacco	19 341	6.60	0.52	0.11
57 Fruit nut (exc oil), fresh or dried	18 745	6.39	0.10	0.04
661 Lime cement construction material	11 840	4.04	0.14	0.07
676 Iron steel bar rod section piling	6 111	2.08	0.05	0.01
81 Animal feed excluding unmilled cereal	5 699	1.94	0.05	0.02
421 Fixed veg fat and oil, "soft"	4 752	1.62	0.07	0.03
971 Gold non-monetary excluding ores	3 856	1.32	0.02	0.01
248 Wood simply worked, railway sleeper	3 849	1.31	0.06	0.01
652 Woven cotton fabrics	3 126	1.07	0.02	0.01
Remainder	30 653	10.45		

Bolivia - Bolivie (**=Developing)

Product	Value	of country total	of ** (1)	of world
All commodity groups	2 525 873	100.00	0.07	0.03
343 Natural gas, liquefied or not	801 834	31.74	2.05	0.72
333 Crude petroleum & bituminous oil	240 661	9.53	0.05	0.04
81 Animal feed excluding unmilled cereal	238 608	9.45	1.98	0.79
287 Base metal ores & concentrates nes	223 469	8.85	2.77	1.55
421 Fixed veg fat and oil, "soft"	133 362	5.28	2.09	0.83
687 Tin	109 160	4.32	4.18	3.61
289 Prec metal ore concentrate excl. gold	88 730	3.51	5.08	2.11
57 Fruit nut (exc oil), fresh or dried	73 954	2.93	0.41	0.17
897 Jewellery nes (667)	65 004	2.57	0.37	0.17
971 Gold non-monetary excluding ores	56 456	2.24	0.29	0.15
Remainder	494 636	19.58		

Bosnia and Herzegovina - Bosnie-Herzégovine (**=Transition)

Product	Value	of country total	of ** (1)	of world
All commodity groups	2 001 924	100.00	0.57	0.02
684 Aluminium	220 928	11.04	3.06	0.31
248 Wood simply worked, railway sleeper	159 234	7.95	5.00	0.46
713 Internal combustion engine part nes	144 329	7.21	21.49	0.13
821 Furniture part; bedding furnishing	110 060	5.50	4.72	0.12
285 Aluminium ore concentrate alumina	96 338	4.81	14.10	1.03
351 Electric current	90 668	4.53	8.09	0.46
851 Footwear	64 445	3.22	2.50	0.10
325 Coke, semi coke, retort carbon	61 386	3.07	6.02	0.84
676 Iron steel bar rod section piling	53 247	2.66	1.11	0.11
691 Iron steel aluminium structures nes	49 260	2.46	7.42	0.20
Remainder	952 029	47.56		

Botswana (**=Developing)

Product	Value	of country total	of ** (1)	of world
All commodity groups	3 549 356	100.00	0.11	0.04
667 Pearls, precious semiprecious stone	3 013 461	84.90	9.66	3.57
284 Nickel ores, concentrates, etc	254 088	7.16	8.59	4.29
283 Copper ores and concentrates	94 159	2.65	0.80	0.64
11 Beef, fresh chilled frozen	61 950	1.75	1.22	0.31
845 Articles of apparel nes	31 213	0.88	0.06	0.04
277 Natural abrasives nes	14 722	0.41	2.11	1.30
773 Electrical distribute equipment nes	13 740	0.39	0.06	0.02
278 Other crude minerals	8 427	0.24	0.26	0.08
611 Leather	4 668	0.13	0.04	0.02
841 Male clothing, woven	3 705	0.10	0.01	0.01
Remainder	49 223	1.39		

For sources and notes, see end of table.

Pour les sources et les notes, se reporter à la fin du tableau.

Leading products exported based on average 2004-2005 values SITC Revision 3 (3-digit level) / Principaux produits exportés d'après la moyenne des valeurs de 2004-2005 CTCI révision 3 (positions à 3 chiffres)	2004-2005			
	Value (f.o.b., thousands of dollars) / Valeur (f.a.b., milliers de dollars)	As percentage / En pourcentage		
		of country total / du total du pays	of ** (1) / des ** (1)	of world / du monde
Brazil - Brésil (=Developing)**				
All commodity groups	105 565 616	100.00	3.13	1.10
281 Iron ore and concentrates	6 027 753	5.71	52.40	26.80
222 Oil seed etc for soft oil	5 408 667	5.12	54.95	25.38
12 Meat nes, fresh chilled frozen	4 153 725	3.93	63.76	11.35
781 Passenger cars and race cars	3 873 457	3.67	6.75	0.82
333 Crude petroleum & bituminous oil	3 346 222	3.17	0.73	0.52
792 Aircraft, spacecraft & equipment	3 337 066	3.16	34.60	2.75
61 Sugar, mollasses and honey	3 325 076	3.15	39.53	20.67
81 Animal feed excluding unmilled cereal	3 199 838	3.03	26.51	10.64
784 Motor vehicle parts and accessories	2 978 227	2.82	7.92	1.33
71 Coffee and coffee substitutes	2 493 219	2.36	28.02	17.81
Remainder	67 422 364	63.87		
Brunei Darussalam - Brunéi Darussalam (=Developing)**				
All commodity groups	5 140 579	100.00	0.15	0.05
333 Crude petroleum & bituminous oil	2 512 430	48.87	0.55	0.39
343 Natural gas, liquefied or not	1 981 378	38.54	5.06	1.79
845 Articles of apparel nes	193 080	3.76	0.34	0.22
793 Ships boats floating structures	165 845	3.23	0.61	0.25
695 Tools for use in hand or in machine	39 016	0.76	0.51	0.13
844 Female clothing, knitted crocheted	32 905	0.64	0.18	0.13
841 Male clothing, woven	26 169	0.51	0.09	0.05
792 Aircraft, spacecraft & equipment	25 971	0.51	0.27	0.02
334 Heavy petroleum & bituminous oil	20 358	0.40	0.01	0.01
728 Special industrial machine part nes	18 512	0.36	0.12	0.02
Remainder	124 915	2.43		
Bulgaria - Bulgarie (=Transition)**				
All commodity groups	10 827 475	100.00	3.08	0.11
334 Heavy petroleum & bituminous oil	991 803	9.16	2.59	0.32
682 Copper	860 894	7.95	17.07	1.52
673 Flat iron non-alloy steel products	534 875	4.94	4.81	0.88
842 Female clothing, woven	492 885	4.55	14.94	0.81
931 Transaction commodity unclassified	455 582	4.21	1.08	0.16
841 Male clothing, woven	437 025	4.04	16.26	0.89
845 Articles of apparel nes	418 557	3.87	21.06	0.48
844 Female clothing, knitted crocheted	277 034	2.56	36.99	1.08
851 Footwear	238 840	2.21	9.28	0.37
821 Furniture part; bedding furnishing	190 298	1.76	8.17	0.20
Remainder	5 929 683	54.77		
Burkina Faso (=Developing)**				
All commodity groups	339 299	100.00	0.01	0.00
263 Cotton	242 418	71.45	5.97	2.16
222 Oil seed etc for soft oil	11 548	3.40	0.12	0.05
122 Manufactured tabacco	9 429	2.78	0.25	0.05
334 Heavy petroleum & bituminous oil	9 413	2.77	0.01	0.00
57 Fruit nut (exc oil), fresh or dried	6 292	1.85	0.03	0.01
1 Live animal excl. fish & crustacean	5 180	1.53	0.22	0.04
61 Sugar, mollasses and honey	4 123	1.22	0.05	0.03
421 Fixed veg fat and oil, "soft"	3 889	1.15	0.06	0.02
658 Made-up textile articles nes	3 637	1.07	0.02	0.01
44 Maize unmilled, excluding sweet corn	3 512	1.03	0.12	0.03
Remainder	39 859	11.75		
Burundi (=Developing)**				
All commodity groups	99 925	100.00	0.00	0.00
971 Gold non-monetary excluding ores	49 703	49.74	0.25	0.13
71 Coffee and coffee substitutes	38 566	38.59	0.43	0.28
61 Sugar, mollasses and honey	2 128	2.13	0.03	0.01
263 Cotton	1 797	1.80	0.04	0.02
112 Alcoholic beverages	1 613	1.61	0.03	0.00
782 Goods and service vehicles	785	0.79	0.00	0.00
122 Manufactured tabacco	781	0.78	0.02	0.00
74 Tea and maté	706	0.71	0.02	0.02
287 Base metal ores & concentrates nes	702	0.70	0.01	0.00
211 Raw hides & skins, excluding furskins	322	0.32	0.04	0.01
Remainder	2 822	2.82		

For sources and notes, see end of table.

Leading products exported based on average 2004-2005 values SITC Revision 3 (3-digit level) / Principaux produits exportés d'après la moyenne des valeurs de 2004-2005 CTCI révision 3 (positions à 3 chiffres)	2004-2005			
	Value (f.o.b., thousands of dollars) / Valeur (f.a.b., milliers de dollars)	As percentage / En pourcentage		
		of country total / du total du pays	of ** (1) / des ** (1)	of world / du monde
Cambodia - Cambodge (=Developing)**				
All commodity groups	2 970 933	100.00	0.09	0.03
844 Female clothing, knitted crocheted	784 795	26.42	4.24	3.07
845 Articles of apparel nes	698 261	23.50	1.24	0.80
892 Printed matter	649 918	21.88	8.94	1.71
843 Male clothing, knitted crocheted	519 196	17.48	4.61	3.61
842 Female clothing, woven	63 073	2.12	0.16	0.10
851 Footwear	43 273	1.46	0.12	0.07
231 Natural rubber, latex, gum, etc	39 224	1.32	0.46	0.44
841 Male clothing, woven	30 307	1.02	0.10	0.06
896 Work of art & collections; antiques	24 807	0.83	2.62	0.18
36 Crustacean mollusc aquat invertebra	11 266	0.38	0.10	0.06
Remainder	106 814	3.60		
Cameroon - Cameroun (=Developing)**				
All commodity groups	2 462 720	100.00	0.07	0.03
333 Crude petroleum & bituminous oil	930 580	37.79	0.20	0.15
931 Transaction commodity unclassified	278 334	11.30	0.66	0.10
72 Cocoa	256 339	10.41	4.80	3.06
334 Heavy petroleum & bituminous oil	255 259	10.36	0.18	0.08
248 Wood simply worked, railway sleeper	240 603	9.77	3.61	0.70
263 Cotton	138 766	5.63	3.42	1.24
684 Aluminium	119 185	4.84	0.69	0.17
57 Fruit nut (exc oil), fresh or dried	72 052	2.93	0.40	0.17
71 Coffee and coffee substitutes	69 905	2.84	0.79	0.50
231 Natural rubber, latex, gum, etc	43 530	1.77	0.51	0.49
Remainder	58 167	2.36		
Canada (=Developed)**				
All commodity groups	338 373 781	100.00	5.73	3.51
781 Passenger cars and race cars	36 931 841	10.91	8.96	7.85
343 Natural gas, liquefied or not	25 218 823	7.45	41.13	22.76
333 Crude petroleum & bituminous oil	22 023 998	6.51	23.33	3.45
931 Transaction commodity unclassified	15 809 103	4.67	7.94	5.58
784 Motor vehicle parts and accessories	13 255 462	3.92	7.20	5.94
641 Paper and paperboard	10 455 527	3.09	12.86	11.08
782 Goods and service vehicles	9 636 872	2.85	14.78	11.39
248 Wood simply worked, railway sleeper	9 179 028	2.71	37.19	26.58
334 Heavy petroleum & bituminous oil	8 301 796	2.45	6.39	2.66
792 Aircraft, spacecraft & equipment	7 618 788	2.25	6.88	6.27
Remainder	179 942 542	53.18		
Cape Verde - Cap-Vert (=Developing)**				
All commodity groups	52 309	100.00	0.00	0.00
334 Heavy petroleum & bituminous oil	41 862	80.03	0.03	0.01
786 Trailer caravan transport container	12 814	24.50	0.16	0.06
34 Fish, fresh live chilled frozen	5 358	10.24	0.04	0.02
851 Footwear	3 776	7.22	0.01	0.01
841 Male clothing, woven	2 989	5.71	0.01	0.01
874 Measure analyze control device nes	2 938	5.62	0.02	0.00
842 Female clothing, woven	2 118	4.05	0.01	0.00
843 Male clothing, knitted crocheted	1 890	3.61	0.02	0.01
793 Ships boats floating structures	1 861	3.56	0.01	0.00
713 Internal combustion engine part nes	1 097	2.10	0.01	0.00
Remainder	-24 394	-46.63		
Central African Republic - République centrafricaine (=Developing)**				
All commodity groups	108 686	100.00	0.00	0.00
667 Pearls, precious semiprecious stone	37 814	34.79	0.12	0.04
277 Natural abrasives nes	28 082	25.84	4.03	2.48
247 Wood in rough or roughly squared	25 363	23.34	1.07	0.26
248 Wood simply worked, railway sleeper	10 444	9.61	0.16	0.03
931 Transaction commodity unclassified	2 715	2.50	0.01	0.00
71 Coffee and coffee substitutes	1 024	0.94	0.01	0.01
782 Goods and service vehicles	790	0.73	0.00	0.00
263 Cotton	709	0.65	0.02	0.01
334 Heavy petroleum & bituminous oil	261	0.24	0.00	0.00
781 Passenger cars and race cars	186	0.17	0.00	0.00
Remainder	1 298	1.19		

Pour les sources et les notes, se reporter à la fin du tableau.

Leading products exported based on average 2004-2005 values SITC Revision 3 (3-digit level) / Principaux produits exportés d'après la moyenne des valeurs de 2004-2005 CTCI révision 3 (positions à 3 chiffres)	Value (f.o.b., thousands of dollars) Valeur (f.a.b., milliers de dollars)	As percentage En pourcentage		
		of country total du total du pays	of ** (1) des ** (1)	of world du monde
Chile - Chili (=Developing)**				
All commodity groups	34 745 214	100.00	1.03	0.36
682 Copper	10 556 003	30.38	40.19	18.58
283 Copper ores and concentrates	5 516 497	15.88	46.77	37.20
287 Base metal ores & concentrates nes	2 027 421	5.84	25.15	14.06
34 Fish, fresh live chilled frozen	1 814 089	5.22	14.43	5.73
57 Fruit nut (exc oil), fresh or dried	1 754 341	5.05	9.75	4.07
251 Pulp and waste paper	1 208 869	3.48	23.94	4.78
248 Wood simply worked, railway sleeper	971 865	2.80	14.57	2.81
112 Alcoholic beverages	869 853	2.50	14.08	1.95
931 Transaction commodity unclassified	729 473	2.10	1.72	0.26
334 Heavy petroleum & bituminous oil	615 597	1.77	0.43	0.20
Remainder	8 681 207	24.99		
China - Chine (=Developing)**				
All commodity groups	677 639 495	100.00	20.08	7.03
752 Computer equipment nes	68 105 303	10.05	47.05	26.13
764 Telecommunicate equipment part nes	53 157 660	7.84	32.72	16.38
759 Office equipment part & accessories	27 293 686	4.03	25.63	14.32
845 Articles of apparel nes	20 849 732	3.08	36.95	23.79
894 Baby carriage toy game sport good	18 498 715	2.73	51.59	30.61
776 Valves tubes; diodes, transistors	18 298 335	2.70	9.23	5.20
763 Sound TV recorder or reproducer	18 141 723	2.68	52.48	30.54
851 Footwear	17 127 558	2.53	46.80	26.50
778 Electrical machinery apparatus nes	15 087 741	2.23	27.56	10.74
821 Furniture part; bedding furnishing	14 595 174	2.15	45.58	15.51
Remainder	406 483 869	59.99		
China, Hong Kong SAR - Chine, Hong Kong RAS (=Developing)**				
All commodity groups	278 830 742	100.00	8.26	2.89
776 Valves tubes; diodes, transistors	28 433 513	10.20	14.34	8.08
764 Telecommunicate equipment part nes	27 280 976	9.78	16.79	8.40
759 Office equipment part & accessories	23 993 425	8.61	22.53	12.59
894 Baby carriage toy game sport good	11 720 327	4.20	32.68	19.39
845 Articles of apparel nes	9 896 716	3.55	17.54	11.29
772 Electrical circuit equipment	9 170 862	3.29	18.47	6.80
763 Sound TV recorder or reproducer	8 444 892	3.03	24.43	14.22
752 Computer equipment nes	7 948 752	2.85	5.49	3.05
778 Electrical machinery apparatus nes	7 421 263	2.66	13.56	5.28
842 Female clothing, woven	6 684 357	2.40	17.32	10.99
Remainder	137 835 661	49.43		
China, Macao SAR - Chine, Macao RAS (=Developing)**				
All commodity groups	2 643 982	100.00	0.08	0.03
845 Articles of apparel nes	608 585	23.02	1.08	0.69
842 Female clothing, woven	469 755	17.77	1.22	0.77
844 Female clothing, knitted crocheted	373 056	14.11	2.02	1.46
841 Male clothing, woven	266 909	10.09	0.87	0.54
843 Male clothing, knitted crocheted	105 808	4.00	0.94	0.74
851 Footwear	97 829	3.70	0.27	0.15
651 Textile yarn	88 286	3.34	0.40	0.22
655 Knitted or crocheted fabrics nes	81 731	3.09	0.65	0.42
652 Woven cotton fabrics	69 644	2.63	0.41	0.24
334 Heavy petroleum & bituminous oil	65 029	2.46	0.05	0.02
Remainder	417 350	15.78		
China, Taiwan Province of - Chine, Taiwan Province de (=Developing)**				
All commodity groups	181 465 910	100.00	5.38	1.88
776 Valves tubes; diodes, transistors	28 504 145	15.71	14.37	8.10
759 Office equipment part & accessories	10 634 493	5.86	9.99	5.58
871 Optical instruments apparatus nes	10 032 665	5.53	36.01	25.96
764 Telecommunicate equipment part nes	8 368 632	4.61	5.15	2.58
778 Electrical machinery apparatus nes	7 257 954	4.00	13.26	5.16
334 Heavy petroleum & bituminous oil	6 826 848	3.76	4.74	2.19
772 Electrical circuit equipment	6 191 870	3.41	12.47	4.59
752 Computer equipment nes	5 964 888	3.29	4.12	2.29
898 Music instrument device recording	3 775 193	2.08	25.57	7.96
699 Base metal manufactures nes	3 002 858	1.65	12.81	3.55
Remainder	90 906 365	50.10		

Leading products exported based on average 2004-2005 values SITC Revision 3 (3-digit level) / Principaux produits exportés d'après la moyenne des valeurs de 2004-2005 CTCI révision 3 (positions à 3 chiffres)	Value (f.o.b., thousands of dollars) Valeur (f.a.b., milliers de dollars)	As percentage En pourcentage		
		of country total du total du pays	of ** (1) des ** (1)	of world du monde
Colombia - Colombie (=Developing)**				
All commodity groups	18 960 050	100.00	0.56	0.20
333 Crude petroleum & bituminous oil	3 513 907	18.53	0.77	0.55
321 Coal excluding non-agglomomeraled	2 102 506	11.09	15.49	5.43
334 Heavy petroleum & bituminous oil	1 361 894	7.18	0.95	0.44
71 Coffee and coffee substitutes	1 343 204	7.08	15.09	9.60
292 Crude vegetable materials nes	813 456	4.29	14.96	3.69
671 Pig & sponge iron, ferro alloys etc	683 924	3.61	5.46	2.93
971 Gold non-monetary excluding ores	601 220	3.17	3.05	1.61
57 Fruit nut (exc oil), fresh or dried	500 000	2.64	2.78	1.16
781 Passenger cars and race cars	339 385	1.79	0.59	0.07
841 Male clothing, woven	305 078	1.61	0.99	0.62
Remainder	7 395 475	39.01		
Congo (=Developing)**				
All commodity groups	4 544 078	100.00	0.13	0.05
333 Crude petroleum & bituminous oil	3 421 025	75.29	0.75	0.54
247 Wood in rough or roughly squared	325 188	7.16	13.75	3.28
334 Heavy petroleum & bituminous oi	211 292	4.65	0.15	0.07
287 Base metal ores & concentrates nes	140 804	3.10	1.75	0.98
342 Liquefied propane and butane	94 459	2.08	0.62	0.40
248 Wood simply worked, railway sleeper	75 983	1.67	1.14	0.22
667 Pearls, precious semiprecious stone	52 724	1.16	0.17	0.06
689 Misc non-ferrous base metals	46 261	1.02	1.87	0.68
61 Sugar, mollasses and honey	35 818	0.79	0.43	0.22
283 Copper ores and concentrates	23 242	0.51	0.20	0.16
Remainder	117 284	2.58		
Costa Rica (=Developing)**				
All commodity groups	6 551 632	100.00	0.19	0.07
57 Fruit nut (exc oil), fresh or dried	908 010	13.86	5.05	2.11
759 Office equipment part & accessories	788 295	12.03	0.74	0.41
776 Valves tubes; diodes, transistors	541 051	8.26	0.27	0.15
872 Medical instruments appliances nes	490 260	7.48	5.72	0.99
71 Coffee and coffee substitutes	232 095	3.54	2.61	1.66
542 Medicines including veterinary	228 279	3.48	2.68	0.12
98 Edible products & preparations nes	202 691	3.09	3.30	0.66
292 Crude vegetable materials nes	184 681	2.82	3.40	0.84
764 Telecommunicate equipment part nes	167 827	2.56	0.10	0.05
841 Male clothing, woven	143 909	2.20	0.47	0.29
Remainder	2 664 535	40.67		
Côte d'Ivoire (=Developing)**				
All commodity groups	6 913 396	100.00	0.20	0.07
72 Cocoa	2 058 597	29.78	38.53	24.54
334 Heavy petroleum & bituminous oil	1 185 255	17.14	0.82	0.38
891 Arms and ammunition	448 807	6.49	48.49	6.10
333 Crude petroleum & bituminous oil	401 343	5.81	0.09	0.06
57 Fruit nut (exc oil), fresh or dried	247 293	3.58	1.38	0.57
248 Wood simply worked, railway sleeper	216 080	3.13	3.24	0.63
231 Natural rubber, latex, gum, etc	182 080	2.63	2.11	2.06
793 Ships boats floating structures	166 377	2.41	0.61	0.25
783 Road motor vehicles nes	159 747	2.31	3.75	0.55
263 Cotton	148 519	2.15	3.66	1.32
Remainder	1 699 297	24.58		
Croatia - Croatie (=Transition)**				
All commodity groups	8 398 355	100.00	2.39	0.09
793 Ships boats floating structures	992 343	11.82	38.25	1.50
334 Heavy petroleum & bituminous oil	704 274	8.39	1.84	0.23
821 Furniture part; bedding furnishing	231 863	2.76	9.95	0.25
845 Articles of apparel nes	228 134	2.72	11.48	0.26
778 Electrical machinery apparatus nes	188 955	2.25	17.40	0.13
248 Wood simply worked, railway sleeper	188 786	2.25	5.93	0.55
851 Footwear	167 731	2.00	6.52	0.26
343 Natural gas, liquefied or not	151 688	1.81	1.46	0.14
684 Aluminium	140 329	1.67	1.94	0.20
562 Manufactured fertilizer excl. crude	138 809	1.65	2.36	0.60
Remainder	5 265 442	62.70		

For sources and notes, see end of table.

Pour les sources et les notes, se reporter à la fin du tableau.

Leading products exported based on average 2004-2005 values SITC Revision 3 (3-digit level) / Principaux produits exportés d'après la moyenne des valeurs de 2004-2005 CTCI révision 3 (positions à 3 chiffres)	2004-2005			
	Value (f.o.b., thousands of dollars) Valeur (f.a.b., milliers de dollars)	As percentage / En pourcentage		
		of country total / du total du pays	of ** (1) / des ** (1)	of world / du monde

Cuba (**=Developing)

All commodity groups	2 291 551	100.00	0.07	0.02
284 Nickel ores, concentrates, etc	1 043 781	45.55	35.27	17.61
61 Sugar, mollasses and honey	275 718	12.03	3.28	1.71
122 Manufactured tabacco	202 678	8.84	5.48	1.18
542 Medicines including veterinary	136 706	5.97	1.61	0.07
36 Crustacean mollusc aquat invertebra	82 981	3.62	0.71	0.43
59 Fruit & vegetable juice unferment	61 771	2.70	1.95	0.73
898 Music instrument device recording	61 761	2.70	0.42	0.13
892 Printed matter	50 380	2.20	0.69	0.13
642 Cut paper and paperboard articles	33 302	1.45	0.43	0.09
288 Non ferrous base metal waste nes	31 960	1.39	0.87	0.20
Remainder	310 512	13.55		

Cyprus - Chypre (**=Developed)

All commodity groups	1 358 919	100.00	0.02	0.01
764 Telecommunicate equipment part nes	208 770	15.36	0.13	0.06
334 Heavy petroleum & bituminous oil	157 739	11.61	0.12	0.05
781 Passenger cars and race cars	144 782	10.65	0.04	0.03
542 Medicines including veterinary	108 139	7.96	0.06	0.06
122 Manufactured tabacco	56 212	4.14	0.43	0.33
782 Goods and service vehicles	48 771	3.59	0.07	0.06
57 Fruit nut (exc oil), fresh or dried	48 515	3.57	0.20	0.11
54 Vegetable & vegetable products nes	44 360	3.26	0.22	0.14
24 Cheese and curd	30 063	2.21	0.19	0.18
34 Fish, fresh live chilled frozen	28 734	2.11	0.15	0.09
Remainder	482 833	35.53		

Czech Republic - République tchèque (**=Developed)

All commodity groups	71 990 041	100.00	1.22	0.75
781 Passenger cars and race cars	5 452 594	7.57	1.32	1.16
784 Motor vehicle parts and accessories	5 072 225	7.05	2.76	2.27
752 Computer equipment nes	3 613 631	5.02	3.12	1.39
699 Base metal manufactures nes	2 403 128	3.34	4.03	2.84
772 Electrical circuit equipment	2 009 170	2.79	2.39	1.49
778 Electrical machinery apparatus nes	1 972 366	2.74	2.33	1.40
821 Furniture part; bedding furnishing	1 737 712	2.41	2.91	1.85
773 Electrical distribute equipment nes	1 687 658	2.34	5.10	2.94
764 Telecommunicate equipment part nes	1 277 569	1.77	0.79	0.39
742 Liquid pump; liquid elevator parts	1 266 279	1.76	4.50	3.88
Remainder	45 497 709	63.20		

Dem. Rep. of the Congo - Rép. dém. du Congo (**=Developing)

All commodity groups	1 971 097	100.00	0.06	0.02
667 Pearls, precious semiprecious stone	856 029	43.43	2.74	1.02
287 Base metal ores & concentrates nes	458 437	23.26	5.69	3.18
689 Misc non-ferrous base metals	189 484	9.61	7.67	2.78
333 Crude petroleum & bituminous oil	145 990	7.41	0.03	0.02
277 Natural abrasives nes	75 924	3.85	10.90	6.70
247 Wood in rough or roughly squared	55 658	2.82	2.35	0.56
248 Wood simply worked, railway sleeper	36 405	1.85	0.55	0.11
334 Heavy petroleum & bituminous oil	30 221	1.53	0.02	0.01
283 Copper ores and concentrates	18 808	0.95	0.16	0.13
71 Coffee and coffee substitutes	12 058	0.61	0.14	0.09
Remainder	92 084	4.67		

Denmark - Danemark (**=Developed)

All commodity groups	78 603 997	100.00	1.33	0.82
333 Crude petroleum & bituminous oil	4 687 545	5.96	4.97	0.74
542 Medicines including veterinary	4 116 262	5.24	2.21	2.11
12 Meat nes, fresh chilled frozen	3 497 602	4.45	11.72	9.56
931 Transaction commodity unclassified	2 926 552	3.72	1.47	1.03
764 Telecommunicate equipment part nes	2 751 662	3.50	1.71	0.85
821 Furniture part; bedding furnishing	2 663 626	3.39	4.46	2.83
716 Rotating electric plant parts nes	2 304 541	2.93	7.19	4.82
541 Pharmaceuticals excluding medicines	1 835 092	2.33	3.22	2.90
334 Heavy petroleum & bituminous oil	1 625 576	2.07	1.25	0.52
893 Articles of plastic nes	1 395 676	1.78	2.56	1.73
Remainder	50 799 862	64.63		

Dominican Republic - République dominicaine (**=Developing)

All commodity groups	1 220 864	100.00	0.04	0.01
841 Male clothing, woven	168 600	13.81	0.55	0.34
845 Articles of apparel nes	138 108	11.31	0.24	0.16
872 Medical instruments appliances nes	103 509	8.48	1.21	0.21
671 Pig & sponge iron, ferro alloys etc	89 194	7.31	0.71	0.38
122 Manufactured tabacco	58 221	4.77	1.57	0.34
843 Male clothing, knitted crocheted	53 266	4.36	0.47	0.37
897 Jewellery nes (667)	52 325	4.29	0.30	0.14
772 Electrical circuit equipment	48 645	3.98	0.10	0.04
842 Female clothing, woven	46 732	3.83	0.12	0.08
851 Footwear	35 499	2.91	0.10	0.05
Remainder	426 765	34.96		

Ecuador - Équateur (**=Developing)

All commodity groups	8 737 737	100.00	0.26	0.09
333 Crude petroleum & bituminous oil	4 647 674	53.19	1.01	0.73
57 Fruit nut (exc oil), fresh or dried	1 103 689	12.63	6.14	2.56
36 Crustacean mollusc aquat invertebra	387 319	4.43	3.32	2.03
37 Fish shellfish, prepared preserved	385 554	4.41	4.42	2.74
292 Crude vegetable materials nes	359 566	4.12	6.61	1.63
334 Heavy petroleum & bituminous oil	291 412	3.34	0.20	0.09
72 Cocoa	155 048	1.77	2.90	1.85
335 Residual petroleum products nes	112 468	1.29	2.10	0.68
71 Coffee and coffee substitutes	84 749	0.97	0.95	0.61
34 Fish, fresh live chilled frozen	80 641	0.92	0.64	0.25
Remainder	1 129 616	12.93		

Egypt - Égypte (**=Developing)

All commodity groups	9 564 035	100.00	0.28	0.10
334 Heavy petroleum & bituminous oil	3 223 250	33.70	2.24	1.03
263 Cotton	583 706	6.10	14.38	5.21
931 Transaction commodity unclassified	549 547	5.75	1.29	0.19
333 Crude petroleum & bituminous oil	487 981	5.10	0.11	0.08
661 Lime cement construction material	405 068	4.24	4.95	2.35
42 Rice	280 557	2.93	4.16	3.12
676 Iron steel bar rod section piling	234 726	2.45	1.76	0.48
571 Primary form ethylene polymers	213 193	2.23	1.68	0.60
54 Vegetable & vegetable products nes	211 314	2.21	2.05	0.68
675 Flat rolled products of alloy steel	192 597	2.01	1.94	0.46
Remainder	3 182 096	33.27		

El Salvador (**=Developing)

All commodity groups	1 486 545	100.00	0.04	0.02
71 Coffee and coffee substitutes	124 781	8.39	1.40	0.89
642 Cut paper and paperboard articles	98 370	6.62	1.27	0.28
542 Medicines including veterinary	71 011	4.78	0.83	0.04
845 Articles of apparel nes	70 898	4.77	0.13	0.08
48 Cereal & preparation flour starch	65 793	4.43	2.00	0.28
673 Flat iron non-alloy steel products	57 000	3.83	0.34	0.09
334 Heavy petroleum & bituminous oil	55 963	3.76	0.04	0.02
893 Articles of plastic nes	50 035	3.37	0.20	0.06
61 Sugar, mollasses and honey	49 373	3.32	0.59	0.31
98 Edible products & preparations nes	39 525	2.66	0.64	0.13
Remainder	803 795	54.07		

Equatorial Guinea - Guinée équatoriale (**=Developing)

All commodity groups	2 399 916	100.00	0.07	0.02
333 Crude petroleum & bituminous oil	2 216 397	92.35	0.48	0.35
512 Alcohols, phenols; derivatives	91 224	3.80	0.70	0.31
247 Wood in rough or roughly squared	59 879	2.50	2.53	0.60
634 Veneer, plywood & other wood nes	13 558	0.56	0.15	0.05
72 Cocoa	4 515	0.19	0.08	0.05
679 Iron steel pipe tube fittings etc	2 798	0.12	0.02	0.01
343 Natural gas, liquefied or not	2 790	0.12	0.01	0.00
248 Wood simply worked, railway sleeper	1 227	0.05	0.02	0.00
342 Liquefied propane and butane	1 096	0.05	0.01	0.00
723 Civil engineering plant & equipment	980	0.04	0.01	0.00
Remainder	5 452	0.23		

For sources and notes, see end of table.   Pour les sources et les notes, se reporter à la fin du tableau.

160

Leading products exported based on average 2004-2005 values SITC Revision 3 (3-digit level) / Principaux produits exportés d'après la moyenne des valeurs de 2004-2005 CTCI révision 3 (positions à 3 chiffres)	Value (f.o.b., thousands of dollars) / Valeur (f.a.b., milliers de dollars)	of country total / du total du pays	of ** (1) / des ** (1)	of world / du monde
Estonia - Estonie (**=Developed)				
All commodity groups	6 624 990	100.00	0.11	0.07
764 Telecommunicate equipment part nes	1 013 240	15.29	0.63	0.31
931 Transaction commodity unclassified	360 546	5.44	0.18	0.13
821 Furniture part; bedding furnishing	340 718	5.14	0.57	0.36
248 Wood simply worked, railway sleeper	292 324	4.41	1.18	0.85
334 Heavy petroleum & bituminous oil	289 258	4.37	0.22	0.09
635 Wood manufactures nes	175 248	2.65	1.33	0.86
781 Passenger cars and race cars	144 434	2.18	0.04	0.03
674 Flat plated iron non-alloy steel	115 906	1.75	0.53	0.36
773 Electrical distribute equipment nes	114 925	1.73	0.35	0.20
691 Iron steel aluminium structures nes	111 304	1.68	0.63	0.45
Remainder	3 667 087	55.35		
Ethiopia - Éthiopie (**=Developing)				
All commodity groups	750 318	100.00	0.02	0.01
71 Coffee and coffee substitutes	268 935	35.84	3.02	1.92
292 Crude vegetable materials nes	170 571	22.73	3.14	0.77
222 Oil seed etc for soft oil	70 874	9.45	0.72	0.33
611 Leather	63 042	8.40	0.57	0.31
54 Vegetable & vegetable products nes	37 110	4.95	0.36	0.12
61 Sugar, mollasses and honey	22 845	3.04	0.27	0.14
263 Cotton	19 312	2.57	0.48	0.17
223 Oil seed for non soft oil	18 478	2.46	5.56	1.46
45 Grain, excl. wheat rice barley maize	16 605	2.21	9.29	1.05
12 Meat nes, fresh chilled frozen	9 363	1.25	0.14	0.03
Remainder	53 184	7.09		
Faeroe Islands - Îles Féroé (**=Developed)				
All commodity groups	605 833	100.00	0.01	0.01
34 Fish, fresh live chilled frozen	371 422	61.31	1.99	1.17
35 Fish, dried salted smoked	101 706	16.79	3.86	2.86
81 Animal feed excluding unmilled cereal	52 917	8.73	0.30	0.18
793 Ships boats floating structures	31 491	5.20	0.09	0.05
37 Fish shellfish, prepared preserved	16 103	2.66	0.31	0.11
291 Crude animal materials nes	12 948	2.14	0.44	0.26
36 Crustacean mollusc aquat invertebra	12 493	2.06	0.17	0.07
411 Animals oils and fats	3 406	0.56	0.16	0.13
657 Special yarn and textile fabric etc	1 726	0.28	0.01	0.01
894 Baby carriage toy game sport good	972	0.16	0.00	0.00
Remainder	648	0.11		
Fiji - Fidji (**=Developing)				
All commodity groups	622 901	100.00	0.02	0.01
334 Heavy petroleum & bituminous oil	164 426	26.40	0.11	0.05
61 Sugar, mollasses and honey	121 891	19.57	1.45	0.76
971 Gold non-monetary excluding ores	44 421	7.13	0.23	0.12
111 Non alcoholic beverage nes	42 119	6.76	2.19	0.42
34 Fish, fresh live chilled frozen	39 957	6.41	0.32	0.13
845 Articles of apparel nes	39 379	6.32	0.07	0.04
842 Female clothing, woven	28 152	4.52	0.07	0.05
841 Male clothing, woven	22 608	3.63	0.07	0.05
48 Cereal & preparation flour starch	19 422	3.12	0.59	0.08
54 Vegetable & vegetable products nes	16 251	2.61	0.16	0.05
Remainder	84 275	13.53		
Finland - Finlande (**=Developed)				
All commodity groups	63 077 082	100.00	1.07	0.65
764 Telecommunicate equipment part nes	10 497 280	16.64	6.51	3.23
641 Paper and paperboard	9 367 090	14.85	11.52	9.93
334 Heavy petroleum & bituminous oil	2 529 394	4.01	1.95	0.81
675 Flat rolled products of alloy steel	2 227 625	3.53	7.24	5.31
248 Wood simply worked, railway sleeper	1 759 551	2.79	7.13	5.09
781 Passenger cars and race cars	1 236 711	1.96	0.30	0.26
251 Pulp and waste paper	1 128 574	1.79	5.80	4.46
744 Mechanical handling equipment nes	1 098 801	1.74	2.67	2.29
728 Special industrial machine part nes	1 011 523	1.60	1.26	1.05
716 Rotating electric plant parts nes	983 352	1.56	3.07	2.06
Remainder	31 237 182	49.52		
France (**=Developed)				
All commodity groups	422 562 325	100.00	7.15	4.39
781 Passenger cars and race cars	34 538 620	8.17	8.38	7.34
792 Aircraft, spacecraft & equipment	23 202 811	5.49	20.97	19.11
542 Medicines including veterinary	18 377 609	4.35	9.87	9.41
784 Motor vehicle parts and accessories	15 699 028	3.72	8.53	7.03
112 Alcoholic beverages	9 889 762	2.34	26.54	22.16
553 Perfume toilet cosmetics, excl. soap	9 756 560	2.31	27.79	23.38
764 Telecommunicate equipment part nes	9 616 660	2.28	5.97	2.96
334 Heavy petroleum & bituminous oil	8 058 963	1.91	6.21	2.58
776 Valves tubes; diodes, transistors	7 625 301	1.80	4.97	2.17
772 Electrical circuit equipment	7 238 623	1.71	8.60	5.37
Remainder	278 558 389	65.92		
French Polynesia - Polynésie française (**=Developing)				
All commodity groups	197 799	100.00	0.01	0.00
667 Pearls, precious semiprecious stone	121 983	61.67	0.39	0.14
792 Aircraft, spacecraft & equipment	17 868	9.03	0.19	0.01
897 Jewellery nes (667)	11 830	5.98	0.07	0.03
58 Fruit preserve preparation excl. juice	11 047	5.58	0.27	0.12
34 Fish, fresh live chilled frozen	3 846	1.94	0.03	0.01
291 Crude animal materials nes	3 311	1.67	0.18	0.07
59 Fruit & vegetable juice unferment	3 303	1.67	0.10	0.04
422 Fixed veg fat and oil, excl. "soft"	3 189	1.61	0.03	0.02
714 Non-electric engines excl. 712 713 718	3 025	1.53	0.07	0.00
75 Spices	2 396	1.21	0.11	0.08
Remainder	16 001	8.09		
Gabon (**=Developing)				
All commodity groups	3 559 909	100.00	0.11	0.04
333 Crude petroleum & bituminous oil	2 662 351	74.79	0.58	0.42
247 Wood in rough or roughly squared	284 959	8.00	12.05	2.88
287 Base metal ores & concentrates nes	193 543	5.44	2.40	1.34
634 Veneer, plywood & other wood nes	128 795	3.62	1.43	0.45
248 Wood simply worked, railway sleeper	62 485	1.76	0.94	0.18
334 Heavy petroleum & bituminous oil	49 686	1.40	0.03	0.02
792 Aircraft, spacecraft & equipment	37 842	1.06	0.39	0.03
36 Crustacean mollusc aquat invertebra	21 667	0.61	0.19	0.11
642 Cut paper and paperboard articles	20 613	0.58	0.27	0.06
122 Manufactured tabacco	15 882	0.45	0.43	0.09
Remainder	82 085	2.31		
Gambia - Gambie (**=Developing)				
All commodity groups	11 588	100.00	0.00	0.00
421 Fixed veg fat and oil, "soft"	5 579	48.14	0.09	0.03
723 Civil engineering plant & equipment	1 900	16.40	0.02	0.00
793 Ships boats floating structures	1 379	11.90	0.01	0.00
111 Non alcoholic beverage nes	1 146	9.89	0.06	0.01
222 Oil seed etc for soft oil	738	6.37	0.01	0.00
54 Vegetable & vegetable products nes	714	6.16	0.01	0.00
81 Animal feed excluding unmilled cereal	666	5.75	0.01	0.00
57 Fruit nut (exc oil), fresh or dried	288	2.48	0.00	0.00
36 Crustacean mollusc aquat invertebra	279	2.40	0.00	0.00
724 Textile leather machinery parts nes	240	2.07	0.00	0.00
Remainder	-1 338	-11.55		
Georgia - Géorgie (**=Transition)				
All commodity groups	757 489	100.00	0.22	0.01
282 Ferrous iron & steel, waste & scrap	90 085	11.89	2.49	0.38
112 Alcoholic beverages	89 714	11.84	7.56	0.20
792 Aircraft, spacecraft & equipment	81 667	10.78	7.17	0.07
671 Pig & sponge iron, ferro alloys etc	61 346	8.10	1.21	0.26
57 Fruit nut (exc oil), fresh or dried	49 088	6.48	7.43	0.11
111 Non alcoholic beverage nes	43 151	5.70	21.95	0.43
283 Copper ores and concentrates	34 106	4.50	11.43	0.23
562 Manufactured fertilizer excl. crude	32 346	4.27	0.55	0.14
61 Sugar, mollasses and honey	32 016	4.23	4.29	0.20
971 Gold non-monetary excluding ores	26 786	3.54	3.88	0.07
Remainder	217 184	28.67		

For sources and notes, see end of table.

Pour les sources et les notes, se reporter à la fin du tableau.

Leading products exported based on average 2004-2005 values SITC Revision 3 (3-digit level) / Principaux produits exportés d'après la moyenne des valeurs de 2004-2005 CTCI révision 3 (positions à 3 chiffres)	Value (f.o.b., thousands of dollars) Valeur (f.a.b., milliers de dollars)	of country total du total du pays	of ** (1) des ** (1)	of world du monde
Germany - Allemagne (**=Developed)				
All commodity groups	946 806 837	100.00	16.02	9.83
781 Passenger cars and race cars	104 290 931	11.02	25.31	22.16
931 Transaction commodity unclassified	49 779 964	5.26	25.01	17.56
784 Motor vehicle parts and accessories	32 574 022	3.44	17.70	14.59
542 Medicines including veterinary	26 657 404	2.82	14.31	13.64
764 Telecommunicate equipment part nes	23 536 743	2.49	14.61	7.25
713 Internal combustion engine part nes	19 016 757	2.01	20.74	17.72
772 Electrical circuit equipment	18 769 734	1.98	22.30	13.91
792 Aircraft, spacecraft & equipment	18 625 683	1.97	16.83	15.34
874 Measure analyze control device nes	18 464 166	1.95	20.26	17.19
752 Computer equipment nes	17 168 143	1.81	14.84	6.59
Remainder	617 923 292	65.26		
Ghana (**=Developing)				
All commodity groups	1 799 563	100.00	0.05	0.02
72 Cocoa	1 082 616	60.16	20.26	12.91
971 Gold non-monetary excluding ores	126 770	7.04	0.64	0.34
634 Veneer, plywood & other wood nes	76 271	4.24	0.84	0.27
37 Fish shellfish, prepared preserved	71 109	3.95	0.82	0.51
334 Heavy petroleum & bituminous oil	55 966	3.11	0.04	0.02
248 Wood simply worked, railway sleeper	55 909	3.11	0.84	0.16
57 Fruit nut (exc oil), fresh or dried	43 729	2.43	0.24	0.10
34 Fish, fresh live chilled frozen	21 924	1.22	0.17	0.07
524 Other inorganic chemicals	16 332	0.91	0.91	0.27
263 Cotton	14 203	0.79	0.35	0.13
Remainder	234 735	13.04		
Gibraltar (**=Developed)				
All commodity groups	142 955	100.00	0.00	0.00
793 Ships boats floating structures	57 827	40.45	0.16	0.09
781 Passenger cars and race cars	26 643	18.64	0.01	0.01
897 Jewellery nes (667)	15 907	11.13	0.08	0.04
667 Pearls, precious semiprecious stone	11 354	7.94	0.02	0.01
792 Aircraft, spacecraft & equipment	5 120	3.58	0.00	0.00
334 Heavy petroleum & bituminous oil	4 426	3.10	0.00	0.00
723 Civil engineering plant & equipment	3 099	2.17	0.01	0.00
896 Work of art & collections; antiques	2 735	1.91	0.02	0.02
562 Manufactured fertilizer excl. crude	1 934	1.35	0.02	0.01
782 Goods and service vehicles	1 067	0.75	0.00	0.00
Remainder	12 843	8.98		
Greece - Grèce (**=Developed)				
All commodity groups	16 329 202	100.00	0.28	0.17
334 Heavy petroleum & bituminous oil	1 267 103	7.76	0.98	0.41
542 Medicines including veterinary	993 925	6.09	0.53	0.51
684 Aluminium	764 549	4.68	1.62	1.06
844 Female clothing, knitted crocheted	691 625	4.24	10.94	2.70
57 Fruit nut (exc oil), fresh or dried	489 497	3.00	2.00	1.14
845 Articles of apparel nes	441 251	2.70	1.51	0.50
931 Transaction commodity unclassified	395 995	2.43	0.20	0.14
263 Cotton	366 672	2.25	6.49	3.27
34 Fish, fresh live chilled frozen	340 088	2.08	1.83	1.07
421 Fixed veg fat and oil, "soft"	334 118	2.05	3.87	2.09
Remainder	10 244 378	62.74		
Greenland - Groenland (**=Developed)				
All commodity groups	425 221	100.00	0.01	0.00
36 Crustacean mollusc aquat invertebra	191 947	45.14	2.59	1.00
37 Fish shellfish, prepared preserved	109 152	25.67	2.11	0.78
34 Fish, fresh live chilled frozen	82 497	19.40	0.44	0.26
35 Fish, dried salted smoked	15 379	3.62	0.58	0.43
792 Aircraft, spacecraft & equipment	12 068	2.84	0.01	0.01
896 Work of art & collections; antiques	1 741	0.41	0.01	0.01
759 Office equipment part & accessories	1 728	0.41	0.00	0.00
212 Raw furskins and furskin pieces	1 461	0.34	0.09	0.06
793 Ships boats floating structures	1 226	0.29	0.00	0.00
848 Headgear, non-textile clothing	889	0.21	0.02	0.00
Remainder	7 133	1.68		

Leading products exported based on average 2004-2005 values SITC Revision 3 (3-digit level) / Principaux produits exportés d'après la moyenne des valeurs de 2004-2005 CTCI révision 3 (positions à 3 chiffres)	Value (f.o.b., thousands of dollars) Valeur (f.a.b., milliers de dollars)	of country total du total du pays	of ** (1) des ** (1)	of world du monde
Grenada - Grenade (**=Developing)				
All commodity groups	29 370	100.00	0.00	0.00
75 Spices	9 916	33.76	0.44	0.32
34 Fish, fresh live chilled frozen	2 762	9.40	0.02	0.01
46 Wheat meal & flour, meslin flour	2 581	8.79	0.30	0.11
642 Cut paper and paperboard articles	1 971	6.71	0.03	0.01
72 Cocoa	1 896	6.45	0.04	0.02
893 Articles of plastic nes	1 373	4.67	0.01	0.00
793 Ships boats floating structures	1 044	3.56	0.00	0.00
764 Telecommunicate equipment part nes	861	2.93	0.00	0.00
551 Essential oils, perfumes & flavours	691	2.35	0.03	0.00
81 Animal feed excluding unmilled cereal	657	2.24	0.01	0.00
Remainder	5 617	19.12		
Guatemala (**=Developing)				
All commodity groups	4 156 304	100.00	0.12	0.04
71 Coffee and coffee substitutes	400 609	9.64	4.50	2.86
844 Female clothing, knitted crocheted	359 003	8.64	1.94	1.40
57 Fruit nut (exc oil), fresh or dried	317 450	7.64	1.77	0.74
61 Sugar, mollasses and honey	239 088	5.75	2.84	1.49
333 Crude petroleum & bituminous oil	202 489	4.87	0.04	0.03
842 Female clothing, woven	187 969	4.52	0.49	0.31
542 Medicines including veterinary	128 473	3.09	1.51	0.07
841 Male clothing, woven	98 982	2.38	0.32	0.20
553 Perfume toilet cosmetics, excl. soap	98 725	2.38	1.60	0.24
843 Male clothing, knitted crocheted	83 361	2.01	0.74	0.58
Remainder	2 040 154	49.09		
Guinea - Guinée (**=Developing)				
All commodity groups	885 715	100.00	0.03	0.01
285 Aluminium ore concentrate alumina	434 362	49.04	13.35	4.64
971 Gold non-monetary excluding ores	219 330	24.76	1.11	0.59
522 Inorganic chemical elem oxide salt	151 862	17.15	1.50	0.57
277 Natural abrasives nes	27 726	3.13	3.98	2.45
681 Silver, platinum, platinum metals	14 945	1.69	0.18	0.08
892 Printed matter	13 627	1.54	0.19	0.04
71 Coffee and coffee substitutes	4 178	0.47	0.05	0.03
231 Natural rubber, latex, gum, etc	3 886	0.44	0.05	0.04
34 Fish, fresh live chilled frozen	2 140	0.24	0.02	0.01
98 Edible products & preparations nes	1 235	0.14	0.02	0.00
Remainder	12 422	1.40		
Guyana (**=Developing)				
All commodity groups	540 957	100.00	0.02	0.01
61 Sugar, mollasses and honey	135 947	25.13	1.62	0.85
971 Gold non-monetary excluding ores	90 226	16.68	0.46	0.24
667 Pearls, precious semiprecious stone	65 708	12.15	0.21	0.08
42 Rice	47 486	8.78	0.70	0.53
36 Crustacean mollusc aquat invertebra	37 862	7.00	0.32	0.20
285 Aluminium ore concentrate alumina	29 043	5.37	0.89	0.31
34 Fish, fresh live chilled frozen	22 883	4.23	0.18	0.07
248 Wood simply worked, railway sleeper	22 273	4.12	0.33	0.06
634 Veneer, plywood & other wood nes	15 224	2.81	0.17	0.05
112 Alcoholic beverages	12 226	2.26	0.20	0.03
Remainder	62 079	11.48		
Haiti - Haïti (**=Developing)				
All commodity groups	429 728	100.00	0.01	0.00
845 Articles of apparel nes	268 838	62.56	0.48	0.31
841 Male clothing, woven	25 314	5.89	0.08	0.05
843 Male clothing, knitted crocheted	25 168	5.86	0.22	0.18
844 Female clothing, knitted crocheted	24 874	5.79	0.13	0.10
773 Electrical distribute equipment nes	10 156	2.36	0.05	0.02
551 Essential oils, perfumes & flavours	9 959	2.32	0.42	0.06
57 Fruit nut (exc oil), fresh or dried	7 820	1.82	0.04	0.02
658 Made-up textile articles nes	7 692	1.79	0.04	0.03
846 Clothing accessory excl. 831 848 851	5 624	1.31	0.06	0.03
894 Baby carriage toy game sport good	4 145	0.96	0.01	0.01
Remainder	40 138	9.34		

For sources and notes, see end of table.

Pour les sources et les notes, se reporter à la fin du tableau.

162

Leading products exported based on average 2004-2005 values SITC Revision 3 (3-digit level) / Principaux produits exportés d'après la moyenne des valeurs de 2004-2005 CTCI révision 3 (positions à 3 chiffres)	Value (f.o.b., thousands of dollars) Valeur (f.a.b., milliers de dollars)	As percentage En pourcentage		
		of country total du total du pays	of ** (1) des ** (1)	of world du monde
Honduras (=Developing)**				
All commodity groups	1 746 998	100.00	0.05	0.02
71 Coffee and coffee substitutes	293 763	16.82	3.30	2.10
57 Fruit nut (exc oil), fresh or dried	198 113	11.34	1.10	0.46
773 Electrical distribute equipment nes	159 824	9.15	0.72	0.28
36 Crustacean mollusc aquat invertebra	135 785	7.77	1.16	0.71
422 Fixed veg fat and oil, excl. "soft"	59 021	3.38	0.51	0.45
122 Manufactured tabacco	58 899	3.37	1.59	0.34
554 Soaps cleansers polishes	47 222	2.70	1.19	0.22
893 Articles of plastic nes	45 197	2.59	0.18	0.06
289 Prec metal ore concentrate excl. gold	43 430	2.49	2.49	1.03
642 Cut paper and paperboard articles	38 644	2.21	0.50	0.11
Remainder	667 101	38.19		
Hungary - Hongrie (=Developed)**				
All commodity groups	59 354 409	100.00	1.00	0.62
764 Telecommunicate equipment part nes	8 006 675	13.49	4.97	2.47
713 Internal combustion engine part nes	5 558 208	9.36	6.06	5.18
752 Computer equipment nes	3 170 917	5.34	2.74	1.22
784 Motor vehicle parts and accessories	2 171 467	3.66	1.18	0.97
781 Passenger cars and race cars	2 085 171	3.51	0.51	0.44
778 Electrical machinery apparatus nes	1 670 166	2.81	1.97	1.19
931 Transaction commodity unclassified	1 631 080	2.75	0.82	0.58
772 Electrical circuit equipment	1 596 657	2.69	1.90	1.18
761 Television video receive project	1 532 928	2.58	6.83	2.89
773 Electrical distribute equipment nes	1 355 971	2.28	4.10	2.36
Remainder	30 575 169	51.51		
Iceland - Islande (=Developed)**				
All commodity groups	2 955 761	100.00	0.05	0.03
34 Fish, fresh live chilled frozen	1 036 696	35.07	5.57	3.28
684 Aluminium	541 298	18.31	1.14	0.75
35 Fish, dried salted smoked	338 881	11.47	12.86	9.52
81 Animal feed excluding unmilled cereal	156 512	5.30	0.89	0.52
37 Fish shellfish, prepared preserved	150 110	5.08	2.90	1.07
542 Medicines including veterinary	107 681	3.64	0.06	0.06
671 Pig & sponge iron, ferro alloys etc	91 204	3.09	1.59	0.39
792 Aircraft, spacecraft & equipment	60 861	2.06	0.05	0.05
899 Manufactured articles nes	51 210	1.73	0.18	0.12
411 Animals oils and fats	44 771	1.51	2.04	1.75
Remainder	376 538	12.74		
India - Inde (=Developing)**				
All commodity groups	91 619 116	100.00	2.71	0.95
667 Pearls, precious semiprecious stone	11 231 303	12.26	36.00	13.32
334 Heavy petroleum & bituminous oil	9 051 037	9.88	6.29	2.90
897 Jewellery nes (667)	3 739 832	4.08	21.15	9.95
281 Iron ore and concentrates	3 447 289	3.76	29.97	15.33
842 Female clothing, woven	2 671 967	2.92	6.92	4.39
658 Made-up textile articles nes	2 095 412	2.29	10.53	7.20
651 Textile yarn	2 084 430	2.28	9.48	5.14
542 Medicines including veterinary	2 071 690	2.26	24.35	1.06
516 Other organic chemicals	1 626 101	1.77	23.25	7.26
845 Articles of apparel nes	1 561 172	1.70	2.77	1.78
Remainder	52 038 882	56.80		
Indonesia - Indonésie (=Developing)**				
All commodity groups	75 071 732	100.00	2.22	0.78
333 Crude petroleum & bituminous oil	6 412 287	8.54	1.40	1.01
343 Natural gas, liquefied or not	5 178 480	6.90	13.23	4.67
422 Fixed veg fat and oil, excl. "soft"	4 486 174	5.98	39.06	33.95
321 Coal excluding non-agglomomerated	3 551 453	4.73	26.17	9.18
283 Copper ores and concentrates	2 557 332	3.41	21.68	17.25
231 Natural rubber, latex, gum, etc	2 382 607	3.17	27.65	26.92
634 Veneer, plywood & other wood nes	1 839 518	2.45	20.35	6.40
641 Paper and paperboard	1 804 006	2.40	16.23	1.91
334 Heavy petroleum & bituminous oil	1 767 335	2.35	1.23	0.57
821 Furniture part; bedding furnishing	1 762 694	2.35	5.50	1.87
Remainder	43 329 845	57.72		

Leading products exported based on average 2004-2005 values SITC Revision 3 (3-digit level) / Principaux produits exportés d'après la moyenne des valeurs de 2004-2005 CTCI révision 3 (positions à 3 chiffres)	Value (f.o.b., thousands of dollars) Valeur (f.a.b., milliers de dollars)	As percentage En pourcentage		
		of country total du total du pays	of ** (1) des ** (1)	of world du monde
Iran, Islamic Republic of - Iran, Rép. islamique d' (=Developing)**				
All commodity groups	52 320 000	100.00	1.55	0.54
333 Crude petroleum & bituminous oil	41 287 500	78.91	9.00	6.48
931 Transaction commodity unclassified	2 983 676	5.70	7.03	1.05
57 Fruit nut (exc oil), fresh or dried	1 031 572	1.97	5.74	2.39
659 Floor coverings etc	633 825	1.21	16.19	5.68
335 Residual petroleum products nes	445 300	0.85	8.31	2.70
342 Liquefied propane and butane	409 126	0.78	2.66	1.73
673 Flat iron non-alloy steel products	352 692	0.67	2.07	0.58
511 Hydrocarbons nes; derivatives	308 082	0.59	2.13	0.66
672 Ingots, Iron steel primary products	294 353	0.56	3.37	1.08
343 Natural gas, liquefied or not	255 470	0.49	0.65	0.23
Remainder	4 318 404	8.25		
Ireland - Irlande (=Developed)**				
All commodity groups	107 151 082	100.00	1.81	1.11
515 Organo-inorganic compound acid salt	16 885 969	15.76	25.83	22.32
542 Medicines including veterinary	15 624 893	14.58	8.39	8.00
752 Computer equipment nes	10 936 946	10.21	9.46	4.20
759 Office equipment part & accessories	6 111 329	5.70	7.28	3.21
551 Essential oils, perfumes & flavours	5 501 562	5.13	42.21	35.59
776 Valves tubes; diodes, transistors	4 828 276	4.51	3.15	1.37
931 Transaction commodity unclassified	4 425 414	4.13	2.22	1.56
872 Medical instruments appliances nes	4 212 326	3.93	10.36	8.53
899 Manufactured articles nes	2 851 435	2.66	9.78	6.76
541 Pharmaceuticals excluding medicines	2 742 426	2.56	4.82	4.34
Remainder	33 030 506	30.83		
Israel - Israël (=Developed)**				
All commodity groups	40 695 372	100.00	0.69	0.42
667 Pearls, precious semiprecious stone	15 025 130	36.92	28.87	17.82
931 Transaction commodity unclassified	2 840 589	6.98	1.43	1.00
764 Telecommunicate equipment part nes	2 433 064	5.98	1.51	0.75
542 Medicines including veterinary	1 594 115	3.92	0.86	0.82
792 Aircraft, spacecraft & equipment	979 838	2.41	0.89	0.81
893 Articles of plastic nes	783 548	1.93	1.44	0.97
874 Measure analyze control device nes	772 453	1.90	0.85	0.72
774 Electrodiagnostic equipment	735 480	1.81	3.27	2.99
776 Valves tubes; diodes, transistors	674 937	1.66	0.44	0.19
562 Manufactured fertilizer excl. crude	674 370	1.66	5.96	2.92
Remainder	14 181 851	34.85		
Italy - Italie (=Developed)**				
All commodity groups	360 679 212	100.00	6.10	3.74
784 Motor vehicle parts and accessories	12 162 942	3.37	6.61	5.45
821 Furniture part; bedding furnishing	10 958 757	3.04	18.34	11.65
728 Special industrial machine part nes	10 385 320	2.88	12.90	10.83
542 Medicines including veterinary	10 040 995	2.78	5.39	5.14
334 Heavy petroleum & bituminous oil	9 436 528	2.62	7.27	3.02
851 Footwear	9 082 397	2.52	35.66	14.05
781 Passenger cars and race cars	8 097 078	2.24	1.97	1.72
699 Base metal manufactures nes	7 567 339	2.10	12.69	8.94
775 Household equipment nes	6 800 800	1.89	19.96	11.20
931 Transaction commodity unclassified	6 525 566	1.81	3.28	2.30
Remainder	269 621 491	74.75		
Jamaica - Jamaïque (=Developing)**				
All commodity groups	1 467 174	100.00	0.04	0.02
285 Aluminium ore concentrate alumina	914 310	62.32	28.11	9.76
61 Sugar, mollasses and honey	102 120	6.96	1.21	0.63
512 Alcohols, phenols; derivatives	57 868	3.94	0.44	0.20
112 Alcoholic beverages	57 665	3.93	0.93	0.13
282 Ferrous iron & steel, waste & scrap	45 638	3.11	1.97	0.19
71 Coffee and coffee substitutes	41 069	2.80	0.46	0.29
334 Heavy petroleum & bituminous oil	34 961	2.38	0.02	0.01
98 Edible products & preparations nes	23 312	1.59	0.38	0.08
54 Vegetable & vegetable products nes	21 565	1.47	0.21	0.07
57 Fruit nut (exc oil), fresh or dried	19 769	1.35	0.11	0.05
Remainder	148 897	10.15		

For sources and notes, see end of table.

Pour les sources et les notes, se reporter à la fin du tableau.

3

Leading products exported based on average 2004-2005 values SITC Revision 3 (3-digit level) / Principaux produits exportés d'après la moyenne des valeurs de 2004-2005 CTCI révision 3 (positions à 3 chiffres)	2004-2005 Value (f.o.b., thousands of dollars) Valeur (f.a.b., milliers de dollars)	of country total du total du pays	of ** (1) des ** (1)	of world du monde
Japan - Japon (=Developed)**				
All commodity groups	580 350 972	100.00	9.82	6.02
781 Passenger cars and race cars	77 296 083	13.32	18.76	16.43
776 Valves tubes; diodes, transistors	40 268 801	6.94	26.27	11.44
784 Motor vehicle parts and accessories	25 023 304	4.31	13.60	11.21
931 Transaction commodity unclassified	24 900 948	4.29	12.51	8.78
728 Special industrial machine part nes	18 430 317	3.18	22.89	19.22
778 Electrical machinery apparatus nes	18 185 296	3.13	21.47	12.94
764 Telecommunicate equipment part nes	17 663 183	3.04	10.96	5.44
759 Office equipment part & accessories	16 648 920	2.87	19.84	8.74
772 Electrical circuit equipment	15 087 867	2.60	17.92	11.18
713 Internal combustion engine part nes	14 295 671	2.46	15.59	13.32
Remainder	312 550 582	53.86		
Jordan - Jordanie (=Developing)**				
All commodity groups	4 084 886	100.00	0.12	0.04
272 Crude fertilizer, excl. manufactured	421 948	10.33	33.20	23.95
844 Female clothing, knitted crocheted	298 200	7.30	1.61	1.17
842 Female clothing, woven	272 000	6.66	0.70	0.45
845 Articles of apparel nes	269 879	6.61	0.48	0.31
542 Medicines including veterinary	260 427	6.38	3.06	0.13
54 Vegetable & vegetable products nes	195 987	4.80	1.90	0.63
562 Manufactured fertilizer excl. crude	180 158	4.41	3.06	0.78
897 Jewellery nes (667)	151 047	3.70	0.85	0.40
841 Male clothing, woven	118 661	2.90	0.39	0.24
431 Processed animal & veg fats & oils	116 308	2.85	4.02	2.07
Remainder	1 800 271	44.07		
Kazakhstan (=Transition)**				
All commodity groups	23 893 829	100.00	6.79	0.25
333 Crude petroleum & bituminous oil	14 406 190	60.29	17.09	2.26
682 Copper	1 345 617	5.63	26.69	2.37
671 Pig & sponge iron, ferro alloys etc	897 934	3.76	17.75	3.85
334 Heavy petroleum & bituminous oil	665 839	2.79	1.74	0.21
673 Flat iron non-alloy steel products	570 900	2.39	5.13	0.94
343 Natural gas, liquefied or not	553 873	2.32	5.35	0.50
281 Iron ore and concentrates	536 560	2.25	26.54	2.39
321 Coal excluding non-agglomomerated	356 419	1.49	9.21	0.92
41 Wheat meslin, incl spelt, unmilled	304 639	1.27	16.69	1.64
342 Liquefied propane and butane	271 478	1.14	45.89	1.15
Remainder	3 984 380	16.68		
Kenya (=Developing)**				
All commodity groups	2 987 547	100.00	0.09	0.03
334 Heavy petroleum & bituminous oil	678 191	22.70	0.47	0.22
74 Tea and maté	521 553	17.46	17.72	13.09
292 Crude vegetable materials nes	322 149	10.78	5.92	1.46
54 Vegetable & vegetable products nes	179 159	6.00	1.74	0.58
71 Coffee and coffee substitutes	105 679	3.54	1.19	0.76
278 Other crude minerals	99 876	3.34	3.09	0.99
674 Flat plated iron non-alloy steel	71 905	2.41	0.76	0.22
34 Fish, fresh live chilled frozen	53 601	1.79	0.43	0.17
58 Fruit preserve preparation excl. juice	51 035	1.71	1.23	0.54
57 Fruit nut (exc oil), fresh or dried	48 219	1.61	0.27	0.11
Remainder	856 182	28.66		
Korea, Republic of - Corée, République de (=Developing)**				
All commodity groups	269 131 361	100.00	7.97	2.79
764 Telecommunicate equipment part nes	32 203 789	11.97	19.82	9.92
776 Valves tubes; diodes, transistors	25 967 070	9.65	13.09	7.38
781 Passenger cars and race cars	25 944 123	9.64	45.20	5.51
793 Ships boats floating structures	16 276 403	6.05	60.08	24.64
334 Heavy petroleum & bituminous oil	12 551 851	4.66	8.72	4.02
752 Computer equipment nes	9 694 639	3.60	6.70	3.72
759 Office equipment part & accessories	9 577 929	3.56	8.99	5.03
784 Motor vehicle parts and accessories	6 557 863	2.44	17.45	2.94
871 Optical instruments apparatus nes	5 803 745	2.16	20.83	15.02
778 Electrical machinery apparatus nes	5 134 780	1.91	9.38	3.65
Remainder	119 419 169	44.37		
Kuwait - Koweït (=Developing)**				
All commodity groups	36 789 623	100.00	1.09	0.38
333 Crude petroleum & bituminous oil	20 366 226	55.36	4.44	3.19
334 Heavy petroleum & bituminous oil	11 826 565	32.15	8.22	3.79
342 Liquefied propane and butane	1 762 541	4.79	11.48	7.47
512 Alcohols, phenols; derivatives	645 076	1.75	4.93	2.23
571 Primary form ethylene polymers	606 976	1.65	4.79	1.71
562 Manufactured fertilizer excl. crude	270 334	0.73	4.59	1.17
575 Other plastics, in primary forms	105 457	0.29	0.85	0.17
274 Sulphur and unroasted iron pyrites	89 462	0.24	16.90	6.81
335 Residual petroleum products nes	86 456	0.24	1.61	0.52
516 Other organic chemicals	86 388	0.23	1.24	0.39
Remainder	944 142	2.57		
Kyrgyzstan - Kirghizistan (=Transition)**				
All commodity groups	695 364	100.00	0.20	0.01
971 Gold non-monetary excluding ores	259 050	37.25	37.50	0.69
334 Heavy petroleum & bituminous oil	58 415	8.40	0.15	0.02
263 Cotton	42 114	6.06	2.80	0.38
664 Glass	29 059	4.18	11.48	0.12
931 Transaction commodity unclassified	21 755	3.13	0.05	0.01
661 Lime cement construction material	21 317	3.07	3.36	0.12
351 Electric current	21 175	3.05	1.89	0.11
778 Electrical machinery apparatus nes	18 873	2.71	1.74	0.01
61 Sugar, mollasses and honey	17 241	2.48	2.31	0.11
842 Female clothing, woven	15 207	2.19	0.46	0.02
Remainder	191 158	27.49		
Lao People's Dem. Rep. - Rép. dém. populaire lao (=Developing)**				
All commodity groups	428 414	100.00	0.01	0.00
248 Wood simply worked, railway sleeper	127 916	29.86	1.92	0.37
845 Articles of apparel nes	78 358	18.29	0.14	0.09
841 Male clothing, woven	59 779	13.95	0.19	0.12
247 Wood in rough or roughly squared	27 087	6.32	1.14	0.27
842 Female clothing, woven	25 721	6.00	0.07	0.04
71 Coffee and coffee substitutes	15 209	3.55	0.17	0.11
843 Male clothing, knitted crocheted	13 555	3.16	0.12	0.09
634 Veneer, plywood & other wood nes	7 501	1.75	0.08	0.04
851 Footwear	6 374	1.49	0.02	0.01
844 Female clothing, knitted crocheted	6 179	1.44	0.03	0.02
Remainder	60 735	14.18		
Latvia - Lettonie (=Developed)**				
All commodity groups	4 840 689	100.00	0.08	0.05
248 Wood simply worked, railway sleeper	597 997	12.35	2.42	1.73
676 Iron steel bar rod section piling	343 645	7.10	1.11	0.70
334 Heavy petroleum & bituminous oil	269 527	5.57	0.21	0.09
247 Wood in rough or roughly squared	181 710	3.75	3.90	1.83
635 Wood manufactures nes	172 782	3.57	1.31	0.85
821 Furniture part; bedding furnishing	159 333	3.29	0.27	0.17
634 Veneer, plywood & other wood nes	157 459	3.25	0.85	0.55
931 Transaction commodity unclassified	146 000	3.02	0.07	0.05
845 Articles of apparel nes	119 572	2.47	0.41	0.14
542 Medicines including veterinary	109 068	2.25	0.06	0.06
Remainder	2 583 597	53.37		
Lebanon - Liban (=Developing)**				
All commodity groups	1 790 278	100.00	0.05	0.02
971 Gold non-monetary excluding ores	185 241	10.35	0.94	0.50
661 Lime cement construction material	118 491	6.62	1.45	0.69
716 Rotating electric plant parts nes	116 817	6.53	0.77	0.24
282 Ferrous iron & steel, waste & scrap	103 917	5.80	4.48	0.44
897 Jewellery nes (667)	78 199	4.37	0.44	0.21
562 Manufactured fertilizer excl. crude	51 950	2.90	0.88	0.23
642 Cut paper and paperboard articles	51 723	2.89	0.67	0.15
288 Non ferrous base metal waste nes	43 098	2.41	1.17	0.27
57 Fruit nut (exc oil), fresh or dried	41 873	2.34	0.23	0.10
522 Inorganic chemical elem oxide salt	39 686	2.22	0.39	0.15
Remainder	959 282	53.58		

For sources and notes, see end of table.

Pour les sources et les notes, se reporter à la fin du tableau.

Leading products exported based on average 2004-2005 values SITC Revision 3 (3-digit level) / Principaux produits exportés d'après la moyenne des valeurs de 2004-2005 CTCI révision 3 (positions à 3 chiffres)	2004-2005			
	Value (f.o.b., thousands of dollars) Valeur (f.a.b., milliers de dollars)	As percentage En pourcentage		
		of country total du total du pays	of ** (1) des ** (1)	of world du monde
Lesotho (=Developing)**				
All commodity groups	632 984	100.00	0.02	0.01
841 Male clothing, woven	262 721	41.51	0.86	0.54
845 Articles of apparel nes	82 635	13.05	0.15	0.09
851 Footwear	42 338	6.69	0.12	0.07
844 Female clothing, knitted crocheted	33 512	5.29	0.18	0.13
652 Woven cotton fabrics	31 305	4.95	0.18	0.11
111 Non alcoholic beverage nes	27 903	4.41	1.45	0.28
211 Raw hides & skins, excluding furskins	25 603	4.04	2.85	0.45
761 Television video receive project	24 532	3.88	0.08	0.05
843 Male clothing, knitted crocheted	24 309	3.84	0.22	0.17
662 Clay and refractory materials	15 198	2.40	0.36	0.09
Remainder	62 929	9.94		
Libyan Arab Jamahiriya - Jamahiriya arabe libyenne (=Developing)**				
All commodity groups	16 500 516	100.00	0.49	0.17
333 Crude petroleum & bituminous oil	14 079 575	85.33	3.07	2.21
334 Heavy petroleum & bituminous oil	1 401 513	8.49	0.97	0.45
512 Alcohols, phenols; derivatives	120 525	0.73	0.92	0.42
511 Hydrocarbons nes; derivatives	115 333	0.70	0.80	0.25
673 Flat iron non-alloy steel products	107 492	0.65	0.63	0.18
562 Manufactured fertilizer excl. crude	103 466	0.63	1.76	0.45
671 Pig & sponge iron, ferro alloys etc	90 932	0.55	0.73	0.39
344 Petroleum and hydrocarbon gas nes	77 457	0.47	3.18	0.81
343 Natural gas, liquefied or not	74 057	0.45	0.19	0.07
342 Liquefied propane and butane	66 068	0.40	0.43	0.28
Remainder	264 098	1.60		
Lithuania - Lituanie (=Developed)**				
All commodity groups	10 686 526	100.00	0.18	0.11
334 Heavy petroleum & bituminous oil	2 479 809	23.21	1.91	0.79
821 Furniture part; bedding furnishing	524 923	4.91	0.88	0.56
562 Manufactured fertilizer excl. crude	466 405	4.36	4.12	2.02
781 Passenger cars and race cars	346 098	3.24	0.08	0.07
842 Female clothing, woven	278 758	2.61	1.47	0.46
793 Ships boats floating structures	265 463	2.48	0.73	0.40
248 Wood simply worked, railway sleeper	227 565	2.13	0.92	0.66
773 Electrical distribute equipment nes	219 077	2.05	0.66	0.38
776 Valves tubes; diodes, transistors	192 097	1.80	0.13	0.05
893 Articles of plastic nes	174 931	1.64	0.32	0.22
Remainder	5 511 399	51.57		
Luxembourg (=Developed)**				
All commodity groups	12 441 204	100.00	0.21	0.13
676 Iron steel bar rod section piling	1 672 321	13.44	5.40	3.40
674 Flat plated iron non-alloy steel	632 809	5.09	2.87	1.95
898 Music instrument device recording	537 306	4.32	1.65	1.13
657 Special yarn and textile fabric etc	483 731	3.89	2.49	1.68
641 Paper and paperboard	425 153	3.42	0.52	0.45
893 Articles of plastic nes	413 114	3.32	0.76	0.51
684 Aluminium	405 855	3.26	0.86	0.56
625 Rubber for wheels, incl inner tube	396 702	3.19	1.45	0.98
781 Passenger cars and race cars	392 751	3.16	0.10	0.08
931 Transaction commodity unclassified	370 942	2.98	0.19	0.13
Remainder	6 710 520	53.94		
Madagascar (=Developing)**				
All commodity groups	369 968	100.00	0.01	0.00
75 Spices	128 107	34.63	5.70	4.19
36 Crustacean mollusc aquat invertebra	51 431	13.90	0.44	0.27
892 Printed matter	37 068	10.02	0.51	0.10
334 Heavy petroleum & bituminous oil	16 256	4.39	0.01	0.01
58 Fruit preserve preparation excl. juice	15 176	4.10	0.37	0.16
61 Sugar, mollasses and honey	8 689	2.35	0.10	0.05
292 Crude vegetable materials nes	8 170	2.21	0.15	0.04
667 Pearls, precious semiprecious stone	8 133	2.20	0.03	0.01
287 Base metal ores & concentrates nes	6 157	1.66	0.08	0.04
652 Woven cotton fabrics	6 008	1.62	0.04	0.02
Remainder	84 775	22.91		

Leading products exported based on average 2004-2005 values SITC Revision 3 (3-digit level) / Principaux produits exportés d'après la moyenne des valeurs de 2004-2005 CTCI révision 3 (positions à 3 chiffres)	2004-2005			
	Value (f.o.b., thousands of dollars) Valeur (f.a.b., milliers de dollars)	As percentage En pourcentage		
		of country total du total du pays	of ** (1) des ** (1)	of world du monde
Malawi (=Developing)**				
All commodity groups	477 096	100.00	0.01	0.00
121 Unmanufactured tabacco and refuse	234 688	49.19	5.83	3.41
61 Sugar, mollasses and honey	60 483	12.68	0.72	0.38
74 Tea and maté	48 436	10.15	1.65	1.22
263 Cotton	18 008	3.77	0.44	0.16
841 Male clothing, woven	14 882	3.12	0.05	0.03
845 Articles of apparel nes	12 779	2.68	0.02	0.01
843 Male clothing, knitted crocheted	10 130	2.12	0.09	0.07
57 Fruit nut (exc oil), fresh or dried	9 520	2.00	0.05	0.02
892 Printed matter	5 594	1.17	0.08	0.01
223 Oil seed for non soft oil	5 489	1.15	1.65	0.43
Remainder	57 087	11.97		
Malaysia - Malaisie (=Developing)**				
All commodity groups	133 731 567	100.00	3.96	1.39
776 Valves tubes; diodes, transistors	23 630 931	17.67	11.92	6.71
752 Computer equipment nes	13 162 744	9.84	9.09	5.05
759 Office equipment part & accessories	8 257 879	6.17	7.75	4.33
764 Telecommunicate equipment part nes	7 037 271	5.26	4.33	2.17
333 Crude petroleum & bituminous oil	6 988 429	5.23	1.52	1.10
343 Natural gas, liquefied or not	4 992 737	3.73	12.76	4.51
422 Fixed veg fat and oil, excl. "soft"	4 976 729	3.72	43.33	37.66
772 Electrical circuit equipment	4 850 601	3.63	9.77	3.60
334 Heavy petroleum & bituminous oil	3 598 330	2.69	2.50	1.15
763 Sound TV recorder or reproducer	2 117 774	1.58	6.13	3.57
Remainder	54 118 141	40.47		
Maldives (=Developing)**				
All commodity groups	161 958	100.00	0.00	0.00
34 Fish, fresh live chilled frozen	64 344	39.73	0.51	0.20
334 Heavy petroleum & bituminous oil	35 934	22.19	0.02	0.01
37 Fish shellfish, prepared preserved	16 261	10.04	0.19	0.12
844 Female clothing, knitted crocheted	14 706	9.08	0.08	0.06
35 Fish, dried salted smoked	12 331	7.61	1.39	0.35
892 Printed matter	6 420	3.96	0.09	0.02
36 Crustacean mollusc aquat invertebra	2 120	1.31	0.02	0.01
81 Animal feed excluding unmilled cereal	1 315	0.81	0.01	0.00
842 Female clothing, woven	1 050	0.65	0.00	0.00
793 Ships boats floating structures	962	0.59	0.00	0.00
Remainder	6 514	4.02		
Mali (=Developing)**				
All commodity groups	1 067 543	100.00	0.03	0.01
971 Gold non-monetary excluding ores	545 890	51.14	2.77	1.46
263 Cotton	382 681	35.85	9.43	3.41
1 Live animal excl. fish & crustacean	59 909	5.61	2.54	0.50
723 Civil engineering plant & equipment	10 418	0.98	0.09	0.02
778 Electrical machinery apparatus nes	7 211	0.68	0.01	0.01
658 Made-up textile articles nes	6 720	0.63	0.03	0.02
931 Transaction commodity unclassified	6 486	0.61	0.02	0.00
334 Heavy petroleum & bituminous oil	3 932	0.37	0.00	0.00
782 Goods and service vehicles	2 971	0.28	0.02	0.00
657 Special yarn and textile fabric etc	2 795	0.26	0.03	0.01
Remainder	38 530	3.61		
Malta - Malte (=Developed)**				
All commodity groups	2 453 628	100.00	0.04	0.03
776 Valves tubes; diodes, transistors	1 153 584	47.02	0.75	0.33
772 Electrical circuit equipment	121 404	4.95	0.14	0.09
892 Printed matter	96 714	3.94	0.32	0.25
841 Male clothing, woven	83 568	3.41	0.53	0.17
894 Baby carriage toy game sport good	81 190	3.31	0.33	0.13
872 Medical instruments appliances nes	61 552	2.51	0.15	0.12
334 Heavy petroleum & bituminous oil	59 358	2.42	0.05	0.02
629 Articles of rubber nes	52 808	2.15	0.38	0.30
98 Edible products & preparations nes	51 952	2.12	0.21	0.17
781 Passenger cars and race cars	45 054	1.84	0.01	0.01
Remainder	646 444	26.35		

For sources and notes, see end of table.

Pour les sources et les notes, se reporter à la fin du tableau.

Leading products exported based on average 2004-2005 values SITC Revision 3 (3-digit level) Principaux produits exportés d'après la moyenne des valeurs de 2004-2005 CTCI révision 3 (positions à 3 chiffres)	Value (f.o.b., thousands of dollars) Valeur (f.a.b., milliers de dollars)	of country total du total du pays	of ** (1) des ** (1)	of world du monde
	2004-2005	As percentage En pourcentage		
Mauritania - Mauritanie (**=Developing)				
All commodity groups	566 299	100.00	0.02	0.01
281 Iron ore and concentrates	280 400	49.51	2.44	1.25
36 Crustacean mollusc aquat invertebra	132 232	23.35	1.13	0.69
34 Fish, fresh live chilled frozen	115 098	20.32	0.92	0.36
81 Animal feed excluding unmilled cereal	13 283	2.35	0.11	0.04
35 Fish, dried salted smoked	3 198	0.56	0.36	0.09
37 Fish shellfish, prepared preserved	2 329	0.41	0.03	0.02
652 Woven cotton fabrics	1 935	0.34	0.01	0.01
776 Valves tubes; diodes, transistors	1 788	0.32	0.00	0.00
282 Ferrous iron & steel, waste & scrap	1 772	0.31	0.08	0.01
841 Male clothing, woven	1 335	0.24	0.00	0.00
Remainder	12 930	2.28		
Mauritius - Maurice (**=Developing)				
All commodity groups	1 964 822	100.00	0.06	0.02
845 Articles of apparel nes	518 413	26.38	0.92	0.59
61 Sugar, mollasses and honey	356 040	18.12	4.23	2.21
841 Male clothing, woven	185 470	9.44	0.60	0.38
764 Telecommunicate equipment part nes	151 415	7.71	0.09	0.05
37 Fish shellfish, prepared preserved	94 898	4.83	1.09	0.68
842 Female clothing, woven	56 810	2.89	0.15	0.09
667 Pearls, precious semiprecious stone	47 450	2.41	0.15	0.06
34 Fish, fresh live chilled frozen	46 743	2.38	0.37	0.15
843 Male clothing, knitted crocheted	44 766	2.28	0.40	0.31
897 Jewellery nes (667)	39 401	2.01	0.22	0.10
Remainder	423 416	21.55		
Mexico - Mexique (**=Developing)				
All commodity groups	201 093 874	100.00	5.96	2.09
333 Crude petroleum & bituminous oil	24 793 654	12.33	5.40	3.89
781 Passenger cars and race cars	12 622 555	6.28	21.99	2.68
764 Telecommunicate equipment part nes	10 994 239	5.47	6.77	3.39
752 Computer equipment nes	10 061 340	5.00	6.95	3.86
734 Motor vehicle parts and accessories	9 054 952	4.50	24.09	4.05
751 Television video receive project	9 005 734	4.48	29.74	16.99
773 Electrical distribute equipment nes	7 028 965	3.50	31.53	12.24
782 Goods and service vehicles	6 911 794	3.44	38.24	8.17
778 Electrical machinery apparatus nes	6 830 411	3.40	12.48	4.86
772 Electrical circuit equipment	5 482 617	2.73	11.04	4.06
Remainder	98 307 613	48.89		
Moldova, Republic of - Moldova, République de (**=Transition)				
All commodity groups	1 038 755	100.00	0.30	0.01
112 Alcoholic beverages	295 962	28.49	24.94	0.66
57 Fruit nut (exc oil), fresh or dried	62 587	6.03	9.47	0.15
211 Raw hides & skins, excluding furskins	60 784	5.85	21.39	1.07
845 Articles of apparel nes	58 627	5.64	2.95	0.07
842 Female clothing, woven	46 155	4.44	1.40	0.08
421 Fixed veg fat and oil, "soft"	39 402	3.79	4.11	0.25
841 Male clothing, woven	37 206	3.58	1.38	0.08
851 Footwear	24 151	2.32	0.94	0.04
59 Fruit & vegetable juice unferment	21 051	2.03	10.95	0.25
222 Oil seed etc for soft oil	20 975	2.02	4.42	0.10
Remainder	371 855	35.80		
Mongolia - Mongolie (**=Developing)				
All commodity groups	960 197	100.00	0.03	0.01
283 Copper ores and concentrates	305 270	31.79	2.59	2.06
971 Gold non-monetary excluding ores	280 504	29.21	1.42	0.75
268 Wool & animal hair, incl wool tops	71 683	7.47	5.09	1.45
287 Base metal ores & concentrates nes	38 823	4.04	0.48	0.27
845 Articles of apparel nes	37 735	3.93	0.07	0.04
842 Female clothing, woven	32 845	3.42	0.09	0.05
841 Male clothing, woven	24 418	2.54	0.08	0.05
278 Other crude minerals	24 229	2.52	0.75	0.24
611 Leather	21 601	2.25	0.20	0.11
321 Coal excluding non-agglomomerated	21 561	2.25	0.16	0.06
Remainder	101 529	10.57		

Leading products exported based on average 2004-2005 values SITC Revision 3 (3-digit level) Principaux produits exportés d'après la moyenne des valeurs de 2004-2005 CTCI révision 3 (positions à 3 chiffres)	Value (f.o.b., thousands of dollars) Valeur (f.a.b., milliers de dollars)	of country total du total du pays	of ** (1) des ** (1)	of world du monde
	2004-2005	As percentage En pourcentage		
Morocco - Maroc (**=Developing)				
All commodity groups	10 277 294	100.00	0.30	0.11
842 Female clothing, woven	1 026 333	9.99	2.66	1.69
845 Articles of apparel nes	846 748	8.24	1.50	0.97
522 Inorganic chemical elem oxide salt	799 706	7.78	7.92	2.99
841 Male clothing, woven	690 623	6.72	2.25	1.41
776 Valves tubes; diodes, transistors	628 276	6.11	0.32	0.18
272 Crude fertilizer, excl. manufactured	466 993	4.54	36.74	26.50
773 Electrical distribute equipment nes	463 473	4.51	2.08	0.81
562 Manufactured fertilizer excl. crude	437 896	4.26	7.44	1.90
37 Fish shellfish, prepared preserved	383 109	3.73	4.40	2.73
57 Fruit nut (exc oil), fresh or dried	375 859	3.66	2.09	0.87
Remainder	4 158 277	40.46		
Mozambique (**=Developing)				
All commodity groups	1 643 421	100.00	0.05	0.02
288 Non ferrous base metal waste nes	511 477	31.12	13.85	3.26
684 Aluminium	457 512	27.84	2.63	0.64
351 Electric current	122 026	7.43	7.04	0.63
36 Crustacean mollusc aquat invertebra	87 519	5.33	0.75	0.46
343 Natural gas, liquefied or not	72 201	4.39	0.18	0.07
931 Transaction commodity unclassified	44 136	2.69	0.10	0.02
121 Unmanufactured tabacco and refuse	42 018	2.56	1.04	0.61
263 Cotton	32 448	1.97	0.80	0.29
334 Heavy petroleum & bituminous oil	31 344	1.91	0.02	0.01
57 Fruit nut (exc oil), fresh or dried	27 073	1.65	0.15	0.06
Remainder	215 666	13.12		
Myanmar (**=Developing)				
All commodity groups	3 341 780	100.00	0.10	0.03
343 Natural gas, liquefied or not	1 032 559	30.90	2.64	0.93
247 Wood in rough or roughly squared	540 421	16.17	22.84	5.46
54 Vegetable & vegetable products nes	266 407	7.97	2.58	0.86
845 Articles of apparel nes	263 390	7.88	0.47	0.30
841 Male clothing, woven	211 893	6.34	0.69	0.43
36 Crustacean mollusc aquat invertebra	166 871	4.99	1.43	0.87
248 Wood simply worked, railway sleeper	140 940	4.22	2.11	0.41
842 Female clothing, woven	134 825	4.03	0.35	0.22
667 Pearls, precious semiprecious stone	53 826	1.61	0.17	0.06
682 Copper	51 780	1.55	0.20	0.09
Remainder	478 866	14.33		
Namibia - Namibie (**=Developing)				
All commodity groups	2 602 979	100.00	0.08	0.03
667 Pearls, precious semiprecious stone	729 914	28.04	2.34	0.87
34 Fish, fresh live chilled frozen	331 292	12.73	2.64	1.05
278 Other crude minerals	252 192	9.69	7.81	2.49
892 Printed matter	114 654	4.40	1.58	0.30
686 Zinc	112 831	4.33	5.36	1.78
112 Alcoholic beverages	79 674	3.06	1.29	0.18
1 Live animal excl. fish & crustacean	78 095	3.00	3.31	0.65
682 Copper	76 443	2.94	0.29	0.13
11 Beef, fresh chilled frozen	71 968	2.76	1.41	0.36
525 Radio active & associated materials	57 095	2.19	12.95	0.85
Remainder	698 822	26.85		
Nepal - Népal (**=Developing)				
All commodity groups	793 056	100.00	0.02	0.01
841 Male clothing, woven	90 254	11.38	0.29	0.18
842 Female clothing, woven	83 223	10.49	0.22	0.14
431 Processed animal & veg fats & oils	61 950	7.81	2.14	1.11
659 Floor coverings etc	49 991	6.30	1.28	0.45
845 Articles of apparel nes	48 808	6.15	0.09	0.06
651 Textile yarn	42 418	5.35	0.19	0.10
553 Perfume toilet cosmetics, excl. soap	36 311	4.58	0.59	0.09
846 Clothing accessory excl. 831 848 851	24 329	3.07	0.27	0.14
674 Flat plated iron non-alloy steel	23 682	2.99	0.25	0.07
893 Articles of plastic nes	19 444	2.45	0.08	0.02
Remainder	312 646	39.42		

For sources and notes, see end of table.

Pour les sources et les notes, se reporter à la fin du tableau.

166

Leading products exported based on average 2004-2005 values SITC Revision 3 (3-digit level) / Principaux produits exportés d'après la moyenne des valeurs de 2004-2005 CTCI révision 3 (positions à 3 chiffres)	Value (f.o.b., thousands of dollars) Valeur (f.a.b., milliers de dollars)	2004-2005 As percentage En pourcentage		
		of country total du total du pays	of ** (1) des ** (1)	of world du monde
Netherlands - Pays-Bas (**=Developed)				
All commodity groups	305 271 025	100.00	5.17	3.17
752 Computer equipment nes	21 093 409	6.91	18.24	8.09
334 Heavy petroleum & bituminous oil	20 558 191	6.73	15.83	6.59
759 Office equipment part & accessories	11 845 388	3.88	14.12	6.22
776 Valves tubes; diodes, transistors	10 273 135	3.37	6.70	2.92
343 Natural gas, liquefied or not	9 357 660	3.07	15.26	8.44
292 Crude vegetable materials nes	7 515 129	2.46	45.64	34.13
764 Telecommunicate equipment part nes	7 498 015	2.46	4.65	2.31
542 Medicines including veterinary	7 488 980	2.45	4.02	3.83
511 Hydrocarbons nes; derivatives	5 252 791	1.72	17.09	11.32
54 Vegetable & vegetable products nes	4 271 492	1.40	21.04	13.74
Remainder	200 116 834	65.55		
Netherlands Antilles - Antilles néerlandaises (**=Developing)				
All commodity groups	1 658 077	100.00	0.05	0.02
334 Heavy petroleum & bituminous oil	1 209 841	72.97	0.84	0.39
793 Ships boats floating structures	79 862	4.82	0.29	0.12
335 Residual petroleum products nes	41 182	2.48	0.77	0.25
278 Other crude minerals	37 129	2.24	1.15	0.37
34 Fish, fresh live chilled frozen	24 319	1.47	0.19	0.08
641 Paper and paperboard	21 450	1.29	0.19	0.02
591 Household and garden chemicals	20 093	1.21	0.54	0.13
897 Jewellery nes (667)	13 433	0.81	0.08	0.04
61 Sugar, mollasses and honey	11 177	0.67	0.13	0.07
333 Crude petroleum & bituminous oil	9 603	0.58	0.00	0.00
Remainder	189 988	11.46		
New Caledonia - Nouvelle-Calédonie (**=Developing)				
All commodity groups	1 063 435	100.00	0.03	0.01
671 Pig & sponge iron, ferro alloys etc	661 482	62.20	5.28	2.83
284 Nickel ores, concentrates, etc	304 228	28.61	10.28	5.13
36 Crustacean mollusc aquat invertebra	25 843	2.43	0.22	0.14
792 Aircraft, spacecraft & equipment	13 741	1.29	0.14	0.01
334 Heavy petroleum & bituminous oil	12 968	1.22	0.01	0.00
679 Iron steel pipe tube fittings etc	6 490	0.61	0.05	0.01
741 Heating cooling equipment parts nes	5 528	0.52	0.03	0.01
34 Fish, fresh live chilled frozen	3 935	0.37	0.03	0.01
892 Printed matter	3 327	0.31	0.05	0.01
764 Telecommunicate equipment part nes	1 800	0.17	0.00	0.00
Remainder	24 092	2.27		
New Zealand - Nouvelle-Zélande (**=Developed)				
All commodity groups	21 037 303	100.00	0.36	0.22
22 Milk products, excl. butter & cheese	2 118 064	10.07	11.61	10.04
12 Meat nes, fresh chilled frozen	1 883 807	8.95	6.31	5.15
11 Beef, fresh chilled frozen	1 265 307	6.01	8.61	6.30
57 Fruit nut (exc oil), fresh or dried	858 654	4.08	3.51	1.99
931 Transaction commodity unclassified	727 671	3.46	0.37	0.26
24 Cheese and curd	723 636	3.44	4.66	4.38
23 Butter fats oils derived from milk	648 845	3.08	16.57	15.54
684 Aluminium	643 036	3.06	1.36	0.89
248 Wood simply worked, railway sleeper	601 270	2.86	2.44	1.74
592 Starches, glutenes, glues, etc	581 695	2.77	5.44	4.28
Remainder	10 985 318	52.22		
Nicaragua (**=Developing)				
All commodity groups	796 743	100.00	0.02	0.01
71 Coffee and coffee substitutes	136 546	17.14	1.53	0.98
11 Beef, fresh chilled frozen	114 751	14.40	2.25	0.57
36 Crustacean mollusc aquat invertebra	74 949	9.41	0.64	0.39
61 Sugar, mollasses and honey	50 410	6.33	0.60	0.31
222 Oil seed etc for soft oil	47 173	5.92	0.48	0.22
971 Gold non-monetary excluding ores	44 672	5.61	0.23	0.12
1 Live animal excl. fish & crustacean	39 975	5.02	1.70	0.33
54 Vegetable & vegetable products nes	29 937	3.76	0.29	0.10
24 Cheese and curd	23 120	2.90	4.52	0.14
57 Fruit nut (exc oil), fresh or dried	19 732	2.48	0.11	0.05
Remainder	215 478	27.04		

Leading products exported based on average 2004-2005 values SITC Revision 3 (3-digit level) / Principaux produits exportés d'après la moyenne des valeurs de 2004-2005 CTCI révision 3 (positions à 3 chiffres)	Value (f.o.b., thousands of dollars) Valeur (f.a.b., milliers de dollars)	2004-2005 As percentage En pourcentage		
		of country total du total du pays	of ** (1) des ** (1)	of world du monde
Niger (**=Developing)				
All commodity groups	313 277	100.00	0.01	0.00
286 Uranium & thorium ore concentrates	141 059	45.03	72.26	22.84
971 Gold non-monetary excluding ores	45 691	14.58	0.23	0.12
1 Live animal excl. fish & crustacean	35 761	11.42	1.52	0.30
54 Vegetable & vegetable products nes	28 622	9.14	0.28	0.09
652 Woven cotton fabrics	10 230	3.27	0.06	0.04
269 Worn clothing, textile article; rag	8 328	2.66	2.00	0.44
723 Civil engineering plant & equipment	5 815	1.86	0.05	0.01
122 Manufactured tabacco	5 718	1.83	0.15	0.03
334 Heavy petroleum & bituminous oil	4 837	1.54	0.00	0.00
931 Transaction commodity unclassified	3 865	1.23	0.01	0.00
Remainder	23 351	7.45		
Nigeria - Nigéria (**=Developing)				
All commodity groups	36 712 442	100.00	1.09	0.38
333 Crude petroleum & bituminous oil	35 390 236	96.40	7.71	5.55
793 Ships boats floating structures	546 156	1.49	2.02	0.83
343 Natural gas, liquefied or not	403 540	1.10	1.03	0.36
344 Petroleum and hydrocarbon gas nes	106 786	0.29	4.38	1.12
743 Gas pump, compressor, fan, filter	83 974	0.23	0.57	0.12
342 Liquefied propane and butane	35 483	0.10	0.23	0.15
625 Rubber for wheels, incl inner tube	21 779	0.06	0.18	0.05
723 Civil engineering plant & equipment	10 099	0.03	0.09	0.02
611 Leather	9 135	0.02	0.08	0.04
656 Tulle lace embroidery trim etc	8 111	0.02	0.19	0.10
Remainder	97 143	0.26		
Norway - Norvège (**=Developed)				
All commodity groups	93 122 202	100.00	1.58	0.97
333 Crude petroleum & bituminous oil	42 084 292	45.19	44.58	6.60
343 Natural gas, liquefied or not	13 500 185	14.50	22.02	12.18
684 Aluminium	3 681 225	3.95	7.79	5.12
334 Heavy petroleum & bituminous oil	3 561 177	3.82	2.74	1.14
931 Transaction commodity unclassified	3 551 840	3.81	1.78	1.25
34 Fish, fresh live chilled frozen	3 504 227	3.76	18.81	11.07
342 Liquefied propane and butane	1 592 711	1.71	20.86	6.75
793 Ships boats floating structures	1 345 986	1.45	3.70	2.04
683 Nickel	1 138 577	1.22	14.05	8.71
641 Paper and paperboard	838 277	0.90	1.03	0.89
Remainder	18 323 706	19.68		
Oman (**=Developing)				
All commodity groups	17 215 668	100.00	0.51	0.18
333 Crude petroleum & bituminous oil	11 132 770	64.67	2.43	1.75
343 Natural gas, liquefied or not	2 693 905	15.65	6.88	2.43
334 Heavy petroleum & bituminous oil	699 607	4.06	0.49	0.22
931 Transaction commodity unclassified	600 881	3.49	1.42	0.21
22 Milk products, excl. butter & cheese	120 588	0.70	5.28	0.57
34 Fish, fresh live chilled frozen	83 532	0.49	0.66	0.26
661 Lime cement construction material	78 492	0.46	0.96	0.45
723 Civil engineering plant & equipment	78 042	0.45	0.67	0.12
562 Manufactured fertilizer excl. crude	76 993	0.45	1.31	0.33
679 Iron steel pipe tube fittings etc	76 852	0.45	0.61	0.16
Remainder	1 574 006	9.14		
Pakistan (**=Developing)				
All commodity groups	14 714 608	100.00	0.44	0.15
658 Made-up textile articles nes	2 701 040	18.36	13.58	9.28
652 Woven cotton fabrics	1 929 592	13.11	11.34	6.72
651 Textile yarn	1 185 892	8.06	5.39	2.93
42 Rice	891 064	6.06	13.21	9.90
843 Male clothing, knitted crocheted	772 585	5.25	6.86	5.38
841 Male clothing, woven	648 800	4.41	2.11	1.32
845 Articles of apparel nes	632 676	4.30	1.12	0.72
848 Headgear, non-textile clothing	523 073	3.55	3.71	2.62
334 Heavy petroleum & bituminous oil	479 798	3.26	0.33	0.15
894 Baby carriage toy game sport good	316 702	2.15	0.88	0.52
Remainder	4 633 387	31.49		

For sources and notes, see end of table.

Pour les sources et les notes, se reporter à la fin du tableau.

167

Leading products exported based on average 2004-2005 values SITC Revision 3 (3-digit level) / Principaux produits exportés d'après la moyenne des valeurs de 2004-2005 CTCI révision 3 (positions à 3 chiffres)	2004-2005			
	Value (f.o.b., thousands of dollars) / Valeur (f.a.b., milliers de dollars)	As percentage En pourcentage		
		of country total / du total du pays	of ** (1) / des ** (1)	of world / du monde
Palau, Pacific Islands (former) - Palaos, Îles du Pacifique (anc.) (**=Developing)				
All commodity groups	12 923	100.00	0.00	0.00
34 Fish, fresh live chilled frozen	10 302	79.72	0.08	0.03
282 Ferrous iron & steel, waste & scrap	2 017	15.61	0.09	0.01
874 Measure analyze control device nes	240	1.86	0.00	0.00
674 Flat plated iron non-alloy steel	80	0.62	0.00	0.00
723 Civil engineering plant & equipment	60	0.46	0.00	0.00
288 Non ferrous base metal waste nes	40	0.31	0.00	0.00
292 Crude vegetable materials nes	32	0.25	0.00	0.00
653 Man-made woven fabrics	23	0.18	0.00	0.00
728 Special industrial machine part nes	22	0.17	0.00	0.00
81 Animal feed excluding unmilled cereal	11	0.09	0.00	0.00
Remainder	96	0.74		
Panama (**=Developing)				
All commodity groups	927 029	100.00	0.03	0.01
34 Fish, fresh live chilled frozen	313 542	33.82	2.49	0.99
57 Fruit nut (exc oil), fresh or dried	213 806	23.06	1.19	0.50
36 Crustacean mollusc aquat invertebra	83 035	8.96	0.71	0.43
35 Fish, dried salted smoked	24 759	2.67	2.79	0.70
282 Ferrous iron & steel, waste & scrap	20 946	2.26	0.90	0.09
54 Vegetable & vegetable products nes	18 285	1.97	0.18	0.06
1 Live animal excl. fish & crustacean	17 355	1.87	0.74	0.14
61 Sugar, mollasses and honey	17 025	1.84	0.20	0.11
11 Beef, fresh chilled frozen	14 697	1.59	0.29	0.07
542 Medicines including veterinary	14 202	1.53	0.17	0.01
Remainder	189 377	20.43		
Papua New Guinea - Papouasie-Nouvelle-Guinée (**=Developing)				
All commodity groups	2 914 517	100.00	0.09	0.03
289 Prec metal ore concentrate excl. gold	833 041	28.58	47.68	19.77
333 Crude petroleum & bituminous oil	591 584	20.30	0.13	0.09
283 Copper ores and concentrates	512 450	17.58	4.34	3.46
422 Fixed veg fat and oil, excl. "soft"	188 793	6.48	1.64	1.43
971 Gold non-monetary excluding ores	185 889	6.38	0.94	0.50
71 Coffee and coffee substitutes	109 047	3.74	1.23	0.78
72 Cocoa	85 087	2.92	1.59	1.01
792 Aircraft, spacecraft & equipment	53 105	1.82	0.55	0.04
247 Wood in rough or roughly squared	48 557	1.67	2.05	0.49
75 Spices	46 933	1.61	2.09	1.53
Remainder	260 032	8.92		
Paraguay (**=Developing)				
All commodity groups	1 656 749	100.00	0.05	0.02
222 Oil seed etc for soft oil	602 049	36.34	6.12	2.82
11 Beef, fresh chilled frozen	201 293	12.15	3.95	1.00
81 Animal feed excluding unmilled cereal	160 851	9.71	1.33	0.53
421 Fixed veg fat and oil, "soft"	111 664	6.74	1.75	0.70
263 Cotton	103 436	6.24	2.55	0.92
41 Wheat meslin, incl spelt, unmilled	53 849	3.25	2.49	0.29
611 Leather	53 519	3.23	0.49	0.26
248 Wood simply worked, railway sleeper	49 932	3.01	0.75	0.14
44 Maize unmilled, excluding sweet corn	38 143	2.30	1.25	0.33
61 Sugar, mollasses and honey	18 556	1.12	0.22	0.12
Remainder	263 457	15.90		
Peru - Pérou (**=Developing)				
All commodity groups	14 774 583	100.00	0.44	0.15
971 Gold non-monetary excluding ores	2 716 376	18.39	13.76	7.28
682 Copper	1 801 752	12.19	6.86	3.17
287 Base metal ores & concentrates nes	1 625 471	11.00	20.16	11.27
283 Copper ores and concentrates	1 254 875	8.49	10.64	8.46
81 Animal feed excluding unmilled cereal	1 090 313	7.38	9.03	3.63
334 Heavy petroleum & bituminous oil	913 751	6.18	0.63	0.29
845 Articles of apparel nes	513 988	3.48	0.91	0.59
71 Coffee and coffee substitutes	298 081	2.02	3.35	2.13
681 Silver, platinum, platinum metals	271 951	1.84	3.37	1.40
54 Vegetable & vegetable products nes	229 509	1.55	2.23	0.74
Remainder	4 058 517	27.47		
Philippines (**=Developing)				
All commodity groups	40 450 891	100.00	1.20	0.42
776 Valves tubes; diodes, transistors	10 795 631	26.69	5.44	3.07
931 Transaction commodity unclassified	7 011 195	17.33	16.51	2.47
752 Computer equipment nes	4 024 411	9.95	2.78	1.54
759 Office equipment part & accessories	3 052 938	7.55	2.87	1.60
778 Electrical machinery apparatus nes	1 295 008	3.20	2.37	0.92
784 Motor vehicle parts and accessories	1 251 754	3.09	3.33	0.56
764 Telecommunicate equipment part nes	1 042 017	2.58	0.64	0.32
773 Electrical distribute equipment nes	833 435	2.06	3.74	1.45
422 Fixed veg fat and oil, excl. "soft"	618 257	1.53	5.38	4.68
842 Female clothing, woven	596 624	1.47	1.55	0.98
Remainder	9 929 620	24.55		
Poland - Fologne (**=Developed)				
All commodity groups	81 578 467	100.00	1.38	0.85
821 Furniture part; bedding furnishing	5 242 498	6.43	8.78	5.57
781 Passenger cars and race cars	4 808 701	5.89	1.17	1.02
713 Internal combustion engine part nes	3 593 420	4.40	3.92	3.35
784 Motor vehicle parts and accessories	3 439 388	4.22	1.87	1.54
793 Ships boats floating structures	2 969 510	3.64	8.16	4.50
699 Base metal manufactures nes	1 862 289	2.28	3.12	2.20
773 Electrical distribute equipment nes	1 822 810	2.23	5.51	3.17
682 Copper	1 534 917	1.88	6.02	2.70
761 Television video receive project	1 511 852	1.85	6.74	2.85
775 Household equipment nes	1 499 793	1.84	4.40	2.47
Remainder	53 293 288	65.33		
Portugal (**=Developed)				
All commodity groups	36 898 944	100.00	0.62	0.38
781 Passenger cars and race cars	2 668 277	7.23	0.65	0.57
931 Transaction commodity unclassified	1 706 380	4.62	0.86	0.60
851 Footwear	1 569 397	4.25	6.16	2.43
845 Articles of apparel nes	1 546 557	4.19	5.29	1.76
784 Motor vehicle parts and accessories	1 505 713	4.08	0.82	0.67
334 Heavy petroleum & bituminous oil	1 047 796	2.84	0.81	0.34
633 Cork manufactures	965 824	2.62	66.94	62.65
821 Furniture part; bedding furnishing	943 778	2.56	1.58	1.00
762 Radio broadcast receivers	873 922	2.37	13.82	4.84
658 Made-up textile articles nes	796 623	2.16	9.15	2.74
Remainder	23 274 677	63.08		
Qatar (**=Developing)				
All commodity groups	22 223 793	100.00	0.66	0.23
333 Crude petroleum & bituminous oil	10 686 294	48.08	2.33	1.68
343 Natural gas, liquefied or not	6 918 468	31.13	17.68	6.24
931 Transaction commodity unclassified	2 318 050	10.43	5.46	0.82
342 Liquefied propane and butane	667 134	3.00	4.34	2.83
334 Heavy petroleum & bituminous oil	586 937	2.64	0.41	0.19
562 Manufactured fertilizer excl. crude	539 813	2.43	9.17	2.34
571 Primary form ethylene polymers	505 434	2.27	3.99	1.43
512 Alcohols, phenols; derivatives	213 414	0.96	1.63	0.74
676 Iron steel bar rod section piling	197 833	0.89	1.48	0.40
511 Hydrocarbons nes; derivatives	144 575	0.65	1.00	0.31
Remainder	-554 159	-2.49		
Romania - Roumanie (**=Transition)				
All commodity groups	25 607 470	100.00	7.28	0.27
334 Heavy petroleum & bituminous oil	2 044 626	7.98	5.35	0.66
842 Female clothing, woven	1 816 586	7.09	55.07	2.99
851 Footwear	1 550 765	6.06	60.26	2.40
841 Male clothing, woven	1 440 290	5.62	53.59	2.93
773 Electrical distribute equipment nes	1 267 172	4.95	61.03	2.21
673 Flat iron non-alloy steel products	1 259 050	4.92	11.31	2.08
821 Furniture part; bedding furnishing	1 080 124	4.22	46.36	1.15
845 Articles of apparel nes	820 281	3.20	41.27	0.94
784 Motor vehicle parts and accessories	721 039	2.82	42.51	0.32
248 Wood simply worked, railway sleeper	543 377	2.12	17.07	1.57
Remainder	13 064 158	51.02		

For sources and notes, see end of table.

Pour les sources et les notes, se reporter à la fin du tableau.

Leading products exported based on average 2004-2005 values SITC Revision 3 (3-digit level) / Principaux produits exportés d'après la moyenne des valeurs de 2004-2005 CTCI révision 3 (positions à 3 chiffres)	Value (f.o.b., thousands of dollars) Valeur (f.a.b., milliers de dollars)	2004-2005 As percentage En pourcentage of country total du total du pays	of ** (1) des ** (1)	of world du monde
Russian Federation - Fédération de Russie (**=Transition)				
All commodity groups	211 438 776	100.00	60.10	2.19
333 Crude petroleum & bituminous oil	67 157 198	31.76	79.67	10.53
931 Transaction commodity unclassified	40 856 536	19.32	97.23	14.41
334 Heavy petroleum & bituminous oil	26 410 456	12.49	69.07	8.46
343 Natural gas. liquefied or not	6 163 218	2.91	59.50	5 56
684 Aluminium	5 241 246	2.48	72.64	7 29
672 Ingots, Iron steel primary products	4 851 987	2.29	57.55	17 80
673 Flat iron non-alloy steel products	4 528 225	2.14	40.69	7 48
683 Nickel	3 432 839	1.62	99.87	26 26
562 Manufactured fertilizer excl. crude	3 359 365	1.59	57.08	14 56
321 Coal excluding non-agglomomerated	3 255 505	1.54	84.16	8 41
Remainder	46 182 201	21.84		
Rwanda (**=Developing)				
All commodity groups	111 644	100.00	0.00	0.00
71 Coffee and coffee substitutes	30 723	27.52	0.35	0.22
74 Tea and maté	26 267	23.53	0.89	0.66
287 Base metal ores & concentrates nes	24 573	22.01	0.30	0.17
334 Heavy petroleum & bituminous oil	7 572	6.78	0.01	0.00
211 Raw hides & skins, excluding furskins	6 226	5.58	0.69	0.11
764 Telecommunicate equipment part nes	2 675	2.40	0.00	0.00
781 Passenger cars and race cars	1 664	1.49	0.00	0.00
269 Worn clothing, textile article; rag	1 311	1.17	0.32	0.07
289 Prec metal ore concentrate excl. gold	1 247	1.12	0.07	0.03
782 Goods and service vehicles	1 115	1.00	0.01	0.00
Remainder	8 271	7.41		
Saint Kitts and Nevis - Saint-Kitts-et-Nevis (**=Developing)				
All commodity groups	38 273	100.00	0.00	0.00
772 Electrical circuit equipment	17 728	46.32	0.04	0.01
778 Electrical machinery apparatus nes	8 214	21.46	0.02	0.01
61 Sugar, mollasses and honey	5 896	15.41	0.07	0.04
716 Rotating electric plant parts nes	762	1.99	0.01	0.00
263 Cotton	740	1.93	0.02	0.01
723 Civil engineering plant & equipment	702	1.83	0.01	0.00
892 Printed matter	686	1.79	0.01	0.00
112 Alcoholic beverages	529	1.38	0.01	0.00
111 Non alcoholic beverage nes	462	1.21	0.02	0.00
764 Telecommunicate equipment part nes	389	1.02	0.00	0.00
Remainder	2 165	5.66		
Saint Lucia - Sainte-Lucie (**=Developing)				
All commodity groups	78 403	100.00	0.00	0.00
334 Heavy petroleum & bituminous oil	20 721	26.43	0.01	0.01
57 Fruit nut (exc oil), fresh or dried	18 019	22.98	0.10	0.04
112 Alcoholic beverages	10 927	13.94	0.18	0.02
642 Cut paper and paperboard articles	3 504	4.47	0.05	0.01
764 Telecommunicate equipment part nes	2 112	2.69	0.00	0.00
772 Electrical circuit equipment	1 762	2.25	0.00	0.00
723 Civil engineering plant & equipment	1 463	1.87	0.01	0.00
897 Jewellery nes (667)	1 141	1.46	0.01	0.00
111 Non alcoholic beverage nes	1 108	1.41	0.06	0.01
781 Passenger cars and race cars	959	1.22	0.00	0.00
Remainder	16 687	21.28		
Saint Vincent and the Grenadines - Saint-Vincent-et-les Grenadines (**=Developing)				
All commodity groups	38 246	100.00	0.00	0.00
57 Fruit nut (exc oil), fresh or dried	13 983	36.56	0.08	0.03
46 Wheat meal & flour, meslin flour	4 972	13.00	0.58	0.21
54 Vegetable & vegetable products nes	3 410	8.92	0.03	0.01
42 Rice	2 891	7.56	0.04	0.03
81 Animal feed excluding unmilled cereal	1 719	4.49	0.01	0.01
111 Non alcoholic beverage nes	1 446	3.78	0.08	0.01
674 Flat plated iron non-alloy steel	1 367	3.57	0.01	0.00
691 Iron steel aluminium structures nes	681	1.78	0.01	0.00
642 Cut paper and paperboard articles	638	1.67	0.01	0.00
845 Articles of apparel nes	605	1.58	0.00	0.00
Remainder	6 534	17.08		

Leading products exported based on average 2004-2005 values SITC Revision 3 (3-digit level) / Principaux produits exportés d'après la moyenne des valeurs de 2004-2005 CTCI révision 3 (positions à 3 chiffres)	Value (f.o.b., thousands of dollars) Valeur (f.a.b., milliers de dollars)	2004-2005 As percentage En pourcentage of country total du total du pays	of ** (1) des ** (1)	of world du monde
Samoa (**=Developing)				
All commodity groups	90 171	100.00	0.00	0.00
773 Electrical distribute equipment nes	63 239	70.13	0.28	0.11
34 Fish, fresh live chilled frozen	11 110	12.32	0.09	0.04
59 Fruit & vegetable juice unferment	2 504	2.78	0.08	0.03
112 Alcoholic beverages	2 143	2.38	0.03	0.00
422 Fixed veg fat and oil, excl. "soft"	1 467	1.63	0.01	0.01
699 Base metal manufactures nes	1 339	1.49	0.01	0.00
54 Vegetable & vegetable products nes	973	1.08	0.01	0.00
57 Fruit nut (exc oil), fresh or dried	734	0.81	0.00	0.00
692 Metal storage transport container	603	0.67	0.03	0.01
846 Clothing accessory excl. 831 848 851	517	0.57	0.01	0.00
Remainder	5 540	6.14		
Saudi Arabia - Arabie saoudite (**=Developing)				
All commodity groups	138 100 583	100.00	4.09	1.43
333 Crude petroleum & bituminous oil	104 859 343	75.93	22.86	16.45
334 Heavy petroleum & bituminous oil	11 567 425	8.38	8.04	3.71
342 Liquefied propane and butane	4 903 401	3.55	31.93	20.79
512 Alcohols, phenols; derivatives	3 484 787	2.52	26.61	12.02
571 Primary form ethylene polymers	3 131 337	2.27	24.70	8.84
511 Hydrocarbons nes; derivatives	1 662 121	1.20	11.48	3.58
516 Other organic chemicals	1 265 351	0.92	18.09	5.65
575 Other plastics, in primary forms	623 115	0.45	5.03	1.03
562 Manufactured fertilizer excl. crude	532 444	0.39	9.04	2.31
344 Petroleum and hydrocarbon gas nes	335 011	0.24	13.75	3.51
Remainder	5 736 247	4.15		
Senegal - Sénégal (**=Developing)				
All commodity groups	1 393 110	100.00	0.04	0.01
334 Heavy petroleum & bituminous oil	221 954	15.93	0.15	0.07
522 Inorganic chemical elem oxide salt	182 984	13.13	1.81	0.68
34 Fish, fresh live chilled frozen	147 320	10.57	1.17	0.47
36 Crustacean mollusc aquat invertebra	108 936	7.82	0.93	0.57
333 Crude petroleum & bituminous oil	57 173	4.10	0.01	0.01
562 Manufactured fertilizer excl. crude	52 065	3.74	0.88	0.23
661 Lime cement construction material	41 543	2.98	0.51	0.24
98 Edible products & preparations nes	37 448	2.69	0.61	0.12
553 Perfume toilet cosmetics, excl. soap	31 029	2.23	0.50	0.07
42 Rice	30 853	2.21	0.46	0.34
Remainder	481 805	34.58		
Serbia and Montenegro - Serbie-et-Monténégro (**=Transition)				
All commodity groups	4 075 679	100.00	1.16	0.04
673 Flat iron non-alloy steel products	379 495	9.31	3.41	0.63
684 Aluminium	255 046	6.26	3.53	0.35
61 Sugar, mollasses and honey	172 225	4.23	23.06	1.07
625 Rubber for wheels, incl inner tube	151 296	3.71	12.82	0.37
58 Fruit preserve preparation excl. juice	150 781	3.70	43.73	1.58
682 Copper	124 056	3.04	2.46	0.22
571 Primary form ethylene polymers	100 897	2.48	13.30	0.28
893 Articles of plastic nes	100 846	2.47	16.32	0.12
674 Flat plated iron non-alloy steel	82 994	2.04	8.93	0.26
851 Footwear	78 243	1.92	3.04	0.12
Remainder	2 479 801	60.84		
Seychelles (**=Developing)				
All commodity groups	315 257	100.00	0.01	0.00
37 Fish shellfish, prepared preserved	173 700	55.10	1.99	1.24
334 Heavy petroleum & bituminous oil	105 015	33.31	0.07	0.03
542 Medicines including veterinary	13 535	4.29	0.16	0.01
36 Crustacean mollusc aquat invertebra	6 819	2.16	0.06	0.04
81 Animal feed excluding unmilled cereal	3 862	1.23	0.03	0.01
34 Fish, fresh live chilled frozen	2 691	0.85	0.02	0.01
899 Manufactured articles nes	2 169	0.69	0.02	0.01
872 Medical instruments appliances nes	1 532	0.49	0.02	0.00
667 Pearls, precious semiprecious stone	805	0.26	0.00	0.00
342 Liquefied propane and butane	774	0.25	0.01	0.00
Remainder	4 356	1.38		

For sources and notes, see end of table.

Pour les sources et les notes, se reporter à la fin du tableau.

Leading products exported based on average 2004-2005 values SITC Revision 3 (3-digit level) / Principaux produits exportés d'après la moyenne des valeurs de 2004-2005 CTCI révision 3 (positions à 3 chiffres)	2004-2005 Value (f.o.b., thousands of dollars) / Valeur (f.a.b., milliers de dollars)	As percentage / En pourcentage: of country total / du total du pays	of ** (1) / des ** (1)	of world / du monde
Singapore - Singapour (=Developing)**				
All commodity groups	214 142 487	100.00	6.35	2.22
776 Valves tubes; diodes, transistors	51 162 444	23.89	25.80	14.54
334 Heavy petroleum & bituminous oil	22 596 495	10.55	15.70	7.24
752 Computer equipment nes	15 971 417	7.46	11.03	6.13
759 Office equipment part & accessories	14 768 589	6.90	13.87	7.75
764 Telecommunicate equipment part nes	12 384 098	5.78	7.62	3.81
931 Transaction commodity unclassified	7 432 334	3.47	17.50	2.62
515 Organo-inorganic compound acid salt	5 414 273	2.53	55.94	7.16
772 Electrical circuit equipment	4 564 696	2.13	9.19	3.38
778 Electrical machinery apparatus nes	4 310 956	2.01	7.88	3.07
723 Civil engineering plant & equipment	2 884 095	1.35	24.64	4.59
Remainder	72 653 091	33.93		
Slovakia - Slovaquie (=Developed)**				
All commodity groups	29 930 633	100.00	0.51	0.31
781 Passenger cars and race cars	4 039 811	13.50	0.98	0.86
784 Motor vehicle parts and accessories	1 941 564	6.49	1.05	0.87
334 Heavy petroleum & bituminous oil	1 648 733	5.51	1.27	0.53
673 Flat iron non-alloy steel products	1 365 953	4.56	4.21	2.26
773 Electrical distribute equipment nes	897 462	3.00	2.71	1.56
761 Television video receive project	769 968	2.57	3.43	1.45
821 Furniture part; bedding furnishing	718 487	2.40	1.20	0.76
752 Computer equipment nes	698 652	2.33	0.60	0.27
699 Base metal manufactures nes	558 461	1.87	0.94	0.66
641 Paper and paperboard	537 158	1.79	0.66	0.57
Remainder	16 754 384	55.98		
Slovenia - Slovénie (=Developed)**				
All commodity groups	17 581 983	100.00	0.30	0.18
781 Passenger cars and race cars	1 706 403	9.71	0.41	0.36
821 Furniture part; bedding furnishing	1 175 060	6.68	1.97	1.25
542 Medicines including veterinary	1 047 590	5.96	0.56	0.54
775 Household equipment nes	999 221	5.68	2.93	1.65
684 Aluminium	555 031	3.16	1.17	0.77
784 Motor vehicle parts and accessories	502 071	2.86	0.27	0.22
778 Electrical machinery apparatus nes	444 526	2.53	0.52	0.32
641 Paper and paperboard	423 414	2.41	0.52	0.45
699 Base metal manufactures nes	352 857	2.01	0.59	0.42
743 Gas pump, compressor, fan, filter	349 704	1.99	0.68	0.52
Remainder	10 026 106	57.02		
South Africa - Afrique du Sud (=Developing)**				
All commodity groups	43 626 474	100.00	1.29	0.45
681 Silver, platinum, platinum metals	5 016 323	11.50	62.08	25.84
321 Coal excluding non-agglomomerated	2 850 468	6.53	21.01	7.37
671 Pig & sponge iron, ferro alloys etc	2 846 871	6.53	22.72	12.20
781 Passenger cars and race cars	2 657 895	6.09	4.63	0.56
667 Pearls, precious semiprecious stone	2 297 789	5.27	7.37	2.72
743 Gas pump, compressor, fan, filter	1 573 668	3.61	10.61	2.34
684 Aluminium	1 498 995	3.44	8.63	2.09
334 Heavy petroleum & bituminous oil	1 230 242	2.82	0.85	0.39
57 Fruit nut (exc oil), fresh or dried	1 207 066	2.77	6.71	2.80
675 Flat rolled products of alloy steel	864 326	1.98	8.70	2.06
Remainder	21 582 829	49.47		
Spain - Espagne (=Developed)**				
All commodity groups	187 762 813	100.00	3.18	1.95
781 Passenger cars and race cars	25 191 795	13.42	6.11	5.35
784 Motor vehicle parts and accessories	10 582 915	5.64	5.75	4.74
334 Heavy petroleum & bituminous oil	5 843 964	3.11	4.50	1.87
57 Fruit nut (exc oil), fresh or dried	5 293 985	2.82	21.67	12.29
542 Medicines including veterinary	4 578 036	2.44	2.46	2.34
782 Goods and service vehicles	4 576 083	2.44	7.02	5.41
54 Vegetable & vegetable products nes	4 237 024	2.26	20.87	13.63
793 Ships boats floating structures	3 149 741	1.68	8.66	4.77
931 Transaction commodity unclassified	2 910 781	1.55	1.46	1.03
792 Aircraft, spacecraft & equipment	2 757 265	1.47	2.49	2.27
Remainder	118 641 223	63.19		

Leading products exported based on average 2004-2005 values SITC Revision 3 (3-digit level) / Principaux produits exportés d'après la moyenne des valeurs de 2004-2005 CTCI révision 3 (positions à 3 chiffres)	2004-2005 Value (f.o.b., thousands of dollars) / Valeur (f.a.b., milliers de dollars)	As percentage / En pourcentage: of country total / du total du pays	of ** (1) / des ** (1)	of world / du monde
Sri Lanka (=Developing)**				
All commodity groups	5 822 495	100.00	0.17	0.06
842 Female clothing, woven	879 103	15.10	2.28	1.44
74 Tea and maté	775 595	13.32	26.35	19.46
845 Articles of apparel nes	658 191	11.30	1.17	0.75
841 Male clothing, woven	513 700	8.82	1.67	1.05
844 Female clothing, knitted crocheted	365 099	6.27	1.97	1.43
667 Pearls, precious semiprecious stone	263 861	4.53	0.85	0.31
625 Rubber for wheels, incl inner tube	210 188	3.61	1.76	0.52
843 Male clothing, knitted crocheted	163 063	2.80	1.45	1.14
682 Copper	124 167	2.13	0.47	0.22
848 Headgear, non-textile clothing	123 481	2.12	0.88	0.62
Remainder	1 746 049	29.99		
Sudan - Soudan (=Developing)**				
All commodity groups	3 871 125	100.00	0.11	0.04
334 Heavy petroleum & bituminous oil	3 259 146	84.19	2.26	1.04
1 Live animal excl. fish & crustacean	121 552	3.14	5.16	1.01
222 Oil seed etc for soft oil	117 975	3.05	1.20	0.55
263 Cotton	95 686	2.47	2.36	0.85
292 Crude vegetable materials nes	78 160	2.02	1.44	0.35
971 Gold non-monetary excluding ores	56 041	1.45	0.28	0.15
54 Vegetable & vegetable products nes	29 198	0.75	0.28	0.09
931 Transaction commodity unclassified	23 207	0.60	0.05	0.01
61 Sugar, mollasses and honey	22 729	0.59	0.27	0.14
12 Meat nes, fresh chilled frozen	18 669	0.48	0.29	0.05
Remainder	48 761	1.26		
Suriname (=Developing)**				
All commodity groups	915 301	100.00	0.03	0.01
285 Aluminium ore concentrate alumina	564 737	61.70	17.36	6.03
971 Gold non-monetary excluding ores	212 402	23.21	1.08	0.57
36 Crustacean mollusc aquat invertebra	42 201	4.61	0.36	0.22
34 Fish, fresh live chilled frozen	22 978	2.51	0.18	0.07
57 Fruit nut (exc oil), fresh or dried	10 403	1.14	0.06	0.02
42 Rice	9 888	1.08	0.15	0.11
333 Crude petroleum & bituminous oil	8 947	0.98	0.00	0.00
515 Organo-inorganic compound acid salt	8 411	0.92	0.09	0.01
892 Printed matter	4 770	0.52	0.07	0.01
54 Vegetable & vegetable products nes	4 214	0.46	0.04	0.01
Remainder	26 350	2.88		
Swaziland (=Developing)**				
All commodity groups	1 697 807	100.00	0.05	0.02
551 Essential oils, perfumes & flavours	794 067	46.77	33.30	5.14
845 Articles of apparel nes	117 175	6.90	0.21	0.13
61 Sugar, mollasses and honey	103 126	6.07	1.23	0.64
251 Pulp and waste paper	98 212	5.78	1.94	0.39
843 Male clothing, knitted crocheted	72 166	4.25	0.64	0.50
844 Female clothing, knitted crocheted	46 007	2.71	0.25	0.18
841 Male clothing, woven	33 326	1.96	0.11	0.07
842 Female clothing, woven	33 223	1.96	0.09	0.05
58 Fruit preserve preparation excl. juice	27 589	1.63	0.67	0.29
62 Sugar confectionery	27 225	1.60	1.30	0.43
Remainder	345 691	20.36		
Sweden - Suède (=Developed)**				
All commodity groups	126 733 687	100.00	2.14	1.32
764 Telecommunicate equipment part nes	11 036 956	8.71	6.85	3.40
641 Paper and paperboard	8 222 200	6.49	10.11	8.71
781 Passenger cars and race cars	8 103 164	6.39	1.97	1.72
931 Transaction commodity unclassified	7 135 834	5.63	3.58	2.52
542 Medicines including veterinary	6 404 627	5.05	3.44	3.28
784 Motor vehicle parts and accessories	5 329 728	4.21	2.90	2.39
334 Heavy petroleum & bituminous oil	4 370 428	3.45	3.37	1.40
675 Flat rolled products of alloy stee	3 356 075	2.65	10.91	8.01
248 Wood simply worked, railway sleeper	2 851 262	2.25	11.55	8.26
713 Internal combustion engine part nes	2 387 235	1.88	2.60	2.22
Remainder	67 536 179	53.29		

For sources and notes, see end of table.

Pour les sources et les notes, se reporter à la fin du tableau.

Leading products exported based on average 2004-2005 values SITC Revision 3 (3-digit level) / Principaux produits exportés d'après la moyenne des valeurs de 2004-2005 CTCI révision 3 (positions à 3 chiffres)	Value (f.o.b., thousands of dollars) Valeur (f.a.b., milliers de dollars)	of country total du total du pays	of ** (1) des ** (1)	of world du monde
Switzerland - Suisse (**=Developed)				
All commodity groups	122 226 902	100.00	2.07	1.27
542 Medicines including veterinary	15 406 216	12.60	8.27	7.89
885 Watches and clocks	9 416 668	7.70	63.92	38.36
541 Pharmaceuticals excluding medicines	9 057 911	7.41	15.92	14.32
515 Organo-inorganic compound acid salt	5 604 138	4.59	8.57	7.41
899 Manufactured articles nes	3 521 796	2.88	12.08	8.35
874 Measure analyze control device nes	3 026 395	2.48	3.32	2.82
728 Special industrial machine part nes	2 844 877	2.33	3.53	2.97
514 Nitrogen function compounds	2 679 241	2.19	10.66	8.24
772 Electrical circuit equipment	2 677 767	2.19	3.18	1.99
897 Jewellery nes (667)	2 533 651	2.07	13.03	6.74
Remainder	65 458 242	53.55		
Syrian Arab Republic - République arabe syrienne (**=Developing)				
All commodity groups	5 995 784	100.00	0.18	0.06
333 Crude petroleum & bituminous oil	3 270 551	54.55	0.71	0.51
334 Heavy petroleum & bituminous oil	783 800	13.07	0.54	0.25
1 Live animal excl. fish & crustacean	297 258	4.96	12.61	2.48
263 Cotton	198 739	3.31	4.90	1.77
41 Wheat meslin, incl spelt, unmilled	139 464	2.33	6.45	0.75
54 Vegetable & vegetable products nes	109 477	1.83	1.06	0.35
651 Textile yarn	102 406	1.71	0.47	0.25
931 Transaction commodity unclassified	100 925	1.68	0.24	0.04
111 Non alcoholic beverage nes	61 272	1.02	3.18	0.61
272 Crude fertilizer, excl. manufactured	51 085	0.85	4.02	2.90
Remainder	880 806	14.69		
Tajikistan - Tadjikistan (**=Transition)				
All commodity groups	894 948	100.00	0.25	0.01
684 Aluminium	435 794	48.69	6.04	0.61
263 Cotton	245 087	27.39	16.27	2.19
57 Fruit nut (exc oil), fresh or dried	33 507	3.74	5.07	0.08
652 Woven cotton fabrics	24 778	2.77	6.11	0.09
671 Pig & sponge iron, ferro alloys etc	18 380	2.05	0.36	0.08
651 Textile yarn	16 388	1.83	1.78	0.04
841 Male clothing, woven	13 668	1.53	0.51	0.03
54 Vegetable & vegetable products nes	12 265	1.37	2.57	0.04
896 Work of art & collections; antiques	8 260	0.92	35.62	0.06
59 Fruit & vegetable juice unferment	5 561	0.62	2.89	0.07
Remainder	81 261	9.08		
Thailand - Thaïlande (**=Developing)				
All commodity groups	103 178 968	100.00	3.06	1.07
752 Computer equipment nes	6 847 123	6.64	4.73	2.63
776 Valves tubes; diodes, transistors	6 429 936	6.23	3.24	1.83
231 Natural rubber, latex, gum, etc	3 554 603	3.45	41.25	40.16
759 Office equipment part & accessories	3 419 366	3.31	3.21	1.79
764 Telecommunicate equipment part nes	2 837 848	2.75	1.75	0.87
782 Goods and service vehicles	2 770 701	2.69	15.33	3.27
772 Electrical circuit equipment	2 729 818	2.65	5.50	2.02
42 Rice	2 506 538	2.43	37.15	27.85
37 Fish shellfish, prepared preserved	2 374 998	2.30	27.26	16.89
741 Heating cooling equipment parts nes	2 306 582	2.24	12.65	3.52
Remainder	67 401 455	65.32		
Macedonia, TFYR - Macédoine, LERY (**=Transition)				
All commodity groups	1 857 374	100.00	0.53	0.02
842 Female clothing, woven	228 701	12.31	6.93	0.38
673 Flat iron non-alloy steel products	195 334	10.52	1.76	0.32
841 Male clothing, woven	162 343	8.74	6.04	0.33
671 Pig & sponge iron, ferro alloys etc	139 062	7.49	2.75	0.60
334 Heavy petroleum & bituminous oil	113 442	6.11	0.30	0.04
121 Unmanufactured tabacco and refuse	76 285	4.11	29.81	1.11
679 Iron steel pipe tube fittings etc	63 749	3.43	2.09	0.13
851 Footwear	54 326	2.92	2.11	0.08
674 Flat plated iron non-alloy steel	49 732	2.68	5.35	0.15
844 Female clothing, knitted crocheted	44 835	2.41	5.99	0.18
Remainder	729 565	39.28		

Leading products exported based on average 2004-2005 values SITC Revision 3 (3-digit level) / Principaux produits exportés d'après la moyenne des valeurs de 2004-2005 CTCI révision 3 (positions à 3 chiffres)	Value (f.o.b., thousands of dollars) Valeur (f.a.b., milliers de dollars)	of country total du total du pays	of ** (1) des ** (1)	of world du monde
Togo (**=Developing)				
All commodity groups	384 098	100.00	0.01	0.00
661 Lime cement construction material	98 494	25.64	1.20	0.57
263 Cotton	44 774	11.66	1.10	0.40
272 Crude fertilizer, excl. manufactured	41 515	10.81	3.27	2.36
72 Cocoa	22 558	5.87	0.42	0.27
893 Articles of plastic nes	22 397	5.83	0.09	0.03
676 Iron steel bar rod section piling	21 276	5.54	0.16	0.04
91 Margarine and shortening	10 940	2.85	1.35	0.42
674 Flat plated iron non-alloy steel	10 349	2.69	0.11	0.03
931 Transaction commodity unclassified	9 924	2.58	0.02	0.00
553 Perfume toilet cosmetics, excl. soap	8 228	2.14	0.13	0.02
Remainder	93 644	24.38		
Trinidad and Tobago - Trinité-et-Tobago (**=Developing)				
All commodity groups	8 064 341	100.00	0.24	0.08
343 Natural gas, liquefied or not	2 013 626	24.97	5.15	1.82
334 Heavy petroleum & bituminous oil	1 918 609	23.79	1.33	0.61
333 Crude petroleum & bituminous oil	1 134 314	14.07	0.25	0.18
522 Inorganic chemical elem oxide salt	902 360	11.19	8.94	3.38
512 Alcohols, phenols; derivatives	614 961	7.63	4.70	2.12
676 Iron steel bar rod section piling	225 260	2.79	1.69	0.46
342 Liquefied propane and butane	216 076	2.68	1.41	0.92
671 Pig & sponge iron, ferro alloys etc	135 434	1.68	1.08	0.58
562 Manufactured fertilizer excl. crude	123 732	1.53	2.10	0.54
111 Non alcoholic beverage nes	52 777	0.65	2.74	0.52
Remainder	727 193	9.02		
Tunisia - Tunisie (**=Developing)				
All commodity groups	10 089 167	100.00	0.30	0.10
845 Articles of apparel nes	1 442 726	14.30	2.56	1.65
841 Male clothing, woven	963 367	9.55	3.14	1.96
333 Crude petroleum & bituminous oil	921 850	9.14	0.20	0.14
842 Female clothing, woven	617 300	6.12	1.60	1.01
773 Electrical distribute equipment nes	562 109	5.57	2.52	0.98
421 Fixed veg fat and oil, "soft"	502 194	4.98	7.87	3.14
772 Electrical circuit equipment	486 684	4.82	0.98	0.36
851 Footwear	435 452	4.32	1.19	0.67
562 Manufactured fertilizer excl. crude	428 710	4.25	7.28	1.86
334 Heavy petroleum & bituminous oil	220 477	2.19	0.15	0.07
Remainder	3 508 299	34.77		
Turkey - Turquie (**=Developing)				
All commodity groups	68 298 678	100.00	2.02	0.71
845 Articles of apparel nes	4 236 115	6.20	7.51	4.83
781 Passenger cars and race cars	4 153 558	6.08	7.24	0.88
676 Iron steel bar rod section piling	3 150 980	4.61	23.57	6.41
761 Television video receive project	2 807 203	4.11	9.27	5.29
842 Female clothing, woven	2 741 072	4.01	7.10	4.51
782 Goods and service vehicles	2 375 723	3.48	13.14	2.81
57 Fruit nut (exc oil), fresh or dried	2 170 963	3.18	12.07	5.04
658 Made-up textile articles nes	1 895 546	2.78	9.53	6.51
841 Male clothing, woven	1 744 134	2.55	5.68	3.55
334 Heavy petroleum & bituminous oil	1 540 700	2.26	1.07	0.49
Remainder	41 482 684	60.74		
Turkmenistan - Turkménistan (**=Transition)				
All commodity groups	3 381 914	100.00	0.96	0.04
343 Natural gas, liquefied or not	2 760 725	81.63	26.65	2.49
334 Heavy petroleum & bituminous oil	259 042	7.66	0.68	0.08
263 Cotton	76 761	2.27	5.10	0.68
333 Crude petroleum & bituminous oil	40 257	1.19	0.05	0.01
652 Woven cotton fabrics	38 251	1.13	9.43	0.13
651 Textile yarn	38 132	1.13	4.13	0.09
575 Other plastics, in primary forms	36 397	1.08	8.34	0.06
658 Made-up textile articles nes	24 754	0.73	4.82	0.09
845 Articles of apparel nes	15 221	0.45	0.77	0.02
351 Electric current	11 294	0.33	1.01	0.06
Remainder	81 080	2.40		

For sources and notes, see end of table.

Pour les sources et les notes, se reporter à la fin du tableau.

3

Leading products exported based on average 2004-2005 values SITC Revision 3 (3-digit level) Principaux produits exportés d'après la moyenne des valeurs de 2004-2005 CTCI révision 3 (positions à 3 chiffres)	2004-2005		
	Value (f.o.b., thousands of dollars) Valeur (f.a.b., milliers de dollars)	As percentage En pourcentage	
		of country total du total du pays	of ** (1) des ** (1)	of world du monde

Turks and Caicos Islands - Îles Turques et Caïques (**=Developing)

Product	Value	of country total	of ** (1)	of world
All commodity groups	12 212	100.00	0.00	0.00
36 Crustacean mollusc aquat invertebra	2 764	22.63	0.02	0.01
37 Fish shellfish, prepared preserved	2 499	20.47	0.03	0.02
381 Photographic device nes	1 121	9.18	0.02	0.01
658 Made-up textile articles nes	858	7.02	0.00	0.00
898 Music instrument device recording	685	5.61	0.00	0.00
716 Rotating electric plant parts nes	417	3.41	0.00	0.00
885 Watches and clocks	346	2.84	0.00	0.00
665 Glassware	292	2.39	0.01	0.00
781 Passenger cars and race cars	278	2.28	0.00	0.00
762 Radio broadcast receivers	278	2.28	0.00	0.00
Remainder	2 673	21.89		

Uganda - Ouganda (**=Developing)

Product	Value	of country total	of ** (1)	of world
All commodity groups	726 141	100.00	0.02	0.01
71 Coffee and coffee substitutes	148 589	20.46	1.67	1.06
34 Fish, fresh live chilled frozen	117 587	16.19	0.94	0.37
971 Gold non-monetary excluding ores	67 113	9.24	0.34	0.18
263 Cotton	41 414	5.70	1.02	0.37
121 Unmanufactured tabacco and refuse	36 020	4.96	0.90	0.52
74 Tea and maté	35 765	4.93	1.22	0.90
292 Crude vegetable materials nes	32 834	4.52	0.60	0.15
334 Heavy petroleum & bituminous oil	23 495	3.24	0.02	0.01
44 Maize unmilled, excluding sweet corn	11 352	1.56	0.37	0.10
674 Flat plated iron non-alloy steel	10 343	1.42	0.11	0.03
Remainder	201 630	27.77		

Ukraine (**=Transition)

Product	Value	of country total	of ** (1)	of world
All commodity groups	33 447 053	100.00	9.51	0.35
673 Flat iron non-alloy steel products	3 649 133	10.91	32.79	6.03
672 Ingots, Iron steel primary products	3 169 782	9.48	37.60	11.63
676 Iron steel bar rod section piling	2 311 477	6.91	48.08	4.70
334 Heavy petroleum & bituminous oil	1 861 364	5.57	4.87	0.60
679 Iron steel pipe tube fittings etc	1 254 983	3.75	41.20	2.63
791 Railway vehicles and equipment	1 214 471	3.63	60.39	7.67
671 Pig & sponge iron, ferro alloys etc	1 092 041	3.26	21.59	4.68
562 Manufactured fertilizer excl. crude	858 332	2.57	14.58	3.72
281 Iron ore and concentrates	759 588	2.27	37.57	3.38
421 Fixed veg fat and oil, "soft"	548 564	1.64	57.18	3.43
Remainder	16 727 317	50.01		

United Arab Emirates - Émirats arabes unis (**=Developing)

Product	Value	of country total	of ** (1)	of world
All commodity groups	95 719 029	100.00	2.84	0.99
333 Crude petroleum & bituminous oil	36 981 743	38.64	8.06	5.80
931 Transaction commodity unclassified	13 457 752	14.06	31.69	4.75
334 Heavy petroleum & bituminous oil	10 852 415	11.34	7.54	3.48
971 Gold non-monetary excluding ores	3 743 026	3.91	18.96	10.03
667 Pearls, precious semiprecious stone	3 612 044	3.77	11.58	4.28
342 Liquefied propane and butane	3 128 171	3.27	20.37	13.26
764 Telecommunicate equipment part nes	2 183 531	2.28	1.34	0.67
343 Natural gas, liquefied or not	1 941 943	2.03	4.96	1.75
684 Aluminium	1 219 216	1.27	7.02	1.70
781 Passenger cars and race cars	864 698	0.90	1.51	0.18
Remainder	17 734 489	18.53		

United Kingdom - Royaume-Uni (**=Developed)

Product	Value	of country total	of ** (1)	of world
All commodity groups	366 688 365	100.00	6.21	3.81
781 Passenger cars and race cars	23 268 509	6.35	5.65	4.94
542 Medicines including veterinary	19 384 630	5.29	10.41	9.92
931 Transaction commodity unclassified	19 326 977	5.27	9.71	6.82
333 Crude petroleum & bituminous oil	18 563 417	5.06	19.66	2.91
764 Telecommunicate equipment part nes	17 577 059	4.79	10.91	5.41
714 Non-electric engines excl. 712 713 718	12 876 412	3.51	21.51	19.69
334 Heavy petroleum & bituminous oil	11 400 756	3.11	8.78	3.65
752 Computer equipment nes	9 458 215	2.58	8.18	3.63
667 Pearls, precious semiprecious stone	8 986 018	2.45	17.27	10.66
784 Motor vehicle parts and accessories	7 752 570	2.11	4.21	3.47
Remainder	218 093 803	59.48		

United Republic of Tanzania - République-Unie de Tanzanie (**=Developing)

Product	Value	of country total	of ** (1)	of world
All commodity groups	1 440 393	100.00	0.04	0.01
971 Gold non-monetary excluding ores	505 108	35.07	2.56	1.35
34 Fish, fresh live chilled frozen	116 326	8.08	0.93	0.37
289 Prec metal ore concentrate excl. gold	99 238	6.89	5.68	2.36
263 Cotton	91 525	6.35	2.26	0.82
121 Unmanufactured tabacco and refuse	89 188	6.19	2.22	1.29
71 Coffee and coffee substitutes	64 997	4.51	0.73	0.46
57 Fruit nut (exc oil), fresh or dried	51 094	3.55	0.28	0.12
667 Pearls, precious semiprecious stone	40 458	2.81	0.13	0.05
54 Vegetable & vegetable products nes	31 714	2.20	0.31	0.10
74 Tea and maté	28 161	1.96	0.96	0.71
Remainder	322 584	22.40		

United States - États-Unis (**=Developed)

Product	Value	of country total	of ** (1)	of world
All commodity groups	861 122 457	100.00	14.57	8.94
776 Valves tubes; diodes, transistors	48 757 128	5.66	31.81	13.85
792 Aircraft, spacecraft & equipment	45 944 196	5.34	41.52	37.83
784 Motor vehicle parts and accessories	31 309 437	3.64	17.01	14.02
781 Passenger cars and race cars	28 220 174	3.28	6.85	6.00
931 Transaction commodity unclassified	27 354 405	3.18	13.74	9.65
764 Telecommunicate equipment part nes	24 829 293	2.88	15.41	7.65
752 Computer equipment nes	24 709 879	2.87	21.36	9.48
874 Measure analyze control device nes	23 840 424	2.77	26.15	22.20
714 Non-electric engines excl. 712 713 718	20 319 526	2.36	33.94	31.07
759 Office equipment part & accessories	19 772 558	2.30	23.57	10.38
Remainder	566 065 435	65.74		

Uruguay (**=Developing)

Product	Value	of country total	of ** (1)	of world
All commodity groups	3 161 369	100.00	0.09	0.03
11 Beef, fresh chilled frozen	668 644	21.15	13.14	3.33
611 Leather	238 865	7.56	2.18	1.17
42 Rice	189 895	6.01	2.81	2.11
334 Heavy petroleum & bituminous oil	137 861	4.36	0.10	0.04
268 Wool & animal hair, incl wool tops	133 845	4.23	9.50	2.70
222 Oil seed etc for soft oil	125 418	3.97	1.27	0.59
22 Milk products, excl. butter & cheese	110 809	3.51	4.86	0.53
34 Fish, fresh live chilled frozen	108 243	3.42	0.86	0.34
48 Cereal & preparation flour starch	78 551	2.48	2.39	0.33
24 Cheese and curd	76 000	2.40	14.85	0.46
Remainder	1 293 173	40.91		

Uzbekistan - Ouzbékistan (**=Transition)

Product	Value	of country total	of ** (1)	of world
All commodity groups	3 184 090	100.00	0.91	0.03
263 Cotton	930 361	29.22	61.77	8.30
343 Natural gas, liquefied or not	330 529	10.38	3.19	0.30
781 Passenger cars and race cars	209 680	6.59	18.50	0.04
682 Copper	205 823	6.46	4.08	0.36
651 Textile yarn	179 562	5.64	19.46	0.44
57 Fruit nut (exc oil), fresh or dried	179 420	5.63	27.15	0.42
971 Gold non-monetary excluding ores	159 310	5.00	23.06	0.43
54 Vegetable & vegetable products nes	92 414	2.90	19.33	0.30
525 Radio active & associated materials	77 244	2.43	23.86	1.16
652 Woven cotton fabrics	74 652	2.34	18.40	0.26
Remainder	745 095	23.40		

Venezuela (Bolivarian Rep. of) - (Rép. Bolivarienne du) (**=Developing)

Product	Value	of country total	of ** (1)	of world
All commodity groups	46 744 042	100.00	1.39	0.49
333 Crude petroleum & bituminous oil	40 283 740	86.18	8.78	6.32
671 Pig & sponge iron, ferro alloys etc	986 546	2.11	7.87	4.23
684 Aluminium	950 807	2.03	5.48	1.32
673 Flat iron non-alloy steel products	510 795	1.09	3.00	0.84
672 Ingots, Iron steel primary products	310 240	0.66	3.55	1.14
321 Coal excluding non-agglomerated	226 179	0.48	1.67	0.58
676 Iron steel bar rod section piling	185 666	0.40	1.39	0.38
784 Motor vehicle parts and accessories	171 615	0.37	0.46	0.08
512 Alcohols, phenols; derivatives	166 577	0.36	1.27	0.57
516 Other organic chemicals	158 475	0.34	2.27	0.71
Remainder	2 793 402	5.98		

For sources and notes, see end of table.

Pour les sources et les notes, se reporter à la fin du tableau.

172

Leading products exported based on average 2004-2005 values SITC Revision 3 (3-digit level) / Principaux produits exportés d'après la moyenne ces valeurs de 2004-2005 CTCI révision 3 (positions à 3 chiffres)	Value (f.o.b., thousands of dollars) Valeur (f.a.b., milliers de dollars)	2004-2005 As percentage / En pourcentage		
		of country total du total du pays	of ** (1) des ** (1)	of world du monde
Viet Nam (=Developing)**				
All commodity groups	31 556 134	100.00	0.94	0.33
333 Crude petroleum & bituminous oil	6 038 452	19.14	1.32	0.95
851 Footwear	5 002 181	15.85	13.67	7.74
821 Furniture part; bedding furnishing	1 638 262	5.19	5.12	1.74
845 Articles of apparel nes	1 526 317	4.84	2.71	1.74
36 Crustacean mollusc aquat invertebra	1 398 875	4.43	12.00	7.32
841 Male clothing, woven	1 370 046	4.34	4.46	2.79
842 Female clothing, woven	1 242 996	3.94	3.22	2.04
71 Coffee and coffee substitutes	794 797	2.52	8.93	5.68
42 Rice	762 628	2.42	11.30	8.47
772 Electrical circuit equipment	620 600	1.97	1.25	0.46
Remainder	11 160 981	35.37		
Yemen - Yémen (=Developing)**				
All commodity groups	4 829 866	100.00	0.14	0.05
333 Crude petroleum & bituminous oil	4 166 893	86.27	0.91	0.65
334 Heavy petroleum & bituminous oil	216 780	4.49	0.15	0.07
34 Fish, fresh live chilled frozen	65 413	1.35	0.52	0.21
335 Residual petroleum products nes	40 998	0.85	0.76	0.25
36 Crustacean mollusc aquat invertebra	28 863	0.60	0.25	0.15
781 Passenger cars and race cars	25 702	0.53	0.04	0.01
971 Gold non-monetary excluding ores	23 508	0.49	0.12	0.06
57 Fruit nut (exc oil), fresh or dried	23 231	0.48	0.13	0.05
343 Natural gas liquefied or not	21 646	0.45	0.06	0.02
122 Manufactured tabacco	16 373	0.34	0.44	0.10
Remainder	200 458	4.15		

Leading products exported based on average 2004-2005 values SITC Revision 3 (3-digit level) / Principaux produits exportés d'après la moyenne des valeurs de 2004-2005 CTCI révision 3 (positions à 3 chiffres)	Value (f.o.b., thousands of dollars) Valeur (f.a.b., milliers de dollars)	2004-2005 As percentage / En pourcentage		
		of country total du total du pays	of ** (1) des ** (1)	of world du monde
Zambia - Zambie (=Developing)**				
All commodity groups	1 656 525	100.00	0.05	0.02
682 Copper	831 900	50.22	3.17	1.46
699 Base metal manufactures nes	198 109	11.96	0.85	0.23
263 Cotton	88 684	5.35	2.19	0.79
121 Unmanufactured tabacco and refuse	59 271	3.58	1.47	0.86
283 Copper ores and concentrates	52 864	3.19	0.45	0.36
61 Sugar, mollasses and honey	51 158	3.09	0.61	0.32
54 Vegetable & vegetable products nes	30 461	1.84	0.30	0.10
44 Maize unmilled, excluding sweet corn	28 168	1.70	0.92	0.25
667 Pearls, precious semiprecious store	22 910	1.38	0.07	0.03
651 Textile yarn	22 409	1.35	0.10	0.06
Remainder	270 591	16.33		
Zimbabwe (=Developing)**				
All commodity groups	1 901 533	100.00	0.06	0.02
121 Unmanufactured tabacco and refuse	394 989	20.77	9.82	5.73
263 Cotton	236 268	12.43	5.82	2.11
284 Nickel ores, concentrates, etc	191 825	10.09	6.48	3.24
683 Nickel	160 925	8.46	10.52	1.23
671 Pig & sponge iron, ferro alloys etc	141 638	7.45	1.13	0.61
892 Printed matter	72 803	3.83	1.00	0.19
278 Other crude minerals	43 138	2.27	1.34	0.43
122 Manufactured tabacco	42 670	2.24	1.15	0.25
61 Sugar, mollasses and honey	37 172	1.95	0.44	0.23
971 Gold non-monetary excluding ores	28 398	1.49	0.14	0.08
Remainder	551 709	29.01		

Sources:
- UNCTAD secretariat calculations based on UN DESA Statistics Division's data

Notes:

(1) The symbol ** indicates the grouping to which the country belongs and the percentage share shown applies. The percentage is the share of exports of each commodity shown by the country in the relevant grouping total exports for that commodity (i.e. "developed", which refers to developed economies; "developing", which refers to developing economies; or "Economies in transition", which refers to economies in transition).

Sources :
- Calculs du secrétariat de la CNUCED sur la base des données de ONU DAES Division de statistique

Notes :

(1) Le symbole ** indique le groupement auquel le pays appartient et par rapport auquel est calculé le pourcentage. Ce pourcentage est la part que représentent les exportations du produit par le pays par rapport aux exportations du même produit par le groupement auquel le pays appartient («developed» se réfère aux économies développées, «developing» aux économies en développement, et " Économies in transition " aux pays en transition).

3.2.E Exports structure by product
Major exporters for leading products among developing economies

3.2.E Structure des exportations par produits
Principaux exportateurs de produits majeurs parmi les économies en développement

Leading exporting developing countries (1) based on average 2004-2005 exports (2) SITC Revision 3 (3-digit level) / Principaux pays en dévelopt exportateurs (1) d'après la moyenne des exportations de 2004-2005 (2) CTCI révision 3 (positions à 3 chiffres)	2004-2005		
	Value (f.o.b., thousands of dollars) Valeur (f.a.b., milliers de dollars)	As percentage En pourcentage		
		of country total du total du pays	of developing countries des pays en dévelop pement	of world du monde

034 - Fish, fresh live chilled frozen

	Value	of country total	of developing countries	of world
World	31 653 134	0.33	_	100.0
Developed economies	18 626 384	0.32	_	58.85
Economies in transition	454 782	0.13	_	1.44
Developing economies	12 571 969	0.37	100.00	39.72
China	2 771 214	0.41	22.04	8.75
Chile	1 814 089	5.22	14.43	5.73
China, Taiwan Province of	1 335 436	0.74	10.62	4.22
Korea, Republic of	590 289	0.22	4.70	1.86
Viet Nam	555 174	1.76	4.42	1.75
Indonesia	468 005	0.62	3.72	1.48
Argentina	450 538	1.21	3.58	1.42
Thailand	449 221	0.44	3.57	1.42
Namibia	331 292	12.73	2.64	1.05
Panama	313 542	33.82	2.49	0.99

036 - Crustacean mollusc aquat invertebra

	Value	of country total	of developing countries	of world
World	19 118 237	0.20	_	100.0
Developed economies	7 404 962	0.13	_	38.73
Economies in transition	57 413	0.02	_	0.30
Developing economies	11 655 862	0.35	100.00	60.97
Viet Nam	1 398 875	4.43	12.00	7.32
Thailand	1 347 184	1.31	11.56	7.05
China	1 218 638	0.18	10.46	6.37
India	1 080 413	1.18	9.27	5.65
Indonesia	963 232	1.28	8.26	5.04
Mexico	426 391	0.21	3.66	2.23
Malaysia	394 376	0.29	3.38	2.06
Ecuador	387 319	4.43	3.32	2.03
Bangladesh	379 767	6.12	3.26	1.99
Morocco	359 673	3.50	3.09	1.88

057 - Fruit nut (exc oil), fresh or dried

	Value	of country total	of developing countries	of world
World	43 077 981	0.45	_	100.0
Developed economies	24 432 631	0.41	_	56.72
Economies in transition	660 921	0.19	_	1.53
Developing economies	17 984 429	0.53	100.00	41.75
Turkey	2 170 963	3.18	12.07	5.04
Chile	1 754 341	5.05	9.75	4.07
Mexico	1 288 778	0.64	7.17	2.99
South Africa	1 207 066	2.77	6.71	2.80
Ecuador	1 103 689	12.63	6.14	2.56
Iran, Islamic Republic of	1 031 572	1.97	5.74	2.39
Costa Rica	908 010	13.86	5.05	2.11
China	838 318	0.12	4.66	1.95
India	772 823	0.84	4.30	1.79
Argentina	679 459	1.83	3.78	1.58

081 - Animal feed excluding unmilled cereal

	Value	of country total	of developing countries	of world
World	30 074 415	0.31	_	100.0
Developed economies	17 593 554	0.30	_	58.50
Economies in transition	409 966	0.12	_	1.36
Developing economies	12 070 895	0.36	100.00	40.14
Argentina	3 933 756	10.57	32.59	13.08
Brazil	3 199 838	3.03	26.51	10.64
Peru	1 090 313	7.38	9.03	3.63
India	913 871	1.00	7.57	3.04
China	509 207	0.08	4.22	1.69
Thailand	465 483	0.45	3.86	1.55
Chile	437 401	1.26	3.62	1.45
Bolivia	238 608	9.43	1.98	0.79
Paraguay	160 851	9.71	1.33	0.53
Indonesia	149 656	0.20	1.24	0.50

281 - Iron ore and concentrates

	Value	of country total	of developing countries	of world
World	22 494 507	0.23	_	100.0
Developed economies	8 968 546	0.15	_	39.87
Economies in transition	2 021 648	0.57	_	8.99
Developing economies	11 504 313	0.34	100.00	51.14
Brazil	6 027 753	5.71	52.40	26.80
India	3 447 289	3.76	29.97	15.33
South Africa	757 341	1.74	6.58	3.37
Mauritania	280 400	49.51	2.44	1.25
Chile	232 574	0.67	2.02	1.03
Bahrain	181 313	2.10	1.58	0.81
Peru	172 588	1.17	1.50	0.77
Viet Nam	60 307	0.19	0.52	0.27
Iran, Islamic Republic of	59 780	0.11	0.52	0.27
United Arab Emirates	59 365	0.06	0.52	0.26

283 - Copper ores and concentrates

	Value	of country total	of developing countries	of world
World	14 827 985	0.15	_	100.0
Developed economies	2 734 294	0.05	_	18.44
Economies in transition	298 418	0.08	_	2.01
Developing economies	11 795 272	0.35	100.00	79.55
Chile	5 516 497	15.88	46.77	37.20
Indonesia	2 557 332	3.41	21.68	17.25
Peru	1 254 875	8.49	10.64	8.46
Argentina	833 128	2.24	7.06	5.62
Papua New Guinea	512 450	17.58	4.34	3.46
Mongolia	305 270	31.79	2.59	2.06
Brazil	237 624	0.23	2.01	1.60
Mexico	128 432	0.06	1.09	0.87
Botswana	94 159	2.65	0.80	0.64
Turkey	83 449	0.12	0.71	0.56

321 - Coal excluding non-agglomomerated

	Value	of country total	of developing countries	of world
World	38 702 101	0.40	_	100.0
Developed economies	21 264 262	0.36	_	54.94
Economies in transition	3 868 150	1.10	_	9.99
Developing economies	13 569 689	0.40	100.00	35.06
China	4 041 690	0.60	29.78	10.44
Indonesia	3 551 453	4.73	26.17	9.18
South Africa	2 850 468	6.53	21.01	7.37
Colombia	2 102 506	11.09	15.49	5.43
Viet Nam	584 869	1.85	4.31	1.51
Venezuela (Bolivarain Republic of)	226 179	0.48	1.67	0.58
India	57 011	0.06	0.42	0.15
Korea, Dem. People's Rep. of	30 555	3.91	0.23	0.08
Myanmar	27 615	0.83	0.20	0.07
Mongolia	21 561	2.25	0.16	0.06

333 - Crude petroleum & bituminous oil

	Value	of country total	of developing countries	of world
World	637 473 180	6.62	_	100.0
Developed economies	94 406 951	1.60	_	14.81
Economies in transition	84 292 968	23.96	_	13.22
Developing economies	458 773 262	13.59	100.00	71.97
Saudi Arabia	104 859 343	75.93	22.86	16.45
Iran, Islamic Republic of	41 287 500	78.91	9.00	6.48
Venezuela (Bolivarain Republic of)	40 283 740	86.18	8.78	6.32
United Arab Emirates	36 981 743	38.64	8.06	5.80
Nigeria	35 390 236	96.40	7.71	5.55
Mexico	24 793 654	12.33	5.40	3.89
Algeria	21 426 804	54.77	4.67	3.36
Kuwait	20 366 226	55.36	4.44	3.19
Iraq	19 556 899	96.37	4.26	3.07
Angola	17 433 148	96.43	3.80	2.73

For sources and notes, see end of table.

Pour les sources et les notes, se reporter à la fin du tableau.

3.2.E Exports structure by product
Major exporters for leading products among developing economies

3.2.E Structure des exportations par produits
Principaux exportateurs de produits majeurs parmi les économies en développement

Leading exporting developing countries (1) based on average 2004-2005 exports (2) SITC Revision 3 (3-digit level) / Principaux pays en dévelopt exportateurs (1) d'après la moyenne des exportations de 2004-2005 (2) CTCI révision 3 (positions à 3 chiffres)	2004-2005			
	Value (f.o.b., thousands of dollars) / Valeur (f.a.b., milliers de dollars)	As percentage / En pourcentage		
		of country total / du total du pays	of developing countries / des pays en dévelop pement	of world / du monde
334 - Heavy petroleum & bituminous oil				
World	312 002 483	3.24	_	100.0
Developed economies	129 861 144	2.20	_	41.62
Economies in transition	38 236 781	10.87	_	12.26
Developing economies	143 904 558	4.26	100.00	46.12
Singapore	22 596 495	10.55	15.70	7.24
Korea, Republic of	12 551 851	4.66	8.72	4.02
Kuwait	11 826 565	32.15	8.22	3.79
Saudi Arabia	11 567 425	8.38	8.04	3.71
United Arab Emirates	10 852 415	11.34	7.54	3.48
India	9 051 037	9.88	6.29	2.90
China, Taiwan Province of	6 826 848	3.76	4.74	2.19
Bahrain	6 669 220	77.33	4.63	2.14
China	5 185 820	0.77	3.60	1.66
Malaysia	3 598 330	2.69	2.50	1.15
342 - Liquefied propane and butane				
World	23 582 840	0.24	_	100.0
Developed economies	7 636 507	0.13	_	32.38
Economies in transition	591 628	0.17	_	2.51
Developing economies	15 354 706	0.45	100.00	65.11
Saudi Arabia	4 903 401	3.55	31.93	20.79
Algeria	3 421 610	8.75	22.28	14.51
United Arab Emirates	3 128 171	3.27	20.37	13.26
Kuwait	1 762 541	4.79	11.48	7.47
Qatar	667 134	3.00	4.34	2.83
Argentina	569 956	1.53	3.71	2.42
Iran, Islamic Republic of	409 126	0.78	2.66	1.73
Indonesia	407 364	0.54	2.65	1.73
Malaysia	403 969	0.30	2.63	1.71
Singapore	369 820	0.17	2.41	1.57
343 - Natural gas, liquefied or not				
World	110 807 378	1.15	_	100.0
Developed economies	61 321 675	1.04	_	55.34
Economies in transition	10 357 534	2.94	_	9.35
Developing economies	39 128 170	1.16	100.00	35.31
Algeria	9 986 296	25.52	25.52	9.01
Qatar	6 918 468	31.13	17.68	6.24
Indonesia	5 178 480	6.90	13.23	4.67
Malaysia	4 992 737	3.73	12.76	4.51
Oman	2 693 905	15.65	6.88	2.43
Trinidad and Tobago	2 013 626	24.97	5.15	1.82
Brunei Darussalam	1 981 378	38.54	5.06	1.79
United Arab Emirates	1 941 943	2.03	4.96	1.75
Myanmar	1 032 559	30.90	2.64	0.93
Bolivia	801 834	31.74	2.05	0.72
511 - Hydrocarbons nes; derivatives				
World	46 412 476	0.48	_	100.0
Developed economies	30 736 581	0.52	_	66.22
Economies in transition	1 198 243	0.34	_	2.58
Developing economies	14 477 652	0.43	100.00	31.19
Korea, Republic of	4 450 309	1.65	30.74	9.59
Singapore	2 079 496	0.97	14.36	4.48
Saudi Arabia	1 662 121	1.20	11.48	3.58
Thailand	970 152	0.94	6.70	2.09
India	923 764	1.01	6.38	1.99
China	807 074	0.12	5.57	1.74
Malaysia	647 065	0.48	4.47	1.39
China, Taiwan Province of	602 648	0.33	4.16	1.30
Brazil	514 015	0.49	3.55	1.11
Iran, Islamic Republic of	308 082	0.59	2.13	0.66

For sources and notes, see end of table.

Leading exporting developing countries (1) based on average 2004-2005 exports (2) SITC Revision 3 (3-digit level) / Principaux pays en dévelopt exportateurs (1) d'après la moyenne des exportations de 2004-2005 (2) CTCI révision 3 (positions à 3 chiffres)	2004-2005			
	Value (f.o.b., thousands of dollars) / Valeur (f.a.b., milliers de dollars)	As percentage / En pourcentage		
		of country total / du total du pays	of developing countries / des pays en dévelop pement	of world / du monde
512 - Alcohols, phenols; derivatives				
World	28 986 890	0.30	_	100.0
Developed economies	14 951 168	0.25	_	51.58
Economies in transition	940 056	0.27	_	3.24
Developing economies	13 095 666	0.39	100.00	45.18
Saudi Arabia	3 484 787	2.52	26.61	12.02
Singapore	1 123 240	0.52	8.58	3.87
China, Taiwan Province of	1 080 933	0.60	8.25	3.73
Malaysia	814 006	0.61	6.22	2.81
Brazil	796 324	0.75	6.08	2.75
Kuwait	645 076	1.75	4.93	2.23
Trinidad and Tobago	614 961	7.63	4.70	2.12
China	584 925	0.09	4.47	2.02
Chile	573 488	1.65	4.38	1.98
Korea, Republic of	546 645	0.20	4.17	1.89
571 - Primary form ethylene polymers				
World	35 412 131	0.37	_	100.0
Developed economies	21 974 395	0.37	_	62.05
Economies in transition	758 478	0.22	_	2.14
Developing economies	12 679 258	0.38	100.00	35.80
Saudi Arabia	3 131 337	2.27	24.70	8.84
Korea, Republic of	2 007 155	0.75	15.83	5.67
Singapore	1 360 215	0.64	10.73	3.84
Thailand	766 797	0.74	6.05	2.17
China, Taiwan Province of	764 956	0.42	6.03	2.16
China, Hong Kong SAR	692 407	0.25	5.46	1.96
Kuwait	606 976	1.65	4.79	1.71
Brazil	591 864	0.56	4.67	1.67
Malaysia	581 180	0.43	4.58	1.64
Qatar	505 434	2.27	3.99	1.43
574 - Polyacetals and polyesters, etc				
World	32 934 483	0.34	_	100.0
Developed economies	20 890 976	0.35	_	63.43
Economies in transition	194 828	0.06	_	0.59
Developing economies	11 848 679	0.35	100.00	35.98
Korea, Republic of	2 427 997	0.90	20.49	7.37
China, Taiwan Province of	1 978 006	1.09	16.69	6.01
Singapore	1 438 257	0.67	12.14	4.37
Thailand	1 255 748	1.22	10.60	3.81
China, Hong Kong SAR	1 169 070	0.42	9.87	3.55
China	1 081 198	0.16	9.13	3.28
Mexico	526 079	0.26	4.44	1.60
Malaysia	411 571	0.31	3.47	1.25
Indonesia	388 011	0.52	3.27	1.18
India	348 455	0.38	2.94	1.06
575 - Other plastics, in primary forms				
World	60 593 937	0.63	_	100.0
Developed economies	47 764 963	0.81	_	78.83
Economies in transition	436 360	0.12	_	0.72
Developing economies	12 392 614	0.37	100.00	20.45
Korea, Republic of	2 306 765	0.86	18.61	3.81
China, Hong Kong SAR	1 809 164	0.65	14.60	2.99
China, Taiwan Province of	1 724 172	0.95	13.91	2.85
Singapore	1 609 441	0.75	12.99	2.66
China	905 960	0.13	7.31	1.50
Thailand	845 724	0.82	6.82	1.40
Saudi Arabia	623 115	0.45	5.03	1.03
India	439 832	0.48	3.55	0.73
Malaysia	402 644	0.30	3.25	0.66
Brazil	375 274	0.36	3.03	0.62

Pour les sources et les notes, se reporter à la fin du tableau.

3.2.E   Exports structure by product
Major exporters for leading products among
developing economies

3.2.E   Structure des exportations par produits
Principaux exportateurs de produits majeurs
parmi les économies en développement

Leading exporting developing countries (1) based on average 2004-2005 exports (2) SITC Revision 3 (3-digit level) / Principaux pays en dévelopt exportateurs (1) d'après la moyenne des exportations de 2004-2005 (2) CTCI révision 3 (positions à 3 chiffres)	Value (f.o.b., thousands of dollars) / Valeur (f.a.b., milliers de dollars)	As percentage / En pourcentage		
		of country total / du total du pays	of developing countries / des pays en dévelop pement	of world / du monde
625 - Rubber for wheels, incl inner tube				
World	40 554 675	0.42	_	100.0
Developed economies	27 434 703	0.46	_	67.65
Economies in transition	1 180 113	0.34	_	2.91
Developing economies	11 939 859	0.35	100.00	29.44
China	3 327 654	0.49	27.87	8.21
Korea, Republic of	2 266 598	0.84	18.98	5.59
Thailand	788 600	0.76	6.60	1.94
Brazil	772 434	0.73	6.47	1.90
China, Taiwan Province of	688 901	0.38	5.77	1.70
Indonesia	599 883	0.80	5.02	1.48
Turkey	589 743	0.86	4.94	1.45
India	513 558	0.56	4.30	1.27
United Arab Emirates	314 912	0.33	2.64	0.78
Mexico	265 751	0.13	2.23	0.66
651 - Textile yarn				
World	40 537 549	0.42	_	100.0
Developed economies	17 616 816	0.30	_	43.46
Economies in transition	922 893	0.26	_	2.28
Developing economies	21 997 839	0.65	100.00	54.27
China	4 820 455	0.71	21.91	11.89
China, Hong Kong SAR	3 693 125	1.32	16.79	9.11
China, Taiwan Province of	2 279 532	1.26	10.36	5.62
India	2 084 430	2.28	9.48	5.14
Korea, Republic of	1 562 772	0.58	7.10	3.86
Indonesia	1 551 257	2.07	7.05	3.83
Pakistan	1 185 892	8.06	5.39	2.93
Turkey	1 007 478	1.48	4.58	2.49
Thailand	782 310	0.76	3.56	1.93
Malaysia	614 642	0.46	2.79	1.52
652 - Woven cotton fabrics				
World	28 724 537	0.30	_	100.0
Developed economies	11 300 632	0.19	_	39.34
Economies in transition	405 786	0.12	_	1.41
Developing economies	17 018 119	0.50	100.00	59.25
China	6 521 253	0.96	38.32	22.70
China, Hong Kong SAR	3 432 621	1.23	20.17	11.95
Pakistan	1 929 592	13.11	11.34	6.72
India	861 066	0.94	5.06	3.00
Turkey	850 830	1.25	5.00	2.96
Korea, Republic of	702 106	0.26	4.13	2.44
China, Taiwan Province of	539 143	0.30	3.17	1.88
Indonesia	390 826	0.52	2.30	1.36
Thailand	347 364	0.34	2.04	1.21
Brazil	282 815	0.27	1.66	0.98
653 - Man-made woven fabrics				
World	31 955 378	0.33	_	100.0
Developed economies	12 714 708	0.22	_	39.79
Economies in transition	167 489	0.05	_	0.52
Developing economies	19 073 181	0.57	100.00	59.69
China	7 538 350	1.11	39.52	23.59
Korea, Republic of	2 444 701	0.91	12.82	7.65
China, Taiwan Province of	2 181 484	1.20	11.44	6.83
China, Hong Kong SAR	1 485 681	0.53	7.79	4.65
Turkey	1 031 748	1.51	5.41	3.23
India	985 555	1.08	5.17	3.08
Indonesia	797 388	1.06	4.18	2.50
United Arab Emirates	657 019	0.69	3.44	2.06
Thailand	525 695	0.51	2.76	1.65
Pakistan	292 578	1.99	1.53	0.92

Leading exporting developing countries (1) based on average 2004-2005 exports (2) SITC Revision 3 (3-digit level) / Principaux pays en dévelopt exportateurs (1) d'après la moyenne des exportations de 2004-2005 (2) CTCI révision 3 (positions à 3 chiffres)	Value (f.o.b., thousands of dollars) / Valeur (f.a.b., milliers de dollars)	As percentage / En pourcentage		
		of country total / du total du pays	of developing countries / des pays en dévelop pement	of world / du monde
655 - Knitted or crocheted fabrics nes				
World	19 621 510	0.20	_	100.0
Developed economies	6 974 246	0.12	_	35.54
Economies in transition	72 990	0.02	_	0.37
Developing economies	12 574 274	0.37	100.00	64.08
China	3 322 910	0.49	26.43	16.94
China, Hong Kong SAR	2 899 630	1.04	23.06	14.78
Korea, Republic of	2 725 005	1.01	21.67	13.89
China, Taiwan Province of	1 920 081	1.06	15.27	9.79
Turkey	506 422	0.74	4.03	2.58
Thailand	149 911	0.15	1.19	0.76
Pakistan	122 800	0.83	0.98	0.63
Singapore	119 836	0.06	0.95	0.61
Malaysia	104 884	0.08	0.83	0.53
Mexico	90 998	0.05	0.72	0.46
658 - Mace-up textile articles nes				
World	29 109 655	0.30	_	100.0
Developed economies	8 703 795	0.15	_	29.90
Economies in transition	513 780	0.15	_	1.76
Developing economies	19 892 080	0.59	100.00	68.33
China	9 001 121	1.33	45.25	30.92
Pakistan	2 701 040	18.36	13.58	9.28
India	2 095 412	2.29	10.53	7.20
Turkey	1 895 564	2.78	9.53	6.51
Mexico	757 946	0.38	3.81	2.60
China, Hong Kong SAR	426 385	0.15	2.14	1.46
Brazil	391 858	0.37	1.97	1.35
Korea, Republic of	389 839	0.14	1.96	1.34
Viet Nam	313 223	0.99	1.57	1.08
Thailand	240 295	0.23	1.21	0.83
667 - Pearls, precious semiprecious stone				
World	84 334 413	0.88	_	100.0
Developed economies	52 042 994	0.88	_	61.71
Economies in transition	1 092 722	0.31	_	1.30
Developing economies	31 198 696	0.92	100.00	36.99
India	11 231 303	12.26	36.00	13.32
China, Hong Kong SAR	4 623 866	1.66	14.82	5.48
United Arab Emirates	3 612 044	3.77	11.58	4.28
Botswana	3 013 461	84.90	9.66	3.57
South Africa	2 297 789	5.27	7.37	2.72
China	1 538 748	0.23	4.93	1.82
Singapore	1 028 318	0.48	3.30	1.22
Thailand	915 838	0.89	2.94	1.09
Dem. Rep. of the Congo	856 029	43.43	2.74	1.02
Namibia	729 914	28.04	2.34	0.87
671 - Pig & sponge iron, ferro alloys etc				
World	23 343 667	0.24	_	100.0
Developed economies	5 754 090	0.10	_	24.65
Economies in transition	5 058 851	1.44	_	21.67
Developing economies	12 530 726	0.37	100.00	53.68
China	3 331 646	0.49	26.59	14.27
South Africa	2 846 871	6.53	22.72	12.20
Brazil	2 157 211	2.04	17.22	9.24
Venezuela (Bolivarain Republic of)	986 546	2.11	7.87	4.23
Colombia	683 924	3.61	5.46	2.93
New Caledonia	661 482	62.20	5.28	2.83
India	397 794	0.43	3.17	1.70
Chile	299 613	0.86	2.39	1.28
Korea, Republic of	143 018	0.05	1.14	0.61
Zimbabwe	141 638	7.45	1.13	0.61

For sources and notes, see end of table.

Pour les sources et les notes, se reporter à la fin du tableau.

3.2.E Exports structure by product
Major exporters for leading products among developing economies

3.2.E Structure des exportations par produits
Principaux exportateurs de produits majeurs parmi les économies en développement

Leading exporting developing countries (1) based on average 2004-2005 exports (2) SITC Revision 3 (3-digit level) / Principaux pays en dévelopt exportateurs (1) d'après la moyenne des exportations de 2004-2005 (2) CTCI révision 3 (positions à 3 chiffres)	2004-2005			
	Value (f.o.b., thousands of dollars) / Valeur (f.a.b., milliers de dollars)	As percentage / En pourcentage		
		of country total / du total du pays	of developing countries / des pays en développement	of world / du monde
673 - Flat iron non-alloy steel products				
World	60 560 340	0.63	_	100.0
Developed economies	32 418 061	0.55	_	53.53
Economies in transition	11 127 802	3.16	_	18.37
Developing economies	17 014 477	0.50	100.00	28.10
Korea, Republic of	3 829 912	1.42	22.51	6.32
China	3 106 837	0.46	18.26	5.13
China, Taiwan Province of	2 338 372	1.29	13.74	3.86
Brazil	1 174 411	1.11	6.90	1.94
India	980 892	1.07	5.77	1.62
South Africa	823 672	1.89	4.84	1.36
China, Hong Kong SAR	712 733	0.26	4.19	1.18
Thailand	601 656	0.58	3.54	0.99
Venezuela (Bolivarain Republic of)	510 795	1.09	3.00	0.84
Turkey	412 874	0.60	2.43	0.68
676 - Iron steel bar rod section piling				
World	49 149 620	0.51	_	100.0
Developed economies	30 975 829	0.52	_	63.02
Economies in transition	4 807 198	1.37	_	9.78
Developing economies	13 366 593	0.40	100.00	27.20
Turkey	3 150 980	4.61	23.57	6.41
China	2 718 085	0.40	20.33	5.53
Korea, Republic of	1 400 687	0.52	10.48	2.85
Brazil	969 258	0.92	7.25	1.97
China, Taiwan Province of	777 455	0.43	5.82	1.58
India	482 931	0.53	3.61	0.98
South Africa	418 926	0.96	3.13	0.85
Mexico	336 890	0.17	2.52	0.69
Singapore	331 527	0.15	2.48	0.67
Thailand	267 121	0.26	2.00	0.54
679 - Iron steel pipe tube fittings etc				
World	47 734 924	0.50	_	100.0
Developed economies	32 192 587	0.54	_	67.44
Economies in transition	3 045 806	0.87	_	6.38
Developing economies	12 496 531	0.37	100.00	26.18
China	3 207 614	0.47	25.67	6.72
Korea, Republic of	1 421 488	0.53	11.38	2.98
India	924 962	1.01	7.40	1.94
Mexico	905 351	0.45	7.24	1.90
Turkey	838 386	1.23	6.71	1.76
Argentina	729 872	1.96	5.84	1.53
Singapore	724 455	0.34	5.80	1.52
Malaysia	717 142	0.54	5.74	1.50
China, Taiwan Province of	701 204	0.39	5.61	1.47
Brazil	453 105	0.43	3.63	0.95
682 - Copper				
World	56 821 290	0.59	_	100.0
Developed economies	25 517 414	0.43	_	44.91
Economies in transition	5 041 851	1.43	_	8.87
Developing economies	26 262 024	0.78	100.00	46.22
Chile	10 556 003	30.38	40.19	18.58
China	2 232 632	0.33	8.50	3.93
Korea, Republic of	1 835 176	0.68	6.99	3.23
Peru	1 801 752	12.19	6.86	3.17
China, Taiwan Province of	1 796 770	0.99	6.84	3.16
China, Hong Kong SAR	1 412 166	0.51	5.38	2.49
India	1 011 153	1.10	3.85	1.78
Indonesia	968 953	1.29	3.69	1.71
Zambia	831 900	50.22	3.17	1.46
Mexico	702 370	0.35	2.67	1.24

Leading exporting developing countries (1) based on average 2004-2005 exports (2) SITC Revision 3 (3-digit level) / Principaux pays en dévelopt exportateurs (1) d'après la moyenne des exportations de 2004-2005 (2) CTCI révision 3 (positions à 3 chiffres)	2004-2005			
	Value (f.o.b., thousands of dollars) / Valeur (f.a.b., milliers de dollars)	As percentage / En pourcentage		
		of country total / du total du pays	of developing countries / des pays en développement	of world / du monde
684 - Aluminium				
World	71 858 397	0.75	_	100.0
Developed economies	47 277 722	0.80	_	65.79
Economies in transition	7 215 515	2.05	_	10.04
Developing economies	17 365 159	0.51	100.00	24.17
China	4 124 621	0.61	23.75	5.74
Brazil	1 821 632	1.73	10.49	2.54
South Africa	1 498 995	3.44	8.63	2.09
Korea, Republic of	1 228 388	0.46	7.07	1.71
United Arab Emirates	1 219 216	1.27	7.02	1.70
Bahrain	981 137	11.38	5.65	1.37
Venezuela (Bolivarain Republic of)	950 807	2.03	5.48	1.32
China, Hong Kong SAR	682 848	0.24	3.93	0.95
China, Taiwan Province of	655 007	0.36	3.77	0.91
Turkey	519 078	0.76	2.99	0.72
699 - Base metal manufactures nes				
World	84 600 950	0.88	_	100.0
Developed economies	59 640 349	1.01	_	70.50
Economies in transition	1 524 419	0.43	_	1.80
Developing economies	23 436 182	0.69	100.00	27.70
China	8 779 837	1.30	37.46	10.38
Mexico	3 155 115	1.57	13.46	3.73
China, Taiwan Province of	3 002 858	1.65	12.81	3.55
China, Hong Kong SAR	1 448 989	0.52	6.18	1.71
Korea, Republic of	1 382 153	0.51	5.90	1.63
India	994 835	1.09	4.24	1.18
Singapore	759 908	0.35	3.24	0.90
Thailand	746 177	0.72	3.18	0.88
Turkey	622 284	0.91	2.66	0.74
Malaysia	572 392	0.43	2.44	0.68
713 - Internal combustion engine part nes				
World	107 309 623	1.11	_	100.0
Developed economies	91 688 486	1.55	_	85.44
Economies in transition	671 756	0.19	_	0.63
Developing economies	14 949 380	0.44	100.00	13.93
Mexico	4 695 516	2.33	31.41	4.38
Brazil	2 242 275	2.12	15.00	2.09
China	1 557 409	0.23	10.42	1.45
Thailand	1 303 112	1.26	8.72	1.21
Korea, Republic of	1 051 279	0.39	7.03	0.98
Singapore	922 841	0.43	6.17	0.86
Turkey	805 146	1.18	5.39	0.75
India	466 684	0.51	3.12	0.43
South Africa	454 358	1.04	3.04	0.42
Malaysia	241 006	0.18	1.61	0.22
716 - Rotating electric plant parts nes				
World	47 827 692	0.50	_	100.0
Developed economies	32 046 332	0.54	_	67.00
Economies in transition	611 868	0.17	_	1.28
Developing economies	15 169 493	0.45	100.00	31.72
China	4 545 317	0.67	29.96	9.50
Mexico	2 559 232	1.27	16.87	5.35
China, Hong Kong SAR	2 302 823	0.83	15.18	4.81
Singapore	1 290 969	0.60	8.51	2.70
Thailand	831 738	0.81	5.48	1.74
Korea, Republic of	773 645	0.29	5.10	1.62
Brazil	585 930	0.56	3.86	1.23
China, Taiwan Province of	526 432	0.29	3.47	1.10
Indonesia	343 251	0.46	2.26	0.72
Malaysia	314 357	0.24	2.07	0.66

For sources and notes, see end of table.

Pour les sources et les notes, se reporter à la fin du tableau.

3.2.E **Exports structure by product**
Major exporters for leading products among developing economies

3.2.E **Structure des exportations par produits**
Principaux exportateurs de produits majeurs parmi les économies en développement

Left table

Leading exporting developing countries (1) based on average 2004-2005 exports (2) SITC Revision 3 (3-digit level) / Principaux pays en dévelopt exportateurs (1) d'après la moyenne des exportations de 2004-2005 (2) CTCI révision 3 (positions à 3 chiffres)	Value (f.o.b., thousands of dollars) Valeur (f.a.b., milliers de dollars)	2004-2005 As percentage / En pourcentage		
		of country total du total du pays	of developing countries des pays en dévelop pement	of world du monde
723 - Civil engineering plant & equipment				
World	62 783 074	0.65	_	100.0
Developed economies	50 353 130	0.85	_	80.20
Economies in transition	727 287	0.21	_	1.16
Developing economies	11 702 657	0.35	100.00	18.64
Singapore	2 884 095	1.35	24.64	4.59
Korea, Republic of	2 425 889	0.90	20.73	3.86
China	1 603 301	0.24	13.70	2.55
Brazil	1 196 483	1.13	10.22	1.91
Mexico	795 711	0.40	6.80	1.27
United Arab Emirates	581 986	0.61	4.97	0.93
China, Hong Kong SAR	512 405	0.18	4.38	0.82
Indonesia	221 458	0.29	1.89	0.35
Turkey	199 878	0.29	1.71	0.32
Thailand	182 592	0.18	1.56	0.29
728 - Special industrial machine part nes				
World	95 903 829	1.00	_	100.0
Developed economies	80 507 655	1.36	_	83.95
Economies in transition	573 530	0.16	_	0.60
Developing economies	14 822 645	0.44	100.00	15.46
Korea, Republic of	3 205 117	1.19	21.62	3.34
China, Taiwan Province of	2 638 531	1.45	17.80	2.75
China	2 290 990	0.34	15.46	2.39
Singapore	1 679 952	0.78	11.33	1.75
China, Hong Kong SAR	1 622 470	0.58	10.95	1.69
Malaysia	655 885	0.49	4.42	0.68
Mexico	540 240	0.27	3.64	0.56
Brazil	429 899	0.41	2.90	0.45
India	384 873	0.42	2.60	0.40
Turkey	276 543	0.40	1.87	0.29
741 - Heating cooling equipment parts nes				
World	65 620 477	0.68	_	100.0
Developed economies	46 730 201	0.79	_	71.21
Economies in transition	661 556	0.19	_	1.01
Developing economies	18 228 721	0.54	100.00	27.78
China	6 347 983	0.94	34.82	9.67
Korea, Republic of	2 443 572	0.91	13.41	3.72
Thailand	2 306 582	2.24	12.65	3.52
Mexico	1 998 002	0.99	10.96	3.04
Malaysia	940 027	0.70	5.16	1.43
China, Hong Kong SAR	743 531	0.27	4.08	1.13
China, Taiwan Province of	733 878	0.40	4.03	1.12
Singapore	630 525	0.29	3.46	0.96
Turkey	366 665	0.54	2.01	0.56
Brazil	336 300	0.32	1.84	0.51
743 - Gas pump, compressor, fan, filter				
World	67 391 676	0.70	_	100.0
Developed economies	51 722 970	0.88	_	76.75
Economies in transition	843 147	0.24	_	1.25
Developing economies	14 825 559	0.44	100.00	22.00
China	3 956 645	0.58	26.69	5.87
Mexico	1 753 326	0.87	11.83	2.60
South Africa	1 573 668	3.61	10.61	2.34
Korea, Republic of	1 180 273	0.44	7.96	1.75
China, Taiwan Province of	1 013 554	0.56	6.84	1.50
China, Hong Kong SAR	975 300	0.35	6.58	1.45
Singapore	869 941	0.41	5.87	1.29
Thailand	824 295	0.80	5.56	1.22
Brazil	820 064	0.78	5.53	1.22
Malaysia	563 122	0.42	3.80	0.84

Right table

Leading exporting developing countries (1) based on average 2004-2005 exports (2) SITC Revision 3 (3-digit level) / Principaux pays en dévelopt exportateurs (1) d'après la moyenne des exportations de 2004-2005 (2) CTCI révision 3 (positions à 3 chiffres)	Value (f.o.b., thousands of dollars) Valeur (f.a.b., milliers de dollars)	2004-2005 As percentage / En pourcentage		
		of country total du total du pays	of developing countries des pays en dévelop pement	of world du monde
752 - Computer equipment nes				
World	260 666 418	2.71	_	100.0
Developed economies	115 663 584	1.96	_	44.37
Economies in transition	245 036	0.07	_	0.09
Developing economies	144 757 798	4.29	100.00	55.53
China	68 105 303	10.05	47.05	26.13
Singapore	15 971 417	7.46	11.03	6.13
Malaysia	13 162 744	9.84	9.09	5.05
Mexico	10 061 340	5.00	6.95	3.86
Korea, Republic of	9 694 639	3.60	6.70	3.72
China, Hong Kong SAR	7 948 752	2.85	5.49	3.05
Thailand	6 847 123	6.64	4.73	2.63
China, Taiwan Province of	5 964 888	3.29	4.12	2.29
Philippines	4 024 411	9.95	2.78	1.54
Indonesia	1 683 803	2.24	1.16	0.65
759 - Office equipment part & accessories				
World	190 557 278	1.98	_	100.0
Developed economies	83 900 634	1.42	_	44.03
Economies in transition	161 304	0.05	_	0.08
Developing economies	106 495 341	3.16	100.00	55.89
China	27 293 686	4.03	25.63	14.32
China, Hong Kong SAR	23 993 425	8.61	22.53	12.59
Singapore	14 768 589	6.90	13.87	7.75
China, Taiwan Province of	10 634 493	5.86	9.99	5.58
Korea, Republic of	9 577 929	3.56	8.99	5.03
Malaysia	8 257 879	6.17	7.75	4.33
Thailand	3 419 366	3.31	3.21	1.79
Philippines	3 052 938	7.55	2.87	1.60
Mexico	2 584 889	1.29	2.43	1.36
Indonesia	1 075 281	1.43	1.01	0.56
761 - Television video receive project				
World	53 018 704	0.55	_	100.0
Developed economies	22 446 958	0.38	_	42.34
Economies in transition	292 333	0.08	_	0.55
Developing economies	30 279 413	0.90	100.00	57.11
Mexico	9 005 734	4.48	29.74	16.99
China	6 952 586	1.03	22.96	13.11
Korea, Republic of	3 203 720	1.19	10.58	6.04
Turkey	2 807 203	4.11	9.27	5.29
China, Taiwan Province of	2 084 871	1.15	6.89	3.93
Malaysia	1 959 996	1.47	6.47	3.70
Thailand	1 650 698	1.60	5.45	3.11
China, Hong Kong SAR	1 099 332	0.39	3.63	2.07
Singapore	589 560	0.28	1.95	1.11
Indonesia	298 678	0.40	0.99	0.56
762 - Radio broadcast receivers				
World	18 074 615	0.19	_	100.0
Developed economies	6 324 894	0.11	_	34.99
Economies in transition	8 131	0.00	_	0.04
Developing economies	11 741 590	0.35	100.00	64.96
China	3 424 389	0.51	29.16	18.95
China, Hong Kong SAR	2 520 723	0.90	21.47	13.95
Malaysia	1 832 695	1.37	15.61	10.14
Mexico	1 635 228	0.81	13.93	9.05
Singapore	649 731	0.30	5.53	3.59
Thailand	635 076	0.62	5.41	3.51
Indonesia	365 965	0.49	3.12	2.02
Korea, Republic of	257 789	0.10	2.20	1.43
United Arab Emirates	128 645	0.13	1.10	0.71
Philippines	78 354	0.19	0.67	0.43

For sources and notes, see end of table.

Pour les sources et les notes, se reporter à la fin du tableau.

3.2.E   Exports structure by product
Major exporters for leading products among
developing economies

3.2.E   Structure des exportations par produits
Principaux exportateurs de produits majeurs
parmi les économies en développement

Left panel

Leading exporting developing countries (1) based on average 2004-2005 exports (2) SITC Revision 3 (3-digit level) / Principaux pays en dévelopt exportateurs (1) d'après la moyenne des exportations de 2004-2005 (2) CTCI révision 3 (positions à 3 chiffres)	Value (f.o.b., thousands of dollars) Valeur (f.a.b., milliers de dollars)	2004-2005 As percentage En pourcentage of country total du total du pays	of developing countries des pays en dévelop pement	of world du monde
763 - Sound TV recorder or reproducer				
World	59 397 537	0.62	_	100.0
Developed economies	24 802 570	0.42	_	41.76
Economies in transition	24 871	0.01	_	0.04
Developing economies	34 570 096	1.02	100.00	58.20
China	18 141 723	2.68	52.48	30.54
China, Hong Kong SAR	8 444 892	3.03	24.43	14.22
Malaysia	2 117 774	1.58	6.13	3.57
Korea, Republic of	1 507 473	0.56	4.36	2.54
Singapore	1 351 983	0.63	3.91	2.28
Indonesia	1 294 893	1.72	3.75	2.18
Thailand	675 811	0.65	1.95	1.14
China, Taiwan Province of	375 541	0.21	1.09	0.63
Mexico	369 415	0.18	1.07	0.62
United Arab Emirates	134 137	0.14	0.39	0.23
764 - Telecommunicate equipment part nes				
World	324 624 671	3.37	_	100.0
Developed economies	161 139 194	2.73	_	49.64
Economies in transition	1 037 171	0.29	_	0.32
Developing economies	162 448 306	4.81	100.00	50.04
China	53 157 660	7.84	32.72	16.38
Korea, Republic of	32 203 789	11.97	19.82	9.92
China, Hong Kong SAR	27 280 976	9.78	16.79	8.40
Singapore	12 384 098	5.78	7.62	3.81
Mexico	10 994 239	5.47	6.77	3.39
China, Taiwan Province of	8 368 632	4.61	5.15	2.58
Malaysia	7 037 271	5.26	4.33	2.17
Thailand	2 837 848	2.75	1.75	0.87
United Arab Emirates	2 183 531	2.28	1.34	0.67
Brazil	2 073 469	1.96	1.28	0.64
771 - Electric power machine part excl. 716				
World	43 638 672	0.45	_	100.0
Developed economies	21 216 140	0.36	_	48.62
Economies in transition	569 713	0.16	_	1.31
Developing economies	21 852 819	0.65	100.00	50.08
China	7 754 896	1.14	35.49	17.77
China, Hong Kong SAR	5 480 020	1.97	25.08	12.56
Mexico	1 911 098	0.95	8.75	4.38
China, Taiwan Province of	1 568 213	0.86	7.18	3.59
Singapore	1 175 546	0.55	5.38	2.69
Korea, Republic of	1 047 714	0.39	4.79	2.40
Thailand	777 310	0.75	3.56	1.78
Malaysia	471 623	0.35	2.16	1.08
Indonesia	321 302	0.43	1.47	0.74
India	285 074	0.31	1.30	0.65
772 - Electrical circuit equipment				
World	134 898 142	1.40	_	100.0
Developed economies	84 182 593	1.42	_	62.40
Economies in transition	1 053 379	0.30	_	0.78
Developing economies	49 662 169	1.47	100.00	36.81
China	9 674 809	1.43	19.48	7.17
China, Hong Kong SAR	9 170 862	3.29	18.47	6.80
China, Taiwan Province of	6 191 870	3.41	12.47	4.59
Mexico	5 482 617	2.73	11.04	4.06
Malaysia	4 850 601	3.63	9.77	3.60
Singapore	4 564 696	2.13	9.19	3.38
Thailand	2 729 818	2.65	5.50	2.02
Korea, Republic of	2 629 667	0.98	5.30	1.95
Indonesia	886 487	1.18	1.79	0.66
Viet Nam	620 600	1.97	1.25	0.46

Right panel

Leading exporting developing countries (1) based on average 2004-2005 exports (2) SITC Revision 3 (3-digit level) / Principaux pays en dévelopt exportateurs (1) d'après la moyenne des exportations de 2004-2005 (2) CTCI révision 3 (positions à 3 chiffres)	Value (f.o.b., thousands of dollars) Valeur (f.a.b., milliers de dollars)	2004-2005 As percentage En pourcentage of country total du total du pays	of developing countries des pays en dévelop pement	of world du monde
773 - Electrical distribute equipment nes				
World	57 433 810	0.60	_	100.0
Developed economies	33 067 644	0.56	_	57.58
Economies in transition	2 076 152	0.59	_	3.61
Developing economies	22 290 014	0.66	100.00	38.81
Mexico	7 028 965	3.50	31.53	12.24
China	4 532 403	0.67	20.33	7.89
China, Hong Kong SAR	1 804 521	0.65	8.10	3.14
Korea, Republic of	1 375 720	0.51	6.17	2.40
Philippines	833 435	2.06	3.74	1.45
China, Taiwan Province of	720 962	0.40	3.23	1.26
Thailand	689 843	0.67	3.09	1.20
Turkey	651 662	0.95	2.92	1.13
Tunisia	562 109	5.57	2.52	0.98
Malaysia	530 649	0.40	2.38	0.92
775 - Household equipment nes				
World	60 739 021	0.63	_	100.0
Developed economies	34 066 571	0.58	_	56.09
Economies in transition	973 797	0.28	_	1.60
Developing economies	25 698 654	0.76	100.00	42.31
China	11 620 048	1.71	45.22	19.13
Korea, Republic of	3 315 612	1.23	12.90	5.46
China, Hong Kong SAR	2 636 988	0.95	10.26	4.34
Mexico	1 882 158	0.94	7.32	3.10
Thailand	1 638 053	1.59	6.37	2.70
Turkey	1 528 293	2.24	5.95	2.52
Singapore	802 466	0.37	3.12	1.32
Malaysia	732 277	0.55	2.85	1.21
Brazil	394 431	0.37	1.53	0.65
United Arab Emirates	202 594	0.21	0.79	0.33
776 - Valves tubes; diodes, transistors				
World	351 934 233	3.65	_	100.0
Developed economies	153 287 820	2.59	_	43.56
Economies in transition	325 983	0.09	_	0.09
Developing economies	198 320 430	5.88	100.00	56.35
Singapore	51 162 444	23.89	25.80	14.54
China, Taiwan Province of	28 504 145	15.71	14.37	8.10
China, Hong Kong SAR	28 433 513	10.20	14.34	8.08
Korea, Republic of	25 967 070	9.65	13.09	7.38
Malaysia	23 630 931	17.67	11.92	6.71
China	18 298 335	2.70	9.23	5.20
Philippines	10 795 631	26.69	5.44	3.07
Thailand	6 429 936	6.23	3.24	1.83
Mexico	2 378 365	1.18	1.20	0.68
Indonesia	750 220	1.00	0.38	0.21
778 - Electrical machinery apparatus nes				
World	140 535 007	1.46	_	100.0
Developed economies	84 713 051	1.43	_	60.28
Economies in transition	1 085 896	0.31	_	0.77
Developing economies	54 736 061	1.62	100.00	38.95
China	15 087 741	2.23	27.56	10.74
China, Hong Kong SAR	7 421 263	2.66	13.56	5.28
China, Taiwan Province of	7 257 954	4.00	13.26	5.16
Mexico	6 830 411	3.40	12.48	4.86
Korea, Republic of	5 134 780	1.91	9.38	3.65
Singapore	4 310 956	2.01	7.88	3.07
Thailand	2 158 075	2.09	3.94	1.54
Malaysia	1 941 728	1.45	3.55	1.38
Philippines	1 295 008	3.20	2.37	0.92
Indonesia	997 135	1.33	1.82	0.71

For sources and notes, see end of table.   Pour les sources et les notes, se reporter à la fin du tableau.

3.2.E   **Exports structure by product**
Major exporters for leading products among
developing economies

3.2.E   **Structure des exportations par produits**
Principaux exportateurs de produits majeurs
parmi les économies en développement

Leading exporting developing countries (1) based on average 2004-2005 exports (2) SITC Revision 3 (3-digit level) / Principaux pays en dévelopt exportateurs (1) d'après la moyenne des exportations de 2004-2005 (2) CTCI révision 3 (positions à 3 chiffres)	2004-2005			
	Value (f.o.b., thousands of dollars) / Valeur (f.a.b., milliers de dollars)	As percentage / En pourcentage		
		of country total / du total du pays	of developing countries / des pays en dévelop pement	of world / du monde
781 - Passenger cars and race cars				
World	470 559 508	4.88	–	100.0
Developed economies	412 024 462	6.97	–	87.56
Economies in transition	1 133 601	0.32	–	0.24
Developing economies	57 401 445	1.70	100.00	12.20
Korea, Republic of	25 944 123	9.64	45.20	5.51
Mexico	12 622 555	6.28	21.99	2.68
Turkey	4 153 558	6.08	7.24	0.88
Brazil	3 873 457	3.67	6.75	0.82
South Africa	2 657 895	6.09	4.63	0.56
Thailand	1 644 637	1.59	2.87	0.35
China, Hong Kong SAR	1 252 993	0.45	2.18	0.27
United Arab Emirates	864 698	0.90	1.51	0.18
India	835 013	0.91	1.45	0.18
Argentina	740 569	1.99	1.29	0.16
782 - Goods and service vehicles				
World	84 619 241	0.88	–	100.0
Developed economies	65 188 329	1.10	–	77.04
Economies in transition	1 354 717	0.39	–	1.60
Developing economies	18 076 195	0.54	100.00	21.36
Mexico	6 911 794	3.44	38.24	8.17
Thailand	2 770 701	2.69	15.33	3.27
Turkey	2 375 723	3.48	13.14	2.81
Brazil	1 413 799	1.34	7.82	1.67
Korea, Republic of	1 404 027	0.52	7.77	1.66
Argentina	813 598	2.19	4.50	0.96
China	583 094	0.09	3.23	0.69
South Africa	390 925	0.90	2.16	0.46
United Arab Emirates	295 928	0.31	1.64	0.35
Singapore	275 553	0.13	1.52	0.33
784 - Motor vehicle parts and accessories				
World	223 312 541	2.32	–	100.0
Developed economies	184 034 962	3.11	–	82.41
Economies in transition	1 695 969	0.48	–	0.76
Developing economies	37 581 610	1.11	100.00	16.83
Mexico	9 054 952	4.50	24.09	4.05
Korea, Republic of	6 557 863	2.44	17.45	2.94
China	5 530 783	0.82	14.72	2.48
Brazil	2 978 227	2.82	7.92	1.33
China, Taiwan Province of	2 700 364	1.49	7.19	1.21
Thailand	1 776 568	1.72	4.73	0.80
Singapore	1 366 573	0.64	3.64	0.61
Turkey	1 364 988	2.00	3.63	0.61
Philippines	1 251 754	3.09	3.33	0.56
India	1 000 925	1.09	2.66	0.45
785 - Motorcycles, mopeds and cycles				
World	31 020 612	0.32	–	100.0
Developed economies	19 037 171	0.32	–	61.37
Economies in transition	114 774	0.03	–	0.37
Developing economies	11 868 666	0.35	100.00	38.26
China	5 556 076	0.82	46.81	17.91
China, Taiwan Province of	2 854 753	1.57	24.05	9.20
Thailand	706 323	0.68	5.95	2.28
India	457 836	0.50	3.86	1.48
Singapore	412 585	0.19	3.48	1.33
Viet Nam	314 537	1.00	2.65	1.01
China, Hong Kong SAR	276 227	0.10	2.33	0.89
Brazil	255 328	0.24	2.15	0.82
Indonesia	252 947	0.34	2.13	0.82
Malaysia	222 283	0.17	1.87	0.72

Leading exporting developing countries (1) based on average 2004-2005 exports (2) SITC Revision 3 (3-digit level) / Principaux pays en dévelopt exportateurs (1) d'après la moyenne des exportations de 2004-2005 (2) CTCI révision 3 (positions à 3 chiffres)	2004-2005			
	Value (f.o.b., thousands of dollars) / Valeur (f.a.b., milliers de dollars)	As percentage / En pourcentage		
		of country total / du total du pays	of developing countries / des pays en dévelop pement	of world / du monde
793 - Ships boats floating structures				
World	66 058 092	0.69	–	100.0
Developed economies	36 371 096	0.62	–	55.06
Economies in transition	2 594 204	0.74	–	3.93
Developing economies	27 092 791	0.80	100.00	41.01
Korea, Republic of	16 276 403	6.05	60.08	24.64
China	3 911 655	0.58	14.44	5.92
Turkey	963 426	1.41	3.56	1.46
Brazil	729 831	0.69	2.69	1.10
Singapore	662 830	0.31	2.45	1.00
China, Taiwan Province of	615 539	0.34	2.27	0.93
India	615 419	0.67	2.27	0.93
Nigeria	546 156	1.49	2.02	0.83
United Arab Emirates	526 345	0.55	1.94	0.80
Malaysia	504 258	0.38	1.86	0.76
821 - Furniture part; bedding furnishing				
World	94 096 503	0.98	–	100.0
Developed economies	59 742 940	1.01	–	63.49
Economies in transition	2 329 862	0.66	–	2.48
Developing economies	32 023 702	0.95	100.00	34.03
China	14 595 174	2.15	45.58	15.51
Mexico	4 373 233	2.17	13.66	4.65
Malaysia	1 963 433	1.47	6.13	2.09
Indonesia	1 762 694	2.35	5.50	1.87
Viet Nam	1 638 262	5.19	5.12	1.74
Thailand	1 241 699	1.20	3.88	1.32
China, Taiwan Province of	1 221 121	0.67	3.81	1.30
Brazil	976 576	0.93	3.05	1.04
China, Hong Kong SAR	709 190	0.25	2.21	0.75
Turkey	655 733	0.96	2.05	0.70
831 - Case bag: storage travel shopping				
World	22 604 053	0.23	–	100.0
Developed economies	8 728 767	0.15	–	38.62
Economies in transition	181 253	0.05	–	0.80
Developing economies	13 694 033	0.41	100.00	60.58
China	6 846 791	1.01	50.00	30.29
China, Hong Kong SAR	4 711 361	1.69	34.40	20.84
Viet Nam	529 950	1.68	3.87	2.34
India	501 049	0.55	3.66	2.22
Thailand	220 456	0.21	1.61	0.98
Singapore	146 949	0.07	1.07	0.65
Korea, Republic of	95 600	0.04	0.70	0.42
Mexico	89 667	0.04	0.65	0.40
Indonesia	79 327	0.11	0.58	0.35
Turkey	70 906	0.10	0.52	0.31
841 - Male clothing, woven				
World	49 101 899	0.51	–	100.0
Developed economies	15 696 648	0.27	–	31.97
Economies in transition	2 687 667	0.76	–	5.47
Developing economies	30 717 584	0.91	100.00	62.56
China	11 088 682	1.64	36.10	22.58
China, Hong Kong SAR	2 897 662	1.04	9.43	5.90
Mexico	2 292 058	1.14	7.46	4.67
Turkey	1 744 134	2.55	5.68	3.55
Viet Nam	1 370 046	4.34	4.46	2.79
India	1 360 913	1.49	4.43	2.77
Bangladesh	1 347 213	21.71	4.39	2.74
Indonesia	1 194 677	1.59	3.89	2.43
Tunisia	963 367	9.55	3.14	1.96
Morocco	690 623	6.72	2.25	1.41

For sources and notes, see end of table.

Pour les sources et les notes, se reporter à la fin du tableau.

3.2.E   Exports structure by product
Major exporters for leading products among
developing economies

3.2.E   Structure des exportations par produits
Principaux exportateurs de produits majeurs
parmi les économies en développement

3

Leading exporting developing countries (1) based on average 2004-2005 exports (2) SITC Revision 3 (3-digit level) / Principaux pays en dévelopt exportateurs (1) d'après la moyenne des exportations de 2004-2005 (2) CTCI révision 3 (positions à 3 chiffres)	Value (f.o.b., thousands of dollars) Valeur (f.a.b., milliers de dollars)	2004-2005		
		As percentage En pourcentage		
		of country total du total du pays	of developing countries des pays en dévelop pement	of world du monde
842 - Female clothing, woven				
World	60 839 837	0.63	_	100.0
Developed economies	18 942 225	0.32	_	31.13
Economies in transition	3 298 828	0.94	_	5.42
Developing economies	38 598 784	1.14	100.00	63.44
China	14 272 459	2.11	36.98	23.46
China, Hong Kong SAR	6 684 357	2.40	17.32	10.99
Turkey	2 741 072	4.01	7.10	4.51
India	2 671 967	2.92	6.92	4.39
Mexico	1 655 731	0.82	4.29	2.72
Indonesia	1 306 449	1.74	3.38	2.15
Viet Nam	1 242 996	3.94	3.22	2.04
Morocco	1 026 333	9.99	2.66	1.69
Sri Lanka	879 103	15.10	2.28	1.44
Thailand	645 622	0.63	1.67	1.06
844 - Female clothing, knitted crocheted				
World	25 569 962	0.27	_	100.0
Developed economies	6 320 962	0.11	_	24.72
Economies in transition	749 009	0.21	_	2.93
Developing economies	18 499 990	0.55	100.00	72.35
China	6 455 835	0.95	34.90	25.25
China, Hong Kong SAR	3 031 130	1.09	16.38	11.85
Turkey	1 315 815	1.93	7.11	5.15
Cambodia	784 795	26.42	4.24	3.07
India	663 424	0.72	3.59	2.59
Mexico	615 719	0.31	3.33	2.41
Viet Nam	469 385	1.49	2.54	1.84
Indonesia	408 898	0.54	2.21	1.60
China, Macao SAR	373 056	14.11	2.02	1.46
Sri Lanka	365 099	6.27	1.97	1.43
845 - Articles of apparel nes				
World	87 624 599	0.91	_	100.0
Developed economies	29 216 334	0.49	_	33.34
Economies in transition	1 987 620	0.56	_	2.27
Developing economies	56 420 645	1.67	100.00	64.39
China	20 849 732	3.08	36.95	23.79
China, Hong Kong SAR	9 896 716	3.55	17.54	11.29
Turkey	4 236 115	6.20	7.51	4.83
Mexico	2 144 426	1.07	3.80	2.45
Bangladesh	1 989 948	32.07	3.53	2.27
India	1 561 172	1.70	2.77	1.78
Viet Nam	1 526 317	4.84	2.71	1.74
Tunisia	1 442 726	14.30	2.56	1.65
Thailand	1 338 679	1.30	2.37	1.53
Indonesia	1 207 760	1.61	2.14	1.38
848 - Headgear, non-textile clothing				
World	19 944 523	0.21	_	100.0
Developed economies	5 698 947	0.10	_	28.57
Economies in transition	157 873	0.04	_	0.79
Developing economies	14 087 703	0.42	100.00	70.63
China	7 666 955	1.13	54.42	38.44
China, Hong Kong SAR	1 691 084	0.61	12.00	8.48
Malaysia	1 188 150	0.89	8.43	5.96
Thailand	583 832	0.57	4.14	2.93
Pakistan	523 073	3.55	3.71	2.62
India	516 339	0.56	3.67	2.59
Turkey	388 856	0.57	2.76	1.95
China, Taiwan Province of	270 730	0.15	1.92	1.36
Korea, Republic of	259 837	0.10	1.84	1.30
Indonesia	185 643	0.25	1.32	0.93

Leading exporting developing countries (1) based on average 2004-2005 exports (2) SITC Revision 3 (3-digit level) / Principaux pays en dévelopt exportateurs (1) d'après la moyenne des exportations de 2004-2005 (2) CTCI révision 3 (positions à 3 chiffres)	Value (f.o.b., thousands of dollars) Valeur (f.a.b., milliers de dollars)	2004-2005		
		As percentage En pourcentage		
		of country total du total du pays	of developing countries des pays en dévelop pement	of world du monde
851 - Footwear				
World	64 642 253	0.67	_	100.0
Developed economies	25 468 303	0.43	_	39.40
Economies in transition	2 573 550	0.73	_	3.98
Developing economies	36 600 400	1.08	100.00	56.62
China	17 127 558	2.53	46.80	26.50
China, Hong Kong SAR	5 921 391	2.12	16.18	9.16
Viet Nam	5 002 181	15.85	13.67	7.74
Brazil	1 939 091	1.84	5.30	3.00
Indonesia	1 374 498	1.83	3.76	2.13
India	949 627	1.04	2.59	1.47
Thailand	826 176	0.80	2.26	1.28
Korea, Republic of	490 881	0.18	1.34	0.76
Tunisia	435 452	4.32	1.19	0.67
China, Taiwan Province of	386 794	0.21	1.06	0.60
871 - Optical instruments apparatus nes				
World	38 644 092	0.40	_	100.0
Developed economies	10 665 883	0.18	_	27.60
Economies in transition	116 827	0.03	_	0.30
Developing economies	27 861 383	0.83	100.00	72.10
China, Taiwan Province of	10 032 665	5.53	36.01	25.96
China	9 436 514	1.39	33.87	24.42
Korea, Republic of	5 803 745	2.16	20.83	15.02
China, Hong Kong SAR	1 682 503	0.60	6.04	4.35
Singapore	684 922	0.32	2.46	1.77
Thailand	65 291	0.06	0.23	0.17
Malaysia	34 652	0.03	0.12	0.09
Mexico	29 769	0.01	0.11	0.08
Viet Nam	15 310	0.05	0.05	0.04
Côte d'Ivoire	12 308	0.18	0.04	0.03
874 - Measure analyze control device nes				
World	107 402 096	1.11	_	100.0
Developed economies	91 153 234	1.54	_	84.87
Economies in transition	1 116 586	0.32	_	1.04
Developing economies	15 132 277	0.45	100.00	14.09
Mexico	2 770 020	1.38	18.31	2.58
China	2 737 627	0.40	18.09	2.55
Singapore	2 343 565	1.09	15.49	2.18
China, Hong Kong SAR	2 282 558	0.82	15.08	2.13
Malaysia	1 768 425	1.32	11.69	1.65
Korea, Republic of	922 828	0.34	6.10	0.86
China, Taiwan Province of	806 310	0.44	5.33	0.75
Thailand	270 284	0.26	1.79	0.25
Brazil	190 371	0.18	1.26	0.18
India	171 479	0.19	1.13	0.16
893 - Articles of plastic nes				
World	80 807 762	0.84	_	100.0
Developed economies	54 545 173	0.92	_	67.50
Economies in transition	617 783	0.18	_	0.76
Developing economies	25 644 806	0.76	100.00	31.74
China	10 226 959	1.51	39.88	12.66
China, Hong Kong SAR	3 014 768	1.08	11.76	3.73
China, Taiwan Province of	2 325 938	1.28	9.07	2.88
Mexico	2 246 144	1.12	8.76	2.78
Korea, Republic of	1 286 287	0.48	5.02	1.59
Thailand	1 075 057	1.04	4.19	1.33
Malaysia	1 008 365	0.75	3.93	1.25
Singapore	748 578	0.35	2.92	0.93
Turkey	607 165	0.89	2.37	0.75
India	392 418	0.43	1.53	0.49

For sources and notes, see end of table.

Pour les sources et les notes, se reporter à la fin du tableau.

3.2.E   Exports structure by product
Major exporters for leading products among developing economies

3.2.E   Structure des exportations par produits
Principaux exportateurs de produits majeurs parmi les économies en développement

Table 1 (left)

Leading exporting developing countries (1) based on average 2004-2005 exports (2) SITC Revision 3 (3-digit level) / Principaux pays en dévelopt exportateurs (1) d'après la moyenne des exportations de 2004-2005 (2) CTCI révision 3 (positions à 3 chiffres)	2004-2005		
	Value (f.o.b., thousands of dollars) Valeur (f.a.b., milliers de dollars)	of country total du total du pays	of developing countries des pays en développement	of world du monde
894 - Baby carriage toy game sport good			
World	60 431 477	0.63	_	100.0
Developed economies	24 240 460	0.41	_	40.11
Economies in transition	331 525	0.09	_	0.55
Developing economies	35 859 492	1.06	100.00	59.34
China	18 498 715	2.73	51.59	30.61
China, Hong Kong SAR	11 720 327	4.20	32.68	19.39
China, Taiwan Province of	1 852 442	1.02	5.17	3.07
Thailand	644 043	0.62	1.80	1.07
Mexico	629 401	0.31	1.76	1.04
Korea, Republic of	444 344	0.17	1.24	0.74
Singapore	370 396	0.17	1.03	0.61
Pakistan	316 702	2.15	0.88	0.52
Malaysia	257 252	0.19	0.72	0.43
Indonesia	251 872	0.34	0.70	0.42
897 - Jewellery nes (667)			
World	37 576 659	0.39	_	100.0
Developed economies	19 451 131	0.33	_	51.76
Economies in transition	441 024	0.13	_	1.17
Developing economies	17 684 504	0.52	100.00	47.06
China, Hong Kong SAR	3 862 551	1.39	21.84	10.28
India	3 739 832	4.08	21.15	9.95
China	2 548 762	0.38	14.41	6.78
Thailand	1 604 744	1.56	9.07	4.27
Turkey	1 067 438	1.56	6.04	2.84
Malaysia	866 925	0.65	4.90	2.31
Singapore	733 911	0.34	4.15	1.95
Korea, Republic of	646 349	0.24	3.65	1.72
Mexico	581 118	0.29	3.29	1.55
United Arab Emirates	522 147	0.55	2.95	1.39
898 - Music instrument device recording			
World	47 409 721	0.49	_	100.0
Developed economies	32 494 671	0.55	_	68.54
Economies in transition	151 574	0.04	_	0.32
Developing economies	14 763 477	0.44	100.00	31.14
China, Taiwan Province of	3 775 193	2.08	25.57	7.96
Singapore	2 870 920	1.34	19.45	6.06
China	2 577 469	0.38	17.46	5.44
Korea, Republic of	1 479 132	0.55	10.02	3.12
China, Hong Kong SAR	1 030 344	0.37	6.98	2.17
Malaysia	876 420	0.66	5.94	1.85
Mexico	672 606	0.33	4.56	1.42
Thailand	358 538	0.35	2.43	0.76
Indonesia	352 012	0.47	2.38	0.74
India	316 126	0.35	2.14	0.67

Table 2 (right)

Leading exporting developing countries (1) based on average 2004-2005 exports (2) SITC Revision 3 (3-digit level) / Principaux pays en dévelopt exportateurs (1) d'après la moyenne des exportations de 2004-2005 (2) CTCI révision 3 (positions à 3 chiffres)	2004-2005		
	Value (f.o.b., thousands of dollars) Valeur (f.a.b., milliers de dollars)	of country total du total du pays	of developing countries des pays en développement	of world du monde
899 - Manufactured articles nes			
World	42 152 357	0.44	_	100.0
Developed economies	29 155 658	0.49	_	69.17
Economies in transition	136 962	0.04	_	0.32
Developing economies	12 859 737	0.38	100.00	30.51
China	6 295 621	0.93	48.96	14.94
China, Hong Kong SAR	2 388 899	0.86	18.58	5.67
Mexico	592 719	0.29	4.61	1.41
Singapore	577 006	0.27	4.49	1.37
China, Taiwan Province of	509 192	0.28	3.96	1.21
Korea, Republic of	448 555	0.17	3.49	1.06
Indonesia	288 563	0.38	2.24	0.68
Thailand	247 338	0.24	1.92	0.59
Viet Nam	238 494	0.76	1.85	0.57
India	206 401	0.23	1.61	0.49
931 - Transaction commodity unclassified			
World	283 547 938	2.94	_	100.0
Developed economies	199 065 322	3.37	_	70.21
Economies in transition	42 020 943	11.94	_	14.82
Developing economies	42 461 673	1.26	100.00	14.98
United Arab Emirates	13 457 752	14.06	31.69	4.75
Singapore	7 432 334	3.47	17.50	2.62
Philippines	7 011 195	17.33	16.51	2.47
Iran, Islamic Republic of	2 983 676	5.70	7.03	1.05
Qatar	2 318 050	10.43	5.46	0.82
Malaysia	1 720 211	1.29	4.05	0.61
Thailand	1 548 879	1.50	3.65	0.55
China	1 356 452	0.20	3.19	0.48
China, Taiwan Province of	986 350	0.54	2.32	0.35
India	946 534	1.03	2.23	0.33
971 - Gold non-monetary excluding ores			
World	37 332 848	0.39	_	100.0
Developed economies	16 904 267	0.29	_	45.28
Economies in transition	690 808	0.20	_	1.85
Developing economies	19 737 773	0.58	100.00	52.87
China, Hong Kong SAR	4 576 199	1.64	23.18	12.26
United Arab Emirates	3 743 026	3.91	18.96	10.03
Peru	2 716 376	18.39	13.76	7.28
Korea, Republic of	1 624 448	0.60	8.23	4.35
Singapore	717 157	0.33	3.63	1.92
Colombia	601 220	3.17	3.05	1.61
Mali	545 890	51.14	2.77	1.46
United Republic of Tanzania	505 108	35.07	2.56	1.35
Brazil	435 847	0.41	2.21	1.17
Malaysia	395 555	0.30	2.00	1.06

Sources:
- UNCTAD secretariat calculations based on UN DESA Statistics Division's data

Notes:
(1) In addition, presented for each product group are the world total exports, the exports from developed, economies in transition and developing economies.
(2) Commodity groups are selected on the basis of ranking by value presented in table 3.2C.

Sources :
- Calculs du secrétariat de la CNUCED sur la base des données de ONU DAES Division de statistique

Notes :
(1) Les exportations mondiales totales, les exportations des économies développées, en transition et en développement sont également présentées pour chaque groupe de produits.
(2) Les groupes de produits sont sélectionnés d'après le classement par valeur présenté dans le tableau 3.2C.

SITC group Revision 3 (3-digit level) (1) Groupes de la CTCI Révision 3 (positions à 3 chiffres) (1)	Concentration index (2) Indice de concentration (2)			Structural change index (3) Indice de changement structurel (3) 1995=0	
	1995	2000	2005	2000	2005
264 Jute, other textile bast fibres n.e.s., raw, processed, not spun; waste of	0.830	0.865	0.849	0.063	0.071
261 Silk	0.592	0.744	0.806	0.233	0.300
345 Coal gas, water gas, producer gas, similar gas (exclude other gas hydrocarbons)	0.525	0.553	0.736	0.394	0.541
286 Uranium or thorium ores and concentrates	0.616	0.690	0.700	0.248	0.257
633 Cork manufactures	0.644	0.612	0.609	0.056	0.074
244 Cork, natural, raw and waste (including natural cork in blocks or sheets)	0.587	0.518	0.607	0.111	0.098
883 Cinematographic film, exposed developed, whether or not incorporating soundtrack	0.321	0.307	0.543	0.310	0.508
422 Fixed vegetable fats and oils, crude, refined or fractionated, other than "soft"	0.492	0.451	0.483	0.194	0.287
231 Natural rubber, balata, gutta-percha, guayule, chicle, natural gums	0.441	0.456	0.479	0.124	0.138
044 Maize (not including sweet corn), unmilled	0.688	0.549	0.462	0.198	0.269
896 Works of art, collectors' pieces and antiques	0.398	0.445	0.454	0.119	0.161
344 Petroleum gases and other gaseous hydrocarbons, n.e.s.	0.366	0.389	0.449	0.346	0.431
885 Watches & clocks	0.376	0.397	0.435	0.081	0.165
792 Aircraft, associated equipment; spacecraft, satellites, launch vehicles; parts	0.403	0.437	0.428	0.135	0.157
891 Arms and ammunition	0.548	0.476	0.415	0.267	0.254
283 Copper ores and concentrates; copper mattes; cement copper	0.355	0.414	0.410	0.205	0.224
281 Iron ore and concentrates	0.372	0.409	0.399	0.076	0.151
325 Coke, semi-coke of coal, lignite, peat, agglomerated or not; retort carbon	0.333	0.417	0.392	0.200	0.253
222 Oil-seed, oleaginous fruit for soft fixed vegetable oils (exclude flours, meals)	0.471	0.428	0.391	0.158	0.295
045 Cereals, unmilled (excluding wheat, rice, barley, maize)	0.436	0.485	0.387	0.140	0.176
263 Cotton	0.353	0.292	0.386	0.220	0.230
265 Vegetable textile fibre (exclu cotton, jute), raw, processed, not spun; waste of	0.384	0.432	0.384	0.132	0.173
551 Essential oils, perfume and flavour materials	0.238	0.267	0.384	0.179	0.330
871 Optical instruments and apparatus, n.e.s.	0.320	0.315	0.384	0.234	0.550
267 Other man-made fibres suitable for spinning; waste of man-made fibres	0.409	0.389	0.380	0.091	0.149
848 Apparel articles accessories other than textile fabrics; headgear (all material)	0.239	0.279	0.378	0.101	0.213
321 Coal, whether or not pulverized, excluding agglomerated	0.343	0.347	0.375	0.146	0.228
285 Aluminium ores and concentrates (including alumina)	0.355	0.369	0.375	0.119	0.156
212 Furskins, raw, other than hides and skins of group 211	0.351	0.364	0.373	0.184	0.229
274 Sulphur and unroasted iron pyrites	0.388	0.354	0.372	0.222	0.262
763 Sound or television image recorder reproducer; prepared unrecorded media	0.295	0.363	0.372	0.210	0.415
714 Engines, motors, non-electric (exclude group 712, 713 and 718); parts of, n.e.s.	0.366	0.378	0.365	0.085	0.120
583 Plastic monofilament, cross-section > 1 mm, rods, sticks, profile shapes	0.378	0.355	0.364	0.128	0.160
831 Cases bags(storage hand executive equipment instrument gun travel shopping back)	0.350	0.353	0.362	0.099	0.216
268 Wool and other animal hair (including wool tops)	0.366	0.401	0.362	0.143	0.152
525 Radio-actives and associated materials	0.353	0.375	0.356	0.152	0.228
726 Printing and bookbinding machinery, and parts thereof	0.337	0.328	0.354	0.053	0.125
272 Fertilizers, crude (excluding those of division 56)	0.324	0.342	0.354	0.232	0.178
961 Coin (other than gold coin), not being legal tender	0.584	0.887	0.351	0.900	0.376
666 Pottery	0.226	0.282	0.348	0.168	0.290
894 Baby carriages, toys, games and sporting goods	0.295	0.329	0.348	0.112	0.235
786 Trailers semi-trailers vehicles not mechanically-propelled; transport containers	0.232	0.289	0.344	0.194	0.245
881 Photographic apparatus and equipment, n.e.s.	0.351	0.327	0.338	0.151	0.219
284 Nickel ores, concentrates; mattes, oxide sinters, intermediate product of	0.391	0.377	0.338	0.232	0.255
712 Steam turbines and other vapour turbines, and parts thereof, n.e.s.	0.338	0.335	0.333	0.220	0.264
774 Electrodiagnostic apparatus, medical surgical dental veterinary radiological	0.350	0.347	0.331	0.118	0.096
613 Furskin, tanned, dressed, unassembled, assembled (without other materials)	0.221	0.249	0.330	0.226	0.403
751 Office machines	0.278	0.281	0.324	0.129	0.373
687 Tin	0.268	0.301	0.324	0.256	0.344
731 Machine tools working by removing metal or other material	0.356	0.345	0.324	0.059	0.032
247 Wood in the rough or roughly squared	0.273	0.245	0.323	0.232	0.230
292 Crude vegetable materials, n.e.s.	0.325	0.298	0.322	0.095	0.038
042 Rice	0.321	0.300	0.322	0.163	0.139
593 Explosives and pyrotechnic products	0.267	0.297	0.321	0.228	0.225
658 Made-up articles, wholly or chiefly of textile materials, n.e.s.	0.193	0.207	0.320	0.131	0.262
072 Cocoa	0.311	0.322	0.312	0.140	0.087
223 Oil-seed, oleaginous fruit to extract other vegetable oil; flour, meal of n.e.s.	0.280	0.185	0.309	0.301	0.401
016 Meat, edible meat offal (salted dried); flours, meals	0.342	0.330	0.308	0.114	0.186
322 Briquettes, lignites and peat	0.356	0.371	0.308	0.214	0.262
041 Wheat (including spelt) and meslin, unmilled	0.370	0.335	0.308	0.159	0.200
696 Cutlery	0.231	0.248	0.303	0.215	0.324
289 Ores and concentrates of precious metals; waste of (excluding gold)	0.323	0.331	0.302	0.391	0.277
683 Nickel	0.279	0.279	0.300	0.147	0.138
667 Pearls and precious or semiprecious stones, unworked or worked	0.320	0.314	0.300	0.119	0.161
662 Clay construction materials and refractory construction materials	0.339	0.351	0.300	0.119	0.226
681 Silver, platinum, other metals of the platinum group	0.250	0.314	0.300	0.232	0.347

For sources and notes, see end of table 3.3 Imports.

Pour les sources et les notes, se reporter à la fin du tableau 3.3 Importations.

SITC group Revision 3 (3-digit level) (1) Groupes de la CTCI Révision 3 (positions à 3 chiffres) (1)	Concentration index (2) Indice de concentration (2)			Structural change index (3) Indice de changement structurel (3) 1995=0	
	1995	2000	2005	2000	2005
343 Natural gas, whether or not liquefied	0.377	0.317	0.297	0.200	0.425
851 Footwear	0.250	0.264	0.297	0.153	0.279
431 Animal, vegetable fats, oils, processed; waxes; inedible preparations of, n.e.s.	0.274	0.264	0.296	0.193	0.205
597 Prepared additives: mineral oil; transmission; anti-freeze, de-ice; lubricating	0.310	0.310	0.295	0.100	0.122
785 Motor cycles, mopeds, cycles, motorized and non-motorized; invalid carriages	0.344	0.333	0.292	0.118	0.238
515 Organo-inorganic and heterocyclic compounds, nucleic acids-salts, sulphonamides	0.238	0.323	0.291	0.230	0.223
793 Ships, boats (including hovercraft) and floating structures	0.312	0.306	0.289	0.159	0.302
752 Automatic data-processing transcibing machines; magnetic optical readers, n.e.s.	0.256	0.215	0.289	0.202	0.435
043 Barley, unmilled	0.282	0.329	0.289	0.176	0.311
689 Miscellaneous non-ferrous base metals employed in metallurgy, and cermets	0.213	0.199	0.289	0.191	0.285
211 Hides and skins (except furskins), raw	0.269	0.287	0.286	0.134	0.190
882 Photographic and cinematographic supplies	0.296	0.289	0.283	0.108	0.146
884 Optical goods, n.e.s.	0.259	0.285	0.281	0.165	0.173
748 Transmission shaft camshaft crankshaft; bearing housing; gearbox speed changer	0.316	0.285	0.281	0.095	0.137
745 Non-electrical machinery, tools and mechanical apparatus, parts thereof, n.e.s.	0.302	0.281	0.280	0.098	0.105
813 Lighting fixtures and fittings, n.e.s.	0.214	0.232	0.279	0.140	0.258
654 Other textile fabrics, woven n.e.s.	0.299	0.254	0.278	0.146	0.183
579 Waste, parings and scrap, of plastics	0.412	0.314	0.276	0.203	0.234
251 Pulp and waste paper	0.349	0.340	0.276	0.101	0.138
874 Measuring, checking, analysing and controlling instruments and apparatus, n.e.s.	0.307	0.328	0.275	0.100	0.117
781 Vehicles to transport less than 10 persons, including station-wagons race cars	0.289	0.284	0.274	0.085	0.116
697 Household equipment of base metal, n.e.s.	0.189	0.200	0.271	0.132	0.295
722 Tractors (excluding headings 714.14 & 744.15)	0.306	0.292	0.270	0.108	0.145
846 Clothing accessories of textiles, knitted or crocheted or not (exluding babies)	0.216	0.221	0.267	0.161	0.250
652 Cotton fabrics, woven (not including narrow or special fabrics)	0.202	0.205	0.266	0.108	0.179
655 Knitted, crocheted fabric (include tubular knit, pile, openwork fabric), n.e.s.	0.256	0.265	0.266	0.121	0.252
524 Other inorganic chemicals; organic and inorganic compounds of precious metals	0.219	0.229	0.263	0.244	0.219
122 Tobacco, manufactured (whether or not containing tobacco substitutes)	0.307	0.293	0.262	0.162	0.399
351 Electric current	0.483	0.365	0.262	0.301	0.341
728 Other machinery or specialized industrial equipment; parts thereof, n.e.s.	0.284	0.302	0.261	0.114	0.085
025 Eggs, birds', yolks, fresh, dried, preserved, sweetened or not; albumin	0.343	0.308	0.261	0.132	0.189
845 Articles of apparel, textile fabrics, knitted or crocheted or not, n.e.s.	0.203	0.207	0.261	0.143	0.232
342 Liquefied propane and butane	0.232	0.249	0.261	0.198	0.230
248 Wood, simply worked, and railway sleepers of wood	0.319	0.328	0.260	0.148	0.198
725 Paper mill pulp mill paper-cutting other paper manufacture machines; parts of	0.262	0.256	0.260	0.074	0.130
843 Men's textile, knitted (coat suit trouser short shirt underwear nightwear)	0.170	0.187	0.258	0.182	0.326
121 Tobacco, unmanufactured; tobacco refuse	0.291	0.262	0.257	0.125	0.234
553 Perfumery, cosmetic or toilet preparations (excluding soaps)	0.319	0.274	0.257	0.112	0.149
733 Machine tool to work metal sintered metal carbide cermet, not removing material	0.288	0.259	0.256	0.089	0.156
074 Tea and maté	0.251	0.288	0.255	0.159	0.177
742 Liquid pump, with without a fitted measuring device; liquid elevator; parts for	0.300	0.287	0.255	0.101	0.155
724 Textile and leather machinery, and parts thereof, n.e.s.	0.317	0.273	0.254	0.107	0.169
112 Alcoholic beverages	0.290	0.281	0.253	0.105	0.141
653 Fabrics, woven, of man-made textiles (excluding narrow or special fabrics)	0.228	0.202	0.253	0.138	0.298
762 Radio-broadcast receivers, with without sound-recording reproducing or clock	0.275	0.254	0.252	0.168	0.314
842 Women's textiles not knitted (articles as code 841, plus dresses skirts)	0.208	0.199	0.252	0.156	0.227
931 Special transactions and commodities not classified according to kind	0.319	0.284	0.251	0.277	0.283
727 Food-processing machines (excluding domestic); parts thereof	0.257	0.247	0.251	0.080	0.102
541 Medicinal and pharmaceutical products, excluding medicines of group 542	0.236	0.243	0.250	0.107	0.121
735 Parts, n.e.s. and accessories for machines of groups 731, 733; tool holder	0.279	0.298	0.249	0.124	0.136
783 Road motor vehicles, n.e.s.	0.302	0.263	0.249	0.150	0.205
721 Agricultural machinery (excluding tractors), and parts thereof	0.270	0.272	0.248	0.062	0.105
872 Instruments and appliances, n.e.s., (medical, surgical, dental or veterinary)	0.274	0.276	0.248	0.116	0.174
037 Fish, crustaceans, molluscs, aquatic invertebrates (prepared preserved) n.e.s.	0.187	0.237	0.247	0.173	0.249
024 Cheese and curd	0.304	0.266	0.245	0.100	0.144
723 Civil engineering and contractors' plant and equipment; parts thereof	0.293	0.287	0.245	0.076	0.118
791 Railway vehicles (including hovertrains) and associated equipment	0.245	0.233	0.243	0.188	0.260
844 Women's textiles, knitted (articles as code 841, plus dresses skirts)	0.184	0.199	0.243	0.183	0.316
287 Ores and concentrates of base metals, n.e.s.	0.225	0.230	0.243	0.153	0.249
659 Floor coverings, etc.	0.287	0.249	0.241	0.095	0.118
575 Other plastics, in primary forms	0.275	0.265	0.241	0.097	0.123
023 Butter and other fats and oils derived from milk	0.257	0.257	0.240	0.143	0.143
246 Wood in chips or particles and wood waste	0.331	0.312	0.240	0.150	0.349
266 Synthetic fibres suitable for spinning	0.249	0.263	0.240	0.112	0.190
713 Internal combustion piston engines, and parts thereof, n.e.s.	0.293	0.273	0.238	0.143	0.198
775 Household-type electrical and non-electrical equipment, n.e.s.	0.224	0.210	0.238	0.133	0.273

For sources and notes, see end of table 3.3 Imports.

Pour les sources et les notes, se reporter à la fin du tableau 3.3 Importations.

SITC group Revision 3 (3-digit level) (1) / Groupes de la CTCI Révision 3 (positions à 3 chiffres) (1)	Concentration index (2) / Indice de concentration (2)			Structural change index (3) / Indice de changement structurel (3) 1995=0	
	1995	2000	2005	2000	2005
531 Synthetic organic colouring matter and colour lakes, preparations based thereon	0.297	0.245	0.238	0.149	0.212
232 Synthetic rubber; reclaimed rubber; waste, parings, scrap of unhardened rubber	0.258	0.265	0.237	0.139	0.169
776 Thermionic cold cathode photo-cathode valves tubes; diodes, transistors	0.293	0.260	0.237	0.138	0.240
598 Miscellaneous chemical products, n.e.s.	0.263	0.257	0.236	0.109	0.117
421 Fixed vegetable fats and oils, "soft", crude, refined or fractionated	0.224	0.237	0.235	0.176	0.207
572 Polymers of styrene, in primary forms	0.235	0.234	0.235	0.129	0.168
047 Other cereal meals and flours	0.243	0.282	0.235	0.198	0.294
971 Gold, non-monetary (excluding gold ores and concentrates)	0.291	0.292	0.233	0.219	0.369
759 Parts, accessories for machines of groups 751, 752	0.252	0.211	0.233	0.190	0.318
542 Medicines (including veterinary medicines)	0.227	0.219	0.233	0.109	0.139
841 Men's textile, not knitted (coat suit trouser short shirt underwear nightwear)	0.185	0.188	0.232	0.148	0.223
685 Lead	0.218	0.220	0.231	0.206	0.192
611 Leather	0.216	0.236	0.229	0.101	0.194
873 Meters and counters, n.e.s.	0.259	0.259	0.229	0.186	0.259
291 Crude animal materials, nes	0.219	0.238	0.228	0.105	0.142
333 Petroleum oils and oils obtained from bituminous minerals, crude	0.219	0.200	0.227	0.137	0.206
771 Electric power machinery parts (excluding rotating electric plant, group 716)	0.191	0.200	0.227	0.148	0.214
746 Ball or roller bearings	0.270	0.246	0.227	0.104	0.138
718 Power-generating machinery, and parts thereof, n.e.s.	0.279	0.218	0.227	0.224	0.160
737 Metalworking machinery (other than machine tools), and parts thereof, n.e.s.	0.262	0.248	0.226	0.131	0.141
672 Ingots, other primary forms of iron or steel; semi-finished products of	0.210	0.230	0.226	0.160	0.196
761 Television receiver, video monitor projector, w wo radio video-record reproduce	0.204	0.227	0.225	0.259	0.361
694 Nails, screws, nuts, bolts, rivets, of iron, steel, copper or aluminium	0.230	0.235	0.224	0.083	0.120
061 Sugar, molasses and honey	0.197	0.185	0.224	0.201	0.298
411 Animals oils and fats	0.356	0.268	0.224	0.155	0.223
011 Meat of bovine animals (fresh chilled frozen)	0.240	0.266	0.224	0.195	0.299
747 Appliances for pipes boiler shells tanks vats; pressure and temperature valves	0.257	0.237	0.223	0.139	0.165
899 Miscellaneous manufactured articles, n.e.s.	0.225	0.220	0.223	0.125	0.233
035 Fish (dried, salted, in brine, smoked); flours, meals, pellets for human consump	0.272	0.232	0.223	0.171	0.236
511 Hydrocarbons, n.e.s., halogenated, sulphonated, nitrated, nitrosated derivatives	0.246	0.229	0.222	0.119	0.152
516 Other organic chemicals	0.225	0.215	0.222	0.110	0.179
612 Manufactures of leather or of composition leather, n.e.s.; saddlery and harness	0.194	0.205	0.222	0.185	0.365
523 Metallic salts and peroxysalts, of inorganic acids	0.231	0.243	0.222	0.114	0.203
782 Motor vehicles for the transport of goods and special-purpose motor vehicles	0.278	0.250	0.221	0.147	0.186
071 Coffee and coffee substitutes	0.188	0.185	0.219	0.139	0.211
743 Pump (non liquid), air gas compressor, fan ventilation filter; centrifuge; parts	0.243	0.240	0.219	0.105	0.152
812 Sanitary, plumbing and heating fixtures and fittings, n.e.s.	0.253	0.230	0.216	0.152	0.191
764 Telecommunications equipment and parts, n.e.s.; accessories within division 76	0.217	0.183	0.216	0.176	0.286
621 Materials of rubber (e.g., pastes, plates, sheets, rods, thread, tubes, of rubber)	0.241	0.230	0.216	0.119	0.135
591 Insecticide, rodenticide, fungicide, herbicide, plant-growth reg, disinfectant	0.255	0.241	0.215	0.123	0.188
269 Worn clothing and other worn textile articles; rags	0.258	0.227	0.215	0.137	0.257
677 Rails or railway track construction material, of iron or steel	0.217	0.224	0.214	0.185	0.215
784 Parts and accessories of the motor vehicles of groups 722, 781, 782 and 783	0.282	0.267	0.214	0.089	0.206
081 Feeding stuff for animals (excluding unmilled cereals)	0.231	0.238	0.214	0.134	0.144
562 Fertilizers (excluding group 272)	0.211	0.216	0.213	0.137	0.193
656 Tulles, lace, embroidery, ribbons, trimmings and other smallwares	0.195	0.203	0.213	0.147	0.219
277 Natural abrasives, n.e.s. (including industrial diamonds)	0.236	0.250	0.213	0.352	0.326
012 Other meat and edible meat offal (fresh chilled frozen)	0.223	0.220	0.212	0.149	0.270
054 Vegetables and veg products (fresh chilled frozen preserved dried edible) n e.s.	0.218	0.214	0.212	0.121	0.138
897 Jewellery, articles of goldsmiths' silversmiths' B2 semiprecious, n.e.s.	0.255	0.257	0.212	0.163	0.243
695 Tools for use in the hand or in machine	0.223	0.201	0.211	0.115	0.128
744 Mechanical handling equipment, and parts thereof, n.e.s.	0.237	0.228	0.211	0.118	0.132
022 Milk, cream and milk products (excluding butter, cheese)	0.267	0.234	0.210	0.124	0.192
892 Printed matter	0.237	0.228	0.209	0.099	0.124
671 Pig-iron, spiegeleisen, sponge iron, iron steel granules, powders, ferro-alloys	0.201	0.205	0.209	0.178	0.203
533 Pigments, paints, varnishes and related materials	0.223	0.216	0.208	0.106	0.095
111 Non-alcoholic beverages, n.e.s.	0.211	0.204	0.208	0.160	0.236
571 Polymers of ethylene, in primary forms	0.217	0.211	0.208	0.118	0.161
581 Tubes, pipes and hoses, and fittings therefor, of plastics	0.224	0.227	0.208	0.164	0.196
282 Ferrous waste and scrap; remelting scrap ingots of iron or steel	0.271	0.199	0.207	0.222	0.230
895 Office and stationery supplies, n.e.s.	0.234	0.222	0.207	0.122	0.211
001 Live animals other than animals of division 03	0.224	0.221	0.207	0.154	0.135
898 Musical instrument, parts accessory; tape, sound recording (excluding 763 & 883)	0.257	0.227	0.206	0.138	0.230
573 Polymers of vinyl chloride or of other halogenated olefins, in primary forms	0.215	0.194	0.205	0.187	0.159
056 Vegetables, roots and tubers (prepared preserved) n.e.s.	0.220	0.207	0.205	0.123	0.154
641 Paper and paperboard	0.226	0.218	0.205	0.066	0.113

For sources and notes, see end of table 3.3 Imports.

Pour les sources et les notes, se reporter à la fin du tableau 3.3 Importations.

SITC group Revision 3 (3-digit level) (1) Groupes de la CTCI Révision 3 (positions à 3 chiffres) (1)	Concentration index (2) Indice de concentration (2)			Structural change index (3) Indice de changement structurel (3) 1995=0	
	1995	2000	2005	2000	2005
749 Non-electric parts and accessories of machinery, n.e.s.	0.251	0.236	0.204	0.093	0.137
073 Chocolate and other food preparations containing cocoa, n.e.s.	0.240	0.216	0.203	0.139	0.175
582 Plates, sheets, film, foil and strip, of plastics	0.222	0.218	0.203	0.093	0.115
711 Steam vapour superheated water boiler, auxiliary plant for use with; parts of	0.245	0.217	0.201	0.207	0.265
821 Furniture and parts; bedding, mattresses, mattress supports, cushions	0.203	0.184	0.200	0.152	0.252
778 Electrical machinery and apparatus, n.e.s.	0.237	0.239	0.199	0.138	0.204
772 Electrical apparatus to switch protect circuits or make circuit connections	0.245	0.220	0.199	0.145	0.189
663 Mineral manufactures, n.e.s.	0.223	0.220	0.199	0.100	0.135
675 Flat-rolled products of alloy steel	0.270	0.226	0.198	0.157	0.226
513 Carboxylic acid, anhydrides, halides, peroxides, peroxyacids, halogenate; derivatives	0.240	0.215	0.198	0.141	0.255
514 Nitrogen-function compounds	0.242	0.223	0.197	0.097	0.229
592 Starches, inulin and wheat gluten; albuminoidal substances; glues	0.212	0.207	0.197	0.120	0.119
046 Meal and flour of wheat and flour of meslin	0.201	0.173	0.196	0.236	0.400
574 Polyacetal, polyether, epoxide resin; polycarbonate, alkyd resin, polyester	0.227	0.217	0.196	0.119	0.170
699 Manufactures of base metal, n.e.s.	0.202	0.209	0.194	0.132	0.158
741 Heating and cooling equipment, and parts thereof, n.e.s.	0.230	0.219	0.193	0.140	0.211
682 Copper	0.174	0.181	0.193	0.125	0.177
017 Meat, edible meat offal (prepared preserved) n.e.s.	0.190	0.187	0.193	0.160	0.242
048 Cereal preparations and preparations of flour or starch of fruits or vegetables	0.204	0.198	0.193	0.106	0.138
629 Articles of rubber, n.e.s.	0.231	0.222	0.191	0.130	0.160
634 Veneers, plywood, particle board, and other wood, worked, n.e.s.	0.240	0.209	0.190	0.160	0.304
059 Fruit and vegetable juice (unfermented, no added spirit, sweetened or not)	0.231	0.218	0.189	0.140	0.184
674 Flat-rolled products of iron or non-alloy steel, clad, plated or coated	0.224	0.206	0.189	0.154	0.201
716 Rotating electric plant, and parts thereof, n.e.s.	0.211	0.187	0.188	0.126	0.186
893 Articles, n.e.s., of plastics	0.183	0.196	0.187	0.146	0.174
664 Glass	0.216	0.211	0.187	0.113	0.146
288 Non-ferrous base metal waste and scrap, n.e.s.	0.209	0.185	0.187	0.156	0.231
532 Dyeing and tanning extracts, and synthetic tanning materials	0.223	0.201	0.186	0.140	0.205
554 Soaps, cleansing and polishing preparations	0.211	0.193	0.186	0.124	0.119
635 Wood manufactures, n.e.s.	0.145	0.155	0.185	0.153	0.241
657 Special yarns, special textile fabrics and related products	0.212	0.205	0.184	0.102	0.162
642 Paper and paperboard, cut to size or shape, and articles of paper or paperboard	0.201	0.191	0.184	0.119	0.168
335 Residual petroleum products, n.e.s., related mater.	0.273	0.225	0.184	0.146	0.202
661 Lime, cement, fabricated construction material (excluding glass, clay material)	0.202	0.194	0.183	0.161	0.288
091 Margarine and shortening	0.233	0.169	0.182	0.266	0.245
665 Glassware	0.209	0.134	0.182	0.127	0.213
522 Inorganic chemical elements, oxides and halogen salts	0.169	0.177	0.181	0.119	0.143
691 Structures and parts of structures, n.e.s., of iron, steel or aluminium	0.184	0.176	0.180	0.195	0.251
512 Alcohol, phenol, phenol-alcohol;halogenate, sulphonate, nitrate, nitrosate deriv	0.208	0.196	0.180	0.156	0.212
679 Tubes, pipes and hollow profiles, and tube or pipe fittings, of iron or steel	0.206	0.184	0.179	0.102	0.159
057 Fruits and nuts (excluding oil nuts), fresh or dried	0.190	0.178	0.178	0.109	0.125
686 Zinc	0.192	0.194	0.175	0.187	0.190
693 Wire products (excluding insulated electrical wiring) and fencing grills	0.174	0.171	0.175	0.156	0.189
625 Rubber tyres, interchangeable tyre treads, tyre flaps, inner tubes for wheels	0.200	0.190	0.174	0.102	0.181
651 Textile yarn	0.157	0.159	0.173	0.127	0.167
075 Spices	0.191	0.179	0.173	0.138	0.233
773 Equipment for distributing electricity, n.e.s.	0.197	0.209	0.171	0.134	0.225
278 Other crude minerals	0.193	0.213	0.171	0.111	0.139
098 Edible products and preparations, n.e.s.	0.220	0.192	0.169	0.181	0.208
673 Flat-rolled products of iron or non-alloy steel, not clad, plated or coated	0.180	0.180	0.168	0.122	0.152
058 Fruit, preserved, and fruit preparations (excluding fruit juices)	0.145	0.148	0.160	0.138	0.189
811 Prefabricated buildings	0.200	0.189	0.159	0.147	0.231
034 Fish, fresh (live dead chilled frozen)	0.158	0.153	0.159	0.134	0.173
692 Metal containers for storage or transport	0.198	0.169	0.158	0.129	0.177
678 Wire of iron or steel	0.170	0.170	0.158	0.126	0.171
684 Aluminium	0.166	0.159	0.153	0.093	0.132
676 Iron and steel bars, rods, angles, shapes and sections (including sheet piling)	0.165	0.160	0.151	0.111	0.162
273 Stone, sand and gravel	0.157	0.158	0.148	0.160	0.220
036 Crustaceans, mollusks and aquatic invertebrates	0.165	0.151	0.148	0.138	0.214
062 Sugar confectionery	0.150	0.146	0.142	0.188	0.193
334 Petroleum oil, oil from bituminous (excl crude); preparations, n.e.s., > 70% oil	0.144	0.129	0.142	0.143	0.199
245 Fuel wood (excluding wood waste) and wood charcoal	0.171	0.180	0.120	0.249	0.314

For sources and notes, see end of table 3.3 Imports.

Pour les sources et les notes, se reporter à la fin du tableau 3.3 Importations.

SITC group Revision 3 (3-digit level) (1) Groupes de la CTCI Révision 3 (positions à 3 chiffres) (1)	Concentration index (2) Indice de concentration (2)			Structural change index (3) Indice de changement structurel (3) 1995=0	
	1995	2000	2005	2000	2005
286 Uranium or thorium ores and concentrates	0.550	0.732	0.898	0.304	0.280
345 Coal gas, water gas, producer gas, similar gas (exclude other gas hydrocarbons)	0.722	0.249	0.604	0.766	0.434
871 Optical instruments and apparatus, n.e.s.	0.242	0.268	0.602	0.291	0.642
246 Wood in chips or particles and wood waste	0.735	0.722	0.532	0.055	0.232
883 Cinematographic film, exposed developed, whether or not incorporating soundtrack	0.316	0.366	0.528	0.213	0.368
244 Cork, natural, raw and waste (including natural cork in blocks or sheets)	0.358	0.462	0.522	0.238	0.289
579 Waste, parings and scrap, of plastics	0.472	0.424	0.507	0.255	0.362
896 Works of art, collectors' pieces and antiques	0.440	0.532	0.449	0.145	0.110
281 Iron ore and concentrates	0.274	0.275	0.445	0.117	0.369
261 Silk	0.306	0.321	0.436	0.203	0.372
613 Furskin, tanned, dressed, unassembled, assembled (without other materials)	0.296	0.307	0.406	0.311	0.401
212 Furskins, raw, other than hides and skins of group 211	0.291	0.356	0.403	0.190	0.299
016 Meat, edible meat offal (salted dried); flours, meals	0.518	0.408	0.393	0.166	0.191
289 Ores and concentrates of precious metals; waste of (excluding gold)	0.389	0.401	0.383	0.138	0.218
264 Jute, other textile bast fibres n.e.s., raw, processed, not spun; waste of	0.251	0.320	0.381	0.280	0.334
344 Petroleum gases and other gaseous hydrocarbons, n.e.s.	0.352	0.273	0.370	0.378	0.595
265 Vegetable textile fibre (exclu cotton, jute), raw, processed, not spun; waste of	0.211	0.240	0.369	0.225	0.397
274 Sulphur and unroasted iron pyrites	0.209	0.205	0.358	0.232	0.426
283 Copper ores and concentrates; copper mattes; cement copper	0.449	0.389	0.357	0.189	0.342
761 Television receiver, video monitor projector, w wo radio video-record reproduce	0.225	0.273	0.348	0.243	0.318
843 Men's textile, knitted (coat suit trouser short shirt underwear nightwear)	0.300	0.346	0.345	0.145	0.169
284 Nickel ores, concentrates; mattes, oxide sinters, intermediate product of	0.375	0.386	0.337	0.179	0.205
525 Radio-actives and associated materials	0.342	0.360	0.326	0.223	0.202
894 Baby carriages, toys, games and sporting goods	0.316	0.359	0.323	0.091	0.096
658 Made-up articles, wholly or chiefly of textile materials, n.e.s.	0.226	0.283	0.316	0.143	0.190
931 Special transactions and commodities not classified according to kind	0.364	0.405	0.315	0.218	0.271
821 Furniture and parts; bedding, mattresses, mattress supports, cushions	0.251	0.318	0.313	0.168	0.209
222 Oil-seed, oleaginous fruit for soft fixed vegetable oils (exclude flours, meals)	0.216	0.229	0.313	0.259	0.374
268 Wool and other animal hair (including wool tops)	0.235	0.294	0.309	0.178	0.269
036 Crustaceans, mollusks and aquatic invertebrates	0.422	0.370	0.301	0.127	0.223
848 Apparel articles accessories other than textile fabrics; headgear (all material)	0.293	0.357	0.300	0.138	0.138
844 Women's textiles, knitted (articles as code 841, plus dresses skirts)	0.293	0.312	0.300	0.150	0.153
667 Pearls and precious or semiprecious stones, unworked or worked	0.314	0.324	0.298	0.136	0.153
263 Cotton	0.165	0.152	0.294	0.240	0.378
897 Jewellery, articles of goldsmiths' silversmiths' B2 semiprecious, n.e.s.	0.291	0.328	0.294	0.144	0.154
842 Women's textiles not knitted (articles as code 841, plus dresses skirts)	0.297	0.342	0.290	0.126	0.166
248 Wood, simply worked, and railway sleepers of wood	0.263	0.287	0.289	0.156	0.216
841 Men's textile, not knitted (coat suit trouser short shirt underwear nightwear)	0.284	0.335	0.288	0.120	0.134
045 Cereals, unmilled (excluding wheat, rice, barley, maize)	0.270	0.339	0.288	0.259	0.225
681 Silver, platinum, other metals of the platinum group	0.300	0.343	0.288	0.199	0.199
813 Lighting fixtures and fittings, n.e.s.	0.221	0.306	0.284	0.158	0.183
211 Hides and skins (except furskins), raw	0.266	0.271	0.281	0.140	0.311
845 Articles of apparel, textile fabrics, knitted or crocheted or not, n.e.s.	0.279	0.318	0.280	0.127	0.153
635 Wood manufactures, n.e.s.	0.257	0.294	0.280	0.182	0.224
697 Household equipment of base metal, n.e.s.	0.213	0.277	0.280	0.140	0.170
762 Radio-broadcast receivers, with without sound-recording reproducing or clock	0.289	0.334	0.280	0.147	0.161
043 Barley, unmilled	0.198	0.232	0.278	0.252	0.241
831 Cases bags(storage hand executive equipment instrument gun travel shopping back)	0.316	0.311	0.272	0.089	0.161
961 Coin (other than gold coin), not being legal tender	0.362	0.915	0.272	0.897	0.475
515 Organo-inorganic and heterocyclic compounds, nucleic acids-salts, sulphonamides	0.193	0.314	0.271	0.200	0.179
342 Liquefied propane and butane	0.354	0.305	0.269	0.137	0.270
343 Natural gas, whether or not liquefied	0.301	0.292	0.267	0.191	0.319
763 Sound or television image recorder reproducer; prepared unrecorded media	0.306	0.389	0.267	0.139	0.131
971 Gold, non-monetary (excluding gold ores and concentrates)	0.218	0.245	0.267	0.327	0.521
689 Miscellaneous non-ferrous base metals employed in metallurgy, and cermets	0.279	0.267	0.266	0.094	0.124
247 Wood in the rough or roughly squared	0.355	0.266	0.265	0.267	0.388
112 Alcoholic beverages	0.215	0.275	0.264	0.141	0.163
851 Footwear	0.290	0.308	0.264	0.104	0.135
288 Non-ferrous base metal waste and scrap, n.e.s.	0.206	0.217	0.262	0.153	0.259
781 Vehicles to transport less than 10 persons, including station-wagons race cars	0.286	0.349	0.261	0.143	0.156
891 Arms and ammunition	0.199	0.245	0.261	0.269	0.318
633 Cork manufactures	0.259	0.259	0.258	0.125	0.151
037 Fish, crustaceans, molluscs, aquatic invertebrates (prepared preserved) n.e.s.	0.273	0.294	0.258	0.109	0.162
666 Pottery	0.298	0.317	0.257	0.090	0.148
572 Polymers of styrene, in primary forms	0.228	0.266	0.256	0.153	0.203
751 Office machines	0.262	0.222	0.255	0.119	0.115

For sources and notes, see end of table.

Pour les sources et les notes, se reporter à la fin du tableau.

SITC group Revision 3 (3-digit level) (1) / Groupes de la CTCI Révision 3 (positions à 3 chiffres) (1)	Concentration index (2) / Indice de concentration (2)			Structural change index (3) / Indice de changement structurel (3) 1995=0	
	1995	2000	2005	2000	2005
776 Thermionic cold cathode photo-cathode valves tubes; diodes, transistors	0.245	0.207	0.253	0.123	0.306
661 Lime, cement, fabricated construction material (excluding glass, clay material)	0.163	0.225	0.253	0.247	0.337
231 Natural rubber, balata, gutta-percha, guayule, chicle, natural gums	0.245	0.239	0.250	0.146	0.185
634 Veneers, plywood, particle board, and other wood, worked, n.e.s.	0.205	0.223	0.250	0.163	0.281
774 Electrodiagnostic apparatus, medical surgical dental veterinary radiological	0.202	0.231	0.246	0.131	0.173
333 Petroleum oils and oils obtained from bituminous minerals, crude	0.246	0.249	0.244	0.102	0.126
285 Aluminium ores and concentrates (including alumina)	0.240	0.224	0.242	0.131	0.270
017 Meat, edible meat offal (prepared preserved) n.e.s.	0.219	0.229	0.241	0.146	0.180
321 Coal, whether or not pulverized, excluding agglomerated	0.284	0.259	0.241	0.112	0.142
885 Watches & clocks	0.269	0.258	0.240	0.096	0.111
611 Leather	0.210	0.221	0.236	0.134	0.218
752 Automatic data-processing transcibing machines; magnetic optical readers, n.e.s.	0.263	0.265	0.235	0.092	0.151
251 Pulp and waste paper	0.204	0.198	0.234	0.115	0.225
659 Floor coverings, etc.	0.243	0.233	0.233	0.195	0.244
714 Engines, motors, non-electric (exclude group 712, 713 and 718); parts of, n.e.s.	0.257	0.290	0.233	0.134	0.148
881 Photographic apparatus and equipment, n.e.s.	0.236	0.261	0.233	0.145	0.250
593 Explosives and pyrotechnic products	0.175	0.201	0.231	0.180	0.253
351 Electric current	0.239	0.298	0.229	0.319	0.342
722 Tractors (excluding headings 714.14 & 744.15)	0.233	0.245	0.227	0.127	0.164
287 Ores and concentrates of base metals, n.e.s.	0.189	0.178	0.226	0.141	0.221
792 Aircraft, associated equipment; spacecraft, satellites, launch vehicles; parts	0.161	0.250	0.225	0.273	0.315
612 Manufactures of leather or of composition leather, n.e.s.; saddlery and harness	0.268	0.242	0.223	0.202	0.287
072 Cocoa	0.240	0.227	0.223	0.127	0.140
071 Coffee and coffee substitutes	0.241	0.247	0.222	0.099	0.102
058 Fruit, preserved, and fruit preparations (excluding fruit juices)	0.229	0.226	0.220	0.104	0.156
513 Carboxylic acid, anhydrides, halides, peroxides, peroxyacids, halogenate; derivatives	0.140	0.169	0.220	0.151	0.235
034 Fish, fresh (live dead chilled frozen)	0.313	0.282	0.219	0.102	0.180
322 Briquettes, lignites and peat	0.207	0.255	0.218	0.231	0.262
884 Optical goods, n.e.s.	0.234	0.239	0.218	0.125	0.296
784 Parts and accessories of the motor vehicles of groups 722, 781, 782 and 783	0.226	0.237	0.216	0.116	0.148
687 Tin	0.225	0.212	0.215	0.132	0.346
001 Live animals other than animals of division 03	0.214	0.233	0.214	0.165	0.205
846 Clothing accessories of textiles, knitted or crocheted or not (exluding babies)	0.190	0.206	0.212	0.185	0.198
512 Alcohol, phenol, phenol-alcohol;halogenate, sulphonate, nitrate, nitrosate deriv	0.160	0.168	0.212	0.158	0.259
713 Internal combustion piston engines, and parts thereof, n.e.s.	0.234	0.248	0.212	0.131	0.186
872 Instruments and appliances, n.e.s., (medical, surgical, dental or veterinary)	0.176	0.199	0.212	0.121	0.169
759 Parts, accessories for machines of groups 751, 752	0.257	0.235	0.210	0.135	0.240
785 Motor cycles, mopeds, cycles, motorized and non-motorized; invalid carriages	0.193	0.217	0.210	0.211	0.226
011 Meat of bovine animals (fresh chilled frozen)	0.238	0.235	0.210	0.188	0.237
025 Eggs, birds', yolks, fresh, dried, preserved, sweetened or not; albumin	0.256	0.194	0.208	0.159	0.174
899 Miscellaneous manufactured articles, n.e.s.	0.199	0.211	0.206	0.095	0.160
731 Machine tools working by removing metal or other material	0.208	0.219	0.205	0.139	0.206
873 Meters and counters, n.e.s.	0.233	0.253	0.205	0.120	0.158
683 Nickel	0.239	0.223	0.205	0.110	0.212
035 Fish (dried, salted, in brine, smoked); flours, meals, pellets for human consump	0.228	0.221	0.205	0.143	0.153
542 Medicines (including veterinary medicines)	0.134	0.154	0.204	0.148	0.163
782 Motor vehicles for the transport of goods and special-purpose motor vehicles	0.211	0.254	0.203	0.169	0.169
223 Oil-seed, oleaginous fruit to extract other vegetable oil; flour, meal of n.e.s.	0.193	0.188	0.202	0.210	0.338
325 Coke, semi-coke of coal, lignite, peat, agglomerated or not; retort carbon	0.179	0.205	0.201	0.250	0.246
541 Medicinal and pharmaceutical products, excluding medicines of group 542	0.164	0.187	0.200	0.132	0.151
771 Electric power machinery parts (excluding rotating electric plant, group 716)	0.184	0.225	0.199	0.143	0.166
696 Cutlery	0.198	0.224	0.198	0.138	0.182
044 Maize (not including sweet corn), unmilled	0.209	0.191	0.198	0.196	0.186
062 Sugar confectionery	0.151	0.193	0.198	0.166	0.182
694 Nails, screws, nuts, bolts, rivets, of iron, steel, copper or aluminium	0.208	0.216	0.197	0.128	0.144
122 Tobacco, manufactured (whether or not containing tobacco substitutes)	0.197	0.193	0.196	0.186	0.256
511 Hydrocarbons, n.e.s., halogenated, sulphonated, nitrated, nitrosated derivatives	0.166	0.168	0.196	0.158	0.178
671 Pig-iron, spiegeleisen, sponge iron, iron steel granules, powders, ferro-alloys	0.222	0.223	0.195	0.147	0.156
775 Household-type electrical and non-electrical equipment, n.e.s.	0.174	0.197	0.195	0.132	0.178
625 Rubber tyres, interchangeable tyre treads, tyre flaps, inner tubes for wheels	0.178	0.202	0.195	0.135	0.143
024 Cheese and curd	0.268	0.211	0.194	0.147	0.176
675 Flat-rolled products of alloy steel	0.159	0.174	0.193	0.154	0.233
733 Machine tool to work metal sintered metal carbide cermet, not removing material	0.170	0.202	0.193	0.212	0.242
551 Essential oils, perfume and flavour materials	0.138	0.152	0.193	0.153	0.227
764 Telecommunications equipment and parts, n.e.s.; accessories within division 76	0.180	0.204	0.193	0.147	0.145
023 Butter and other fats and oils derived from milk	0.259	0.221	0.192	0.155	0.224

For sources and notes, see end of table.

Pour les sources et les notes, se reporter à la fin du tableau.

SITC group Revision 3 (3-digit level) (1) / Groupes de la CTCI Révision 3 (positions à 3 chiffres) (1)		Concentration index (2) / Indice de concentration (2)			Structural change index (3) / Indice de changement structurel (3) 1995=0	
		1995	2000	2005	2000	2005
292	Crude vegetable materials, n.e.s.	0.217	0.203	0.192	0.115	0.127
056	Vegetables, roots and tubers (prepared preserved) n.e.s.	0.212	0.202	0.192	0.123	0.142
059	Fruit and vegetable juice (unfermented, no added spirit, sweetened or not)	0.220	0.207	0.191	0.124	0.133
266	Synthetic fibres suitable for spinning	0.191	0.195	0.191	0.092	0.165
054	Vegetables and veg products (fresh chilled frozen preserved dried edible) n.e.s.	0.208	0.194	0.191	0.131	0.173
655	Knitted, crocheted fabric (include tubular knit, pile, openwork fabric), n.e.s.	0.215	0.187	0.190	0.203	0.291
718	Power-generating machinery, and parts thereof, n.e.s.	0.165	0.179	0.190	0.260	0.218
277	Natural abrasives, n.e.s. (including industrial diamonds)	0.204	0.201	0.190	0.193	0.251
773	Equipment for distributing electricity, n.e.s.	0.196	0.221	0.190	0.113	0.147
291	Crude animal materials, nes	0.226	0.221	0.189	0.140	0.199
682	Copper	0.161	0.184	0.189	0.167	0.221
012	Other meat and edible meat offal (fresh chilled frozen)	0.283	0.230	0.186	0.156	0.234
282	Ferrous waste and scrap; remelting scrap ingots of iron or steel	0.205	0.185	0.185	0.192	0.231
686	Zinc	0.210	0.211	0.184	0.131	0.237
812	Sanitary, plumbing and heating fixtures and fittings, n.e.s.	0.213	0.178	0.184	0.190	0.233
747	Appliances for pipes boiler shells tanks vats; pressure and temperature valves	0.165	0.204	0.183	0.137	0.154
895	Office and stationery supplies, n.e.s.	0.187	0.200	0.183	0.111	0.143
737	Metalworking machinery (other than machine tools), and parts thereof, n.e.s.	0.163	0.163	0.182	0.165	0.203
684	Aluminium	0.188	0.182	0.181	0.110	0.151
111	Non-alcoholic beverages, n.e.s.	0.176	0.188	0.180	0.193	0.219
893	Articles, n.e.s., of plastics	0.171	0.184	0.180	0.115	0.142
748	Transmission shaft camshaft crankshaft; bearing housing; gearbox speed changer	0.194	0.203	0.180	0.115	0.164
046	Meal and flour of wheat and flour of meslin	0.139	0.091	0.179	0.394	0.448
724	Textile and leather machinery, and parts thereof, n.e.s.	0.158	0.151	0.179	0.132	0.208
334	Petroleum oil, oil from bituminous (excl crude); preparations, n.e.s., > 70% oil	0.137	0.174	0.178	0.170	0.235
245	Fuel wood (excluding wood waste) and wood charcoal	0.196	0.222	0.177	0.224	0.214
522	Inorganic chemical elements, oxides and halogen salts	0.159	0.161	0.177	0.098	0.137
057	Fruits and nuts (excluding oil nuts), fresh or dried	0.210	0.191	0.177	0.125	0.147
267	Other man-made fibres suitable for spinning; waste of man-made fibres	0.142	0.164	0.176	0.182	0.246
874	Measuring, checking, analysing and controlling instruments and apparatus, n.e.s.	0.165	0.188	0.175	0.120	0.122
772	Electrical apparatus to switch protect circuits or make circuit connections	0.166	0.180	0.175	0.125	0.219
716	Rotating electric plant, and parts thereof, n.e.s.	0.154	0.188	0.175	0.161	0.168
735	Parts, n.e.s. and accessories for machines of groups 731, 733; tool holder	0.203	0.210	0.174	0.092	0.153
898	Musical instrument, parts accessory; tape, sound recording (excluding 763 & 883)	0.179	0.180	0.174	0.121	0.159
629	Articles of rubber, n.e.s.	0.169	0.184	0.174	0.119	0.131
699	Manufactures of base metal, n.e.s.	0.162	0.193	0.173	0.143	0.123
335	Residual petroleum products, n.e.s., related mater.	0.151	0.155	0.173	0.205	0.248
778	Electrical machinery and apparatus, n.e.s.	0.177	0.184	0.173	0.122	0.163
524	Other inorganic chemicals; organic and inorganic compounds of precious metals	0.171	0.215	0.172	0.209	0.140
075	Spices	0.183	0.194	0.172	0.118	0.126
712	Steam turbines and other vapour turbines, and parts thereof, n.e.s.	0.166	0.192	0.172	0.465	0.404
672	Ingots, other primary forms of iron or steel; semi-finished products of	0.201	0.221	0.171	0.237	0.223
786	Trailers semi-trailers vehicles not mechanically-propelled; transport containers	0.166	0.203	0.169	0.160	0.185
232	Synthetic rubber; reclaimed rubber; waste, parings, scrap of unhardened rubber	0.145	0.165	0.168	0.137	0.165
571	Polymers of ethylene, in primary forms	0.150	0.155	0.168	0.139	0.196
422	Fixed vegetable fats and oils, crude, refined or fractionated, other than "soft"	0.168	0.165	0.168	0.184	0.195
663	Mineral manufactures, n.e.s.	0.173	0.202	0.167	0.148	0.160
695	Tools for use in the hand or in machine	0.167	0.183	0.167	0.113	0.135
516	Other organic chemicals	0.179	0.206	0.165	0.095	0.140
641	Paper and paperboard	0.183	0.183	0.165	0.098	0.120
685	Lead	0.175	0.167	0.164	0.197	0.254
743	Pump (non liquid), air gas compressor, fan ventilation filter; centrifuge; parts	0.149	0.173	0.164	0.109	0.135
728	Other machinery or specialized industrial equipment; parts thereof, n.e.s.	0.161	0.173	0.163	0.167	0.156
744	Mechanical handling equipment, and parts thereof, n.e.s.	0.141	0.191	0.163	0.205	0.172
272	Fertilizers, crude (excluding those of division 56)	0.139	0.152	0.163	0.175	0.232
746	Ball or roller bearings	0.167	0.166	0.162	0.091	0.139
693	Wire products (excluding insulated electrical wiring) and fencing grills	0.162	0.170	0.161	0.144	0.162
514	Nitrogen-function compounds	0.170	0.170	0.161	0.106	0.159
723	Civil engineering and contractors' plant and equipment; parts thereof	0.144	0.164	0.160	0.174	0.181
892	Printed matter	0.158	0.166	0.159	0.111	0.131
745	Non-electrical machinery, tools and mechanical apparatus, parts thereof, n.e.s.	0.137	0.165	0.159	0.118	0.137
665	Glassware	0.171	0.187	0.158	0.138	0.166
048	Cereal preparations and preparations of flour or starch of fruits or vegetables	0.168	0.161	0.158	0.169	0.202
273	Stone, sand and gravel	0.183	0.167	0.157	0.203	0.236
073	Chocolate and other food preparations containing cocoa, n.e.s.	0.185	0.173	0.157	0.124	0.170
121	Tobacco, unmanufactured; tobacco refuse	0.169	0.156	0.157	0.179	0.270

For sources and notes, see end of table.

Pour les sources et les notes, se reporter à la fin du tableau.

SITC group Revision 3 (3-digit level) (1) / Groupes de la CTCI Révision 3 (positions à 3 chiffres) (1)	Concentration index (2) / Indice de concentration (2)			Structural change index (3) / Indice de changement structurel (3) 1995=0	
	1995	2000	2005	2000	2005
573 Polymers of vinyl chloride or of other halogenated olefins, in primary forms	0.150	0.180	0.157	0.215	0.263
742 Liquid pump, with without a fitted measuring device; liquid elevator; parts for	0.148	0.157	0.156	0.120	0.158
651 Textile yarn	0.158	0.156	0.156	0.124	0.184
621 Materials of rubber (e.g., pastes, plates, sheets, rods, thread, tubes, of rubber)	0.156	0.165	0.154	0.139	0.173
562 Fertilizers (excluding group 272)	0.190	0.144	0.152	0.196	0.219
278 Other crude minerals	0.163	0.164	0.152	0.103	0.185
642 Paper and paperboard, cut to size or shape, and articles of paper or paperboard	0.144	0.157	0.152	0.116	0.127
662 Clay construction materials and refractory construction materials	0.173	0.170	0.152	0.203	0.242
678 Wire of iron or steel	0.176	0.171	0.152	0.137	0.147
721 Agricultural machinery (excluding tractors), and parts thereof	0.162	0.171	0.151	0.111	0.140
726 Printing and bookbinding machinery, and parts thereof	0.163	0.170	0.151	0.138	0.169
749 Non-electric parts and accessories of machinery, n.e.s.	0.164	0.156	0.150	0.126	0.160
575 Other plastics, in primary forms	0.150	0.141	0.149	0.112	0.164
882 Photographic and cinematographic supplies	0.174	0.171	0.149	0.106	0.197
421 Fixed vegetable fats and oils, "soft", crude, refined or fractionated	0.144	0.125	0.149	0.231	0.220
583 Plastic monofilament, cross-section > 1 mm, rods, sticks, profile shapes	0.179	0.194	0.148	0.220	0.307
598 Miscellaneous chemical products, n.e.s.	0.140	0.145	0.148	0.134	0.144
664 Glass	0.158	0.166	0.148	0.142	0.165
574 Polyacetal, polyether, epoxide resin; polycarbonate, alkyd resin, polyester	0.140	0.141	0.148	0.147	0.226
783 Road motor vehicles, n.e.s.	0.212	0.187	0.148	0.243	0.278
677 Rails or railway track construction material, of iron or steel	0.153	0.174	0.147	0.324	0.280
652 Cotton fabrics, woven (not including narrow or special fabrics)	0.155	0.160	0.147	0.158	0.231
074 Tea and maté	0.153	0.146	0.147	0.138	0.221
674 Flat-rolled products of iron or non-alloy steel, clad, plated or coated	0.138	0.145	0.146	0.144	0.197
654 Other textile fabrics, woven n.e.s.	0.176	0.165	0.145	0.166	0.234
592 Starches, inulin and wheat gluten; albuminoidal substances; glues	0.157	0.151	0.144	0.108	0.130
532 Dyeing and tanning extracts, and synthetic tanning materials	0.130	0.135	0.143	0.127	0.186
656 Tulles, lace, embroidery, ribbons, trimmings and other smallwares	0.149	0.155	0.143	0.176	0.222
725 Paper mill pulp mill paper-cutting other paper manufacture machines; parts of	0.150	0.176	0.142	0.202	0.223
673 Flat-rolled products of iron or non-alloy steel, not clad, plated or coated	0.143	0.152	0.142	0.171	0.244
791 Railway vehicles (including hovertrains) and associated equipment	0.175	0.223	0.141	0.247	0.303
679 Tubes, pipes and hollow profiles, and tube or pipe fittings, of iron or steel	0.121	0.146	0.140	0.174	0.174
793 Ships, boats (including hovercraft) and floating structures	0.152	0.177	0.139	0.447	0.415
811 Prefabricated buildings	0.242	0.190	0.139	0.309	0.424
582 Plates, sheets, film, foil and strip, of plastics	0.151	0.145	0.137	0.116	0.165
657 Special yarns, special textile fabrics and related products	0.136	0.133	0.137	0.115	0.157
553 Perfumery, cosmetic or toilet preparations (excluding soaps)	0.142	0.140	0.137	0.116	0.139
022 Milk, cream and milk products (excluding butter, cheese)	0.175	0.132	0.134	0.151	0.220
411 Animals oils and fats	0.141	0.126	0.134	0.223	0.253
691 Structures and parts of structures, n.e.s., of iron, steel or aluminium	0.158	0.152	0.133	0.214	0.258
711 Steam vapour superheated water boiler, auxiliary plant for use with; parts of	0.147	0.178	0.132	0.325	0.339
531 Synthetic organic colouring matter and colour lakes, preparations based thereon	0.142	0.138	0.131	0.091	0.144
581 Tubes, pipes and hoses, and fittings therefor, of plastics	0.139	0.140	0.130	0.151	0.159
653 Fabrics, woven, of man-made textiles (excluding narrow or special fabrics)	0.173	0.152	0.130	0.170	0.229
741 Heating and cooling equipment, and parts thereof, n.e.s.	0.116	0.131	0.130	0.155	0.186
047 Other cereal meals and flours	0.098	0.093	0.129	0.267	0.334
431 Animal, vegetable fats, oils, processed; waxes; inedible preparations of, n.e.s.	0.154	0.114	0.126	0.220	0.207
676 Iron and steel bars, rods, angles, shapes and sections (including sheet piling)	0.154	0.166	0.126	0.187	0.200
091 Margarine and shortening	0.144	0.110	0.124	0.323	0.328
554 Soaps, cleansing and polishing preparations	0.125	0.116	0.121	0.102	0.118
692 Metal containers for storage or transport	0.126	0.129	0.120	0.148	0.150
081 Feeding stuff for animals (excluding unmilled cereals)	0.150	0.127	0.119	0.110	0.146
041 Wheat (including spelt) and meslin, unmilled	0.140	0.111	0.117	0.205	0.251
591 Insecticide, rodenticide, fungicide, herbicide, plant-growth reg, disinfectant	0.139	0.124	0.117	0.115	0.148
098 Edible products and preparations, n.e.s.	0.137	0.112	0.116	0.152	0.151
061 Sugar, molasses and honey	0.118	0.113	0.115	0.149	0.197
597 Prepared additives: mineral oil; transmission; anti-freeze, de-ice; lubricating	0.109	0.109	0.113	0.121	0.154
533 Pigments, paints, varnishes and related materials	0.115	0.116	0.111	0.104	0.124
523 Metallic salts and peroxysalts, of inorganic acids	0.112	0.118	0.108	0.102	0.112
727 Food-processing machines (excluding domestic); parts thereof	0.117	0.107	0.106	0.180	0.184
042 Rice	0.104	0.094	0.103	0.263	0.297
269 Worn clothing and other worn textile articles; rags	0.119	0.086	0.087	0.306	0.349
911 Postal packages not classified according to kind	0.433	..	..	..	..

For sources and notes, see end of table.

Pour les sources et les notes, se reporter à la fin du tableau.

Sources:
- UNCTAD secretariat calculations based on UN DESA Statistics Division's data

Notes:

(1) Product groups are ranked according to the concentration index in 2005.

(2) Concentration index:
   The Herfindahl-Hirschmann index is a measure of the degree of market concentration. It has been normalized to obtain values ranking from 0 to 1 (maximum concentration), according to the following formula:

$$H_i = \frac{\sqrt{\sum_{j=1}^{n}(\frac{x_{ij}}{X_i})^2} - \sqrt{\frac{1}{n}}}{1 - \sqrt{\frac{1}{n}}}$$

where

   H_i = value of concentration index for product i

   x_{ij} = value of exports or imports for country j and product i

$$X_i = \sum_{j=1}^{n} x_{ij} \quad \text{and}$$

n = maximum number of individual economies over the period from 1995 to 2005.

An index value that is close to 1 indicates a very concentrated market. On the contrary, values closer to 0 reflect a more equal distribution of market shares among exporters or importers.

(3) Structural change index:
   This index, ranging from 0 to 1 reveals the structural change in trade for a particular product as compared to the reference year (1995 = 0).

An index value close to 1 indicates a significant change in the composition of exporters (importers). On the contrary, values closer to 0 would demonstrate a higher degree of "traditionality" in the markets over the period concerned.

The value is calculated as follows:

$$I_i = \frac{\sum_{j=1}^{}\left| S^1_{ij} - S^0_{ij} \right|}{2}$$

where

   I_i = Value of structure index for product i

   S^0_{ij} = Share of trade of product i for country j in 1995

   S^1_{ij} = Share of trade of product i for the country j in the concerned year

Sources :
- Calculs du secrétariat de la CNUCED sur la base des données de ONU DAES Division de statistique

Notes :

(1) Les groupes de produits sont classés d'après l'indice de concentration en 2005.

(2) Indice de concentration :
   L'indice Herfindahl-Hirschmann mesure le degré de concentration des marchés. Il a été normalisé afin d'obtenir des valeurs comprises entre 0 et 1 (concentration maximale), d'après la formule suivante:

$$H_i = \frac{\sqrt{\sum_{j=1}^{n}(\frac{x_{ij}}{X_i})^2} - \sqrt{\frac{1}{n}}}{1 - \sqrt{\frac{1}{n}}}$$

où

   H_i = Valeur de l'indice de concentration pour le produit i

   x_{ij} = Valeur des exportations ou des importations du pays j pour le produit i

$$X_i = \sum_{j=1}^{n} x_{ij} \quad \text{et}$$

n = nombre maximum d'économies individuelles sur la période allant de 1995 à 2005.

Un indice proche de 1 indique une concentration très forte du marché pour ce produit en particulier. En revanche, une valeur proche de 0 démontre une répartition plus homogène du commerce entre les exportateurs ou les importateurs.

(3) Indice de changement structurel :
   Cet indice, dont la valeur est comprise entre 0 et 1, représente les changements de structure du commerce par rapport à une année de référence(1995 = 0).

Une valeur proche de 1 indique un important changement structurel du commerce de ce produit, c'est à dire, une grande variation des parts de marché au sein des exportateurs ou importateurs, par rapport à l'année de référence. Plus la valeur de l'indice est proche de 0, plus la structure du commerce de ce produit est stable.

Il est calculé comme suit :

$$I_i = \frac{\sum_{j=1}^{}\left| S^1_{ij} - S^0_{ij} \right|}{2}$$

où

   I_i = Valeur de l'indice de changement structurel, pour le produit i

   S^0_{ij} = Part du commerce du produit i pour le pays j par rapport au commerce total de ce produit pour l'année 1995

   S^1_{ij} = Part du commerce du produit i pour le pays j, par rapport au commerce total de ce produit pour l'année concernée

4

INTERNATIONAL **MERCHANDISE** TRADE INDICATORS

INDICATEURS DU COMMERCE INTERNATIONAL DES **MARCHANDISES**

Region, country or territory	Exports - Exportations					
	1995			2005		
	Number of products exported	Diversification index	Concentration index	Number of products exported	Diversification index	Concentration index
	Nombre de produits exportés (1)	Indice de diversification (2)	Indice de concentration (3)	Nombre de produits exportés (1)	Indice de diversification (2)	Indice de concentration (3)
WORLD	**261**	**0.000**	**0.053**	**260**	**0.000**	**0.067**
DEVELOPED ECONOMIES	261	0.117	0.057	260	0.138	0.067
DEVELOPING ECONOMIES	261	0.281	0.092	260	0.239	0.096
ECONOMIES IN TRANSITION	257	0.556	0.158	259	0.568	0.277
Developed economies: America	**259**	**0.235**	**0.073**	**260**	**0.209**	**0.072**
Bermuda	4	0.484	0.984	..	..	..
Canada	259	0.403	0.132	260	0.377	0.126
Greenland	117	0.782	0.550	..	..	..
Saint Pierre and Miquelon	20	0.609	0.522	..	..	..
United States	258	0.268	0.075	258	0.249	0.074
Developed economies: Asia	**256**	**0.389**	**0.119**	**257**	**0.379**	**0.128**
Israel	238	0.555	0.275	235	0.607	0.368
Japan	253	0.384	0.124	255	0.396	0.135
Developed economies: Europe	**261**	**0.154**	**0.052**	**260**	**0.158**	**0.066**
Andorra	50	0.570	0.226	160	0.631	0.281
Austria	257	0.371	0.078	258	0.348	0.074
Belgium	–	–	–	259	0.353	0.106
Belgium-Luxembourg	258	0.363	0.102	–	–	–
Cyprus	161	0.641	0.280	219	0.557	0.249
Czech Republic	258	0.367	0.045	257	0.384	0.094
Denmark	254	0.469	0.093	258	0.399	0.084
Estonia	221	0.520	0.082	246	0.472	0.148
Faeroe Islands	14	0.544	0.617	13	0.556	0.622
Finland	256	0.529	0.204	257	0.516	0.195
France	258	0.262	0.059	259	0.283	0.082
Germany	259	0.281	0.094	258	0.282	0.105
Gibraltar	59	0.695	0.321	..	..	..
Greece	250	0.589	0.106	251	0.500	0.101
Hungary	228	0.414	0.061	253	0.384	0.139
Iceland	85	0.777	0.407	200	0.791	0.391
Ireland	253	0.551	0.170	256	0.642	0.224
Italy	258	0.352	0.055	260	0.357	0.054
Latvia	245	0.624	0.139	247	0.517	0.125
Lithuania	226	0.535	0.089	252	0.529	0.214
Luxembourg	–	–	–	252	0.560	0.136
Malta	138	0.707	0.506	214	0.642	0.426
Netherlands	257	0.337	0.058	255	0.366	0.085
Norway	256	0.639	0.352	254	0.675	0.454
Poland	249	0.492	0.081	257	0.426	0.081
Portugal	241	0.483	0.105	253	0.392	0.103
Slovakia	228	0.469	0.094	246	0.449	0.124
Slovenia	224	0.460	0.095	240	0.474	0.119
Spain	259	0.362	0.142	259	0.337	0.110
Sweden	259	0.426	0.127	258	0.366	0.118
Switzerland	241	0.519	0.091	242	0.548	0.142
United Kingdom	257	0.233	0.070	258	0.244	0.098
Developed economies: Oceania	**259**	**0.543**	**0.101**	**259**	**0.573**	**0.140**
Australia	259	0.552	0.120	259	0.585	0.168
New Zealand	252	0.648	0.118	254	0.626	0.133
Developing economies: Africa	**261**	**0.592**	**0.209**	**260**	**0.556**	**0.190**
Eastern Africa	*242*	*0.714*	*0.176*	*257*	*0.691*	*0.130*
Burundi	18	0.642	0.631	21	0.780	0.607
Comoros	45	0.628	0.769	..	..	..
Djibouti	27	0.549	0.133	..	..	..
Eritrea	39	0.612	0.378	..	..	..
Ethiopia	25	0.549	0.647	..	..	..
Kenya	186	0.714	0.232	198	0.762	0.276
Madagascar	201	0.759	0.280	208	0.783	0.356

For sources and notes, see end of table 4.1.2

Imports - Importations						Régions, pays ou territoires
1995			2005			
Number of products exported	Diversification index	Concentration index	Number of products exported	Diversification index	Concentration index	
Nombre de produits exportés (1)	Indice de diversification (2)	Indice de concentration (3)	Nombre de produits exportés (1)	Indice de diversification (2)	Indice de concentration (3)	
261	**0.000**	**0.052**	**260**	**0.000**	**0.077**	**MONDE**
261	0.073	0.058	260	0.090	0.081	ÉCONOMIES DÉVELOPPÉES
261	0.174	0.056	260	0.194	0.098	ÉCONOMIES EN DÉVELOPPEMENT
260	0.348	0.064	259	0.258	0.065	ÉCONOMIES EN TRANSITION
260	**0.186**	**0.092**	**260**	**0.164**	**0.105**	**Économies développées : Amérique**
111	0.355	0.110	..	..	..	Bermudes
260	0.218	0.091	260	0.214	0.082	Canada
230	0.479	0.171	..	..	..	Groenland
115	0.416	0.083	..	..	..	Saint-Pierre-et-Miquelon
259	0.207	0.097	260	0.185	0.112	États-Unis
257	**0.286**	**0.075**	**258**	**0.266**	**0.127**	**Économies développées : Asie**
249	0.261	0.144	254	0.297	0.198	Israël
257	0.305	0.078	258	0.280	0.132	Japon
261	**0.094**	**0.049**	**260**	**0.109**	**0.070**	**Économies développées : Europe**
176	0.530	0.094	183	0.519	0.111	Andorre
259	0.222	0.052	259	0.233	0.064	Autriche
			260	0.284	0.104	Belgique
260	0.239	0.071	_	_	_	Belgique-Luxembourg
229	0.360	0.095	254	0.373	0.153	Chypre
258	0.248	0.042	259	0.245	0.062	République tchèque
258	0.240	0.061	259	0.259	0.059	Danemark
236	0.379	0.077	256	0.330	0.102	Estonie
169	0.431	0.122	252	0.405	0.126	Îles Féroé
258	0.195	0.054	258	0.199	0.085	Finlande
259	0.146	0.048	259	0.161	0.073	France
258	0.177	0.076	258	0.166	0.094	Allemagne
140	0.675	0.482	..	..	..	Gibraltar
256	0.259	0.054	254	0.283	0.116	Grèce
244	0.280	0.052	255	0.279	0.119	Hongrie
221	0.330	0.069	229	0.404	0.102	Islande
260	0.323	0.123	260	0.300	0.113	Irlande
259	0.194	0.058	258	0.205	0.097	Italie
231	0.421	0.107	255	0.346	0.099	Lettonie
251	0.367	0.084	256	0.332	0.179	Lituanie
			259	0.379	0.104	Luxembourg
229	0.400	0.254	221	0.358	0.194	Malte
257	0.197	0.057	257	0.220	0.097	Pays-Bas
258	0.266	0.046	257	0.302	0.060	Norvège
253	0.292	0.050	259	0.241	0.061	Pologne
252	0.218	0.059	257	0.185	0.084	Portugal
248	0.305	0.061	258	0.284	0.076	Slovaquie
254	0.242	0.057	251	0.317	0.068	Slovénie
258	0.197	0.064	260	0.178	0.091	Espagne
257	0.204	0.055	259	0.176	0.076	Suède
252	0.256	0.055	251	0.298	0.079	Suisse
259	0.169	0.064	259	0.214	0.088	Royaume-Uni
253	**0.220**	**0.065**	**259**	**0.233**	**0.092**	**Économies développées : Océanie**
252	0.225	0.064	259	0.235	0.092	Australie
244	0.253	0.073	255	0.271	0.096	Nouvelle-Zélande
261	**0.275**	**0.045**	**260**	**0.250**	**0.070**	**Économies en développement : Afrique**
260	*0.368*	*0.060*	*260*	*0.390*	*0.098*	*Afrique orientale*
220	0.510	0.120	227	0.507	0.128	Burundi
200	0.610	0.240	..	..	..	Comores
142	0.572	0.120	..	..	..	Djibouti
149	0.507	0.134	..	..	..	Érythrée
192	0.498	0.126	..	..	..	Éthiopie
216	0.415	0.099	231	0.431	0.143	Kenya
240	0.439	0.104	247	0.540	0.195	Madagascar

Pour les sources et les notes, se reporter à la fin du tableau 4.1.2

Region, country or territory	Exports - Exportaticns					
	1995			2005		
	Number of products exported Nombre de produits exportés (1)	Diversification index Indice de diversification (2)	Concentration index Indice de concentration (3)	Numbe· of products exported Nombre de produits exportés (1)	Diversification index Indice de diversification (2)	Concentration index Indice de concentration (3)
Malawi	70	0.822	0.663	74	0.825	0.525
Mauritius	109	0.805	0.363	168	0.735	0.299
Mozambique	64	0.721	0.448	213	0.791	0.560
Rwanda	16	0.582	0.464	..	..	..
Seychelles	18	0.708	0.557	21	0.726	0.615
Uganda	81	0.865	0.650	127	0.733	0.259
United Republic of Tanzania	80	0.755	0.276	130	0.828	0.345
Zambia	86	0.857	0.829	117	0.870	0.544
Zimbabwe	191	0.727	0.252	158	0.765	0.247
Middle Africa	*155*	*0.850*	*0.643*	*222*	*0.791*	*0.578*
Angola	35	0.767	0.897	..	..	..
Cameroon	77	0.801	0.326	207	0.791	0.379
Central African Republic	28	0.698	0.450	68	0.671	0.451
Congo	34	0.788	0.854	..	..	..
Dem. Rep. of the Congo	60	0.814	0.499	..	..	..
Equatorial Guinea	10	0.638	0.559	..	..	..
Gabon	61	0.803	0.812	76	0.809	0.739
São Tome and Principe	6	0.559	0.524	..	..	..
Northern Africa	*230*	*0.729*	*0.374*	*254*	*0.707*	*0.351*
Algeria	99	0.828	0.530	118	0.832	0.591
Egypt	164	0.678	0.247	240	0.674	0.319
Libyan Arab Jamahiriya	29	0.537	0.768	..	..	..
Morocco	169	0.751	0.179	198	0.704	0.158
Sudan	19	0.571	0.351	41	0.530	0.851
Tunisia	193	0.677	0.216	200	0.623	0.182
Western Sahara	7	0.486	0.605	..	..	..
Southern Africa	*258*	*0.617*	*0.257*	*255*	*0.558*	*0.133*
Namibia	..	..	..	259	0.789	0.293
South Africa	258	0.617	0.257	253	0.559	0.138
Western Africa	*216*	*0.796*	*0.228*	*214*	*0.727*	*0.260*
Benin	53	0.756	0.517	51	0.731	0.566
Burkina Faso	40	0.781	0.573	58	0.756	0.699
Cape Verde	17	0.679	0.392	39	0.733	0.475
Côte d'Ivoire	232	0.820	0.345	230	0.753	0.322
Gambia	99	0.583	0.314	9	0.583	0.438
Ghana	95	0.853	0.444	117	0.801	0.585
Guinea	40	0.806	0.644	..	..	..
Guinea-Bissau	..	..	..	..	..	..
Mali	41	0.762	0.587	173	0.833	0.603
Mauritania	30	0.706	0.501	..	..	..
Niger	32	0.761	0.552	179	0.785	0.459
Saint Helena	1	0.527	0.405	..	..	..
Senegal	104	0.769	0.288	160	0.660	0.201
Sierra Leone	19	0.794	0.555	..	..	..
Togo	92	0.726	0.327	69	0.695	0.288
Developing economies: America	**261**	**0.365**	**0.089**	**259**	**0.366**	**0.145**
Caribbean	*258*	*0.660*	*0.188*	*214*	*0.753*	*0.275*
Anguilla	1	0.542	0.200	10	0.577	0.323
Antigua and Barbuda	41	0.694	0.358	36	0.725	0.690
Aruba	..	..	..	..	..	..
Bahamas	67	0.670	0.339	..	..	..
Barbados	101	0.652	0.184	220	0.659	0.270
British Virgin Islands	16	0.690	0.291	..	..	..
Cayman Islands	10	0.667	0.264	..	..	..
Cuba	89	0.832	0.616	119	0.806	0.454
Dominica	25	0.764	0.527	21	0.736	0.375
Dominican Republic	121	0.754	0.223	..	..	..
Grenada	18	0.692	0.299	24	0.671	0.342
Haiti	24	0.559	0.326	..	..	..
Jamaica	107	0.774	0.481	107	0.800	0.608
Montserrat	2	0.680	0.744	55	0.512	0.353

For sources and notes, see end of table 4.1.2

Imports - Importations						Régions, pays ou territoires
1995			2005			
Number of products exported	Diversification index	Concentration index	Number of products exported	Diversification index	Concentration index	
Nombre de produits exportés (1)	Indice de diversification (2)	Indice de concentration (3)	Nombre de produits exportés (1)	Indice de diversification (2)	Indice de concentration (3)	
171	0.533	0.131	194	0.565	0.133	Malawi
216	0.459	0.089	218	0.456	0.141	Maurice
222	0.526	0.100	252	0.568	0.302	Mozambique
140	0.503	0.123	..	..	..	Rwanda
170	0.447	0.143	248	0.606	0.254	Seychelles
186	0.482	0.072	204	0.495	0.146	Ouganda
203	0.518	0.097	217	0.468	0.098	République-Unie de Tanzanie
202	0.470	0.100	218	0.488	0.108	Zambie
255	0.398	0.084	256	0.506	0.112	Zimbabwe
233	*0.440*	*0.064*	*219*	*0.437*	*0.140*	*Afrique centrale*
202	0.530	0.143	..	..	..	Angola
195	0.491	0.071	198	0.497	0.213	Cameroun
129	0.531	0.141	195	0.564	0.213	République centrafricaine
160	0.575	0.173	..	..	..	Congo
204	0.483	0.094	..	..	..	Rép. dém. du Congo
75	0.562	0.126	..	..	..	Guinée équatoriale
193	0.430	0.064	243	0.460	0.066	Gabon
66	0.469	0.100	..	..	..	Sao Tomé-et-Principe
256	*0.368*	*0.052*	*259*	*0.339*	*0.055*	*Afrique septentrionale*
231	0.468	0.084	235	0.469	0.083	Algérie
237	0.444	0.076	253	0.448	0.107	Égypte
188	0.408	0.080	207	0.592	0.125	Jamahiriya arabe libyenne
236	0.422	0.082	248	0.356	0.112	Maroc
185	0.503	0.133	243	0.449	0.087	Soudan
242	0.400	0.076	242	0.399	0.088	Tunisie
17	0.489	0.270	..	..	..	Sahara occidental
255	*0.251*	*0.076*	*260*	*0.245*	*0.125*	*Afrique australe*
..	..	..	258	0.420	0.075	Namibie
255	0.251	0.076	257	0.247	0.130	Afrique du Sud
261	*0.445*	*0.095*	*260*	*0.419*	*0.111*	*Afrique occidentale*
147	0.561	0.141	227	0.583	0.171	Bénin
167	0.543	0.129	178	0.590	0.229	Burkina Faso
145	0.525	0.125	173	0.487	0.087	Cap-Vert
251	0.454	0.146	248	0.526	0.255	Côte d'Ivoire
237	0.594	0.174	239	0.591	0.187	Gambie
198	0.467	0.103	218	0.443	0.094	Ghana
238	0.557	0.194	..	..	..	Guinée
59	0.591	0.321	..	..	..	Guinée-Bissau
168	0.589	0.151	238	0.563	0.194	Mali
135	0.576	0.179	167	0.675	0.446	Mauritanie
152	0.592	0.135	172	0.598	0.158	Niger
31	0.474	0.141	..	..	..	Sainte-Hélène
181	0.481	0.115	217	0.449	0.145	Sénégal
150	0.463	0.118	..	..	..	Sierra Leone
166	0.570	0.269	158	0.632	0.265	Togo
260	**0.200**	**0.049**	**260**	**0.211**	**0.063**	**Économies en développement : Amérique**
260	*0.337*	*0.080*	*258*	*0.351*	*0.131*	*Caraïbes*
8	0.785	0.659	118	0.522	0.100	Anguilla
168	0.497	0.172	161	0.525	0.307	Antigua-et-Barbuda
69	0.402	0.134	77	0.507	0.615	Aruba
200	0.468	0.111	..	..	..	Bahamas
206	0.355	0.072	253	0.398	0.151	Barbade
27	0.826	0.587	..	..	..	Îles Vierges britanniques
138	0.631	0.222	..	..	..	Îles Caïmanes
235	0.483	0.140	236	0.403	0.126	Cuba
133	0.517	0.075	226	0.420	0.105	Dominique
230	0.452	0.081	..	..	..	République dominicaine
137	0.454	0.075	160	0.501	0.084	Grenade
191	0.486	0.106	..	..	..	Haïti
254	0.394	0.098	252	0.397	0.149	Jamaïque
61	0.598	0.431	209	0.515	0.207	Montserrat

Pour les sources et les notes, se reporter à la fin du tableau 4.1.2

4

Region, country or territory	Exports - Exportations					
	1995			2005		
	Number of products exported	Diversification index	Concentration index	Number of products exported	Diversification index	Concentration index
	Nombre de produits exportés (1)	Indice de diversification (2)	Indice de concentration (3)	Nombre de produits exportés (1)	Indice de diversification (2)	Indice de concentration (3)
Netherlands Antilles	134	0.798	0.529	..	..	..
Saint Kitts and Nevis	15	0.724	0.439	13	0.732	0.575
Saint Lucia	51	0.704	0.509	179	0.618	0.307
Saint Vincent and the Grenadines	36	0.717	0.445	27	0.741	0.349
Trinidad and Tobago	207	0.731	0.361	172	0.809	0.383
Turks and Caicos Islands	5	0.624	0.445	100	0.616	0.296
Central America	*249*	*0.381*	*0.112*	*252*	*0.382*	*0.132*
Belize	34	0.738	0.376	34	0.799	0.385
Costa Rica	219	0.681	0.304	199	0.623	0.177
El Salvador	130	0.689	0.354	175	0.630	0.116
Guatemala	162	0.708	0.284	211	0.664	0.159
Honduras	95	0.822	0.536	170	0.737	0.204
Mexico	249	0.391	0.123	252	0.402	0.144
Nicaragua	93	0.773	0.272	113	0.791	0.225
Panama	78	0.569	0.364	75	0.629	0.384
South America	*260*	*0.511*	*0.109*	*258*	*0.526*	*0.187*
Argentina	240	0.574	0.125	254	0.573	0.137
Bolivia	105	0.732	0.217	150	0.789	0.357
Brazil	255	0.521	0.087	249	0.484	0.089
Chile	250	0.780	0.306	252	0.773	0.318
Colombia	216	0.662	0.244	231	0.609	0.211
Ecuador	161	0.787	0.376	170	0.778	0.537
Falkland Islands (Malvinas)	6	0.623	0.591	..	..	..
Guyana	58	0.774	0.383	221	0.829	0.325
Paraguay	98	0.717	0.337	116	0.808	0.366
Peru	175	0.802	0.245	215	0.791	0.244
Suriname	33	0.798	0.631	..	..	..
Uruguay	163	0.641	0.165	181	0.698	0.212
Venezuela (Bolivarian Republic of)	209	0.773	0.517	209	0.863	0.870
Developing economies: Asia	**261**	**0.325**	**0.098**	**260**	**0.277**	**0.101**
Eastern Asia	*258*	*0.380*	*0.075*	*258*	*0.381*	*0.108*
China	260	0.477	0.070	256	0.447	0.110
China, Hong Kong SAR	253	0.449	0.093	242	0.515	0.151
China, Macao SAR	143	0.761	0.293	129	0.777	0.306
China, Taiwan Province of	236	0.446	0.111	254	0.463	0.157
Korea, Dem. People's Rep. of	201	0.509	0.138	..	..	..
Korea, Republic of	240	0.410	0.149	242	0.430	0.162
Mongolia	47	0.744	0.496	68	0.818	0.416
Southern Asia	*257*	*0.635*	*0.223*	*259*	*0.563*	*0.232*
Bangladesh	123	0.670	0.352	112	0.735	0.378
Bhutan	38	0.633	0.327	..	..	..
India	250	0.583	0.139	259	0.541	0.134
Iran, Islamic Republic of	175	0.832	0.835	247	0.797	0.793
Maldives	9	0.498	0.410	23	0.779	0.501
Nepal	35	0.511	0.473	..	..	..
Pakistan	139	0.783	0.244	207	0.771	0.229
Sri Lanka	172	0.757	0.221	247	0.748	0.213
South-Eastern Asia	*261*	*0.386*	*0.124*	*260*	*0.346*	*0.152*
Brunei Darussalam	87	0.821	0.606	..	..	..
Cambodia	..	..	..	78	0.813	0.416
Indonesia	230	0.605	0.144	247	0.521	0.130
Lao People's Dem. Rep.	59	0.750	0.259	..	..	..
Malaysia	257	0.517	0.180	258	0.469	0.187
Myanmar	88	0.820	0.308	..	..	..
Philippines	233	0.620	0.363	227	0.615	0.358
Singapore	259	0.489	0.213	257	0.477	0.246
Thailand	256	0.481	0.090	259	0.377	0.087
Timor-Leste	25	0.491	0.270	..	..	..
Viet Nam	198	0.690	0.211	235	0.692	0.229
Western Asia	*253*	*0.680*	*0.552*	*259*	*0.545*	*0.286*
Bahrain	138	0.770	0.481	138	0.851	0.795
Iraq	29	0.724	0.735	..	..	..
Jordan	221	0.637	0.214	200	0.621	0.150

For sources and notes, see end of table 4.1.2

Imports - Importations						Régions, pays ou territoires
1995			2005			
Number of products exported	Diversification index	Concentration index	Number of products exported	Diversification index	Concentration index	
Nombre de produits exportés	Indice de diversification	Indice de concentration	Nombre de produits exportés	Indice de diversification	Indice de concentration	
(1)	(2)	(3)	(1)	(2)	(3)	
206	0.617	0.364	..	..		Antilles néerlandaises
142	0.470	0.072	144	0.416	0.087	Saint-Kitts-et-Nevis
167	0.458	0.073	169	0.449	0.110	Sainte-Lucie
137	0.484	0.070	155	0.442	0.105	Saint-Vincent-et-les Grenadines
228	0.480	0.193	226	0.447	0.276	Trinité-et-Tobago
73	0.519	0.148	149	0.476	0.083	Îles Turques et Caïques
259	*0.288*	*0.073*	*259*	*0.266*	*0.075*	*Amérique centrale*
158	0.466	0.090	239	0.457	0.175	Belize
222	0.357	0.069	234	0.377	0.155	Costa Rica
226	0.354	0.069	232	0.381	0.080	El Salvador
228	0.390	0.088	235	0.434	0.112	Guatemala
218	0.487	0.108	224	0.474	0.160	Honduras
258	0.323	0.089	258	0.243	0.079	Mexique
201	0.457	0.119	245	0.377	0.106	Nicaragua
224	0.334	0.086	220	0.365	0.144	Panama
260	*0.225*	*0.053*	*258*	*0.213*	*0.068*	*Amérique du Sud*
246	0.297	0.057	256	0.327	0.072	Argentine
210	0.419	0.090	220	0.455	0.090	Bolivie
251	0.289	0.072	251	0.286	0.098	Brésil
256	0.291	0.066	257	0.307	0.111	Chili
255	0.325	0.066	255	0.345	0.073	Colombie
227	0.391	0.076	232	0.391	0.080	Équateur
44	0.558	0.322	..	..	..	Îles Falkland (Malvinas)
176	0.465	0.074	241	0.552	0.247	Guyana
206	0.456	0.095	213	0.438	0.126	Paraguay
239	0.327	0.063	242	0.341	0.115	Pérou
158	0.463	0.121	237	0.413	0.126	Suriname
224	0.315	0.074	233	0.367	0.157	Uruguay
238	0.338	0.053	236	0.361	0.078	Venezuela (République bolivarienne du)
261	**0.207**	**0.065**	**260**	**0.238**	**0.115**	**Économies en développement : Asie**
260	*0.248*	*0.061*	*259*	*0.306*	*0.129*	*Asie orientale*
260	0.409	0.067	259	0.387	0.140	Chine
254	0.360	0.076	249	0.443	0.154	Chine, Hong Kong RAS
206	0.533	0.141	208	0.499	0.117	Chine, Macao RAS
257	0.318	0.114	257	0.372	0.156	Chine, Taiwan Province de
238	0.443	0.097	..	..	..	Corée, Rép. populaire dém. de
256	0.350	0.087	256	0.350	0.155	Corée, République de
165	0.517	0.151	188	0.505	0.227	Mongolie
260	*0.380*	*0.081*	*258*	*0.394*	*0.165*	*Asie méridionale*
219	0.570	0.136	232	0.602	0.102	Bangladesh
95	0.486	0.111	..	..	..	Bhoutan
252	0.481	0.137	255	0.475	0.244	Inde
215	0.477	0.083	246	0.444	0.113	Iran, Rép. islamique d'
151	0.499	0.098	170	0.518	0.127	Maldives
123	0.493	0.243	..	..	..	Népal
226	0.506	0.113	243	0.439	0.129	Pakistan
236	0.460	0.086	234	0.445	0.095	Sri Lanka
261	*0.261*	*0.108*	*260*	*0.289*	*0.165*	*Asie du Sud-Est*
212	0.464	0.083	..	..	..	Brunéi Darussalam
128	0.600	0.170	190	0.643	0.220	Cambodge
255	0.433	0.062	250	0.439	0.181	Indonésie
168	0.552	0.117	..	..	..	Rép. dém. populaire lao
258	0.385	0.178	259	0.372	0.221	Malaisie
201	0.492	0.078	..	..	..	Myanmar
254	0.367	0.174	250	0.456	0.292	Philippines
259	0.368	0.161	257	0.379	0.217	Singapour
258	0.311	0.079	257	0.320	0.135	Thaïlande
50	0.486	0.217	..	..	..	Timor-Leste
234	0.479	0.096	251	0.421	0.091	Viet Nam
260	*0.244*	*0.045*	*260*	*0.254*	*0.071*	*Asie occidentale*
208	0.500	0.318	226	0.591	0.529	Bahreïn
76	0.748	0.369	..	..	..	Iraq
247	0.389	0.083	247	0.349	0.145	Jordanie

Pour les sources et les notes, se reporter à la fin du tableau 4.1.2

Region, country or territory	Exports - Exportations					
	1995			2005		
	Number of products exported Nombre de produits exportés (1)	Diversification index Indice de diversification (2)	Concentration index Indice de concentration (3)	Number of products exported Nombre de produits exportés (1)	Diversification index Indice de diversification (2)	Concentration index Indice de concentration (3)
Kuwait	135	0.845	0.940	..	..	..
Lebanon	180	0.608	0.102	240	0.653	0.125
Oman	189	0.710	0.766	202	0.741	0.658
Qatar	102	0.837	0.641	227	0.852	0.568
Saudi Arabia	220	0.862	0.736	..	..	..
Syrian Arab Republic	131	0.700	0.539	161	0.585	0.537
Turkey	233	0.634	0.112	258	0.522	0.091
United Arab Emirates	242	0.699	0.562	254	0.670	0.412
Yemen	70	0.764	0.891	109	0.819	0.840
Developing economies: Oceania	**153**	**0.792**	**0.216**	**161**	**0.795**	**0.346**
Cook Islands	7	0.570	0.325	5	0.508	0.483
Fiji	70	0.804	0.385	232	0.750	0.289
French Polynesia	52	0.718	0.640	38	0.799	0.603
Kiribati	12	0.485	0.637	33	0.522	0.362
Marshall Islands	10	0.603	0.630	..	..	..
Micronesia, Federated States of	6	0.549	0.898	..	..	..
Nauru	7	0.710	0.707	..	..	..
New Caledonia	36	0.796	0.618	68	0.870	0.670
Niue	2	0.467	0.417	..	..	..
Norfolk Island	1	0.539	0.988	..	..	..
Northern Mariana Islands	45	0.468	0.256	..	..	..
Palau, Pacific Islands (former)	12	0.658	0.685	..	..	..
Papua New Guinea	57	0.847	0.376	..	..	..
Samoa	6	0.611	0.716	29	0.809	0.695
Solomon Islands	18	0.701	0.601	..	..	..
Tokelau	1	0.547	0.499	..	..	..
Tonga	5	0.617	0.579	..	..	..
Vanuatu	15	0.592	0.302	..	..	..
Wallis and Futuna Islands	3	0.469	0.304	..	..	..
Economies in transition: Asia	**244**	**0.705**	**0.205**	**232**	**0.759**	**0.546**
Armenia	102	0.676	0.246	106	0.801	0.358
Azerbaijan	105	0.698	0.609	123	0.786	0.546
Georgia	91	0.659	0.168	122	0.746	0.204
Kazakhstan	206	0.747	0.206	196	0.803	0.606
Kyrgyzstan	200	0.658	0.137	209	0.702	0.331
Tajikistan	110	0.782	0.469	..	..	..
Turkmenistan	58	0.576	0.454	..	..	..
Uzbekistan	171	0.804	0.487	..	..	..
Economies in transition: Europe	**256**	**0.555**	**0.166**	**259**	**0.563**	**0.262**
Albania	77	0.727	0.241	117	0.747	0.283
Bosnia and Herzegovina	105	0.580	0.164	198	0.648	0.142
Belarus	..	..	..	236	0.571	0.279
Bulgaria	228	0.507	0.091	250	0.507	0.122
Croatia	226	0.535	0.103	232	0.486	0.111
Moldova, Republic of	160	0.740	0.229	157	0.723	0.272
Macedonia, TFYR	170	0.608	0.126	185	0.661	0.177
Romania	238	0.585	0.127	247	0.517	0.126
Serbia and Montenegro	216	0.561	0.091	252	0.561	0.101
Russian Federation	250	0.674	0.260	254	0.698	0.379
Ukraine	233	0.584	0.109	253	0.608	0.145

For sources and notes, see end cf table 4.1.2

Imports - Importations						Régions, pays ou territoires
1995			2005			
Number of products exported	Diversification index	Concentration index	Number of products exported	Diversification index	Concentration index	
Nombre de produits exportés	Indice de diversification	Indice de concentration	Nombre de produits exportés	Indice de diversification	Indice de concentration	
(1)	(2)	(3)	(1)	(2)	(3)	
205	0.393	0.110	..	..	..	Koweït
236	0.372	0.086	238	0.434	0.175	Liban
244	0.459	0.099	257	0.434	0.136	Oman
212	0.462	0.113	258	0.446	0.106	Qatar
251	0.367	0.062	249	0.353	0.093	Arabie saoudite
217	0.492	0.089	214	0.430	0.080	République arabe syrienne
249	0.385	0.077	257	0.285	0.084	Turquie
249	0.363	0.061	257	0.419	0.121	Émirats arabes unis
180	0.480	0.087	215	0.530	0.189	Yémen
236	**0.411**	**0.088**	**231**	**0.414**	**0.139**	**Économies en développement : Océanie**
93	0.504	0.127	111	0.503	0.078	Îles Cook
209	0.441	0.113	247	0.484	0.245	Fidji
189	0.387	0.072	201	0.431	0.105	Polynésie française
208	0.575	0.119	220	0.582	0.183	Kiribati
19	0.816	0.878	..	..	..	Îles Marshall
91	0.567	0.128	..	..	..	Micronésie, États fédérés de
74	0.481	0.111	..	..	..	Nauru
199	0.393	0.105	208	0.422	0.130	Nouvelle-Calédonie
4	0.666	0.516	..	..	..	Nioué
49	0.430	0.072	..	..	..	Île Norfolk
134	0.574	0.222	..	..	..	Îles Mariannes du Nord
87	0.483	0.090	..	..	..	Palaos, Îles du Pacifique (anc.)
203	0.469	0.119	..	..	..	Papouasie-Nouvelle-Guinée
98	0.570	0.253	159	0.530	0.128	Samoa
141	0.444	0.131	..	..	..	Îles Salomon
3	0.544	0.377	..	..	..	Tokélaou
116	0.467	0.093	..	..	..	Tonga
106	0.527	0.413	..	..	..	Vanuatu
33	0.535	0.203	..	..	..	Îles Wallis et Futuna
252	**0.452**	**0.065**	**252**	**0.396**	**0.074**	**Économies en transition : Asie**
180	0.644	0.181	212	0.491	0.162	Arménie
187	0.521	0.098	216	0.490	0.129	Azerbaïdjan
150	0.683	0.256	215	0.467	0.128	Géorgie
230	0.497	0.099	244	0.402	0.075	Kazakhstan
159	0.576	0.201	206	0.535	0.203	Kirghizistan
177	0.610	0.161	..	..	..	Tadjikistan
177	0.547	0.108	..	..	..	Turkménistan
225	0.447	0.062	..	..	..	Ouzbékistan
260	**0.348**	**0.068**	**259**	**0.256**	**0.068**	**Économies en transition : Europe**
208	0.520	0.095	225	0.465	0.072	Albanie
137	0.530	0.073	239	0.390	0.071	Bosnie-Herzégovine
..	..	..	247	0.411	0.226	Bélarus
235	0.449	0.181	253	0.335	0.139	Bulgarie
255	0.298	0.080	249	0.259	0.076	Croatie
212	0.586	0.219	226	0.492	0.110	Moldova, République de
251	0.420	0.114	234	0.391	0.104	Macédoine, LERY
250	0.394	0.092	251	0.287	0.075	Roumanie
242	0.373	0.068	257	0.284	0.068	Serbie-et-Monténégro
250	0.423	0.045	255	0.371	0.083	Fédération de Russie
243	0.517	0.302	256	0.334	0.136	Ukraine

Pour les sources et les notes, se reporter à la fin du tableau 4.1.2

Region country or territory	Exports - Exportations					
	1995			2005		
	Number of products exported Nombre de produits exportés (1)	Diversification index Indice de diversification (2)	Concentration index Indice de concentration (3)	Number of products exported Nombre de produits exportés (1)	Diversification index Indice de diversification (2)	Concentration index Indice de concentration (3)
DEVELOPING ECONOMIES	**261**	**0.281**	**0.092**	**260**	**0.239**	**0.096**
Developing economies excluding China	261	0.282	0.102	260	0.239	0.111
Developing economies excluding LDCs	261	0.278	0.091	260	0.238	0.096
High-income countries	261	0.312	0.122	260	0.268	0.128
Middle-income countries	261	0.343	0.089	260	0.308	0.124
Low-income countries	261	0.423	0.064	260	0.362	0.083
Heavily indebted poor countries	248	0.722	0.154	259	0.674	0.193
Landlocked countries	256	0.638	0.143	256	0.691	0.377
Small island developing states	256	0.697	0.168	223	0.700	0.265
Least developed countries	*247*	*0.736*	*0.242*	*260*	*0.727*	*0.213*
Africa and Haiti	239	0.789	0.267	258	0.765	0.271
Asia	241	0.765	0.287	178	0.803	0.355
Islands	79	0.732	0.306	73	0.788	0.374
Major petroleum exporters	*256*	*0.696*	*0.539*	*260*	*0.636*	*0.460*
Africa	152	0.860	0.684	144	0.847	0.596
America	255	0.744	0.477	226	0.810	0.758
Asia	254	0.681	0.537	260	0.596	0.388
Major exporters of manufactured goods	*260*	*0.302*	*0.073*	*260*	*0.283*	*0.097*
America	258	0.328	0.078	255	0.332	0.102
Asia	260	0.343	0.083	260	0.328	0.108
Emerging economies	*260*	*0.281*	*0.093*	*260*	*0.260*	*0.108*
America	258	0.344	0.069	259	0.339	0.086
Asia	260	0.361	0.127	260	0.359	0.151
Newly industrialized economies	*260*	*0.349*	*0.098*	*260*	*0.337*	*0.138*
First tier	260	0.382	0.107	259	0.381	0.151
Second tier	260	0.406	0.100	260	0.367	0.128
Developing economies: Africa	**261**	**0.592**	**0.209**	**260**	**0.556**	**0.190**
Northern Africa excluding Sudan	229	0.734	0.383	254	0.704	0.358
Sub-Saharan Africa	261	0.594	0.162	260	0.531	0.111
Sub-Saharan Africa excluding South Africa	251	0.720	0.231	260	0.662	0.188
Developing economies: America	**261**	**0.365**	**0.089**	**259**	**0.366**	**0.145**
Central America and Greater Carribean Islands excluding Puerto Rico	251	0.381	0.105	253	0.380	0.129
Central America and Greater Carribean Islands excluding Mexico and Puerto Rico	254	0.692	0.195	236	0.589	0.109
South America and Central America	260	0.367	0.091	259	0.371	0.147
South America excluding Brazil	256	0.606	0.171	258	0.630	0.298
Developing economies: Asia	**261**	**0.325**	**0.098**	**260**	**0.277**	**0.101**
Eastern and South-Eastern Asia excluding China	261	0.348	0.096	260	0.333	0.133
Southern Asia excluding India	228	0.761	0.433	258	0.735	0.520

For sources and notes, see next page.

Imports - Importations						Régions, pays ou territoires
1995			2005			
Number of products exported	Diversification index	Concentration index	Number of products exported	Diversification index	Concentration index	
Nombre de produits exportés	Indice de diversification	Indice de concentration	Nombre de produits exportés	Indice de diversification	Indice de concentration	
(1)	(2)	(3)	(1)	(2)	(3)	
261	0.174	0.056	260	0.194	0.098	ÉCONOMIES EN DÉVELOPPEMENT
261	0.160	0.057	260	0.166	0.092	Économies en développement sans la Chine
261	0.174	0.057	260	0.195	0.099	Économies en développement sans les PMA
261	0.177	0.067	260	0.186	0.100	Pays à revenu élevé
261	0.204	0.058	260	0.179	0.080	Pays à revenu intermédiaire
261	0.303	0.055	260	0.308	0.119	Pays à revenu faible
257	0.402	0.071	260	0.383	0.085	Pays pauvres très endettés
260	0.362	0.057	256	0.368	0.074	Pays sans littoral
260	0.363	0.065	257	0.356	0.134	Petits états insulaires en développement
256	0.431	0.064	260	0.451	0.084	Pays les moins avancés
252	0.448	0.072	260	0.431	0.087	Afrique et Haïti
244	0.474	0.081	245	0.554	0.105	Asie
206	0.470	0.089	198	0.508	0.103	Îles
260	0.260	0.038	260	0.275	0.068	Principaux exportateurs de pétrole
244	0.413	0.063	247	0.474	0.077	Afrique
258	0.275	0.056	242	0.299	0.080	Amérique
259	0.268	0.039	260	0.291	0.074	Asie
260	0.203	0.072	260	0.248	0.122	Principaux exportateurs d'articles manufacturés
259	0.258	0.063	260	0.249	0.072	Amérique
260	0.223	0.076	260	0.277	0.134	Asie
260	0.216	0.090	260	0.217	0.122	Économies émergentes
259	0.222	0.055	260	0.222	0.067	Amérique
259	0.268	0.110	260	0.286	0.158	Asie
260	0.221	0.085	260	0.259	0.145	Économies nouvellement industrialisées
260	0.235	0.086	260	0.277	0.143	Premier tier
260	0.291	0.092	260	0.300	0.154	Deuxième tier
261	0.275	0.045	260	0.250	0.070	Économies en développement : Afrique
255	0.371	0.052	259	0.337	0.056	Afrique septentrionale sans le Soudan
261	0.260	0.056	260	0.250	0.091	Afrique subsaharienne
261	0.380	0.065	260	0.365	0.082	Afrique sub-saharienne sans l'Afrique du Sud
260	0.200	0.049	260	0.211	0.063	Économies en développement : Amérique
260	0.269	0.067	259	0.261	0.074	Amérique centrale et Grandes Antilles sans Porto Rico
259	0.329	0.067	259	0.330	0.103	Amérique centrale et Grandes Antilles sans le Mexique et Porto Rico
260	0.209	0.049	260	0.215	0.063	Amérique du Sud et Amérique centrale
260	0.240	0.048	259	0.242	0.063	Amérique du Sud sans le Brésil
261	0.207	0.065	260	0.238	0.115	Économies en développement : Asie
261	0.218	0.083	260	0.254	0.140	Asie orientale et Asie du Sud-Est sans la Chine
255	0.411	0.062	258	0.402	0.082	Asie méridionale sans l'Inde

Pour les sources et les notes, se reporter à la page suivante.

Sources:
- UNCTAD secretariat calculations based on UN DESA Statistics Division's data

Notes:

(1) Number of products (at SITC, Revision 3, 3-digit group level) exported or imported by country or country grouping; this figure includes only those products that are greater than 100,000 dollars or more than 0.3 per cent of the country's or country group's total exports or imports.

(2) Diversification index that ranges from 0 to 1, reveals the extent of the differences between the structure of trade of the country or country group and the world average. The index value closer to 1 indicates a bigger difference from the world average.

Diversification index is computed by measuring absolute deviation of the country share from world structure, as follows:

$$S_j = \frac{\sum_i \left| h_{ij} - h_i \right|}{2}$$

where h_{ij} = share of product i in total exports or imports of country or country group j
h_i = share of product i in total world exports or imports.

This index is a modified Finger-Kreinin measure of similarity in trade. For more information, please consult the article of Finger, J. M. and M. E. Kreinin (1979), "A measure of 'export similarity' and its possible uses" in the *Economic Journal*, 89: 905-12.

(3) The Herfindahl-Hirschmann index is a measure of the degree of market concentration. It has been normalized to obtain values ranking from 0 to 1 (maximum concentration), according to the following formula:

$$H_j = \frac{\sqrt{\sum_{i=1}^{n} \left(\frac{x_i}{X} \right)^2} - \sqrt{1/n}}{1 - \sqrt{1/n}}$$

where H_j = country or country group index
x_i = value of exports of product i

$$X = \sum_{i=1}^{n} x_i$$

and n = number of products (at SITC Revision 3, 3-digit group level) .

Sources :
- Calculs du secrétariat de la CNUCED sur la base des données de ONU DAES Division de statistique

Notes :

(1) Nombre de produits (au niveau de la CTCI révision 3, position à 3 chiffres) exportés ou importés par chaque pays ou groupes de pays; cependant, seuls les produits ayant une valeur supérieure à 100.000 dollars ou comptant pour plus de 0,3 pour cent des exportations ou des importations totales du pays ou groupe de pays sont inclus.

(2) L'indice de diversification, dont la valeur est comprise entre 0 et 1, indique si la structure par produits des exportations d'un pays ou groupe de pays diverge peu ou beaucoup de la structure par produits des exportations totales dans le monde. Plus l'indice est proche de 1, plus la divergence est forte

L'indice de diversification mesure la déviation absolue de la structure du pays par rapport à la structure mondiale comme ci-dessous :

$$S_j = \frac{\sum_i \left| h_{ij} - h_i \right|}{2}$$

où h_{ij} = part du produit i dans le total des exportations (ou importations) du pays j
h_i = part du produit i dans le total des exportations (ou importations) mondiales.

Cet indice est une variante de l'indicateur de Finger-Kreinin sur la similarité de la structure du commerce. Pour plus d'information, veuillez consulter l'article de Finger, J. M. et M. E. Kreinin (1979), "A measure of 'export similarity' and its possible uses", dans l'*Economic Journal*, 89: 905-12.

(3) L'indice Herfindahl-Hirschmann mesure le degré de concentration des marchés. Il a été normalisé afin d'obtenir des valeurs comprises entre 0 et 1 (concentration maximale), d'après la formule suivante:

$$H_j = \frac{\sqrt{\sum_{i=1}^{n} \left(\frac{x_i}{X} \right)^2} - \sqrt{1/n}}{1 - \sqrt{1/n}}$$

où H_j = indice du pays
x_i = valeur des exportations du produit i

$$X = \sum_{i=1}^{n} x_i$$

et n = nombre de groupes de produits (de la CTCI révision 3, position à 3 chiffres).

4

Region, country or territory	Exports (1) - Exportations (1)										
	1980	1985	1990	1995	1998	1999	2001	2002	2003	2004	2005
WORLD	31	35	48	67	81	86	99	104	110	122	129
DEVELOPED ECONOMIES	34	40	52	69	84	88	99	101	104	113	119
DEVELOPING ECONOMIES	24	25	40	63	76	85	99	107	120	139	149
ECONOMIES IN TRANSITION	..	..	..	..	..	..	105	116	128	144	143
Developing economies: Africa	65	64	69	70	79	88	101	106	110	118	120
Eastern Africa	40	37	50	71	88	97	113	126	125	132	129
Burundi	19	37	34	48	63	83	93	75	80	90	87
Ethiopia	−	−	−	55	79	80	108	114	108	134	145
Kenya	52	54	63	101	95	99	124	137	145	143	148
Madagascar	89	59	57	75	73	81	132	72	112	134	92
Malawi	79	79	87	95	114	115	120	118	152	134	131
Mauritius	38	50	87	99	109	107	98	103	95	92	101
Mozambique	45	15	21	32	56	64	212	253	304	375	367
Rwanda	232	310	297	91	119	138	168	125	119	183	169
Seychelles	..	12	32	25	61	68	127	139	157	145	130
Uganda	..	28	20	48	78	96	110	106	122	144	149
United Republic of Tanzania	..	..	49	106	72	76	121	135	153	163	151
Zambia	99	97	93	71	136	181	160	155	152	178	186
Zimbabwe	30	37	46	74	82	98	66	126	85	84	77
Middle Africa	21	40	52	54	68	94	103	117	121	143	161
Angola	..	46	60	75	104	103	94	118	117	127	162
Cameroon	59	45	125	94	132	128	103	98	110	104	103
Central African Republic	21	17	17	43	67	76	92	98	74	69	69
Congo	40	57	53	74	112	94	92	102	101	118	105
Dem. Rep. of the Congo	84	156	136	81	56	111	125	157	180	221	203
Equatorial Guinea	..	4	7	16	77	82	169	192	184	312	349
Gabon	36	46	54	77	74	93	109	103	105	104	118
Northern Africa	67	63	82	72	73	81	98	105	108	117	118
Algeria	48	61	77	78	93	92	91	101	97	106	109
Egypt	61	81	127	74	67	82	93	108	128	129	146
Libyan Arab Jamahiriya	144	97	..	..	..	..	102	103	109	119	121
Morocco	32	40	57	87	95	99	102	107	102	105	128
Sudan	21	11	16	28	31	47	103	120	130	155	139
Tunisia	35	38	56	82	91	94	114	119	135	154	155
Southern Africa	59	63	66	76	85	90	103	102	103	110	115
Botswana	23	58	63	72	71	96	92	89	113	121	148
Lesotho	20	16	27	59	84	75	132	170	225	334	312
Namibia	..	..	64	94	90	94	91	84	96	128	135
South Africa	59	63	66	76	85	89	103	104	100	105	110
Swaziland	42	34	71	83	104	102	119	118	177	206	173
Western Africa	115	113	80	82	91	95	98	99	110	114	109
Benin	28	62	69	83	91	96	101	131	129	133	137
Burkina Faso	57	42	52	89	125	112	117	135	141	210	158
Cape Verde	51	109	52	62	83	92	92	100	118	140	132
Côte d'Ivoire	56	63	77	80	100	102	96	100	107	121	114
Gambia	221	260	191	93	123	99	73	94	78	137	129
Ghana	171	50	54	92	91	100	101	86	112	124	122
Guinea	..	..	56	76	90	87	117	107	80	72	78
Mali	25	22	42	59	89	102	137	152	133	132	150
Mauritania	55	101	86	100	79	95	98	94	85	90	102
Niger	106	87	73	86	118	104	102	101	111	104	122
Nigeria	141	188	84	96	125	106	96	100	111	111	108
Senegal	32	48	45	62	88	96	114	122	133	145	128
Togo	76	53	53	92	100	95	170	202	268	199	229
Developing economies: America	24	30	42	60	81	89	100	102	105	115	119
Caribbean	112	75	59	64	74	81	101	89	91	94	88
Aruba	..	..	..	..	..	..	106	67	77	80	70
Barbados	..	..	..	..	..	..	97	92	88	93	101
Cuba	..	..	..	..	..	..	102	92	100	108	90
Dominican Republic	82	68	78	85	91	84	90	88	93	96	91
Grenada	59	105	..	84	..	..	87	57	52	45	38
Haiti	49	34	40	34	94	103	87	88	110	122	144
Jamaica	63	56	78	100	108	103	97	93	93	93	100
Montserrat	..	..	..	..	..	..	67	132	152	345	101
Netherlands Antilles	..	..	..	..	..	..	134	93	57	54	29

For sources and notes, see end of table.

4.2.1 Indices du volume des exportations et importations des pays et des régions géographiques
2000 = 100

					Imports (1) - Importations (1)						Régions, pays ou territoires
1980	1985	1990	1995	1998	1999	2001	2002	2003	2004	2005	
31	34	48	69	83	88	99	104	112	125	133	**MONDE**
34	36	52	67	83	89	99	103	108	117	124	ÉCONOMIES DÉVELOPPÉES
25	27	41	73	82	86	99	106	118	139	149	ÉCONOMIES EN DÉVELOPPEMENT
..	..	..	..	..	..	117	133	162	195	219	ÉCONOMIES EN TRANSITION
77	79	70	85	97	97	107	114	122	134	147	**Économies en développement : Afrique**
47	41	59	79	96	99	109	111	113	132	143	*Afrique orientale*
37	51	45	59	63	71	96	89	101	106	149	Burundi
–	–	–	87	123	127	148	132	162	220	272	Éthiopie
50	35	53	94	93	88	108	108	114	124	145	Kenya
116	58	68	61	72	75	100	63	62	133	103	Madagascar
138	113	127	84	100	129	109	132	141	155	177	Malawi
37	36	81	84	96	110	93	99	94	98	104	Maurice
96	56	79	65	71	102	94	136	146	156	176	Mozambique
71	106	78	114	155	133	136	120	118	120	165	Rwanda
..	28	46	64	119	116	145	127	117	127	113	Seychelles
..	22	16	65	92	90	107	74	78	118	99	Ouganda
..	..	95	111	76	94	116	111	136	144	143	République-Unie de Tanzanie
123	112	120	61	108	82	134	126	152	179	208	Zambie
28	31	51	95	129	114	95	136	92	103	116	Zimbabwe
30	64	56	48	57	94	120	139	167	179	219	*Afrique centrale*
..	87	60	62	71	97	108	128	180	184	260	Angola
56	57	73	58	92	80	129	129	142	143	149	Cameroun
53	73	72	116	110	100	92	103	95	112	117	République centrafricaine
83	123	74	76	76	110	151	149	177	218	240	Congo
35	65	64	30	28	100	80	107	149	172	181	Rép. dém. du Congo
..	4	6	20	50	94	184	114	273	327	415	Guinée équatoriale
87	120	91	81	114	89	107	101	109	118	126	Gabon
74	89	89	91	104	98	105	116	113	131	146	*Afrique septentrionale*
145	149	89	121	106	94	108	123	135	179	190	Algérie
69	152	146	98	114	119	93	91	75	79	113	Égypte
..	103	112	129	143	91	131	285	147	167	168	Jamahiriya arabe libyenne
30	34	48	68	87	84	98	105	113	127	139	Maroc
64	27	30	73	114	100	150	161	182	213	299	Soudan
46	46	66	78	87	90	114	114	124	137	128	Tunisie
58	47	54	89	100	92	100	104	121	134	144	*Afrique australe*
29	43	74	63	96	88	74	79	100	128	120	Botswana
53	67	82	110	111	101	93	117	145	176	155	Lesotho
..	..	54	76	98	99	102	87	125	145	135	Namibie
58	47	54	89	99	92	102	107	121	133	146	Afrique du Sud
61	52	74	84	101	101	111	91	149	160	160	Swaziland
208	178	70	84	100	103	114	118	132	133	134	*Afrique occidentale*
82	82	43	101	104	109	104	122	140	125	110	Bénin
50	58	75	66	122	114	111	125	146	182	160	Burkina Faso
38	67	58	87	84	92	103	120	144	150	157	Cap-Vert
175	152	121	122	137	116	92	93	116	138	142	Côte d'Ivoire
173	66	95	85	110	95	73	89	82	109	100	Gambie
181	49	41	61	91	125	104	95	107	135	157	Ghana
..	..	77	87	60	63	101	112	100	98	101	Guinée
43	44	65	77	93	101	127	119	151	142	155	Mali
64	62	46	112	92	89	105	81	82	114	148	Mauritanie
184	184	119	97	119	96	108	120	148	163	155	Niger
398	443	74	87	108	99	137	147	164	144	137	Nigéria
69	71	74	83	104	102	115	135	148	157	169	Sénégal
94	72	99	93	104	107	64	55	53	56	54	Togo
34	24	31	60	89	88	99	94	95	107	112	**Économies en développement : Amérique**
135	77	61	58	86	89	103	97	93	92	96	*Caraïbes*
..	..	..	..	..	..	101	101	99	95	108	Aruba
..	..	..	..	..	..	94	95	101	114	117	Barbade
..	..	..	..	..	..	112	89	93	100	120	Cuba
30	24	31	51	81	87	96	96	78	75	75	République dominicaine
..	..	..	..	..	..	86	82	100	94	101	Grenade
56	55	33	69	79	105	99	109	109	112	118	Haïti
..	..	..	..	..	..	104	110	107	101	105	Jamaïque
..	..	..	..	..	..	90	120	127	104	106	Montserrat
..	..	..	..	..	..	112	88	90	61	64	Antilles néerlandaises

Pour les sources et les notes, se reporter à la fin du tableau.

4.2.1 Volume indices of exports and imports
of countries and geographical regions
2000 = 100

Region, country or territory	Exports (1) - Exportations (1)										
	1980	1985	1990	1995	1998	1999	2001	2002	2003	2004	2005
Saint Kitts and Nevis	..	..	..	..	..	..	105	123	109	106	115
Saint Lucia	134	..	..	..	..	..	93	93	122	131	95
Saint Vincent and the Grenadines	..	..	..	..	..	..	78	75	79	57	64
Trinidad and Tobago	79	42	46	..	..	..	106	101	110	118	134
Central America	*8*	*15*	*27*	*50*	*76*	*87*	*96*	*98*	*100*	*108*	*112*
Belize	..	..	..	..	..	..	72	82	104	99	88
Costa Rica	21	20	31	52	86	108	83	89	107	101	107
El Salvador	93	89	68	69	87	87	95	98	95	97	100
Guatemala	52	46	44	64	89	90	94	97	100	100	106
Honduras	58	59	85	84	101	84	95	101	116	109	90
Mexico	6	13	26	49	75	86	97	99	100	108	113
Nicaragua	58	49	41	62	83	87	97	93	95	106	107
Panama	–	55	60	76	91	95	103	100	106	102	99
South America	*33*	*42*	*57*	*71*	*88*	*93*	*105*	*107*	*113*	*127*	*133*
Argentina	36	40	63	73	101	97	104	105	110	118	135
Bolivia	51	36	75	89	90	89	114	131	144	143	153
Brazil	32	52	58	72	83	89	111	121	131	154	162
Chile	17	22	38	59	90	98	100	101	113	126	129
Colombia	36	34	67	84	98	101	106	107	115	129	146
Ecuador	31	44	57	100	105	109	108	109	119	134	137
Guyana	48	27	41	91	106	..	103	105	102	108	86
Paraguay	40	56	120	96	107	84	116	109	123	146	157
Peru	34	39	41	60	76	89	119	126	133	144	140
Suriname	80	65	..	..	..	..	45	34	35	104	140
Uruguay	38	42	63	75	103	95	90	78	89	106	115
Venezuela (Bolivarian Republic of)	46	44	64	82	104	93	96	85	79	90	95
Developing economies: Asia	**21**	**20**	**37**	**63**	**75**	**84**	**98**	**109**	**124**	**148**	**162**
Eastern Asia	*9*	*15*	*34*	*64*	*77*	*83*	*99*	*114*	*138*	*171*	*200*
China	7	13	26	57	71	77	108	135	181	239	302
China, Hong Kong SAR	11	17	40	78	83	85	96	104	118	135	149
China, Macao SAR	..	..	..	..	..	..	91	93	101	108	93
China, Taiwan Province of	..	18	65	94	81	88	85	93	102	118	129
Korea, Republic of	8	14	24	45	75	83	100	113	132	161	178
Mongolia	..	..	..	..	..	..	101	95	99	113	119
Southern Asia	*26*	*33*	*46*	*66*	*66*	*80*	*102*	*118*	*125*	*137*	*151*
Bangladesh	14	18	32	69	81	85	96	98	113	129	145
India	21	22	35	67	74	83	108	129	134	155	190
Iran, Islamic Republic of	36	50	..	..	..	..	94	110	117	119	117
Maldives	..	..	..	..	..	..	102	122	139	153	115
Nepal	..	..	..	..	..	..	94	73	82	88	93
Pakistan	29	36	62	75	80	86	109	122	137	144	172
Sri Lanka	29	38	47	71	81	84	92	95	98	106	113
South-Eastern Asia	*12*	*17*	*32*	*64*	*78*	*88*	*96*	*103*	*110*	*129*	*146*
Brunei Darussalam	..	..	..	..	..	..	96	108	100	96	89
Cambodia	..	..	..	..	..	..	127	89	104	128	142
Indonesia	25	26	44	71	97	121	101	98	98	96	169
Lao People's Dem. Rep.	..	..	..	..	..	..	102	92	112	103	140
Malaysia	18	21	27	59	70	84	93	101	104	125	133
Myanmar	..	13	15	35	55	63	144	198	137	120	168
Philippines	4	14	25	54	76	86	99	119	116	134	121
Singapore	11	15	33	72	82	87	95	100	117	156	174
Thailand	10	14	35	70	74	83	93	103	111	118	123
Viet Nam	..	..	..	..	..	..	111	122	143	165	182
Western Asia	*76*	*33*	*53*	*70*	*79*	*90*	*97*	*102*	*106*	*123*	*119*
Bahrain	..	..	..	..	..	..	97	104	103	94	88
Jordan	32	48	63	84	89	92	119	143	159	182	173
Kuwait	93	55	..	..	..	..	94	90	100	110	123
Lebanon	..	..	..	..	..	..	125	144	198	206	204
Oman	17	34	..	88	108	98	114	109	99	91	88
Qatar	46	30	..	..	..	..	93	112	108	124	125
Saudi Arabia	131	33	67	104	111	101	84	91	103	114	104
Syrian Arab Republic	14	12	83	78	104	100	128	158	122	94	89
Turkey	9	21	39	60	87	91	116	130	159	182	200
United Arab Emirates	39	30	..	..	..	..	106	109	110	146	146
Yemen	–	–	..	..	..	..	95	100	95	87	86

For sources and notes, see end of table.

1980	1985	1990	1995	1998	1999	2001	2002	2003	2004	2005	Régions, pays ou territoires
..	..	..	..	..	..	97	104	99	93	91	Saint-Kitts-et-Nevis
..	..	..	..	..	..	101	89	111	111	96	Sainte-Lucie
..	..	..	..	..	..	107	112	120	126	122	Saint-Vincent-et-les Grenadines
139	54	34	..	..	..	113	115	115	129	127	Trinité-et-Tobago
22	*17*	*27*	*42*	*74*	*83*	*98*	*100*	*99*	*109*	*112*	*Amérique centrale*
..	..	..	..	..	..	101	103	102	87	89	Belize
24	17	29	59	97	101	106	117	122	124	137	Costa Rica
31	29	44	84	84	86	104	106	112	114	115	El Salvador
41	27	40	65	100	95	111	125	126	135	138	Guatemala
39	31	36	53	92	99	106	108	112	124	130	Honduras
22	15	26	39	72	81	98	99	97	108	110	Mexique
66	69	44	60	87	111	101	99	100	108	114	Nicaragua
—	60	47	77	104	110	91	92	90	99	104	Panama
40	*26*	*31*	*84*	*111*	*94*	*98*	*86*	*90*	*108*	*117*	*Amérique du Sud*
52	18	14	67	119	101	83	38	58	87	108	Argentine
45	49	38	69	106	98	95	99	86	92	107	Bolivie
27	17	26	87	106	93	100	97	100	111	101	Brésil
52	34	41	83	114	95	96	95	102	119	137	Chili
55	47	50	113	123	93	113	115	127	140	161	Colombie
79	59	60	103	150	84	146	176	174	200	232	Équateur
..	..	..	..	..	..	92	91	85	86	88	Guyana
21	23	69	154	132	90	102	79	109	129	145	Paraguay
41	32	39	98	114	97	85	86	91	100	110	Pérou
..	..	..	..	..	..	89	96	130	137	152	Suriname
56	21	38	79	112	104	91	58	61	78	85	Uruguay
86	69	47	70	96	87	106	73	51	84	126	Venezuela (République bolivarienne du)
18	**23**	**41**	**75**	**78**	**85**	**98**	**108**	**124**	**149**	**160**	**Économies en développement : Asie**
12	*17*	*37*	*72*	*75*	*83*	*99*	*112*	*133*	*159*	*168*	*Asie orientale*
10	20	25	57	66	76	113	139	186	233	251	Chine
11	17	38	82	85	84	98	105	117	133	143	Chine, Hong Kong RAS
..	..	..	..	..	..	108	115	121	146	156	Chine, Macao RAS
..	12	54	83	82	88	79	85	93	113	112	Chine, Taiwan Province de
12	19	37	72	67	86	97	108	117	130	139	Corée, République de
..	..	..	..	..	..	106	115	126	146	147	Mongolie
38	*42*	*50*	*78*	*95*	*96*	*105*	*115*	*133*	*144*	*178*	*Asie méridionale*
52	57	63	102	96	100	104	98	108	132	136	Bangladesh
22	26	32	67	92	95	101	106	130	139	191	Inde
..	..	..	..	..	..	122	157	182	200	204	Iran, Rép. islamique d'
..	..	..	..	..	..	103	103	119	150	158	Maldives
..	..	..	..	..	..	98	94	106	102	91	Népal
63	74	74	107	100	101	100	109	111	136	170	Pakistan
42	43	47	83	..	..	103	114	104	113	113	Sri Lanka
13	*22*	*45*	*86*	*78*	*85*	*94*	*101*	*109*	*130*	*136*	*Asie du Sud-Est*
..	..	..	..	..	..	105	141	118	120	122	Brunéi Darussalam
..	..	..	..	..	..	113	129	137	158	177	Cambodge
..	41	66	106	82	73	97	99	123	142	153	Indonésie
..	..	..	..	..	..	101	83	96	85	123	Rép. dém. populaire lao
13	16	32	81	71	81	93	103	105	128	132	Malaisie
..	29	21	80	110	98	124	101	85	82	65	Myanmar
7	15	37	76	77	85	113	121	130	143	136	Philippines
18	23	46	80	84	89	89	90	96	124	134	Singapour
23	24	66	114	71	86	92	103	116	127	137	Thaïlande
..	..	..	..	..	..	106	127	156	177	189	Viet Nam
43	*34*	*46*	*59*	*84*	*89*	*97*	*103*	*113*	*154*	*171*	*Asie occidentale*
..	..	..	..	..	..	97	116	119	119	107	Bahreïn
48	60	60	84	83	82	104	105	108	136	154	Jordanie
..	..	..	..	..	..	110	126	151	166	223	Koweït
..	..	..	..	..	..	120	107	112	133	117	Liban
..	..	..	..	..	..	115	128	147	153	145	Oman
..	..	..	..	..	..	116	124	147	170	271	Qatar
..	..	..	..	..	..	105	108	111	137	174	Arabie saoudite
..	..	..	..	..	..	124	123	132	165	172	République arabe syrienne
13	15	37	54	83	78	76	93	113	148	142	Turquie
..	..	..	..	..	..	108	113	115	192	233	Émirats arabes unis
—	—	50	42	106	96	107	127	151	150	159	Yémen

Pour les sources et les notes, se reporter à la fin du tableau.

Imports (1) - Importations (1)

4.2.1 Volume indices of exports and imports of countries and geographical regions
2000 = 100

Region, country or territory	Exports (1) - Exportations (1)										
	1980	1985	1990	1995	1998	1999	2001	2002	2003	2004	2005
Developing economies: Oceania	**67**	**81**	**169**	**162**	**103**	**98**	**92**	**93**	**109**	**99**	**85**
Fiji	47	53	..	..	..	..	99	101	126	125	105
French Polynesia	..	..	..	..	..	..	77	72	64	76	84
New Caledonia	..	..	..	..	..	..	78	85	123	108	110
Papua New Guinea	159	128	148	183	98	92	96	92	104	97	82
Samoa	..	99	102	76	98	117	111	99	108	75	78
Solomon Islands	40	56	108	..	..	..	74	88	102	118	124

Sources:
- UN, Economic Commission for Latin America and the Caribbean (ECLAC)
- UN DESA Statistics Division, *Monthly Bulletin of Statistics (MBS)*
- IMF, *International Financial Statistics (IFS)*
- World Bank, *World Bank Africa Database*
- National sources
- USA BLS external trade prices indices
- Unit value indices of Japan Customs
- UNCTAD Commodity Price Statistics

Notes:

(1)   The volume index is the percentage ratio of the export or import value index to the corresponding unit value index.

4.2.1   Indices du volume des exportations et importations
des pays et des régions géographiques
2000 = 100

Imports (1) - Importations (1)											Régions, pays ou territoires
1980	1985	1990	1995	1998	1999	2001	2002	2003	2004	2005	
50	**60**	..	..	..	..	**102**	**110**	**133**	**136**	**134**	**Économies en développement : Océanie**
53	54	..	..	..	..	106	109	139	153	145	Fidji
..	..	..	..	..	..	101	119	143	127	136	Polynésie française
..	..	..	..	..	..	103	112	164	164	161	Nouvelle-Calédonie
..	..	..	..	..	..	96	110	116	131	122	Papouasie-Nouvelle-Guinée
..	..	..	..	..	..	135	147	140	154	167	Samoa
67	90	..	..	..	..	95	78	98	115	151	Îles Salomon

Sources :
- ONU, Commission Economique pour l'Amérique latine et les Caraïbes (CEPALC)
- ONU DAES Division de statistique : *Monthly Bulletin of Statistics (MBS)*
- FMI, *International Financial Statistics (IFS*
- Banque mondiale, *World Bank Africa Database*
- Sources nationales
- USA BLS external trade prices indices
- Unit value indices of Japan Customs
- CNUCED, Statistiques des prix des produits de base

Notes :

(1)   L'Indice de volume des exportations ou des importations est le rapport de l'indice de la valeur des exportations ou des importations à l'indice de la valeur unitaire correspondant exprimé en pourcentage.

4

4.2.1 Unit value indices of exports and imports
of countries and geographical regions
2000 = 100

Region, country or territory	Exports - Exportations										
	1980	1985	1990	1995	1998	1999	2001	2002	2003	2004	2005
WORLD	98	84	111	119	105	103	97	97	107	117	126
DEVELOPED ECONOMIES	88	78	114	123	108	106	98	99	111	121	125
DEVELOPING ECONOMIES	120	100	103	111	98	95	95	93	99	109	123
ECONOMIES IN TRANSITION	..	..	..	..	..	..	96	93	107	129	164
Developing economies: Africa	129	90	110	109	93	90	93	94	111	133	168
Eastern Africa	173	140	149	137	114	101	92	92	100	112	127
Burundi	702	603	440	440	206	131	83	83	94	106	131
Ethiopia	—	—	—	157	147	120	87	87	95	105	125
Kenya	139	102	94	107	122	102	90	89	96	108	128
Madagascar	55	56	68	82	90	88	85	81	93	94	100
Malawi	98	82	126	112	100	104	99	91	91	95	100
Mauritius	74	57	88	100	97	95	92	97	110	120	117
Mozambique	173	140	168	142	112	113	94	88	94	110	131
Rwanda	99	81	70	109	96	83	95	85	91	101	139
Seychelles	..	116	92	110	103	111	88	85	90	104	126
Uganda	..	303	169	209	139	117	91	91	100	107	126
United Republic of Tanzania	..	..	101	97	123	108	96	99	109	123	134
Zambia	198	121	211	220	114	88	93	90	97	124	150
Zimbabwe	241	157	196	149	109	100	94	96	102	119	127
Middle Africa	244	119	133	123	92	79	90	91	104	131	182
Angola	..	63	82	63	43	63	88	89	103	134	188
Cameroon	154	105	104	113	91	78	93	101	112	130	165
Central African Republic	344	343	437	247	141	120	96	94	102	112	115
Congo	92	76	74	64	49	67	90	90	104	133	183
Dem. Rep. of the Congo	355	156	225	268	276	111	99	95	100	110	142
Equatorial Guinea	..	37	87	50	52	79	88	90	104	134	186
Gabon	248	171	166	143	105	104	89	90	103	130	178
Northern Africa	122	97	93	93	86	87	94	91	109	132	175
Algeria	133	98	88	66	55	63	97	86	114	141	196
Egypt	107	98	83	100	99	93	94	93	106	125	155
Libyan Arab Jamahiriya	119	100	..	..	..	..	88	88	103	134	189
Morocco	110	78	107	114	108	107	94	99	116	127	111
Sudan	144	184	131	108	108	91	91	90	108	135	192
Tunisia	110	78	107	114	108	107	99	99	102	107	116
Southern Africa	144	87	120	123	103	100	95	96	119	140	149
Botswana	81	53	105	109	101	102	99	96	98	105	109
Lesotho	131	63	102	124	105	105	100	100	99	99	99
Namibia	156	76	128	114	104	99	98	96	99	108	116
South Africa	144	87	120	123	103	100	94	96	122	147	156
Swaziland	98	58	86	115	103	101	99	96	97	104	110
Western Africa	94	56	94	90	79	82	91	100	111	133	176
Benin	57	62	107	129	114	112	94	87	107	109	106
Burkina Faso	76	80	139	148	122	109	93	89	110	111	107
Cape Verde	78	56	102	126	118	117	100	99	100	101	126
Côte d'Ivoire	144	121	103	122	119	117	106	135	139	147	169
Gambia	93	64	106	115	111	108	91	92	102	107	111
Ghana	44	74	98	112	118	103	102	129	137	132	137
Guinea	..	..	180	138	116	110	94	99	115	152	175
Mali	149	103	155	137	114	102	97	105	128	136	139
Mauritania	99	103	145	139	124	110	102	100	105	115	156
Niger	189	105	137	119	100	97	95	98	112	148	167
Nigeria	87	33	77	60	43	59	87	88	102	132	186
Senegal	160	126	186	175	120	116	95	95	102	113	131
Togo	123	98	140	113	116	113	58	58	63	83	71
Developing economies: America	130	102	94	105	96	93	96	95	100	113	132
Caribbean	121	112	105	107	99	98	96	94	104	121	152
Aruba	..	..	..	..	..	..	90	88	105	134	198
Barbados	..	..	..	..	..	..	98	96	104	110	130
Cuba	..	..	..	..	..	..	97	92	101	129	149
Dominican Republic	121	112	97	106	100	99	102	102	102	108	111
Grenada	112	82	..	100	..	..	89	89	96	95	95
Haiti	146	157	127	103	107	102	100	100	99	101	102
Jamaica	118	78	115	111	94	93	97	92	98	115	115
Montserrat	..	..	..	..	..	..	97	95	104	110	128
Netherlands Antilles	..	..	..	..	..	..	90	87	102	126	173

For sources and notes, see end of table.

4.2.1 Indices de la valeur unitaire des exportations et importations des pays et des régions géographiques
2000 = 100

1980	1985	1990	1995	1998	1999	2001	2002	2003	2004	2005	Régions, pays ou territoires
				Imports - Importations							
94	86	109	114	102	100	97	96	104	114	121	**MONDE**
91	85	111	117	103	101	97	97	107	116	123	ÉCONOMIES DÉVELOPPÉES
103	90	102	108	98	96	97	95	99	109	118	ÉCONOMIES EN DÉVELOPPEMENT
..	..	..	..	..	..	99	97	102	111	121	ÉCONOMIES EN TRANSITION
98	74	111	114	106	101	96	95	107	119	128	**Économies en développement : Afrique**
140	110	128	117	107	101	97	98	105	115	128	*Afrique orientale*
304	248	343	269	170	113	98	98	105	113	121	Burundi
–	–	–	104	98	96	97	98	104	111	120	Éthiopie
138	133	134	103	111	104	95	97	105	118	136	Kenya
66	58	84	103	96	99	96	96	103	113	130	Madagascar
60	49	85	106	97	98	97	99	105	113	123	Malawi
80	71	95	113	103	98	97	99	113	128	138	Maurice
72	65	96	94	96	96	97	97	103	112	118	Mozambique
174	133	174	99	87	89	97	97	103	111	123	Rwanda
..	104	118	107	94	109	96	97	103	114	130	Seychelles
..	96	116	106	100	97	97	97	104	112	125	Ouganda
..	..	94	99	125	109	97	98	105	115	127	République-Unie de Tanzanie
89	65	102	116	101	101	98	100	104	114	124	Zambie
284	162	201	154	112	103	97	97	103	115	127	Zimbabwe
238	107	149	149	160	106	97	98	101	108	114	*Afrique centrale*
..	53	87	78	97	105	97	97	100	105	106	Angola
192	136	128	125	109	111	96	97	103	114	131	Cameroun
132	133	184	128	114	112	99	100	106	113	125	République centrafricaine
95	68	117	123	125	104	99	99	103	109	115	Congo
422	184	261	336	421	107	98	98	104	112	121	Rép. dém. du Congo
..	98	231	136	140	100	98	98	100	106	113	Guinée équatoriale
81	75	106	114	102	99	98	98	101	108	114	Gabon
87	74	104	109	104	103	97	94	105	114	121	*Afrique septentrionale*
79	72	119	114	108	106	100	101	104	110	115	Algérie
50	52	82	86	101	96	98	99	106	116	125	Égypte
..	98	117	98	96	114	83	47	105	112	115	Jamahiriya arabe libyenne
122	99	126	128	102	103	97	98	109	121	127	Maroc
158	184	131	108	108	91	99	99	103	108	114	Soudan
89	70	98	119	112	110	98	98	102	110	120	Tunisie
114	82	115	116	100	99	94	93	112	131	140	*Afrique australe*
97	64	107	122	101	102	99	99	101	105	110	Botswana
100	63	102	124	105	106	99	99	104	111	118	Lesotho
139	71	138	138	109	105	98	97	102	107	112	Namibie
114	82	115	116	99	98	93	92	114	135	143	Afrique du Sud
98	58	86	115	103	101	98	98	104	112	122	Swaziland
58	40	95	110	101	101	98	99	107	117	132	*Afrique occidentale*
66	66	100	121	115	112	98	97	104	116	133	Bénin
117	94	117	113	98	97	97	97	104	114	131	Burkina Faso
78	56	102	126	118	117	99	99	106	112	121	Cap-Vert
71	48	72	100	102	99	94	95	100	112	129	Côte d'Ivoire
51	75	106	115	111	108	98	97	102	113	127	Gambie
21	60	98	105	95	94	96	96	102	107	114	Ghana
..	..	148	154	145	143	97	97	104	115	133	Guinée
128	85	115	125	102	101	97	97	103	113	129	Mali
137	117	149	136	120	106	98	97	104	108	112	Mauritanie
82	51	83	98	101	104	96	99	106	117	131	Niger
48	23	87	108	98	99	97	97	104	113	127	Nigéria
101	77	108	112	92	101	96	97	104	116	133	Sénégal
104	71	105	114	101	99	154	192	260	281	330	Togo
93	89	106	107	100	98	99	96	99	106	118	**Économies en développement : Amérique**
69	81	100	106	99	97	96	97	103	112	126	*Caraïbes*
..	..	..	..	..	..	100	100	103	110	115	Aruba
..	..	..	..	..	..	98	98	103	107	118	Barbade
..	..	..	..	..	..	97	97	104	115	131	Cuba
69	77	101	108	99	97	97	97	103	111	120	République dominicaine
..	..	..	..	..	..	99	98	102	108	115	Grenade
65	77	96	91	97	94	99	100	105	112	119	Haïti
..	..	..	..	..	..	98	97	103	113	129	Jamaïque
..	..	..	..	..	..	99	98	103	113	130	Montserrat
..	..	..	..	..	..	89	90	102	112	127	Antilles néerlandaises

Pour les sources et les notes, se reporter à la fin du tableau.

4

213

4.2.1   Unit value indices of exports and imports
of countries and geographical regions
2000 = 100

Region, country or territory	Exports - Exportations										
	1980	1985	1990	1995	1998	1999	2001	2002	2003	2004	2005
Saint Kitts and Nevis	..	..	..	..	..	..	102	101	102	102	102
Saint Lucia	100	..	..	..	..	..	117	112	108	129	144
Saint Vincent and the Grenadines	..	..	..	..	..	..	113	111	102	125	132
Trinidad and Tobago	121	118	100	..	..	..	94	90	110	127	169
Turks and Caicos Islands	..	..	..	..	..	..	91	88	90	92	95
Central America	*156*	*115*	*94*	*100*	*95*	*96*	*98*	*98*	*99*	*105*	*114*
Belize	..	..	..	..	..	..	107	92	88	98	111
Costa Rica	83	84	81	114	110	105	103	101	98	107	112
El Salvador	78	57	64	109	109	101	95	95	100	107	118
Guatemala	109	86	98	125	108	99	97	94	97	109	121
Honduras	103	96	71	105	110	101	101	95	82	102	135
Mexico	171	120	95	98	94	95	98	98	100	105	114
Nicaragua	120	95	124	116	108	98	95	94	99	111	125
Panama	—	71	66	96	100	101	103	99	95	108	119
South America	*122*	*95*	*94*	*109*	*97*	*90*	*93*	*91*	*101*	*119*	*144*
Argentina	85	80	75	109	99	91	97	93	102	111	113
Bolivia	150	142	101	101	100	96	92	81	90	122	142
Brazil	116	90	99	117	112	98	95	91	101	114	132
Chile	146	91	116	141	94	91	96	94	100	133	164
Colombia	84	79	78	92	85	88	89	85	87	96	111
Ecuador	164	135	96	87	81	83	88	94	107	118	150
Guyana	162	122	127	100	92	..	95	94	100	109	128
Paraguay	90	62	92	110	109	101	98	100	116	128	124
Peru	167	111	113	132	109	98	85	88	98	126	170
Suriname	127	100	..	..	..	..	88	91	107	149	172
Uruguay	121	94	117	122	117	103	100	104	109	121	129
Venezuela (Bolivarian Republic of)	131	103	86	71	52	68	89	90	103	133	183
Developing economies: Asia	**114**	**102**	**104**	**112**	**99**	**97**	**95**	**93**	**97**	**105**	**116**
Eastern Asia	*106*	*102*	*106*	*114*	*101*	*99*	*96*	*93*	*94*	*97*	*99*
China	101	87	97	105	104	101	98	97	97	100	101
China, Hong Kong SAR	92	86	101	110	104	101	98	95	94	95	96
China, Macao SAR	..	..	..	..	..	..	100	100	100	103	105
China, Taiwan Province of	..	113	70	80	92	93	97	95	96	100	104
Korea, Republic of	128	122	156	162	102	100	87	83	85	92	93
Mongolia	..	..	..	..	..	..	97	103	116	144	167
Southern Asia	*108*	*96*	*111*	*107*	*108*	*102*	*93*	*92*	*102*	*118*	*138*
Bangladesh	82	86	81	85	99	100	99	98	97	99	100
India	96	98	121	108	107	101	94	92	104	116	124
Iran, Islamic Republic of	122	100	..	..	..	..	89	90	103	132	180
Maldives	..	..	..	..	..	..	100	100	101	109	129
Nepal	..	..	..	..	..	..	97	97	100	106	111
Pakistan	101	85	100	118	117	109	94	90	96	103	103
Sri Lanka	68	64	75	99	110	101	96	91	96	100	103
South-Eastern Asia	*141*	*97*	*106*	*116*	*98*	*96*	*94*	*92*	*96*	*102*	*104*
Brunei Darussalam	..	..	..	..	..	..	97	87	113	134	181
Cambodia	..	..	..	..	..	..	100	100	102	103	104
Indonesia	157	116	93	103	81	65	90	96	103	120	81
Lao People's Dem. Rep.	..	..	..	..	..	..	98	98	103	106	109
Malaysia	75	73	113	127	107	103	96	94	97	102	108
Myanmar	..	139	136	150	118	109	100	94	110	120	138
Philippines	337	81	83	81	97	107	83	77	78	74	83
Singapore	123	108	115	120	97	96	93	91	90	93	96
Thailand	97	72	96	116	106	102	101	96	105	118	130
Viet Nam	..	..	..	..	..	..	94	94	98	107	120
Western Asia	*107*	*110*	*95*	*82*	*71*	*78*	*96*	*95*	*109*	*132*	*177*
Bahrain	..	..	..	..	..	..	93	90	104	129	183
Jordan	95	86	89	111	107	105	101	102	102	114	131
Kuwait	109	100	..	..	..	..	89	88	105	134	189
Lebanon	..	..	..	..	..	..	100	102	108	119	126
Oman	121	101	..	61	45	65	86	91	104	129	188
Qatar	109	100	..	..	..	..	96	84	109	132	181
Saudi Arabia	100	107	86	62	45	65	104	103	117	143	206
Syrian Arab Republic	329	300	110	99	60	75	88	89	101	124	161
Turkey	120	134	120	129	112	105	97	96	105	122	129
United Arab Emirates	112	100	..	..	..	..	92	91	104	124	160
Yemen	—	—	..	..	..	..	87	89	102	131	182

For sources and notes, see end of table.

Imports - Importations											Régions, pays ou territoires
1980	1985	1990	1995	1998	1999	2001	2002	2003	2004	2005	
..	..	..	..	..	..	99	99	102	109	117	Saint-Kitts-et-Nevis
..	..	..	..	..	..	99	98	102	111	122	Sainte-Lucie
..	..	..	..	..	..	99	98	103	110	121	Saint-Vincent-et-les Grenadines
69	86	100	..	..	..	95	96	102	114	136	Trinité-et-Tobago
..	..	..	..	..	..	99	98	101	108	115	Îles Turques et Caïques
63	*73*	*93*	*105*	*100*	*99*	*99*	*97*	*100*	*105*	*112*	**Amérique centrale**
..	..	..	..	..	..	98	97	103	113	127	Belize
102	100	108	109	101	98	97	96	99	105	112	Costa Rica
83	88	76	90	98	96	98	97	103	112	123	El Salvador
82	92	85	106	97	96	98	97	103	112	124	Guatemala
91	100	91	109	97	95	97	97	102	111	124	Honduras
56	69	93	106	100	100	99	98	100	105	110	Mexique
74	77	80	90	95	93	97	98	104	114	126	Nicaragua
–	69	96	96	97	95	97	96	101	108	119	Panama
108	*100*	*120*	*108*	*100*	*96*	*99*	*93*	*95*	*107*	*124*	**Amérique du Sud**
80	85	118	119	104	100	97	94	94	102	105	Argentine
80	77	99	113	102	98	98	98	103	110	120	Bolivie
157	145	149	106	98	95	100	87	86	102	131	Brésil
60	49	102	104	94	91	98	97	103	113	129	Chili
75	76	96	106	103	99	98	96	95	104	114	Colombie
77	80	84	108	100	97	99	98	104	110	119	Équateur
..	..	..	..	..	..	98	97	104	117	136	Guyana
132	100	89	93	100	97	97	96	102	110	120	Paraguay
68	65	99	107	98	95	97	98	104	114	127	Pérou
..	..	..	..	..	..	98	97	103	111	122	Suriname
86	95	101	105	98	93	97	97	104	116	132	Uruguay
85	72	96	112	102	100	105	100	112	123	126	Venezuela (République bolivarienne du)
112	*96*	*100*	*108*	*96*	*95*	*96*	*95*	*99*	*108*	*117*	**Économies en développement : Asie**
97	*98*	*98*	*107*	*95*	*95*	*95*	*93*	*97*	*105*	*113*	**Asie orientale**
86	94	95	103	94	97	96	95	99	107	117	Chine
92	83	101	111	102	100	97	93	93	96	98	Chine, Hong Kong RAS
..	..	..	..	..	..	98	97	101	106	111	Chine, Macao RAS
..	122	72	89	91	90	97	95	98	107	117	Chine, Taiwan Province de
112	101	117	117	87	87	91	88	96	107	117	Corée, République de
..	..	..	..	..	..	98	98	104	113	131	Mongolie
110	*100*	*121*	*97*	*90*	*95*	*96*	*100*	*107*	*129*	*137*	**Asie méridionale**
60	53	69	76	87	92	96	97	105	114	122	Bangladesh
134	121	141	100	91	96	96	104	108	139	141	Inde
..	..	..	..	..	..	98	100	105	116	128	Iran, Rép. islamique d'
..	..	..	..	..	..	99	98	102	110	121	Maldives
..	..	..	..	..	..	95	96	105	117	131	Népal
78	73	92	99	86	93	94	95	109	122	138	Pakistan
78	68	91	100	..	..	92	85	103	113	124	Sri Lanka
131	*82*	*97*	*111*	*98*	*96*	*97*	*95*	*98*	*106*	*118*	**Asie du Sud-Est**
..	..	..	..	..	..	99	100	102	107	111	Brunéi Darussalam
..	..	..	..	..	..	96	95	100	107	114	Cambodge
..	74	98	114	99	98	95	95	102	115	136	Indonésie
..	..	..	..	..	..	97	97	102	111	123	Rép. dém. populaire lao
105	91	110	117	100	98	97	94	95	100	106	Malaisie
..	41	54	70	102	99	96	97	102	111	123	Myanmar
340	101	95	101	111	104	83	83	82	80	93	Philippines
97	86	99	115	93	93	96	96	99	104	111	Singapour
64	61	81	100	98	95	109	101	106	120	140	Thaïlande
..	..	..	..	..	..	96	96	102	112	124	Viet Nam
110	*132*	*110*	*121*	*100*	*96*	*99*	*99*	*103*	*113*	*120*	**Asie occidentale**
..	..	..	..	..	..	94	93	103	119	152	Bahreïn
108	99	95	96	100	98	102	105	115	130	148	Jordanie
..	..	..	..	..	..	100	100	102	106	110	Koweït
..	..	..	..	..	..	97	97	103	113	128	Liban
..	..	..	..	..	..	100	93	89	115	121	Oman
..	..	..	..	..	..	100	100	102	109	114	Qatar
..	..	..	..	..	..	99	99	102	108	113	Arabie saoudite
..	..	..	..	..	..	97	96	101	112	124	République arabe syrienne
110	140	110	122	101	96	100	98	106	120	128	Turquie
..	..	..	..	..	..	99	99	102	107	112	Émirats arabes unis
–	–	135	161	88	90	99	99	105	114	131	Yémen

Pour les sources et les notes, se reporter à la fin du tableau.

Region, country or territory	Exports - Exportat ons										
	1980	1985	1990	1995	1998	1999	2001	2002	2003	2004	2005
Developing economies: Oceania	**86**	**59**	**41**	**69**	**86**	**97**	**93**	**90**	**102**	**126**	**171**
Fiji	174	100	..	..	..	..	100	96	99	103	125
French Polynesia	..	..	..	..	..	..	97	95	96	100	103
Micronesia, Federated States of	..	..	..	..	..	..	96	93	94	94	104
New Caledonia	..	..	..	..	..	..	94	97	106	149	167
Palau, Pacific Islands (former)	..	..	..	..	..	..	98	96	97	107	120
Papua New Guinea	31	34	37	69	86	97	89	85	101	126	190
Samoa	..	115	61	82	105	123	98	97	97	100	108
Solomon Islands	288	191	100	..	..	..	98	100	112	126	130

Sources:
- UN, Economic Commission for Latin America and the Caribbean (ECLAC)
- UN DESA Statistics Division, *Monthly Bulletin of Statistics (MBS)*
- IMF, *International Financial Statistics (IFS)*
- World Bank, *World Bank Africa Database*
- National sources
- USA BLS external trade prices indices
- Unit value indices of Japan Customs
- UNCTAD Commodity Price Statistics

Imports - Importations											Régions, pays ou territoires
1980	1985	1990	1995	1998	1999	2001	2002	2003	2004	2005	
131	**100**	..	..	..	..	**98**	**98**	**102**	**110**	**122**	**Économies en développement : Océanie**
128	100	..	..	..	..	97	97	102	111	129	Fidji
..	..	..	..	..	..	99	99	102	109	117	Polynésie française
..	..	..	..	..	..	97	96	100	108	114	Micronésie, États fédérés de
..	..	..	..	..	..	98	98	102	108	120	Nouvelle-Calédonie
..	..	..	..	..	..	99	99	101	106	110	Palaos, Îles du Pacifique (anc.)
..	..	..	..	..	..	97	97	102	111	123	Papouasie-Nouvelle-Guinée
..	..	..	..	..	..	98	96	102	112	124	Samoa
145	100	..	..	..	..	97	96	104	115	133	Îles Salomon

Sources :
- ONU, Commission Economique pour l'Amérique latine et les Caraïbes (CEPALC)
- ONU DAES Division de statistique : *Monthly Bulletin of Statistics (MBS)*
- FMI, *International Financial Statistics (IFS)*
- Banque mondiale, *World Bank Africa Database*
- Sources nationales
- USA BLS external trade prices indices
- Unit value indices of Japan Customs
- CNUCED, Statistiques des prix des produits de base

4

Region, country or territory	Terms of trade (1) - Termes de l'échange (1)										
	1980	1985	1990	1995	1998	1999	2001	2002	2003	2004	2005
WORLD	**104**	**97**	**102**	**104**	**103**	**103**	**100**	**101**	**102**	**103**	**104**
DEVELOPED ECONOMIES	97	92	103	105	105	105	101	103	104	104	102
DEVELOPING ECONOMIES	117	111	101	102	100	99	98	98	99	100	104
ECONOMIES IN TRANSITION	..	..	..	..	..	..	97	96	105	117	135
Developing economies: Africa	**132**	**122**	**99**	**95**	**88**	**89**	**97**	**99**	**103**	**111**	**131**
Eastern Africa	*123*	*127*	*116*	*118*	*107*	*100*	*95*	*94*	*95*	*97*	*100*
Burundi	231	243	128	164	121	116	85	84	90	94	108
Ethiopia	–	–	–	151	150	125	89	89	91	94	104
Kenya	101	77	70	104	110	98	95	92	92	91	94
Madagascar	83	97	81	80	94	89	89	85	90	83	77
Malawi	163	167	148	106	103	106	102	92	87	84	82
Mauritius	93	80	93	88	94	97	95	98	97	94	85
Mozambique	240	215	175	151	117	118	97	90	91	98	111
Rwanda	57	61	40	110	110	93	98	88	89	90	113
Seychelles	..	112	78	103	110	102	91	88	88	92	97
Uganda	..	316	146	197	139	121	94	93	96	96	101
United Republic of Tanzania	..	..	107	98	98	99	99	101	103	107	106
Zambia	222	186	207	190	113	87	94	90	93	109	120
Zimbabwe	85	97	98	97	97	97	98	99	99	104	100
Middle Africa	*102*	*112*	*89*	*82*	*58*	*75*	*92*	*93*	*102*	*121*	*160*
Angola	..	119	94	81	44	60	91	92	103	128	178
Cameroon	80	77	81	90	83	70	96	103	109	114	126
Central African Republic	261	258	238	193	124	107	97	94	96	99	92
Congo	97	112	63	52	39	64	91	90	101	121	159
Dem. Rep. of the Congo	84	85	86	80	66	104	101	97	97	98	117
Equatorial Guinea	..	38	38	37	37	79	90	91	103	126	165
Gabon	306	228	157	125	103	105	91	92	102	120	156
Northern Africa	*140*	*131*	*90*	*85*	*82*	*84*	*97*	*97*	*104*	*116*	*145*
Algeria	168	136	74	58	51	59	97	86	110	128	171
Egypt	214	188	101	116	98	97	96	94	100	107	124
Libyan Arab Jamahiriya	..	102	..	..	..	..	106	188	99	120	164
Morocco	90	79	85	89	106	104	97	101	107	104	87
Sudan	91	100	100	100	100	100	93	90	105	125	169
Tunisia	124	111	109	96	96	97	102	102	100	98	97
Southern Africa	*126*	*106*	*104*	*106*	*103*	*101*	*101*	*103*	*106*	*107*	*107*
Botswana	84	83	98	89	100	100	100	97	97	100	100
Lesotho	131	100	100	100	100	99	101	101	95	89	84
Namibia	112	107	93	83	95	94	100	99	97	101	104
South Africa	126	106	104	106	104	102	101	104	107	108	109
Swaziland	100	100	100	100	100	100	100	98	94	93	91
Western Africa	*162*	*140*	*99*	*82*	*78*	*82*	*93*	*100*	*103*	*113*	*133*
Benin	86	94	107	107	99	100	96	90	103	93	79
Burkina Faso	65	85	119	131	124	112	96	91	106	97	81
Cape Verde	100	100	100	100	100	100	101	100	95	90	104
Côte d'Ivoire	203	252	143	122	117	118	112	143	139	131	131
Gambia	182	85	100	100	100	100	93	95	100	95	87
Ghana	210	123	100	107	124	110	106	134	134	123	120
Guinea	..	..	122	90	80	77	96	102	110	132	132
Mali	116	121	135	110	112	101	100	109	124	120	107
Mauritania	72	88	97	102	103	104	104	103	101	106	140
Niger	230	206	165	121	99	93	98	99	106	127	128
Nigeria	181	143	89	56	44	60	89	90	98	117	146
Senegal	158	164	172	156	130	115	99	98	98	98	98
Togo	118	138	133	99	115	114	38	30	24	30	21
Developing economies: America	**140**	**114**	**88**	**99**	**96**	**95**	**97**	**99**	**101**	**106**	**112**
Caribbean	*177*	*139*	*104*	*101*	*100*	*102*	*100*	*97*	*101*	*107*	*120*
Aruba	..	..	..	..	..	..	91	88	103	122	173
Barbados	..	..	..	..	..	..	99	98	101	103	110
Cuba	..	..	..	..	..	..	100	95	97	112	114
Dominican Republic	175	145	96	98	101	102	105	105	99	97	92
Grenada	..	..	..	..	..	..	90	91	94	88	83
Haiti	225	204	132	113	110	109	101	100	95	90	86
Jamaica	..	..	..	..	..	..	100	95	95	101	89
Montserrat	..	..	..	..	..	..	98	97	101	97	99
Netherlands Antilles	..	..	..	..	..	..	102	97	101	113	136

For sources and notes, see end of table.

Purchasing power (2) - Pouvoir d'achat (2)											Régions, pays ou territoires
1980	1985	1990	1995	1998	1999	2001	2002	2003	2004	2005	
32	34	49	70	84	89	99	105	112	125	134	**MONDE**
33	37	54	73	88	92	100	104	108	117	121	ÉCONOMIES DÉVELOPPÉES
29	27	40	64	76	84	97	106	119	139	155	ÉCONOMIES EN DÉVELOPPEMENT
..	..	..	..	..	..	102	111	134	168	194	ÉCONOMIES EN TRANSITION
86	79	68	67	69	78	97	104	113	132	158	**Économies en développement : Afrique**
50	*47*	*58*	*83*	*94*	*96*	*107*	*118*	*118*	*129*	*129*	*Afrique orientale*
43	90	44	79	76	96	79	63	72	85	94	Burundi
–	–	–	84	118	100	97	101	99	126	151	Éthiopie
52	42	44	105	104	97	118	126	133	131	140	Kenya
74	57	46	60	68	72	118	62	101	112	71	Madagascar
130	132	129	101	117	122	122	109	132	112	107	Malawi
35	40	81	87	103	104	93	101	92	86	86	Maurice
107	32	36	49	66	75	205	228	277	368	406	Mozambique
132	189	119	100	131	128	165	109	106	166	191	Rwanda
..	14	25	26	67	69	116	122	138	132	126	Seychelles
..	88	29	94	109	116	103	99	118	138	150	Ouganda
..	..	53	104	71	75	119	136	158	173	159	République-Unie de Tanzanie
220	181	193	135	154	158	150	140	141	193	224	Zambie
26	36	45	71	80	95	65	125	84	87	77	Zimbabwe
22	*45*	*46*	*45*	*39*	*70*	*95*	*109*	*124*	*174*	*257*	*Afrique centrale*
..	55	56	60	46	62	85	108	120	163	288	Angola
47	35	102	85	110	90	99	101	119	119	129	Cameroun
55	43	41	83	83	81	89	91	71	69	64	République centrafricaine
39	64	34	38	44	60	83	93	102	143	166	Congo
71	133	117	65	37	115	126	152	174	218	238	Rép. dém. du Congo
..	2	2	6	29	65	151	175	191	394	578	Guinée equatoriale
109	106	84	97	76	98	99	94	108	125	184	Gabon
93	*83*	*73*	*61*	*60*	*68*	*96*	*102*	*112*	*135*	*171*	*Afrique septentrionale*
81	83	57	45	47	55	89	86	107	136	187	Algérie
130	152	129	86	66	79	90	102	127	138	182	Égypte
..	99	89	69	50	55	108	194	108	143	198	Jamahirya arabe libyenne
29	31	49	77	101	103	99	108	109	110	112	Maroc
19	11	16	28	31	47	95	109	137	193	234	Soudan
43	42	62	79	88	91	116	120	134	151	149	Tunisie
75	*66*	*68*	*80*	*87*	*91*	*104*	*105*	*109*	*117*	*123*	*Afrique australe*
19	48	61	65	71	96	91	87	110	121	148	Botswana
26	16	27	59	84	74	133	171	215	298	261	Lesotho
..	..	60	77	86	89	91	83	94	129	140	Namibie
75	66	68	80	89	91	105	107	107	114	120	Afrique du Sud
42	34	71	83	104	102	119	115	166	191	157	Swaziland
186	*158*	*80*	*67*	*72*	*78*	*91*	*99*	*113*	*129*	*145*	*Afrique occidentale*
24	58	73	88	90	96	97	118	133	124	109	Bénin
37	36	62	117	156	126	112	123	150	204	129	Burkina Faso
51	109	52	62	83	92	93	100	113	126	138	Cap-Vert
114	159	110	98	116	121	108	143	149	159	150	Côte d'Ivoire
403	222	191	93	123	99	68	89	78	130	113	Gambie
358	62	54	98	113	110	107	116	151	153	147	Ghana
..	..	68	68	72	67	113	109	88	95	103	Guinée
29	26	57	64	100	103	137	166	165	159	161	Mali
40	89	84	102	81	98	102	97	87	96	143	Mauritanie
244	180	120	104	117	97	100	100	117	133	156	Niger
255	269	74	54	55	63	86	90	109	130	157	Nigéria
51	79	77	96	114	111	113	119	131	141	125	Sénégal
89	74	70	91	115	109	64	61	65	59	49	Togo
33	34	37	59	78	85	98	100	107	122	133	**Économies en développement : Amérique**
198	*105*	*61*	*64*	*74*	*82*	*101*	*87*	*92*	*101*	*105*	*Caraïbes*
..	..	..	..	..	..	96	59	79	98	120	Aruba
..	..	..	..	..	..	97	91	89	96	111	Barbade
..	..	..	..	..	..	102	87	97	120	103	Cuba
144	99	75	84	92	86	95	93	93	93	84	République dominicaine
..	..	..	..	..	..	78	51	49	39	32	Grenade
110	69	53	38	104	112	87	88	104	110	124	Haïti
..	..	..	..	..	..	96	88	88	95	90	Jamaïque
..	..	..	..	..	..	65	129	154	336	99	Montserrat
..	..	..	..	..	..	136	90	57	61	40	Antilles néerlandaises

Pour les sources et les notes, se reporter à la fin du tableau.

Region, country or territory	Terms of trade (1) - Termes de l'échange (1)										
	1980	1985	1990	1995	1998	1999	2001	2002	2003	2004	2005
Saint Kitts and Nevis	..	..	..	..	..	..	102	102	99	94	87
Saint Lucia	..	..	..	..	..	..	118	115	106	116	118
Saint Vincent and the Grenadines	..	..	..	..	..	..	115	113	100	113	109
Trinidad and Tobago	176	137	100	..	..	..	99	94	108	111	124
Turks and Caicos Islands	..	..	..	..	..	..	92	90	89	86	82
Central America	*248*	*156*	*101*	*95*	*96*	*96*	*100*	*100*	*99*	*100*	*102*
Belize	..	..	..	..	..	..	109	94	85	87	87
Costa Rica	81	84	75	105	109	107	106	105	99	102	100
El Salvador	94	65	84	121	111	105	98	97	97	95	96
Guatemala	133	93	115	118	111	103	99	96	94	97	97
Honduras	113	96	78	96	113	106	104	99	81	92	109
Mexico	305	174	102	92	94	95	100	100	99	101	103
Nicaragua	162	123	155	129	114	105	98	96	95	97	99
Panama	–	103	69	100	103	106	106	102	94	100	100
South America	*113*	*95*	*78*	*101*	*97*	*94*	*94*	*98*	*105*	*111*	*117*
Argentina	106	94	64	92	95	91	99	99	108	110	107
Bolivia	188	184	102	89	98	98	93	82	88	111	118
Brazil	74	62	66	110	114	103	95	105	117	112	101
Chile	243	186	114	136	100	100	98	97	97	118	127
Colombia	112	104	81	87	83	89	91	89	92	93	97
Ecuador	213	169	114	81	81	86	89	96	103	107	126
Guyana	..	..	..	..	..	..	97	97	96	94	94
Paraguay	68	62	103	118	109	104	101	104	113	116	104
Peru	246	171	114	123	111	103	87	90	94	110	134
Suriname	..	..	..	..	..	..	90	94	104	134	141
Uruguay	141	99	116	116	119	111	103	107	104	104	98
Venezuela (Bolivarian Republic of)	154	143	90	63	51	68	85	90	92	108	146
Developing economies: Asia	**102**	**107**	**105**	**104**	**103**	**102**	**99**	**98**	**98**	**97**	**99**
Eastern Asia	*110*	*105*	*108*	*107*	*107*	*105*	*100*	*101*	*97*	*93*	*88*
China	117	93	102	102	111	104	103	103	99	93	87
China, Hong Kong SAR	100	104	100	99	102	101	101	102	101	99	98
China, Macao SAR	..	..	..	..	..	..	102	102	100	97	94
China, Taiwan Province of	..	93	97	90	101	103	101	100	98	93	89
Korea, Republic of	114	121	133	138	117	115	95	95	89	85	79
Mongolia	..	..	..	..	..	..	99	106	112	127	128
Southern Asia	*98*	*96*	*92*	*110*	*120*	*107*	*97*	*91*	*95*	*91*	*101*
Bangladesh	137	162	117	112	114	109	104	101	93	87	82
India	72	81	86	108	118	105	98	89	96	83	87
Iran, Islamic Republic of	..	..	..	..	..	..	91	91	98	114	141
Maldives	..	..	..	..	..	..	101	102	99	99	107
Nepal	..	..	..	..	..	..	102	100	95	91	85
Pakistan	129	116	109	119	136	117	100	95	89	85	75
Sri Lanka	87	94	82	99	..	..	104	107	94	89	83
South-Eastern Asia	*108*	*118*	*109*	*105*	*100*	*99*	*96*	*97*	*97*	*97*	*88*
Brunei Darussalam	..	..	..	..	..	..	98	88	111	126	164
Cambodia	..	..	..	..	..	..	104	106	102	97	91
Indonesia	..	157	95	90	82	66	94	101	100	105	60
Lao People's Dem. Rep.	..	..	..	..	..	..	101	101	100	96	89
Malaysia	71	80	103	109	107	105	100	100	102	102	102
Myanmar	..	339	252	214	116	110	104	97	108	108	112
Philippines	99	80	87	80	87	103	99	93	96	93	89
Singapore	127	126	116	104	104	103	96	94	91	89	87
Thailand	152	118	119	116	108	107	93	95	99	98	93
Viet Nam	..	..	..	..	..	..	98	98	96	96	97
Western Asia	*98*	*83*	*86*	*68*	*71*	*81*	*97*	*96*	*105*	*117*	*147*
Bahrain	..	..	..	..	..	..	98	96	101	108	121
Jordan	88	87	94	116	107	107	99	97	88	87	89
Kuwait	..	..	..	..	..	..	89	88	103	126	171
Lebanon	..	..	..	..	..	..	103	105	105	105	98
Oman	..	..	..	..	..	..	86	97	117	112	156
Qatar	..	..	..	..	..	..	96	84	106	121	159
Saudi Arabia	..	..	..	..	..	..	106	104	115	133	182
Syrian Arab Republic	..	..	..	..	..	..	92	93	100	111	130
Turkey	109	96	109	106	111	109	98	97	99	102	101
United Arab Emirates	..	..	..	..	..	..	93	91	101	116	143
Yemen	–	..	..	..	..	..	88	89	97	115	139

For sources and notes, see end of table.

Purchasing power (2) - Pouvoir d'achat (2)											Régions, pays ou territoires
1980	1985	1990	1995	1998	1999	2001	2002	2003	2004	2005	
..	..	..	..	..	..	107	126	109	100	100	Saint-Kitts-et-Nevis
..	..	..	..	..	..	110	107	129	152	112	Sainte-Lucie
..	..	..	..	..	..	89	85	79	64	70	Saint-Vincent-et-les Grenadines
138	58	46	..	..	..	105	95	119	131	166	Trinité-et-Tobago
..	..	..	..	..	..	..	..	..	..	..	Îles Turques et Caïques
20	*24*	*27*	*47*	*73*	*84*	*96*	*99*	*99*	*108*	*115*	*Amérique centrale*
..	..	..	..	..	..	79	77	88	87	77	Belize
17	17	23	55	94	116	88	94	106	103	107	Costa Rica
87	58	57	83	96	92	93	95	91	92	96	El Salvador
69	43	51	75	99	93	93	94	94	97	104	Guatemala
66	57	66	81	115	89	99	99	94	101	98	Honduras
19	23	26	45	71	82	97	99	· 99	109	117	Mexique
95	61	64	81	94	91	94	89	90	104	106	Nicaragua
_	57	41	76	94	101	109	102	99	102	99	Panama
37	*40*	*45*	*72*	*85*	*87*	*99*	*105*	*119*	*141*	*155*	*Amérique du Sud*
38	37	40	67	96	88	104	104	119	129	144	Argentine
96	66	76	79	88	87	107	108	126	159	181	Bolivie
23	32	38	80	95	92	106	126	154	172	164	Brésil
41	40	43	80	90	98	97	98	110	149	164	Chili
40	36	54	73	81	90	96	95	106	120	142	Colombie
65	74	66	81	85	93	96	104	122	142	172	Équateur
..	..	..	..	..	..	100	102	98	101	81	Guyana
27	35	124	114	117	88	117	113	140	170	163	Paraguay
82	66	47	74	84	92	104	114	125	159	187	Pérou
..	..	..	..	..	..	40	32	36	139	197	Suriname
54	42	73	87	123	105	92	83	92	110	113	Uruguay
71	63	57	52	53	63	82	77	72	97	139	Venezuela (République bolivarienne du)
21	*21*	*38*	*66*	*77*	*85*	*97*	*107*	*122*	*144*	*160*	**Économies en développement : Asie**
10	*16*	*37*	*68*	*82*	*87*	*99*	*114*	*134*	*159*	*176*	*Asie orientale*
8	12	26	58	78	81	111	138	178	222	262	Chine
11	18	40	78	85	86	97	107	119	134	146	Chine, Hong Kong RAS
..	..	..	..	..	..	93	95	100	104	87	Chine, Macao RAS
..	17	63	85	82	91	86	93	100	110	115	Chine, Taiwan Province de
9	17	32	62	88	96	96	108	118	137	141	Corée, République de
..	..	..	..	..	..	100	100	111	143	152	Mongolie
26	*31*	*42*	*72*	*79*	*86*	*99*	*108*	*119*	*125*	*152*	*Asie méridionale*
20	29	38	77	92	93	99	99	105	112	119	Bangladesh
15	18	30	72	87	88	106	115	129	130	166	Inde
..	..	..	..	..	..	86	100	114	135	165	Iran, Rép. islamique d'
..	..	..	..	..	..	103	125	138	152	123	Maldives
..	..	..	..	..	..	96	73	79	80	79	Népal
37	42	67	89	109	100	109	116	122	122	129	Pakistan
25	36	39	70	..	..	96	102	92	94	94	Sri Lanka
13	*20*	*35*	*68*	*78*	*87*	*93*	*100*	*107*	*125*	*129*	*Asie du Sud-Est*
..	..	..	..	..	..	94	95	112	121	145	Brunéi Darussalam
..	..	..	..	..	..	132	95	106	124	130	Cambodge
..	40	42	64	79	80	96	99	99	100	101	Indonésie
..	..	..	..	..	..	103	93	112	99	125	Rép. dém. populaire lao
13	17	27	64	75	88	92	100	106	128	136	Malaisie
..	45	37	75	64	70	150	191	148	130	189	Myanmar
4	11	21	44	67	88	98	110	111	124	108	Philippines
14	19	39	75	86	89	92	95	106	139	151	Singapour
15	17	41	82	80	89	87	97	110	116	114	Thaïlande
..	..	..	..	..	..	108	119	137	158	177	Viet Nam
74	*28*	*45*	*47*	*56*	*73*	*94*	*98*	*112*	*143*	*176*	*Asie occidentale*
..	..	..	..	..	..	95	100	104	102	107	Bahreïn
28	42	59	97	95	98	118	139	141	159	153	Jordanie
..	..	..	..	..	..	84	79	103	138	210	Koweït
..	..	..	..	..	..	128	151	207	216	201	Liban
..	..	..	..	..	..	98	106	116	103	137	Oman
..	..	..	..	..	..	89	94	114	151	198	Qatar
..	..	..	..	..	..	89	94	118	151	190	Arabie saoudite
..	..	..	..	..	..	117	147	122	104	115	République arabe syrienne
10	20	42	64	96	100	113	126	158	186	202	Turquie
..	..	..	..	..	..	99	100	111	170	208	Émirats arabes unis
_	_	13	30	42	66	84	90	92	100	120	Yémen

Pour les sources et les notes, se reporter à la fin du tableau.

4.2.1 Terms of trade indices and purchasing power indices of exports of countries and geographical regions
2000 = 100

Region, country or territory	Terms of trade (1) - Termes de l'échange (1)										
	1980	1985	1990	1995	1998	1999	2001	2002	2003	2004	2005
Developing economies: Oceania	**65**	**59**	**..**	**..**	**..**	**..**	**95**	**93**	**100**	**115**	**141**
Fiji	135	100	..	..	..	..	103	99	97	93	96
French Polynesia	..	..	..	..	..	..	99	96	94	92	88
Micronesia, Federated States of	..	..	..	..	..	..	99	97	93	88	92
New Caledonia	..	..	..	..	..	..	96	99	104	138	140
Palau, Pacific Islands (former)	..	..	..	..	..	..	99	97	96	101	109
Papua New Guinea	..	..	..	..	..	..	92	88	99	113	155
Samoa	..	..	..	..	..	..	100	101	96	90	87
Solomon Islands	198	191	..	..	..	..	100	105	108	109	98

Sources:
- UN, Economic Commission for Latin America and the Caribbean (ECLAC)
- UN DESA Statistics Division, *Monthly Bulletin of Statistics (MBS)*
- IMF, *International Financial Statistics (IFS)*
- World Bank, *World Bank Africa Database*
- National sources
- USA BLS external trade prices indices
- Unit value indices of Japan Customs
- UNCTAD Commodity Price Statistics

Notes:
(1) The terms of trade or "net barter" terms of trade is the percentage ratio of the export unit value index to the import unit value index.
(2) The purchasing power index of exports is the value index of exports deflated by the import unit value index.

Purchasing power (2) - Pouvoir d'achat (2)											Régions, pays ou territoires
1980	1985	1990	1995	1998	1999	2001	2002	2003	2004	2005	
44	48	..	..	..	..	87	86	109	114	120	Économies en développement : Océanie
63	53	..	..	..	..	102	100	123	117	101	Fidji
..	..	..	..	..	..	76	69	61	70	74	Polynésie française
..	..	..	..	..	..	..	..	..	..	..	Micronésie, États fédérés de
..	..	..	..	..	..	74	84	128	149	154	Nouvelle-Calédonie
..	..	..	..	..	..	..	..	..	..	..	Palaos, Îles du Pacifique (anc.)
..	..	..	..	..	..	89	81	103	110	127	Papouasie-Nouvelle-Guinée
..	..	..	..	..	..	111	100	103	67	67	Samoa
78	108	..	..	..	..	74	92	110	130	121	Îles Salomon

Sources :
- ONU, Commission Économique pour l'Amérique latine et les Caraïbes (CEPALC)
- ONU DAES Division de statistique : *Monthly Bulletin of Statistics (MBS)*
- FMI, *International Financial Statistics (IFS)*
- Banque mondiale, *World Bank Africa Database*
- Sources nationales
- USA BLS external trade prices indices
- Unit value indices of Japan Customs
- CNUCED, Statistiques des prix des produits de base

Notes :
(1)   Le terme de l'échange, appelé aussi "troc net", est le rapport de l'indice de la valeur unitaire des exportations à l'indice de la valeur unitaire des importations exprimé en pourcentage.
(2)   Le pouvoir d'achat des exportations est l'indice de la valeur des exportations corrigé par l'indice de la valeur unitaire des importations.

4

Economic grouping	Exports (1) - Exportations (1)										
	1980	1985	1990	1995	1998	1999	2001	2002	2003	2004	2005
DEVELOPING ECONOMIES	**24**	**25**	**40**	**63**	**76**	**85**	**99**	**107**	**120**	**139**	**149**
Developing economies excluding China	27	26	42	64	77	86	97	104	111	126	130
Developing economies excluding LDCs	25	24	40	63	77	85	98	107	120	139	150
High-income countries	26	22	40	64	78	85	95	101	110	127	129
Middle-income countries	26	34	47	67	76	86	100	108	115	127	131
Low-income countries	21	23	35	58	73	83	105	121	144	175	211
Heavily indebted poor countries	46	48	61	66	82	92	107	107	118	135	128
Landlocked countries	41	42	55	55	77	87	106	115	126	145	144
Small island developing states	98	76	69	95	81	86	99	98	104	103	104
Least developed countries	*23*	*32*	*38*	*51*	*65*	*84*	*108*	*118*	*122*	*138*	*144*
Africa and Haiti	29	41	53	54	68	91	112	126	133	157	164
Asia	22	19	24	55	61	72	104	106	108	113	122
Islands	27	44	80	113	106	101	97	108	127	134	117
Major petroleum exporters	*69*	*43*	*61*	*76*	*92*	*104*	*96*	*98*	*99*	*109*	*111*
Africa	86	80	81	83	99	97	96	103	106	113	117
America	58	44	64	83	106	95	99	87	81	91	96
Asia	67	35	56	73	87	107	96	99	100	110	112
Major exporters of manufactured goods	*10*	*17*	*33*	*62*	*77*	*84*	*99*	*110*	*127*	*153*	*173*
America	12	22	34	54	77	87	100	104	108	119	125
Asia	9	16	33	64	77	84	98	111	130	160	183
Emerging economies	*12*	*19*	*35*	*61*	*78*	*86*	*96*	*103*	*112*	*132*	*142*
America	15	24	36	56	80	89	101	105	109	120	125
Asia	11	16	34	64	77	85	94	102	114	139	151
Newly industrialized economies	*10*	*17*	*36*	*66*	*79*	*87*	*95*	*103*	*114*	*134*	*150*
First tier	10	16	37	68	80	86	95	103	118	142	157
Second tier	12	19	32	63	77	89	95	103	105	115	133
Developing economies: Africa	**65**	**64**	**69**	**70**	**79**	**88**	**101**	**106**	**110**	**118**	**120**
Northern Africa excluding Sudan	68	65	84	73	74	82	98	105	108	116	118
Sub-Saharan Africa	63	64	63	70	82	91	102	107	111	120	122
Sub-Saharan Africa excluding South Africa	66	65	62	68	81	93	102	108	117	128	127
Developing economies: America	**24**	**30**	**42**	**60**	**81**	**89**	**100**	**102**	**105**	**115**	**119**
Central America and Greater Caribbean Islands excluding Puerto Rico	11	18	30	51	77	87	96	98	100	107	111
Central America and Greater Caribbean Islands excluding Mexico and Puerto Rico	57	60	59	65	89	96	91	92	100	100	99
South America and Central America	20	27	41	60	82	90	100	102	106	116	120
South America excluding Brazil	34	37	56	71	92	95	102	99	103	114	118
Developing economies: Asia	**21**	**20**	**37**	**63**	**75**	**84**	**98**	**109**	**124**	**148**	**162**
Eastern and South-Eastern Asia excluding China	11	17	35	66	79	86	95	103	114	134	149
Southern Asia excluding India	31	42	63	65	58	77	97	108	117	121	121

Sources:
- UN, Economic Commission for Latin America and the Caribbean (ECLAC)
- UN DESA Statistics Division, *Monthly Bulletin of Statistics (MBS)*
- IMF, *International Financial Statistics (IFS)*
- World Bank, *World Bank Africa Database*
- National sources
- USA BLS external trade prices indices
- Unit value indices of Japan Customs
- UNCTAD Commodity Price Statistics

Notes:

(1) The volume index is the percentage ratio of the export or import value index to the corresponding unit value index.

Imports (1) - Importations (1)											Groupements économiques
1980	1985	1990	1995	1998	1999	2001	2002	2003	2004	2005	
25	27	41	73	82	86	99	106	118	139	149	**ÉCONOMIES EN DÉVELOPPEMENT**
27	28	43	75	84	88	97	101	109	127	136	Économies en développement sans la Chine
25	27	41	73	82	86	98	105	118	139	149	Économies en développement sans les PMA
26	22	40	71	82	87	95	98	104	124	133	Pays à revenu élevé
32	34	50	84	89	88	96	104	112	128	133	Pays à revenu intermédiaire
22	32	36	65	76	83	109	124	153	183	202	Pays à revenu faible
56	54	54	69	85	101	108	111	118	135	146	Pays pauvres très endettés
36	52	55	75	99	93	110	117	129	156	169	Pays sans littoral
116	65	61	68	90	92	102	105	107	113	114	Petits états insulaires en développement
41	*49*	*49*	*69*	*87*	*98*	*111*	*116*	*127*	*142*	*155*	*Pays les moins avancés*
50	54	56	66	78	97	111	119	134	152	172	Afrique et Haïti
46	58	47	79	109	100	111	112	118	130	133	Asie
33	49	53	76	86	97	106	112	128	147	156	Îles
107	*90*	*63*	*77*	*88*	*87*	*108*	*112*	*119*	*152*	*175*	*Principaux exportateurs de pétrole*
223	165	82	101	107	96	122	145	151	165	176	Afrique
113	66	49	65	91	84	108	81	65	87	118	Amérique
..	72	64	73	86	88	106	111	122	159	183	Asie
13	*17*	*36*	*70*	*77*	*84*	*96*	*106*	*120*	*141*	*149*	*Principaux exportateurs d'articles manufacturés*
18	14	24	51	80	84	98	98	98	109	107	Amérique
12	18	38	75	76	84	96	107	125	148	158	Asie
18	*17*	*38*	*73*	*79*	*86*	*92*	*96*	*101*	*118*	*122*	*Économies émergentes*
23	15	25	55	86	87	96	93	94	107	109	Amérique
15	18	44	81	75	86	90	97	104	124	129	Asie
13	*18*	*43*	*82*	*78*	*85*	*93*	*100*	*109*	*127*	*133*	*Économies nouvellement industrialisées*
14	17	42	79	79	86	92	98	107	126	133	Premier tier
11	22	47	93	74	82	96	105	114	130	134	Deuxième tier
77	**79**	**70**	**85**	**97**	**97**	**107**	**114**	**122**	**134**	**147**	**Économies en développement : Afrique**
77	93	91	92	103	98	104	115	111	128	142	Afrique septentrionale sans le Soudan
80	70	58	80	94	97	108	113	128	138	150	Afrique subsaharienne
95	85	61	75	91	99	112	117	131	143	154	Afrique sub-saharienne sans l'Afrique du Sud
34	**24**	**31**	**60**	**89**	**88**	**99**	**94**	**95**	**107**	**112**	**Économies en développement : Amérique**
27	22	30	43	75	84	99	100	98	108	110	Amérique centrale et Grandes Antilles sans Porto Rico
50	50	50	62	89	95	103	105	103	105	111	Amérique centrale et Grandes Antilles sans le Mexique et Porto Rico
28	20	28	60	90	88	98	94	95	109	114	Amérique du Sud et Amérique centrale
57	37	37	83	115	95	97	79	84	106	128	Amérique du Sud sans le Brésil
18	**23**	**41**	**75**	**78**	**85**	**98**	**108**	**124**	**149**	**160**	**Économies en développement : Asie**
13	18	43	82	78	85	93	101	110	128	134	Asie orientale et Asie du Sud-Est sans la Chine
76	81	90	93	102	99	110	126	135	154	164	Asie méridionale sans l'Inde

Sources :
- ONU, Commission Economique pour l'Amérique latine et les Caraïbes (CEPALC)
- ONU DAES Division de statistique : *Monthly Bulletin of Statistics (MBS)*
- FMI, *International Financial Statistics (IFS)*
- Banque mondiale, *World Bank Africa Database*
- Sources nationales
- USA BLS external trade prices indices
- Unit value indices of Japan Customs
- CNUCED, Statistiques des prix des produits de base

Notes :

(1) L'Indice de volume des exportations ou des importations est le rapport de l'indice de la valeur des exportations ou des importations à l'indice de la valeur unitaire correspondant exprimé en pourcentage.

4.2.2   Unit value indices of exports and imports
of economic groupings
2000 = 100

Economic grouping	Exports - Exportat ons										
	1980	1985	1990	1995	1998	1999	2001	2002	2003	2004	2005
DEVELOPING ECONOMIES	**120**	**100**	**103**	**111**	**98**	**95**	**95**	**93**	**99**	**109**	**123**
Developing economies excluding China	121	101	104	111	97	95	95	93	99	111	128
Developing economies excluding LDCs	119	100	102	110	98	95	95	93	99	108	122
High-income countries	113	106	103	111	94	94	95	93	97	106	125
Middle-income countries	126	96	104	117	104	99	96	94	104	118	137
Low-income countries	128	92	101	104	99	95	95	95	98	105	111
Heavily indebted poor countries	162	124	137	137	118	102	96	103	111	125	152
Landlocked countries	190	156	163	152	111	102	94	92	106	125	156
Small island developing states	110	90	88	89	92	96	94	92	105	121	157
Least developed countries	*196*	*120*	*140*	*129*	*108*	*94*	*93*	*93*	*102*	*120*	*157*
Africa and Haiti	205	123	148	140	110	91	91	91	102	125	169
Asia	82	98	90	97	102	102	97	95	101	111	130
Islands	259	158	106	116	111	119	95	98	102	111	124
Major petroleum exporters	*114*	*100*	*89*	*78*	*60*	*65*	*93*	*93*	*107*	*132*	*175*
Africa	113	80	88	70	52	64	91	88	106	135	190
America	129	105	87	71	52	68	90	90	104	132	181
Asia	113	108	90	81	64	65	94	94	108	132	170
Major exporters of manufactured goods	*123*	*101*	*106*	*114*	*102*	*99*	*96*	*93*	*95*	*100*	*105*
America	142	105	97	105	99	96	97	96	100	108	120
Asia	116	100	107	116	102	100	95	93	95	99	103
Emerging economies	*123*	*104*	*107*	*119*	*100*	*97*	*95*	*92*	*95*	*102*	*109*
America	136	102	96	110	99	95	97	95	100	111	126
Asia	111	106	111	122	100	98	94	91	93	98	102
Newly industrialized economies	*130*	*103*	*107*	*117*	*99*	*97*	*94*	*91*	*93*	*98*	*99*
First tier	114	107	109	118	100	98	94	91	91	94	97
Second tier	148	91	100	114	99	95	94	93	98	107	106
Developing economies: Africa	**129**	**90**	**110**	**109**	**93**	**90**	**93**	**94**	**111**	**133**	**168**
Northern Africa excluding Sudan	122	96	92	92	85	87	94	91	109	132	174
Sub-Saharan Africa	133	86	117	115	96	91	93	96	111	133	165
Sub-Saharan Africa excluding South Africa	127	85	115	109	92	87	92	95	106	127	169
Developing economies: America	**130**	**102**	**94**	**105**	**96**	**93**	**96**	**95**	**100**	**113**	**132**
Central America and Greater Caribbean Islands excluding Puerto Rico	153	114	94	100	96	96	99	98	99	106	114
Central America and Greater Caribbean Islands excluding Mexico and Puerto Rico	105	88	91	111	105	101	100	98	98	110	119
South America and Central America	131	101	94	105	96	93	96	95	100	113	132
South America excluding Brazil	125	98	91	105	87	86	92	91	100	122	152
Developing economies: Asia	**114**	**102**	**104**	**112**	**99**	**97**	**95**	**93**	**97**	**105**	**116**
Eastern and South-Eastern Asia excluding China	130	103	107	117	99	97	94	91	93	98	100
Southern Asia excluding India	113	95	91	105	110	104	93	91	100	120	153

Sources:
- UN, Economic Commission for Latin America and the Caribbean (ECLAC)
- UN DESA Statistics Division, *Monthly Bulletin of Statistics (MBS)*
- IMF, *International Financial Statistics (IFS)*
- World Bank, *World Bank Africa Database*
- National sources
- USA BLS external trade prices indices
- Unit value indices of Japan Customs
- UNCTAD Commodity Price Statistics

				Imports - Importations							Groupements économiques
1980	1985	1990	1995	1998	1999	2001	2002	2003	2004	2005	
103	90	102	108	98	96	97	95	99	109	118	ÉCONOMIES EN DÉVELOPPEMENT
104	90	103	109	98	96	97	95	99	109	118	Économies en développement sans la Chine
102	90	102	108	97	96	97	95	99	108	118	Économies en développement sans les PMA
86	90	99	109	96	95	97	94	98	104	111	Pays à revenu élevé
106	92	106	110	100	97	99	96	102	114	126	Pays à revenu intermédiaire
120	89	106	105	98	98	95	95	100	111	122	Pays à revenu faible
121	94	119	119	115	100	98	99	106	115	127	Pays pauvres très endettés
149	101	132	118	103	100	98	98	103	111	122	Pays sans littoral
80	86	100	115	103	102	97	97	104	114	129	Petits états insulaires en développement
129	88	117	112	111	99	98	99	106	114	124	*Pays les moins avancés*
144	98	127	123	122	102	99	100	107	115	124	Afrique et Haïti
60	52	87	91	91	93	96	97	104	113	123	Asie
118	81	120	131	118	116	98	98	103	111	122	Îles
68	65	103	113	100	101	98	97	103	111	121	*Principaux exportateurs de pétrole*
61	58	108	108	102	105	96	91	104	110	117	Afrique
82	74	97	112	102	100	101	98	108	120	127	Amérique
..	74	100	116	98	97	98	98	102	111	121	Asie
113	99	102	108	97	96	97	94	98	107	116	*Principaux exportateurs d'articles manufacturés*
110	102	112	106	99	99	99	95	97	104	115	Amérique
115	98	100	108	96	95	96	94	98	107	116	Asie
99	96	100	108	95	94	97	94	98	106	117	*Économies émergentes*
99	95	111	107	99	98	99	95	98	105	116	Amérique
99	96	97	108	93	92	97	94	98	107	117	Asie
118	92	98	109	96	95	96	93	96	104	113	*Économies nouvellement industrialisées*
100	96	99	109	95	93	95	92	96	103	110	Premier tier
161	80	95	109	101	98	98	95	98	106	122	Deuxième tier
98	74	111	114	106	101	96	95	107	119	128	Économies en développement : Afrique
82	71	103	109	104	103	97	93	105	114	121	Afrique septentrionale sans le Soudan
104	75	117	117	107	100	96	96	108	122	132	Afrique subsaharienne
99	73	118	118	111	102	98	98	105	114	125	Afrique sub-saharienne sans l'Afrique du Sud
93	89	106	107	100	98	99	96	99	106	118	Économies en développement : Amérique
63	74	93	105	100	99	98	97	101	106	113	Amérique centrale et Grandes Antilles sans Porto Rico
82	84	94	103	98	96	97	97	102	111	122	Amérique centrale et Grandes Antilles sans le Mexique et Porto Rico
95	89	107	107	100	98	99	96	98	106	117	Amérique du Sud et Amérique centrale
78	73	100	109	101	97	99	97	101	111	120	Amérique du Sud sans le Brésil
112	96	100	108	96	95	96	95	99	108	117	Économies en développement : Asie
118	92	98	109	96	95	96	93	96	104	113	Asie orientale et Asie du Sud-Est sans la Chine
73	67	86	93	86	93	96	96	106	116	129	Asie méridionale sans l'Inde

Sources :
- ONU, Commission Economique pour l'Amérique latine et les Caraïbes (CEPALC)
- ONU DAES Division de statistique : *Monthly Bulletin of Statistics (MBS)*
- FMI, *International Financial Statistics (IFS)*
- Banque mondiale, *World Bank Africa Database*
- Sources nationales
- USA BLS external trade prices indices
- Unit value indices of Japan Customs
- CNUCED, Statistiques des prix des produits de base

4.2.2 Terms of trade indices and purchasing power indices of exports of economic groupings
2000 = 100

Economic grouping	Terms of trade (1) - Termes de l'échange (1)										
	1980	1985	1990	1995	1998	1999	2001	2002	2003	2004	2005
DEVELOPING ECONOMIES	**117**	**111**	**101**	**102**	**100**	**99**	**98**	**98**	**99**	**100**	**104**
Developing economies excluding China	116	112	101	102	99	98	97	98	99	102	108
Developing economies excluding LDCs	117	110	100	102	100	99	98	99	99	100	104
High-income countries	131	118	105	102	98	99	98	99	99	102	112
Middle-income countries	118	104	98	107	104	102	96	97	102	104	109
Low-income countries	107	103	95	99	101	97	99	99	98	95	91
Heavily indebted poor countries	134	132	116	114	102	102	98	104	104	109	119
Landlocked countries	127	154	124	128	108	102	96	95	102	112	128
Small island developing states	138	105	88	77	89	95	97	94	101	107	122
Least developed countries	*152*	*137*	*120*	*115*	*97*	*95*	*96*	*94*	*97*	*106*	*127*
Africa and Haiti	143	125	116	113	90	89	92	91	96	109	136
Asia	137	190	103	106	113	109	100	98	97	98	105
Islands	221	195	88	89	95	103	97	100	99	100	102
Major petroleum exporters	*168*	*154*	*86*	*69*	*60*	*65*	*95*	*96*	*104*	*119*	*144*
Africa	185	137	81	65	51	62	94	97	103	123	162
America	158	141	91	63	51	68	89	92	96	110	142
Asia	..	146	89	70	65	67	96	96	105	119	140
Major exporters of manufactured goods	*109*	*102*	*104*	*106*	*105*	*104*	*99*	*99*	*98*	*94*	*91*
America	130	104	86	99	100	97	99	101	103	104	104
Asia	102	102	107	107	106	105	99	99	97	93	89
Emerging economies	*124*	*109*	*107*	*110*	*105*	*103*	*97*	*98*	*97*	*96*	*94*
America	137	107	87	102	100	97	98	100	103	106	108
Asia	112	110	115	113	108	107	97	97	94	92	87
Newly industrialized economies	*110*	*111*	*109*	*107*	*103*	*103*	*98*	*98*	*97*	*94*	*88*
First tier	113	111	111	108	105	105	98	98	95	92	88
Second tier	92	113	104	105	98	97	96	98	101	101	87
Developing economies: Africa	**132**	**122**	**99**	**95**	**88**	**89**	**97**	**99**	**103**	**111**	**131**
Northern Africa excluding Sudan	148	135	90	85	82	84	98	98	104	115	143
Sub-Saharan Africa	128	114	100	98	89	91	96	99	103	109	125
Sub-Saharan Africa excluding South Africa	128	118	97	93	82	86	94	97	101	112	135
Developing economies: America	**140**	**114**	**88**	**99**	**96**	**95**	**97**	**99**	**101**	**106**	**112**
Central America and Greater Carribean Islands excluding Puerto Rico	242	155	101	95	96	96	100	100	99	100	101
Central America and Greater Carribean Islands excluding Mexico and Puerto Rico	128	104	97	108	107	105	103	101	96	99	97
South America and Central America	139	113	88	99	96	95	97	99	101	106	112
South America excluding Brazil	160	134	91	96	87	88	93	94	99	110	126
Developing economies: Asia	**102**	**107**	**105**	**104**	**103**	**102**	**99**	**98**	**98**	**97**	**99**
Eastern and South-Eastern Asia excluding China	110	112	109	107	103	103	98	98	97	95	88
Southern Asia excluding India	155	141	107	114	127	113	96	95	95	103	118

Sources:
- UN, Economic Commission for Latin America and the Caribbean (ECLAC)
- UN DESA Statistics Division, *Monthly Bulletin of Statistics (MBS)*
- IMF, *International Financial Statistics (IFS)*
- World Bank, *World Bank Africa Database*
- National sources
- USA BLS external trade prices indices
- Unit value indices of Japan Customs
- UNCTAD Commodity Price Statistics

Notes:

(1) The terms of trade or "net barter" terms of trade is the percentage ratio of the export unit value index to the import unit value index.
(2) The purchasing power index of exports is the value index of exports deflated by the import unit value index.

4.2.2 Indices des termes de l'échange et du pouvoir d'achat des exportations des groupements économiques
2000 = 100

				Purchasing power (2) - Pouvoir d'achat (2)							Groupements économiques
1980	1985	1990	1995	1998	1999	2001	2002	2003	2004	2005	
29	**27**	**40**	**64**	**76**	**84**	**97**	**106**	**119**	**139**	**155**	**ÉCONOMIES EN DÉVELOPPEMENT**
31	29	42	65	76	85	95	101	110	128	141	Économies en développement sans la Chine
29	27	40	65	77	84	97	106	119	139	155	Économies en développement sans les PMA
34	25	42	65	76	84	94	100	109	130	145	Pays à revenu élevé
30	36	47	71	79	88	96	105	116	132	142	Pays à revenu intermédiaire
23	24	33	58	74	81	104	120	141	166	192	Pays à revenu faible
62	63	70	76	84	94	105	112	124	147	153	Pays pauvres très endettés
53	64	68	71	83	88	102	109	129	163	184	Pays sans littoral
136	79	61	73	73	81	96	92	105	110	127	Petits états insulaires en développement
34	*44*	*46*	*59*	*62*	*80*	*104*	*110*	*118*	*146*	*183*	*Pays les moins avancés*
41	51	61	61	61	81	103	115	127	171	223	Afrique et Haïti
30	36	25	59	69	79	105	104	105	111	128	Asie
59	86	70	101	100	104	94	109	126	135	119	Îles
116	*66*	*53*	*52*	*55*	*68*	*91*	*94*	*104*	*129*	*161*	*Principaux exportateurs de pétrole*
159	110	66	54	51	60	90	100	109	138	190	Afrique
92	62	58	53	54	65	88	80	78	100	136	Amérique
..	51	50	51	57	72	91	95	105	131	158	Asie
11	*17*	*34*	*66*	*81*	*87*	*98*	*109*	*124*	*144*	*157*	*Principaux exportateurs d'articles manufacturés*
16	23	29	54	77	84	99	105	111	124	130	Amérique
10	16	35	68	82	88	97	110	126	148	162	Asie
15	*20*	*37*	*67*	*81*	*89*	*93*	*101*	*109*	*127*	*133*	*Économies émergentes*
20	26	32	57	80	86	99	104	112	127	135	Amérique
12	18	39	72	83	91	91	99	108	127	132	Asie
11	*19*	*39*	*71*	*82*	*89*	*93*	*101*	*110*	*127*	*131*	*Économies nouvellement industrialisées*
12	18	41	73	84	90	93	101	112	131	138	Premier tier
11	21	34	66	75	86	92	101	106	116	115	Deuxième tier
86	**79**	**68**	**67**	**69**	**78**	**97**	**104**	**113**	**132**	**158**	**Économies en développement : Afrique**
101	88	75	62	61	69	96	102	112	133	169	Afrique septentrionale sans le Soudan
81	73	63	69	73	83	98	106	114	131	153	Afrique subsaharienne
85	77	61	63	66	79	95	105	118	143	172	Afrique sub-saharienne sans l'Afrique du Sud
33	**34**	**37**	**59**	**78**	**85**	**98**	**100**	**107**	**122**	**133**	**Économies en développement : Amérique**
26	28	30	48	73	84	96	98	99	107	113	Amérique centrale et Grandes Antilles sans Porto Rico
72	63	57	70	95	100	94	93	96	99	96	Amérique centrale et Grandes Antilles sans le Mexique et Porto Rico
27	31	36	59	78	85	98	101	108	124	135	Amérique du Sud et Amérique centrale
54	49	51	68	80	84	95	94	102	126	150	Amérique du Sud sans le Brésil
21	**21**	**38**	**66**	**77**	**85**	**97**	**107**	**122**	**144**	**160**	**Économies en développement : Asie**
12	19	39	71	81	89	93	102	111	127	132	Asie orientale et Asie du Sud-Est sans la Chine
48	59	67	74	74	87	93	103	111	125	143	Asie méridionale sans l'Inde

Sources :
- ONU, Commission Economique pour l'Amérique latine et les Caraïbes (CEPALC)
- ONU DAES Division de statistique : *Monthly Bulletin of Statistics (MBS)*
- FMI, *International Financial Statistics (IFS)*
- Banque mondiale, *World Bank Africa Database*
- Sources nationales
- USA BLS external trade prices indices
- Unit value indices of Japan Customs
- CNUCED, Statistiques des prix des produits de base

Notes :

(1)   Le terme de l'échange, appelé aussi "troc net", est le rapport de l'indice de la valeur unitaire des exportations à l'indice de la valeur unitaire des importations exprimé en pourcentage.
(2)   Le pouvoir d'achat des exportations est l'indice de la valeur des exportations corrigé par l'indice de la valeur unitaire des importations.

229

Market / Marchés	Year / Année	MFN rate - Simple average (2) / Droit NPF - Moyenne simple (2)						MFN rate - Weighted average (3) / Droit NPF - Moyenne pondérée (3)					
		Total of non-agricultural and non-fuel products / Total des produits non-agricoles et non-pétroliers	Ores and metals / Minérais et métaux	Manu-factured products / Produits manu-facturés	Of which: / dont : Chemical products / Produits chimiques	Machinery and transport equipment / Machines et matériel de transport	Other manu-factured products / Produits manu-facturés divers	Total of non-agricultural and non-fuel products / Total des produits non-agricoles et non-pétroliers	Ores and metals / Minérais et métaux	Manu-factured products / Produits manu-facturés	Of which: / dont : Chemical products / Produits chimiques	Machinery and transport equipment / Machines et matériel de transport	Other manu-factured products / Produits manu-facturés divers
SITC Rev.2 (1) / CTCI Rév.2 (1)		5+6+7+8 +27+28	27+28+68	(5+6+7+8) - 68	5	7	(6+8) - 68	5+6+7+8 +27+28	27+28+68	(5+6+7+8) - 68	5	7	(6+8) - 68
Albania - Albanie	1997	16.1	12.2	16.2	12.4	8.9	20.6	15.2	15.1	15.2	12.3	9.8	18.7
	2001	10.5	8.3	10.6	7.6	6.0	13.6	11.6	9.5	11.6	8.1	7.2	14.9
	2002	7.2	5.1	7.3	3.8	3.5	10.1	8.6	7.9	8.7	4.8	3.9	11.8
	2005	5.8	2.5	5.9	2.0	2.5	8.7	7.6	1.1	7.6	2.9	4.7	10.2
Algeria - Algérie	1993	24.4	12.1	24.8	13.2	16.8	32.1	18.7	11.5	18.8	13.7	16.5	23.8
	1997	23.5	11.5	23.9	15.5	17.3	29.6	19.4	12.1	19.4	10.0	18.3	25.2
	1998	23.3	11.4	23.7	15.1	17.1	29.4	18.6	12.1	18.6	9.0	17.2	25.3
	2001	21.7	11.4	22.0	13.8	16.8	27.1	17.2	12.7	17.2	9.2	17.0	21.4
	2002	18.6	12.3	18.9	15.7	12.2	22.7	13.1	13.8	13.1	11.6	11.5	16.2
	2003	18.1	11.9	18.4	14.3	11.9	22.5	12.5	10.9	12.5	8.5	11.3	16.3
	2005	18.1	11.9	18.4	14.3	11.8	22.5	12.5	9.6	12.5	8.6	11.7	16.2
Angola	2002	8.0	9.5	7.9	4.8	3.8	10.6	5.9	6.4	5.9	7.0	4.1	8.7
	2005	6.4	7.2	6.2	4.7	3.0	8.1	4.4	7.1	4.4	7.3	2.7	10.2
Antigua and Barbuda - Antigua-et-Barbuda	1996	20.6	16.0	20.7	14.5	20.6	21.6	25.0	13.6	25.1	19.1	31.0	20.7
	1999	17.2	12.8	17.2	11.3	17.9	18.0	22.1	11.4	22.2	14.7	29.8	16.4
	2000	10.1	4.3	10.3	6.3	8.9	12.3	15.3	10.0	15.3	16.0	13.6	17.1
	2001	8.6	3.9	8.8	5.7	8.0	10.2	12.4	7.8	12.5	12.4	12.0	13.1
	2002	8.6	3.9	8.8	5.7	8.0	10.2	12.4	7.8	12.5	12.4	12.0	13.1
	2003	8.6	3.9	8.8	5.7	8.0	10.2	12.4	7.8	12.5	12.4	12.0	13.1
Argentina - Argentine	1992	13.8	8.1	14.1	9.4	13.6	16.0	13.5	6.5	13.6	8.5	14.5	14.8
	1993	12.5	6.0	12.8	7.6	14.6	13.9	13.4	5.2	13.5	7.7	14.7	14.2
	1995	12.7	6.5	13.0	8.3	9.9	15.9	12.0	5.9	12.1	8.9	11.3	15.8
	1996	13.5	6.3	13.8	8.3	13.4	15.9	14.2	5.8	14.4	8.8	15.5	16.2
	1997	13.6	6.3	13.9	8.3	14.5	15.7	14.7	6.0	14.9	9.3	16.1	15.9
	1998	15.9	9.1	16.3	11.3	15.2	18.4	16.3	8.5	16.4	12.4	16.8	18.2
	1999	15.8	9.1	16.1	11.4	14.9	18.2	15.3	8.6	15.4	12.5	15.2	17.7
	2000	15.7	9.0	16.0	11.4	14.7	18.1	15.1	8.4	15.2	12.4	15.0	17.6
	2001	13.0	8.5	13.2	11.0	14.5	13.5	14.1	7.3	14.2	12.1	15.4	14.1
	2002	14.5	7.3	14.8	9.7	15.0	16.5	12.7	5.1	13.1	10.9	13.9	15.0
	2003	15.2	5.9	15.6	8.3	14.0	18.8	13.6	4.0	14.0	9.5	16.1	15.8
	2004	12.7	7.0	13.0	9.0	8.8	16.1	14.2	4.8	14.4	9.5	15.5	14.7
	2005	11.6	5.8	11.9	8.0	8.5	14.6	13.5	4.2	13.6	8.4	15.0	13.3
Armenia - Arménie	2001	2.2	0.0	2.3	0.1	1.4	3.5	1.3	0.0	1.3	0.0	2.4	1.2
Australia - Australie	1991	13.6	2.6	14.1	5.0	11.5	18.2	11.7	5.1	11.8	5.5	9.9	16.6
	1993	10.1	2.4	10.4	4.4	9.3	13.0	10.0	4.9	10.1	5.0	9.4	12.9
	1996	6.5	1.2	6.7	1.9	4.0	9.5	5.4	2.2	5.4	1.8	4.5	8.4
	1997	6.1	1.2	6.3	1.9	4.0	8.8	5.4	2.2	5.4	1.9	4.6	8.0
	1998	5.8	1.2	6.0	1.9	3.9	8.2	5.2	2.1	5.2	1.8	4.5	7.6
	1999	5.5	1.2	5.6	1.9	3.9	7.7	4.9	2.4	4.9	1.8	4.2	7.3
	2000	5.2	1.2	5.3	1.9	3.9	7.1	4.7	2.4	4.7	1.7	4.2	7.0
	2001	4.8	1.1	5.0	1.5	3.2	6.9	4.5	2.3	4.5	1.7	3.9	6.8
	2002	4.9	1.0	5.0	1.5	3.2	7.0	4.6	2.2	4.6	1.7	4.0	6.8
	2003	4.9	1.0	5.0	1.5	3.2	7.0	4.7	2.2	4.7	1.7	4.2	6.8
	2004	4.9	1.0	5.0	1.5	3.2	7.0	4.7	2.5	4.7	1.6	4.2	6.8
	2005	4.0	1.0	4.1	1.5	3.0	5.5	3.8	2.5	3.8	1.6	3.4	5.5
Azerbaijan - Azerbaïdjan	2002	8.3	4.4	8.4	3.9	5.2	11.3	6.9	3.4	7.0	6.0	4.0	10.5
	2005	8.6	4.3	8.8	4.0	6.0	11.3	6.9	2.4	7.1	5.9	3.7	10.6
Bahamas	1999	32.1	34.3	32.1	34.0	35.6	30.0	32.1	28.7	32.1	26.9	38.5	27.6
	2002	31.6	33.3	31.6	33.5	34.6	29.6	30.3	26.9	30.4	24.6	36.8	26.1
Bahrain - Bahreïn	1999	7.7	5.4	7.8	5.3	9.5	8.1	9.0	5.4	9.6	6.2	12.4	7.9
	2001	7.7	5.4	7.8	5.3	9.5	8.1	9.3	5.3	10.0	6.2	13.0	8.0
	2005	4.9	4.8	4.9	4.9	4.9	5.0	4.9	5.0	4.9	3.9	5.0	5.0
Bangladesh	1989	118.1	45.0	121.3	62.7	69.2	160.5	108.8	57.5	110.1	52.5	74.7	143.6
	1994	82.7	61.2	83.8	68.6	77.3	91.6	86.3	67.5	86.5	70.1	78.0	92.7

For sources and notes, see end of table.   Pour les sources et les notes, se reporter à la fin du tableau.

Market / Marchés	Year / Année	MFN rate - Simple average (2) / Droit NPF - Moyenne simple (2)						MFN rate - Weighted average (3) / Droit NPF - Moyenne pondérée (3)					
		Total of non-agricultural and non-fuel products / Total des produits non-agricoles et non-pétroliers	Ores and metals / Minérais et métaux	Manufactured products / Produits manufacturés	Chemical products / Produits chimiques	Machinery and transport equipment / Machines et matériel de transport	Other manufactured products / Produits manufacturés divers	Total of non-agricultural and non-fuel products / Total des produits non-agricoles et non-pétroliers	Ores and metals / Minérais et métaux	Manufactured products / Produits manufacturés	Chemical products / Produits chimiques	Machinery and transport equipment / Machines et matériel de transport	Other manufactured products / Produits manufacturés divers
SITC Rev.2 (1) / CTCI Rév.2 (1)		5+6+7+8 +27+28	27+28+68	(5+6+7+8) - 68	5	7	(6+8) - 68	5+6+7+8 +27+28	27+28+68	(5+6+7+8) - 68	5	7	(6+8) - 68
Bangladesh	1999	21.6	14.4	22.0	16.7	13.4	27.4	20.3	11.6	20.4	11.8	12.9	26.6
	2000	21.6	14.4	22.0	16.7	13.3	27.4	19.8	11.6	19.9	11.8	11.9	26.6
	2002	20.4	12.8	20.7	14.9	12.4	26.2	20.1	8.3	20.2	10.8	12.8	27.1
	2003	19.2	13.0	19.5	14.6	12.9	23.9	19.4	11.5	19.5	10.8	13.5	25.5
	2004	18.1	13.0	18.4	14.2	12.5	22.3	17.0	12.8	17.1	10.5	11.1	23.4
	2005	15.2	9.9	15.5	11.5	11.7	18.4	75.8	10.4	76.7	9.7	164.0	41.8
Barbados - Barbade	1996	21.2	19.4	21.2	14.5	18.9	22.7	23.5	43.6	23.3	15.9	24.9	24.6
	1999	17.9	16.2	17.9	11.4	16.4	19.2	22.4	19.1	22.4	14.2	27.8	21.5
	2000	17.9	16.2	17.9	11.4	16.4	19.2	21.6	18.2	21.6	14.3	26.1	21.1
	2001	9.5	5.8	9.6	6.5	8.0	11.3	14.8	8.9	14.8	13.8	11.3	17.9
	2002	9.5	5.8	9.6	6.5	8.0	11.3	14.3	9.6	14.3	14.0	11.2	17.1
	2003	9.5	5.8	9.6	6.5	8.0	11.3	14.9	9.0	14.9	14.1	12.0	17.6
Belarus - Bélarus	1996	12.4	9.9	12.6	6.0	11.9	15.2	10.3	5.0	10.5	7.0	11.1	11.5
	1997	13.0	8.9	13.2	7.0	12.7	15.5	11.0	7.0	11.2	8.6	11.6	12.0
	2002	11.1	8.2	11.2	6.7	10.6	13.1	10.2	8.1	10.4	8.0	10.6	11.2
Belize	1996	21.2	19.6	21.2	14.5	18.8	22.8	18.9	22.8	18.8	12.6	21.0	20.2
	1999	17.8	16.4	17.8	11.1	16.1	19.2	17.1	21.6	16.6	14.2	27.4	14.5
	2001	8.9	4.4	9.0	5.6	7.5	10.9	11.2	15.8	11.2	9.7	10.4	12.3
	2002	8.9	4.4	9.0	5.6	7.5	10.9	11.0	15.0	10.9	9.3	10.2	12.3
	2003	8.9	4.4	9.0	5.6	7.5	10.9	10.8	11.8	10.8	9.3	10.7	11.3
Benin - Bénin	2001	11.8	7.5	12.0	6.3	8.5	15.4	12.3	6.6	12.4	4.8	10.3	16.4
	2002	11.7	7.5	11.9	6.3	8.5	15.3	12.4	7.1	12.5	5.2	11.7	16.5
	2003	11.7	7.3	11.9	6.3	8.6	15.3	12.4	7.0	12.4	5.2	11.7	16.4
	2004	11.7	7.4	11.9	6.3	8.6	15.3	12.4	7.1	12.5	5.2	11.7	16.5
	2005	11.7	7.4	11.9	6.3	8.6	15.3	12.4	7.1	12.5	5.2	11.6	16.5
Bermuda - Bermudes	2001	19.3	19.9	19.3	20.1	23.9	17.1	26.2	20.3	26.2	1.9	32.3	18.8
	2005	19.3	20.0	19.3	20.2	23.7	17.2	27.6	18.6	27.6	11.4	31.8	14.7
Bhutan - Bhoutan	1996	15.5	17.8	15.5	9.2	12.0	19.5	16.7	12.3	16.8	28.8	14.3	19.0
	2002	16.5	17.4	16.5	12.7	11.3	20.0	15.0	16.3	15.0	26.3	11.2	19.2
	2004	19.0	24.0	18.7	13.5	11.6	23.3	14.7	26.0	14.5	26.8	9.1	21.5
	2005	19.0	24.0	18.7	13.5	11.6	23.3	14.7	26.0	14.5	26.8	9.1	21.5
Bolivia - Bolivie	1993	9.8	10.0	9.8	10.0	9.0	10.0	9.3	10.0	9.3	10.0	8.8	9.9
	1994	10.0	10.0	10.0	10.0	10.0	10.0	9.9	10.0	9.9	10.0	10.0	9.8
	1995	9.7	10.0	9.7	10.0	8.6	10.0	9.4	10.0	9.4	10.0	8.9	9.9
	1996	9.7	10.0	9.7	10.0	8.6	10.0	9.1	10.0	9.1	10.0	8.7	9.7
	1997	9.7	10.0	9.7	10.0	8.6	10.0	9.1	10.0	9.1	10.0	8.7	9.7
	1998	9.7	10.0	9.7	10.0	8.6	10.0	8.9	10.0	8.9	10.0	8.3	9.6
	1999	9.7	10.0	9.7	10.0	8.6	10.0	9.0	10.0	9.0	10.0	8.2	9.8
	2000	9.2	9.9	9.2	9.9	6.7	9.9	8.2	10.0	8.2	9.7	6.4	9.7
	2001	9.2	9.9	9.2	9.9	6.7	9.9	8.6	10.0	8.6	9.7	6.8	9.8
	2002	9.6	10.0	9.6	10.7	7.1	10.2	9.0	10.0	9.0	10.3	6.3	10.6
	2004	9.3	10.0	9.2	10.0	6.7	9.9	8.7	10.0	8.7	10.0	6.8	9.8
	2005	8.1	8.2	8.0	7.4	5.6	9.3	8.3	9.2	8.3	9.5	6.5	9.5
Bosnia and Herzegovina - Bosnie-Herzégovine	2001	6.4	1.8	6.6	2.8	6.2	8.2	7.8	5.0	7.8	6.5	7.6	8.4
Botswana	2001	7.9	1.4	8.2	2.5	3.2	12.4	9.7	0.5	9.9	7.5	9.4	11.0
	2004	8.1	1.3	8.3	2.4	3.0	12.5	13.4	0.9	13.5	0.9	12.4	18.4
	2005	8.0	1.2	8.3	2.5	3.0	12.4	13.0	0.9	13.0	1.0	12.0	18.0
Brazil - Brésil	1989	46.7	22.6	47.6	38.7	44.5	52.0	35.3	12.8	37.1	33.9	40.9	33.7
	1990	34.0	10.7	34.8	25.0	38.5	36.9	27.0	6.9	28.1	21.5	32.9	25.8
	1991	27.6	6.9	28.4	18.4	31.2	30.8	22.2	5.0	23.1	16.3	28.4	20.7
	1992	22.7	5.4	23.4	15.1	26.8	25.0	19.8	3.4	20.7	13.4	25.9	17.4
	1993	15.0	2.9	15.5	11.3	19.6	15.4	15.8	1.6	16.3	10.7	20.4	13.0
	1994	13.7	3.3	14.1	7.9	19.5	14.2	15.5	2.8	16.0	6.9	21.1	12.7
	1995	13.8	6.0	14.2	8.4	16.8	15.2	13.7	5.4	13.9	8.1	16.2	13.9

For sources and notes, see end of table. Pour les sources et les notes, se reporter à la fin du tableau.

231

Market / Marchés	Year / Année	MFN rate - Simple average (2) / Droit NPF - Moyenne simple (2)						MFN rate - Weighted average (3) / Droit NPF - Moyenne pondérée (3)					
		Total of non-agricultural and non-fuel products / Total des produits non-agricoles et non-pétroliers	Ores and metals / Minérais et métaux	Manufactured products / Produits manufacturés	Of which / dont : Chemical products / Produits chimiques	Of which / dont : Machinery and transport equipment / Machines et matériel de transport	Of which / dont : Other manufactured products / Produits manufacturés divers	Total of non-agricultural and non-fuel products / Total des produits non-agricoles et non-pétroliers	Ores and metals / Minérais et métaux	Manufactured products / Produits manufacturés	Of which / dont : Chemical products / Produits chimiques	Of which / dont : Machinery and transport equipment / Machines et matériel de transport	Of which / dont : Other manufactured products / Produits manufacturés divers
SITC Rev.2 (1) / CTCI Rév.2 (1)		5+6+7+8 +27+28	27+28+68	(5+6+7+8) - 68	5	7	(6+8) - 68	5+6+7+8 +27+28	27+28+68	(5+6+7+8) - 68	5	7	(6+8) - 68
Brazil - Brésil	1996	14.2	6.3	14.6	8.3	17.7	15.5	16.0	5.3	16.2	8.0	20.3	14.6
	1997	13.9	6.2	14.2	8.5	16.9	15.2	16.1	5.8	16.3	8.5	20.1	13.9
	1998	16.8	9.2	17.1	11.5	19.3	18.2	17.8	9.2	17.9	11.3	20.9	16.5
	1999	16.5	9.1	16.8	11.5	18.4	18.2	15.4	8.6	15.6	11.4	17.2	16.1
	2000	16.3	9.0	16.6	11.4	17.6	18.1	14.7	8.2	14.8	11.0	16.1	15.7
	2001	14.7	8.6	15.0	10.9	12.8	17.4	12.2	7.8	12.3	10.1	12.5	14.4
	2002	14.4	7.5	14.7	9.8	14.8	16.4	11.9	6.8	12.0	8.7	12.8	14.3
	2003	14.0	7.4	14.3	9.7	14.6	15.9	11.5	6.5	11.6	8.5	12.5	13.7
	2004	14.0	7.4	14.3	9.5	14.7	15.8	11.1	6.0	11.3	8.1	12.2	13.6
	2005	13.0	5.8	13.3	8.1	13.9	14.9	10.1	4.6	10.3	7.0	11.3	12.7
Brunei Darussalam - Brunéi Darussalam	1992	2.5	0.0	2.6	0.6	2.5	3.3	4.4	0.0	4.4	2.3	6.2	2.6
	2001	3.1	0.0	3.2	0.3	9.6	1.6	10.6	0.0	10.6	1.1	19.0	0.9
	2002	3.1	0.0	3.2	0.3	9.6	1.6	10.6	0.0	10.6	1.1	19.0	0.9
	2003	3.1	0.0	3.2	0.3	9.6	1.6	12.3	0.0	12.4	1.0	27.1	1.0
	2004	3.1	0.0	3.1	0.2	9.5	1.7	6.5	0.0	6.5	1.1	11.0	2.4
	2005	3.1	0.0	3.1	0.2	9.5	1.7	6.8	0.0	6.8	1.1	11.1	2.6
Bulgaria - Bulgarie	2001	11.4	3.9	11.7	8.2	7.9	14.5	10.3	1.6	10.9	8.5	7.4	14.9
	2003	9.0	2.7	9.2	7.4	5.8	11.2	8.8	1.8	9.3	7.4	6.6	12.3
	2004	9.0	2.7	9.2	7.4	5.8	11.2	8.6	1.6	9.1	6.8	7.1	11.8
	2005	9.0	2.7	9.2	7.4	5.8	11.2	8.6	1.6	9.1	6.8	7.1	11.8
Burkina Faso	1993	24.6	20.1	25.0	28.3	17.0	27.0	20.2	10.3	20.3	16.5	21.1	21.8
	2001	11.8	7.5	12.0	6.3	8.5	15.4	11.4	8.0	11.5	5.3	11.2	15.3
	2002	11.7	7.5	11.9	6.3	8.5	15.3	11.5	8.7	11.5	5.0	12.1	15.5
	2003	11.7	7.3	11.9	6.3	8.6	15.3	12.1	7.9	12.2	4.9	13.4	14.2
	2004	11.7	7.4	11.9	6.3	8.6	15.3	12.6	8.4	12.6	5.5	13.9	14.8
	2005	11.7	7.4	11.9	6.3	8.6	15.3	12.6	8.4	12.6	5.5	13.9	14.8
Burundi	2002	21.8	11.9	22.1	12.3	17.0	27.6	20.1	14.6	20.2	14.2	22.8	21.0
	2005	18.1	11.3	18.3	12.0	14.8	22.0	18.6	14.7	18.7	15.6	16.3	22.3
Cambodia - Cambodge	2001	16.2	11.6	16.3	10.7	17.9	17.7	16.8	11.4	16.8	6.8	18.9	17.5
	2002	16.2	11.6	16.3	10.7	17.9	17.7	16.7	11.4	16.7	6.2	18.8	17.2
	2003	16.2	11.6	16.3	10.7	17.9	17.7	16.9	9.8	16.9	5.9	18.8	17.4
Cameroon - Cameroun	1994	18.0	15.4	18.2	11.3	14.1	22.1	13.6	11.3	13.8	7.3	15.2	16.3
	1995	17.5	12.1	17.7	10.6	14.0	21.7	13.3	10.8	13.5	8.1	14.9	15.3
	2001	17.3	11.7	17.5	10.6	14.0	21.4	13.5	11.6	13.5	9.7	12.0	16.9
	2002	17.3	11.7	17.5	10.6	14.0	21.4	14.4	11.0	14.5	9.5	13.7	18.0
	2005	17.3	11.8	17.5	10.8	14.1	21.3	15.5	11.9	15.6	8.1	15.6	19.5
Canada	1989	10.2	3.8	10.5	8.5	7.3	12.5	7.6	2.3	7.7	8.7	6.4	10.3
	1993	10.0	3.8	10.3	8.4	7.1	12.1	7.5	2.0	7.7	8.8	6.3	10.1
	1995	9.1	3.4	9.3	7.4	6.5	11.1	6.6	2.0	6.8	7.6	5.6	9.0
	1996	7.4	1.4	7.6	4.4	4.9	9.8	5.4	0.9	5.5	5.7	4.4	7.7
	1997	6.9	1.3	7.1	4.2	4.4	9.2	4.9	0.9	5.0	5.4	4.0	7.1
	1998	5.1	0.7	5.2	3.1	2.3	7.2	3.5	0.6	3.5	3.7	2.8	5.1
	1999	4.8	0.7	5.0	2.9	2.2	6.8	3.2	0.6	3.3	3.3	2.6	4.7
	2000	4.7	0.7	4.8	2.8	2.2	6.6	3.1	0.6	3.1	3.2	2.5	4.5
	2001	4.6	0.7	4.7	2.7	2.2	6.4	3.2	0.6	3.2	3.0	2.6	4.5
	2002	4.4	0.7	4.6	2.7	2.2	6.1	3.2	0.7	3.3	2.9	2.8	4.4
	2003	4.3	0.7	4.4	2.6	2.2	5.9	3.2	0.6	3.3	2.7	2.9	4.2
	2004	4.2	0.7	4.3	2.6	2.2	5.7	3.1	0.6	3.2	2.6	2.9	4.0
	2005	4.1	0.7	4.3	2.6	2.2	5.7	3.1	0.6	3.2	2.6	2.9	4.0
Central African Republic - République centrafricaine	1995	17.5	12.1	17.7	10.6	14.0	21.7	14.6	19.0	14.6	7.8	14.4	18.7
	1997	17.5	12.1	17.7	10.6	14.0	21.7	14.6	16.7	14.6	7.0	14.9	19.3
	2001	17.3	11.7	17.5	10.6	14.0	21.4	15.9	21.0	15.9	9.3	17.1	18.7
	2002	17.3	11.7	17.5	10.6	14.0	21.4	15.1	18.3	15.2	9.7	16.4	17.0
	2005	17.3	11.8	17.5	10.8	14.1	21.3	13.2	11.0	13.2	5.6	12.7	19.2

For sources and notes, see end of table.

Pour les sources et les notes, se reporter à la fin du tableau.

232

Market / Marchés	Year / Année	MFN rate - Simple average (2) / Droit NPF - Moyenne simple (2)						MFN rate - Weighted average (3) / Droit NPF - Moyenne pondérée (3)					
		Total of non-agricultural and non-fuel products / Total des produits non-agricoles et non-pétroliers	Ores and metals / Minérais et métaux	Manufactured products / Produits manufacturés	Chemical products / Produits chimiques	Machinery and transport equipment / Machines et matériel de transport	Other manufactured products / Produits manufacturés divers	Total of non-agricultural and non-fuel products / Total des produits non-agricoles et non-pétroliers	Ores and metals / Minérais et métaux	Manufactured products / Produits manufacturés	Chemical products / Produits chimiques	Machinery and transport equipment / Machines et matériel de transport	Other manufactured products / Produits manufacturés divers
SITC Rev.2 (1) / CTCI Rév.2 (1)		5+6+7+8 +27+28	27+28+68	(5+6+7+8) - 68	5	7	(6+8) - 68	5+6+7+8 +27+28	27+28+68	(5+6+7+8) - 68	5	7	(6+8) - 68
Chad - Tchad	1995	17.5	12.1	17.7	10.6	14.0	21.7	15.1	12.4	15.1	7.5	14.8	17.7
	1997	17.5	12.1	17.7	10.6	14.0	21.7	15.1	12.4	15.1	7.5	14.8	17.7
	2001	17.3	11.7	17.5	10.6	14.0	21.4	11.8	10.4	11.9	8.0	11.5	14.4
	2002	17.3	11.7	17.5	10.6	14.0	21.4	13.0	8.7	13.0	8.3	11.9	15.5
	2005	17.3	11.8	17.5	10.8	14.1	21.3	10.3	9.6	10.3	5.6	9.0	18.9
Chile - Chili	1992	11.0	11.0	11.0	11.0	10.9	11.0	10.9	11.0	10.9	11.0	10.9	11.0
	1993	11.0	11.0	11.0	11.0	10.9	11.0	10.9	11.0	10.9	11.0	10.9	11.0
	1994	11.0	11.0	11.0	11.0	10.9	11.0	10.9	11.0	10.9	11.0	10.9	11.0
	1995	11.0	11.0	11.0	11.0	10.9	11.0	10.9	11.0	10.9	11.0	10.9	11.0
	1997	11.0	11.0	11.0	11.0	10.9	11.0	11.0	11.0	11.0	11.0	10.9	11.0
	1998	11.0	11.0	11.0	11.0	10.9	11.0	10.9	11.0	10.9	11.0	10.9	11.0
	1999	10.0	10.0	10.0	10.0	9.9	10.0	10.0	10.0	10.0	10.0	9.9	10.0
	2000	9.0	9.0	9.0	9.0	9.0	9.0	9.0	9.0	9.0	9.0	9.0	9.0
	2001	8.0	8.0	8.0	8.0	8.0	8.0	8.0	8.0	8.0	8.0	8.0	8.0
	2002	7.0	7.0	7.0	7.0	6.9	7.0	6.9	7.0	6.9	7.0	6.9	7.0
	2004	6.0	6.0	6.0	6.0	5.9	6.0	6.0	6.0	6.0	6.0	6.0	6.0
	2005	6.0	6.0	6.0	6.0	5.9	6.0	6.0	6.0	6.0	6.0	6.0	6.0
China - Chine	1992	42.2	17.7	43.0	27.2	32.6	52.6	34.8	7.7	35.6	22.2	34.0	43.5
	1993	39.3	16.8	39.9	26.1	31.3	48.1	32.1	7.4	32.8	24.1	34.1	33.7
	1994	35.2	15.4	35.8	23.3	27.9	43.4	29.8	7.8	30.4	21.5	29.8	34.3
	1996	22.0	7.5	22.5	14.1	19.7	26.7	17.8	5.8	18.2	14.6	16.1	22.6
	1997	16.5	5.3	17.0	11.1	16.2	19.4	14.3	4.8	14.7	12.8	13.2	17.4
	1998	16.5	5.3	16.9	11.1	16.3	19.3	14.2	5.2	14.6	12.9	13.5	17.0
	1999	16.1	5.3	16.5	11.1	16.2	18.7	13.5	5.3	13.8	12.8	12.8	16.0
	2000	15.8	5.3	16.2	11.1	16.2	18.0	13.1	5.2	13.5	13.0	12.8	14.9
	2001	14.7	4.5	15.1	10.2	15.4	16.7	12.4	4.2	12.8	12.5	12.5	13.7
	2003	10.6	3.8	10.8	7.4	10.0	12.4	6.4	2.7	6.6	8.9	5.3	8.0
	2004	9.8	3.7	10.0	7.1	9.4	11.3	5.6	2.0	5.8	8.2	4.5	7.4
	2005	9.2	3.7	9.4	6.9	9.1	10.4	5.3	2.0	5.5	7.4	4.4	6.9
China, Taiwan Province of - Chine, Taiwan Province de	1989	10.2	4.0	10.5	9.0	11.6	10.5	10.2	4.5	10.5	6.5	12.8	9.1
	1992	6.5	1.7	6.7	4.1	6.8	7.5	6.3	1.8	6.4	3.7	7.8	5.4
	1996	6.3	1.5	6.5	4.0	6.5	7.4	4.2	1.4	4.3	3.5	4.3	4.6
	1999	6.3	1.5	6.5	4.0	6.6	7.4	4.5	1.4	4.6	3.8	4.7	4.7
	2000	6.1	1.5	6.2	3.9	6.0	7.2	2.9	1.4	3.0	3.3	2.5	3.8
	2001	6.0	1.5	6.2	3.9	6.0	7.2	2.9	1.3	3.0	3.6	2.4	3.9
	2002	5.9	1.4	6.1	3.8	5.7	7.0	3.0	1.2	3.1	3.4	2.8	3.6
	2003	5.2	1.1	5.4	3.4	5.1	6.2	2.8	1.1	2.9	2.8	2.8	3.0
	2005	4.4	0.8	4.5	2.8	4.4	5.2	2.2	0.7	2.2	1.8	2.5	1.9
Colombia - Colombie	1991	6.3	2.2	6.4	3.4	5.1	8.1	6.0	1.1	6.0	3.9	8.7	4.6
	1992	12.0	6.7	12.2	8.2	10.2	14.5	10.3	7.7	10.4	7.7	11.2	11.8
	1994	12.0	6.7	12.2	8.1	10.3	14.4	11.4	7.9	11.5	7.7	12.5	12.3
	1995	13.5	7.2	13.8	10.6	12.7	15.4	12.0	5.5	12.1	9.4	12.8	12.9
	1996	11.7	6.4	11.9	7.7	9.8	14.2	10.7	6.1	10.8	7.3	11.5	12.2
	1997	11.7	6.4	11.9	7.7	9.8	14.2	10.9	6.0	11.0	7.6	11.7	12.2
	1999	11.8	6.4	12.0	7.8	9.9	14.3	9.9	6.4	10.0	7.9	9.4	12.6
	2000	11.8	6.4	12.0	7.8	9.9	14.3	10.4	6.6	10.5	7.9	10.7	12.5
	2001	11.8	6.4	12.0	7.8	9.9	14.3	10.2	7.0	10.3	8.1	9.8	12.8
	2002	11.8	6.4	12.0	7.8	9.9	14.3	10.6	6.9	10.6	7.9	11.0	12.9
	2004	11.8	6.3	12.0	7.8	9.9	14.3	10.9	6.8	10.9	7.9	11.6	12.5
	2005	11.8	6.3	12.0	7.8	9.8	14.3	10.9	6.8	10.9	7.9	11.5	12.5
Congo	1994	17.4	13.6	17.6	10.9	14.1	21.5	14.6	16.1	14.6	9.6	14.4	17.3
	1997	15.3	10.9	15.5	6.6	13.0	19.7	17.8	10.8	17.8	16.0	13.8	21.1
	2001	17.3	11.7	17.5	10.6	14.0	21.4	16.2	11.7	16.2	11.2	13.5	22.5
	2002	17.3	11.7	17.5	10.6	14.0	21.4	16.5	10.9	16.5	11.2	14.5	21.5
	2005	17.3	11.8	17.5	10.8	14.1	21.3	16.2	11.3	16.2	8.5	14.6	21.2
Costa Rica	1995	9.5	5.8	9.6	5.8	4.6	12.9	8.3	6.1	8.3	6.4	7.7	9.9
	1999	5.4	1.3	5.6	1.3	2.5	8.3	4.5	2.5	4.5	3.6	2.6	7.1

For sources and notes, see end of table.

Pour les sources et les notes, se reporter à la fin du tableau.

Market / Marchés	Year / Année	MFN rate - Simple average (2) / Droit NPF - Moyenne simple (2)						MFN rate - Weighted average (3) / Droit NPF - Moyenne pondérée (3)					
		Total of non-agricultural and non-fuel products / Total des produits non-agricoles et non-pétroliers	Ores and metals / Minérais et métaux	Manufactured products / Produits manu-facturés	Chemical products / Produits chimiques	Machinery and transport equipment / Machines et matériel de transport	Other manu-factured products / Produits manu-facturés divers	Total of non-agricultural and non-fuel products / Total des produits non-agricoles et non-pétroliers	Ores and metals / Minérais et métaux	Manufactured products / Produits manu-facturés	Chemical products / Produits chimiques	Machinery and transport equipment / Machines et matériel de transport	Other manu-factured products / Produits manu-facturés divers
SITC Rev.2 (1) / CTCI Rév.2 (1)		5+6+7+8 +27+28	27+28+68	(5+6+7+8) - 68	5	7	(6+8) - 68	5+6+7+8 +27+28	27+28+68	(5+6+7+8) - 68	5	7	(6+8) - 68
Costa Rica	2000	4.6	1.4	4.7	1.2	2.1	6.9	3.8	1.6	3.8	2.9	1.9	6.6
	2001	4.5	1.3	4.6	1.2	2.0	6.8	3.7	2.0	3.7	3.1	1.6	6.8
	2002	4.8	1.0	4.9	1.3	2.2	7.3	3.6	1.5	3.6	3.0	2.1	6.1
	2004	4.8	1.0	5.0	1.3	2.3	7.3	3.9	1.3	3.9	2.9	2.7	5.9
	2005	4.8	1.0	4.9	1.3	2.2	7.3	3.7	1.3	3.7	2.9	2.4	6.0
Côte d'Ivoire	1993	21.7	16.4	21.8	13.0	19.3	25.8	22.4	17.0	22.5	8.6	28.9	23.7
	1996	18.6	12.8	18.8	12.4	12.0	23.8	14.3	14.0	14.3	9.7	12.3	20.0
	2001	11.8	7.5	12.0	6.3	8.5	15.4	10.7	7.6	10.8	5.3	10.1	14.6
	2002	11.7	7.5	11.9	6.3	8.5	15.3	10.6	7.6	10.6	5.5	10.3	14.2
	2003	11.7	7.3	11.9	6.3	8.6	15.3	10.0	7.7	10.1	5.4	10.1	13.8
	2004	11.7	7.4	11.9	6.3	8.6	15.3	9.8	6.9	9.9	4.8	9.9	13.6
	2005	11.7	7.4	11.9	6.3	8.6	15.3	9.8	6.9	9.9	4.8	9.9	13.6
Croatia - Croatie	2001	10.1	5.6	10.2	7.0	8.8	11.9	11.0	5.9	11.1	10.1	9.8	12.7
	2004	4.0	1.5	4.0	1.3	3.1	5.4	4.0	2.2	4.0	2.6	3.7	4.9
	2005	3.9	1.5	3.9	1.2	3.1	5.3	3.9	2.1	3.9	2.3	3.6	4.6
Cuba	1993	12.8	5.6	13.1	11.1	11.0	14.6	12.9	5.1	12.9	10.0	12.3	14.7
	1997	11.1	5.4	11.3	9.3	9.8	12.7	10.3	3.7	10.3	7.2	9.9	11.8
	2002	11.2	5.3	11.4	9.1	9.9	12.8	10.9	3.9	10.9	7.1	11.2	12.1
	2003	11.3	5.1	11.5	9.0	10.0	13.0	10.8	3.9	10.9	9.7	10.5	11.7
	2004	11.2	5.1	11.4	9.0	9.9	12.9	10.5	3.8	10.6	9.9	9.9	11.6
	2005	11.2	5.1	11.4	9.0	9.9	12.9	10.4	3.8	10.5	9.9	9.8	11.5
Cyprus - Chypre	2002	4.2	1.6	4.3	4.7	2.3	5.0	5.0	4.8	5.0	2.8	5.6	5.1
Czech Republic - République tchèque	1996	5.9	1.6	6.1	5.3	5.6	6.6	6.1	1.9	6.2	5.0	6.2	6.7
	1999	5.2	2.2	5.4	4.5	5.9	5.5	5.8	2.8	5.8	4.0	6.2	6.0
	2002	4.5	1.2	4.6	4.1	3.8	5.1	4.3	1.6	4.3	3.5	3.8	5.3
	2003	4.5	1.2	4.6	4.1	3.8	5.1	4.3	1.7	4.3	3.4	3.9	5.2
Czechoslovakia (former) - Tchécoslovaquie (anc.)	1992	8.9	1.6	9.2	5.2	11.4	9.7	8.6	2.2	8.7	5.0	9.2	9.0
Dem. Rep. of the Congo - Rép. dém. du Congo	2003	11.8	8.8	11.9	7.7	8.3	15.0	13.3	13.5	13.3	13.6	8.8	16.8
Djibouti	2002	32.9	32.5	32.9	31.2	33.3	33.3	32.3	31.9	32.3	27.1	34.5	31.8
Dominica - Dominique	1996	20.3	17.1	20.3	14.5	18.5	21.6	18.7	22.3	18.7	14.1	23.5	18.4
	1999	16.9	13.8	16.9	11.3	16.0	18.0	16.5	16.9	16.5	11.6	22.0	15.0
	2000	13.2	13.7	13.2	8.7	12.4	14.7	15.0	14.4	15.0	9.0	21.8	12.6
	2001	8.0	3.7	8.1	6.1	5.8	9.7	11.2	5.2	11.2	10.1	10.1	12.3
	2002	8.0	3.7	8.1	6.2	5.8	9.7	12.5	5.0	12.5	11.0	10.7	14.4
	2003	8.0	3.7	8.1	6.2	5.8	9.7	12.0	4.8	12.0	10.7	10.4	13.7
Dominican Republic - République dominicaine	1997	14.1	7.6	14.4	8.3	10.2	18.2	13.7	11.0	13.8	8.6	14.3	15.5
	2000	17.5	9.2	17.9	9.9	13.1	22.6	17.5	13.6	17.5	9.5	17.8	21.0
	2001	7.7	4.5	7.8	4.4	5.5	10.1	8.6	5.1	8.7	4.0	8.6	11.0
	2002	7.8	4.5	7.9	4.4	5.4	10.1	9.3	4.2	9.3	4.7	9.6	10.9
	2003	7.8	4.5	7.9	4.4	5.4	10.1	8.6	5.2	8.6	3.9	8.6	11.0
	2004	7.7	4.6	7.8	4.3	5.5	10.1	8.7	5.3	8.7	3.9	8.6	11.2
	2005	7.7	4.5	7.8	4.5	5.4	10.0	9.0	6.0	9.0	5.7	6.8	10.8
Ecuador - Équateur	1993	9.4	3.7	9.6	6.0	6.7	12.1	8.3	4.3	8.3	4.7	9.8	7.7
	1994	12.0	6.5	12.2	7.5	9.5	15.0	11.6	7.3	11.7	6.9	13.7	11.0
	1995	12.6	6.5	12.9	9.4	11.0	14.9	11.3	5.7	11.3	6.5	12.9	11.9
	1996	11.5	5.9	11.7	7.1	8.9	14.4	11.3	5.7	11.3	5.8	14.2	11.4
	1997	11.5	5.9	11.7	7.1	8.9	14.4	10.9	5.6	10.9	6.0	13.2	11.6
	1998	11.5	5.9	11.7	7.1	9.0	14.4	10.8	5.8	10.8	6.2	12.2	11.9
	1999	13.4	7.9	13.6	8.5	10.8	16.5	11.3	7.5	11.3	7.5	12.0	13.8
	2002	11.4	5.9	11.6	7.2	8.7	14.4	10.8	6.2	10.8	7.0	10.9	12.8
	2004	11.4	5.9	11.6	7.2	8.7	14.4	10.5	6.1	10.5	6.8	10.8	12.6
	2005	11.2	5.9	11.4	7.0	8.3	14.3	10.3	6.1	10.3	6.7	10.7	12.2

For sources and notes, see end of table.

Pour les sources et les notes, se reporter à la fin du tableau.

		MFN rate - Simple average (2) / Droit NPF - Moyenne simple (2)						MFN rate - Weighted average (3) / Droit NPF - Moyenne pondérée (3)					
				of which / dont :						of which: / dont :			
		Total of non-agricultural and non-fuel products	Ores and metals	Manu-factured products	Of which: / dont :			Total of non-agricultural and non-fuel products	Ores and metals	Manu-factured products	Of which: / dont :		
Market / Marchés	Year / Année	Total des produits non-agricoles et non-pétroliers	Minérais et métaux	Produits manu-facturés	Chemical products / Produits chimiques	Machinery and transport equipment / Machines et matériel de transport	Other manu-factured products / Produits manu-facturés divers	Total des produits non-agricoles et non-pétroliers	Minérais et métaux	Produits manu-facturés	Chemical products / Produits chimiques	Machinery and transport equipment / Machines et matériel de transport	Other manu-factured products / Produits manu-facturés divers
SITC Rev.2 (1) / CTCI Rév.2 (1)		5+6+7+8 +27+28	27+28+68	(5+6+7+8) - 68	5	7	(6+8) - 68	5+6+7+8 +27+28	27+28+68	(5+6+7+8) - 68	5	7	(6+8) - 68
Egypt - Égypte	1995	28.4	13.8	28.9	14.1	19.1	37.9	21.9	11.2	22.2	11.4	27.2	22.9
	1998	21.7	12.8	22.1	13.0	12.6	28.4	17.2	9.6	17.5	10.9	19.4	18.9
	2002	19.9	12.6	20.3	12.7	14.0	26.2	16.6	10.8	16.9	11.0	15.9	21.3
	2004	13.2	6.0	13.5	6.7	8.2	18.1	11.1	4.4	11.4	15.8	8.3	14.3
	2005	12.9	5.1	13.2	6.3	8.0	17.7	10.6	2.6	10.9	15.0	8.1	13.5
El Salvador	1995	9.5	5.9	9.6	6.0	4.0	13.0	8.7	6.0	8.7	7.6	7.1	11.1
	1997	7.4	1.7	7.6	1.9	2.8	11.5	6.7	2.8	6.7	5.2	5.4	9.3
	1998	3.8	1.7	3.9	1.8	2.7	5.1	5.6	3.0	5.6	5.5	4.7	6.5
	2000	6.6	1.1	6.7	1.4	2.2	10.5	5.4	1.6	5.4	4.5	3.5	8.1
	2001	6.6	1.1	6.8	1.4	2.2	10.5	5.9	1.7	6.0	4.6	3.9	8.5
	2002	6.3	1.0	6.5	1.5	2.2	10.0	6.5	1.3	6.5	5.3	4.8	8.7
	2004	6.6	1.0	6.8	1.5	2.2	10.5	6.4	1.4	6.4	5.1	4.7	8.7
	2005	5.0	1.0	5.1	1.5	2.2	7.5	5.7	1.4	5.8	5.1	4.7	7.1
Equatorial Guinea - Guinée équatoriale	1998	17.4	12.0	17.6	10.3	13.8	21.6	13.6	7.1	13.6	15.1	11.7	17.6
	2001	17.3	11.7	17.5	10.5	14.0	21.4	12.7	9.9	12.7	14.8	10.4	17.3
	2002	17.3	11.7	17.5	10.5	14.0	21.4	13.9	8.3	14.0	15.6	12.5	16.8
	2005	17.3	11.8	17.5	10.3	14.1	21.3	14.3	9.1	14.3	15.7	12.4	17.5
Estonia - Estonie	1995	0.1	0.0	0.1	0.0	0.1	0.1	0.5	0.0	0.5	0.0	1.3	0.0
	2000	0.1	0.0	0.1	0.4	0.0	0.0	0.0	0.0	0.0	0.1	0.0	0.0
	2001	0.1	0.0	0.1	0.4	0.0	0.0	0.0	0.0	0.0	0.1	0.0	0.0
	2002	0.1	0.0	0.1	0.4	0.0	0.0	0.0	0.0	0.0	0.1	0.0	0.0
	2003	0.1	0.0	0.1	0.4	0.0	0.0	0.0	0.0	0.0	0.1	0.0	0.0
Ethiopia - Éthiopie	1995	27.4	13.6	27.9	16.5	14.6	37.1	18.0	11.0	18.0	9.5	19.3	21.2
	2001	18.6	10.0	18.9	10.8	12.4	24.5	15.1	9.1	15.2	8.8	13.9	19.2
	2002	18.6	10.0	18.9	10.8	12.4	24.5	15.6	8.6	15.7	7.9	14.8	20.0
EU 15 - UE 15	1988	5.8	2.5	6.0	7.6	4.9	5.9	5.4	1.7	5.7	7.8	5.7	5.0
	1989	5.8	2.5	6.0	7.6	4.9	5.9	5.3	1.7	5.6	7.7	5.6	5.0
	1990	8.1	2.5	8.4	7.5	5.0	10.0	7.1	1.7	7.4	7.4	5.9	8.9
	1991	6.7	2.5	6.9	7.5	5.0	7.4	6.4	1.7	6.6	7.6	5.9	7.3
	1992	6.8	2.5	7.0	7.7	5.1	7.5	6.8	1.7	7.0	7.7	6.3	7.5
	1993	6.7	2.5	7.0	7.5	5.1	7.5	6.7	1.7	6.9	7.5	6.0	7.6
	1994	6.7	2.5	6.9	7.5	5.0	7.4	6.5	1.9	6.7	7.6	5.9	7.3
	1995	6.1	2.3	6.3	6.6	4.5	6.9	6.1	2.0	6.2	5.9	5.8	6.8
	1996	5.2	2.0	5.4	5.0	3.5	6.2	4.8	1.8	5.0	4.0	4.2	6.0
	1997	5.3	1.9	5.5	5.7	3.5	6.2	4.8	1.8	5.0	4.7	4.2	6.0
	1998	4.8	1.8	4.9	4.8	2.8	5.8	4.0	1.9	4.1	3.7	2.9	5.6
	1999	4.4	1.6	4.5	4.4	2.3	5.4	3.4	1.8	3.5	3.0	2.4	5.1
	2000	4.2	1.6	4.3	4.1	2.3	5.2	3.1	1.7	3.1	2.7	2.0	4.8
	2001	4.3	1.6	4.4	4.9	2.3	5.0	3.2	1.8	3.3	3.4	2.1	4.8
	2002	4.4	1.6	4.6	4.7	2.3	5.4	3.4	1.9	3.5	3.1	2.3	5.1
	2003	4.2	1.6	4.3	4.6	2.3	5.0	3.4	1.9	3.5	3.2	2.4	5.0
	2004	3.9	1.6	4.1	4.5	2.3	4.6	3.4	1.9	3.4	3.1	2.4	4.8
	2005	3.9	1.6	4.0	4.5	2.3	4.6	3.5	2.0	3.6	3.2	2.8	4.7
Gabon	1995	17.5	12.1	17.7	10.6	14.0	21.7	15.1	16.5	15.2	9.9	14.8	17.8
	1998	17.4	12.0	17.6	10.3	13.8	21.6	14.2	16.7	14.2	7.9	13.6	18.1
	2001	17.3	11.7	17.5	10.6	14.0	21.4	15.1	17.9	15.1	11.1	14.4	17.9
	2002	17.3	11.7	17.5	10.6	14.0	21.4	13.4	10.6	13.5	9.9	12.8	16.1
	2005	17.3	11.8	17.5	10.8	14.1	21.3	15.7	14.4	15.8	9.6	15.5	18.7
Georgia - Géorgie	1999	10.3	11.8	10.2	11.7	5.8	11.5	8.3	10.6	8.3	6.9	6.7	11.0
	2002	10.2	11.8	10.2	11.7	5.9	11.3	8.4	11.4	8.4	7.2	7.3	10.8
	2003	7.6	8.7	7.5	7.7	4.4	8.7	6.9	9.9	6.8	4.6	5.4	9.2
	2004	7.0	7.9	6.9	6.6	4.2	8.0	6.3	8.8	6.3	4.3	5.2	8.4
Ghana	1993	14.0	11.0	14.1	11.1	10.1	16.7	9.2	9.8	9.2	9.7	8.4	10.4
	2000	13.8	11.7	13.9	11.7	5.3	17.9	8.9	10.2	8.9	11.2	5.2	13.3
	2004	12.5	11.5	12.5	10.9	5.7	15.8	8.9	11.1	8.8	10.1	5.9	13.2

For sources and notes see end of table.

Pour les sources et les notes, se reporter à la fin du tableau.

4

Market / Marchés	Year / Année	MFN rate - Simple average (2) / Droit NPF - Moyenne simple (2)						MFN rate - Weighted average (3) / Droit NPF - Moyenne pondérée (3)					
		Total of non-agricultural and non-fuel products / Total des produits non-agricoles et non-pétroliers	of which: / dont :					Total of non-agricultural and non-fuel products / Total des produits non-agricoles et non-pétroliers	of which: / dont :				
			Ores and metals / Minérais et métaux	Manufactured products / Produits manufacturés	Of which: / dont :				Ores and metals / Minérais et métaux	Manufactured products / Produits manufacturés	Of which: / dont :		
					Chemical products / Produits chimiques	Machinery and transport equipment / Machines et matériel de transport	Other manufactured products / Produits manufacturés divers				Chemical products / Produits chimiques	Machinery and transport equipment / Machines et matériel de transport	Other manufactured products / Produits manufacturés divers
SITC Rev.2 (1) / CTCI Rév.2 (1)		5+6+7+8 +27+28	27+28+68	(5+6+7+8) - 68	5	7	(6+8) - 68	5+6+7+8 +27+28	27+28+68	(5+6+7+8) - 68	5	7	(6+8) - 68
Grenada - Grenade	1996	20.4	16.5	20.4	14.5	19.2	21.6	21.5	14.3	21.6	18.4	28.0	19.4
	1999	17.0	13.3	17.0	11.4	16.8	18.0	16.7	10.5	16.8	14.2	21.2	15.4
	2001	17.0	13.3	17.1	11.5	16.8	18.0	16.2	12.4	16.3	14.3	20.3	15.1
	2002	9.0	5.6	9.1	6.3	7.8	10.4	11.3	7.7	11.3	13.2	9.8	12.0
	2003	9.0	5.6	9.1	6.3	7.8	10.4	10.3	6.2	10.4	12.7	10.0	10.3
Guatemala	1995	9.5	5.9	9.6	6.0	4.2	12.9	8.0	6.4	8.0	6.3	7.4	10.0
	1997	7.9	2.5	8.0	2.6	3.6	11.7	6.5	3.2	6.5	4.4	5.7	9.0
	1998	7.8	1.4	8.0	1.6	2.8	12.5	6.0	2.9	6.0	3.8	5.5	7.9
	2000	6.6	1.1	6.8	1.4	2.5	10.4	5.1	2.0	5.1	3.4	4.7	6.8
	2001	6.3	1.1	6.4	1.4	2.5	9.8	5.8	2.1	5.8	3.7	5.6	7.5
	2002	5.6	1.0	5.7	1.5	2.5	8.6	5.7	2.0	5.7	3.6	5.4	7.5
	2004	5.0	1.0	5.1	1.5	2.4	7.5	5.9	1.4	6.0	3.7	6.0	7.3
	2005	4.9	1.0	5.1	1.5	2.5	7.4	5.8	1.4	5.9	3.5	6.1	7.2
Guinea - Guinée	2005	11.6	7.5	11.8	6.3	8.4	15.1	11.2	8.8	11.2	3.8	11.8	15.0
Guinea-Bissau - Guinée-Bissau	2001	11.8	7.5	12.0	6.3	8.5	15.4	12.5	8.7	12.5	5.7	10.1	15.9
	2002	11.7	7.5	11.9	6.3	8.5	15.3	12.6	9.4	12.6	8.6	10.9	15.9
	2003	11.7	7.3	11.9	6.3	8.6	15.3	12.9	11.8	12.9	7.2	9.7	16.7
	2004	11.7	7.4	11.9	6.3	8.6	15.3	14.7	11.0	14.7	14.2	11.3	17.1
	2005	11.7	7.4	11.9	6.3	8.6	15.3	14.6	11.0	14.7	14.2	11.3	17.0
Guyana	1996	21.4	19.0	21.4	15.6	18.9	22.9	18.4	21.2	18.4	13.9	20.4	18.9
	1999	18.0	15.8	18.0	12.5	16.4	19.3	15.6	16.5	15.6	10.7	19.7	14.7
	2000	18.0	15.8	18.0	12.5	16.4	19.2	16.1	16.2	16.1	12.1	20.3	14.9
	2001	9.2	5.7	9.3	6.3	7.7	11.0	9.7	6.6	9.8	8.7	9.6	10.5
	2002	9.2	5.7	9.3	6.3	7.7	11.0	10.0	9.2	10.0	9.1	9.7	10.8
	2003	9.2	5.7	9.3	6.3	7.7	11.0	9.7	10.6	9.7	9.7	9.1	10.1
Honduras	1995	9.4	5.8	9.5	5.7	4.0	13.0	7.5	6.6	7.5	5.0	4.7	12.0
	1999	6.9	2.0	7.1	2.3	3.4	10.2	5.9	3.3	5.9	3.9	4.1	9.2
	2000	6.7	2.0	6.9	2.2	3.5	9.9	6.0	3.8	6.0	2.4	8.0	8.5
	2001	6.4	2.0	6.5	2.1	3.3	9.4	5.4	3.9	5.4	2.2	8.0	7.6
	2002	5.2	1.0	5.4	1.3	2.4	8.0	5.6	3.0	5.6	2.9	5.0	7.7
	2004	5.2	1.0	5.4	1.3	2.4	8.0	5.7	2.7	5.7	2.9	5.2	7.7
	2005	4.9	1.0	5.0	1.3	2.4	7.4	5.5	2.7	5.5	2.9	5.0	7.5
Hungary - Hongrie	1991	11.5	3.9	11.7	9.6	16.4	10.7	11.7	4.1	11.9	6.8	15.2	10.5
	1993	9.7	4.0	9.9	8.5	10.7	10.1	10.4	2.8	10.4	6.3	12.9	9.7
	1996	8.7	3.2	8.8	7.1	9.9	9.1	9.1	2.4	9.2	6.1	11.1	8.7
	1997	8.3	3.0	8.4	6.6	9.6	8.6	8.7	2.7	8.7	5.6	9.8	8.3
	2002	7.0	2.5	7.1	5.2	8.8	7.1	8.0	2.8	8.0	4.2	9.0	7.3
Iceland - Islande	1993	3.4	0.0	3.5	0.8	3.9	4.3	4.9	0.0	5.1	3.4	4.6	5.9
	1996	2.5	0.0	2.6	0.7	1.3	3.7	2.8	0.0	2.9	3.1	0.8	5.1
	2001	2.5	0.0	2.6	1.0	1.3	3.8	2.9	0.0	3.1	3.3	0.8	5.4
	2003	2.5	0.0	2.6	0.7	1.3	3.7	2.8	0.0	2.9	3.1	0.7	5.4
India - Inde	1990	83.0	67.8	83.7	77.5	75.8	89.0	70.5	74.1	70.8	78.7	74.0	64.0
	1992	59.1	55.4	59.4	62.0	51.3	61.6	41.5	25.8	44.2	60.0	51.6	29.8
	1997	30.8	24.0	31.1	29.7	26.1	33.6	21.0	25.2	21.1	25.2	21.4	18.6
	1999	33.7	27.1	34.1	34.6	29.2	35.8	31.1	28.1	31.6	28.7	26.9	36.1
	2001	31.3	26.4	31.6	34.1	28.2	32.1	28.0	25.1	28.4	30.3	22.8	31.7
	2004	28.1	22.2	28.4	29.4	26.7	28.7	24.9	22.8	25.1	26.3	21.2	28.4
	2005	15.3	13.7	15.3	15.9	15.1	15.2	12.7	13.7	12.7	14.7	9.8	14.8
Indonesia - Indonésie	1989	22.5	7.1	23.1	9.4	18.1	30.0	14.7	4.2	15.3	6.3	19.3	15.6
	1990	18.6	6.9	19.0	9.4	16.9	23.3	15.1	3.9	15.6	7.1	19.5	13.7
	1993	17.9	6.9	18.3	8.9	16.1	22.5	14.0	4.2	14.3	8.5	16.3	14.2
	1995	15.6	6.4	16.0	7.5	13.1	20.1	12.6	3.6	12.9	6.7	15.8	11.6
	1996	11.9	5.4	12.2	7.1	8.4	15.5	9.0	2.9	9.2	8.1	9.3	9.8
	1999	10.8	5.0	11.0	6.8	8.1	13.7	7.8	3.0	8.0	6.9	7.6	9.6
	2000	8.7	4.9	8.9	5.9	5.4	11.4	6.5	2.9	6.6	5.5	6.1	8.5

For sources and notes, see end of table.

Pour les sources et les notes, se reporter à la fin du tableau.

Market / Marchés	Year / Année	MFN rate - Simple average (2) / Droit NPF - Moyenne simple (2)						MFN rate - Weighted average (3) / Droit NPF - Moyenne pondérée (3)					
					of which: / dont :						of which: / dont :		
		Total of non-agricultural and non-fuel products / Total des produits non-agricoles et non-pétroliers	Ores and metals / Minérais et métaux	Manu-factured products / Produits manu-facturés	Of which: / dont :			Total of non-agricultural and non-fuel products / Total des produits non-agricoles et non-pétroliers	Ores and metals / Minérais et métaux	Manu-factured products / Produits manu-facturés	Of which: / dont :		
					Chemical products / Produits chimiques	Machinery and transport equipment / Machines et matériel de transport	Other manu-factured products / Produits manu-facturés divers				Chemical products / Produits chimiques	Machinery and transport equipment / Machines et matériel de transport	Other manu-factured products / Produits manu-facturés divers
SITC Rev.2 (1) / CTCI Rév.2 (1)		5+6+7+8 +27+28	27+28+68	(5+6+7+8) - 68	5	7	(6+8) - 68	5+6+7+8 +27+28	27+28+68	(5+6+7+8) - 68	5	7	(6+8) - 68
Indonesia - Indonésie	2001	6.8	4.3	6.9	4.9	4.6	8.6	5.3	2.5	5.4	4.2	5.3	6.8
	2002	6.9	4.3	7.0	4.9	4.7	8.6	6.1	2.9	6.2	5.4	5.2	8.3
	2003	6.9	4.3	7.0	4.9	4.7	8.6	6.4	3.4	6.5	5.3	5.9	8.2
	2004	7.0	4.4	7.1	5.0	4.7	8.8	6.8	3.6	6.9	6.3	5.9	8.8
	2005	7.0	4.4	7.1	5.0	4.7	8.8	6.8	3.6	6.9	6.3	5.9	8.8
Iran, Islamic Republic of - Iran, Rép. islamique d'	2000	64.7	18.9	65.9	19.1	43.9	91.6	28.1	13.3	28.6	11.9	34.8	29.4
	2003	27.0	8.5	27.6	11.4	16.1	38.0	17.9	9.9	18.0	20.7	18.6	15.5
	2004	20.9	7.9	21.3	11.6	16.4	26.8	14.5	8.5	14.6	15.5	14.8	13.7
Israel - Israël	1993	8.4	1.0	8.7	3.4	5.1	11.9	5.4	2.0	5.4	5.2	4.7	6.0
	2004	4.5	0.6	4.6	1.8	3.6	6.1	2.7	0.5	2.7	3.0	2.7	2.7
	2005	4.4	0.6	4.6	1.8	3.6	6.0	2.7	0.5	2.7	3.0	2.6	2.7
Jamaica - Jamaïque	1996	20.1	16.5	20.1	14.6	17.9	21.5	20.8	17.2	20.9	16.9	22.3	20.9
	1999	16.7	13.2	16.7	11.5	15.4	17.9	18.4	14.7	18.4	14.1	21.2	18.1
	2000	5.4	1.4	5.5	1.9	3.8	7.5	9.9	1.1	9.9	6.6	10.5	10.7
	2001	5.4	1.4	5.5	1.9	3.8	7.5	9.1	0.7	9.1	5.7	9.5	10.2
	2002	5.4	1.4	5.5	1.9	3.8	7.5	9.3	0.7	9.3	6.0	9.1	10.8
	2003	5.4	1.4	5.5	1.9	3.8	7.5	9.3	0.7	9.3	6.0	9.1	10.8
Japan - Japon	1988	4.5	2.0	4.7	4.4	1.9	5.9	3.4	0.4	3.8	4.1	1.2	5.0
	1989	4.5	2.0	4.6	4.4	1.8	5.8	3.4	0.4	3.8	4.2	1.0	5.2
	1990	3.7	1.8	3.8	4.3	0.2	5.1	2.7	0.4	3.0	3.9	0.1	4.5
	1991	3.7	1.8	3.8	4.2	0.1	5.1	2.8	0.4	3.1	3.7	0.1	4.9
	1992	3.7	1.8	3.8	4.2	0.1	5.1	3.1	0.4	3.3	3.6	0.1	5.5
	1993	3.7	1.8	3.8	4.2	0.1	5.1	3.2	0.4	3.4	3.6	0.1	5.7
	1994	3.7	1.8	3.8	4.2	0.1	5.1	3.1	0.4	3.3	3.7	0.1	5.7
	1995	3.5	1.8	3.6	3.6	0.0	5.0	2.7	0.2	2.9	2.8	0.0	5.4
	1996	3.3	1.7	3.4	3.3	0.1	4.7	2.7	0.2	2.8	2.5	0.1	5.4
	1997	3.1	1.5	3.2	3.2	0.1	4.6	2.4	0.2	2.5	2.2	0.1	4.9
	1998	3.0	1.3	3.1	3.0	0.1	4.4	2.2	0.2	2.3	2.1	0.1	4.7
	1999	2.9	1.1	3.0	2.8	0.1	4.2	2.1	0.2	2.2	1.9	0.1	4.6
	2000	2.8	1.1	2.9	2.8	0.1	4.1	2.0	0.1	2.1	1.8	0.1	4.5
	2001	2.7	1.1	2.8	2.8	0.1	3.9	2.0	0.2	2.1	1.9	0.1	4.5
	2002	2.6	1.1	2.7	2.7	0.1	3.8	1.9	0.2	2.0	1.8	0.1	4.3
	2003	2.5	1.1	2.6	2.7	0.1	3.6	1.8	0.2	1.9	1.7	0.1	4.1
	2004	2.4	1.1	2.5	2.8	0.1	3.4	1.7	0.2	1.8	1.8	0.1	3.8
	2005	2.4	1.1	2.5	2.7	0.1	3.4	1.7	0.2	1.8	1.7	0.1	3.8
Jordan - Jordanie	2000	21.8	16.0	22.1	18.0	14.4	26.6	19.8	14.3	19.8	13.9	18.7	24.2
	2001	14.0	11.0	14.2	7.5	11.5	17.6	12.8	9.3	12.8	7.3	12.9	15.1
	2002	14.1	11.0	14.2	7.5	11.5	17.7	13.0	8.7	13.1	7.7	12.9	15.6
	2003	12.0	6.6	12.2	2.7	10.4	16.4	10.9	4.8	11.0	4.5	11.4	13.3
	2005	12.4	7.4	12.6	2.5	10.9	17.0	11.9	6.3	12.0	4.1	12.8	14.1
Kazakhstan	1996	9.2	8.5	9.4	3.7	1.1	14.5	8.4	3.6	8.5	17.8	1.0	13.3
	2004	2.8	4.1	2.8	3.5	0.3	3.5	1.6	1.8	1.6	1.6	0.4	3.2
Kenya	1994	34.4	28.3	34.6	30.0	25.5	39.8	23.7	26.3	23.7	18.1	24.5	28.1
	2000	17.7	12.7	17.9	11.7	13.4	23.1	12.9	7.7	12.9	7.1	12.3	19.0
	2001	18.9	12.0	19.2	10.9	11.8	25.2	11.5	6.3	11.5	6.1	9.6	19.2
	2004	16.0	12.2	16.2	9.2	9.6	21.3	10.2	4.0	10.2	3.8	11.2	13.7
	2005	11.6	6.6	11.8	3.1	6.2	17.2	7.2	3.8	7.2	3.3	6.8	10.2
Korea, Republic of - Corée, République de	1988	18.2	13.4	18.6	18.6	18.2	18.7	16.1	8.5	17.0	17.3	16.4	17.7
	1989	14.3	7.4	14.6	14.3	14.8	14.7	12.5	4.5	13.5	12.4	14.4	13.0
	1990	12.3	7.0	12.6	12.4	12.6	12.7	10.9	4.7	11.4	11.4	11.5	11.3
	1992	10.5	6.0	10.8	10.6	10.7	10.8	9.4	4.4	9.8	10.1	9.7	9.9
	1995	7.6	4.5	7.7	7.8	7.7	7.7	7.1	3.7	7.3	7.5	7.4	7.2
	1996	8.3	4.4	8.5	11.8	7.6	7.7	7.3	3.6	7.5	9.6	7.3	7.2
	1999	7.8	4.3	8.0	7.6	7.2	8.4	5.9	2.9	6.2	7.1	5.5	7.0
	2002	7.9	4.2	8.0	11.0	5.9	7.8	4.9	2.8	5.0	8.5	3.3	6.3
	2004	7.2	4.1	7.4	9.4	5.9	7.2	4.3	2.7	4.5	7.4	3.5	4.9

For sources and notes, see end of table.

Pour les sources et les notes, se reporter à la fin du tableau.

4

237

Market / Marchés	Year / Année	MFN rate - Simple average (2) / Droit NPF - Moyenne simple (2)						MFN rate - Weighted average (3) / Droit NPF - Moyenne pondérée (3)					
		Total of non-agricultural and non-fuel products / Total des produits non-agricoles et non-pétroliers	Ores and metals / Minérais et métaux	Manufactured products / Produits manufacturés	Chemical products / Produits chimiques	Machinery and transport equipment / Machines et matériel de transport	Other manufactured products / Produits manufacturés divers	Total of non-agricultural and non-fuel products / Total des produits non-agricoles et non-pétroliers	Ores and metals / Minérais et métaux	Manufactured products / Produits manufacturés	Chemical products / Produits chimiques	Machinery and transport equipment / Machines et matériel de transport	Other manufactured products / Produits manufacturés divers
SITC Rev.2 (1) / CTCI Rév 2 (1)		5+6+7+8 +27+28	27+28+68	(5+6+7+8) - 68	5	7	(6+8) - 68	5+6+7+8 +27+28	27+28+68	(5+6+7+8) - 68	5	7	(6+8) - 68
Kuwait - Koweït	2002	4.0	4.0	4.0	4.0	4.0	4.0	4.0	4.0	4.0	4.0	4.0	4.0
	2005	4.9	4.8	4.9	4.8	4.9	5.0	4.8	5.0	4.8	3.0	5.0	5.0
Kyrgyzstan - Kirghizistan	2002	8.4	7.0	8.5	7.6	7.0	9.4	7.1	5.4	7.1	4.8	6.9	8.8
	2003	4.8	3.6	4.8	2.8	4.6	5.6	2.9	3.2	2.9	0.8	3.3	3.7
Lao People's Dem. Rep. - Rép. dém. populaire lao	2000	7.9	5.8	8.0	6.3	7.2	8.9	12.6	5.0	12.6	9.2	16.6	8.5
	2001	8.0	5.9	8.1	6.3	7.5	8.9	11.9	5.0	11.9	10.6	14.7	8.4
	2004	8.0	5.9	8.1	6.3	7.5	8.9	10.5	5.0	10.5	8.9	11.7	8.5
	2005	8.0	6.0	8.1	6.3	7.6	9.0	10.4	5.0	10.4	8.9	11.5	8.2
Latvia - Lettonie	1996	2.7	0.5	2.7	1.1	1.7	3.7	2.6	0.5	2.6	1.8	0.9	4.2
	1997	3.6	0.5	3.7	1.1	1.4	5.5	2.8	0.5	2.8	1.9	0.9	4.9
	2001	2.1	0.5	2.2	0.8	0.4	3.4	1.5	0.5	1.5	0.6	0.1	3.2
Lebanon - Liban	1999	9.8	4.1	10.0	4.7	7.7	12.8	12.6	4.6	12.7	6.7	13.5	14.4
	2000	13.6	6.5	13.9	7.4	11.5	17.2	16.0	6.4	16.2	10.6	15.7	18.7
	2001	4.8	2.0	4.9	2.3	3.8	6.2	6.7	2.1	6.8	5.6	5.3	8.2
	2002	4.1	1.9	4.2	2.3	3.6	5.1	6.2	2.0	6.2	5.7	5.1	7.4
	2004	4.1	1.9	4.2	2.3	3.6	5.1	6.0	1.6	6.1	5.5	4.9	7.3
	2005	4.1	1.8	4.2	2.3	3.6	5.1	6.2	1.5	6.3	5.6	5.1	7.6
Lesotho	2001	7.9	1.4	8.2	2.5	3.2	12.4	17.6	0.0	17.6	1.4	5.9	21.5
	2004	8.1	1.3	8.3	2.4	3.0	12.5	18.2	4.2	18.3	3.6	7.4	20.4
	2005	8.0	1.2	8.3	2.5	3.0	12.4	17.5	3.9	17.5	5.4	7.5	20.2
Libyan Arab Jamahiriya - Jamahiriya arabe libyenne	1996	18.6	8.3	18.8	6.9	21.3	22.1	25.1	3.4	25.6	10.3	35.1	17.8
	2002	16.8	7.7	17.0	6.5	19.3	19.9	28.5	7.4	28.5	9.0	38.8	16.2
Lithuania - Lituanie	1995	2.8	0.0	2.9	0.7	0.5	4.5	2.0	0.0	2.1	0.4	0.7	4.0
	1997	2.7	0.0	2.8	0.6	0.4	4.5	2.0	0.0	2.0	0.7	0.6	4.3
	2002	2.6	0.0	2.6	0.5	0.4	4.3	1.9	0.0	1.9	0.5	0.6	4.2
	2003	2.4	0.0	2.5	0.5	0.4	4.1	1.9	0.0	1.9	0.6	0.7	4.1
Madagascar	1995	7.3	2.1	7.5	0.9	7.7	9.7	6.3	0.7	6.3	0.8	9.0	6.3
	2001	4.6	1.5	4.7	0.6	4.5	6.3	4.6	0.7	4.6	0.9	5.3	5.3
	2005	11.1	11.0	11.1	9.9	6.7	13.3	6.2	7.9	6.2	6.6	3.5	9.6
Malawi	1994	31.8	15.4	32.7	25.0	26.8	36.8	26.3	10.9	26.6	13.4	26.7	34.1
	1996	27.4	14.8	28.0	20.1	23.2	32.7	19.4	13.3	19.5	6.8	19.9	31.1
	1997	25.7	13.9	26.2	19.8	22.1	30.1	21.0	4.1	21.2	11.9	20.1	27.3
	1998	20.3	10.4	20.6	11.1	17.2	25.3	16.4	2.4	16.6	8.2	14.8	23.3
	2001	13.0	8.0	13.1	6.1	9.4	17.0	11.6	5.7	11.7	5.5	11.8	14.5
Malaysia - Malaisie	1988	14.1	5.9	14.5	5.5	11.1	18.9	10.8	4.8	11.0	4.7	10.9	13.6
	1991	14.3	6.0	14.6	6.9	10.4	19.0	10.9	5.7	11.0	9.9	10.3	13.2
	1993	11.8	5.4	12.1	6.0	9.2	15.4	9.3	5.5	9.4	9.3	8.9	10.9
	1996	9.0	2.4	9.3	2.7	5.9	13.0	6.2	4.2	6.3	4.7	5.6	8.8
	1997	9.4	2.4	9.7	3.7	6.5	13.2	5.7	4.4	5.8	4.8	5.2	8.1
	2001	9.3	2.4	9.6	3.0	7.0	12.9	5.2	4.3	5.2	4.4	4.3	9.2
	2002	9.3	2.4	9.6	3.0	7.0	12.9	5.1	4.6	5.2	4.4	4.2	9.1
	2003	9.3	2.4	9.6	3.0	7.0	12.9	5.1	4.4	5.2	4.5	4.2	9.2
	2005	8.3	2.3	8.6	2.6	5.6	11.9	4.6	4.2	4.7	4.7	2.7	11.4
Maldives	2000	20.6	24.3	20.5	14.7	23.9	21.1	21.4	19.2	21.5	19.8	23.8	19.9
	2001	20.6	24.3	20.5	14.7	23.9	21.1	21.4	18.3	21.5	20.5	23.8	19.9
	2002	20.6	24.2	20.5	14.7	23.9	21.1	21.6	18.1	21.7	20.1	23.4	20.7
	2003	20.6	24.3	20.4	14.7	23.9	21.2	21.9	19.8	21.9	20.7	24.0	20.3
	2004	20.6	24.3	20.5	14.7	24.1	21.2	21.5	19.7	21.6	21.2	23.8	19.9
	2005	20.6	24.3	20.5	14.7	23.9	21.2	21.9	19.7	22.0	21.3	24.4	20.2
Mali	1995	14.8	16.9	14.7	3.3	8.4	21.2	8.6	12.0	8.5	2.0	9.0	11.7
	2001	11.8	7.5	12.0	6.3	8.5	15.4	10.6	9.0	10.7	5.2	9.3	15.2
	2002	11.7	7.5	11.9	6.3	8.5	15.3	10.6	9.0	10.7	5.2	9.3	15.2
	2003	11.7	7.3	11.9	6.3	8.6	15.3	10.5	9.9	10.5	5.4	9.4	15.1

For sources and notes, see end of table.

Pour les sources et les notes, se reporter à la fin du tableau.

Market / Marchés	Year / Année	MFN rate - Simple average (2) / Droit NPF - Moyenne simple (2)						MFN rate - Weighted average (3) / Droit NPF - Moyenne pondérée (3)					
		Total of non-agricultural and non-fuel products / Total des produits non-agricoles et non-pétroliers	Ores and metals / Minérais et métaux	Manu-factured products / Produits manu-facturés	Chemical products / Produits chimiques	Machinery and transport equipment / Machines et matériel de transport	Other manu-factured products / Produits manu-facturés divers	Total of non-agricultural and non-fuel products / Total des produits non-agricoles et non-pétroliers	Ores and metals / Minérais et métaux	Manu-factured products / Produits manu-facturés	Chemical products / Produits chimiques	Machinery and transport equipment / Machines et matériel de transport	Other manu-factured products / Produits manu-facturés divers
SITC Rev.2 (1) / CTCI Rév.2 (1)		5+6+7+8 +27+28	27+28+68	(5+6+7+8) - 68	5	7	(6+8) - 68	5+6+7+8 +27+28	27+28+68	(5+6+7+8) - 68	5	7	(6+8) - 68
Mali	2004	11.7	7.4	11.9	6.3	8.6	15.3	10.6	9.4	10.6	5.3	9.1	16.5
	2005	11.7	7.4	11.9	6.3	8.6	15.3	10.4	9.4	10.4	5.3	8.8	16.4
Malta - Malte	1997	7.9	7.9	7.9	7.3	7.2	8.4	9.3	4.6	9.3	4.4	10.9	7.9
	2000	7.8	7.9	7.8	7.3	7.1	8.4	10.3	4.5	10.3	4.2	11.7	8.0
	2002	6.2	2.5	6.3	6.5	4.7	6.9	6.4	5.0	6.4	4.7	6.3	7.2
	2003	6.2	2.5	6.3	6.5	4.7	6.9	6.0	6.0	6.0	4.8	5.6	7.1
Mauritania - Mauritanie	2001	10.5	5.6	10.7	4.9	8.4	13.7	9.9	5.1	9.9	9.4	8.9	12.1
Mauritius - Maurice	1995	31.7	15.9	32.2	22.0	31.5	36.1	23.0	16.4	23.1	20.6	38.6	17.0
	1997	30.6	16.1	31.1	22.0	30.7	34.5	19.0	12.3	19.1	19.8	25.5	15.1
	1998	30.6	22.6	31.1	24.9	30.0	33.7	27.0	23.8	27.1	36.6	27.9	25.1
	2002	18.7	1.0	19.2	6.1	14.2	26.0	14.2	2.2	14.4	14.1	13.5	14.9
	2005	5.5	1.1	5.6	3.3	5.3	6.5	4.9	1.8	4.9	4.8	4.6	5.2
Mexico - Mexique	1991	13.7	10.0	13.9	11.2	13.7	14.9	12.9	8.1	13.0	9.8	13.7	13.3
	1995	13.1	9.8	13.2	10.8	11.3	14.8	11.7	8.9	11.8	9.5	11.1	13.6
	1997	13.9	9.6	14.1	9.9	11.1	16.8	12.4	8.3	12.4	8.8	11.3	15.4
	1998	13.8	9.4	14.0	9.6	10.9	16.8	12.1	8.8	12.2	8.7	10.8	15.4
	1999	17.0	12.4	17.2	12.3	14.3	20.2	15.1	12.0	15.2	11.5	14.0	18.3
	2000	17.0	12.4	17.2	12.3	14.1	20.1	14.6	11.9	14.6	11.4	13.2	18.1
	2001	17.0	12.4	17.2	12.3	14.0	20.2	14.5	12.2	14.5	11.6	12.9	18.3
	2002	17.1	12.4	17.3	12.6	14.0	20.3	14.5	12.3	14.6	11.9	12.8	18.7
	2003	17.1	12.3	17.3	12.4	14.0	20.4	14.4	12.2	14.5	11.7	12.6	18.8
	2004	16.4	12.3	16.6	12.3	13.5	19.3	12.8	11.8	12.8	11.4	10.8	16.9
	2005	13.5	9.4	13.7	9.4	10.4	16.5	11.5	8.9	11.6	8.5	10.6	14.5
Moldova, Republic of - Moldova, République de	1996	4.9	2.9	4.9	3.4	1.0	7.0	2.3	1.9	2.3	1.4	1.1	3.6
	2000	4.3	2.0	4.3	3.5	1.5	5.7	2.8	1.8	2.8	1.5	1.3	4.0
	2001	4.1	1.3	4.2	3.4	1.5	5.5	2.9	1.6	2.9	1.7	1.1	4.2
Mongolia - Mongolie	2005	4.4	5.0	4.3	5.0	2.1	5.0	3.9	5.0	3.9	5.0	2.7	5.0
Montserrat	1996	19.8	15.8	19.8	14.5	16.7	21.3	15.4	7.0	15.6	19.8	10.7	18.7
	1999	16.4	12.9	16.4	11.2	14.3	17.7	12.1	6.9	12.2	15.1	9.1	14.4
Morocco - Maroc	1993	64.5	28.0	65.9	49.5	55.3	75.7	53.6	17.8	55.1	45.9	51.9	64.1
	1997	18.4	9.3	18.7	12.5	10.7	24.2	17.7	3.9	18.1	12.2	10.9	25.8
	2000	27.9	23.8	28.1	26.2	13.1	34.9	25.9	12.8	26.3	25.6	15.5	35.6
	2001	27.7	23.7	27.9	25.8	13.0	34.6	25.6	12.9	26.0	25.3	14.4	35.8
	2002	27.5	24.1	27.7	24.6	13.0	34.7	25.4	12.7	25.8	24.1	15.2	35.1
	2003	27.1	23.9	27.3	23.2	12.7	34.5	24.1	10.7	24.6	21.1	14.5	34.6
	2005	23.0	12.8	23.4	16.8	10.8	30.8	21.2	7.0	21.7	18.2	13.5	30.6
Mozambique	1994	5.0	5.0	5.0	5.0	5.0	5.0	5.0	5.0	5.0	5.0	5.0	5.0
	1997	14.5	4.4	14.9	4.9	9.4	20.6	15.4	4.3	15.5	12.0	10.6	21.3
	2001	12.9	4.4	13.2	4.7	8.8	17.9	12.3	6.8	12.4	5.5	9.2	17.6
	2002	11.2	4.3	11.5	4.4	8.1	15.4	8.9	6.4	9.0	7.8	7.4	10.9
	2003	11.2	4.3	11.5	4.4	8.1	15.4	10.2	6.3	10.2	7.3	8.2	13.3
	2005	11.2	4.3	11.5	4.4	8.1	15.4	10.6	4.5	10.6	7.1	8.8	13.5
Myanmar	2001	5.0	3.2	5.1	1.9	2.9	7.1	4.9	2.9	4.9	2.5	2.8	6.9
	2002	5.0	3.2	5.1	1.9	2.9	7.1	4.8	3.2	4.8	2.3	2.9	7.0
	2003	5.0	3.2	5.1	1.9	2.9	7.1	4.1	2.7	4.1	2.4	2.6	6.2
	2004	5.0	3.2	5.1	1.9	2.9	7.1	3.9	3.0	3.9	2.2	2.7	5.6
	2005	5.1	3.1	5.2	1.8	3.0	7.2	3.9	3.0	4.0	2.2	2.9	5.7
Namibia - Namibie	2001	7.9	1.4	8.2	2.5	3.2	12.4	11.3	0.7	11.5	10.4	10.2	13.4
	2004	8.1	1.3	8.3	2.4	3.0	12.5	10.4	0.3	10.8	6.6	9.8	12.9
	2005	8.0	1.2	8.3	2.5	3.0	12.4	10.2	0.3	10.6	6.7	9.5	12.7
Nepal - Népal	1993	18.0	7.4	18.4	8.9	18.0	21.9	20.8	5.2	21.0	8.5	25.6	22.7
	1998	17.5	7.5	17.9	8.8	17.4	21.4	29.2	5.1	29.9	9.2	44.9	22.8
	1999	12.9	7.2	13.2	9.7	12.1	14.9	15.1	7.2	15.2	10.9	21.9	12.1

For sources and notes, see end of table.   Pour les sources et les notes, se reporter à la fin du tableau.

239

Market / Marchés	Year / Année	MFN rate - Simple average (2) / Droit NPF - Moyenne simple (2)						MFN rate - Weighted average (3) / Droit NPF - Moyenne pondérée (3)					
		Total of non-agricultural and non-fuel products / Total des produits non-agricoles et non-pétroliers	Ores and metals / Minérais et métaux	Manu-factured products / Produits manu-facturés	Chemical products / Produits chimiques	Machinery and transport equipment / Machines et matériel de transport	Other manu-factured products / Produits manu-facturés divers	Total of non-agricultural and non-fuel products / Total des produits non-agricoles et non-pétroliers	Ores and metals / Minérais et métaux	Manu-factured products / Produits manu-facturés	Chemical products / Produits chimiques	Machinery and transport equipment / Machines et matériel de transport	Other manu-factured products / Produits manu-facturés divers
SITC Rev.2 (1) / CTCI Rév 2 (1)		5+6+7+8 +27+28	27+28+68	(5+6+7+8) - 68	5	7	(6+8) - 68	5+6+7+8 +27+28	27+28+68	(5+6+7+8) - 68	5	7	(6+8) - 68
Nepal - Népal	2000	13.4	9.5	13.5	12.1	11.8	14.6	19.5	5.4	19.9	12.0	33.2	11.8
	2002	13.6	10.2	13.7	12.2	11.9	15.0	16.8	7.3	17.0	13.9	22.7	15.2
	2003	13.7	10.2	13.8	12.3	12.0	15.2	17.0	7.3	17.2	14.1	23.0	15.4
	2004	13.8	10.4	13.9	12.5	11.4	15.4	16.1	7.2	16.3	14.5	18.8	15.7
	2005	13.8	10.4	13.9	12.5	11.4	15.4	16.4	7.2	16.5	14.5	19.6	15.7
New Zealand - Nouvelle-Zélande	1992	8.9	2.4	9.1	2.4	10.9	10.8	9.3	3.5	9.6	5.5	9.5	11.3
	1993	8.4	2.4	8.6	2.1	9.7	10.5	9.0	3.4	9.3	4.4	9.7	10.9
	1996	6.1	1.7	6.3	1.4	6.6	7.8	7.3	2.2	7.5	2.9	8.1	8.6
	1997	5.3	1.3	5.5	1.2	5.8	6.9	6.2	2.4	6.4	2.3	6.4	8.0
	1998	4.5	1.0	4.6	0.9	4.9	5.8	5.3	1.8	5.5	1.8	5.4	7.1
	1999	3.7	0.8	3.9	0.8	4.1	4.9	4.6	1.7	4.7	1.7	4.8	5.8
	2000	2.9	0.6	3.0	0.6	3.1	3.8	3.6	1.3	3.7	1.3	3.8	4.5
	2002	3.6	0.8	3.7	0.8	3.9	4.8	4.6	1.8	4.7	1.8	4.8	5.8
	2003	3.6	0.8	3.7	0.8	3.9	4.7	4.6	1.9	4.7	1.9	4.9	5.5
	2004	3.5	0.8	3.6	0.8	3.9	4.5	4.5	2.0	4.6	1.7	4.8	5.4
	2005	3.6	0.8	3.7	0.8	3.9	4.7	4.5	2.0	4.6	1.7	4.8	5.5
Nicaragua	1995	9.4	5.8	9.5	5.8	4.1	12.9	7.6	6.3	7.6	6.5	5.1	10.9
	1998	4.8	1.2	4.9	1.3	1.9	7.4	5.1	3.8	5.1	3.9	4.0	7.2
	1999	9.7	6.2	9.8	6.2	6.9	12.3	9.6	10.0	9.6	8.0	8.2	12.1
	2000	3.1	0.9	3.2	0.9	1.5	4.7	3.9	2.3	3.9	3.0	3.5	4.8
	2001	3.9	0.9	4.0	1.1	1.8	6.0	4.5	2.2	4.5	3.8	3.6	5.6
	2002	3.9	0.9	4.0	1.1	1.8	5.9	4.5	2.2	4.5	3.9	3.7	5.5
	2004	4.3	1.0	4.4	1.4	2.2	6.4	5.5	4.5	5.5	3.7	5.3	6.8
	2005	4.8	1.0	4.9	1.4	2.2	7.3	5.5	4.6	5.5	3.7	4.2	7.8
Niger	2001	11.8	7.5	12.0	6.3	8.5	15.4	12.4	5.5	12.7	6.2	12.9	16.2
	2002	11.7	7.5	11.9	6.3	8.5	15.3	12.4	5.4	12.6	6.0	11.5	16.8
	2003	11.7	7.3	11.9	6.3	8.6	15.3	13.0	8.4	13.0	4.0	13.4	15.9
	2004	11.7	7.4	11.9	6.3	8.6	15.3	12.0	6.2	12.1	4.9	12.2	13.7
	2005	11.7	7.4	11.9	6.3	8.6	15.3	12.0	6.2	12.1	4.7	12.1	13.8
Nigeria - Nigéria	1988	33.6	22.5	34.2	18.5	18.2	45.9	21.3	18.7	21.4	18.5	18.9	27.1
	1989	35.6	29.9	36.1	19.1	19.5	48.5	22.3	15.8	22.4	19.0	19.8	28.5
	1990	35.8	30.0	36.2	19.0	20.2	48.6	22.5	16.6	22.6	18.9	20.6	28.1
	1992	34.5	23.2	35.0	22.6	20.2	45.2	23.1	16.6	23.3	22.3	20.6	27.8
	1995	27.0	11.4	27.7	11.5	12.3	34.9	19.5	10.3	19.6	12.4	17.8	23.9
	1996	23.4	16.6	23.7	13.2	12.7	31.9	14.9	9.8	15.1	14.4	12.9	17.9
	1997	23.4	16.6	23.7	13.2	12.7	31.9	15.1	10.0	15.3	15.1	12.9	18.0
	1998	23.4	16.6	23.7	13.2	12.7	31.9	15.1	10.0	15.3	15.1	12.9	18.0
	1999	25.3	18.8	25.6	17.6	16.3	32.2	18.5	14.6	18.6	18.9	16.7	20.6
	2000	25.3	18.8	25.6	17.6	16.3	32.2	18.2	15.4	18.2	17.0	17.5	20.3
	2001	25.3	18.8	25.6	17.6	16.3	32.2	18.6	16.9	18.7	17.5	17.4	21.1
	2002	26.7	17.4	27.1	16.1	15.4	35.7	15.7	10.0	15.7	12.4	14.6	19.5
	2005	11.4	6.9	11.6	6.8	5.9	15.6	9.3	9.8	9.3	9.5	6.7	14.1
Norway - Norvège	1988	6.5	0.5	6.8	5.0	5.1	8.2	5.5	0.4	5.8	6.2	3.6	8.5
	1993	6.6	0.4	6.8	5.0	5.2	8.2	5.7	0.3	6.1	6.0	4.2	8.5
	1995	6.2	0.4	6.4	4.7	4.8	7.7	5.4	0.4	5.7	5.8	4.3	7.3
	1996	5.7	0.4	5.9	4.8	4.0	7.2	4.6	0.3	4.9	6.7	3.1	6.9
	1998	3.6	0.3	3.7	3.5	0.7	5.0	2.3	0.3	2.4	5.2	0.7	4.1
	2000	2.4	0.3	2.5	1.4	0.3	3.8	1.6	0.3	1.7	3.2	0.2	3.7
	2001	2.3	0.3	2.3	1.0	0.3	3.6	1.5	0.3	1.6	2.1	0.2	3.5
	2002	1.8	0.2	1.9	0.7	0.2	3.0	1.3	0.2	1.3	1.4	0.1	2.9
	2003	0.8	0.0	0.8	0.3	0.0	1.3	0.6	0.0	0.7	0.7	0.0	1.5
Oman	1992	5.1	5.0	5.1	5.0	5.0	5.2	5.4	5.7	5.4	4.5	5.0	6.5
	1997	4.9	4.9	4.9	4.8	4.8	5.0	4.9	4.9	4.9	4.7	5.0	4.8
	2002	7.1	5.4	7.1	5.6	7.0	7.8	6.5	5.2	6.5	7.4	6.1	7.1
	2005	4.9	4.8	4.9	4.8	4.9	5.0	4.9	5.0	4.9	4.0	5.0	4.9

For sources and notes, see end of table.

Pour les sources et les notes, se reporter à la fin du tableau.

Market / Marchés	Year / Année	MFN rate - Simple average (2) / Droit NPF - Moyenne simple (2)						MFN rate - Weighted average (3) / Droit NPF - Moyenne pondérée (3)					
		Total of non-agricultural and non-fuel products / Total des produits non-agricoles et non-pétroliers	Ores and metals / Minérais et métaux	Manufactured products / Produits manufacturés	Chemical products / Produits chimiques	Machinery and transport equipment / Machines et matériel de transport	Other manufactured products / Produits manufacturés divers	Total of non-agricultural and non-fuel products / Total des produits non-agricoles et non-pétroliers	Ores and metals / Minérais et métaux	Manufactured products / Produits manufacturés	Chemical products / Produits chimiques	Machinery and transport equipment / Machines et matériel de transport	Other manufactured products / Produits manufacturés divers
SITC Rev.2 (1) / CTCI Rév.2 (1)		5+6+7+8 +27+28	27+28+68	(5+6+7+8) - 68	5	7	(6+8) - 68	5+6+7+8 +27+28	27+28+68	(5+6+7+8) - 68	5	7	(6+8) - 68
Pakistan	1995	51.9	37.2	52.4	43.3	45.6	58.3	48.8	29.3	49.2	41.6	51.1	56.0
	1998	47.7	36.8	48.1	42.0	38.7	53.8	43.5	28.7	43.8	38.9	43.8	50.7
	2001	20.4	12.1	20.6	14.9	19.6	23.1	20.8	9.6	21.1	13.8	25.7	21.6
	2002	17.4	10.6	17.5	13.9	16.4	19.3	17.5	8.9	17.8	13.2	20.5	18.3
	2003	17.1	9.9	17.3	13.6	16.1	19.1	17.2	8.6	17.4	13.0	20.0	18.0
	2004	16.6	9.7	16.8	12.7	15.4	18.9	15.6	8.3	15.7	10.8	18.2	17.6
	2005	14.3	8.4	14.5	9.7	13.5	16.7	13.2	10.0	13.3	8.6	15.7	14.8
Panama	1997	10.9	12.9	11.0	6.4	9.5	13.1	11.0	11.5	11.0	6.7	9.6	14.4
	1998	7.6	8.9	7.6	4.9	7.0	8.9	8.5	5.6	8.5	5.4	9.1	8.7
	2000	7.1	8.7	7.1	4.1	6.9	8.3	7.7	6.9	7.7	4.9	7.8	8.6
	2001	6.8	8.4	6.8	3.4	6.9	8.0	7.4	6.5	7.4	4.7	7.8	8.2
	2005	6.2	8.3	6.2	1.9	6.8	7.5	6.5	5.6	6.6	2.8	7.4	7.5
Papua New Guinea - Papouasie-Nouvelle-Guinée	1997	16.7	13.3	16.9	9.5	9.9	22.3	13.2	20.1	13.1	10.5	11.9	15.8
	2002	4.9	0.0	5.1	1.1	0.3	8.4	2.5	0.0	2.5	2.2	0.1	5.3
	2003	4.1	0.0	4.2	0.9	0.3	7.0	1.7	0.0	1.7	2.5	0.1	3.7
	2004	4.1	0.0	4.2	0.9	0.3	7.0	1.7	0.0	1.7	2.5	0.1	3.7
	2005	4.1	0.0	4.2	0.9	0.3	7.0	1.7	0.0	1.7	2.5	0.1	3.7
Paraguay	1991	15.0	5.6	15.3	5.4	11.8	20.2	14.4	3.1	14.5	8.8	14.0	17.4
	1994	7.7	2.1	7.9	1.1	7.1	10.5	8.1	0.8	8.1	3.1	9.0	8.9
	1995	11.1	6.0	11.3	8.0	6.6	14.4	10.4	6.9	10.4	9.3	9.5	12.4
	1996	11.2	6.0	11.4	7.8	6.1	14.8	9.4	8.1	9.4	8.2	8.7	11.4
	1997	11.4	6.0	11.6	7.9	7.1	14.8	10.4	7.6	10.4	8.8	9.7	12.2
	1998	11.4	6.0	11.7	7.9	7.6	14.7	10.2	8.2	10.2	8.8	9.6	12.1
	1999	13.4	8.8	13.6	10.6	8.1	16.9	10.5	10.7	10.5	10.3	9.1	12.8
	2000	13.4	8.8	13.7	10.7	8.7	16.7	11.7	8.8	11.7	11.1	10.0	14.0
	2001	13.1	7.9	13.4	9.8	9.8	16.1	11.9	8.5	11.9	10.3	10.8	14.1
	2002	12.8	7.3	13.1	9.2	9.8	15.8	11.3	7.2	11.4	9.7	9.9	14.3
	2003	12.9	7.3	13.1	9.3	9.8	15.8	11.8	7.4	11.9	9.4	11.3	14.6
	2004	12.1	7.3	12.3	9.4	6.4	15.7	12.3	7.6	12.4	9.8	11.5	15.2
	2005	10.9	5.8	11.1	7.7	5.9	14.4	10.8	6.5	10.9	7.3	10.9	13.3
Peru - Pérou	1993	17.9	15.4	18.0	15.5	16.0	19.7	16.6	15.0	16.6	15.7	16.0	18.3
	1995	16.5	15.0	16.6	15.0	15.3	17.6	15.4	15.0	15.4	15.0	15.2	15.8
	1997	13.2	12.0	13.3	12.0	12.3	14.1	12.3	12.0	12.3	12.0	12.2	12.7
	1998	13.2	12.0	13.2	12.0	12.3	14.1	12.3	12.0	12.3	12.0	12.2	12.7
	1999	13.2	12.0	13.2	12.0	12.3	14.1	12.3	12.0	12.3	12.0	12.2	12.8
	2000	13.2	12.0	13.2	12.0	12.3	14.1	12.3	12.0	12.3	12.0	12.2	12.8
	2004	10.2	8.8	10.2	6.7	7.7	12.4	8.9	9.4	8.9	7.2	8.4	10.7
	2005	9.6	8.7	9.6	6.6	6.1	12.1	8.3	9.4	8.3	6.9	7.4	10.4
Philippines	1988	27.5	17.2	28.0	16.9	23.7	33.6	23.1	12.8	23.4	19.6	22.5	27.7
	1989	27.6	17.2	28.0	16.9	23.7	33.6	23.1	12.8	23.4	19.6	22.5	27.7
	1990	19.2	13.8	19.5	12.5	15.1	23.6	14.8	10.8	14.9	12.7	13.4	20.1
	1992	19.2	13.8	19.5	12.5	15.1	23.6	14.8	10.8	14.9	12.7	13.4	20.1
	1993	21.8	11.4	22.3	12.7	15.2	28.3	15.1	9.5	15.2	12.2	13.3	21.9
	1994	21.3	11.3	21.6	12.7	14.8	27.5	14.8	9.5	15.0	12.2	13.2	21.2
	1995	19.4	12.9	19.7	12.5	14.1	24.4	14.1	9.5	14.2	12.1	12.4	20.3
	1998	10.0	3.9	10.2	4.6	7.0	13.5	5.6	3.9	5.7	5.9	4.3	10.6
	1999	9.1	3.8	9.2	4.5	6.9	11.9	5.7	3.9	5.7	5.8	4.5	9.7
	2000	7.2	3.3	7.3	3.9	5.0	9.5	3.5	3.4	3.5	5.1	2.1	7.3
	2001	6.8	3.3	7.0	3.8	4.6	9.0	3.2	3.7	3.2	4.9	1.8	6.9
	2002	5.2	2.7	5.3	3.2	3.5	6.8	2.1	2.9	2.1	4.3	1.1	5.3
	2003	4.3	2.7	4.3	3.1	3.1	5.2	2.0	2.9	2.0	4.3	1.2	4.3
	2004	5.8	2.5	5.9	3.5	3.5	7.7	2.9	2.5	2.9	4.9	1.6	5.9
	2005	5.8	2.5	5.9	3.4	3.5	7.7	2.9	2.5	2.9	4.8	1.6	5.8
Poland - Pologne	1991	11.8	6.7	12.0	11.4	9.3	13.3	10.6	3.9	10.9	12.2	9.4	11.6
	1992	11.8	6.7	12.0	11.3	9.3	13.3	10.6	3.9	10.9	12.2	9.4	11.6
	1995	9.6	6.5	9.7	12.7	13.1	7.4	10.2	5.5	10.4	11.4	12.2	8.2
	1996	13.7	6.8	14.0	11.8	12.5	15.4	12.9	5.1	13.1	10.5	13.9	13.4

For sources and notes, see end of table.

Pour les sources et les notes, se reporter à la fin du tableau.

Market / Marchés	Year / Année	MFN rate - Simple average (2) / Droit NPF - Moyenne simple (2)						MFN rate - Weighted average (3) / Droit NPF - Moyenne pondérée (3)					
		Total of non-agricultural and non-fuel products / Total des produits non-agricoles et non-pétroliers	Ores and metals / Minérais et métaux	Manufactured products / Produits manufacturés	Chemical products / Produits chimiques	Machinery and transport equipment / Machines et matériel de transport	Other manufactured products / Produits manufacturés divers	Total of non-agricultural and non-fuel products / Total des produits non-agricoles et non-pétroliers	Ores and metals / Minérais et métaux	Manufactured products / Produits manufacturés	Chemical products / Produits chimiques	Machinery and transport equipment / Machines et matériel de transport	Other manufactured products / Produits manufacturés divers
SITC Rev.2 (1) / CTCI Rév 2 (1)		5+6+7+8 +27+28	27+28+68	(5+6+7+8) - 68	5	7	(6+8) - 68	5+6+7+8 +27+28	27+28+68	(5+6+7+8) - 68	5	7	(6+8) - 68
Poland - Pologne	1997	12.0	5.8	12.3	11.3	9.9	13.5	10.2	4.6	10.4	9.1	9.7	11.7
	1998	11.4	5.7	11.7	11.0	9.2	12.9	9.6	5.1	9.7	8.8	8.5	11.3
	1999	10.9	5.5	11.2	10.7	8.8	12.3	9.1	5.8	9.2	8.5	7.9	10.9
	2000	10.5	5.4	10.8	9.7	9.2	11.8	10.0	5.6	10.1	7.8	10.7	10.5
	2001	10.0	5.1	10.3	10.3	8.1	11.1	8.1	5.5	8.2	7.5	6.5	10.1
	2002	10.0	5.1	10.2	10.2	8.1	11.0	8.2	5.9	8.3	7.4	6.7	10.3
	2003	10.0	5.1	10.2	10.2	8.1	11.0	8.2	5.9	8.3	7.5	6.6	10.2
Qatar	2002	4.1	4.0	4.1	4.0	4.0	4.1	4.0	4.0	4.0	4.0	4.0	4.0
	2005	4.9	4.8	4.9	4.9	4.9	5.0	3.6	5.0	3.5	2.7	3.1	5.0
Romania - Roumanie	1991	17.3	6.8	17.7	16.5	16.3	18.7	15.8	2.8	17.9	15.4	20.1	16.6
	1999	16.0	6.7	16.4	15.9	14.6	17.3	14.1	5.6	14.3	13.9	12.1	15.9
	2001	16.1	6.6	16.4	14.5	14.0	18.1	14.7	3.9	15.0	10.9	12.6	17.7
	2004	16.0	6.5	16.3	15.2	13.3	18.0	14.8	4.4	15.1	12.0	13.9	17.0
	2005	15.3	6.3	15.7	14.2	12.8	17.3	13.8	4.4	14.0	9.7	13.5	15.7
Russian Federation - Fédération de Russie	1993	8.7	7.1	8.8	5.3	6.3	10.9	7.2	3.7	7.5	7.6	6.4	8.7
	1994	12.1	6.9	12.4	5.7	12.1	14.9	9.2	3.5	9.5	5.8	8.8	11.8
	1996	11.4	10.0	11.5	5.7	11.4	13.9	9.1	5.4	9.3	7.7	8.1	11.9
	1997	13.0	9.0	13.2	7.1	12.8	15.6	11.5	5.7	11.8	9.3	11.2	13.9
	2001	10.0	8.2	10.2	6.5	10.2	11.8	9.0	6.4	9.3	8.5	8.6	10.8
	2002	9.7	8.6	9.8	6.6	8.9	11.6	8.8	6.8	9.0	8.7	7.9	11.0
	2005	9.6	8.6	9.7	6.6	8.5	11.6	8.3	5.2	8.6	9.0	7.4	10.6
Rwanda	1993	33.1	24.9	33.6	17.8	24.8	42.6	25.2	17.2	25.5	15.2	25.2	29.4
	2001	9.5	6.7	9.7	5.7	7.2	12.1	7.0	5.4	7.1	4.8	8.2	6.9
	2003	9.5	6.7	9.7	5.7	7.2	12.1	8.8	5.5	8.9	4.7	9.1	10.6
	2005	19.6	10.9	20.0	14.8	18.4	22.5	16.8	8.8	17.0	7.8	17.1	22.8
Saint Kitts and Nevis - Saint-Kitts-et-Nevis	1996	20.8	16.0	20.8	14.5	21.3	21.6	23.7	15.7	23.8	17.6	34.2	19.9
	1999	17.3	12.8	17.4	11.0	18.5	18.1	19.1	10.9	19.1	14.4	32.6	15.7
	2000	8.8	2.4	9.1	5.1	7.8	11.0	13.3	4.4	13.4	13.1	12.5	14.0
	2001	8.8	2.4	9.1	5.1	7.8	11.0	12.1	5.6	12.1	12.0	11.2	12.9
	2002	8.8	2.4	9.1	5.1	7.8	11.0	13.4	2.7	13.6	12.0	11.9	15.1
	2003	8.8	2.4	9.1	5.1	7.8	11.0	13.4	3.9	13.4	12.1	12.2	14.6
Saint Lucia - Sainte-Lucie	1996	20.5	16.5	20.6	14.5	20.5	21.5	20.8	14.1	20.9	15.8	25.7	20.1
	1999	17.1	13.3	17.1	11.3	17.3	18.0	17.6	13.1	17.6	13.5	24.3	15.5
	2000	17.1	13.3	17.1	11.5	17.3	17.9	17.7	13.1	17.7	14.2	24.3	15.6
	2001	7.5	2.2	7.6	5.6	5.2	9.4	11.6	1.5	11.7	13.2	11.6	11.4
	2002	7.5	2.2	7.6	5.6	5.2	9.4	12.4	1.4	12.5	13.3	10.7	13.5
	2003	7.5	2.2	7.6	5.6	5.2	9.4	12.4	1.6	12.5	12.8	10.5	14.1
	2005	7.5	2.2	7.6	5.6	5.0	9.4	12.9	4.7	13.0	13.2	11.7	13.8
Saint Vincent and the Grenadines - Saint-Vincent-et-les Grenadines	1996	20.1	15.5	20.1	14.5	18.4	21.4	20.2	18.8	20.2	16.0	23.3	19.9
	1999	16.7	12.2	16.7	11.3	15.9	17.7	16.5	13.0	16.5	12.0	20.1	16.4
	2000	16.7	12.2	16.7	11.5	15.9	17.7	16.5	14.5	16.6	12.6	22.3	15.5
	2001	8.5	4.4	8.6	5.7	7.4	10.2	12.2	6.9	12.3	10.1	11.4	13.3
	2002	8.5	4.4	8.6	5.7	7.4	10.2	11.3	7.0	11.3	11.2	10.5	11.9
	2003	8.5	4.4	8.6	5.7	7.4	10.2	11.2	5.5	11.2	11.2	10.6	11.6
Saudi Arabia - Arabie saoudite	1994	12.2	12.2	12.2	11.8	11.8	12.5	11.5	13.4	11.5	9.0	11.0	12.9
	1999	12.1	12.2	12.1	11.8	11.8	12.4	11.5	13.3	11.5	8.3	11.3	13.0
	2000	12.1	12.2	12.1	11.8	11.8	12.3	11.4	13.1	11.4	8.4	11.4	12.6
	2003	6.1	5.5	6.1	6.0	5.4	6.4	6.6	7.9	6.6	5.2	5.8	8.2
	2004	6.1	5.5	6.1	6.0	5.4	6.4	6.6	7.9	6.6	5.2	5.8	8.2
Senegal - Sénégal	2001	11.8	7.5	12.0	6.3	8.5	15.4	10.3	6.8	10.4	5.7	10.5	13.1
	2002	11.7	7.5	11.9	6.3	8.5	15.3	10.9	8.5	11.0	5.6	12.4	13.2
	2003	11.7	7.3	11.9	6.3	8.6	15.3	10.2	6.4	10.4	5.7	10.4	13.4
	2004	11.7	7.4	11.9	6.3	8.6	15.3	10.3	6.2	10.5	5.5	10.5	13.4
	2005	11.7	7.4	11.9	6.3	8.6	15.3	10.3	6.2	10.5	5.5	10.5	13.4

For sources and notes, see end of table.

Pour les sources et les notes, se reporter à la fin du tableau.

Market / Marchés	Year / Année	MFN rate - Simple average (2) / Droit NPF - Moyenne simple (2)						MFN rate - Weighted average (3) / Droit NPF - Moyenne pondérée (3)					
		Total of non-agricultural and non-fuel products / Total des produits non-agricoles et non-pétroliers	of which: / dont :					Total of non-agricultural and non-fuel products / Total des produits non-agricoles et non-pétroliers	of which: / dont :				
			Ores and metals / Minérais et métaux	Manu-factured products / Produits manu-facturés	Of which: / dont :				Ores and metals / Minérais et métaux	Manu-factured products / Produits manu-facturés	Of which: / dont :		
					Chemical products / Produits chimiques	Machinery and transport equipment / Machines et matériel de transport	Other manu-factured products / Produits manu-facturés divers				Chemical products / Produits chimiques	Machinery and transport equipment / Machines et matériel de transport	Other manu-factured products / Produits manu-facturés divers
SITC Rev.2 (1) / CTCI Rév.2 (1)		5+6+7+8 +27+28	27+28+68	(5+6+7+8) - 68	5	7	(6+8) - 68	5+6+7+8 +27+28	27+28+68	(5+6+7+8) - 68	5	7	(6+8) - 68
Seychelles	2000	25.1	22.5	25.1	28.7	20.8	25.6	18.5	21.3	18.5	22.7	17.3	21.0
	2001	24.8	22.5	24.8	28.7	20.8	25.1	18.5	21.3	18.5	22.7	17.3	21.0
	2005	13.1	11.1	13.2	4.5	17.2	14.9	17.6	11.6	17.7	10.1	32.1	11.1
Singapore - Singapour	1989	0.4	0.0	0.5	0.0	0.6	0.6	0.6	0.0	0.6	0.0	0.9	0.3
Slovakia - Slovaquie	2002	20.7	6.6	21.3	19.2	18.6	23.0	23.1	5.6	23.6	18.7	21.5	28.0
Slovenia - Slovénie	1999	10.0	3.2	10.3	7.5	10.7	11.1	11.9	4.4	12.1	9.0	13.6	11.6
	2001	9.7	3.0	9.9	7.5	9.5	11.0	10.4	4.8	10.6	9.0	10.4	11.3
	2002	9.6	3.0	9.9	7.5	9.4	10.9	10.3	4.9	10.5	9.0	10.1	11.3
	2003	9.6	3.0	9.9	7.5	9.4	10.9	10.3	4.7	10.5	9.0	10.5	11.2
Solomon Islands - Îles Salomon	1995	39.1	7.9	40.3	16.3	20.4	56.5	34.0	10.9	34.0	24.8	27.4	42.4
South Africa - Afrique du Sud	1988	(a)11.85	(a)3.85	a)12.18	(a)8.82	(a)7.55	a)15.41	(a)12.21	(a)4.43	(a)12.31	(a)7.03	(a)14.61	(a)9.87
	1990	(a)10.76	(a)3.84	a)11.07	(a)8.64	(a)7.7	a)13.59	(a)10.88	(a)5.9	(a)10.95	(a)7.12	(a)12.27	(a)10.52
	1991	(a)10.46	(a)3.49	a)10.77	(a)8.44	(a)7.89	a)13.05	(a)11.77	(a)5.66	(a)11.85	(a)6.94	(a)14.2	(a)9.93
	1993	(a)17.17	(a)3.92	a)17.66	(a)8.91	(a)8.17	a)24.44	(a)13.97	(a)5.66	(a)14.11	(a)7.81	(a)15.2	(a)15.39
	1996	(a)14.95	(a)1.8	a)15.58	(a)3.19	(a)4.56	a)24.38	(a)8.77	(a)1.08	(a)9.02	(a)3.53	(a)7.4	(a)14.69
	1997	(a)6.97	(a)1.98	(a)7.18	(a)3.03	(a)5.71	(a)9.77	(a)6.04	(a)1.78	(a)6.17	(a)2.91	(a)5.64	(a)8.97
	1999	(a)5.68	(a)1.68	(a)5.85	(a)2.9	(a)3.44	(a)8.42	(a)4.94	(a)1.35	(a)5.03	(a)3	(a)4.65	(a)6.89
	2001	7.9	1.4	8.2	2.5	3.2	12.4	5.9	0.9	6.0	2.6	5.4	9.1
	2004	8.1	1.3	8.3	2.4	3.0	12.5	6.5	0.5	6.6	2.8	6.1	9.6
	2005	8.0	1.2	8.3	2.5	3.0	12.4	6.2	0.5	6.4	2.9	5.8	9.2
Sri Lanka	1990	26.0	11.4	26.4	12.3	14.1	36.4	24.1	7.4	24.3	7.8	14.4	35.9
	1993	22.5	12.0	22.8	12.2	15.7	29.3	26.4	11.8	26.5	9.5	18.4	34.2
	1994	22.5	12.0	22.8	12.2	15.7	29.3	26.9	11.6	27.0	9.8	20.2	34.2
	1997	18.2	11.7	18.4	11.6	14.4	22.3	21.5	10.7	21.5	9.9	20.2	24.3
	2000	7.9	5.5	7.9	6.1	6.1	9.3	5.5	5.3	5.5	5.3	7.0	4.8
	2001	7.9	5.5	7.9	6.1	6.1	9.3	5.2	6.3	5.1	5.4	6.5	4.6
	2004	8.3	5.1	8.4	5.1	6.8	10.1	6.4	4.2	6.4	5.2	9.3	5.2
	2005	9.4	5.3	9.5	4.9	7.8	11.8	6.8	4.1	6.8	5.0	10.3	5.5
Sudan - Soudan	1996	4.3	1.8	4.4	2.3	1.6	6.3	4.0	3.9	4.0	3.2	1.8	7.6
	2002	22.6	16.9	22.9	14.5	14.5	29.3	18.9	11.2	18.9	15.2	15.5	29.7
Suriname	1996	20.0	17.1	20.1	14.9	16.9	21.6	18.5	17.1	18.5	18.8	17.4	20.0
	1999	16.6	13.8	16.7	11.9	14.2	18.0	15.3	12.0	15.3	14.1	14.4	16.1
	2000	12.5	13.7	12.5	9.3	8.7	14.6	12.1	14.8	12.1	8.9	10.0	14.5
Swaziland	2001	7.9	1.4	8.2	2.5	3.2	12.4	11.3	3.3	11.4	4.9	10.6	14.7
	2004	8.1	1.3	8.3	2.4	3.0	12.5	11.9	2.1	11.9	1.8	4.7	15.9
	2005	8.0	1.2	8.3	2.5	3.0	12.4	10.8	2.1	10.8	2.1	3.6	15.2
Syrian Arab Republic - République arabe syrienne	2002	19.8	6.9	20.3	5.5	15.1	27.6	16.6	5.6	16.6	3.6	30.6	10.8
Tajikistan - Tadjikistan	2002	8.1	8.7	8.1	5.2	5.3	10.3	7.5	6.2	8.4	5.1	5.0	11.9
Thailand - Thaïlande	1989	39.9	17.8	40.9	32.0	35.2	48.3	34.1	10.7	34.9	31.0	39.7	25.9
	1991	39.9	17.8	40.9	32.2	35.2	48.3	33.8	12.2	34.2	31.4	37.9	26.6
	1993	45.4	18.8	46.5	36.7	34.0	55.1	36.1	14.1	36.5	38.4	34.9	38.9
	1995	20.2	10.3	20.6	14.0	13.3	26.0	15.6	8.7	15.6	15.2	15.6	15.9
	2000	15.5	6.5	15.8	11.1	12.1	19.1	10.0	5.4	10.1	10.5	8.8	12.3
	2001	14.6	6.1	14.9	6.2	12.4	19.0	10.5	4.2	10.6	9.8	8.8	14.7
	2003	13.7	4.7	14.0	5.6	12.3	17.8	10.7	3.7	10.8	9.6	10.0	12.9
	2005	10.2	2.4	10.5	4.6	8.0	13.5	6.6	2.2	6.7	6.9	6.1	7.7
Macedonia, TFYR - Macédoine, LERY	2001	13.6	7.6	13.8	7.3	11.5	17.1	12.9	8.4	13.0	10.8	11.6	15.5
	2004	8.8	3.9	9.0	3.8	6.6	11.8	7.1	3.3	7.2	6.0	7.1	7.7
	2005	8.0	3.0	8.1	3.5	6.1	10.5	6.1	2.5	6.2	5.4	6.0	6.6

For sources and notes, see end of table.

Pour les sources et les notes, se reporter à la fin du tableau.

Market / Marchés	Year / Année	MFN rate - Simple average (2) / Droit NPF - Moyenne simple (2)						MFN rate - Weighted average (3) / Droit NPF - Moyenne pondérée (3)					
		Total of non-agricultural and non-fuel products / Total des produits non-agricoles et non-pétroliers	of which: / dont :					Total of non-agricultural and non-fuel products / Total des produits non-agricoles et non-pétroliers	of which: / dont :				
			Ores and metals / Minérais et métaux	Manufactured products / Produits manufacturés	Of which: / dont :				Ores and metals / Minérais et métaux	Manufactured products / Produits manufacturés	Of which: / dont :		
					Chemical products / Produits chimiques	Machinery and transport equipment / Machines et matériel de transport	Other manufactured products / Produits manufacturés divers				Chemical products / Produits chimiques	Machinery and transport equipment / Machines et matériel de transport	Other manufactured products / Produits manufacturés divers
SITC Rev.2 (1) / CTCI Rév.2 (1)		5+6+7+8 +27+28	27+28+68	(5+6+7+8) - 68	5	7	(6+8) - 68	5+6+7+8 +27+28	27+28+68	(5+6+7+8) - 68	5	7	(6+8) - 68
Togo	2001	11.8	7.5	12.0	6.3	8.5	15.4	11.1	5.9	11.2	6.1	11.2	12.8
	2002	11.7	7.5	11.9	6.3	8.5	15.3	10.1	5.8	10.2	5.4	9.7	12.2
	2003	11.7	7.3	11.9	6.3	8.6	15.3	11.1	5.6	11.3	5.4	11.0	13.0
	2004	11.7	7.4	11.9	6.3	8.6	15.3	11.1	5.6	11.3	5.4	11.0	13.1
	2005	11.7	7.4	11.9	6.3	8.6	15.3	11.1	5.6	11.3	5.4	11.0	13.1
Trinidad and Tobago - Trinité-et-Tobago	1991	16.4	8.0	16.5	11.3	12.7	19.9	13.7	6.8	14.1	13.0	14.0	14.7
	1992	16.4	8.0	16.5	11.3	12.7	19.9	13.9	7.7	14.2	13.2	14.3	14.5
	1996	8.3	3.6	8.5	4.5	6.3	10.7	7.0	3.4	7.2	8.0	6.7	7.6
	1999	17.3	15.5	17.4	11.4	17.0	18.3	16.7	15.6	16.7	13.4	19.0	15.7
	2001	6.2	1.4	6.3	2.1	4.9	8.4	4.5	3.2	4.5	6.3	3.3	6.5
	2002	6.3	1.4	6.4	2.1	5.1	8.5	5.4	1.4	5.5	7.2	4.5	6.8
	2003	6.3	1.4	6.4	2.1	5.1	8.5	5.6	0.8	5.9	7.4	4.8	7.1
Tunisia - Tunisie	1990	28.5	21.4	28.8	24.2	25.0	31.9	28.1	19.7	28.5	22.6	24.8	33.0
	1992	28.6	21.5	28.9	23.6	25.3	32.1	28.3	20.0	28.6	22.6	24.7	32.7
	1995	28.9	21.5	29.2	21.2	26.4	33.2	30.2	20.2	30.4	20.6	26.4	35.4
	1998	28.4	24.2	28.6	23.5	19.8	34.0	27.8	21.9	27.9	22.3	21.0	35.5
	2002	27.4	24.3	27.5	23.3	18.7	32.6	25.7	22.9	25.7	21.1	18.2	32.5
	2003	22.1	15.8	22.4	14.5	14.5	28.3	22.2	13.8	22.4	12.4	16.9	29.4
	2004	22.4	15.6	22.7	14.3	14.1	29.1	23.2	9.9	23.5	12.4	17.4	31.3
	2005	21.3	15.6	21.5	14.2	14.0	27.1	20.9	9.9	21.2	12.1	17.4	26.6
Turkey - Turquie	1993	9.3	6.1	9.5	8.0	7.9	10.6	7.4	1.9	7.8	8.1	7.4	8.2
	1995	8.4	4.0	8.6	7.8	6.3	9.8	6.9	2.3	7.3	8.3	6.1	8.2
	1997	5.6	1.9	5.8	5.7	3.7	6.7	5.6	1.6	5.8	5.8	5.3	6.5
	1999	6.3	1.6	6.5	5.4	2.5	8.5	5.1	1.9	5.3	5.1	4.0	7.7
	2003	4.3	1.6	4.5	4.7	2.2	5.2	4.5	1.4	4.7	4.1	4.1	6.0
	2005	4.1	1.6	4.2	4.6	2.3	4.9	4.1	1.3	4.4	4.0	4.3	4.6
Turkmenistan - Turkménistan	2002	4.0	1.4	4.0	0.7	1.2	6.3	1.1	2.9	1.1	0.5	0.9	1.6
Uganda - Ouganda	1994	16.1	11.8	16.2	11.0	13.7	19.0	14.9	15.3	14.9	6.2	15.2	17.2
	2000	8.5	8.0	8.5	7.1	3.8	10.9	7.0	7.2	7.0	4.7	6.3	8.6
	2001	8.4	8.0	8.4	7.1	3.6	10.7	6.8	7.1	6.8	4.2	5.9	8.9
	2002	8.3	8.0	8.3	7.0	3.5	10.6	6.7	6.9	6.7	4.2	6.2	8.4
	2003	7.9	7.7	7.9	5.9	3.2	10.5	6.2	5.7	6.2	2.8	5.8	8.1
	2004	7.0	7.5	7.0	1.9	3.2	10.4	5.5	5.1	5.5	1.7	4.8	7.9
	2005	11.6	6.6	11.8	3.1	6.2	17.2	11.4	14.1	11.3	6.1	7.6	17.3
Ukraine	1995	6.6	1.9	6.7	5.3	4.7	8.0	4.3	3.0	4.3	2.5	3.9	5.6
	1997	7.4	1.9	7.5	6.0	5.4	8.9	5.1	1.6	5.2	4.2	4.8	6.3
	2002	7.0	3.6	7.1	5.3	5.8	8.2	6.2	2.2	6.4	5.5	5.6	7.7
United Arab Emirates - Émirats arabes unis	2005	4.9	4.8	4.9	4.8	4.9	5.0	4.9	4.8	4.9	4.2	4.8	5.0
United Republic of Tanzania - République-Unie de Tanzanie	1993	19.0	19.2	19.0	17.2	11.1	22.8	15.0	18.1	15.0	22.2	10.1	16.5
	1997	22.6	28.9	22.4	27.0	17.7	22.7	18.3	24.3	18.3	16.2	16.2	22.5
	1998	22.9	29.3	22.7	27.2	18.0	23.0	19.7	26.6	19.7	19.6	17.9	22.5
	2000	15.9	12.0	16.2	7.9	13.1	20.5	13.0	10.4	13.0	8.4	11.0	18.3
	2003	12.9	7.0	13.3	3.7	8.9	18.5	9.1	7.0	9.1	4.8	7.0	14.5
	2005	11.6	6.6	11.8	3.1	6.2	17.2	8.4	9.0	8.4	3.5	6.9	13.3
United States - États-Unis	1989	5.9	2.3	6.1	5.0	3.7	7.4	4.5	1.4	4.6	5.2	3.1	6.7
	1990	5.9	2.3	6.1	5.0	3.7	7.4	4.6	1.3	4.7	5.2	3.1	6.9
	1991	5.9	2.3	6.0	5.0	3.7	7.4	4.7	1.2	4.7	5.3	3.1	7.1
	1992	5.9	2.3	6.0	5.0	3.7	7.4	4.8	1.4	4.8	5.3	3.1	7.2
	1993	5.9	2.3	6.1	5.0	3.7	7.4	4.7	1.4	4.7	5.2	3.1	7.1
	1995	5.3	2.1	5.5	4.0	3.4	6.8	4.1	1.4	4.2	3.8	3.0	6.2
	1996	5.0	1.9	5.2	4.0	3.0	6.5	4.0	1.4	4.0	3.7	2.8	6.0
	1997	4.9	1.6	5.1	4.3	2.7	6.3	3.9	1.4	3.9	4.0	2.6	5.9
	1998	4.4	1.5	4.5	3.6	2.2	5.7	3.4	1.3	3.4	3.2	2.2	5.4
	1999	4.0	1.3	4.1	3.5	1.8	5.3	3.1	1.2	3.2	3.1	2.1	5.0

For sources and notes, see end of table.

Pour les sources et les notes, se reporter à la fin du tableau.

Market / Marchés	Year / Année	MFN rate - Simple average (2) / Droit NPF - Moyenne simple (2)						MFN rate - Weighted average (3) / Droit NPF - Moyenne pondérée (3)					
		Total of non-agricultural and non-fuel products / Total des produits non-agricoles et non-pétroliers	of which: / dont :					Total of non-agricultural and non-fuel products / Total des produits non-agricoles et non-pétroliers	of which: / dont :				
			Ores and metals / Minérais et métaux	Manu-factured products / Produits manu-facturés	Of which: / dont :				Ores and metals / Minérais et métaux	Manu-factured products / Produits manu-facturés	Of which: / dont :		
					Chemical products / Produits chimiques	Machinery and transport equipment / Machines et matériel de transport	Other manu-factured products / Produits manu-facturés divers				Chemical products / Produits chimiques	Machinery and transport equipment / Machines et matériel de transport	Other manu-factured products / Produits manu-facturés divers
SITC Rev.2 (1) / CTCI Rév.2 (1)		5+6+7+8+27+28	27+28+68	(5+6+7+8)-68	5	7	(6+8)-68	5+6+7+8+27+28	27+28+68	(5+6+7+8)-68	5	7	(6+8)-68
United States - États-Unis	2000	3.9	1.3	4.0	3.4	1.7	5.2	2.9	1.1	3.0	3.0	1.8	4.8
	2001	3.8	1.3	3.9	3.3	1.7	5.0	3.1	1.1	3.1	2.8	2.0	4.7
	2002	3.7	1.3	3.8	3.1	1.7	4.9	3.0	1.4	3.0	2.6	2.1	4.6
	2003	3.6	1.3	3.7	3.0	1.7	4.7	3.0	1.4	3.0	2.3	2.0	4.5
	2004	3.5	1.3	3.6	3.0	1.7	4.6	2.8	1.3	2.8	2.3	1.9	4.1
	2005	3.5	1.3	3.6	3.0	1.7	4.6	2.8	1.3	2.8	2.3	1.9	4.1
Uruguay	1992	5.6	4.9	5.6	4.2	5.4	6.2	5.8	5.4	5.8	4.7	5.1	7.4
	1995	11.3	6.1	11.5	8.1	6.3	14.8	11.9	7.7	11.9	8.7	11.3	14.5
	1996	11.6	6.1	11.9	8.1	6.5	15.4	11.2	6.7	11.3	8.6	9.5	15.4
	1997	11.8	6.1	12.1	8.1	7.6	15.3	11.5	6.7	11.6	8.7	10.2	15.3
	1998	14.0	8.8	14.3	10.7	9.1	17.7	13.6	8.9	13.6	11.0	12.1	17.2
	1999	14.2	8.8	14.4	10.8	9.7	17.6	13.7	8.8	13.7	11.8	11.6	17.5
	2000	14.4	9.0	14.6	10.9	10.4	17.8	14.4	9.6	14.4	12.5	12.8	17.4
	2001	14.2	8.4	14.5	10.7	11.1	17.3	14.1	9.3	14.2	12.4	12.7	16.9
	2002	13.3	7.3	13.6	9.4	10.7	16.3	12.7	6.4	12.8	10.7	11.7	15.5
	2004	13.3	7.3	13.6	9.4	10.7	16.3	12.3	5.4	12.5	10.1	11.6	15.5
	2005	11.1	5.8	11.4	7.9	6.3	14.6	10.5	4.3	10.6	9.0	8.7	13.9
Uzbekistan - Ouzbékistan	2001	11.7	9.3	11.8	8.9	4.9	15.6	6.2	7.0	6.2	8.0	3.0	10.9
Vanuatu	2002	13.3	9.5	13.4	10.5	12.5	14.7	6.7	11.8	6.7	3.3	4.8	16.1
Venezuela (Bolivarian Republic of) - Venezuela (République bolivarienne du)	1992	16.5	8.2	16.7	10.2	12.7	20.7	16.4	6.9	16.5	9.5	18.1	16.7
	1995	13.5	7.4	13.8	10.6	12.6	15.4	13.2	7.5	13.3	10.7	13.6	14.5
	1997	12.0	6.7	12.2	8.1	10.2	14.4	13.4	7.3	13.5	8.8	14.9	13.2
	1998	12.0	6.6	12.2	8.1	10.3	14.5	13.2	7.0	13.3	8.9	14.3	13.2
	1999	12.0	6.7	12.3	8.1	10.4	14.5	12.7	7.2	12.7	9.1	12.6	14.5
	2000	12.0	6.7	12.2	8.1	10.3	14.5	13.2	8.5	13.3	9.3	14.0	14.2
	2002	12.4	6.7	12.6	8.2	10.4	15.1	13.5	8.5	13.6	10.0	13.9	15.2
	2004	12.0	6.7	12.2	8.1	10.4	14.5	12.9	8.3	13.0	9.7	13.9	13.7
	2005	12.0	6.7	12.2	8.1	10.4	14.5	12.9	8.3	13.0	9.6	13.9	13.7
Viet Nam	1994	13.5	1.2	13.9	3.8	6.4	20.4	13.5	0.5	13.6	2.6	13.7	19.4
	1999	15.4	1.7	15.8	3.8	9.4	22.7	14.5	1.6	14.5	4.6	13.4	20.9
	2001	15.4	1.8	15.8	3.7	9.9	22.6	16.1	1.5	16.2	3.9	19.6	18.3
	2002	15.4	1.8	15.8	3.7	9.7	22.6	15.5	1.1	15.6	4.1	15.5	19.7
	2003	15.7	1.9	16.1	4.2	9.9	22.8	14.4	1.4	14.4	4.1	12.2	20.5
	2004	15.7	1.9	16.1	4.1	9.9	22.9	14.3	1.1	14.3	3.7	13.1	19.3
	2005	15.7	1.9	16.1	4.2	9.9	22.8	13.6	1.1	13.7	3.8	12.5	18.6
Yemen - Yémen	2000	12.2	12.7	12.3	9.5	11.2	13.7	12.4	10.5	12.4	8.2	13.2	12.9
Zambia - Zambie	1993	25.6	20.6	25.8	20.5	22.9	28.8	20.0	20.1	20.0	11.3	21.2	23.2
	1997	13.4	9.6	13.6	7.0	10.8	17.1	11.6	6.6	11.9	6.5	11.9	15.5
	2002	11.4	6.8	11.5	6.2	6.5	15.3	8.3	4.8	8.3	5.5	7.8	10.2
	2003	13.0	9.3	13.2	6.3	10.5	16.8	10.6	4.6	10.8	5.6	10.7	14.1
	2005	12.9	9.1	13.1	6.2	10.3	16.7	9.4	3.4	9.6	4.4	10.6	11.1
Zimbabwe	1996	41.9	30.5	42.3	33.0	37.9	47.3	39.2	31.9	39.3	32.1	39.6	43.0
	1997	24.0	9.4	24.5	8.3	15.7	33.9	17.4	8.3	17.5	9.8	16.8	23.1
	1998	21.2	9.6	21.7	8.4	15.2	29.0	16.1	9.7	16.3	9.2	15.8	21.6
	1999	18.6	9.6	19.0	9.3	14.1	25.2	16.9	8.8	17.1	9.6	18.0	21.6
	2001	19.1	8.6	19.5	7.9	13.3	26.1	13.9	7.8	14.2	7.4	16.2	18.1
	2002	15.3	8.5	15.6	7.9	11.9	20.4	18.9	7.3	19.3	7.0	26.9	18.3
	2003	15.0	8.2	15.3	7.7	11.6	20.0	14.0	6.2	14.7	8.4	16.7	15.9

For sources and notes, see next page.

Pour les sources et les notes, se reporter à la page suivante.

Sources:
- UNCTAD TRAINS database

Notes:
(1) Product categories are defined in terms of SITC Revision 2, and all corresponding Harmonized System (HS) 6-digit codes have been aggregated for each category.
(2) Simple average for each product group calculated from simple average at HS 6-digit level.
(3) Weighted average for each product group calculated from simple average at HS 6-digit level. Country's own imports at HS 6-digit level for corresponding years are used as weights. Where imports are not reported, mirror imports have been compiled using exports of partner countries.

Sources :
- Base de données TRAINS de la CNUCED

Notes :
(1) Les catégories de produits sont définies sur la base de la CTCI, révision 2, et pour chaque catégorie, les codes à 6 chiffres du Système harmonisé (SH) correspondants ont été agrégés.
(2) Moyenne arithmétique, pour chaque catégorie de produits, calculée à partir des moyennes arithmétiques au niveau du code à 6 chiffres du SH.
(3) Moyenne arithmétique pondérée, pour chaque catégorie de produits, calculée à partir des moyennes simples au niveau du code à 6 chiffres du SH. Pour chaque année, les coefficients de pondération sont les importations de chaque marché au niveau du code à 6 chiffres du SH. Lorsque les importations n'étaient pas disponibles, elles ont été évaluées par les données miroir basées sur les exportations des pays partenaires.

5 | INTERNATIONAL TRADE IN SERVICES

COMMERCE INTERNATIONAL DES SERVICES

Region, country or territory	Exports - Exportations Millions of dollars							
	1980	1990	2000	2002	2003	2004	2005	2006
WORLD	**391 080**	**830 805**	**1 529 340**	**1 640 038**	**1 880 017**	**2 249 718**	**2 494 520**	**2 735 658**
DEVELOPED ECONOMIES	309 811	668 605	1 149 189	1 237 176	1 422 328	1 685 240	1 835 024	1 987 600
DEVELOPING ECONOMIES	74 442	154 347	353 258	366 925	412 872	508 286	593 426	669 748
ECONOMIES IN TRANSITION	6 826	7 853	26 893	35 937	44 818	56 193	66 070	78 311
Developed economies: America	**54 995**	**165 670**	**336 195**	**329 269**	**343 170**	**390 043**	**430 435**	**472 843**
Canada	7 445	19 210	40 230	40 481	43 778	49 111	53 647	(e)58 732
United States (1)	47 550	146 460	295 965	288 788	299 392	340 932	376 788	414 111
Developed economies: Asia	**22 962**	**45 953**	**84 293**	**77 510**	**90 943**	**113 714**	**127 983**	**134 868**
Israel	2 722	4 569	15 055	11 798	13 322	16 102	17 773	(e)18 568
Japan	20 240	41 384	69 238	65 712	77 621	97 611	110 210	116 300
Developed economies: Europe	**226 983**	**444 285**	**705 231**	**806 392**	**959 345**	**1 147 131**	**1 239 660**	**1 340 828**
Austria	9 423	23 279	31 342	35 386	42 964	49 153	53 921	(e)58 801
Belgium				37 822	44 708	52 708	55 754	(e)59 917
Belgium-Luxembourg	12 925	28 417	49 789					
Cyprus	482	2 004	4 068	4 531	5 372	6 235	6 478	(e)7 382
Czechoslovakia (former)	-	2 673						
Czech Republic			6 839	7 083	7 789	9 699	10 764	(e)11 218
Denmark	-	12 830	23 721	26 667	31 672	36 304	42 384	(e)49 575
Estonia			1 486	1 706	2 224	2 830	3 156	(e)3 373
Faeroe Islands	..	..	54	71	78	-	-	-
Finland	2 733	4 649	6 177	10 441	11 471	15 170	17 007	(e)16 718
France	43 506	76 457	80 917	86 130	98 759	109 516	115 986	113 533
Germany, Federal Rep. (former)	32 817							
Germany		62 662	83 150	103 140	'23 272	143 189	154 935	(e)163 083
Greece	3 947	6 560	19 239	20 142	24 283	33 085	34 159	(e)38 049
Hungary	-	2 884	5 901	7 417	8 701	10 751	12 321	(e)12 744
Iceland	280	560	1 044	1 118	1 378	1 623	1 999	-
Ireland	1 381	3 445	18 538	29 901	42 061	52 718	57 287	(e)66 066
Italy	19 192	49 666	56 556	60 439	71 767	84 535	89 960	(e)103 926
Latvia			1 150	1 238	1 506	1 780	2 165	2 640
Lithuania			1 059	1 464	1 878	2 444	3 104	(e)3 300
Luxembourg				20 280	25 447	33 574	40 612	(e)49 110
Malta	481	752	1 092	1 199	1 376	1 573	1 582	-
Netherlands	17 150	29 302	49 319	56 138	63 227	73 774	80 087	83 630
Norway	8 615	12 765	17 263	18 689	20 982	25 572	29 305	(e)32 023
Poland	2 018	3 200	10 398	10 037	11 174	13 471	16 227	(e)19 867
Portugal	2 006	5 096	9 016	10 357	12 354	14 840	15 105	17 790
Slovakia			2 241	2 812	3 297	3 725	4 407	(e)5 204
Slovenia			1 888	2 315	2 791	3 455	3 975	(e)4 388
Spain	11 593	27 937	52 453	60 247	74 308	86 078	93 540	(e)101 510
Sweden	7 489	13 726	20 252	24 009	30 654	38 719	43 167	49 827
Switzerland	6 888	19 001	29 884	30 306	35 237	43 085	47 106	(e)51 026
United Kingdom	36 452	56 422	120 397	135 308	158 615	197 431	203 068	(e)212 943
Developed economies: Oceania	**4 871**	**12 698**	**23 470**	**24 005**	**28 871**	**34 353**	**36 946**	**39 062**
Australia	3 862	10 204	19 062	18 680	22 138	26 362	28 436	31 311
New Zealand	1 009	2 494	4 408	5 325	6 733	7 991	8 510	-
Developing economies: Africa	**13 392**	**21 474**	**32 910**	**36 149**	**44 821**	**53 573**	**59 931**	**65 203**
Eastern Africa	*1 777*	*2 968*	*5 077*	*5 501*	*6 123*	*7 338*	*8 297*	*8 708*
Burundi	-	17	4	8	7	16	35	(e)43
Comoros	2	17	17	20	29	41	45	(p)47
Djibouti	..	..	-	-	211	213	224	-
Ethiopia (former)	125	305						
Eritrea			61	(e)117	(e)137	(e)146	(e)149	(e)154
Ethiopia			506	585	762	1 005	1 012	(e)1 076
Kenya	577	1 138	993	1 054	1 198	1 557	1 886	1 974
Madagascar	79	153	364	224	186	154	168	-
Malawi	32	37	34	49	40	41	47	78
Mauritius	140	484	1 070	1 149	1 280	1 456	1 618	(e)1 580
Mozambique	118	103	325	339	304	256	342	(e)401
Rwanda	34	42	59	65	76	103	129	(e)142
Seychelles	91	172	287	313	330	327	368	-
Somalia	66	..	..	..	..	..	..	-
Uganda	10	..	213	225	266	358	478	(e)542
United Republic of Tanzania	165	131	627	920	948	1 117	1 226	-

For sources and notes, see end of table.

1980	1990	2000	2002	2003	2004	2005	2006	Régions, pays ou territoires
Imports - Importations Millions de dollars								

1980	1990	2000	2002	2003	2004	2005	2006	Régions, pays ou territoires
436 051	860 477	1 518 794	1 624 975	1 853 521	2 196 614	2 404 156	2 616 583	**MONDE**
293 659	659 935	1 090 269	1 167 093	1 340 571	1 567 412	1 682 967	1 808 492	ÉCONOMIES DÉVELOPPÉES
135 569	184 114	397 846	414 326	461 134	562 474	641 835	718 693	ÉCONOMIES EN DÉVELOPPEMENT
6 823	16 428	30 679	43 557	51 816	66 727	79 354	89 398	ÉCONOMIES EN TRANSITION
51 636	145 353	267 857	276 119	302 466	349 192	379 531	415 150	**Économies développées : Amérique**
10 666	28 303	44 118	45 070	52 227	58 914	64 956	(e)73 528	Canada
40 970	117 050	223 739	231 049	250 239	290 278	314 575	(a)341 622	États-Unis (1)
34 670	89 203	128 702	118 777	122 718	148 339	147 912	149 463	**Économies développées : Asie**
2 310	4 921	11 838	10 837	11 190	12 825	13 656	(e)14 863	Israël
32 360	84 281	116 864	107 940	111 528	135 514	134 256	134 600	Japon
198 942	408 283	670 563	749 315	888 182	1 035 591	1 117 937	1 205 349	**Économies développées : Europe**
6 204	14 197	29 653	34 996	41 261	46 737	49 107	(e)53 002	Autriche
			35 863	42 862	49 023	51 294	(e)56 908	Belgique
12 827	26 581	41 868						Belgique-Luxembourg
268	674	1 585	1 742	2 237	2 644	2 700	(e)2 796	Chypre
-	2 472							Tchécoslovaquie (anc.)
-		5 436	6 439	7 320	9 218	9 954	(e)10 595	République tchèque
-	10 218	21 063	24 305	28 254	33 401	37 841	(e)42 271	Danemark
		886	1 106	1 393	1 756	2 156	(e)2 303	Estonie
..	..	97	132	147	-	-	-	Îles Féroé
2 555	7 627	8 440	8 073	10 007	12 285	15 203	(e)14 754	Finlande
32 148	61 052	61 044	68 907	82 863	98 462	106 102	109 242	France
45 110								Allemagne, Rép. Fédérale d' (anc.)
	85 052	137 254	144 811	172 240	194 816	202 855	(e)215 571	Allemagne
1 428	3 000	11 286	9 819	11 250	14 020	14 742	(e)15 830	Grèce
-	2 400	4 775	6 849	9 150	10 605	11 760	(e)11 448	Hongrie
263	556	1 164	1 123	1 501	1 835	2 550	(e)2 638	Islande
1 593	5 178	31 272	42 829	54 597	65 384	69 810	(e)75 926	Irlande
16 249	46 795	55 601	63 166	74 332	83 255	90 605	(e)102 942	Italie
-	-	690	701	929	1 178	1 557	1 968	Lettonie
-	-	679	915	1 264	1 632	2 055	(e)2 385	Lituanie
			12 254	15 378	20 910	24 853	(e)29 797	Luxembourg
243	514	758	776	861	981	965		Malte
18 148	29 708	51 339	57 204	63 897	69 443	73 308	78 565	Pays-Bas
6 996	12 358	14 465	16 910	19 179	23 069	29 549	(e)31 747	Norvège
2 023	2 847	8 993	9 186	10 647	12 457	14 315	(e)17 889	Pologne
1 525	4 005	7 053	7 146	8 293	9 688	10 056	11 656	Portugal
-	-	1 805	2 351	3 056	3 458	4 087	(e)4 699	Slovaquie
		1 438	1 732	2 182	2 603	2 916	(e)3 258	Slovénie
5 732	16 055	33 171	38 712	47 951	59 188	65 548	(e)75 665	Espagne
7 018	17 058	23 440	23 958	28 771	33 056	35 155	39 365	Suède
4 885	11 202	15 561	17 286	19 112	24 401	26 242	(e)28 172	Suisse
27 933	48 737	99 747	110 023	127 250	149 916	160 470	(e)162 896	Royaume-Uni
8 411	17 096	23 146	22 882	27 204	34 290	37 587	38 530	**Économies développées : Océanie**
6 568	13 772	18 666	18 095	21 444	27 040	29 349	30 696	Australie
1 843	3 324	4 481	4 788	5 761	7 250	8 238	-	Nouvelle-Zélande
29 749	29 960	39 866	44 051	49 951	61 308	74 407	82 153	**Économies en développement : Afrique**
3 413	*3 944*	*5 632*	*5 825*	*6 069*	*7 083*	*8 343*	*9 136*	*Afrique orientale*
-	129	44	44	46	74	112	(e)155	Burundi
12	44	23	24	37	38	42	(p)45	Comores
..	..	-	-	67	77	84	-	Djibouti
208	359							Éthiopie (anc.)
-	-	28	(e)34	(e)37	(e)37	(e)39	(e)41	Érythrée
		490	580	709	958	1 194	(e)1 342	Éthiopie
502	700	719	708	691	939	1 132	(e)1 173	Kenya
311	242	522	398	357	236	208	-	Madagascar
179	268	167	222	189	211	242	216	Malawi
174	421	763	793	906	1 023	1 216	(e)1 252	Maurice
124	206	446	577	574	531	648	(e)764	Mozambique
133	129	200	202	204	240	304	(e)333	Rwanda
40	80	190	217	220	216	255	-	Seychelles
133	..	..	..	..	..	..	-	Somalie
123	195	459	558	502	666	799	(e)926	Ouganda
295	288	682	633	726	965	1 164	-	République-Unie de Tanzanie

Pour les sources et les notes, se reporter à la fin du tableau.

Region, country or territory	Exports - Exportations Millions of dollars							
	1980	1990	2000	2002	2003	2004	2005	2006
Zambia	151	107	114	(e)137	(e)165	(e)232	(e)272	(e)294
Zimbabwe	169	264	-	-	-	-	-	-
Middle Africa	*1 168*	*1 180*	*1 334*	*1 608*	*1 282*	*1 522*	*1 548*	*1 681*
Angola	-	109	267	207	201	323	177	-
Cameroon	401	382	590	939	445	-	-	-
Central African Republic	54	69	-	-	-	-	-	-
Chad	0	41	51	67	71	90	126	-
Congo	111	99	137	165	194	197	235	-
Equatorial Guinea	-	5	18	25	34	50	71	(e)71
Gabon	325	242	178	86	172	156	-	-
São Tome and Principe	3	4	14	13	14	17	18	-
Northern Africa	*5 175*	*10 455*	*16 730*	*18 086*	*21 253*	*26 533*	*29 064*	*31 976*
Algeria	476	497	-	-	-	-	-	-
Egypt	2 393	5 971	9 803	9 320	11 073	14 197	14 643	(e)16 234
Libyan Arab Jamahiriya	164	117	172	401	442	437	534	(e)553
Morocco	783	2 009	3 034	4 360	5 478	6 710	8 098	(e)8 926
Sudan	292	173	27	132	36	44	114	-
Tunisia	1 067	1 688	2 767	2 681	2 937	3 629	4 004	4 221
Southern Africa	*2 632*	*3 897*	*5 863*	*5 895*	*9 667*	*11 440*	*12 772*	*13 406*
Botswana	101	210	325	490	643	748	856	(e)909
Lesotho	32	41	43	35	50	64	55	(e)57
Namibia	..	132	222	283	420	482	(e)421	(e)486
South Africa	2 463	3 407	5 046	4 985	8 298	9 682	11 157	(e)11 634
Swaziland	36	108	228	102	255	464	282	-
Western Africa	*2 639*	*2 975*	*3 906*	*5 059*	*6 495*	*6 740*	*8 250*	*9 431*
Benin	62	126	136	152	172	216	-	-
Burkina Faso	49	69	31	(e)59	(e)46	(e)47	(e)58	(e)83
Cape Verde	10	35	108	153	224	242	277	(e)275
Côte d'Ivoire	564	590	482	585	664	763	801	-
Gambia	18	57	-	-	84	73	80	-
Ghana	107	86	504	555	630	702	1 066	(e)1 394
Guinea	-	157	68	90	134	85	(e)87	(e)87
Guinea-Bissau	-	7	6	6	6	8	13	-
Liberia	13	..	..	..	..	..	..	..
Mali	58	85	99	169	224	241	-	-
Mauritania	56	27	47	74	44	52	63	-
Niger	41	44	38	51	63	93	-	-
Nigeria	1 127	965	1 833	2 524	3 473	3 336	4 164	-
Senegal	337	515	387	456	569	670	-	-
Sierra Leone	49	61	42	38	66	61	78	-
Togo	74	149	62	90	95	150	-	-
Developing economies: America	**18 615**	**31 508**	**62 090**	**59 544**	**63 993**	**73 007**	**84 600**	**93 787**
Caribbean	*3 511*	*7 473*	*15 595*	*15 319*	*16 579*	*17 897*	*19 399*	*21 381*
Anguilla	..	41	65	66	69	78	95	116
Antigua and Barbuda	45	312	415	394	413	468	461	508
Aruba	-	411	1 008	997	1 048	1 244	1 304	(e)1 378
Bahamas	746	1 500	1 973	2 062	2 055	2 244	2 482	(e)2 685
Barbados	345	654	1 090	1 041	1 165	1 224	1 457	-
Dominica	6	33	90	80	77	88	84	97
Dominican Republic	309	1 097	3 228	3 071	3 469	3 504	3 910	(e)4 246
Grenada	21	64	153	131	134	157	128	132
Haiti	90	52	172	148	136	113	134	(e)197
Jamaica	401	1 027	2 026	1 912	2 138	2 297	2 330	(e)2 709
Montserrat	-	18	16	14	12	15	15	14
Netherlands Antilles	878	1 161	1 614	1 626	1 701	1 799	1 847	(e)2 122
Saint Kitts and Nevis	8	54	99	90	108	135	143	157
Saint Lucia	41	151	324	250	318	367	390	405
Saint Vincent and the Grenadines	18	45	128	137	133	145	157	171
Trinidad and Tobago	411	329	554	637	685	851	974	(e)974
Central America	*6 196*	*10 793*	*20 014*	*19 746*	*20 223*	*22 521*	*25 657*	*27 004*
Belize	-	115	153	176	212	235	293	(e)389
Costa Rica	194	609	1 936	1 868	2 021	2 242	2 616	-
El Salvador	139	329	698	783	948	1 075	1 141	(e)1 205
Guatemala	211	356	777	1 145	1 059	1 178	1 238	(e)1 298
Honduras	82	137	479	530	598	719	779	-
Mexico	4 591	8 094	13 756	12 740	12 617	14 047	16 137	(e)16 319
Nicaragua	44	60	221	226	258	286	309	(e)339
Panama-Canal-Zone (former)	902	—	—	—	—	—	—	—
Panama	—	1 092	1 994	2 278	2 510	2 739	3 144	(e)3 661

For sources and notes, see end of table.

Imports - Importations Millions de dollars								Régions, pays ou territoires
1980	1990	2000	2002	2003	2004	2005	2006	
651	386	340	(e)382	(e)403	(e)447	(e)509	(e)724	Zambie
395	496	-	-	-	-	-	-	Zimbabwe
4 011	*5 828*	*6 424*	*7 962*	*8 486*	*11 322*	*14 759*	*15 668*	*Afrique centrale*
-	1 807	2 699	3 322	3 321	4 803	6 791	-	Angola
717	1 045	957	1 212	1 098	-		-	Cameroun
142	169	-	-	-	-		-	République centrafricaine
24	228	241	670	828	1 366	1 522	-	Tchad
480	769	738	927	875	1 016	1 560	-	Congo
-	36	567	615	1 017	1 243	1 518	(e)1 680	Guinée équatoriale
789	1 007	858	759	840	939	-	-	Gabon
6	9	11	13	19	21	23	-	Sao Tomé-et-Principe
9 733	*9 013*	*13 577*	*14 366*	*14 884*	*18 431*	*23 010*	*25 003*	*Afrique septentrionale*
2 697	1 321	-	-	-	-	-		Algérie
2 343	3 788	7 513	6 629	6 474	8 020	10 508	(e)11 187	Égypte
2 303	1 385	895	1 544	1 597	1 914	2 349	(e)2 619	Jamahiriya arabe libyenne
1 436	1 445	1 892	2 413	2 861	3 451	3 845	(e)4 509	Maroc
353	228	648	818	830	1 065	1 844	-	Soudan
600	846	1 218	1 450	1 612	1 936	2 182	2 343	Tunisie
3 641	*4 728*	*7 053*	*6 489*	*9 331*	*12 234*	*13 930*	*16 005*	*Afrique australe*
216	376	547	510	652	793	857	(e)884	Botswana
50	81	43	55	85	96	94	(e)89	Lesotho
..	354	333	224	249	385	(e)366	(e)368	Namibie
3 295	3 738	5 823	5 504	8 045	10 328	12 155	(e)14 083	Afrique du Sud
80	179	308	196	299	632	458	-	Swaziland
8 951	*6 448*	*7 179*	*9 410*	*11 181*	*12 238*	*14 366*	*16 340*	*Afrique occidentale*
109	131	192	209	254	287	-	-	Bénin
209	216	140	(e)163	(e)196	(e)203	(e)287	(e)348	Burkina Faso
7	28	100	142	203	199	208	(e)211	Cap-Vert
1 531	1 626	1 227	1 545	1 780	2 033	2 080	-	Côte d'Ivoire
42	52	-	-	36	46	45	-	Gambie
270	301	584	621	900	1 058	1 264	(e)2 171	Ghana
-	367	285	331	307	275	(e)291	(e)314	Guinée
-	20	40	27	36	44	47	-	Guinée-Bissau
73	..	..	..	..	..	..	..	Libéria
212	374	335	387	482	532	-	-	Mali
128	137	149	154	189	296	390	-	Mauritanie
279	227	132	152	193	262	-	-	Niger
5 285	1 976	3 300	4 922	5 715	5 973	7 321	-	Nigéria
340	676	405	474	591	698	-	-	Sénégal
85	74	113	81	94	92	91	-	Sierra Leone
167	244	118	148	204	239	-	-	Togo
29 679	**37 040**	**74 493**	**68 667**	**71 645**	**80 726**	**95 344**	**106 568**	**Économies en développement : Amérique**
2 600	*4 108*	*7 791*	*7 722*	*7 939*	*8 385*	*9 278*	*10 653*	*Caraïbes*
..	15	41	39	44	47	52	66	Anguilla
17	105	156	171	182	190	205	234	Antigua-et-Barbuda
-	135	646	608	728	794	927	(e)1 050	Aruba
226	573	1 026	1 016	1 092	1 231	1 373	(e)1 842	Bahamas
129	250	487	491	519	556	680	-	Barbade
6	30	53	54	44	46	50	54	Dominique
399	440	1 373	1 314	1 219	1 213	1 457	(e)1 529	République dominicaine
11	33	89	91	83	94	107	93	Grenade
162	72	282	270	301	315	447	(e)501	Haïti
370	697	1 423	1 597	1 586	1 725	1 729	(e)1 928	Jamaïque
-	12	23	16	18	23	20	26	Montserrat
529	518	732	793	812	801	813	(e)888	Antilles néerlandaises
6	35	76	79	80	83	92	112	Saint-Kitts-et-Nevis
22	81	133	129	145	151	164	187	Sainte-Lucie
11	32	56	57	65	73	82	92	Saint-Vincent-et-les Grenadines
645	479	388	373	371	371	330	(e)330	Trinité-et-Tobago
8 460	*12 652*	*22 596*	*23 326*	*24 055*	*26 375*	*28 790*	*30 700*	*Amérique centrale*
-	60	123	130	139	146	158	(e)144	Belize
286	550	1 273	1 183	1 245	1 384	1 499	-	Costa Rica
273	315	933	1 023	1 055	1 153	1 213	(e)1 323	El Salvador
487	384	825	1 066	1 126	1 308	1 477	(e)1 699	Guatemala
174	220	597	617	673	757	848	-	Honduras
6 514	10 323	17 360	17 660	18 141	19 779	21 440	(e)22 821	Mexique
104	112	343	337	363	388	426	(e)437	Nicaragua
588								Panama, Zone du canal de (anc.)
—	689	1 141	1 310	1 312	1 460	1 729	(e)1 736	Panama

Pour les sources et les notes, se reporter à la fin du tableau.

Region, country or territory	Exports - Exportations Millions of dollars							
	1980	1990	2000	2002	2003	2004	2005	2006
South America	*8 908*	*13 242*	*26 481*	*24 480*	*27 191*	*32 589*	*39 544*	*45 402*
Argentina	1 876	2 446	4 936	3 459	4 427	5 146	6 236	(e)6 850
Bolivia	88	146	224	257	364	416	489	-
Brazil	1 737	3 762	9 498	9 551	10 447	12 584	16 095	(e)19 998
Chile	1 263	1 848	4 083	4 386	4 986	6 063	7 172	(e)7 470
Colombia	1 342	1 600	2 049	1 867	1 921	2 255	2 664	(e)3 166
Ecuador	367	538	849	884	881	1 014	1 012	(e)999
Guyana	20	..	169	172	157	161	147	
Paraguay	164	418	595	568	574	629	661	(e)790
Peru	715	798	1 529	1 530	1 695	1 914	2 179	(e)2 452
Suriname	176	37	91	39	59	141	204	-
Uruguay	468	466	1 276	754	803	1 151	1 329	(e)1 450
Venezuela (Bolivarian Republic of)	693	1 183	1 182	1 013	878	1 115	1 356	(e)1 408
Developing economies: Asia	**42 131**	**100 587**	**257 334**	**270 413**	**302 995**	**380 582**	**447 528**	**509 425**
Eastern Asia	*12 649*	*42 149*	*125 068*	*139 310*	*155 224*	*193 664*	*216 809*	*247 362*
China	-	5 855	30 431	39 745	46 734	62 434	74 404	(e)86 376
China, Hong Kong SAR	-	-	40 430	44 601	46 555	55 157	62 175	(e)69 059
China, Macao SAR	-	-	3 586	4 758	5 605	8 063	8 614	(e)10 226
China, Taiwan Province of	1 944	7 008	20 010	21 635	23 166	25 789	25 827	29 381
Korea, Republic of	2 570	9 637	30 534	28 388	32 957	41 882	45 375	51 874
Mongolia	-	48	78	184	208	338	(e)414	(e)447
Southern Asia	*5 040*	*7 655*	*22 070*	*28 209*	*34 641*	*42 254*	*70 235*	*87 172*
Afghanistan	36	..	..	..	..	..	..	..
Bangladesh	211	392	815	849	1 012	1 083	1 245	1 296
India	2 971	4 625	16 684	19 478	23 397	(e)29 235	-	-
Iran, Islamic Republic of	731	436	1 382	3 488	5 025	6 663	(e)6 839	-
Maldives	52	101	348	363	432	507	317	478
Nepal	155	204	506	305	372	461	380	(e)335
Pakistan	652	1 429	1 380	2 429	2 968	2 749	3 677	-
Sri Lanka	231	440	939	1 268	1 411	1 527	1 540	(e)1 676
South-Eastern Asia	*9 373*	*29 121*	*68 552*	*74 498*	*78 948*	*104 316*	*115 279*	*128 294*
Brunei Darussalam	..	..	-	437	435	543	617	-
Cambodia	..	..	428	604	545	801	1 107	(e)1 321
Indonesia (2)	-	2 488	5 214	6 663	5 293	12 045	12 926	(e)12 760
Lao People's Dem. Rep.	-	24	176	(e)174	(e)126	(e)176	(e)184	(e)192
Malaysia	1 135	3 859	13 941	14 878	13 578	16 768	19 576	(e)20 618
Myanmar	53	94	478	426	249	255	(e)277	
Philippines	1 447	3 244	3 377	3 428	3 389	4 043	4 462	(e)5 320
Singapore	4 856	12 811	28 171	29 549	36 263	46 778	51 308	58 794
Thailand	1 490	6 419	13 868	15 391	15 798	19 040	20 647	(e)23 707
Viet Nam	..	-	2 702	2 948	3 272	3 867	4 176	(e)4 594
Western Asia	*15 069*	*21 662*	*41 643*	*28 396*	*34 181*	*40 349*	*45 206*	*46 597*
Bahrain	333	359	933	1 068	1 260	1 558	1 662	(e)1 879
Jordan	1 003	1 447	1 637	1 775	1 740	2 057	2 283	(e)2 461
Kuwait	1 225	1 279	1 803	1 647	3 146	3 741	4 700	(e)5 640
Palestinian territory	..	..	462	192	214	181	-	
Oman	9	68	452	606	645	726	822	(e)910
Saudi Arabia	5 191	3 027	4 779	5 177	5 713	5 852	5 916	
Syrian Arab Republic	365	874	1 699	1 559	1 331	2 766	3 227	-
Turkey	711	8 016	19 519	14 040	18 006	22 947	25 857	(e)24 307
Yemen Arab Republic (former)	164	—	—	—	—	—	—	—
Yemen, Democratic (former)	87	—	—	—	—	—	—	—
Yemen	—	106	211	166	318	370	372	(e)477
Developing economies: Oceania	**305**	**778**	**925**	**819**	**1 063**	**1 123**	**1 367**	**1 333**
Fiji	201	417	432	486	593	669	783	(e)737
Kiribati	4	8	..	..	..	..	..	..
Papua New Guinea	43	206	243	162	233	203	302	(e)308
Samoa	8	36	-	-	(e)87	95	112	(e)107
Solomon Islands	12	25	49	16	25	31	36	(e)51
Tonga	9	26	(e)16	23	(e)26	(e)23	(e)26	(e)25
Vanuatu	-	60	130	84	99	101	109	(e)105
Economies in transition: Asia	**—**	**—**	**2 532**	**3 583**	**4 064**	**4 818**	**5 801**	**7 035**
Armenia	—	—	137	184	207	247	332	-
Azerbaijan	—	—	260	362	432	492	683	(e)902
Georgia	—	—	206	392	443	540	698	(e)894
Kazakhstan	—	—	1 053	1 540	1 712	2 009	2 248	(e)2 773

For sources and notes, see end of table.

	Imports - Importations Millions de dollars							Régions, pays ou territoires
1980	1990	2000	2002	2003	2004	2005	2006	
18 620	*20 280*	*44 105*	*37 619*	*39 651*	*45 967*	*57 276*	*65 215*	*Amérique du Sud*
3 788	3 120	9 219	4 978	5 713	6 628	7 615	(e)8 168	Argentine
259	311	468	433	551	607	683	(e)705	Bolivie
4 871	7 523	16 660	14 509	15 378	17 260	24 243	(e)29 568	Brésil
1 583	2 076	4 802	5 087	5 631	6 752	7 760	(e)8 497	Chili
1 170	1 750	3 307	3 302	3 360	3 934	4 766	(e)5 186	Colombie
704	804	1 269	1 600	1 624	1 968	2 112	(e)2 221	Équateur
107	..	193	196	172	208	197	-	Guyana
165	434	420	355	329	301	340	(e)457	Paraguay
880	1 164	2 234	2 471	2 549	2 756	3 092	(e)3 314	Pérou
364	171	216	166	195	271	352	-	Suriname
476	393	882	600	636	786	896	(e)851	Uruguay
4 253	2 534	4 435	3 922	3 512	4 497	5 222	(e)5 656	Venezuela (République bolivarienne du)
75 646	**116 284**	**282 221**	**300 507**	**338 109**	**418 783**	**470 212**	**527 852**	**Économies en développement : Asie**
10 983	*40 673*	*121 824*	*135 133*	*148 880*	*185 796*	*209 313*	*240 246*	*Asie orientale*
-	4 352	36 031	46 528	55 306	72 133	83 796	(e)98 597	Chine
-	-	24 698	25 964	26 126	31 138	32 384	(e)34 890	Chine, Hong Kong RAS
-	-	904	1 071	1 175	1 364	1 576	(e)1 880	Chine, Macao RAS
2 554	14 658	26 647	24 719	25 635	30 731	32 480	33 563	Chine, Taiwan Province de
3 293	10 252	33 381	36 585	40 381	49 928	58 467	70 637	Corée, République de
	155	163	266	257	504	-	-	Mongolie
10 189	*13 697*	*27 313*	*30 637*	*41 351*	*53 468*	*59 645*	*71 182*	*Asie méridionale*
144	..	..	..	..	..	..	..	Afghanistan
481	700	1 620	1 406	1 711	1 931	2 164	2 406	Bangladesh
2 981	6 090	19 187	21 041	25 710	(e)31 888	-	-	Inde
5 223	3 962	2 296	3 983	-	-	-	-	Iran, Rép. islamique d'
43	38	110	111	121	158	190	256	Maldives
88	167	200	237	266	385	435	(e)478	Népal
877	2 073	2 252	2 241	3 294	5 333	7 482	(e)8 213	Pakistan
351	639	1 621	1 584	1 679	1 908	2 089	-	Sri Lanka
13 668	*28 478*	*87 318*	*94 341*	*104 154*	*125 662*	*140 905*	*154 687*	*Asie du Sud-Est*
..	..	-	896	1 029	1 074	1 111	-	Brunéi Darussalam
..	..	329	377	434	513	631	(e)732	Cambodge
-	6 056	15 637	17 045	17 400	20 856	23 728	(e)25 394	Indonésie (2)
-	26	43	(e)28	(e)39	(e)43	(e)47	(e)52	Rép. dém. populaire lao
2 957	5 485	16 747	16 448	17 532	19 078	21 956	(e)22 775	Malaisie
74	73	328	309	420	460	(e)428	-	Myanmar
1 439	1 761	5 247	5 430	5 352	5 815	5 858	(e)5 334	Philippines
2 912	8 642	29 506	33 389	39 729	50 006	54 260	61 651	Singapour
1 644	6 309	15 460	16 720	18 169	23 077	27 605	(e)31 178	Thaïlande
..	-	3 252	3 698	4 050	4 739	5 282	(e)5 916	Viet Nam
40 807	*33 437*	*45 766*	*40 396*	*43 725*	*53 857*	*60 350*	*61 738*	*Asie occidentale*
474	474	738	927	886	933	977	(e)1 285	Bahreïn
1 094	1 268	1 722	1 883	1 889	2 146	2 542	(e)2 690	Jordanie
3 067	3 359	4 894	5 837	6 614	7 583	8 842	(e)8 002	Koweït
..	..	566	651	516	490	-	-	Territoire palestinien
518	719	1 759	1 880	2 180	2 756	3 052	(e)3 598	Oman
30 231	22 384	25 228	19 980	20 857	25 696	27 947	-	Arabie saoudite
521	892	1 667	1 883	1 806	2 058	2 236	-	République arabe syrienne
569	3 071	8 153	6 161	7 502	10 163	11 891	(e)10 768	Turquie
375	—	—	—	—	—	—	—	Rép. arabe du Yémen (anc.)
130	—	—	—	—	—	—	—	Yémen dém. (anc.)
—	683	809	935	1 004	1 059	1 161	(e)1 527	Yémen
495	**830**	**1 267**	**1 101**	**1 429**	**1 658**	**1 872**	**2 120**	**Économies en développement : Océanie**
124	257	302	278	378	479	516	(e)538	Fidji
9	19	..	..	..	..	..	..	Kiribati
302	403	772	678	868	998	1 167	(e)1 395	Papouasie-Nouvelle-Guinée
15	25	-	-	(e)26	42	53	(e)52	Samoa
28	79	73	42	52	41	29	(e)32	Îles Salomon
6	23	(e)26	32	(e)44	(e)32	(e)34	(e)33	Tonga
-	24	70	51	61	66	73	(e)70	Vanuatu
—	**—**	**3 943**	**7 053**	**8 327**	**11 144**	**14 193**	**16 157**	**Économies en transition : Asie**
—	—	193	225	276	317	391	-	Arménie
—	—	485	1 298	2 047	2 730	2 653	(e)2 878	Azerbaïdjan
—	—	216	357	390	483	625	(e)724	Géorgie
—	—	1 850	3 538	3 753	5 108	7 524	(e)8 647	Kazakhstan

Pour les sources et les notes, se reporter à la fin du tableau.

Region, country or territory	Exports - Exportations Millions of dollars							
	1980	1990	2000	2002	2003	2004	2005	2006
Kyrgyzstan	–	–	62	142	158	210	256	(e)295
Tajikistan			-	69	89	123	146	(e)169
Economies in transition: Europe	**6 826**	**7 853**	**24 361**	**32 355**	**40 754**	**51 374**	**60 269**	**71 275**
Albania	11	32	448	585	720	1 003	1 165	(e)1 328
Belarus	–	–	1 000	1 341	1 500	1 747	1 959	(e)2 229
Bosnia and Herzegovina	–	–	450	524	721	900	1 013	(e)1 021
Bulgaria	1 211	837	2 175	2 203	2 961	4 029	4 303	4 872
Croatia	–	–	4 071	5 582	8 569	9 373	9 921	(e)12 606
Macedonia, TFYR	–	–	317	253	327	408	472	(e)572
Moldova, Republic of	–	–	165	217	254	355	424	(e)497
Romania	1 063	610	1 747	2 347	3 028	3 614	5 083	5 513
Russian Federation	–	–	9 565	13 611	16 229	20 290	24 566	(e)28 929
Serbia and Montenegro	–	–	624	1 010	1 232	1 797	2 010	(e)2 619
Yugoslavia, SFR (former)	4 541	6 374	–	–	–	–	–	–
Ukraine	–	–	3 800	4 682	5 214	7 859	9 354	(e)11 089

Sources:
- UNCTAD secretariat calculations based on International Monteray Fund (IMF) *Balance of Payments Statistics* on CD-ROM
- Other international and national sources

Notes:

(1)   Including United States Virgin Islands
(2)   Year 2004: break in series; change in classification of services.

Imports - Importations Millions de dollars								Régions, pays ou territoires
1980	1990	2000	2002	2003	2004	2005	2006	
–	–	148	148	160	224	291	(e)374	Kirghizistan
–	–	-	105	122	213	252	(e)392	Tadjikistan
6 823	**16 428**	**26 736**	**36 504**	**43 489**	**55 584**	**65 161**	**73 241**	**Économies en transition : Europe**
18	29	429	590	803	1 055	1 383	(e)1 535	Albanie
–	–	563	908	915	1 058	1 250	(e)1 499	Bélarus
–	–	263	305	384	432	460	(e)390	Bosnie-Herzégovine
549	600	1 670	1 755	2 447	3 193	3 479	4 148	Bulgarie
–	–	1 822	2 414	2 982	3 565	3 400	(e)3 446	Croatie
–	–	268	275	337	462	505	(e)547	Macédoine. LERY
–	–	202	257	300	376	447	(e)489	Moldova, République de
1 045	787	1 993	2 338	2 958	3 879	5 518	5 507	Roumanie
–	–	16 230	23 497	27 122	33 732	39 415	(e)44 084	Fédération de Russie
–	–	293	629	798	1 208	1 756	(e)2 456	Serbie-et-Monténégro
5 211	15 012	–	–	–	–	–	–	Yougoslavie, RSF (anc.)
–	–	3 004	3 535	4 444	6 622	7 548	(e)9 140	Ukraine

Sources :
- Calculs du secrétariat de la CNUCED, basés sur les *Statistiques de la balance des paiements* sur CD-ROM du Fonds monétaire international (FMI)
- Autres sources internationales et nationales

Notes :

(1)　Y compris les Îles Vierges américaines
(2)　Année 2004 : rupture de série ; changement de la classification des services.

5

Economic grouping	Exports - Exportations Millions of dollars							
	1980	1990	2000	2002	2003	2004	2005	2006
DEVELOPING ECONOMIES	**74 442**	**154 347**	**353 258**	**366 925**	**412 872**	**508 286**	**593 426**	**669 748**
Developing economies excluding China	72 464	148 447	322 700	327 043	366 005	445 706	518 865	583 201
Developing economies excluding LDCs	71 215	150 259	345 764	358 825	403 898	497 732	581 848	657 003
High-income countries	34 104	72 808	163 896	168 239	187 935	226 955	249 445	279 778
Middle-income countries	20 333	49 006	105 720	105 961	120 457	146 777	164 950	179 770
Low-income countries	20 005	32 533	83 642	92 725	104 479	134 553	179 031	210 199
Heavily indebted poor countries	3 745	4 482	7 023	8 274	8 671	10 034	11 448	12 573
Landlocked countries	1 395	2 305	6 488	7 443	8 730	10 918	12 223	13 871
Small island developing states	2 643	5 758	9 619	9 565	10 599	11 688	12 616	13 533
Least developed countries	*3 210*	*4 043*	*7 366*	*7 962*	*8 841*	*10 409*	*11 421*	*12 574*
Africa and Haiti	2 373	2 910	4 015	4 711	5 284	6 200	6 897	7 546
Asia	717	848	2 630	2 554	2 647	3 174	3 611	3 944
Islands	120	285	721	698	911	1 034	913	1 084
Major petroleum exporters	*18 817*	*19 824*	*33 682*	*30 826*	*34 008*	*44 144*	*48 377*	*53 385*
Africa	2 368	2 028	3 514	4 573	5 770	5 965	6 952	7 934
America	1 982	2 673	3 350	3 276	3 264	3 765	4 178	4 503
Asia	14 467	15 123	26 819	22 977	24 975	34 414	37 247	40 947
Major exporters of manufactured goods	*31 176*	*91 457*	*240 217*	*253 423*	*282 906*	*350 703*	*418 051*	*478 496*
America	6 328	11 856	23 254	22 291	23 064	26 630	32 232	36 317
Asia	24 848	79 601	216 963	231 131	259 842	324 073	385 820	442 179
Emerging economies	*22 176*	*56 682*	*140 324*	*141 506*	*155 933*	*190 009*	*210 551*	*237 463*
America	10 182	16 948	33 801	31 666	34 172	39 753	47 818	53 089
Asia	11 994	39 734	106 523	109 840	121 762	150 257	162 733	184 374
Newly industrialized economies	*19 586*	*63 593*	*155 544*	*164 532*	*176 999*	*221 502*	*242 295*	*271 513*
First tier	15 133	47 583	119 144	124 172	138 941	169 606	184 684	209 108
Second tier	4 453	16 010	36 400	40 360	38 058	51 896	57 611	62 406
Developing economies: Africa	**13 392**	**21 474**	**32 910**	**36 149**	**44 821**	**53 573**	**59 931**	**65 203**
Northern Africa excluding Sudan	4 883	10 283	16 703	17 953	21 217	26 489	28 950	31 856
Sub-Saharan Africa	8 509	11 192	16 207	18 195	23 604	27 084	30 981	33 346
Sub-Saharan Africa excluding South Africa	6 046	7 785	11 161	13 210	15 305	17 402	19 824	21 713
Developing economies: America	**18 615**	**31 508**	**62 090**	**59 544**	**63 993**	**73 007**	**84 600**	**93 787**
Central America and Greater Carribean Islands excluding Puerto Rico	6 996	13 494	28 082	27 540	28 884	31 604	35 518	38 052
Central America and Greater Carribean Islands excluding Mexico and Puerto Rico	2 405	5 400	14 326	14 800	16 267	17 557	19 381	21 733
South America and Central America	15 104	24 035	46 495	44 226	47 414	55 109	65 201	72 406
South America excluding Brazil	7 171	9 480	16 983	14 928	16 744	20 005	23 449	25 403
Developing economies: Asia	**42 131**	**100 587**	**257 334**	**270 413**	**302 995**	**380 582**	**447 528**	**509 425**
Eastern and South-Eastern Asia excluding China	20 061	65 414	163 190	174 063	187 439	235 546	257 683	289 280
Southern Asia excluding India	2 069	3 030	5 387	8 731	11 244	13 019	14 045	14 429

Sources:
- UNCTAD secretariat calculations based on International Monetary Fund (IMF) *Balance of Payments Statistics* on CD-ROM
- Other international and national sources

Imports - Importations Millions de dollars								Groupements économiques
1980	1990	2000	2002	2003	2004	2005	2006	
135 569	**184 114**	**397 846**	**414 326**	**461 134**	**562 474**	**641 835**	**718 693**	**ÉCONOMIES EN DÉVELOPPEMENT**
133 769	179 730	361 759	367 741	405 763	490 269	557 958	620 004	Économies en développement sans la Chine
127 356	174 040	383 780	398 479	443 368	540 490	614 482	688 396	Économies en développement sans les PMA
66 974	93 892	190 103	189 062	204 137	246 122	271 395	300 960	Pays à revenu élevé
34 771	50 845	101 058	100 162	113 668	136 888	163 011	178 536	Pays à revenu intermédiaire
33 824	39 377	106 685	125 102	143 329	179 465	207 430	239 197	Pays à revenu faible
9 411	10 779	12 359	14 321	15 673	18 754	22 644	25 528	Pays pauvres très endettés
3 765	4 933	9 571	13 190	15 337	20 387	24 507	27 697	Pays sans littoral
2 223	3 765	6 350	6 460	7 103	7 833	8 618	9 962	Petits états insulaires en développement
8 201	*10 043*	*14 010*	*15 789*	*17 701*	*21 911*	*27 272*	*30 205*	*Pays les moins avancés*
6 731	8 100	10 243	12 060	13 267	16 919	21 731	23 779	Afrique et Haïti
1 337	1 678	3 357	3 326	3 916	4 428	4 922	5 733	Asie
133	265	410	404	519	564	619	694	Îles
66 906	*50 912*	*69 482*	*71 697*	*79 327*	*97 127*	*110 835*	*117 599*	*Principaux exportateurs de pétrole*
12 516	8 265	9 901	12 984	13 857	16 641	21 377	22 811	Afrique
5 427	3 531	5 554	5 088	4 695	5 670	6 365	6 874	Amérique
48 963	39 116	54 026	53 625	60 775	74 816	83 093	87 914	Asie
34 819	*89 483*	*249 077*	*265 154*	*294 961*	*360 996*	*408 679*	*465 506*	*Principaux exportateurs d'articles manufacturés*
11 385	17 846	34 020	32 169	33 519	37 039	45 683	52 389	Amérique
23 434	71 637	215 057	232 986	261 441	323 957	362 996	413 118	Asie
30 995	*69 551*	*172 017*	*172 566*	*188 858*	*225 995*	*258 916*	*292 171*	*Économies émergentes*
17 636	24 206	50 275	44 705	47 413	53 175	64 149	72 367	Amérique
13 360	45 345	121 742	127 862	141 445	172 820	194 767	219 804	Asie
22 692	*64 180*	*167 324*	*176 301*	*190 323*	*230 629*	*256 737*	*285 421*	*Économies nouvellement industrialisées*
12 055	44 570	114 232	120 658	131 870	161 803	177 590	200 740	Premier tier
10 636	19 611	53 092	55 643	58 453	68 827	79 146	84 681	Deuxième tier
29 749	**29 960**	**39 866**	**44 051**	**49 951**	**61 308**	**74 407**	**82 153**	**Économies en développement : Afrique**
9 380	8 785	12 929	13 548	14 054	17 366	21 166	23 079	Afrique septentrionale sans le Soudan
20 369	21 176	26 936	30 503	35 898	43 942	53 241	59 074	Afrique subsaharienne
17 074	17 438	21 114	24 999	27 853	33 614	41 087	44 991	Afrique sub-saharienne sans l'Afrique du Sud
29 679	**37 040**	**74 493**	**68 667**	**71 645**	**80 726**	**95 344**	**106 568**	**Économies en développement : Amérique**
9 391	14 462	26 482	27 131	27 811	30 298	33 172	35 468	Amérique centrale et Grandes Antilles sans Porto Rico
2 877	4 139	9 122	9 471	9 670	10 520	11 733	12 647	Amérique centrale et Grandes Antilles sans le Mexique et Porto Rico
27 079	32 932	66 702	60 945	63 705	72 342	86 066	95 915	Amérique du Sud et Amérique centrale
13 749	12 757	27 445	23 111	24 272	28 707	33 033	35 647	Amérique du Sud sans le Brésil
75 646	**116 284**	**282 221**	**300 507**	**338 109**	**418 783**	**470 212**	**527 852**	**Économies en développement : Asie**
22 862	64 798	173 111	182 946	197 727	239 325	266 422	296 335	Asie orientale et Asie du Sud-Est sans la Chine
7 208	7 608	8 126	9 596	15 641	21 580	25 344	27 456	Asie méridionale sans l'Inde

Sources :
- Calculs du secrétariat de la CNUCED, basés sur les *Statistiques de la balance des paiements* sur CD-ROM du Fonds monétaire international (FMI)
- Autres sources internationales et nationales

Trade group	Exports - Exportations Millions of dollars							
	1980	1990	2000	2002	2003	2004	2005	2006
AFRICA								
CEPGL	154	289	134	172	228	290	351	381
COMESA	4 417	9 324	14 521	14 102	16 582	21 164	22 132	24 093
ECCAS	1 219	1 238	1 397	1 680	1 366	1 640	1 712	1 866
ECOWAS	2 583	2 948	3 859	4 985	6 451	6 688	8 188	9 365
MRU	130	219	110	129	200	147	165	175
SADC	3 754	5 514	9 068	9 236	13 120	15 508	17 107	17 914
CEMAC (UDEAC)	897	837	982	1 288	923	1 011	1 166	1 262
UEMOA	1 191	1 585	1 241	1 569	1 840	2 188	2 436	2 642
UMA	2 547	4 339	6 947	8 707	10 188	12 345	14 370	15 688
AMERICA								
ANCOM	3 204	4 265	5 833	5 551	5 739	6 714	7 699	8 460
CACM	670	1 491	4 112	4 553	4 884	5 500	6 083	6 635
CARICOM	2 367	4 390	7 451	7 283	7 803	8 641	9 399	10 397
FTAA	72 538	195 021	392 940	383 449	401 415	456 745	508 287	559 106
LAIA	13 303	21 824	42 618	39 672	42 511	49 502	58 817	65 233
MERCOSUR	4 245	7 092	16 305	14 333	16 250	19 509	24 322	29 089
NAFTA	59 586	173 764	349 950	342 009	355 787	404 089	446 572	489 162
OECS	146	717	1 288	1 162	1 264	1 453	1 473	1 599
ASIA								
APTA	7 957	20 972	79 577	89 901	105 635	136 337	178 938	214 156
ASEAN	9 373	29 121	68 552	74 498	78 948	104 316	115 279	128 294
ECO	2 130	9 881	24 470	22 964	29 412	36 391	41 144	40 745
GCC	6 757	4 733	7 967	8 498	10 764	11 877	13 101	15 233
SAARC	4 273	7 219	20 688	24 721	29 616	35 591	63 396	79 307
EUROPE								
EFTA	15 783	32 325	48 190	50 113	57 597	70 280	78 410	84 834
EU 25	211 201	411 960	656 987	756 208	901 670	1 076 759	1 161 150	1 255 887
Euro Zone	156 672	317 470	456 495	530 423	634 621	748 341	808 352	872 131
OCEANIA								
MSG	283	708	854	747	950	1 005	1 230	1 201
INTERREGIONAL								
ACP	11 481	17 964	30 436	32 017	38 845	43 507	49 130	53 203
APEC	108 265	300 328	646 952	659 075	712 860	852 869	949 438	1 046 875
BSEC	6 943	16 055	57 260	58 765	71 776	94 460	106 623	116 683
CIS	..	..	17 062	23 433	27 260	35 069	42 104	49 780

Sources:
- UNCTAD secretariat calculations based on International Monetary Fund (IMF) *Balance of Payments Statistics* on CD-ROM
- Other international and national sources

Imports - Importations Millions de dollars								Groupements commerciaux
1980	1990	2000	2002	2003	2004	2005	2006	
								AFRIQUE
1 101	1 017	483	599	648	819	1 009	1 107	CEPGL
7 433	10 210	15 911	15 934	16 092	20 611	26 725	28 676	COMESA
4 278	6 086	6 667	8 207	8 736	11 635	15 175	16 156	CEEAC
8 823	6 311	7 031	9 256	10 992	11 942	13 976	15 933	CEDEAO
356	442	398	411	401	368	382	429	UFM
7 564	9 600	13 407	13 567	16 607	21 381	25 696	28 598	SADC
2 209	3 253	3 474	4 272	4 748	5 993	7 352	7 814	CEMAC (UDEAC)
2 863	3 513	2 588	3 106	3 737	4 299	4 755	5 295	UEMOA
7 164	5 134	5 565	7 073	7 769	9 642	11 048	12 299	UMA
								AMÉRIQUE
7 266	6 563	11 713	11 729	11 597	13 762	15 875	17 082	ANCOM
1 325	1 580	3 973	4 226	4 462	4 989	5 463	5 999	MCAC
2 119	2 631	4 723	4 836	4 993	5 485	5 985	7 046	CARICOM
80 721	181 113	340 101	342 705	371 859	427 583	472 313	518 877	ZLEA
24 662	31 031	61 865	55 542	58 075	65 937	78 917	88 255	ALADI
9 300	11 470	27 182	20 442	22 055	24 975	33 093	39 044	MERCOSUR
58 150	155 676	285 217	293 779	320 607	368 971	400 971	437 970	ALENA
82	343	627	636	660	708	772	863	OECO
								ASIE
8 941	22 059	91 883	107 172	124 826	157 831	180 864	217 740	ACAP
13 668	28 478	87 318	94 341	104 154	125 662	140 905	154 687	ANASE
6 813	9 106	16 235	18 857	26 985	37 667	45 477	47 780	ECO
34 289	26 936	32 619	28 624	30 538	36 968	40 818	42 543	CCG
4 822	9 735	25 017	26 654	32 823	41 640	46 718	57 463	SAARC
								EUROPE
12 144	24 116	31 191	35 319	39 792	49 305	58 341	62 557	AELE
186 799	384 167	639 275	713 864	848 244	986 115	1 059 411	1 142 598	UE 25
143 519	299 248	467 981	523 780	624 930	723 211	773 482	839 859	Zone Euro
								OCÉANIE
466	763	1 218	1 049	1 359	1 584	1 786	2 036	MSG
								INTERRÉGIONAUX
23 374	25 664	35 085	38 362	44 170	52 944	63 285	70 554	ACP
126 165	329 355	656 640	683 757	746 219	891 588	971 173	1 059 504	CEAP
3 609	7 487	43 860	49 831	59 539	76 571	88 092	95 454	CEMN
..	..	23 941	35 250	41 108	52 933	62 852	71 369	CEI

Sources :
- Calculs du secrétariat de la CNUCED, basés sur les *Statistiques de la balance des paiements* sur CD-ROM du Fonds monétaire international (FMI)
- Autres sources internationales et nationales

5

Ranking based on average 2004-2005 exports Classement d'après la moyenne des exportations de 2004-2005	2003			2004			2005		
	Millions of dollars Millions de dollars	As % of country's total En % du total du pays	Annual change in % Variation annuelle en %	Millions of dollars Millions de dollars	As % of country's total En % du total du pays	Annual change in % Variation annuelle en %	Millions of dollars Millions de dollars	As % of country's total En % du total du pays	Annual change in % Variation annuelle en %
TRANSPORT (1) - TRANSPORT (1)									
Korea, Republic of - Corée, République de	17 180	52.1	30.0	22 529	53.8	31.1	23 884	52.6	6.0
China, Hong Kong SAR - Chine, Hong Kong RAS	13 832	29.7	4.0	17 358	31.5	25.5	..	..	..
Singapore - Singapour	13 557	37.4	12.8	16 923	36.2	24.8	17 904	34.9	5.8
China - Chine	7 906	16.9	38.2	12 068	19.3	52.6	15 427	20.7	27.8
China, Taiwan Province of - Chine, Taiwan Province de (5)	4 387	18.9	17.0	5 294	20.5	20.7	5 924	22.9	11.9
Thailand - Thaïlande	3 503	22.2	7.3	4 350	22.8	24.2	4 626	22.4	6.3
Egypt - Égypte	3 299	29.8	17.9	4 016	28.3	21.7	4 746	32.4	18.2
Chile - Chili	2 692	54.0	22.0	3 388	55.9	25.9	4 193	58.5	23.8
Turkey - Turquie	2 184	12.1	-21.9	3 267	14.2	49.6	4 027	15.6	23.3
Malaysia - Malaisie	2 767	20.4	-3.1	3 163	18.9	14.3	4 056	20.7	28.2
Brazil - Brésil	1 822	17.4	18.6	2 467	19.6	35.4	3 186	19.8	29.2
Indonesia - Indonésie	856	16.2	-19.1	2 279	18.9	166.3	2 841	22.0	24.7
Kuwait - Koweït	1 517	48.2	34.4	1 683	45.0	11.0	2 212	47.1	31.4
Panama	1 354	53.9	11.9	1 519	55.5	12.2	1 776	56.5	16.9
South Africa - Afrique du Sud	1 261	15.2	23.4	1 417	14.6	12.4	1 533	13.7	8.2
Mexico - Mexique	1 113	8.8	-2.6	1 362	9.7	22.4	1 753	10.9	28.7
Argentina - Argentine	944	21.3	22.7	1 155	22.4	22.4	1 297	20.8	12.3
Morocco - Maroc	910	16.6	16.6	1 025	15.3	12.6	1 300	16.1	26.8
Philippines	951	28.1	8.4	1 001	24.8	5.3	1 041	23.3	4.0
Pakistan	836	28.2	5.6	940	34.2	12.4	1 076	29.3	14.5
TRAVEL (2) - VOYAGES (2)									
China - Chine	17 406	37.2	-14.6	25 739	41.2	47.9	29 296	39.4	13.8
Turkey - Turquie	13 203	73.3	55.7	15 888	69.2	20.3	18 152	70.2	14.2
Mexico - Mexique	9 362	74.2	5.7	10 796	76.9	15.3	11 803	73.1	9.3
Thailand - Thaïlande	7 856	49.7	-0.6	10 043	52.7	27.8	10 104	48.9	0.6
China, Hong Kong SAR - Chine, Hong Kong RAS	7 141	15.3	-4.2	8 999	16.3	26.0	..	..	..
Malaysia - Malaisie	5 901	43.5	-17.1	8 198	48.9	38.9	8 846	45.2	7.9
China, Macao SAR - Chine, Macao RAS	5 155	92.0	19.7	7 479	92.8	45.1	7 980	92.6	6.7
South Africa - Afrique du Sud	5 571	67.1	90.6	6 322	65.3	13.5	7 335	65.7	16.0
Egypt - Égypte	4 584	41.4	21.8	6 125	43.1	33.6	6 851	46.8	11.8
Korea, Republic of - Corée, République de	5 358	16.3	-9.7	6 069	14.5	13.3	5 660	12.5	-6.7
Lebanon - Liban	6 374	67.4	48.8	5 411	55.8	-15.1	5 432	50.5	0.4
Singapore - Singapour	3 783	10.4	-14.6	5 224	11.2	38.1	5 736	11.2	9.8
Indonesia - Indonésie	4 037	76.3	-23.6	4 798	39.8	18.8	4 522	35.0	-5.8
China, Taiwan Province of - Chine, Taiwan Province de (5)	2 977	12.9	-35.0	4 054	15.7	36.2	4 977	19.3	22.8
Morocco - Maroc	3 221	58.8	21.7	3 922	58.5	21.8	4 610	56.9	17.5
Brazil - Brésil	2 479	23.7	24.1	3 222	25.6	30.0	3 861	24.0	19.8
Dominican Republic - République dominicaine	3 128	90.2	14.6	3 152	89.9	0.8	3 508	89.7	11.3
Argentina - Argentine	2 006	45.3	30.6	2 235	43.4	11.4	2 753	44.1	23.2
Philippines	1 544	45.6	-12.3	2 017	49.9	30.6	2 130	47.7	5.6
Tunisia - Tunisie	1 583	53.9	3.9	1 970	54.3	24.5	2 124	53.1	7.8
COMMUNICATIONS (3)									
China, Hong Kong SAR - Chine, Hong Kong RAS	756	1.6	7.1	852	1.5	12.8	..	..	..
Indonesia - Indonésie	248	4.7	42.7	835	6.9	>200.0	998	7.7	19.5
Kuwait - Koweït	..	..	..	506	13.5	..	1 295	27.5	156.0
Philippines	433	12.8	14.6	487	12.0	12.5	520	11.7	6.8
Korea, Republic of - Corée, République de	341	1.0	-9.7	446	1.1	30.6	435	1.0	-2.3
China - Chine	638	1.4	16.1	440	0.7	-31.0	485	0.7	10.2
Mexico - Mexique	423	3.3	-24.2	423	3.0	0.0	548	3.4	29.6
Egypt - Égypte	309	2.8	40.1	405	2.9	31.0	362	2.5	-10.6
Malaysia - Malaisie	201	1.5	-14.3	390	2.3	94.1	615	3.1	57.5
Turkey - Turquie	224	1.2	..	346	1.5	54.5	412	1.6	19.1
Morocco - Maroc	250	4.6	7.9	342	5.1	36.9	446	5.5	30.6
China, Taiwan Province of - Chine, Taiwan Province de (5)	338	1.5	19.4	333	1.3	-1.5	320	1.2	-3.9
Brazil - Brésil	449	4.3	>200.0	243	1.9	-45.8	239	1.5	-1.7
Pakistan	190	6.4	-42.8	233	8.5	22.6	284	7.7	21.9
Lebanon - Liban	163	1.7	172.1	229	2.4	41.0	241	2.2	4.8
Thailand - Thaïlande	148	0.9	14.5	201	1.1	35.7	258	1.2	28.1
Jamaica - Jamaïque	145	6.8	-15.5	193	8.4	33.4	148	6.4	-23.0
South Africa - Afrique du Sud	136	1.6	46.2	189	1.9	38.4	231	2.1	22.4
Colombia - Colombie	133	6.9	-8.7	183	8.1	37.1	217	8.2	18.8
Argentina - Argentine	146	3.3	-2.4	163	3.2	11.2	209	3.3	28.2

For sources and notes, see end of table.

Pour les sources et les notes, se reporter à la fin du tableau.

Ranking based on average 2004-2005 exports / Classement d'après la moyenne des exportations de 2004-2005	2003 Millions of dollars / Millions de dollars	2003 As % of country's total / En % du total du pays	2003 Annual change in % / Variation annuelle en %	2004 Millions of dollars / Millions de dollars	2004 As % of country's total / En % du total du pays	2004 Annual change in % / Variation annuelle en %	2005 Millions of dollars / Millions de dollars	2005 As % of country's total / En % du total du pays	2005 Annual change in % / Variation annuelle en %
CONSTRUCTION - BÂTIMENTS ET TRAVAUX PUBLICS									
China - Chine	1 290	2.8	3.5	1 467	2.4	13.8	2 593	3.5	76.7
Turkey - Turquie	743	4.1	-12.3	743	3.2	0.0	882	3.4	18.7
Singapore - Singapour	426	1.2	40.6	562	1.2	31.8	566	1.1	0.6
Indonesia - Indonésie	..	..	..	463	3.8	..	484	3.7	4.6
Egypt - Égypte	222	2.0	29.2	406	2.9	33.1	503	3.4	23.7
China, Hong Kong SAR - Chine, Hong Kong RAS	510	1.1	48.4	378	0.7	-25.9	..	..	..
Malaysia - Malaisie	262	1.9	-38.5	327	1.9	24.5	811	4.1	148.2
Thailand - Thaïlande	188	1.2	-23.3	236	1.2	25.7	255	1.2	8.2
China, Taiwan Province of - Chine, Taiwan Province de (5)	118	0.5	18.0	152	0.6	28.8	121	0.5	-20.4
Tunisia - Tunisie	122	4.1	36.4	148	4.1	21.2	143	3.6	-3.0
Korea, Republic of - Corée, République de	37	0.1	-5.3	99	0.2	166.7	76	0.2	-23.7
Senegal - Sénégal	36	6.4	>200.0	72	10.7	98.9	..	..	..
Philippines	48	1.4	60.0	71	1.8	47.9	66	1.5	-7.0
Argentina - Argentine	41	0.9	149.7	61	1.2	50.6	46	0.7	-25.4
Syrian Arab Republic - République arabe syrienne	2	0.2	..	58	2.1	>200.0	14	0.4	-75.9
Papua New Guinea - Papouasie-Nouvelle-Guinée	96	41.4	..	28	13.8	-70.8	15	5.1	-45.5
South Africa - Afrique du Sud	21	0.3	47.0	28	0.3	31.3	35	0.3	23.5
Sri Lanka	38	2.7	11.4	26	1.7	-32.5	29	1.9	13.4
Pakistan	4	0.1	..	24	0.9	>200.0	18	0.5	-25.0
El Salvador	10	1.1	-54.5	19	1.7	86.0	24	2.1	29.6
COMPUTER AND INFORMATION SERVICES - INFORMATIQUE ET INFORMATION									
China - Chine	1 102	2.4	72.7	1 637	2.6	48.5	1 840	2.5	12.4
Singapore - Singapour	351	1.0	-0.5	447	1.0	27.3	476	0.9	6.4
Malaysia - Malaisie	216	1.6	19.0	349	2.1	61.6	435	2.2	24.7
China, Hong Kong SAR - Chine, Hong Kong RAS	245	0.5	18.2	245	0.4	-0.3	..	..	..
Costa Rica	167	8.3	8.7	200	8.9	20.1	255	9.7	27.2
Argentina - Argentine	166	3.7	30.4	192	3.7	15.5	245	3.9	27.9
Indonesia - Indonésie	..	..	..	138	1.1	..	147	1.1	7.0
China, Taiwan Province of - Chine, Taiwan Province de (5)	110	0.5	-4.3	110	0.4	0.0	105	0.4	-4.5
South Africa - Afrique du Sud	66	0.8	48.6	89	0.9	34.0	109	1.0	22.9
Sri Lanka	65	4.6	30.0	72	4.7	10.8	82	5.4	14.5
Chile - Chili	81	1.6	29.4	70	1.2	-13.4	74	1.0	5.3
Uruguay	12	1.4	-14.7	69	6.0	>200.0	79	5.9	14.5
Syrian Arab Republic - République arabe syrienne	50	3.8	..	55	2.0	10.0	60	1.9	9.1
Brazil - Brésil	29	0.3	-20.2	53	0.4	83.6	88	0.5	64.4
Pakistan	34	1.1	61.9	38	1.4	11.8	59	1.6	55.3
Egypt - Égypte	23	0.2	-16.5	33	0.2	46.7	25	0.2	-25.2
Jamaica - Jamaïque	36	1.7	5.4	33	1.4	-8.1	34	1.5	4.1
Philippines	28	0.8	-24.3	33	0.8	17.9	89	2.0	169.7
Korea, Republic of - Corée, République de	30	0.1	52.3	25	0.1	-14.8	54	0.1	113.8
Barbados - Barbade	18	1.5	2.6	20	1.6	10.0	23	1.6	14.1
INSURANCE - ASSURANCE									
Singapore - Singapour	1 229	3.4	54.1	1 314	2.8	6.9	1 122	2.2	-14.6
Mexico - Mexique	1 163	9.2	-4.1	864	6.2	-25.7	1 550	9.6	79.4
China, Hong Kong SAR - Chine, Hong Kong RAS	394	0.8	-10.3	411	0.7	4.3	..	..	..
China, Taiwan Province of - Chine, Taiwan Province de (5)	451	1.9	-19.9	382	1.5	-15.3	365	1.4	-4.5
China - Chine	313	0.7	49.7	381	0.6	21.7	549	0.7	44.3
Turkey - Turquie	211	1.2	>200.0	274	1.2	29.9	323	1.2	17.9
Malaysia - Malaisie	223	1.6	43.1	273	1.6	22.4	278	1.4	2.0
Chile - Chili	145	2.9	5.1	144	2.4	-0.4	150	2.1	3.7
Lebanon - Liban	124	1.3	89.5	141	1.5	13.8	209	1.9	48.7
Korea, Republic of - Corée, République de	34	0.1	-7.9	139	0.3	>200.0	391	0.9	182.0
Thailand - Thaïlande	134	0.8	45.7	135	0.7	0.8	280	1.4	106.9
Trinidad and Tobago - Trinité-et-Tobago	108	15.8	8.4	113	13.3	4.6	..	..	..
South Africa - Afrique du Sud	77	0.9	45.4	106	1.1	37.3	124	1.1	17.6
Brazil - Brésil	124	1.2	-39.9	105	0.8	-14.9	134	0.8	27.5
Morocco - Maroc	76	1.4	168.3	95	1.4	24.3	72	0.9	-24.1
Barbados - Barbade	90	7.7	3.3	91	7.4	1.0	143	9.8	57.4
Peru - Pérou	88	5.2	-6.1	82	4.3	-7.5	118	5.4	44.8
Kuwait - Koweït	83	2.6	-23.8	79	2.1	-5.4	83	1.8	5.7
Libyan Arab Jamahiriya - Jamahiriya arabe libyenne	55	12.4	48.6	60	13.7	9.1	43	8.1	-28.3
Guatemala	59	5.6	20.1	58	4.9	-2.1	61	5.0	5.8

For sources and notes, see end of table.

Pour les sources et les notes, se reporter à la fin du tableau.

5

Ranking based on average 2004-2005 exports / Classement d'après la moyenne des exportations de 2004-2005	2003			2004			2005		
	Millions of dollars / Millions de dollars	As % of country's total / En % du total du pays	Annual change in % / Variation annuelle en %	Millions of dollars / Millions de dollars	As % of country's total / En % du total du pays	Annual change in % / Variation annuelle en %	Millions of dollars / Millions de dollars	As % of country's total / En % du total du pays	Annual change in % / Variation annuelle en %
FINANCIAL SERVICES - SERVICES FINANCIERS									
China, Hong Kong SAR - Chine, Hong Kong RAS	3 763	8.1	-10.3	4 553	8.3	21.0	..	..	..
Singapore - Singapour	1 838	5.1	39.8	2 460	5.3	33.8	3 695	7.2	50.2
China, Taiwan Province of - Chine, Taiwan Province de (5)	863	3.7	14.0	1 142	4.4	32.3	1 517	5.9	32.8
Korea, Republic of - Corée, République de	699	2.1	0.5	1 083	2.6	55.1	1 612	3.6	48.8
South Africa - Afrique du Sud	295	3.6	31.2	426	4.4	44.4	534	4.8	25.5
Brazil - Brésil	363	3.5	-7.0	423	3.4	16.5	507	3.2	20.0
Indonesia - Indonésie	..	..	..	297	2.5	..	367	2.8	23.8
Swaziland	98	38.2	..	291	62.7	198.0	151	53.5	-48.0
Turkey - Turquie	291	1.6	31.7	288	1.3	-1.0	345	1.3	19.8
Panama	293	11.7	8.0	240	8.8	-18.0	197	6.3	-17.8
Malaysia - Malaisie	109	0.8	115.0	180	1.1	64.6	60	0.3	-66.7
China - Chine	152	0.3	197.9	94	0.2	-38.2	145	0.2	54.6
Barbados - Barbade	74	6.3	5.1	80	6.5	8.4	117	8.0	46.9
Egypt - Égypte	80	0.7	-6.1	74	0.5	-7.3	137	0.9	85.6
Tunisia - Tunisie	55	1.9	30.6	55	1.5	0.5	58	1.4	4.3
Uruguay	58	7.2	7.0	53	4.6	-7.9	65	4.9	22.0
Côte d'Ivoire	47	7.2	22.6	53	6.9	11.6	..	..	..
Philippines	38	1.1	18.8	42	1.0	10.5	53	1.2	26.2
Kuwait - Koweït	47	1.5	185.5	41	1.1	-13.3	34	0.7	-15.9
Pakistan	12	0.4	-29.4	40	1.5	>200.0	47	1.3	17.5
ROYALTIES AND LICENSE FEES - REDEVANCES ET DROITS DE LICENCE									
Korea, Republic of - Corée, République de	1 311	4.0	57.0	1 861	4.4	41.9	1 827	4.0	-1.8
Singapore - Singapour	196	0.5	-3.6	494	1.1	151.7	544	1.1	10.1
China, Taiwan Province of - Chine, Taiwan Province de (5)	215	0.9	-15.7	290	1.1	34.9	234	0.9	-19.3
China - Chine	107	0.2	-19.5	236	0.4	120.9	157	0.2	-33.4
Angola	..	..	..	227	70.3	..	49	28.0	-78.2
Indonesia - Indonésie	..	..	..	221	1.8	..	263	2.0	19.1
China, Hong Kong SAR - Chine, Hong Kong RAS	341	0.7	48.8	218	0.4	-36.0	..	..	..
Paraguay	193	33.7	3.4	208	33.0	7.5	196	29.7	-5.7
Brazil - Brésil	108	1.0	7.8	114	0.9	5.9	102	0.6	-11.2
Egypt - Égypte	121	1.1	>200.0	100	0.7	-17.2	136	0.9	36.0
Mexico - Mexique	84	0.7	73.9	92	0.7	8.9	70	0.4	-23.1
Argentina - Argentine	52	1.2	54.1	61	1.2	17.6	54	0.9	-10.6
Chile - Chili	45	0.9	10.6	48	0.8	6.6	54	0.8	11.5
Malaysia - Malaisie	20	0.1	67.6	41	0.2	103.2	27	0.1	-34.4
South Africa - Afrique du Sud	27	0.3	36.5	37	0.4	40.8	45	0.4	21.2
Guyana	32	20.5	-6.7	34	20.9	5.0	35	24.1	5.0
Tunisia - Tunisie	18	0.6	10.3	18	0.5	-1.0	14	0.3	-21.5
Lesotho	15	29.9	41.3	17	26.6	14.3	18	32.6	6.1
Kenya	12	1.0	17.1	17	1.1	42.8	18	0.9	5.2
Morocco - Maroc	26	0.5	132.4	16	0.2	-36.9	13	0.2	-21.9
OTHER BUSINESS SERVICES (4) - AUTRES SERVICES AUX ENTREPRISES (4)									
China, Hong Kong SAR - Chine, Hong Kong RAS	19 382	41.6	10.4	21 798	39.5	12.5	..	..	..
China - Chine	17 427	37.3	67.3	19 952	32.0	14.5	23 283	31.3	16.7
Singapore - Singapour	14 266	39.3	25.4	16 538	35.4	15.9	..	..	..
China, Taiwan Province of - Chine, Taiwan Province de (5)	13 529	58.4	22.5	13 739	53.3	1.6	11 950	46.3	-13.0
Korea, Republic of - Corée, République de	6 687	20.3	11.4	8 125	19.4	21.5	9 727	21.4	19.7
Saudi Arabia - Arabie saoudite	5 713	100.0	10.4	5 852	100.0	2.4	5 916	100.0	1.1
Brazil - Brésil	4 133	39.6	-4.3	4 938	39.2	19.5	6 720	41.8	36.1
Thailand - Thaïlande	3 858	24.4	5.3	3 952	20.8	2.5	4 955	24.0	25.4
Lebanon - Liban	2 351	24.8	>200.0	3 340	34.4	42.1	4 381	40.7	31.1
Egypt - Égypte	2 092	18.9	7.4	2 780	19.6	32.9	..	..	..
Indonesia - Indonésie	..	..	..	2 669	22.2	..	2 881	22.3	8.0
Nigeria - Nigéria	3 078	88.6	49.4	2 637	79.0	-14.3	..	..	..
Malaysia - Malaisie	1 924	14.2	-10.6	2 078	12.4	8.0	..	..	..
Argentina - Argentine	857	19.3	28.7	994	19.3	16.0	1 181	18.9	18.9
Chile - Chili	830	16.6	11.4	951	15.7	14.5	1 088	15.2	14.4
Morocco - Maroc	643	11.7	60.4	904	13.5	40.6	..	..	..
Netherlands Antilles - Antilles néerlandaises	637	37.5	11.6	699	38.9	9.8	..	..	..
South Africa - Afrique du Sud	461	5.6	46.6	555	5.7	20.3	628	5.6	13.2
Turkey - Turquie	272	1.5	7.1	482	2.1	77.2	332	1.3	-31.1
Côte d'Ivoire	208	31.4	-4.5	415	54.4	99.3	..	..	..

For sources and notes, see end of table.

Pour les sources et les notes, se reporter à la fin du tableau.

5.2   Trade in services by sector:
Leading exporters among developing
economies

5.2   Commerce des services par secteurs :
Principaux exportateurs parmi les
économies en développement

	2003			2004			2005		
Ranking based on average 2004-2005 exports Classement d'après la moyenne des exportations de 2004-2005	Millions of dollars Millions de dollars	As % of country's total En % du total du pays	Annual change in % Variation annuelle en %	Millions of dollars Millions de dollars	As % of country's total En % du total du pays	Annual change in % Variation annuelle en %	Millions of dollars Millions de dollars	As % of country's total En % du total du pays	Annual change in % Variation annuelle en %
PERSONAL, CULTURAL AND RECREATIONAL SERVICES - **SERVICES PERSONNELS, CULTURELS ET RELATIFS AUX LOISIRS**									
Malaysia - Malaisie	1 835	13.5	17.1	1 657	9.9	-9.7	1 562	8.0	-5.8
Turkey - Turquie	781	4.3	-42.4	1 418	6.2	81.6	1 079	4.2	-23.9
Mexico - Mexique	293	2.3	-26.7	358	2.5	22.1	373	2.3	4.3
China, Hong Kong SAR - Chine, Hong Kong RAS	137	0.3	22.8	290	0.5	110.8	..	..	..
Singapore - Singapour	154	0.4	21.8	189	0.4	22.5	197	0.4	4.1
Argentina - Argentine	116	2.6	26.1	136	2.6	17.4	149	2.4	9.8
Korea, Republic of - Corée, République de	76	0.2	-58.8	128	0.3	68.0	261	0.6	104.2
South Africa - Afrique du Sud	60	0.7	57.2	88	0.9	46.1	114	1.0	29.5
Syrian Arab Republic - République arabe syrienne	..	..	..	75	2.7	..	95	2.9	26.7
Chile - Chili	68	1.4	75.2	73	1.2	7.9	86	1.2	18.2
Egypt - Égypte	72	0.7	34.1	69	0.5	-4.0	83	0.6	19.8
China, Taiwan Province of - Chine, Taiwan Province de (5)	40	0.2	-14.9	49	0.2	22.5	61	0.2	24.5
Indonesia - Indonésie	..	..	..	47	0.4	..	57	0.4	20.9
Brazil - Brésil	54	0.5	-7.4	47	0.4	-13.2	56	0.3	20.0
China - Chine	33	0.1	12.7	41	0.1	22.6	134	0.2	>200.0
Colombia - Colombie	31	1.6	15.3	39	1.7	24.3	41	1.6	7.0
Ecuador - Équateur	34	3.8	6.7	36	3.6	6.7	39	3.8	6.7
Jamaica - Jamaïque	20	1.0	121.7	28	1.2	39.4	30	1.3	4.3
Congo	9	4.8	-56.6	11	5.5	16.1	..	..	..
Tunisia - Tunisie	5	0.2	93.1	10	0.3	92.1	4	0.1	-63.1

Sources:
- International Monetary Fund (IMF), *Balance of Payments Statistics* on CD-ROM

Notes:

(1)   Excludes freight insurance, which is included with insurance services.
(2)   Includes goods and services acquired from an economy by non-resident travelers during visits shorter than one year.
(3)   Postal, courier and telecommunications services between residents and non-residents.
(4)   Includes merchanting and other trade-related services, operational leasing services, and miscellaneous business, professional and technical services.
(5)   National data sources.

Sources :
- Fonds monétaire international (FMI), *Statistiques de la balance des paiements* sur CD-ROM

Notes :

(1)   Non-compris l'assurance du fret, incluse dans la rubrique des services d'assurance.
(2)   Comprend les biens et services acquis dans une économie par les voyageurs non-résidents, au cours d'un séjour inférieur à un an.
(3)   Services postaux (y compris les messageries) et les services de télécommunication, entre résidents et non-résidents.
(4)   Y compris le négoce international et les autres services liés au commerce, la location-exploitation et divers services aux entreprises, spécialisés et techniques.
(5)   Données des sources nationales.

5

	2003			2004			2005		
Ranking based on average 2004-2005 imports Classement d'après la moyenne des importations de 2004-2005	Millions of dollars Millions de dollars	As % of country's total En % du total du pays	Annual change in % Variation annuelle en %	Millions of dollars Millions de dollars	As % of country's total En % du total du pays	Annual change in % Variation annuelle en %	Millions of dollars Millions de dollars	As % of country's total En % du total du pays	Annual change in % Variation annuelle en %
TRANSPORT (1) - TRANSPORTS (1)									
China - Chine	18 233	33.0	33.9	24 544	34.0	34.6	28 448	33.9	15.9
Singapore - Singapour	13 308	33.5	22.0	17 815	35.6	33.9	19 876	36.6	11.6
Korea, Republic of - Corée, République de	13 613	33.7	20.5	17 655	35.4	29.7	19 966	34.1	13.1
Thailand - Thaïlande	8 484	46.7	19.1	10 830	46.9	27.7	13 999	50.7	29.3
China, Hong Kong SAR - Chine, Hong Kong RAS	6 719	25.7	8.0	8 687	27.9	29.3	..	..	..
China, Taiwan Province of - Chine, Taiwan Province de (5)	6 714	26.2	12.5	8 132	26.5	21.1	8 439	26.0	3.8
Malaysia - Malaisie	6 260	35.7	6.2	7 842	41.1	25.3	8 396	38.2	7.1
Indonesia - Indonésie	4 824	27.7	-6.3	5 474	26.2	13.5	7 030	29.6	28.4
Brazil - Brésil	3 412	22.2	-2.4	4 452	25.8	30.5	4 976	20.5	11.8
South Africa - Afrique du Sud	3 174	39.5	38.4	4 401	42.6	38.6	5 328	43.8	21.1
Turkey - Turquie	2 707	36.1	40.0	4 331	42.6	60.0	5 324	44.8	22.9
Chile - Chili	2 546	45.2	10.7	3 345	49.5	31.4	4 112	53.0	22.9
Saudi Arabia - Arabie saoudite	2 743	13.2	14.3	3 325	12.9	21.2	4 157	14.9	25.0
Philippines	2 419	45.2	5.0	3 095	53.2	27.9	3 125	53.3	1.0
Egypt - Égypte	2 013	31.1	12.9	2 986	37.2	48.4	3 731	35.5	24.9
Kuwait - Koweït	2 027	30.6	16.0	2 294	30.3	13.2	3 014	34.1	31.4
Mexico - Mexique	1 930	10.6	-3.0	2 127	10.8	10.2	2 716	12.7	27.7
Pakistan	1 585	48.1	14.2	2 076	38.9	31.0	2 601	34.8	25.3
Venezuela (Bolivarian Rep. of) - (Rép. bolivarienne du)	1 261	35.9	-18.4	1 730	38.5	37.2	2 178	41.7	25.9
Argentina - Argentine	1 146	20.1	20.8	1 622	24.5	41.5	1 971	25.9	21.5
TRAVEL (2) - VOYAGES (2)									
China - Chine	15 187	27.5	-1.4	19 149	26.5	26.1	21 759	26.0	13.6
China, Hong Kong SAR - Chine, Hong Kong RAS	11 448	43.8	-7.8	13 269	42.6	15.9	..	..	..
Korea, Republic of - Corée, République de	10 103	25.0	-3.5	12 350	24.7	22.2	15 314	26.2	24.0
Singapore - Singapour	7 991	20.1	-2.0	9 585	19.2	20.0	9 853	18.2	2.8
China, Taiwan Province of - Chine, Taiwan Province de (5)	6 480	25.3	-6.8	8 170	26.6	26.1	8 682	26.7	6.3
Mexico - Mexique	6 253	34.5	3.2	6 959	35.2	11.3	7 600	35.4	9.2
Thailand - Thaïlande	2 921	16.1	-11.6	4 514	19.6	54.6	4 995	18.1	10.7
Kuwait - Koweït	3 348	50.6	10.8	3 701	48.8	10.6	4 277	48.4	15.6
Indonesia - Indonésie	3 082	17.7	-6.3	3 507	16.8	13.8	3 584	15.1	2.2
Lebanon - Liban	2 943	45.4	9.7	3 170	38.5	7.7	2 878	36.6	-9.2
South Africa - Afrique du Sud	2 889	35.9	59.5	3 157	30.6	9.3	3 373	27.8	6.9
Malaysia - Malaisie	2 846	16.2	8.7	3 093	16.2	8.7	3 711	16.9	20.0
Brazil - Brésil	2 261	14.7	-5.6	2 871	16.6	27.0	4 720	19.5	64.4
Argentina - Argentine	2 511	44.0	7.9	2 604	39.3	3.7	2 817	37.0	8.2
Turkey - Turquie	2 113	28.2	12.4	2 524	24.8	19.5	2 872	24.2	13.8
Philippines	1 413	26.4	-13.1	1 275	21.9	-9.8	1 279	21.8	0.3
Pakistan	925	28.1	>200.0	1 268	23.8	37.1	1 275	17.0	0.6
Egypt - Égypte	1 321	20.4	4.3	1 257	15.7	-4.8	1 629	15.5	29.5
Nigeria - Nigéria	1 795	31.4	103.7	1 161	19.4	-35.3	1 109	15.1	-4.5
Colombia - Colombie	1 062	31.6	-1.2	1 108	28.2	4.3	1 127	23.6	1.7
COMMUNICATIONS (3)									
China, Hong Kong SAR - Chine, Hong Kong RAS	941	3.6	13.4	1 124	3.6	19.4	..	..	..
Korea, Republic of - Corée, République de	693	1.7	1.1	636	1.3	-8.3	702	1.2	10.5
Malaysia - Malaisie	252	1.4	8.6	529	2.8	110.0	680	3.1	28.6
China, Taiwan Province of - Chine, Taiwan Province de (5)	460	1.8	-2.7	496	1.6	7.8	505	1.6	1.8
China - Chine	427	0.8	-9.1	472	0.7	10.5	603	0.7	27.8
Indonesia - Indonésie	131	0.8	-23.3	359	1.7	173.5	495	2.1	37.7
Argentina - Argentine	228	4.0	1.8	225	3.4	-1.5	267	3.5	18.9
Egypt - Égypte	148	2.3	18.5	224	2.8	51.3	406	3.9	80.9
Turkey - Turquie	231	3.1	>200.0	207	2.0	-10.4	228	1.9	10.1
Lebanon - Liban	97	1.5	>200.0	203	2.5	110.4	138	1.8	-31.9
Mexico - Mexique	310	1.7	57.6	176	0.9	-43.4	119	0.6	-32.4
South Africa - Afrique du Sud	100	1.2	40.3	147	1.4	47.7	198	1.6	34.4
Colombia - Colombie	108	3.2	-4.2	144	3.7	33.8	152	3.2	5.0
Thailand - Thaïlande	180	1.0	107.7	141	0.6	-21.2	214	0.8	51.1
Philippines	81	1.5	-4.7	128	2.2	58.0	115	2.0	-10.2
Kuwait - Koweït	..	..	..	122	1.6	..	96	1.1	-21.5
Chile - Chili	111	2.0	-19.4	110	1.6	-0.3	126	1.6	14.7
Kenya	6	0.9	-3.4	108	11.5	>200.0	108	9.5	-0.8
Brazil - Brésil	366	2.4	>200.0	70	0.4	-81.0	112	0.5	60.7
Venezuela (Bolivarian Rep. of) - (Rép. bolivarienne du)	58	1.7	-6.5	68	1.5	17.2	76	1.5	11.8

For sources and notes, see end of table.   Pour les sources et les notes, se reporter à la fin du tableau.

5.2　Trade in services by sector:
Leading importers among developing
economies

5.2　Commerce des services par secteurs :
Principaux importateurs parmi les
économies en développement

	2003			2004			2005		
Ranking based on average 2004-2005 imports Classement d'après la moyenne des importations de 2004-2005	Millions of dollars Millions de dollars	As % of country's total En % du total du pays	Annual change in % Variation annuelle en %	Millions of dollars Millions de dollars	As % of country's total En % du total du pays	Annual change in % Variation annuelle en %	Millions of dollars Millions de dollars	As % of country's total En % du total du pays	Annual change in % Variation annuelle en %
CONSTRUCTION - BÂTIMENTS ET TRAVAUX PUBLICS									
China - Chine	1 183	2.1	22.8	1 339	1.9	-3.1	1 619	1.9	21.0
Angola	150	4.5	-73.0	866	18.0	>200.0	1 323	19.5	52.7
Indonesia - Indonésie	..	..	..	708	3.4	..	726	3.1	2.5
China, Taiwan Province of - Chine, Taiwan Province de (5)	457	1.8	-5.8	558	1.8	22.1	376	1.2	-32.6
Malaysia - Malaisie	410	2.3	-13.9	467	2.4	14.0	1 087	5.0	132.7
China, Hong Kong SAR - Chine, Hong Kong RAS	399	1.5	14.1	346	1.1	-13.3	..	..	..
Singapore - Singapour	142	0.4	7.1	269	0.5	90.0	271	0.5	0.7
Thailand - Thaïlande	152	0.8	110.4	229	1.0	51.2	314	1.1	37.2
Tunisia - Tunisie	160	9.9	0.1	183	9.2	14.5	197	9.0	7.4
Libyan Arab Jamahiriya - Jamahiriya arabe libyenne	168	10.5	-10.6	183	9.6	8.9	149	6.3	-18.6
Egypt - Égypte	108	1.7	-13.5	171	2.1	59.3	231	2.2	34.8
Yemen - Yémen	34	3.4	14.7	108	10.2	>200.0	108	9.3	0.0
United Republic of Tanzania - République-Unie de Tanzanie	10	1.4	-4.8	93	9.6	>200.0	143	12.3	53.8
Ethiopia - Éthiopie	67	9.5	-16.7	78	8.1	15.3	121	10.1	55.7
Mozambique	61	10.6	-33.2	52	9.8	-14.3	79	12.1	50.6
Philippines	64	1.2	-48.0	48	0.8	-25.0	7	0.1	-85.4
Cambodia - Cambodge	44	10.0	118.2	42	8.2	-3.9	43	6.8	2.2
Kuwait - Koweït	40	0.6	2.0	41	0.5	1.1	41	0.5	0.9
Papua New Guinea - Papouasie-Nouvelle-Guinée	40	4.6	..	38	3.8	-5.0	58	5.0	54.0
Honduras	35	5.2	0.0	36	4.8	3.1	38	4.5	5.3
COMPUTER AND INFORMATION SERVICES - INFORMATIQUE ET INFORMATION									
Brazil - Brésil	1 063	6.9	-8.0	1 281	7.4	20.6	1 713	7.1	33.7
China - Chine	1 036	1.9	-8.6	1 253	1.7	20.9	1 623	1.9	29.5
Indonesia - Indonésie	..	..	..	468	2.2	..	561	2.4	19.9
China, Hong Kong SAR - Chine, Hong Kong RAS	282	1.1	25.3	395	1.3	40.0	..	..	..
Malaysia - Malaisie	197	1.1	14.7	315	1.6	59.4	379	1.7	20.6
Singapore - Singapour	330	0.8	21.3	314	0.6	-4.9	334	0.6	6.4
China, Taiwan Province of - Chine, Taiwan Province de (5)	248	1.0	-18.7	238	0.8	-4.0	315	1.0	32.4
Korea, Republic of - Corée, République de	134	0.3	7.6	157	0.3	17.3	182	0.3	16.0
Argentina - Argentine	135	2.4	6.7	153	2.3	13.5	179	2.4	17.0
South Africa - Afrique du Sud	59	0.7	35.9	84	0.8	41.9	114	0.9	35.1
Jamaica - Jamaïque	20	1.3	75.9	75	4.4	>200.0	17	1.0	-77.1
Venezuela (Bolivarian Rep. of) - (Rép. bolivarienne du)	58	1.7	-10.8	69	1.5	19.0	83	1.6	20.3
Colombia - Colombie	72	2.1	148.9	66	1.7	-9.2	118	2.5	80.3
Chile - Chili	60	1.1	46.4	63	0.9	5.9	68	0.9	8.3
Philippines	46	0.9	-42.5	49	0.8	6.5	62	1.1	26.5
China, Macao SAR - Chine, Macao RAS	17	1.4	2.3	24	1.8	48.3	25	1.6	3.0
Egypt - Égypte	27	0.4	94.2	24	0.3	-10.9	27	0.3	15.2
Pakistan	6	0.2	..	18	0.3	200.0	34	0.5	88.9
Costa Rica	10	0.8	-31.0	16	1.2	60.7	11	0.7	-32.7
Libyan Arab Jamahiriya - Jamahiriya arabe libyenne	12	0.8	>200.0	15	0.8	25.0	25	1.1	66.7
INSURANCE - ASSURANCE									
Mexico - Mexique	6 755	37.2	3.6	7 666	38.8	13.5	8 714	40.6	13.7
China - Chine	4 564	8.3	40.6	6 124	8.5	34.2	7 200	8.6	17.6
Singapore - Singapour	1 800	4.5	16.9	2 187	4.4	21.5	2 240	4.1	2.5
Thailand - Thaïlande	1 125	6.2	15.7	1 290	5.6	14.7	1 656	6.0	28.3
China, Taiwan Province of - Chine, Taiwan Province de (5)	1 236	4.8	29.7	1 205	3.9	-2.5	967	3.0	-19.8
Turkey - Turquie	622	8.3	67.2	839	8.3	34.9	891	7.5	6.2
Brazil - Brésil	560	3.6	-10.6	649	3.8	16.0	702	2.9	8.1
China, Hong Kong SAR - Chine, Hong Kong RAS	622	2.4	5.0	611	2.0	-1.7	..	..	..
Egypt - Égypte	423	6.5	6.2	588	7.3	39.1	781	7.4	32.9
Malaysia - Malaisie	480	2.7	10.7	475	2.5	-1.0	518	2.4	9.0
Korea, Republic of - Corée, République de	390	1.0	-31.6	461	0.9	18.2	638	1.1	38.4
Chile - Chili	434	7.7	23.0	451	6.7	3.9	419	5.4	-7.2
South Africa - Afrique du Sud	297	3.7	31.7	391	3.8	31.8	478	3.9	22.3
Saudi Arabia - Arabie saoudite	305	1.5	14.3	369	1.4	21.2	462	1.7	25.0
Indonesia - Indonésie	300	1.7	-4.4	353	1.7	17.7	338	1.4	-4.1
Oman	221	10.1	28.8	257	9.3	16.5	299	9.8	16.2
Colombia - Colombie	233	7.1	-15.6	249	6.3	4.8	290	6.1	16.2
Peru - Pérou	263	10.3	8.1	206	7.5	-21.5	231	7.5	12.1
Philippines	182	3.4	4.0	199	3.4	9.3	203	3.5	2.0
Lebanon - Liban	217	3.3	-63.9	176	2.1	-18.9	237	3.0	34.7

For sources and notes, see end of table.

Pour les sources et les notes, se reporter à la fin du tableau.

5

	2003			2004			2005		
Ranking based on average 2004-2005 imports Classement d'après la moyenne des importations de 2004-2005	Millions of dollars Millions de dollars	As % of country's total En % du total du pays	Annual change in % Variation annuelle en %	Millions of dollars Millions de dollars	As % of country's total En % du total du pays	Annual change in % Variation annuelle en %	Millions of dollars Millions de dollars	As % of country's total En % du total du pays	Annual change in % Variation annuelle en %
FINANCIAL SERVICES - SERVICES FINANCIERS									
China, Hong Kong SAR - Chine, Hong Kong RAS	878	3.4	-11.0	1 165	3.7	32.7	..	..	..
China, Taiwan Province of - Chine, Taiwan Province de (5)	1 112	4.3	29.9	884	2.9	-20.5	1 370	4.2	55.0
Singapore - Singapour	502	1.3	17.3	668	1.3	32.9	788	1.5	18.1
Indonesia - Indonésie	..	..	..	594	2.8	..	539	2.3	-9.2
Brazil - Brésil	745	4.8	19.7	499	2.9	-33.0	737	3.0	47.5
Mexico - Mexique	400	2.2	99.7	412	2.1	3.1	550	2.6	33.3
Turkey - Turquie	374	5.0	-39.8	377	3.7	0.8	386	3.2	2.4
Chile - Chili	257	4.6	11.5	275	4.1	7.2	313	4.0	13.7
Swaziland	35	11.8	>200.0	250	39.6	>200.0	123	26.9	-50.9
South Africa - Afrique du Sud	102	1.3	37.8	149	1.4	45.2	184	1.5	23.3
Malaysia - Malaisie	117	0.7	14.7	148	0.8	26.6	119	0.5	-19.5
China - Chine	233	0.4	158.8	138	0.2	-40.6	159	0.2	15.5
Panama	169	12.9	-12.3	138	9.5	-18.4	158	9.1	14.1
Korea, Republic of - Corée, République de	101	0.3	45.5	127	0.3	25.1	177	0.3	39.9
Côte d'Ivoire	110	6.2	22.4	124	6.1	12.7	..	..	..
Venezuela (Bolivarian Rep. of) - (Rép. bolivarienne du)	157	4.5	25.6	110	2.4	-29.9	243	4.7	120.9
Argentina - Argentine	113	2.0	126.2	105	1.6	-6.9	210	2.8	99.5
Colombia - Colombie	101	3.0	-10.9	95	2.4	-5.4	145	3.0	52.0
Philippines	54	1.0	-22.9	76	1.3	40.7	93	1.6	22.4
Pakistan	73	2.2	37.7	75	1.4	2.7	124	1.7	65.3
ROYALTIES AND LICENSE FEES - REDEVANCES ET DROITS DE LICENCE									
Singapore - Singapour	6 635	16.7	38.4	7 851	15.7	18.3	8 647	15.9	10.1
China - Chine	3 548	6.4	13.9	4 497	6.2	26.7	5 321	6.4	18.3
Korea, Republic of - Corée, République de	3 570	8.8	18.9	4 446	8.9	24.5	4 398	7.5	-1.1
China, Taiwan Province of - Chine, Taiwan Province de (5)	1 689	6.6	-1.8	1 677	5.5	-0.7	1 796	5.5	7.1
Thailand - Thaïlande	1 268	7.0	14.8	1 584	6.9	24.9	1 674	6.1	5.7
Brazil - Brésil	1 228	8.0	-0.1	1 197	6.9	-2.5	1 404	5.8	17.3
China, Hong Kong SAR - Chine, Hong Kong RAS	864	3.3	24.2	1 111	3.6	28.6	..	..	..
Indonesia - Indonésie	..	..	..	990	4.7	..	961	4.0	-3.0
Malaysia - Malaisie	782	4.5	24.5	911	4.8	16.5	1 370	6.2	50.4
South Africa - Afrique du Sud	617	7.7	38.1	891	8.6	44.5	1 071	8.8	20.2
Mexico - Mexique	608	3.4	-15.5	805	4.1	32.4	111	0.5	-86.2
Argentina - Argentine	399	7.0	13.6	518	7.8	29.8	635	8.3	22.5
Turkey - Turquie	167	2.2	56.1	362	3.6	116.8	439	3.7	21.3
Chile - Chili	257	4.6	2.6	283	4.2	10.1	322	4.1	13.7
Philippines	278	5.2	17.8	273	4.7	-1.8	265	4.5	-2.9
Venezuela (Bolivarian Rep. of) - (Rép. bolivarienne du)	183	5.2	-13.3	219	4.9	19.7	239	4.6	9.1
Egypt - Égypte	165	2.5	-3.6	108	1.3	-34.5	182	1.7	68.4
Pakistan	36	1.1	100.0	86	1.6	138.9	110	1.5	27.9
Colombia - Colombie	76	2.2	-12.5	82	2.1	8.9	118	2.5	43.3
Swaziland	114	38.1	111.3	76	12.0	-33.8	88	19.2	16.0
OTHER BUSINESS SERVICES (4) - AUTRES SERVICES AUX ENTREPRISES (4)									
China - Chine	10 371	18.8	30.3	13 911	19.3	34.1	16 287	19.4	17.1
Korea, Republic of - Corée, République de	11 049	27.4	15.0	13 163	26.4	19.1	15 881	27.2	20.6
China, Taiwan Province of - Chine, Taiwan Province de (5)	6 201	24.2	4.7	8 261	26.9	33.2	8 669	26.7	4.9
Singapore - Singapour	7 241	18.2	14.6	8 222	16.4	13.5	..	..	..
Indonesia - Indonésie	8 834	50.8	12.6	7 984	38.3	-9.6	10 526	44.4	31.8
Saudi Arabia - Arabie saoudite	4 888	23.4	9.0	7 363	28.7	50.6	9 620	34.4	30.6
Brazil - Brésil	4 379	28.5	23.6	4 682	27.1	6.9	7 480	30.9	59.8
Thailand - Thaïlande	3 870	21.3	-1.1	4 320	18.7	11.6	4 606	16.7	6.6
China, Hong Kong SAR - Chine, Hong Kong RAS	3 772	14.4	9.5	4 223	13.6	12.0	..	..	..
Lebanon - Liban	2 310	35.6	>200.0	3 426	41.6	48.3	3 245	41.3	-5.3
Malaysia - Malaisie	3 057	17.4	5.2	3 097	16.2	1.3	..	..	..
Angola	2 151	64.8	7.9	2 731	56.9	27.0	..	..	..
Nigeria - Nigéria	2 587	45.3	-5.8	2 280	38.2	-11.9	..	..	..
Egypt - Égypte	1 793	27.7	-14.2	2 069	25.8	15.4	..	..	..
Pakistan	347	10.5	21.3	1 431	26.8	>200.0	2 689	35.9	87.9
Chile - Chili	938	16.7	1.4	1 068	15.8	13.9	1 117	14.4	4.6
Mexico - Mexique	1 094	6.0	0.8	880	4.4	-19.6	830	3.9	-5.7
Oman	525	24.1	42.0	817	29.6	55.6	..	..	..
Argentina - Argentine	654	11.5	6.5	815	12.3	24.5	872	11.4	7.0
Venezuela (Bolivarian Rep. of) - (Rép. bolivarienne du)	508	14.5	-19.9	690	15.3	35.8	641	12.3	-7.1

For sources and notes, see end of table.

Pour les sources et les notes, se reporter à la fin du tableau.

5.2   Trade in services by sector:
Leading importers among developing
economies

5.2   Commerce des services par secteurs :
Principaux importateurs parmi les
économies en développement

Ranking based on average 2004-2005 imports Classement d'après la moyenne des importations de 2004-2005	2003			2004			2005		
	Millions of dollars Millions de dollars	As % of country's total En % du total du pays	Annual change in % Variation annuelle en %	Millions of dollars Millions de dollars	As % of country's total En % du total du pays	Annual change in % Variation annuelle en %	Millions of dollars Millions de dollars	As % of country's total En % du total du pays	Annual change in % Variation annuelle en %
PERSONAL, CULTURAL AND RECREATIONAL SERVICES - SERVICES PERSONNELS, CULTURELS ET RELATIFS AUX LOISIRS									
Malaysia - Malaisie	2 922	16.7	4.7	1 899	10.0	-35.0	1 855	8.4	-2.4
Brazil - Brésil	337	2.2	9.0	409	2.4	21.5	451	1.9	10.4
Korea, Republic of - Corée, République de	261	0.6	-7.8	376	0.8	43.9	473	0.8	25.8
Singapore - Singapour	241	0.6	-9.2	267	0.5	11.0	278	0.5	4.1
China, Taiwan Province of - Chine, Taiwan Province de (5)	206	0.8	-5.1	238	0.8	15.5	301	0.9	26.5
Mexico - Mexique	221	1.2	-15.0	225	1.1	2.1	275	1.3	22.2
Indonesia - Indonésie	..	..	..	184	0.9	..	166	0.7	-9.8
Turkey - Turquie	117	1.6	-42.9	176	1.7	50.4	88	0.7	-50.0
China - Chine	70	0.1	-27.6	176	0.2	152.9	154	0.2	-12.4
Venezuela (Bolivarian Rep. of) - (Rép. bolivarienne du)	52	1.5	-10.3	165	3.7	>200.0	101	1.9	-38.8
Argentina - Argentine	108	1.9	14.0	140	2.1	28.8	153	2.0	9.5
Ecuador - Équateur	92	5.7	7.0	98	5.0	6.6	106	5.0	8.2
China, Hong Kong SAR - Chine, Hong Kong RAS	68	0.3	0.7	52	0.2	-24.6	..	..	..
Chile - Chili	47	0.8	7.3	52	0.8	9.1	56	0.7	8.2
Colombia - Colombie	29	0.9	4.2	31	0.8	6.1	44	0.9	40.5
Angola	11	0.3	-27.9	28	0.6	164.0	45	0.7	57.6
Mauritius - Maurice	14	1.5	45.2	21	2.1	54.3	31	2.5	43.4
Palestinian territory - Territoire palestinien	36	7.0	-6.3	16	3.2	-55.9	..	..	..
Egypt - Égypte	15	0.2	11.8	15	0.2	0.0	22	0.2	45.4
Philippines	15	0.3	-11.8	15	0.3	0.0	9	0.2	-40.0

Sources:
- International Monetary Fund (IMF), *Balance of Payments Statistics* on CD-ROM

Sources :
- Fonds monétaire international (FMI), *Statistiques de la balance des paiements*
  sur CD-ROM

Notes:

(1)   Excludes freight insurance, which is included with insurance services.
(2)   Includes goods and services acquired from an economy by non-resident travelers during visits shorter than one year.
(3)   Postal, courier and telecommunications services between residents and non-residents.
(4)   Includes merchanting and other trade-related services, operational leasing services, and miscellaneous business, professional and technical services.
(5)   National data sources.

Notes :

(1)   Non-compris l'assurance du fret, incluse dans la rubrique des services d'assurance.
(2)   Comprend les biens et services acquis dans une économie par les voyageurs non-résidents, au cours d'un séjour inférieur à un an.
(3)   Services postaux (y compris les messageries) et les services de télécommunication, entre résidents et non-résidents.
(4)   Y compris le négoce international et les autres services liés au commerce, la location-exploitation et divers services aux entreprises, spécialisés et techniques.
(5)   Données des sources nationales.

5

	1990	1995	2000	2001	2002	2003	2004	2005
				Afghanistan				
Arrivals of visitors (thousands)	8	..	..	..	..	..	..	..
Tourists' overnight stays (thousands)	..	..	..	..	..	..	..	..
Total expenditure of visitors (millions of dollars)	..	..	..	..	..	..	..	..
Expenditure excluding transport (millions of dollars)	..	..	..	..	..	..	..	..
				Albania - Albanie (1)				
Arrivées des visiteurs (milliers)	30	(d)304	(d)317	(d)354	(d)470	(d)557	(d)645	..
Nuitées des touristes (milliers)	..	..	..	..	..	..	..	..
Dépenses totales des visiteurs (millions de dollars)	..	70	398	451	492	537	756	880
Dépenses sans transport (millions de dollars)	4	65	389	446	487	522	735	854
				Algeria - Algérie				
Arrivals of visitors (thousands)	1 137	(d)520	(d)866	(d)901	(d)988	(d)1 166	(d)1 234	..
Tourists' overnight stays (thousands)	..	..	..	..	..	..	..	..
Total expenditure of visitors (millions of dollars)	150	32	102	100	110	112	178	..
Expenditure excluding transport (millions of dollars)	64	..	..	..	..	..	..	..
				American Samoa - Samoa américaines				
Arrivées des visiteurs (milliers)	26	(a)34	(a)44	(a)36	..	..	..	..
Nuitées des touristes (milliers)	..	..	..	..	..	..	..	..
Dépenses totales des visiteurs (millions de dollars)	..	..	..	..	..	..	..	..
Dépenses sans transport (millions de dollars)	..	..	..	..	..	..	..	..
				Andorra - Andorre				
Arrivals of visitors (thousands)	..	..	..	..	..	..	..	(a)2 418
Tourists' overnight stays (thousands)	..	..	..	..	..	..	..	..
Total expenditure of visitors (millions of dollars)	..	..	..	..	..	..	..	..
Expenditure excluding transport (millions of dollars)	..	..	..	..	..	..	..	..
				Angola				
Arrivées des visiteurs (milliers)	67	(a)9	(a)51	(a)67	(a)91	(a)107	(a)194	..
Nuitées des touristes (milliers)	..	..	77	112	207	217	149	..
Dépenses totales des visiteurs (millions de dollars)	27	27	34	36	51	63	82	..
Dépenses sans transport (millions de dollars)	13	10	18	22	37	49	66	..
				Anguilla				
Arrivals of visitors (thousands)	31	(a)39	(a)44	(a)48	(a)44	(a)47	(a)54	(a)62
Tourists' overnight stays (thousands)	..	366	377	411	369	399	410	..
Total expenditure of visitors (millions of dollars)	..	..	..	..	..	..	..	..
Expenditure excluding transport (millions of dollars)	36	50	56	62	57	60	69	..
				Antigua and Barbuda - Antigua-et-Barbuda				
Arrivées des visiteurs (milliers)	206	(a)220	(a)207	(a)193	(a)198	(a)224	(a)245	..
Nuitées des touristes (milliers)	..	..	..	..	..	..	..	..
Dépenses totales des visiteurs (millions de dollars)	273	..	..	..	..	..	..	..
Dépenses sans transport (millions de dollars)	231	247	291	272	274	300	337	..
				Argentina - Argentine				
Arrivals of visitors (thousands)	1 930	(a)2 289	(a)2 909	(a)2 620	(a)2 820	(a)2 995	(a)3 353	..
Tourists' overnight stays (thousands)	..	..	..	..	..	..	..	..
Total expenditure of visitors (millions of dollars)	1 292	2 550	3 195	2 756	1 716	2 306	2 990	..
Expenditure excluding transport (millions of dollars)	903	2 222	2 904	2 642	1 535	2 006	2 563	..
				Armenia - Arménie				
Arrivées des visiteurs (milliers)	—	(b)12	(b)45	(b)123	(b)162	(b)206	(b)263	..
Nuitées des touristes (milliers)	—	78	151	200	202	343	385	..
Dépenses totales des visiteurs (millions de dollars)	—	14	52	81	82	90	103	173
Dépenses sans transport (millions de dollars)	—	1	38	65	63	73	86	154
				Aruba				
Arrivals of visitors (thousands)	433	(a)619	(a)721	(a)691	(a)643	(a)642	(a)728	(a)733
Tourists' overnight stays (thousands)	3 380	4 473	5 248	5 145	4 863	5 098	5 640	5 695
Total expenditure of visitors (millions of dollars)	..	554	850	828	833	861	1 052	..
Expenditure excluding transport (millions of dollars)	349	521	814	824	832	861	1 052	1 096
				Australia - Australie				
Arrivées des visiteurs (milliers)	2 215	(d)3 726	(d)4 931	(d)4 856	(d)4 841	(d)4 746	(d)5 215	(d)5 497
Nuitées des touristes (milliers)	22 950	26 645	67 037	69 849	74 610	70 688	76 247	..
Dépenses totales des visiteurs (millions de dollars)	5 461	11 658	12 196	11 629	12 230	14 521	17 946	20 617
Dépenses sans transport (millions de dollars)	4 247	7 873	8 469	8 049	8 577	10 312	12 703	14 935

For sources and notes, see end of table.

Pour les sources et les notes, se reporter à la fin du tableau.

	1990	1995	2000	2001	2002	2003	2004	2005
				Austria - Autriche				
Arrivals of visitors (thousands)	19 011	(b)17 173	(b)17 982	(b)18 180	(b)18 611	(b)19 078	(b)19 373	(b)19 952
Tourists' overnight stays (thousands)	94 788	63 840	64 468	65 523	67 346	68 217	68 270	..
Total expenditure of visitors (millions of dollars)	..	14 529	11 483	12 033	13 047	16 342	18 401	19 311
Expenditure excluding transport (millions of dollars)	13 417	13 435	9 998	10 291	11 137	13 842	15 306	15 589
				Azerbaijan - Azerbaïdjan				
Arrivées des visiteurs (milliers)	–	(a)93	(a)681	(a)767	(a)834	(a)1 014	(a)1 349	..
Nuitées des touristes (milliers)	–	..	..	..	..	..	..	..
Dépenses totales des visiteurs (millions de dollars)	–	88	68	57	63	70	79	99
Dépenses sans transport (millions de dollars)	–	70	63	43	51	58	65	78
				Bahamas				
Arrivals of visitors (thousands)	1 562	(a)1 598	(a)1 544	(a)1 538	(a)1 513	(a)1 510	(a)1 561	..
Tourists' overnight stays (thousands)	8 963	9 031	9 048	8 973	8 704	8 957	9 898	..
Total expenditure of visitors (millions of dollars)	1 337	1 356	1 753	1 665	1 773	1 770	1 897	..
Expenditure excluding transport (millions of dollars)	1 324	1 346	1 738	1 648	1 760	1 757	1 884	2 072
				Bahrain - Bahreïn				
Arrivées des visiteurs (milliers)	1 376	(a)1 396	(a)2 420	(a)2 789	(a)3 167	(a)2 955	(a)3 514	..
Nuitées des touristes (milliers)	..	..	..	..	..	..	..	..
Dépenses totales des visiteurs (millions de dollars)	332	593	854	886	986	1 206	1 504	..
Dépenses sans transport (millions de dollars)	136	247	573	630	741	720	864	..
				Bangladesh				
Arrivals of visitors (thousands)	115	(a)156	(a)199	(a)207	(a)207	(a)245	(a)271	(a)208
Tourists' overnight stays (thousands)	..	..	..	..	..	..	..	..
Total expenditure of visitors (millions of dollars)	..	..	..	..	59	59	76	..
Expenditure excluding transport (millions of dollars)	19	25	50	48	57	57	67	70
				Barbados - Barbade				
Arrivées des visiteurs (milliers)	432	(a)442	(a)545	(a)507	(a)498	(a)531	(a)552	(a)547
Nuitées des touristes (milliers)	2 337	2 488	2 695	2 460	2 031	2 459	2 463	..
Dépenses totales des visiteurs (millions de dollars)	..	630	734	706	666	767	784	..
Dépenses sans transport (millions de dollars)	508	622	723	697	658	758	776	..
				Belarus - Bélarus				
Arrivals of visitors (thousands)	–	(a)161	(a)60	(a)61	(a)63	(a)64	(a)67	..
Tourists' overnight stays (thousands)	–	.	..	..	..	..	..	..
Total expenditure of visitors (millions of dollars)	–	28	188	272	295	339	379	344
Expenditure excluding transport (millions of dollars)	–	23	93	211	234	267	287	251
				Belgium - Belgique				
Arrivées des visiteurs (milliers)	–	–	–	–	(b)6 720	(ɔ)6 690	(b)6 710	..
Nuitées des touristes (milliers)	–	–	–	–	15 895	15 929	15 545	..
Dépenses totales des visiteurs (millions de dollars)	–	–	–	–	7 590	8 802	10 044	10 802
Dépenses sans transport (millions de dollars)	–	–	–	–	6 931	8 163	9 171	9 793
				Belgium-Luxembourg - Belgique-Luxembourg				
Arrivals of visitors (thousands)	5 967	(b)6 328	(b)7 309	(b)7 288	–	–	–	–
Tourists' overnight stays (thousands)	15 316	16 256	17 934	17 795	–	–	–	–
Total expenditure of visitors (millions of dollars)	..	..	..	..	–	–	–	–
Expenditure excluding transport (millions of dollars)	..	6 243	8 278	8 683	–	–	–	–
				Belize				
Arrivées des visiteurs (milliers)	88	(a)131	(a)196	(a)196	(a)200	(a)221	(a)231	..
Nuitées des touristes (milliers)	..	..	..	..	..	..	..	..
Dépenses totales des visiteurs (millions de dollars)	38	..	..	..	..	..	..	..
Dépenses sans transport (millions de dollars)	38	78	116	103	103	117	133	..
				Benin - Bénin				
Arrivals of visitors (thousands)	110	(a)138	(a)96	(a)88	(a)72	(a)175	(a)174	..
Tourists' overnight stays (thousands)	406	314	200	190	144	219	215	..
Total expenditure of visitors (millions of dollars)	..	..	77	86	95	108	..	..
Expenditure excluding transport (millions of dollars)	55	85	77	85	93	106	..	..
				Bermuda - Bermudes				
Arrivées des visiteurs (milliers)	435	(a)387	(a)332	(a)278	(a)284	(a)257	(a)272	(a)270
Nuitées des touristes (milliers)	2 739	2 421	1 966	1 775	1 822	1 598	1 733	..
Dépenses totales des visiteurs (millions de dollars)	..	438	431	351	378	342	354	393
Dépenses sans transport (millions de dollars)	..	..	..	..	..	..	..	..

For sources and notes, see end of table.   Pour les sources et les notes, se reporter à la fin du tableau.

	1990	1995	2000	2001	2002	2003	2004	2005
				Bhutan - Bhoutan				
Arrivals of visitors (thousands)	2	(a)5	(a)8	(a)6	(a)6	(a)6	(a)9	(a)14
Tourists' overnight stays (thousands)	..	..	..	..	..	..	..	..
Total expenditure of visitors (millions of dollars)	..	5	10	9	8	8	13	19
Expenditure excluding transport (millions of dollars)	..	..	..	..	..	..	..	..
				Bolivia - Bolivie				
Arrivées des visiteurs (milliers)	254	(a)284	(a)319	(a)316	(a)334	(a)370	(a)405	..
Nuitées des touristes (milliers)	..	..	..	..	..	..	..	..
Dépenses totales des visiteurs (millions de dollars)	79	92	101	119	144	244	265	..
Dépenses sans transport (millions de dollars)	58	55	68	76	101	167	177	..
				Bosnia and Herzegovina - Bosnie-Herzégovine				
Arrivals of visitors (thousands)	—	..	..	..	..	..	..	..
Tourists' overnight stays (thousands)	—	..	..	..	..	..	..	..
Total expenditure of visitors (millions of dollars)	—	..	..	..	..	..	..	604
Expenditure excluding transport (millions of dollars)	—	..	..	..	..	..	..	565
				Botswana				
Arrivées des visiteurs (milliers)	543	(a)521	(a)1 104	(a)1 049	(a)1 037	(a)975	..	..
Nuitées des touristes (milliers)	..	..	..	..	..	..	..	..
Dépenses totales des visiteurs (millions de dollars)	129	176	227	235	324	459	..	..
Dépenses sans transport (millions de dollars)	117	162	222	230	319	457	549	..
				Brazil - Brésil				
Arrivals of visitors (thousands)	1 091	(a)1 991	(a)5 313	(a)4 773	(a)3 785	(a)4 133	(a)4 794	(a)5 358
Tourists' overnight stays (thousands)	..	..	..	..	..	..	..	..
Total expenditure of visitors (millions of dollars)	1 415	1 085	1 969	1 845	2 142	2 673	3 389	4 169
Expenditure excluding transport (millions of dollars)	1 383	972	1 810	1 731	1 998	2 479	3 222	3 861
				British Virgin Islands - Îles Vierges britanniques				
Arrivées des visiteurs (milliers)	160	(a)219	(a)272	(a)296	(a)282	(a)318	(a)305	(a)337
Nuitées des touristes (milliers)	..	..	117	106	105	..	..	..
Dépenses totales des visiteurs (millions de dollars)	..	211	345	374	357	425	391	..
Dépenses sans transport (millions de dollars)	..	..	..	..	..	..	..	..
				Brunei Darussalam - Brunéi Darussalam				
Arrivals of visitors (thousands)	377	(d)498	(d)984	(d)840	..	..	..	(d)815
Tourists' overnight stays (thousands)	..	..	..	..	..	..	..	..
Total expenditure of visitors (millions of dollars)	..	..	..	..	..	..	..	..
Expenditure excluding transport (millions of dollars)	..	..	..	..	..	..	..	..
				Bulgaria - Bulgarie				
Arrivées des visiteurs (milliers)	1 586	(a)3 466	(a)2 785	(a)3 186	(a)3 433	(a)4 048	(a)4 630	(a)4 837
Nuitées des touristes (milliers)	12 759	5 438	5 170	6 190	7 055	9 142	10 303	11 624
Dépenses totales des visiteurs (millions de dollars)	..	662	1 364	1 223	1 466	2 106	2 718	3 026
Dépenses sans transport (millions de dollars)	320	473	1 074	963	1 154	1 658	2 140	2 383
				Burkina Faso				
Arrivals of visitors (thousands)	74	(c)124	(c)126	(c)128	(c)150	(c)163	(c)222	..
Tourists' overnight stays (thousands)	..	..	..	..	..	..	..	..
Total expenditure of visitors (millions of dollars)	15	..	23	25	..	..	..	..
Expenditure excluding transport (millions of dollars)	11	..	19	20	..	..	..	..
				Burundi				
Arrivées des visiteurs (milliers)	109	(a)34	(a)29	(a)36	..	..	..	..
Nuitées des touristes (milliers)	..	..	..	..	..	..	..	..
Dépenses totales des visiteurs (millions de dollars)	5	2	1	1	2	1	..	..
Dépenses sans transport (millions de dollars)	3	1	1	1	1	1	..	..
				Cambodia - Cambodge				
Arrivals of visitors (thousands)	17	(a)220	(a)466	(a)605	(a)787	(a)701	(a)1 055	(a)1 422
Tourists' overnight stays (thousands)	..	..	..	..	..	..	..	..
Total expenditure of visitors (millions of dollars)	..	71	345	429	509	441	674	..
Expenditure excluding transport (millions of dollars)	..	53	304	380	454	389	604	..
				Cameroon - Cameroun				
Arrivées des visiteurs (milliers)	89	(c)100	(c)277	(c)221	(c)226	..	(c)190	..
Nuitées des touristes (milliers)	..	..	..	..	..	..	..	..
Dépenses totales des visiteurs (millions de dollars)	97	75	39	..	..	..	..	..
Dépenses sans transport (millions de dollars)	53	36	..	..	..	..	..	..

For sources and notes, see end of table.   Pour les sources et les notes, se reporter à la fin du tableau.

	1990	1995	2000	2001	2002	2003	2004	2005
Canada								
Arrivals of visitors (thousands)	15 209	(a)16 932	(a)19 627	(a)19 679	(a)20 057	(a)17 534	(a)19 095	..
Tourists' overnight stays (thousands)	82 177	91 983	119 381	125 022	122 150	107 698	121 595	..
Total expenditure of visitors (millions of dollars)	7 391	9 176	13 035	12 680	12 748	12 236	14 925	15 842
Expenditure excluding transport (millions of dollars)	6 360	7 917	10 778	10 623	10 691	10 602	12 817	13 615
Cape Verde - Cap-Vert								
Arrivées des visiteurs (milliers)	24	(a)28	(a)115	(a)134	(a)126	(a)150	(a)157	(a)198
Nuitées des touristes (milliers)	..	..	..	..	..	..	..	..
Dépenses totales des visiteurs (millions de dollars)	10	29	64	77	101	137	..	..
Dépenses sans transport (millions de dollars)	6	10	41	54	66	85	125	..
Cayman Islands - Îles Caïmanes								
Arrivals of visitors (thousands)	253	(a)361	(a)354	(a)334	(a)303	(a)294	(a)260	(a)168
Tourists' overnight stays (thousands)	..	..	..	..	..	..	..	..
Total expenditure of visitors (millions of dollars)	..	394	559	585	607	518	519	..
Expenditure excluding transport (millions of dollars)	..	..	..	..	..	..	..	..
Central African Republic - République centrafricaine								
Arrivées des visiteurs (milliers)	6	(a)26	(a)11	(a)10	(a)3	(a)6	(a)8	..
Nuitées des touristes (milliers)	..	..	..	..	..	..	..	..
Dépenses totales des visiteurs (millions de dollars)	..	4	5	5	3	4	4	..
Dépenses sans transport (millions de dollars)	3	..	..	..	..	..	..	..
Chad - Tchad								
Arrivals of visitors (thousands)	9	(c)19	(c)43	(c)57	(c)32	(c)21	..	..
Tourists' overnight stays (thousands)	..	..	..	..	..	..	..	..
Total expenditure of visitors (millions of dollars)	12	43	14	23	25	..	..	..
Expenditure excluding transport (millions of dollars)	8	..	..	..	..	..	..	..
Chile - Chili								
Arrivées des visiteurs (milliers)	943	(a)1 540	(a)1 742	(a)1 723	(a)1 412	(a)1 614	(a)1 785	(a)2 027
Nuitées des touristes (milliers)	..	..	..	..	..	..	..	..
Dépenses totales des visiteurs (millions de dollars)	666	1 186	1 179	1 184	1 221	1 241	1 554	1 779
Dépenses sans transport (millions de dollars)	531	911	819	799	898	859	1 091	1 256
China - Chine								
Arrivals of visitors (thousands)	10 484	(a)20 034	(a)31 229	(a)33 167	(a)36 803	(a)32 970	(a)41 761	..
Tourists' overnight stays (thousands)	..	..	..	..	..	..	..	..
Total expenditure of visitors (millions of dollars)	2 218	..	17 318	19 006	21 742	18 708	27 755	..
Expenditure excluding transport (millions of dollars)	1 738	8 730	16 231	17 792	20 385	17 406	25 739	..
China, Hong Kong SAR - Chine, Hong Kong RAS								
Arrivées des visiteurs (milliers)	6 581	(d)10 200	(d)13 059	(d)13 725	(d)16 566	(d)15 537	(d)21 811	(d)23 359
Nuitées des touristes (milliers)	..	..	..	..	..	..	..	..
Dépenses totales des visiteurs (millions de dollars)	..	..	8 198	7 924	9 850	9 020	11 893	13 586
Dépenses sans transport (millions de dollars)	..	9 604	5 868	5 905	7 411	7 084	8 932	10 209
China, Macao SAR - Chine, Macao RAS								
Arrivals of visitors (thousands)	2 513	(a)4 202	(a)5 197	(a)5 842	(a)6 565	(a)6 309	(a)8 324	(a)9 014
Tourists' overnight stays (thousands)	..	..	..	..	..	..	..	..
Total expenditure of visitors (millions of dollars)	..	3 233	3 205	3 745	4 440	5 303	7 344	..
Expenditure excluding transport (millions of dollars)	..	..	..	..	4 306	5 155	7 479	..
China, Taiwan Province of - Chine, Taiwan Province de								
Arrivées des visiteurs (milliers)	1 934	(d)2 332	(d)2 624	(d)2 831	(d)2 978	(d)2 248	(d)2 950	(d)3 378
Nuitées des touristes (milliers)	12 494	14 834	16 487	16 987	16 856	14 461	18 838	20 593
Dépenses totales des visiteurs (millions de dollars)	..	..	4 253	4 849	5 077	3 578	4 670	..
Dépenses sans transport (millions de dollars)	..	3 286	3 738	4 335	4 583	2 977	4 054	4 977
Colombia - Colombie								
Arrivals of visitors (thousands)	813	(d)1 433	(d)557	(d)616	(c)567	(d)625	(d)791	..
Tourists' overnight stays (thousands)	..	..	..	..	..	..	..	..
Total expenditure of visitors (millions of dollars)	574	887	1 313	1 483	1 237	1 167	1 340	1 570
Expenditure excluding transport (millions of dollars)	406	657	1 030	1 217	967	869	1 032	1 218
Comoros - Comores								
Arrivées des visiteurs (milliers)	8	(a)23	(a)24	(a)19	(a)19	(a)14	(a)18	..
Nuitées des touristes (milliers)	..	181	161	135	133	123	123	..
Dépenses totales des visiteurs (millions de dollars)	3	22	15	9	11	8	10	..
Dépenses sans transport (millions de dollars)	2	21	..	..	..	..	..	..

For sources and notes, see end of table.   Pour les sources et les notes, se reporter à la fin du tableau.

	1990	1995	2000	2001	2002	2003	2004	2005
				Congo				
Arrivals of visitors (thousands)	33	(c)37	(c)19	(c)27	(c)22	..	..	..
Tourists' overnight stays (thousands)	..	..	..	..	..	..	..	..
Total expenditure of visitors (millions of dollars)	..	15	12	23	26	..	..	..
Expenditure excluding transport (millions of dollars)	8	14	12	22	25	20		..
				Cook Islands - Îles Cook				
Arrivées des visiteurs (milliers)	34	(a)48	(a)73	(a)75	(a)73	(a)78	(a)83	(a)88
Nuitées des touristes (milliers)	..	..	..	..	..	..	..	..
Dépenses totales des visiteurs (millions de dollars)	..	28	36	38	46	69	72	92
Dépenses sans transport (millions de dollars)	..	..	..	..	..	..	..	..
				Costa Rica				
Arrivals of visitors (thousands)	435	(a)785	(a)1 088	(a)1 131	(a)1 113	(a)1 239	(a)1 453	..
Tourists' overnight stays (thousands)	..	..	..	..	..	..	..	..
Total expenditure of visitors (millions of dollars)	330	763	1 477	1 339	1 292	1 424	1 585	..
Expenditure excluding transport (millions of dollars)	285	681	1 302	1 173	1 161	1 293	1 459	..
				Côte d'Ivoire				
Arrivées des visiteurs (milliers)	196	(a)188	..	..	..	..	..	..
Nuitées des touristes (milliers)	..	..	..	..	..	..	..	..
Dépenses totales des visiteurs (millions de dollars)	55	103	53	58	56	76	..	..
Dépenses sans transport (millions de dollars)	51	89	49	53	51	69	76	..
				Croatia - Croatie				
Arrivals of visitors (thousands)	–	(b)1 485	(b)5 831	(b)6 544	(b)6 944	(b)7 409	(b)7 912	(b)8 467
Tourists' overnight stays (thousands)	–	8 763	34 045	38 384	39 711	41 323	42 516	45 987
Total expenditure of visitors (millions of dollars)	–	..	2 871	3 463	3 953	6 581	7 191	7 625
Expenditure excluding transport (millions of dollars)	–	1 349	2 758	3 335	3 812	6 377	6 973	7 370
				Cuba				
Arrivées des visiteurs (milliers)	327	(a)742	(a)1 741	(a)1 736	(a)1 656	(a)1 847	(a)2 017	..
Nuitées des touristes (milliers)	3 703	6 394	11 557	11 250	10 486	12 684	15 041	..
Dépenses totales des visiteurs (millions de dollars)	..	963	1 737	1 692	1 633	1 846	1 915	..
Dépenses sans transport (millions de dollars)	..	..	..	..	..	..	..	..
				Cyprus - Chypre				
Arrivals of visitors (thousands)	1 561	(a)2 100	(a)2 686	(a)2 697	(a)2 418	(a)2 303	(a)2 349	(a)2 470
Tourists' overnight stays (thousands)	9 426	14 222	16 816	18 093	15 289	13 490	13 637	14 006
Total expenditure of visitors (millions of dollars)	1 440	2 018	2 137	2 203	2 146	2 244	2 564	2 643
Expenditure excluding transport (millions of dollars)	1 254	1 798	1 941	1 993	1 927	2 016	2 253	2 318
				Czech Republic - République tchèque				
Arrivées des visiteurs (milliers)	–	(b)3 381	(b)4 666	(b)5 194	(b)4 579	(b)5 076	(b)6 061	..
Nuitées des touristes (milliers)	–	10 327	15 831	16 564	14 589	16 511	18 980	..
Dépenses totales des visiteurs (millions de dollars)	–	..	..	..	3 376	4 069	4 956	..
Dépenses sans transport (millions de dollars)	–	2 880	2 973	3 104	2 964	3 566	4 183	..
				Dem. Rep. of the Congo - Rép. dém. du Congo				
Arrivals of visitors (thousands)	55	(a)35	(a)103	(a)55	(a)28	(a)35	..	..
Tourists' overnight stays (thousands)	..	120	46	175	163	150	..	..
Total expenditure of visitors (millions of dollars)	..	..	..	..	..	..	..	..
Expenditure excluding transport (millions of dollars)	..	..	..	..	..	..	..	..
				Denmark - Danemark (2)				
Arrivées des visiteurs (milliers)	1 838	(b)2 124	(b)3 535	(b)3 684	(b)3 436	(b)3 474	(b)3 358	..
Nuitées des touristes (milliers)	9 338	10 790	26 280	25 456	25 663	26 152	24 560	..
Dépenses totales des visiteurs (millions de dollars)	3 471	..	..	..	..	..	..	..
Dépenses sans transport (millions de dollars)	3 338	3 691	3 671	4 003	4 791	5 271	5 652	..
				Djibouti				
Arrivals of visitors (thousands)	33	(c)21	(c)20	(c)22	(c)23	(c)23	(c)26	..
Tourists' overnight stays (thousands)	..	..	..	..	..	..	..	..
Total expenditure of visitors (millions of dollars)	..	6	..	..	..	..	..	..
Expenditure excluding transport (millions of dollars)	..	4	..	..	..	7	7	..
				Dominica - Dominique				
Arrivées des visiteurs (milliers)	45	(a)60	(a)70	(a)66	(a)69	(a)73	(a)79	..
Nuitées des touristes (milliers)	..	..	..	..	..	..	..	..
Dépenses totales des visiteurs (millions de dollars)	..	..	..	..	..	..	..	..
Dépenses sans transport (millions de dollars)	20	42	48	46	46	52	60	..

For sources and notes, see end of table.   Pour les sources et les notes, se reporter à la fin du tableau.

	1990	1995	2000	2001	2002	2003	2004	2005
Dominican Republic - République dominicaine								
Arrivals of visitors (thousands)	1 305	(a)1 776	(a)2 978	(a)2 882	(a)2 811	(a)3 282	(a)3 450	(a)3 691
Tourists' overnight stays (thousands)	..	..	..	..	..	..	..	..
Total expenditure of visitors (millions of dollars)	..	..	..	..	..	..	..	..
Expenditure excluding transport (millions of dollars)	726	1 571	2 860	2 798	2 730	3 128	3 152	3 508
Ecuador - Équateur								
Arrivées des visiteurs (milliers)	362	(d)440	(d)627	(d)641	(d)683	(d)761	(d)819	..
Nuitées des touristes (milliers)	..	..	..	..	..	..	..	..
Dépenses totales des visiteurs (millions de dollars)	266	315	451	438	449	408	369	..
Dépenses sans transport (millions de dollars)	188	255	402	430	447	406	367	..
Egypt - Égypte								
Arrivals of visitors (thousands)	2 411	(a)2 871	(a)5 116	(a)4 357	(a)4 906	(a)5 746	(a)7 795	..
Tourists' overnight stays (thousands)	..	.	..	..	..	..	..	..
Total expenditure of visitors (millions of dollars)	1 530	2 954	4 657	4 119	4 133	4 704	6 328	..
Expenditure excluding transport (millions of dollars)	1 100	2 684	4 345	3 800	3 764	4 584	6 125	..
El Salvador								
Arrivées des visiteurs (milliers)	194	(a)235	(a)795	(a)735	(a)951	(a)857	(a)966	(a)1 154
Nuitées des touristes (milliers)	..	..	..	..	..	..	..	..
Dépenses totales des visiteurs (millions de dollars)	130	152	437	452	521	569	632	..
Dépenses sans transport (millions de dollars)	76	85	217	201	245	288	337	..
Eritrea - Érythrée								
Arrivals of visitors (thousands)	–	(d)315	(d)70	(d)113	(d)101	(d)80	(d)87	..
Tourists' overnight stays (thousands)	–	..	..	..	..	..	..	..
Total expenditure of visitors (millions of dollars)	–	58	36	74	73	..	73	..
Expenditure excluding transport (millions of dollars)	–	2	35			..		..
Estonia - Estonie								
Arrivées des visiteurs (milliers)	–	(a)530	(a)1 220	(a)1 320	(a)1 362	(a)1 462	(a)1 750	..
Nuitées des touristes (milliers)	–	789	1 598	1 911	1 998	2 268	2 747	2 982
Dépenses totales des visiteurs (millions de dollars)	–	452	654	661	737	881	1 102	1 194
Dépenses sans transport (millions de dollars)	–	357	505	507	555	669	878	935
Ethiopia - Éthiopie								
Arrivals of visitors (thousands)	–	(a)103	(a)136	(a)148	(a)156	(a)180	(a)210	..
Tourists' overnight stays (thousands)	–	..	..	..	..	..	..	..
Total expenditure of visitors (millions of dollars)	–	177	205	218	261	336	457	..
Expenditure excluding transport (millions of dollars)	–	16	57	51	72	114	173	..
Ethiopia (former) - Éthiopie (anc.)								
Arrivées des visiteurs (milliers)	79	–	–	–	–	–	–	–
Nuitées des touristes (milliers)	..	–	–	–	–	–	–	–
Dépenses totales des visiteurs (millions de dollars)	143	–	–	–	–	–	–	–
Dépenses sans transport (millions de dollars)	5	–	–	–	–	–	–	–
Fiji - Fidji								
Arrivals of visitors (thousands)	279	(a)318	(a)294	(a)348	(a)398	(a)431	(a)499	(a)550
Tourists' overnight stays (thousands)	..	..	..	..	..	..	..	..
Total expenditure of visitors (millions of dollars)	271	369	..	..	..	521	575	..
Expenditure excluding transport (millions of dollars)	200	291	182	197	254	337	414	431
Finland - Finlande								
Arrivées des visiteurs (milliers)	1 572	(b)1 779	(a)2 714	(a)2 826	(a)2 875	(a)2 601	(a)2 840	..
Nuitées des touristes (milliers)	2 830	3 292	4 066	4 183	4 290	4 331	4 383	..
Dépenses totales des visiteurs (millions de dollars)	1 742	2 384	2 035	2 066	2 242	2 677	2 867	..
Dépenses sans transport (millions de dollars)	1 179	1 641	1 406	1 438	1 578	1 870	2 050	..
France								
Arrivals of visitors (thousands)	53 555	(a)61 667	(a)79 049	(a)76 877	(a)78 148	(a)76 607	(a)76 728	(a)76 485
Tourists' overnight stays (thousands)	393 511	501 687	592 399	586 593	594 452	573 142	568 064	566 927
Total expenditure of visitors (millions of dollars)	23 856	32 353	..	..	..	..	..	..
Expenditure excluding transport (millions of dollars)	20 270	27 587	30 981	30 363	32 437	36 617	40 686	42 170
French Polynesia - Polynésie française								
Arrivées des visiteurs (milliers)	132	(a)172	(a)252	(a)228	(a)189	(a)213	(a)212	(a)208
Nuitées des touristes (milliers)	1 399	2 067	..	2 875	2 592	2 888	2 861	2 787
Dépenses totales des visiteurs (millions de dollars)	..	326	..	..	471	651	767	..
Dépenses sans transport (millions de dollars)	..	..	..	..	372	480	553	..

For sources and notes, see end of table.   Pour les sources et les notes, se reporter à la fin du tableau.

	1990	1995	2000	2001	2002	2003	2004	2005
Gabon								
Arrivals of visitors (thousands)	109	(a)125	(a)155	(a)169	(a)208	(a)222	..	..
Tourists' overnight stays (thousands)	..	..	..	..	..	..	..	..
Total expenditure of visitors (millions of dollars)	33	94	99	46	77	84	..	..
Expenditure excluding transport (millions of dollars)	3	17	20	15	18	15	..	..
Gambia - Gambie								
Arrivées des visiteurs (milliers)	100	(a)45	(a)79	(a)57	(a)81	(a)73	(a)90	..
Nuitées des touristes (milliers)	..	..	..	..	..	..	..	..
Dépenses totales des visiteurs (millions de dollars)	..	..	..	48	48	51	59	..
Dépenses sans transport (millions de dollars)	46	28	..	..	..	..	..	..
Georgia - Géorgie								
Arrivals of visitors (thousands)	—	..	..	..	..	..	..	..
Tourists' overnight stays (thousands)	—	..	..	..	..	..	..	..
Total expenditure of visitors (millions of dollars)	—	..	..	..	..	..	..	284
Expenditure excluding transport (millions of dollars)	—	..	..	..	..	..	..	239
Germany - Allemagne								
Arrivées des visiteurs (milliers)	17 045	(b)14 847	(b)18 983	(b)17 861	(b)17 969	(b)18 399	(b)20 137	..
Nuitées des touristes (milliers)	39 146	35 481	42 629	40 798	40 655	41 746	45 374	..
Dépenses totales des visiteurs (millions de dollars)	19 502	24 052	24 943	24 175	26 680	30 149	35 589	38 381
Dépenses sans transport (millions de dollars)	14 330	18 036	18 611	18 031	19 278	23 125	27 601	29 151
Ghana								
Arrivals of visitors (thousands)	146	(a)286	(a)399	(a)439	(a)483	(a)531	(a)584	..
Tourists' overnight stays (thousands)	..	2 906	..	..	..	..	..	..
Total expenditure of visitors (millions of dollars)	15	30	357	374	383	441	495	..
Expenditure excluding transport (millions of dollars)	4	11	335	351	358	414	466	..
Greece - Grèce								
Arrivées des visiteurs (milliers)	8 873	(a)10 130	(a)13 096	(a)14 057	(a)14 180	(a)13 969	..	..
Nuitées des touristes (milliers)	..	38 227	47 024	42 494	40 953	40 407	38 796	..
Dépenses totales des visiteurs (millions de dollars)	2 617	4 182	9 262	9 216	10 005	10 842	12 809	..
Dépenses sans transport (millions de dollars)	2 587	4 135	9 219	9 155	9 909	10 766	12 715	..
Grenada - Grenade								
Arrivals of visitors (thousands)	76	(a)108	(a)129	(a)123	(ε)132	(a)142	(a)134	..
Tourists' overnight stays (thousands)	..	..	626	..	..	..	..	..
Total expenditure of visitors (millions of dollars)	..	..	..	..	..	..	..	..
Expenditure excluding transport (millions of dollars)	50	76	93	84	92	104	92	..
Guam								
Arrivées des visiteurs (milliers)	780	(a)1 362	(a)1 287	(a)1 159	(a)1 059	(a)910	(a)1 157	..
Nuitées des touristes (milliers)	..	..	..	..	..	..	..	..
Dépenses totales des visiteurs (millions de dollars)	..	..	..	..	..	..	..	..
Dépenses sans transport (millions de dollars)	..	..	..	..	..	..	..	..
Guatemala								
Arrivals of visitors (thousands)	509	(a)563	(a)826	(a)835	(a)884	(a)880	(a)1 182	(a)1 316
Tourists' overnight stays (thousands)	3 201	3 674	..	..	..	..	..	..
Total expenditure of visitors (millions of dollars)	..	216	498	588	647	646	806	..
Expenditure excluding transport (millions of dollars)	118	213	482	562	620	621	776	869
Guyana								
Arrivées des visiteurs (milliers)	64	(a)106	(a)105	(a)99	(a)104	(a)101	(a)122	(a)117
Nuitées des touristes (milliers)	..	..	..	..	..	..	..	..
Dépenses totales des visiteurs (millions de dollars)	..	..	80	65	53	28	30	..
Dépenses sans transport (millions de dollars)	..	33	75	61	49	26	28	..
Haiti - Haïti								
Arrivals of visitors (thousands)	144	(a)145	(a)140	(a)142	(a)140	(a)136	(a)96	..
Tourists' overnight stays (thousands)	1 150	968	..	..	..	..	..	..
Total expenditure of visitors (millions of dollars)	37	..	..	..	..	..	..	..
Expenditure excluding transport (millions of dollars)	34	90	128	105	112	93	..	..
Honduras								
Arrivées des visiteurs (milliers)	290	(a)271	(a)471	(a)518	(a)550	(a)611	(a)672	..
Nuitées des touristes (milliers)	..	..	..	..	..	..	..	..
Dépenses totales des visiteurs (millions de dollars)	44	85	263	260	305	358	403	..
Dépenses sans transport (millions de dollars)	29	80	260	256	301	350	396	..

For sources and notes, see end of table.   Pour les sources et les notes, se reporter à la fin du tableau.

	1990	1995	2000	2001	2002	2003	2004	2005
	Hungary - Hongrie							
Arrivals of visitors (thousands)	3 693	(b)2 878	(b)2 992	(b)3 070	(b)3 013	(b)2 948	(b)3 270	..
Tourists' overnight stays (thousands)	13 618	9 998	10 514	10 894	10 361	10 040	10 508	..
Total expenditure of visitors (millions of dollars)	..	2 938	3 809	4 191	3 774	4 119	4 084	4 581
Expenditure excluding transport (millions of dollars)	985	2 928	3 733	4 154	3 728	4 061	4 034	4 279
	Iceland - Islande							
Arrivées des visiteurs (milliers)	142	..	(b)634	(b)672	(b)705	(b)771	(b)836	(b)871
Nuitées des touristes (milliers)	..	815	1 142	1 184	1 257	1 377	1 479	1 550
Dépenses totales des visiteurs (millions de dollars)	234	309	386	383	415	486	558	630
Dépenses sans transport (millions de dollars)	152	186	227	232	256	319	370	408
	India - Inde							
Arrivals of visitors (thousands)	1 707	(a)2 124	(a)2 649	(a)2 537	(a)2 384	(a)2 726	(a)3 457	(a)3 915
Tourists' overnight stays (thousands)	..	..	..	..	..	..	..	..
Total expenditure of visitors (millions of dollars)	..	..	3 718	3 497	3 476	4 128		..
Expenditure excluding transport (millions of dollars)	1 558	2 582	3 460	3 198	3 102	3 887	..	..
	Indonesia - Indonésie							
Arrivées des visiteurs (milliers)	2 178	(a)4 324	(a)5 064	(a)5 153	(a)5 033	(a)4 467	(a)5 321	(a)5 002
Nuitées des touristes (milliers)	..	44 151	62 087	54 062	..	..	..	..
Dépenses totales des visiteurs (millions de dollars)	..	..	..	..	5 797	4 461	5 226	..
Dépenses sans transport (millions de dollars)	2 153	5 229	4 975	5 277	5 285	4 037	4 798	4 522
	Iran, Islamic Republic of - Iran, Rép. islamique d'							
Arrivals of visitors (thousands)	154	(a)489	(a)1 342	(a)1 402	(a)1 585	(a)1 546	(a)1 659	..
Tourists' overnight stays (thousands)	..	..	..	..	..	..	..	..
Total expenditure of visitors (millions of dollars)	64	205	677	1 122	1 607	1 266	1 324	..
Expenditure excluding transport (millions of dollars)	28	67	467	891	1 357	1 033	1 074	..
	Iraq							
Arrivées des visiteurs (milliers)	748	(d)61	(d)78	(d)127	..	..	..	..
Nuitées des touristes (milliers)	..	..	..	..	..	..	..	..
Dépenses totales des visiteurs (millions de dollars)	..	..	..	..	..	..	..	..
Dépenses sans transport (millions de dollars)	..	18	2	15	45	..	..	..
	Ireland - Irlande							
Arrivals of visitors (thousands)	3 666	(a)4 818	(a)6 646	(a)6 353	(a)6 476	(a)6 764	(a)6 982	..
Tourists' overnight stays (thousands)	36 183	13 902	21 516	18 332	17 677	..	..	..
Total expenditure of visitors (millions of dollars)	1 897	2 698	3 517	3 789	4 229	5 206	5 962	6 555
Expenditure excluding transport (millions of dollars)	1 459	2 211	2 615	2 791	3 098	3 862	4 262	4 549
	Israel - Israël							
Arrivées des visiteurs (milliers)	1 063	(a)2 215	(a)2 417	(a)1 196	(a)862	(a)1 063	(a)1 506	(a)1 903
Nuitées des touristes (milliers)	6 167	10 084	10 352	4 637	2 745	3 438	5 040	..
Dépenses totales des visiteurs (millions de dollars)	1 757	3 491	4 585	2 769	2 325	2 401	2 813	3 425
Dépenses sans transport (millions de dollars)	1 396	2 993	4 088	2 475	2 044	2 060	2 380	2 842
	Italy - Italie							
Arrivals of visitors (thousands)	26 679	(a)31 052	(a)41 181	(a)39 563	(a)39 799	(a)39 604	(a)37 071	(a)36 513
Tourists' overnight stays (thousands)	84 720	113 001	140 357	146 672	145 560	139 653	141 169	..
Total expenditure of visitors (millions of dollars)	18 300	30 426	28 706	26 916	28 192	32 592	37 872	38 694
Expenditure excluding transport (millions of dollars)	16 460	28 731	27 493	25 822	26 873	31 247	35 378	35 745
	Jamaica - Jamaïque							
Arrivées des visiteurs (milliers)	989	(a)1 147	(a)1 323	(a)1 277	(a)1 266	(a)1 350	(a)1 415	(a)1 479
Nuitées des touristes (milliers)	9 194	11 107	12 327	12 109	12 038	12 844	13 134	..
Dépenses totales des visiteurs (millions de dollars)	869	1 199	1 577	1 494	1 482	1 621	1 733	..
Dépenses sans transport (millions de dollars)	751	1 069	1 333	1 232	1 209	1 355	1 438	..
	Japan - Japon							
Arrivals of visitors (thousands)	3 236	(a)3 345	(a)4 757	(a)4 772	(a)5 239	(a)5 212	(a)6 138	(a)6 728
Tourists' overnight stays (thousands)	..	..	..	..	..	..	..	..
Total expenditure of visitors (millions of dollars)	..	4 894	5 970	5 750	6 069	11 476	14 343	15 554
Expenditure excluding transport (millions of dollars)	..	3 224	3 373	3 306	3 497	8 849	11 265	12 430
	Jordan - Jordanie							
Arrivées des visiteurs (milliers)	572	(a)1 075	(a)1 580	(a)1 672	(a)2 384	(a)2 353	(a)2 853	(a)2 987
Nuitées des touristes (milliers)	..	..	..	..	..	..	..	..
Dépenses totales des visiteurs (millions de dollars)	788	973	935	884	1 254	1 266	1 621	1 759
Dépenses sans transport (millions de dollars)	511	660	723	700	1 048	1 062	1 330	1 441

For sources and notes, see end of table.   Pour les sources et les notes, se reporter à la fin du tableau.

	1990	1995	2000	2001	2002	2003	2004	2005
Kazakhstan								
Arrivals of visitors (thousands)	–	..	..	..	..	..	..	..
Tourists' overnight stays (thousands)	–	..	..	..	..	..	..	..
Total expenditure of visitors (millions of dollars)	–	..	..	..	..	..	..	792
Expenditure excluding transport (millions of dollars)	–	..	..	..	..	..	..	685
Kenya								
Arrivées des visiteurs (milliers)	814	(a)896	(a)899	(a)841	(a)838	(a)927	(a)1 199	..
Nuitées des touristes (milliers)	..	..	..	..	..	..	..	..
Dépenses totales des visiteurs (millions de dollars)	578	590	500	536	513	611	808	..
Dépenses sans transport (millions de dollars)	465	486	283	309	276	339	495	..
Kiribati								
Arrivals of visitors (thousands)	3	(a)4	(a)5	(a)5	(a)5	(a)5	(a)3	..
Tourists' overnight stays (thousands)	..	..	..	..	..	..	..	..
Total expenditure of visitors (millions of dollars)	2	2	3	3	..	..	..	..
Expenditure excluding transport (millions of dollars)	1	..	..	..	..	..	..	..
Korea, Dem. People's Rep. of - Corée, Rép. populaire dém. de								
Arrivées des visiteurs (milliers)	115	..	..	..	..	..	..	..
Nuitées des touristes (milliers)	..	..	..	..	..	..	..	..
Dépenses totales des visiteurs (millions de dollars)	..	..	..	..	..	..	..	..
Dépenses sans transport (millions de dollars)	..	..	..	..	..	..	..	..
Korea, Republic of - Corée, République de								
Arrivals of visitors (thousands)	2 959	(d)3 753	(d)5 322	(d)5 147	(d)5 347	(d)4 753	(d)5 818	(d)6 022
Tourists' overnight stays (thousands)	9 952	8 768	..	..	..	..	..	..
Total expenditure of visitors (millions of dollars)	4 010	6 670	8 527	7 919	7 621	7 005	7 870	..
Expenditure excluding transport (millions of dollars)	3 161	5 150	6 834	6 384	5 936	5 358	5 713	..
Kuwait - Koweït								
Arrivées des visiteurs (milliers)	15	(d)1 443	(d)1 944	(d)2 072	(d)2 316	(d)2 602	(d)3 056	..
Nuitées des touristes (milliers)	..	..	..	..	..	..	..	..
Dépenses totales des visiteurs (millions de dollars)	471	309	395	283	323	328	414	..
Dépenses sans transport (millions de dollars)	132	121	98	104	119	117	180	..
Lao People's Dem. Rep. - Rép. dém. populaire lao								
Arrivals of visitors (thousands)	14	(a)60	(a)191	(a)173	(a)215	(a)196	(a)407	(a)672
Tourists' overnight stays (thousands)	..	..	..	..	..	..	..	..
Total expenditure of visitors (millions of dollars)	..	52	..	..	..	..	..	..
Expenditure excluding transport (millions of dollars)	3	51	114	104	113	87	119	146
Latvia - Lettonie								
Arrivées des visiteurs (milliers)	–	(a)539	(a)509	(a)591	(a)848	(a)971	(a)1 079	..
Nuitées des touristes (milliers)	–	668	697	847	871	983	1 201	..
Dépenses totales des visiteurs (millions de dollars)	–	37	172	154	200	271	343	447
Dépenses sans transport (millions de dollars)	–	20	131	120	161	222	267	341
Lebanon - Liban								
Arrivals of visitors (thousands)	..	(a)450	(a)742	(a)837	(a)956	(a)1 016	(a)1 278	(a)1 140
Tourists' overnight stays (thousands)	..	..	..	..	..	..	..	..
Total expenditure of visitors (millions of dollars)	..	710	742	837	4 284	6 782	5 931	..
Expenditure excluding transport (millions of dollars)	..	..	..	..	4 284	6 374	5 411	..
Lesotho (3)								
Arrivées des visiteurs (milliers)	171	(d)209	(d)302	(d)295	(d)287	(d)329	(d)304	..
Nuitées des touristes (milliers)	359	..	..	..	..	..	..	..
Dépenses totales des visiteurs (millions de dollars)	22	29	24	..	..	..	..	..
Dépenses sans transport (millions de dollars)	17	27	24	23	20	28	34	..
Libyan Arab Jamahiriya - Jamahiriya arabe libyenne								
Arrivals of visitors (thousands)	96	(a)56	(a)174	(a)169	(a)135	(a)142	(a)149	..
Tourists' overnight stays (thousands)	..	..	..	..	..	..	..	..
Total expenditure of visitors (millions of dollars)	15	4	84	90	202	243	261	..
Expenditure excluding transport (millions of dollars)	6	2	75	78	181	205	218	..
Lithuania - Lituanie								
Arrivées des visiteurs (milliers)	–	(a)650	(a)1 083	(a)1 271	(a)1 428	(a)1 491	(a)1 800	..
Nuitées des touristes (milliers)	–	762	963	1 073	1 145	1 170	1 526	..
Dépenses totales des visiteurs (millions de dollars)	–	102	430	425	556	700	874	975
Dépenses sans transport (millions de dollars)	–	77	391	383	505	638	816	921

For sources and notes, see end of table.   Pour les sources et les notes, se reporter à la fin du tableau.

	1990	1995	2000	2001	2002	2003	2004	2005
				Luxembourg				
Arrivals of visitors (thousands)	–	–	–	–	(b)885	(b)867	(b)878	(b)913
Tourists' overnight stays (thousands)	–	–	–	–	2 469	2 541	2 514	2 468
Total expenditure of visitors (millions of dollars)	–	–	–	–	2 577	3 134	3 889	..
Expenditure excluding transport (millions of dollars)	–	–	–	–	2 436	2 979	3 659	3 630
				Madagascar				
Arrivées des visiteurs (milliers)	53	(a)75	(a)160	(a)170	(a)62	(a)139	(a)229	..
Nuitées des touristes (milliers)	..	..	..	..	..	..	..	..
Dépenses totales des visiteurs (millions de dollars)	79	106	152	149	62	118	265	..
Dépenses sans transport (millions de dollars)	40	58	121	115	36	76	105	..
				Malawi				
Arrivals of visitors (thousands)	130	(a)192	(a)228	(a)266	(a)383	(a)424	(a)471	..
Tourists' overnight stays (thousands)	1 178	1 345	1 325	2 029	2 893	3 259	3 617	..
Total expenditure of visitors (millions of dollars)	26	22	29	41	39	35	36	36
Expenditure excluding transport (millions of dollars)	16	18	25	26	29	23	24	23
				Malaysia - Malaisie				
Arrivées des visiteurs (milliers)	7 446	(a)7 469	(a)10 222	(a)12 775	(a)13 292	(a)10 577	(a)15 703	(a)16 431
Nuitées des touristes (milliers)	..	..	..	..	..	..	..	..
Dépenses totales des visiteurs (millions de dollars)	2 131	5 044	5 873	7 627	8 084	6 799	9 181	..
Dépenses sans transport (millions de dollars)	1 684	3 969	5 011	6 863	7 118	5 901	8 198	8 543
				Maldives				
Arrivals of visitors (thousands)	195	(a)315	(a)467	(a)461	(a)485	(a)564	(a)617	..
Tourists' overnight stays (thousands)	..	..	..	..	..	..	..	..
Total expenditure of visitors (millions of dollars)	..	..	..	..	..	..	..	..
Expenditure excluding transport (millions of dollars)	89	211	321	327	337	402	471	..
				Mali				
Arrivées des visiteurs (milliers)	44	(c)42	(c)86	(c)89	(c)96	(c)110	(c)113	(c)143
Nuitées des touristes (milliers)	..	..	..	..	..	..	..	..
Dépenses totales des visiteurs (millions de dollars)	40	26	47	91	105	136	148	..
Dépenses sans transport (millions de dollars)	38	25	40	88	104	128	130	..
				Malta - Malte				
Arrivals of visitors (thousands)	872	(a)1 116	(a)1 216	(a)1 180	(a)1 134	(a)1 127	(a)1 158	..
Tourists' overnight stays (thousands)	9 604	10 919	10 266	11 067	10 599	11 115	10 973	..
Total expenditure of visitors (millions of dollars)	613	818	754	721	714	856	963	909
Expenditure excluding transport (millions of dollars)	495	661	610	578	571	696	780	789
				Marshall Islands - Îles Marshall				
Arrivées des visiteurs (milliers)	5	(a)6	(a)5	(a)5	(a)6	(a)7	(a)9	(a)9
Nuitées des touristes (milliers)	..	..	32	30	37	40	38	41
Dépenses totales des visiteurs (millions de dollars)	..	3	4	4	4	..	..	..
Dépenses sans transport (millions de dollars)	..	..	..	..	..	..	..	..
				Mauritius - Maurice				
Arrivals of visitors (thousands)	292	(a)422	(a)656	(a)660	(a)682	(a)702	(a)719	(a)761
Tourists' overnight stays (thousands)	..	..	..	..	..	..	..	..
Total expenditure of visitors (millions of dollars)	385	616	732	820	829	960	1 156	..
Expenditure excluding transport (millions of dollars)	244	430	542	623	612	697	856	871
				Mexico - Mexique				
Arrivées des visiteurs (milliers)	17 176	(a)20 241	(a)20 641	(a)19 810	(a)19 667	(a)18 665	(a)20 618	(a)21 959
Nuitées des touristes (milliers)	..	..	..	..	..	..	..	..
Dépenses totales des visiteurs (millions de dollars)	5 968	6 847	9 133	9 190	9 547	10 058	11 566	12 794
Dépenses sans transport (millions de dollars)	5 527	6 179	8 294	8 401	8 858	9 362	10 753	11 795
				Moldova, Republic of - Moldova, République de				
Arrivals of visitors (thousands)	–	(a)32	(a)18	(a)16	(a)18	(a)21	(a)24	..
Tourists' overnight stays (thousands)	..	..	..	..	..	..	..	..
Total expenditure of visitors (millions of dollars)	–	71	57	58	72	83	119	163
Expenditure excluding transport (millions of dollars)	–	57	39	39	50	58	95	128
				Mongolia - Mongolie				
Arrivées des visiteurs (milliers)	147	(a)108	(a)137	(a)166	(a)229	(a)201	(a)301	..
Nuitées des touristes (milliers)	..	..	..	..	..	..	..	..
Dépenses totales des visiteurs (millions de dollars)	..	33	43	49	143	154	205	..
Dépenses sans transport (millions de dollars)	5	21	36	39	130	143	185	..

For sources and notes, see end of table.

Pour les sources et les notes, se reporter à la fin du tableau.

	1990	1995	2000	2001	2002	2003	2004	2005
				Montserrat				
Arrivals of visitors (thousands)	13	(a)19	(a)10	(a)10	(a)10	(a)8	(a)10	..
Tourists' overnight stays (thousands)	..	..	..	..	..	..	..	..
Total expenditure of visitors (millions of dollars)	..	..	..	..	..	..	..	..
Expenditure excluding transport (millions of dollars)	11	17	9	8	9	7	9	..
				Morocco - Maroc				
Arrivées des visiteurs (milliers)	4 024	(a)2 602	(a)4 278	(a)4 380	(a)4 453	(a)4 761	(a)5 477	(a)5 843
Nuitées des touristes (milliers)	18 720	18 436	21 152	20 349	18 478	18 190	20 951	..
Dépenses totales des visiteurs (millions de dollars)	1 318	1 469	2 280	2 966	3 157	3 802	4 541	..
Dépenses sans transport (millions de dollars)	1 280	1 296	2 039	2 583	2 646	3 221	3 923	..
				Myanmar				
Arrivals of visitors (thousands)	21	(a)117	(a)208	(a)205	(a)217	(a)206	(a)242	..
Tourists' overnight stays (thousands)	..	..	..	..	..	..	..	..
Total expenditure of visitors (millions of dollars)	21	169	195	132	136	70	98	..
Expenditure excluding transport (millions of dollars)	20	151	162	109	120	56	84	..
				Namibia - Namibie				
Arrivées des visiteurs (milliers)	..	(a)272	(a)656	(a)670	(a)757	(a)695	..	..
Nuitées des touristes (milliers)	..	700	619	800	1 006	424	..	..
Dépenses totales des visiteurs (millions de dollars)	..	..	..	264	251	383	426	..
Dépenses sans transport (millions de dollars)	86	278	160	236	218	333	405	..
				Nepal - Népal				
Arrivals of visitors (thousands)	255	(a)363	(a)464	(a)361	(a)275	(a)338	(a)385	..
Tourists' overnight stays (thousands)	..	..	..	..	..	..	..	..
Total expenditure of visitors (millions of dollars)	115	232	219	191	135	233	260	..
Expenditure excluding transport (millions of dollars)	109	177	158	144	104	200	230	..
				Netherlands - Pays-Bas				
Arrivées des visiteurs (milliers)	5 795	(b)6 574	(b)10 003	(b)9 500	(b)9 595	(b)9 181	(b)9 646	..
Nuitées des touristes (milliers)	16 459	19 741	27 261	25 502	26 368	25 342	25 385	..
Dépenses totales des visiteurs (millions de dollars)	5 944	10 611	11 285	11 147	11 745	..	..	..
Dépenses sans transport (millions de dollars)	4 155	6 578	7 197	6 708	7 710	9 249	10 417	10 449
				Netherlands Antilles - Antilles néerlandaises (4)				
Arrivals of visitors (thousands)	..	(a)751	(a)692	(a)677	(a)672	(a)731	(a)783	..
Tourists' overnight stays (thousands)	..	2 241	2 038	2 194	2 301	2 493	2 498	..
Total expenditure of visitors (millions of dollars)	..	..	..	..	..	..	..	..
Expenditure excluding transport (millions of dollars)	..	..	..	..	..	..	..	..
				New Caledonia - Nouvelle-Calédonie				
Arrivées des visiteurs (milliers)	87	(a)86	(a)110	(a)101	(a)104	(a)102	(a)100	(a)101
Nuitées des touristes (milliers)	..	..	..	..	..	..	..	..
Dépenses totales des visiteurs (millions de dollars)	..	108	110	93	..	..	..	..
Dépenses sans transport (millions de dollars)	..	108	111	94	156	196	241	..
				New Zealand - Nouvelle-Zélande				
Arrivals of visitors (thousands)	976	(d)1 409	(d)1 787	(d)1 909	(d)2 045	(d)2 104	(d)2 334	(d)2 365
Tourists' overnight stays (thousands)	20 654	..	9 115	10 452	11 625	11 683	12 927	..
Total expenditure of visitors (millions of dollars)	1 499	..	..	..	..	..	..	..
Expenditure excluding transport (millions of dollars)	1 030	2 318	2 267	2 360	3 006	3 976	5 069	..
				Nicaragua				
Arrivées des visiteurs (milliers)	106	(a)281	(a)486	(a)483	(a)472	(a)526	(a)615	..
Nuitées des touristes (milliers)	88	210	375	339	423	412	527	..
Dépenses totales des visiteurs (millions de dollars)	..	51	133	138	138	164	191	..
Dépenses sans transport (millions de dollars)	12	50	129	135	135	160	187	..
				Niger				
Arrivals of visitors (thousands)	21	(c)35	(c)50	(c)53	(c)58	(c)55	..	..
Tourists' overnight stays (thousands)	105	200	215	218	199	245	..	..
Total expenditure of visitors (millions of dollars)	13	15	28	32	28	29	..	..
Expenditure excluding transport (millions of dollars)	13	7	23	30	20	28	..	..
				Nigeria - Nigéria				
Arrivées des visiteurs (milliers)	190	(a)656	(a)813	(a)850	(a)887	(a)924	(a)962	..
Nuitées des touristes (milliers)	..	..	..	..	..	..	..	..
Dépenses totales des visiteurs (millions de dollars)	30	47	186	168	256	58	49	..
Dépenses sans transport (millions de dollars)	25	17	101	91	139	30	21	..

For sources and notes, see end of table.   Pour les sources et les notes, se reporter à la fin du tableau.

	1990	1995	2000	2001	2002	2003	2004	2005
Niue - Nioué								
Arrivals of visitors (thousands)	1	(a)2	(a)2	(a)1	(a)2	(a)3	(a)3	(a)3
Tourists' overnight stays (thousands)	..	..	..	..	..	..	..	..
Total expenditure of visitors (millions of dollars)	..	2	..	..	..	..	..	..
Expenditure excluding transport (millions of dollars)	..	..	..	..	..	..	..	..
Northern Mariana Islands - Îles Mariannes du Nord								
Arrivées des visiteurs (milliers)	426	(a)669	(a)517	(a)438	(a)466	(a)452	(a)525	..
Nuitées des touristes (milliers)	..	..	..	..	..	..	..	..
Dépenses totales des visiteurs (millions de dollars)	..	655	..	..	..	..	..	..
Dépenses sans transport (millions de dollars)	..	..	..	..	..	..	..	..
Norway - Norvège								
Arrivals of visitors (thousands)	1 955	(a)2 880	(a)3 104	(a)3 073	(a)3 111	(a)3 269	(a)3 600	..
Tourists' overnight stays (thousands)	5 840	7 060	7 469	7 322	7 275	6 956	7 442	7 651
Total expenditure of visitors (millions of dollars)	2 167	2 730	2 521	2 380	2 581	2 955	3 400	3 884
Expenditure excluding transport (millions of dollars)	1 570	2 238	2 050	1 958	2 179	2 506	2 931	3 278
Oman								
Arrivées des visiteurs (milliers)	149	(c)279	(c)571	(c)647	(c)643	(c)630	(c)909	(c)772
Nuitées des touristes (milliers)	..	..	..	3 815	3 965	..	..	..
Dépenses totales des visiteurs (millions de dollars)	..	..	377	419	447	547	708	..
Dépenses sans transport (millions de dollars)	58	..	221	265	302	385	518	..
Pakistan								
Arrivals of visitors (thousands)	424	(a)378	(a)557	(a)500	(a)498	(a)501	(a)648	(a)798
Tourists' overnight stays (thousands)	..	..	1 901	1 583	1 096	1 577	2 773	..
Total expenditure of visitors (millions of dollars)	617	582	551	533	562	620	763	..
Expenditure excluding transport (millions of dollars)	147	110	81	88	97	122	178	185
Palau, Pacific Islands (former) - Palaos, Îles cu Pacifique (anc.)								
Arrivées des visiteurs (milliers)	33	(a)53	(a)58	(a)54	(a)59	(a)68	(a)95	(a)86
Nuitées des touristes (milliers)	..	..	..	..	..	..	..	..
Dépenses totales des visiteurs (millions de dollars)	..	..	53	59	47	76	97	..
Dépenses sans transport (millions de dollars)	..	..	..	..	..	..	..	..
Panama								
Arrivals of visitors (thousands)	214	(a)345	(a)484	(a)519	(a)534	(a)566	(a)621	..
Tourists' overnight stays (thousands)	..	..	..	..	..	..	..	..
Total expenditure of visitors (millions of dollars)	179	372	628	665	710	809	903	1 108
Expenditure excluding transport (millions of dollars)	172	309	458	477	513	585	651	780
Papua New Guinea - Papouasie-Nouvelle-Guinée								
Arrivées des visiteurs (milliers)	41	(a)42	(a)58	(a)54	(a)54	(a)56	(a)59	(a)69
Nuitées des touristes (milliers)	..	..	..	..	..	..	..	..
Dépenses totales des visiteurs (millions de dollars)	38	..	..	..	..	..	..	..
Dépenses sans transport (millions de dollars)	24	25	7	5	..	..	..	..
Paraguay								
Arrivals of visitors (thousands)	280	(a)438	(a)289	(a)279	(a)250	(a)268	(a)309	..
Tourists' overnight stays (thousands)	..	..	..	..	..	..	..	..
Total expenditure of visitors (millions of dollars)	140	162	88	91	76	81	84	..
Expenditure excluding transport (millions of dollars)	85	137	73	69	62	64	67	..
Peru - Pérou								
Arrivées des visiteurs (milliers)	317	(a)479	(a)800	(a)901	(a)998	(a)1 070	(a)1 277	(a)1 486
Nuitées des touristes (milliers)	..	..	..	..	..	..	..	..
Dépenses totales des visiteurs (millions de dollars)	262	521	861	763	863	1 001	1 169	1 370
Dépenses sans transport (millions de dollars)	217	428	837	733	814	941	1 079	1 241
Philippines								
Arrivals of visitors (thousands)	1 025	(a)1 760	(a)1 992	(a)1 797	(a)1 933	(a)1 907	(a)2 291	(a)2 623
Tourists' overnight stays (thousands)	..	..	..	..	..	..	..	..
Total expenditure of visitors (millions of dollars)	506	1 141	2 377	1 822	1 827	1 820	2 412	..
Expenditure excluding transport (millions of dollars)	466	1 136	2 134	1 723	1 740	1 545	2 012	..
Poland - Pologne								
Arrivées des visiteurs (milliers)	3 400	(a)19 215	(a)17 400	(a)15 000	(a)13 980	(a)13 720	(a)14 290	(a)15 200
Nuitées des touristes (milliers)	5 350	5 480	6 891	6 991	7 085	7 828	9 313	..
Dépenses totales des visiteurs (millions de dollars)	692	6 927	6 128	5 121	4 971	4 733	6 499	7 137
Dépenses sans transport (millions de dollars)	358	6 614	5 677	4 646	4 314	4 069	5 833	6 284

For sources and notes, see end of table.   Pour les sources et les notes, se reporter à la fin du tableau.

	1990	1995	2000	2001	2002	2003	2004	2005
				Portugal				
Arrivals of visitors (thousands)	8 020	(a)9 511	(a)12 097	(a)12 167	(a)11 644	(a)11 707	(a)11 617	..
Tourists' overnight stays (thousands)	19 349	22 241	25 785	25 229	24 574	24 369	23 922	..
Total expenditure of visitors (millions of dollars)	3 652	5 646	6 027	6 238	6 559	7 565	8 922	9 222
Expenditure excluding transport (millions of dollars)	3 556	4 831	5 243	5 470	5 762	6 580	7 758	7 893
				Qatar				
Arrivées des visiteurs (milliers)	136	(c)309	(c)378	(c)376	(c)587	(c)557	(c)732	..
Nuitées des touristes (milliers)	795		..	..	..	..	..	..
Dépenses totales des visiteurs (millions de dollars)	..	..	128	272	285	369	..	..
Dépenses sans transport (millions de dollars)	..	..	128	272	285	369	498	..
			Romania - Roumanie (3)					
Arrivals of visitors (thousands)	3 009	(d)5 445	(d)5 264	(d)4 938	(d)4 794	(d)5 595	(d)6 600	(d)5 839
Tourists' overnight stays (thousands)	4 238	2 381	2 149	2 391	2 534	2 766	3 333	..
Total expenditure of visitors (millions of dollars)	..	689	394	419	400	523	607	..
Expenditure excluding transport (millions of dollars)	106	590	359	362	335	449	503	1 051
		Russian Federation - Fédération de Russie						
Arrivées des visiteurs (milliers)	—	(d)10 290	(d)21 169	(d)21 595	(d)23 309	(d)22 521	(d)22 064	..
Nuitées des touristes (milliers)	—	..	..	..	11 357	10 858	11 516	..
Dépenses totales des visiteurs (millions de dollars)	—	..	..	4 726	5 429	5 879	6 958	7 401
Dépenses sans transport (millions de dollars)	—	4 312	3 430	3 572	4 168	4 502	5 226	5 466
			Saint Kitts and Nevis - Saint-Kitts-et-Nevis					
Arrivals of visitors (thousands)	73	(a)79	(a)73	(a)71	(a)69	(a)91	(a)118	..
Tourists' overnight stays (thousands)	..	..	..	..	..	..	..	..
Total expenditure of visitors (millions of dollars)	..	..	..	..	..	..	..	..
Expenditure excluding transport (millions of dollars)	44	63	58	62	57	75	107	..
				Saint Lucia - Sainte-Lucie				
Arrivées des visiteurs (milliers)	141	(a)231	(a)270	(a)250	(a)253	(a)277	(a)298	..
Nuitées des touristes (milliers)	..	..	..	..	..	..	..	..
Dépenses totales des visiteurs (millions de dollars)	121	..	..	..	..	..	..	..
Dépenses sans transport (millions de dollars)	121	230	279	237	215	282	326	..
		Saint Vincent and the Grenadines - Saint-Vincent-et-les Grenadines						
Arrivals of visitors (thousands)	54	(a)60	(a)73	(a)71	(a)78	(a)79	(a)87	..
Tourists' overnight stays (thousands)	..	..	..	..	..	..	..	..
Total expenditure of visitors (millions of dollars)	31	..	..	..	..	..	..	..
Expenditure excluding transport (millions of dollars)	29	53	75	80	83	85	96	..
				Samoa				
Arrivées des visiteurs (milliers)	48	(a)68	(a)88	(a)88	(a)89	(a)92	(a)98	(a)102
Nuitées des touristes (milliers)	..	..	..	..	..	..	..	..
Dépenses totales des visiteurs (millions de dollars)	22	36	..	..	..	..	..	..
Dépenses sans transport (millions de dollars)	21	35	41	39	45	54	70	77
			São Tome and Principe - Sao Tomé-et-Principe					
Arrivals of visitors (thousands)	4	(a)6	(a)7	(a)8	..	..	..	(a)11
Tourists' overnight stays (thousands)	..	..	..	..	..	..	..	..
Total expenditure of visitors (millions of dollars)	2	..	..	..	..	..	..	..
Expenditure excluding transport (millions of dollars)	2	..	10	10	10	..	..	..
				Saudi Arabia - Arabie saoudite				
Arrivées des visiteurs (milliers)	2 209	(a)3 325	(a)6 585	(a)6 727	(a)7 511	(a)7 332	(a)8 599	..
Nuitées des touristes (milliers)	..	..	..	..	..	..	111 810	..
Dépenses totales des visiteurs (millions de dollars)	..	..	..	..	3 418	..	6 540	..
Dépenses sans transport (millions de dollars)	..	..	..	..	..	..	..	..
				Senegal - Sénégal				
Arrivals of visitors (thousands)	246	(c)280	(c)389	(c)396	(c)427	(c)354	(c)363	..
Tourists' overnight stays (thousands)	1 068	1 139	1 401	1 499	1 569	1 451	..	..
Total expenditure of visitors (millions of dollars)	154	168	152	175	210	269	..	..
Expenditure excluding transport (millions of dollars)	152	168	144	174	190	209	..	..
		Serbia and Montenegro - Serbie-et-Monténégro						
Arrivées des visiteurs (milliers)	—	(b)228	(b)239	(b)351	(b)448	(b)481	(b)580	..
Nuitées des touristes (milliers)	—	776	865	1 281	1 650	1 707	2 075	..
Dépenses totales des visiteurs (millions de dollars)	—	..	..	..	..	..	..	..
Dépenses sans transport (millions de dollars)	—	42	30	54	97	201	..	..

For sources and notes, see end of table.   Pour les sources et les notes, se reporter à la fin du tableau.

	1990	1995	2000	2001	2002	2003	2004	2005
	Seychelles							
Arrivals of visitors (thousands)	104	(a)121	(a)130	(a)130	(a)132	(a)122	(a)121	(a)129
Tourists' overnight stays (thousands)	1 048	1 147	..	..	..	..	..	..
Total expenditure of visitors (millions of dollars)	141	224	221	210	242	258	256	..
Expenditure excluding transport (millions of dollars)	122	129	139	139	161	171	172	..
	Sierra Leone							
Arrivées des visiteurs (milliers)	98	(a)38	(a)16	(a)24	(a)28	(a)38	(a)44	(a)40
Nuitées des touristes (milliers)	..	..	..	..	..	..	..	..
Dépenses totales des visiteurs (millions de dollars)	..	..	..	..	..	..	58	..
Dépenses sans transport (millions de dollars)	34	57	11	14	38	60	58	83
	Singapore - Singapour							
Arrivals of visitors (thousands)	4 842	(a)6 422	(a)6 917	(a)6 725	(a)6 997	(a)5 705	..	..
Tourists' overnight stays (thousands)	..	..	..	..	..	..	..	..
Total expenditure of visitors (millions of dollars)	..	..	..	..	..	..	..	..
Expenditure excluding transport (millions of dollars)	4 650	7 646	5 142	4 627	4 437	3 790	5 093	..
	Slovakia - Slovaquie							
Arrivées des visiteurs (milliers)	–	(b)903	(b)1 053	(b)1 219	(b)1 399	(b)1 387	(b)1 401	(b)1 515
Nuitées des touristes (milliers)	–	3 069	3 743	4 378	5 043	4 964	4 675	4 872
Dépenses totales des visiteurs (millions de dollars)	–	630	441	649	742	876	932	..
Dépenses sans transport (millions de dollars)	–	623	433	641	736	865	901	1 210
	Slovenia - Slovénie							
Arrivals of visitors (thousands)	–	(b)732	(b)1 090	(b)1 219	(b)1 302	(b)1 373	(b)1 499	..
Tourists' overnight stays (thousands)	–	2 322	3 277	3 653	3 847	4 009	4 198	..
Total expenditure of visitors (millions of dollars)	–	1 128	1 016	1 059	1 152	1 427	1 726	1 893
Expenditure excluding transport (millions of dollars)	–	1 084	961	1 001	1 086	1 342	1 625	1 794
	Solomon Islands - Îles Salomon							
Arrivées des visiteurs (milliers)	9	(a)12	..	..	..	..	..	..
Nuitées des touristes (milliers)	..	..	..	..	..	..	..	..
Dépenses totales des visiteurs (millions de dollars)	8	17	..	..	..	..	..	..
Dépenses sans transport (millions de dollars)	7	16	4	5	1	2	4	..
	South Africa - Afrique du Sud							
Arrivals of visitors (thousands)	1 029	(a)4 488	(a)5 872	(a)5 787	(a)6 430	(a)6 505	(a)6 678	(a)7 369
Tourists' overnight stays (thousands)	..	..	..	..	..	..	..	..
Total expenditure of visitors (millions of dollars)	2 167	2 655	3 338	3 256	3 695	6 147	6 729	8 448
Expenditure excluding transport (millions of dollars)	1 835	2 126	2 677	2 569	2 923	5 185	5 672	7 335
	Spain - Espagne							
Arrivées des visiteurs (milliers)	34 085	(a)34 920	(a)47 898	(a)50 094	(a)52 327	(a)50 854	(a)52 430	..
Nuitées des touristes (milliers)	68 630	107 787	233 897	232 035	220 707	217 852	209 081	..
Dépenses totales des visiteurs (millions de dollars)	..	27 510	33 833	35 970	37 371	45 967	51 125	52 960
Dépenses sans transport (millions de dollars)	18 581	25 510	30 979	32 691	33 783	41 770	46 202	47 681
	Sri Lanka							
Arrivals of visitors (thousands)	298	(a)403	(a)400	(a)337	(a)393	(a)501	(a)566	(a)549
Tourists' overnight stays (thousands)	3 225	4 024	4 056	3 342	3 989	5 093	5 742	4 754
Total expenditure of visitors (millions of dollars)	224	367	388	347	594	709	808	..
Expenditure excluding transport (millions of dollars)	128	226	248	213	363	441	513	..
	Sudan - Soudan							
Arrivées des visiteurs (milliers)	33	(a)29	(a)38	(a)50	(a)52	(a)52	(a)61	..
Nuitées des touristes (milliers)	..	..	..	..	..	..	..	..
Dépenses totales des visiteurs (millions de dollars)	34	..	..	..	..	..	..	..
Dépenses sans transport (millions de dollars)	21	8	5	3	23	18	21	89
	Suriname							
Arrivals of visitors (thousands)	46	(a)43	(a)57	(a)54	(a)60	(a)82	(a)138	..
Tourists' overnight stays (thousands)	..	..	..	..	..	..	..	..
Total expenditure of visitors (millions of dollars)	4	52	42	26	17	18	52	..
Expenditure excluding transport (millions of dollars)	1	21	16	14	3	4	17	..
	Swaziland							
Arrivées des visiteurs (milliers)	263	(c)300	(c)281	(c)283	(c)256	(c)461	(c)459	..
Nuitées des touristes (milliers)	..	..	..	..	..	..	..	..
Dépenses totales des visiteurs (millions de dollars)	35	54	40	32	68	113	109	..
Dépenses sans transport (millions de dollars)	30	48	37	30	62	101	95	..

For sources and notes, see end of table.   Pour les sources et les notes, se reporter à la fin du tableau.

	1990	1995	2000	2001	2002	2003	2004	2005
				Sweden - Suède				
Arrivals of visitors (thousands)	1 900	(b)2 310	(b)2 746	(a)7 431	(a)7 458	(a)7 627	..	..
Tourists' overnight stays (thousands)	6 575	7 861	8 654	9 133	9 768	9 715	9 724	..
Total expenditure of visitors (millions of dollars)	3 900	4 390	4 825	5 200	5 671	6 548	7 245	..
Expenditure excluding transport (millions of dollars)	2 915	3 471	4 064	4 253	4 710	5 304	6 056	..
				Switzerland - Suisse (5)				
Arrivées des visiteurs (milliers)	13 278	(c)7 005	(c)7 883	(c)7 511	(c)6 917	(c)6 579	..	(c)7 279
Nuitées des touristes (milliers)	36 889	33 984	32 844	32 111	29 641	28 569	..	..
Dépenses totales des visiteurs (millions de dollars)	9 042	11 354	10 124	10 013	9 742	11 048	12 208	..
Dépenses sans transport (millions de dollars)	7 411	9 459	7 788	7 505	7 885	9 169	10 399	..
				Syrian Arab Republic - République arabe syrienne				
Arrivals of visitors (thousands)	562	(b)815	(b)1 416	(b)1 318	(a)2 870	(a)2 788	(a)3 032	..
Tourists' overnight stays (thousands)	..	3 160	5 997	..	..	20 700	27 930	..
Total expenditure of visitors (millions of dollars)	..	..	..	..	..	877	1 888	..
Expenditure excluding transport (millions of dollars)	320	1 258	1 082	1 150	970	773	1 800	..
				Thailand - Thaïlande				
Arrivées des visiteurs (milliers)	5 299	(a)6 952	(a)9 579	(a)10 133	(a)10 873	(a)10 082	(a)11 737	..
Nuitées des touristes (milliers)	..	..	..	..	..	..	..	..
Dépenses totales des visiteurs (millions de dollars)	4 987	9 257	9 936	9 380	10 388	10 456	13 054	12 629
Dépenses sans transport (millions de dollars)	4 325	8 035	7 483	7 076	7 901	7 856	10 043	10 104
				Macedonia, TFYR - Macédoine, LERY				
Arrivals of visitors (thousands)	–	(b)147	(b)224	(b)99	(b)123	(b)158	(b)165	..
Tourists' overnight stays (thousands)	–	276	494	213	275	346	361	..
Total expenditure of visitors (millions of dollars)	–	..	88	49	55	65	77	..
Expenditure excluding transport (millions of dollars)	–	19	38	26	39	57	72	..
				Togo				
Arrivées des visiteurs (milliers)	103	(c)53	(c)60	(c)57	(c)58	(c)61	(c)83	(c)81
Nuitées des touristes (milliers)	..	..	..	..	..	..	..	..
Dépenses totales des visiteurs (millions de dollars)	..	..	11	14	16	26	..	..
Dépenses sans transport (millions de dollars)	58	13	8	11	13	15	..	..
				Tonga				
Arrivals of visitors (thousands)	21	(a)29	(a)35	(a)32	(a)37	(a)40	(a)41	..
Tourists' overnight stays (thousands)	328	488	..	..	..	..	..	..
Total expenditure of visitors (millions of dollars)	7	..	..	..	..	..	..	..
Expenditure excluding transport (millions of dollars)	7	10	7	6	8	15	15	..
				Trinidad and Tobago - Trinité-et-Tobago				
Arrivées des visiteurs (milliers)	195	(a)260	(a)399	(a)383	(a)384	(a)409	(a)443	..
Nuitées des touristes (milliers)	..	..	..	..	..	..	..	..
Dépenses totales des visiteurs (millions de dollars)	221	232	371	361	402	437	568	..
Dépenses sans transport (millions de dollars)	95	77	213	201	242	249	341	..
				Tunisia - Tunisie				
Arrivals of visitors (thousands)	3 204	(a)4 120	(a)5 058	(a)5 387	(a)5 064	(a)5 114	(a)5 998	..
Tourists' overnight stays (thousands)	..	..	..	..	..	..	..	..
Total expenditure of visitors (millions of dollars)	1 197	1 838	1 978	2 061	1 832	1 935	2 432	..
Expenditure excluding transport (millions of dollars)	1 020	1 530	1 682	1 751	1 524	1 583	1 970	..
				Turkey - Turquie				
Arrivées des visiteurs (milliers)	4 799	(a)7 083	(a)9 586	(a)10 783	(a)12 790	(a)13 341	(a)16 826	(a)20 270
Nuitées des touristes (milliers)	13 271	18 477	28 511	36 368	43 312	40 866	49 728	..
Dépenses totales des visiteurs (millions de dollars)	..	..	..	..	..	..	..	..
Dépenses sans transport (millions de dollars)	3 225	4 957	7 636	10 067	11 901	13 203	15 888	..
				Turkmenistan - Turkménistan				
Arrivals of visitors (thousands)	–	(a)218	..	..	..	..	..	..
Tourists' overnight stays (thousands)	–	..	..	..	..	..	..	..
Total expenditure of visitors (millions of dollars)	–	..	..	..	..	..	..	..
Expenditure excluding transport (millions of dollars)	–	..	..	..	..	..	..	..
				Turks and Caicos Islands - Îles Turques et Caïques				
Arrivées des visiteurs (milliers)	49	(a)79	(a)152	(a)166	(a)155	(a)164	..	..
Nuitées des touristes (milliers)	..	600	1 142	1 239	1 172	..	..	..
Dépenses totales des visiteurs (millions de dollars)	..	53	285	311	292	..	..	..
Dépenses sans transport (millions de dollars)	..	..	..	..	..	..	..	..

For sources and notes, see end of table.

Pour les sources et les notes, se reporter à la fin du tableau.

	1990	1995	2000	2001	2002	2003	2004	2005
				Tuvalu				
Arrivals of visitors (thousands)	1	(a)1	(a)1	(a)1	(a)1	(a)1	(a)1	..
Tourists' overnight stays (thousands)	..	..	..	..	..	..	..	..
Total expenditure of visitors (millions of dollars)	..	..	..	..	..	..	..	..
Expenditure excluding transport (millions of dollars)	..	..	..	..	..	..	..	..
				Uganda - Ouganda				
Arrivées des visiteurs (milliers)	69	(a)160	(a)193	(a)205	(a)254	(a)305	(a)512	(a)468
Nuitées des touristes (milliers)	..	640	772	820	1 016	..	..	..
Dépenses totales des visiteurs (millions de dollars)	..	..	..	193	202	219	306	275
Dépenses sans transport (millions de dollars)	..	78	165	165	172	184	266	233
				Ukraine				
Arrivals of visitors (thousands)	—	(a)3 716	(a)6 431	(a)9 174	(a)10 517	(a)12 514	(a)15 629	..
Tourists' overnight stays (thousands)	—	5 332	5 053	5 177	4 757	4 479	..	..
Total expenditure of visitors (millions of dollars)	—	.	563	759	1 001	1 204	1 512	3 542
Expenditure excluding transport (millions of dollars)	—	191	394	573	788	935	1 141	3 125
				United Arab Emirates - Émirats arabes unis				
Arrivées des visiteurs (milliers)	633	(c)2 315	(c)3 907	(c)4 134	(c)5 445	(c)5 871	..	..
Nuitées des touristes (milliers)	..	..	..	..	..	..	..	..
Dépenses totales des visiteurs (millions de dollars)	..	632	1 063	1 200	1 332	1 439	1 594	..
Dépenses sans transport (millions de dollars)	..	..	..	..	..	..	..	..
				United Kingdom - Royaume-Uni				
Arrivals of visitors (thousands)	18 013	(d)23 537	(d)25 209	(d)22 835	(d)24 180	(d)24 715	(d)27 755	(d)29 971
Tourists' overnight stays (thousands)	196 100	220 300	203 759	189 516	199 285	203 432	227 406	247 587
Total expenditure of visitors (millions of dollars)	21 268	27 624	29 978	26 137	27 819	30 738	37 193	38 853
Expenditure excluding transport (millions of dollars)	15 588	20 487	21 769	18 864	20 549	22 668	28 188	30 281
				United Republic of Tanzania - République-Unie de Tanzanie				
Arrivées des visiteurs (milliers)	153	(a)285	(a)459	(a)501	(a)550	(a)552	(a)566	..
Nuitées des touristes (milliers)	1 265	417	1 957	2 015	2 100	2 200	..	..
Dépenses totales des visiteurs (millions de dollars)	..	..	381	444	448	468	610	..
Dépenses sans transport (millions de dollars)	48	502	377	432	444	461	594	..
				United States - États-Unis				
Arrivals of visitors (thousands)	41 922	(a)46 621	(a)54 579	(a)50 478	(a)46 668	(a)44 456	(a)49 625	(a)49 402
Tourists' overnight stays (thousands)	..	..	..	..	..	..	..	..
Total expenditure of visitors (millions of dollars)	65 700	95 523	121 018	109 433	104 284	101 624	115 804	124 264
Expenditure excluding transport (millions of dollars)	50 400	74 791	97 943	88 779	84 752	83 254	93 922	102 774
				United States Virgin Islands - Îles Vierges américaines				
Arrivées des visiteurs (milliers)	463	(a)454	(a)546	(a)527	(a)520	(a)538	(a)544	..
Nuitées des touristes (milliers)	..	1 049	1 060	1 040	1 057	1 052	1 104	..
Dépenses totales des visiteurs (millions de dollars)	..	822	1 206	1 234	1 195	1 257	1 357	..
Dépenses sans transport (millions de dollars)	..	..	..	..	..	..	..	..
				Uruguay				
Arrivals of visitors (thousands)	1 267	(a)2 022	(a)1 968	(a)1 892	(a)1 258	(a)1 420	(a)1 756	..
Tourists' overnight stays (thousands)	..	..	3 319	2 992	2 927	3 531	2 938	..
Total expenditure of visitors (millions of dollars)	303	725	827	700	409	419	579	..
Expenditure excluding transport (millions of dollars)	238	611	713	611	351	345	494	..
				Uzbekistan - Ouzbékistan				
Arrivées des visiteurs (milliers)	—	(a)92	(a)302	(a)345	(a)332	(a)231	(a)262	..
Nuitées des touristes (milliers)	—	1 315	918	1 082	1 069	935	964	..
Dépenses totales des visiteurs (millions de dollars)	—	..	63	72	68	48	57	..
Dépenses sans transport (millions de dollars)	—	..	27	22	22	24	28	..
				Vanuatu				
Arrivals of visitors (thousands)	35	(a)44	(a)58	(a)53	(a)49	(a)50	(a)61	..
Tourists' overnight stays (thousands)	..	..	..	..	..	..	..	..
Total expenditure of visitors (millions of dollars)	..	..	69	58	62	71	..	..
Expenditure excluding transport (millions of dollars)	39	45	56	46	44	52	..	.
				Venezuela (Bolivarian Republic of) - Venezuela (République bolivarienne du)				
Arrivées des visiteurs (milliers)	525	(a)700	(a)469	(a)584	(a)432	(a)337	(a)486	(a)706
Nuitées des touristes (milliers)	..	..	8 456	10 512	9 126	9 819	..	..
Dépenses totales des visiteurs (millions de dollars)	649	995	469	677	484	378	531	713
Dépenses sans transport (millions de dollars)	496	849	423	615	434	331	477	641

For sources and notes, see end of table.   Pour les sources et les notes, se reporter à la fin du tableau.

	1990	1995	2000	2001	2002	2003	2004	2005
				Viet Nam				
Arrivals of visitors (thousands)	250	(d)1 351	(d)2 140	(d)2 330	(d)2 628	(d)2 429	(d)2 928	(d)3 468
Tourists' overnight stays (thousands)	..	..	..	..	..	..	..	..
Total expenditure of visitors (millions of dollars)	..	..	..	..	..	..	..	..
Expenditure excluding transport (millions of dollars)	..	..	..	..	..	..	..	..
				Yemen - Yémen				
Arrivées des visiteurs (milliers)	52	(c)61	(c)73	(c)76	(c)98	(c)155	(c)274	..
Nuitées des touristes (milliers)	..	..	..	..	..	..	..	..
Dépenses totales des visiteurs (millions de dollars)	..	..	..	..	..	..	..	..
Dépenses sans transport (millions de dollars)	40	50	73	38	38	139	139	181
				Zambia - Zambie				
Arrivals of visitors (thousands)	141	(a)163	(a)457	(a)492	(a)565	(a)413	(a)515	..
Tourists' overnight stays (thousands)	..	..	..	..	..	..	..	..
Total expenditure of visitors (millions of dollars)	41	47	111	117	134	149	161	..
Expenditure excluding transport (millions of dollars)	13	..	67	..	..	..	..	..
				Zimbabwe				
Arrivées des visiteurs (milliers)	605	(d)1 416	(d)1 967	(d)2 217	(d)2 041	(d)2 256	(d)1 854	(d)1 559
Nuitées des touristes (milliers)	..	6 270	..	..	..	..	..	..
Dépenses totales des visiteurs (millions de dollars)	112	145	125	81	76	61	194	99
Dépenses sans transport (millions de dollars)	64	..	..	..	..	..	..	..

Sources:
- World Tourism Organisation (UNWTO), database
- International Monetary Fund (IMF), Balance of Payments Statistics on CD-ROM

Notes:
Arrivals of visitors represent the total number of non-resident visitors who arrived in a reporting economy during a given year. When the same person visits a country several times in a year, the total number of arrivals is counted. Similarly, when a person travels to several countries during one trip, her/his arrival in each country is recorded separately. Countries differ in the way in which they count arrivals. Most take into account arrivals of non-resident tourists at national borders. Exceptions are marked by a note.

Tourists' overnight stays refer to the number of nights spent by non-resident tourists in a reporting country and concern all types of tourism accommodation.

Total expenditure of visitors corresponds to the sum of items "Travel receipts" and "Passenger transport" in IMF balance-of-payments data. It refers to expenditures of non-resident visitors within the territory of a reporting economy, including the costs they pay for transportation.

Expenditure excluding transport corresponds to the item "Travel receipts" in IMF balance-of-payments data. It refers to expenditures of non-resident visitors within the territory of a reporting economy. Transport expenditures are not included.

(a)   Arrivals of non-resident tourists at national borders
(b)   Arrivals of non-resident tourists in all types of accommodation establishments
(c)   Arrivals of non-resident tourists in hotels and similar establishments
(d)   Arrivals of non-resident visitors at national borders

(1)   Arrivals - From 1995 onwards: break in series. Data until 1994 (inclusive) concern only arrivals at hotels and similar establishments, while later figures cover arrivals at national borders.
(2)   Arrivals - From 2000 onwards: break in series owing to new accommodation coverage.
(3)   Arrivals - From 1995 onwards: break in series. Data until 1994 (inclusive) concern only arrivals of tourists at national borders, while later figures cover arrivals of visitors at national borders.
(4)   Data for overnight stays of tourists include only Bonaire and Curaçao, while figures referring to visitors' arrivals cover all of the Netherlands Antilles.
(5)   Arrivals - From 1995 onwards: break in series. Data until 1994 (inclusive) concern arrivals at national borders, while later figures cover only arrivals at hotels and similar establishments.

Sources :
- Organisation mondiale du tourisme (UNWTO), base de données
- Statistiques de la balance des paiements sur CD-ROM du Fonds monétaire international (FMI)

Notes :
Les **Arrivées des visiteurs** représentent le nombre total de visiteurs qui sont arrivés dans l'économie déclarante durant une année. Quand une personne visite un pays plusieurs fois par an, chaque visite est comptée séparément. De même, si quelqu'un se rend dans plusieurs pays durant un voyage, son arrivée dans chaque pays est prise en compte. Les pays déclarent les arrivées des visiteurs de manières différentes. La plupart de pays prennent en compte les arrivées des touristes aux frontières nationales. Les exceptions sont repérées par les notes.

Les **Nuitées des touristes** se réfèrent au nombre de nuits que les touristes non-résidents ont passées dans le pays déclarant et concernent tout type d'établissement touristique.

Les **Dépenses totales des visiteurs** correspondent à la somme des rubriques "Revenus des voyages" et "Transport des passagers" de la balance des paiements du FMI. Les dépenses totales des visiteurs se réfèrent aux dépenses ces visiteurs non-résidents sur le territoire de l'économie déclarante, y compris les dépenses pour le transport.

Les **Dépenses sans transport** correspondent à la rubrique "Revenus des voyages" de la balance des paiements du FMI. Elles se réfèrent aux dépenses des visiteurs non-résidents sur le territoire de l'économie déclarante. Les dépenses pour le transport n'y sont pas incluses.

(a)   Arrivées de touristes non-résidents aux frontières nationales
(b)   Arrivées de touristes non-résidents à tout type de logement
(c)   Arrivées de touristes non-résidents aux hôtels et autres types de logement similaire
(d)   Arrivées de visiteurs non-résidents aux frontières nationales

(1)   Arrivées - À partir de 1995 : rupture de série. Les données jusqu'à l'année 1994 (incluse) concernent seulement les arrivées aux hôtels, tandis que les chiffres des années d'après couvrent les arrivées aux frontières nationales.
(2)   Arrivées - À partir de l'année 2000 : rupture de série, suite à la nouvelle classification de logements.
(3)   Arrivées - À partir de 1995 : rupture de série. Les données jusqu'à l'année 1994 (incluse) concernent seulement les arrivées des touristes, tandis que les chiffres des années d'après couvrent les arrivées des visiteurs.
(4)   Les données sur les nuitées des touristes comprennent Bonaire et Curaçao seulement, tandis que les chiffres concernant les arrivés des visiteurs couvrent la totalité des Antilles Néerlandaises.
(5)   Arrivées - À partir de 1995 : rupture de série. Les données jusqu'à l'année 1994 (incluse) concernent les arrivées aux frontières nationales, tandis que les chiffres des années d'après couvrent seulement les arrivées aux hôtels et autres types de logement similaires.

5.4 World merchant fleet by flag of registration and type of ship of countries and geographical regions

5.4 Flotte marchande mondiale par pavillons d'immatriculation et par types de navires des pays et des régions géographiques

Region, country or territory / Régions pays ou territoires	Year / Année	Total fleet (thousands of DWT) (1) / Flotte totale (milliers de TPL) (1)	As percentage of world total fleet / En pourcentage de la flotte mondiale					As percentage of the country or region total fleet / En pourcentage de la flotte totale du pays ou de la région				
			Oil tankers Pétroliers	Bulk carriers Vraquiers	General cargo Navires de charge classique	Container ships Porte-conteneurs	Other types Autres navires	Oil tankers Pétroliers	Bulk carriers Vraquiers	General cargo Navires de charge classique	Container ships Porte-conteneurs	Other types Autres navires
WORLD - MONDE	**1990**	**651 282.0**	**100.0**	**100.0**	**100.0**	**100.0**	**100.0**	**37.6**	**35.3**	**15.7**	**3.6**	**7.8**
	1995	**722 617.3**	**100.0**	**100.0**	**100.0**	**100.0**	**100.0**	**36.7**	**35.5**	**14.2**	**5.7**	**7.9**
	2000	**794 963.6**	**100.0**	**100.0**	**100.0**	**100.0**	**100.0**	**35.6**	**34.8**	**12.5**	**8.4**	**8.6**
	2005	**959 963.8**	**100.0**	**100.0**	**100.0**	**100.0**	**100.0**	**36.9**	**36.0**	**10.0**	**11.6**	**5.5**
DEVELOPED ECONOMIES - ÉCONOMIES DÉVELOPPÉES	1990	269 315.0	45.2	38.9	30.9	52.4	50.1	41.0	33.2	11.7	4.6	9.4
	1995	273 542.3	40.4	35.0	30.2	45.5	46.8	39.2	32.9	11.4	6.8	9.8
	2000	288 175.0	41.3	30.9	29.7	41.1	42.0	40.6	29.6	10.3	9.6	10.0
	2005	327 807.9	36.7	30.1	26.7	40.0	44.5	39.7	31.8	7.8	13.6	7.1
DEVELOPING ECONOMIES - ÉCONOMIES EN DÉVELOPPEMENT	1990	338 462.0	51.5	54.9	54.2	44.2	40.0	37.3	37.3	16.4	3.1	6.0
	1995	421 250.5	57.6	62.5	58.4	53.0	46.5	36.2	38.0	14.2	5.2	6.3
	2000	491 810.6	57.7	68.0	64.1	58.2	54.5	33.3	38.2	13.0	7.9	7.6
	2005	617 331.3	62.4	68.8	67.6	59.7	51.7	35.8	38.5	10.5	10.8	4.4
ECONOMIES IN TRANSITION - ÉCONOMIES EN TRANSITION	1990	43 505.0	3.3	6.2	14.9	3.4	10.0	18.7	33.0	34.9	1.9	11.6
	1995	27 824.6	2.0	2.5	11.4	1.5	6.7	18.8	23.2	42.0	2.2	13.7
	2000	14 978.0	1.0	1.2	6.2	0.7	3.5	18.3	21.3	41.6	3.0	15.8
	2005	14 824.7	0.9	1.1	5.7	0.2	3.8	21.1	26.6	37.0	1.8	13.6
Developed economies: America - Économies développées : Amérique	**1990**	**33 535.0**	**9.3**	**1.0**	**2.3**	**11.8**	**6.9**	**67.8**	**6.6**	**6.9**	**8.3**	**10.4**
	1995	**26 706.5**	**5.6**	**1.1**	**2.0**	**9.3**	**5.9**	**55.3**	**10.3**	**7.6**	**14.3**	**12.5**
	2000	**39 231.0**	**7.5**	**3.0**	**2.0**	**6.5**	**4.8**	**54.3**	**21.2**	**5.0**	**11.1**	**8.3**
	2005	**72 311.3**	**11.3**	**4.9**	**2.6**	**7.1**	**9.7**	**55.1**	**23.4**	**3.5**	**10.9**	**7.0**
Bermuda - Bermudes	1990	7 800.0	2.7	0.1	0.2	0.1	1.3	85.0	3.7	2.4	0.4	8.5
	1995	4 797.0	1.2	0.2	0.2	0.4	1.4	67.5	9.1	3.5	3.2	16.6
	2000	9 398.0	1.5	1.3	0.3	0.7	0.8	46.3	39.4	3.4	4.9	6.1
	2005	8 582.3	0.7	1.0	0.2	0.7	3.2	27.1	41.7	2.7	8.7	19.8
Canada	1990	700.0	0.1	0.0	0.1	0.0	0.5	40.7	8.1	13.4	1.0	36.7
	1995	666.7	0.1	0.0	0.1	0.0	0.5	25.3	19.1	13.6	0.3	41.8
	2000	1 168.0	0.2	0.1	0.1	0.0	0.5	46.1	14.0	10.4	0.2	29.4
	2005	3 054.0	0.3	0.5	0.1	0.0	0.8	29.1	53.4	3.3	0.5	13.7
United States - États-Unis	1990	25 035.0	6.5	0.8	2.0	11.7	5.1	63.2	7.5	8.1	11.0	10.2
	1995	21 242.8	4.3	0.9	1.7	8.9	4.0	53.5	10.3	8.3	17.3	10.7
	2000	28 665.0	5.8	1.6	1.5	5.8	3.4	57.3	15.6	5.3	13.6	8.2
	2005	60 675.0	10.3	3.4	2.3	6.4	5.6	60.4	19.3	3.6	11.8	4.9
Developed economies: Asia - Économies développées : Asie	**1990**	**41 437.0**	**5.6**	**7.2**	**5.9**	**6.9**	**6.7**	**33.3**	**39.9**	**14.6**	**3.9**	**8.2**
	1995	**29 504.2**	**4.1**	**3.9**	**3.2**	**4.3**	**6.1**	**36.8**	**34.2**	**11.2**	**5.9**	**11.8**
	2000	**20 163.0**	**2.4**	**2.1**	**2.6**	**2.1**	**5.0**	**33.8**	**29.4**	**12.8**	**6.9**	**17.1**
	2005	**15 973.8**	**1.3**	**1.3**	**2.2**	**1.2**	**6.1**	**29.7**	**29.0**	**13.2**	**8.0**	**20.0**
Israel - Israël	1990	609.0	0.0	0.0	0.1	1.9	0.0	0.2	8.5	18.6	72.2	0.5
	1995	720.7	0.0	0.0	0.1	1.5	0.0	0.3	2.5	9.8	86.9	0.5
	2000	712.0	0.0	..	0.0	1.0	0.0	0.4	..	1.0	98.2	0.4
	2005	873.8	0.0	..	0.0	0.8	0.0	2.7	..	0.6	96.1	0.5
Japan - Japon	1990	40 828.0	5.6	7.2	5.8	5.1	6.7	33.8	40.4	14.6	2.9	8.3
	1995	28 783.5	4.1	3.9	3.1	2.7	6.1	37.8	35.0	11.2	3.9	12.1
	2000	19 451.0	2.4	2.1	2.6	1.0	5.0	35.0	30.5	13.2	3.6	17.7
	2005	15 099.9	1.3	1.3	2.2	0.4	6.1	31.3	30.7	13.9	2.9	21.2
Developed economies: Europe - Économies développées : Europe	**1990**	**190 311.0**	**29.7**	**29.9**	**22.4**	**33.1**	**35.7**	**38.2**	**36.1**	**12.0**	**4.1**	**9.5**
	1995	**213 048.1**	**30.3**	**29.3**	**24.9**	**31.6**	**32.9**	**37.7**	**35.3**	**12.0**	**6.1**	**8.8**
	2000	**226 258.0**	**31.2**	**25.3**	**25.0**	**32.4**	**30.9**	**39.0**	**30.9**	**11.0**	**9.6**	**9.4**
	2005	**237 064.0**	**24.0**	**23.7**	**21.7**	**31.7**	**26.7**	**35.9**	**34.5**	**8.8**	**14.9**	**5.9**
Austria - Autriche	1990	234.0	..	0.1	0.1	..	..	..	52.1	47.9	..	..
	1995	130.0	..	0.0	0.1	..	..	..	5.2	94.8	..	..
	2000	121.0	..	..	0.1	..	..	..	..	100.0	..	..
	2005	44.4	..	..	0.0	0.0	..	..	..	85.6	14.4	..
Belgium - Belgique	2005	6 502.8	0.9	0.7	0.0	0.3	1.4	46.6	36.5	0.6	5.2	11.0
Belgium-Luxembourg - Belgique-Luxembourg	1990	3 122.0	0.1	0.8	0.1	0.9	1.5	6.6	59.1	2.9	7.0	24.4
	1995	1 546.8	0.0	0.2	0.1	0.2	1.7	0.6	24.9	5.0	5.0	64.5
	2000	1 598.0	0.2	0.0	0.1	0.0	1.4	35.2	0.6	3.6	1.8	58.8

For sources and notes, see end of table.

Pour les sources et les notes, se reporter à la fin du tableau.

5.4 World merchant fleet by flag of registration and type of ship of countries and geographical regions

5.4 Flotte marchande mondiale par pavillons d'immatriculation et par types de navires des pays et des régions géographiques

Region, country or territory / Régions pays ou territoires	Year / Année	Total fleet (thousands of DWT) (1) / Flotte totale (milliers de TPL) (1)	As percentage of world total fleet / En pourcentage de la flotte mondiale					As percentage of the country or region total fleet / En pourcentage de la flotte totale du pays ou de la région				
			Oil tankers / Pétroliers	Bulk carriers / Vraquiers	General cargo / Navires de charge classique	Container ships / Porte-conteneurs	Other types / Autres navires	Oil tankers / Pétroliers	Bulk carriers / Vraquiers	General cargo / Navires de charge classique	Container ships / Porte-conteneurs	Other types / Autres navires
Cyprus - Chypre	1990	32 985.0	4.3	7.3	4.7	1.4	1.2	31.8	50.7	14.7	1.0	1.9
	1995	40 378.0	3.1	8.9	6.5	4.2	1.6	20.1	56.9	16.4	4.3	2.3
	2000	36 165.0	2.5	7.2	5.2	4.2	1.8	19.7	54.7	14.4	7.8	3.4
	2005	30 316.1	1.7	5.4	2.5	3.0	0.3	19.5	61.2	7.8	11.0	0.5
Czechoslovakia (former) - Tchécoslovaquie (anc.)	1990	510.0	..	0.2	0.1	..	..	..	77.5	22.5	..	..
Czech Republic - République tchèque	1995	226.5	..	0.1	0.1	..	..	..	73.1	26.9		..
Denmark - Danemark	1990	8 787.0	1.2	0.3	0.8	6.0	6.0	32.8	7.5	9.2	16.0	34.5
	1995	7 617.2	0.8	0.4	0.8	5.2	3.0	26.2	12.1	11.0	28.3	22.5
	2000	8 455.0	0.7	0.2	0.8	5.4	1.9	24.6	7.9	9.6	42.8	15.2
	2005	9 764.0	0.8	0.1	0.4	5.0	0.9	29.1	5.0	4.1	57.0	4.9
Estonia - Estonie	1995	595.2	0.0	0.1	0.2	..	0.2	2.6	43.5	37.9	..	16.0
	2000	281.0	0.0	0.0	0.2	..	0.1	3.9	17.1	58.0	..	21.0
	2005	101.1	0.0	..	0.0	..	0.1	12.3	..	24.2	..	63.6
Finland - Finlande	1990	983.0	0.1	0.1	0.3	..	0.5	24.8	18.9	29.0	..	27.3
	1995	1 158.0	0.2	0.0	0.3	..	0.3	44.0	10.4	29.9	..	15.7
	2000	1 215.0	0.2	0.0	0.4	..	0.3	42.0	11.0	30.2	..	16.8
	2005	1 121.1	0.1	0.0	0.4	0.0	0.3	47.2	7.6	31.9	1.2	12.0
France	1990	5 574.0	1.4	0.3	0.5	2.3	1.0	60.3	11.0	9.7	9.6	9.5
	1995	6 201.6	1.5	0.2	0.4	1.5	1.1	65.3	8.7	6.4	10.0	9.7
	2000	6 883.0	1.5	0.4	0.3	0.7	1.3	60.3	14.8	4.9	6.7	13.4
	2005	7 297.4	1.3	0.1	0.2	1.1	1.6	64.5	4.8	3.1	16.2	11.4
Germany - Allemagne	1990	7 100.0	0.1	0.5	2.5	9.9	1.7	2.7	16.1	35.9	33.0	12.3
	1995	6 599.7	0.0	0.2	1.4	10.0	1.1	0.3	6.0	21.6	62.5	9.5
	2000	7 773.0	0.0	0.0	0.9	9.6	0.5	0.6	0.1	11.6	82.9	4.8
	2005	13 578.2	0.2	0.1	0.5	10.5	0.4	6.4	2.4	3.8	85.8	1.6
Gibraltar	1990	3 849.0	1.3	0.3	0.1	..	0.1	79.6	15.9	3.7	..	0.8
	1995	579.4	0.2	..	0.0	..	0.0	92.5	..	5.9	..	1.6
	2000	922.0	0.2	0.0	0.1	0.1	0.1	70.5	2.9	10.3	7.6	8.7
	2005	1 418.0	0.1	0.0	0.7	0.2	0.0	35.1	0.2	44.2	18.7	1.7
Greece - Grèce	1990	37 205.0	6.2	7.9	2.5	1.3	1.8	41.0	48.9	6.8	0.8	2.5
	1995	52 064.7	9.4	8.9	2.0	2.0	2.4	48.1	43.8	3.9	1.6	2.6
	2000	44 618.0	9.1	5.3	0.8	3.1	1.8	57.9	32.8	1.9	4.6	2.8
	2005	52 135.6	7.8	6.2	0.5	2.0	0.7	53.2	41.0	0.8	4.2	0.7
Hungary - Hongrie	1990	143.0	..	0.0	0.1	..	..	..	20.3	79.7	..	..
	1995	65.0	..	..	0.1	..	..	..	..	100.0	..	..
Iceland - Islande	1990	135.0	0.0	0.0	0.1	..	0.1	0.7	4.4	52.6	..	43.0
	1995	107.0	0.0	0.0	0.0	..	0.1	2.1	0.6	34.4	..	62.9
	2000	15.0	0.0	0.0	0.0	..	0.0	20.0	6.7	20.0	..	53.3
	2005	78.1	0.0	0.0	0.0	..	0.1	0.6	0.8	1.4	..	97.2
Ireland - Irlande	1990	188.0	0.0	0.0	0.1	0.1	0.1	5.9	7.4	49.5	13.3	23.9
	1995	199.9	0.0	..	0.1	0.0	0.1	7.1	..	60.0	5.1	27.8
	2000	176.0	..	0.0	0.1	0.0	0.1	..	20.5	49.4	4.0	26.1
	2005	306.4	0.0	0.0	0.1	0.0	0.1	3.0	32.0	46.3	2.4	16.2
Italy - Italie	1990	(a)11 840.0	1.8	1.8	1.3	1.7	2.9	37.8	35.6	10.9	3.4	12.3
	1995	(a)8 843.8	1.3	1.1	0.7	1.0	2.8	37.5	32.0	7.7	4.5	18.3
	2000	(a)10 366.0	1.0	1.4	1.0	1.2	2.8	27.2	37.1	9.6	7.7	18.3
	2005	(a)12 074.1	1.5	0.9	1.5	0.8	2.2	44.5	26.8	11.8	7.4	9.5
Latvia - Lettonie	1995	881.0	0.2	..	0.3	..	0.2	56.1	..	33.5	..	10.4
	2000	81.0	0.0	..	0.0	..	0.1	14.8	..	40.7	..	44.4
	2005	366.1	0.1	..	0.0	..	0.2	68.7	..	8.1	..	23.2
Lithuania - Lituanie	1995	562.4	0.0	0.1	0.2	..	0.3	2.4	28.5	42.1	..	27.1
	2000	420.0	0.0	0.1	0.2	..	0.1	1.7	34.8	51.7	..	11.9
	2005	445.8	0.0	0.0	0.2	0.0	0.2	1.4	26.1	52.4	0.9	19.3
Luxembourg	2005	644.6	0.1	0.0	0.0	0.1	0.3	39.3	15.3	6.5	16.3	22.7

For sources and notes, see end of table.

Pour les sources et les notes, se reporter à la fin du tableau.

286

5.4 World merchant fleet by flag of registration and type of ship of countries and geographical regions

5.4 Flotte marchande mondiale par pavillons d'immatriculation et par types de navires des pays et des régions géographiques

Region, country or territory / Régions pays ou territoires	Year / Année	Total fleet (thousands of DWT) (1) / Flotte totale (milliers de TPL) (1)	As percentage of world total fleet / En pourcentage de la flotte mondiale					As percentage of the country or region total fleet / En pourcentage de la flotte totale du pays ou de la région				
			Oil tankers / Pétroliers	Bulk carriers / Vraquiers	General cargo / Navires de charge classique	Container ships / Porte-conteneurs	Other types / Autres navires	Oil tankers / Pétroliers	Bulk carriers / Vraquiers	General cargo / Navires de charge classique	Container ships / Porte-conteneurs	Other types / Autres navires
Malta - Malte	1990	7 756.0	1.2	1.4	1.5	0.0	0.3	38.4	40.2	19.5	0.1	1.8
	1995	29 629.1	4.7	4.6	3.8	1.3	1.2	42.4	40.2	13.2	1.8	2.4
	2000	46 330.0	7.4	6.6	5.2	1.4	1.6	45.0	39.4	11.2	2.0	2.4
	2005	36 942.4	3.5	5.5	3.7	1.4	0.9	33.8	51.2	9.6	4.2	1.2
Netherlands - Pays-Bas	1990	4 725.0	0.2	0.2	1.8	2.5	2.4	12.0	11.6	38.0	12.5	26.0
	1995	5 315.4	0.3	0.1	2.0	2.4	2.1	15.5	4.9	38.3	18.6	22.7
	2000	6 911.0	0.1	0.0	3.2	2.8	2.3	4.0	0.2	45.9	27.2	22.7
	2005	7 625.6	0.2	0.1	3.7	1.7	2.3	8.7	4.0	47.1	24.3	15.9
Norway - Norvège	1990	41 207.0	8.2	5.8	2.1	0.6	10.5	48.9	32.6	5.3	0.3	12.9
	1995	32 867.2	6.4	2.8	3.3	0.2	9.4	51.4	21.7	10.3	0.3	16.3
	2000	31 994.0	5.3	2.6	3.8	0.2	8.8	46.9	22.2	11.9	0.3	18.8
	2005	23 237.4	2.5	2.0	3.3	0.1	7.4	38.7	30.5	13.8	0.3	16.8
Poland - Pologne	1990	4 442.0	0.1	1.1	1.3	0.2	0.4	4.9	58.1	30.9	1.1	5.0
	1995	3 176.7	0.0	0.9	0.6	..	0.3	0.3	75.4	19.3	..	5.0
	2000	1 561.0	0.0	0.5	0.0	..	0.2	0.6	90.6	1.9	..	6.9
	2005	124.4	0.0	..	0.0	..	0.1	10.7	..	34.9	..	54.4
Portugal	1990	1 322.0	0.3	0.2	0.1	0.1	0.2	54.2	28.0	8.4	1.7	7.8
	1995	1 417.9	0.3	0.1	0.2	0.0	0.2	62.3	16.5	11.9	1.0	8.3
	2000	1 718.0	0.2	0.2	0.4	0.1	0.3	37.6	27.5	21.2	2.1	11.6
	2005	1 527.0	0.3	0.0	0.2	0.0	0.3	62.7	11.2	12.6	2.9	10.7
Slovakia - Slovaquie	2000	19.0	..	..	0.0	..	..	..	..	100.0	..	..
	2005	298.8	0.0	0.0	0.2	..	0.0	1.4	20.1	78.2	..	0.4
Slovenia - Slovénie	1995	1.1	..	..	0.0	..	0.0	..	..	20.8	..	79.2
	2005	0.4	..	..	..	..	0.0	..	..	..	..	100.0
Spain - Espagne	1990	6 185.0	1.2	0.7	0.7	0.4	1.5	49.2	25.3	11.7	1.6	12.0
	1995	1 282.4	0.1	0.0	0.2	0.2	0.9	27.6	7.2	19.1	7.8	38.3
	2000	2 142.0	0.4	0.0	0.3	0.2	0.7	51.8	3.3	15.1	6.3	23.5
	2005	2 540.7	0.3	0.0	0.3	0.2	1.7	42.9	1.7	11.1	9.9	34.4
Sweden - Suède	1990	2 942.0	0.3	0.3	1.0	0.3	1.1	24.5	21.8	33.1	2.4	18.2
	1995	2 384.3	0.3	0.0	1.0	..	1.1	28.4	3.1	43.4	..	25.2
	2000	1 822.0	0.1	0.0	1.0	..	0.9	8.9	2.2	53.8	..	35.0
	2005	2 235.3	0.2	0.0	1.2	..	0.3	37.6	2.1	52.6	..	7.6
Switzerland - Suisse	1990	483.0	..	0.2	0.0	..	0.0	..	88.4	7.0	..	4.6
	1995	660.2	..	0.2	0.0	..	0.0	..	93.9	1.9	..	4.2
	2000	834.0	..	0.3	0.0	..	0.0	..	91.7	5.5	..	2.8
	2005	790.6	0.0	0.2	0.1	0.1	0.0	1.1	67.0	11.4	19.9	0.6
United Kingdom - Royaume-Uni	1990	8 594.0	1.7	0.6	0.7	5.3	2.3	49.0	15.0	7.8	14.5	13.7
	1995	8 557.5	1.5	0.4	0.5	3.3	2.8	47.0	12.3	6.3	15.9	18.6
	2000	13 838.0	2.3	0.6	0.8	3.5	3.9	46.7	11.2	5.8	17.1	19.2
	2005	25 547.8	2.2	2.2	1.7	5.2	4.9	31.1	29.7	6.5	22.6	10.1
Developed economies: Oceania - Économies développées : Océanie	**1990**	**4 032.0**	**0.5**	**0.8**	**0.3**	**0.6**	**0.9**	**30.4**	**48.5**	**6.6**	**3.5**	**11.0**
	1995	**4 283.4**	**0.4**	**0.7**	**0.2**	**0.3**	**1.9**	**26.6**	**40.2**	**4.2**	**3.1**	**25.9**
	2000	**2 523.0**	**0.2**	**0.4**	**0.1**	**0.1**	**1.3**	**19.8**	**40.2**	**3.0**	**1.9**	**35.2**
	2005	**2 458.9**	**0.1**	**0.2**	**0.2**	**0.0**	**2.0**	**19.9**	**29.9**	**6.3**	**0.4**	**43.5**
Australia - Australie	1990	3 730.0	0.5	0.8	0.2	0.5	0.8	29.5	51.3	4.8	3.4	11.0
	1995	3 975.9	0.4	0.7	0.1	0.3	1.8	25.5	42.4	3.0	3.3	25.8
	2000	2 356.0	0.1	0.4	0.1	0.1	1.2	17.3	42.4	2.5	2.0	35.8
	2005	2 279.3	0.1	0.2	0.1	0.0	1.9	17.7	31.5	5.7	0.4	44.6
New Zealand - Nouvelle-Zélande	1990	302.0	0.1	0.0	0.1	0.1	0.1	41.4	13.9	29.1	4.6	10.9
	1995	307.6	0.0	0.0	0.1	..	0.1	41.2	12.1	19.5	..	27.2
	2000	167.0	0.0	0.0	0.0	..	0.1	54.5	10.2	9.0	..	26.3
	2005	179.5	0.0	0.0	0.0	..	0.1	47.9	9.5	13.9	..	28.6
Developing economies: Africa - Économies en développement : Afrique	**1990**	**106 851.0**	**23.6**	**13.8**	**7.6**	**9.6**	**14.2**	**54.2**	**29.7**	**7.2**	**2.1**	**6.8**
	1995	**104 832.7**	**21.3**	**11.6**	**6.1**	**10.2**	**14.6**	**53.8**	**28.3**	**6.0**	**4.0**	**8.0**
	2000	**86 383.3**	**13.5**	**8.5**	**6.4**	**11.9**	**15.2**	**44.2**	**27.1**	**7.4**	**9.3**	**12.0**
	2005	**98 562.9**	**14.5**	**6.0**	**4.5**	**15.0**	**10.3**	**52.0**	**21.2**	**4.4**	**17.0**	**5.5**

For sources and notes, see end of table.

Pour les sources et les notes, se reporter à la fin du tableau.

5.4 World merchant fleet by flag of registration and type of ship of countries and geographical regions

5.4 Flotte marchande mondiale par pavillons d'immatriculation et par types de navires des pays et des régions géographiques

Region, country or territory / Régions pays ou territoires	Year / Année	Total fleet (thousands of DWT) (1) / Flotte totale (milliers de TPL) (1)	As percentage of world total fleet / En pourcentage de la flotte mondiale					As percentage of the country or region total fleet / En pourcentage de la flotte totale du pays ou de la région				
			Oil tankers / Pétroliers	Bulk carriers / Vraquiers	General cargo / Navires de charge classique	Container ships / Porte-conteneurs	Other types / Autres navires	Oil tankers / Pétroliers	Bulk carriers / Vraquiers	General cargo / Navires de charge classique	Container ships / Porte-conteneurs	Other types / Autres navires
Eastern Africa - Afrique orientale	*1990*	*413.0*	*0.0*	*0.0*	*0.2*	*0.1*	*0.1*	*4.6*	*19.1*	*60.3*	*7.0*	*9.0*
	1995	*588.4*	*0.0*	*0.0*	*0.3*	*0.2*	*0.1*	*21.0*	*0.4*	*59.8*	*11.7*	*7.1*
	2000	*410.0*	*0.0*	*0.0*	*0.2*	*0.1*	*0.1*	*9.5*	*1.2*	*57.6*	*16.8*	*14.9*
	2005	*1 241.2*	*0.1*	*0.1*	*0.6*	*0.0*	*0.3*	*29.4*	*14.4*	*43.8*	*0.4*	*11.9*
Comoros - Comores	1990	3.0	..	..	0.0	..	..	..	..	100.0	..	..
	1995	3.0	..	..	0.0	..	0.0	..	..	77.6	..	22.4
	2000	31.0	..	..	0.0	..	..	..	..	100.0	..	..
	2005	810.8	0.1	0.0	0.4	0.0	0.1	27.8	21.1	45.4	0.6	5.2
Djibouti	1995	4.8	..	..	0.0	..	0.0	..	..	92.7	..	7.3
	2000	4.0	..	..	0.0	..	..	..	..	100.0	..	..
	2005	3.7	..	..	0.0	..	0.0	..	..	81.4	..	18.6
Ethiopia (former) - Éthiopie (anc.)	1990	91.0	0.0	..	0.1	..	0.0	6.6	..	92.3	..	1.1
Ethiopia - Éthiopie	1995	98.7	0.0	..	0.1	..	..	5.9	..	94.1	..	..
	2000	110.0	0.0	..	0.1	..	..	3.6	..	96.4	..	..
	2005	97.7	..	..	0.1	..	..	..	..	100.0	..	..
Kenya	1990	4.0	..	..	..	..	0.0	..	..	..	..	100.0
	1995	17.0	0.0	..	0.0	..	0.0	37.8	..	9.0	..	53.2
	2000	19.0	0.0	..	0.0	..	0.0	42.1	..	10.5	..	47.4
	2005	16.5	0.0	..	0.0	..	0.0	46.2	..	12.0	..	41.9
Madagascar	1990	92.0	0.0	..	0.1	..	0.0	7.6	..	82.6	..	9.8
	1995	40.8	0.0	..	0.0	..	0.0	41.5	..	43.2	..	15.3
	2000	48.0	0.0	..	0.0	..	0.0	35.4	..	50.0	..	14.6
	2005	31.5	0.0	..	0.0	..	0.0	22.3	..	57.5	..	20.3
Mauritius - Maurice	1990	141.0	..	0.0	0.0	0.1	0.0	..	56.0	19.9	20.6	3.5
	1995	324.7	0.0	0.0	0.2	0.2	0.0	26.0	0.8	50.1	21.2	1.9
	2000	106.0	..	0.0	0.0	0.1	0.0	..	4.7	13.2	65.1	17.0
	2005	72.4	..	0.0	0.0	..	0.1	..	11.0	21.0	..	68.0
Mozambique	1990	29.0	0.0	..	0.0	..	0.0	6.9	..	69.0	..	24.1
	1995	27.2	0.0	..	0.0	..	0.0	1.5	..	60.9	..	37.6
	2000	24.0	..	..	0.0	..	0.0	..	..	45.8	..	54.2
	2005	27.5	..	..	0.0	..	0.0	..	..	38.5	..	61.5
Seychelles	1990	2.0	..	..	0.0	..	..	..	..	100.0	..	..
	1995	4.2	..	..	0.0	..	0.0	..	..	78.5	..	21.5
	2000	21.0	..	..	0.0	..	0.0	..	..	57.1	..	42.9
	2005	135.9	0.0	..	0.0	..	0.0	80.9	..	2.9	..	16.2
Somalia - Somalie	1990	19.0	..	..	0.0	..	0.0	..	..	68.4	..	31.6
	1995	16.5	..	..	0.0	..	0.0	..	..	68.0	..	32.0
	2000	8.0	0.0	..	0.0	..	0.0	25.0	..	62.5	..	12.5
	2005	6.5	0.0	..	0.0	..	0.0	23.5	..	37.6	..	39.0
Uganda - Ouganda	2000	3.0	..	..	0.0	..	..	..	..	100.0	..	..
United Republic of Tanzania - République-Unie de Tanzanie	1990	32.0	0.0	..	0.0	..	0.0	12.5	..	71.9	..	15.6
	1995	51.5	0.0	..	0.0	..	0.0	18.0	..	76.5	..	5.5
	2000	36.0	0.0	..	0.0	..	0.0	22.2	..	66.7	..	11.1
	2005	38.6	0.0	..	0.0	..	0.0	35.9	..	59.8	..	4.2
Middle Africa - Afrique centrale	*1990*	*285.0*	*0.0*	*..*	*0.2*	*..*	*0.1*	*0.7*	*..*	*82.5*	*..*	*16.8*
	1995	*236.9*	*0.0*	*0.0*	*0.1*	*..*	*0.1*	*1.4*	*16.3*	*61.2*	*..*	*21.1*
	2000	*305.3*	*0.0*	*0.0*	*0.2*	*0.0*	*0.1*	*5.6*	*5.2*	*72.8*	*1.6*	*14.7*
	2005	*223.7*	*0.0*	*0.0*	*0.1*	*..*	*0.1*	*33.6*	*12.9*	*27.3*	*..*	*26.2*
Angola	1990	122.0	0.0	..	0.1	..	0.0	1.6	..	87.7	..	10.7
	1995	116.1	0.0	..	0.1	..	0.0	2.3	..	85.9	..	11.8
	2000	70.0	0.0	..	0.0	..	0.0	7.1	..	68.6	..	24.3
	2005	42.8	0.0	..	0.0	..	0.1	9.4	..	28.8	..	61.8
Cameroon - Cameroun	1990	39.0	..	..	0.0	..	0.0	..	..	87.2	..	12.8
	1995	40.2	..	..	0.0	..	0.0	..	..	83.4	..	16.6
	2000	5.3	..	..	0.0	..	0.0	..	..	5.7	..	94.3
	2005	78.6	0.0	..	0.0	..	0.0	87.6	..	4.4	..	8.0

For sources and notes, see end of table.

Pour les sources et les notes, se reporter à la fin du tableau.

5.4 World merchant fleet by flag of registration and type of ship of countries and geographical regions

5.4 Flotte marchande mondiale par pavillons d'immatriculation et par types de navires des pays et des régions géographiques

Region, country or territory / Régions pays ou territoires	Year / Année	Total fleet (thousands of DWT) (1) / Flotte totale (milliers de TPL) (1)	As percentage of world total fleet / En pourcentage de la flotte mondiale — Oil tankers / Pétroliers	Bulk carriers / Vraquiers	General cargo / Navires de charge classique	Container ships / Porte-conteneurs	Other types / Autres navires	As percentage of the country or region total fleet / En pourcentage de la flotte totale du pays ou de la région — Oil tankers / Pétroliers	Bulk carriers / Vraquiers	General cargo / Navires de charge classique	Container ships / Porte-conteneurs	Other types / Autres navires
Congo	1990	11.0	..	..	..	..	0.0	..	..	..	..	100.0
	1995	15.1	..	..	0.0	..	0.0	..	..	27.1	..	72.9
	2005	0.7	..	..	..	..	0.0	..	..	..	..	100.0
Dem. Rep. of the Congo - Rép. dém. du Congo	1990	76.0	..	..	0.1	..	0.0	..	..	80.3	..	19.7
	1995	15.8	..	..	0.0	..	0.0	..	..	3.8	..	96.2
Equatorial Guinea - Guinée équatoriale	1990	7.0	..	..	0.0	..	..	..	..	100.0	..	..
	1995	3.3	..	..	0.0	..	..	..	..	100.0	..	..
	2000	25.0	..	..	0.0	..	0.0	..	..	68.0	..	32.0
	2005	26.4	0.0	..	0.0	..	0.0	2.1	..	24.5	..	73.4
Gabon	1990	29.0	..	..	0.0	..	0.0	..	..	89.7	..	10.3
	1995	43.8	0.0	0.0	0.0	..	0.0	1.7	87.9	5.7	..	4.8
	2000	8.0	0.0	..	0.0	..	0.0	12.5	..	50.0	..	37.5
	2005	8.2	0.0	..	0.0	..	0.0	9.1	..	47.5	..	43.4
São Tome and Principe - Sao Tomé-et-Principe	1990	1.0	..	..	..	..	0.0	..	..	..	..	100.0
	1995	2.5	..	..	0.0	..	0.0	..	..	51.6	..	48.4
	2000	197.0	0.0	0.0	0.2	0.0	0.0	5.6	8.1	77.7	2.5	6.1
	2005	67.1	0.0	0.0	0.0	..	0.0	1.5	43.0	52.1	..	3.4
Northern Africa - Afrique septentrionale	*1990*	*5 494.0*	*0.8*	*0.5*	*1.3*	*0.0*	*2.2*	*35.5*	*18.9*	*24.6*	*0.2*	*20.7*
	1995	*4 871.9*	*0.6*	*0.5*	*1.1*	*0.0*	*1.6*	*32.2*	*24.8*	*23.6*	*0.2*	*19.2*
	2000	*4 361.0*	*0.3*	*0.4*	*1.1*	*0.1*	*1.4*	*22.5*	*28.3*	*25.5*	*2.1*	*21.5*
	2005	*3 131.8*	*0.2*	*0.3*	*0.6*	*0.1*	*1.4*	*18.8*	*33.7*	*18.6*	*4.9*	*24.0*
Algeria - Algérie	1990	1 062.0	0.0	0.1	0.3	..	0.9	4.3	23.9	27.9	..	43.9
	1995	1 111.1	0.0	0.1	0.3	..	0.8	4.7	25.9	26.7	..	42.7
	2000	1 063.0	0.0	0.1	0.3	..	0.7	2.8	27.1	26.2	..	43.9
	2005	881.6	0.0	0.1	0.1	..	0.8	5.4	32.7	12.2	..	49.7
Egypt - Égypte	1990	1 825.0	0.2	0.2	0.7	..	0.2	27.2	31.0	36.6	..	5.3
	1995	1 919.3	0.1	0.3	0.5	..	0.2	20.0	44.9	28.3	..	6.8
	2000	2 010.0	0.1	0.3	0.5	0.1	0.2	18.0	45.9	26.9	2.9	6.3
	2005	1 615.7	0.1	0.2	0.4	0.1	0.3	21.3	45.8	21.1	3.6	8.2
Libyan Arab Jamahiriya - Jamahiriya arabe libyenne	1990	1 468.0	0.5	..	0.1	..	0.0	91.6	..	6.8	..	1.6
	1995	1 222.5	0.4	..	0.1	..	0.1	89.4	..	7.2	..	3.4
	2000	661.0	0.2	..	0.1	..	0.1	81.2	..	12.9	..	5.9
	2005	103.5	0.0	..	0.1	..	0.1	12.8	..	60.7	..	26.5
Morocco - Maroc	1990	618.0	0.0	0.1	0.1	0.0	0.5	3.1	26.4	24.4	1.6	44.5
	1995	380.1	0.0	..	0.1	0.0	0.4	6.6	..	26.7	2.6	64.1
	2000	398.0	0.0	..	0.1	0.1	0.3	5.0	..	30.2	8.5	56.3
	2005	389.8	0.0	..	0.1	0.1	0.2	28.9	..	14.1	24.7	32.3
Sudan - Soudan	1990	79.0	0.0	..	0.1	..	0.0	1.3	..	97.5	..	1.3
	1995	61.8	0.0	..	0.1	..	0.0	2.0	..	96.7	..	1.3
	2000	52.0	0.0	..	0.1	..	..	1.9	..	98.1	..	..
	2005	16.7	0.0	..	0.0	..	..	7.3	..	84.4	..	8.2
Tunisia - Tunisie	1990	442.0	0.0	0.0	0.1	..	0.5	10.6	13.1	13.8	..	62.4
	1995	177.1	0.0	0.0	0.1	..	0.1	7.4	33.1	34.0	..	25.6
	2000	177.0	0.0	0.0	0.0	..	0.1	18.1	14.7	21.5	..	45.8
	2005	124.5	0.0	0.0	0.0	..	0.0	56.4	21.2	2.6	..	19.8
Southern Africa - Afrique australe	*1990*	*299.0*	*0.0*	*..*	*..*	*0.9*	*0.2*	*0.3*	*..*	*..*	*72.2*	*27.4*
	1995	*293.7*	*0.0*	*..*	*0.0*	*0.5*	*0.2*	*0.8*	*..*	*0.0*	*67.6*	*31.6*
	2000	*368.0*	*0.0*	*..*	*..*	*0.4*	*0.1*	*1.4*	*..*	*..*	*71.2*	*27.4*
	2005	*114.0*	*0.0*	*..*	*0.0*	*0.0*	*0.1*	*8.9*	*..*	*0.1*	*26.0*	*65.0*
South Africa - Afrique du Sud	1990	299.0	0.0	..	..	0.9	0.2	0.3	..	..	72.2	27.4
	1995	293.7	0.0	..	0.0	0.5	0.2	0.3	..	0.0	67.6	31.6
	2000	368.0	0.0	..	..	0.4	0.1	1.4	..	..	71.2	27.4
	2005	114.0	0.0	..	0.0	0.0	0.1	8.9	..	0.1	26.0	65.0
Western Africa - Afrique occidentale	*1990*	*100 360.0*	*22.8*	*13.3*	*5.8*	*8.5*	*11.7*	*55.7*	*30.5*	*5.9*	*2.0*	*5.9*
	1995	*98 841.8*	*20.6*	*11.1*	*4.5*	*9.6*	*12.7*	*55.3*	*28.8*	*4.6*	*4.0*	*7.3*
	2000	*80 939.0*	*13.1*	*8.0*	*4.8*	*11.3*	*13.5*	*45.9*	*27.4*	*5.9*	*9.4*	*11.4*
	2005	*93 852.2*	*14.2*	*5.7*	*3.2*	*14.9*	*8.4*	*53.5*	*20.9*	*3.3*	*17.6*	*4.7*

For sources and notes, see end of table.

Pour les sources et les notes, se reporter à la fin du tableau.

5.4 World merchant fleet by flag of registration and type of ship of countries and geographical regions

5.4 Flotte marchande mondiale par pavillons d'immatriculation et par types de navires des pays et des régions géographiques

Region, country or territory / Régions pays ou territoires	Year / Année	Total fleet (thousands of DWT) (1) / Flotte totale (milliers de TPL) (1)	As percentage of world total fleet / En pourcentage de la flotte mondiale					As percentage of the country or region total fleet / En pourcentage de la flotte totale du pays ou de la région				
			Oil tankers / Pétroliers	Bulk carriers / Vraquiers	General cargo / Navires de charge classique	Container ships / Porte-conteneurs	Other types / Autres navires	Oil tankers / Pétroliers	Bulk carriers / Vraquiers	General cargo / Navires de charge classique	Container ships / Porte-conteneurs	Other types / Autres navires
Benin - Bénin	1990	5.0	..	..	0.0	..	0.0	..	..	80.0	..	20.0
	1995	0.2	..	..	..	..	0.0	..	..	..	..	100.0
	2005	0.2	..	..	..	..	0.0	..	..	..	..	100.0
Cape Verde - Cap-Vert	1990	30.0	0.0	..	0.0	..	0.0	3.3	..	90.0	..	6.7
	1995	21.5	0.0	..	0.0	..	0.0	2.6	..	79.9	..	17.5
	2000	24.0	0.0	..	0.0	..	0.0	4.2	..	79.2	..	16.7
	2005	22.1	0.0	..	0.0	..	0.0	15.9	..	60.1	..	24.0
Côte d'Ivoire	1990	100.0	..	..	0.1	..	0.0	..	..	85.0	..	15.0
	1995	41.9	0.0	..	0.0	..	0.0	2.8	..	82.2	..	15.0
	2000	5.0	0.0	..	..	..	0.0	20.0	..	..	..	80.0
	2005	5.1	0.0	..	..	..	0.0	22.8	..	..	..	77.2
Gambia - Gambie	1990	2.0	..	..	..	..	0.0	..	..	..	..	100.0
	1995	2.7	..	..	..	..	0.0	..	..	..	..	100.0
	2000	2.0	..	..	..	..	0.0	..	..	..	..	100.0
	2005	11.2	0.0	..	0.0	..	0.0	44.5	..	40.1	..	15.4
Ghana	1990	110.0	0.0	..	0.1	..	0.1	0.9	..	66.4	..	32.7
	1995	96.0	0.0	0.0	0.0	..	0.1	1.2	0.3	42.6	..	55.9
	2000	94.0	0.0	..	0.0	..	0.1	9.6	..	19.1	..	71.3
	2005	88.8	0.0	0.0	0.0	..	0.1	5.1	0.3	17.4	..	77.2
Guinea - Guinée	1990	3.0	..	..	..	..	0.0	..	..	..	..	100.0
	1995	2.4	..	..	0.0	..	0.0	..	..	11.8	..	88.2
	2000	5.0	..	..	..	..	0.0	..	..	..	..	100.0
	2005	7.2	..	..	0.0	..	0.0	..	..	4.0	..	96.0
Guinea-Bissau - Guinée-Bissau	1990	2.0	..	..	..	..	0.0	..	..	..	..	100.0
	1995	2.7	..	..	0.0	..	0.0	..	..	20.0	..	80.0
	2000	3.0	..	..	0.0	..	0.0	..	..	33.3	..	66.7
	2005	2.2	..	..	0.0	..	0.0	..	..	10.2	..	89.8
Liberia - Libéria	1990	99 226.0	22.7	13.3	5.3	8.5	11.2	55.9	30.9	5.5	2.0	5.7
	1995	97 888.6	20.4	11.1	4.2	9.6	12.4	55.3	29.0	4.4	4.0	7.2
	2000	80 062.0	12.9	8.0	4.6	11.3	13.2	45.7	27.7	5.8	9.5	11.3
	2005	93 026.1	14.0	5.7	3.1	14.9	7.9	53.4	21.1	3.3	17.8	4.5
Mauritania - Mauritanie	1990	22.0	..	..	0.0	..	0.0	..	..	9.1	..	90.9
	1995	19.4	..	..	0.0	..	0.0	..	..	9.6	..	90.4
	2000	23.0	..	..	0.0	..	0.0	..	..	4.3	..	95.7
	2005	24.5	..	..	0.0	..	0.0	..	..	2.9	..	97.1
Nigeria - Nigéria	1990	727.0	0.2	..	0.2	..	0.1	60.0	..	33.8	..	6.2
	1995	724.6	0.2	..	0.2	..	0.1	68.6	..	25.2	..	6.2
	2000	685.0	0.2	..	0.1	..	0.1	75.6	..	16.9	..	7.4
	2005	530.1	0.1	0.0	0.0	..	0.2	74.9	2.5	5.2	..	17.4
Saint Helena - Sainte-Hélène	1990	2.0	..	..	..	..	0.0	..	..	..	..	100.0
	2005	1.1	..	..	..	..	0.0	..	..	..	..	100.0
Senegal - Sénégal	1990	38.0	..	..	0.0	..	0.0	..	..	44.7	..	55.3
	1995	26.5	..	..	0.0	..	0.0	..	..	25.2	..	74.8
	2000	25.0	..	..	0.0	..	0.0	..	..	8.0	..	92.0
	2005	17.7	0.0	..	0.0	..	0.0	1.6	..	8.8	..	89.7
Sierra Leone	1990	15.0	0.0	..	0.0	..	0.0	6.7	..	20.0	..	73.3
	1995	15.1	0.0	..	0.0	..	0.0	12.1	..	6.2	..	81.6
	2000	8.0	..	..	0.0	..	0.0	..	..	50.0	..	50.0
	2005	100.6	0.0	..	0.0	..	0.0	75.2	..	13.8	..	11.0
Togo	1990	78.0	0.0	..	0.0	..	0.1	1.3	..	26.9	..	73.1
	1995	0.1	..	..	..	..	0.0	..	..	..	..	100.0
	2000	3.0	..	..	0.0	..	..	..	..	100.0	..	..
	2005	15.4	..	..	0.0	..	0.0	..	..	28.6	..	71.4
Developing economies: America - Économies en développement : Amérique	**1990**	**110 078.0**	**15.3**	**17.1**	**22.3**	**14.8**	**14.2**	**33.9**	**35.6**	**20.7**	**3.2**	**6.6**
	1995	**176 029.3**	**24.3**	**24.7**	**27.1**	**24.2**	**18.0**	**36.6**	**36.0**	**15.8**	**5.7**	**5.8**
	2000	**252 859.3**	**29.5**	**36.3**	**31.8**	**29.5**	**25.5**	**33.1**	**39.6**	**12.5**	**7.8**	**6.9**
	2005	**299 772.0**	**26.0**	**37.9**	**32.8**	**28.1**	**26.0**	**30.8**	**43.7**	**10.5**	**10.4**	**4.6**

For sources and notes, see end of table.

Pour les sources et les notes, se reporter à la fin du tableau.

5.4 World merchant fleet by flag of registration and type of ship of countries and geographical regions

5.4 Flotte marchande mondiale par pavillons d'immatriculation et par types de navires des pays et des régions géographiques

Region, country or territory Régions pays ou territoires	Year Année	Total fleet (thousands of DWT) (1) Flotte totale (milliers de TPL) (1)	As percentage of world total fleet En pourcentage de la flotte mondiale					As percentage of the country or region total fleet En pourcentage de la flotte totale du pays ou de la région				
			Oil tankers Pétroliers	Bulk carriers Vraquiers	General cargo Navires de charge classique	Container ships Porte-conteneurs	Other types Autres navires	Oil tankers Pétroliers	Bulk carriers Vraquiers	General cargo Navires de charge classique	Container ships Porte-conteneurs	Other types Autres navires
Caribbean - Caraïbes	*1990*	*27 769.0*	*5.5*	*3.4*	*4.6*	*1.6*	*2.9*	*48.4*	*28.0*	*16.9*	*1.4*	*5.2*
	1995	*50 164.5*	*8.3*	*4.8*	*11.1*	*4.4*	*4.5*	*44.0*	*24.5*	*22.7*	*3.6*	*5.1*
	2000	*65 869.3*	*9.7*	*5.4*	*14.0*	*7.1*	*7.0*	*41.9*	*22.5*	*21.1*	*7.3*	*7.3*
	2005	*76 535.5*	*8.1*	*6.0*	*14.8*	*6.9*	*10.2*	*37.5*	*26.9*	*18.5*	*10.1*	*7.0*
Anguilla	1990	4.0	..	..	0.0	..	0.0	..	..	75.0	..	25.0
	1995	3.6	..	..	0.0	..	0.0	..	..	97.4	..	2.6
	2000	1.3	..	..	0.0	..	..	..	..	100.0	..	..
	2005	0.9	..	..	0.0	..	..	..	..	100.0	..	..
Antigua and Barbuda - Antigua-et-Barbuda	1990	608.0	0.0	0.0	0.5	0.1	0.1	1.0	0.8	83.2	5.1	9.9
	1995	2 441.2	0.0	0.1	1.4	2.0	0.1	0.2	6.7	58.5	33.1	1.4
	2000	5 462.0	0.0	0.1	2.2	4.3	0.1	0.1	5.6	39.8	53.3	1.1
	2005	9 466.4	0.0	0.3	3.4	4.7	0.2	0.3	9.6	34.2	54.9	1.1
Bahamas	1990	22 365.0	5.2	2.8	2.0	1.1	1.9	56.5	28.6	9.3	1.2	4.3
	1995	36 717.0	7.5	3.1	6.1	2.0	3.4	54.1	21.4	17.0	2.3	5.3
	2000	46 453.0	9.0	3.1	7.4	2.4	5.0	55.1	18.4	15.8	3.5	7.3
	2005	51 922.2	7.1	3.7	6.9	2.1	9.1	48.7	24.9	12.8	4.5	9.2
Barbados - Barbade	1990	8.0	..	..	0.0	..	..	..	..	100.0	..	..
	1995	414.1	0.0	0.0	0.2	..	0.1	18.4	20.4	54.0	..	7.2
	2000	1 172.0	0.2	0.1	0.1	0.1	0.1	54.6	22.5	12.0	3.0	7.8
	2005	783.8	0.1	0.1	0.2	..	0.1	31.8	39.7	20.8	..	7.7
British Virgin Islands - Îles Vierges britanniques	1990	5.0	..	..	0.0	..	0.0	..	..	80.0	..	20.0
	1995	4.1	..	..	0.0	..	0.0	..	..	79.0	..	21.0
	2000	8.0	..	..	0.0	..	0.0	..	..	12.5	..	87.5
	2005	11.5	..	..	0.0	..	0.0	..	..	10.7	..	89.3
Cayman Islands - Îles Caïmanes	1990	570.0	0.0	0.1	0.2	..	0.2	20.4	27.2	34.7	..	17.7
	1995	487.7	0.0	0.1	0.2	0.0	0.1	1.8	39.0	42.1	0.4	16.7
	2000	2 805.0	0.2	0.4	0.3	0.1	1.1	19.3	39.9	11.9	1.4	27.5
	2005	4 387.4	0.5	0.5	0.7	..	0.3	40.8	41.0	14.7	..	3.5
Cuba	1990	1 115.0	0.0	0.0	0.7	..	0.3	10.5	9.0	65.2	..	15.3
	1995	490.2	0.0	0.0	0.3	..	0.2	18.7	0.1	53.1	..	28.1
	2000	80.0	0.0	..	0.1	..	0.0	6.3	..	86.3	..	7.5
	2005	82.2	0.0	0.0	0.0	..	0.1	39.4	10.9	12.4	..	37.3
Dominica - Dominique	1990	4.0	..	..	0.0	..	..	.	..	100.0	..	..
	1995	1.9	..	..	0.0	..	..	.	..	100.0	..	..
	2000	2.0	..	..	0.0	..	..	.	..	100.0	..	..
	2005	868.4	0.2	0.0	0.2	0.0	0.0	76.4	4.0	17.4	0.9	1.3
Dominican Republic - République dominicaine	1990	52.0	0.0	0.0	0.0	..	..	3.8	36.5	59.6	..	..
	1995	11.2	0.0	..	0.0	..	0.0	14.5	..	76.9	..	8.6
	2000	8.0	..	..	0.0	..	0.0	..	..	87.5	..	12.5
	2005	7.1	..	..	0.0	..	0.0	..	..	89.1	..	10.9
Grenada - Grenade	1990	1.0	..	..	..	..	0.0	.	..	..	..	100.0
	1995	8.4	..	..	0.0	..	..	.	..	100.0	..	..
	2000	1.0	..	..	0.0	..	..	.	..	100.0	..	..
	2005	1.0	..	..	0.0	..	0.0	.	..	95.5	..	4.5
Haiti - Haïti	1990	1.0	..	..	..	..	0.0	.	..	..	..	100.0
	1995	0.2	..	..	..	..	0.0	.	..	..	..	100.0
	2000	1.0	..	..	0.0	..	..	.	..	100.0	..	..
	2005	1.0	..	..	0.0	..	0.0	.	..	82.3	..	17.7
Jamaica - Jamaïque	1990	21.0	0.0	0.0	0.0	0.0	0.0	14.3	19.0	38.1	23.8	4.8
	1995	6.1	0.0	..	0.0	..	..	53.9	..	46.1	..	..
	2000	3.0	0.0	..	..	..	..	100.0	..	..	..	..
	2005	197.7	0.0	0.0	0.0	..	0.0	1.6	86.4	11.8	..	0.2
Montserrat	1990	1.0	..	..	0.0	..	..	.	..	100.0	..	..
Saint Kitts and Nevis - Saint-Kitts-et-Nevis	1990	1.0	..	..	..	..	0.0	.	..	..	..	100.0
	1995	0.6	..	..	0.0	..	..	.	..	100.0	..	..
	2000	1.0	..	..	0.0	..	..	.	..	100.0	..	..
	2005	265.6	0.0	0.0	0.1	..	0.0	39.7	7.5	49.1	..	3.7
Saint Lucia - Sainte-Lucie	1990	2.0	..	..	0.0	..	..	.	..	100.0	..	..
	1995	1.7	..	..	0.0	..	..	.	..	100.0	..	..

For sources and notes, see end of table.

Pour les sources et les notes, se reporter à la fin du tableau.

5

5.4 World merchant fleet by flag of registration and type of ship of countries and geographical regions

5.4 Flotte marchande mondiale par pavillons d'immatriculation et par types de navires des pays et des régions géographiques

Region, country or territory / Régions pays ou territoires	Year / Année	Total fleet (thousands of DWT) (1) / Flotte totale (milliers de TPL) (1)	As percentage of world total fleet / En pourcentage de la flotte mondiale					As percentage of the country or region total fleet / En pourcentage de la flotte totale du pays ou de la région				
			Oil tankers Pétroliers	Bulk carriers Vraquiers	General cargo Navires de charge classique	Container ships Porte-conteneurs	Other types Autres navires	Oil tankers Pétroliers	Bulk carriers Vraquiers	General cargo Navires de charge classique	Container ships Porte-conteneurs	Other types Autres navires
Saint Vincent and the Grenadines - Saint-Vincent-et-les Grenadines	1990	2 995.0	0.2	0.5	1.1	0.4	0.3	18.6	36.9	36.9	2.9	4.6
	1995	9 556.3	0.8	1.6	2.9	0.4	0.6	21.5	41.7	31.6	1.7	3.5
	2000	9 866.0	0.3	1.7	3.9	0.3	0.7	8.0	46.4	39.1	2.0	4.6
	2005	8 524.2	0.2	1.3	3.3	0.1	0.4	6.5	52.0	37.6	1.6	2.3
Trinidad and Tobago - Trinité-et-Tobago	1990	13.0	..	..	0.0	..	0.0	..	..	46.2	..	53.8
	1995	19.9	..	..	0.0	..	0.0	..	..	37.9	..	62.1
	2000	6.0	0.0	..	..	..	0.0	16.7	..	..	..	83.3
	2005	16.2	0.0	..	0.0	..	0.0	25.5	..	2.5	..	72.0
Turks and Caicos Islands - Îles Turques et Caïques	1990	3.0	..	..	0.0	..	0.0	..	..	33.3	..	66.7
	1995	0.4	..	..	0.0	..	0.0	..	..	39.8	..	60.2
	2005	0.2	..	..	0.0	..	..	..	..	100.0	..	..
Central America - Amérique centrale	*1990*	*65 049.0*	*7.4*	*10.5*	*14.8*	*12.2*	*9.1*	*28.0*	*37.2*	*23.3*	*4.4*	*7.1*
	1995	*113 418.7*	*14.1*	*18.2*	*14.9*	*19.0*	*11.2*	*32.9*	*41.1*	*13.5*	*6.9*	*5.6*
	2000	*177 450.0*	*18.4*	*29.7*	*16.8*	*22.0*	*17.0*	*29.3*	*46.3*	*9.5*	*8.3*	*6.6*
	2005	*215 156.9*	*16.8*	*31.5*	*17.3*	*21.0*	*13.3*	*27.6*	*50.6*	*7.7*	*10.8*	*3.3*
Belize	1995	710.7	0.0	0.0	0.5	0.0	0.1	4.6	4.4	78.2	1.7	11.2
	2000	2 589.0	0.2	0.1	1.5	0.1	0.2	24.0	11.4	56.2	3.2	5.2
	2005	1 730.7	0.0	0.1	1.1	0.0	0.3	7.4	18.2	63.0	1.6	9.7
Costa Rica	1990	6.0	..	..	0.0	..	0.0	..	..	33.3	..	66.7
	1995	2.2	..	..	..	..	0.0	..	..	..	..	100.0
	2000	4.0	..	0.0	..	..	0.0	..	75.0	..	..	25.0
	2005	0.8	..	..	..	..	0.0	..	..	..	..	100.0
El Salvador	2005	1.7	..	..	..	..	0.0	..	..	..	..	100.0
Guatemala	1990	7.0	..	..	0.0	..	0.0	..	..	85.7	..	14.3
	2000	4.0	..	..	..	..	0.0	..	..	..	..	100.0
	2005	4.5	0.0	..	..	..	0.0	21.1	..	..	..	78.9
Honduras	1990	1 046.0	0.1	0.0	0.7	0.1	0.1	17.1	9.0	67.7	1.2	5.0
	1995	1 695.8	0.1	0.1	1.1	0.0	0.2	10.4	13.3	69.6	0.4	6.4
	2000	1 317.0	0.1	0.1	0.8	0.0	0.2	19.7	12.7	57.3	0.4	10.0
	2005	931.4	0.1	0.0	0.4	0.0	0.2	31.7	18.3	38.8	0.2	11.1
Mexico - Mexique	1990	1 803.0	0.3	0.1	0.1	0.1	1.2	46.6	14.8	4.4	0.7	33.5
	1995	1 494.1	0.3	..	0.1	0.4	1.0	47.2	..	5.0	9.8	38.0
	2000	1 180.0	0.3	..	0.0	..	0.6	64.0	..	1.9	..	34.1
	2005	1 364.5	0.3	0.0	0.1	..	0.5	75.3	2.0	4.5	..	18.2
Nicaragua	1990	3.0	..	..	0.0	..	..	..	..	100.0	..	..
	1995	1.5	..	..	0.0	..	0.0	..	..	79.2	..	20.8
	2000	1.0	..	..	0.0	..	..	..	..	100.0	..	..
	2005	2.7	0.0	..	0.0	..	0.0	33.9	..	43.4	..	22.7
Panama	1990	62 184.0	7.0	10.4	14.1	12.1	7.8	27.7	38.3	23.1	4.6	6.4
	1995	109 514.4	13.7	18.1	13.2	18.5	9.8	33.2	42.3	12.3	7.0	5.1
	2000	172 355.0	17.8	29.6	14.6	21.9	16.0	29.3	47.4	8.4	8.5	6.4
	2005	211 120.6	16.4	31.3	15.7	21.0	12.3	27.5	51.3	7.1	11.0	3.1
South America - Amérique du Sud	*1990*	*17 260.0*	*2.3*	*3.2*	*2.9*	*0.9*	*2.3*	*32.9*	*42.2*	*17.1*	*1.3*	*6.6*
	1995	*12 446.2*	*1.9*	*1.8*	*1.1*	*0.9*	*2.3*	*40.8*	*36.6*	*9.0*	*2.8*	*10.8*
	2000	*9 540.0*	*1.4*	*1.2*	*1.0*	*0.4*	*1.5*	*42.2*	*33.6*	*10.6*	*2.9*	*10.7*
	2005	*8 079.6*	*1.2*	*0.5*	*0.8*	*0.2*	*2.5*	*50.8*	*20.1*	*9.7*	*3.0*	*16.3*
Argentina - Argentine	1990	2 872.0	0.4	0.4	0.7	0.3	0.5	33.1	30.6	25.0	2.3	8.9
	1995	757.5	0.1	0.0	0.2	0.1	0.4	24.5	13.9	24.2	6.5	30.9
	2000	384.0	0.1	0.0	0.1	..	0.1	39.1	13.5	34.4	..	13.0
	2005	917.6	0.1	0.0	0.1	..	0.4	57.6	5.7	12.2	..	24.5
Bolivia - Bolivie	1990	16.0	..	..	0.0	..	..	..	..	100.0	..	..
	2000	259.0	0.0	0.0	0.1	0.0	0.0	15.8	19.3	54.4	1.5	8.9
	2005	211.7	0.0	0.0	0.0	0.0	0.0	73.3	3.2	17.4	1.0	5.1
Brazil - Brésil	1990	10 005.0	1.4	2.3	0.9	0.5	1.0	33.1	51.7	8.8	1.1	5.2
	1995	8 543.3	1.4	1.4	0.4	0.6	0.7	44.2	43.1	5.0	2.9	4.8
	2000	6 152.0	1.0	0.9	0.4	0.3	0.3	46.0	41.0	6.0	3.1	3.9
	2005	3 449.6	0.5	0.3	0.3	0.2	0.5	48.5	28.8	8.8	6.2	7.7

For sources and notes, see end of table.

Pour les sources et les notes, se reporter à la fin du tableau.

5.4 World merchant fleet by flag of registration and type of ship of countries and geographical regions

5.4 Flotte marchande mondiale par pavillons d'immatriculation et par types de navires des pays et des régions géographiques

Region, country or territory / Régions pays ou territoires	Year / Année	Total fleet (thousands of DWT) (1) / Flotte totale (milliers de TPL) (1)	As percentage of world total fleet / En pourcentage de la flotte mondiale					As percentage of the country or region total fleet / En pourcentage de la flotte totale du pays ou de la région				
			Oil tankers / Pétroliers	Bulk carriers / Vraquiers	General cargo / Navires de charge classique	Container ships / Porte-conteneurs	Other types / Autres navires	Oil tankers / Pétroliers	Bulk carriers / Vraquiers	General cargo / Navires de charge classique	Container ships / Porte-conteneurs	Other types / Autres navires
Chile - Chili	1990	883.0	0.0	0.2	0.2	..	0.2	0.7	62.7	22.9	..	13.7
	1995	1 038.8	0.1	0.2	0.1	0.1	0.4	13.2	51.1	10.5	2.1	23.1
	2000	881.0	0.1	0.1	0.1	0.1	0.3	18.8	42.0	10.1	8.7	20.3
	2005	1 074.0	0.1	0.1	0.1	0.0	0.4	39.7	29.7	9.8	2.0	18.9
Colombia - Colombie	1990	541.0	0.0	0.1	0.3	..	0.0	3.0	29.0	64.3	..	3.7
	1995	171.4	0.0	..	0.1	..	0.0	5.6	..	83.0	..	11.3
	2000	103.0	0.0	..	0.1	..	0.0	9.7	..	60.2	..	30.1
	2005	119.7	0.0	..	0.1	..	0.1	10.8	..	52.6	..	36.6
Ecuador - Équateur	1990	523.0	0.1	0.0	0.2	..	0.1	40.0	8.8	46.1	..	5.2
	1995	209.3	0.0	..	0.0	..	0.1	62.5	..	21.9	..	15.6
	2000	440.0	0.1	..	0.0	..	0.1	86.4	..	0.9	..	12.7
	2005	356.6	0.1	..	0.0	..	0.1	82.1	..	0.7	..	17.1
Falkland Islands (Malvinas) - Îles Falkland (Malvinas)	1990	4.0	..	..	..	..	0.0	..	..	..	..	100.0
	1995	11.8	..	..	0.0	..	0.0	..	..	5.4	..	94.6
	2000	36.0	..	..	0.0	..	0.1	..	..	2.8	..	97.2
	2005	36.1	..	..	0.0	..	0.1	..	..	1.4	..	98.6
Guyana	1990	11.0	..	..	0.0	..	0.0	..	..	45.5	..	54.5
	1995	12.9	..	..	0.0	..	0.0	..	..	54.7	..	45.3
	2000	15.0	..	..	0.0	..	0.0	..	..	60.0	..	40.0
	2005	37.9	0.0	..	0.0	..	0.0	18.1	..	63.0	..	18.9
Paraguay	1990	42.0	0.0	..	0.0	..	0.0	2.4	..	57.1	..	40.5
	1995	40.0	0.0	..	0.0	..	0.0	7.1	..	83.9	..	8.9
	2000	52.0	0.0	..	0.0	0.0	0.0	17.3	..	76.9	3.8	1.9
	2005	49.2	0.0	..	0.0	..	0.0	7.9	..	85.3	4.4	2.3
Peru - Pérou	1990	807.0	0.1	0.1	0.2	..	0.1	40.5	26.8	26.6	..	6.1
	1995	343.7	0.1	0.0	0.1	..	0.1	43.8	14.7	21.7	..	19.8
	2000	222.0	0.0	..	0.1	..	0.1	26.6	..	36.5	..	36.9
	2005	148.8	0.0	..	0.0	..	0.2	18.2	..	24.9	..	56.9
Suriname	1990	16.0	0.0	..	0.0	0.0	0.0	18.8	..	62.5	12.5	6.3
	1995	9.0	0.0	..	0.0	0.0	0.0	33.6	..	38.3	19.6	8.5
	2000	6.0	0.0	..	0.0	..	..	50.0	..	50.0	..	..
	2005	6.8	0.0	..	0.0	..	0.0	49.9	..	46.4	..	3.7
Uruguay	1990	157.0	0.0	..	0.0	0.1	0.0	59.9	..	2.5	21.7	15.9
	1995	149.5	0.0	..	0.0	0.1	0.0	62.4	..	1.8	18.8	16.9
	2000	40.0	0.0	..	0.0	..	0.0	20.0	..	10.0	..	70.0
	2005	57.3	0.0	..	0.0	..	0.1	19.1	..	15.2	..	65.7
Venezuela (Bolivarian Republic of) - Venezuela (République bolivarienne du)	1990	1 383.0	0.3	0.1	0.3	0.0	0.2	54.9	17.9	20.0	0.1	7.2
	1995	1 159.1	0.2	0.1	0.1	0.0	0.5	51.1	16.2	7.9	0.1	24.7
	2000	950.0	0.1	0.1	0.1	0.0	0.4	38.8	22.0	8.1	0.1	30.9
	2005	1 614.4	0.3	0.1	0.1	0.0	0.6	59.8	15.9	3.0	0.2	21.1
Developing economies: Asia - Économies en développement : Asie	**1990**	**117 993.0**	**12.5**	**23.1**	**23.5**	**19.5**	**11.2**	**25.9**	**45.1**	**20.3**	**3.9**	**4.8**
	1995	**137 823.1**	**12.0**	**25.6**	**24.6**	**18.5**	**13.0**	**23.0**	**47.7**	**18.3**	**5.5**	**5.4**
	2000	**150 954.0**	**14.7**	**23.0**	**25.5**	**16.7**	**13.4**	**27.6**	**42.0**	**16.8**	**7.4**	**6.1**
	2005	**216 235.7**	**21.9**	**24.4**	**29.6**	**16.5**	**14.1**	**35.8**	**39.1**	**13.2**	**8.5**	**3.4**
Eastern Asia - Asie orientale	*1990*	*45 049.0*	*2.3*	*10.8*	*9.9*	*10.4*	*3.7*	*12.6*	*55.4*	*22.3*	*5.5*	*4.2*
	1995	*51 839.7*	*2.2*	*11.8*	*9.5*	*9.7*	*3.4*	*11.4*	*58.2*	*18.9*	*7.7*	*3.8*
	2000	*51 487.0*	*2.3*	*10.7*	*9.5*	*6.3*	*2.5*	*12.6*	*57.4*	*18.4*	*8.2*	*3.4*
	2005	*99 297.4*	*5.8*	*15.7*	*13.8*	*8.6*	*3.5*	*20.6*	*54.5*	*13.4*	*9.6*	*1.9*
China - Chine	1990	(b)20 755.0	1.1	3.6	7.6	4.6	1.7	13.0	40.3	37.3	5.3	4.2
	1995	(b)24 933.6	1.4	4.4	7.2	4.1	1.7	14.9	44.8	29.7	6.7	3.9
	2000	(b)23 808.0	1.3	4.0	6.4	2.6	1.4	15.4	46.5	26.6	7.4	4.1
	2005	(b)32 773.9	2.0	4.1	6.8	3.3	1.8	22.1	43.8	19.9	11.3	2.8
China, Hong Kong SAR - Chine, Hong Kong RAS	1990	11 176.0	0.8	3.5	0.5	2.5	0.5	16.7	71.0	4.4	5.3	2.5
	1995	15 257.2	0.5	4.7	0.8	2.3	0.2	7.9	79.4	5.5	6.3	0.9
	2000	17 778.0	0.6	4.7	1.3	2.5	0.2	9.3	73.7	7.0	9.3	0.6
	2005	50 443.4	3.2	8.7	4.3	4.0	0.5	22.7	59.9	8.2	8.7	0.5
Korea, Dem. People's Rep. of - Corée, Rép. populaire dém. de	1990	656.0	0.0	0.1	0.5	..	0.1	3.0	19.1	70.6	..	7.3
	1995	1 011.9	0.1	0.1	0.5	..	0.1	23.3	17.2	54.4	..	5.1
	2000	843.0	0.0	0.0	0.7	..	0.1	1.4	12.3	79.4	..	6.9
	2005	1 733.0	0.0	0.1	1.3	0.0	0.1	6.6	16.3	72.6	1.5	2.9

For sources and notes, see end of table.

Pour les sources et les notes, se reporter à la fin du tableau.

5.4   World merchant fleet by flag of registration and type of ship of countries and geographical regions

5.4   Flotte marchande mondiale par pavillons d'immatriculation et par types de navires des pays et des régions géographiques

Region, country or territory / Régions pays ou territoires	Year / Année	Total fleet (thousands of DWT) (1) / Flotte totale (milliers de TPL) (1)	As percentage of world total fleet / En pourcentage de la flotte mondiale					As percentage of the country or region total fleet / En pourcentage de la flotte totale du pays ou de la région				
			Oil tankers / Pétroliers	Bulk carriers / Vraquiers	General cargo / Navires de charge classique	Container ships / Porte-conteneurs	Other types / Autres navires	Oil tankers / Pétroliers	Bulk carriers / Vraquiers	General cargo / Navires de charge classique	Container ships / Porte-conteneurs	Other types / Autres navires
Korea, Republic of - Corée, République de	1990	12 462.0	0.5	3.7	1.3	3.2	1.4	8.9	68.5	10.9	6.1	5.5
	1995	10 637.0	0.3	2.6	0.9	3.2	1.4	7.3	63.4	9.2	12.6	7.6
	2000	9 058.0	0.4	1.9	1.2	1.2	0.9	12.7	58.2	13.6	9.0	6.5
	2005	14 347.1	0.5	2.7	1.4	1.2	1.2	11.7	64.9	9.6	9.5	4.3
Southern Asia - Asie méridionale	*1990*	*20 968.0*	*3.8*	*3.3*	*3.3*	*..*	*1.4*	*44.9*	*35.7*	*16.0*	*..*	*3.4*
	1995	*18 189.7*	*2.7*	*2.9*	*2.4*	*0.3*	*1.6*	*39.8*	*41.1*	*13.5*	*0.6*	*5.0*
	2000	*19 013.0*	*3.1*	*2.4*	*2.3*	*0.6*	*1.6*	*45.8*	*34.7*	*11.8*	*2.0*	*5.7*
	2005	*23 960.0*	*4.2*	*1.6*	*1.9*	*0.6*	*1.6*	*62.5*	*23.6*	*7.6*	*2.7*	*3.6*
Bangladesh	1990	620.0	0.0	..	0.5	..	0.0	13.5	..	84.4	..	2.1
	1995	520.5	0.0	0.0	0.4	..	0.0	16.3	1.7	78.6	..	3.4
	2000	505.0	0.0	0.0	0.4	0.0	0.0	21.0	1.8	71.7	1.6	4.0
	2005	663.9	0.0	0.0	0.4	0.1	0.0	17.7	13.3	57.1	9.3	2.6
India - Inde	1990	10 497.0	1.2	2.4	1.6	..	1.0	27.5	52.1	15.3	..	5.1
	1995	11 613.6	1.7	2.1	0.8	0.3	1.3	39.5	46.1	7.3	1.0	6.2
	2000	10 570.0	1.6	1.6	0.6	0.2	1.3	42.6	42.4	5.3	1.4	8.2
	2005	13 295.1	2.3	1.1	0.3	0.1	1.3	62.5	29.1	2.2	1.1	5.2
Iran, Islamic Republic of - Iran, Rép. islamique d'	1990	8 692.0	2.5	0.8	0.6	..	0.3	71.3	20.4	6.6	..	1.7
	1995	4 975.0	0.9	0.7	0.6	0.0	0.3	49.3	34.2	13.3	0.0	3.1
	2000	7 207.0	1.4	0.7	0.9	0.3	0.2	55.6	27.1	12.6	2.5	2.2
	2005	9 009.3	1.7	0.5	0.8	0.4	0.2	68.1	18.1	8.1	4.3	1.4
Maldives	1990	123.0	0.0	0.0	0.1	..	0.0	8.1	43.9	45.5	..	2.4
	1995	130.7	0.0	0.0	0.1	..	0.0	9.7	15.0	69.5	..	5.9
	2000	112.0	0.0	..	0.1	..	0.0	6.3	..	90.2	..	3.6
	2005	118.1	0.0	..	0.1	..	0.0	14.9	..	80.6	..	4.5
Pakistan	1990	508.0	0.0	..	0.4	..	0.0	17.7	..	80.1	..	2.2
	1995	624.2	0.0	0.1	0.3	..	0.0	14.6	34.0	49.6	..	1.8
	2000	381.0	0.0	..	0.2	0.1	0.0	23.9	..	61.7	11.0	3.4
	2005	651.7	0.1	0.0	0.2	..	0.0	59.5	10.1	28.2	..	2.2
Sri Lanka	1990	528.0	0.1	0.1	0.2	..	0.0	26.3	35.6	37.1	..	0.6
	1995	325.7	0.0	0.1	0.1	..	0.0	1.3	55.3	42.2	..	1.2
	2000	238.0	0.0	0.1	0.1	..	0.0	1.3	63.0	32.4	..	3.4
	2005	221.9	0.0	..	0.1	0.0	0.0	6.9	..	63.9	24.1	5.1
South-Eastern Asia - Asie du Sud-Est	*1990*	*35 717.0*	*3.2*	*7.4*	*6.9*	*6.9*	*4.3*	*21.8*	*47.7*	*19.9*	*4.5*	*6.1*
	1995	*47 679.3*	*4.4*	*8.0*	*8.7*	*7.5*	*6.1*	*24.5*	*43.1*	*18.8*	*6.4*	*7.3*
	2000	*61 147.0*	*7.2*	*7.6*	*9.6*	*7.9*	*7.3*	*33.4*	*34.1*	*15.6*	*8.7*	*8.2*
	2005	*76 892.2*	*10.1*	*5.8*	*10.8*	*6.3*	*7.4*	*46.4*	*26.0*	*13.5*	*9.1*	*5.0*
Brunei Darussalam - Brunéi Darussalam	1990	349.0	..	..	0.0	..	0.7	..	..	0.9	..	99.1
	1995	352.5	0.0	..	0.0	..	0.6	0.1	..	1.2	..	98.7
	2000	349.0	..	..	0.0	..	0.5	..	..	0.9	..	99.1
	2005	421.2	0.0	..	0.0	..	0.8	0.4	..	0.6	..	99.0
Cambodia - Cambodge	1990	4.0	..	..	0.0	..	0.0	..	..	25.0	..	75.0
Indonesia - Indonésie	1990	2 910.0	0.4	0.1	1.3	0.4	0.5	33.2	6.9	47.2	3.4	9.3
	1995	3 626.2	0.5	0.1	1.7	0.2	0.6	33.0	8.7	47.2	2.2	8.8
	2000	4 262.0	0.5	0.2	2.0	0.2	0.5	30.2	12.5	46.2	2.8	8.3
	2005	5 308.3	0.5	0.2	2.4	0.3	0.7	30.1	14.1	42.8	5.9	7.1
Malaysia - Malaisie	1990	2 460.0	0.1	0.3	0.7	1.0	1.2	12.5	25.8	27.5	9.5	24.8
	1995	4 748.4	0.3	0.7	0.8	1.0	1.9	14.7	37.0	16.4	9.0	22.9
	2000	7 692.0	0.5	1.0	0.8	1.3	2.5	20.0	36.1	10.8	11.1	22.0
	2005	7 755.3	1.2	0.2	0.7	0.8	2.6	53.1	9.3	9.2	10.8	17.6
Myanmar	1990	1 246.0	0.0	0.4	0.2	0.1	0.0	0.8	75.1	20.1	2.0	1.9
	1995	696.2	0.0	0.1	0.2	0.1	0.2	0.7	53.7	28.9	3.6	13.0
	2000	656.0	0.0	0.1	0.2	..	0.0	0.8	60.1	37.2	..	2.0
	2005	645.5	0.0	0.1	0.2	..	0.0	0.7	67.1	30.0	..	2.1
Philippines	1990	14 159.0	0.3	4.9	1.9	0.4	0.4	5.0	79.4	13.6	0.7	1.3
	1995	13 504.2	0.1	4.2	2.0	0.5	0.4	1.8	79.9	15.0	1.6	1.8
	2000	9 956.0	0.1	2.7	1.9	0.1	0.6	2.2	74.3	18.9	0.8	3.8
	2005	7 128.9	0.2	1.3	1.6	0.2	0.5	10.1	62.0	21.2	2.8	3.9

For sources and notes, see end of table.   Pour les sources et les notes, se reporter à la fin du tableau.

5.4 World merchant fleet by flag of registration and type of ship of countries and geographical regions

5.4 Flotte marchande mondiale par pavillons d'immatriculation et par types de navires des pays et des régions géographiques

Region, country or territory / Régions pays ou territoires	Year / Année	Total fleet (thousands of DWT) (1) / Flotte totale (milliers de TPL) (1)	As percentage of world total fleet / En pourcentage de la flotte mondiale					As percentage of the country or region total fleet / En pourcentage de la flotte totale du pays ou de la région				
			Oil tankers / Pétroliers	Bulk carriers / Vraquiers	General cargo / Navires de charge classique	Container ships / Porte-conteneurs	Other types / Autres navires	Oil tankers / Pétroliers	Bulk carriers / Vraquiers	General cargo / Navires de charge classique	Container ships / Porte-conteneurs	Other types / Autres navires
Singapore - Singapour	1990	12 965.0	2.3	1.7	1.7	4.7	1.0	43.4	30.6	13.5	8.5	4.1
	1995	21 020.7	3.4	2.6	2.1	5.4	1.6	43.4	31.5	10.2	10.6	4.3
	2000	33 742.0	5.8	3.2	2.5	6.0	2.7	48.8	26.2	7.5	11.9	5.5
	2005	48 562.1	7.9	3.3	2.6	4.7	2.0	57.9	23.8	5.2	10.9	2.2
Thailand - Thaïlande	1990	912.0	0.1	0.0	0.6	0.3	0.1	16.7	1.9	69.4	7.0	5.0
	1995	2 670.0	0.1	0.3	1.4	0.2	0.2	13.6	24.3	55.3	3.0	3.8
	2000	3 034.0	0.2	0.3	1.3	0.3	0.2	22.8	24.1	42.7	6.1	4.3
	2005	4 591.4	0.2	0.5	1.9	0.3	0.3	13.9	36.2	40.3	6.5	3.1
Viet Nam	1990	712.0	0.0	0.0	0.5	..	0.3	4.8	3.4	68.1	..	23.7
	1995	1 061.1	0.0	0.0	0.6	..	0.6	3.1	3.4	58.8	..	34.7
	2000	1 456.0	0.1	0.1	0.8	0.0	0.3	15.0	13.4	53.3	2.2	16.1
	2005	2 479.4	0.1	0.1	1.4	0.1	0.4	18.6	17.4	53.4	2.3	8.4
Western Asia - Asie occidentale	*1990*	*16 259.0*	*3.1*	*1.6*	*3.4*	*2.3*	*1.7*	*47.0*	*22.9*	*21.5*	*3.3*	*5.4*
	1995	*20 114.3*	*2.6*	*3.0*	*4.0*	*1.1*	*1.9*	*34.3*	*37.7*	*20.3*	*2.3*	*5.5*
	2000	*19 307.0*	*2.1*	*2.3*	*4.1*	*1.9*	*2.0*	*31.5*	*33.2*	*21.4*	*6.7*	*7.1*
	2005	*16 086.1*	*1.8*	*1.3*	*3.1*	*1.1*	*1.6*	*39.8*	*28.9*	*18.4*	*7.6*	*5.2*
Bahrain - Bahreïn	1990	49.0	0.0	..	0.0	..	0.0	4.1	..	55.1	..	40.8
	1995	242.1	0.0	0.0	0.1	..	0.1	40.1	5.4	40.8	..	13.7
	2000	450.0	0.1	0.0	0.1	0.1	0.1	34.0	13.3	21.8	22.2	8.7
	2005	395.8	0.0	0.0	0.0	0.1	0.1	38.9	21.5	1.0	25.2	13.3
Iraq	1990	1 797.0	0.6	..	0.1	..	0.2	86.4	..	6.7	..	7.0
	1995	1 503.8	0.5	..	0.1	..	0.1	87.4	..	7.2	..	5.3
	2000	835.0	0.2	..	0.1	..	0.1	79.0	..	12.6	..	8.4
	2005	175.4	0.0	..	0.1	..	0.1	29.0	..	31.3	..	39.6
Jordan - Jordanie	1990	64.0	..	0.0	0.0	..	0.0	.	68.8	25.0	..	6.3
	1995	33.6	..	0.0	..	..	0.0	.	99.3	..	..	0.7
	2000	59.0	..	0.0	0.0	0.0	..	.	30.5	57.6	11.9	..
	2005	224.9	0.0	0.0	0.1	0.0	0.0	3.1	23.4	58.3	6.9	8.3
Kuwait - Koweït	1990	2 944.0	0.8	..	0.5	0.6	0.5	68.5	..	17.5	5.0	9.1
	1995	3 250.1	0.9	..	0.4	0.2	0.6	74.5	..	11.5	2.8	11.2
	2000	3 813.0	1.0	0.0	0.3	0.3	0.5	76.9	0.7	6.8	6.0	9.6
	2005	3 706.4	0.9	0.0	0.1	0.2	0.5	82.1	2.5	2.3	6.1	6.9
Lebanon - Liban	1990	473.0	0.0	0.0	0.4	..	0.0	4.9	15.6	78.0	..	1.5
	1995	424.0	0.0	0.1	0.3	0.0	0.0	0.5	32.5	65.6	0.3	1.1
	2000	546.0	0.0	0.1	0.2	..	0.0	0.2	57.1	40.8	..	1.8
	2005	215.4	0.0	0.0	0.1	..	0.0	0.7	37.3	60.6	..	1.5
Oman	1990	12.0	..	..	0.0	..	0.0	.	..	58.3	..	41.7
	1995	11.1	0.0	..	0.0	..	0.0	4.1	..	26.9	..	68.9
	2000	13.0	..	..	0.0	..	0.0	.	..	46.2	..	53.8
	2005	11.1	0.0	..	0.0	..	0.0	11.1	..	14.8	..	74.1
Qatar	1990	556.0	0.1	..	0.1	0.4	0.0	53.6	..	27.0	16.4	3.1
	1995	773.6	0.1	0.1	0.2	0.2	0.0	25.1	34.9	26.5	11.8	1.6
	2000	1 079.0	0.1	0.1	0.2	0.3	0.0	34.3	25.0	19.1	18.9	2.2
	2005	794.6	0.1	..	0.1	0.2	0.1	60.7	..	6.6	24.3	8.5
Saudi Arabia - Arabie saoudite	1990	2 716.0	0.7	0.0	0.6	0.3	0.4	63.1	1.7	24.2	2.8	8.3
	1995	1 414.7	0.2	..	0.6	0.3	0.4	29.4	..	44.9	8.3	17.4
	2000	1 523.0	0.1	..	0.6	0.3	0.5	27.6	..	37.2	13.2	21.9
	2005	1 277.6	0.2	..	0.3	0.1	0.1	59.4	..	23.2	12.2	5.2
Syrian Arab Republic - République arabe syrienne	1990	116.0	..	..	0.1	..	0.0	.	..	96.6	..	3.4
	1995	558.7	..	0.0	0.5	..	..	.	15.1	84.9	..	..
	2000	697.0	0.0	0.0	0.7	..	0.0	0.3	5.7	93.8	..	0.1
	2005	598.2	0.0	0.0	0.5	0.0	0.0	0.4	10.2	87.8	1.4	0.2
Turkey - Turquie	1990	6 360.0	0.6	1.5	1.3	..	0.2	22.3	55.0	20.4	..	1.8
	1995	10 345.1	0.6	2.7	1.6	0.0	0.3	14.4	67.5	16.1	0.1	1.9
	2000	9 159.0	0.4	2.1	1.8	0.3	0.5	12.4	62.1	19.2	2.3	3.9
	2005	7 621.1	0.4	1.2	1.6	0.3	0.3	19.1	54.3	20.7	4.0	1.9
United Arab Emirates - Émirats arabes unis	1990	1 158.0	0.2	0.0	0.2	0.9	0.2	50.2	4.7	18.7	18.8	7.6
	1995	1 530.9	0.4	0.0	0.2	0.3	0.2	62.7	4.0	15.3	9.3	8.7
	2000	1 102.0	0.1	0.0	0.2	0.5	0.2	36.1	0.1	19.6	31.7	12.5
	2005	1 065.6	0.1	0.0	0.1	0.2	0.3	41.2	13.3	9.4	21.3	14.8

For sources and notes, see end of table.   Pour les sources et les notes, se reporter à la fin du tableau.

5

295

5.4 World merchant fleet by flag of registration and type of ship of countries and geographical regions

5.4 Flotte marchande mondiale par pavillons d'immatriculation et par types de navires des pays et des régions géographiques

Region, country or territory / Régions pays ou territoires	Year / Année	Total fleet (thousands of DWT) (1) / Flotte totale (milliers de TPL) (1)	As percentage of world total fleet / En pourcentage de la flotte mondiale					As percentage of the country or region total fleet / En pourcentage de la flotte totale du pays ou de la région				
			Oil tankers / Pétroliers	Bulk carriers / Vraquiers	General cargo / Navires de charge classique	Container ships / Porte-conteneurs	Other types / Autres navires	Oil tankers / Pétroliers	Bulk carriers / Vraquiers	General cargo / Navires de charge classique	Container ships / Porte-conteneurs	Other types / Autres navires
Yemen - Yémen	1990	14.0	0.0	..	..	0.0	0.0	21.4	..	35.7	..	42.9
	1995	26.6	0.0	..	0.0	..	0.0	12.0	..	11.5	..	76.5
	2000	31.0	0.0	..	0.0	..	0.0	25.8	..	9.7	..	64.5
Developing economies: Oceania - Économies en développement : Océanie	**1990**	**3 540.0**	**0.2**	**0.9**	**0.8**	**0.3**	**0.4**	**11.0**	**58.0**	**23.8**	**2.1**	**5.1**
	1995	**2 565.4**	**0.0**	**0.5**	**0.6**	**0.1**	**0.8**	**2.9**	**54.2**	**23.9**	**1.2**	**17.8**
	2000	**1 614.0**	**0.0**	**0.3**	**0.4**	**0.1**	**0.4**	**1.5**	**52.0**	**25.7**	**2.2**	**18.6**
	2005	**2 748.6**	**0.0**	**0.4**	**0.7**	**0.0**	**1.2**	**0.7**	**51.2**	**24.0**	**1.2**	**22.8**
Fiji - Fidji	1990	53.0	0.0	..	0.0	..	0.0	11.3	..	69.8	..	18.9
	1995	26.9	0.0	..	0.0	..	0.0	13.4	..	40.3	..	46.3
	2000	25.0	0.0	..	0.0	..	0.0	16.0	..	24.0	..	60.0
	2005	14.9	..	..	0.0	..	0.0	..	..	45.6	..	54.4
Kiribati	1990	3.0	..	..	0.0	..	..	..	..	100.0	..	..
	1995	7.1	0.0	..	0.0	..	0.0	43.0	..	47.3	..	9.8
	2000	3.0	..	..	0.0	..	..	..	..	100.0	..	..
	2005	6.7	..	..	0.0	..	0.0	..	..	90.3	..	9.7
Nauru	1990	41.0	..	0.0	0.0	..	..	..	65.9	34.1	..	..
Papua New Guinea - Papouasie-Nouvelle-Guinée	1990	35.0	0.0	0.0	0.0	..	0.0	8.6	14.3	48.6	..	28.6
	1995	52.3	0.0	..	0.0	..	0.0	9.7	..	84.3	..	6.1
	2000	80.0	0.0	..	0.1	..	0.0	3.8	..	80.0	..	16.3
	2005	95.1	0.0	0.0	0.1	..	0.0	7.0	5.7	81.0	..	6.2
Samoa	1990	35.0	..	..	0.0	..	0.0	..	..	97.1	..	2.9
	1995	6.5	..	..	0.0	..	0.0	..	..	93.3	..	6.7
Solomon Islands - Îles Salomon	1990	6.0	..	..	0.0	..	0.0	..	..	66.7	..	33.3
	1995	5.7	..	..	0.0	..	0.0	..	..	54.9	..	45.1
	2000	6.0	..	..	0.0	..	0.0	..	..	33.3	..	66.7
	2005	5.4	..	..	0.0	..	0.0	..	..	34.6	..	65.4
Tonga	1990	50.0	..	..	0.0	0.1	0.0	..	..	34.0	60.0	6.0
	1995	15.3	..	..	0.0	..	0.0	..	..	72.4	..	27.6
	2000	30.0	..	..	0.0	..	0.0	..	..	63.3	..	36.7
	2005	96.9	0.0	0.0	0.1	..	0.0	4.3	6.9	79.9	..	8.9
Tuvalu	1990	1.0	..	..	0.0	..	..	..	..	100.0	..	..
	1995	93.1	..	..	0.0	..	0.1	..	..	37.8	..	62.2
	2000	78.0	..	..	0.0	..	0.1	..	..	44.9	..	55.1
	2005	310.4	0.0	0.0	0.3	0.0	0.0	3.0	11.5	78.0	1.4	6.1
Vanuatu	1990	3 316.0	0.2	0.9	0.7	0.2	0.3	11.5	60.9	21.5	1.4	4.6
	1995	2 358.6	0.0	0.5	0.5	0.1	0.7	2.7	59.0	21.2	1.3	15.9
	2000	1 392.0	0.0	0.3	0.3	0.1	0.3	1.2	60.3	20.5	2.5	15.4
	2005	2 219.1	..	0.4	0.3	0.0	1.1	..	61.3	11.2	1.3	26.2
Developing Economies: Unspecified - Économies en développement : non spécifiées ailleurs	2005	12.2	..	..	0.0	..	..	..	..	100.0	..	..
Economies in transition: Asia - Économies en transition : Asie	**1995**	**939.9**	**0.2**	**0.1**	**0.1**	**..**	**0.3**	**50.0**	**17.0**	**12.4**	**..**	**20.5**
	2000	**684.0**	**0.1**	**0.0**	**0.2**	**..**	**0.3**	**36.3**	**0.4**	**33.5**	**..**	**29.8**
	2005	**2 158.2**	**0.1**	**0.2**	**0.9**	**0.0**	**0.5**	**17.5**	**29.3**	**40.7**	**0.6**	**11.9**
Azerbaijan - Azerbaïdjan	1995	504.1	0.1	..	0.1	..	0.3	48.2	..	20.6	..	31.2
	2000	503.0	0.1	..	0.1	..	0.2	46.3	..	20.5	..	33.2
	2005	568.3	0.1	..	0.1	..	0.3	50.9	..	19.9	..	29.2
Georgia - Géorgie	1995	407.7	0.1	0.1	0.0	..	0.0	54.4	39.2	0.9	..	5.4
	2000	142.0	0.0	..	0.1	..	0.0	8.5	..	77.5	..	14.1
	2005	1 501.5	0.0	0.2	0.8	0.0	0.1	3.7	41.9	49.3	0.9	4.2
Kazakhstan	1995	5.8	..	..	0.0	..	0.0	..	..	22.2	..	77.8
	2000	6.0	..	..	0.0	..	0.0	..	..	16.7	..	83.3
	2005	46.8	0.0	..	0.0	..	0.0	53.9	..	19.5	..	26.5
Turkmenistan - Turkménistan	1995	22.3	0.0	..	0.0	..	0.0	22.4	..	36.1	..	41.5
	2000	33.0	0.0	0.0	0.0	..	0.0	9.1	9.1	45.5	..	36.4
	2005	41.6	0.0	0.0	0.0	..	0.0	20.2	8.0	37.2	..	34.6

For sources and notes, see end of table.

Pour les sources et les notes, se reporter à la fin du tableau.

5.4 World merchant fleet by flag of registration and type of ship of countries and geographical regions

5.4 Flotte marchande mondiale par pavillons d'immatriculation et par types de navires des pays et des régions géographiques

Region, country or territory / Régions pays ou territoires	Year / Année	*Total fleet (thousands of DWT) (1) / Flotte totale (milliers de TPL) (1)	As percentage of world total fleet / En pourcentage de la flotte mondiale					As percentage of the country or region total fleet / En pourcentage de la flotte totale du pays ou de la région				
			Oil tankers / Pétroliers	Bulk carriers / Vraquiers	General cargo / Navires de charge classique	Container ships / Porte-conteneurs	Other types / Autres navires	Oil tankers / Pétroliers	Bulk carriers / Vraquiers	General cargo / Navires de charge classique	Container ships / Porte-conteneurs	Other types / Autres navires
Economies in transition: Europe - Économies en transition : Europe	**1990**	**43 505.0**	**3.3**	**6.2**	**14.9**	**3.4**	**10.0**	**18.7**	**33.0**	**34.9**	**1.9**	**11.6**
	1995	**26 884.7**	**1.8**	**2.5**	**11.3**	**1.5**	**6.3**	**17.7**	**23.5**	**43.1**	**2.3**	**13.5**
	2000	**14 294.0**	**0.9**	**1.2**	**6.0**	**0.7**	**3.2**	**17.4**	**22.3**	**42.0**	**3.1**	**15.2**
	2005	**12 666.5**	**0.8**	**1.0**	**4.8**	**0.2**	**3.3**	**21.7**	**26.1**	**36.4**	**2.0**	**13.9**
Albania - Albanie	1990	75.0	..	..	0.1	..	..	..	..	100.0	..	..
	1995	81.0	..	..	0.1	..	..	..	..	100.0	..	..
	2000	24.0	..	..	0.0	..	0.0	..	..	95.8	..	4.2
	2005	107.6	..	..	0.1	..	0.0	..	..	98.7	..	1.3
Bulgaria - Bulgarie	1990	1 954.0	0.2	0.4	0.4	0.1	0.1	23.5	49.6	22.5	0.9	3.4
	1995	1 642.3	0.1	0.3	0.4	0.2	0.1	21.2	47.5	24.1	4.1	3.1
	2000	1 445.0	0.1	0.3	0.3	0.1	0.1	18.5	56.2	18.0	4.6	2.7
	2005	1 307.7	0.0	0.3	0.2	0.1	0.0	2.3	79.3	11.3	5.9	1.2
Croatia - Croatie	1995	372.8	0.0	0.0	0.2	0.2	0.0	2.4	8.4	66.3	16.8	6.0
	2000	1 036.0	0.0	0.3	0.2	0.0	0.0	1.2	73.5	19.7	2.7	3.0
	2005	1 740.6	0.2	0.3	0.2	..	0.1	31.5	57.6	9.0	..	1.9
Romania - Roumanie	1990	6 089.0	0.5	1.4	1.6	0.1	0.3	18.8	51.9	26.8	0.3	2.3
	1995	3 718.8	0.3	0.5	1.3	0.0	0.3	20.4	37.9	36.6	0.4	4.6
	2000	956.0	0.0	0.1	0.5	0.0	0.2	10.7	23.2	49.6	0.8	15.7
	2005	372.2	0.0	0.0	0.1	..	0.2	24.3	6.7	34.8	..	34.3
Russian Federation - Fédération de Russie	1995	15 794.1	1.3	1.1	6.1	0.8	4.9	22.3	18.1	39.5	2.1	17.9
	2000	9 393.0	0.7	0.4	4.2	0.5	2.3	21.5	13.1	45.1	3.3	16.9
	2005	8 006.2	0.6	0.3	3.5	0.1	2.6	25.3	13.5	42.3	1.8	17.1
Yugoslavia, SFR (former) - Yougoslavie, RSF (anc.)	1990	6 027.0	0.2	1.5	1.8	0.6	0.1	8.6	58.0	30.2	2.4	0.8
USSR (former) - URSS (anc.)	1990	29 360.0	2.4	2.9	11.0	2.7	9.5	20.4	22.9	38.2	2.2	16.3
Ukraine	1995	5 275.8	0.0	0.5	3.2	0.3	1.0	2.3	23.2	61.6	2.5	10.5
	2000	1 440.0	0.0	0.1	0.8	0.0	0.5	6.3	11.1	55.9	2.1	24.7
	2005	1 132.1	0.0	0.0	0.7	0.0	0.4	4.2	14.2	60.0	3.0	18.7
MEMO ITEM												
Major open-registry countries - Principaux pays de libre immatriculation	*1990*	*232 316.0*	*43.1*	*35.2*	*27.8*	*23.2*	*23.7*	*45.4*	*34.9*	*12.2*	*2.4*	*5.2*
	1995	*318 924.1*	*50.7*	*45.9*	*33.8*	*36.0*	*29.9*	*42.1*	*37.0*	*10.9*	*4.6*	*5.3*
	2000	*390 763.0*	*51.2*	*55.8*	*37.3*	*41.8*	*38.4*	*37.1*	*39.4*	*9.5*	*7.2*	*6.7*
	2005	*431 909.6*	*43.4*	*52.6*	*32.1*	*43.0*	*33.7*	*35.6*	*42.1*	*7.2*	*11.1*	*4.1*
Developed economies excluding Bermuda, Cyprus and Malta - Économies développées sans les Bermudes, Chypre et Malte	1990	220 774.0	36.9	30.1	24.5	50.9	47.3	41.0	31.4	11.3	5.4	10.9
	1995	198 738.1	31.4	21.3	19.8	39.6	42.5	41.9	27.5	10.2	8.2	12.2
	2000	196 282.0	29.9	15.8	18.9	34.8	37.8	43.1	22.2	9.6	11.9	13.2
	2005	251 967.2	30.9	18.2	20.3	34.9	40.1	43.4	25.0	7.8	15.4	8.4
Developing economies excluding Bahamas, Liberia and Panama - Économies en développement sans les Bahamas, le Libéria et Panama	1990	154 687.0	16.7	28.4	32.8	22.5	19.0	26.4	42.3	21.7	3.4	6.2
	1995	177 130.5	15.9	30.3	35.0	22.9	20.9	23.8	43.8	20.3	5.3	6.7
	2000	192 940.6	18.0	27.3	37.5	22.7	20.3	26.4	39.1	19.4	7.9	7.2
	2005	261 262.4	24.9	28.0	41.9	21.8	22.4	33.7	37.1	15.4	9.3	4.5
Developing economies Africa excluding Liberia - Économies en développement Afrique sans le Libéria	1990	7 625.0	1.0	0.5	2.3	1.1	3.0	31.7	14.7	30.4	3.3	20.0
	1995	6 944.0	0.8	0.5	1.9	0.7	2.3	31.7	18.0	27.8	4.0	18.5
	2000	6 321.3	0.6	0.5	1.7	0.6	1.9	24.9	19.9	27.5	6.8	21.0
	2005	5 536.8	0.4	0.4	1.3	0.2	2.4	27.6	23.0	22.9	3.4	23.0
Developing economies America excluding Bahamas and Panama - Économies en développement Amérique sans les Bahamas et le Panama	1990	25 529.0	3.1	3.9	6.2	1.5	4.5	29.4	35.4	24.9	1.4	9.0
	1995	29 798.0	3.1	3.6	7.9	3.6	4.8	27.6	31.0	27.2	5.0	9.2
	2000	34 051.3	2.7	3.6	9.9	5.3	4.5	22.5	29.2	28.9	10.4	9.1
	2005	36 729.2	2.5	2.8	10.3	5.1	4.6	24.5	26.8	26.9	15.3	6.6

Sources:
- UNCTAD *Review of Maritime Transport*, various editions
- *Lloyd's Register-Fairplay*, from 2003 onwards
- *Lloyd's Maritime Information Services* (London), from 1994 to 2002
- *Lloyd's Register of Shipping* (London) - Statistical tables and supplementary data regarding the Great Lakes Fleet of the United States and Canada and the United States Reserve Fleet, from 1979 to 1993

Notes:
- Major open-registry countries include: Bahamas, Bermuda, Cyprus, Liberia, Malta, and Panama.
(a) Including San Marino.
(b) Including Taïwan.
(1) Weight measure of a vessel's carrying capacity. It includes cargo, fuel and stores.

Sources :
- *Étude sur les transports maritimes* de la CNUCED, diverses éditions
- *Lloyd's Registry-Fairplay*, à partir de 2003
- *Services d'informations maritimes de Lloyd* (Londres), de 1994 à 2002
- *Le registre maritime de la Lloyd* (Londres) - Tableaux statistiques et les données supplémentaires concernant les flottes des Grands Lacs des États-Unis et du Canada et la flotte de réserve des États-Unis, de 1979 à 1993

Notes :
- Les pays de libre immatriculation comprennent : Bahamas, Bermudes, Chypre, Libéria, Malte et Panama.
(a) Y compris Saint-Marin.
(b) Y compris Taïwan.
(1) Mesure de poids de la capacité de charge d'un navire. Inclut la cargaison, le carburant et les magasins.

6

COMMODITIES

PRODUITS DE BASE

Commodity	Level (1) Niveau (1) 2000	1985	1990	1995	1998	1999	2001	2002	2003	2004	2005	2006
ALL COMMODITIES	–	**96.0**	**124.3**	**138.0**	**114.4**	**98.4**	**96.4**	**97.2**	**105.1**	**125.5**	**140.8**	**183.6**
All food	–	**103.4**	**121.8**	**138.9**	**126.3**	**102.8**	**99.6**	**102.5**	**106.8**	**120.8**	**128.4**	**149.4**
Food and tropical beverages	–	*98.8*	*123.5*	*135.5*	*121.0*	*100.1*	*100.4*	*100.8*	*103.1*	*116.7*	*127.0*	*149.6*
Food	–	*89.6*	*125.4*	*132.3*	*117.8*	*98.0*	*102.8*	*102.2*	*104.1*	*118.6*	*127.2*	*151.3*
1. Wheat*	119.6	91.4	88.9	139.4	99.3	96.0	99.5	108.2	126.8	114.9	109.2	128.5
2. Wheat	119.2	115.6	114.8	150.0	108.6	96.7	109.0	127.1	126.2	134.8	132.9	168.2
3. Maize	86.8	..	123.9	142.7	117.2	108.7	101.1	111.0	117.9	120.3	103.8	138.6
4. Maize*	90.0	..	121.9	139.0	114.3	102.9	101.2	111.7	118.9	124.9	109.9	136.8
5. Rice	203.8	106.7	140.9	157.8	149.9	122.3	84.7	94.1	97.9	120.6	141.2	149.0
6. Sugar (2)	8.2	49.6	153.4	162.4	109.6	76.7	105.6	84.2	86.7	87.6	120.9	180.6
7. Beef (2)	87.8	111.2	131.5	98.5	89.2	94.7	110.0	109.7	110.2	129.8	135.2	131.9
8. Bananas (2)	19.0	90.7	123.6	104.7	113.7	102.4	138.8	125.5	89.4	125.1	137.4	162.8
9. Pepper	4 341.6	93.0	41.3	87.3	163.7	157.2	57.0	53.1	64.7	59.1	57.1	74.5
10. Soybean meal	199.7	78.7	107.1	105.5	94.9	82.4	99.1	95.7	112.4	128.6	116.5	110.3
11. Fish meal	413.0	67.8	99.8	119.9	160.3	95.0	117.8	146.7	147.9	157.1	172.2	281.9
Tropical beverages	–	*179.1*	*107.6*	*163.3*	*149.6*	*118.2*	*79.4*	*88.7*	*94.1*	*100.2*	*125.7*	*134.1*
12. Coffee (2)	102.6	151.9	94.1	154.3	139.2	113.5	70.4	63.6	65.6	82.0	114.0	115.4
13. Coffee (2)	79.9	190.0	103.7	182.7	152.5	111.2	63.3	56.5	63.6	85.4	126.9	128.8
14. Coffee (2)	85.1	171.1	104.7	175.4	155.4	119.3	72.8	71.0	75.3	94.2	134.3	133.9
15. Coffee (2)	42.1	288.2	130.5	301.0	199.3	160.6	64.8	73.2	91.2	88.5	126.7	166.9
16. Coffee* (2)	63.6	209.8	113.3	217.0	171.2	133.0	70.2	71.8	80.6	92.3	131.8	144.8
17. Cocoa (2)	40.3	254.0	143.2	161.5	189.2	128.4	122.7	200.3	197.7	174.5	173.3	179.4
18. Tea (3)	248.1	..	..	71.1	100.7	93.7	79.9	72.2	78.3	79.9	87.2	97.4
Vegetable oilseeds and oils	–	*141.2*	*107.0*	*167.1*	*169.9*	*125.4*	*93.6*	*116.9*	*137.2*	*155.3*	*140.6*	*147.7*
19. Soybeans	211.8	106.3	116.5	122.4	114.7	95.2	92.5	100.4	124.6	144.7	129.7	126.8
20. Soybean oil	338.1	169.2	132.3	184.9	185.1	126.4	104.7	134.4	163.8	182.2	161.2	177.1
21. Sunflower oil	391.8	153.7	124.9	176.9	185.9	129.5	123.6	151.7	151.4	174.6	172.9	167.9
22. Groundnut oil	713.7	126.8	135.0	138.8	127.4	110.4	95.3	96.3	174.2	162.7	148.6	135.9
23. Copra	304.8	126.7	75.7	143.9	134.9	151.4	66.3	87.4	98.4	147.7	135.8	132.1
24. Coconut oil	450.3	131.1	74.8	148.7	146.1	163.7	70.6	93.5	103.8	146.7	137.0	134.8
25. Palm kernel oil	443.5	124.3	75.3	152.8	154.8	156.5	69.5	93.8	103.4	146.1	141.4	131.0
26. Palm oil	310.3	161.3	93.4	202.5	216.3	140.5	92.1	125.8	142.9	151.9	136.1	154.2
Agricultural raw materials	–	**92.5**	**130.2**	**153.1**	**107.8**	**97.0**	**96.1**	**93.8**	**112.4**	**123.5**	**132.3**	**152.2**
27. Linseed oil	398.4	157.5	177.9	165.0	177.6	128.5	96.2	130.4	170.2	218.5	276.5	168.6
28. Tobacco	2 988.1	87.4	113.7	88.5	111.7	103.8	100.0	91.8	88.6	91.7	93.4	99.4
29. Cotton (2)	83.8	117.6	112.1	133.8	98.0	84.9	94.8	79.4	88.8	97.1	88.0	102.5
30. Cotton (2)	65.5	108.9	127.9	159.4	114.7	85.1	81.0	72.5	105.9	95.8	89.9	92.8
31. Cotton (2)	57.3	111.8	138.4	176.0	125.3	96.6	79.1	76.5	105.5	107.3	97.6	101.6
32. Cotton* (2)	51.7	90.7	150.3	161.5	138.2	85.2	89.4	80.5	120.7	92.5	101.1	110.9
33. Cotton* (2)	59.2	101.0	139.5	164.4	110.2	89.7	81.0	78.1	107.1	103.6	91.5	97.0
34. Cotton (2)	108.5	147.9	236.0	..	120.1	106.6	108.6	94.4	103.5	109.5	93.2	126.3
35. Wool (4)	733.5	..	..	..	75.4	84.4	85.0	87.9	95.7	97.2	92.4	97.6
36. Wool (4)	281.0	..	..	..	119.7	98.4	118.3	201.3	234.5	196.9	188.8	192.4
37. Jute	278.8	204.2	146.5	131.2	92.9	98.9	118.2	97.2	86.8	100.5	104.0	104.0
38. Sisal	782.1	79.2	95.0	97.4	123.3	112.4	107.7	99.4	102.1	122.9	126.0	126.0
39. Sisal	628.7	83.6	113.7	113.0	130.7	110.7	111.2	105.0	111.1	137.0	140.8	140.8
40. Hides (2)	80.2	63.8	115.0	109.9	95.6	89.9	105.5	102.4	85.2	83.7	82.0	86.1
41. Non-coniferous woods*	100.0	..	..	107.8	102.5	104.0	98.0	105.4	118.0	136.0	143.9	165.3
42. Tropical logs (5)	244.6	71.1	140.4	139.4	103.9	96.4	106.4	95.2	114.3	136.3	136.7	130.2
43. Tropical sawnwood* (5)	531.8	51.9	98.6	144.2	83.4	97.8	95.7	94.3	102.2	103.4	103.4	103.4
44. Plywood* (6)	448.5	47.0	79.1	129.9	83.7	98.4	91.4	89.8	97.2	103.6	113.4	132.8
45. Rubber	669.2	112.8	129.4	239.2	106.1	92.7	85.9	114.3	162.0	194.9	224.4	315.2

For sources and notes, see end of table.

	2004				2005				2006				Produits
	I	II	III	IV	I	II	III	IV	I	II	III	IV	
126.0	**127.0**	**123.0**	**126.1**	**138.8**	**137.9**	**139.8**	**146.7**	**167.2**	**187.6**	**189.0**	**190.5**	**TOTAL DES PRODUITS**
122.2	**125.5**	**117.7**	**118.0**	**130.4**	**127.3**	**125.9**	**130.2**	**143.0**	**150.7**	**147.3**	**151.5**	**Total des produits alimentaires**
115.9	*121.2*	*114.6*	*115.2*	*129.3*	*125.2*	*124.3*	*129.2*	*149.3*	*151.9*	*147.1*	*150.0*	***Produits alimentaires et boissons tropicales***
117.8	*124.1*	*116.3*	*116.1*	*129.1*	*124.5*	*124.8*	*130.3*	*150.8*	*154.5*	*148.7*	*151.3*	*Produits alimentaires*
128.4	127.9	106.9	96.6	97.3	110.2	117.4	111.7	112.8	117.0	127.1	157.2	1. Blé*
140.7	138.1	126.8	133.5	131.1	125.1	133.1	142.1	150.5	166.1	173.1	182.9	2. Blé
128.4	136.1	114.0	102.6	94.6	100.2	112.7	107.6	119.1	126.4	129.9	179.1	3. Maïs
136.8	143.2	113.8	105.6	108.2	107.4	112.6	111.5	117.8	122.9	130.8	175.5	4. Maïs*
108.0	122.6	121.9	129.9	143.1	144.1	138.9	138.6	143.7	148.2	153.4	150.5	5. Riz
73.8	80.9	94.5	101.3	108.8	106.9	121.8	145.9	207.6	202.6	169.5	142.6	6. Sucre (2)
115.4	126.8	142.4	134.8	133.6	136.3	137.8	132.8	129.5	128.3	133.3	136.7	7. Viande de boeuf (2)
114.8	133.8	133.6	118.2	182.4	135.6	110.2	121.4	189.0	185.1	133.2	143.9	8. Bananes (2)
59.8	61.0	58.5	57.1	58.7	57.6	56.6	55.6	57.6	60.3	81.5	98.7	9. Poivre
151.2	147.7	109.9	105.7	118.0	120.2	117.4	110.2	108.2	105.0	107.7	120.4	10. Farine de soja
163.8	156.6	152.3	155.5	155.1	160.6	172.5	200.6	217.8	285.3	323.1	301.2	11. Farine de poisson
98.9	*95.5*	*99.5*	*106.8*	*131.4*	*131.8*	*119.9*	*119.6*	*136.2*	*129.1*	*132.5*	*138.7*	*Boissons tropicales*
76.7	79.0	78.9	93.5	120.7	123.7	105.6	106.2	120.1	110.4	109.8	121.1	12. Café (2)
81.9	81.3	78.9	99.3	133.2	137.7	115.8	121.1	137.3	123.6	119.9	134.5	13. Café (2)
89.7	91.2	89.2	106.5	142.6	146.9	123.4	124.4	139.0	126.8	127.0	142.7	14. Café (2)
94.2	92.7	84.1	82.9	106.8	138.5	131.6	130.1	154.2	152.4	175.9	184.9	15. Café (2)
91.2	91.7	87.5	98.7	130.7	144.1	126.1	126.3	144.1	135.3	143.2	156.7	16. Café* (2)
176.4	159.9	181.3	180.1	185.5	174.1	168.0	165.4	175.3	179.3	182.3	180.7	17. Cacao (2)
79.7	74.2	85.7	80.2	99.0	82.5	85.6	81.8	102.7	96.5	99.6	90.9	18. Thé (3)
174.7	*162.2*	*143.3*	*141.1*	*139.5*	*144.2*	*139.7*	*139.0*	*137.1*	*140.7*	*149.3*	*163.5*	***Graines oléagineuses et huiles végétales***
178.0	152.5	126.5	121.8	127.9	137.2	131.4	122.2	121.3	124.5	124.6	136.9	19. Fèves de soja
200.9	185.8	176.7	165.4	154.2	162.1	163.2	165.2	158.3	170.5	183.5	196.1	20. Huile de soja
181.4	171.2	162.8	183.1	179.3	178.7	176.4	157.0	152.5	170.5	168.6	180.2	21. Huile de tournesol
167.8	167.9	156.6	158.4	161.5	154.3	143.6	134.9	128.6	125.6	132.5	157.0	22. Huile d'arachide
137.1	160.7	145.8	147.1	147.0	146.4	124.9	124.7	125.9	125.7	131.4	145.6	23. Coprah
141.5	156.2	144.6	144.7	148.2	145.5	126.9	127.4	128.4	128.5	133.1	149.1	24. Huile de coprah
139.6	155.9	141.8	147.2	149.3	147.9	131.3	137.0	136.8	125.6	126.1	135.7	25. Huile de palmiste
169.9	160.2	139.3	138.3	133.2	135.9	133.8	141.3	140.6	141.4	158.8	175.9	26. Huile de palme
130.0	*119.7*	*119.3*	*124.9*	*126.1*	*128.5*	*136.9*	*137.7*	*148.5*	*161.6*	*155.4*	*143.2*	***Matières premières d'origine agricole***
168.3	191.6	235.0	279.2	312.4	380.2	223.4	189.9	165.4	166.9	166.2	175.8	27. Huile de lin
92.8	92.7	90.7	90.7	91.5	93.7	92.6	95.7	96.4	96.9	101.7	104.5	28. Tabac
111.5	100.2	94.9	81.2	86.6	89.4	87.8	..	102.4	102.4	102.7	..	29. Coton (2)
114.7	106.9	84.1	80.9	85.9	90.9	88.8	93.4	94.4	90.2	94.9	91.7	30. Coton (2)
125.9	114.5	96.4	92.2	93.7	97.5	96.5	102.8	101.6	97.5	104.9	102.3	31. Coton (2)
..	..	98.3	90.6	97.4	103.5	97.6	104.7	110.9	..	..	..	32. Coton* (2)
125.1	114.8	92.2	82.2	88.3	91.9	90.4	95.5	98.8	93.3	98.0	97.9	33. Coton* (2)
131.2	124.2	100.8	81.6	89.7	95.1	98.0	..	126.9	129.7	129.8	119.8	34. Coton (2)
98.1	95.0	97.0	98.7	99.7	96.8	91.3	81.8	93.1	97.4	96.7	103.2	35. Laine (4)
215.1	195.5	187.8	189.1	195.9	194.6	191.4	173.4	183.4	184.3	187.3	214.6	36. Laine (4)
90.0	104.0	104.0	104.0	104.0	104.0	104.0	104.0	104.0	104.0	104.0	104.0	37. Jute
113.7	126.0	126.0	126.0	126.0	126.0	126.0	126.0	126.0	126.0	126.0	126.0	38. Sisal
125.6	140.8	140.8	140.8	140.8	140.8	140.8	140.8	140.8	140.8	140.8	140.8	39. Sisal
86.8	79.8	85.2	83.1	82.3	81.4	82.3	81.9	82.7	85.6	86.4	89.7	40. Cuirs (2)
136.5	133.8	135.3	138.5	143.7	145.4	142.5	144.1	148.6	159.2	170.1	183.3	41. Bois non conifères*
131.7	131.6	136.1	145.6	144.8	135.6	135.1	131.2	129.0	129.3	128.7	133.9	42. Grumes tropicales (5)
103.4	103.4	103.4	103.4	103.4	103.4	103.4	103.4	103.4	103.4	103.4	103.4	43. Grumes tropicales sciées* (5)
104.0	101.7	101.4	107.5	114.9	114.3	112.9	111.5	117.9	128.8	142.3	142.1	44. Contre-plaqué* (6)
195.1	206.0	191.0	187.5	189.1	207.0	250.3	251.3	302.4	367.2	328.1	262.9	45. Caoutchouc

Pour les sources et les notes, se reporter à la fin du tableau.

6

6.1 Annual and quaterly indices of free-market prices of selected primary commodities
2000 = 100

Commodity	Level (1) Niveau (1) 2000	1985	1990	1995	1998	1999	2001	2002	2003	2004	2005	2006
Minerals, ores and metals	_	**81.2**	**127.0**	**128.1**	**90.7**	**89.0**	**89.2**	**86.8**	**97.6**	**137.3**	**173.2**	**277.7**
46. Phosphate rock	43.8	76.6	92.6	80.0	96.0	100.4	95.5	92.3	86.9	93.7	96.0	101.1
47. Manganese ore	186.0	74.5	213.1	109.7	109.5	102.6	106.7	106.7	106.7	106.7	175.8	139.7
48. Iron ore (7)	27.7	96.0	111.3	97.4	107.3	97.4	104.5	103.4	112.2	131.7	225.9	268.8
49. Iron ore* (7)	27.5	96.5	109.8	97.4	108.1	99.8	104.3	103.5	109.8	126.2	201.0	256.4
50. Aluminium	1 549.2	69.8	105.8	116.6	87.6	87.9	93.2	87.1	92.4	110.8	122.5	165.9
51. Copper	1 813.1	78.2	146.8	161.8	91.2	86.7	87.0	86.0	98.1	158.0	202.9	370.7
52. Copper* (2)	86.8	75.6	140.4	158.4	88.4	85.9	87.0	85.8	96.6	152.8	198.4	361.2
53. Nickel*	8 637.7	56.8	102.6	95.3	53.6	69.6	68.8	78.4	111.5	160.0	170.6	280.7
54. Nickel (2)	397.9	56.8	102.3	98.1	53.9	69.1	69.0	77.8	111.7	159.4	171.2	276.0
55. Lead	454.0	86.1	178.5	138.9	116.5	110.7	104.9	99.7	113.5	195.2	215.0	283.8
56. Lead* (2)	43.6	43.8	103.4	96.3	103.9	100.4	100.2	100.0	100.4	126.6	140.1	178.0
57. Zinc	1 128.1	67.0	134.6	91.4	90.8	95.4	78.5	69.0	73.4	92.9	122.5	290.3
58. Zinc* 2	55.6	72.6	134.1	95.9	92.0	96.2	79.0	69.5	73.1	94.4	120.7	285.7
59. Tin	5 432.8	221.8	114.8	114.3	101.9	99.4	82.5	74.7	90.0	156.5	135.8	161.5
60. Tin*	5 382.0	221.5	113.1	113.1	99.8	98.6	81.9	74.9	90.9	157.8	136.7	162.9
61. Tungsten (8)	44.9	150.9	103.4	141.2	98.4	89.2	145.6	84.8	100.0	122.9	271.3	369.7
62. Gold* (9)	279.0	113.7	137.4	137.7	105.4	99.9	97.1	111.1	130.3	146.6	159.4	216.6
63. Silver* (10)	499.9	122.9	96.4	103.8	110.7	105.0	87.8	92.6	98.2	133.3	146.8	231.4
MEMO ITEM:												
64. Crude petroleum (11)	28.2	95.6	78.1	59.9	46.3	64.3	86.7	88.4	102.4	133.8	189.1	227.8
65. Manufactures export unit value	100.0	70.9	110.9	122.3	109.1	105.2	97.9	98.5	107.6	116.5	119.4	122.5

Sources:
- The prices used in the calculation of the indices shown in this table are extracted from
  the UNCTAD *Commodity Price Statistics* on-line.

Notes:

- The group indices have been re-based on 2000 using new weights. These indices include all commodities shown except for those with an asterisk (*).
- The average annual indices are calculated from monthly data and may not correspond to the average from quarterly data.
(1) Dollars per metric ton (if not indicated otherwise).
(2) Cents per pound.
(3) Cents per kilogram.
(4) Dollars per 100 kilograms.
(5) Dollars per cubic meter.
(6) Cents per sheet.
(7) Cents per Fe unit.
(8) Dollars per metric ton unit of WO3.
(9) Dollars per troy ounce.
(10) Cents per troy ounce.
(11) Dollars per barrel.

- For specifications, see next page.

	2004				2005				2006			Produits
I	II	III	IV	I	II	III	IV	I	II	III	IV	
132.8	**133.9**	**137.2**	**145.2**	**164.5**	**166.9**	**172.8**	**188.6**	**220.5**	**285.1**	**301.2**	**304.0**	**Minéraux, minerais et métaux**
88.6	94.1	96.0	96.0	96.0	96.0	96.0	96.0	96.8	99.4	104.0	104.0	46. Phosphate brut
106.7	106.7	106.7	106.7	143.3	204.3	195.4	160.4	146.8	145.2	131.1	135.8	47. Minerai de manganèse
131.7	131.7	131.7	131.7	225.9	225.9	225.9	225.9	268.8	268.8	268.8	268.8	48. Minerai de fer (7)
112.1	130.9	130.9	130.9	130.9	224.4	224.4	224.4	224.4	267.1	267.1	267.1	49. Minerai de fer* (7)
106.5	108.3	110.3	118.0	122.6	115.5	118.0	134.0	156.3	171.3	160.2	175.8	50. Aluminium
150.6	153.8	157.1	170.6	180.2	186.9	207.1	237.2	272.4	397.6	423.0	389.8	51. Cuivre
145.1	146.6	152.7	166.6	173.6	181.0	200.5	238.3	264.7	394.1	413.0	372.9	52. Cuivre* (2)
170.5	144.7	162.0	162.9	177.6	189.9	168.6	146.4	171.4	230.6	337.3	383.4	53. Nickel*
168.1	145.0	162.7	161.6	178.6	192.4	170.0	144.0	170.0	228.4	328.3	377.1	54. Nickel (2)
185.9	178.6	205.3	211.1	215.6	217.3	196.3	231.0	273.4	242.5	262.2	357.0	55. Plomb
113.4	123.2	130.3	139.3	139.4	139.5	138.8	142.7	171.2	174.9	175.7	190.4	56. Plomb* (2)
94.8	91.0	86.8	98.7	116.7	112.8	115.0	145.4	198.7	291.8	298.2	372.6	57. Zinc
95.3	93.0	89.2	99.9	115.4	111.0	113.0	143.3	194.5	287.2	296.2	364.8	58. Zinc* (2)
127.4	169.2	166.0	163.5	148.7	146.4	129.6	118.3	139.9	156.8	159.1	190.1	59. Etain
128.5	171.7	166.1	165.0	149.7	147.3	130.3	119.5	140.9	159.4	160.2	191.2	60. Etain*
104.4	120.6	130.3	136.4	162.1	277.4	322.9	322.9	368.6	381.0	361.6	367.4	61. Tungstène (8)
146.4	140.9	143.8	155.5	153.1	153.1	157.5	174.0	198.6	224.8	222.8	220.2	62. Or* (9)
134.3	125.7	128.1	145.3	140.1	143.7	141.8	161.7	193.9	245.3	233.8	252.7	63. Argent* (10)
												POUR MÉMOIRE :
113.9	126.2	143.7	151.4	163.5	179.9	212.6	200.4	216.1	242.0	243.7	209.2	64. Pétrole brut (11)
115.4	114.4	116.0	120.4	123.0	120.0	118.0	117.0	119.0	123.0	124.0	124.0	65. Valeur unitaire des exportations d'articles manufacturés

Sources :
- Les prix utilisés pour le calcul des indices présentés dans ce tableau sont extraits des
  Statistiques des prix des produits de base en ligne de la CNUCED.

Notes :

- Les indices agrégés ont été calculés en utilisant 2000=100 comme année de base et une nouvelle
  pondération; ils recouvrent tous les produits présentés à l'exception de ceux munis d'un astérisque (*).
- Les indices moyens annuels sont calculés sur la base de données mensuelles et peuvent ne pas
  correspondre aux moyennes calculées sur la base des trimestres.
(1) Dollars par tonne métrique (sauf mention spéciale).
(2) Cents par livre.
(3) Cents par kilogramme.
(4) Dollars par 100 kilogrammes.
(5) Dollars par mètre cube.
(6) Cents par feuille.
(7) Cents par unité de Fe.
(8) Dollars par tonne métrique d'unité de WO3.
(9) Dollars par once "troy".
(10) Cents par once "troy".
(11) Dollars par baril.

- Pour les spécifications, se reporter à la page suivante.

6

Specifications

Food

1. Wheat: Argentina, Trigo Pan Upriver, f.o.b.
2. Wheat: United States, No. 2, Hard Red Winter (ordinary), f.o.b. Gulf ports.
3. Maize: Argentina, Rosario, f.o.b.
4. Maize: United States, No. 3 yellow, f.o.b. Gulf ports.
5. Rice: Thailand, white milled, 5 % broken, f.o.b. Bangkok.
6. Sugar: Caribbean ports, f.o.b. bulk basis (I.S.A.).
7. Beef: Australia and New-Zealand, frozen and boneless, 85 % visible lean, f.o.b. United States ports.
8. Bananas: Central America and Ecuador, fresh, f.o.b. United States ports.
9. Pepper: White Sarawak/Muntok, European market and spot London. Prior to June 2003, Singapore.
10. Soybean meal: Hamburg, 44/45 %, f.o.b. ex-mill.
11. Fish meal: Any origin, 64/65 %, Bremen free carrier price. Prior to March 2006, cost and freight Hamburg.

Tropical beverages

12. Coffee: Colombian mild Arabicas, ex-dock New York (I.C.A.).
13. Coffee: Brazilian and other natural Arabicas, ex-dock New York (I.C.A.).
14. Coffee: Other mild Arabicas, ex-dock New York (I.C.A.).
15. Coffee: Robustas, ex-dock New York (I.C.A.).
16. Coffee: Composite indicator price 1976 (I.C.A.).
17. Cocoa: Average of daily prices, New York/London, 3 months futures (I.C.C.A.).
18. Tea: Mombasa auction prices, Best Pekoe Fannings 1.

Vegetable oils and oilseeds

19. Soybeans: United States, No. 2 yellow, c.i.f. Rotterdam.
20. Soybean oil: Any origin, crude oil, the Netherlands, f.o.b. ex-mill.
21. Sunflower oil: European Union, f.o.b. N.W. European ports.
22. Groundnut oil: Any origin, c.i.f. Rotterdam.
23. Copra: Philippines/Indonesia, bulk, c.i.f. N.W. European ports.
24. Coconut oil: Philippines, c.i.f. Rotterdam.
25. Palm kernel oil: Malaysia, c.i.f. Rotterdam.
26. Palm oil: generally Indonesia, 5%, c.i.f. N.W. European ports.

Agricultural raw materials

27. Linseed oil: Any origin, ex-tank, c.i.f. Rotterdam.
28. Tobacco: Unmanufactured tobacco, US general import price.
29. Cotton: Sudan, Barakat, X4B, C/F Far Eastern quotations. Prior to August 2005, c.i.f. North Europe.
30. Cotton: United States, Memphis/Eastern Midd 1-3/32", c.i.f. North Europe.
31. Cotton: United States; Memphis/Orleans/Texas, Midd 1-3/32", C/F Far Eastern quotations. Prior to June 2005, Memphis/Orleans/Texas, Midd 1-3/32", c.i.f. North Europe.
32. Cotton: Pakistan, Sind/Punjab, Afzal 1-1/32", c.i.f. North Europe.
33. Cotton: Cotton Outlook Index A, Middling 1-3/32", C/F Far Eastern quotations. Prior to August 2004, c.i.f. North Europe.
34. Cotton: Egypt, Giza 88, good + 3/8, C/F Far Eastern quotations. Prior to August 2005, Giza 70, good + 3/8, f.o.b. Alexandria.
35. Wool: Australia, 19 microns.
36. Wool: Australia, 23 microns.
37. Jute: Bangladesh, B.W.D., f.o.b. Mongla.
38. Sisal: Tanzania/Kenya, No. 2 & 3 long, c.i.f. European ports. Prior to 1997, c.i.f. London.
39. Sisal: Tanzania/Kenya, No. 3 & UG, c.i.f. European ports. Prior to 1997, c.i.f. London.
40. Hides: US, Chicago packer's heavy native steers, wholesale dealer's price, f.o.b. shipping point.
41. Non-coniferous woods: United Kingdom, import price index 2000 = 100, dollar equivalent.
42. Tropical logs: Sapele, loyal and marchand, UK import price. Prior to June 2000, Cameroon f.o.b.
43. Tropical sawnwood: Malaysia, Dark Red Meranti, select and better, c.i.f. French ports.
44. Plywood: Southeast Asia, Lauan, 3-ply, Extra, 182 cm x 91 cm x 4 mm, wholesale price, spot Tokyo.
45. Rubber: Singapore, No. 1 RSS, f.o.b. in bales.

Spécifications

Produits alimentaires

1. Blé: Argentine, Trigo Pan Upriver, f.a.b.
2. Blé: États-Unis, Hard Red Winter, n° 2 (ordinaire), f.a.b. ports du Golfe.
3. Maïs: Argentine, Rosario, f.a.b.
4. Maïs: États-Unis, jaune n° 3, f.a.b. ports du Golfe.
5. Riz: Thaïlande, blanchi, 5 % brisures, f.a.b. Bangkok.
6. Sucre: Ports des Caraïbes, f.a.b. en vrac (A.I.S.).
7. Viande de boeuf: Australie et Nouvelle-Zélande, désossée et congelée, maigres à 85 % visibles, f.a.b. ports des États-Unis.
8. Bananes: Amérique centrale et Equateur, fraîches, f.a.b. ports des États-Unis.
9. Poivre: Sarawak blanc/Muntok, cours du disponible sur le marché européen et à Londres. Avant juin 2003, Singapour.
10. Farine de soja: Hambourg, 44/45 %, f.a.b. départ moulin.
11. Farine de poisson: Toutes origines, 64/65 %, Brême, prix franco transporteur. Avant mars 2006, coût et fret Hambourg.

Boissons tropicales

12. Café: Arabicas doux colombiens, ex-dock New York (A.I.C.).
13. Café: Brésilien et autres Arabicas naturels, ex-dock New York (A.I.C.).
14. Café: Autres Arabicas doux, ex-dock New York (A.I.C.).
15. Café: Robustas, ex-dock New York (A.I.C.).
16. Café: Prix indicatif composite de 1976 (A.I.C.).
17. Cacao: Moyenne des cours quotidiens New York/Londres, 3 mois à terme (A.I.C.C.).
18. Thé: Cours aux enchères à Mombasa, Best Pekoe Fannings 1.

Huiles végétales et graines oléagineuses

19. Fèves de soja: États-Unis, n° 2 jaune, c.a.f. Rotterdam.
20. Huile de soja: Toutes origines, huile brute, f.a.b. Pays-Bas, départ raffinerie.
21. Huile de tournesol: Union européenne, f.a.b. ports de l'Europe du Nord-Ouest.
22. Huile d'arachide: Toutes origines, c.a.f. Rotterdam.
23. Coprah: Philippines/Indonésie, en vrac, c.a.f. ports de l'Europe du Nord-Ouest.
24. Huile de coprah: Philippines, c.a.f. Rotterdam.
25. Huile de palmiste: Malaisie, c.a.f. Rotterdam.
26. Huile de palme: généralement Indonésie, 5 %, c.a.f. ports de l'Europe du Nord-Ouest.

Matières premières d'origine agricole

27. Huile de lin: Toutes origines, cours du disponible, c.a.f. Rotterdam.
28. Tabac: Tabac non fabrique, prix général à l'importation aux États-Unis.
29. Coton: Soudan, Barakat, classe X4B, cotations coût et fret Extrême Orient. Avant août 2005, c.a.f. Europe septentrionale.
30. Coton: États-Unis, Memphis, oriental Midd 1-3/32", c.a.f. Europe septentrionale.
31. Coton: États-Unis, Memphis/Orléans/Texas, Midd 1-3/32", cotations coût et fret Extrême Orient. Avant juin 2005, Memphis/Orléans/Texas, Midd 1-3/32", c.a.f. Europe septentrionale.
32. Coton: Pakistan, Sind/Punjab, Afzal 1-1/32", c.a.f. Europe septentrionale.
33. Coton: Indice A de "Cotton Outlook", Middling 1-3/32", cotations coût et fret Extrême Orient. Avant août 2005, c.a.f. Europe septentrionale.
34. Coton: Égypte, Giza 88, good + 3/8, cotations coût et fret Extrême Orient. Avant août 2005, Giza 70, good + 3/8, f.a.b. Alexandrie.
35. Laine: Australie, 19 microns.
36. Laine: Australie, 23 microns.
37. Jute: Bangladesh, B.W.D., f.a.b. Mongla.
38. Sisal: Tanzanie/Kenya, n° 2 & 3 long, c.a.f. ports européens. Avant 1997, c.a.f. Londres.
39. Sisal: Tanzanie/Kenya, n° 3 & UG, c.a.f. ports européens. Avant 1997, c.a.f. Londres.
40. Peaux: États-Unis, bouvillons abattus à Chicago, prix de gros, f.a.b. point d'expédition.
41. Bois non conifères: Royaume-Uni, indice des prix à l'importation 2000 = 100, équivalent collar.
42. Grumes tropicales: Sapelli, loyal et marchand, prix d'importation au Royaume-Uni. Avant juin 2000, Cameroun, f.a.b.
43. Grumes tropicales sciées: Malaisie, Meranti rouge foncé, select and better, c.a.f. ports français.
44. Contre-plaqué: Asie du Sud-Est, Lauan, 3-feuilles, extra, 182 cm x 91 cm x 4 mm, prix de gros, cours du disponible à Tokyo.
45. Caoutchouc: Singapour, n° 1 RSS, f.a.b. en balles.

Minerals, ores and metals

46. Phosphate rock: Khouribga, 70 % BPL, f.a.s. Casablanca.
47. Manganese ore: Metallurgical 48/50 % Mn content, f.o.b. United Kingdom.
48. Iron ore: Brazilian to Europe, fines, C.V.R.D., f.o.b.
49. Iron ore: Australian to Japan, fines, Hamersley, f.o.b.
50. Aluminium: London Metal Exchange, high grade, cash.
51. Copper: London Metal Exchange, grade A, cash.
52. Copper: United States producer, wire bars, f.o.b. refinery.
53. Nickel: London Metal Exchange, cash.
54. Nickel: New York dealer, 4x4 cathodes, free market.
55. Lead: London Metal Exchange, settlement and cash seller's price in warehouse, excluding duty, range main United Kingdom ports; purity 99.97 % Pb.
56. Lead: North America, producer price, refined.
57. Zinc: London Metal Exchange, cash settlement.
58. Zinc: North America, high grade, daily weighted average, delivered basis.
59. Tin: London Metal Exchange, high grade, cash.
60. Tin: Ex-smelter price Kuala Lumpur market.
61. Tungsten ore: wolframite and sheelite, c.i.f. European ports, basis minimum 65 % WO3. Prior to April 1992, Wolfram.
62. Gold: United Kingdom, 99.5 % fine, London afternoon fixing, average of daily rates.
63. Silver: Handy & Harman, 99.9 % grade refined, average of daily quotations, New York.

MEMO ITEM:

64. Crude petroleum: Average of Dubai, United Kingdom Brent and West Texas crude prices, reflecting relatively equal consumption of medium, light and heavy crudes worldwide.
65. Manufactures export unit value: Developed economies, sections 5-8 of the Standard International Trade Classification (SITC), Revision 2, 2000=100.

Minéraux, minerais et métaux

46. Phosphate brut: Khouribga, 70 % BPL, f.a.s. Casablanca.
47. Minerai de manganèse: 48/50 % teneur en Mn, f.a.b. Royaume-Uni.
48. Minerai de fer: Brésilien vers l'Europe, minerai fin, C.V.R.D., f.a.b.
49. Minerai de fer: Australien vers le Japon, minerai fin, Hamersley, f.a.b.
50. Aluminium: Bourse des métaux de Londres, haute qualité, cours au comptant.
51. Cuivre: Bourse des métaux de Londres, grade A, comptant.
52. Cuivre: Producteur États-Unis, barres à fil, f.a.b. sortie affinerie.
53. Nickel: Bourse des métaux de Londres, cours au comptant.
54. Nickel: Prix du négociant à New York, cathodes 4x4, marché libre.
55. Plomb: Bourse des métaux de Londres, prix vendeur, à terme et au comptant, à l'entrepôt, droits non acquittés, principaux ports du Royaume-Uni; pureté: 99,97 % Pb.
56. Plomb: Amérique du Nord, prix des producteurs, raffiné.
57. Zinc: Bourse des métaux de Londres, cours de vente au comptant.
58. Zinc: Amérique du Nord, haute qualité, moyenne pondérée des prix journaliers à la livraison.
59. Étain: Bourse des métaux de Londres, haute qualité, cours au comptant.
60. Étain: Prix départ fonderie, marché de Kuala Lumpur.
61. Minerai de tungstène: wolframite et scheelite, c.a.f. ports européens, minimum 65 % de WO3. Avant avril 1992, Wolfram.
62. Or: Royaume-Uni, 99,5 % fin, cotation de l'après-midi à Londres, moyenne des taux journaliers.
63. Argent: Handy & Harman, 99,9 % raffiné, moyenne des cotations journalières à New York.

POUR MÉMOIRE :

64. Pétrole brut: moyenne des prix du Dubaï, brent du Royaume-Uni et du Texas de l'Ouest, correspondant aux parts relatives de la consommation mondiale du brut moyen, léger et lourd.
65. Valeur unitaire des exportations des produits manufacturés: Économies développées, sections 5 à 8 de la Classification type pour le commerce international (CTCI), révision 2, 2000=100.

6

6.2 **Instability indices and trends in free-market prices for selected primary commodities** 2000 = 100

6.2 **Indices d'instabilité et tendances des prix sur le marché libre d'une sélection de produits de base** 2000 = 100

Commodity	Price instability indices (1), (2) / Indices d'instabilité des prix (1), (2)			Price trends (1), (3) / Tendances des prix (1), (3) — In current dollars / En dollars courants			In constant dollars (4) / En dollars constants (4)			Produits
	1992-96	1997-01	2002-06	1992-96	1997-01	2002-06	1992-96	1997-01	2002-06	
				Annual average rate of change in percentage / Taux de variation annuel en pourcentage						
ALL COMMODITIES	**5.1**	**4.6**	**5.0**	**5.5**	**-7.6**	**15.5**	**3.4**	**-4.4**	**10.1**	**TOTAL DES PRODUITS**
All food	**4.2**	**5.4**	**3.9**	**6.2**	**-9.4**	**9.2**	**4.1**	**-6.2**	**3.8**	**Total des produits alimentaires**
Food and tropical beverages	*4.3*	*6.3*	*4.4*	*5.9*	*-8.7*	*9.7*	*3.8*	*-5.4*	*4.3*	*Produits alimentaires et boissons tropicales*
Food	*5.1*	*6.9*	*4.6*	*5.0*	*-7.3*	*9.6*	*2.9*	*-4.1*	*4.2*	*Produits alimentaires*
Wheat	10.2	9.5	8.7	8.2	-5.1	6.8	6.1	-1.9	1.5	Blé
Maize	12.2	6.2	9.7	9.5	-6.8	3.3	7.4	-3.6	-2.0	Maïs
Rice	10.4	6.8	5.0	4.8	-15.3	12.6	2.7	-12.1	7.2	Riz
Sugar	9.4	20.0	16.8	8.1	-6.4	17.8	6.0	-3.2	12.4	Sucre
Beef	6.8	4.9	6.0	-9.3	3.8	5.7	-11.4	7.1	0.4	Viande de bœuf
Bananas	18.2	15.6	19.1	-1.3	1.1	8.0	-3.4	4.4	2.6	Bananes
Pepper	16.0	23.1	13.8	23.9	-23.8	6.1	21.8	-20.6	0.8	Poivre
Soybean meal	8.2	15.5	10.2	4.3	-7.0	3.1	2.2	-3.8	-2.2	Farine de soja
Fishmeal	14.9	16.1	12.3	6.8	-8.4	14.5	4.7	-5.2	9.1	Farine de poisson
Tropical beverages	*18.4*	*5.3*	*6.1*	*15.0*	*-19.8*	*10.9*	*12.9*	*-16.6*	*5.5*	*Boissons tropicales*
Coffee	25.8	9.3	9.7	20.3	-25.8	17.9	18.2	-22.6	12.5	Café
Cocoa	7.4	14.7	8.3	8.3	-13.9	-3.1	6.2	-10.7	-8.4	Cacao
Tea	6.8	10.9	5.7	-4.1	-3.8	6.7	-7.8	-0.5	1.3	Thé
Vegetable oilseeds and oils	**6.5**	**10.2**	**7.7**	**8.5**	**-15.5**	**5.2**	**6.4**	**-12.3**	**-0.1**	**Graines oléagineuses et huiles végétales**
Soybeans	5.9	6.9	10.4	5.2	-9.6	5.2	3.1	-6.4	-0.1	Fèves de soja
Soybean oil	9.7	13.8	9.4	7.6	-14.9	6.1	5.5	-11.7	0.8	Huile de soja
Sunflower oil	10.9	16.1	5.7	7.5	-9.3	3.4	5.4	-6.1	-2.0	Huile de tournesol
Groundnut oil	12.4	5.0	18.5	10.7	-9.9	5.5	8.5	-6.7	0.1	Huile d'arachide
Copra	10.9	17.8	13.3	9.0	-18.3	11.5	6.9	-15.1	6.1	Coprah
Coconut oil	10.4	19.4	11.2	9.2	-18.2	10.1	7.1	-15.0	4.7	Huile de coprah
Palm kernel oil	11.2	18.8	11.5	9.2	-19.3	9.9	7.1	-16.1	4.5	Huile de palmiste
Palm oil	12.4	17.4	8.2	11.1	-20.4	3.9	9.0	-17.2	-1.4	Huile de palme
Cottonseed oil	9.3	8.9	20.2	-0.2	-11.6	1.7	-2.2	-8.4	-3.6	Huile de graines de coton
Agricultural raw materials	**7.0**	**5.2**	**4.4**	**5.7**	**-5.8**	**11.3**	**3.6**	**-2.5**	**5.9**	**Matières premières d'origine agricole**
Linseed oil	8.6	12.3	22.1	11.0	-13.3	10.2	8.9	-10.1	4.8	Huile de lin
Tobacco	9.1	2.9	2.3	-2.7	-4.4	1.8	-4.8	-1.1	-3.5	Tabac
Cotton	11.6	9.3	11.5	11.1	-11.4	2.9	9.0	-8.2	-2.5	Coton
Wool	..	13.3	6.0	..	-2.0	1.7	..	1.2	-3.6	Laine
Jute	17.6	9.9	6.8	12.3	2.4	3.7	10.2	5.7	-1.5	Jute
Sisal	6.3	5.2	5.0	13.3	-3.9	6.8	11.2	-0.7	1.4	Sisal
Hides and skins	6.2	8.9	6.2	3.9	-0.7	-3.4	1.8	2.5	-8.7	Cuirs et peaux
Non-coniferous woods	3.9	2.2	3.1	5.0	-1.7	11.0	2.8	1.6	5.6	Bois non conifères
Tropical logs	6.3	6.3	7.5	-2.9	-0.3	8.1	-5.0	2.9	2.7	Grumes tropicales
Tropical sawnwood	12.0	9.1	2.5	9.1	-2.5	2.1	7.0	0.7	-3.2	Grumes tropicales sciées
Plywood	16.5	7.3	4.0	5.0	-1.6	9.4	2.9	1.7	4.1	Contre-plaqué
Rubber	13.6	10.4	10.0	15.9	-11.9	23.5	13.8	-8.7	18.1	Caoutchouc
Minerals, ores and metals	**10.4**	**8.1**	**8.6**	**3.5**	**-3.6**	**28.8**	**1.4**	**-0.4**	**23.3**	**Minéraux, minerais et métaux**
Phosphate rock	8.6	2.6	3.2	-1.6	0.7	2.8	-3.7	4.0	-2.5	Phosphate brut
Manganese ore	13.1	3.1	12.9	-14.1	-1.7	9.8	-16.1	1.6	4.5	Minerai de manganèse
Iron ore	5.4	2.9	10.8	-2.4	-0.6	25.3	-4.4	2.6	19.9	Minerai de fer
Aluminium	11.5	7.6	5.8	7.9	-0.9	15.5	5.8	2.4	10.1	Aluminium
Copper	13.7	11.1	11.7	4.1	-6.4	36.3	2.0	-3.2	30.8	Cuivre
Nickel	14.1	21.3	12.6	5.3	2.4	29.3	3.2	5.7	23.8	Nickel
Lead	13.3	5.5	11.8	11.5	-6.9	27.1	9.4	-3.6	21.6	Plomb
Zinc	7.7	10.6	19.9	-3.0	-6.8	33.4	-5.1	-3.6	28.0	Zinc
Tin	7.6	6.3	14.0	2.0	-4.9	19.4	-0.1	-1.7	14.0	Étain
Tungsten ore	20.9	13.8	16.9	4.1	6.1	39.2	2.0	9.4	33.7	Minerai de tungstène
Gold	2.9	4.0	4.9	3.0	-4.5	15.4	0.9	-1.3	10.0	Or
Silver	7.7	6.8	9.7	7.2	-3.3	22.1	5.1	-0.1	16.7	Argent
Crude petroleum	9.6	21.3	8.8	2.9	12.2	25.1	0.8	15.5	19.7	Pétrole brut

For sources and notes, see next page.

Pour les sources et les notes, se reporter à la page suivante.

6.2 **Instability indices and trends in free-market prices for selected primary commodities**
2000 = 100

6.2 **Indices d'instabilité et tendances des prix sur le marché libre d'une sélection de produits de base**
2000 = 100

Sources:
- UNCTAD calculations based on UNCTAD *Commodity Price Statistics* on-line

Notes:

(1) Price instability indices and price trends reported here may not correspond to those published in the earlier issues of the Handbook of Statistics, since revised price indices, with a new base year (2000=100), have been used for their calculations.

(2) The measure of price instability is

$$1/n\sum_{t=1}^{n}\left[\left(\left|Y(t) - y(t)\right|\right)/y(t)\right]*100$$

where

$Y(t)$ is the observed magnitude of the variable.

$y(t)$ is the magnitude estimated by fitting an exponential trend to the observed value and

n is the number of observations.

Accordingly, instability is measured as the percentage deviation of the variables concerned from their exponential trend levels for a given period.

(3) The growth rate of each period has been calculated using the formula:

$$\log(p) = a + b(t)$$

where

p is the price index and t is time.

(4) Constant 2000 dollars (current dollars divided by the United Nations unit value index of manufactured goods exported by developed economies)

Sources :
- Calculs du secrétariat de la CNUCED fondés sur les *Statistiques des prix des produits de base* en ligne de la CNUCED.

Notes :

(1) Les indices d'instabilité et les tendances des prix présentés ici ne correpondent pas à ceux publiés dans les versions antérieures du Manuel de Statistiques, car les indices des prix ont été révisés en utilisant comme nouvelle année de base l'année 2000=100.

(2) L'indice d'instabilité des prix est calculé selon

$$1/n\sum_{t=1}^{n}\left[\left(\left|Y(t) - y(t)\right|\right)/y(t)\right]*100$$

où

$Y(t)$ est la valeur observée de la variable.

$y(t)$ est la valeur estimée par ajustement à la tendance exponentielle des valeurs observées et

n est le nombre d'observations.

L'instabilité est le pourcentage de déviation des variables en question par rapport à la ligne de tendance exponentielle pour une période donnée.

(3) Le taux de croissance de chaque période a été calculé selon la formule :

$$\log(p) = a + b(t)$$

où

p est l'indice de prix et t le temps.

(4) Dollars constants 2000 (dollar courant divisé par l'index des Nations Unies de la valeur unitaire des exportations des produits manufacturés par les économies développées)

6

Region, country or territory / Régions, pays ou territoires	Year / Année	Aluminium (Quantity) - Aluminium (Quantité)				Copper (Quantity) - Cuivre (Quantité)			
		Bauxite production / Production de bauxite (1)	Alumina production / Production d'alumine (2)	Primary aluminium production / Production d'aluminium de première fusion	Primary aluminium consumption / Consommation d'aluminium de première fusion (3)	Copper ore production / Production de minerai de cuivre (4)	Unrefined copper production / Production de cuivre non affiné (5)	Refined copper production / Production de cuivre affiné	Refined copper consumption / Consommation de cuivre affiné (3)
WORLD - MONDE	1990	115 099 268	21 965 247	19 286 485	17 921 000	9 327 399	9 763 500	10 678 541	10 773 800
	1995	120 177 863	22 095 290	19 946 044	20 022 000	10 223 686	10 393 423	11 906 668	12 185 000
	2000	139 162 577	27 734 840	24 642 989	25 451 513	13 207 328	12 284 739	14 773 972	15 360 835
	2004	162 589 898	32 446 098	29 912 199	30 325 066	14 538 003	12 767 566	15 848 720	16 914 088
	2005	..	..	..	31 825 489	..	..	..	16 971 648
DEVELOPED ECONOMIES - ÉCONOMIES DÉVELOPPÉES	1990	47 446 279	12 315 116	10 855 413	11 226 000	3 390 709	4 495 900	5 731 241	7 486 100
	1995	46 273 015	12 565 952	10 490 051	14 009 000	3 595 065	4 979 228	6 378 889	7 998 000
	2000	57 051 995	14 791 355	12 227 700	15 971 557	3 560 835	5 462 308	6 618 431	9 168 468
	2004	60 051 726	15 817 542	12 083 390	16 386 827	3 304 162	4 860 205	6 079 134	8 188 933
	2005	..	..	..	16 392 933	..	..	..	7 697 043
DEVELOPING ECONOMIES - ÉCONOMIES EN DÉVELOPPEMENT	1990	55 183 640	5 859 688	4 400 985	3 646 800	4 818 995	3 543 200	3 575 972	2 117 800
	1995	66 644 348	6 932 749	6 131 393	5 386 200	5 636 535	4 329 225	4 499 188	3 829 700
	2000	72 402 282	9 599 781	8 379 742	8 055 786	8 429 760	5 255 143	6 750 383	5 770 196
	2004	90 725 172	12 731 503	13 278 246	12 094 365	9 837 074	6 193 600	8 199 103	7 856 497
	2005	..	..	..	13 484 695	..	..	..	8 142 522
ECONOMIES IN TRANSITION - ÉCONOMIES EN TRANSITION	1990	12 469 349	3 790 443	4 030 087	3 027 900	1 117 295	1 724 400	1 371 328	1 159 800
	1995	7 260 500	2 596 589	3 324 600	619 300	992 086	1 084 970	1 028 591	339 300
	2000	9 708 300	3 343 704	4 035 547	993 377	1 216 733	1 567 288	1 405 158	250 884
	2004	11 813 000	3 897 053	4 550 563	1 353 542	1 396 767	1 713 761	1 570 483	695 282
	2005	..	..	..	1 440 134	..	..	..	971 661
Developed economies: America - Économies développées : Amérique	1990	495 000	3 341 708	5 615 395	4 717 600	2 381 477	1 993 000	2 533 225	2 331 000
	1995	258 000	2 960 813	5 547 092	5 666 700	2 575 393	2 217 690	2 852 516	2 724 100
	2000	200 000	3 072 961	6 041 860	6 960 811	2 077 955	1 603 702	2 353 493	3 297 541
	2004	200 000	3 451 109	5 108 560	6 560 475	1 723 471	1 018 183	1 837 767	2 707 345
	2005	..	..	..	6 917 493	..	..	..	2 559 544
Canada	1990	..	575 038	1 567 395	387 200	793 735	523 000	515 835	180 600
	1995	..	562 856	2 171 992	611 900	726 293	613 690	572 616	189 700
	2000	..	541 167	2 373 460	799 466	633 855	603 702	551 393	272 076
	2004	..	618 843	2 592 160	760 475	563 471	476 183	526 967	297 345
	2005	..	..	..	803 116	..	..	..	289 544
United States - États-Unis	1990	(e)495 000	(e)2 766 670	4 048 000	4 330 400	1 587 742	1 470 000	2 017 390	2 150 400
	1995	258 000	(e)2 397 957	3 375 100	5 054 800	1 849 100	1 604 000	2 279 900	2 534 400
	2000	(e)200 000	2 531 794	3 668 400	6 161 345	1 444 100	1 000 000	1 802 100	3 025 465
	2004	(e)200 000	2 832 266	2 516 400	5 800 000	1 160 000	(e)542 000	1 310 800	2 410 000
	2005	..	..	..	6 114 377	..	..	..	2 270 000
Developed economies: Asia - Économies développées : Asie	1990	..	242 754	34 224	2 433 900	12 927	1 040 000	1 007 976	1 576 500
	1995	..	256 988	18 034	2 375 400	2 376	1 168 481	1 187 959	1 414 500
	2000	..	413 519	6 536	2 270 824	1 211	1 480 634	1 437 351	1 349 208
	2004	..	383 525	6 433	2 364 632	1 000	1 465 422	1 380 144	1 278 578
	2005	..	..	..	2 321 538	..	..	..	1 226 746
Japan - Japon	1990	..	242 754	34 224	2 414 300	12 927	1 040 000	1 007 976	1 576 500
	1995	..	256 988	18 034	2 335 600	2 376	1 168 481	1 187 959	1 414 500
	2000	..	413 519	6 536	2 224 890	1 211	1 480 634	1 437 351	1 349 208
	2004	..	(e)383 525	6 433	2 318 632	1 000	1 465 422	1 380 144	1 278 578
	2005	..	..	..	2 276 338	..	..	..	1 226 746
Developed economies: Europe - Économies développées : Europe	1990	5 560 279	2 789 455	3 712 094	3 759 800	666 305	1 260 900	1 916 040	3 453 900
	1995	3 360 015	2 385 982	3 354 629	5 585 000	638 296	1 360 457	2 048 414	3 685 100
	2000	3 049 995	3 010 155	4 081 904	6 347 497	649 669	1 983 972	2 318 587	4 353 830
	2004	3 258 726	3 241 183	4 722 997	7 025 028	725 691	1 933 600	2 346 223	4 034 434
	2005	..	..	..	6 702 461	..	..	..	3 755 851
Austria - Autriche	1990	..	..	89 434	..	..	41 000	49 703	..
	1995	..	..	..	..	..	53 400	53 408	..
	2000	..	..	..	..	..	70 000	73 873	..
	2004	..	..	..	..	..	(e)88 000	74 200	..
Belgium - Belgique	2004	..	..	..	401 764	..	120 700	402 300	310 000
	2005	..	..	..	441 956	..	..	..	320 400
Belgium-Luxembourg - Belgique-Luxembourg	1990	..	..	..	317 800	..	105 000	331 857	389 500
	1995	..	..	..	355 600	..	180 200	376 000	362 400
	2000	..	..	..	340 624	..	144 700	423 000	347 000

For sources and notes, see end of table.

Pour les sources et les notes, se reporter à la fin du tableau.

Region, country or territory / Régions, pays ou territoires	Year / Année	Aluminium (Quantity) - Aluminium (Quantité)				Copper (Quantity) - Cuivre (Quantité)			
		Bauxite production / Production de bauxite (1)	Alumina production / Production d'alumine (2)	Primary aluminium production / Production d'aluminium de première fusion	Primary aluminium consumption / Consommation d'aluminium de première fusion (3)	Copper ore production / Production de minerai de cuivre (4)	Unrefined copper production / Production de cuivre non affiné (5)	Refined copper production / Production de cuivre affiné	Refined copper consumption / Consommation de cuivre affiné (3)
Cyprus - Chypre	1990	..	..	..	..	472	..	..	..
	2000	..	..	..	..	5 200	..	5 088	..
	2004	..	..	..	..	..	..	1 344	..
Czechoslovakia (former) - Tchécoslovaquie (anc.)	1990	..	110 682	30 076	..	2 884	8 200	24 606	..
Finland - Finlande	1990	..	..	..	..	17 482	102 000	69 030	..
	1995	..	..	..	..	9 049	132 577	73 665	..
	2000	..	..	..	..	11 500	157 400	114 000	..
	2004	..	..	..	..	15 500	172 400	132 384	..
France	1990	489 805	246 800	330 824	723 000	483	6 600	44 034	477 600
	1995	131 000	224 984	364 500	743 800	..	2 580	42 500	539 500
	2000	185 000	268 732	441 100	782 300	..	..	..	574 165
	2004	168 000	(e)269 790	447 000	748 533	..	..	..	535 798
	2005	..	..	..	718 945	..	..	..	472 216
Germany - Allemagne	1990	..	634 698	(e)735 946	83 100	3 564	(e)275 900	531 900	1 027 800
	1995	..	396 773	575 200	1 491 300	..	308 000	616 390	1 065 800
	2000	..	(e)386 170	643 545	1 490 481	..	709 472	709 472	1 307 103
	2004	..	(e)441 715	667 800	1 794 594	..	541 200	652 600	1 100 214
	2005	..	..	..	1 773 005	..	..	..	1 117 603
Greece - Grèce	1990	2 511 036	200 277	152 362	110 500	..	..	..	..
	1995	2 200 215	316 141	144 430	162 800	..	..	..	..
	2000	1 818 525	(e)238 579	168 000	230 497	..	..	..	..
	2004	2 444 000	271 906	166 634	265 634	..	..	..	..
	2005	..	..	..	281 157	..	..	..	..
Hungary - Hongrie	1990	2 559 100	436 954	75 162	..	..	(e)100	12 817	..
	1995	1 017 600	97 336	34 900	..	..	100	..	..
	2000	1 046 470	188 906	33 850	..	..	..	..	..
	2004	646 726	160 816	34 300	..	..	..	..	..
Iceland - Islande	1990	..	..	86 773	..	..	..	..	..
	1995	..	..	100 101	..	..	..	..	..
	2000	..	..	225 721	..	..	..	..	..
	2004	..	..	271 300	..	..	..	..	..
Ireland - Irlande	1990	..	490 118	..	..	..	..	..	..
	1995	..	627 182	..	..	..	..	..	..
	2000	..	746 247	..	..	..	..	..	..
	2004	..	(e)793 500	..	..	..	..	..	..
Italy - Italie	1990	338	259 951	231 800	652 000	..	..	83 000	474 800
	1995	11 200	296 293	177 800	665 400	..	..	98 000	498 000
	2000	..	540 638	189 800	780 349	..	..	33 000	673 944
	2004	..	562 856	195 400	986 603	..	..	33 600	715 008
	2005	..	..	..	976 789	..	..	..	676 084
Netherlands - Pays-Bas	1990	..	..	257 884	..	..	..	..	..
	1995	..	..	216 000	..	..	..	..	..
	2000	..	..	301 689	..	..	..	..	..
	2004	..	..	331 000	..	..	..	..	..
Norway - Norvège	1990	..	..	867 061	..	23 041	36 500	33 514	..
	1995	..	..	846 794	..	6 799	..	34 332	..
	2000	..	..	1 031 000	..	..	..	25 300	..
	2004	..	..	1 370 438	..	..	..	35 643	..
Poland - Pologne	1990	..	..	45 974	..	370 000	351 000	346 000	170 700
	1995	..	..	50 800	..	384 200	410 000	405 700	213 000
	2000	..	..	55 473	..	454 100	482 500	486 002	246 324
	2004	..	..	58 931	..	530 768	571 000	550 066	274 300
	2005	..	..	..	..	..	..	..	270 560
Portugal	1990	..	..	..	..	159 841	2 000	(e)100	..
	1995	..	..	..	..	129 726	..	..	..
	2000	..	..	..	..	76 300	..	..	..
	2004	..	..	..	..	95 700	..	..	..

For sources and notes, see end of table.

Pour les sources et les notes, se reporter à la fin du tableau.

309

Region, country or territory Régions, pays ou territoires	Year Année	Aluminium (Quantity) - Aluminium (Quantité)				Copper (Quantity) - Cuivre (Quantité)			
		Bauxite production Production de bauxite (1)	Alumina production Production d'alumine (2)	Primary aluminium production Production d'aluminium de première fusion	Primary aluminium consumption Consommation d'aluminium de première fusion (3)	Copper ore production Production de minerai de cuivre (4)	Unrefined copper production Production de cuivre non affiné (5)	Refined copper production Production de cuivre affiné	Refined copper consumption Consommation de cuivre affiné (3)
Slovakia - Slovaquie	1995	..	..	60 600	..	400	9 600	21 400	..
	2000	..	..	109 000	..	..	..	..	..
	2004	..	..	156 893	..	..	..	..	..
Slovenia - Slovénie	1995	..	..	70 200		..	..	..	..
	2000	..	..	75 600	..	..	..	..	..
	2004	..	..	120 700	..	..	..	..	..
Spain - Espagne	1990	..	346 495	355 300	288 000	13 300	150 000	170 567	146 100
	1995	..	370 141	361 882	350 000	24 519	159 000	164 213	174 500
	2000	..	594 067	365 700	525 562	24 804	289 900	315 734	289 271
	2004	..	(e)740 600	397 500	603 101	1 308	224 300	228 466	331 000
	2005	..	..	..	624 274	..	..	..	291 974
Sweden - Suède	1990	..	..	92 100	..	74 283	108 000	97 278	..
	1995	..	..	92 797	..	83 603	105 000	110 939	..
	2000	..	..	100 788	..	77 765	(e)130 000	133 118	..
	2004	..	..	100 591	..	82 415	(e)216 000	235 620	..
Switzerland - Suisse	1990	..	..	71 602	..	..	..	..	..
	1995	..	..	20 726	..	..	..	..	..
	2000	..	..	35 539	..	..	..	..	..
	2004	..	..	44 879	..	..	..	..	..
United Kingdom - Royaume-Uni	1990	..	63 480	289 796	453 700	955	74 600	121 634	..
	1995	..	57 132	237 899	620 000	..	..	51 867	..
	2000	..	46 816	305 099	575 499	..	..	..	..
	2004	..	..	359 631	438 937	..	..	..	..
	2005	..	..	..	353 249	..	..	..	..
Developed economies: Oceania - **Économies développées : Océanie**	**1990**	**41 391 000**	**5 941 199**	**1 493 700**	**314 700**	**330 000**	**202 000**	**274 000**	**124 700**
	1995	**42 655 000**	**6 962 169**	**1 570 296**	**381 900**	**379 000**	**232 600**	**290 000**	**174 300**
	2000	**53 802 000**	**8 294 720**	**2 097 400**	**392 425**	**832 000**	**394 000**	**509 000**	**167 889**
	2004	**56 593 000**	**8 741 725**	**2 245 400**	**436 692**	**854 000**	**443 000**	**515 000**	**168 576**
	2005	**..**	**..**	**..**	**451 441**	**..**	**..**	**..**	**154 902**
Australia - Australie	1990	41 391 000	5 941 199	1 234 000	287 800	330 000	202 000	(e)274 000	..
	1995	42 655 000	6 962 169	1 297 000	343 100	379 000	232 600	290 000	..
	2000	53 802 000	8 294 720	1 769 000	346 425	832 000	394 000	509 000	..
	2004	56 593 000	8 741 725	1 895 000	361 800	854 000	443 000	515 000	..
	2005	..	..	..	380 200	..	..	..	..
New Zealand - Nouvelle-Zélande	1990	..	..	259 700	..	..	..	..	..
	1995	..	..	273 296	..	..	..	..	..
	2000	..	..	328 400	..	..	..	..	..
	2004	..	..	350 400	..	..	..	..	..
Developing economies: Africa - **Économies en développement : Afrique**	**1990**	**17 984 406**	**339 671**	**560 281**	**217 000**	**1 163 655**	**953 300**	**760 818**	**96 000**
	1995	**18 257 015**	**325 879**	**589 992**	**247 200**	**623 532**	**542 108**	**499 969**	**115 400**
	2000	**18 503 854**	**286 148**	**1 158 070**	**338 823**	**460 782**	**520 582**	**375 969**	**131 610**
	2004	**19 299 783**	**411 562**	**1 712 596**	**396 729**	**611 062**	**394 000**	**522 019**	**162 785**
	2005	**..**	**..**	**..**	**409 950**	**..**	**..**	**..**	**165 893**
Eastern Africa - Afrique orientale	*1990*	*7 186*	*..*	*..*	*..*	*560 577*	*398 100*	*450 643*	*21 700*
	1995	*10 663*	*..*	*..*	*..*	*349 983*	*307 900*	*331 181*	*28 600*
	2000	*8 130*	*..*	*53 800*	*..*	*249 862*	*372 800*	*240 569*	*23 034*
	2004	*6 723*	*..*	*547 100*	*..*	*418 983*	*280 000*	*412 900*	*25 608*
	2005	*..*	*..*	*..*	*..*	*..*	*..*	*..*	*25 608*
Mozambique	1990	7 186	..	..	..	100	..	..	..
	1995	10 663	..	..	..	..	..	..	..
	2000	8 130	..	53 800	..	..	..	..	..
	2004	6 723	..	547 100	..	..	..	..	..
United Republic of Tanzania - République-Unie de Tanzanie	2004	..	..	..	..	4 300	..	..	..
Zambia - Zambie	1990	..	..	..	..	545 677	384 000	426 243	..
	1995	..	..	..	..	341 938	299 900	307 181	..
	2000	..	..	..	..	249 304	358 300	226 169	..
	2004	..	..	..	..	412 300	(e)280 000	407 900	..

For sources and notes, see end of table.

Pour les sources et les notes, se reporter à la fin du tableau.

310

Region, country or territory / Régions, pays ou territoires	Year / Année	Aluminium (Quantity) - Aluminium (Quantité)				Copper (Quantity) - Cuivre (Quantité)			
		Bauxite production / Production de bauxite (1)	Alumina production / Production d'alumine (2)	Primary aluminium production / Production d'aluminium de première fusion	Primary aluminium consumption / Consommation d'aluminium de première fusion (3)	Copper ore production / Production de minerai de cuivre (4)	Unrefined copper production / Production de cuivre non affiné (5)	Refined copper production / Production de cuivre affiné	Refined copper consumption / Consommation de cuivre affiné (3)
Zimbabwe	1990	..	..	..	..	14 800	14 100	24 400	..
	1995	..	..	..	..	8 045	8 000	24 000	..
	2000	..	..	..	..	558	14 500	14 400	..
	2004	..	..	..	..	2 383	..	5 000	..
Middle Africa - Afrique centrale	*1990*	*..*	*..*	*87 500*	*20 100*	*352 400*	*346 000*	*173 175*	*2 300*
	1995	*..*	*..*	*79 300*	*21 000*	*34 958*	*28 800*	*33 088*	*..*
	2000	*..*	*..*	*86 384*	*24 200*	*33 000*	*..*	*29 000*	*..*
	2004	*..*	*..*	*85 900*	*19 200*	*69 600*	*..*	*20 000*	*..*
	2005	*..*	*..*	*..*	*19 200*	*..*	*..*	*..*	*..*
Cameroon - Cameroun	1990	..	..	87 500	..	..	..	..	..
	1995	..	..	79 300	..	..	..	..	..
	2000	..	..	86 384	..	..	..	..	..
	2004	..	..	85 900	..	..	..	..	..
Dem. Rep. of the Congo - Rép. dém. du Congo	1990	..	..	..	..	352 400	346 000	173 175	..
	1995	..	..	..	..	34 958	28 800	33 088	..
	2000	..	..	..	..	33 000	..	29 000	..
	2004	..	..	..	..	69 600	..	20 000	..
Northern Africa - Afrique septentrionale	*1990*	*..*	*..*	*141 081*	*83 700*	*13 901*	*..*	*4 000*	*4 200*
	1995	*..*	*..*	*180 000*	*85 400*	*13 600*	*..*	*4 000*	*4 000*
	2000	*..*	*..*	*188 900*	*93 513*	*6 528*	*..*	*..*	*23 256*
	2004	*..*	*..*	*216 000*	*110 037*	*4 400*	*..*	*14 119*	*49 000*
	2005	*..*	*..*	*..*	*109 950*	*..*	*..*	*..*	*50 160*
Egypt - Égypte	1990	..	..	141 081	..	..	..	(e)4 000	..
	1995	..	..	(e)180 000	..	..	..	(e)4 000	..
	2000	..	..	188 900	..	..	..	..	..
	2004	..	..	216 000	..	..	..	14 119	..
Morocco - Maroc	1990	..	..	..	..	13 901	..	..	..
	1995	..	..	..	..	13 600	..	..	..
	2000	..	..	..	..	6 528	..	..	..
	2004	..	..	..	..	4 400	..	..	..
Southern Africa - Afrique australe	*1990*	*..*	*..*	*157 500*	*91 000*	*236 777*	*209 200*	*133 000*	*67 600*
	1995	*..*	*..*	*195 292*	*119 700*	*224 991*	*205 408*	*131 700*	*81 600*
	2000	*..*	*..*	*673 486*	*186 296*	*171 392*	*147 782*	*106 400*	*82 791*
	2004	*..*	*..*	*863 596*	*222 000*	*118 079*	*114 000*	*75 000*	*85 577*
	2005	*..*	*..*	*..*	*240 000*	*..*	*..*	*..*	*87 525*
Botswana	1990	..	..	..	..	20 612	..	..	..
	1995	..	..	..	..	20 461	21 209	..	..
	2000	..	..	..	..	18 722	(e)18 722	..	..
	2004	..	..	..	..	21 195	..	..	..
Namibia - Namibie	1990	..	..	..	..	27 797	33 200	..	..
	1995	..	..	..	..	22 530	29 799	..	..
	2000	..	..	..	..	5 070	5 082	..	..
	2004	..	..	..	..	11 174	24 700	..	..
South Africa - Afrique du Sud	1990	..	..	157 500	..	188 368	176 000	133 000	..
	1995	..	..	195 292	..	182 000	154 400	131 700	..
	2000	..	..	673 486	..	147 600	123 978	106 400	..
	2004	..	..	863 596	..	85 710	(e)89 300	75 000	..
Western Africa - Afrique occidentale	*1990*	*17 977 220*	*339 671*	*174 200*	*22 200*	*..*	*..*	*..*	*..*
	1995	*18 246 352*	*325 879*	*135 400*	*21 100*	*..*	*..*	*..*	*..*
	2000	*18 495 724*	*286 148*	*155 500*	*26 854*	*..*	*..*	*..*	*..*
	2004	*19 293 060*	*411 562*	*..*	*27 000*	*..*	*..*	*..*	*..*
	2005	*..*	*..*	*..*	*27 000*	*..*	*..*	*..*	*..*
Ghana	1990	382 100	..	174 200	..	..	..	..	..
	1995	512 900	..	135 400	..	..	..	..	..
	2000	503 824	..	155 500	..	..	..	..	..
	2004	498 060	..	..	..	..	..	..	..

For sources and notes, see end of table.   Pour les sources et les notes, se reporter à la fin du tableau.

Region, country or territory / Régions, pays ou territoires	Year / Année	Aluminium (Quantity) - Aluminium (Quantité)				Copper (Quantity) - Cuivre (Quantité)			
		Bauxite production / Production de bauxite (1)	Alumina production / Production d'alumine (2)	Primary aluminium production / Production d'aluminium de première fusion	Primary aluminium consumption / Consommation d'aluminium de première fusion (3)	Copper ore production / Production de minerai de cuivre (4)	Unrefined copper production / Production de cuivre non affiné (5)	Refined copper production / Production de cuivre affiné	Refined copper consumption / Consommation de cuivre affiné (3)
Guinea - Guinée	1990	16 150 000	339 671	..	..	..	..	..	..
	1995	17 733 452	325 879	..	..	..	..	..	..
	2000	17 991 900	286 148	..	..	..	..	..	..
	2004	18 795 000	411 562	..	..	..	..	..	..
Sierra Leone	1990	1 445 120	..	..	..	..	..	..	..
Developing economies: America - Économies en développement : Amérique	1990	26 261 271	3 946 272	1 794 470	727 300	2 247 593	1 733 400	1 701 515	368 100
	1995	33 052 624	4 455 598	2 038 120	859 000	3 285 496	2 125 633	2 225 839	553 000
	2000	35 761 556	5 827 233	2 167 933	913 081	5 700 837	2 314 445	3 663 485	988 668
	2004	45 615 102	6 923 616	2 363 888	1 166 875	7 135 510	2 437 600	3 899 726	1 012 772
	2005	..	..	..	1 282 493	..	..	..	1 018 853
Caribbean - Caraïbes	1990	11 050 164	1 517 618	..	2 500	2 000	..	..	..
	1995	10 857 492	1 602 958	..	1 000	1 858	..	..	..
	2000	11 126 524	1 904 466	..	1 200	1 346	..	..	1 000
	2004	13 296 481	2 128 020	..	1 200	..	..	..	1 000
	2005	..	..	..	3 600	..	..	..	..
Cuba	1990				..	(e)2 000	..	..	..
	1995					1 858			
	2000					1 346			
Dominican Republic - République dominicaine	1990	85 164	..	..	..	..	..	..	..
Jamaica - Jamaïque	1990	10 965 000	1 517 618	..	..	..	..	..	..
	1995	10 857 492	1 602 958	..	..	..	..	..	..
	2000	11 126 524	1 904 466	..	..	..	..	..	..
	2004	13 296 481	2 128 020	..	..	..	..	..	..
Central America - Amérique centrale	1990	..	..	67 515	91 900	298 695	175 400	157 108	127 200
	1995	..	..	10 413	39 800	333 565	288 456	258 200	171 900
	2000	..	..	61 200	87 454	364 566	302 000	343 200	463 914
	2004	..	..	..	129 802	405 540	290 000	333 700	475 423
	2005	..	..	..	158 400	..	..	..	471 188
Mexico - Mexique	1990	..	..	67 515	..	298 695	175 400	157 108	127 200
	1995	..	..	10 413	..	333 565	288 456	258 200	171 900
	2000	..	..	61 200	..	364 566	(e)302 000	343 200	463 914
	2004	..	..	..	..	405 540	(e)290 000	333 700	475 423
	2005								471 188
South America - Amérique du Sud	1990	15 211 107	2 428 654	1 726 955	632 900	1 946 898	1 558 000	1 544 407	240 900
	1995	22 195 132	2 852 640	2 027 707	818 200	2 950 073	1 837 177	1 967 639	381 100
	2000	24 635 032	3 922 767	2 106 733	824 427	5 334 925	2 012 445	3 320 285	523 754
	2004	32 318 621	4 795 596	2 363 888	1 035 873	6 729 970	2 147 600	3 566 026	536 349
	2005	..	..	..	1 120 493	..	..	..	547 665
Argentina - Argentine	1990	..	..	165 608	..	357	..	(e)15 000	..
	1995	..	..	183 113	..	..	..	(e)16 000	..
	2000	..	..	263 870	..	145 197	..	(e)16 000	..
	2004	..	..	275 388	..	177 143	..	(e)16 000	..
Bolivia - Bolivie	1990	..	..	..	..	200	..	..	..
	1995	..	..	..	..	100	..	..	..
Brazil - Brésil	1990	9 748 948	875 389	930 585	341 200	34 441	152 000	152 117	128 700
	1995	11 616 402	1 133 594	1 188 100	500 600	48 933	164 966	164 996	197 600
	2000	13 974 480	1 985 919	1 271 400	513 775	31 786	185 345	184 257	331 179
	2004	20 948 800	2 711 918	1 457 400	651 002	103 153	(e)186 000	208 020	332 446
	2005	..	..	..	759 275	..	..	..	333 850
Chile - Chili	1990	..	..	..	..	1 588 400	1 210 000	1 191 600	..
	1995	..	..	..	..	2 488 600	1 293 700	1 491 500	..
	2000	..	..	..	..	4 602 000	1 460 400	2 668 300	..
	2004	..	..	..	..	5 412 500	1 563 800	2 836 700	..
Colombia - Colombie	1990	..	..	..	..	..	..	3 900	..
	1995	..	..	..	..	2 747	..	..	..
	2000	..	..	..	..	2 018	..	..	..
	2004	..	..	..	..	1 600	..	..	..

For sources and notes, see end of table.

Pour les sources et les notes, se reporter à la fin du tableau.

Region, country or territory / Régions, pays ou territoires	Year / Année	Aluminium (Quantity) - Aluminium (Quantité)				Copper (Quantity) - Cuivre (Quantité)			
		Bauxite production / Production de bauxite (1)	Alumina production / Production d'alumine (2)	Primary aluminium production / Production d'aluminium de première fusion	Primary aluminium consumption / Consommation d'aluminium de première fusion (3)	Copper ore production / Production de minerai de cuivre (4)	Unrefined copper production / Production de cuivre non affiné (5)	Refined copper production / Production de cuivre affiné	Refined copper consumption / Consommation de cuivre affiné (3)
Ecuador - Équateur	1990	..	..	..	..	100	..	..	..
Guyana	1990	1 423 978	..	..	..				
	1995	2 028 080	..	..	..				
	2000	2 689 451	..	..	..				
	2004	1 503 416	..	..	..	..	..	..	..
Peru - Pérou	1990	..	..	..	..	323 400	196 000	181 790	..
	1995	..	..	..	..	409 693	378 511	295 143	..
	2000	..	..	..	..	553 924	366 700	451 728	..
	2004	..	..	..	..	1 035 574	397 800	505 306	..
Suriname	1990	3 266 759	810 142	31 282	..	..	..	..	..
	1995	3 530 210	840 489	26 667	..	..	..	..	..
	2000	3 610 381	1 008 313	..	..	..	..	..	..
	2004	4 051 700	1 078 578	..	..	..	..	..	..
Venezuela (Bolivarian Republic of) - Venezuela (République bolivarienne du)	1990	771 422	743 123	599 480	..	..	..	..	..
	1995	5 020 440	878 557	629 827	..	..	..	..	..
	2000	4 360 720	928 535	571 463	..	..	..	..	..
	2004	5 814 705	(e)1 005 100	631 100	..	..	..	..	..
Developing economies: Asia - Économies en développement : Asie	**1990**	**10 937 963**	**1 573 745**	**2 046 234**	**2 702 500**	**1 237 536**	**856 500**	**1 113 639**	**1 653 700**
	1995	**15 334 709**	**2 151 272**	**3 503 281**	**4 280 000**	**1 514 770**	**1 661 484**	**1 773 380**	**3 161 300**
	2000	**18 136 872**	**3 486 400**	**5 053 739**	**6 803 882**	**2 065 080**	**2 420 116**	**2 710 929**	**4 649 918**
	2004	**25 810 287**	**5 396 325**	**9 201 762**	**10 530 761**	**1 913 302**	**3 362 000**	**3 777 358**	**6 680 940**
	2005	**..**	**..**	**..**	**11 792 252**	**..**	**..**	**..**	**6 957 776**
Eastern Asia - Asie orientale	*1990*	*3 655 200*	*774 350*	*878 585*	*1 506 400*	*692 993*	*565 600*	*796 286*	*1 130 900*
	1995	*8 255 500*	*1 175 808*	*1 879 700*	*2 591 600*	*573 800*	*1 189 000*	*1 332 471*	*2 280 200*
	2000	*7 900 000*	*2 289 565*	*2 989 200*	*4 895 011*	*730 468*	*1 639 100*	*1 857 697*	*3 439 439*
	2004	*12 000 000*	*3 699 826*	*6 589 000*	*7 704 866*	*792 000*	*2 285 000*	*2 683 328*	*5 018 475*
	2005	*..*	*..*	*..*	*8 783 814*	*..*	*..*	*..*	*5 149 347*
China - Chine	1990	3 655 200	774 350	854 300	(e)861 000	557 000	358 500	558 000	(e)512 000
	1995	8 255 500	1 175 808	1 869 700	1 491 600	441 900	1 000 000	1 079 700	1 143 400
	2000	(e)7 900 000	2 289 565	2 989 200	3 499 085	592 600	(e)1 200 000	1 371 100	1 928 057
	2004	(e)12 000 000	3 699 826	6 589 000	6 042 670	650 000	(e)1 840 000	2 170 000	3 363 887
	2005	..	..	..	7 118 592	..	..	..	3 639 133
China, Taiwan Province of - Chine, Taiwan Province de	1990	..	..	..	197 700	..	16 100	16 090	264 700
	1995	..	..	..	362 600	..	..	(e)9 600	563 200
	2000	..	..	..	501 568	..	..	..	628 385
	2004	..	..	..	496 721	..	..	..	689 472
	2005	..	..	..	412 176	..	..	..	638 417
Korea, Dem. People's Rep. of - Corée, Rép. populaire dém. de	1990	..	..	(e)11 000	..	(e)12 000	30 000	(e)30 000	..
	1995	..	..	(e)10 000	..	10 000	29 000	(e)10 000	..
	2000	..	..	..	..	(e)12 000	(e)15 000	(e)15 000	..
	2004	..	..	..	..	(e)12 000	(e)15 000	(e)15 000	..
Korea, Republic of - Corée, République de	1990	..	..	13 285	368 900	100	161 000	192 196	324 200
	1995	..	..	..	675 400	..	160 000	233 171	539 600
	2000	..	..	..	822 641	..	424 100	470 956	862 197
	2004	..	..	..	1 118 275	..	430 000	495 952	939 516
	2005	..	..	..	1 201 044	..	..	..	852 597
Mongolia - Mongolie	1990	..	..	..	..	123 893	..	..	..
	1995	..	..	..	..	121 900	..	..	..
	2000	..	..	..	..	125 868	..	641	..
	2004	..	..	..	..	130 000	..	2 376	..
Southern Asia - Asie méridionale	*1990*	*4 948 090*	*705 686*	*527 847*	*578 300*	*118 566*	*100 100*	*94 200*	*178 000*
	1995	*5 763 463*	*884 488*	*632 685*	*724 000*	*148 800*	*161 496*	*161 200*	*169 000*
	2000	*8 488 289*	*1 114 603*	*765 700*	*719 134*	*184 711*	*391 000*	*440 921*	*351 531*
	2004	*12 091 620*	*1 606 574*	*1 096 562*	*1 021 565*	*180 600*	*609 900*	*589 130*	*470 318*
	2005	*..*	*..*	*..*	*1 094 855*	*..*	*..*	*..*	*501 000*

For sources and notes, see end of table.

Pour les sources et les notes, se reporter à la fin du tableau.

Region, country or territory Régions, pays ou territoires	Year Année	Aluminium (Quantity) - Aluminium (Quantité)				Copper (Quantity) - Cuivre (Quantité)			
		Bauxite production Production de bauxite (1)	Alumina production Production d'alumine (2)	Primary aluminium production Production d'aluminium de première fusion	Primary aluminium consumption Consommation d'aluminium de première fusion (3)	Copper ore production Production de minerai de cuivre (4)	Unrefined copper production Production de cuivre non affiné (5)	Refined copper production Production de cuivre affiné	Refined copper consumption Consommation de cuivre affiné (3)
India - Inde	1990	4 853 000	705 686	433 200	433 300	51 566	40 700	46 400	135 000
	1995	5 564 775	884 488	517 806	581 000	46 600	39 496	39 569	116 400
	2000	7 992 782	1 114 603	624 206	602 398	37 511	(e)256 000	259 683	240 246
	2004	11 696 773	(e)1 534 100	883 960	860 565	32 500	400 900	406 316	341 611
	2005	..	..	..	940 883	..	..	..	398 025
Iran, Islamic Republic of - Iran, Rép. islamique d'	1990	92 509	..	94 647	..	67 000	(e)59 400	47 800	..
	1995	192 790	..	114 879	..	102 200	122 000	121 631	..
	2000	485 130	..	141 494	..	147 200	(e)135 000	181 238	..
	2004	390 000	72 474	212 602	..	141 000	(e)209 000	182 814	..
Pakistan	1990	2 581	..	..	..	..	..	..	..
	1995	5 898	..	..	..	..	..	..	..
	2000	10 377	..	..	..	..	..	..	..
	2004	4 847	..	..	..	7 100	..	..	..
South-Eastern Asia - Asie du Sud-Est	*1990*	*1 562 000*	*..*	*192 100*	*320 200*	*371 552*	*153 500*	*125 938*	*172 400*
	1995	*1 083 468*	*..*	*228 100*	*622 800*	*746 670*	*242 171*	*158 109*	*422 700*
	2000	*1 290 046*	*..*	*192 300*	*559 616*	*1 073 011*	*333 726*	*323 811*	*438 858*
	2004	*1 352 867*	*..*	*240 800*	*845 105*	*890 102*	*431 600*	*424 900*	*736 041*
	2005	*..*	*..*	*..*	*910 873*	*..*	*..*	*..*	*806 090*
Indonesia - Indonésie	1990	1 163 820	..	192 100	..	162 366	..	..	49 300
	1995	899 035	..	228 100	..	618 000	..	..	85 000
	2000	1 150 776	..	192 300	..	1 012 000	173 726	158 400	59 756
	2004	1 330 827	..	240 800	..	840 318	211 600	210 500	203 000
	2005	..	..	..	..	..	..	..	246 030
Malaysia - Malaisie	1990	398 180	..	..	..	24 327	..	..	48 500
	1995	184 433	..	..	..	20 751	..	..	113 600
	2000	123 270	..	..	..	..	..	..	166 209
	2004	2 040	..	..	..	..	..	..	185 692
	2005	..	..	..	..	..	..	..	224 400
Myanmar	1990	..	..	..	..	4 400	..	..	..
	1995	..	..	..	..	5 282	..	..	..
	2000	..	..	..	..	26 711	..	26 711	..
	2004	..	..	..	..	31 800	..	31 800	..
Philippines	1990	..	..	..	..	180 459	153 500	125 938	..
	1995	..	..	..	..	102 637	242 171	158 109	..
	2000	..	..	..	..	31 900	160 000	138 700	..
	2004	..	..	..	..	15 984	(e)220 000	174 600	..
Thailand - Thaïlande	1990	..	..	..	128 100	..	..	..	52 300
	1995	..	..	..	253 200	..	..	..	147 500
	2000	..	..	..	195 154	..	..	..	150 579
	2004	..	..	..	378 404	..	..	8 000	247 349
	2005	..	..	..	373 628	..	..	..	240 783
Viet Nam	2000	16 000	..	..	..	2 400	..	..	..
	2004	(e)20 000	..	..	..	2 000	..	..	..
Western Asia - Asie occidentale	*1990*	*772 673*	*93 709*	*447 702*	*297 600*	*54 425*	*37 300*	*97 215*	*158 100*
	1995	*232 278*	*90 976*	*762 796*	*341 600*	*45 500*	*68 817*	*121 600*	*264 200*
	2000	*458 537*	*82 232*	*1 106 539*	*544 468*	*76 890*	*56 290*	*88 500*	*415 025*
	2004	*365 800*	*89 925*	*1 275 400*	*838 325*	*50 600*	*35 500*	*80 000*	*444 106*
	2005	*..*	*..*	*..*	*881 810*	*..*	*..*	*..*	*486 939*
Bahrain - Bahreïn	1990	..	..	212 500	103 800	..	..	..	..
	1995	..	..	453 883	135 000	..	..	..	..
	2000	..	..	509 038	239 248	..	..	..	..
	2004	..	..	530 000	353 362	..	..	..	..
	2005	..	..	..	355 000	..	..	..	..
Oman	1990	..	..	..	..	13 700	12 100	12 015	..
	1995	..	..	..	..	..	34 200	21 300	..
	2000	..	..	..	..	..	23 790	24 400	..
	2004	..	..	..	..	..	(e)24 000	17 000	..

For sources and notes, see end of table.   Pour les sources et les notes, se reporter à la fin du tableau.

Region, country or territory / Régions, pays ou territoires	Year / Année	Aluminium (Quantity) - Aluminium (Quantité)				Copper (Quantity) - Cuivre (Quantité)			
		Bauxite production / Production de bauxite (1)	Alumina production / Production d'alumine (2)	Primary aluminium production / Production d'aluminium de première fusion	Primary aluminium consumption / Consommation d'aluminium de première fusion (3)	Copper ore production / Production de minerai de cuivre (4)	Unrefined copper production / Production de cuivre non affiné (5)	Refined copper production / Production de cuivre affiné	Refined copper consumption / Consommation de cuivre affiné (3)
Saudi Arabia - Arabie saoudite	1990	..	..	..	..	(e)900	..	..	..
	1995	..	..	..	..	1 000	917	..	..
	2000	..	..	..	..	837	..	..	..
	2004	..	..	..	..	700	..	..	..
Turkey - Turquie	1990	772 673	93 709	60 902	152 000	39 825	25 200	85 200	108 900
	1995	232 278	(e)90 976	61 513	144 000	44 500	33 700	100 300	139 200
	2000	458 537	82 232	61 501	211 220	76 053	32 500	64 100	247 990
	2004	365 800	89 925	62 400	350 963	49 900	(e)11 500	63 000	273 946
	2005	..	..	..	389 810	..	..	..	316 779
United Arab Emirates - Émirats arabes unis	1990	..	..	174 300		..			..
	1995	..	..	247 400		..			..
	2000	..	..	536 000		..			..
	2004	..	..	683 000		..			..
Developing economies: Oceania - Économies en développement : Océanie	**1990**	..	..	..	..	**170 211**	..	..	..
	1995	..	..	..	..	**212 737**	..	..	..
	2000	..	..	..	..	**203 061**	..	..	..
	2004	..	..	..	..	**177 200**	..	..	..
Papua New Guinea - Papouasie-Nouvelle-Guinée	1990	..	..	..	..	170 211	..	..	..
	1995	..	..	..	..	212 737	..	..	..
	2000	..	..	..	..	203 061	..	..	..
	2004	..	..	..	..	177 200	..	..	..
Economies in transition: Asia - Économies en transition : Asie	**1995**	**3 318 500**	**554 445**	**248 000**	..	**275 997**	**317 800**	**350 559**	**52 000**
	2000	**3 729 600**	**676 950**	**300 002**	..	**521 434**	**502 859**	**469 723**	**26 000**
	2004	**4 705 400**	**899 373**	**387 619**	..	**574 500**	**527 700**	**530 300**	**81 408**
	2005	..	..	..	..	..	..	..	**75 303**
Armenia - Arménie	1995	..	..	..	..	1 697	..	..	..
	2000	..	..	..	..	12 234	(e)4 000	..	..
	2004	..	..	..	..	17 700	(e)7 500	..	..
Azerbaijan - Azerbaïdjan	1995	..	13 807	(e)11 000	..	..			..
	2000	..	33 327	2	..	..			..
	2004	..	122 887	29 537	..	..			..
Georgia - Géorgie	1995	..	..	..	..	5 800	..	..	..
	2000	..	..	..	..	(e)9 000	..	..	..
	2004	..	..	..	..	(e)12 000	..	..	..
Kazakhstan	1995	3 318 500	540 638	..	..	228 500	242 800	255 559	..
	2000	3 729 600	643 623	..	..	430 200	413 859	394 723	..
	2004	4 705 400	776 486	..	..	461 800	445 200	445 300	..
Tajikistan - Tadjikistan	1995	..	..	237 000	..	..			..
	2000	..	..	300 000	..	..			..
	2004	..	..	358 082	..	..			..
Uzbekistan - Ouzbékistan	1995	..	..	..	..	40 000	75 000	95 000	..
	2000	..	..	..	..	(e)70 000	(e)85 000	75 000	..
	2004	..	..	..	..	83 000	(e)75 000	85 000	..
Economies in transition: Europe - Économies en transition : Europe	**1990**	**12 469 349**	**3 790 443**	**4 030 087**	**3 027 900**	**1 117 295**	**1 724 400**	**1 371 328**	**1 159 800**
	1995	**3 942 000**	**2 042 144**	**3 076 600**	**619 300**	**716 089**	**767 170**	**678 032**	**287 300**
	2000	**5 978 700**	**2 666 754**	**3 735 545**	**993 377**	**695 299**	**1 064 429**	**935 435**	**224 884**
	2004	**7 107 600**	**2 997 680**	**4 162 944**	**1 353 542**	**822 267**	**1 186 061**	**1 040 183**	**613 874**
	2005	..	..	..	**1 440 134**	..	..	..	**896 358**
Albania - Albanie	1990	23 489	..	..		12 250	11 800	10 900	..
	1995	..	..	..	..	3 650	2 900	2 100	..
	2000	(e)5 000	..	..	..	..			..
Bosnia and Herzegovina - Bosnie-Herzégovine	1995	..	(e)26 450	..	..	..			..
	2000	254 700	110 244	94 751	..	..			..
	2004	480 000	15 870	120 900	..	..			..

For sources and notes, see end of table.

Pour les sources et les notes, se reporter à la fin du tableau.

315

Region, country or territory / Régions, pays ou territoires	Year / Année	Aluminium (Quantity) - Aluminium (Quantité)				Copper (Quantity) - Cuivre (Quantité)			
		Bauxite production / Production de bauxite (1)	Alumina production / Production d'alumine (2)	Primary aluminium production / Production d'aluminium de première fusion	Primary aluminium consumption / Consommation d'aluminium de première fusion (3)	Copper ore production / Production de minerai de cuivre (4)	Unrefined copper production / Production de cuivre non affiné (5)	Refined copper production / Production de cuivre affiné	Refined copper consumption / Consommation de cuivre affiné (3)
Bulgaria - Bulgarie	1990	..	..	..	..	32 900	30 300	24 333	..
	1995	..	..	..	..	77 400	107 560	25 468	..
	2000	..	..	..	..	93 200	178 000	32 500	..
	2004	..	..	..	..	79 600	(e)227 000	55 300	..
Croatia - Croatie	1995	(e)1 000	..	(e)26 000		..	..	..	..
Macedonia, TFYR - Macédoine, LERY	1995	..	..	..	..	(e)10 000	..	..	..
	2000	..	..	..	..	10 000	..	..	..
Romania - Roumanie	1990	247 400	232 760	168 000	..	32 000	28 300	(e)24 700	..
	1995	175 000	170 747	140 500	..	24 520	24 300	22 013	..
	2000	..	220 375	179 039	..	16 099	18 429	15 303	..
	2004	..	295 873	218 534	..	18 767	61	24 383	..
Russian Federation - Fédération de Russie	1995	3 706 000	1 192 525	2 789 000	475 900	525 900	545 000	(e)550 000	187 000
	2000	5 089 000	1 515 585	3 247 000	748 428	(e)530 000	(e)820 000	842 000	183 000
	2004	6 017 600	1 729 521	3 594 747	1 020 000	(e)700 000	919 000	919 000	525 588
	2005	..	..	..	1 020 000	..	..	..	792 000
Serbia and Montenegro - Serbie-et-Monténégro	1995	60 000	18 680	26 000	..	74 619	87 410	78 451	..
	2000	630 000	98 465	95 465	..	46 000	(e)48 000	45 632	..
	2004	610 000	129 605	115 551	..	23 900	(e)40 000	36 000	..
Ukraine	1995	..	633 742	95 100	..	..	..	..	..
	2000	..	722 085	119 290	..	..	..	..	..
	2004	..	826 811	113 212	..	..	..	5 500	..
Yugoslavia, SFR (former) - Yougoslavie, RSF (anc.)	1990	2 952 460	574 652	349 087	..	140 145	174 000	151 395	..
USSR (former) - URSS (anc.)	1990	9 246 000	2 983 031	3 513 000	..	(e)900 000	1 480 000	1 160 000	..

Sources:
- UNCTAD, *Commodity Yearbook*
- National sources
- British Geological Survey, *World Mineral Production*
- British Geological Survey, *World Mineral Statistics*
- Metallgesellschaft, *Metal Statistics*
- World Bureau of Metal Statistics, *World Metal Statistics Quarterly Summary*
- World Bureau of Metal Statistics, *World Metal Statistics Yearbook*
- United States Geological Survey (on-line) - *Minerals Yearbook Volume III. -- Area Reports: International*

Sources :
- CNUCED, *Annuaire des produits de base*
- Sources nationales
- British Geological Survey, *World Mineral Production*
- British Geological Survey, *World Mineral Statistics*
- Metallgesellschaft, *Metal Statistics*
- World Bureau of Metal Statistics, *World Metal Statistics Quarterly Summary*
- World Bureau of Metal Statistics, *World Metal Statistics Yearbook*
- Service géologique des États-Unis (en ligne) - *Minerals Yearbook Volume III. -- Area Reports: International*

Notes:
-   Quantities are expressed in metric ton, unless otherwise indicated.
(1)   Volume in gross weight.
(2)   UNCTAD estimates based on the data from *World Mineral Production* and *World Mineral Statistics*. Volume in metal content.
(3)   Only major consuming countries are reported. World and regional totals have been calculated by the UNCTAD secretariat, and include the data for countries which are not reported in this *Handbook*.
(4)   Volume in metal content.
(5)   Includes production from both primary and secondary copper smelters.

Notes :
-   Les quantités sont indiquées en tonne métrique, sauf indication contraire.
(1)   Volume en poids brut.
(2)   Les estimations de la CNUCED sont fondées sur les données des *World Mineral Production* et *World Mineral Statistics*. Les volumes sont exprimés en métal contenu.
(3)   Seuls les principaux pays consommateurs sont rapportés. Les totaux pour le monde et les totaux régionaux ont été calculés par le secrétariat de la CNUCED et incluent les données des pays qui ne sont pas déclarés dans ce *Manuel*.
(4)   Les volumes sont indiqués en métal contenu.
(5)   Inclut la production des fonderies de cuivre de première et seconde fusion.

7

INTERNATIONAL **FINANCE**

FLUX **FINANCIERS** INTERNATIONAUX

1
2
3
4
5
6
7
8

Country or territory / Pays ou territoires	Year / Année	Goods and services / Biens et services			Income / Revenu				Current transfers (net) / Transferts courants (nets)	Current account balance / Solde du compte des transactions courantes
		Exports / Exportations	Imports / Importations	Balance on goods and services / Balance des biens et services	Debit / Débit		Credit / Crédit			
					Total	of which: / dont : Direct investment income / Revenu d'investissement direct	Total	of which: / dont : Direct investment income / Revenu d'investissement direct		
		(1)	(2)	(3)=(1)+(2)	(4)	(5)	(6)	(7)	(8)	
		Millions of dollars / Millions de dollars								
Albania - Albanie	1990	354	-485	-131	-2	..	..	..	15	-118
	2000	704	-1 499	-796	-9	0	49	..	533	-156
	2004	1 607	-3 250	-1 643	-23	0	71	..	1 110	-358
	2005	1 821	-3 860	-2 040	-46	-2	98	0	1 294	-571
Algeria - Algérie	1990	13 462	-10 107	3 355	-2 341	-151	73	5	333	1 420
Angola	1990	3 992	-3 386	607	-766	-314	11	..	-77	-236
	2000	8 188	-5 739	2 449	-1 525	-929	34	..	28	796
	2004	13 798	-10 635	3 163	-2 338	-1 950	33	..	7	686
	2005	24 286	-15 144	9 142	-3 959	-3 406	26	18	27	5 138
Anguilla	1990	41	-43	-2	-8	-7	2	..	0	-9
	2000	69	-124	-55	-13	-10	4	0	3	-61
	2004	84	-137	-53	-7	-5	4	..	5	-48
	2005	110	-166	-56	-7	-5	4	..	1	-53
Antigua and Barbuda - Antigua-et-Barbuda	1990	345	-341	5	-46	-19	2	..	10	-31
	2000	467	-498	-32	-60	-22	9	..	9	-67
	2004	523	-569	-46	-57	-25	5	..	8	-83
	2005	518	-620	-102	-51	-26	3	..	8	-136
Argentina - Argentine	1990	14 800	-6 846	7 954	-6 254	-637	1 854	2	998	4 552
	2000	31 277	-33 108	-1 832	-14 940	-3 086	7 384	978	399	-8 981
	2004	39 721	-27 939	11 783	-12 341	-2 556	3 445	625	591	3 446
	2005	46 343	-34 917	11 426	-10 240	-3 640	4 068	826	570	5 789
Armenia - Arménie	2000	447	-966	-519	-50	-22	26	..	188	-278
	2004	985	-1 514	-529	-158	-139	16	..	330	-162
	2005	1 337	-1 984	-647	-192	-170	29	0	409	-193
Aruba	1990	566	-716	-149	-23	..	15	..	-1	-158
	2000	3 534	-3 228	306	-72	-23	53	1	-76	211
	2004	3 967	-3 792	175	-95	-35	36	2	-101	14
	2005	4 788	-4 464	324	-495	-434	39	2	-127	-259
Australia - Australie	1990	49 846	-53 056	-3 210	-16 063	-4 488	2 880	760	439	-15 948
	2000	83 087	-87 531	-4 444	-19 213	-7 290	8 473	5 468	-47	-15 306
	2004	113 569	-132 278	-18 709	-33 762	-16 923	13 439	8 295	-269	-39 745
	2005	135 505	-149 738	-14 233	-42 596	-22 004	15 375	9 026	-363	-42 286
Austria - Autriche	1990	63 694	-61 580	2 114	-10 087	-933	9 145	313	-6	1 166
	2000	96 026	-97 074	-1 048	-14 073	-2 598	11 081	1 279	-1 352	-4 864
	2004	161 223	-155 757	5 466	-20 284	-5 010	18 326	5 215	-2 759	1 382
	2005	171 154	-162 913	8 241	-24 346	-6 939	22 305	7 014	-2 652	4 252
Azerbaijan - Azerbaïdjan	2000	2 118	-2 024	95	-344	-317	56	..	73	-168
	2004	4 235	-6 312	-2 077	-658	-581	53	..	188	-2 589
	2005	8 332	-7 003	1 329	-1 735	-1 582	69	0	484	167
Bahamas	1990	1 784	-1 653	131	-370	..	232	..	6	-37
	2000	2 438	-3 009	-571	-406	..	317	..	78	-633
	2004	2 722	-3 138	-417	-158	..	80	..	251	-307
	2005	3 031	-3 775	-744	-206	..	173	..	85	-765
Bahrain - Bahreïn	1990	4 119	-3 999	120	-5 275	-112	5 497	83	-272	70
	2000	7 176	-5 132	2 044	-6 552	-881	6 328	209	-990	830
	2004	9 179	-7 069	2 110	-3 119	-1 006	2 544	347	-1 120	415
	2005	11 794	-8 583	3 211	-5 428	-1 158	5 016	471	-1 223	1 575
Bangladesh	1990	2 064	-3 960	-1 896	-180	..	64	..	1 613	-398
	2000	7 214	-9 673	-2 459	-343	-149	69	2	2 420	-306
	2004	9 234	-13 089	-3 855	-471	-247	91	3	3 948	-279
	2005	10 432	-14 456	-4 024	-908	-659	102	2	4 691	-132

For sources and notes, see end of table.

Pour les sources et les notes, se reporter à la fin du tableau.

Country or territory / Pays ou territoires	Year / Année	Goods and services / Biens et services			Income / Revenu				Current transfers (net) / Transferts courants (nets)	Current account balance / Solde du compte des transactions courantes
		Exports / Exportations	Imports / Importations	Balance on goods and services / Balance des biens et services	Debit / Débit		Credit / Crédit			
					Total	of which: / dont : Direct investment income / Revenu d'investissement direct	Total	of which: / dont : Direct investment income / Revenu d'investissement direct		
		(1)	(2)	(3)=(1)+(2)	(4)	(5)	(6)	(7)	(8)	
		Millions of dollars / Millions de dollars								
Barbados - Barbade	1990	873	-878	-5	-75	-9	18	1	43	-8
	2000	1 377	-1 518	-141	-150	-17	54	6	78	-145
	2004	1 517	-1 820	-303	-195	-76	66	20	88	-337
	2005	1 836	-2 144	-308	-254	-82	76	27	95	-385
Belarus - Bélarus	2000	7 641	-8 087	-446	-70	-5	12	0	155	-338
	2004	15 689	-17 185	-1 495	-159	-76	31	1	303	-1 194
	2005	18 068	-17 859	209	-227	-135	48	1	169	434
Belgium - Belgique	2004	298 134	-284 741	13 392	-41 272	-17 260	42 355	13 862	-6 478	12 537
	2005	318 775	-308 430	10 345	-50 544	-21 310	51 172	16 381	-6 411	9 328
Belgium-Luxembourg - Belgique-Luxembourg	1990	138 605	-135 098	3 507	-62 073	..	62 723	..	-2 197	3 627
	2000	214 466	-203 954	10 512	-67 693	-11 488	71 954	5 138	-4 179	11 381
	2001	213 811	-203 106	10 705	-72 726	-13 739	75 244	6 909	-4 220	9 392
Belize	1990	245	-248	-4	-14	-7	6	..	29	15
	2000	434	-601	-167	-54	-31	5	..	58	-162
	2004	543	-627	-84	-111	-42	2	0	46	-152
	2005	615	-714	-99	-112	-35	3	0	51	-159
Benin - Bénin	1990	364	-454	-90	-37	0	7	..	97	-18
	2000	528	-708	-179	-41	-7	26	8	111	-81
	2003	713	-1 073	-360	-63	-26	20	4	66	-331
	2004	784	-1 129	-345	-73	-30	30	17	93	-288
Bolivia - Bolivie	1990	977	-1 086	-110	-261	-17	17	..	159	-199
	2000	1 470	-2 078	-608	-359	-148	114	3	387	-446
	2004	2 562	-2 331	231	-453	-292	44	3	491	337
	2005	3 160	-2 872	287	-487	-270	88	3	584	498
Bosnia and Herzegovina - Bosnie-Herzégovine	2000	1 580	-4 157	-2 578	-74	..	36	..	1 591	-396
	2004	2 986	-7 089	-4 102	-149	-51	66	..	1 851	-1 840
	2005	3 602	-8 004	-4 402	-209	-78	112	..	1 841	-2 156
Botswana	1990	2 005	-1 987	18	-463	-407	335	30	69	-19
	2000	3 000	-2 321	679	-675	-658	360	25	217	545
	2004	4 444	-3 657	787	-1 165	-1 092	198	10	526	287
	2005	5 285	-3 683	1 603	-1 177	-1 066	426	194	678	1 469
Brazil - Brésil	1990	35 170	-28 184	6 986	-12 760	-1 892	1 147	27	799	-3 823
	2000	64 584	-72 444	-7 860	-21 348	-4 238	3 383	999	1 521	-24 225
	2004	109 059	-80 069	28 990	-23 546	-6 860	2 845	1 061	3 268	11 738
	2005	134 403	-97 794	36 609	-29 050	-10 976	2 869	724	3 558	14 199
Bulgaria - Bulgarie	1990	6 950	-8 027	-1 077	-878	..	120	..	125	-1 710
	2000	7 000	-7 670	-670	-618	-107	263	-2	290	-703
	2004	13 960	-16 812	-2 852	-1 192	-756	248	0	1 107	-1 451
	2005	16 057	-20 601	-4 543	-1 146	-658	347	2	1 229	-3 004
Burkina Faso	1990	349	-758	-409	-18	-6	18	..	332	-77
	2000	237	-658	-421	-26	-3	9	0	122	-319
	2001	260	-650	-390	-32	-5	9	0	124	-291
Burundi	1990	89	-318	-229	-18	-3	8	..	174	-69
	2000	53	-152	-99	-12	-12	2	2	59	-51
	2004	64	-236	-173	-20	-20	1	1	22	-171
	2005	92	-353	-261	-21	-21	3	3	23	-256
Cambodia - Cambodge	2000	1 826	-2 265	-439	-138	-123	64	5	425	-138
	2004	3 390	-3 782	-392	-225	-205	45	8	428	-185
	2005	4 017	-4 559	-542	-250	-227	64	8	440	-356
Cameroon - Cameroun	1990	2 508	-2 475	32	-552	-138	4	2	-26	-551
	2000	2 576	-2 441	135	-503	-41	16	11	109	-249
	2002	2 903	-3 023	-120	-391	-90	27	6	52	-445
	2003	2 894	-3 239	-345	-467	-105	35	28	116	-675

For sources and notes, see end of table.

Pour les sources et les notes, se reporter à la fin du tableau.

7.1 Balance of payments: current account summaries

7.1 Balance des paiements : sommaires des comptes des transactions courantes

Country or territory / Pays ou territoires	Year / Année	Goods and services / Biens et services			Income / Revenu				Current transfers (net) / Transferts courants (nets)	Current account balance / Solde du compte des transactions courantes
		Exports / Exportations	Imports / Importations	Balance on goods and services / Balance des biens et services	Debit / Débit		Credit / Crédit			
					Total	of which: / dont : Direct investment income / Revenu d'investissement direct	Total	of which: / dont : Direct investment income / Revenu d'investissement direct		
		(1)	(2)	(3)=(1)+(2)	(4)	(5)	(6)	(7)	(8)	
		Millions of dollars / Millions de dollars								
Canada	1990	149 538	-149 118	419	-34 460	-5 730	15 072	3 890	-796	-19 764
	2000	329 252	-288 093	41 159	-47 036	-16 468	24 746	10 164	754	19 622
	2004	379 216	-338 794	40 422	-47 930	-21 088	28 905	15 906	-240	21 157
	2005	427 955	-385 473	42 482	-55 341	-25 579	39 832	21 483	-419	26 555
Cape Verde - Cap-Vert	1990	57	-149	-92	-3	0	3	0	86	-4
	2000	146	-326	-180	-17	-5	4	2	135	-58
	2004	300	-590	-290	-34	-3	19	7	247	-58
	2005	366	-646	-280	-51	-10	19	0	279	-34
Central African Republic - République centrafricaine	1990	220	-410	-191	-22	-2	1	..	123	-89
Chad - Tchad	1990	271	-488	-216	-24	..	3	..	192	-46
Chile - Chili	1990	10 221	-9 166	1 055	-2 214	-387	484	2	198	-485
	2000	23 293	-21 893	1 400	-4 438	-2 539	1 584	568	558	-898
	2004	38 278	-29 771	8 507	-9 805	-8 231	1 809	951	1 079	1 586
	2005	47 746	-38 154	9 591	-12 778	-11 071	2 158	1 052	1 735	703
China - Chine	1990	57 374	-46 706	10 668	-1 962	-46	3 017		274	11 997
	2000	279 561	-250 688	28 874	-26 537	-20 198	12 348	62	6 311	20 518
	2004	655 827	-606 543	49 284	-22 685	-17 415	18 530	218	22 898	68 659
	2005	836 888	-712 090	124 798	-26 507	-21 040	35 622	3 385	25 386	160 818
China, Hong Kong SAR - Chine, Hong Kong RAS	2000	243 127	-235 589	7 538	-53 133	-34 183	54 348	19 748	-1 670	6 993
	2004	315 420	-300 712	14 708	-48 677	-40 269	51 763	29 543	-1 985	15 728
	2005	351 754	-329 590	22 164	-64 084	-50 507	64 491	35 056	-2 192	20 284
China, Macao SAR - Chine, Macao RAS	2004	10 879	-6 022	4 857	-933	-899	381	-8	-27	4 253
	2005	11 092	-6 847	4 246	-1 527	-1 407	801	29	-100	3 367
Colombia - Colombie	1990	8 679	-6 858	1 821	-2 609	-964	340	20	1 026	542
	2000	15 771	-14 397	1 374	-3 325	-655	1 022	31	1 673	764
	2004	19 479	-19 812	-333	-4 984	-2 466	651	152	3 727	-938
	2005	24 393	-24 901	-507	-6 619	-3 668	1 043	166	4 089	-1 981
Comoros - Comores	1990	35	-89	-54	-4	-1	3	0	45	-10
Congo	1990	1 488	-1 282	206	-475	.	15	..	3	-251
	2000	2 628	-1 194	1 435	-787	-466	5	0	19	648
	2004	3 630	-1 985	1 645	-919	-647	4	1	-22	674
	2005	4 964	-2 917	2 048	-1 093	-1 093	4	4	-22	903
Costa Rica	1990	1 963	-2 346	-383	-363	-60	118	3	192	-424
	2000	7 750	-7 297	452	-1 461	-1 141	227	11	93	-707
	2004	8 611	-9 175	-564	-552	-330	127	5	212	-796
	2005	9 716	-10 730	-1 014	-436	-170	214	19	270	-959
Côte d'Ivoire	1990	3 503	-3 445	58	-1 136	-75	14	..	-181	-1 214
	2000	4 370	-3 629	742	-783	-284	22	3	-330	-241
	2004	7 682	-6 324	1 358	-825	-364	31	3	-465	241
	2005	8 289	-7 174	1 115	-838	..	32	..	-465	-12
Croatia - Croatie	2000	8 638	-9 592	-954	-727	-150	274	10	880	-458
	2004	17 583	-20 126	-2 543	-1 556	-740	481	214	1 486	-1 842
	2005	18 876	-21 702	-2 825	-2 024	-1 053	466	129	1 475	-2 585
Cyprus - Chypre	1990	2 955	-3 178	-223	-205	-4	159	..	127	-154
	2000	5 019	-5 142	-123	-1 067	-846	527	39	177	-488
	2004	7 408	-7 866	-458	-1 538	-962	1 127	390	168	-827
	2005	8 023	-8 476	-453	-1 999	-1 160	1 561	499	93	-929
Czech Republic - République tchèque	2000	35 859	-37 551	-1 692	-2 720	-1 379	1 658	-11	373	-2 690
	2004	76 918	-77 483	-565	-8 070	-6 089	2 599	387	165	-6 538
	2005	89 007	-86 461	2 546	-8 462	-6 176	3 658	675	888	-2 495
Czechoslovakia (former) - Tchécoslovaquie (anc.)	1990	14 307	-15 529	-1 222	-709	..	498	..	206	-1 227

For sources and notes, see end of table.

Pour les sources et les notes, se reporter à la fin du tableau.

320

Country or territory / Pays ou territoires	Year / Année	Goods and services / Biens et services			Income / Revenu				Current transfers (net) / Transferts courants (nets)	Current account balance / Solde du compte des transactions courantes
		Exports / Exportations	Imports / Importations	Balance on goods and services / Balance des biens et services	Debit / Débit		Credit / Crédit			
					Total	of which: / dont : Direct investment income / Revenu d'investissement direct	Total	of which: / dont : Direct investment income / Revenu d'investissement direct		
		(1)	(2)	(3)=(1)+(2)	(4)	(5)	(6)	(7)	(8)	
		Millions of dollars / Millions de dollars								
Denmark - Danemark	1990	48 902	-41 415	7 487	-11 719	..	6 011	..	-408	1 372
	2000	73 805	-64 506	9 300	-15 245	-6 539	11 217	5 108	-3 014	2 262
	2004	111 355	-98 925	12 430	-13 888	-4 715	11 709	4 163	-4 159	5 941
	2005	125 046	-112 482	12 564	..	..	..	..	-4 223	8 616
Dominica - Dominique	1990	89	-134	-45	-9	-5	4	0	6	-44
	2000	145	-183	-39	-44	-33	4	0	18	-60
	2004	130	-174	-44	-35	-19	2	..	17	-59
	2005	126	-196	-70	-31	-20	2	..	17	-80
Dominican Republic - République dominicaine	1990	1 832	-2 233	-402	-335	-90	86	..	371	-280
	2000	8 964	-10 852	-1 888	-1 322	-1 068	150	..	1 902	-1 027
	2004	9 440	-9 101	339	-2 131	-1 664	65	..	2 528	1 047
	2005	10 056	-11 333	-1 277	-2 347	-1 825	128	..	2 734	-500
Ecuador - Équateur	1990	3 262	-2 519	743	-1 233	-125	24	..	107	-360
	2000	5 987	-5 012	975	-1 470	-280	65	..	1 352	921
	2004	8 982	-9 651	-670	-1 934	-715	29	..	2 025	-551
	2005	11 439	-11 826	-387	-2 015	-789	76	..	2 267	-59
Egypt - Égypte	1990	9 895	-14 091	-4 196	-1 852	-14	857	247	7 545	2 327
	2000	16 864	-22 895	-6 031	-983	-92	1 871	71	4 172	-971
	2004	26 516	-26 915	-399	-818	-56	572	16	4 567	3 922
	2005	30 716	-34 326	-3 611	-1 460	-647	1 425	92	5 748	2 103
El Salvador	1990	973	-1 624	-651	-158	-31	21	..	631	-152
	2000	3 662	-5 636	-1 975	-375	-60	128	..	1 797	-431
	2004	4 412	-7 151	-2 739	-571	-82	128	5	2 568	-632
	2005	4 573	-7 652	-3 080	-730	-187	171	14	2 865	-786
Equatorial Guinea - Guinée équatoriale	1990	42	-89	-47	-10	..	..	..	38	-19
Eritrea - Érythrée	2000	98	-500	-402	-9	-4	6	0	299	-105
Estonia - Estonie	2000	4 784	-4 965	-182	-320	-205	115	13	86	-299
	2004	8 813	-9 758	-945	-1 048	-862	281	152	124	-1 458
	2005	10 939	-11 784	-845	-1 320	-1 066	415	256	100	-1 445
Ethiopia - Éthiopie	2000	992	-1 621	-629	-52	-9	16	..	678	13
	2004	1 684	-3 727	-2 043	-60	-28	32	1	1 404	-668
	2005	1 929	-4 895	-2 965	-48	-21	43	0	1 402	-1 568
Ethiopia (former) - Éthiopie (anc.)	1990	597	-1 271	-674	-78	..	4	..	449	-294
Faeroe Islands - Îles Féroé	2000	531	-612	-81	-61	-4	59	1	146	99
	2002	609	-604	5	-64	-9	52	1	102	126
	2003	671	-830	-159	-71	-6	62	2	123	-7
Fiji - Fidji	1990	833	-899	-67	-75	-49	28	10	-1	-94
Finland - Finlande	1990	31 180	-33 456	-2 276	-7 224	-277	3 442	-340	-952	-6 962
	2000	51 880	-40 459	11 421	-8 889	-2 837	6 793	3 825	-723	8 975
	2004	76 309	-60 654	15 656	-12 655	-4 914	12 462	6 471	-1 078	14 826
	2005	82 457	-71 091	11 367	-14 067	-4 390	13 343	6 659	-1 572	9 517
France	1990	285 389	-283 238	2 151	-55 646	-2 698	52 704	2 267	-8 199	-9 944
	2000	379 115	-362 861	16 255	-55 714	-5 400	64 440	14 749	-13 256	18 581
	2004	530 791	-528 403	2 389	-102 005	-13 110	104 272	32 523	-21 902	-6 808
	2005	555 204	-577 463	-22 260	-117 440	-13 072	123 269	35 472	-27 344	-33 289
Gabon	1990	2 730	-1 812	919	-633	-116	20	13	-134	168
	2000	3 498	-1 656	1 843	-792	-473	45	12	-63	1 001
	2003	3 351	-1 882	1 468	-564	-359	46	41	-181	766
	2004	4 228	-2 155	2 073	-959	-722	8	2	-184	924
Gambia - Gambie	1990	168	-192	-24	-13	..	2	..	59	23
	2004	182	-253	-71	-29	-22	1	..	67	-31
	2005	181	-261	-80	-35	-26	2	..	69	-44

For sources and notes, see end of table.

Pour les sources et les notes, se reporter à la fin du tableau.

Country or territory Pays ou territoires	Year Année	Goods and services Biens et services			Income Revenu				Current transfers (net) Transferts courants (nets)	Current account balance Solde du compte des transactions courantes
		Exports Exportations	Imports Importations	Balance on goods and services Balance des biens et services	Debit / Débit		Credit / Crédit			
					Total	of which: / dont : Direct investment income Revenu d'investissement direct	Total	of which: / dont : Direct investment income Revenu d'investissement direct		
		(1)	(2)	(3)=(1)+(2)	(4)	(5)	(6)	(7)	(8)	
		Millions of dollars / Millions de dollars								
Georgia - Géorgie	2000	665	-1 187	-521	-47	0	..	..	135	-269
	2004	1 632	-2 491	-859	-139	-80	15	10	414	-347
	2005	2 171	-3 312	-1 141	-153	-87	16	4	359	-690
Germany - Allemagne	1990	473 672	-427 547	46 125	-47 046	-6 892	66 924	6 078	-21 954	46 745
	2000	626 435	-625 074	1 361	-109 133	-12 890	103 031	16 847	-25 654	-31 955
	2004	1 044 500	-908 564	135 937	-140 727	-30 912	142 842	34 555	-35 117	101 792
	2005	1 127 020	-985 673	141 347	-153 574	-35 795	166 210	42 583	-35 989	116 035
Ghana	1990	983	-1 506	-522	-77	-7	-34	..	411	-223
	2000	2 441	-3 350	-910	-123	..	16	..	631	-387
	2004	3 407	-5 356	-1 949	-242	..	45	..	1 831	-316
	2005	3 869	-6 610	-2 741	-230	..	43	..	2 117	-812
Greece - Grèce	1990	13 018	-19 564	-6 546	-1 902	-78	273	19	4 718	-3 537
	2000	29 440	-41 727	-12 286	-3 442	-319	2 227	48	3 352	-9 820
	2004	48 824	-61 380	-12 556	-8 685	-1 307	3 148	578	4 504	-13 476
	2005	51 790	-66 626	-14 836	-10 829	-1 697	3 715	657	3 987	-17 879
Grenada - Grenade	1990	93	-139	-46	-14	-8	2	0	11	-46
	2000	236	-310	-74	-39	-28	5	0	20	-88
	2004	190	-331	-140	-45	-14	6	..	121	-59
	2005	167	-387	-220	-28	-8	4	..	114	-129
Guatemala	1990	1 568	-1 812	-244	-213	-37	9	1	227	-213
	2000	3 862	-5 567	-1 705	-408	-248	182	78	865	-1 050
	2004	4 546	-8 483	-3 937	-488	-291	133	94	3 045	-1 211
	2005	4 939	-9 547	-4 608	-585	-375	209	124	3 558	-1 387
Guinea - Guinée	1990	829	-953	-124	-162	-61	13	..	70	-203
	2000	734	-872	-138	-100	-8	23	..	75	-140
	2003	743	-952	-209	-120	-79	13	0	135	-185
	2004	811	-964	-153	-35	..	10	..	18	-162
Guinea-Bissau - Guinée-Bissau	1990	26	-88	-62	-11	..	..	..	39	-45
	2003	71	-102	-31	-11	0	0	..	39	0
	2004	83	-127	-44	-11	0	1	..	67	14
Guyana	2000	672	-743	-71	-66	-6	12	..	47	-82
	2004	745	-799	-55	-38	-3	4	..	74	-20
	2005	693	-917	-224	-36	-7	3	..	167	-96
Haiti - Haïti	1990	318	-515	-197	-25	..	7	7	193	-22
	2000	504	-1 369	-865	-9	..	..	..	760	-114
	2004	491	-1 525	-1 035	-12	..	..	..	993	-54
	2005	593	-1 756	-1 163	-39	..	2	..	1 254	54
Honduras	1990	1 033	-1 127	-94	-258	-72	8	..	280	-51
	2000	2 491	-3 267	-777	-252	-70	112	..	648	-262
	2004	3 112	-4 434	-1 321	-410	-290	44	..	1 254	-426
	2005	3 427	-5 035	-1 608	-434	-313	95	..	1 854	-86
Hungary - Hongrie	1990	12 035	-11 017	1 019	-1 707	-37	280	27	787	379
	2000	34 663	-36 449	-1 787	-3 670	-2 023	945	73	357	-4 004
	2004	66 816	-69 676	-2 860	-7 869	-5 461	1 617	698	317	-8 639
	2005	74 168	-75 596	-1 428	-8 491	-5 430	1 450	386	237	-8 106
Iceland - Islande	1990	2 149	-2 065	83	-285	-3	38	6	-4	-134
	2000	2 946	-3 540	-595	-380	-16	77	13	-10	-847
	2004	4 519	-5 250	-731	-1 036	-493	385	210	-17	-1 330
	2005	5 106	-7 140	-2 033	-2 045	-1 005	1 429	1 005	-27	-2 627
India - Inde	1990	22 911	-29 527	-6 616	-3 588	..	405	..	2 837	-7 036
	2000	59 930	-73 073	-13 143	-5 566	-4 163	2 376	414	13 435	-4 601
	2002	70 619	-75 741	-5 122	-6 549	-4 964	3 081	1 438	16 091	7 060
	2003	82 735	-93 918	-11 184	-7 485	-5 989	3 647	1 448	22 488	6 853

For sources and notes, see end cf table.

Pour les sources et les notes, se reporter à la fin du tableau.

322

Country or territory Pays ou territoires	Year Année	Goods and services Biens et services			Income Revenu				Current transfers (net) Transferts courants (nets)	Current account balance Solde du compte des transactions courantes
		Exports Exportations	Imports Importations	Balance on goods and services Balance des biens et services	Debit / Débit		Credit / Crédit			
					Total	of which: / dont : Direct investment income Revenu d'investissement direct	Total	of which: / dont : Direct investment income Revenu d'investissement direct		
		(1)	(2)	(3)=(1)+(2)	(4)	(5)	(6)	(7)	(8)	
		Millions of dollars / Millions de dollars								
Indonesia - Indonésie	1990	29 295	-27 511	1 784	-5 599	-2 192	409	..	418	-2 988
	2000	70 622	-56 003	14 619	-10 901	-3 574	2 458	..	1 816	7 992
	2004	82 813	-71 471	11 341	-12 774	-8 323	1 329	103	1 139	1 563
	2005	99 104	-87 584	11 520	-13 838	-9 665	2 210	209	1 258	929
Iran, Islamic Republic of - Iran, Rép. islamique d'	1990	19 741	-22 292	-2 551	-78	..	456	..	2 500	327
	2000	29 727	-17 503	12 224	-604	..	404	..	457	12 481
Ireland - Irlande	1990	26 786	-24 576	2 211	-8 169	-4 350	2 994	395	2 384	-361
	2000	92 068	-79 792	12 276	-41 053	-21 707	27 417	3 061	915	-356
	2004	152 834	-126 486	26 348	-70 655	-39 681	43 068	7 489	503	-1 081
	2005	161 366	-137 081	24 286	-83 325	-40 583	53 276	8 279	691	-5 331
Israel - Israël	1990	17 312	-20 228	-2 916	-2 721	-162	1 490	17	5 061	163
	2000	46 243	-46 566	-323	-7 468	-2 466	3 442	591	6 482	-854
	2004	52 761	-52 313	448	-4 424	-1 298	2 700	1 131	6 286	3 159
	2005	57 874	-57 525	349	-4 948	-1 041	4 298	1 420	6 029	3 756
Italy - Italie	1990	219 971	-218 573	1 397	-30 069	-613	15 233	264	-3 164	-16 479
	2000	297 030	-286 526	10 504	-48 720	-3 535	37 160	1 936	-4 276	-5 781
	2004	436 707	-424 531	12 176	-69 392	-5 503	51 312	5 006	-9 551	-15 713
	2005	462 709	-463 295	-585	-75 717	-5 819	59 330	4 974	-10 061	-27 724
Jamaica - Jamaïque	1990	2 217	-2 390	-173	-532	-189	15	1	291	-312
	2000	3 589	-4 427	-838	-522	-290	105	9	821	-367
	2004	3 899	-5 272	-1 373	-801	-362	134	25	1 446	-509
	2005	3 994	-5 975	-1 981	-952	-454	188	24	1 578	-1 079
Japan - Japon	1990	323 692	-297 306	26 386	..	..	..	..	-4 800	44 078
	2000	528 751	-459 660	69 091	-36 527	-2 615	96 931	8 241	-9 831	119 660
	2004	636 611	-542 380	94 231	-27 343	-6 343	113 158	18 957	-7 875	172 059
	2005	677 782	-607 869	69 912	-37 319	-9 484	140 890	30 373	-7 573	165 783
Jordan - Jordanie	1990	2 511	-3 569	-1 058	-282	..	67	..	1 045	-227
	2000	3 536	-5 796	-2 260	-512	-1	486	..	2 184	59
	2004	5 940	-9 407	-3 467	-293	-1	286	..	3 216	-18
	2005	6 584	-11 859	-5 275	-341	-1	437	..	2 588	-2 311
Kazakhstan	2000	10 341	-8 970	1 371	-1 346	-1 046	135	..	249	366
	2004	22 612	-18 926	3 687	-2 872	-2 347	419	-30	-488	335
	2005	30 548	-25 503	5 046	-5 632	-4 630	674	-162	-412	-724
Kenya	1990	2 228	-2 705	-477	-419	-132	5	..	368	-527
	2000	2 776	-3 763	-987	-178	-29	45	..	921	-199
	2004	4 277	-5 289	-1 012	-172	-31	45	..	786	-353
	2005	5 126	-6 540	-1 415	-182	-35	73	..	1 028	-495
Kiribati	1990	11	-46	-35	-2	-2	17	..	9	-9
Korea, Republic of - Corée, République de	1990	73 297	-76 373	-3 076	-2 956	-266	2 352	373	1 150	-2 014
	2000	206 754	-192 648	14 106	-8 746	-1 194	5 794	449	566	12 251
	2004	299 592	-270 069	29 523	-8 202	-2 533	8 697	1 559	-2 432	28 174
	2005	334 370	-313 989	20 381	-11 447	-4 499	9 573	1 543	-2 502	16 559
Kuwait - Koweït	1990	8 268	-7 169	1 099	-846	..	8 584	..	-4 951	3 886
	2000	21 281	-11 346	9 935	-616	..	7 315	..	-1 956	14 679
	2004	33 831	-19 246	14 584	-456	..	6 584	..	-2 550	18 163
	2005	51 574	-24 513	27 061	-555	..	9 389	..	-3 261	32 634
Kyrgyzstan - Kirghizistan	2000	573	-654	-81	-89	-37	17	..	87	-76
	2004	943	-1 127	-184	-97	-58	11	..	209	-76
	2005	942	-1 397	-455	-80	-34	17	..	332	-203
Lao People's Dem. Rep. - Rép. dém. populaire lao	1990	102	-212	-110	-3	..	2	..	56	-55
	2000	506	-578	-72	-59	..	7	..	116	-8
	2001	477	-560	-82	-39	..	5	..	34	-82

For sources and notes, see end of table.

Pour les sources et les notes, se reporter à la fin du tableau.

Country or territory Pays ou territoires	Year Année	Goods and services Biens et services			Income Revenu				Current transfers (net) Transferts courants (nets)	Current account balance Solde du compte des transactions courantes
					Debit / Débit		Credit / Crédit			
		Exports Exportations	Imports Importations	Balance on goods and services Balance des biens et services	Total	of which: / dont : Direct investment income Revenu d'investissement direct	Total	of which: / dont : Direct investment income Revenu d'investissement direct		
		(1)	(2)	(3)=(1)+(2)	(4)	(5)	(6)	(7)	(8)	
		Millions of dollars / Millions de dollars								
Latvia - Lettonie	2000	3 229	-3 813	-583	-194	-92	146	1	195	-371
	2004	6 001	-8 180	-2 179	-778	-541	272	6	694	-1 774
	2005	7 526	-9 936	-2 410	-940	-632	389	32	596	-2 002
Lebanon - Liban	2004	11 754	-16 736	-4 982	-1 507	-91	903	63	1 716	-4 122
	2005	13 037	-16 222	-3 185	-1 689	-95	2 000	122	1 057	-1 881
Lesotho	1990	100	-754	-654	-22	-13	27	..	286	65
	2000	254	-770	-516	-35	-15	37	..	139	-151
	2004	771	-1 398	-627	-47	-21	39	..	248	-76
	2005	705	-1 354	-649	-48	-11	50	..	301	-44
Libyan Arab Jamahiriya - Jamahiriya arabe libyenne	1990	11 468	-8 960	2 508	-493	-436	666	18	-481	2 201
	2000	13 680	-5 024	8 656	-1 143	-1 143	720	..	-487	7 740
	2004	17 862	-10 682	7 180	-2 657	-2 657	1 334	156	-2 324	3 503
	2005	29 383	-13 523	15 860	-2 058	-2 058	1 829	224	-634	14 945
Lithuania - Lituanie	2000	5 109	-5 833	-724	-342	-123	138	15	243	-675
	2004	11 751	-13 321	-1 570	-941	-649	192	16	458	-1 725
	2005	14 879	-16 745	-1 866	-1 030	-711	224	10	662	-1 831
Luxembourg	2004	47 163	-38 038	9 125	-59 811	-9 474	60 437	3 642	-985	3 982
	2005	54 983	-43 455	11 528	-72 452	-11 756	71 442	5 969	-925	4 267
Madagascar	1990	471	-809	-338	-174	-1	15	..	234	-265
	2000	1 188	-1 520	-332	-63	-4	11	..	113	-260
	2004	515	-766	-251	-30	-7	3	..	119	-158
	2005	450	-691	-241	-30	-13	5	..	80	-188
Malawi	1990	443	-549	-106	-89	-5	9	..	99	-86
	2000	437	-629	-192	-51	-15	33	..	135	-73
	2001	472	-644	-172	-43	-14	12	..	143	-60
	2002	472	-795	-323	-45	-22	6	..	161	-201
Malaysia - Malaisie	1990	32 665	-31 765	900	-3 539	-1 926	1 664	63	102	-870
	2000	112 370	-94 350	18 020	-8 995	-7 173	1 644	-222	-1 924	8 488
	2004	143 410	-118 227	25 183	-9 687	-7 757	3 527	1 126	-3 851	14 872
	2005	161 384	-130 609	30 776	-10 446	-8 330	4 256	1 087	-4 477	19 980
Maldives	1990	179	-159	20	-18	-14	3	..	4	10
	2000	457	-452	6	-40	-34	8	..	-27	-51
	2004	688	-725	-37	-51	-44	5	..	-54	-134
	2005	479	-846	-367	-37	-27	8	..	63	-330
Mali	1990	420	-830	-410	-59	-4	23	..	225	-221
	2000	644	-927	-283	-116	-76	17	1	126	-255
	2003	1 152	-1 471	-318	-172	-120	6	1	207	-271
	2004	1 218	-1 625	-407	-207	-152	7	0	193	-409
Malta - Malte	1990	1 950	-2 283	-333	-75	-74	248	248	87	-56
	2000	3 571	-3 990	-419	-1 002	-998	885	885	27	-500
	2004	4 257	-4 592	-336	-980	-288	925	24	-71	-444
	2005	4 063	-4 628	-565	-1 232	-358	1 156	25	34	-594
Mauritania - Mauritanie	1990	471	-520	-49	-50	-1	4	..	86	-10
Mauritius - Maurice	1990	1 722	-1 916	-194	-79	-22	56	2	97	-119
	2000	2 622	-2 707	-85	-65	-3	49	1	64	-37
	2004	3 449	-3 596	-147	-56	-14	51	4	49	-112
	2005	3 762	-4 154	-393	-142	-34	142	4	61	-340
Mexico - Mexique	1990	48 805	-51 915	-3 110	-11 589	-2 304	2 667	..	3 975	-7 451
	2000	179 876	-191 818	-11 942	-19 712	-6 017	5 025	..	6 994	-18 683
	2004	202 045	-216 588	-14 543	-14 799	-3 577	4 087	1 876	17 044	-6 682
	2005	230 369	-243 259	-12 890	-17 965	-5 705	3 986	975	20 484	-4 647
Moldova, Republic of - Moldova, République de	2000	641	-972	-331	-89	-3	14	..	211	-98
	2004	1 349	-2 125	-776	-92	-50	10	..	366	-53
	2005	1 528	-2 743	-1 215	-93	-50	19	..	570	-242

For sources and notes, see end of table.

Pour les sources et les notes, se reporter à la fin du tableau.

Country or territory / Pays ou territoires	Year / Année	Goods and services / Biens et services			Income / Revenu				Current transfers (net) / Transferts courants (nets)	Current account balance / Solde du compte des transactions courantes
		Exports / Exportations	Imports / Importations	Balance on goods and services / Balance des biens et services	Debit / Débit		Credit / Crédit			
					Total	of which: / dont : Direct investment income / Revenu d'investissement direct	Total	of which: / dont : Direct investment income / Revenu d'investissement direct		
		(1)	(2)	(3)=(1)+(2)	(4)	(5)	(6)	(7)	(8)	
		Millions of dollars / Millions de dollars								
Mongolia - Mongolie	1990	493	-1 096	-603	-49	..	5	..	7	-640
	2000	614	-771	-158	-20	-9	13	..	94	-70
	2003	835	-1 084	-249	-25	-5	14	..	162	-99
	2004	1 211	-1 405	-194	-28	-10	9	..	269	63
Montserrat	1990	19	-55	-36	-2	-2	2	..	14	-23
	2000	17	-42	-24	-4	-3	1	..	19	-8
	2004	20	-48	-29	-4	-2	1	..	23	-9
	2005	17	-46	-29	-4	-2	2	..	16	-16
Morocco - Maroc	1990	6 239	-7 783	-1 544	-1 071	-69	83	..	2 336	-196
	2000	10 453	-12 546	-2 093	-1 140	-268	276	13	2 483	-475
	2004	16 632	-19 860	-3 228	-1 176	-670	505	60	4 868	970
	2005	18 788	-22 739	-3 951	-1 003	-525	689	59	5 375	1 110
Mozambique	1990	229	-996	-766	-142	..	..	..	448	-415
	2000	689	-1 492	-802	-218	0	43	..	231	-764
	2004	1 759	-2 381	-622	-365	-168	20	0	314	-607
	2005	2 087	-2 891	-804	-448	-284	48	..	403	-761
Myanmar	1990	319	-603	-283	-194	-147	2	..	39	-436
	2000	2 139	-2 493	-354	-169	-137	9	..	276	-212
	2003	2 959	-2 332	627	-771	-752	3	..	95	-19
	2004	3 181	-2 458	723	-786	-762	4	..	134	112
Namibia - Namibie	1990	1 220	-1 584	-364	-128	-67	178	3	354	28
	2000	1 531	-1 643	-111	-220	-194	243	1	436	347
	2003	1 682	-1 975	-293	-43	3	276	3	460	397
	2004	2 310	-2 495	-185	-205	-144	360	6	669	634
Nepal - Népal	1990	422	-834	-412	-11	..	25	..	109	-289
	2000	1 282	-1 790	-508	-35	..	72	..	340	-131
	2004	1 234	-2 293	-1 059	-77	-45	33	..	1 174	100
	2005	1 283	-2 711	-1 428	-86	-57	54	..	1 533	153
Netherlands - Pays-Bas	1990	159 304	-147 652	11 652	-26 249	-7 053	25 783	6 334	-2 943	8 089
	2000	254 590	-238 810	15 779	-46 879	-16 144	45 080	20 254	-6 219	7 264
	2004	392 171	-345 979	46 192	-63 718	-19 926	80 071	41 438	-9 400	52 108
	2005	427 949	-374 710	53 239	-88 406	-29 330	95 788	48 536	-10 497	48 936
Netherlands Antilles - Antilles néerlandaises	1990	1 464	-1 631	-166	-101	-73	122	15	106	-44
	2000	2 289	-2 388	-99	-65	-4	119	2	39	-37
	2004	2 576	-2 757	-181	-70	-10	91	14	78	-113
	2005	2 818	-3 098	-280	-66	-6	96	1	136	-148
New Zealand - Nouvelle-Zélande	1990	11 683	-11 699	-15	-2 295	-129	719	305	138	-1 453
	2000	17 870	-17 331	539	-4 141	-1 148	693	92	236	-2 672
	2004	28 457	-29 137	-680	-7 587	-4 493	1 530	360	202	-6 535
	2005	30 467	-32 921	-2 454	-9 077	-5 199	1 451	126	459	-9 622
Nicaragua	1990	392	-682	-290	-229	..	12	..	202	-305
	2000	1 102	-2 145	-1 043	-233	-69	31	..	406	-839
	2004	1 651	-2 827	-1 177	-202	-80	9	..	673	-696
	2005	1 861	-3 292	-1 431	-142	-82	22	..	750	-800
Niger	1990	533	-728	-196	-72	-23	20	0	14	-236
	2000	321	-456	-135	-28	-2	3	-1	47	-104
	2003	415	-681	-266	-41	-9	3	0	73	-219
	2004	530	-852	-322	-36	-16	10	6	104	-231
Nigeria - Nigéria	1990	14 550	-6 909	7 642	-2 949	-135	211	..	85	4 988
	2000	20 965	-12 017	8 948	-3 365	-2 279	218	..	1 629	7 429
	2004	38 102	-20 982	17 120	-2 689	-2 689	157	157	2 252	16 840
	2005	52 233	-24 609	27 624	-7 437	-7 437	705	705	3 310	24 202
Norway - Norvège	1990	47 078	-38 911	8 168	-6 515	-798	3 870	86	-1 476	3 992
	2000	77 726	-48 953	28 773	-7 560	-2 418	6 395	1 479	-1 285	25 851
	2004	108 449	-72 327	36 121	-12 018	-6 157	13 668	4 776	-2 585	34 712
	2005	133 484	-84 039	49 446	-16 649	-8 231	18 259	8 344	-2 831	46 560

For sources and notes, see end of table.

Pour les sources et les notes, se reporter à la fin du tableau.

Country or territory / Pays ou territoires	Year / Année	Goods and services / Biens et services			Income / Revenu				Current transfers (net)	Current account balance
		Exports Exportations (1)	Imports Importations (2)	Balance on goods and services / Balance des biens et services (3)=(1)+(2)	Debit / Débit		Credit / Crédit		Transfers courants (nets) (8)	Solde du compte des transactions courantes
					Total (4)	of which: / dont : Direct investment income / Revenu d'investissement direct (5)	Total (6)	of which: / dont : Direct investment income / Revenu d'investissement direct (7)		
					Millions of dollars / Millions de dollars					
Oman	1990	5 577	-3 342	2 235	-629	-390	375	..	-874	1 106
	2000	11 770	-6 352	5 418	-1 129	-830	252	..	-1 451	3 129
	2004	14 107	-10 629	3 478	-1 343	-1 199	221	..	-1 826	569
	2005	19 514	-11 080	8 433	-1 862	-1 667	364	..	-2 257	4 717
Pakistan	1990	6 835	-10 205	-3 371	-1 181	-53	96	..	2 794	-1 661
	2000	10 119	-12 148	-2 029	-2 336	-429	118	2	4 162	-85
	2004	16 046	-22 026	-5 980	-2 583	-1 486	219	18	7 526	-817
	2005	19 059	-29 042	-9 983	-3 172	-1 871	654	18	9 036	-3 463
Palestinian territory - Territoire palestinien	2000	1 022	-3 498	-2 476	-42	-34	90	28	640	-1 012
	2003	587	-2 806	-2 218	-1	..	55	6	764	-998
	2004	586	-3 260	-2 674	-32	-18	58	20	765	-1 483
Panama	1990	4 438	-4 193	245	-1 395	-196	1 047	..	219	209
	2000	7 833	-8 122	-289	-2 136	-562	1 575	..	177	-673
	2004	8 817	-9 077	-260	-1 808	-964	787	..	220	-1 061
	2005	10 736	-10 636	99	-2 184	-1 041	1 060	..	243	-782
Papua New Guinea - Papouasie-Nouvelle-Guinée	1990	1 381	-1 509	-128	-210	-158	107	..	156	-76
	2000	2 337	-1 771	566	-242	-198	32	1	-5	351
	2004	2 758	-2 457	301	-400	-361	18	2	257	122
	2005	3 580	-2 692	888	-511	-475	25	1	291	640
Paraguay	1990	2 514	-2 169	345	-115	-17	83	..	43	390
	2000	2 924	-3 286	-362	-238	-84	134	12	177	-163
	2004	3 492	-3 409	83	-304	-193	59	29	194	138
	2005	3 927	-4 098	-171	-268	-157	85	25	223	-22
Peru - Pérou	1990	4 120	-4 087	33	-1 928	-15	195	..	281	-1 419
	2000	8 484	-9 600	-1 115	-2 146	-344	737	..	999	-1 526
	2004	14 530	-12 581	1 949	-3 753	-2 304	332	..	1 461	-11
	2005	19 426	-15 176	4 250	-5 629	-3 960	618	..	1 791	1 030
Philippines	1990	11 430	-13 967	-2 537	-2 465	-311	395	17	714	-2 695
	2000	40 724	-48 565	-7 841	-3 363	-230	1 573	57	5 643	-2 225
	2004	42 837	-50 293	-7 456	-3 796	-1 373	874	27	9 160	1 633
	2005	44 693	-53 635	-8 942	-4 060	-1 253	1 044	19	11 403	2 338
Poland - Pologne	1990	19 037	-15 095	3 942	-3 989	-20	603	..	2 511	3 067
	2000	46 300	-57 202	-10 902	-3 497	-700	2 058	24	2 380	-9 981
	2004	95 333	-99 941	-4 608	-13 098	-9 557	1 658	32	5 451	-10 676
	2005	112 622	-113 476	-854	-13 132	-9 293	2 067	-155	6 935	-5 105
Portugal	1990	21 554	-27 146	-5 592	-1 380	-102	1 144	1	5 507	-181
	2000	33 680	-46 248	-12 569	-6 974	-1 717	4 418	494	3 352	-11 748
	2004	51 968	-65 459	-13 492	-10 618	-2 722	7 764	2 027	3 471	-12 962
	2005	53 272	-69 078	-15 806	-11 357	-2 449	7 553	1 381	2 731	-17 007
Romania - Roumanie	1990	6 380	-9 901	-3 521	-14	..	175	1	106	-3 254
	2000	12 113	-14 043	-1 930	-605	-72	231	8	860	-1 355
	2004	27 099	-34 029	-6 930	-3 577	-2 594	320	9	3 697	-6 382
	2005	32 813	-42 866	-10 053	-4 409	-2 926	579	-76	4 449	-8 504
Russian Federation - Fédération de Russie	2000	114 598	-61 091	53 507	-11 257	-887	4 253	62	69	46 839
	2004	203 497	-131 114	72 383	-23 303	-10 294	10 792	6 336	-677	58 592
	2005	268 136	-164 718	103 417	-33 466	-19 506	16 225	8 649	-1 122	83 184
Rwanda	1990	143	-354	-211	-16	-6	4	..	143	-85
	2000	128	-423	-296	-16	-3	11	..	216	-94
	2004	201	-516	-315	-23	-3	5	..	314	-35
	2005	257	-659	-402	-23	-5	15	2	366	-52
Saint Kitts and Nevis - Saint-Kitts-et-Nevis	1990	82	-132	-50	-8	-5	3	..	7	-47
	2000	150	-249	-99	-33	-21	5	..	63	-66
	2004	193	-259	-66	-47	-23	7	0	18	-90
	2005	201	-285	-84	-47	-25	8	0	18	-107

For sources and notes, see end of table.

Pour les sources et les notes, se reporter à la fin du tableau.

Country or territory / Pays ou territoires	Year / Année	Goods and services / Biens et services			Income / Revenu				Current transfers (net) / Transferts courants (nets)	Current account balance / Solde du compte des transactions courantes
		Exports / Exportations	Imports / Importations	Balance on goods and services / Balance des biens et services	Debit / Débit		Credit / Crédit			
					Total	of which: / dont : Direct investment income / Revenu d'investissement direct	Total	of which: / dont : Direct investment income / Revenu d'investissement direct		
		(1)	(2)	(3)=(1)+(2)	(4)	(5)	(6)	(7)	(8)	
		Millions of dollars / Millions de dollars								
Saint Lucia - Sainte-Lucie	1990	282	-320	-38	-32	-26	5	..	8	-57
	2000	377	-446	-69	-48	-33	4	..	19	-95
	2004	476	-520	-43	-77	-49	6	0	14	-100
	2005	459	-578	-119	-81	-51	2	0	16	-183
Saint Vincent and the Grenadines - Saint-Vincent-et-les Grenadines	1990	130	-152	-22	-16	-13	4	0	10	-24
	2000	179	-200	-21	-22	-13	3	..	16	-24
	2004	184	-272	-88	-34	-25	4	..	14	-103
	2005	199	-294	-95	-44	-24	11	..	18	-110
Samoa	1990	45	-95	-50	-2	..	7	..	54	9
	2004	107	-197	-91	-10	-8	3	..	90	-17
	2005	124	-240	-116	-9	-8	5	..	106	-24
São Tome and Principe - Sao Tomé-et-Principe	1990	8	-22	-14	0	..	0	..	2	-12
	2000	16	-36	-20	-3	..	..	..	4	-19
	2001	16	-36	-20	-4	..	..	..	4	-21
	2002	19	-41	-23	-4	..	..	..	5	-23
Saudi Arabia - Arabie saoudite	1990	47 381	-43 880	3 501	-1 219	-1 219	9 187	..	-15 616	-4 147
	2000	82 260	-52 932	29 328	-2 865	-2 865	3 345	..	-15 490	14 317
	2004	131 849	-66 746	65 103	-3 800	-3 800	4 278	..	-13 655	51 926
	2005	180 551	-79 274	101 277	-4 671	-4 671	4 943	..	-14 418	87 132
Senegal - Sénégal	1990	1 453	-1 840	-387	-213	-60	33	31	153	-363
	2000	1 307	-1 742	-435	-180	-75	22	2	214	-332
	2003	1 826	-2 657	-831	-214	-89	24	4	530	-437
	2004	2 180	-3 194	-1 014	-216	-68	26	6	632	-513
Seychelles	1990	229	-247	-18	-18	-8	4	1	18	-13
	2000	482	-502	-20	-41	-8	10	4	10	-43
	2004	628	-672	-44	-38	-17	9	2	18	-60
	2005	724	-875	-151	-48	-20	10	3	31	-165
Sierra Leone	1990	210	-215	-5	-72	-51	1	1	7	-69
	2000	55	-250	-195	-13	-2	7	1	88	-112
	2004	215	-367	-151	-69	-32	4	..	119	-99
	2005	263	-452	-189	-54	-41	5	..	137	-103
Singapore - Singapour	1990	67 489	-64 953	2 537	-5 502	..	6 508	..	-421	3 122
	2000	181 266	-168 644	12 622	..	..	..	..	-1 160	10 728
	2004	247 804	-218 106	29 698	..	..	..	..	-1 150	26 318
	2005	283 565	-248 627	34 938	..	..	..	..	-1 184	33 212
Slovakia - Slovaquie	2000	14 137	-14 596	-459	-616	-43	250	27	120	-694
	2002	17 272	-18 977	-1 705	-779	-154	317	10	199	-1 955
	2003	25 241	-25 649	-408	-1 011	-178	482	21	245	-282
Slovenia - Slovénie	2000	10 696	-11 385	-689	-381	-90	246	23	115	-548
	2004	19 520	-19 925	-406	-982	-474	418	32	-94	-892
	2005	22 121	-22 320	-199	-1 053	-458	526	82	-120	-682
Yugoslavia, SFR (former) - Yougoslavie, RSF (anc.)	1990	20 682	-31 996	-11 314	-1 667	..	789	..	9 828	-2 364
Solomon Islands - Îles Salomon	1990	95	-156	-61	-7	-2	2	..	38	-28
South Africa - Afrique du Sud	1990	27 160	-21 017	6 143	-3 813	-962	549	353	-321	1 552
	2000	36 995	-33 075	3 920	-5 081	-2 329	2 187	878	-926	-191
	2004	57 919	-58 846	-928	-6 642	-3 892	2 790	1 020	-1 758	-7 003
	2005	66 437	-68 639	-2 201	-8 528	-5 090	4 027	1 459	-2 011	-9 142
Spain - Espagne	1990	83 595	-100 870	-17 275	-11 339	-2 455	7 588	357	2 799	-18 009
	2000	168 221	-186 027	-17 805	-24 911	-6 121	18 207	5 477	1 469	-23 185
	2004	271 287	-311 128	-39 841	-47 645	-13 109	32 791	12 998	14	-54 865
	2005	288 042	-345 642	-57 599	-58 679	-16 001	37 452	15 329	-4 084	-83 136

For sources and notes, see end of table.   Pour les sources et les notes, se reporter à la fin du tableau.

Country or territory / Pays ou territoires	Year / Année	Goods and services / Biens et services			Income / Revenu				Current transfers (net) / Transferts courants (nets)	Current account balance / Solde du compte des transactions courantes
		Exports / Exportations (1)	Imports / Importations (2)	Balance on goods and services / Balance des biens et services (3)=(1)+(2)	Debit / Débit		Credit / Crédit			
					Total (4)	of which: / dont : Direct investment income / Revenu d'investissement direct (5)	Total (6)	of which: / dont : Direct investment income / Revenu d'investissement direct (7)	(8)	
		Millions of dollars / Millions de dollars								
Sri Lanka	1990	2 293	-2 965	-672	-260	-25	93	0	541	-298
	2000	6 378	-8 105	-1 727	-435	-109	137	2	983	-1 044
	2004	7 284	-9 108	-1 824	-344	-95	147	3	1 380	-648
	2005	7 887	-10 066	-2 179	-316	-115	28	3	1 828	-647
Sudan - Soudan	1990	499	-877	-378	-148	..	12	..	141	-372
	2000	1 834	-2 014	-180	-575	..	2	..	237	-518
	2004	3 822	-4 651	-829	-1 132	-1 122	20	..	1 123	-818
	2005	4 938	-7 790	-2 852	-1 404	-1 399	42	..	1 446	-2 768
Suriname	1990	869	-840	29	-17	-3	4	..	53	67
	2000	490	-462	28	-6	..	13	..	-2	32
	2004	924	-1 011	-88	-73	..	14	..	13	-138
	2005	1 416	-1 541	-125	-60	-45	22	..	22	-144
Swaziland	1990	658	-768	-110	-103	-85	51	9	102	51
	2000	1 133	-1 349	-216	-119	-88	79	1	107	-75
	2004	2 202	-2 231	-28	-122	-87	56	1	125	115
	2005	2 110	-2 212	-102	-108	-68	57	1	128	46
Sweden - Suède	1990	70 561	-70 490	70	-13 915	-473	9 608	3 690	-1 936	-6 339
	2000	107 683	-95 656	12 027	-21 648	-8 867	19 770	12 880	-3 348	6 617
	2004	163 934	-134 855	29 079	-24 971	-9 505	28 440	19 018	-4 818	27 485
	2005	178 072	-150 358	27 713	-33 911	-15 477	34 653	22 358	-4 616	23 643
Switzerland - Suisse	1990	97 033	-96 389	644	-14 756	-1 286	27 899	2 829	-2 398	6 124
	2000	124 694	-108 300	16 394	-34 578	-10 616	60 849	26 388	-4 210	33 562
	2004	184 958	-150 483	34 475	-34 424	-15 811	70 723	39 353	-5 946	56 688
	2005	198 414	-171 665	26 750	-53 483	-27 637	105 003	64 403	-8 977	60 973
Syrian Arab Republic - République arabe syrienne	1990	5 030	-2 955	2 075	-831	..	45	..	88	1 762
	2000	6 845	-5 390	1 455	-1 195	..	165	..	485	1 061
	2004	8 026	-8 600	-574	-1 073	-931	220	220	679	-624
	2005	9 769	-10 718	-949	-1 220	-1 088	335	..	751	-1 061
Tajikistan - Tadjikistan	2004	1 220	-1 445	-225	-59	-1	2	..	226	-57
	2005	1 254	-1 682	-428	-49	-2	8	..	450	-19
Thailand - Thaïlande	1990	29 230	-35 871	-6 641	-2 715	-312	1 086	1	213	-7 281
	2000	81 762	-71 653	10 109	-5 616	..	2 538	..	586	9 313
	2004	114 019	-107 271	6 748	-5 142	..	1 497	..	2 131	6 857
	2005	129 847	-133 599	-3 753	-6 312	..	2 204	..	3 004	-3 671
Macedonia, TFYR - Macédoine, LERY	2000	1 637	-2 279	-642	-87	-7	41	0	615	-72
	2004	2 080	-3 247	-1 166	-122	-66	33	0	791	-415
	2005	2 511	-3 602	-1 091	-151	-86	40	1	1 065	-81
Togo	1990	663	-847	-184	-65	-15	33	..	132	-84
	2000	424	-602	-179	-59	-17	14	2	68	-140
	2003	693	-959	-266	-49	-18	6	1	128	-162
	2004	751	-1 093	-342	-71	-37	13	5	169	-206
Tonga	1990	38	-74	-36	-1	0	4	0	37	6
	2001	26	-91	-65	..	..	..	..	51	-11
	2002	41	-105	-65	-3	-1	2	0	58	-3
Trinidad and Tobago - Trinité-et-Tobago	1990	2 289	-1 427	862	-434	-197	40	..	-6	459
	2000	4 844	-3 709	1 135	-709	..	81	..	38	544
	2003	5 890	-4 283	1 607	-759	-366	78	..	59	985
	2004	7 254	-5 266	1 988	-664	-253	66	..	56	1 447
Tunisia - Tunisie	1990	5 203	-6 039	-836	-552	-97	97	1	828	-463
	2000	8 607	-9 311	-705	-1 036	-468	94	3	825	-821
	2004	13 308	-14 095	-787	-1 412	-678	114	12	1 534	-551
	2005	14 493	-14 638	-146	-1 777	-990	118	12	1 501	-303

For sources and notes, see end of table.

Pour les sources et les notes, se reporter à la fin du tableau.

Country or territory / Pays ou territoires	Year / Année	Goods and services / Biens et services			Income / Revenu				Current transfers (net) / Transferts courants (nets)	Current account balance / Solde du compte des transactions courantes
					Debit / Débit		Credit / Crédit			
		Exports / Exportations	Imports / Importations	Balance on goods and services / Balance des biens et services	Total	of which: / dont : Direct investment income / Revenu d'investissement direct	Total	of which: / dont : Direct investment income / Revenu d'investissement direct		
		(1)	(2)	(3)=(1)+(2)	(4)	(5)	(6)	(7)	(8)	
		Millions of dollars / Millions de dollars								
Turkey - Turquie	1990	21 042	-25 524	-4 482	-3 425	-161	917	..	4 365	-2 625
	2000	50 240	-60 833	-10 593	-6 839	-279	2 836	368	4 774	-9 822
	2004	89 994	-101 088	-11 094	-8 288	-1 040	2 651	244	1 127	-15 604
	2005	102 806	-121 766	-18 960	-9 347	-1 011	3 684	277	1 468	-23 155
Uganda - Ouganda	1990	178	-686	-509	-48	..	..	..	293	-263
	2000	663	-1 409	-745	-120	-19	53	..	499	-359
	2004	1 067	-2 133	-1 066	-151	-95	36	..	1 044	-192
	2005	1 343	-2 584	-1 241	-155	-112	50	..	1 139	-259
Ukraine	2000	19 522	-17 947	1 575	-1 083	-43	110	..	848	1 481
	2004	41 291	-36 313	4 978	-1 028	-180	171	2	2 576	6 909
	2005	44 378	-43 707	671	-1 733	-268	399	5	2 845	2 531
United Kingdom - Royaume-Uni	1990	239 226	-264 089	-24 863	-143 819	-13 960	138 860	29 032	-8 794	-38 811
	2000	404 775	-433 976	-29 201	-195 953	-41 526	202 688	68 175	-15 106	-37 357
	2004	547 088	-611 049	-63 961	-209 695	-51 185	258 398	118 111	-20 053	-35 184
	2005	587 541	-669 823	-82 282	-282 887	-62 461	337 594	143 854	-21 991	-49 459
United Republic of Tanzania - République-Unie de Tanzanie	1990	538	-1 474	-936	-191	..	6	..	562	-559
	2000	1 291	-2 050	-759	-160	-13	42	..	391	-499
	2004	2 590	-3 305	-715	-232	-145	74	..	646	-246
	2005	2 890	-3 825	-935	-259	-146	71	..	603	-536
United States - États-Unis	1990	535 260	-616 120	-80 860	-139 730	-3 450	170 580	65 980	-26 660	-78 960
	2000	1 070 600	-1 448 160	-377 559	-322 344	-56 910	348 084	151 839	-58 645	-415 148
	2004	1 151 940	-1 763 240	-611 296	-338 401	-102 358	372 034	226 223	-81 582	-665 288
	2005	1 275 240	-1 991 970	-716 730	-454 124	-116 953	471 723	251 372	-86 073	-791 509
Uruguay	1990	2 158	-1 659	499	-580	..	258	..	8	186
	2000	3 660	-4 193	-533	-842	-89	782	1	28	-566
	2004	4 296	-3 778	517	-960	-229	373	8	113	43
	2005	5 087	-4 626	462	-1 152	-295	567	10	121	-2
Vanuatu	1990	74	-103	-29	-21	-15	32	..	25	-6
	2000	157	-147	10	-29	-22	16	..	8	5
	2004	140	-179	-39	-43	-27	22	1	14	-43
	2005	147	-205	-58	-51	-35	23	1	20	-64
Venezuela (Bolivarian Republic of) - Venezuela (République bolivarienne du)	1990	18 806	-9 451	9 355	-3 422	-224	2 657	231	-302	8 279
	2000	34 711	-21 300	13 411	-4 408	-1 424	3 032	296	-170	11 853
	2004	40 783	-21 518	19 265	-5 695	-3 498	2 032	725	-72	15 522
	2005	56 829	-28 915	27 914	-6 413	-3 964	4 139	1 338	-99	25 533
Viet Nam	2000	17 150	-17 325	-175	..	..	..	..	1 732	1 106
	2004	30 352	-33 511	-3 159	..	..	..	..	3 093	-957
	2005	36 618	-38 562	-1 944	..	..	..	..	3 380	217
Yemen - Yémen	1990	1 490	-2 170	-680	-409	-283	38	..	1 790	739
	2000	4 008	-3 294	714	-927	-855	150	..	1 399	1 337
	2004	5 045	-4 918	127	-1 378	-1 289	104	..	1 444	225
	2005	6 752	-5 285	1 467	-1 763	-1 648	178	..	1 406	1 215
Zambia - Zambie	1990	1 360	-1 897	-537	-439	-115	2	..	380	-594
	2000	871	-1 318	-447	-160	..	46	..	14	-553
Zimbabwe	1990	2 012	-2 001	11	-279	-92	22	1	112	-140

For sources and notes, see next page.

Pour les sources et les notes, se reporter à la page suivante.

7

Sources:
- International Monetary Fund (IMF), *Balance of Payments Statistics* on CD-ROM.

Notes:
- (1), (2) and (3): Goods (f.o.b.) and services
  The goods component - data on f.o.b. basis - includes general merchandise, goods for processing (gross value of goods before and after processing), repairs on goods (value of repairs only), goods procured in ports and non-monetary gold. The services component comprises 11 main BPM5 categories: transportation, travel, communications, construction, insurance, financial services, computer and information services, royalties and licence fees, other business services, personal-cultural-recreational services, and government services n.i.e. The statistics on services trade are presented separately in table 5.1.
  The credit (export) figures related to goods in table 7.1 differ from those reported in table 1.1 because of adjustments for coverage, valuation, timing, inland freight, etc. Such adjustments are necessary to make the trade statistics compatible with the concepts used in the balance of payments. Further adjustments are applied in cases in which the market price for goods differs from the price used for customs purposes. The valuation problem is probably more important for imports (debits) than for exports and is likely to be a factor whenever there is a long delay between the date of sale and the date on which the import duty becomes payable. In addition, an adjustment is made to convert imports from a c.i.f. to an f.o.b. basis for those countries reporting imports c.i.f. The balance of trade is also evaluated f.o.b./f.o.b.

- (4) and (6): Income
  Income figures shown on the debit side comprise compensation of non-resident employees and investment income payments on external financial assets and liabilities. Included in the investment income are payments on direct investment (columns 5 and 7), and portfolio and other investments. Column 4 presents total payments for income. Column 6 is a counterpart to column 4 and shows total receipts for income.

- (5) and (7): Direct investment income
  The heading includes two categories: income on equity and income on debt, as income accruing to a direct investor residing in one economy from the ownership of direct investment capital in another economy. Income on direct investment is presented on a net basis for both direct investment abroad and in the reporting economy (i.e. receipts of income on equity and income on debt less payments on income on equity and income on debt for each).

- (8): Current transfers
  Transfers are defined as economic values exchanged without quid pro quo (without reciprocity). BPM5 distinguishes current and capital transfers. Current transfers comprise two main categories: general government and other transfers. General government transfers include transfers – in cash or in kind – between governments of different economies or between governments and international organizations (international cooperation). Other transfers occur between other sectors of the economy and non-residents of that economy and can take place between individuals, non-governmental institutions, organizations and groups. Workers' remittances also fall into this category.

Sources :
- Fonds monétaire international (FMI), *Statistiques de la balance des paiements* sur CD-ROM.

Notes :
- (1), (2) et (3) : Biens (f.a.b.) et services
  La partie relative aux biens comprend les marchandises générales, les biens importés ou exportés pour subir une transformation (valeur brute des biens avant et après transformation), la valeur des réparations de biens (seulement la valeur des réparations), les biens achetés dans les ports et l'or non-monétaire. La partie relative aux services couvre les 11 principales catégories selon le MBP5 : transports, voyages, communications, services de bâtiment et travaux publics, assurances, services financiers, services informatiques et d'information, redevances et droits de licence, autres services aux entreprises, services personnels, culturels et relatifs aux loisirs et services fournis ou reçus par les administrations publiques, n.c.a. Les données sur le commerce des services sont présentées séparément dans le tableau 5.1.
  Les chiffres relatifs aux exportations de biens dans le tableau 7.1 sont différents des données présentées dans le tableau 1.1. Ces différences sont dues principalement aux ajustements effectués sur la couverture, l'évaluation, la date d'enregistrement des transactions, le fret terrestre, etc. Les ajustements des données relatives aux importations et aux exportations sont nécessaires, car ils permettent de rendre les données du commerce extérieur compatibles avec les concepts employés dans les statistiques de balance des paiements. Les ajustements d'évaluation sont requis, en particulier dans les cas où les prix du marché auxquels les marchandises ont été vendues diffèrent des prix utilisés par les autorités douanières. Ce problème d'évaluation est probablement plus important pour les importations que pour les exportations et devient un facteur sérieux lorsque s'écoule une longue période entre la date de vente et la date à laquelle les importations sont soumises aux droits de douane. Par ailleurs, les importations déclarées sur la base c.a.f. sont converties sur la base f.a.b. pour les pays qui rapportent c.a.f. La balance du commerce est aussi évaluée f.a.b./f.a.b.

- (4) et (6) : Revenu
  Les chiffres relatifs au revenu et présentés comme débit, comprennent la rémunération des salariés non-résidents et les paiements du revenu des investissements afférents aux avoirs ou engagements financiers extérieurs. Le revenu des investissements se subdivise en paiements provenant d'investissement direct (colonnes 5 et 7), d'investissement de portefeuille et d'autres investissements. La colonne 4 présente les paiements totaux du revenu et la colonne 6 les recettes totales des revenus.

- (5) et (7) : Revenu d'investissement direct
  Deux catégories figurent sous cette rubrique : titres de participation et titres de créance. Ils recouvrent les revenus qui rapportent à un investisseur direct, résidant dans une économie, des capitaux d'investissement direct qu'il possède dans une entreprise située dans une autre économie. Aussi bien pour les investissements directs à l'étranger que pour ceux de l'étranger, c'est le montant net des revenus que l'on reporte (autrement dit : dans chaque cas, les revenus perçus moins les revenus versés).

- (8) : Transferts courants
  Les transferts sont définis comme des valeurs économiques échangées sans quid pro quo (sans réciprocité). MBP5 distingue les transferts courants et les transferts de capitaux. Les transferts courants se répartissent en deux grandes catégories sectorielles : les administrations publiques et les autres secteurs. Parmi les transferts courants des administrations publiques, on trouve les transferts – en espèces ou en nature – entre les administrations publiques de différentes économies ou entre les administrations publiques et les organisations internationales (coopération internationale). Les transferts d'autres secteurs s'opèrent entre tous les autres secteurs d'une économie et les non-résidents de celle-ci. Ils peuvent avoir lieu entre les particuliers, les institutions non-gouvernementales, les organisations et les groupes. Les envois de fonds des travailleurs sont également inclus sous cette rubrique.

Country or territory / Pays ou territoires	Year / Année	Capital account, net / Compte de capital, net (1)	Direct investment / Investissement direct		Portfolio investment / Investissement de portefeuille		Other investment / Autres investissements		Reserve assets / Avoirs de réserve (8)	Financial account, net / Compte financier, net (9)	Capital and financial account, net / Compte de capital et compte financier, net (10)=(1)+(9)
			Abroad / À l'étranger (2)	In reporting economy / Dans l'économie déclarante (3)	Assets / Avoirs (4)	Liabilities / Engagements (5)	Assets / Avoirs (6)	Liabilities / Engagements (7)			
					Millions of dollars / Millions de dollars						
Albania - Albanie	1990	..	..	..	..	..	..	88	32	120	120
	2000	78	..	143	-25	..	-40	123	-132	69	147
	2004	132	-14	341	-4	..	-114	188	-288	110	243
	2005	123	-4	262	-6	..	7	136	-151	245	368
Algeria - Algérie	1990	..	-5	0	..	..	-229	-712	-138	-1 084	-1 084
Angola	1990	..	-1	-335	..	..	-349	941	-2	255	255
	2000	18	..	879	..	..	-702	-309	-631	-763	-745
	2004	440	-35	1 449	-2	..	-1 952	-83	-780	-1 403	-963
	2005	172	-219	-1 304	-1 267	..	-1 850	1 525	-1 817	-4 932	-4 760
Anguilla	1990	3	..	11	..	..	10	1	-3	19	23
	2000	10	..	40	..	..	-1	6	0	44	54
	2004	8	..	87	..	1	-14	-32	-1	41	50
	2005	9	..	78	..	1	0	-28	-5	45	53
Antigua and Barbuda - Antigua-et-Barbuda	1990	5	..	61	..	..	-2	2	1	61	66
	2000	39	..	43	0	2	0	-3	6	48	88
	2004	21	..	77	-1	8	-10	-11	-6	56	78
	2005	214	..	114	1	-1	-2	-170	-7	-65	149
Argentina - Argentine	1990	..	..	1 836	-241	-1 068	661	-3 333	-3 121	-5 267	-5 267
	2000	106	-901	10 418	-1 252	-1 331	-1 368	3 060	403	9 029	9 135
	2004	43	-442	4 274	-77	-9 339	-2 352	9 640	-5 283	-3 579	-3 536
	2005	91	-1 151	4 730	1 368	-1 922	1 934	-2 022	-9 088	-6 151	-6 060
Armenia - Arménie	2000	28	..	104	-19	0	-9	177	-20	233	261
	2004	34	-2	219	0	-2	-142	83	-26	128	163
	2005	51	-7	258	-3	1	-36	88	-162	139	190
Aruba	1990	..	..	131	9	-15	-10	58	-12	161	161
	2000	11	-6	-122	-46	44	14	-87	15	-189	-177
	2004	18	1	143	-27	61	-111	-105	-2	-39	-21
	2005	18	-5	119	-12	21	91	-23	22	214	232
Australia - Australie	1990	1 516	-1 013	8 111	380	6 971	-2 735	4 521	-1 740	14 495	16 011
	2000	615	-3 275	13 618	-10 919	14 874	-4 887	4 416	1 365	14 318	14 933
	2004	817	-10 906	36 613	-25 081	39 403	-5 991	3 992	-1 166	37 470	38 287
	2005	886	35 292	-34 420	-21 111	57 401	-3 410	14 551	-7 256	40 161	41 048
Austria - Autriche	1990	8	-1 701	653	-1 608	3 239	-1 433	831	15	-4	4
	2000	-432	-5 599	8 523	-27 145	30 360	-16 334	13 790	746	4 153	3 721
	2004	-341	-8 664	3 892	-32 677	31 695	-21 178	24 983	1 849	-769	-1 110
	2005	-237	-10 078	9 057	-44 060	30 396	-29 966	42 870	750	-878	-1 115
Azerbaijan - Azerbaïdjan	2000	..	-1	130	..	..	-114	427	-274	168	168
	2004	-4	-1 205	3 556	-18	..	-360	928	-257	2 643	2 639
	2005	41	-1 221	1 680	-48	78	-1 365	925	-132	-83	-42
Bahamas	1990	-8	0	-17	..	..	2 283	-2 199	-12	55	47
	2000	-16	..	250	..	..	-19 067	19 247	61	491	475
	2004	-48	..	274	..	..	19 293	-19 209	-183	175	127
	2005	-60	..	360	..	..	-11 064	11 194	88	578	518
Bahrain - Bahreïn	1990	457	-25	-183	698	..	10 769	-10 102	-796	361	818
	2000	50	-10	364	-88	282	-3 834	3 256	-200	-230	-180
	2004	50	-1 036	865	-3 893	388	-9 784	13 064	-158	-553	-503
	2005	50	-1 123	1 049	-7 036	2 422	-11 562	14 884	-294	-1 662	-1 612
Bangladesh	1990	..	..	3	..	0	-208	757	-79	474	474
	2000	249	..	280	..	1	-1 247	619	121	-225	23
	2004	142	-4	449	..	4	-495	857	-650	162	304
	2005	75	..	802	..	1	-789	118	407	539	614
Barbados - Barbade	1990	..	-1	11	-3	-22	-22	76	48	86	86
	2000	2	-1	19	-29	100	53	147	-178	111	113
	2004	..	-4	-12	-58	-10	30	189	157	291	291
	2005	..	-9	62	-76	98	-239	548	-24	367	367

For sources and notes, see end of table.   Pour les sources et les notes, se reporter à la fin du tableau.

331

Country or territory / Pays ou territoires	Year / Année	Capital account, net / Compte de capital, net (1)	Direct investment / Investissement direct		Portfolio investment / Investissement de portefeuille		Other investment / Autres investissements		Reserve assets / Avoirs de réserve (8)	Financial account, net / Compte financier, net (9)	Capital and financial account, net / Compte de capital et compte financier, net (10)=(1)+(9)
			Abroad / À l'étranger (2)	In reporting economy / Dans l'économie déclarante (3)	Assets / Avoirs (4)	Liabilities / Engagements (5)	Assets / Avoirs (6)	Liabilities / Engagements (7)			
					Millions of dollars / Millions de dollars						
Belarus - Bélarus	2000	69	0	119	-6	50	42	-114	-76	15	84
	2004	49	-1	164	3	60	-151	1 053	-256	871	920
	2005	41	-3	305	-3	-39	-492	185	-539	-586	-545
Belgium - Belgique	2004	-497	-34 682	44 415	-35 558	5 070	-64 685	80 365	723	-9 937	-10 434
	2005	-844	-30 084	31 959	-43 525	-1 215	-87 540	125 123	2 176	-8 476	-9 320
Belgium-Luxembourg - Belgique-Luxembourg	1990	..	-6 314	8 047	-9 443	7 946	-64 422	62 536	-404	-2 055	-2 055
	2000	-213	-207 472	214 941	-122 814	132 547	-39 033	14 999	959	-8 274	-8 487
	2001	26	-86 091	73 635	-125 068	140 588	-70 053	63 158	-1 442	-9 420	-9 395
Belize	1990	..	..	17	..	..	..	5	-12	10	10
	2000	-2	..	23	..	113	-51	119	-52	153	151
	2004	10	0	111	0	72	-4	12	32	223	233
	2005	3	-1	126	0	13	-9	50	-19	155	158
Benin - Bénin	1990	125	..	62	-5	..	-6	-111	-58	-118	7
	2000	73	-11	67	6	-2	25	3	-87	1	74
	2003	64	-4	48	-7	-1	26	30	-6	86	149
	2004	80	-15	108	3	-3	-19	47	127	246	327
Bolivia - Bolivie	1990	7	-1	27	..	..	-32	214	-5	203	210
	2000	..	-3	736	55	..	-146	-180	39	501	501
	2004	8	-3	65	-35	..	94	316	-157	280	288
	2005	9	-3	-277	-153	..	124	388	-463	-385	-376
Bosnia and Herzegovina - Bosnie-Herzégovine	2000	546	..	146	..	..	-675	628	-77	23	569
	2004	498	-2	669	..	..	319	359	-427	918	1 416
	2005	455	-1	521	..	..	353	861	-458	1 276	1 731
Botswana	1990	65	-7	96	..	1	-137	130	-307	-225	-160
	2000	38	-2	57	-34	-6	-264	38	-367	-581	-543
	2004	32	-39	391	-438	-29	-86	-84	57	-229	-197
	2005	31	56	279	-404	16	-152	260	-1 363	-1 310	-1 278
Brazil - Brésil	1990	35	-665	989	-67	579	-2 864	6 587	-474	4 084	4 119
	2000	273	-2 282	32 779	-1 696	8 651	-2 989	-15 131	2 260	21 395	21 667
	2004	339	-9 471	18 166	-755	-3 996	-2 196	-8 766	-2 238	-9 932	-9 593
	2005	663	-2 517	15 193	-1 771	6 655	-3 792	-23 171	-4 324	-13 766	-13 104
Bulgaria - Bulgarie	1990	..	..	4	..	..	384	374	878	1 640	1 640
	2000	25	-3	1 002	-62	-115	-332	566	-409	644	669
	2004	0	217	2 653	-10	-692	-964	2 562	-1 846	1 913	1 913
	2005	-1	-308	3 275	35	-1 706	82	1 782	-415	2 710	2 709
Burkina Faso	1990	..	..	..	..	..	-7	89	-7	75	75
	2000	186	0	23	6	0	-10	77	31	127	314
	2001	197	-1	9	10	2	6	95	-31	90	288
Burundi	1990	-1	0	1	..	..	4	72	4	81	81
	2000	0	..	12	..	..	7	65	1	84	84
	2004	132	..	0	..	..	-22	60	-2	36	168
	2005	192	..	1	..	..	-3	130	-34	89	281
Cambodia - Cambodge	2000	36	-7	149	-7	..	-176	236	-109	86	122
	2004	68	-10	131	-8	..	-24	191	-128	152	220
	2005	95	-6	379	-7	..	-331	258	-10	283	378
Cameroon - Cameroun	1990	3	-15	-113	56	..	482	160	65	634	637
	2000	17	-10	159	-2	0	64	114	-206	120	137
	2002	61	33	602	5	1	-272	356	-211	514	575
	2003	198	-4	220	-3	0	-115	169	106	373	571
Canada	1990	5 331	-5 229	7 581	-2 239	15 964	-8 442	9 648	-1 139	16 144	21 475
	2000	3 581	-44 487	66 144	-42 975	10 259	-4 195	754	-3 720	-18 220	-14 639
	2004	3 424	-42 528	1 249	-18 924	41 586	-7 899	-4 742	2 836	-28 422	-24 999
	2005	4 881	-34 196	34 146	-42 728	6 978	-16 572	24 860	-1 335	-28 847	-23 966

For sources and notes, see end of table.   Pour les sources et les notes, se reporter à la fin du tableau.

Country or territory / Pays ou territoires	Year / Année	Capital account, net / Compte de capital, net (1)	Direct investment / Investissement direct		Portfolio investment / Investissement de portefeuille		Other investment / Autres investissements		Reserve assets / Avoirs de réserve (8)	Financial account, net / Compte financier, net (9)	Capital and financial account, net / Compte de capital et compte financier, net (10)=(1)+(9)
			Abroad / À l'étranger (2)	In reporting economy / Dans l'économie déclarante (3)	Assets / Avoirs (4)	Liabilities / Engagements (5)	Assets / Avoirs (6)	Liabilities / Engagements (7)			
					Millions of dollars / Millions de dollars						
Cape Verde - Cap-Vert	1990	2	0	0	..	..	-29	4	12	-12	-11
	2000	11	-1	33	0	..	-22	39	10	59	70
	2004	18	0	20	..	..	11	38	-37	32	51
	2005	20	0	54	..	..	-55	95	-56	38	58
Central African Republic - République centrafricaine	1990	..	-4	1	-	..	-16	98	9	88	88
Chad - Tchad	1990	..	..	..	..	..	..	75	4	79	79
Chile - Chili	1990	..	-8	661	..	361	355	1 287	-2 121	535	535
	2000	..	-3 987	4 860	766	-127	-2 065	1 338	-317	471	471
	2004	5	-1 527	7 173	-4 674	1 122	-3 389	-829	191	-2 017	-2 012
	2005	..	-2 146	6 667	-4 003	1 470	-2 047	2 267	-1 711	434	434
China - Chine	1990	..	-830	3 487	-241	..	-231	578	-11 555	-8 792	-8 792
	2000	-35	-916	38 399	-11 308	7 317	-43 864	12 329	-10 693	-8 735	-8 770
	2004	-69	-1 805	54 937	6 486	13 203	1 980	35 928	-206 153	-95 424	-95 493
	2005	4 102	-11 306	79 127	-26 157	21 224	-48 947	44 921	-207 342	-148 480	-144 378
China, Hong Kong SAR - Chine, Hong Kong RAS	2000	-1 546	-59 352	61 924	-22 022	46 508	18 279	-41 376	-10 044	-5 878	-7 424
	2004	-329	-45 715	34 032	-43 214	3 882	-32 609	57 838	-3 286	-23 380	-23 708
	2005	-672	-32 560	35 897	-30 648	9 076	-7 628	5 452	-1 378	-20 020	-20 693
China, Macao SAR - Chine, Macao RAS	2004	274	95	768	-2 181	0	-196	563	-1 098	-2 633	-2 359
	2005	515	-47	1 848	-617	0	-4 396	3 317	-1 234	-1 651	-1 137
Colombia - Colombie	1990	..	-16	500	..	-4	-102	-380	-610	-612	-612
	2000	..	-325	2 395	-1 173	1 453	-551	-1 622	-862	-811	-811
	2004	..	-142	3 117	-1 565	1 136	432	380	-2 470	698	698
	2005	..	-4 623	10 375	-1 530	-53	-181	-542	-1 726	1 658	1 658
Comoros - Comores	1990	..	-1	0	..	..	1	14	5	19	19
Congo	1990	..	..	..	..	..	-68	473	-113	292	292
	2000	17	-4	166	-4	0	-74	-488	-184	-588	-571
	2004	201	-5	-9	..	2	-441	-256	-75	-783	-582
	2005	6	..	724	..	-13	..	-1 326	-619	-1 235	-1 229
Costa Rica	1990	..	-2	163	..	-28	-125	176	197	381	381
	2000	18	-5	409	-18	-50	-344	154	153	298	316
	2004	13	-61	794	53	88	-309	234	-80	719	732
	2005	..	43	861	-681	336	141	508	-393	815	815
Côte d'Ivoire	1990	..	..	48	4	..	-92	1 347	16	1 324	1 324
	2000	8	..	235	-13	5	-182	293	-89	246	254
	2004	146	..	283	-37	19	-402	-20	-250	-403	-257
	2005	181	..	266	-43	35	-415	-130	148	-189	-8
Croatia - Croatie	2000	21	-9	1 087	-23	730	-916	938	-627	1 180	1 201
	2004	28	-350	1 225	-948	1 209	-522	2 357	-68	2 903	2 931
	2005	61	-228	1 761	-625	-721	1 325	3 402	-1 022	3 893	3 954
Cyprus - Chypre	1990	..	-5	127	..	-38	-115	467	-294	142	142
	2000	5	-172	855	-453	170	-1 285	1 413	8	538	543
	2004	134	-712	1 119	-1 813	2 979	-3 134	2 517	-371	541	675
	2005	87	-474	1 181	-1 620	1 567	-7 239	8 030	-703	727	814
Czech Republic - République tchèque	2000	-5	-43	4 987	-2 236	482	984	-300	-844	2 991	2 986
	2004	-595	-1 038	4 978	-2 565	4 795	-1 072	2 325	-263	7 014	6 420
	2005	211	-842	10 973	-3 080	79	-4 322	3 010	-3 879	1 828	2 039
Czechoslovakia (former) - Tchécoslovaquie (anc.)	1990	..	-20	207	..	..	-711	1 166	1 127	1 770	1 770
Denmark - Danemark	1990	..	-1 482	1 132	-1 168	4 068	-5 442	7 312	-3 385	1 035	1 035
	2000	-11	-28 381	36 013	-23 582	5 783	-2 025	8 554	5 521	2 210	2 199
	2004	13	9 930	-8 804	-24 768	10 055	-9 021	378	1 426	-17 598	-17 585
	2005	283	-9 570	5 238	-31 318	21 012	-18 523	21 619	1 506	-8 361	-8 078

For sources and notes, see end of table.

Pour les sources et les notes, se reporter à la fin du tableau.

Country or territory / Pays ou territoires	Year / Année	Capital account, net / Compte de capital, net (1)	Direct investment / Investissement direct — Abroad / À l'étranger (2)	Direct investment — In reporting economy / Dans l'économie déclarante (3)	Portfolio investment / Investissement de portefeuille — Assets / Avoirs (4)	Portfolio investment — Liabilities / Engagements (5)	Other investment / Autres investissements — Assets / Avoirs (6)	Other investment — Liabilities / Engagements (7)	Reserve assets / Avoirs de réserve (8)	Financial account, net / Compte financier, net (9)	Capital and financial account, net / Compte de capital et compte financier, net (10)=(1)+(9)
					Millions of dollars / Millions de dollars						
Dominica - Dominique	1990	14	..	13	..	0	11	5	-4	24	38
	2000	11	..	18	0	14	-10	35	0	55	66
	2004	27	..	24	-2	0	-2	-5	6	20	47
	2005	18	..	26	0	..	-5	42	-14	49	67
Dominican Republic - République dominicaine	1990	..	..	133	..	..	89	129	49	400	400
	2000	2	..	953	268	-4	-165	521	70	1 643	1 645
	2004	4	..	909	-8	-17	-429	20	-540	-65	-60
	2005	..	..	1 023	-82	-13	277	364	-1 110	458	458
Ecuador - Équateur	1990	..	..	126	..	..	..	369	-261	234	234
	2000	1 977	..	720	..	-1 725	-1 274	-297	-307	-2 883	-906
	2004	14	..	1 160	..	0	-1 803	868	-275	-50	-36
	2005	62	..	1 646	..	594	-2 366	382	-714	-457	-395
Egypt - Égypte	1990	10 610	-12	734	15	..	-1 921	-9 875	-2 508	-13 567	-2 957
	2000	..	-51	1 235	-3	269	-2 991	619	1 306	384	384
	2004	..	-159	1 253	324	-85	-5 888	1 363	-684	-3 876	-3 876
	2005	-40	-92	5 376	-60	3 528	-3 246	1 178	-6 319	364	324
El Salvador	1990	..	..	2	..	..	-21	36	-165	-148	-148
	2000	109	5	173	-9	-17	-245	380	46	333	442
	2004	100	53	376	-210	182	-134	-169	53	151	251
	2005	136	-217	517	94	86	-163	410	59	782	917
Equatorial Guinea - Guinée équatoriale	1990	..	..	11	..	..	10	..	-3	17	17
Eritrea - Érythrée	2000	..	..	28	..	..	-26	64	61	128	128
Estonia - Estonie	2000	26	-63	387	16	76	-167	139	-122	265	291
	2004	93	-268	972	-381	1 114	-901	1 086	-271	1 351	1 444
	2005	140	-609	2 997	-872	-1 360	-887	2 441	-386	1 316	1 456
Ethiopia - Éthiopie	2000	..	..	..	..	..	113	210	-109	218	218
	2004	..	..	..	..	..	-262	739	544	1 022	1 022
	2005	..	..	265	..	..	302	184	330	1 081	1 081
Ethiopia (former) - Éthiopie (anc.)	1990	..	..	..	..	..	87	307	35	428	428
Fiji - Fidji	1990	48	-13	92	..	..	-18	-10	-34	17	65
Finland - Finlande	1990	..	-2 782	812	-469	5 696	720	8 428	-3 931	8 474	8 474
	2000	103	-23 898	9 125	-18 920	17 116	-5 636	14 002	-351	-9 192	-9 089
	2004	187	1 146	3 037	-24 505	10 991	-11 851	9 355	-907	-12 210	-12 022
	2005	174	-4 538	3 978	-17 642	11 830	-1 302	1 784	197	-3 525	-3 350
France	1990	-4 133	-34 824	13 183	-8 409	43 219	-61 543	73 137	-10 947	13 817	9 684
	2000	1 392	-174 320	42 370	-97 435	132 332	632	59 088	2 433	-30 116	-28 724
	2004	1 810	-76 654	38 709	-224 638	165 695	-116 143	193 860	-4 108	-17 068	-15 258
	2005	661	-133 600	70 686	-238 214	226 378	-278 173	304 535	9 047	-29 443	-28 782
Gabon	1990	..	-29	73	..	..	-285	330	-219	-130	-130
	2000	0	-25	-43	-9	-2	-729	131	-172	-848	-849
	2003	43	21	158	3	4	-355	-353	-25	-549	-506
	2004	..	25	320	-9	-1	-512	-178	-211	-567	-567
Gambia - Gambie	1990	..	..	..	..	..	-1	-8	-3	-12	-12
	2004	5	..	57	..	..	-15	25	-31	35	40
	2005	1	..	52	..	..	14	41	-9	97	98
Georgia - Géorgie	2000	-5	1	131	3	..	-8	-60	20	86	82
	2004	41	-10	499	-13	..	-27	33	-179	304	345
	2005	59	89	450	13	2	-15	192	-111	620	679
Germany - Allemagne	1990	-3 113	-24 484	3 004	-13 991	12 291	-74 663	42 552	-7 254	-62 582	-65 695
	2000	6 188	-59 745	210 085	-191 545	40 882	-80 178	120 924	5 222	34 209	40 398
	2004	513	-1 077	-15 104	-136 850	149 238	-181 660	49 458	1 807	-141 168	-140 655
	2005	-1 689	-47 087	32 034	-263 770	248 707	-156 964	62 167	2 601	-128 394	-130 083

For sources and notes, see end of table.

Pour les sources et les notes, se reporter à la fin du tableau.

Country or territory / Pays ou territoires	Year / Année	Capital account, net / Compte de capital, net (1)	Direct investment / Investissement direct Abroad / À l'étranger (2)	Direct investment In reporting economy / Dans l'économie déclarante (3)	Portfolio investment / Investissement de portefeuille Assets / Avoirs (4)	Portfolio investment Liabilities / Engagements (5)	Other investment / Autres investissements Assets / Avoirs (6)	Other investment Liabilities / Engagements (7)	Reserve assets / Avoirs de réserve (8)	Financial account, net / Compte financier, net (9)	Capital and financial account, net / Compte de capital et compte financier, net (10)=(1)+(9)
						Millions of dollars / Millions de dollars					
Ghana	1990	-1	..	15	..	..	-94	242	26	189	188
	2000	..	..	166	..	..	70	158	345	739	739
	2004	..	..	139	..	..	-88	341	-114	279	279
	2005	..	..	107	..	..	107	793	-220	786	786
Greece - Grèce	1990	..	..	1 005	..	..	..	2 757	-40	3 722	3 722
	2000	2 112	-2 099	1 083	-1 184	9 262	6 970	-3 551	-2 573	8 257	10 370
	2004	2 990	-1 028	2 105	-13 835	31 301	-7 464	-3 813	3 277	10 113	13 103
	2005	2 563	-1 458	640	-23 194	32 308	-8 740	16 064	104	15 737	18 300
Grenada - Grenade	1990	22	..	13	..	0	-11	17	-2	16	38
	2000	32	..	37	0	20	-11	18	-7	57	89
	2004	40	..	54	-7	37	-4	-29	-46	5	45
	2005	44	..	26	1	9	-4	26	27	86	130
Guatemala	1990	..	..	48	-2	-15	-78	182	42	177	177
	2000	86	..	230	-36	79	213	1 035	-643	878	964
	2004	135	..	155	111	349	252	842	-608	1 101	1 236
	2005	125	..	208	..	0	328	1 069	-255	1 350	1 475
Guinea - Guinée	1990	7	..	18	..	..	-53	182	-3	144	151
	2000	..	..	10	9	..	-17	4	50	56	56
	2003	58	..	79	-5	..	-4	83	132	285	342
	2004	-30	..	..	15	..	50	48	12	124	94
Guinea-Bissau - Guinée-Bissau	1990	29	..	..	..	..	..	23	-5	18	47
	2003	43	-1	4	1	0	-19	4	-38	-49	-6
	2004	27	8	2	1	..	-8	-7	-33	-37	-10
Guyana	2000	16	..	67	3	-12	66	-30	-24	70	87
	2004	46	..	30	-16	11	61	-59	-11	16	62
	2005	52	..	77	-34	17	103	-25	6	143	195
Haiti - Haïti	1990	..	8	..	..	..	-23	44	39	68	68
	2000	..	..	13	..	..	-43	14	57	41	41
	2004	..	..	6	..	..	25	30	-51	9	9
	2005	..	..	10	..	..	8	4	-21	1	1
Honduras	1990	..	..	44	0	..	-40	175	-20	159	159
	2000	129	..	282	-59	-1	-204	44	-32	29	158
	2004	113	..	325	-4	..	35	432	-520	267	380
	2005	826	..	464	-5	..	-31	-729	-350	-651	175
Hungary - Hongrie	1990	..	..	..	..	..	-524	-423	558	-388	-388
	2000	270	-589	2 770	-309	-141	939	2 232	-1 052	3 908	4 178
	2004	328	-1 118	4 666	-442	7 353	-1 824	2 977	-1 981	10 044	10 372
	2005	883	-1 322	6 436	-1 140	5 774	-1 429	6 529	-4 904	9 727	10 610
Iceland - Islande	1990	2	-12	22	..	25	-49	251	-74	163	165
	2000	-3	-375	155	-667	1 142	-79	671	74	920	917
	2004	-3	-2 567	759	-1 561	8 403	-3 447	427	-202	1 813	1 810
	2005	-27	-6 998	2 472	-4 528	16 956	-10 936	5 057	-71	1 952	1 925
India - Inde	1990	..	..	..	..	..	-611	5 281	2 798	7 468	7 468
	2000	716	-510	3 584	..	2 345	1 712	2 440	-6 017	3 555	4 270
	2002	102	-1 678	5 626	..	1 022	3 699	3 213	-18 853	-6 971	-6 869
	2003	3 839	-1 324	4 585	..	8 216	-3 259	6 574	-25 667	-10 875	-7 036
Indonesia - Indonésie	1990	..	..	1 093	..	-93	..	3 332	-2 088	2 244	2 244
	2000	..	..	-4 550	..	-1 911	-150	-160	-5 051	-11 821	-11 821
	2004	..	-3 408	1 896	353	4 056	-716	-3 037	686	-170	-170
	2005	334	-3 065	5 260	-1 078	5 315	-4 471	-2 688	1 488	761	1 095
Iran, Islamic Republic of - Iran, Rép. islamique d'	1990	..	..	..	..	..	-1 510	1 805	325	620	620
	2000	..	..	39	..	..	-8 257	-1 971	-1 083	-11 273	-11 273
Ireland - Irlande	1990	387	-365	627	-465	266	-5 284	3 212	-626	-2 635	-2 248
	2000	1 074	-4 641	25 501	-83 075	77 906	-37 036	28 883	-121	7 791	8 865
	2004	368	-18 107	-10 994	-168 940	136 471	-57 406	71 236	1 435	4 735	5 104
	2005	324	-13 760	-29 730	-148 435	213 540	-134 057	117 696	1 776	-1 209	-885

For sources and notes, see end of table.

Pour les sources et les notes, se reporter à la fin du tableau.

Country or territory / Pays ou territoires	Year / Année	Capital account, net / Compte de capital, net (1)	Direct investment / Investissement direct — Abroad / À l'étranger (2)	Direct investment — In reporting economy / Dans l'économie déclarante (3)	Portfolio investment / Investissement de portefeuille — Assets / Avoirs (4)	Portfolio investment — Liabilities / Engagements (5)	Other investment / Autres investissements — Assets / Avoirs (6)	Other investment — Liabilities / Engagements (7)	Reserve assets / Avoirs de réserve (8)	Financial account, net / Compte financier, net (9)	Capital and financial account, net / Compte de capital et compte financier, net (10)=(1)+(9)
					Millions of dollars / Millions de dollars						
Israel - Israël	1990	728	-199	151	-368	-171	-632	1 677	-511	-53	675
	2000	466	-3 338	5 066	-2 883	5 047	-3 552	2 050	-943	1 448	1 914
	2004	667	-4 544	1 757	-2 381	6 871	-6 228	498	-279	-4 332	-3 665
	2005	727	-2 491	5 585	-8 054	4 618	-5 133	284	-1 972	-7 135	-6 408
Italy - Italie	1990	759	-7 394	6 411	-19 325	19 216	-13 894	57 542	-11 623	31 016	31 775
	2000	2 879	-12 078	13 176	-80 263	57 020	242	27 074	-3 247	4 257	7 136
	2004	2 324	-19 144	16 772	-26 394	58 551	-48 904	24 195	2 844	10 204	12 527
	2005	2 195	-40 714	19 585	-108 081	164 403	-101 379	86 101	1 030	24 074	26 269
Jamaica - Jamaïque	1990	-16	..	138	..	..	-3	229	-65	299	283
	2000	2	-74	468	-70	6	-96	600	-499	336	338
	2004	2	-60	602	-1 133	1 229	-127	697	-686	521	523
	2005	-3	-101	682	-1 406	1 280	-289	1 096	-228	1 035	1 033
Japan - Japon	1990	-1 062	-50 497	1 777	-37 798	46 680	..	9 120	9 085	-30 710	-31 772
	2000	-9 259	-31 534	8 227	-83 362	47 387	-4 148	-10 211	-48 955	-127 268	-136 526
	2004	-4 787	-30 958	7 805	-173 773	196 721	-48 008	68 306	-160 854	-138 354	-143 141
	2005	-4 878	-45 438	3 214	-196 397	183 129	-106 598	45 938	-22 325	-145 007	-149 885
Jordan - Jordanie	1990	..	31	38	..	..	222	272	-412	152	152
	2000	65	-2	815	-45	-141	-942	589	-682	-408	-343
	2004	2	..	651	-217	-120	-660	-30	-80	-456	-454
	2005	8	..	1 532	72	60	-589	206	-2	1 279	1 288
Kazakhstan	2000	-291	-4	1 283	-85	30	43	-400	-129	737	446
	2004	-21	1 279	4 157	-1 092	675	-4 466	4 194	-3 999	702	680
	2005	14	146	1 975	-5 157	1 225	-4 296	7 149	1 944	2 873	2 887
Kenya	1990	7	..	57	..	..	73	265	59	453	460
	2000	50	..	111	-11	-4	-56	343	-107	277	327
	2004	145	-4	46	-72	5	-307	422	-37	53	199
	2005	103	-10	21	-46	15	-201	895	-281	394	498
Kiribati	1990	12	..	0	-8	..	..	3	7	2	14
Korea, Republic of - Corée, République de	1990	-331	-1 052	789	-500	662	-2 425	5 500	1 208	4 103	3 772
	2000	-615	-4 999	9 283	-520	12 697	-2 289	-1 268	-23 790	-11 065	-11 680
	2004	-1 753	-4 650	9 246	-9 918	18 375	-8 138	4 282	-38 675	-29 316	-31 069
	2005	-2 313	-4 312	4 339	-13 554	13 899	-3 975	8 071	-19 864	-17 061	-19 374
Kuwait - Koweït	1990	..	-239	..	-919	537	829	205	897	1 310	1 310
	2000	2 217	303	16	-12 923	254	-1 109	-321	-2 268	-16 047	-13 830
	2004	433	-2 526	24	-14 217	288	-292	-107	-629	-17 459	-17 026
	2005	797	-4 708	250	-7 157	-542	-20 228	4 255	-621	-28 751	-27 954
Kyrgyzstan - Kirghizistan	2000	-11	-5	-2	-2	0	-29	102	-21	69	58
	2004	-20	-44	175	-3	0	-36	93	-166	-1	-21
	2005	-21	..	43	-4	0	-61	24	-80	-79	-100
Lao People's Dem. Rep. - Rép. dém. populaire lao	1990	11	..	6	..	..	-5	83	-1	84	95
	2000	..	..	34	..	..	19	66	-36	83	83
	2001	..	..	24	..	..	25	83	7	140	140
Latvia - Lettonie	2000	36	-12	413	-351	27	-389	714	7	410	446
	2004	144	-103	638	-21	260	-1 779	3 009	-398	1 559	1 703
	2005	212	-127	730	-268	150	-400	2 620	-524	2 106	2 318
Lebanon - Liban	2004	50	-827	1 899	-614	160	4 995	815	-782	5 647	5 698
	2005	27	-715	2 573	-93	960	2 295	-1 263	455	4 213	4 240
Lesotho	1990	..	..	17	..	..	-110	51	-21	-62	-62
	2000	22	..	118	..	..	-19	-19	-13	67	89
	2004	33	0	123	..	..	-49	-1	-15	58	92
	2005	21	..	92	..	..	0	-44	-40	8	29
Libyan Arab Jamahiriya - Jamahiriya arabe libyenne	1990	..	-105	159	-115	..	-715	-230	-1 158	-2 164	-2 164
	2000	..	-98	141	-706	..	-333	847	-6 458	-6 607	-6 607
	2004	..	210	1 146	-187	..	-1 767	1 574	-5 661	-4 685	-4 685
	2005	..	-128	1 038	-393	..	-418	291	-15 411	-15 019	-15 019

For sources and notes, see end of table.

Pour les sources et les notes, se reporter à la fin du tableau.

Country or territory Pays ou territoires	Year Année	Capital account, net Compte de capital, net (1)	Direct investment Investissement direct		Portfolio investment Investissement de portefeuille		Other investment Autres investissements		Reserve assets Avoirs de réserve (8)	Financial account, net Compte financier, net (9)	Capital and financial account, net Compte de capital et compte financier, net (10)=(1)+(9)
			Abroad À l'étranger (2)	In reporting economy Dans l'économie déclarante (3)	Assets Avoirs (4)	Liabilities Engagements (5)	Assets Avoirs (6)	Liabilities Engagements (7)			
					Millions of dollars / Millions de dollars						
Lithuania - Lituanie	2000	2	-4	379	-141	406	40	-5	-131	544	547
	2004	287	-263	773	-220	431	-684	1 081	124	1 246	1 533
	2005	331	-343	1 032	-779	542	-786	2 557	-687	1 549	1 881
Luxembourg	2004	-695	-82 795	78 594	-87 546	139 604	-117 126	69 775	-8	-2 772	-3 467
	2005	1 305	-117 189	109 888	-267 098	316 105	-214 020	170 187	48	-5 220	-3 915
Madagascar	1990	3	..	22	..	..	-7	78	167	260	263
	2000	115	..	83	..	..	-87	142	-30	107	222
	2004	65	..	20	..	..	104	136	-140	119	184
	2005	65	..	29	..	..	4	66	-4	95	160
Malawi	1990	..	..	..	..	1	34	100	-34	100	100
	2000	..	..	26	..	..	..	162	-91	97	97
	2001	..	..	19	..	..	..	187	75	281	281
	2002	..	..	6	..	..	..	144	-105	44	44
Malaysia - Malaisie	1990	-48	..	2 332	..	-255	-205	-89	-1 951	-167	-215
	2000	..	-2 026	3 788	-387	-2 145	-5 565	..	1 009	-5 267	-5 267
	2004	..	-2 061	4 624	-287	8 895	-11 166	3 670	-21 875	-17 905	-17 905
	2005	..	-2 972	3 966	-715	-2 985	-4 877	-2 164	-3 644	-13 450	-13 450
Maldives	1990	..	..	6	..	..	-2	5	0	8	8
	2000	..	..	13	..	..	23	4	4	45	45
	2004	..	..	15	..	..	107	31	-44	108	108
	2005	..	..	9	..	..	162	96	17	284	284
Mali	1990	117	..	6	..	..	-30	192	-55	112	229
	2000	105	-4	82	15	1	-87	204	-58	154	259
	2003	166	-1	132	-27	28	4	142	-217	60	226
	2004	206	-1	101	-3	1	-131	103	160	230	435
Malta - Malte	1990	..	..	46	-2	..	-243	156	96	53	53
	2000	19	-21	600	-782	71	-221	585	222	454	472
	2004	84	2	398	-2 104	10	-1 261	2 961	206	195	278
	2005	193	29	536	-2 605	40	-2 731	5 230	-218	259	452
Mauritania - Mauritanie	1990	..	..	7	..	..	206	-181	41	72	72
Mauritius - Maurice	1990	-1	-1	41	-2	..	-7	64	-188	-93	-94
	2000	-1	-13	266	-19	-120	-308	452	-231	27	27
	2004	-2	-32	14	-52	15	-49	112	27	36	34
	2005	-2	-47	39	-42	25	-284	358	165	215	214
Mexico - Mexique	1990	..	..	2 634	-7 354	3 369	-1 345	12 180	-3 261	6 223	6 223
	2000	..	..	17 773	1 290	-1 134	5 809	-4 182	-2 862	16 694	16 694
	2004	..	-4 432	18 941	1 718	5 942	-6 413	-4 643	-4 120	6 994	6 994
	2005	..	-6 474	18 772	..	10 189	-6 368	-2 947	-6 980	6 192	6 192
Moldova, Republic of - Moldova, République de	2000	-12	0	128	..	117	-36	-43	-47	119	107
	2004	-13	-3	149	-1	-8	-32	1	-148	-42	-55
	2005	-4	0	199	-1	-6	-78	76	-128	60	56
Mongolia - Mongolie	1990	..	..	..	..	..	-2	543	102	643	643
	2000	..	..	54	..	..	-44	82	-2	89	89
	2003	..	..	132	50	..	10	-183	97	105	105
	2004	..	..	93	-3	-50	-132	61	-34	-65	-65
Montserrat	1990	5	..	10	..	..	15	-1	-3	21	26
	2000	4	..	2	..	1	-5	4	4	6	10
	2004	12	..	2	..	0	1	-5	-1	-3	9
	2005	10	..	1	..	0	1	5	-1	6	15
Morocco - Maroc	1990	-5	..	165	..	..	-267	1 830	-1 537	191	186
	2000	-6	-59	427	..	18	..	-435	416	367	361
	2004	-8	-31	893	..	597	-454	217	-1 901	-680	-688
	2005	-5	-78	1 602	2	64	-891	958	-2 349	-691	-696

For sources and notes, see end of table.

Pour les sources et les notes, se reporter à la fin du tableau.

337

Country or territory / Pays ou territoires	Year / Année	Capital account, net / Compte de capital, net (1)	Direct investment / Investissement direct		Portfolio investment / Investissement de portefeuille		Other investment / Autres investissements		Reserve assets / Avoirs de réserve (8)	Financial account, net / Compte financier, net (9)	Capital and financial account, net / Compte de capital et compte financier, net (10)=(1)+(9)
			Abroad / À l'étranger (2)	In reporting economy / Dans l'économie déclarante (3)	Assets / Avoirs (4)	Liabilities / Engagements (5)	Assets / Avoirs (6)	Liabilities / Engagements (7)			
					Millions of dollars / Millions de dollars						
Mozambique	1990	22	..	9	..	..	.	301	-18	293	315
	2000	306	..	139	..	..	-145	503	-77	420	726
	2004	578	..	245	-25	..	-89	-149	-169	-187	391
	2005	194	..	108	-89	0	-73	215	130	286	480
Myanmar	1990	235	..	163	..	..	.	22	-6	179	414
	2000	..	..	258	..	..	.	-45	23	236	236
	2003	..	..	251	..	..	.	-114	-39	98	98
	2004	..	..	214	..	..	.	-88	-94	31	31
Namibia - Namibie	1990	42	-1	30	-5	15	-323	86	-37	-240	-197
	2000	113	-3	186	-118	-20	-502	109	-11	-359	-247
	2003	68	7	146	-217	-81	-453	102	97	-399	-331
	2004	77	17	222	-250	-86	-463	-98	16	-646	-569
Nepal - Népal	1990	..	..	..	..	..	116	176	-8	284	284
	2000	..	..	0	..	..	129	148	-291	-15	-15
	2004	16	..	0	..	..	-343	-5	-178	-532	-516
	2005	40	..	2	..	..	-242	78	-171	-332	-292
Netherlands - Pays-Bas	1990	-301	-13 718	10 676	-3 547	-1 367	-25 277	28 376	-268	-5 190	-5 491
	2000	-97	-74 510	63 119	-65 635	55 242	-28 347	46 507	-219	-7 824	-7 921
	2004	-1 670	-26 415	2 038	-105 083	68 098	-67 053	77 021	911	-52 001	-53 671
	2005	-1 835	-140 461	40 416	-81 774	158 993	-52 564	35 083	1 790	-42 699	-44 533
Netherlands Antilles - Antilles néerlandaises	1990	-2	-2	8	-50	1	-249	302	30	39	38
	2000	30	2	-13	-38	0	-41	36	48	-6	24
	2004	79	-25	26	-94	93	1	28	-37	-8	71
	2005	96	-72	73	-26	2	44	24	-74	-28	68
New Zealand - Nouvelle-Zélande	1990	213	-1 594	1 735	-111	282	-81	1 479	-1 014	696	909
	2000	-180	-752	3 994	-2 318	102	-22	961	143	2 109	1 929
	2004	156	885	2 506	-2 001	8 320	54	-894	-629	8 241	8 398
	2005	-197	1 110	1 979	-587	502	4 633	3 546	-2 410	8 775	8 578
Nicaragua	1990	..	..	..	..	..	.	447	7	454	454
	2000	322	..	267	..	35	80	81	17	479	801
	2004	1 952	..	250	..	-1	-3	-1 258	-169	-1 187	766
	2005	470	..	241	..	-8	-21	136	-46	303	774
Niger	1990	202	0	41	..	..	-2	23	-10	52	254
	2000	55	1	8	0	9	-15	104	-44	62	118
	2003	92	0	15	-4	7	-42	137	29	141	233
	2004	249	-13	26	0	5	-73	-121	41	-134	115
Nigeria - Nigéria	1990	..	..	588	..	-197	-2 886	-250	-2 478	-5 223	-5 223
	2000	33	..	1 140	502	..	-4 534	-1 958	-4 459	-9 309	-9 276
	2004	36	..	1 874	178	..	-7 301	-6 772	-9 531	-21 552	-21 516
	2005	23	..	2 013	2 869	..	-15 786	-11 722	-11 357	-33 983	-33 960
Norway - Norvège	1990	31	-1 470	1 003	-987	1 548	-1 502	648	-414	-1 175	-1 144
	2000	-91	-8 511	5 806	-25 143	9 843	-14 100	19 171	-3 686	-17 081	-17 171
	2004	-154	-3 607	2 474	-38 031	9 353	-16 177	25 458	-5 227	-25 614	-25 768
	2005	-633	-18 261	7 806	-39 515	32 581	-37 652	21 664	-4 511	-37 887	-38 520
Oman	1990	..	..	142	..	..	-270	-369	-135	-633	-633
	2000	8	..	82	..	-36	-497	81	-2 263	-2 633	-2 626
	2004	21	-250	200	-62	148	-850	1 399	-510	75	96
	2005	-16	-44	715	-122	15	-2 042	497	-2 788	-3 770	-3 785
Pakistan	1990	8	-2	245	..	87	-365	1 321	471	1 758	1 766
	2000	..	-11	308	..	9	-437	-348	7	-472	-472
	2004	591	-56	1 118	9	237	-1 339	-2 157	1 728	-459	132
	2005	202	-44	2 183	18	751	146	764	-176	3 642	3 844
Palestinian territory - Territoire palestinien	2000	198	-213	62	-113	12	1 071	57	-91	784	982
	2003	305	-49	18	-38	13	1 028	-78	-100	795	1 099
	2004	670	51	49	54	8	530	57	-27	721	1 392

For sources and notes, see end of table.

Pour les sources et les notes, se reporter à la fin du tableau.

7.2 Balance of payments: capital and financial account summaries

7.2 Balance des paiements : sommaires des comptes de capital et d'opérations financières

Country or territory / Pays ou territoires	Year / Année	Capital account, net / Compte de capital, net (1)	Direct investment / Investissement direct — Abroad / À l'étranger (2)	Direct investment / Investissement direct — In reporting economy / Dans l'économie déclarante (3)	Portfolio investment / Investissement de portefeuille — Assets / Avoirs (4)	Portfolio investment / Investissement de portefeuille — Liabilities / Engagements (5)	Other investment / Autres investissements — Assets / Avoirs (6)	Other investment / Autres investissements — Liabilities / Engagements (7)	Reserve assets / Avoirs de réserve (8)	Financial account, net / Compte financier, net (9)	Capital and financial account, net / Compte de capital et compte financier, net (10)=(1)+(9)
		Millions of dollars / Millions de dollars									
Panama	1990	..	..	136	-200	-36	-1 422	1 806	-356	-72	-72
	2000	2	..	624	-93	184	489	-904	108	408	410
	2004	9	..	1 004	-609	776	-1 571	781	397	778	787
	2005	..	..	1 027	-1 109	258	-486	1 960	-523	1 128	1 128
Papua New Guinea - Papouasie-Nouvelle-Guinée	1990	-37	0	155	..	..	..	113	-75	193	155
	2000	..	..	96	-124	..	-41	-167	-128	-364	-364
	2004	..	..	55	-104	..	34	-31	-102	-148	-148
	2005	..	-7	34	27	-2	-640	-18	-82	-687	-687
Paraguay	1990	13	..	77	..	..	-50	-71	-220	-264	-252
	2000	3	-6	104	2	1	-212	305	210	403	406
	2004	16	-6	44	..	0	-8	-71	-181	-223	-207
	2005	20	-6	64	..	..	107	98	-149	112	132
Peru - Pérou	1990	-25	..	41	-48	..	468	1 384	-287	1 558	1 533
	2000	-251	..	810	-481	75	191	221	329	1 145	894
	2004	-60	..	1 816	-425	1 244	13	-313	-2 442	-107	-167
	2005	-51	..	2 519	-817	2 585	-1 037	-3 207	-1 472	-1 429	-1 480
Philippines	1990	..	..	530	..	-50	..	1 234	388	2 102	2 102
	2000	138	-125	2 240	-812	259	2 454	-418	69	3 711	3 849
	2004	17	-579	688	-862	-803	-907	-515	1 637	-1 368	-1 351
	2005	40	-162	1 132	-1 153	3 988	-3 532	-219	-1 600	-1 589	-1 549
Poland - Pologne	1990	..	..	89	..	..	-4 504	3 603	-2 418	-3 229	-3 229
	2000	34	-16	9 343	-84	3 423	-3 870	1 156	-624	9 597	9 631
	2004	1 180	-793	12 890	-1 331	10 612	-11 809	-1 351	-801	7 617	8 797
	2005	995	-3 024	9 602	-2 485	15 139	-2 856	-2 105	-8 146	6 378	7 373
Portugal	1990	..	-163	2 610	..	961	-2 442	1 598	-3 542	-979	-979
	2000	1 512	-8 183	6 682	-4 582	2 792	-10 823	24 664	-371	10 501	12 013
	2004	2 808	-7 892	2 103	-13 598	14 706	147	14 095	1 863	11 334	14 142
	2005	2 139	-1 195	3 200	-19 031	17 004	-94	14 783	1 741	16 188	18 327
Romania - Roumanie	1990	..	-18	..	..	..	562	1 069	1 494	3 107	3 107
	2000	36	11	1 037	28	73	-407	1 380	-928	1 194	1 230
	2004	643	-70	6 443	-559	28	-212	4 960	-6 018	4 572	5 215
	2005	731	30	6 482	-140	1 089	-1 078	7 579	-6 777	7 160	7 891
Russian Federation - Fédération de Russie	2000	10 955	-3 177	2 714	-411	-9 923	-17 086	-4 166	-16 009	-48 058	-37 103
	2004	-1 624	-13 782	15 444	-3 820	4 406	-25 290	17 676	-45 236	-50 700	-52 324
	2005	-12 764	-12 900	15 151	-10 666	-854	-30 060	42 340	-61 461	-58 684	-71 448
Rwanda	1990	-1	..	8	0	..	8	39	1	55	55
	2000	63	..	8	0	..	23	31	-53	10	73
	2004	61	..	8	..	..	8	67	-99	-17	44
	2005	93	..	8	..	..	-14	31	-92	-67	26
Saint Kitts and Nevis - Saint-Kitts-et-Nevis	1990	2	..	49	..	..	-1	3	0	51	53
	2000	6	..	96	0	5	-11	-14	4	81	87
	2004	5	..	46	0	-9	-22	81	-14	82	87
	2005	14	..	47	0	-12	-6	38	7	74	89
Saint Lucia - Sainte-Lucie	1990	4	..	45	..	0	2	5	-6	45	49
	2000	14	..	54	-1	29	-15	19	-13	73	87
	2004	3	..	80	1	15	-30	60	-27	99	103
	2005	7	..	108	0	7	-29	94	15	195	202
Saint Vincent and the Grenadines - Saint-Vincent-et-les Grenadines	1990	19	..	8	..	..	-11	5	-5	-3	15
	2000	6	..	38	-1	2	-9	-6	-14	11	16
	2004	19	..	66	-10	43	-9	-8	-25	56	75
	2005	14	..	56	0	32	-37	15	4	69	83
Samoa	1990	..	..	..	..	..	0	9	-12	-3	-3
	2004	44	0	2	0	0	-9	0	-8	-15	29
	2005	41	-2	-4	0	0	-1	-4	1	-9	31

For sources and notes, see end of table.

Pour les sources et les notes, se reporter à la fin du tableau.

Country or territory / Pays ou territoires	Year / Année	Capital account, net / Compte de capital, net (1)	Direct investment / Investissement direct — Abroad / À l'étranger (2)	Direct investment — In reporting economy / Dans l'économie déclarante (3)	Portfolio investment / Investissement de portefeuille — Assets / Avoirs (4)	Portfolio investment — Liabilities / Engagements (5)	Other investment / Autres investissements — Assets / Avoirs (6)	Other investment — Liabilities / Engagements (7)	Reserve assets / Avoirs de réserve (8)	Financial account, net / Compte financier, net (9)	Capital and financial account, net / Compte de capital et compte financier, net (10)=(1)+(9)
					Millions of dollars / Millions de dollars						
São Tome and Principe - Sao Tomé-et-Principe	1990	..	..	..	..	..	..	14	1	15	15
	2000	12	..	4	..	..	-5	11	-2	9	21
	2001	18	..	3	..	..	-5	6	-4	1	18
	2002	15	..	3	..	..	0	7	-2	8	23
Saudi Arabia - Arabie saoudite	1990	..	..	1 861	-3 337	..	1 435	-1 181	5 373	4 150	4 150
	2000	..	..	-1 881	-9 378	..	-3 937	3 544	-2 665	-14 317	-14 317
	2004	..	..	-334	-26 654	..	-21 955	1 516	-4 498	-51 926	-51 926
	2005	..	..	-2 351	-48 013	..	-42 380	5 149	464	-87 132	-87 132
Senegal - Sénégal	1990	172	10	57	-1	2	58	58	10	193	364
	2000	83	-1	63	11	12	-4	191	-14	258	341
	2003	150	-3	52	-56	11	58	229	-18	275	426
	2004	750	-13	77	-48	1	6	-121	-155	-253	497
Seychelles	1990	..	-1	20	2	0	-3	5	-4	19	19
	2000	1	-11	24	0	1	-15	58	-19	39	39
	2004	1	-8	38	0	1	-12	6	33	59	60
	2005	6	-8	82	0	1	-10	110	-22	154	160
Sierra Leone	1990	0	..	32	..	..	-20	13	-5	20	20
	2000	..	..	39	..	..	44	30	2	115	115
	2004	81	..	61	..	..	10	45	-45	71	153
	2005	68	8	59	..	..	-2	63	-56	71	139
Singapore - Singapour	1990	-22	-2 034	5 575	-1 610	573	-220	1 664	-5 431	-1 484	-1 506
	2000	-163	-5 899	16 479	-13 371	-1 243	-15 824	14 097	-6 751	-12 510	-12 673
	2004	-184	-8 516	14 839	-13 680	2 435	-22 047	12 614	-12 087	-26 442	-26 626
	2005	-202	-5 527	20 071	-18 182	4 521	-41 097	20 227	-12 074	-32 060	-32 262
Slovakia - Slovaquie	2000	91	-22	2 052	-195	1 016	-973	-533	-794	553	644
	2002	110	-3	4 104	265	289	738	-165	-3 684	1 547	1 657
	2003	102	-24	559	-742	168	-20	1 703	-1 508	153	255
Slovenia - Slovénie	2000	4	-65	136	-58	246	-519	941	-178	502	506
	2004	-123	-550	831	-809	37	-1 608	2 793	297	998	875
	2005	-138	-629	541	-2 100	102	-1 899	4 842	-206	637	499
Yugoslavia, SFR (former) - Yougoslavie, RSF (anc.)	1990	..	..	..	..	..	496	2 742	-1 102	2 136	2 136
Solomon Islands - Îles Salomon	1990	0	..	10	..	..	-1	18	9	37	36
South Africa - Afrique du Sud	1990	-56	-28	-76	-332	338	367	-1 650	-11	-1 391	-1 447
	2000	-52	-277	969	-3 672	1 807	34	1 354	-480	-406	-458
	2004	52	-1 305	701	-950	7 357	-216	2 065	-6 324	1 327	1 380
	2005	30	-909	6 133	-911	5 698	-3 503	4 896	-5 766	5 638	5 668
Spain - Espagne	1990	1 451	-3 522	13 984	-1 357	10 382	-13 175	16 665	-7 188	15 782	17 232
	2000	4 797	-57 411	38 835	-59 318	58 146	-18 475	51 665	2 880	18 141	22 938
	2004	10 450	-61 504	24 792	-39 651	141 686	-52 659	24 226	6 412	43 376	53 826
	2005	9 862	-38 953	22 789	-118 259	170 429	-40 989	77 641	1 919	74 427	84 289
Sri Lanka	1990	..	-1	43	..	..	-116	619	-132	413	413
	2000	49	..	173	19	-63	-244	477	447	808	857
	2004	64	-6	233	111	-100	-354	755	133	773	837
	2005	250	-38	272	276	-216	-223	941	-540	473	723
Sudan - Soudan	1990	..	..	..	..	..	-29	385	5	361	361
	2000	-119	..	392	..	..	-53	38	-108	269	149
	2004	..	..	1 511	20	..	599	-807	-730	593	593
	2005	..	..	2 305	51	..	1 135	-637	-828	2 025	2 025
Suriname	1990	-5	..	-77	..	1	28	21	-18	-45	-50
	2000	2	..	-148	..	..	25	-16	-10	-149	-147
	2004	19	..	-37	..	..	-2	16	-76	-100	-81
	2005	15	..	28	..	-2	-32	-15	-20	-40	-26

For sources and notes, see end of table.

Pour les sources et les notes, se reporter à la fin du tableau.

Country or territory / Pays ou territoires	Year / Année	Capital account, net / Compte de capital, net (1)	Direct investment / Investissement direct — Abroad / À l'étranger (2)	Direct investment — In reporting economy / Dans l'économie déclarante (3)	Portfolio investment / Investissement de portefeuille — Assets / Avoirs (4)	Portfolio investment — Liabilities / Engagements (5)	Other investment / Autres investissements — Assets / Avoirs (6)	Other investment — Liabilities / Engagements (7)	Reserve assets / Avoirs de réserve (8)	Financial account, net / Compte financier, net (9)	Capital and financial account, net / Compte de capital et compte financier, net (10)=(1)+(9)
					Millions of dollars / Millions de dollars						
Swaziland	1990	2	-8	30	-1	-2	-39	-20	-11	-50	-48
	2000	0	-17	91	-2	1	-98	41	6	23	23
	2004	-2	1	71	-11	0	-167	-46	19	-133	-135
	2005	1	25	-16	4	0	41	27	2	83	84
Sweden - Suède	1990	-353	-14 629	1 982	-3 644	6 112	-9 618	39 074	-7 552	11 726	11 373
	2000	384	-39 962	22 125	-12 772	9 017	-16 000	34 609	-170	-3 467	-3 083
	2004	94	-15 369	-588	-24 796	-265	-16 930	23 417	1 100	-33 669	-33 576
	2005	309	-27 560	10 679	-13 019	17 099	-18 297	9 678	-249	-22 475	-22 166
Switzerland - Suisse	1990	..	-5 530	5 545	-746	-551	-28 697	19 920	-1 169	-11 227	-11 227
	2000	-3 541	-43 990	19 788	-23 169	10 247	-101 376	108 372	4 214	-25 913	-29 455
	2004	-1 400	-26 073	2 296	-42 412	2 858	-27 882	28 129	-1 618	-64 701	-66 102
	2005	-783	-54 069	-600	-53 263	5 636	-71 373	81 785	17 691	-74 192	-74 975
Syrian Arab Republic - République arabe syrienne	1990	..	..	..	..	..	-2 008	172	-36	-1 872	-1 872
	2000	63	..	270	..	..	1 206	-1 615	-814	-953	-890
	2004	18	..	275	..	..	1 818	-2 287	-218	-412	-394
	2005	18	..	427	..	..	1 899	-2 175	439	590	608
Tajikistan - Tadjikistan	2004	26	..	272	..	5	-28	-138	-46	64	90
	2005	..	..	54	..	..	-71	138	-26	95	95
Thailand - Thaïlande	1990	-1	-140	2 444	..	-38	-164	6 722	-2 961	5 863	5 862
	2000	..	23	3 366	-160	-546	-2 203	-10 716	1 608	-8 628	-8 628
	2004	..	-110	1 718	1 233	1 855	-1 560	-3 224	-5 713	-5 908	-5 908
	2005	..	-299	4 527	-1 452	7 614	-1 726	232	-5 417	2 954	2 954
Macedonia, TFYR - Macédoine, LERY	2000	0	1	175	-1	0	-78	178	-264	11	11
	2004	-5	-1	157	-1	15	7	255	-19	412	407
	2005	-2	-3	100	1	235	-89	268	-415	96	94
Togo	1990	..	.	18	-2	4	25	87	-29	104	104
	2000	9	0	42	1	6	9	96	-28	126	135
	2003	21	6	34	-5	19	-29	104	22	152	172
	2004	40	13	57	-26	26	6	200	-125	151	191
Tonga	1990	0	0	0	0	-8	5	1	-6	-8	-8
	2001	10	..	..	..	..	..	1	-2	-1	9
	2002	13	..	..	..	..	..	-3	-7	-10	3
Trinidad and Tobago - Trinité-et-Tobago	1990	-19	..	109	..	..	63	-303	-198	-328	-347
	2000	..	-25	680	-30	..	398	-848	-441	-267	-267
	2003	..	225	808	-509	..	-257	-233	-409	-374	-374
	2004	..	25	1 098	-690	..	-389	-245	-710	-910	-910
Tunisia - Tunisie	1990	-7	1	76	-1	3	-343	476	-220	-7	-14
	2000	3	-1	752	..	-20	-624	500	245	851	854
	2004	108	-2	593	..	24	-205	1 028	-977	462	569
	2005	127	-10	723	..	12	17	407	-936	213	340
Turkey - Turquie	1990	..	16	684	-134	681	-409	3 151	-895	3 094	3 094
	2000	..	-870	982	-593	1 615	-1 939	13 705	-383	12 518	12 518
	2004	..	-859	2 930	-1 388	9 411	-6 955	11 140	-787	13 492	13 492
	2005	..	-1 078	9 805	-1 233	14 670	250	16 380	-17 854	20 940	20 940
Uganda - Ouganda	1990	..	..	..	..	..	..	249	5	254	254
	2000	70	..	161	..	..	-1	134	-45	249	318
	2004	64	..	222	..	-17	0	89	-162	132	196
	2005	64	..	257	..	-12	-1	53	-92	206	270
Ukraine	2000	-8	-1	595	-4	-197	-449	-868	-401	-1 325	-1 333
	2004	7	-4	1 715	-6	2 073	-12 313	3 898	-2 226	-6 862	-6 855
	2005	-65	-275	7 808	..	2 757	-7 936	5 450	-10 425	-2 622	-2 687
United Kingdom - Royaume-Uni	1990	888	-20 124	33 504	-29 952	23 846	-94 789	114 100	-131	26 454	27 341
	2000	2 569	-246 265	122 157	-97 188	255 647	-426 811	414 585	-5 300	19 088	21 657
	2004	3 777	-98 188	77 949	-259 157	159 880	-596 925	741 155	-407	10 035	13 812
	2005	4 411	-103 534	158 801	-290 622	230 599	-913 396	955 365	-1 732	32 055	36 466

For sources and notes, see end of table.

Pour les sources et les notes, se reporter à la fin du tableau.

Country or territory / Pays ou territoires	Year / Année	Capital account, net / Compte de capital, net (1)	Direct investment / Investissement direct		Portfolio investment / Investissement de portefeuille		Other investment / Autres investissements		Reserve assets / Avoirs de réserve (8)	Financial account, net / Compte financier, net (9)	Capital and financial account, net / Compte de capital et compte financier, net (10)=(1)+(9)
			Abroad / À l'étranger (2)	In reporting economy / Dans l'économie déclarante (3)	Assets / Avoirs (4)	Liabilities / Engagements (5)	Assets / Avoirs (6)	Liabilities / Engagements (7)			
					Millions of dollars / Millions de dollars						
United Republic of Tanzania - République-Unie de Tanzanie	1990	338	..	..	..	..	..	324	-141	183	521
	2000	420	..	463	..	..	-134	364	-199	494	914
	2004	460	..	470	..	2	-1	-29	-257	175	635
	2005	617	..	473	..	3	-92	-24	247	607	1 224
United States - États-Unis	1990	-6 578	-37 200	48 490	-28 771	22 010	-13 140	71 047	-2 233	60 203	53 625
	2000	-1 010	-159 212	321 274	-127 908	436 573	-273 1?3	289 049	-295	486 368	485 358
	2004	-2 262	-244 128	133 163	-146 549	766 181	-479 930	550 879	2 804	582 420	580 158
	2005	-4 351	-9 072	109 754	-180 125	908 546	-251 699	193 949	14 100	785 454	781 103
Uruguay	1990	..	..	..	..	108	-632	343	-40	-222	-222
	2000	..	1	274	-98	290	-690	1 004	-166	613	613
	2004	..	-18	333	-696	273	-260	434	-454	-387	-387
	2005	..	4	711	266	530	-1 087	270	-621	74	74
Vanuatu	1990	16	..	13	..	..	-1	2	-5	9	26
	2000	-24	..	20	1	..	-14	11	1	19	-4
	2004	-2	-1	20	0	1	-9	44	-15	40	38
	2005	-2	-1	13	-1	0	55	-10	-9	48	46
Venezuela (Bolivarian Republic of) - Venezuela (République bolivarienne du)	1990	..	-375	451	-1 952	17 928	-2 305	-15 908	-4 376	-6 537	-6 537
	2000	..	-521	4 701	-954	-2 180	-4 839	316	-5 449	-8 927	-8 927
	2004	..	-619	1 483	-813	-1 271	-8 233	-1 408	-2 155	-13 016	-13 016
	2005	..	-1 183	2 583	-4 077	3 289	-16 171	-1 315	-5 425	-22 299	-22 299
Viet Nam	2000	..	..	1 298	..	..	-2 039	454	-89	-426	-426
	2004	..	..	1 610	..	..	35	1 035	-808	1 872	1 872
	2005	..	-65	1 954	750	..	-634	913	-2 077	842	842
Yemen - Yémen	1990	..	..	-131	2	..	-351	468	-51	-62	-62
	2000	339	..	6	0	..	-178	-370	-1 429	-1 971	-1 632
	2004	163	..	144	-6	..	-25	-21	-532	-441	-278
	2005	202	..	-266	-14	..	-82	72	-713	-1 003	-801
Zambia - Zambie	1990	-3	..	203	..	..	-275	467	-119	275	272
	2000	153	..	122	..	-1	-85	270	-90	215	368
Zimbabwe	1990	-7	..	-12	10	-32	..	254	-63	157	150

For sources and notes, see next page.

Pour les sources et les notes, se reporter à la page suivante.

Sources:
- International Monetary Fund (IMF), *Balance of Payments Statistics* on CD-ROM.

Notes:
- (1): Capital account
  The capital account consists of capital transfers and of acquisition or disposal of non-produced, non-financial assets. Transfers refer to transactions exchanged without quid-pro-quo (without reciprocity). Capital transfers include transfers of ownership of fixed assets or of funds linked to acquisition or disposal of fixed assets. They further incorporate cancellations of liabilities by creditors, where the later receive no counterpart value. Acquisitions/disposals of non-produced, non-financial assets mainly refer to intangibles such as patents, leases, and goodwill. Items are entered in capital account as net credits or debits. Column 1, as presented here, shows the total net amounts (net credits less net debits).

- (2) and (3): Direct investment
  Within the financial account, direct investment is firstly split according to its direction into direct investment abroad (column 2) and direct investment in reporting economy (column 3). Further subdivisions include: direct investment in equity capital, reinvested earnings and other direct investment capital (inter-company transactions.). Direct investment is defined as investment that reflects a lasting interest of a resident entity of one economy (direct investor) in an entity resident in another economy (direct investment enterprise). It covers all the transactions between direct investors and direct investment enterprises. Direct investment implies a significant degree of influence by the investor on the management of the direct investment enterprise.

- (4) and (5): Portfolio investment
  Within portfolio investment the distinction is being made between assets (column 4) and liabilities (column 5). Assets are claims on the rest of the world and liabilities represent indebtedness to the rest of the world. Portfolio investment covers transactions in equity securities and debt securities. The later are subdivided into bonds, notes, money market instruments and financial derivatives (when the derivatives generate financial claims or liabilities).

- (6) and (7): Other investment
  Other investment is a residual category that covers all financial transactions not included under direct investment, portfolio investment or reserve assets. Assets (column 6) and liabilities (column 7) in this category are classified primarily on an instrument bases, such as trade credits, loans, currency and deposits.

- (8): Reserve assets
  Includes: monetary gold, special drawing rights, reserve position in the IMF, foreign exchange and other claims.

- (9): Financial account
  The financial account constituents are classified according to the type of investment or by a functional breakdown into four main components: direct investment, portfolio investment, other investment and reserve assets. Each component is further divided into relevant subcomponents. The sum of figures in columns 2 to 8 is equal to column 9 (financial account balance). Where the financial account subcomponents do not add up to the total net financial account, the difference can be attributed to financial derivatives that are not shown within this table.

Sources :
- Fonds monétaire international (FMI), *Statistiques de la balance des paiements* sur CD-ROM.

Notes :
- (1) : Compte de capital
  Le compte de capital est subdivisé en transferts de capital et en acquisitions ou cessions d'avoirs non-financiers non-produits. Les transferts sont les transactions échangées sans quid-pro-quo (sans réciprocité.) Les transferts de capitaux comprennent les transferts de propriété d'un actif fixe ou les transferts de fonds liés à l'acquisition ou à la cession d'un actif fixe. De plus, ils incorporent la remise d'une dette par un créancier, sans que celui-ci ne reçoive une valeur équivalente. Les acquisitions ou cession d'avoirs non-financiers non-produits se réfèrent aux avoirs incorporels tels que les brevets, les contrats de location et marques. Les éléments du compte de capital sont reportés comme les crédits ou les débits nets. La colonne (1) présente les totaux (crédits nets moins débits nets).

- (2) et (3) : Investissement direct
  Dans le Compte financier, l'investissement direct est d'abord divisé en fonction du sens des mouvements de capitaux entre investissement de l'économie déclarante à l'étranger (colonne 2) et celui en provenance de l'étranger investi dans l'économie déclarante (colonne 3). Les subdivisions suivantes incluent : capital social, bénéfices réinvestis et autres transactions. L'investissement direct étranger est accompagné d'un intérêt durable de la part d'une entité résidente d'une économie (l'investisseur direct) pour une entité résidente d'une autre économie (l'entreprise d'investissement direct.) Il recouvre toutes les transactions entre les investisseurs directs et les entreprises d'investissement direct. L'investissement direct donne à l'investisseur le privilège d'exercer une influence significative sur la gestion de l'entreprise dans laquelle il a investi.

- (4) et (5) : Investissement de portefeuille
  En investissement de portefeuille on distingue les avoirs (colonne 4) et les engagements (colonne 5). Les avoirs représentent les créances sur les non-résidents et les engagements les endettements envers les non-résidents. Les investissements de portefeuille couvrent les transactions portant sur les titres de participation et les titres de créances, ces dernières étant subdivisées en trois catégories : obligations et autres titres d'emprunt, instruments du marché monétaire et produits financiers dérivés (lorsque les dérivés résultent en créances ou en engagements financiers).

- (6) et (7) : Autres investissements
  Les autres investissements constituent une catégorie résiduelle qui comprend toutes les opérations sur actifs et passifs financiers qui ne figurent pas parmi les investissements directs, les investissements de portefeuille ou les avoirs de réserve. Les avoirs (colonne 6) et les engagements (colonne 7) sont répartis par instruments tels que les crédits commerciaux, les prêts, la monnaie fiduciaire et les dépôts.

- (8) : Avoirs de réserve
  Comprend : l'or monétaire, droits de tirage spéciaux, position de réserve dans le FMI, devises et autres créances.

- (9) : Compte financier
  Les éléments qui constituent le compte financier se divisent selon le type d'investissement ou selon une ventilation fonctionnelle en quatre principaux composants : investissements directs, investissements de portefeuille, autres investissements et avoirs de réserve. Chaque composant comprend plusieurs sous-groupes. La somme de tous les chiffres des colonnes 2 à 8 est égale à la colonne 9 (balance du compte financier). Dans le cas où la somme des éléments du compte financier ne correspond pas au total, la différence peut être attribuée aux instruments financiers dérivés, qui ne sont pas présentés dans ce tableau.

7

7.3.1 Foreign direct investment: inward and outward flows of countries and geographical regions

Region, country or territory	Inward flows - Flux entrants Millions of dollars							
	1980	1990	2000	2001	2002	2003	2004	2005
WORLD	**55 272**	**201 614**	**1 409 568**	**832 248**	**617 732**	**557 869**	**710 755**	**916 277**
DEVELOPED ECONOMIES	47 575	165 637	1 145 913	610 181	442 766	360 831	410 941	555 927
DEVELOPING ECONOMIES	7 674	35 897	254 593	210 538	162 055	172 846	260 236	320 670
ECONOMIES IN TRANSITION	24	79	9 062	11 529	12 911	24 192	39 577	39 679
Developed economies: America	**23 665**	**56 823**	**393 026**	**198 032**	**98 140**	**63 053**	**138 707**	**146 880**
Bermuda	940	819	12 238	10 888	1 533	2 292	14 772	13 615
Canada	5 807	7 582	66 791	27 663	22 156	7 615	1 533	33 822
United States	16 918	48 422	313 997	159 481	74 452	53 146	122 401	99 443
Developed economies: Asia	**287**	**1 904**	**13 389**	**9 872**	**11 004**	**10 265**	**9 569**	**8 363**
Israel	9	151	5 067	3 630	1 765	3 941	1 753	5 587
Japan	278	1 753	8 323	6 241	9 239	6 324	7 816	2 775
Developed economies: Europe	**21 578**	**97 054**	**721 616**	**393 144**	**314 168**	**274 095**	**217 696**	**433 628**
Austria	239	653	8 840	5 919	357	7 144	3 685	8 919
Belgium	—	—	—	—	16 251	33 375	42 044	23 691
Belgium-Luxembourg	1 545	8 047	88 739	88 203				
Cyprus	85	127	855	944	1 057	891	1 079	1 166
Czechoslovakia (former)	..	165	—	—	—	—	—	—
Czech Republic	—	—	4 986	5 641	8 483	2 101	4 974	10 991
Denmark	52	1 132	33 818	11 525	6 630	2 595	-10 722	5 309
Estonia	—	—	387	542	284	919	1 049	2 853
Finland	28	786	8 834	3 732	7 919	3 319	3 537	4 561
France	3 328	9 056	43 252	50 477	49 035	42 498	31 371	63 576
Germany, Federal Rep. (former)	342							
Germany	—	2 962	198 276	26 414	53 520	29 202	-15 113	32 663
Gibraltar	2	36	138	12	83	62	102	192
Greece	672	1 005	1 108	1 589	50	1 275	2 101	607
Hungary	1	623	2 764	3 936	2 994	2 137	4 654	6 699
Iceland	22	22	171	174	91	318	645	2 329
Ireland	286	622	25 779	9 651	29 324	22 781	11 159	-22 773
Italy	577	6 345	13 375	14 871	14 545	16 415	16 815	19 971
Latvia	—	—	413	132	254	292	699	632
Lithuania	—	—	379	446	732	179	773	1 009
Luxembourg	—	—	—	—	3 992	3 943	3 958	3 685
Malta	27	46	618	247	-448	958	309	562
Netherlands	2 278	10 515	63 854	51 927	25 038	21 742	442	43 630
Norway	60	1 003	5 967	2 127	637	3 484	2 473	3 413
Poland	10	89	9 343	5 714	4 131	4 589	12 873	7 724
Portugal	157	2 610	6 635	6 231	1 799	8 593	2 367	3 113
Slovakia	—	—	1 925	1 584	4 094	756	1 261	1 908
Slovenia	—	—	136	370	1 636	333	827	496
Spain	1 493	13 294	39 575	28 342	39 214	25 926	24 761	22 987
Sweden	251	1 971	23 427	10 915	12 160	4 986	12 609	13 389
Switzerland	..	5 484	19 255	8 856	6 276	16 503	750	5 795
United Kingdom	10 123	30 461	118 764	52 623	24 029	16 778	56 214	164 530
Developed economies: Oceania	**2 044**	**9 856**	**17 882**	**9 133**	**19 453**	**13 417**	**44 970**	**-32 944**
Australia	1 866	8 121	14 019	8 314	17 698	9 722	42 390	-34 547
New Zealand	178	1 735	3 863	820	1 755	3 695	2 580	1 603
Developing economies: Africa	**400**	**2 826**	**9 577**	**19 894**	**12 999**	**18 513**	**17 199**	**30 672**
Eastern Africa	*197*	*409*	*1 443*	*1 489*	*1 473*	*2 050*	*1 936*	*1 651*
Burundi	5	1	12	0	0	0	-2	-1
Comoros	..	0	0	1	0	1	0	1
Djibouti	0	0	3	3	4	14	39	23
Ethiopia (former)	1	12	—	—	—	—	—	—
Eritrea	—	—	28	12	20	22	-8	11
Ethiopia	—	—	135	349	255	465	545	205
Kenya	79	57	111	5	28	82	46	21
Madagascar	-1	22	83	93	8	95	53	48
Malawi	9	23	26	34	6	4	-1	3
Mauritius	1	41	266	-28	32	63	14	24
Mayotte	..	..	0	..	..	..	..	..
Mozambique	4	9	139	255	347	337	245	108
Rwanda	16	8	8	4	3	5	8	8
Seychelles	10	20	24	65	48	58	37	82

For sources and notes, see end of table.

1980	1990	2000	2001	2002	2003	2004	2005	Régions, pays ou territoires
53 825	229 887	1 244 465	764 197	539 540	561 104	813 068	778 725	**MONDE**
50 676	217 669	1 107 815	681 683	489 441	510 631	685 724	640 733	ÉCONOMIES DÉVELOPPÉES
3 148	11 945	133 463	79 818	45 413	39 742	113 371	122 936	ÉCONOMIES EN DÉVELOPPEMENT
0	273	3 187	2 696	4 687	10 731	13 973	15 056	ÉCONOMIES EN TRANSITION
23 601	36 982	197 595	157 798	166 048	146 693	265 153	15 896	Économies développées : Amérique
273	763	10 294	-3 103	4 329	-4 175	-538	-5 473	Bermudes
4 098	5 237	44 675	36 028	26 773	21 516	43 254	34 083	Canada
19 230	30 982	142 626	124 873	134 946	129 352	222 437	-12 714	États-Unis
2 382	48 223	34 893	39 020	33 262	30 864	35 494	48 273	Économies développées : Asie
-3	199	3 335	687	981	2 064	4 543	2 492	Israël
2 385	48 024	31 558	38 333	32 281	28 800	30 951	45 781	Japon
24 126	129 876	871 401	473 957	281 692	316 956	367 989	618 810	Économies développées : Europe
101	1 701	5 740	3 137	5 807	7 136	7 388	9 293	Autriche
				12 277	38 899	33 526	22 925	Belgique
196	6 314	86 362	100 646	—	—	—	—	Belgique-Luxembourg
..	5	172	250	461	490	619	432	Chypre
..	20							Tchécoslovaquie (anc.)
—	—	43	165	207	206	1 014	856	République tchèque
94	1 482	26 558	13 374	5 686	1 126	-10 363	9 328	Danemark
—	—	63	200	132	156	268	603	Estonie
137	2 702	24 030	8 371	7 622	-2 280	-1 075	2 705	Finlande
3 137	26 924	177 449	86 767	50 441	53 147	57 006	115 668	France
4 699								Allemagne, Rép. Fédérale d' (anc.)
—	24 235	56 557	39 684	18 946	6 174	1 883	45 634	Allemagne
0	0	0	0	0	0	0	0	Gibraltar
..	11	2 137	616	655	412	1 029	1 451	Grèce
..	16	620	368	278	1 644	1 122	1 346	Hongrie
..	12	394	346	323	372	2 561	6 690	Islande
..	364	4 629	4 065	11 025	5 549	15 804	12 938	Irlande
740	7 614	12 316	21 472	17 123	9 071	19 262	39 671	Italie
—	—	12	18	3	36	103	135	Lettonie
—	—	4	7	18	37	263	329	Lituanie
—	—	—	—	9 295	-53	4 245	2 935	Luxembourg
..	..	21	9	-28	550	0	-26	Malte
5 918	13 660	75 635	50 592	32 019	44 181	17 282	119 454	Pays-Bas
253	1 431	13 197	19 903	7 351	15 037	3 675	14 461	Norvège
21	5	16	-90	230	305	794	1 455	Pologne
14	163	8 132	6 262	-149	8 028	7 958	1 146	Portugal
—	—	21	35	5	22	-141	146	Slovaquie
—	—	65	145	148	472	551	568	Slovénie
311	3 349	58 213	33 106	32 715	27 529	60 532	38 772	Espagne
625	14 746	40 971	7 335	10 599	21 080	20 985	25 938	Suède
..	7 176	44 673	18 320	8 203	15 442	26 838	42 858	Suisse
7 881	17 948	233 371	58 855	50 300	62 187	94 862	101 099	Royaume-Uni
567	2 587	3 926	10 908	8 439	16 118	17 089	-42 246	Économies développées : Océanie
460	993	3 174	11 986	8 045	15 602	17 995	-40 946	Australie
107	1 594	752	-1 078	394	516	-906	-1 300	Nouvelle-Zélande
1 089	689	1 524	-2 663	334	1 159	1 885	1 054	Économies en développement : Afrique
4	21	0	20	29	5	44	66	*Afrique orientale*
..	0	0	0	0	0	..	..	Burundi
..	1	..	..	..	..	..	..	Comores
0	0	0	0	0	0	0	0	Djibouti
0	0							Éthiopie (anc.)
—	—	0	0	0	0	0	0	Érythrée
—	—	0	0	0	0	0	0	Éthiopie
1	0	0	0	7	2	4	10	Kenya
..	1	..	..	..	..	..	..	Madagascar
..	..	..	5	..	..	..	..	Malawi
..	1	13	3	9	-6	32	48	Maurice
0	0	0	0	0	0	0	0	Mayotte
..	0	0	0	0	0	0	..	Mozambique
-1	0	0	0	0	0	0	0	Rwanda
4	1	8	9	9	8	8	8	Seychelles

Pour les sources et les notes, se reporter à la fin du tableau.

Region, country or territory	Inward flows - Flux entrants Millions of dollars							
	1980	1990	2000	2001	2002	2003	2004	2005
Somalia	0	6	0	0	0	-1	21	24
Uganda	4	-6	181	151	185	202	222	258
United Republic of Tanzania	5	0	282	467	430	527	470	473
Zambia	62	203	122	72	82	172	239	259
Zimbabwe	2	12	23	4	26	4	9	103
Middle Africa	*353*	*-345*	*1 252*	*3 629*	*3 212*	*6 340*	*4 584*	*4 618*
Angola	37	-335	879	2 146	1 672	3 505	1 449	-24
Cameroon	130	-113	0	0	0	0	0	18
Central African Republic	5	1	1	5	6	3	-13	6
Chad	0	9	115	460	924	713	478	705
Congo	40	23	166	77	137	323	668	402
Dem. Rep. of the Congo	110	-14	23	82	117	158	15	1 344
Equatorial Guinea	..	11	108	945	323	1 431	1 664	1 860
Gabon	32	73	-43	-89	30	206	323	300
São Tome and Principe	..	..	4	3	3	1	-2	7
Northern Africa	*152*	*1 116*	*3 456*	*5 425*	*3 925*	*5 376*	*5 905*	*12 738*
Algeria	349	0	438	1 113	1 065	634	882	1 081
Egypt	548	734	1 235	510	647	237	2 157	5 376
Libyan Arab Jamahiriya	-1 089	159	141	-133	145	142	-354	261
Morocco	89	165	471	2 875	534	2 429	1 070	2 933
Sudan	9	-31	392	574	713	1 349	1 511	2 305
Tunisia	246	89	779	486	821	584	639	782
Southern Africa	*132*	*92*	*1 255*	*7 264*	*1 459*	*1 281*	*1 530*	*7 108*
Botswana	112	96	57	31	403	418	391	346
Lesotho	4	16	31	28	27	42	53	47
Namibia	..	30	188	365	182	149	226	349
South Africa	-10	-78	888	6 789	757	734	799	6 379
Swaziland	26	28	91	51	90	-61	60	-14
Western Africa	*-434*	*1 553*	*2 171*	*2 087*	*2 930*	*3 466*	*3 244*	*4 557*
Benin	4	62	60	44	14	45	64	21
Burkina Faso	0	0	23	6	15	29	14	19
Cape Verde	..	0	32	9	12	14	20	19
Côte d'Ivoire	95	48	235	273	213	165	283	192
Gambia	0	14	44	35	43	-1	2	24
Ghana	16	15	166	89	59	137	139	156
Guinea	1	18	10	2	30	83	98	102
Guinea-Bissau	..	2	1	0	4	4	2	10
Liberia	72	225	21	8	3	372	207	194
Mali	2	6	82	122	244	132	101	159
Mauritania	27	7	40	92	118	214	5	115
Niger	49	41	8	23	5	11	20	12
Nigeria	-739	1 003	1 310	1 277	2 040	2 171	2 127	3 403
Saint Helena	0	..	-4	0	..	..	-1	..
Senegal	14	57	63	32	78	52	77	54
Sierra Leone	-19	32	39	10	2	3	26	27
Togo	43	23	42	64	53	34	59	49
Developing economies: America	**6 492**	**9 733**	**96 763**	**78 488**	**52 812**	**43 845**	**85 710**	**90 047**
Caribbean	*390*	*828*	*19 355*	*10 633*	*4 307*	*3 601*	*26 754*	*24 620*
Anguilla	..	11	43	35	38	34	92	103
Antigua and Barbuda	20	59	67	112	80	179	91	129
Aruba	..	131	-122	-260	331	156	143	119
Bahamas	4	-17	250	102	153	190	274	360
Barbados	3	11	19	19	17	58	-12	159
British Virgin Islands	-1	18	9 877	3 483	1 472	3 111	17 580	9 620
Cayman Islands	20	49	6 922	4 356	-242	-2 575	5 969	11 222
Cuba	0	1	-10	4	3	-9	4	-1
Dominica	..	8	20	18	18	30	25	27
Dominican Republic	93	133	953	1 079	917	613	758	899
Grenada	..	13	39	61	62	91	55	28
Haiti	13	8	13	4	6	14	6	10
Jamaica	28	175	469	614	481	721	602	601
Montserrat	..	10	2	1	1	2	3	1
Netherlands Antilles	35	8	-63	-5	8	-81	-26	48
Saint Kitts and Nevis	1	49	99	90	81	78	53	50
Saint Lucia	31	46	58	63	57	112	84	112
Saint Vincent and the Grenadines	1	8	38	21	34	55	66	34
Trinidad and Tobago	143	109	680	835	791	808	1 001	1 100
Turks and Caicos Islands	..	..	0	..	0	14	-15	..

For sources and notes, see end of table.

1980	1990	2000	2001	2002	2003	2004	2005	Régions, pays ou territoires
				Outward flows - Flux sortants Millions de dollars				
0	0	0	0	0	0	0	0	Somalie
..	..	-28	..	..	..	..	..	Ouganda
0	0	0	0	0	0	0	0	République-Unie de Tanzanie
..	..	..	..	..	..	..	..	Zambie
..	17	8	4	3	0	0	1	Zimbabwe
0	*52*	*32*	*58*	*9*	*4*	*40*	*1*	*Afrique centrale*
..	1	20	15	29	24	35	29	Angola
-8	15	-12	29	7	36	..	..	Cameroun
..	4	0	0	1	0	..	..	République centrafricaine
0	0	0	0	0	0	..	..	Tchad
..	3	4	6	6	2	..	..	Congo
..	..	-2	1	-2	..	..	..	Rép. dém. du Congo
..	0	-4	4	0	0	..	..	Guinée équatoriale
8	29	25	4	-32	-57	5	-28	Gabon
0	0	0	0	0	0	0	0	Sao Tomé-et-Principe
87	*135*	*227*	*302*	*52*	*123*	*182*	*439*	*Afrique septentrionale*
34	5	18	9	100	14	258	23	Algérie
7	12	51	12	28	21	159	92	Égypte
47	105	98	175	-136	63	-271	138	Jamahiriya arabe libyenne
..	13	60	100	54	20	32	174	Maroc
0	0	0	0	0	0	0	0	Soudan
..	0	0	6	7	5	4	13	Tunisie
766	*39*	*292*	*-2 832*	*-361*	*750*	*1 292*	*134*	*Afrique australe*
2	7	2	380	43	206	-39	57	Botswana
..	..	..	..	0	0	0	..	Lesotho
..	1	3	-13	-5	-10	-22	-12	Namibie
755	27	271	-3 180	-399	565	1 352	68	Afrique du Sud
9	3	17	-18	0	-11	1	21	Swaziland
232	*442*	*972*	*-212*	*606*	*277*	*328*	*414*	*Afrique occidentale*
..	0	4	2	1	0	-1	0	Bénin
0	-1	0	1	2	2	-9	-3	Burkina Faso
..	0	1	1	0	..	..	..	Cap-Vert
..	31	8	-5	-4	23	-26	-4	Côte d'Ivoire
..	3	5	5	5	7	10	13	Gambie
..	0	0	0	0	0	0	0	Ghana
..	0	..	5	7	..	..	..	Guinée
..	..	..	0	1	1	-8	-4	Guinée-Bissau
231	-3	780	-313	386	80	92	186	Libéria
..	0	4	17	2	1	1	2	Mali
..	..	1	..	..	-1	..	..	Mauritanie
-4	0	-1	-4	-2	0	7	3	Niger
3	415	169	94	172	167	261	200	Nigéria
0	0	0	0	0	0	0	0	Sainte-Hélène
2	-10	1	-7	34	3	13	30	Sénégal
..	0	..	..	..	..	..	..	Sierra Leone
..	5	0	-7	2	-6	-13	-10	Togo
901	**300**	**49 727**	**35 283**	**10 353**	**19 587**	**28 040**	**38 298**	**Économies en développement : Amérique**
121	*-1 718*	*42 160*	*29 897*	*3 352*	*10 483*	*10 707*	*18 458*	*Caraïbes*
..	..	..	..	..	..	..	..	Anguilla
..	..	2	12	15	..	..	..	Antigua-et-Barbuda
..	487	6	1	-1	2	-1	5	Aruba
115	0	..	..	..	..	..	..	Bahamas
1	1	1	1	0	1	4	3	Barbade
..	-2 520	34 400	22 544	8 980	5 285	5 880	15 994	Îles Vierges britanniques
5	282	7 593	7 219	-5 837	4 892	4 679	2 241	Îles Caïmanes
..	..	..	1	0	..	..	..	Cuba
0	0	0	0	0	0	0	0	Dominique
..	..	61	-28	12	-38	..	..	République dominicaine
0	0	0	0	0	0	0	0	Grenade
..	-8	0	0	0	0	..	..	Haïti
..	37	74	89	74	116	91	94	Jamaïque
0	0	0	0	0	0	0	0	Montserrat
1	2	-2	-1	1	-1	25	1	Antilles néerlandaises
..	..	..	0	..	..	..	..	Saint-Kitts-et-Nevis
0	0	0	0	0	0	0	0	Sainte-Lucie
0	0	0	0	0	0	0	0	Saint-Vincent-et-les Grenadines
..	..	25	58	106	225	29	120	Trinité-et-Tobago
0	0	0	0	0	0	0	0	Îles Turques et Caïques

Pour les sources et les notes, se reporter à la fin du tableau.

Region, country or territory	Inward flows - Flux entrants Millions of dollars							
	1980	1990	2000	2001	2002	2003	2004	2005
Central America	**2 505**	**3 056**	**19 595**	**29 216**	**20 017**	**16 250**	**21 537**	**20 730**
Belize	..	19	23	60	24	-1	128	107
Costa Rica	53	162	409	460	659	575	617	653
El Salvador	6	2	173	279	470	142	376	518
Guatemala	111	59	230	456	111	131	155	208
Honduras	6	44	282	193	176	247	325	272
Mexico	2 099	2 633	17 588	27 151	18 275	14 184	18 674	18 055
Nicaragua	13	1	267	150	204	201	250	241
Panama-Canal-Zone (former)	219							
Panama	—	136	624	467	99	771	1 012	677
South America	**3 597**	**5 849**	**57 812**	**38 639**	**23 488**	**23 994**	**37 419**	**44 697**
Argentina	678	1 836	10 418	2 166	2 149	1 652	4 274	4 662
Bolivia	50	67	736	706	677	197	65	-277
Brazil	1 910	989	32 779	22 457	16 590	10 144	18 146	15 066
Chile	287	1 315	4 860	4 200	2 550	4 307	7 173	6 667
Colombia	157	500	2 395	2 525	2 139	1 758	3 117	10 192
Ecuador	70	126	720	1 330	1 275	1 555	1 160	1 913
Falkland Islands (Malvinas)	0	..	45	18	..	..	..	..
Guyana	1	8	67	56	44	26	30	77
Paraguay	30	71	104	84	6	21	41	219
Peru	27	41	810	1 144	2 156	1 335	1 599	2 579
Suriname	18	77	-97	-27	-74	-76	-37	41
Uruguay	290	42	273	297	194	416	332	600
Venezuela (Bolivarian Republic of)	80	778	4 701	3 683	782	2 659	1 518	2 957
Developing economies: Asia	**663**	**22 642**	**147 993**	**112 045**	**96 125**	**110 137**	**156 622**	**199 554**
Eastern Asia	**950**	**8 791**	**116 275**	**78 829**	**67 350**	**72 174**	**105 074**	**118 192**
China	57	3 487	40 715	46 878	52 743	53 505	60 630	72 406
China, Hong Kong SAR	710	3 275	61 924	23 777	9 682	13 624	34 032	35 897
China, Macao SAR	..	0	-1	160	375	411	498	770
China, Taiwan Province of	166	1 330	4 928	4 109	1 445	453	1 898	1 625
Korea, Dem. People's Rep. of	..	-61	5	-4	-15	158	197	113
Korea, Republic of	17	759	8 651	3 866	3 043	3 892	7 727	7 198
Mongolia	..	..	54	43	78	132	93	182
Southern Asia	**284**	**213**	**4 697**	**6 476**	**7 530**	**6 211**	**7 401**	**9 795**
Afghanistan	9	..	0	1	1	2	1	1
Bangladesh	9	3	579	355	328	350	460	692
Bhutan	..	2	0	0	0	1	1	1
India	79	237	3 585	5 472	5 627	4 585	5 474	6 598
Iran, Islamic Republic of	81	-362	39	61	548	482	100	30
Maldives	0	6	13	12	12	14	15	14
Nepal	0	6	0	21	-6	15	0	5
Pakistan	64	278	309	383	823	534	1 118	2 183
Sri Lanka	43	43	173	172	197	229	233	272
South-Eastern Asia	**2 756**	**12 821**	**23 541**	**19 582**	**15 774**	**19 920**	**25 666**	**37 136**
Brunei Darussalam	-20	7	549	526	1 035	3 375	212	275
Cambodia	1	..	149	149	145	84	131	381
Indonesia	300	1 092	-4 550	-2 978	145	-597	1 896	5 260
Lao People's Dem. Rep.	..	6	34	24	25	19	17	28
Malaysia	934	2 611	3 788	554	3 203	2 473	4 624	3 967
Myanmar	0	225	208	192	191	291	251	300
Philippines	114	550	2 240	195	1 542	491	688	1 132
Singapore	1 236	5 575	16 484	15 649	7 338	10 376	14 820	20 083
Thailand	189	2 575	3 350	3 886	947	1 952	1 414	3 687
Timor-Leste	0	0	0	84	1	5	2	3
Viet Nam	2	180	1 289	1 300	1 200	1 450	1 610	2 020
Western Asia	**-3 328**	**818**	**3 479**	**7 159**	**5 471**	**11 832**	**18 481**	**34 431**
Bahrain	-418	-183	364	80	217	517	865	1 049
Iraq	2	0	-3	-6	-2	0	90	300
Jordan	34	38	815	138	75	436	651	1 532
Kuwait	1	6	16	-111	3	-67	24	250
Lebanon	-12	6	964	1 451	1 336	2 860	1 899	2 573
Palestinian territory	..	..	62	20	-5	..	-3	..
Oman	98	125	83	5	109	489	200	715
Qatar	11	5	252	296	624	625	1 199	1 469
Saudi Arabia	-3 192	312	183	504	453	778	1 942	4 628
Syrian Arab Republic	0	71	270	110	115	180	275	500
Turkey	18	684	982	3 352	1 137	1 752	2 837	9 681

For sources and notes, see end of table.

Outward flows - Flux sortants Millions de dollars								Régions, pays ou territoires
1980	1990	2000	2001	2002	2003	2004	2005	
358	*907*	*-312*	*5 564*	*2 901*	*4 136*	*5 951*	*7 874*	**Amérique centrale**
..	2	0	0	0	0	0	0	Belize
5	2	8	10	34	27	61	-43	Costa Rica
..	..	-5	-10	-26	19	-53	217	El Salvador
2	0	40	18	15	2	..	..	Guatemala
1	-1	-2	4	2	20	26	28	Honduras
3	223	363	4 404	891	1 253	4 432	6 171	Mexique
..	..	5	15	12	10	..	..	Nicaragua
347								Panama, Zone du canal de (anc.)
–	681	-722	1 124	1 974	2 804	1 485	1 500	Panama
422	*1 111*	*7 879*	*-178*	*4 100*	*4 968*	*11 382*	*11 966*	**Amérique du Sud**
-110	35	901	161	-627	774	442	1 157	Argentine
1	1	3	3	3	3	3	3	Bolivie
367	625	2 282	-2 258	2 482	249	9 807	2 517	Brésil
44	8	3 987	1 610	343	1 606	1 527	2 146	Chili
106	16	325	16	857	938	142	4 623	Colombie
1	2	..	..	..	..	..	..	Équateur
0	0	0	0	0	0	0	0	Îles Falkland (Malvinas)
..	..	2	0	0	..	..	..	Guyana
2	..	6	6	2	6	6	5	Paraguay
..	50	-146	74	0	60	-215	60	Pérou
0	0	0	0	0	0	0	0	Suriname
..	..	-1	6	14	15	18	-4	Uruguay
12	375	521	204	1 026	1 318	-348	1 460	Venezuela (République bolivarienne du)
1 141	*10 946*	*82 211*	*47 140*	*34 721*	*18 979*	*83 429*	*83 557*	**Économies en développement : Asie**
150	*9 574*	*71 974*	*26 145*	*27 556*	*14 441*	*59 211*	*54 189*	**Asie orientale**
..	830	916	6 885	2 518	-152	1 805	11 306	Chine
82	2 448	59 352	11 345	17 463	5 492	45 716	32 560	Chine. Hong Kong RAS
..	..	..	11	71	-5	-116	-17	Chine. Macao RAS
42	5 243	6 701	5 480	4 886	5 632	7 145	6 028	Chine. Taiwan Province de
..	1	6	3	0	-1	2	..	Corée, Rép. populaire dém. de
26	1 052	4 999	2 420	2 617	3 426	4 658	4 312	Corée, République de
0	0	0	..	0	1	..	..	Mongolie
6	*10*	*545*	*1 423*	*1 761*	*1 022*	*2 111*	*1 532*	**Asie méridionale**
0	0	0	0	0	0	0	0	Afghanistan
..	1	2	21	4	6	6	10	Bangladesh
0	0	0	0	0	0	0	0	Bhoutan
4	6	509	1 397	1 679	1 325	2 024	1 364	Inde
7	0	21	-26	39	-356	19	76	Iran, Rép. islamique d'
..	0	0	0	0	0	0	0	Maldives
0	0	0	0	0	0	0	0	Népal
-5	2	11	31	28	19	56	44	Pakistan
..	1	2	0	11	27	6	38	Sri Lanka
394	*2 328*	*8 231*	*20 782*	*4 574*	*5 402*	*14 700*	*11 970*	**Asie du Sud-Est**
..	..	20	9	24	76	4	..	Brunéi Darussalam
..	..	7	7	6	10	10	6	Cambodge
6	-11	150	125	182	15	3 408	3 065	Indonésie
..	0	10	0	..	0	..	..	Rép. dém. populaire lao
201	129	2 026	267	1 905	1 370	2 061	2 971	Malaisie
0	0	0	0	0	0	0	0	Myanmar
86	22	125	-140	65	303	579	162	Philippines
98	2 034	5 915	20 168	2 287	3 143	8 512	5 519	Singapour
3	154	-22	346	106	486	125	246	Thaïlande
0	0	0	0	0	0	0	0	Timor-Leste
0	0	0	0	0	0	0	0	Viet Nam
591	*-966*	*1 461*	*-1 210*	*830*	*-1 886*	*7 408*	*15 866*	**Asie occidentale**
..	25	10	216	190	741	1 036	1 123	Bahreïn
0	0	0	0	0	0	0	0	Iraq
3	-31	2	6	0	0	0	0	Jordanie
407	-239	-303	-1 915	-76	-4 962	2 528	4 709	Koweït
2	-16	108	1	0	611	827	715	Liban
..	..	213	380	..	..	..	..	Territoire palestinien
1	0	-1	..	..	153	250	44	Oman
2	2	18	17	-21	-2	192	352	Qatar
178	-634	126	-612	143	83	709	1 183	Arabie saoudite
0	0	0	0	0	0	0	0	République arabe syrienne
..	-16	870	497	175	499	859	1 078	Turquie

Pour les sources et les notes, se reporter à la fin du tableau.

7

Region, country or territory	Inward flows - Flux entrants Millions of dollars							
	1980	1990	2000	2001	2002	2003	2004	2005
United Arab Emirates	98	-116	-515	1 184	1 307	4 256	8 359	12 000
Yemen Arab Republic (former)	34		_	_	_	_	_	_
Yemen	_	-131	6	136	102	6	144	-266
Developing economies: Oceania	**118**	**696**	**260**	**111**	**119**	**352**	**705**	**397**
Cook Islands	..	4	-28	1	0	..	-1	..
Fiji	36	84	-18	43	21	26	94	-4
French Polynesia	..	22	2	-19	11	58	6	45
Kiribati	..	0	18	15	15	16	19	17
Marshall Islands	0	1	125	-1	-47	5	513	157
Micronesia, Federated States of	0	0	..	0	..	..	..	..
Nauru	..	0	0	0	1	2	1	1
New Caledonia	2	31	22	-1	59	116	27	122
Niue	0	0	0	0	9	..	..	..
Northern Mariana Islands	-1	124	12	..	..	..	..	..
Palau, Pacific Islands (former)	0	1	15	11	1	2	7	3
Papua New Guinea	76	398	96	63	18	101	26	32
Samoa	0	7	-2	1	0	1	-11	-4
Solomon Islands	2	10	1	-12	-1	-2	1	-1
Tokelau	0	0	0	1	0	0	0	0
Tonga	..	0	5	1	1	12	1	5
Tuvalu	..	..	-1	1	25	0	0	8
Vanuatu	3	13	13	9	7	15	22	15
Economies in transition: Asia	**_**	**_**	**1 895**	**3 550**	**4 501**	**6 103**	**8 818**	**4 296**
Armenia	_	_	125	88	144	157	217	220
Azerbaijan	_	_	130	227	1 393	3 285	3 556	1 680
Georgia	_	_	135	133	167	340	499	450
Kazakhstan	_	_	1 283	2 835	2 590	2 092	4 113	1 738
Kyrgyzstan	_	_	-2	5	5	46	175	47
Tajikistan	_	_	24	9	36	14	272	54
Turkmenistan	_	_	126	170	100	100	-15	62
Uzbekistan	_	_	75	83	65	70	1	45
Economies in transition: Europe	**24**	**79**	**7 167**	**7 978**	**8 410**	**18 089**	**30 760**	**35 383**
Albania	..	..	143	207	135	178	332	260
Belarus	_	_	119	96	247	172	164	305
Bosnia and Herzegovina	_	_	146	119	265	381	606	298
Bulgaria	..	4	1 002	813	905	2 097	3 443	2 223
Croatia	_	_	1 085	1 338	1 213	2 133	1 262	1 695
Macedonia, TFYR	_	_	175	442	78	95	157	100
Moldova, Republic of	_	_	127	102	133	78	154	225
Romania	..	0	1 037	1 157	1 144	2 213	6 517	6 388
Russian Federation	_	_	2 714	2 748	3 461	7 958	15 444	14 600
Serbia and Montenegro	_	_	25	165	137	1 360	966	1 481
Yugoslavia, SFR (former)	24	71	_	_	_	_	_	_
USSR (former)	..	4	_	_	_	_	_	_
Ukraine	_	_	595	792	693	1 424	1 715	7 808

Sources:
- UNCTAD, *World Investment Report 2006: FDI from Developing and Transition Economies: Implications for Development*

Outward flows - Flux sortants Millions de dollars								Régions, pays ou territoires
1980	1990	2000	2001	2002	2003	2004	2005	
-2	-58	429	201	407	931	1 007	6 661	Émirats arabes unis
..	–	–	–	–	–	–	–	Rép. arabe du Yémen (anc.)
–	..	-10	-1	11	..	..	..	Yémen
18	**11**	**2**	**59**	**5**	**16**	**17**	**27**	**Économies en développement : Océanie**
0	0	..	1	1	0	2	0	Îles Cook
2	3	2	3	1	4	3	10	Fidji
0	0	0	0	0	0	0	0	Polynésie française
0	0	0	0	0	0	0	0	Kiribati
0	0	0	0	0	0	0	0	Îles Marshall
0	0	0	0	0	0	0	0	Micronésie, États fédérés de
0	0	0	0	0	0	0	0	Nauru
0	0	0	0	4	14	11	10	Nouvelle-Calédonie
0	0	0	0	0	0	0	0	Nioué
0	0	0	0	0	0	0	0	Îles Mariannes du Nord
0	0	0	0	0	0	0	0	Palaos, Îles du Pacifique (anc.)
16	8	-1	55	-1	-3	0	6	Papouasie-Nouvelle-Guinée
0	0	0	0	0	0	0	0	Samoa
0	0	0	0	0	0	0	0	Îles Salomon
0	0	0	0	0	0	0	0	Tokélaou
..	0	..	..	.	..	..	..	Tonga
0	0	0	0	0	0	0	0	Tuvalu
..	..	..	..	1	1	1	1	Vanuatu
–	**–**	**8**	**-7**	**776**	**816**	**-18**	**1 156**	**Économies en transition : Asie**
–	–	-1	0	19	0	2	7	Arménie
–	–	1	12	326	933	1 205	1 221	Azerbaïdjan
–	–	0	0	4	4	10	-89	Géorgie
–	–	4	-26	426	-121	-1 279	17	Kazakhstan
–	–	5	6	0	0	44	0	Kirghizistan
–	–	0	0	0	0	0	0	Tadjikistan
–	–	0	0	0	0	0	0	Turkménistan
–	–	0	0	0	0	0	0	Ouzbekistan
0	**273**	**3 178**	**2 703**	**3 911**	**9 915**	**13 991**	**13 900**	**Économies en transition : Europe**
..	..	6	0	..	..	..	..	Albanie
–	–	0	0	-206	2	1	3	Bélarus
–	–	..	..	..	..	-2	3	Bosnie-Herzégovine
..	-3	3	8	29	27	-217	316	Bulgarie
–	–	3	154	539	108	348	187	Croatie
–	–	-1	1	0	0	1	3	Macédoine, LERY
–	–	0	0	0	0	3	0	Moldova, République de
..	18	-11	-17	16	39	70	-13	Roumanie
–	–	3 177	2 533	3 533	9 727	13 782	13 126	Fédération de Russie
–	–	..	..	5	..	..	..	Serbie-et-Monténégro
0	258	–	–	–	–	–	–	Yougoslavie, RSF (anc.)
0	0	–	–	–	–	–	–	URSS (anc.)
–	–	1	23	-5	13	4	275	Ukraine

Sources :
- CNUCED, *World Investment Report 2006: FDI from Developing and Transition Economies: Implications for Development*

Economic grouping	Inward flows - Flux entrants Millions of dollars							
	1980	1990	2000	2001	2002	2003	2004	2005
DEVELOPING ECONOMIES	**7 674**	**35 897**	**254 593**	**210 538**	**162 055**	**172 846**	**260 236**	**320 670**
Developing economies excluding China	7 616	32 403	213 840	163 639	109 278	119 286	199 540	248 231
Developing economies excluding LDCs	7 136	35 311	250 488	203 392	155 426	161 923	251 431	310 957
High-income countries	1 304	18 559	149 857	97 825	54 028	67 361	130 664	145 036
Middle-income countries	5 459	9 494	54 295	52 923	36 531	32 147	46 611	72 483
Low-income countries	910	7 844	50 441	59 790	71 495	73 338	82 961	103 151
Heavily indebted poor countries	785	837	3 911	4 576	5 218	6 403	6 398	7 693
Landlocked countries	387	603	3 903	6 179	7 593	8 463	10 972	6 447
Small island developing states	358	1 042	2 331	2 212	1 923	2 654	2 999	2 980
Least developed countries	*536*	*579*	*4 067*	*7 125*	*6 595*	*10 868*	*8 740*	*9 680*
Africa and Haiti	478	431	3 013	6 124	5 734	10 035	7 669	8 459
Asia	53	111	975	877	786	768	1 004	1 142
Islands	5	37	79	124	74	64	66	79
Major petroleum exporters	*-4 118*	*2 646*	*4 902*	*8 711*	*11 326*	*20 411*	*22 894*	*35 738*
Africa	-1 371	923	2 890	4 391	5 089	6 981	5 095	5 424
America	259	896	5 318	4 513	1 580	3 387	2 494	4 105
Asia	-3 006	827	-3 305	-193	4 657	10 043	15 305	26 210
Major exporters of manufactured goods	*7 529*	*24 705*	*197 014*	*157 345*	*121 572*	*117 430*	*170 964*	*195 396*
America	4 010	3 622	50 367	49 608	34 865	24 327	36 820	33 121
Asia	3 520	21 083	146 647	107 737	86 707	93 103	134 144	162 275
Emerging economies	*7 542*	*19 664*	*103 656*	*85 183*	*57 696*	*50 768*	*80 349*	*83 589*
America	5 001	6 814	66 455	57 118	41 720	31 622	49 866	47 029
Asia	2 541	12 850	37 201	28 064	15 976	19 146	30 483	36 560
Newly industrialized economies	*3 665*	*17 767*	*96 815*	*49 057*	*27 345*	*32 664*	*67 099*	*78 850*
First tier	2 128	10 939	91 987	47 401	21 508	28 345	58 477	64 803
Second tier	1 537	6 828	4 828	1 657	5 838	4 319	8 622	14 047
Developing economies: Africa	**400**	**2 826**	**9 577**	**19 894**	**12 999**	**18 513**	**17 199**	**30 672**
Northern Africa excluding Sudan	144	1 147	3 064	4 851	3 212	4 027	4 394	10 433
Sub-Saharan Africa	257	1 679	6 514	15 043	9 787	14 486	12 805	20 239
Sub-Saharan Africa excluding South Africa	267	1 757	5 626	8 254	9 031	13 752	12 006	13 859
Developing economies: America	**6 492**	**9 733**	**96 763**	**78 488**	**52 812**	**43 845**	**85 710**	**90 047**
Central America and Greater Carribean Islands excluding Puerto Rico	2 639	3 372	21 020	30 918	21 423	17 588	22 906	22 239
Central America and Greater Carribean Islands excluding Mexico and Puerto Rico	539	739	3 432	3 767	3 149	3 405	4 232	4 184
South America and Central America	6 103	8 905	77 407	67 855	48 505	40 244	58 956	65 428
South America excluding Brazil	1 687	4 861	25 033	16 182	11 898	13 851	19 273	29 631
Developing economies: Asia	**663**	**22 642**	**147 993**	**112 045**	**96 125**	**110 137**	**156 622**	**199 554**
Eastern and South-Eastern Asia excluding China	3 649	18 125	99 101	51 533	30 381	38 589	70 110	82 922
Southern Asia excluding India	205	-24	1 112	1 004	1 903	1 626	1 927	3 197

Sources:
- UNCTAD, *World Investment Report 2006: FDI from Developing and Transition Economies: Implications for Development*

Outward flows - Flux sortants Millions de dollars								Groupements économiques
1980	1990	2000	2001	2002	2003	2004	2005	
3 148	**11 945**	**133 463**	**79 818**	**45 413**	**39 742**	**113 371**	**122 936**	**ÉCONOMIES EN DÉVELOPPEMENT**
3 148	11 115	132 548	72 933	42 895	39 894	111 566	111 630	Économies en développement sans la Chine
2 921	11 950	132 673	80 067	44 924	39 614	113 227	122 672	Économies en développement sans les PMA
957	8 857	125 276	73 744	32 780	30 834	88 902	92 639	Pays à revenu élevé
1 860	1 754	5 496	-2 175	7 456	6 937	16 178	13 814	Pays à revenu intermédiaire
331	1 335	2 691	8 250	5 177	1 921	8 290	16 483	Pays à revenu faible
221	43	775	-239	463	131	140	246	Pays pauvres très endettés
9	33	28	387	826	1 021	-53	1 338	Pays sans littoral
137	53	126	231	213	346	167	289	Petits états insulaires en développement
228	*-4*	*790*	*-249*	*489*	*128*	*144*	*264*	*Pays les moins avancés*
228	-7	780	-277	467	110	128	247	Afrique et Haïti
0	1	9	27	21	16	16	16	Asie
0	2	1	1	0	1	1	1	Îles
704	*21*	*1 337*	*-1 422*	*2 172*	*-1 506*	*9 147*	*19 156*	*Principaux exportateurs de pétrole*
91	558	334	302	139	212	288	362	Afrique
13	377	544	261	1 133	1 543	-294	1 582	Amérique
599	-914	459	-1 985	900	-3 261	9 153	17 213	Asie
912	*12 749*	*84 036*	*50 812*	*37 073*	*23 075*	*87 723*	*74 234*	*Principaux exportateurs d'articles manufacturés*
370	848	2 645	2 146	3 373	1 503	14 239	8 687	Amérique
542	11 901	81 391	48 665	33 700	21 572	73 484	65 547	Asie
673	*9 551*	*27 005*	*32 672*	*14 889*	*18 049*	*38 494*	*31 128*	*Économies émergentes*
303	940	7 386	3 991	3 089	3 943	15 993	12 050	Amérique
370	8 611	19 619	28 681	11 800	14 106	22 501	19 077	Asie
544	*11 070*	*79 246*	*40 011*	*29 510*	*19 916*	*72 204*	*54 864*	*Économies nouvellement industrialisées*
248	10 776	76 967	39 413	27 252	17 742	66 031	48 419	Premier tier
296	294	2 279	598	2 257	2 173	6 173	6 445	Deuxième tier
1 089	**689**	**1 524**	**-2 663**	**334**	**1 159**	**1 885**	**1 054**	**Économies en développement : Afrique**
87	135	227	302	52	123	182	439	Afrique septentrionale sans le Soudan
1 002	554	1 296	-2 965	282	1 036	1 704	616	Afrique subsaharienne
247	526	1 026	215	681	471	352	548	Afrique sub-saharienne sans l'Afrique du Sud
901	**300**	**49 727**	**35 283**	**10 353**	**19 537**	**28 040**	**38 298**	**Économies en développement : Amérique**
358	936	-177	5 626	2 988	4 214	6 042	7 968	Amérique centrale et Grandes Antilles sans Porto Rico
354	713	-540	1 222	2 097	2 961	1 610	1 797	Amérique centrale et Grandes Antilles sans le Mexique et Porto Rico
779	2 018	7 567	5 386	7 001	9 104	17 332	19 840	Amérique du Sud et Amérique centrale
55	486	5 597	2 080	1 617	4 719	1 575	9 449	Amérique du Sud sans le Brésil
1 141	**10 946**	**82 211**	**47 140**	**34 721**	**18 979**	**83 429**	**83 557**	**Économies en développement : Asie**
544	11 072	79 289	40 041	29 611	19 995	72 105	54 854	Asie orientale et Asie du Sud-Est sans la Chine
2	4	36	26	82	-303	87	168	Asie meridionale sans l'Inde

Sources :
- CNUCED, *World Investment Report 2006: FDI from Developing and Transition Economies: Implications for Development*

7

Trade group	Inward flows - Flux entrants Millions of dollars							
	1980	1990	2000	2001	2002	2003	2004	2005
AFRICA								
CEPGL	131	-6	43	86	120	163	21	1 351
COMESA	919	777	3 641	4 129	3 935	6 375	6 394	10 032
ECCAS	374	-336	1 272	3 633	3 215	6 344	4 589	4 625
ECOWAS	-461	1 547	2 135	1 994	2 813	3 252	3 240	4 442
MRU	54	276	70	20	34	458	331	323
SADC	361	54	3 098	10 389	4 179	6 145	4 022	9 446
CEMAC (UDEAC)	206	4	347	1 398	1 420	2 676	3 121	3 291
UEMOA	208	239	514	563	624	473	620	516
UMA	-378	420	1 868	4 434	2 683	4 003	2 241	5 173
AMERICA								
ANCOM	384	1 512	9 362	9 388	7 029	7 504	7 460	17 364
CACM	188	268	1 360	1 538	1 620	1 296	1 723	1 892
CARICOM	262	581	1 748	2 029	1 775	2 286	2 369	2 835
FTAA	29 164	65 510	460 856	258 000	147 809	103 954	185 894	202 201
LAIA	5 678	8 399	75 375	65 747	46 795	38 220	56 104	62 633
MERCOSUR	2 907	2 937	43 575	25 004	18 939	12 233	22 793	20 548
NAFTA	24 825	58 638	398 376	214 295	114 882	74 945	142 609	151 320
OECS	51	221	10 244	3 884	1 843	3 691	18 050	10 104
ASIA								
APTA	204	4 536	53 736	56 766	61 962	62 580	74 541	87 194
ASEAN	2 756	12 821	23 541	19 497	15 773	19 915	25 664	37 133
ECO	172	600	2 965	7 126	6 698	8 376	12 157	15 522
GCC	-3 403	149	383	1 959	2 713	6 598	12 590	20 111
SAARC	194	575	4 658	6 414	6 982	5 727	7 301	9 764
EUROPE								
EFTA	82	6 509	25 393	11 157	7 005	20 305	3 868	11 537
EU 25	21 494	90 509	696 085	381 975	307 081	253 728	213 726	421 899
Euro Zone	10 945	55 895	498 268	287 356	241 043	216 213	127 126	204 631
OCEANIA								
MSG	117	506	92	103	45	141	142	43
INTERREGIONAL								
ACP	729	2 903	9 431	18 370	12 531	17 557	16 607	24 203
APEC	31 241	93 441	572 428	335 586	234 084	199 382	349 187	298 579
BSEC	690	1 693	8 097	11 209	9 362	20 758	36 816	44 141
CIS	..	..	5 449	7 288	9 035	15 736	26 295	27 234

Sources:
- UNCTAD, *World Investment Report 2006: FDI from Developing and Transition Economies: Implications for Development*

Outward flows - Flux sortants Millions de dollars								Groupements commerciaux
1980	1990	2000	2001	2002	2003	2004	2005	
								AFRIQUE
-1	0	-2	1	-1	0	0	0	CEPGL
20	37	86	30	83	39	239	209	COMESA
-1	52	31	59	10	5	40	1	CEEAC
232	442	972	-212	606	278	328	414	CEDEAO
231	-3	780	-308	393	80	92	186	UFM
766	59	331	-2 805	-322	768	1 359	212	SADC
0	51	14	42	-18	-19	5	-28	CEMAC (UDEAC)
-3	26	16	-3	36	24	-35	15	UEMOA
80	123	177	290	24	101	23	347	UMA
								AMÉRIQUE
120	444	703	297	1 886	2 318	-418	6 146	ANCOM
8	1	46	36	37	78	34	203	MCAC
116	32	104	160	196	343	124	217	CARICCM
24 224	38 267	195 031	166 419	168 928	160 276	283 147	41 425	ZLEA
425	1 334	8 240	4 227	4 990	6 222	15 814	18 137	ALADI
258	660	3 188	-2 085	1 871	1 044	10 272	3 674	MERCOSUR
23 332	36 442	187 665	165 305	162 609	152 121	270 123	27 539	ALENA
0	-2 520	34 402	22 556	8 995	5 285	5 880	15 994	OECO
								ASIE
30	1 889	6 437	10 723	6 829	4 632	8 499	17 030	ACAP
394	2 328	8 231	20 782	4 574	5 402	14 700	11 970	ANASE
2	-14	912	495	994	974	904	2 436	ECO
586	-903	278	-2 092	644	-2 996	5 722	14 072	CCG
-1	10	524	1 449	1 722	1 378	2 092	1 456	SAARC
								EUROPE
253	8 618	58 264	38 569	15 877	30 850	33 073	64 008	AELE
23 872	121 258	813 137	435 388	265 815	286 106	334 915	554 802	UE 25
15 253	87 036	511 199	354 718	197 776	197 795	224 839	412 593	Zone Euro
								OCÉANIE
18	11	2	58	1	1	4	17	MSG
								INTERRÉGIONAUX
1 135	597	1 463	-2 773	492	1 343	1 834	850	ACP
26 887	99 019	310 347	265 724	239 256	228 269	407 271	112 583	CEAP
..	10	6 182	3 672	4 753	11 654	16 747	17 372	CEMN
..	..	3 186	2 549	4 097	10 558	13 772	14 560	CEI

Sources :
- CNUCED, *World Investment Report 2006: FDI from Developing and Transition Economies: Implications for Development*

Developing countries ranked by 2004 values / Pays en développemnt classés d'après les valeurs de 2004	Total amount (millions of dollars) / Montant total (millions de dollars)						As percentage of exports of goods and services (1) / En pourcentage des exportations de biens et services (1)					
	1990	1995	2000	2003	2004	2005	1990	1995	2000	2003	2004	2005
India - Inde	2 384	6 223	12 890	21 727	(e)19 736	(e)23 499	10.4	16.4	21.5	26.3	..	..
Mexico - Mexique	3 098	4 368	7 525	14 911	18 143	21 772	6.3	4.9	4.2	8.4	9.0	9.5
Philippines	1 465	5 360	6 924	10 239	11 468	13 561	12.8	20.0	17.0	26.4	26.8	30.3
China - Chine	124	350	758	4 625	6 641	8 832	0.2	0.2	0.3	1.0	1.0	1.1
Lebanon - Liban	..	..	..	4 743	5 591	4 924	..	..	..	42.4	47.6	37.8
Morocco - Maroc	2 006	1 970	2 161	3 614	4 221	(e)4 482	32.2	21.8	20.7	25.4	25.4	23.9
Pakistan	2 006	1 712	1 075	3 964	3 945	4 280	29.4	16.8	10.6	26.7	24.6	22.5
Bangladesh	779	1 202	1 968	3 192	3 584	4 252	37.7	27.1	27.3	39.6	38.8	40.8
Egypt - Égypte	4 284	3 226	2 852	2 961	3 341	(a)(p)4 330	43.3	24.3	16.9	14.8	12.6	14.1
Colombia - Colombie	495	815	1 610	3 076	3 190	3 345	5.7	6.6	10.2	19.6	16.4	13.7
Brazil - Brésil	537	2 952	1 350	2 287	2 813	2 805	1.5	5.6	2.1	2.7	2.6	2.1
Guatemala	119	358	596	2 147	2 591	..	7.6	12.7	15.4	52.1	57.0	..
El Salvador	366	1 064	1 764	2 121	2 563	(a)2 830	37.6	52.2	48.2	51.7	58.1	61.9
Dominican Republic - République dominicaine	315	839	1 839	2 325	2 501	2 700	17.2	14.6	20.5	26.0	26.5	26.9
Jordan - Jordanie	499	1 244	1 845	2 201	2 287	(a)2 500	19.9	35.8	52.2	45.7	38.5	38.0
Nigeria - Nigéria	10	804	1 392	1 063	2 273	..	0.1	6.5	6.6	3.9	6.0	..
Indonesia - Indonésie	166	651	1 190	1 489	1 866	1 865	0.6	1.2	1.7	2.1	2.3	1.9
Thailand - Thaïlande	973	1 695	1 697	1 607	1 622	1 187	3.3	2.4	2.1	1.7	1.4	0.9
Ecuador - Équateur	51	386	1 322	1 545	1 610	..	1.6	7.4	22.1	21.1	17.9	..
Jamaica - Jamaïque	229	639	878	1 380	1 601	..	10.3	18.8	24.5	39.2	41.1	..
Sri Lanka	401	801	1 154	1 423	1 574	..	17.5	17.3	18.1	21.8	21.6	..
Tunisia - Tunisie	551	680	796	1 250	1 432	..	10.6	8.5	9.2	11.4	10.8	..
Sudan - Soudan	62	346	641	1 224	1 403	1 016	12.4	50.8	34.9	47.5	36.7	20.6
Yemen - Yémen	1 498	1 081	1 288	1 270	1 283	1 283	100.6	50.0	32.1	29.9	25.4	19.0
Honduras	63	124	416	867	1 151	1 796	6.1	7.6	16.7	32.3	37.0	52.4
Peru - Pérou	87	599	718	860	1 123	1 440	2.1	9.0	8.5	8.0	7.7	7.4
Syrian Arab Republic - République arabe syrienne	385	339	180	889	855	..	7.7	5.9	2.6	12.5	10.7	..
Nepal - Népal	..	57	111	771	823	..	..	5.5	8.7	71.7	66.7	..
Turkey - Turquie	3 246	3 327	4 560	729	804	851	15.4	9.1	9.1	1.1	0.9	0.8
Korea, Republic of - Corée, République de	1 030	1 065	645	775	743	738	1.4	0.7	0.3	0.3	0.2	0.2
Malaysia - Malaisie	185	116	342	571	689	..	0.6	0.1	0.3	0.5	0.5	..
Nicaragua	..	75	320	439	519	600	..	11.3	29.0	33.6	31.4	32.3
South Africa - Afrique du Sud	108	83	325	391	468	614	0.4	0.2	0.9	0.8	0.8	0.9
Lesotho	428	411	252	288	355	..	427.6	206.3	99.4	54.8	46.0	..
Uganda - Ouganda	..	..	238	285	347	642	..	..	35.9	34.3	32.5	47.8
Costa Rica	12	123	136	321	320	420	0.6	2.8	1.8	3.9	3.7	4.3
Argentina - Argentine	..	64	86	256	292	413	..	0.3	0.3	0.7	0.7	0.9
China, Taiwan Province of - Chine, Taiwan Province de (1)	..	(a)142	(a)274	(a)261	(a)278	(a)323	..	..	..	..	..	..
Paraguay	34	287	278	222	260	..	1.3	6.0	9.5	8.1	7.4	..
China, Hong Kong SAR - Chine, Hong Kong RAS	..	..	136	120	240	240	..	..	0.1	0.0	0.1	0.1
Bolivia - Bolivie	4	5	127	158	211	337	0.4	0.4	8.6	8.1	8.2	10.7
Mongolia - Mongolie	..	..	12	129	203	..	..	..	2.0	15.4	16.7	..
Côte d'Ivoire	44	151	119	142	148	..	1.3	3.5	2.7	2.2	1.9	..
Cambodia - Cambodge	..	12	103	128	147	164	..	1.2	5.6	4.9	4.3	4.1
Ethiopia - Éthiopie	..	27	53	46	134	..	..	3.6	5.4	3.7	7.9	..
Panama	110	112	16	94	127	126	2.5	1.5	0.2	1.2	1.4	1.2
Myanmar	6	81	104	85	118	..	1.9	6.2	4.8	2.9	3.7	..
Barbados - Barbade	38	53	100	113	109	..	4.3	4.7	7.3	7.9	7.2	..
Guyana	..	..	27	99	100	..	..	..	4.1	14.9	13.5	..
Swaziland	111	82	74	88	89	..	16.8	8.1	6.5	4.7	4.0	..

Sources:
- International Monetary Fund (IMF), *Balance of Payments Statistics* on CD-ROM
- National sources

Sources :
- Fonds monétaire international (FMI), *Statistiques de la balance des paiements* sur CD-ROM
- Sources nationales

Notes:
- This table includes workers' remittances and compensation of employees in the values shown.
(1) Trade data in this calculation correspond to IMF balance-of-payments series.

(a) National sources.

Notes :
- Les valeurs dans ce tableau incluent les envois de fonds des travailleurs et la rémunération des salariés.
(1) Les données du commerce utilisées dans ce calcul proviennent de la série de la balance des paiements du FMI.

(a) Sources nationales.

Developing countries ranked by 2004 values Pays en développemnt classés d'après les valeurs de 2004	Total amount (millions of dollars) Montant total (millions de dollars)						As percentage of exports of goods and services (1) En pourcentage des exportations de biens et services (1)					
	1990	1995	2000	2003	2004	2005	1990	1995	2000	2003	2004	2005
Saudi Arabia - Arabie saoudite	11 221	16 594	15 390	14 783	13 555	14 318	25.6	37.0	29.1	27.0	20.3	18.1
Malaysia - Malaisie	(b)182	1 329	(b)599	3 464	4 990	..	0.6	1.5	0.6	3.6	4.2	..
Lebanon - Liban	..	..	..	4 081	4 233	4 018	..	..	..	31.4	25.3	24.8
Kuwait - Koweït	770	1 354	1 734	2 144	2 402	..	10.7	10.7	15.3	13.0	12.5	..
China - Chine	5	..	754	1 597	1 998	2 550	0.0	..	0.3	0.4	0.3	0.4
Oman	856	1 537	1 451	1 672	1 826	(a)(p)2 258	25.6	30.5	22.8	20.2	17.2	20.4
China, Taiwan Province of - Chine, Taiwan Province de	..	(a)945	(a)1 544	(a)1 172	(a)1 251	(a)1 342	..	..	..	..	..	..
Bahrain - Bahreïn	332	500	1 013	1 082	1 120	..	8.3	12.1	19.7	17.4	15.8	..
South Africa - Afrique du Sud	1 116	567	614	706	935	1 042	5.3	1.7	1.9	1.6	1.6	1.5
Indonesia - Indonésie	..	..	..	..	913	1 200	..	..	..	..	1.3	1.4
Libyan Arab Jamahiriya - Jamahiriya arabe libyenne	446	222	463	676	790	..	5.0	3.9	9.2	7.7	7.4	..
Korea, Republic of - Corée, République de	26	132	278	457	685	950	0.0	0.1	0.1	0.2	0.3	0.3
Côte d'Ivoire	471	457	390	628	635	..	13.7	12.0	10.7	12.5	10.0	..
Jamaica - Jamaïque	11	50	152	322	391	..	0.5	1.3	3.4	6.6	7.4	..
Brazil - Brésil	11	336	338	296	339	374	0.0	0.5	0.5	0.5	0.4	0.4
China, Hong Kong SAR - Chine, Hong Kong RAS	..	..	225	317	321	335	..	..	0.1	0.1	0.1	0.1
Angola	150	210	266	230	296	..	4.4	6.0	4.6	2.6	2.8	..
Jordan - Jordanie	71	107	197	227	272	..	2.0	2.2	3.4	3.3	2.9	0.3
Uganda - Ouganda	..	..	353	257	258	369	..	..	25.1	14.7	12.1	14.3
Sri Lanka	..	13	14	224	230	..	..	0.2	0.2	2.9	2.5	..
Venezuela (Bolivarian Republic of) - Venezuela (République bolivarienne du)	701	203	331	209	214	211	7.4	1.2	1.6	1.5	1.0	0.7
Argentina - Argentine	..	195	268	158	205	279	..	0.7	0.8	0.8	0.7	0.8
Costa Rica	..	36	142	192	192	209	..	0.8	2.0	2.3	2.1	1.9
China, Macao SAR - Chine, Macao RAS	..	..	..	94	132	..	..	..	..	1.9	2.2	..
Swaziland	4	3	21	130	130	..	0.5	0.3	1.5	7.2	5.8	..
Yemen - Yémen	106	61	61	60	108	109	4.9	2.5	1.8	1.3	2.2	2.1
Panama	22	20	22	57	87	91	0.5	0.3	0.3	0.7	1.0	0.9
Bahamas	39	32	56	63	71	..	2.3	1.8	1.9	2.2	2.3	..
Nepal - Népal	..	9	17	26	64	..	..	0.6	0.9	1.4	2.8	..
Maldives	8	27	46	55	62	..	5.2	3.6	10.3	10.3	8.5	..
Guyana	..	9	27	50	57	..	..	1.3	3.7	7.2	7.1	..
Cambodia - Cambodge	..	52	60	56	56	88	..	3.8	2.6	1.8	1.5	1.9
Netherlands Antilles - Antilles néerlandaises	8	9	46	52	52	..	0.5	0.4	1.9	2.1	1.9	..
Aruba	..	5	44	53	51	61	..	0.2	1.4	1.7	1.3	1.4
Bolivia - Bolivie	8	9	37	46	51	67	0.7	0.6	1.8	2.2	2.2	2.3
Colombia - Colombie	44	150	219	65	50	56	0.6	0.9	1.5	0.4	0.3	0.2
Mongolia - Mongolie	..	..	3	54	49	..	..	..	0.4	5.0	3.5	..
Guinea - Guinée	20	10	27	46	48	..	2.1	1.0	3.1	4.9	5.0	..
Syrian Arab Republic - République arabe syrienne	..	15	29	40	42	..	..	0.3	0.5	0.6	0.5	..
Guatemala	14	8	56	86	36	..	0.7	0.2	1.0	1.2	0.4	..
Morocco - Maroc	11	15	23	34	34	(e)41	0.1	0.1	0.2	0.2	0.2	0.2
United Republic of Tanzania - République-Unie de Tanzanie	..	1	20	28	32	..	..	0.0	1.0	1.0	1.0	..
El Salvador	3	..	19	24	32	(a)24	0.2	..	0.3	0.4	0.5	0.3
Rwanda	19	1	28	30	31	35	5.4	0.3	6.6	6.9	5.9	5.2
Lesotho	..	75	28	27	29	..	..	7.2	3.6	2.5	2.1	..
Myanmar	..	..	14	23	25	..	..	..	0.6	1.0	1.0	..
Dominican Republic - République dominicaine	..	7	19	23	24	25	..	0.1	0.2	0.3	0.3	0.2
Nigeria - Nigéria	9	5	1	12	21	..	0.1	0.0	0.0	0.1	0.1	..
Mozambique	25	21	156	29	20	21	2.6	2.0	10.5	1.3	0.9	0.7
Barbados - Barbade	6	14	16	19	18	..	0.7	1.3	1.1	1.2	1.0	..

Sources:
- International Monetary Fund (IMF), *Balance of Payments Statistics* on CD-ROM
- National sources

Sources :
- Fonds monetaire international (FMI), *Statistiques de la balance des paiements* sur CD-ROM
- Sources nationales

Notes:
- Includes workers' remittances and compensation of employees.

(1) Trade data in this calculation correspond to IMF balance-of-payments series.

(a) National sources.
(b) Includes compensation of employees only.

Notes :
- Les valeurs dans ce tableau incluent les envois de fonds des travailleurs et la rémunération des salariés.

(1) Les données du commerce utilisées dans ce calcul proviennent de la série de la balance des paiements du FMI.

(a) Sources nationales.
(b) Comprend uniquement la rémunération des salariés.

357

Region, country or territory	Total reserves minus gold (1) - Réserves totales moins l'or (1) Millions of dollars - Millions de dollars							
	1980	1990	2000	2001	2002	2003	2004	2005
DEVELOPING ECONOMIES	157 092	308 199	1 028 706	1 120 969	1 329 181	1 676 500	2 128 534	2 489 938
Developing economies: Africa	33 208	25 252	79 075	91 500	98 788	122 492	164 866	219 171
Eastern Africa	*1 385*	*2 293*	*5 977*	*6 475*	*8 142*	*9 423*	*10 973*	*10 672*
Burundi	95	105	33	18	59	67	66	100
Comoros	6	30	43	62	80	94	104	86
Djibouti	..	94	68	70	74	100	94	89
Ethiopia (former)	80	20	–	–	–	–	–	–
Eritrea	–	–	26	40	30	25	35	28
Ethiopia	–	–	306	433	882	956	1 497	1 121
Kenya	492	205	898	1 065	1 068	1 482	1 519	1 799
Madagascar	9	92	285	398	363	414	504	481
Malawi	68	137	243	203	161	122	128	159
Mauritius	91	738	897	836	1 227	1 577	1 606	1 340
Mozambique	..	232	723	713	802	937	1 131	1 054
Rwanda	196	44	191	212	244	215	315	406
Seychelles	18	17	44	37	70	67	35	56
Somalia	15	..	..	..	..	..	..	..
Uganda	3	44	808	983	934	1 080	1 308	1 344
United Republic of Tanzania	20	193	974	1 157	1 529	2 038	2 296	2 049
Zambia	78	193	245	183	535	248	337	560
Zimbabwe	213	149	193	65	83	..	..	..
Middle Africa	*646*	*771*	*2 101*	*1 470*	*1 624*	*2 088*	*4 101*	*8 041*
Angola	..	..	1 198	732	376	634	1 374	3 197
Cameroon	189	26	212	332	630	640	829	949
Central African Republic	55	119	133	119	123	132	148	139
Chad	5	128	111	122	219	187	222	226
Congo	86	6	222	69	32	35	120	732
Dem. Rep. of the Congo	204	219	..	..	..	..	..	..
Equatorial Guinea	..	1	23	71	89	238	945	2 102
Gabon	108	274	190	10	140	197	443	669
São Tome and Principe	..	..	12	15	17	25	20	27
Northern Africa	*18 947*	*12 120*	*44 374*	*56 321*	*63 459*	*83 624*	*104 819*	*138 913*
Algeria	3 773	725	12 024	18 081	23 237	33 125	43 246	56 303
Egypt	1 046	2 684	13 118	12 926	13 242	13 589	14 273	20 609
Libyan Arab Jamahiriya	13 091	5 839	12 461	14 801	14 307	19 584	25 689	39 508
Morocco	399	2 066	4 823	8 474	10 133	13 851	16 337	16 187
Sudan	49	11	138	50	249	529	1 338	1 869
Tunisia	590	795	1 811	1 989	2 290	2 945	3 936	4 437
Southern Africa	*1 269*	*4 629*	*13 431*	*12 835*	*12 384*	*12 898*	*19 973*	*25 963*
Botswana	334	3 331	6 318	5 897	5 474	5 340	5 661	6 309
Lesotho	50	72	418	386	406	460	502	519
Namibia	..	..	260	234	323	325	345	312
South Africa	726	1 008	6 083	6 045	5 904	6 496	13 141	18 579
Swaziland	159	216	352	272	276	278	324	244
Western Africa	*10 961*	*5 440*	*13 192*	*14 399*	*13 179*	*14 459*	*25 000*	*35 582*
Benin	8	65	458	578	616	718	640	657
Burkina Faso	68	300	244	261	313	752	669	438
Cape Verde	42	77	28	45	80	94	140	174
Côte d'Ivoire	20	4	668	1 019	1 863	1 304	1 694	1 322
Gambia	6	55	109	106	107	59	84	98
Ghana	180	219	232	298	540	1 353	1 627	1 753
Guinea	..	..	148	200	171	..	110	95
Guinea-Bissau	..	18	67	69	103	33	73	80
Liberia	5	..	0	0	3	7	19	25
Mali	15	191	381	349	594	952	861	855
Mauritania	140	54	280	284	396	415	..	..
Niger	126	222	80	107	134	260	258	250
Nigeria	10 235	3 864	9 911	10 457	7 331	7 128	16 956	28 280
Senegal	8	11	384	447	637	1 111	1 386	1 191
Sierra Leone	31	5	49	51	85	67	125	171
Togo	78	353	152	126	205	205	360	195
Developing economies: America	38 877	47 448	156 425	158 707	160 787	195 485	220 615	255 378
Caribbean	*3 411*	*1 478*	*4 901*	*7 071*	*6 493*	*6 374*	*8 511*	*11 509*
Anguilla	..	7	20	24	26	33	34	40
Antigua and Barbuda	8	28	64	80	88	114	120	127
Aruba	..	98	208	294	340	295	295	274
Bahamas	92	158	350	319	381	491	674	586
Barbados	79	118	473	690	669	738	580	603
Dominica	5	14	29	31	45	48	42	49
Dominican Republic	202	62	627	1 099	468	253	798	1 843
Grenada	13	18	58	64	88	83	122	94
Haiti	16	3	182	141	82	62	114	133

For sources and notes, see end of table.

Annual change in reserves (millions of dollars) Variations annuelles des réserves (millions de dollars)				Number of months of imports (2) Nombre de mois d'importations (2)								Régions, pays ou territoires
2001-2002	2002-2003	2003-2004	2004-2005	1980	1990	2000	2001	2002	2003	2004	2005	
208 212	347 319	452 033	361 404	3.6	4.4	6.6	7.2	7.7	7.9	8.2	8.2	ÉCONOMIES EN DÉVELOPPEMENT
7 288	23 704	42 374	54 305	4.0	3.2	7.1	7.9	7.6	7.7	8.7	10.0	Économies en développement : Afrique
1 667	1 281	1 550	-301	1.6	2.3	4.1	4.3	5.1	4.9	4.6	3.9	Afrique orientale
41	8	-1	34	6.9	5.2	2.8	1.6	4.9	4.8	3.6	3.8	Burundi
18	14	9	-18	2.5	6.5	11.1	14.5	15.7	14.6	14.3	11.0	Comores
3	26	-6	-5	..	5.2	3.1	3.1	3.4	4.8	4.2	..	Djibouti
—	—	—	—	1.3	0.3							Éthiopie (anc.)
-9	-6	10	-7	—	—	0.7	1.0	0.7	0.6	0.9	0.6	Érythrée
449	74	541	-375	—	—	2.4	3.0	5.7	4.4	5.0	3.0	Éthiopie
3	414	37	280	2.9	1.2	3.4	4.0	3.7	4.3	3.4	3.2	Kenya
-35	51	89	-22	0.2	2.2	3.5	6.1	7.0	4.7	4.3	4.2	Madagascar
-41	-39	6	31	2.1	2.6	5.3	3.9	2.6	1.7	1.5	1.8	Malawi
392	350	29	-266	1.8	5.6	5.1	4.8	6.5	7.4	6.5	4.9	Maurice
89	135	193	-77	..	3.1	7.8	6.6	5.8	5.9	6.1	5.2	Mozambique
32	-29	100	91	8.8	1.8	9.3	9.6	11.5	9.5	10.5	10.3	Rwanda
33	-2	-33	22	2.3	1.1	1.3	1.0	2.0	1.8	0.8	0.9	Seychelles
..	..	..	..	0.4								Somalie
-49	146	228	36	. 0.1	2.2	6.2	8.7	9.5	7.9	8.0	7.3	Ouganda
372	510	257	-247	0.2	1.6	7.2	8.2	9.5	10.4	10.4	7.5	République-Unie de Tanzanie
352	-287	89	223	0.9	2.3	2.6	1.7	4.5	1.7	1.8	2.7	Zambie
19	..	..	..	1.6	0.9	1.3	0.4	0.5	..	..	..	Zimbabwe
154	464	2 013	3 940	1.3	1.5	2.8	1.7	1.6	1.7	2.7	4.4	Afrique centrale
-356	. 259	740	1 823	..	..	4.6	2.5	1.0	1.3	2.3	3.9	Angola
298	10	190	120	1.5	0.2	1.5	2.1	3.7	3.4	3.8	3.7	Cameroun
4	9	16	-9	7.5	11.5	14.3	12.5	12.4	12.0	11.2	9.4	République centrafricaine
96	-32	35	4	0.7	5.7	2.7	1.3	2.2	2.7	2.7	2.3	Tchad
-37	3	85	612	2.0	0.1	2.9	0.8	0.3	0.3	0.8	4.5	Congo
..	..	..	..	1.7	1.7	..	..	..	..	..	..	Rép. dém. du Congo
18	149	707	1 158	..	0.1	0.4	1.3	1.2	2.0	6.2	12.2	Guinée équatoriale
130	57	247	225	1.7	3.7	2.3	0.1	1.7	2.1	4.1	5.5	Gabon
2	8	-6	7	..	..	4.8	6.2	5.8	7.4	5.1	5.5	Sao Tomé-et-Principe
7 139	20 165	21 195	34 094	6.5	3.5	10.8	13.1	13.6	15.3	15.8	18.4	Afrique septentrionale
5 156	9 888	10 121	13 057	4.1	0.8	15.1	20.3	22.9	25.6	27.2	32.9	Algérie
317	346	684	6 336	1.8	2.6	11.8	12.3	13.4	13.6	10.5	12.2	Égypte
-493	5 277	6 105	13 819	20.7	13.1	35.1	35.9	29.2	33.8	39.9	52.3	Jamahiriya arabe libyenne
1 659	3 718	2 485	-149	1.1	3.6	5.1	8.9	9.3	10.4	10.3	9.0	Maroc
199	281	809	531	0.4	0.2	0.9	0.2	1.1	2.0	3.6	4.4	Soudan
301	655	990	501	1.9	1.8	2.4	2.5	2.7	3.0	3.6	3.8	Tunisie
-452	515	7 074	5 990	0.7	3.0	4.7	4.6	3.6	2.8	3.6	4.2	Afrique australe
-423	-134	322	648	..	..	35.4	37.9	29.7	21.9	20.6	24.5	Botswana
20	54	41	18	..	..	7.3	6.2	5.1	4.5	4.4	4.5	Lesotho
89	2	20	-33	..	..	2.0	2.0	2.4	1.8	1.7	1.6	Namibie
-141	591	6 646	5 438	0.4	0.7	2.5	2.5	2.0	1.6	2.7	3.4	Afrique du Sud
4	2	46	-80	..	..	3.8	3.1	2.6	1.9	2.0	1.4	Swaziland
-1 220	1 279	10 542	10 582	4.8	4.1	7.0	7.1	5.7	5.5	8.5	10.1	Afrique occidentale
38	102	-78	17	0.2	3.1	8.9	10.3	9.1	9.6	8.6	8.9	Bénin
53	439	-83	-231	2.4	6.8	4.6	4.5	4.5	8.2	6.3	4.0	Burkina Faso
34	14	46	34	7.3	6.5	1.5	2.1	3.1	3.0	4.1	4.1	Cap-Vert
844	-559	390	-372	0.1	0.0	3.1	5.0	7.9	4.2	4.3	2.9	Côte d'Ivoire
1	-48	24	15	0.5	3.4	8.2	8.6	8.1	3.7	4.3	5.0	Gambie
242	813	274	126	1.9	2.3	0.9	1.3	2.2	4.3	4.0	3.6	Ghana
-29	..	..	-15	..	..	2.9	3.8	3.1	..	1.8	..	Guinée
33	-70	40	7	..	2.7	14.5	13.9	19.9	5.3	8.7	7.9	Guinée-Bissau
3	4	11	7	0.1	..	0.0	0.0	0.2	0.3	0.7	0.9	Libéria
246	358	-92	-6	0.4	4.3	5.1	4.4	6.5	9.0	7.1	6.9	Mali
112	19	..	..	6.1	2.1	7.3	8.3	12.8	10.6	..	..	Mauritanie
27	126	-2	-8	2.7	7.2	2.4	2.9	2.9	4.5	4.0	3.8	Niger
-3 125	-203	9 827	11 324	6.5	6.3	11.7	10.4	6.4	5.9	13.9	18.0	Nigéria
190	474	275	-195	0.1	0.1	2.8	2.9	3.5	5.1	5.3	4.0	Sénégal
33	-18	58	45	1.0	0.4	3.6	2.8	3.6	2.7	4.8	5.5	Sierra Leone
79	0	155	-165	1.9	8.3	3.3	2.7	3.6	3.0	4.6	2.3	Togo
2 080	34 699	25 130	34 763	3.6	4.2	4.9	5.2	5.4	5.8	5.5	5.5	Économies en développement : Amérique
-579	-118	2 137	2 998	1.5	1.0	1.9	2.9	2.7	2.5	3.0	3.5	Caraïbes
2	7	1	5	..	..	..	..	..	..	..	..	Anguilla
8	26	6	7	0.9	1.2	2.0	2.5	2.6	3.1	2.7	..	Antigua-et-Barbuda
46	-45	0	-22	..	2.3	3.0	4.2	4.8	4.1	3.7	..	Aruba
61	110	183	-88	0.1	1.7	2.1	2.1	2.6	3.2	3.9	2.8	Bahamas
-22	69	-158	24	1.7	2.0	5.1	7.7	7.1	6.8	4.6	4.7	Barbade
14	2	-5	7	1.3	1.5	2.5	3.0	4.5	4.2	3.3	3.6	Dominique
-631	-215	545	1 045	1.2	0.2	0.8	1.5	0.7	0.4	1.2	..	République dominicaine
24	-5	39	-27	3.0	1.8	3.0	3.7	4.7	4.0	5.4	4.1	Grenade
-60	-20	52	19	0.5	0.1	2.1	1.6	0.8	0.6	1.0	1.0	Haïti

Pour les sources et les notes, se reporter à la fin du tableau.

Region, country or territory	Total reserves minus gold (1) - Réserves totales moins l'or (1) Millions of dollars - Millions de dollars							
	1980	1990	2000	2001	2002	2003	2004	2005
Jamaica	105	168	1 054	1 901	1 645	1 195	1 846	2 170
Montserrat	..	10	10	12	14	15	14	14
Netherlands Antilles	95	215	261	301	406	373	415	462
Saint Kitts and Nevis	..	16	45	56	66	65	78	72
Saint Lucia	8	45	79	89	94	107	133	116
Saint Vincent and the Grenadines	7	26	55	61	53	51	75	70
Trinidad and Tobago	2 781	492	1 386	1 907	2 028	2 451	3 168	4 856
Central America	*3 972*	*11 641*	*42 993*	*52 956*	*59 138*	*68 448*	*74 560*	*86 090*
Belize	13	70	123	112	115	85	48	71
Costa Rica	146	521	1 318	1 330	1 502	1 839	1 922	2 313
El Salvador	78	415	1 773	1 594	1 473	1 792	1 754	1 723
Guatemala	445	282	1 746	2 292	2 299	2 833	3 426	3 664
Honduras	150	40	1 313	1 416	1 524	1 430	1 970	2 327
Mexico	2 960	9 863	35 509	44 741	50 594	58 956	64 141	74 054
Nicaragua	65	107	488	380	448	502	668	728
Panama-Canal-Zone (former)	117							
Panama	–	344	723	1 092	1 183	1 011	631	1 211
South America	*31 493*	*34 329*	*108 532*	*98 680*	*95 156*	*120 663*	*137 543*	*157 778*
Argentina	6 719	4 592	25 147	14 553	10 489	14 153	18 884	27 179
Bolivia	106	167	926	886	580	717	872	1 328
Brazil	5 769	7 441	32 488	35 739	37 683	49 111	52 740	53 574
Chile	3 123	6 068	15 035	14 379	15 341	15 840	15 994	16 929
Colombia	4 831	4 628	8 916	10 154	10 732	10 784	13 394	14 787
Ecuador	1 013	838	947	840	715	813	1 070	1 714
Guyana	13	29	305	287	284	276	232	252
Paraguay	762	661	763	714	629	969	1 168	1 297
Peru	1 980	1 040	8 374	8 672	9 339	9 777	12 176	13 599
Suriname	189	21	63	119	106	106	129	126
Uruguay	384	524	2 479	3 097	769	2 083	2 508	3 074
Venezuela (Bolivarian Republic of)	6 604	8 321	13 089	9 239	8 487	16 035	18 375	23 919
Developing economies: Asia	**84 370**	**234 680**	**792 235**	**869 738**	**1 068 666**	**1 357 311**	**1 741 595**	**2 014 005**
Eastern Asia	*7 676*	*141 909*	*482 194*	*555 438*	*690 175*	*893 006*	*1 184 447*	*1 416 485*
China	2 546	29 586	168 277	215 605	291 128	408 151	614 500	821 514
China, Hong Kong SAR	..	24 568	107 542	111 155	111 896	118 360	123 540	124 244
China, Macao SAR	..	521	3 323	3 508	3 800	4 343	5 436	6 689
China, Taiwan Province of	2 205	72 441	106 742	122 211	161 656	206 632	241 738	253 290
Korea, Republic of	2 925	14 793	96 131	102 753	121 345	155 284	198 996	210 317
Mongolia	..	..	179	206	350	236	236	430
Southern Asia	*18 763*	*3 543*	*43 326*	*53 527*	*80 564*	*116 470*	*143 761*	*149 528*
Afghanistan	371	266	..	..	..	..	..	..
Bangladesh	300	629	1 486	1 275	1 683	2 578	3 172	2 767
Bhutan	..	89	318	323	355	367	399	467
India	6 944	1 521	37 902	45 871	67 665	98 938	126 593	131 924
Iran, Islamic Republic of	10 223	..	..	..	..	..	..	..
Maldives	1	24	123	93	133	159	204	186
Nepal	183	295	945	1 038	1 018	1 222	1 462	1 499
Pakistan	496	296	1 513	3 640	8 078	10 941	9 799	10 033
Sri Lanka	245	423	1 039	1 287	1 631	2 265	2 132	2 651
South-Eastern Asia	*21 013*	*59 506*	*186 758*	*183 159*	*203 725*	*237 542*	*284 231*	*296 753*
Brunei Darussalam	..	..	408	391	438	482	505	494
Cambodia	..	..	502	587	776	816	943	953
Indonesia	5 392	7 459	28 502	27 246	30 971	34 962	34 953	32 989
Lao People's Dem. Rep.	..	2	139	131	192	209	223	234
Malaysia	4 387	9 754	28 330	29 522	33 361	43 822	65 881	69 850
Myanmar	261	313	223	400	470	550	672	771
Philippines	2 846	924	13 090	13 476	13 329	13 655	13 116	15 926
Singapore	6 567	27 748	80 132	75 375	82 021	95 746	112 232	115 794
Thailand	1 560	13 305	32 016	32 355	38 046	41 077	48 664	50 691
Viet Nam	..	..	3 417	3 675	4 121	6 224	7 041	9 051
Western Asia	*36 919*	*29 722*	*79 956*	*77 614*	*94 203*	*110 293*	*129 156*	*151 240*
Bahrain	953	1 235	1 564	1 684	1 726	1 778	1 941	..
Iraq	..	..	..	..	..	..	7 824	12 104
Jordan	1 143	849	3 331	3 062	3 976	5 194	5 267	5 250
Kuwait	3 929	1 952	7 082	9 897	9 208	7 577	8 242	8 863
Lebanon	1 588	660	5 944	5 014	7 244	12 519	11 735	11 887
Oman	581	1 672	2 380	2 365	3 173	3 593	3 597	4 358
Qatar	343	631	1 158	1 313	1 567	2 944	3 396	4 542
Saudi Arabia (3)	23 437	11 668	19 585	17 596	20 610	22 620	27 291	26 530
Syrian Arab Republic	337	..	..	..	.	..	..	..
Turkey	1 077	6 050	22 488	18 879	27 069	33 991	35 669	50 579
United Arab Emirates	2 015	4 584	13 523	14 146	15 219	15 088	18 530	21 010
Yemen Arab Republic (former)	1 283							
Yemen, Democratic (former)	234	–	–	–	–	–	–	–
Yemen	–	422	2 900	3 658	4 411	4 987	5 665	6 115

For sources and notes, see end of table.

Annual change in reserves (millions of dollars) Variations annuelles des réserves (millions de dollars)				Number of months of imports (2) Nombre de mois d'importations (2)								Régions, pays ou territoires
2001-2002	2002-2003	2003-2004	2004-2005	1980	1990	2000	2001	2002	2003	2004	2005	
-255	-450	652	323	1.0	1.1	3.8	6.6	5.5	3.9	5.4	5.2	Jamaïque
2	1	-1	0	..	2.9	6.1	6.7	6.4	6.8	6.1	6.1	Montserrat
105	-33	43	46	0.2	1.2	1.1	1.4	2.0	2.0	2.3	..	Antilles néerlandaises
9	-1	14	-7	..	1.8	3.2	3.9	4.5	4.4	5.2	4.6	Saint-Kitts-et-Nevis
5	13	26	-16	0.8	1.9	2.7	3.2	3.2	3.1	3.7	3.3	Sainte-Lucie
-8	-2	24	-5	1.5	2.3	4.0	4.2	3.4	2.9	3.9	3.3	Saint-Vincent-et-les Grenadines
121	423	717	1 688	10.6	4.3	4.8	6.3	6.5	6.7	7.2	9.5	Trinité-et-Tobago
6 182	*9 311*	*6 112*	*11 530*	*1.5*	*2.5*	*2.5*	*3.2*	*3.5*	*3.7*	*3.6*	*3.7*	*Amérique centrale*
2	-30	-36	23	1.0	3.6	2.8	2.6	2.6	1.9	1.0	1.4	Belize
172	337	83	391	1.3	3.2	2.4	2.3	2.4	2.8	2.6	2.6	Costa Rica
-121	320	-38	-31	1.0	3.7	5.6	4.9	4.3	4.7	4.1	3.5	El Salvador
7	534	593	238	3.2	1.9	3.9	4.6	4.2	4.7	4.9	4.6	Guatemala
109	-94	540	357	1.8	0.5	5.4	5.7	5.8	4.8	5.5	5.6	Honduras
5 854	8 361	5 185	9 913	1.4	2.5	2.4	3.0	3.4	3.7	3.6	3.7	Mexique
68	54	166	60	0.8	1.8	3.3	2.6	3.0	2.9	3.3	3.1	Nicaragua
				..								Panama, Zone du canal de (anc.)
91	-172	-380	580	_	2.5	2.7	4.4	4.7	3.6	1.9	3.3	Panama
-3 523	*25 506*	*16 881*	*20 235*	*5.6*	*6.7*	*8.7*	*8.8*	*9.1*	*9.5*	*8.3*	*7.8*	*Amérique du Sud*
-4 064	3 664	4 731	8 295	8.1	9.0	13.2	11.9	11.0	9.4	8.9	10.4	Argentine
-306	136	156	455	1.6	2.4	6.3	6.1	4.1	5.0	5.0	6.2	Bolivie
1 944	11 427	3 629	834	2.8	3.9	6.6	7.9	9.0	10.1	8.8	7.6	Brésil
962	498	154	935	5.8	9.1	10.0	10.0	10.1	8.6	6.7	5.7	Chili
579	51	2 610	1 393	11.7	10.5	8.8	9.5	9.7	8.4	8.5	7.5	Colombie
-125	98	257	645	5.4	4.7	2.5	1.7	1.3	1.3	1.4	1.8	Équateur
-3	-8	-45	20	0.4	1.1	5.9	5.9	5.9	5.4	3.9	3.7	Guyana
-84	340	199	129	15.1	5.6	4.2	4.4	3.7	4.2	4.1	3.2	Paraguay
667	438	2 400	1 423	7.9	3.3	12.4	14.1	14.1	12.7	12.9	11.7	Pérou
-13	0	24	-4	4.2	0.5	1.5	3.0	2.1	1.7	1.7	..	Suriname
-2 328	1 314	425	566	2.8	4.2	9.1	14.8	4.4	9.4	8.6	8.5	Uruguay
-752	7 548	2 341	5 543	6.4	10.8	9.2	7.4	9.6	14.8	10.4	9.5	Venezuela (République bolivarienne du)
198 929	**288 645**	**384 284**	**272 410**	**3.4**	**4.6**	**7.1**	**7.7**	**8.3**	**8.3**	**8.7**	**8.6**	**Économies en développement : Asie**
134 737	*202 831*	*291 441*	*232 038*	*1.0*	*5.9*	*8.0*	*9.1*	*9.6*	*9.8*	*10.8*	*11.1*	*Asie orientale*
75 523	117 024	206 348	207 015	1.5	6.1	8.6	9.6	9.9	10.1	12.1	13.6	Chine
741	6 464	5 180	704	..	3.2	6.2	6.5	6.1	5.6	5.2	4.7	Chine, Hong Kong RAS
292	543	1 093	1 253	..	3.7	17.2	17.1	17.3	16.7	17.7	18.5	Chine, Macao RAS
39 445	44 975	35 107	11 551	1.3	14.7	10.4	13.3	16.2	16.8	16.5	15.8	Chine, Taiwan Province de
18 592	33 939	43 713	11 321	1.4	2.3	7.7	8.4	8.8	9.2	9.8	8.8	Corée, République de
144	-114	0	194		3.4	3.7	5.6	3.1	2.6	3.9		Mongolie
27 037	*35 907*	*27 291*	*5 767*	*5.5*	*0.7*	*5.4*	*6.2*	*7.9*	*8.9*	*8.4*	*7.1*	*Asie méridionale*
				5.2	4.1							Afghanistan
408	895	595	-405	1.4	2.1	2.1	1.9	2.3	2.8	2.9	2.2	Bangladesh
32	12	32	69	..	13.0	20.8	20.1	19.1	13.3	10.5	..	Bhoutan
21 795	31 272	27 655	5 331	5.5	0.8	8.9	10.3	12.6	13.8	12.7	10.2	Inde
..	..	..	..	8.3								Iran, Rép. islamique d'
40	26	44	-17	0.4	2.0	3.8	2.8	3.7	3.4	3.5	2.7	Maldives
-20	205	240	37	6.2	5.0	7.4	8.6	7.7	8.1	9.4	8.1	Népal
4 438	2 863	-1 142	234	1.1	0.4	1.7	4.1	8.0	8.5	5.4	4.5	Pakistan
344	634	-133	519	1.5	1.8	2.0	2.6	3.1	3.7	3.0	3.3	Sri Lanka
20 566	*33 817*	*46 689*	*12 522*	*3.6*	*4.1*	*6.3*	*6.3*	*6.5*	*6.3*	*6.2*	*5.6*	*Asie du Sud-Est*
46	44	24	-11	..	..	4.3	3.5	3.6	4.2	4.2	..	Brunéi Darussalam
189	39	128	10	..	..	3.0	3.2	3.3	3.3	3.1	2.7	Cambodge
3 725	3 992	-10	-1 963	5.4	3.8	10.6	10.5	10.1	8.7	6.7	5.4	Indonésie
61	17	15	11	..	0.1	3.1	3.3	4.8	4.9	4.1	3.1	Rép. dém. populaire lao
3 838	10 461	22 059	3 969	4.7	3.6	4.4	4.6	4.9	5.6	7.2	6.8	Malaisie
70	80	122	99	8.5	8.1	1.0	1.8	2.5	3.1	3.9	4.8	Myanmar
-147	326	-539	2 810	4.1	0.9	4.4	4.5	4.2	4.0	3.5	3.8	Philippines
6 646	13 725	16 486	3 562	3.1	5.2	7.7	7.8	8.1	7.6	7.2	6.4	Singapour
5 692	3 031	7 587	2 027	2.0	4.5	6.2	6.1	6.5	5.8	5.5	5.0	Thaïlande
446	2 103	817	2 009	..	..	2.6	2.5	2.3	2.7	2.5	3.0	Viet Nam
16 588	*16 090*	*18 863*	*22 084*	*4.8*	*4.1*	*5.7*	*5.5*	*6.1*	*5.4*	*4.8*	*4.6*	*Asie occidentale*
42	53	162	..	3.0	3.8	4.2	4.4	3.9	3.5	3.3	..	Bahreïn
..	..	..	4 280	..	..	..	..	..	.	4.3	6.1	Iraq
914	1 218	72	-16	4.9	4.0	8.4	7.4	8.8	9.0	6.8	5.7	Jordanie
-689	-1 631	665	621	7.0	5.4	11.3	14.1	11.1	7.7	6.5	6.5	Koweït
2 230	5 276	-785	153	5.3	2.5	10.5	8.8	12.8	18.1	15.0	15.4	Liban
809	420	4	761	3.5	6.8	5.3	4.8	6.1	5.6	4.9	5.4	Oman
254	1 377	452	1 146	2.8	4.4	4.0	4.0	4.2	6.5	5.1	4.8	Qatar
3 015	2 010	4 671	-761	8.6	5.3	7.7	6.7	7.5	6.9	6.3	5.2	Arabie saoudite (3)
..	..	..	..	0.9								République arabe syrienne
8 189	6 922	1 678	14 910	1.5	3.3	5.6	5.0	5.6	5.0	4.4	5.1	Turquie
1 073	-132	3 442	2 480	2.6	4.4	4.5	4.4	4.6	3.2	2.7	2.3	Émirats arabes unis
_	_	_	_	15.5	_	_	_	_	_	_	_	Rép. arabe du Yémen (anc.)
				1.9								Yémen dém. (anc.)
752	576	678	451	_	2.8	14.5	16.3	16.0	15.6	15.4	15.7	Yémen

Pour les sources et les notes, se reporter à la fin du tableau.

Region, country or territory	Total reserves minus gold (1) - Réserves totales moins l'or (1) Millions of dollars - Millions de dollars							
	1980	1990	2000	2001	2002	2003	2004	2005
Developing economies: Oceania	**637**	**820**	**971**	**1 025**	**940**	**1 212**	**1 459**	**1 385**
Fiji	168	261	412	366	359	424	478	315
Micronesia, Federated States of	..	..	113	98	117	90	55	50
Papua New Guinea	423	403	287	423	322	494	633	718
Samoa	3	69	64	57	62	84	96	92
Solomon Islands	30	18	32	19	18	37	81	95
Tonga	14	31	25	24	25	40	55	47
Vanuatu	..	38	39	38	37	44	62	67

Sources:
- International Monetary Fund (IMF), *International Financial Statistics* on CD-ROM

Notes:
(1)   End of year data.
(2)   Reserve stock of the year, divided by the average monthly imports of the current and following year. Data on imports are based on figures shown in table 1.1.1. Year 2005 data were calculated on the basis of monthly imports of the current year.
(3)   Reserves data have been revised starting with 1996 because national financial authorities modified their methodolgy for classification of foreign assests.

Annual change in reserves (millions of dollars) Variations annuelles des réserves (millions de dollars)				Number of months of imports (2) Nombre de mois d'importations (2)								Régions, pays ou territoires
2001-2002	2002-2003	2003-2004	2004-2005	1980	1990	2000	2001	2002	2003	2004	2005	
-85	**272**	**247**	**-74**	**2.2**	**1.9**	**2.2**	**2.2**	**1.7**	**1.9**	**2.1**	**1.8**	**Économies en développement : Océanie**
-8	65	54	-163	3.4	4.5	5.7	4.9	4.1	3.8	3.8	2.2	Fidji
19	-28	-35	-5	..	..	..	..	..	..	..	..	Micronésie, États fédérés de
-101	173	138	86	4.2	3.5	3.1	4.4	3.0	3.9	4.5	4.6	Papouasie-Nouvelle-Guinée
6	21	12	-3	0.6	9.5	7.3	5.5	5.8	7.1	6.7	4.7	Samoa
-1	19	43	15	3.9	2.1	4.3	3.0	2.7	4.1	6.3	5.7	Îles Salomon
1	15	15	-8	4.2	6.2	4.2	3.5	3.3	4.8	6.2	5.0	Tonga
-1	7	18	5	..	5.1	5.3	5.0	4.5	4.5	5.7	6.0	Vanuatu

Sources :
- Fonds monétaire international (FMI), *International Financial Statistics* sur CD-ROM

Notes :
(1) Données de fin d'année.
(2) Montant des réserves de l'année, divisé par la moyenne mensuelle des importations de l'année en cours et de l'année suivante. Les connées des importations se basent sur les chiffres présentés dans le tableau 1.1.1. Les chiffres de l'année 2005 ont été calculés sur la base des importations mensuelles de l'année en cours.
(3) Les données des réserves ont été révisées à partir de 1996, en raison d'une modification par les autorités financières nationales, de leur méthodologie de classification des avoirs extérieurs.

7

Economic grouping	Total reserves minus gold (end-of-year data) (1) - Réserves totales moins l'or (données de fin d'année) (1) Millions de dollars - Millions of dollars							
	1980	1990	2000	2001	2002	2003	2004	2005
DEVELOPING ECONOMIES	**157 092**	**308 199**	**1 028 706**	**1 120 969**	**1 329 181**	**1 676 500**	**2 128 534**	**2 489 938**
Developing economies excluding China	154 539	278 587	860 373	905 303	1 038 001	1 268 298	1 513 959	1 668 354
Developing economies excluding LDCs	152 944	302 919	1 013 339	1 104 553	1 309 275	1 652 158	2 098 281	2 456 704
High-income countries	80 518	198 900	552 230	572 093	644 162	778 450	908 440	979 983
Middle-income countries	41 946	58 993	192 793	206 011	234 169	284 360	348 919	403 931
Low-income countries	34 628	50 307	283 683	342 865	450 351	613 690	871 175	1 106 025
Heavily indebted poor countries	2 375	3 738	12 357	13 419	16 383	19 556	24 148	25 294
Landlocked countries	2 967	6 753	16 885	17 277	18 622	21 986	28 812	28 421
Small island developing states	3 894	2 788	5 710	7 313	7 703	8 572	10 405	11 998
Least developed countries	*4 140*	*5 254*	*15 311*	*16 355*	*19 853*	*24 292*	*30 178*	*33 165*
Africa and Haiti	1 428	2 983	8 458	8 612	10 522	13 026	16 937	19 630
Asia	2 631	2 016	6 513	7 412	8 904	10 728	12 537	12 807
Islands	82	255	341	330	427	538	704	728
Major petroleum exporters	*85 496*	*49 358*	*127 845*	*133 894*	*143 667*	*173 594*	*221 730*	*274 931*
Africa	27 291	10 708	36 006	44 149	45 423	60 703	87 828	128 688
America	9 479	9 028	14 736	11 448	10 921	18 859	21 959	29 237
Asia	48 726	29 623	77 103	78 297	87 323	94 032	111 943	117 006
Major exporters of manufactured goods	*39 786*	*217 994*	*760 648*	*847 682*	*1 035 795*	*1 323 722*	*1 697 811*	*1 971 757*
America	8 729	17 304	67 997	80 480	88 278	108 066	116 881	127 628
Asia	31 057	200 691	692 651	767 202	947 517	1 215 655	1 580 930	1 844 129
Emerging economies	*38 196*	*167 046*	*459 903*	*480 300*	*559 877*	*690 396*	*831 447*	*885 277*
America	20 552	29 004	116 553	118 084	123 447	147 836	163 935	185 336
Asia	17 644	138 042	343 350	362 216	436 430	542 560	667 512	699 941
Newly industrialized economies	*25 882*	*170 993*	*492 484*	*514 094*	*592 626*	*709 537*	*839 121*	*873 100*
First tier	11 697	139 550	390 547	411 494	476 919	576 021	676 507	703 644
Second tier	14 185	31 443	101 938	102 600	115 707	133 516	162 614	169 456
Developing economies: Africa	**33 208**	**25 252**	**79 075**	**91 500**	**98 788**	**122 492**	**164 866**	**219 171**
Northern Africa excluding Sudan	18 898	12 109	44 237	56 271	63 210	83 095	103 481	137 044
Sub-Saharan Africa	14 310	13 144	34 838	35 229	35 578	39 398	61 385	82 127
Sub-Saharan Africa excluding South Africa	13 584	12 135	28 756	29 184	29 674	32 902	48 244	63 548
Developing economies: America	**38 877**	**47 448**	**156 425**	**158 707**	**160 787**	**195 485**	**220 615**	**255 378**
Central America and Greater Carribean Islands excluding Puerto Rico	4 295	11 874	44 856	56 097	61 333	69 958	77 319	90 236
Central America and Greater Carribean Islands excluding Mexico and Puerto Rico	1 335	2 011	9 347	11 356	10 738	11 002	13 179	16 182
South America and Central America	35 466	45 970	151 524	151 635	154 294	189 111	212 104	243 868
South America excluding Brazil	25 724	26 889	76 043	62 940	57 473	71 552	84 803	104 204
Developing economies: Asia	**84 370**	**234 680**	**792 235**	**869 738**	**1 068 666**	**1 357 311**	**1 741 595**	**2 014 005**
Eastern and South-Eastern Asia excluding China	26 143	171 828	500 675	522 992	602 772	722 397	854 178	891 723
Southern Asia excluding India	11 819	2 022	5 424	7 656	12 898	17 532	17 168	17 604

Sources:
- International Monetary Fund (IMF), *International Financial Statistics* on CD-ROM

Notes:
(1)   End of year data.
(2)   Reserve stock of the year, divided by the average monthly imports of the current and following year. Data on imports are based on figures shown in table 1.1. Year 2005 data were calculated on the basis of monthly imports of the current year.

7.5.2 Réserves internationales des économies en développement par groupements économiques

Annual change in reserves (millions of dollars) Variations annuelles des réserves (millions de dollars)				Number of months of imports (2) Nombre de mois d'importations (2)								Groupements économiques
2001-2002	2002-2003	2003-2004	2004-2005	1980	1990	2000	2001	2002	2003	2004	2005	
208 212	**347 319**	**452 033**	**361 404**	**3.6**	**4.4**	**6.6**	**7.2**	**7.7**	**7.9**	**8.2**	**8.2**	**ÉCONOMIES EN DÉVELOPPEMENT**
132 697	230 297	245 661	154 395	3.7	4.3	6.3	6.8	7.3	7.4	7.2	6.9	Économies en développement sans la Chine
204 722	342 883	446 123	358 423	3.7	4.4	6.7	7.3	7.8	8.0	8.3	8.3	Économies en développement sans les PMA
72 069	134 289	129 990	71 543	4.1	5.5	6.9	7.4	7.9	8.0	7.8	7.3	Pays à revenu élevé
28 158	50 191	64 559	55 011	3.3	3.1	5.5	5.9	6.1	6.1	6.2	6.2	Pays à revenu intermédiaire
107 986	162 839	257 485	234 850	3.1	3.3	7.2	8.0	8.5	8.8	10.0	10.7	Pays à revenu faible
3 464	2 674	4 592	1 145	1.2	2.0	3.9	4.0	4.6	4.5	4.6	4.2	Pays pauvres très endettés
1 345	3 364	6 826	-392	3.8	7.0	5.3	5.1	4.9	4.7	4.9	4.1	Pays sans littoral
391	869	1 832	1 593	3.0	3.1	4.0	5.1	5.1	5.1	5.3	5.3	Petits états insulaires en développement
3 499	*4 438*	*5 887*	*2 987*	*2.1*	*2.6*	*4.0*	*4.0*	*4.4*	*4.5*	*4.7*	*4.5*	*Pays les moins avancés*
1 909	2 504	3 912	2 693	1.0	2.2	4.0	3.7	4.0	4.0	4.3	4.3	Afrique et Haïti
1 492	1 824	1 808	270	4.5	3.1	4.1	4.5	5.0	5.2	5.2	4.8	Asie
98	110	166	23	2.6	4.5	4.0	3.7	4.2	4.4	4.8	4.1	Îles
9 774	*29 926*	*48 136*	*53 201*	*6.2*	*4.1*	*7.3*	*7.3*	*7.3*	*7.0*	*6.9*	*7.1*	*Principaux exportateurs de pétrole*
1 274	15 280	27 125	40 860	8.2	5.0	14.9	16.0	14.1	16.1	20.3	25.0	Afrique
-526	7 938	3 100	7 278	5.3	8.5	7.6	6.5	7.8	11.5	9.2	9.1	Amérique
9 026	6 709	17 911	5 063	5.6	3.3	5.9	5.7	5.8	4.8	4.4	3.8	Asie
188 113	*287 927*	*374 089*	*273 946*	*2.2*	*4.8*	*6.7*	*7.5*	*8.2*	*8.5*	*9.0*	*9.0*	*Principaux exportateurs d'articles manufacturés*
7 798	19 789	8 814	10 748	2.1	2.9	3.4	4.2	4.6	5.2	4.9	4.7	Amérique
180 315	268 138	365 275	263 199	2.2	5.1	7.5	8.2	8.8	9.0	9.6	9.6	Asie
79 577	*130 519*	*141 051*	*53 830*	*2.9*	*5.6*	*6.7*	*7.4*	*8.2*	*8.5*	*8.5*	*7.9*	*Économies émergentes*
5 363	24 389	16 099	21 401	3.6	3.9	4.9	5.3	5.6	5.9	5.6	5.5	Amérique
74 214	106 130	124 952	32 429	2.3	6.2	7.6	8.5	9.4	9.6	9.8	8.9	Asie
78 532	*116 912*	*129 583*	*33 980*	*2.3*	*5.2*	*7.3*	*7.9*	*8.3*	*8.3*	*8.3*	*7.6*	*Économies nouvellement industrialisées*
65 425	99 103	100 485	27 138	1.5	5.8	7.7	8.6	9.1	9.2	9.1	8.3	Premier tier
13 108	17 809	29 098	6 842	4.1	3.6	5.9	5.9	6.1	6.0	6.0	5.5	Deuxième tier
7 288	**23 704**	**42 374**	**54 305**	**4.0**	**3.2**	**7.1**	**7.9**	**7.6**	**7.7**	**8.7**	**10.0**	**Économies en développement : Afrique**
6 939	19 884	20 386	33 564	6.8	3.6	11.2	13.7	14.3	16.0	16.5	19.3	Afrique septentrionale sans le Soudan
349	3 820	21 987	20 742	2.6	2.9	4.9	4.7	4.1	3.7	4.8	5.6	Afrique subsaharienne
490	3 228	15 342	15 304	3.6	4.2	6.1	5.8	5.2	4.9	6.1	6.8	Afrique sub-saharienne sans l'Afrique du Sud
2 080	**34 699**	**25 130**	**34 763**	**3.6**	**4.2**	**4.9**	**5.2**	**5.4**	**5.8**	**5.5**	**5.5**	**Économies en développement : Amérique**
5 236	8 625	7 361	12 917	1.2	2.1	2.4	3.1	3.3	3.5	3.5	3.6	Amérique centrale et Grandes Antilles sans Porto Rico
-618	264	2 176	3 004	0.9	1.3	2.6	3.2	2.9	2.8	2.9	3.1	Amérique centrale et Grandes Antilles sans le Mexique et Porto Rico
2 659	34 817	22 993	31 765	4.2	4.7	5.1	5.4	5.6	6.1	5.7	5.6	Amérique du Sud et Amérique centrale
-5 467	14 079	13 252	19 401	7.2	8.3	10.0	9.4	9.2	9.1	8.1	7.8	Amérique du Sud sans le Brésil
198 929	**288 645**	**384 284**	**272 410**	**3.4**	**4.6**	**7.1**	**7.7**	**8.3**	**8.3**	**8.7**	**8.6**	**Économies en développement : Asie**
79 780	119 625	131 781	37 545	2.3	5.1	7.1	7.7	8.1	8.2	8.1	7.5	Asie orientale et Asie du Sud-Est sans la Chine
5 242	4 634	-364	436	5.4	0.6	1.4	1.8	2.7	3.0	2.4	2.2	Asie méridionale sans l'Inde

Sources :
- Fonds monétaire international (FMI), *International Financial Statistics* sur CD-ROM

Notes :
(1) Données de fin d'année.
(2) Montant des réserves de l'année, divisé par la moyenne mensuelle des importations de l'année en cours et de l'année suivante. Les données des importations se basent sur les chiffres présentés dans le tableau 1.1. Les chiffres de l'année 2005 ont été calculés sur la base des importations mensuelles de l'année en cours.

7

7.6.1 Official financial flows from bilateral and multilateral sources to developing economies by country and geographical region

7.6.1 Flux financiers publics bilatéraux et multilatéraux à destination des économies en développement par pays et régions géographiques

Region, country or territory / Régions, pays ou territoires	Year / Année	Total Official Net (1) / Total secteur officiel net (1)	Total ODA Net / Total OA Net (2) / APD totale nette / AP totale nette (2)			Total OOF Net (3) / Flux AASP nets (3)		
			Total Donors / Tous donneurs	of which: / dont :		Total Donors / Tous donneurs	of which: / dont :	
				DAC Bilateral Donors / Donneurs bilatéraux du CAD	Multilateral Donors / Donneurs multilatéraux		DAC Bilateral Donors / Donneurs bilatéraux du CAD	Multilateral Donors / Donneurs multilatéraux
		Millions of dollars / Millions de dollars						
Developing economies - Économies en développement	1990	74 171.0	56 004.3	36 861.8	13 260.0	18 166.7	8 065.1	10 128.2
	1995	68 631.1	56 302.8	38 535.0	17 068.0	12 328.3	8 847.3	2 897.7
	2000	51 353.7	46 459.0	34 109.0	11 695.0	4 894.7	-2 577.4	8 141.6
	2005	103 234.6	101 104.5	78 797.5	20 277.6	2 130.1	2 052.6	-685.1
Developing economies: Africa - Économies en développement : Afrique	1990	28 258.9	25 312.0	15 817.3	6 361.1	2 946.9	847.9	1 950.3
	1995	25 328.5	21 958.7	13 223.1	8 588.2	3 369.8	3 574.0	-203.6
	2000	14 458.1	15 732.4	10 384.4	5 047.7	-1 274.2	-333.3	-930.8
	2005	35 061.1	35 211.9	24 717.2	10 268.9	-150.8	-494.5	348.3
Eastern Africa - Afrique orientale	*1990*	*8 392.5*	*8 239.9*	*5 169.1*	*2 762.5*	*152.6*	*137.0*	*11.9*
	1995	*8 980.5*	*9 273.9*	*4 786.1*	*4 460.2*	*-293.4*	*-41.7*	*-251.7*
	2000	*6 487.9*	*6 591.8*	*4 295.8*	*2 241.7*	*-103.9*	*-37.7*	*-65.8*
	2005	*11 031.8*	*11 400.4*	*7 027.6*	*4 310.5*	*-368.5*	*-308.5*	*-60.0*
Burundi	1990	260.7	264.1	157.6	106.3	-3.4	1.0	-4.4
	1995	286.0	287.7	108.4	182.1	-1.8	0.2	-2.0
	2000	92.7	92.7	40.9	51.7	0.0	0.0	0.0
	2005	365.0	365.0	180.7	184.1	0.0	0.0	0.0
Comoros - Comores	1990	45.4	45.3	30.6	14.5	0.1	0.1	0.0
	1995	41.6	41.8	21.7	20.0	-0.1	-0.1	0.0
	2000	18.7	18.8	10.8	7.8	0.0	0.0	0.0
	2005	25.2	25.2	17.2	8.1	0.0	0.0	0.0
Djibouti	1990	193.7	193.8	88.3	17.4	-0.1	-0.1	0.0
	1995	105.3	105.1	79.6	22.3	0.2	0.2	0.0
	2000	71.4	71.4	42.1	19.7	0.0	0.0	0.0
	2005	78.6	78.6	53.7	23.1	0.0	0.0	0.0
Ethiopia (former) - Éthiopie (anc.)	1990	1 013.6	1 015.7	509.7	438.1	-2.0	-2.3	0.3
Eritrea - Érythrée	1995	149.0	149.0	94.6	49.1	0.0	0.0	0.0
	2000	176.0	176.0	111.9	54.9	0.0	0.0	0.0
	2005	355.2	355.2	226.4	131.9	0.0	0.0	0.0
Ethiopia - Éthiopie	1995	905.7	883.2	525.5	357.1	22.5	5.5	17.1
	2000	674.2	693.0	379.5	298.4	-18.8	-1.0	-17.9
	2005	1 845.3	1 937.3	1 201.7	705.9	-92.0	-69.3	-22.7
Kenya	1990	1 145.8	1 185.8	735.2	446.1	-40.0	15.4	-55.4
	1995	632.3	734.0	458.7	270.1	-101.7	-16.4	-85.3
	2000	478.3	512.1	293.0	214.3	-33.8	-4.6	-29.0
	2005	788.5	768.3	494.6	259.7	20.2	16.6	3.6
Madagascar	1990	413.3	398.4	268.2	131.4	14.9	11.2	3.2
	1995	301.5	301.2	194.9	106.1	0.3	4.8	-4.5
	2000	316.7	322.2	138.7	184.6	-5.5	1.4	-6.9
	2005	802.4	929.2	500.5	428.7	-126.7	-126.5	-0.3
Malawi	1990	489.3	503.4	216.2	286.6	-14.1	-5.8	-8.3
	1995	417.0	435.0	220.9	211.4	-18.0	-1.0	-17.0
	2000	443.9	446.3	269.2	170.9	-2.4	-0.1	-2.3
	2005	572.8	575.3	322.1	250.8	-2.6	0.1	-2.6
Mauritius - Maurice	1990	107.6	88.7	75.7	12.3	18.9	16.2	2.7
	1995	3.9	23.4	11.0	13.8	-19.5	-1.2	-18.3
	2000	-17.8	20.5	12.4	7.5	-38.3	-20.7	-17.5
	2005	15.8	31.9	22.2	9.8	-16.1	-1.8	-14.3
Mayotte	1990	60.5	60.5	58.5	2.0	0.0	0.0	0.0
	1995	107.8	107.8	106.2	1.5	0.0	0.0	0.0
	2000	103.2	103.2	103.0	0.2	0.0	0.0	0.0
	2005	190.2	201.3	201.9	-0.5	-11.1	-11.1	0.0

For sources and notes, see end of table.   Pour les sources et les notes, se reporter à la fin du tableau.

7.6.1 Official financial flows from bilateral and multilateral sources to developing economies by country and geographical region

7.6.1 Flux financiers publics bilatéraux et multilatéraux à destination des économies en développement par pays et régions géographiques

Region, country or territory / Régions, pays ou territoires	Year / Année	Total Official Net (1) / Total secteur officiel net (1)	Total ODA Net / Total OA Net (2) APD totale nette / AP totale nette (2)			Total OOF Net (3) Flux AASP nets (3)		
			Total Donors / Tous donneurs	of which: / dont :		Total Donors / Tous donneurs	of which: / dont :	
				DAC Bilateral Donors / Donneurs bilatéraux du CAD	Multilateral Donors / Donneurs multilatéraux		DAC Bilateral Donors / Donneurs bilatéraux du CAD	Multilateral Donors / Donneurs multilatéraux
			Millions of dollars / Millions de dollars					
Mozambique	1990	1 004.4	1 002.6	750.3	252.0	1.9	3.3	-1.5
	1995	1 037.4	1 064.2	698.3	363.7	-26.8	-23.4	-3.4
	2000	1 043.5	877.0	623.5	253.5	166.5	105.2	61.2
	2005	1 268.1	1 285.9	770.8	513.3	-17.8	-21.1	3.3
Rwanda	1990	290.2	291.2	183.2	97.8	-1.0	-0.1	-0.9
	1995	702.4	702.1	339.2	363.1	0.3	0.1	0.2
	2000	324.1	322.0	175.4	146.5	2.1	2.2	-0.2
	2005	570.6	576.0	292.0	283.8	-5.4	-5.4	0.0
Seychelles	1990	37.8	35.9	32.7	3.4	1.9	-0.8	-0.4
	1995	16.4	13.0	11.0	2.5	3.4	-0.4	3.9
	2000	14.5	18.3	3.3	8.4	-3.8	-0.7	-3.1
	2005	17.6	18.8	7.9	10.8	-1.3	0.0	-1.3
Somalia - Somalie	1990	492.3	493.5	269.6	142.0	-1.2	-0.8	-0.4
	1995	189.1	188.9	119.2	69.7	0.2	0.2	0.0
	2000	103.8	103.8	56.4	47.3	0.0	0.0	0.0
	2005	236.4	236.4	146.1	90.2	0.0	0.0	0.0
Uganda - Ouganda	1990	670.2	668.1	244.4	381.0	2.1	9.4	-7.3
	1995	819.3	834.9	423.1	400.1	-15.7	-5.7	-9.9
	2000	775.9	819.4	578.2	235.6	-43.6	-46.3	2.8
	2005	1 196.1	1 198.0	704.3	491.8	-2.0	-0.1	-1.9
United Republic of Tanzania - République-Unie de Tanzanie	1990	1 173.2	1 173.3	844.1	326.0	-0.1	28.2	-28.2
	1995	845.5	877.4	586.7	286.2	-31.9	-9.0	-22.9
	2000	1 049.1	1 022.0	778.7	246.0	27.1	32.1	-4.9
	2005	1 498.7	1 505.1	871.0	621.8	-6.5	-7.8	1.4
Zambia - Zambie	1990	546.1	480.1	408.9	71.2	66.0	47.2	18.8
	1995	1 966.7	2 033.8	439.5	1 594.1	-67.1	3.7	-70.8
	2000	675.0	795.1	486.2	308.6	-120.1	-104.4	-15.8
	2005	847.9	945.0	835.9	108.6	-97.2	-79.2	-18.0
Zimbabwe	1990	448.3	339.6	295.9	34.6	108.7	14.9	93.8
	1995	453.7	491.6	347.7	147.3	-37.8	1.0	-38.8
	2000	144.8	178.1	192.6	-13.9	-33.2	-0.9	-32.3
	2005	357.6	367.7	178.8	188.8	-10.1	-2.9	-7.2
Middle Africa - Afrique centrale	*1990*	*3 600.9*	*2 641.0*	*1 821.6*	*738.3*	*960.0*	*675.6*	*284.4*
	1995	*2 439.8*	*1 849.6*	*1 278.0*	*566.4*	*590.1*	*667.4*	*-77.3*
	2000	*985.0*	*1 177.6*	*658.8*	*514.7*	*-192.6*	*-52.5*	*-140.2*
	2005	*5 092.5*	*4 731.9*	*3 294.6*	*1 435.0*	*360.6*	*520.9*	*-160.4*
Angola	1990	345.9	268.3	163.2	103.3	77.7	76.2	1.5
	1995	491.1	417.9	241.7	176.1	73.1	73.1	0.0
	2000	260.8	306.7	189.1	111.5	-45.9	-23.3	-22.6
	2005	434.0	441.8	258.2	183.0	-7.9	-6.3	-1.6
Cameroon - Cameroun	1990	608.5	445.7	339.1	109.2	162.8	75.1	87.7
	1995	579.2	443.8	345.5	96.8	135.4	235.2	-99.8
	2000	309.3	379.9	213.5	169.1	-70.6	9.4	-80.0
	2005	321.6	413.8	336.0	76.9	-92.2	-35.5	-56.7
Central African Republic - République centrafricaine	1990	250.1	250.4	99.9	148.2	-0.3	0.9	-1.1
	1995	167.8	168.6	122.4	42.8	-0.8	-0.8	0.0
	2000	74.1	75.4	53.1	22.5	-1.3	-1.3	0.0
	2005	95.3	95.3	62.2	33.0	0.0	0.0	0.0
Chad - Tchad	1990	313.7	313.8	183.3	128.2	-0.1	-0.1	0.0
	1995	238.6	236.4	127.0	108.8	2.2	2.2	0.0
	2000	129.8	130.8	53.3	76.7	-0.9	-0.9	0.0
	2005	375.2	379.8	166.6	213.2	-4.6	-0.2	-4.4
Congo	1990	227.2	218.1	202.0	16.1	9.1	13.2	-4.1
	1995	394.6	125.4	105.0	20.4	269.2	287.2	-18.0
	2000	17.7	33.3	23.0	10.2	-15.6	-12.4	-3.2
	2005	1 879.0	1 448.9	1 359.5	89.3	430.2	458.7	-28.5

For sources and notes, see end of table.

Pour les sources et les notes, se reporter à la fin du tableau.

7

7.6.1 Official financial flows from bilateral and multilateral sources to developing economies by country and geographical region

7.6.1 Flux financiers publics bilatéraux et multilatéraux à destination des économies en développement par pays et régions géographiques

Region, country or territory / Régions, pays ou territoires	Year / Année	Total Official Net (1) / Total secteur officiel net (1)	Total ODA Net / Total OA Net (2) / APD totale nette / AP totale nette (2)			Total OOF Net (3) / Flux AASP nets (3)		
			Total Donors / Tous donneurs	of which: / dont :		Total Donors / Tous donneurs	of which: / dont :	
				DAC Bilateral Donors / Donneurs bilatéraux du CAD	Multilateral Donors / Donneurs multilatéraux		DAC Bilateral Donors / Donneurs bilatéraux du CAD	Multilateral Donors / Donneurs multilatéraux
			Millions of dollars / Millions de dollars					
Dem. Rep. of the Congo - Rép. dém. du Congo	1990	1 421.0	897.1	632.7	187.2	523.9	380.6	143.3
	1995	189.4	195.7	117.7	77.9	-6.3	-5.1	-1.2
	2000	180.1	183.5	102.7	80.7	-3.4	0.0	-3.4
	2005	1 863.2	1 827.6	1 034.3	792.8	35.6	60.2	-24.6
Equatorial Guinea - Guinée équatoriale	1990	61.3	60.8	43.6	17.1	0.6	0.0	0.6
	1995	35.3	33.6	21.7	11.9	1.8	1.8	0.0
	2000	20.3	21.3	18.2	3.3	-1.1	-0.7	-0.4
	2005	54.9	39.0	29.6	9.4	15.9	15.9	0.0
Gabon	1990	318.6	132.4	126.9	5.5	186.3	129.7	56.5
	1995	285.3	144.0	135.6	9.2	141.4	99.7	41.7
	2000	-42.0	11.8	-11.7	23.4	-53.7	-23.2	-30.5
	2005	37.4	53.9	29.8	24.0	-16.5	28.1	-44.6
São Tome and Principe - Sao Tomé-et-Principe	1990	54.7	54.7	31.0	23.7	0.0	0.0	0.0
	1995	58.5	84.3	61.5	22.7	-25.8	-25.8	0.0
	2000	35.0	35.0	17.7	17.3	0.0	0.0	0.0
	2005	31.9	31.9	18.4	13.5	0.0	0.0	0.0
Northern Africa - Afrique septentrionale	*1990*	*8 019.7*	*7 843.5*	*4 501.3*	*678.9*	*176.2*	*-949.7*	*977.3*
	1995	*6 323.7*	*3 133.0*	*2 504.2*	*522.9*	*3 190.7*	*2 709.3*	*481.9*
	2000	*2 042.3*	*2 412.3*	*1 750.0*	*440.7*	*-370.0*	*101.0*	*-461.4*
	2005	*4 030.2*	*4 177.8*	*2 995.7*	*1 042.0*	*-147.6*	*-786.4*	*638.8*
Algeria - Algérie	1990	675.9	132.0	102.2	21.8	543.9	114.2	283.3
	1995	1 989.8	297.7	275.3	34.4	1 692.2	1 325.6	366.6
	2000	-40.4	201.0	65.7	64.1	-241.4	-143.4	-98.0
	2005	-1 135.9	370.6	289.7	71.4	-1 506.5	-813.4	-693.1
Egypt - Égypte	1990	4 157.7	5 429.5	3 163.1	80.0	-1 271.8	-1 234.0	-37.6
	1995	2 654.3	2 016.3	1 691.2	208.2	638.0	775.7	-137.7
	2000	1 368.3	1 328.4	1 138.9	135.6	39.9	220.5	-180.0
	2005	1 993.7	925.9	658.8	237.8	1 067.8	131.6	936.2
Libyan Arab Jamahiriya - Jamahiriya arabe libyenne	1990	19.5	19.5	7.6	11.8	0.0	0.0	0.0
	1995	6.3	6.3	3.2	3.0	0.0	0.0	0.0
	2000	15.4	15.4	11.9	3.1	0.0	0.0	0.0
	2005	24.4	24.4	16.8	3.6	0.0	0.0	0.0
Morocco - Maroc	1990	1 696.9	1 048.8	595.4	92.4	648.1	164.5	486.2
	1995	488.3	495.2	347.4	127.9	-6.9	-163.6	156.7
	2000	276.3	419.3	293.1	130.4	-143.0	-47.3	-95.7
	2005	990.2	651.8	289.3	308.8	338.4	-47.2	385.6
Sudan - Soudan	1990	819.7	822.3	420.0	394.4	-2.6	2.7	-5.2
	1995	256.1	242.4	130.6	108.2	13.7	-4.3	18.1
	2000	216.0	225.4	90.3	35.7	-9.5	0.0	-0.4
	2005	1 854.8	1 828.6	1 472.0	315.2	26.2	0.1	26.2
Tunisia - Tunisie	1990	649.9	391.4	212.9	78.5	258.5	2.9	250.7
	1995	929.0	75.2	56.5	41.2	853.7	775.9	78.3
	2000	206.7	222.8	150.3	71.9	-16.0	71.2	-87.2
	2005	303.0	376.5	269.1	105.2	-73.5	-57.5	-16.0
Southern Africa - Afrique australe	*1990*	*467.0*	*463.8*	*281.9*	*183.9*	*3.2*	*-2.2*	*5.4*
	1995	*1 171.4*	*842.6*	*620.0*	*216.4*	*328.7*	*359.7*	*-30.9*
	2000	*844.0*	*720.8*	*498.5*	*221.2*	*123.2*	*-83.3*	*206.7*
	2005	*1 065.5*	*1 009.1*	*695.9*	*310.7*	*56.4*	*-110.3*	*171.2*
Botswana	1990	169.0	146.8	121.2	27.4	22.2	4.6	17.6
	1995	69.2	90.1	54.5	35.2	-20.9	18.5	-39.4
	2000	34.3	30.7	23.5	8.1	3.6	23.1	-19.5
	2005	86.8	70.9	51.9	19.0	15.9	2.0	13.9
Lesotho	1990	142.2	141.7	85.2	56.9	0.5	-1.5	2.0
	1995	135.2	113.7	61.6	52.1	21.5	12.6	8.9
	2000	47.1	36.7	21.8	16.1	10.4	-8.2	18.6
	2005	60.1	68.8	39.1	29.7	-8.8	-0.5	-8.3

For sources and notes, see end of table.

Pour les sources et les notes, se reporter à la fin du tableau.

7.6.1 Official financial flows from bilateral and multilateral sources to developing economies by country and geographical region

7.6.1 Flux financiers publics bilatéraux et multilatéraux à destination des économies en développement par pays et régions géographiques

Region, country or territory / Régions, pays ou territoires	Year / Année	Total Official Net (1) / Total secteur officiel net (1)	Total ODA Net / Total OA Net (2) APD totale nette / AP totale nette (2)			Total OOF Net (3) Flux AASP nets (3)		
			Total Donors / Tous donneurs	of which: / dont :		Total Donors / Tous donneurs	of which: / dont :	
				DAC Bilateral Donors / Donneurs bilatéraux du CAD	Multilateral Donors / Donneurs multilatéraux		DAC Bilateral Donors / Donneurs bilatéraux du CAD	Multilateral Donors / Donneurs multilatéraux
			Millions of dollars / Millions de dollars					
Namibia - Namibie	1990	121.2	121.2	39.4	81.9	0.0	0.0	0.0
	1995	193.8	191.8	147.7	43.9	2.1	2.1	0.0
	2000	154.3	152.7	96.8	54.8	1.6	-0.5	2.1
	2005	140.2	123.4	98.8	22.8	16.9	-3.1	20.0
South Africa - Afrique du Sud	1995	715.5	388.9	318.5	67.4	326.6	326.6	0.0
	2000	592.3	487.5	353.6	132.0	104.8	-94.3	199.3
	2005	742.0	700.0	486.0	213.5	42.0	-108.7	155.2
Swaziland	1990	34.5	54.0	36.1	17.8	-19.5	-5.3	-14.2
	1995	57.6	58.1	37.7	17.8	-0.5	0.0	-0.5
	2000	15.9	13.2	2.8	10.3	2.8	-3.5	6.2
	2005	36.4	46.0	20.2	25.8	-9.6	0.0	-9.6
Western Africa - Afrique occidentale	*1990*	*6 767.7*	*5 129.2*	*3 203.0*	*1 852.6*	*1 638.5*	*981.3*	*660.7*
	1995	*5 312.4*	*5 793.1*	*3 212.3*	*2 578.4*	*-480.7*	*-151.7*	*-329.0*
	2000	*2 900.4*	*3 633.0*	*2 333.6*	*1 293.1*	*-732.6*	*-267.6*	*-465.0*
	2005	*11 758.8*	*11 940.2*	*9 111.3*	*2 810.9*	*-181.4*	*104.1*	*-285.6*
Benin - Bénin	1990	295.9	268.0	125.7	142.6	27.9	26.2	1.7
	1995	282.6	280.5	177.4	96.3	2.1	2.9	-0.8
	2000	227.6	238.6	190.5	49.2	-11.0	-11.0	0.0
	2005	348.4	349.1	206.9	142.0	-0.7	-0.3	-0.3
Burkina Faso	1990	332.4	331.0	238.7	81.0	1.4	1.3	0.1
	1995	488.6	491.0	252.3	230.9	-2.4	0.1	-2.5
	2000	330.5	336.0	227.8	104.5	-5.5	-3.5	-2.0
	2005	660.5	659.6	338.5	319.3	1.0	-0.3	1.2
Cape Verde - Cap-Vert	1990	106.5	107.9	75.9	31.6	-1.4	-0.2	-1.1
	1995	117.3	117.3	76.9	40.2	0.1	0.4	-0.3
	2000	92.5	94.1	69.7	24.7	-1.6	-0.1	-1.4
	2005	167.2	160.6	104.2	56.4	6.6	0.0	6.6
Côte d'Ivoire	1990	1 123.2	687.7	530.6	157.1	435.5	134.2	301.3
	1995	1 148.4	1 212.9	726.6	485.8	-64.5	31.6	-96.1
	2000	276.9	351.8	250.1	101.2	-74.9	17.8	-92.7
	2005	103.0	119.1	151.0	-32.4	-16.1	-10.0	-6.1
Gambia - Gambie	1990	107.2	99.1	56.9	41.8	8.0	8.5	-0.5
	1995	44.4	46.7	25.1	23.0	-2.3	-0.4	-1.9
	2000	48.4	49.1	14.6	32.0	-0.7	0.0	-0.7
	2005	58.2	58.2	15.0	43.0	0.0	0.0	0.0
Ghana	1990	719.2	562.6	264.9	296.6	156.6	26.4	130.2
	1995	581.5	650.8	358.6	298.2	-69.3	10.7	-80.0
	2000	583.7	600.4	376.0	222.1	-16.8	8.6	-25.3
	2005	1 101.1	1 119.9	602.7	503.4	-18.9	-14.1	-4.8
Guinea - Guinée	1990	301.6	292.8	139.0	149.7	8.8	19.6	-10.8
	1995	433.7	416.9	220.4	190.7	16.8	-2.3	19.1
	2000	141.6	153.0	92.8	57.6	-11.4	-1.4	-10.0
	2005	173.5	182.1	127.8	54.1	-8.6	-0.3	-8.3
Guinea-Bissau - Guinée-Bissau	1990	127.3	128.6	75.4	53.2	-1.3	0.0	-1.3
	1995	115.2	118.5	76.9	38.6	-3.3	0.0	-3.3
	2000	80.4	80.4	41.6	38.8	0.0	0.1	-0.1
	2005	79.0	79.1	39.4	39.6	-0.1	-0.1	0.0
Liberia - Libéria	1990	67.0	114.2	42.3	69.7	-47.3	-12.5	-34.8
	1995	120.1	123.5	31.1	91.1	-3.4	-3.1	-0.4
	2000	69.4	67.8	23.8	44.0	1.6	-1.9	3.5
	2005	235.5	236.2	148.6	87.5	-0.7	0.0	-0.7
Mali	1990	482.8	481.7	312.5	153.8	1.1	1.9	-0.8
	1995	586.3	541.3	285.1	269.8	45.0	21.3	23.8
	2000	343.3	359.7	299.8	61.3	-16.4	-6.9	-9.5
	2005	686.4	691.5	378.2	313.1	-5.1	-4.1	-1.0

For sources and notes, see end of table.

Pour les sources et les notes, se reporter à la fin du tableau.

7

7.6.1 Official financial flows from bilateral and multilateral sources to developing economies by country and geographical region

7.6.1 Flux financiers publics bilatéraux et multilatéraux à destination des économies en développement par pays et régions géographiques

Region, country or territory / Régions, pays ou territoires	Year / Année	Total Official Net (1) Total secteur officiel net (1)	Total ODA Net / Total OA Net (2) APD totale nette / AP totale nette (2)			Total OOF Net (3) Flux AASP nets (3)		
			Total Donors Tous donneurs	of which: / dont :		Total Donors Tous donneurs	of which: / dont :	
				DAC Bilateral Donors Donneurs bilatéraux du CAD	Multilateral Donors Donneurs multilatéraux		DAC Bilateral Donors Donneurs bilatéraux du CAD	Multilateral Donors Donneurs multilatéraux
			Millions of dollars / Millions de dollars					
Mauritania - Mauritanie	1990	225.9	237.2	106.4	106.2	-11.3	0.8	-12.1
	1995	219.0	230.4	126.0	120.2	-11.4	-9.0	-2.4
	2000	207.8	211.9	82.5	129.3	-4.2	6.8	-11.0
	2005	194.6	190.4	124.5	65.6	4.3	0.0	4.3
Niger	1990	401.8	396.5	254.6	138.3	5.3	6.7	-1.4
	1995	201.8	274.4	193.9	79.6	-72.6	-71.3	-1.2
	2000	186.7	211.0	105.8	105.1	-24.3	-24.3	0.0
	2005	507.2	515.4	255.7	259.4	-8.2	-5.8	-2.4
Nigeria - Nigéria	1990	1 310.9	258.2	172.7	76.6	1 052.6	739.4	313.2
	1995	-66.2	211.9	72.6	139.8	-278.1	-125.3	-152.8
	2000	-379.5	184.8	84.3	100.2	-564.3	-260.5	-303.8
	2005	6 337.1	6 437.3	5 966.3	471.2	-100.2	154.8	-255.0
Saint Helena - Sainte-Hélène	1990	24.7	24.7	23.3	1.4	0.0	0.0	0.0
	1995	12.6	12.6	12.4	0.2	0.0	0.0	0.0
	2000	18.7	18.7	18.4	0.3	0.0	0.0	0.0
	2005	22.6	22.6	22.5	0.1	0.0	0.0	0.0
Senegal - Sénégal	1990	830.2	818.1	589.2	226.6	12.0	31.1	-15.6
	1995	639.3	665.8	399.4	253.8	-26.5	-0.4	-26.1
	2000	417.5	423.5	288.4	139.7	-6.0	9.2	-15.2
	2005	658.5	689.3	440.1	248.8	-30.8	-15.0	-15.8
Sierra Leone	1990	56.6	60.9	39.9	20.9	-4.3	-3.4	-0.9
	1995	201.4	206.4	59.6	146.1	-4.9	-1.4	-3.5
	2000	180.6	182.4	115.6	66.8	-1.8	-0.9	-0.9
	2005	342.3	343.4	130.4	212.8	-1.2	0.0	-1.1
Togo	1990	254.6	260.0	155.0	105.6	-5.4	1.3	-6.7
	1995	186.3	192.3	117.8	74.1	-6.0	-5.4	-0.6
	2000	74.3	69.8	51.9	16.4	4.5	0.4	4.1
	2005	83.8	86.7	59.4	27.1	-2.9	-0.6	-2.3
Developing Economies: Africa Unallocated - Économies en développement Afrique : non ventilé	1990	1 011.1	994.6	840.4	145.0	16.5	5.8	10.6
	1995	1 100.8	1 066.5	822.6	243.9	34.3	30.9	3.5
	2000	1 198.5	1 196.9	847.7	336.4	1.7	6.9	-5.2
	2005	2 082.2	1 952.5	1 592.1	359.7	129.8	85.6	44.2
Developing economies: America - Économies en développement : Amérique	**1990**	**13 580.8**	**5 246.4**	**4 146.3**	**1 088.0**	**8 334.4**	**3 730.0**	**4 634.3**
	1995	**8 096.8**	**6 461.3**	**4 809.4**	**1 618.0**	**1 635.6**	**81.2**	**1 557.5**
	2000	**11 255.3**	**5 161.2**	**4 034.0**	**1 076.5**	**6 094.2**	**-465.3**	**6 551.9**
	2005	**3 046.3**	**6 293.5**	**4 574.3**	**1 679.3**	**-3 247.1**	**-1 487.7**	**-1 658.0**
Caribbean - Caraïbes	*1990*	*1 019.3*	*812.9*	*624.6*	*183.7*	*206.4*	*94.4*	*130.5*
	1995	*1 428.5*	*1 328.5*	*857.4*	*463.2*	*100.1*	*-75.9*	*176.0*
	2000	*1 339.2*	*622.4*	*466.9*	*137.0*	*716.8*	*468.3*	*250.8*
	2005	*924.1*	*835.1*	*582.5*	*250.7*	*89.0*	*54.8*	*45.1*
Anguilla	1990	3.9	3.8	2.4	1.4	0.1	0.0	0.1
	1995	3.5	3.4	2.5	0.8	0.1	0.0	0.1
	2000	7.7	3.5	3.8	-0.3	4.2	0.0	4.2
	2005	3.7	4.0	4.3	-0.3	-0.3	0.0	-0.3
Antigua and Barbuda - Antigua-et-Barbuda	1990	-2.6	4.7	2.9	1.7	-7.3	-7.3	0.0
	1995	-0.8	2.3	0.8	0.7	-3.1	-3.1	0.0
	2000	9.9	9.8	3.7	1.1	0.1	0.0	0.1
	2005	6.5	7.2	6.9	0.2	-0.7	-0.6	-0.2
Aruba	1990	30.0	30.0	28.9	1.1	0.0	0.0	0.0
	1995	29.7	25.8	18.0	7.9	3.9	4.0	-0.1
	2000	10.0	11.5	10.7	0.8	-1.5	-1.5	0.0
Bahamas	1990	30.9	3.5	0.4	2.2	27.4	-0.6	28.0
	1995	6.9	4.6	1.3	2.5	2.4	-4.6	7.0
	2000	10.2	5.5	5.2	0.3	4.7	-3.6	8.3

For sources and notes, see end of table.

Pour les sources et les notes, se reporter à la fin du tableau.

7.6.1 Official financial flows from bilateral and multilateral sources to developing economies by country and geographical region

7.6.1 Flux financiers publics bilatéraux et multilatéraux à destination des économies en développement par pays et régions géographiques

Region, country or territory / Régions, pays ou territoires	Year / Année	Total Official Net (1) / Total secteur officiel net (1)	Total ODA Net / Total OA Net (2) / APD totale nette / AP totale nette (2)			Total OOF Net (3) / Flux AASP nets (3)		
			Total Donors / Tous donneurs	of which: / dont :		Total Donors / Tous donneurs	of which: / dont :	
				DAC Bilateral Donors / Donneurs bilatéraux du CAD	Multilateral Donors / Donneurs multilatéraux		DAC Bilateral Donors / Donneurs bilatéraux du CAD	Multilateral Donors / Donneurs multilatéraux
		Millions of dollars / Millions de collars						
Barbados - Barbade	1990	21.7	2.9	1.4	1.5	18.8	10.7	8.1
	1995	8.6	-0.7	0.1	-0.9	9.4	-3.0	12.3
	2000	16.1	0.3	1.0	-0.8	15.9	3.1	12.8
	2005	-3.1	-2.1	6.1	-8.2	-1.0	5.8	-6.8
British Virgin Islands - Îles Vierges britanniques	1990	9.4	5.6	3.0	2.5	3.9	1.6	2.3
	1995	2.6	1.4	0.3	1.1	1.2	0.0	1.2
	2000	8.5	4.8	1.2	3.6	3.7	4.4	-0.7
Cayman Islands - Îles Caïmanes	1990	11.9	3.0	2.1	0.9	8.9	2.4	6.5
	1995	-0.1	-0.6	-0.6	0.0	0.5	0.7	-0.3
	2000	550.0	-3.6	-3.2	-0.5	553.6	553.1	0.5
Cuba	1990	60.3	52.0	33.6	17.4	8.3	8.3	0.0
	1995	56.5	63.6	33.7	29.8	-7.1	-7.1	0.0
	2000	47.5	44.0	30.8	12.9	3.5	3.5	0.0
	2005	108.4	87.8	68.7	18.9	20.6	20.6	0.0
Dominica - Dominique	1990	19.5	19.7	10.8	8.5	-0.3	-0.4	0.1
	1995	24.3	25.1	9.5	14.5	-0.8	-1.2	0.4
	2000	18.5	15.2	5.9	6.5	3.3	-0.1	3.4
	2005	18.2	15.2	4.5	10.5	3.1	0.0	3.1
Dominican Republic - République dominicaine	1990	136.7	102.0	72.7	28.2	34.7	1.4	33.3
	1995	165.8	119.8	81.2	37.2	46.0	-12.1	58.1
	2000	79.3	62.4	44.6	17.8	16.9	-34.0	53.1
	2005	260.5	77.0	56.6	19.9	183.5	51.4	143.0
Grenada - Grenade	1990	13.0	13.8	5.0	8.7	-0.9	-1.1	0.2
	1995	8.4	10.9	5.6	4.5	-2.5	-0.6	-1.9
	2000	19.9	16.5	9.9	3.2	3.4	-0.2	3.6
	2005	53.9	44.9	20.0	24.8	9.1	0.0	9.1
Haiti - Haïti	1990	168.0	168.5	117.1	51.2	-0.5	0.0	-0.4
	1995	719.9	725.9	510.0	215.8	-6.0	-6.0	0.0
	2000	207.2	208.3	153.9	54.4	-1.1	-1.1	0.0
	2005	514.9	515.0	354.4	160.5	-0.1	-0.1	0.0
Jamaica - Jamaïque	1990	325.7	271.0	251.9	19.3	54.7	55.8	17.3
	1995	88.3	108.5	67.5	41.2	-20.1	-8.7	-11.5
	2000	130.2	10.0	-26.4	30.0	120.2	-19.9	140.1
	2005	-60.5	35.7	11.2	24.3	-96.3	-5.8	-90.5
Montserrat	1990	8.3	8.4	7.8	0.5	-0.1	0.0	-0.1
	1995	9.8	9.5	9.1	0.4	0.3	0.0	0.3
	2000	30.9	30.9	30.9	0.1	-0.1	0.0	-0.1
	2005	27.6	27.8	27.0	0.9	-0.2	0.0	-0.2
Netherlands Antilles - Antilles néerlandaises	1990	50.2	58.1	53.0	5.1	-7.9	-10.9	3.0
	1995	97.0	98.4	94.0	4.4	-1.4	0.0	-1.4
	2000	178.5	177.0	173.8	3.1	1.5	2.4	-0.9
Saint Kitts and Nevis - Saint-Kitts-et-Nevis	1990	8.2	8.1	5.0	2.9	0.1	0.0	0.1
	1995	5.6	3.9	1.7	0.7	1.7	0.2	1.5
	2000	6.0	3.9	0.1	4.1	2.1	-1.3	3.3
	2005	2.7	3.5	1.6	1.8	-0.8	-2.0	1.2
Saint Lucia - Sainte-Lucie	1990	15.9	12.4	6.2	5.9	3.5	-0.4	3.9
	1995	52.9	48.3	12.7	34.6	4.6	0.1	4.5
	2000	13.5	11.0	7.1	4.4	2.5	0.0	2.5
	2005	12.1	11.1	6.5	4.5	1.0	0.0	1.0
Saint Vincent and the Grenadines - Saint-Vincent-et-les Grenadines	1990	15.4	15.4	5.2	9.7	0.0	0.0	0.0
	1995	48.3	47.7	6.3	40.7	0.6	0.4	0.2
	2000	9.7	6.2	3.8	1.1	3.5	0.0	3.5
	2005	7.7	4.9	5.7	-0.9	2.8	0.0	2.8
Trinidad and Tobago - Trinité-et-Tobago	1990	81.2	18.2	6.1	12.1	63.0	34.8	28.2
	1995	95.6	25.4	-1.8	27.1	70.2	-35.1	105.4
	2000	-21.6	-1.5	4.4	-5.9	-20.1	-36.7	16.5
	2005	-34.4	-2.1	6.1	-8.2	-32.3	-14.7	-17.6

For sources and notes, see end of table.

Pour les sources et les notes, se reporter à la fin du tableau.

7

7.6.1 Official financial flows from bilateral and multilateral sources to developing economies by country and geographical region

7.6.1 Flux financiers publics bilatéraux et multilatéraux à destination des économies en développement par pays et régions géographiques

Region, country or territory / Régions, pays ou territoires	Year / Année	Total Official Net (1) / Total secteur officiel net (1)	Total ODA Net / Total OA Net (2) APD totale nette / AP totale nette (2)			Total OOF Net (3) Flux AASP nets (3)		
			Total Donors / Tous donneurs	of which: / dont :		Total Donors / Tous donneurs	of which: / dont :	
				DAC Bilateral Donors / Donneurs bilatéraux du CAD	Multilateral Donors / Donneurs multilatéraux		DAC Bilateral Donors / Donneurs bilatéraux du CAD	Multilateral Donors / Donneurs multilatéraux
			Millions of dollars / Millions de dollars					
Turks and Caicos Islands - Îles Turques et Caïques	1990	11.8	11.8	8.9	3.0	0.0	0.0	0.0
	1995	5.7	5.6	5.5	0.1	0.1	0.0	0.1
	2000	7.3	6.7	5.6	1.1	0.6	0.0	0.6
	2005	5.8	5.2	3.1	2.1	0.6	0.0	0.6
Central America - Amérique centrale	*1990*	*6 624.2*	*1 850.2*	*1 599.5*	*244.7*	*4 774.0*	*2 027.8*	*2 751.0*
	1995	*2 394.8*	*2 043.2*	*1 553.9*	*466.3*	*351.6*	*-834.9*	*1 187.7*
	2000	*1 733.9*	*1 444.0*	*1 002.4*	*425.4*	*289.9*	*-778.0*	*1 029.9*
	2005	*1 357.0*	*2 125.2*	*1 556.7*	*558.7*	*-768.2*	*-397.9*	*-345.0*
Belize	1990	38.6	30.4	18.8	11.4	8.1	4.1	4.1
	1995	23.7	18.6	8.8	6.6	5.2	-2.0	7.2
	2000	31.8	14.7	2.9	11.2	17.2	3.5	13.7
	2005	11.6	12.9	7.5	5.4	-1.3	-0.1	-1.2
Costa Rica	1990	240.3	229.5	206.6	21.7	10.8	21.1	-10.3
	1995	84.1	34.2	16.6	4.6	49.9	-28.2	78.1
	2000	-37.4	11.8	17.2	-6.2	-49.2	-26.8	-22.3
	2005	-98.9	29.5	25.0	3.9	-128.4	7.1	-135.5
El Salvador	1990	308.7	347.7	312.0	34.7	-39.0	-0.9	-38.1
	1995	382.9	297.2	243.7	52.4	85.7	0.1	85.6
	2000	283.7	180.0	172.3	7.1	103.7	-13.1	117.2
	2005	318.3	199.4	162.4	34.3	119.0	-14.6	133.5
Guatemala	1990	222.3	202.1	149.5	51.3	20.1	6.2	13.9
	1995	207.4	209.8	161.4	46.6	-2.4	11.6	-14.0
	2000	321.7	263.6	230.3	32.8	58.0	7.5	51.4
	2005	248.7	253.6	218.5	33.3	-4.9	-5.5	0.6
Honduras	1990	434.0	449.2	383.5	64.7	-15.2	-0.7	-14.6
	1995	397.1	405.6	232.9	171.3	-8.4	26.1	-33.9
	2000	397.8	450.0	310.6	134.8	-52.2	20.2	-71.7
	2005	501.0	680.8	456.1	223.0	-179.9	-82.9	-97.0
Mexico - Mexique	1990	5 027.3	159.3	144.7	14.5	4 868.0	2 034.9	2 837.9
	1995	408.8	385.1	365.1	20.0	23.7	-990.4	1 014.6
	2000	77.8	-54.1	-68.4	13.7	131.9	-751.7	842.6
	2005	-195.3	189.4	160.6	27.5	-384.7	-184.6	-175.4
Nicaragua	1990	329.5	332.4	288.5	43.9	-2.9	-1.8	-1.1
	1995	826.8	652.9	492.1	159.7	173.9	165.1	8.8
	2000	553.3	561.5	325.9	235.3	-8.3	-6.2	-2.0
	2005	613.4	740.1	509.5	229.6	-126.7	-115.0	-11.7
Panama	1990	23.7	99.6	96.0	2.6	-75.8	-35.0	-40.8
	1995	64.0	39.9	33.5	5.2	24.2	-17.2	41.3
	2000	105.2	16.5	11.7	-3.3	88.7	-11.5	101.1
	2005	-41.8	19.5	17.3	1.6	-61.3	-2.5	-58.2
South America - Amérique du Sud	*1990*	*5 262.7*	*2 047.5*	*1 569.5*	*476.6*	*3 215.2*	*1 608.0*	*1 613.8*
	1995	*3 613.3*	*2 479.8*	*1 910.0*	*567.7*	*1 133.5*	*864.1*	*271.4*
	2000	*7 024.9*	*1 974.7*	*1 562.0*	*396.8*	*5 050.3*	*-157.0*	*5 235.5*
	2005	*-60.0*	*2 439.6*	*1 806.5*	*614.4*	*-2 499.5*	*-1 144.6*	*-1 289.7*
Argentina - Argentine	1990	905.0	169.9	166.2	3.7	735.1	411.9	323.2
	1995	2 530.4	143.5	110.3	33.2	2 386.9	719.6	1 667.1
	2000	700.9	76.3	43.5	25.3	624.6	-550.3	1 178.0
	2005	-432.2	99.7	77.9	20.0	-531.9	-106.2	-425.6
Bolivia - Bolivie	1990	578.1	547.3	364.7	182.6	30.8	10.4	20.4
	1995	719.7	718.8	518.0	200.5	0.9	-18.8	19.7
	2000	438.8	474.6	336.1	138.3	-35.8	-25.4	-10.4
	2005	558.7	582.9	388.3	190.1	-24.1	-30.1	5.9
Brazil - Brésil	1990	530.6	155.5	142.1	13.4	375.2	715.4	-334.5
	1995	-38.5	273.1	204.1	72.4	-311.6	-32.0	-278.6
	2000	4 188.7	322.4	222.5	98.4	3 866.3	440.5	3 435.4
	2005	128.7	191.9	170.9	19.7	-63.2	-360.8	362.7

For sources and notes, see end of table.

Pour es sources et les notes, se reporter à la fin du tableau.

7.6.1 Official financial flows from bilateral and multilateral sources to developing economies by country and geographical region
7.6.1 Flux financiers publics bilatéraux et multilatéraux à destination des économies en développement par pays et régions géographiques

Region, country or territory / Régions, pays ou territoires	Year / Année	Total Official Net (1) / Total secteur officiel net (1)	Total ODA Net / Total OA Net (2) — APD totale nette / AP totale nette (2)			Total OOF Net (3) — Flux AASP nets (3)		
			Total Donors / Tous donneurs	of which: / dont :		Total Donors / Tous donneurs	of which: / dont :	
				DAC Bilateral Donors / Donneurs bilatéraux du CAD	Multilateral Donors / Donneurs multilatéraux		DAC Bilateral Donors / Donneurs bilatéraux du CAD	Multilateral Donors / Donneurs multilatéraux
			Millions of dollars / Millions de dollars					
Chile - Chili	1990	787.6	103.9	83.3	20.6	683.7	207.9	475.8
	1995	-1 626.5	157.4	143.3	14.1	-1 783.9	-98.2	-1 685.8
	2000	-207.2	49.3	41.0	7.7	-256.5	-175.6	-80.8
	2005	12.9	151.7	75.6	75.0	-138.8	50.7	-189.5
Colombia - Colombie	1990	-0.5	89.5	86.6	2.9	-90.0	-93.2	3.2
	1995	73.7	171.1	160.7	10.1	-97.4	131.3	-228.7
	2000	-23.9	186.9	178.5	7.8	-210.9	-276.7	66.0
	2005	-355.0	511.1	457.9	51.9	-866.1	-119.6	-746.5
Ecuador - Équateur	1990	354.2	160.9	122.2	38.3	193.3	112.7	80.6
	1995	637.2	227.1	160.7	65.6	410.1	85.3	324.8
	2000	227.1	146.8	137.4	8.6	80.3	-16.0	108.7
	2005	29.2	209.5	174.8	35.0	-180.3	-68.7	-111.7
Falkland Islands (Malvinas) - Îles Falkland (Malvinas)	1990	1.8	1.8	1.8	..	0.0	0.0	..
	1995	1.7	1.7	0.1	1.6	0.0	0.0	0.0
	2000	0.7	-0.2	..	-0.2	1.0	-0.4	1.4
Guyana	1990	222.0	168.8	35.8	132.9	53.2	72.0	-18.8
	1995	81.5	86.0	23.2	62.7	-4.6	11.3	-15.8
	2000	95.3	107.3	51.9	55.4	-11.9	-0.7	-11.2
	2005	139.3	136.8	38.7	98.0	2.5	0.0	2.5
Paraguay	1990	29.8	57.5	47.6	9.0	-27.8	1.6	-29.4
	1995	153.7	139.6	105.8	30.3	14.1	-20.1	34.2
	2000	202.3	81.8	72.9	8.5	120.5	8.3	112.2
	2005	46.0	51.1	55.3	-6.7	-5.1	-3.9	-1.2
Peru - Pérou	1990	401.4	400.2	350.4	49.8	1.2	-2.0	3.2
	1995	819.7	372.9	327.0	45.5	446.9	65.4	381.5
	2000	1 116.2	401.1	372.7	26.0	715.1	515.7	201.9
	2005	178.1	397.8	310.2	82.8	-219.7	-399.6	179.9
Suriname	1990	64.8	61.7	51.2	10.5	3.1	-0.1	4.0
	1995	75.3	77.1	70.3	6.7	-1.8	0.0	-0.7
	2000	36.2	34.4	29.1	5.2	1.8	0.0	1.8
	2005	42.5	44.0	33.5	10.4	-1.5	-0.6	-0.8
Uruguay	1990	87.3	53.1	41.7	11.3	34.2	1.1	33.1
	1995	54.7	67.8	57.5	10.2	-13.0	-2.6	-10.4
	2000	198.7	17.5	15.3	1.4	181.3	2.0	179.2
	2005	62.7	14.6	2.8	11.2	48.1	4.2	43.9
Venezuela (Bolivarian Republic of) - Venezuela (République bolivarienne du)	1990	1 300.7	77.5	75.7	1.8	1 223.2	170.3	1 052.9
	1995	130.8	43.8	29.0	14.9	86.9	22.9	64.0
	2000	51.1	76.6	61.3	14.6	-25.5	-78.5	53.3
	2005	-470.8	48.7	20.8	27.1	-519.4	-110.0	-409.4
Developing Economies: America Unallocated - Économies en développement Amérique : non ventilé	1990	674.6	535.8	352.8	183.0	138.8	-0.2	139.1
	1995	660.2	609.9	488.1	120.9	50.4	127.9	-77.6
	2000	1 157.3	1 120.1	1 002.7	117.4	37.2	1.5	35.7
	2005	825.2	893.6	628.5	255.5	-68.4	0.0	-68.4
Developing economies: Asia - Économies en développement : Asie	**1990**	**24 391.7**	**17 980.7**	**10 544.6**	**4 752.6**	**6 411.1**	**3 075.4**	**3 481.1**
	1995	**24 307.9**	**17 506.7**	**11 754.6**	**5 322.2**	**6 801.2**	**5 104.2**	**1 555.2**
	2000	**13 004.5**	**14 925.4**	**10 146.9**	**4 358.6**	**-1 920.8**	**-3 775.0**	**2 518.1**
	2005	**48 951.8**	**43 840.4**	**36 431.6**	**6 659.2**	**5 111.5**	**3 816.5**	**569.6**
Eastern Asia - Asie orientale	*1990*	*2 887.7*	*2 186.1*	*1 553.3*	*613.5*	*701.6*	*662.3*	*39.3*
	1995	*6 916.9*	*3 771.6*	*2 688.1*	*1 051.5*	*3 145.4*	*1 766.2*	*1 275.8*
	2000	*1 176.8*	*1 841.3*	*1 251.4*	*568.4*	*-664.4*	*-2 060.8*	*1 439.5*
	2005	*636.1*	*2 049.8*	*1 860.7*	*134.6*	*-1 413.7*	*-1 072.8*	*-452.6*
China - Chine	1990	3 301.8	2 037.6	1 465.5	577.4	1 264.1	835.9	428.2
	1995	7 047.1	3 476.2	2 476.6	958.0	3 571.0	1 839.6	1 627.9
	2000	1 180.7	1 731.9	1 256.2	460.4	-551.2	-2 141.3	1 639.1
	2005	2 058.2	1 756.9	1 689.4	39.2	301.3	-1 073.6	1 263.4
China, Hong Kong SAR - Chine, Hong Kong RAS	1990	31.4	38.2	19.4	18.7	-6.8	-6.8	0.0
	1995	2.3	17.7	11.5	6.2	-15.5	-15.5	0.0
	2000	-8.4	4.3	4.2	0.1	-12.8	-21.6	0.0

For sources and notes, see end of table.

Pour les sources et les notes, se reporter à la fin du tableau.

7

7.6.1 Official financial flows from bilateral and multilateral sources to developing economies by country and geographical region

7.6.1 Flux financiers publics bilatéraux et multilatéraux à destination des économies en développement par pays et régions géographiques

Region, country or territory / Régions, pays ou territoires	Year / Année	Total Official Net (1) / Total secteur officiel net (1)	Total ODA Net / Total OA Net (2) / APD totale nette / AP totale nette (2)			Total OOF Net (3) / Flux AASP nets (3)		
			Total Donors / Tous donneurs	of which: / dont :		Total Donors / Tous donneurs	of which: / dont :	
				DAC Bilateral Donors / Donneurs bilatéraux du CAD	Multilateral Donors / Donneurs multilatéraux		DAC Bilateral Donors / Donneurs bilatéraux du CAD	Multilateral Donors / Donneurs multilatéraux
			Millions of dollars / Millions de dollars					
China, Macao SAR - Chine, Macao RAS	1990	0.2	0.2	0.1	0.1	0.0	0.0	0.0
	1995	-4.0	-4.0	0.1	-4.1	0.0	0.0	0.0
	2000	0.7	0.7	0.2	0.5	0.0	0.0	0.0
China, Taiwan Province of - Chine, Taiwan Province de	1990	24.6	36.3	6.3	..	-11.7	-3.1	-8.6
	1995	10.1	0.2	11.0	..	9.9	9.9	..
	2000	6.8	9.7	9.7	..	-2.9	0.0	..
Korea, Dem. People's Rep. of - Corée, Rép. populaire dém. de	1990	7.4	8.2	0.9	7.4	-0.9	-0.9	0.0
	1995	17.2	13.7	1.5	12.2	3.5	3.5	0.0
	2000	36.4	75.2	26.9	48.3	-38.8	0.9	-39.7
	2005	-1 634.2	81.1	39.4	41.5	-1 715.3	0.6	-1 715.9
Korea, Republic of - Corée, République de	1990	-490.8	52.4	54.8	3.1	-543.2	-162.9	-380.3
	1995	-354.0	57.1	60.4	0.6	-411.1	-59.0	-352.1
	2000	-256.8	-198.0	-196.6	-1.5	-58.7	101.2	-159.9
Mongolia - Mongolie	1990	13.1	13.1	6.3	6.8	0.0	0.0	0.0
	1995	198.2	210.6	126.9	78.7	-12.4	-12.4	0.0
	2000	217.5	217.5	150.8	60.6	0.0	0.0	0.0
	2005	212.1	211.9	131.9	54.0	0.2	0.3	0.0
Southern Asia - Asie méridionale	*1990*	*7 918.5*	*6 090.7*	*3 318.3*	*2 768.9*	*1 827.9*	*177.2*	*1 654.6*
	1995	*6 033.8*	*5 378.6*	*3 138.9*	*2 334.7*	*655.2*	*469.5*	*185.6*
	2000	*3 575.7*	*4 368.7*	*2 460.6*	*1 869.9*	*-793.1*	*-593.4*	*-130.9*
	2005	*11 819.9*	*9 364.5*	*5 813.6*	*3 275.7*	*2 455.4*	*209.2*	*1 776.6*
Afghanistan	1990	130.8	130.8	100.4	31.7	0.0	0.0	0.0
	1995	214.3	214.3	106.1	108.2	0.0	0.0	0.0
	2000	140.9	140.9	87.5	52.7	0.0	0.0	0.0
	2005	2 830.3	2 775.3	2 191.7	536.4	54.9	12.9	42.0
Bangladesh	1990	2 114.7	2 095.1	1 103.3	1 002.1	19.7	21.9	-2.2
	1995	1 283.5	1 292.3	727.4	573.9	-8.8	-3.3	-5.5
	2000	1 170.6	1 171.3	616.5	519.5	-0.7	-2.4	4.6
	2005	1 461.5	1 320.5	562.9	726.7	140.9	-12.6	153.7
Bhutan - Bhoutan	1990	46.9	46.9	20.1	27.6	0.0	0.0	0.0
	1995	71.8	71.8	55.2	16.2	0.0	0.0	0.0
	2000	53.2	53.3	33.7	20.0	-0.1	-0.1	0.0
	2005	94.8	90.0	57.0	32.8	4.8	4.4	0.4
India - Inde	1990	2 907.7	1 406.4	751.8	652.1	1 501.2	255.5	1 248.3
	1995	1 780.0	1 739.5	1 060.8	705.6	40.6	41.4	-0.8
	2000	1 344.9	1 485.2	650.3	846.5	-140.3	20.7	-191.9
	2005	2 876.1	1 724.1	846.3	874.6	1 152.0	-258.2	1 318.7
Iran, Islamic Republic of - Iran, Rép. islamique d'	1990	-95.7	105.2	34.8	36.0	-200.9	-133.9	-67.0
	1995	400.3	191.3	158.9	32.4	209.0	129.6	79.4
	2000	-582.3	130.1	112.8	17.2	-712.4	-668.8	44.4
	2005	1 039.5	104.0	78.2	21.0	935.4	481.9	104.1
Maldives	1990	25.3	21.2	11.6	10.2	4.1	4.1	0.0
	1995	59.3	57.9	30.4	21.5	1.3	1.3	0.0
	2000	16.3	19.3	13.3	7.2	-3.0	-1.8	-1.2
	2005	109.8	66.8	39.7	22.5	43.0	-1.1	44.0
Nepal - Népal	1990	435.3	426.0	239.0	184.7	9.3	0.0	9.2
	1995	432.3	432.6	266.1	166.9	-0.3	0.7	-1.0
	2000	412.6	389.6	231.2	154.9	23.0	2.7	20.2
	2005	420.1	427.9	348.7	77.4	-7.9	-0.6	-7.2
Pakistan	1990	1 633.8	1 129.3	653.5	494.9	504.5	31.2	474.7
	1995	1 244.7	823.8	360.1	528.5	421.0	299.9	121.1
	2000	766.1	702.8	475.1	226.7	63.3	81.1	-11.4
	2005	1 736.8	1 666.5	832.2	699.9	70.3	-22.4	65.1
Sri Lanka	1990	719.8	729.8	403.8	329.5	-10.0	-1.6	-8.5
	1995	547.5	555.1	374.0	181.5	-7.6	-0.1	-7.6
	2000	253.5	276.3	240.2	25.2	-22.8	-24.8	4.4
	2005	1 251.2	1 189.3	857.1	284.5	61.9	4.9	55.8

For sources and notes, see end of table.

Pour les sources et les notes, se reporter à la fin du tableau.

7.6.1 Official financial flows from bilateral and multilateral sources to developing economies by country and geographical region

7.6.1 Flux financiers publics bilatéraux et multilatéraux à destination des économies en développement par pays et régions géographiques

Region, country or territory / Régions, pays ou territoires	Year / Année	Total Official Net (1) / Total secteur officiel net (1)	Total ODA Net / Total OA Net (2) — APD totale nette / AP totale nette (2)			Total OOF Net (3) — Flux AASP nets (3)		
			Total Donors / Tous donneurs	of which: / dont : DAC Bilateral Donors / Donneurs bilatéraux du CAD	Multilateral Donors / Donneurs multilatéraux	Total Donors / Tous donneurs	of which: / dont : DAC Bilateral Donors / Donneurs bilatéraux du CAD	Multilateral Donors / Donneurs multilatéraux
		Millions of dollars / Millions de dollars						
South-Eastern Asia - Asie du Sud-Est	*1990*	*7 804.2*	*4 810.1*	*4 085.8*	*704.7*	*2 994.1*	*1 561.3*	*1 456.8*
	1995	*7 587.1*	*5 032.1*	*4 099.6*	*929.6*	*2 555.0*	*2 021.7*	*488.8*
	2000	*4 172.4*	*5 682.4*	*4 742.9*	*916.7*	*-1 510.0*	*-1 295.2*	*334.6*
	2005	*4 961.5*	*6 013.7*	*4 567.3*	*1 324.0*	*-1 052.2*	*-376.7*	*-833.9*
Brunei Darussalam - Brunéi Darussalam	1990	-4.5	3.9	3.7	0.1	-8.4	-8.4	0.0
	1995	4.3	4.3	4.2	0.1	0.0	0.0	0.0
	2000	0.7	0.6	0.6	0.0	0.1	0.1	0.0
Cambodia - Cambodge	1990	41.6	41.6	28.5	13.1	0.0	0.0	0.0
	1995	559.0	556.0	341.2	214.8	3.0	3.0	0.0
	2000	398.0	398.4	248.0	149.7	-0.4	-0.2	0.0
	2005	553.1	537.8	344.4	175.5	15.3	1.5	13.0
Indonesia - Indonésie	1990	3 261.7	1 722.1	1 520.1	177.5	1 539.6	534.3	1 029.3
	1995	2 707.6	1 303.5	1 215.8	98.5	1 404.1	820.8	545.2
	2000	2 321.4	1 657.8	1 544.0	109.5	663.6	-6.7	721.0
	2005	859.3	2 523.5	2 247.2	230.1	-1 664.3	-1 503.1	-317.4
Lao People's Dem. Rep. - Rép. dém. populaire lao	1990	150.6	150.6	51.2	98.4	0.0	0.0	0.0
	1995	308.7	308.6	170.0	138.5	0.1	0.1	0.0
	2000	281.4	281.8	194.9	86.1	-0.4	-0.3	0.2
	2005	355.3	295.7	159.0	126.3	59.6	10.2	49.4
Malaysia - Malaisie	1990	538.9	468.8	458.6	13.6	70.1	-6.3	76.4
	1995	400.6	108.8	106.9	8.0	291.8	412.8	-121.0
	2000	-117.6	45.4	43.3	3.3	-163.0	-80.2	-73.9
	2005	-524.0	31.6	20.1	7.4	-555.6	-423.8	-131.8
Myanmar	1990	186.7	163.5	83.1	80.4	23.2	23.6	-0.4
	1995	155.6	151.4	126.3	23.2	4.2	5.1	-0.9
	2000	127.0	106.8	68.1	37.8	20.2	1.3	0.0
	2005	116.8	144.7	77.8	58.7	-27.9	-27.9	0.0
Philippines	1990	2 180.6	1 274.3	1 102.1	171.0	906.3	411.7	494.6
	1995	679.1	905.9	764.5	132.6	-226.8	-169.5	-57.2
	2000	359.1	577.5	502.1	72.2	-218.4	-10.3	-198.1
	2005	49.7	561.8	526.4	27.4	-512.1	-569.0	62.5
Singapore - Singapour	1990	152.1	-3.1	-3.2	0.1	155.2	193.2	-38.1
	1995	-49.0	16.7	13.9	2.8	-65.6	-65.6	0.0
	2000	-157.9	1.1	0.7	0.4	-159.0	-157.6	0.0
Thailand - Thaïlande	1990	1 107.7	799.4	733.7	69.5	308.2	413.2	-104.9
	1995	1 768.3	839.6	807.2	37.7	928.7	821.9	106.9
	2000	-1 244.9	698.4	682.9	17.7	-1 943.2	-1 329.1	-159.7
	2005	1 337.4	-171.1	-219.9	40.3	1 508.4	2 001.9	-492.3
Timor-Leste	1990	0.1	0.1	..	0.1	0.0	..	0.0
	1995	0.0	0.0	0.0	..	0.0	0.0	..
	2000	650.7	232.9	212.3	20.6	417.8	417.8	0.0
	2005	185.8	184.7	160.1	24.3	1.1	1.1	0.0
Viet Nam	1990	188.9	188.9	107.9	80.9	0.0	0.2	-0.1
	1995	1 052.9	837.3	549.7	273.4	215.6	193.2	15.8
	2000	1 554.3	1 681.8	1 246.2	419.5	-127.5	-129.9	45.1
	2005	2 028.1	1 904.9	1 252.1	634.1	123.3	132.4	-17.4
Western Asia - Asie occidentale	*1990*	*4 636.5*	*3 748.9*	*1 349.7*	*243.0*	*887.5*	*674.6*	*330.4*
	1995	*3 002.5*	*2 543.2*	*1 356.8*	*696.7*	*459.3*	*846.8*	*-381.4*
	2000	*3 419.7*	*2 373.7*	*1 260.7*	*850.4*	*1 046.0*	*165.5*	*883.0*
	2005	*29 592.4*	*24 554.9*	*22 776.5*	*1 484.2*	*5 037.5*	*4 974.8*	*77.1*
Bahrain - Bahreïn	1990	136.2	137.0	1.9	2.4	-0.8	-0.8	0.0
	1995	47.4	49.2	1.8	0.5	-1.8	-1.8	0.0
	2000	48.9	49.1	1.6	0.0	-0.2	-0.2	0.0
Iraq	1990	700.3	63.4	-8.6	16.6	636.9	642.3	-5.4
	1995	328.8	339.3	238.9	88.3	-10.5	-10.5	0.0
	2000	100.8	100.8	84.1	16.6	0.0	0.0	0.0
	2005	26 852.8	21 653.5	21 426.6	53.2	5 199.3	5 199.3	0.0

For sources and notes, see end of table.

Pour les sources et les notes, se reporter à la fin du tableau.

7.6.1 Official financial flows from bilateral and multilateral sources to developing economies by country and geographical region

7.6.1 Flux financiers publics bilatéraux et multilatéraux à destination des économies en développement par pays et régions géographiques

Region, country or territory / Régions, pays ou territoires	Year / Année	Total Official Net (1) / Total secteur officiel net (1)	Total ODA Net / Total OA Net (2) APD totale nette / AP totale nette (2)			Total OOF Net (3) Flux AASP nets (3)		
			Total Donors / Tous donneurs	of which: / dont :		Total Donors / Tous donneurs	of which: / dont :	
				DAC Bilateral Donors / Donneurs bilatéraux du CAD	Multilateral Donors / Donneurs multilatéraux		DAC Bilateral Donors / Donneurs bilatéraux du CAD	Multilateral Donors / Donneurs multilatéraux
			Millions of dollars / Millions de dollars					
Jordan - Jordanie	1990	1 081.8	887.7	435.0	26.8	194.1	126.1	75.5
	1995	1 032.8	540.1	392.1	145.0	492.7	410.0	82.7
	2000	552.2	552.5	385.3	168.0	-0.2	-21.4	21.2
	2005	700.4	622.0	440.8	145.4	78.4	26.3	52.2
Kuwait - Koweït	1990	5.8	5.8	2.2	3.6	0.0	0.0	0.0
	1995	19.7	3.2	2.1	1.1	16.5	16.5	0.0
	2000	-20.9	2.9	2.0	0.9	-23.8	-23.8	0.0
Lebanon - Liban	1990	229.9	252.4	64.9	39.3	-22.5	-13.6	-8.9
	1995	310.5	187.2	57.2	73.3	123.4	2.2	121.2
	2000	268.5	199.7	93.7	91.3	68.8	2.8	66.0
	2005	195.3	243.0	129.8	115.0	-47.7	-2.7	-45.0
Palestinian territory - Territoire palestinien	1995	498.6	498.6	183.2	262.9	0.0	0.0	0.0
	2000	682.6	637.3	306.4	226.1	45.3	-0.1	45.4
	2005	1 101.1	1 101.6	569.4	516.0	-0.5	0.2	-0.8
Oman	1990	57.7	61.2	11.3	2.3	-3.5	6.0	-9.6
	1995	52.1	58.7	11.9	2.5	-6.6	-10.8	4.1
	2000	50.6	45.6	9.2	2.3	5.0	9.7	-4.7
	2005	275.4	30.7	3.9	1.3	244.7	191.0	53.8
Qatar	1990	1.6	1.7	1.3	0.3	0.0	0.0	0.0
	1995	618.0	2.3	2.1	0.2	615.7	615.7	0.0
	2000	-108.4	0.5	1.1	-0.6	-108.9	-108.9	0.0
Saudi Arabia - Arabie saoudite	1990	39.4	40.0	12.8	27.1	-0.6	-0.6	0.0
	1995	6.7	17.3	14.5	2.2	-10.6	-10.6	0.0
	2000	57.1	31.0	18.0	11.2	26.1	26.5	0.0
	2005	-33.5	26.3	13.8	2.0	-59.8	-109.5	49.7
Syrian Arab Republic - République arabe syrienne	1990	674.3	683.4	69.4	34.8	-9.1	0.5	-10.3
	1995	326.1	359.3	158.9	73.1	-33.2	-5.1	-21.9
	2000	486.4	158.5	97.3	38.7	327.9	342.1	-14.2
	2005	109.3	77.9	5.9	74.6	31.4	-17.5	48.9
Turkey - Turquie	1990	1 297.9	1 207.8	587.9	-10.7	90.0	-88.5	289.1
	1995	-328.1	313.7	180.7	-11.7	-641.8	-74.2	-567.5
	2000	1 082.6	327.2	99.7	190.7	755.5	-4.1	761.6
	2005	56.9	464.0	51.8	410.2	-407.1	-312.3	-80.5
United Arab Emirates - Émirats arabes unis	1990	4.2	4.0	2.8	1.1	0.3	0.3	0.0
	1995	-77.6	5.5	4.8	0.4	-83.0	-83.0	0.0
	2000	-53.1	4.0	2.7	1.3	-57.1	-57.1	0.0
Yemen - Yémen	1990	407.5	404.7	168.8	99.3	2.8	2.8	0.0
	1995	167.6	169.1	108.6	59.0	-1.6	-1.6	0.0
	2000	272.5	264.8	159.6	104.0	7.6	0.0	7.7
	2005	334.7	335.9	134.7	166.7	-1.2	0.0	-1.2
Developing Economies: Asia Unallocated - Économies en développement Asie : non ventilé	1990	1 144.9	1 144.9	237.5	422.6	0.0	0.0	0.0
	1995	767.6	781.3	471.3	309.7	-13.7	0.0	-13.7
	2000	660.0	659.3	431.4	153.2	0.7	8.9	-8.2
	2005	1 941.9	1 857.4	1 413.6	440.6	84.5	82.0	2.5
Developing economies: Oceania - Économies en développement : Océanie	**1990**	**1 497.3**	**1 374.8**	**1 214.7**	**156.8**	**122.5**	**60.0**	**62.5**
	1995	**1 975.9**	**1 867.7**	**1 710.9**	**152.3**	**108.3**	**119.6**	**-11.3**
	2000	**1 620.3**	**1 569.4**	**1 459.2**	**106.8**	**50.9**	**51.4**	**2.4**
	2005	**1 136.8**	**1 144.5**	**977.2**	**165.2**	**-7.7**	**-12.6**	**8.5**
Cook Islands - Îles Cook	1990	11.4	12.2	10.1	2.1	-0.8	-0.8	0.0
	1995	13.1	13.1	10.4	2.6	0.0	0.0	0.0
	2000	4.2	4.3	3.4	0.9	-0.2	-0.2	0.0
	2005	7.4	7.8	7.0	0.8	-0.3	-0.3	0.0
Fiji - Fidji	1990	35.8	50.5	43.5	6.5	-14.7	-0.4	-14.3
	1995	42.4	44.9	39.1	4.4	-2.5	3.6	-6.0
	2000	22.8	29.1	28.7	0.2	-6.3	-0.1	-6.2
	2005	74.2	64.0	38.8	24.8	10.2	2.2	8.1

For sources and notes, see end of table.

Pour les sources et les notes, se reporter à la fin du tableau.

7.6.1 Official financial flows from bilateral and multilateral sources to developing economies by country and geographical region

7.6.1 Flux financiers publics bilatéraux et multilatéraux à destination des économies en développement par pays et régions géographiques

Region, country or territory / Régions, pays ou territoires	Year / Année	Total Official Net (1) / Total secteur officiel net (1)	Total ODA Net / Total OA Net (2) APD totale nette / AP totale nette (2)			Total OOF Net (3) Flux AASP nets (3)		
			Total Donors / Tous donneurs	of which: / dont :		Total Donors / Tous donneurs	of which: / dont :	
				DAC Bilateral Donors / Donneurs bilatéraux du CAD	Multilateral Donors / Donneurs multilatéraux		DAC Bilateral Donors / Donneurs bilatéraux du CAD	Multilateral Donors / Donneurs multilatéraux
			Millions of dollars / Millions de dollars					
French Polynesia - Polynésie française	1990	304.0	259.7	258.0	1.7	44.3	44.7	-0.4
	1995	434.3	450.9	444.4	6.5	-16.6	-16.1	-0.5
	2000	381.0	402.6	400.2	2.4	-21.6	-21.6	0.0
Kiribati	1990	20.2	20.2	17.7	2.5	0.0	0.0	0.0
	1995	15.4	15.4	11.4	4.0	0.0	0.0	0.0
	2000	17.9	17.9	14.8	3.1	0.0	0.0	0.0
	2005	28.1	27.8	21.3	6.5	0.2	0.2	0.0
Marshall Islands - Îles Marshall	1995	38.9	38.9	32.1	6.8	0.0	0.0	0.0
	2000	57.2	57.2	47.1	10.1	0.0	0.0	0.0
	2005	56.5	56.6	55.8	0.7	-0.1	0.0	-0.1
Micronesia, Federated States of - Micronésie, États fédérés de	1995	78.3	77.3	71.8	5.5	1.0	1.0	0.0
	2000	101.5	101.6	96.6	5.0	-0.1	0.0	0.0
	2005	106.6	106.4	104.4	1.9	0.3	0.4	0.0
Nauru	1990	0.2	0.2	0.2	..	0.0	0.0	..
	1995	2.8	2.8	2.2	0.0	0.0	0.0	0.0
	2000	4.0	4.0	3.9	0.1	0.0	0.0	0.0
	2005	9.3	9.1	8.9	0.1	0.2	0.2	0.0
New Caledonia - Nouvelle-Calédonie	1990	325.8	302.4	300.2	2.2	23.4	24.0	-0.6
	1995	548.8	451.2	442.3	9.0	97.6	98.7	-1.1
	2000	351.8	350.2	348.7	1.4	1.6	1.6	0.0
Niue - Nioué	1990	7.2	7.2	7.0	0.2	0.0	0.0	0.0
	1995	8.3	8.3	8.1	0.2	0.0	0.0	0.0
	2000	3.2	3.2	3.0	0.2	0.0	0.0	0.0
	2005	21.1	21.1	20.1	1.0	0.0	0.0	0.0
Northern Mariana Islands - Îles Mariannes du Nord	1990	63.1	63.1	61.9	1.2	0.0	0.0	0.0
	1995	18.8	-0.7	-0.2	-0.5	19.5	19.5	0.0
Palau, Pacific Islands (former) - Palaos, Îles du Pacifique (anc.)	1995	156.3	142.3	141.7	0.1	14.0	14.0	0.0
	2000	37.7	39.1	38.9	0.2	-1.5	-1.5	0.0
	2005	21.4	23.5	23.4	0.1	-2.1	-2.1	0.0
Papua New Guinea - Papouasie-Nouvelle-Guinée	1990	475.6	413.2	320.0	91.6	62.5	-15.3	77.8
	1995	366.1	371.0	300.5	69.6	-5.0	-1.3	-3.7
	2000	357.3	275.4	268.6	5.2	81.9	75.3	9.2
	2005	263.1	266.1	245.3	21.2	-3.0	-0.2	0.6
Samoa	1990	47.6	47.7	27.7	19.6	-0.1	-0.1	0.0
	1995	43.4	43.4	31.3	12.3	0.0	0.0	0.0
	2000	27.8	27.4	18.1	9.2	0.4	0.3	0.1
	2005	44.4	44.0	29.9	13.9	0.4	0.5	-0.1
Solomon Islands - Îles Salomon	1990	46.2	45.8	31.1	14.3	0.5	0.5	0.0
	1995	47.0	47.8	36.5	10.2	-0.7	-0.7	0.0
	2000	69.6	68.4	20.8	46.3	1.2	1.2	0.0
	2005	186.6	198.2	172.3	25.9	-11.7	-11.7	0.0
Tokelau - Tokélaou	1990	4.8	4.8	4.4	0.4	0.0	0.0	0.0
	1995	3.7	3.7	3.5	0.3	0.0	0.0	0.0
	2000	3.5	3.5	3.4	0.1	0.0	0.0	0.0
	2005	16.0	16.0	15.9	0.1	0.0	0.0	0.0
Tonga	1990	29.6	29.8	24.2	5.5	-0.2	-0.2	0.0
	1995	38.9	38.9	28.8	10.0	0.0	0.0	0.0
	2000	18.9	18.8	14.8	4.0	0.0	0.0	0.0
	2005	32.2	31.8	24.7	7.0	0.4	0.4	0.0
Tuvalu	1990	5.1	5.1	4.8	0.3	0.0	0.0	0.0
	1995	7.9	7.9	6.3	1.6	0.0	0.0	0.0
	2000	4.0	4.0	3.8	0.2	0.0	0.0	0.0
	2005	9.0	9.0	5.9	3.1	0.0	0.0	0.0
Vanuatu	1990	54.4	49.8	42.1	7.7	4.6	4.6	0.0
	1995	45.2	45.6	39.6	6.1	-0.5	-0.5	0.0
	2000	45.2	45.8	28.3	17.5	-0.7	0.0	-0.7
	2005	40.3	39.5	33.4	6.1	0.8	0.8	0.0

For sources and notes, see end of table.

Pour es sources et les notes, se reporter à la fin du tableau.

7.6.1 Official financial flows from bilateral and multilateral sources to developing economies by country and geographical region

7.6.1 Flux financiers publics bilatéraux et multilatéraux à destination des économies en développement par pays et régions géographiques

Region, country or territory / Régions, pays ou territoires	Year / Année	Total Official Net (1) / Total secteur officiel net (1)	Total ODA Net / Total OA Net (2) APD totale nette / AP totale nette (2)			Total OOF Net (3) Flux AASP nets (3)		
			Total Donors / Tous donneurs	of which: / dont :		Total Donors / Tous donneurs	of which: / dont :	
				DAC Bilateral Donors / Donneurs bilatéraux du CAD	Multilateral Donors / Donneurs multilatéraux		DAC Bilateral Donors / Donneurs bilatéraux du CAD	Multilateral Donors / Donneurs multilatéraux
		Millions of dollars / Millions de dollars						
Wallis and Futuna Islands - Îles Wallis et Futuna	1990	3.9	0.9	0.0	0.9	3.0	3.0	0.0
	1995	0.5	1.0	0.1	0.8	-0.4	-0.4	0.0
	2000	53.3	52.1	52.1	0.0	1.2	1.2	0.0
	2005	69.0	72.0	71.7	0.4	-3.0	-3.0	0.0
Developing Economies: Oceania Unallocated - Économies en développement Océanie : non ventilé	1990	62.4	62.4	61.9	0.1	0.0	0.0	0.0
	1995	65.9	64.0	61.1	3.0	1.9	1.9	0.0
	2000	59.5	64.7	64.0	0.7	-5.2	-5.0	0.0
	2005	151.8	151.8	98.4	51.8	0.0	0.0	0.0
Developing Economies: Unspecified - Économies en développement : non spécifiées ailleurs	1990	6 442.3	6 090.4	5 139.0	901.6	351.9	351.9	0.0
	1995	8 921.9	8 508.4	7 037.0	1 387.3	413.5	-31.7	0.0
	2000	11 015.4	9 070.7	8 084.5	1 105.4	1 944.7	1 944.7	0.0
	2005	15 038.5	14 614.3	12 097.2	1 505.1	424.3	230.8	46.5

Sources:
- Organisation for Economic Co-operation and Development (OECD): *OLISNET*, online statistical database

Notes:

(1) Sum of "Total ODA/OA Net; total donors" and "Total OOF Net; total donors". It represents the total net disbursements by the official sector at large to the recipient country.

(2) Total ODA Net; total donors:
The Total Official Development Assistance (ODA) includes grants and loans to countries and territories on Part I of the "DAC List of Aid Recipients" which are:
undertaken by the official sector; with promotion of economic development and welfare as the main objective and at concessional financial terms (if a loan, have a grant element of at least 25 per cent).
Grants, loans and credits for military purposes are excluded.

"Total Donors" is the sum of the three following donor types:
- DAC Bilateral Donors: The Development Assistance Committee (DAC) is the Committee of the OECD which deals with development co-operation matters. It consists of 23 Member countries.
- Multilateral Donors (i.e. African Development Bank, International Bank for Reconstruction and Development, International Monetary Fund, United Nations Development Programme).
- Other Donors: the Non-DAC Bilateral Donors (i.e Hungary, Lithuania, Turkey).

(3) Total OOF Net; total donors:
The Other Official Flows (OOF) are transactions by the official sector whose main objective is other than development motivated, or, if development motivated, whose grant element is below the 25% threshold which would make them eligible to be recorded as ODA. The main classes of transactions included here are official export credits, official sector equity and portfolio investment, and debt reorganisation undertaken by the official sector at non-concessional terms (irrespective of the nature or the identity of the original creditor)

Total Donors is the sum of the three following donor types:
- DAC Bilateral Donors: The Development Assistance Committee (DAC) is the Committee of the OECD which deals with development co-operation matters. It consists of 23 Member countries.
- Multilateral Donors (i.e. African Development Bank, International Bank for Reconstruction and Development, International Monetary Fund, United Nations Development Programme).
- Other Donors: the Non-DAC Bilateral Donors (i.e Hungary, Lithuania, Turkey).

Sources :
- Organisation de coopération et de développement économique (OECD) : *OLISNET*, base de données statistique en ligne

Notes :

(1) Somme de "APD/AP totale nette ; tous donneurs" et de "Flux AASP nets ; tous donneurs". Cet agrégat correspond aux versements nets effectués par le secteur public dans son ensemble aux pays bénéficiaires considérés.

(2) AP totale nette ; tous donneurs :
Par aide publique (AP), on entend l'ensemble des apports de ressources qui sont fournis aux pays qui figurent à la Partie II de la "Liste des bénéficiaires de l'aide établie par le CAD" et qui répondent aux critères suivants :
a) être dispensés dans le but essentiel de favoriser le développement économique et l'amélioration du niveau de vie dans les pays en développement ; et
b) revêtir un caractère de faveur et comporter un élément de libéralité d'au moins 25 pour cent.

"Tous Donneurs" est la somme des 3 types de donneurs suivants :
- Donneurs Bilatéraux du CAD : Le Comité d'aide au développement (CAD) est la principale instance chargée, à l'OCDE, des questions relatives à la coopération avec les pays en développement. Le CAD regroupe 23 pays membres.
- Donneurs Multilatéraux (i.e. Banque africaine de développement, Banque internationale pour la reconstruction et le développement, Fonds monétaire international, Programme des Nations Unies pour le développement).
- Autres Donneurs : les Donneurs Bilatéraux non-membres du CAD (i.e. Hongrie, Lituanie, Turquie).

(3) Flux AASP nets ; tous donneurs :
Autres apports du secteur public (AASP) : il s'agit des opérations du secteur public dont le but essentiel est autre que le développement ou qui, tout en visant à favoriser le développement, sont assorties d'un élément de libéralité inférieur au seuil de 25 pour cent à partir duquel elles auraient pu être notifiées comme de l'APD. Les principales catégories d'opérations couvertes dans les AASP sont les crédits publics à l'exportation, les prises de participation et les investissements de portefeuille du secteur public et le réaménagement de la dette effectué par le secteur public aux conditions du marché (et ce, quelle que soit la nature ou l'identité du créancier initial).

Tous Donneurs est la somme des 3 types de donneurs suivants :
- Donneurs Bilatéraux du CAD : Le Comité d'aide au développement (CAD) est la principale instance chargée, à l'OCDE, des questions relatives à la coopération avec les pays en développement. Le CAD regroupe 23 pays membres.
- Donneurs Multilatéraux (i.e. Banque africaine de développement, Banque internationale pour la reconstruction et le développement, Fonds monétaire international, Programme des Nations Unies pour le développement).
- Autres Donneurs : les Donneurs Bilatéraux non-membres du CAD (i.e. Hongrie, Lituanie, Turquie).

7.6.2 Official financial flows from bilateral and multilateral sources to developing economies by economic grouping
7.6.2 Flux financiers publics bilatéraux et multilatéraux à destination des économies en développement par groupements économiques

Economic grouping / Groupements économiques	Year / Année	Total Official Net (1) / Total secteur officiel net (1)	Total ODA Net / Total OA Net (2) — APD totale nette / AP totale nette (2) — Total Donors / Tous donneurs	of which: / dont : — DAC Bilateral Donors / Donneurs bilatéraux du CAD	of which: / dont : — Multilateral Donors / Donneurs multilatéraux	Total OOF Net (3) / Flux AASP nets (3) — Total Donors / Tous donneurs	of which: / dont : — DAC Bilateral Donors / Donneurs bilatéraux du CAD	of which: / dont : — Multilateral Donors / Donneurs multilatéraux
			Millions of dollars / Millions de dollars					
DEVELOPING ECONOMIES -	**1990**	**74 171.0**	**56 004.3**	**36 861.8**	**13 260.0**	**18 166.7**	**8 065.1**	**10 128.2**
ÉCONOMIES EN DÉVELOPPEMENT	**1995**	**68 631.1**	**56 302.8**	**38 535.0**	**17 068.0**	**12 328.3**	**8 847.3**	**2 897.7**
	2000	**51 353.7**	**46 459.0**	**34 109.0**	**11 695.0**	**4 894.7**	**-2 577.4**	**8 141.6**
	2005	**103 234.6**	**101 104.5**	**78 797.5**	**20 277.6**	**2 130.1**	**2 052.6**	**-685.1**
Developing economies excluding China -	1990	61 518.5	45 123.1	28 759.8	11 020.7	16 395.4	6 871.7	9 550.3
Économies en développement sans la Chine	1995	50 019.2	41 748.9	27 172.0	14 004.6	8 270.3	6 878.3	1 357.4
	2000	36 072.6	32 609.4	22 418.7	9 520.6	3 463.2	-2 393.1	6 476.7
	2005	81 129.1	79 873.1	61 272.6	17 626.6	1 256.0	2 727.8	-1 975.9
Developing economies excluding LDCs -	1990	47 348.6	30 409.1	20 337.3	5 311.0	16 939.5	7 019.0	9 944.0
Économies en développement sans les PMA	1995	39 961.1	27 983.4	20 304.6	7 110.7	11 977.7	8 759.4	3 080.2
	2000	24 230.0	21 658.8	15 727.7	5 439.5	2 571.2	-4 873.1	8 120.1
	2005	57 275.4	55 650.5	46 697.4	8 202.5	1 624.9	1 943.2	-933.4
High-income countries - Pays à revenu élevé	1990	9 341.3	2 060.2	1 485.5	220.0	7 281.1	2 926.6	4 356.2
	1995	3 592.6	2 515.6	2 092.3	284.1	1 077.0	123.7	953.7
	2000	2 297.0	1 418.3	1 096.8	198.3	878.7	-1 285.6	2 122.7
	2005	-447.3	970.1	614.6	311.0	-1 417.4	-280.7	-1 111.9
Middle-income countries -	1990	16 303.3	14 961.8	9 432.6	1 202.0	1 341.6	319.2	1 016.2
Pays à revenu intermédiaire	1995	15 619.2	10 122.7	7 686.5	1 980.6	5 496.5	5 008.1	497.3
	2000	11 075.9	8 214.0	6 117.9	1 785.1	2 861.9	-1 225.5	4 671.0
	2005	9 270.9	9 070.6	5 942.3	2 935.4	200.3	-29.7	-22.5
Low-income countries - Pays à revenu faible	1990	39 130.6	30 093.7	19 253.8	10 183.9	9 036.9	4 461.8	4 606.2
	1995	37 795.1	32 526.7	19 770.0	12 737.1	5 268.4	3 586.5	1 534.5
	2000	23 786.9	24 612.0	16 361.0	7 998.5	-825.1	-2 023.4	1 325.7
	2005	74 181.1	71 392.8	56 208.9	14 419.0	2 788.3	1 975.6	424.7
Heavily indebted poor countries -	1990	17 585.9	16 168.1	10 150.3	5 656.5	1 417.8	885.7	535.2
Pays pauvres très endettés	1995	18 309.5	18 053.5	9 971.0	8 041.3	256.1	615.4	-365.8
	2000	12 140.7	12 493.1	7 865.0	4 470.3	-352.4	-33.5	-309.0
	2005	24 313.8	24 631.2	15 757.8	8 697.6	-317.4	-105.7	-266.4
Landlocked countries - Pays sans littoral	1990	7 229.5	7 050.2	4 176.7	2 707.9	179.3	84.9	94.4
	1995	11 229.2	10 681.2	5 283.6	5 352.4	548.0	159.3	400.1
	2000	8 001.4	7 655.2	4 831.6	2 685.1	346.2	27.3	334.6
	2005	14 191.9	14 705.0	9 411.9	4 969.4	-513.1	-19.2	-752.2
Small island developing states -	1990	1 620.8	1 385.6	1 063.7	316.2	235.2	99.9	150.5
Petits états insulaires en développement	1995	1 517.7	1 489.5	1 057.4	416.6	28.2	-65.3	93.5
	2000	1 786.0	1 204.3	938.5	238.4	581.7	411.2	173.3
	2005	1 428.0	1 514.2	1 202.3	305.1	-86.2	-28.2	-54.4
Least developed countries -	*1990*	*17 471.7*	*16 751.7*	*9 888.0*	*6 287.1*	*720.0*	*688.6*	*34.5*
Pays les moins avancés	*1995*	*17 105.3*	*17 241.7*	*9 344.1*	*7 851.9*	*-136.4*	*-41.5*	*-94.9*
	2000	*13 023.3*	*12 682.5*	*7 947.2*	*4 541.4*	*340.8*	*338.7*	*-4.3*
	2005	*25 911.9*	*25 979.5*	*16 264.6*	*9 463.3*	*-67.6*	*-289.1*	*220.8*
Africa and Haiti - Afrique et Haïti	1990	13 552.2	12 894.8	7 821.1	4 625.1	657.3	631.5	28.9
	1995	13 476.9	13 584.3	7 127.6	6 412.7	-107.4	-20.1	-87.3
	2000	9 189.5	9 312.2	5 898.1	3 262.9	-122.7	-79.6	-33.8
	2005	18 917.1	19 263.7	11 786.1	7 382.9	-346.6	-266.8	-79.8
Asia - Asie	1990	3 514.1	3 459.1	1 794.4	1 537.4	55.0	48.2	6.7
	1995	3 192.8	3 196.1	1 900.9	1 300.7	-3.3	4.0	-7.3
	2000	2 856.2	2 806.9	1 639.6	1 124.6	49.2	1.0	32.7
	2005	6 166.6	5 928.0	3 876.2	1 900.4	238.6	-12.1	250.1
Islands - Îles	1990	405.4	397.7	272.5	124.6	7.8	8.9	-1.1
	1995	435.6	461.3	315.6	138.4	-25.7	-25.4	-0.3
	2000	977.6	563.4	409.5	153.9	414.2	417.4	-3.2
	2005	828.2	787.8	602.4	180.1	40.4	-10.2	50.5

For sources and notes, see end of table.   Pour les sources et les notes, se reporter à la fin du tableau.

7

7.6.2 Official financial flows from bilateral and multilateral sources to developing economies by economic grouping

7.6.2 Flux financiers publics bilatéraux et multilatéraux à destination des économies en développement par groupements économiques

Economic grouping / Groupements économiques	Year / Année	Total Official Net (1) / Total secteur officiel net (1)	Total ODA Net / Total OA Net (2) APD totale nette / AP totale nette (2)			Total OOF Net (3) Flux AASP nets (3)		
			Total Donors / Tous donneurs	of which: / dont : DAC Bilateral Donors / Donneurs bilatéraux du CAD	Multilateral Donors / Donneurs multilatéraux	Total Donors / Tous donneurs	of which: / dont : DAC Bilateral Donors / Donneurs bilatéraux du CAD	Multilateral Donors / Donneurs multilatéraux
				Millions of dollars / Millions de dollars				
Major petroleum exporters -	*1990*	*9 518.5*	*4 414.4*	*2 730.1*	*655.2*	*5 104.1*	*2 309.6*	*2 671.4*
Principaux exportateurs de pétrole	*1995*	*8 025.1*	*3 873.6*	*2 877.0*	*787.4*	*4 151.5*	*3 107.4*	*1 012.3*
	2000	*2 613.5*	*3 450.7*	*2 634.5*	*625.3*	*-837.2*	*-1 062.6*	*365.0*
	2005	*36 508.4*	*33 575.2*	*31 857.4*	*1 410.2*	*2 933.1*	*3 939.5*	*-1 511.9*
Africa - Afrique	1990	2 898.0	1 028.4	774.6	235.0	1 869.6	1 072.8	650.4
	1995	3 100.9	1 203.2	833.4	382.8	1 897.8	1 660.3	237.5
	2000	-168.0	753.0	362.2	312.5	-921.0	-462.8	-458.2
	2005	7 576.1	8 776.9	7 920.4	842.5	-1 200.8	-178.1	-1 022.7
America - Amérique	1990	1 432.1	153.9	134.9	19.0	1 278.3	194.2	1 084.1
	1995	323.4	167.6	121.2	46.4	155.8	-12.2	168.0
	2000	208.0	252.0	239.4	11.8	-44.1	-112.7	68.9
	2005	-505.1	46.6	26.8	18.9	-551.7	-124.7	-427.1
Asia - Asie	1990	5 188.4	3 232.2	1 820.6	401.3	1 956.2	1 042.5	937.0
	1995	4 600.8	2 502.8	1 922.4	358.3	2 098.0	1 459.3	606.8
	2000	2 573.5	2 445.7	2 032.9	301.0	127.8	-487.2	754.2
	2005	29 437.4	24 751.8	23 910.2	548.8	4 685.6	4 242.2	-62.1
Major exporters of manufactured goods -	*1990*	*16 609.5*	*7 632.9*	*5 463.8*	*1 522.7*	*8 976.6*	*4 592.2*	*4 508.2*
Principaux exportateurs d'articles	*1995*	*11 326.8*	*8 133.5*	*6 062.6*	*1 932.1*	*3 193.3*	*1 719.4*	*1 372.1*
manufacturés	*2000*	*6 455.2*	*4 951.0*	*3 206.6*	*1 701.9*	*1 504.3*	*-3 933.4*	*5 895.3*
	2005	*5 787.7*	*4 748.6*	*3 245.4*	*1 446.1*	*1 039.1*	*-1 180.3*	*2 127.4*
America - Amérique	1990	5 557.9	314.7	286.8	27.9	5 243.2	2 750.3	2 503.4
	1995	370.4	658.3	569.2	92.4	-287.9	-1 022.4	736.0
	2000	4 266.5	268.3	154.1	112.1	3 998.2	-311.2	4 278.0
	2005	-66.6	381.2	331.5	47.1	-447.8	-545.3	187.3
Asia - Asie	1990	11 051.6	7 318.2	5 177.0	1 494.8	3 733.4	1 841.9	2 004.7
	1995	10 956.4	7 475.3	5 493.5	1 839.6	3 481.2	2 741.8	636.1
	2000	2 188.7	4 682.6	3 052.5	1 589.9	-2 493.9	-3 622.2	1 617.3
	2005	5 854.3	4 367.3	2 914.0	1 398.9	1 487.0	-635.0	1 940.1
Emerging economies -	*1990*	*8 984.3*	*2 342.6*	*2 137.1*	*188.3*	*6 641.7*	*3 802.1*	*2 850.1*
Économies émergentes	*1995*	*3 869.9*	*2 354.4*	*2 149.2*	*234.1*	*1 515.5*	*784.4*	*732.7*
	2000	*4 106.3*	*1 351.6*	*1 151.2*	*191.1*	*2 754.6*	*-1 987.2*	*5 183.6*
	2005	*505.5*	*890.9*	*595.3*	*272.6*	*-385.4*	*577.6*	*-871.8*
America - Amérique	1990	7 651.9	988.8	886.8	102.0	6 663.1	3 368.0	3 305.7
	1995	2 094.0	1 332.0	1 149.8	185.1	761.9	-335.6	1 098.9
	2000	5 876.5	795.1	611.3	171.1	5 081.4	-521.4	5 577.1
	2005	-307.9	1 030.3	795.1	225.0	-1 338.2	-1 000.5	-247.8
Asia - Asie	1990	1 332.4	1 353.9	1 250.3	86.3	-21.5	434.1	-455.6
	1995	1 776.0	1 022.4	999.4	49.0	753.6	1 120.0	-366.3
	2000	-1 770.2	556.6	539.9	20.0	-2 326.8	-1 465.7	-393.5
	2005	813.4	-139.5	-199.8	47.7	952.9	1 578.1	-624.0
Newly industrialized economies -	*1990*	*6 806.0*	*4 388.4*	*3 892.0*	*453.5*	*2 417.6*	*1 373.3*	*1 068.3*
Économies nouvellement industrialisées	*1995*	*5 165.0*	*3 249.5*	*2 991.2*	*286.3*	*1 915.5*	*1 755.8*	*121.7*
	2000	*901.9*	*2 796.2*	*2 590.2*	*201.7*	*-1 894.3*	*-1 504.3*	*129.5*
	2005	*1 722.4*	*2 945.9*	*2 573.8*	*305.1*	*-1 223.5*	*-494.0*	*-878.9*
First tier - Premier tier	1990	-282.7	123.8	77.4	21.9	-406.5	20.5	-427.0
	1995	-390.6	91.7	96.9	9.5	-482.3	-130.2	-352.1
	2000	-416.2	-182.8	-182.0	-0.9	-233.4	-78.0	-159.9
Second tier - Deuxième tier	1990	7 088.8	4 264.6	3 814.6	431.6	2 824.1	1 352.8	1 495.3
	1995	5 555.6	3 157.8	2 894.3	276.8	2 397.8	1 886.0	473.8
	2000	1 318.1	2 979.0	2 772.2	202.7	-1 660.9	-1 426.3	289.4
	2005	1 722.4	2 945.9	2 573.8	305.1	-1 223.5	-494.0	-878.9
Developing economies: Africa -	1990	28 258.9	25 312.0	15 817.3	6 361.1	2 946.9	847.9	1 950.3
Économies en développement : Afrique	1995	25 328.5	21 958.7	13 223.1	8 588.2	3 369.8	3 574.0	-203.6
	2000	14 458.1	15 732.4	10 384.4	5 047.7	-1 274.2	-333.3	-930.8
	2005	35 061.1	35 211.9	24 717.2	10 268.9	-150.8	-494.5	348.3

For sources and notes, see end of table.

Pour les sources et les notes, se reporter à la fin du tableau.

7.6.2 Official financial flows from bilateral and multilateral sources to developing economies by economic grouping

7.6.2 Flux financiers publics bilatéraux et multilatéraux à destination des économies en développement par groupements économiques

Economic grouping / Groupements économiques	Year / Année	Total Official Net (1) / Total secteur officiel net (1)	Total ODA Net / Total OA Net (2) APD totale nette / AP totale nette (2)			Total OOF Net (3) Flux AASP nets (3)		
			Total Donors / Tous donneurs	of which: / dont :		Total Donors / Tous donneurs	of which: / dont :	
				DAC Bilateral Donors / Donneurs bilatéraux du CAD	Multilateral Donors / Donneurs multilatéraux		DAC Bilateral Donors / Donneurs bilatéraux du CAD	Multilateral Donors / Donneurs multilatéraux
		Millions of dollars / Millions de dollars						
Northern Africa excluding Sudan - Afrique septentrionale sans le Soudan	1990	7 200.0	7 021.2	4 081.3	284.5	178.7	-952.3	982.5
	1995	6 067.6	2 890.6	2 373.6	414.8	3 177.0	2 713.7	463.9
	2000	1 826.4	2 186.9	1 659.7	405.0	-360.5	101.0	-461.0
	2005	2 175.4	2 349.2	1 523.7	726.8	-173.8	-786.5	612.7
Sub-Saharan Africa - Afrique subsaharienne	1990	20 047.9	17 296.2	10 895.6	5 931.7	2 751.7	1 794.4	957.1
	1995	18 160.1	18 001.6	10 027.0	7 929.5	158.5	829.4	-670.9
	2000	11 433.2	12 348.6	7 876.9	4 306.3	-915.4	-441.1	-464.6
	2005	30 803.5	30 910.2	21 601.4	9 182.4	-106.7	206.3	-308.6
Sub-Saharan Africa excluding South Africa - Afrique sub-saharienne sans l'Afrique du Sud	1990	20 047.9	17 296.2	10 895.6	5 931.7	2 751.7	1 794.4	957.1
	1995	17 444.6	17 612.7	9 708.5	7 862.1	-168.1	502.9	-670.9
	2000	10 840.9	11 861.1	7 523.4	4 174.4	-1 020.2	-346.8	-664.0
	2005	30 061.4	30 210.2	21 115.4	8 968.9	-148.8	315.0	-463.8
Developing economies: America - Économies en développement : Amérique	**1990**	**13 580.8**	**5 246.4**	**4 146.3**	**1 088.0**	**8 334.4**	**3 730.0**	**4 634.3**
	1995	**8 096.8**	**6 461.3**	**4 809.4**	**1 618.0**	**1 635.6**	**81.2**	**1 557.5**
	2000	**11 255.3**	**5 161.2**	**4 034.0**	**1 076.5**	**6 094.2**	**-465.3**	**6 551.9**
	2005	**3 046.3**	**6 293.5**	**4 574.3**	**1 679.3**	**-3 247.1**	**-1 487.7**	**-1 658.0**
Central America and Greater Carribean Islands excluding Puerto Rico - Amérique centrale et Grandes Antilles sans Porto Rico	1990	7 314.8	2 443.7	2 074.9	360.7	4 871.2	2 093.3	2 801.2
	1995	3 425.3	3 060.8	2 246.3	790.4	364.5	-868.7	1 234.4
	2000	2 198.1	1 768.7	1 205.3	540.3	429.3	-829.5	1 223.1
	2005	2 180.3	2 840.7	2 047.5	782.3	-660.4	-331.7	-292.5
Central America and Greater Carribean Islands excluding Mexico and Puerto Rico - Amérique centrale et Grandes Antilles sans le Mexique et Porto Rico	1990	2 287.6	2 284.4	1 930.2	346.1	3.2	58.4	-36.7
	1995	3 016.5	2 675.7	1 881.3	770.3	340.8	121.7	219.8
	2000	2 120.3	1 822.8	1 273.6	526.7	297.5	-77.9	380.5
	2005	2 375.6	2 651.3	1 887.0	754.8	-275.7	-147.1	-117.1
South America and Central America - Amérique du Sud et Amérique centrale	1990	11 886.9	3 897.8	3 168.9	721.3	7 989.2	3 635.8	4 364.7
	1995	6 008.1	4 523.0	3 463.9	1 034.0	1 485.1	29.2	1 459.0
	2000	8 758.8	3 418.7	2 564.4	822.2	5 340.2	-935.1	6 265.5
	2005	1 297.1	4 564.7	3 363.3	1 173.1	-3 267.7	-1 542.5	-1 634.6
South America excluding Brazil - Amérique du Sud sans le Brésil	1990	4 732.1	1 892.1	1 427.4	463.3	2 840.0	892.6	1 948.2
	1995	3 651.8	2 206.7	1 705.9	495.3	1 445.1	896.1	550.0
	2000	2 836.2	1 652.3	1 339.6	298.4	1 184.0	-597.5	1 800.1
	2005	-188.6	2 247.7	1 635.7	594.8	-2 436.4	-783.8	-1 652.4
Developing economies: Asia - Économies en développement : Asie	**1990**	**24 391.7**	**17 980.7**	**10 544.6**	**4 752.6**	**6 411.1**	**3 075.4**	**3 481.1**
	1995	**24 307.9**	**17 506.7**	**11 754.6**	**5 322.2**	**6 801.2**	**5 104.2**	**1 555.2**
	2000	**13 004.5**	**14 925.4**	**10 146.9**	**4 358.6**	**-1 920.8**	**-3 775.0**	**2 518.1**
	2005	**48 951.8**	**43 840.4**	**36 431.6**	**6 659.2**	**5 111.5**	**3 816.5**	**569.6**
Eastern and South-Eastern Asia excluding China - Asie orientale et Asie du Sud-Est sans la Chine	1990	7 390.2	4 958.6	4 173.7	740.8	2 431.6	1 387.7	1 067.9
	1995	7 456.9	5 327.5	4 311.0	1 023.1	2 129.4	1 948.2	136.6
	2000	4 168.5	5 791.8	4 738.1	1 024.7	-1 623.3	-1 214.7	135.0
	2005	3 539.4	6 306.7	4 738.6	1 419.5	-2 767.3	-375.9	-2 549.9
Southern Asia excluding India - Asie méridionale sans l'Inde	1990	5 010.9	4 684.2	2 566.5	2 116.8	326.6	-78.4	406.3
	1995	4 253.7	3 639.1	2 078.1	1 629.2	614.6	428.2	186.4
	2000	2 230.8	2 883.5	1 810.3	1 023.4	-652.8	-614.1	61.0
	2005	8 943.8	7 640.4	4 967.3	2 401.1	1 303.4	467.4	457.9

For sources and notes, see next page.

Pour les sources et les notes, se reporter à la page suivante.

7.6.2 Official financial flows from bilateral and multilateral sources to developing economies by economic grouping

7.6.2 Flux financiers publics bilatéraux et multilatéraux à destination des économies en développement par groupements économiques

Sources:
- Organisation for Economic Co-operation and Development (OECD):
  OLISNET, online statistical database

Notes:

- The groupings presented in this table do not include Unallocated/Unspecified recipient countries.

(1) Sum of "Total ODA/OA Net; total donors" and "Total OOF Net; total donors". It represents the total net disbursements by the official sector at large to the recipient country.

(2) Total ODA Net; total donors:
The Total Official Development Assistance (ODA) includes grants and loans to countries and territories on Part I of the "DAC List of Aid Recipients" which are:
undertaken by the official sector; with promotion of economic development and welfare as the main objective and at concessional financial terms (if a loan, have a grant element of at least 25 per cent).
Grants, loans and credits for military purposes are excluded.

"Total Donors" is the sum of the three following donor types:
- DAC Bilateral Donors: The Development Assistance Committee (DAC) is the Committee of the OECD which deals with development co-operation matters. It consists of 23 Member countries.
- Multilateral Donors (i.e. African Development Bank, International Bank for Reconstruction and Development, International Monetary Fund, United Nations Development Programme).
- Other Donors: the Non-DAC Bilateral Donors (i.e Hungary, Lithuania, Turkey).

(3) Total OOF Net; total donors:
The Other Official Flows (OOF) are transactions by the official sector whose main objective is other than development motivated, or, if development motivated, whose grant element is below the 25% threshold which would make them eligible to be recorded as ODA. The main classes of transactions included here are official export credits, official sector equity and portfolio investment, and debt reorganisation undertaken by the official sector at non-concessional terms (irrespective of the nature or the identity of the original creditor).

Total Donors is the sum of the three following donor types:
- DAC Bilateral Donors: The Development Assistance Committee (DAC) is the Committee of the OECD which deals with development co-operation matters. It consists of 23 Member countries.
- Multilateral Donors (i.e. African Development Bank, International Bank for Reconstruction and Development, International Monetary Fund, United Nations Development Programme).
- Other Donors: the Non-DAC Bilateral Donors (i.e Hungary, Lithuania, Turkey).

Sources :
- Organisation de coopération et de développement économique (OECD) :
  OLISNET, base de données statistique en ligne

Notes :

- Les groupements présentés dans ce tableau n'incluent pas les pays bénéficiaires non-ventilé/non-spécifié.

(1) Somme de "APD/AP totale nette ; tous donneurs" et de "Flux AASP nets ; tous donneurs". Cet agrégat correspond aux versements nets effectués par le secteur public dans son ensemble aux pays bénéficiaires considérés.

(2) AP totale nette ; tous donneurs :
Par aide publique (AP), on entend l'ensemble des apports de ressources qui sont fournis aux pays qui figurent à la Partie II de la "Liste des bénéficiaires de l'aide établie par le CAD" et qui répondent aux critères suivants :
a) être dispensés dans le but essentiel de favoriser le développement économique et l'amélioration du niveau de vie dans les pays en développement ; et
b) revêtir un caractère de faveur et comporter un élément de libéralité d'au moins 25 pour cent.

"Tous Donneurs" est la somme des 3 types de donneurs suivants :
- Donneurs Bilatéraux du CAD : Le Comité d'aide au développement (CAD) est la principale instance chargée, à l'OCDE, des questions relatives à la coopération avec les pays en développement. Le CAD regroupe 23 pays membres.
- Donneurs Multilatéraux (i.e. Banque africaine de développpement, Banque internationale pour la reconstruction et le développement, Fonds monétaire international, Programme des Nations Unies pour le développement).
- Autres Donneurs : les Donneurs Bilatéraux non-membres du CAD (i.e. Hongrie, Lituanie, Turquie).

(3) Flux AASP nets ; tous donneurs :
Autres apports du secteur public (AASP) : il s'agit des opérations du secteur public dont le but essentiel est autre que le développement ou qui, tout en visant à favoriser le développement, sont assorties d'un élément de libéralité inférieur au seuil de 25 pour cent à partir duquel elles auraient pu être notifiées comme de l'APD. Les principales catégories d'opérations couvertes dans les AASP sont les crédits publics à l'exportation, les prises de participation et les investissements de portefeuille du secteur public et le réaménagement de la dette effectué par le secteur public aux conditions du marché (et ce, quelle que soit la nature ou l'identité du créancier initial).

Tous Donneurs est la somme des 3 types de donneurs suivants :
- Donneurs Bilatéraux du CAD : Le Comité d'aide au développement (CAD) est la principale instance chargée, à l'OCDE, des questions relatives à la coopération avec les pays en développement. Le CAD regroupe 23 pays membres.
- Donneurs Multilatéraux (i.e. Banque africaine de développpement, Banque internationale pour la reconstruction et le développement, Fonds monétaire international, Programme des Nations Unies pour le développement).
- Autres Donneurs : les Donneurs Bilatéraux non-membres du CAD (i.e. Hongrie, Lituanie, Turquie).

Debt stocks and flows / Stocks et flux de la dette	Public and publicly guaranteed debt (1) / Dette publique et garantie par l'état (1)										Private non-guaranteed debt (4) / Dette privée non garantie (4)
	Total creditors / Total créanciers	Official creditors (2) / Créanciers publics (2)						Private creditors (3) / Créanciers (3)			
		Total	Bilateral / Bilatéraux				Multilateral / Multilatéraux	Total	Bonds / Obligations	Commercial banks / Banques commerciales	
			Total	DAC / CAD	OPEC / OPEP	Other / Autres					
	Millions of dollars / Millions de dollars										
1990											
Debt Outstanding (5)	906 003	505 270	309 077	209 456	18 403	81 218	196 194	400 733	97 364	197 138	56 140
Disbursments (6)	79 659	45 313	19 182	16 345	572	2 265	26 131	34 346	3 862	13 707	16 058
Debt Service (7)	95 212	39 001	17 759	13 432	1 114	3 212	21 242	56 211	8 389	29 129	10 266
Principal Repayments	54 684	21 812	10 557	7 549	861	2 147	11 255	32 872	4 367	15 154	6 069
Interest Payments	40 528	17 189	7 201	5 883	253	1 066	9 987	23 339	4 022	13 975	4 196
Net Transfers on Debt (8)	-15 554	6 312	1 424	2 913	-542	-948	4 888	-21 866	-4 527	-15 423	5 792
1995											
Dette totale (5)	1 126 759	684 485	414 564	307 788	13 966	92 810	269 920	442 274	213 167	130 042	208 335
Décaissements (6)	120 825	60 558	32 133	26 205	526	5 402	28 425	60 266	22 001	22 062	53 384
Service de la dette (7)	134 467	66 511	34 718	26 254	932	7 533	31 792	67 956	24 241	22 630	37 276
Remboursement du principal	81 574	41 076	22 130	15 509	725	5 896	18 946	40 499	10 039	15 270	26 212
Paiement des intérêts	52 892	25 435	12 589	10 745	207	1 637	12 846	27 457	14 202	7 360	11 064
Transfers nets (8)	-13 642	-5 952	-2 585	-49	-406	-2 131	-3 367	-7 690	-2 240	-568	16 108
1999											
Debt Outstanding (5)	1 160 517	671 495	367 174	282 468	14 646	70 060	304 321	489 022	290 464	127 584	455 687
Disbursments (6)	124 836	53 817	21 260	16 842	701	3 717	32 557	71 019	45 657	15 585	92 506
Debt Service (7)	152 458	64 835	33 539	25 725	742	7 072	31 295	87 624	39 821	33 224	122 299
Principal Repayments	98 002	40 896	23 072	17 125	561	5 386	17 824	57 106	20 409	25 690	93 494
Interest Payments	54 457	23 939	10 468	8 600	182	1 686	13 471	30 518	19 412	7 535	28 805
Net Transfers on Debt (8)	-27 623	-11 018	-12 279	-8 883	-41	-3 355	1 262	-16 605	5 837	-17 640	-29 793
2000											
Dette totale (5)	1 137 246	649 423	345 567	250 583	14 243	80 741	303 856	487 822	304 260	122 810	453 140
Décaissements (6)	130 176	48 882	17 243	14 615	446	2 182	31 639	81 294	55 566	17 958	84 269
Service de la dette (7)	166 793	67 327	31 794	24 836	767	6 191	35 533	99 467	53 713	31 770	121 338
Remboursement du principal	108 292	43 581	22 136	16 931	584	4 621	21 445	64 710	31 225	22 775	92 622
Paiement des intérêts	58 501	23 745	9 658	7 905	182	1 570	14 087	34 756	22 488	8 995	28 716
Transfers nets (8)	-36 617	-18 444	-14 551	-10 221	-321	-4 009	-3 894	-18 172	1 852	-13 812	-37 069
2001											
Debt Outstanding (5)	1 113 910	632 155	323 492	217 622	13 834	92 036	308 663	481 755	304 403	120 766	438 029
Disbursments (6)	108 616	46 996	15 896	11 835	542	3 519	31 100	61 620	39 563	16 316	83 537
Debt Service (7)	154 801	57 881	27 011	19 400	774	6 837	30 870	96 920	49 623	33 972	118 980
Principal Repayments	101 744	35 057	18 010	12 607	604	4 799	17 047	66 686	30 833	25 418	92 692
Interest Payments	53 057	22 824	9 001	6 793	169	2 039	13 823	30 233	18 790	8 554	26 289
Net Transfers on Debt (8)	-46 184	-10 885	-11 115	-7 565	-232	-3 318	231	-35 300	-10 060	-17 656	-35 443
2002											
Dette totale (5)	1 158 390	661 677	337 551	244 458	13 969	79 123	324 126	496 713	323 850	119 410	419 089
Décaissements (6)	100 728	41 932	12 679	11 267	382	1 030	29 253	58 796	35 355	19 130	84 015
Service de la dette (7)	155 503	68 385	27 301	21 056	728	5 517	41 084	87 118	41 537	34 054	116 760
Remboursement du principal	108 184	48 523	19 880	15 178	574	4 128	28 643	59 661	23 462	26 637	96 258
Paiement des intérêts	47 319	19 862	7 421	5 878	153	1 389	12 441	27 457	18 076	7 417	20 501
Transfers nets (8)	-54 774	-26 452	-14 622	-9 789	-345	-4 487	-11 830	-28 322	-6 183	-14 925	-32 744
2003											
Debt Outstanding (5)	1 215 749	699 500	355 539	284 599	13 257	57 683	343 961	516 250	350 501	116 671	425 589
Disbursments (6)	111 585	45 191	10 756	9 216	387	1 153	34 435	66 394	41 874	20 321	99 157
Debt Service (7)	173 839	75 287	31 034	25 864	743	4 427	44 253	98 552	51 362	36 148	121 426
Principal Repayments	123 503	56 064	22 830	19 051	595	3 184	33 233	67 440	30 130	28 378	99 692
Interest Payments	50 336	19 223	8 203	6 813	148	1 243	11 020	31 112	21 232	7 770	21 734
Net Transfers on Debt (8)	-62 254	-30 096	-20 278	-16 648	-356	-3 274	-9 813	-32 158	-9 488	-15 827	-22 269
2004											
Dette totale (5)	1 240 796	704 959	351 655	281 043	12 585	58 027	353 304	535 837	372 643	117 649	429 510
Décaissements (6)	123 534	39 950	10 917	7 920	729	2 268	29 034	83 583	50 913	29 108	117 007
Service de la dette (7)	164 579	67 617	30 709	25 872	1 088	3 750	36 907	96 962	51 591	36 731	132 079
Remboursement du principal	116 001	49 127	22 131	18 827	950	2 354	26 996	66 875	29 903	30 172	112 564
Paiement des intérêts	48 577	18 490	8 578	7 045	138	1 396	9 912	30 087	21 689	6 559	19 515
Transfers nets (8)	-41 045	-27 666	-19 793	-17 952	-359	-1 482	-7 874	-13 379	-678	-7 623	-15 072

For sources and notes, see end of table 7.G.

Pour les sources et les notes, se reporter à la fin du tableau 7.G.

Debt stocks and flows / Stocks et flux de la dette	Total creditors / Total créanciers	Public and publicly guaranted debt (1) / Dette publique et garantie par l'état (1)									Private non-guaranteed debt (4) / Dette privée non garantie (4)
		Official creditors (2) / Créanciers publics (2)						Private creditors (3) / Créanciers (3)			
		Total	Bilateral / Bilatéraux				Multilateral / Multilatéraux	Total	Bonds / Obligations	Commercial banks / Banques commerciales	
			Total	DAC / CAD	OPEC / OPEP	Other / Autres					
					Millions of dollars / Millions de dcllars						
1990											
Debt Outstanding (5)	235 549	228 855	157 978	107 455	77 623	11 468	18 3€4	50 523	70 877	1 721	25 454
Disbursments (6)	21 552	20 833	12 177	5 535	4 733	204	5S7	6 642	8 656	0	1 232
Debt Service (7)	23 025	21 947	9 970	5 729	4 758	295	676	4 241	11 977	231	3 805
Principal Repayments	14 674	14 031	5 395	3 015	2 522	210	283	2 380	8 636	108	2 532
Interest Payments	8 351	7 916	4 575	2 713	2 236	85	393	1 861	3 341	123	1 273
Net Transfers on Debt (8)	-1 472	-1 114	2 207	-194	-25	-91	-78	2 401	-3 321	-231	-2 573
1995											
Dette totale (5)	281 374	268 825	206 679	133 216	106 228	8 497	18 492	73 464	62 145	5 319	23 146
Décaissements (6)	19 178	18 297	10 283	3 203	2 917	130	153	7 080	8 014	1 129	2 235
Service de la dette (7)	22 246	20 336	11 738	5 518	4 778	318	422	6 220	8 598	667	2 760
Remboursement du principal	13 410	12 038	6 475	2 702	2 157	246	299	3 773	5 563	318	1 730
Paiement des intérêts	8 836	8 298	5 263	2 816	2 621	72	123	2 446	3 035	348	1 030
Transfers nets (8)	-3 068	-2 039	-1 455	-2 316	-1 861	-188	-266	861	-584	463	-525
1999											
Debt Outstanding (5)	250 026	236 286	192 139	117 417	94 531	9 454	13 431	74 723	44 147	10 587	16 448
Disbursments (6)	12 868	10 996	6 593	1 553	1 192	221	140	5 041	4 403	1 867	1 506
Debt Service (7)	22 875	19 097	11 774	6 142	5 115	330	697	5 632	7 323	776	3 410
Principal Repayments	15 432	12 043	7 052	3 556	2 717	235	604	3 496	4 990	127	2 610
Interest Payments	7 443	7 054	4 721	2 586	2 399	95	93	2 135	2 333	650	800
Net Transfers on Debt (8)	-10 007	-8 101	-5 180	-4 589	-3 923	-109	-557	-591	-2 921	1 091	-1 903
2000											
Dette totale (5)	249 844	235 233	195 369	122 896	77 860	9 445	35 591	72 473	39 864	10 630	15 781
Décaissements (6)	14 647	11 362	6 506	1 725	1 310	257	158	4 781	4 856	765	2 605
Service de la dette (7)	22 262	20 170	11 343	6 237	4 418	340	1 479	5 106	8 827	1 555	4 180
Remboursement du principal	15 322	13 733	6 960	3 718	2 452	255	1 011	3 242	6 774	881	3 442
Paiement des intérêts	6 940	6 437	4 384	2 519	1 966	85	468	1 865	2 053	674	738
Transfers nets (8)	-7 615	-8 808	-4 837	-4 512	-3 108	-83	-1 321	-325	-3 971	-789	-1 575
2001											
Debt Outstanding (5)	241 150	225 247	186 857	115 018	72 138	9 233	33 647	71 839	38 390	12 511	13 413
Disbursments (6)	15 543	12 351	6 520	1 327	873	169	285	5 193	5 831	3 175	1 422
Debt Service (7)	21 804	19 389	11 839	7 222	4 464	340	2 418	4 617	7 550	1 117	3 524
Principal Repayments	15 383	13 527	7 685	4 675	2 593	260	1 822	3 010	5 842	518	2 921
Interest Payments	6 421	5 862	4 154	2 547	1 872	80	596	1 607	1 708	599	603
Net Transfers on Debt (8)	-6 261	-7 038	-5 320	-5 895	-3 591	-171	-2 133	576	-1 718	2 058	-2 102
2002											
Dette totale (5)	254 097	237 549	199 123	119 730	76 820	9 406	33 504	79 393	38 426	13 981	12 326
Décaissements (6)	15 525	12 645	7 120	1 162	769	243	151	5 958	5 524	3 122	1 446
Service de la dette (7)	22 558	18 172	11 351	5 789	5 003	355	432	5 561	6 822	1 731	2 774
Remboursement du principal	16 243	12 472	7 177	3 487	2 928	276	282	3 690	5 295	972	2 414
Paiement des intérêts	6 315	5 701	4 173	2 303	2 075	79	149	1 871	1 527	759	360
Transfers nets (8)	-7 032	-5 528	-4 230	-4 627	-4 234	-112	-281	397	-1 297	1 391	-1 328
2003											
Debt Outstanding (5)	276 824	256 465	217 027	128 285	107 384	8 671	12 231	88 742	39 438	15 576	12 287
Disbursments (6)	19 172	13 659	7 590	1 086	749	191	146	6 504	6 069	2 498	2 388
Debt Service (7)	24 048	20 391	12 882	7 153	6 361	337	455	5 729	7 509	1 633	3 215
Principal Repayments	17 303	14 419	8 514	4 443	3 877	260	306	4 070	5 905	816	2 870
Interest Payments	6 744	5 972	4 368	2 710	2 483	78	149	1 659	1 604	817	345
Net Transfers on Debt (8)	-4 875	-6 733	-5 292	-6 067	-5 612	-146	-309	774	-1 440	865	-826
2004											
Dette totale (5)	278 897	259 359	219 168	124 057	102 060	8 233	13 764	95 110	40 191	16 174	13 595
Décaissements (6)	17 086	15 043	8 413	1 480	615	584	281	6 933	6 630	1 559	3 931
Service de la dette (7)	25 031	21 418	14 842	8 852	6 973	745	1 134	5 990	6 577	1 540	2 699
Remboursement du principal	18 486	15 688	10 641	6 307	4 700	668	940	4 334	5 047	689	2 421
Paiement des intérêts	6 545	5 730	4 201	2 545	2 274	77	194	1 656	1 529	851	278
Transfers nets (8)	-7 945	-6 375	-6 429	-7 372	-6 358	-161	-852	944	54	20	1 232

For sources and notes, see end of table 7.G.

Pour les sources et les notes, se reporter à la fin du tableau 7.G.

Debt stocks and flows / Stocks et flux de la dette	Total creditors / Total créanciers	Public and publicly guaranted debt (1) / Dette publique et garantie par l'état (1)									Private non-guaranteed debt (4) / Dette privée non garantie (4)
		Official creditors (2) / Créanciers publics (2)						Private creditors (3) / Créanciers (3)			
		Total	Bilateral / Bilatéraux				Multilateral / Multilatéraux	Total	Bonds / Obligations	Commercial banks / Banques commerciales	
			Total	DAC CAD	OPEC OPEP	Other Autres					
				Millions of dollars / Millions de dollars							
1990											
Debt Outstanding (5)	327 952	121 502	61 522	48 116	1 761	11 645	59 980	206 450	75 976	101 797	25 029
Disbursments (6)	23 035	13 185	4 199	3 246	211	742	8 986	9 850	1 938	4 803	4 702
Debt Service (7)	32 107	11 940	3 065	2 368	172	524	8 876	20 166	4 406	11 910	4 478
Principal Repayments	16 239	6 442	1 692	1 215	123	353	4 751	9 797	2 008	5 214	2 216
Interest Payments	15 868	5 498	1 373	1 153	49	171	4 125	10 370	2 398	6 697	2 262
Net Transfers on Debt (8)	-9 072	1 245	1 134	877	39	218	110	-10 316	-2 468	-7 107	224
1995											
Dette totale (5)	375 048	160 841	88 057	77 415	1 401	9 242	72 783	214 207	165 605	35 461	87 394
Décaissements (6)	46 615	23 750	13 726	13 434	95	197	10 024	22 865	13 694	7 463	27 530
Service de la dette (7)	50 644	23 570	10 347	9 664	274	409	13 223	27 074	17 127	5 970	18 562
Remboursement du principal	27 843	14 614	6 278	5 784	220	273	8 336	13 229	5 839	4 332	12 725
Paiement des intérêts	22 801	8 956	4 069	3 880	53	135	4 887	13 845	11 289	1 638	5 836
Transfers nets (8)	-4 029	181	3 379	3 770	-179	-212	-3 199	-4 210	-3 434	1 493	8 968
1999											
Debt Outstanding (5)	399 121	141 887	50 608	39 372	1 055	10 180	91 279	257 234	216 317	32 339	242 384
Disbursments (6)	57 264	17 649	2 803	1 902	254	648	14 846	39 615	30 694	6 172	64 209
Debt Service (7)	71 026	23 853	9 961	8 396	102	1 464	13 891	47 173	28 664	16 097	73 453
Principal Repayments	44 202	15 131	7 331	6 452	76	802	7 800	29 071	13 666	13 475	55 543
Interest Payments	26 823	8 722	2 631	1 943	26	662	6 091	18 102	14 998	2 622	17 910
Net Transfers on Debt (8)	-13 761	-6 203	-7 159	-6 494	152	-816	955	-7 558	2 030	-9 925	-9 243
2000											
Dette totale (5)	400 133	140 887	47 605	36 134	913	10 557	93 282	259 246	218 671	32 488	241 455
Décaissements (6)	59 896	16 492	2 883	2 237	39	607	13 609	43 404	35 604	7 033	57 823
Service de la dette (7)	82 226	25 467	9 254	8 217	122	916	16 213	56 759	44 063	10 311	76 091
Remboursement du principal	52 238	16 883	7 035	6 467	81	487	9 848	35 355	26 718	7 047	58 048
Paiement des intérêts	29 988	8 584	2 219	1 749	41	429	6 365	21 404	17 345	3 264	18 043
Transfers nets (8)	-22 331	-8 975	-6 371	-5 980	-82	-308	-2 605	-13 355	-8 459	-3 278	-18 268
2001											
Debt Outstanding (5)	396 032	138 388	40 459	30 553	650	9 257	97 929	257 644	215 840	35 341	238 493
Disbursments (6)	51 463	15 698	2 868	2 689	27	151	12 830	35 765	26 233	8 811	53 175
Debt Service (7)	72 949	18 905	6 264	4 453	156	1 656	12 641	54 044	37 052	13 811	70 264
Principal Repayments	47 942	10 901	4 503	3 262	119	1 123	6 398	37 041	24 341	10 341	52 775
Interest Payments	25 007	8 004	1 761	1 191	37	533	6 243	17 003	12 712	3 470	17 490
Net Transfers on Debt (8)	-21 486	-3 207	-3 397	-1 763	-129	-1 505	189	-18 278	-10 819	-4 999	-17 089
2002											
Dette totale (5)	406 066	144 003	41 613	32 737	601	8 280	102 385	262 063	224 942	32 108	225 796
Décaissements (6)	43 208	16 094	4 131	3 925	28	178	11 963	27 114	16 616	9 946	37 790
Service de la dette (7)	67 596	22 273	7 028	5 443	98	1 487	15 245	45 324	25 495	17 319	59 753
Remboursement du principal	45 204	15 140	5 391	4 289	78	1 025	9 749	30 064	13 793	14 041	45 895
Paiement des intérêts	22 393	7 133	1 636	1 154	20	462	5 497	15 260	11 702	3 278	13 859
Transfers nets (8)	-24 388	-6 179	-2 897	-1 518	-70	-1 309	-3 282	-18 209	-8 880	-7 373	-21 963
2003											
Debt Outstanding (5)	426 312	148 216	40 323	32 386	549	7 388	107 893	278 096	245 044	28 987	223 225
Disbursments (6)	54 731	19 156	1 708	1 539	49	119	17 448	35 575	26 680	8 209	41 170
Debt Service (7)	73 280	26 568	6 182	4 917	125	1 140	20 386	46 712	30 958	13 978	56 112
Principal Repayments	50 496	19 871	4 766	3 915	106	745	15 105	30 625	18 139	10 896	42 451
Interest Payments	22 783	6 697	1 416	1 002	18	395	5 281	16 087	12 819	3 082	13 660
Net Transfers on Debt (8)	-18 549	-7 412	-4 474	-3 378	-75	-1 021	-2 938	-11 137	-4 277	-5 769	-14 942
2004											
Dette totale (5)	432 820	143 544	36 583	29 382	430	6 770	106 961	289 276	256 169	29 318	205 989
Décaissements (6)	48 830	12 332	1 754	1 536	36	181	10 579	36 498	22 935	12 676	48 857
Service de la dette (7)	67 991	22 256	5 646	4 758	62	826	16 611	45 735	29 392	15 308	72 619
Remboursement du principal	45 101	16 548	4 397	3 893	49	454	12 151	28 553	15 463	12 205	60 644
Paiement des intérêts	22 890	5 708	1 249	864	13	372	4 460	17 182	13 930	3 103	11 975
Transfers nets (8)	-19 162	-9 924	-3 892	-3 222	-26	-645	-6 032	-9 237	-6 457	-2 632	-23 763

For sources and notes, see end of table 7.G.

Pour les sources et les notes, se reporter à la fin du tableau 7.G.

7

Debt stocks and flows / Stocks et flux de la dette	Total creditors / Total créanciers	Public and publicly guaranteed debt (1) / Dette publique et garantie par l'état (1)									Private non-guaranteed debt (4) / Dette privée non garantie (4)
		Official creditors (2) / Créanciers publics (2)						Private creditors (3) / Créanciers (3)			
		Total	Bilateral / Bilatéraux				Multilateral / Multilatéraux	Total	Bonds / Obligations	Commercial banks / Banques commerciales	
			Total	DAC CAD	OPEC OPEP	Other Autres					
Millions of dollars / Millions de dollars											
1990											
Debt Outstanding (5)	347 088	224 184	139 641	83 296	5 164	51 181	84 543	122 904	19 628	69 557	23 384
Disbursments (6)	35 459	19 666	9 383	8 305	157	921	10 282	15 793	1 923	7 651	10 279
Debt Service (7)	40 792	16 927	8 918	6 261	646	2 010	8 009	23 865	3 749	13 239	4 411
Principal Repayments	24 163	9 876	5 824	3 786	527	1 511	4 052	14 287	2 251	7 271	2 989
Interest Payments	16 629	7 051	3 094	2 475	119	499	3 957	9 578	1 498	5 968	1 422
Net Transfers on Debt (8)	-5 333	2 739	465	2 044	-490	-1 089	2 273	-8 071	-1 826	-5 588	5 868
1995											
Dette totale (5)	480 675	314 992	192 716	123 600	4 057	65 058	122 276	165 683	42 243	71 278	107 564
Décaissements (6)	55 733	26 363	15 137	9 788	300	5 049	11 226	29 370	7 178	12 350	24 916
Service de la dette (7)	63 146	31 005	18 791	11 752	338	6 701	12 214	32 141	6 412	13 827	16 458
Remboursement du principal	41 449	19 866	13 109	7 529	257	5 323	6 757	21 584	3 850	9 145	11 802
Paiement des intérêts	21 697	11 140	5 683	4 223	81	1 378	5 457	10 557	2 562	4 683	4 656
Transfers nets (8)	-7 413	-4 642	-3 654	-1 964	-38	-1 652	-988	-2 771	766	-1 477	8 459
1999											
Debt Outstanding (5)	523 065	335 496	198 566	148 036	4 127	46 404	136 930	187 568	63 560	78 745	198 444
Disbursments (6)	56 476	29 478	16 874	13 718	227	2 929	12 604	26 998	13 096	7 904	26 422
Debt Service (7)	62 130	29 028	17 377	12 167	309	4 902	11 651	33 102	10 381	13 703	45 035
Principal Repayments	41 615	18 589	12 141	7 922	248	3 972	6 448	23 026	6 616	9 595	34 535
Interest Payments	20 515	10 439	5 236	4 245	61	930	5 203	10 076	3 765	4 108	10 500
Net Transfers on Debt (8)	-5 654	450	-503	1 552	-82	-1 973	953	-6 104	2 716	-5 799	-18 612
2000											
Dette totale (5)	499 889	311 240	174 444	136 028	3 874	34 542	136 796	188 649	74 960	74 488	196 010
Décaissements (6)	58 662	25 642	12 489	10 935	148	1 406	13 152	33 020	19 196	8 306	23 126
Service de la dette (7)	64 189	30 333	16 234	12 142	304	3 788	14 099	33 856	8 095	17 266	43 032
Remboursement du principal	42 176	19 615	11 333	7 969	248	3 117	8 281	22 561	3 626	12 276	32 895
Paiement des intérêts	22 013	10 719	4 901	4 173	56	671	5 818	11 294	4 470	4 990	10 137
Transfers nets (8)	-5 527	-4 691	-3 745	-1 207	-156	-2 382	-947	-835	11 101	-8 960	-19 906
2001											
Debt Outstanding (5)	490 746	305 093	167 458	114 443	3 940	49 076	137 634	185 653	76 052	71 948	182 660
Disbursments (6)	44 587	24 594	11 640	8 234	345	3 061	12 953	19 994	10 156	6 052	27 160
Debt Service (7)	62 291	26 976	13 466	10 431	278	2 757	13 510	35 315	11 454	16 627	46 172
Principal Repayments	40 159	16 364	8 791	6 717	225	1 848	7 572	23 795	5 974	12 150	37 960
Interest Payments	22 132	10 612	4 675	3 714	52	908	5 937	11 520	5 480	4 478	8 213
Net Transfers on Debt (8)	-17 703	-2 382	-1 826	-2 198	68	304	-556	-15 321	-1 299	-10 575	-19 013
2002											
Dette totale (5)	512 750	316 617	175 612	134 386	3 952	37 274	141 005	196 133	84 927	74 890	175 893
Décaissements (6)	44 783	18 652	7 360	6 560	112	688	11 292	26 131	15 617	7 711	43 344
Service de la dette (7)	69 567	34 606	14 426	10 557	274	3 595	20 180	34 961	14 311	13 951	52 479
Remboursement du principal	50 396	26 102	10 963	7 925	220	2 818	15 139	24 295	8 697	10 175	46 470
Paiement des intérêts	19 171	8 504	3 463	2 632	55	776	5 041	10 667	5 614	3 776	6 009
Transfers nets (8)	-24 784	-15 954	-7 066	-3 997	-163	-2 906	-8 888	-8 830	1 306	-6 240	-9 135
2003											
Debt Outstanding (5)	530 867	332 250	186 314	144 288	4 027	37 998	145 936	198 618	89 881	75 303	181 251
Disbursments (6)	43 123	18 387	7 948	6 917	147	885	10 439	24 736	12 695	9 708	52 473
Debt Service (7)	79 967	35 662	17 622	14 514	281	2 827	18 040	44 305	18 771	18 929	61 538
Principal Repayments	58 442	27 555	13 564	11 205	229	2 130	13 991	30 887	11 175	14 589	54 261
Interest Payments	21 525	8 107	4 058	3 309	52	697	4 050	13 418	7 596	4 340	7 277
Net Transfers on Debt (8)	-36 844	-17 275	-9 673	-7 597	-134	-1 943	-7 602	-19 568	-6 076	-9 221	-9 064
2004											
Dette totale (5)	546 548	340 261	190 445	149 102	3 914	37 429	149 816	206 287	100 300	74 658	203 435
Décaissements (6)	59 605	19 155	7 680	5 766	109	1 806	11 475	40 450	26 418	12 496	66 107
Service de la dette (7)	74 967	30 343	16 127	14 063	280	1 784	14 216	44 624	20 659	18 697	55 598
Remboursement du principal	55 060	21 809	11 362	10 174	232	956	10 448	33 251	13 751	15 523	48 913
Paiement des intérêts	19 907	8 533	4 765	3 889	48	828	3 768	11 373	6 908	3 175	6 685
Transfers nets (8)	-15 362	-11 187	-8 447	-8 297	-171	21	-2 740	-4 174	5 760	-6 202	10 509

For sources and notes, see end of table 7.G.

Pour les sources et les notes, se reporter à la fin du tableau 7.G.

Debt stocks and flows / Stocks et flux de la dette	Total creditors / Total créanciers	Public and publicly guaranteed debt (1) / Dette publique et garantie par l'état (1)										Private non-guaranteed debt (4) / Dette privée non garantie (4)
		Official creditors (2) / Créanciers publics (2)						Private creditors (3) / Créanciers (3)				
		Total	Bilateral / Bilatéraux				Multilateral / Multilatéraux	Total	Bonds / Obligations	Commercial banks / Banques commerciales		
			Total	DAC CAD	OPEC OPEP	Other Autres						
						Millions of dollars / Millions de dollars						
1990												
Debt Outstanding (5)	2 108	1 606	458	421	10	27	1 147	502	39	330		1 033
Disbursments (6)	332	286	66	61	0	4	220	46	0	21		358
Debt Service (7)	367	164	47	44	0	3	116	203	3	175		299
Principal Repayments	251	99	26	25	0	0	73	152	0	137		222
Interest Payments	116	65	21	19	0	2	44	51	3	38		77
Net Transfers on Debt (8)	-36	122	18	17	0	2	104	-157	-3	-155		59
1995												
Dette totale (5)	2 212	1 973	576	546	11	19	1 397	239	0	157		828
Décaissements (6)	180	162	67	67	0	1	95	18	0	13		57
Service de la dette (7)	341	198	62	60	1	1	136	143	35	73		347
Remboursement du principal	244	121	41	39	1	1	80	124	32	63		313
Paiement des intérêts	97	77	21	21	0	0	56	20	2	9		34
Transfers nets (8)	-161	-36	5	7	-1	0	-41	-126	-35	-59		-290
1999												
Debt Outstanding (5)	2 045	1 972	584	529	9	46	1 389	73	..	53		1 118
Disbursments (6)	99	96	30	30	0	0	66	3	..	3		2
Debt Service (7)	206	180	59	47	2	10	121	25	..	15		34
Principal Repayments	141	123	44	34	2	8	79	19	..	10		27
Interest Payments	64	58	15	13	0	1	42	7	..	5		7
Net Transfers on Debt (8)	-107	-84	-29	-18	-2	-9	-55	-23	..	-12		-31
2000												
Dette totale (5)	1 991	1 927	622	562	10	49	1 305	64	..	54		1 064
Décaissements (6)	256	243	146	134	2	10	97	13	..	13		35
Service de la dette (7)	208	183	68	60	1	8	114	25	..	13		123
Remboursement du principal	144	124	50	43	1	6	74	20	..	10		89
Paiement des intérêts	64	59	19	17	0	2	40	5	..	3		33
Transfers nets (8)	48	60	77	74	1	2	-18	-11	..	0		-88
2001												
Debt Outstanding (5)	1 885	1 817	556	489	10	57	1 261	68	..	63		973
Disbursments (6)	215	185	61	39	1	22	124	30	..	30		10
Debt Service (7)	172	161	59	52	1	7	101	12	..	9		129
Principal Repayments	116	107	41	35	1	5	66	9	..	7		101
Interest Payments	56	53	18	17	0	1	35	3	..	3		28
Net Transfers on Debt (8)	43	24	2	-13	0	15	22	18	..	20		-119
2002												
Dette totale (5)	2 026	1 934	591	515	10	66	1 343	92	..	87		851
Décaissements (6)	92	66	26	14	0	12	40	27	..	27		0
Service de la dette (7)	167	155	58	54	1	4	97	12	..	10		142
Remboursement du principal	112	104	39	36	1	2	65	8	..	7		122
Paiement des intérêts	55	51	19	18	0	1	32	4	..	4		20
Transfers nets (8)	-75	-89	-32	-40	-1	8	-57	15	..	16		-142
2003												
Debt Outstanding (5)	2 104	2 006	616	541	9	66	1 390	98	..	94		754
Disbursments (6)	72	58	13	11	0	3	45	15	..	15		0
Debt Service (7)	201	175	77	72	1	4	98	26	..	26		120
Principal Repayments	146	124	57	54	1	2	67	23	..	23		95
Interest Payments	55	51	20	18	0	2	31	4	..	4		25
Net Transfers on Debt (8)	-129	-117	-64	-61	-1	-2	-53	-12	..	-12		-120
2004												
Dette totale (5)	2 069	1 987	570	498	9	63	1 417	82	..	78		549
Décaissements (6)	55	50	3	3	0	0	47	5	..	5		0
Service de la dette (7)	202	176	85	78	1	6	91	26	..	26		249
Remboursement du principal	152	129	65	61	1	4	63	23	..	23		208
Paiement des intérêts	51	47	19	17	0	2	28	3	..	3		41
Transfers nets (8)	-147	-126	-81	-75	-1	-6	-45	-21	..	-21		-249

For sources and notes, see end of table 7.G.　　　　　　　　　　　　　　　Pour les sources et les notes, se reporter à la fin du tableau 7.G.

Debt stocks and flows / Stocks et flux de la dette	Total creditors / Total créanciers	Official creditors (2) / Créanciers publics (2)		Bilateral / Bilatéraux				Multilateral / Multilatéraux	Private creditors (3) / Créanciers (3)			Private non-guaranteed debt (4) / Dette privée non garantie (4)
		Total	Total	DAC / CAD	OPEC / OPEP	Other / Autres			Total	Bonds / Obligations	Commercial banks / Banques commerciales	
											Millions of dollars / Millions de dollars	
1990												
Debt Outstanding (5)	171 435	83 465	58 671	39 619	2 122	16 930		24 794	87 969	22 095	25 316	14 574
Disbursments (6)	17 380	8 402	4 149	3 723	90	336		4 253	8 978	599	1 110	5 015
Debt Service (7)	26 787	8 528	5 540	3 819	107	1 614		2 988	18 259	741	8 941	2 490
Principal Repayments	16 761	4 975	3 516	2 178	86	1 252		1 459	11 786	415	4 895	1 456
Interest Payments	10 026	3 554	2 025	1 641	21	362		1 529	6 472	327	4 046	1 034
Net Transfers on Debt (8)	-9 408	-126	-1 391	-96	-17	-1 278		1 265	-9 281	-142	-7 830	2 525
1995												
Dette totale (5)	213 391	134 519	97 485	66 705	2 306	28 474		37 034	78 872	23 950	16 624	38 440
Décaissements (6)	14 993	8 159	4 030	3 712	195	123		4 129	6 833	954	2 305	7 358
Service de la dette (7)	26 137	13 814	8 795	4 258	102	4 434		5 019	12 323	2 807	3 567	6 892
Remboursement du principal	15 927	8 536	5 884	2 175	72	3 638		2 651	7 392	1 095	2 354	5 403
Paiement des intérêts	10 210	5 279	2 910	2 084	30	797		2 368	4 931	1 712	1 213	1 489
Transfers nets (8)	-11 144	-5 655	-4 765	-546	93	-4 311		-890	-5 489	-1 853	-1 262	467
1999												
Debt Outstanding (5)	196 008	130 060	93 973	69 487	2 389	22 097		36 087	65 948	21 203	24 119	57 424
Disbursments (6)	13 046	8 336	4 211	3 649	91	470		4 125	4 710	230	2 679	3 564
Debt Service (7)	25 797	12 794	7 925	4 784	169	2 973		4 869	13 003	2 946	5 943	9 981
Principal Repayments	16 882	7 874	5 244	2 569	106	2 570		2 630	9 008	1 258	4 559	8 560
Interest Payments	8 914	4 920	2 681	2 215	63	403		2 239	3 994	1 689	1 384	1 421
Net Transfers on Debt (8)	-12 751	-4 459	-3 715	-1 135	-77	-2 503		-744	-8 293	-2 716	-3 264	-6 417
2000												
Dette totale (5)	195 432	136 234	100 499	53 894	2 204	44 401		35 735	59 197	20 655	21 997	50 185
Décaissements (6)	10 870	5 949	2 928	2 321	47	560		3 021	4 921	814	2 464	2 483
Service de la dette (7)	23 663	11 929	6 886	3 714	181	2 990		5 043	11 734	2 827	5 705	9 350
Remboursement du principal	14 720	6 777	4 144	1 661	120	2 362		2 633	7 943	1 241	4 263	6 662
Paiement des intérêts	8 943	5 152	2 742	2 053	61	627		2 410	3 791	1 587	1 442	2 687
Transfers nets (8)	-12 793	-5 980	-3 957	-1 393	-135	-2 430		-2 022	-6 813	-2 013	-3 241	-6 867
2001												
Debt Outstanding (5)	188 120	130 368	95 631	47 717	2 543	45 371		34 737	57 752	19 962	23 138	42 949
Disbursments (6)	9 675	4 045	1 505	1 298	57	150		2 540	5 630	763	3 206	2 714
Debt Service (7)	23 930	12 137	7 175	3 711	178	3 286		4 962	11 793	2 645	5 795	7 685
Principal Repayments	15 136	6 966	4 222	1 725	122	2 375		2 745	8 170	1 044	4 488	6 166
Interest Payments	8 794	5 171	2 954	1 986	57	911		2 217	3 623	1 601	1 307	1 519
Net Transfers on Debt (8)	-14 254	-8 092	-5 670	-2 413	-121	-3 136		-2 422	-6 162	-1 881	-2 589	-4 971
2002												
Dette totale (5)	189 012	134 677	99 554	51 196	2 569	45 789		35 123	54 335	18 367	21 424	38 101
Décaissements (6)	8 431	3 622	1 189	1 028	43	117		2 433	4 809	512	2 782	2 621
Service de la dette (7)	22 198	10 105	4 805	3 328	193	1 284		5 300	12 093	3 327	5 937	9 522
Remboursement du principal	15 787	6 419	3 283	2 163	135	984		3 137	9 368	2 090	4 893	8 188
Paiement des intérêts	6 411	3 685	1 522	1 165	58	300		2 163	2 725	1 236	1 044	1 333
Transfers nets (8)	-13 767	-6 483	-3 616	-2 299	-149	-1 167		-2 866	-7 285	-2 815	-3 155	-6 901
2003												
Debt Outstanding (5)	201 479	144 137	108 188	80 091	2 561	25 535		35 950	57 342	20 685	21 270	37 787
Disbursments (6)	15 849	3 425	1 170	992	69	108		2 255	12 424	4 963	5 133	5 776
Debt Service (7)	24 873	10 715	5 198	3 992	187	1 019		5 518	14 158	4 360	6 759	10 864
Principal Repayments	18 270	6 833	3 309	2 464	133	712		3 523	11 437	3 074	5 759	9 378
Interest Payments	6 603	3 883	1 888	1 528	54	307		1 994	2 720	1 286	1 000	1 486
Net Transfers on Debt (8)	-9 023	-7 290	-4 028	-3 000	-118	-911		-3 262	-1 733	603	-1 625	-5 088
2004												
Dette totale (5)	201 841	142 704	108 359	84 463	2 683	21 213		34 345	59 137	23 277	20 948	41 161
Décaissements (6)	14 710	3 980	1 569	876	432	261		2 411	10 730	3 500	5 098	8 931
Service de la dette (7)	27 882	15 784	9 452	7 692	376	1 383		6 332	12 099	2 740	5 923	11 147
Remboursement du principal	20 140	11 055	6 422	5 030	326	1 066		4 633	9 085	1 138	5 083	9 622
Paiement des intérêts	7 743	4 729	3 030	2 662	50	317		1 699	3 014	1 601	841	1 524
Transfers nets (8)	-13 173	-11 804	-7 883	-6 816	56	-1 123		-3 921	-1 369	760	-825	-2 216

For sources and notes, see end of table 7.G.

Pour les sources et les notes, se reporter à la fin du tableau 7.G.

Debt stocks and flows Stocks et flux de la dette	Total creditors Total créanciers	Public and publicly guaranted debt (1) Dette publique et garantie par l'état (1)									Private non-guaranteed debt (4) Dette privée non garantie (4)
		Official creditors (2) / Créanciers publics (2)						Private creditors (3) / Créanciers (3)			
		Total	Bilateral / Bilatéraux				Multilateral Multilatéraux	Total	Bonds Obligations	Commercial banks Banques commerciales	
			Total	DAC CAD	OPEC OPEP	Other Autres					
							Millions of dollars / Millions de dollars				
1990											
Debt Outstanding (5)	367 183	160 745	85 744	68 748	1 337	15 659	75 002	206 437	61 108	109 215	25 390
Disbursments (6)	38 239	18 061	7 572	6 730	48	795	10 488	20 178	3 098	10 415	8 160
Debt Service (7)	41 702	15 988	6 242	5 212	326	704	9 746	25 714	5 239	14 045	4 775
Principal Repayments	22 593	8 842	3 592	3 066	260	266	5 251	13 751	2 693	6 794	2 929
Interest Payments	19 108	7 145	2 650	2 146	66	438	4 495	11 963	2 546	7 251	1 846
Net Transfers on Debt (8)	-3 463	2 073	1 331	1 518	-278	91	742	-5 536	-2 141	-3 631	3 386
1995											
Dette totale (5)	478 892	217 559	120 907	100 746	469	19 691	96 652	261 334	139 790	77 985	118 975
Décaissements (6)	72 506	31 820	21 532	16 670	6	4 856	10 288	40 686	14 992	16 395	35 207
Service de la dette (7)	71 470	27 896	14 738	12 432	157	2 148	13 159	43 573	18 111	14 136	22 781
Remboursement du principal	43 657	17 413	9 583	7 916	120	1 547	7 830	26 244	8 303	9 617	16 107
Paiement des intérêts	27 812	10 483	5 154	4 516	37	601	5 329	17 329	9 808	4 520	6 674
Transfers nets (8)	1 036	3 924	6 794	4 238	-151	2 707	-2 871	-2 887	-3 118	2 259	12 426
1999											
Debt Outstanding (5)	502 501	221 061	110 482	96 059	684	13 739	110 579	281 440	166 505	76 883	308 664
Disbursments (6)	66 769	25 514	13 211	10 192	307	2 712	12 303	41 255	27 023	8 934	71 181
Debt Service (7)	83 908	30 328	16 045	13 153	163	2 729	14 283	53 580	24 676	20 995	89 443
Principal Repayments	56 949	20 217	11 814	9 531	137	2 146	8 403	36 732	13 990	16 681	67 327
Interest Payments	26 959	10 110	4 231	3 622	26	583	5 880	16 848	10 685	4 314	22 116
Net Transfers on Debt (8)	-17 139	-4 813	-2 834	-2 961	145	-17	-1 980	-12 326	2 348	-12 061	-18 262
2000											
Dette totale (5)	492 714	210 054	98 779	88 276	600	9 903	111 275	282 660	174 493	75 323	311 194
Décaissements (6)	77 692	25 038	9 660	8 579	75	1 006	15 378	52 654	35 521	12 583	65 763
Service de la dette (7)	94 922	34 087	16 061	13 987	155	1 919	18 026	60 835	33 249	19 162	93 186
Remboursement du principal	64 606	24 023	12 260	10 615	121	1 524	11 763	40 583	20 734	13 367	72 879
Paiement des intérêts	30 316	10 064	3 801	3 372	34	395	6 263	20 252	12 515	5 796	20 306
Transfers nets (8)	-17 230	-9 049	-6 401	-5 408	-80	-913	-2 648	-8 182	2 272	-6 580	-27 423
2001											
Debt Outstanding (5)	478 836	204 551	91 060	78 973	386	11 702	113 491	274 285	165 573	77 023	293 065
Disbursments (6)	60 546	22 453	10 531	7 768	48	2 714	11 923	38 093	24 725	10 609	69 242
Debt Service (7)	91 709	25 570	11 482	9 235	137	2 111	14 088	66 139	36 509	21 900	93 535
Principal Repayments	61 246	16 060	8 394	6 636	108	1 650	7 666	45 186	23 170	15 988	73 719
Interest Payments	30 463	9 510	3 088	2 599	28	461	6 422	20 953	13 339	5 912	19 817
Net Transfers on Debt (8)	-31 164	-3 117	-951	-1 467	-88	604	-2 165	-28 047	-11 784	-11 291	-24 293
2002											
Dette totale (5)	489 333	207 256	93 463	84 959	364	8 140	113 793	282 077	172 882	79 774	282 494
Décaissements (6)	55 161	19 746	7 875	7 477	53	346	11 871	35 415	19 036	14 199	69 760
Service de la dette (7)	94 566	35 989	14 797	11 775	96	2 925	21 192	58 577	28 877	22 977	92 047
Remboursement du principal	67 081	27 918	11 992	9 290	80	2 621	15 925	39 163	16 104	17 445	76 140
Paiement des intérêts	27 485	8 071	2 804	2 485	16	304	5 267	19 414	12 773	5 531	15 908
Transfers nets (8)	-39 405	-16 243	-6 921	-4 299	-43	-2 580	-9 321	-23 162	-9 841	-8 778	-22 287
2003											
Debt Outstanding (5)	493 729	206 379	93 503	85 109	331	8 064	112 876	287 350	183 688	78 895	284 646
Disbursments (6)	56 309	16 517	5 701	5 140	51	510	10 815	39 792	25 582	13 212	79 125
Debt Service (7)	104 596	37 348	16 890	14 927	105	1 858	20 458	67 248	36 278	24 734	93 802
Principal Repayments	75 183	30 290	14 044	12 397	92	1 556	16 245	44 893	21 354	18 563	76 845
Interest Payments	29 413	7 059	2 846	2 530	13	302	4 213	22 354	14 924	6 171	16 958
Net Transfers on Debt (8)	-48 287	-20 831	-11 189	-9 787	-54	-1 348	-9 643	-27 456	-10 697	-11 522	-14 678
2004											
Dette totale (5)	498 887	207 663	95 877	81 792	267	13 818	111 786	291 223	189 592	79 390	292 106
Décaissements (6)	70 638	16 097	5 975	4 700	32	1 243	10 122	54 541	33 570	20 316	93 282
Service de la dette (7)	97 092	28 232	12 539	11 546	106	886	15 693	68 860	38 162	26 869	98 013
Remboursement du principal	69 635	21 675	9 776	9 183	96	496	11 899	47 960	23 424	21 690	84 110
Paiement des intérêts	27 457	6 557	2 764	2 363	10	390	3 793	20 900	14 739	5 179	13 904
Transfers nets (8)	-26 453	-12 135	-6 564	-6 846	-74	356	-5 571	-14 318	-4 593	-6 552	-4 731

For sources and notes, see next page.

Pour les sources et les notes, se reporter à la page suivante.

7

7.7.G External long-term debt by lending source
Major exporters of manufactures

7.7.G Dette extérieure à long terme par catégories de prêt
Principaux exportateurs d'articles manufacturés

Sources:
- World Bank, *Global Development Finance 2006*

Notes:

(1) Public and publicly guaranteed debt (PPG) are aggregated.
- Public debt is an obligation of a public debtor, including the national government, a political subdivision (or an agency of either), and autonomous public bodies.
- Publicly guaranteed debt is an external obligation of a private debtor that is guaranteed for repayment by a public entity.
Data is shown by type of creditor: official creditors and private creditors.

(2) Public and publicly guaranteed debt from official creditors includes loans from Governments and loans from international organizations .
Government loans include loans from governments and their agencies (including central banks), loans from autonomous bodies, and direct loans from official export credit agencies.
Loans from international organizations include loans and credits from the World Bank, regional development banks, and other multilateral and intergovernmental agencies. Excluded are loans from funds administered by an international organization on behalf of a single donor Government; these are classified as loans from Governments.
In this table, governments are treated as bilateral creditors and international organizations are treated as multilateral creditors.

(3) Public and publicly guaranteed debt from private creditors includes:
- Bonds that are either publicly issued or privately placed;
- Commercial bank loans from private banks and other private financial institutions;
- Other private credits from manufacturers, exporters, and other suppliers of goods, and bank credits covered by a guarantee of an export credit agency.

(4) Private nonguaranteed debt (PNG) is an obligation of a private debtor that is not guaranteed for repayment by a public entity.

(5) Long-term debt is defined as debt that has an original or extended maturity of more than one year and that is owed to nonresidents and repayable in foreign currency, goods, or services. Long-term debt has three components: Public debt, Publicly guaranteed debt, and Private nonguaranteed debt.
Total outstanding long term debt at year end is long-term debt outstanding and disbursed.

(6) Disbursements on long-term debt are drawings on loan commitments during the year specified.

(7) Long-term debt service payments are the sum of principal repayments and interest payments in the year specified.

(8) Net transfers are disbursements minus debt service payments.

Sources :
- Banque mondiale, *Global Development Finance 2006*

Notes :

(1) La dette publique et garantie par l'État est une aggrégation de 2 composantes : .
- La dette publique qui est une dette contractée par le secteur public, y compris le gouvernement, une entité politique et d'autres organismes publics autonomes.
- La dette garantie par l'État qui est une dette contractée par le secteur privé, dont l'amortissement est garanti par une entité publique.
Les données sont indiquées par type de créanciers : créanciers publics et créanciers privés.

(2) La dette publique et garantie par l'État octroyée par les créanciers publics inclut les prêts des gouvernements et les prêts des organisations internationales.
Les prêts des gouvernements incluent les prêts des gouvernements et des organismes publics (y compris les banques centrales), les prêts provenant d'entités autonomes et les prêts octroyés directement par des organismes publics de crédits à l'exportation.
Les prêts des organisations internationales incluent les prêts et les crédits de la Banque mondiale, des banques régionales de développement, et d'autres organismes multilatéraux et intergouvernementaux. Ne sont pas compris les prêts provenant des fonds administrés par une organisation internationale, pour le compte d'un gouvernement ; ceux-ci sont classés sous la rubrique des prêts des gouvernements.
Dans ce tableau, les gouvernements sont appelés créditeurs bilatéraux et les organisations internationales sont appelées créditeurs multilatéraux.

(3) La dette publique et garantie par l'État octroyée par les créanciers privés, comprend :
- Obligations qui sont soit des émissions publiques, soit des placements privés ;
- Prêts des banques commerciales octroyés par des banques privées et par d'autres entités financières ;
- Autres crédits privés provenant du secteur manufacturier, du secteur des exportations, et d'autres fournisseurs de biens, ainsi que des crédits bancaires couverts par un organisme de crédits à l'exportation.

(4) La dette du secteur privé non garantie est une dette contractée par le secteur privé, dont l'amortissement n'est pas garanti par une entité publique.

(5) La dette à long terme a une durée de remboursement (d'origine ou différée) supérieure à une année, et son amortissement est dû, en monnaies convertibles ou en nature, à des créanciers non-résidents. La dette à long terme a trois composantes : dette publique, dette garantie par l'État et dette du secteur privé non garantie.
L'encours total de la dette à long terme à la fin de l'année est la somme de l'encours de la dette à long terme et de la dette décaissée à long terme.

(6) Les décaissements de la dette à long terme sont les tirages sur les engagements de la dette effectués au cours de l'année spécifiée.

(7) Les paiements du service de la dette à long terme sont la somme du remboursement du principal et du paiement des intérêts, effectués au cours de l'année spécifiée.

(8) Les transferts nets sont les décaissements moins les paiements du service de la dette.

DEVELOPMENT INDICATORS

INDICATEURS DU DÉVELOPPEMENT

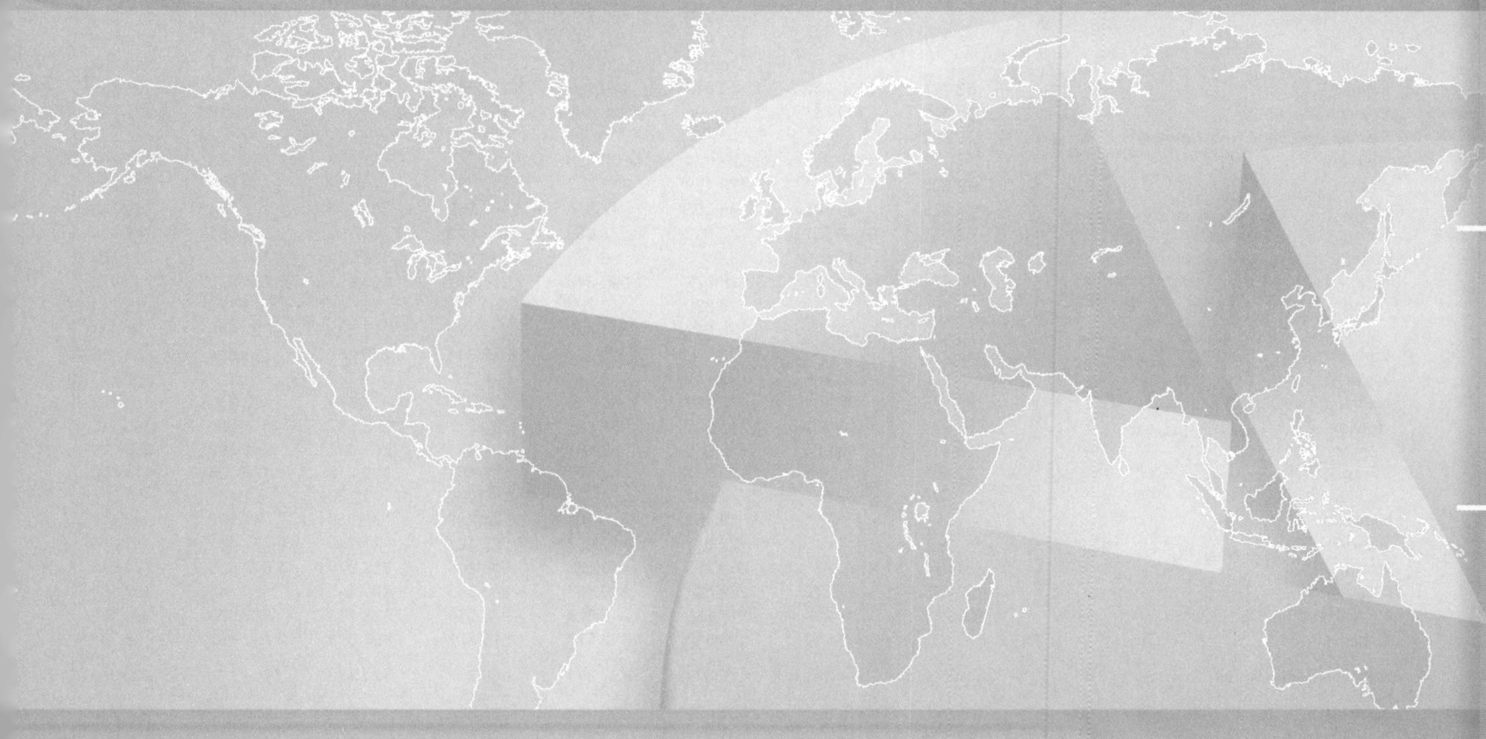

1

2

3

4

5

6

7

8

Region, country or territory	Total gross domestic product / Produit intérieur brut total (1) Millions of dollars / Millions de dollars							
	1980	1990	1995	2000	2002	2003	2004	2005
WORLD	**11 858 462**	**22 059 825**	**29 556 282**	**31 678 619**	**32 717 346**	**36 756 087**	**41 278 164**	**44 475 204**
DEVELOPED ECONOMIES	8 200 587	17 304 955	23 287 869	24 577 132	25 431 032	28 627 503	31 782 615	33 314 361
DEVELOPING ECONOMIES	2 611 798	3 810 973	5 653 956	6 659 394	6 712 239	7 414 587	8 549 776	9 962 981
ECONOMIES IN TRANSITION	1 046 077	943 896	614 457	442 093	574 024	713 997	945 773	1 197 861
Developed economies: America	**3 051 058**	**6 365 714**	**7 971 882**	**10 551 983**	**11 220 226**	**11 856 446**	**12 742 479**	**13 678 531**
Bermuda	931	2 023	2 577	3 522	3 960	4 288	4 505	4 090
Canada	265 272	574 204	581 664	714 453	724 304	854 711	976 742	1 131 760
United States	2 784 856	5 789 487	7 387 641	9 834 008	10 491 962	10 997 447	11 761 233	12 542 682
Developed economies: Asia	**1 070 752**	**3 052 658**	**5 301 247**	**4 770 639**	**4 013 749**	**4 346 227**	**4 707 274**	**4 688 598**
Israel	23 369	56 923	94 588	121 023	108 923	114 976	122 389	129 648
Japan	1 047 383	2 995 736	5 206 658	4 649 615	3 904 826	4 231 250	4 584 885	4 558 950
Developed economies: Europe	**3 889 832**	**7 532 437**	**9 569 362**	**8 802 179**	**9 711 283**	**11 800 341**	**13 578 741**	**14 128 179**
Andorra	595	1 371	1 554	1 360	1 809	2 378	2 786	3 091
Austria	81 176	164 988	239 576	193 838	207 696	256 162	294 324	306 065
Belgium	–	–	–	–	251 826	309 900	357 712	370 815
Belgium-Luxembourg	131 170	215 359	305 002	252 203				
Cyprus	2 230	5 777	9 168	9 124	10 431	13 211	15 561	16 723
Czechoslovakia (former)	48 582	53 350			–	–	–	–
Czech Republic	–	–	55 262	55 703	73 756	90 602	107 694	122 345
Denmark	69 727	135 839	181 985	160 082	173 881	213 909	244 917	258 718
Estonia	–	–	4 359	5 477	7 038	9 190	11 234	12 762
Finland	52 761	138 238	130 913	120 563	132 561	162 304	185 909	193 155
France	689 350	1 239 858	1 570 990	1 328 689	1 458 201	1 800 951	2 061 118	2 127 781
Germany, Federal Rep. (former)	912 585							
Germany	–	1 707 359	2 522 624	1 900 220	2 018 744	2 441 667	2 751 113	2 794 856
Greece	49 898	85 931	120 159	115 997	135 035	175 549	209 119	225 201
Hungary	24 929	36 385	45 008	47 035	65 592	83 148	100 764	109 239
Iceland	3 331	6 367	7 013	8 628	8 723	10 792	13 061	15 814
Ireland	21 107	47 856	67 106	96 166	122 832	156 988	184 459	201 763
Italy	458 471	1 133 465	1 126 077	1 097 343	1 218 977	1 507 113	1 724 523	1 762 475
Latvia	–	–	4 890	7 726	9 203	11 055	13 597	15 244
Lithuania	–	–	6 392	11 462	14 128	18 548	22 456	24 864
Luxembourg	–	–	–	–	22 614	28 987	33 594	36 468
Malta	1 206	2 458	3 449	3 793	4 031	4 753	5 304	5 573
Netherlands	185 779	307 381	432 563	386 510	437 827	537 619	606 734	624 187
Norway	63 646	116 107	147 975	166 905	190 277	222 697	254 706	295 513
Poland	56 516	63 084	135 905	166 561	191 448	209 541	241 592	290 006
Portugal	31 458	75 278	112 958	112 650	127 461	155 212	177 595	183 300
San Marino	228	565	692	774	880	1 123	1 287	1 315
Slovakia	–	–	19 402	20 291	24 239	32 665	41 092	46 417
Slovenia	–	–	20 019	19 098	22 121	27 749	32 494	34 030
Spain	228 371	526 441	596 755	580 673	686 104	880 948	1 039 673	1 124 612
Sweden	130 795	242 179	250 641	242 003	243 563	304 145	350 145	357 683
Switzerland	109 788	237 236	317 236	248 527	278 914	325 769	362 023	369 369
United Kingdom	536 132	989 564	1 133 690	1 442 777	1 571 372	1 805 663	2 132 156	2 198 796
Developed economies: Oceania	**188 945**	**354 146**	**445 378**	**452 331**	**485 824**	**624 489**	**754 120**	**819 053**
Australia	166 090	310 528	384 096	399 658	425 304	543 643	655 652	709 446
New Zealand	22 854	43 618	61 282	52 673	60 520	80 846	98 469	109 607
Developing economies: Africa	**513 234**	**508 443**	**531 146**	**599 779**	**573 932**	**686 557**	**815 252**	**947 747**
Eastern Africa	*45 100*	*55 962*	*55 521*	*63 636*	*66 090*	*72 402*	*77 982*	*88 110*
Burundi	951	1 148	1 003	711	630	597	681	845
Comoros	135	250	232	204	247	318	368	380
Djibouti	301	457	510	553	592	625	664	705
Ethiopia (former)	4 106	8 128			–	–	–	–
Eritrea	–	–	598	634	623	742	933	1 077
Ethiopia	–	–	5 502	6 473	6 041	6 623	8 013	9 297
Kenya	9 221	11 104	11 772	12 705	13 191	15 036	16 088	19 184
Madagascar	3 265	3 080	3 160	3 878	4 397	5 473	4 364	4 950
Malawi	1 238	1 752	1 423	1 744	1 935	1 764	1 903	2 140
Mauritius	1 146	2 588	4 042	4 552	4 744	5 634	6 317	6 288
Mozambique	4 401	2 708	2 291	3 832	4 092	4 789	5 912	6 682
Rwanda	1 383	2 541	1 283	1 732	1 669	1 684	1 823	2 118
Seychelles	147	369	508	618	699	703	703	699

For sources and notes, see end of table.

Per capita gross domestic product / Produit intérieur brut par habitant Dollars								Régions, pays ou territoires
1980	1990	1995	2000	2002	2003	2004	2005	
2 664	**4 166**	**5 168**	**5 173**	**5 209**	**5 780**	**6 413**	**6 827**	**MONDE**
9 914	19 701	25 397	26 096	26 677	29 841	32 927	34 314	ÉCONOMIES DÉVELOPPÉES
791	937	1 267	1 374	1 344	1 464	1 664	1 912	ÉCONOMIES EN DÉVELOPPEMENT
3 263	2 716	1 811	1 316	1 716	2 140	2 841	3 605	ÉCONOMIES EN TRANSITION
11 792	**22 146**	**26 278**	**33 026**	**34 402**	**35 983**	**38 283**	**40 687**	**Économies développées : Amérique**
16 602	33 824	41 952	56 026	62 438	67 324	70 452	63 731	Bermudes
10 820	20 729	19 851	23 280	23 135	27 020	30 566	35 071	Canada
11 895	22 299	26 968	34 064	35 601	36 936	39 104	41 287	États-Unis
8 881	**23 839**	**40 515**	**35 838**	**29 994**	**32 407**	**35 032**	**34 836**	**Économies développées : Asie**
6 209	12 611	17 601	19 891	17 194	17 811	18 617	19 374	Israël
8 967	24 250	41 497	36 601	30 630	33 145	35 876	35 646	Japon
9 045	**17 018**	**20 759**	**18 881**	**20 672**	**25 008**	**28 654**	**29 700**	**Économies développées : Europe**
15 927	25 970	24 015	20 470	26 206	33 623	38 535	42 063	Andorre
10 753	21 346	29 774	23 897	25 416	31 193	35 661	36 911	Autriche
				24 518	30 040	34 529	35 662	Belgique
12 870	20 878	29 069	23 726	–	–	–	–	Belgique-Luxembourg
3 650	8 488	12 542	11 603	12 924	16 168	18 821	19 996	Chypre
3 184	3 429							Tchécoslovaquie (anc.)
		5 360	5 450	7 230	8 885	10 564	12 004	République tchèque
13 611	26 428	34 811	30 004	32 369	39 702	45 331	47 761	Danemark
		3 030	3 998	5 187	6 795	8 331	9 494	Estonie
11 039	27 723	25 630	23 293	25 480	31 113	35 539	36 820	Finlande
12 503	21 290	26 263	21 812	23 663	29 031	33 006	33 863	France
11 657								Allemagne, Rép. Fédérale d' (anc.)
	21 494	30 891	23 086	24 474	29 572	33 295	33 815	Allemagne
5 175	8 457	11 277	10 570	12 233	15 873	18 875	20 289	Grèce
2 328	3 510	4 357	4 605	6 453	8 201	9 964	10 830	Hongrie
14 601	24 991	26 221	30 695	30 396	37 218	44 591	53 474	Islande
6 206	13 616	18 595	25 281	31 291	39 299	45 347	48 696	Irlande
8 124	19 984	19 652	19 021	20 997	25 864	29 492	30 053	Italie
–	–	1 964	3 248	3 925	4 745	5 873	6 623	Lettonie
–	–	1 761	3 272	4 074	5 370	6 528	7 259	Lituanie
				50 809	64 607	74 255	79 866	Luxembourg
3 722	6 825	9 130	9 754	10 222	11 963	13 255	13 843	Malte
13 129	20 559	27 981	24 272	27 189	33 212	37 306	38 229	Pays-Bas
15 578	27 374	33 946	37 183	41 843	48 646	55 268	63 704	Norvège
1 589	1 655	3 521	4 334	4 994	5 472	6 317	7 593	Pologne
3 221	7 540	11 262	11 015	12 319	14 910	16 960	17 410	Portugal
10 665	23 371	26 926	28 708	31 202	38 807	43 418	43 534	Saint-Marin
–	–	3 617	3 766	4 499	6 064	7 628	8 616	Slovaquie
		10 192	9 628	11 112	13 914	16 270	17 020	Slovénie
6 086	13 550	15 151	14 434	16 577	20 923	24 294	25 914	Espagne
15 739	28 296	28 395	27 290	27 305	33 955	38 915	39 575	Suède
17 304	34 567	44 279	34 063	37 909	44 071	48 749	49 520	Suisse
9 488	17 225	19 487	24 416	26 359	30 144	35 423	36 361	Royaume-Uni
10 644	**17 459**	**20 482**	**19 673**	**20 628**	**26 191**	**31 251**	**33 558**	**Économies développées : Océanie**
11 346	18 403	21 254	20 882	21 695	27 396	32 651	34 930	Australie
7 342	12 789	16 682	13 667	15 329	20 213	24 312	26 752	Nouvelle-Zélande
1 071	**798**	**732**	**731**	**668**	**780**	**905**	**1 029**	**Économies en développement : Afrique**
310	*285*	*248*	*248*	*244*	*261*	*274*	*302*	*Afrique orientale*
230	202	161	107	89	82	90	107	Burundi
350	475	382	292	334	419	473	477	Comores
886	815	817	758	776	805	840	877	Djibouti
104	150		–	–	–	–	–	Éthiopie (anc.)
		186	172	156	178	214	238	Érythrée
–	–	91	93	83	88	104	118	Éthiopie
566	474	430	407	401	445	464	539	Kenya
360	256	227	240	256	310	241	266	Madagascar
199	186	141	150	158	140	148	162	Malawi
1 186	2 449	3 594	3 839	3 925	4 619	5 134	5 066	Maurice
363	200	144	211	214	244	294	325	Mozambique
266	348	227	212	190	189	201	229	Rwanda
2 229	5 118	6 713	7 619	8 407	8 367	8 288	8 173	Seychelles

Pour les sources et les notes, se reporter à la fin du tableau.

Region, country or territory	Total gross domestic product / Produit intérieur brut total (1) Millions of dollars / Millions de dollars							
	1980	1990	1995	2000	2002	2003	2004	2005
Somalia	593	994	1 122	2 070	2 056	2 100	2 213	2 182
Uganda	2 747	3 652	6 046	5 734	6 015	6 435	7 820	9 115
United Republic of Tanzania	6 226	4 683	5 404	9 331	10 037	10 573	11 668	12 937
Zambia	3 885	3 742	3 471	3 239	3 697	4 305	5 440	7 315
Zimbabwe	5 355	8 767	7 153	5 628	5 427	5 000	3 071	2 198
Middle Africa	*29 573*	*45 106*	*29 500*	*35 466*	*40 407*	*49 476*	*63 243*	*78 325*
Angola	5 415	10 295	4 994	9 130	10 960	13 825	19 498	28 853
Cameroon	9 676	14 310	9 074	9 287	10 830	13 723	15 806	16 823
Central African Republic	693	1 297	1 058	906	934	1 126	1 246	1 325
Chad	918	1 539	1 444	1 386	1 977	2 727	4 399	4 942
Congo	1 706	2 799	2 116	3 220	3 018	3 481	4 137	5 528
Dem. Rep. of the Congo	6 139	9 187	5 643	5 256	5 548	5 634	6 507	7 212
Equatorial Guinea	53	133	166	1 216	2 186	2 976	4 523	5 651
Gabon	4 927	5 489	4 959	5 019	4 800	5 926	7 063	7 919
São Tome and Principe	47	58	45	46	54	59	64	73
Northern Africa	*138 678*	*184 653*	*201 224*	*252 983*	*237 971*	*253 275*	*294 270*	*346 013*
Algeria	42 348	61 891	42 066	54 790	56 948	68 017	85 021	102 257
Egypt	24 057	39 412	68 653	99 601	90 064	77 109	84 019	101 406
Libyan Arab Jamahiriya	35 721	28 905	25 540	34 265	19 131	23 273	28 025	37 173
Morocco	18 821	25 824	32 985	33 335	36 094	43 813	50 031	51 461
Sudan	8 989	16 307	13 950	11 549	14 718	16 108	19 040	24 667
Tunisia	8 743	12 314	18 030	19 444	21 016	24 955	28 134	29 049
Southern Africa	*84 527*	*119 332*	*161 337*	*143 427*	*120 939*	*180 964*	*232 595*	*257 729*
Botswana	993	3 489	4 423	4 889	5 045	7 341	8 498	8 850
Lesotho	380	618	933	859	699	1 077	1 324	1 335
Namibia	2 021	2 340	3 503	3 414	3 122	4 473	5 713	6 130
South Africa	80 544	112 014	151 113	132 878	110 882	166 169	214 663	238 825
Swaziland	590	871	1 364	1 388	1 192	1 904	2 396	2 588
Western Africa	*215 356*	*103 390*	*83 564*	*104 266*	*108 525*	*130 442*	*147 162*	*177 569*
Benin	1 374	1 845	2 170	2 359	2 808	3 557	4 060	4 378
Burkina Faso	1 287	3 120	2 665	2 415	3 006	4 028	4 945	5 397
Cape Verde	142	308	491	539	621	814	930	1 038
Côte d'Ivoire	10 176	11 893	11 105	10 682	11 692	14 255	16 064	16 785
Gambia	239	333	382	421	370	366	415	480
Ghana	3 252	6 226	6 458	4 978	6 160	7 624	8 620	10 393
Guinea	1 360	2 818	3 923	3 134	3 044	3 446	3 788	3 058
Guinea-Bissau	158	233	248	215	204	239	281	298
Liberia	917	384	135	561	559	435	492	561
Mali	1 422	2 510	2 721	2 670	3 304	4 291	4 831	5 181
Mauritania	829	1 022	1 058	928	983	1 180	1 351	1 672
Niger	2 538	2 506	1 672	1 666	2 065	2 523	2 792	3 245
Nigeria	186 312	61 873	43 881	67 359	66 218	78 441	87 845	113 461
Senegal	2 988	5 698	4 476	4 374	4 982	6 410	7 617	8 274
Sierra Leone	1 231	992	871	636	1 033	1 073	1 071	1 162
Togo	1 131	1 628	1 309	1 329	1 476	1 759	2 061	2 187
Developing economies: America	**765 506**	**1 123 193**	**1 720 950**	**2 009 383**	**1 736 090**	**1 805 358**	**2 067 916**	**2 486 993**
Caribbean	*43 026*	*60 260*	*71 162*	*89 519*	*96 492*	*95 504*	*104 058*	*125 729*
Anguilla	9	54	75	108	113	118	146	157
Antigua and Barbuda	110	392	494	665	715	754	818	856
Aruba	493	828	1 321	1 859	1 91·	2 011	2 134	2 258
Bahamas	1 454	3 166	3 429	5 004	5 389	5 503	5 661	5 870
Barbados	865	1 720	1 871	2 559	2 476	2 695	2 816	2 996
British Virgin Islands	29	108	397	784	813	782	873	972
Cayman Islands	132	708	960	1 323	1 415	1 468	1 533	1 593
Cuba	21 490	30 914	32 838	32 685	36 089	38 625	41 065	46 932
Dominica	59	167	219	269	252	258	271	283
Dominican Republic	6 761	7 074	11 935	19 772	21 625	16 325	18 452	29 101
Grenada	84	221	277	410	408	444	437	454
Haiti	1 384	2 614	2 334	3 515	3 077	2 708	3 501	3 884
Jamaica	2 689	4 271	5 796	7 889	8 471	8 190	8 825	10 063
Montserrat	24	67	60	35	38	38	41	42
Netherlands Antilles	943	1 980	2 571	2 798	2 905	3 002	3 081	3 204
Saint Kitts and Nevis	48	159	230	329	351	365	405	453
Saint Lucia	117	432	571	707	703	739	787	851
Saint Vincent and the Grenadines	59	198	264	335	365	380	408	428
Trinidad and Tobago	6 236	5 068	5 329	8 154	9 008	10 691	12 319	14 763
Turks and Caicos Islands	39	119	191	319	367	410	486	570

For sources and notes, see end of table.

Per capita gross domestic product / Produit intérieur brut par habitant Dollars								Régions, pays ou territoires
1980	1990	1995	2000	2002	2003	2004	2005	
91	148	180	293	274	272	278	266	Somalie
217	205	285	232	229	237	279	315	Ouganda
333	184	181	276	282	289	311	336	République-Unie de Tanzanie
653	461	375	310	340	389	483	637	Zambie
735	836	607	445	422	386	236	168	Zimbabwe
540	*613*	*340*	*363*	*392*	*466*	*579*	*696*	*Afrique centrale*
691	977	405	655	744	911	1 247	1 793	Angola
1 066	1 169	645	586	654	806	908	945	Cameroun
298	431	307	234	246	277	302	316	République centrafricaine
199	252	202	164	217	288	448	487	Tchad
946	1 156	758	1 005	896	1 009	1 172	1 531	Congo
219	242	124	104	104	102	114	123	Rép. dém. du Congo
251	392	435	2 824	4 844	6 442	9 565	11 672	Guinée équatoriale
7 226	5 980	4 696	4 245	3 910	4 744	5 561	6 136	Gabon
495	496	356	331	369	400	429	476	Sao Tomé-et-Principe
1 245	*1 283*	*1 262*	*1 450*	*1 319*	*1 381*	*1 578*	*1 825*	*Afrique septentrionale*
2 251	2 448	1 488	1 796	1 813	2 133	2 627	3 112	Algérie
551	715	1 132	1 497	1 305	1 097	1 174	1 392	Égypte
11 662	6 624	5 285	6 410	3 436	4 095	4 832	6 281	Jamahiriya arabe libyenne
962	1 041	1 224	1 156	1 224	1 469	1 659	1 688	Maroc
458	629	473	346	424	455	527	668	Soudan
1 354	1 498	2 009	2 033	2 149	2 524	2 815	2 875	Tunisie
2 563	*2 853*	*3 403*	*2 761*	*2 268*	*3 357*	*4 273*	*4 695*	*Afrique australe*
997	2 552	2 824	2 828	2 842	4 089	4 682	4 821	Botswana
293	386	542	456	362	552	674	674	Lesotho
2 035	1 651	2 114	1 816	1 607	2 272	2 865	3 035	Namibie
2 770	3 062	3 641	2 927	2 380	3 529	4 515	4 982	Afrique du Sud
959	1 007	1 423	1 311	1 094	1 727	2 151	2 302	Swaziland
1 598	*572*	*401*	*435*	*430*	*503*	*554*	*652*	*Afrique occidentale*
370	356	349	326	364	447	494	516	Bénin
189	352	259	203	237	308	366	387	Burkina Faso
492	867	1 223	1 197	1 315	1 683	1 877	2 048	Cap-Vert
1 220	931	741	627	661	793	879	903	Côte d'Ivoire
357	346	329	304	250	240	264	297	Gambie
285	400	361	247	292	353	391	461	Ghana
297	467	536	382	358	397	429	340	Guinée
199	230	208	157	140	159	181	186	Guinée-Bissau
491	180	63	183	172	132	147	163	Libéria
234	327	311	267	312	393	429	446	Mali
552	525	476	362	361	421	469	564	Mauritanie
439	320	180	150	173	204	218	245	Niger
2 622	655	403	540	504	583	637	803	Nigéria
509	722	494	423	457	573	664	703	Sénégal
380	243	210	141	210	208	199	208	Sierra Leone
406	411	290	246	257	298	339	351	Togo
2 124	*2 553*	*3 591*	*3 877*	*3 261*	*3 348*	*3 787*	*4 497*	*Économies en développement : Amérique*
1 654	*2 004*	*2 217*	*2 635*	*2 781*	*2 725*	*2 939*	*3 518*	*Caraïbes*
1 240	6 033	7 246	9 617	9 716	9 934	12 148	12 786	Anguilla
1 523	6 324	7 263	8 665	8 977	9 334	9 988	10 310	Antigua-et-Barbuda
8 097	13 003	15 895	20 576	20 009	20 410	21 103	21 940	Aruba
6 920	12 406	12 231	16 506	17 307	17 448	17 728	18 155	Bahamas
3 474	6 341	6 685	8 933	8 576	9 298	9 681	10 264	Barbade
2 632	6 568	21 508	38 203	38 385	36 425	40 147	44 150	Îles Vierges britanniques
7 579	26 919	29 199	32 882	33 189	33 585	34 306	34 935	Îles Caïmanes
2 188	2 915	3 004	2 933	3 221	3 440	3 651	4 168	Cuba
809	2 430	3 190	3 931	3 693	3 789	3 985	4 166	Dominique
1 139	970	1 489	2 261	2 393	1 778	1 979	3 073	République dominicaine
940	2 305	2 818	4 079	3 980	4 286	4 181	4 318	Grenade
243	368	298	410	347	301	383	418	Haïti
1 261	1 803	2 332	3 047	3 223	3 094	3 311	3 752	Jamaïque
2 033	6 253	5 863	7 014	8 106	7 608	7 683	7 535	Montserrat
5 433	10 388	13 486	15 489	16 047	16 460	16 720	17 188	Antilles néerlandaises
1 109	3 910	5 336	7 149	7 424	7 624	8 339	9 220	Saint-Kitts-et-Nevis
993	3 135	3 909	4 627	4 512	4 685	4 935	5 277	Sainte-Lucie
589	1 812	2 337	2 891	3 116	3 221	3 441	3 594	Saint-Vincent-et-les Grenadines
5 765	4 142	4 196	6 270	6 876	8 132	9 339	11 153	Trinité-et-Tobago
5 223	10 321	12 430	16 931	17 331	18 283	20 621	23 316	Îles Turques et Caïques

Pour les sources et les notes, se reporter à la fin du tableau.

Region, country or territory	Total gross domestic product / Produit intérieur brut total (1) Millions of dollars / Millions de dollars							
	1980	1990	1995	2000	2002	2003	2004	2005
Central America	**234 085**	**295 544**	**338 845**	**651 545**	**726 894**	**721 097**	**771 999**	**866 788**
Belize	195	405	620	832	927	981	1 036	1 105
Costa Rica	6 139	7 254	11 716	15 947	16 844	17 514	18 557	19 818
El Salvador	3 214	4 801	9 501	13 134	14 312	14 941	15 824	16 980
Guatemala	7 879	7 650	14 656	19 289	23 304	24 884	27 276	31 923
Honduras	2 566	3 049	3 960	6 025	6 530	6 945	7 536	8 374
Mexico	207 663	262 710	286 166	580 792	648 629	638 797	683 069	768 437
Nicaragua	2 375	3 598	3 185	3 907	4 026	4 102	4 496	4 910
Panama-Canal-Zone (former)	4 054							
Panama	_	6 077	9 042	11 621	12 272	12 933	14 204	15 241
South America	**488 396**	**767 389**	**1 310 943**	**1 268 319**	**912 704**	**988 757**	**1 191 859**	**1 494 475**
Argentina	75 494	141 353	258 096	284 346	102 042	129 596	153 129	183 310
Bolivia	2 696	4 868	6 715	8 398	7 924	8 089	8 773	9 728
Brazil	227 565	438 228	704 169	601 732	460 838	505 732	603 948	799 413
Chile	29 479	33 507	72 065	75 196	67 266	73 370	94 125	111 339
Colombia	39 590	47 743	92 503	83 766	81 243	80 348	98 281	121 877
Ecuador	12 351	11 248	20 196	15 934	24 899	28 691	32 964	33 062
Guyana	591	396	622	713	726	743	788	786
Paraguay	4 095	4 904	8 066	7 095	5 092	5 552	6 950	7 684
Peru	16 740	29 281	53 635	53 131	56 554	60 800	68 634	76 607
Suriname	891	467	691	775	955	1 122	1 285	1 503
Uruguay	9 636	8 366	19 298	20 086	12 277	11 191	13 216	16 792
Venezuela (Bolivarian Republic of)	69 268	47 028	74 889	117 148	92 869	83 522	109 764	132 373
Developing economies: Asia	**1 325 918**	**2 168 131**	**3 386 090**	**4 036 872**	**4 388 584**	**4 906 053**	**5 647 554**	**6 508 128**
Eastern Asia	**450 743**	**909 162**	**1 649 670**	**2 098 447**	**2 327 897**	**2 557 033**	**2 911 994**	**3 312 024**
China	303 744	382 996	700 606	1 079 191	1 303 590	1 470 699	1 720 401	1 981 648
China, Hong Kong SAR	28 818	76 890	144 230	168 754	163 710	158 364	165 743	172 649
China, Macao SAR	1 030	3 263	6 945	6 102	6 824	7 925	10 359	10 992
China, Taiwan Province of	42 943	166 281	274 698	321 187	294 812	299 574	322 218	344 981
Korea, Dem. People's Rep. of	9 879	14 702	4 849	10 608	10 910	11 051	11 168	12 260
Korea, Republic of	63 834	263 776	517 116	511 659	546 935	608 146	680 492	787 627
Mongolia	494	1 254	1 227	946	1 118	1 274	1 612	1 867
Southern Asia	**341 207**	**520 038**	**619 778**	**723 057**	**801 521**	**910 769**	**1 059 056**	**1 231 100**
Afghanistan	3 639	3 622	3 236	2 963	4 411	4 585	5 319	6 504
Bangladesh	19 749	31 830	41 294	48 626	51 924	57 261	61 916	64 058
Bhutan	139	285	295	447	539	613	708	917
India	183 321	324 250	366 364	464 937	506 743	592 493	688 803	800 783
Iran, Islamic Republic of	96 893	95 903	116 203	112 695	141 265	147 020	179 521	216 713
Maldives	42	215	399	624	641	691	753	770
Nepal	1 946	3 521	4 224	5 338	5 429	5 998	6 727	7 412
Pakistan	31 203	52 207	74 401	70 709	73 701	83 510	94 969	110 017
Sri Lanka	4 273	8 204	13 363	16 717	16 861	18 600	20 341	23 927
South-Eastern Asia	**194 933**	**354 303**	**676 101**	**594 296**	**643 505**	**717 365**	**795 708**	**882 071**
Brunei Darussalam	4 929	3 591	5 217	4 316	4 273	4 773	5 530	6 280
Cambodia	735	1 698	3 309	3 668	4 088	4 357	4 888	5 397
Indonesia	79 637	125 720	222 082	165 021	200 111	237 416	253 022	281 276
Lao People's Dem. Rep.	322	866	1 778	1 733	1 830	2 130	2 512	2 872
Malaysia	24 488	44 025	88 833	90 320	95 266	103 952	118 318	130 770
Myanmar	5 905	5 179	7 761	7 275	10 369	10 000	10 062	10 938
Philippines	32 450	44 312	74 120	75 031	76 814	79 202	86 123	97 653
Singapore	11 718	36 901	83 932	92 717	88 468	92 727	107 502	116 775
Thailand	32 354	85 361	168 019	122 725	126 877	142 920	161 688	176 602
Timor-Leste	..	179	315	316	343	336	339	354
Viet Nam	2 395	6 472	20 736	31 173	35 064	39 553	45 724	53 153
Western Asia	**339 036**	**384 628**	**440 541**	**621 072**	**615 661**	**720 885**	**880 795**	**1 082 933**
Bahrain	3 292	4 293	5 848	7 971	8 447	9 699	11 013	13 348
Iraq	21 225	29 980	6 187	20 969	17 437	10 621	27 366	33 379
Jordan	4 013	4 020	6 732	8 461	9 561	10 161	11 515	12 535
Kuwait	28 691	18 471	26 554	37 718	38 119	46 200	55 718	74 214
Lebanon	4 074	2 812	10 965	16 679	18 462	19 396	20 856	21 184
Palestinian territory	1 073	1 936	3 220	4 116	3 484	3 921	4 068	4 179
Oman	6 326	11 685	13 803	19 868	20 325	21 784	24 778	30 269
Qatar	7 838	7 360	8 138	17 760	19 707	23 701	31 591	42 113
Saudi Arabia	147 574	104 531	127 641	188 442	188 551	214 573	250 558	314 021
Syrian Arab Republic	13 062	11 152	13 538	19 651	21 659	20 724	23 318	25 812
Turkey	68 794	150 676	169 319	199 264	184 162	239 700	301 999	362 614
United Arab Emirates	29 626	33 780	42 807	70 522	74 959	88 536	104 204	133 757

For sources and notes, see end of table.

396

Per capita gross domestic product / Produit intérieur brut par habitant Dollars								Régions, pays ou territoires
1980	1990	1995	2000	2002	2003	2004	2005	
2 537	2 622	2 731	4 805	5 228	5 130	5 433	6 029	*Amérique centrale*
1 354	2 183	2 896	3 402	3 604	3 726	3 844	4 010	Belize
2 616	2 359	3 372	4 059	4 111	4 194	4 363	4 580	Costa Rica
701	939	1 687	2 120	2 239	2 304	2 406	2 546	El Salvador
1 123	859	1 465	1 718	1 976	2 058	2 200	2 512	Guatemala
706	623	711	972	1 021	1 057	1 124	1 225	Honduras
2 995	3 127	3 117	5 823	6 376	6 231	6 610	7 370	Mexique
729	869	683	765	766	770	834	899	Nicaragua
2 080		–	–	–	–	–	–	Panama, Zone du canal de (anc.)
–	2 520	3 386	3 939	4 007	4 146	4 473	4 716	Panama
2 016	2 583	4 057	3 637	2 544	2 719	3 234	4 001	*Amérique du Sud*
2 687	4 339	7 409	7 707	2 711	3 410	3 991	4 731	Argentine
503	730	898	1 010	915	916	974	1 059	Bolivie
1 871	2 931	4 357	3 455	2 571	2 782	3 277	4 279	Brésil
2 638	2 543	5 006	4 879	4 264	4 600	5 838	6 833	Chili
1 396	1 369	2 418	2 010	1 889	1 840	2 218	2 712	Colombie
1 551	1 095	1 772	1 295	1 973	2 247	2 552	2 531	Équateur
777	542	841	970	986	1 007	1 067	1 063	Guyana
1 281	1 155	1 681	1 326	914	977	1 200	1 301	Paraguay
966	1 345	2 248	2 070	2 149	2 282	2 546	2 809	Pérou
2 500	1 160	1 662	1 775	2 152	2 512	2 859	3 322	Suriname
3 307	2 694	5 996	6 053	3 691	3 366	3 976	5 049	Uruguay
4 590	2 383	3 392	4 801	3 667	3 238	4 180	4 953	Venezuela (République bolivarienne du)
539	726	1 042	1 153	1 221	1 348	1 533	1 746	**Économies en développement : Asie**
425	745	1 279	1 555	1 701	1 856	2 101	2 375	*Asie orientale*
310	339	588	865	1 030	1 154	1 342	1 536	Chine
5 720	13 479	23 241	25 330	23 982	22 935	23 740	24 463	Chine, Hong Kong RAS
4 088	8 769	16 871	13 834	15 016	17 179	22 152	23 235	Chine, Macao RAS
2 434	8 200	12 916	14 478	13 124	13 277	14 228	15 177	Chine, Taiwan Province de
573	730	223	462	469	472	475	519	Corée, Rép. populaire dém. de
1 674	6 153	11 490	10 937	11 568	12 806	14 271	16 454	Corée, République de
297	566	513	383	445	503	631	724	Mongolie
363	436	466	495	530	593	678	776	*Asie méridionale*
261	286	177	143	199	198	221	259	Afghanistan
222	282	327	349	358	388	411	418	Bangladesh
330	520	581	801	913	1 009	1 136	1 440	Bhoutan
266	377	384	444	468	539	617	706	Inde
2 464	1 692	1 868	1 704	2 096	2 162	2 614	3 122	Iran, Rép. islamique d'
269	997	1 610	2 287	2 274	2 414	2 592	2 606	Maldives
128	184	195	219	213	230	253	274	Népal
394	462	582	490	491	547	611	696	Pakistan
286	479	739	893	893	981	1 068	1 251	Sri Lanka
543	804	1 405	1 143	1 202	1 322	1 446	1 582	*Asie du Sud-Est*
25 534	13 972	17 686	12 944	12 229	13 350	15 122	16 799	Brunéi Darussalam
109	175	290	287	308	323	356	387	Cambodge
527	688	1 125	780	920	1 077	1 133	1 244	Indonésie
104	212	379	332	339	388	451	507	Rép. dém. populaire lao
1 779	2 432	4 314	3 881	3 927	4 204	4 697	5 098	Malaisie
177	129	180	159	222	212	212	228	Myanmar
675	724	1 081	984	966	976	1 039	1 155	Philippines
4 853	12 234	24 132	23 079	21 247	21 968	25 152	26 985	Singapour
691	1 572	2 921	2 023	2 057	2 300	2 584	2 803	Thaïlande
..	242	371	386	383	352	335	332	Timor-Leste
45	98	283	394	431	479	545	625	Viet Nam
3 459	2 906	2 925	3 663	3 474	3 982	4 764	5 738	*Asie occidentale*
9 487	8 709	10 124	12 261	12 422	13 952	15 507	18 416	Bahreïn
1 506	1 619	286	837	663	395	997	1 192	Iraq
1 803	1 235	1 564	1 763	1 891	1 952	2 144	2 261	Jordanie
20 867	8 619	15 394	16 926	15 627	18 254	21 291	27 487	Koweït
1 463	945	3 141	4 421	4 772	4 951	5 260	5 282	Liban
727	899	1 230	1 307	1 029	1 117	1 119	1 111	Territoire palestinien
5 327	6 340	6 355	8 271	8 316	8 858	9 997	12 074	Oman
34 161	15 747	15 479	28 797	28 685	32 609	41 335	52 893	Qatar
15 365	6 430	6 994	9 057	8 603	9 545	10 872	13 299	Arabie saoudite
1 456	877	927	1 190	1 244	1 158	1 268	1 366	République arabe syrienne
1 485	2 628	2 699	2 924	2 626	3 372	4 193	4 969	Turquie
29 182	18 093	17 605	21 718	20 805	23 429	26 400	32 589	Émirats arabes unis

Pour les sources et les notes, se reporter à la fin du tableau.

Region, country or territory	Total gross domestic product / Produit intérieur brut total (1) Millions of dollars / Millions de dollars							
	1980	1990	1995	2000	2002	2003	2004	2005
Yemen Arab Republic (former)	668	–	–	–	–	–	–	–
Yemen, Democratic (former)	2 779	–	–	–	–	–	–	–
Yemen	–	3 930	5 789	9 652	10 737	11 870	13 811	15 508
Developing economies: Oceania	**7 139**	**11 207**	**15 769**	**13 361**	**13 632**	**16 619**	**19 055**	**20 114**
Cook Islands	24	59	93	81	102	143	173	183
Fiji	1 203	1 337	1 990	1 686	1 843	2 309	2 728	2 998
French Polynesia	1 260	2 930	3 750	3 242	3 564	4 471	5 144	5 388
Kiribati	24	28	41	47	50	57	66	72
Marshall Islands	23	69	105	99	105	105	108	111
Micronesia, Federated States of	61	146	209	214	223	232	228	239
Nauru	36	51	41	33	36	44	52	55
New Caledonia	1 182	2 529	3 628	3 003	3 233	3 939	4 326	4 341
Palau, Pacific Islands (former)	26	77	95	117	115	117	120	123
Papua New Guinea	2 823	3 286	4 840	3 864	3 434	4 169	4 935	5 330
Samoa	155	201	200	231	262	319	375	406
Solomon Islands	144	208	365	338	274	256	276	299
Tonga	60	124	156	148	142	163	189	214
Tuvalu	5	10	12	12	15	18	23	26
Vanuatu	113	153	243	245	235	276	311	329
Economies in transition: Asia	**–**	**–**	**46 007**	**48 676**	**53 876**	**63 313**	**82 034**	**102 997**
Armenia	–	–	1 287	1 912	2 376	2 807	3 555	4 868
Azerbaijan	–	–	3 079	5 273	6 236	7 276	8 680	12 561
Georgia	–	–	2 721	3 044	3 396	3 991	5 202	6 490
Kazakhstan	–	–	20 547	18 292	24 637	30 834	43 152	56 088
Kyrgyzstan	–	–	1 492	1 370	1 606	1 922	2 212	2 441
Tajikistan	–	–	1 230	870	1 218	1 554	2 073	2 342
Turkmenistan	–	–	2 188	4 157	4 531	4 774	5 145	5 826
Uzbekistan	–	–	13 465	13 759	9 877	10 155	12 016	12 381
Economies in transition: Europe	**1 046 077**	**943 896**	**568 450**	**393 416**	**520 148**	**650 684**	**863 739**	**1 094 864**
Albania	2 219	2 184	2 479	3 709	4 505	5 859	7 549	8 538
Bosnia and Herzegovina (2)	–	–	2 043	4 527	5 606	7 100	8 569	9 132
Belarus	–	–	13 845	10 418	14 595	17 825	23 142	29 566
Bulgaria	18 620	20 726	13 106	12 600	15 568	19 938	24 131	26 419
Croatia	–	–	18 811	18 428	22 798	28 801	34 309	36 947
Macedonia, TFYR	–	–	4 475	3 587	3 791	4 630	5 369	5 651
Moldova, Republic of	–	–	1 766	1 288	1 662	1 981	2 598	2 917
Romania	26 927	38 242	35 478	37 025	45 825	59 507	75 489	98 566
Serbia and Montenegro	–	–	28 673	10 855	17 917	23 422	27 416	29 493
Russian Federation	–	–	399 166	259 718	345 483	431 488	590 287	765 968
USSR (former)	928 352	776 920	–	–	–	–	–	–
Yugoslavia, SFR (former)	69 959	105 824	–	–	–	–	–	–
Ukraine	–	–	48 608	31 262	42 393	50 133	64 881	81 669

Sources:
- UN DESA Population Division
- UN DESA Statistics Division

Notes:

(1)   GDP by expenditure, in current prices and current exchange rates.
(2)   GDP data include the Federation of Bosnia and Herzegovina only. Data for the Republika Srpska are excluded.

Per capita gross domestic product / Produit intérieur brut par habitant Dollars								Régions, pays ou territoires
1980	1990	1995	2000	2002	2003	2004	2005	
80	–	–	–	–	–	–	–	Rép. arabe du Yémen (anc.)
..	–	–	–	–	–	–	–	Yémen dém. (anc.)
–	319	373	531	559	597	674	735	Yémen
1 400	**1 738**	**2 175**	**1 647**	**1 609**	**1 921**	**2 159**	**2 234**	**Économies en développement : Océanie**
1 332	3 300	5 168	5 055	6 748	9 687	12 087	13 098	Îles Cook
1 898	1 848	2 592	2 103	2 268	2 824	3 315	3 620	Fidji
8 341	14 995	17 376	13 732	14 598	18 026	20 423	21 077	Polynésie française
435	396	536	561	574	647	733	779	Kiribati
765	1 453	2 063	1 896	1 958	1 925	1 947	1 956	Îles Marshall
842	1 512	1 948	1 998	2 069	2 138	2 087	2 176	Micronésie, États fédérés de
4 796	5 588	4 074	3 283	3 546	4 368	5 139	5 486	Nauru
8 285	14 786	18 792	13 967	14 503	17 375	18 774	18 536	Nouvelle-Calédonie
2 128	5 150	5 584	6 081	5 820	5 867	5 978	6 096	Palaos, Îles du Pacifique (anc.)
882	795	1 028	718	607	719	832	878	Papouasie-Nouvelle-Guinée
997	1 247	1 191	1 301	1 455	1 758	2 054	2 210	Samoa
627	664	1 008	814	625	570	598	633	Îles Salomon
622	1 309	1 599	1 513	1 444	1 651	1 906	2 151	Tonga
564	1 012	1 199	1 204	1 421	1 780	2 209	2 516	Tuvalu
968	1 023	1 412	1 289	1 181	1 351	1 483	1 527	Vanuatu
–	**–**	**662**	**683**	**745**	**869**	**1 115**	**1 387**	**Économies en transition : Asie**
–	–	399	620	779	924	1 174	1 613	Arménie
–	–	395	647	758	880	1 045	1 504	Azerbaïdjan
–	–	541	645	736	875	1 152	1 451	Géorgie
–	–	1 291	1 223	1 650	2 055	2 856	3 687	Kazakhstan
–	–	325	277	317	376	429	469	Kirghizistan
–	–	213	141	193	243	321	358	Tadjikistan
–	–	522	923	979	1 016	1 079	1 205	Turkménistan
–	–	588	557	388	393	458	466	Ouzbékistan
3 263	**2 716**	**2 107**	**1 486**	**1 984**	**2 495**	**3 330**	**4 243**	**Économies en transition : Europe**
831	664	787	1 204	1 454	1 881	2 408	2 707	Albanie
–	–	597	1 195	1 445	1 822	2 194	2 332	Bosnie-Herzégovine (2)
–	–	1 349	1 036	1 467	1 801	2 350	3 018	Bélarus
2 101	2 350	1 568	1 574	1 972	2 542	3 096	3 411	Bulgarie
–	–	4 029	4 090	5 060	6 368	7 557	8 118	Croatie
–	–	2 279	1 785	1 875	2 285	2 644	2 779	Macédoine, LERY
–	–	403	311	412	498	662	752	Moldova, République de
1 213	1 648	1 564	1 673	2 090	2 726	3 475	4 557	Roumanie
–	–	2 650	1 005	1 680	2 213	2 607	2 817	Serbie-et-Monténégro
–	–	2 677	1 762	2 364	2 967	4 080	5 321	Fédération de Russie
3 498	2 685	–	–	–	–	–	–	URSS (anc.)
3 263	4 638	–	–	–	–	–	–	Yougoslavie, RSF (anc.)
–	–	953	640	883	1 052	1 372	1 741	Ukraine

Sources :
- ONU DAES Division de la population
- ONU DAES Division de statistique

Notes :

(1)   PIB par dépenses, aux prix et taux de change courants.
(2)   Y compris le PIB de la Fédération de Bosnie-Herzégovine seulement. Non compris le PIB de la Republika Srpska.

Economic grouping	Total gross domestic product / Produit intérieur brut total (1) Millions of dollars / Millions de dollars							
	1980	1990	1995	2000	2002	2003	2004	2005
DEVELOPING ECONOMIES	2 611 798	3 810 973	5 653 956	6 659 394	6 712 239	7 414 587	8 549 776	9 962 981
Developing economies excluding China	2 307 995	3 427 779	4 953 086	5 579 867	5 408 234	5 943 509	6 828 967	7 980 905
Developing economies excluding LDCs	2 506 510	3 660 270	5 499 697	6 482 298	6 513 937	7 193 054	8 294 744	9 672 078
High-income countries	821 155	1 276 432	2 029 702	2 607 559	2 450 049	2 593 395	2 913 721	3 363 222
Middle-income countries	783 252	1 267 658	1 883 670	1 814 272	1 694 558	1 907 194	2 269 429	2 717 769
Low-income countries	1 007 392	1 266 884	1 740 584	2 237 563	2 567 633	2 913 998	3 366 626	3 881 991
Heavily indebted poor countries	97 556	137 429	126 591	136 862	149 671	169 954	194 760	220 213
Landlocked countries	41 815	65 000	117 230	118 867	125 961	145 598	176 583	207 951
Small island developing states	18 055	25 448	32 812	40 255	42 220	46 640	51 633	56 821
Least developed countries	*105 229*	*150 505*	*153 994*	*176 761*	*197 887*	*221 154*	*254 624*	*290 475*
Africa and Haiti	68 540	97 965	83 966	94 454	105 768	121 198	145 177	173 122
Asia	35 882	50 931	67 685	79 704	89 378	96 813	105 942	113 606
Islands	807	1 610	2 343	2 603	2 741	3 144	3 505	3 747
Major petroleum exporters	*795 416*	*675 726*	*800 151*	*976 467*	*1 011 519*	*1 127 095*	*1 337 183*	*1 632 219*
Africa	276 429	171 252	123 555	173 783	161 075	192 962	231 589	295 190
America	76 448	54 076	82 789	128 100	104 803	97 216	125 164	150 340
Asia	442 540	450 399	593 806	674 585	745 642	836 917	980 430	1 186 689
Major exporters of manufactured goods	*1 227 693*	*2 276 405*	*3 577 570*	*4 308 308*	*4 496 850*	*4 932 306*	*5 640 307*	*6 539 953*
America	435 227	700 937	990 334	1 182 524	1 109 467	1 144 529	1 287 017	1 567 851
Asia	792 466	1 575 467	2 587 236	3 125 784	3 387 383	3 787 777	4 353 290	4 972 102
Emerging economies	*732 278*	*1 501 423*	*2 506 727*	*2 733 804*	*2 487 686*	*2 655 614*	*2 993 125*	*3 495 861*
America	556 941	905 079	1 374 131	1 595 197	1 335 329	1 408 296	1 602 907	1 939 106
Asia	175 337	596 344	1 132 597	1 138 608	1 152 358	1 247 318	1 390 219	1 556 755
Newly industrialized economies	*316 242*	*843 265*	*1 573 028*	*1 547 413*	*1 592 993*	*1 722 301*	*1 895 107*	*2 108 332*
First tier	147 314	543 848	1 019 975	1 094 316	1 093 924	1 158 811	1 275 956	1 422 031
Second tier	168 929	299 417	553 053	453 097	499 068	563 490	619 151	686 301
Developing economies: Africa	*513 234*	*508 443*	*531 146*	*599 779*	*573 932*	*686 557*	*815 252*	*947 747*
Northern Africa excluding Sudan	129 689	168 346	187 274	241 434	223 252	237 167	275 231	321 346
Sub-Saharan Africa	383 545	340 097	343 872	358 344	350 680	449 391	540 021	626 401
Sub-Saharan Africa excluding South Africa	303 002	228 083	192 759	225 467	239 798	283 222	325 358	387 576
Developing economies: America	**765 506**	**1 123 193**	**1 720 950**	**2 009 383**	**1 736 090**	**1 805 358**	**2 067 916**	**2 486 993**
Central America and Greater Carribean Islands excluding Puerto Rico	266 409	340 416	391 748	715 406	796 156	786 945	843 842	956 768
Central America and Greater Carribean Islands excluding Mexico and Puerto Rico	58 746	77 706	105 583	134 615	147 527	148 148	160 773	188 331
South America and Central America	722 481	1 062 933	1 649 788	1 919 864	1 639 598	1 709 854	1 963 857	2 361 263
South America excluding Brazil	260 832	329 161	606 775	666 586	451 866	483 025	587 910	695 062
Developing economies: Asia	**1 325 918**	**2 168 131**	**3 386 090**	**4 036 872**	**4 388 584**	**4 906 053**	**5 647 554**	**6 508 128**
Eastern and South-Eastern Asia excluding China	341 931	880 469	1 625 165	1 613 551	1 667 812	1 803 699	1 987 301	2 212 447
Southern Asia excluding India	157 885	195 788	253 414	258 120	294 772	318 277	370 252	430 317

Sources:
- UN DESA Population Division
- UN DESA Statistics Division

Notes:

(1)   GDP by expenditure, in current prices and current exchange rates.

Per capita gross domestic product / Produit intérieur brut par habitant Dollars								Groupements économiques
1980	1990	1995	2000	2002	2003	2004	2005	
791	937	1 267	1 374	1 344	1 464	1 664	1 912	ÉCONOMIES EN DÉVELOPPEMENT
994	1 166	1 515	1 551	1 451	1 568	1 771	2 035	Économies en développement sans la Chine
865	1 033	1 424	1 556	1 522	1 659	1 889	2 176	Économies en développement sans les PMA
3 862	4 934	7 238	8 611	7 898	8 271	9 195	10 499	Pays à revenu élevé
1 564	2 011	2 725	2 425	2 201	2 443	2 867	3 387	Pays à revenu intermédiaire
389	398	499	590	656	734	835	949	Pays à revenu faible
344	364	290	274	285	315	352	388	Pays pauvres très endettés
274	325	393	357	361	409	485	558	Pays sans littoral
1 594	1 880	2 212	2 511	2 542	2 757	2 998	3 243	Petits états insulaires en développement
259	*286*	*256*	*260*	*277*	*303*	*340*	*379*	*Pays les moins avancés*
293	315	235	231	245	273	319	370	Afrique et Haïti
211	241	280	298	322	341	366	385	Asie
389	605	775	799	795	882	952	988	Îes
2 238	*1 452*	*1 541*	*1 705*	*1 702*	*1 862*	*2 169*	*2 601*	*Principaux exportateurs de pétrole*
2 677	1 241	781	971	858	1 004	1 178	1 468	Afrique
4 677	2 557	3 517	4 949	3 907	3 562	4 508	5 324	Amérique
1 876	1 470	1 760	1 834	1 962	2 168	2 500	2 979	Asie
591	*916*	*1 332*	*1 498*	*1 527*	*1 656*	*1 873*	*2 149*	*Principaux exportateurs d'articles manufacturés*
2 279	3 002	3 908	4 317	3 949	4 026	4 474	5 386	Amérique
420	700	1 064	1 201	1 271	1 406	1 598	1 806	Asie
1 999	*3 415*	*5 284*	*5 373*	*4 779*	*5 048*	*5 632*	*6 510*	*Économies émergentes*
2 250	3 006	4 208	4 534	3 702	3 859	4 343	5 193	Amérique
1 476	4 304	7 659	7 256	7 209	7 741	8 562	9 517	Asie
979	*2 171*	*3 745*	*3 427*	*3 436*	*3 668*	*3 986*	*4 381*	*Économies nouvellement industrialisées*
2 330	7 567	13 428	13 740	13 550	14 275	15 639	17 345	Premier tier
650	946	1 607	1 219	1 303	1 451	1 572	1 719	Deuxième tier
1 071	*798*	*732*	*731*	*668*	*780*	*905*	*1 029*	*Économies en développement : Afrique*
1 416	1 429	1 444	1 715	1 537	1 607	1 837	2 111	Afrique septentrionale sans le Soudan
989	655	577	527	491	614	720	815	Afrique subsaharienne
845	473	348	356	359	413	463	538	Afrique sub-saharienne sans l'Afrique du Sud
2 124	*2 553*	*3 591*	*3 877*	*3 261*	*3 348*	*3 787*	*4 497*	*Économies en développement : Amérique*
2 300	2 430	2 555	4 293	4 662	4 559	4 836	5 421	Amérique centrale et Grandes Antilles sans Porto Rico
1 263	1 385	1 717	2 012	2 137	2 114	2 260	2 608	Amérique centrale et Grandes Antilles sans le Mexique et Porto Rico
2 160	2 594	3 690	3 964	3 294	3 391	3 846	4 565	Amérique du Sud et Amérique centrale
2 163	2 231	3 758	3 820	2 518	2 656	3 191	3 724	Amérique du Sud sans le Brésil
539	*726*	*1 042*	*1 153*	*1 221*	*1 348*	*1 533*	*1 746*	*Économies en développement : Asie*
779	1 655	2 810	2 596	2 614	2 792	3 038	3 342	Asie orientale et Asie du Sud-Est sans la Chine
626	589	676	623	686	728	832	950	Asie méridionale sans l'Inde

Sources :
- ONU DAES Division de la population
- ONU DAES Division de statistique

Notes :

(1)   PIB par dépenses, aux prix et taux de change courants.

Region, country or territory	Total real product / Produit réel total Percentage										
	80 -90	80 -00	80 -05	90 -00	90 -05	95 -05	C0 -05	01 -02	02 -03	03 -04	04 -05
WORLD	**3.1**	**2.6**	**2.7**	**2.8**	**2.8**	**2.9**	**2.8**	**1.9**	**2.8**	**4.0**	**3.4**
DEVELOPED ECONOMIES	3.2	2.8	2.7	2.5	2.5	2.5	2.0	1.2	1.9	3.1	2.5
DEVELOPING ECONOMIES	3.9	4.5	4.5	4.9	4.7	4.5	5.2	4.1	5.4	6.9	6.3
ECONOMIES IN TRANSITION	-0.2	-6.4	-4.4	-4.5	-0.3	4.3	6.2	4.9	6.8	7.5	6.2
Developed economies: America	**3.6**	**3.2**	**3.2**	**3.5**	**3.2**	**3.2**	**2.6**	**1.7**	**2.7**	**4.1**	**3.3**
Bermuda	1.4	1.6	2.0	3.0	3.2	3.3	3.2	5.8	4.4	1.6	2.5
Canada	3.2	2.6	2.8	3.1	3.3	3.6	2.8	3.1	2.0	2.9	4.6
United States	3.6	3.2	3.2	3.5	3.2	3.2	2.6	1.6	2.7	4.2	3.2
Developed economies: Asia	**3.9**	**2.9**	**2.4**	**1.1**	**1.1**	**1.0**	**1.4**	**0.1**	**1.8**	**2.4**	**2.7**
Israel	3.6	4.8	4.4	5.4	4.1	2.8	1.7	-1.5	1.3	4.7	4.9
Japan	3.9	2.8	2.3	1.0	1.0	0.9	1.4	0.1	1.8	2.3	2.6
Developed economies: Europe	**2.5**	**2.4**	**2.3**	**2.2**	**2.2**	**2.3**	**1.6**	**1.1**	**1.1**	**2.4**	**1.6**
Andorra	3.1	2.5	3.1	1.4	3.5	5.1	7.1	8.1	6.6	3.0	7.2
Austria	2.2	2.5	2.4	2.4	2.2	2.2	1.5	1.0	1.4	2.4	1.8
Belgium									0.9	2.6	1.2
Belgium-Luxembourg	2.2	2.3	–	2.2					–	–	–
Cyprus	6.3	5.6	5.1	4.6	4.2	3.6	3.0	2.1	1.9	3.8	3.9
Czechoslovakia (former)	1.9	–	–	–	–				–	–	–
Czech Republic		–	–	–	–	2.2	3.5	1.5	3.2	4.7	6.0
Denmark	2.0	2.1	2.1	2.7	2.3	1.9	1.2	0.5	0.7	1.9	3.1
Estonia		–	–	–	–	6.2	7.3	7.2	6.7	7.8	8.4
Finland	3.3	1.9	2.2	2.5	2.9	3.4	2.4	2.2	2.4	3.6	2.1
France	2.5	2.2	2.2	2.0	2.1	2.3	1.5	1.0	1.1	2.3	1.2
Germany	–	–	–	1.8	1.6	1.4	0.7	0.1	-0.2	1.6	1.0
Greece	0.9	1.5	2.1	2.2	3.1	4.1	4.4	3.8	4.8	4.7	3.7
Hungary	1.3	0.1	1.0	1.5	2.8	4.3	4.1	3.8	3.4	5.2	4.1
Iceland	3.1	2.2	2.5	2.7	3.2	4.0	3.7	-1.0	3.0	8.2	5.5
Ireland	3.2	5.1	5.8	7.5	7.4	7.5	5.1	6.1	4.4	4.5	4.8
Italy	2.6	2.0	1.9	1.5	1.5	1.4	0.6	0.3	0.0	1.1	0.0
Latvia	–	–	–	–	–	6.5	7.7	6.4	7.2	8.5	9.1
Lithuania	–	–	–	–	–	5.7	7.7	6.8	10.5	7.0	7.0
Luxembourg	–	–	–	–	–	–	–	–	2.0	4.2	4.0
Malta	3.6	4.9	4.4	5.1	3.7	2.6	0.4	1.1	-2.1	0.2	4.7
Netherlands	2.4	2.7	2.6	2.9	2.5	2.3	0.7	0.1	-0.1	1.7	1.1
Norway	3.0	3.2	3.1	4.0	3.3	2.6	2.0	1.1	1.1	3.1	2.3
Poland	1.6	1.7	2.2	4.6	4.1	3.7	3.1	1.4	3.8	5.3	3.2
Portugal	3.2	3.2	3.0	2.8	2.5	2.4	0.5	0.8	-1.1	1.2	0.4
San Marino	2.6	5.5	5.6	9.7	7.2	4.0	2.3	0.3	3.9	2.0	0.0
Slovakia	–	–	–	–	–	3.9	4.9	4.6	4.5	5.5	6.1
Slovenia	–	–	–	–	–	3.9	3.6	3.3	2.5	5.6	3.9
Spain	3.1	2.8	3.0	2.5	3.1	3.8	3.1	2.7	3.0	3.1	3.4
Sweden	2.5	2.0	2.1	2.3	2.5	2.8	2.3	2.0	1.7	3.7	2.7
Switzerland	2.2	1.6	1.6	1.0	1.2	1.6	0.9	0.3	-0.3	2.1	1.9
United Kingdom	3.2	2.5	2.6	2.7	2.8	2.8	2.4	2.0	2.5	3.1	1.8
Developed economies: Oceania	**3.2**	**3.2**	**3.3**	**3.9**	**3.7**	**3.5**	**3.3**	**3.4**	**3.9**	**2.5**	**2.6**
Australia	3.4	3.4	3.4	3.9	3.7	3.6	3.2	3.2	4.0	2.3	2.7
New Zealand	1.9	2.1	2.5	3.3	3.3	3.2	3.7	4.7	3.6	3.7	2.0
Developing economies: Africa	**2.6**	**2.3**	**2.6**	**2.4**	**3.1**	**3.8**	**4.7**	**3.6**	**5.4**	**5.3**	**4.9**
Eastern Africa	*2.8*	*3.0*	*3.1*	*3.3*	*3.3*	*3.3*	*3.4*	*1.7*	*1.8*	*5.7*	*4.4*
Burundi	4.2	1.0	0.7	-2.6	-0.9	1.1	2.7	4.5	-1.2	4.4	5.0
Comoros	2.8	1.7	1.7	1.3	1.7	2.1	2.2	2.3	2.1	1.9	2.8
Djibouti	0.5	1.0	1.3	1.3	1.6	1.8	2.9	2.6	3.5	3.0	3.2
Ethiopia (former)	1.7	–	–	–	–						
Eritrea	–	–	–	–	–	1.1	2.7	0.7	3.0	1.8	0.8
Ethiopia	–	–	–	–	–	4.2	3.9	1.6	-4.2	11.5	7.3
Kenya	4.4	3.2	3.0	2.2	2.4	2.5	3.1	0.4	2.8	4.3	4.7
Madagascar	1.2	1.4	1.7	2.0	2.3	2.9	2.2	-12.7	9.7	5.3	6.4
Malawi	3.2	4.9	4.6	7.0	4.8	2.3	2.9	2.7	6.1	5.1	1.9
Mauritius	6.3	5.8	5.6	5.2	5.0	4.9	3.7	1.7	4.2	4.5	3.0
Mozambique	-0.1	3.1	4.4	5.9	7.1	8.4	8.6	8.2	7.9	7.5	7.7
Rwanda	1.8	-0.5	0.9	0.1	3.2	7.2	4.8	9.3	0.7	3.8	5.0
Seychelles	4.2	4.8	3.9	4.6	2.6	1.5	-2.5	1.3	-6.3	-2.0	-2.7
Somalia	1.1	-1.7	-1.0	-3.2	-0.5	2.6	2.9	3.5	2.1	2.8	2.8
Uganda	3.5	5.7	5.9	7.4	6.8	6.1	5.7	4.7	6.3	5.7	5.6

For sources and notes, see end of table.

Per capita real product / Produit réel par habitant En pourcentage											Régions, pays ou territoires
80-90	80-00	80-05	90-00	90-05	95-05	00-05	01-02	02-03	03-04	04-05	
1.3	1.0	1.1	1.3	1.4	1.6	1.5	0.7	1.5	2.8	2.2	**MONDE**
2.5	2.1	2.0	1.9	1.8	1.9	1.4	0.6	1.2	2.4	1.9	ÉCONOMIES DÉVELOPPÉES
1.8	2.5	2.6	3.1	3.0	2.9	3.7	2.6	3.9	5.4	4.8	ÉCONOMIES EN DÉVELOPPEMENT
-1.0	-6.6	-4.5	-4.2	0.0	4.5	6.5	5.1	7.0	7.7	6.4	ÉCONOMIES EN TRANSITION
2.5	2.1	2.1	2.4	2.2	2.1	1.6	0.7	1.6	3.0	2.3	**Économies développées : Amérique**
0.7	1.0	1.5	2.5	2.7	2.9	2.8	5.3	4.0	1.2	2.1	Bermudes
1.9	1.4	1.7	2.1	2.3	2.6	1.8	2.0	1.0	1.9	3.6	Canada
2.6	2.2	2.1	2.4	2.2	2.1	1.5	0.6	1.7	3.2	2.2	États-Unis
3.3	2.4	1.9	0.7	0.8	0.7	1.2	-0.2	1.5	2.2	2.5	**Économies développées : Asie**
1.8	2.2	1.8	2.2	1.4	0.6	-0.2	-3.4	-0.6	2.8	3.0	Israël
3.3	2.4	2.0	0.8	0.8	0.8	1.3	0.0	1.6	2.2	2.5	Japon
2.3	1.9	1.9	1.7	1.8	2.0	1.1	0.7	0.6	1.9	1.2	**Économies développées : Europe**
-0.3	-0.5	0.5	-0.8	1.6	3.8	4.9	5.8	4.0	0.8	5.5	Andorre
2.0	2.0	2.0	1.9	1.8	1.9	1.1	0.5	0.9	1.9	1.3	Autriche
								0.5	2.2	0.9	Belgique
2.1	2.1	—	1.9					—	—	—	Belgique-Luxembourg
5.1	4.2	3.8	3.1	2.7	2.2	1.7	0.8	0.7	2.6	2.7	Chypre
1.8	—	—	—	—							Tchécoslovaquie (anc.)
—	—	—	—	—	2.3	3.5	1.6	3.3	4.7	6.0	République tchèque
2.0	1.8	1.8	2.3	1.9	1.6	0.9	0.1	0.4	1.6	2.8	Danemark
—	—	—	—	—	6.9	7.7	7.7	7.0	8.1	8.7	Estonie
2.9	1.5	1.8	2.1	2.5	3.1	2.1	1.9	2.2	3.3	1.8	Finlande
1.9	1.7	1.7	1.5	1.6	1.8	0.8	0.4	0.4	1.6	0.6	France
—	—	—	1.4	1.3	1.3	0.6	0.0	-0.3	1.6	0.9	Allemagne
0.4	0.8	1.5	1.4	2.5	3.7	4.2	3.6	4.6	4.5	3.5	Grèce
1.7	0.3	1.2	1.7	3.0	4.5	4.4	4.1	3.6	5.5	4.4	Hongrie
1.9	1.2	1.5	1.7	2.2	2.9	2.6	-2.1	2.0	7.1	4.5	Islande
2.9	4.7	5.1	6.6	6.2	6.1	3.3	4.4	2.6	2.6	2.9	Irlande
2.5	1.9	1.7	1.3	1.3	1.2	0.2	0.0	-0.3	0.7	-0.3	Italie
—	—	—	—	—	7.3	8.4	7.2	7.9	9.2	9.7	Lettonie
—	—	—	—	—	6.3	8.2	7.2	10.9	7.4	7.5	Lituanie
—	—	—	—	—				1.2	3.4	3.1	Luxembourg
2.6	4.0	3.6	4.3	3.0	1.9	-0.3	0.3	-2.9	-0.5	4.0	Malte
1.8	2.1	2.0	2.3	1.9	1.7	0.2	-0.5	-0.7	1.2	0.7	Pays-Bas
2.6	2.7	2.6	3.4	2.7	2.0	1.3	0.4	0.5	2.4	1.6	Norvège
0.9	1.3	2.0	4.5	4.1	3.8	3.2	1.5	4.0	5.5	3.4	Pologne
3.0	3.1	2.8	2.5	2.1	1.9	-0.1	0.2	-1.7	0.6	-0.2	Portugal
1.3	4.3	4.3	8.5	5.7	2.3	-0.1	-2.1	1.2	-0.4	-1.9	Saint-Marin
—	—	—	—	—	3.9	4.9	4.6	4.5	5.5	6.1	Slovaquie
—	—	—	—	—	3.7	3.4	3.1	2.3	5.4	3.8	Slovénie
2.8	2.5	2.5	2.2	2.4	2.7	1.5	1.1	1.2	1.4	2.0	Espagne
2.2	1.5	1.7	1.9	2.2	2.6	1.9	1.6	1.3	3.3	2.2	Suède
1.4	0.8	0.9	0.4	0.7	1.2	0.4	-0.1	-0.8	1.6	1.4	Suisse
3.0	2.3	2.3	2.4	2.4	2.4	1.9	1.5	2.0	2.6	1.4	Royaume-Uni
1.9	1.8	2.0	2.6	2.4	2.3	2.0	2.2	2.7	1.3	1.5	**Économies développées : Océanie**
2.0	2.0	2.1	2.7	2.5	2.3	2.0	2.0	2.7	1.1	1.5	Australie
1.0	1.0	1.3	2.0	2.1	2.1	2.4	3.4	2.2	2.4	0.9	Nouvelle-Zélande
-0.3	-0.5	-0.1	-0.1	0.6	1.4	2.3	1.2	2.9	2.9	2.5	**Économies en développement : Afrique**
-0.3	0.2	0.3	0.6	0.6	0.6	0.8	-0.9	-0.7	3.1	1.7	*Afrique orientale*
0.8	-1.4	-1.6	-4.0	-2.7	-1.1	-0.6	1.4	-4.5	0.6	1.0	Burundi
-0.3	-1.3	-1.2	-1.6	-1.1	-0.7	-0.4	-0.4	-0.6	-0.7	0.2	Comores
-4.5	-2.9	-2.3	-1.2	-0.9	-0.7	0.9	0.5	1.6	1.2	1.4	Djibouti
-1.5	—	—	—	—							Éthiopie (anc.)
—	—	—	—	—	-2.4	-1.4	-3.5	-1.3	-2.4	-3.0	Érythrée
					1.4	1.2	-1.0	-6.7	8.6	4.6	Éthiopie
0.6	-0.1	-0.2	-0.7	-0.4	-0.2	0.4	-2.2	0.1	1.6	2.0	Kenya
-1.6	-1.5	-1.2	-1.0	-0.7	-0.1	-0.6	-15.1	6.7	2.4	3.5	Madagascar
-1.2	1.6	1.5	4.9	2.4	-0.5	0.2	0.0	3.4	2.5	-0.7	Malawi
5.4	4.7	4.5	4.0	3.9	3.9	2.7	0.8	3.3	3.6	2.2	Maurice
-1.0	1.1	2.2	2.7	4.1	5.7	6.0	5.5	5.3	5.0	5.3	Mozambique
-1.9	-1.6	-0.9	-0.9	0.4	1.7	2.4	6.5	-1.0	2.2	3.0	Rwanda
3.3	3.7	2.8	3.4	1.4	0.2	-3.6	0.1	-7.3	-3.0	-3.5	Seychelles
0.9	-1.8	-1.6	-3.5	-2.0	-0.3	-0.2	0.4	-0.9	-0.2	-0.2	Somalie
0.0	2.1	2.4	4.0	3.4	2.9	2.4	1.5	2.9	2.3	2.2	Ouganda

Pour les sources et les notes, se reporter à la fin du tableau.

Region, country or territory	Total real product / Produit réel total Percentage									
	80 -90	80 -00	80 -05	90 -00	90 -05	95 -05	00 -05	01 -02	02 -03	03 -04	04 -05
United Republic of Tanzania	2.8	3.8	4.2	3.7	4.6	5.5	6.9	7.3	7.1	6.7	6.9
Zambia	1.0	0.6	1.2	0.5	1.9	3.4	4.7	3.3	4.3	6.2	5.1
Zimbabwe	3.6	2.9	1.4	1.5	-1.0	-3.3	-4.9	-4.9	-9.7	0.7	-7.1
Middle Africa	*2.7*	*0.7*	*1.4*	*1.2*	*2.7*	*4.2*	*6.1*	*6.4*	*4.3*	*8.4*	*7.3*
Angola	3.4	1.0	2.2	1.6	4.1	6.8	9.2	14.4	3.4	11.2	14.7
Cameroon	3.4	1.0	1.7	2.6	3.6	4.6	4.4	4.0	4.2	5.1	3.9
Central African Republic	1.4	0.9	1.0	1.9	1.6	1.4	-0.1	0.4	-4.5	1.3	2.2
Chad	6.1	4.4	5.1	3.2	5.7	8.0	15.7	8.4	15.5	33.2	7.7
Congo	3.5	1.7	2.0	1.2	2.2	3.2	4.1	5.4	0.8	4.0	9.2
Dem. Rep. of the Congo	1.6	-2.9	-2.6	-4.9	-2.7	-0.6	4.4	3.5	5.7	6.8	6.6
Equatorial Guinea	1.7	9.0	13.8	23.7	26.1	29.4	22.9	20.2	13.6	24.1	6.2
Gabon	0.9	2.1	1.7	2.0	1.1	-0.1	1.4	-0.3	2.0	1.6	2.0
São Tome and Principe	-0.4	1.0	1.5	1.8	2.5	3.2	4.2	4.1	4.5	4.5	3.2
Northern Africa	*2.7*	*2.5*	*2.8*	*2.8*	*3.4*	*4.1*	*5.1*	*3.4*	*7.6*	*5.1*	*4.8*
Algeria	2.7	1.7	2.1	1.9	2.8	3.9	5.1	4.1	7.3	5.2	5.3
Egypt	7.0	5.6	5.3	4.9	4.6	4.5	4.3	4.1	4.1	5.0	5.0
Libyan Arab Jamahiriya	-1.8	-0.5	0.3	1.4	2.3	3.1	6.3	-0.2	19.3	4.4	4.3
Morocco	4.2	3.3	3.2	2.3	2.9	3.5	4.2	3.2	5.5	4.2	1.2
Sudan	2.9	2.9	3.5	2.2	3.9	5.5	6.7	6.5	6.1	7.2	8.0
Tunisia	3.3	4.1	4.3	4.7	4.7	4.9	4.5	1.7	5.6	5.8	5.0
Southern Africa	*1.6*	*1.7*	*2.0*	*2.2*	*2.8*	*3.2*	*3.7*	*3.7*	*3.1*	*4.6*	*4.2*
Botswana	10.9	8.0	7.3	4.8	5.3	5.9	5.5	2.2	6.7	6.6	3.8
Lesotho	4.5	5.0	4.4	3.9	3.1	2.1	2.5	3.5	3.3	2.0	-0.7
Namibia	2.3	3.5	3.7	4.0	4.0	4.0	4.6	6.7	3.5	5.9	3.5
South Africa	1.4	1.4	1.8	2.1	2.6	3.1	3.6	3.7	3.0	4.5	4.3
Swaziland	7.7	5.7	4.9	3.3	3.0	2.7	2.3	2.8	2.4	2.2	2.2
Western Africa	*3.6*	*3.0*	*3.2*	*2.0*	*3.1*	*4.2*	*5.1*	*4.1*	*6.1*	*5.2*	*5.2*
Benin	3.3	3.7	4.0	4.6	4.7	4.7	4.2	4.4	3.9	3.4	3.5
Burkina Faso	2.5	4.4	4.6	5.4	5.0	4.7	6.3	4.6	7.9	6.6	5.9
Cape Verde	5.4	5.4	5.8	7.1	6.9	7.0	5.2	5.3	4.7	4.4	6.3
Côte d'Ivoire	3.3	2.8	2.5	3.3	2.3	1.3	0.5	0.0	0.0	1.8	0.5
Gambia	3.8	3.3	3.5	3.2	3.7	4.4	4.3	-3.2	6.7	8.3	4.6
Ghana	3.0	4.0	4.1	4.3	4.4	4.6	5.0	4.5	5.2	5.2	5.8
Guinea	3.2	3.9	3.9	4.4	3.9	3.6	2.9	4.2	1.2	2.7	3.0
Guinea-Bissau	4.3	3.0	2.1	1.1	0.3	-1.0	-0.2	-7.2	0.6	4.3	2.3
Liberia	-5.0	-10.3	-6.2	3.9	6.1	12.6	-6.5	3.7	-31.3	2.4	8.5
Mali	3.8	3.7	4.2	4.1	5.1	6.1	6.0	4.2	7.4	2.2	6.4
Mauritania	1.6	3.2	3.6	4.7	4.7	4.7	5.1	2.3	6.4	6.9	5.4
Niger	-0.1	1.2	1.9	2.9	3.4	4.1	4.1	5.3	3.8	-0.6	7.1
Nigeria	4.3	3.0	3.3	0.4	2.6	4.6	6.6	4.6	9.6	6.6	6.2
Senegal	3.1	2.8	3.3	3.6	4.3	5.1	4.7	5.6	1.1	6.5	6.0
Sierra Leone	2.2	-1.7	-0.3	-5.1	0.6	5.4	13.7	27.4	9.2	7.4	7.5
Togo	1.5	1.9	2.1	3.5	3.0	2.6	2.5	4.1	2.7	3.0	1.8
Developing economies: America	**1.7**	**2.4**	**2.4**	**3.2**	**2.7**	**2.3**	**2.4**	**-0.4**	**2.1**	**5.7**	**4.6**
Caribbean	*2.2*	*0.8*	*1.5*	*1.8*	*2.8*	*4.1*	*3.8*	*2.3*	*3.3*	*3.9*	*8.0*
Anguilla	9.4	7.8	6.8	5.1	4.4	4.3	3.9	-1.4	2.2	12.7	3.5
Antigua and Barbuda	6.7	4.7	4.3	3.4	3.5	3.8	4.3	2.5	5.2	7.2	3.0
Aruba	10.0	8.3	6.7	5.4	3.6	2.2	0.9	-2.5	1.5	3.5	3.2
Bahamas	3.1	1.9	2.1	2.8	2.8	2.9	1.8	2.3	1.4	1.8	2.7
Barbados	1.7	1.1	1.2	2.0	1.8	1.9	1.5	0.5	2.0	3.7	3.1
British Virgin Islands	6.2	6.7	6.5	7.5	6.3	5.9	1.4	-3.5	-7.2	10.5	9.2
Cayman Islands	9.2	8.4	7.2	7.4	5.2	3.2	1.6	1.7	2.0	1.7	1.4
Cuba	3.4	-0.9	0.1	-0.7	1.6	4.2	4.7	1.8	3.8	5.4	11.8
Dominica	5.2	3.4	2.6	2.0	1.2	0.7	0.9	-4.0	2.2	6.8	2.6
Dominican Republic	2.8	4.1	4.4	6.6	5.8	5.4	2.8	4.4	-1.9	2.0	9.3
Grenada	6.1	4.4	3.9	3.6	3.2	3.3	0.6	1.5	7.5	-4.1	0.9
Haiti	0.2	-0.8	-0.6	-0.8	-0.3	0.6	-0.8	-0.5	0.5	-3.8	1.5
Jamaica	1.5	1.6	1.4	0.5	0.7	0.7	1.4	1.1	2.3	0.9	0.7
Montserrat	2.7	-0.5	-1.8	-6.6	-5.7	-6.1	0.4	3.2	-0.7	4.6	-0.7
Netherlands Antilles	-0.5	1.3	1.1	1.5	0.8	-0.3	1.0	0.3	1.4	1.1	0.9
Saint Kitts and Nevis	6.3	5.3	4.8	5.1	4.1	3.2	2.8	1.0	0.6	6.6	4.1
Saint Lucia	7.4	4.8	3.8	2.2	1.7	1.5	2.6	1.6	3.2	6.3	5.1
Saint Vincent and the Grenadines	6.0	5.7	5.1	5.1	4.2	3.3	3.7	3.7	4.1	4.9	3.6
Trinidad and Tobago	-3.4	0.2	2.0	4.6	6.0	7.7	7.9	4.0	13.4	6.5	6.7
Turks and Caicos Islands	6.7	7.0	7.2	8.5	8.0	7.6	8.2	1.2	9.3	11.4	13.9
Central America	*1.1*	*2.4*	*2.6*	*3.2*	*3.1*	*3.4*	*2.0*	*1.0*	*1.7*	*4.2*	*3.0*
Belize	4.7	5.3	5.3	3.9	4.6	5.1	5.6	4.7	9.2	4.6	3.1
Costa Rica	3.0	4.4	4.4	5.3	4.7	4.4	4.0	2.9	6.4	4.1	4.1

For sources and notes, see end of table.

Per capita real product / Produit réel par habitant En pourcentage											Régions, pays ou territoires
80 -90	80 -00	80 -05	90 -00	90 -05	95 -05	00 -05	01 -02	02 -03	03 -04	04 -05	
-0.4	0.7	1.2	0.9	1.9	2.9	4.2	4.6	4.3	4.0	4.2	République-Unie de Tanzanie
-2.1	-2.2	-1.5	-2.0	-0.4	1.2	2.8	1.4	2.4	4.3	3.2	Zambie
-0.2	0.0	-1.0	-0.4	-2.4	-4.3	-5.6	-5.6	-10.3	0.0	-7.8	Zimbabwe
-0.3	*-2.3*	*-1.5*	*-1.6*	*0.0*	*1.6*	*3.2*	*3.5*	*1.3*	*5.3*	*4.3*	*Afrique centrale*
0.4	-1.8	-0.7	-1.2	1.3	4.0	6.0	11.1	0.4	8.0	11.4	Angola
0.3	-1.8	-1.0	0.0	1.0	2.1	2.0	1.6	1.8	2.8	1.7	Cameroun
-1.2	-1.6	-1.4	-0.7	-0.6	-0.5	-1.7	-1.2	-6.0	-0.3	0.6	République centrafricaine
3.1	1.3	1.8	0.0	2.2	4.2	11.5	4.4	11.3	28.5	4.1	Tchad
0.5	-1.1	-0.8	-1.6	-0.5	0.6	1.7	2.8	-1.6	1.6	6.7	Congo
-1.4	-5.9	-5.5	-7.6	-5.3	-3.1	1.4	0.6	2.6	3.5	3.3	Rép. dém. du Congo
-3.1	5.7	10.6	20.8	23.1	26.4	20.1	17.4	11.0	21.2	3.7	Guinée équatoriale
-2.1	-0.8	-1.0	-0.6	-1.2	-2.1	-0.4	-2.1	0.2	-0.1	0.4	Gabon
-2.4	-1.0	-0.4	-0.1	0.7	1.4	2.4	2.3	2.7	2.8	1.5	Sao Tomé-et-Principe
0.0	*0.2*	*0.7*	*0.8*	*1.5*	*2.3*	*3.3*	*1.7*	*5.9*	*3.4*	*3.0*	*Afrique septentrionale*
-0.3	-0.8	-0.1	0.0	1.1	2.4	3.6	2.6	5.7	3.6	3.7	Algérie
4.6	3.4	3.2	2.9	2.7	2.6	2.4	2.2	2.2	3.1	3.1	Égypte
-5.2	-3.1	-2.1	-0.6	0.2	1.1	4.2	-2.3	16.9	2.3	2.2	Jamahiriya arabe libyenne
1.8	1.3	1.5	0.8	1.5	2.3	3.0	2.0	4.4	3.1	0.0	Maroc
0.1	0.3	0.9	-0.4	1.4	3.2	4.6	4.3	4.1	5.1	5.8	Soudan
0.8	2.0	2.4	3.1	3.3	3.7	3.4	0.6	4.4	4.7	3.8	Tunisie
-0.8	*-0.7*	*-0.1*	*0.0*	*0.9*	*1.7*	*2.6*	*2.4*	*2.0*	*3.6*	*3.3*	*Afrique australe*
7.5	5.0	4.7	2.4	3.2	4.2	4.2	1.0	5.5	5.5	2.7	Botswana
2.3	3.2	2.7	2.2	1.6	0.7	1.5	2.4	2.3	1.2	-1.4	Lesotho
-1.4	0.0	0.5	1.1	1.6	1.9	3.1	5.1	2.1	4.6	2.2	Namibie
-0.9	-0.9	-0.3	-0.1	0.8	1.6	2.5	2.4	1.9	3.5	3.4	Afrique du Sud
4.1	2.8	2.3	1.3	1.2	1.1	1.1	1.4	1.2	1.1	1.3	Swaziland
0.6	*0.0*	*0.3*	*-0.8*	*0.3*	*1.4*	*2.4*	*1.4*	*3.4*	*2.6*	*2.6*	*Afrique occidentale*
-0.1	0.3	0.6	1.2	1.3	1.5	0.9	1.1	0.5	0.1	0.3	Bénin
-0.1	1.5	1.6	2.4	1.9	1.6	3.0	1.3	4.5	3.2	2.6	Burkina Faso
3.2	3.1	3.4	4.6	4.4	4.5	2.7	2.8	2.2	2.0	3.9	Cap-Vert
-1.0	-0.8	-0.7	0.4	-0.3	-0.8	-1.2	-1.7	-1.6	0.1	-1.2	Côte d'Ivoire
0.1	-0.4	-0.2	-0.5	0.1	1.0	1.1	-6.3	3.4	5.1	1.6	Gambie
-0.3	1.1	1.3	1.6	1.9	2.2	2.7	2.2	2.9	2.9	3.6	Ghana
0.5	0.7	0.9	1.2	1.3	1.5	1.0	2.3	-0.6	0.8	1.0	Guinée
1.8	0.2	-0.7	-1.9	-2.6	-3.9	-3.2	-10.0	-2.5	1.1	-0.7	Guinée-Bissau
-6.3	-11.7	-8.3	-0.2	1.8	7.4	-8.4	1.6	-32.2	0.7	5.6	Libéria
1.4	1.1	1.6	1.4	2.2	3.1	2.9	1.1	4.3	-0.9	3.3	Mali
-1.0	0.5	0.8	1.9	1.8	1.7	2.1	-0.6	3.3	3.9	2.6	Mauritanie
-3.1	-2.0	-1.4	-0.7	-0.2	0.5	0.5	1.7	0.2	-4.0	3.4	Niger
1.4	0.1	0.5	-2.3	-0.2	1.9	3.9	2.0	6.9	4.0	3.7	Nigéria
0.1	-0.1	0.4	0.8	1.5	2.4	2.0	2.9	-1.5	3.8	3.3	Sénégal
-0.2	-3.2	-2.1	-5.9	-1.4	2.1	8.9	21.7	4.2	2.9	3.8	Sierra Leone
-2.0	-1.3	-1.1	0.3	-0.2	-0.7	-0.3	1.1	-0.1	0.2	-1.0	Togo
-0.3	*0.5*	*0.6*	*1.5*	*1.1*	*0.9*	*1.1*	*-1.7*	*0.8*	*4.4*	*3.3*	**Économies en développement : Amérique**
0.8	*-0.5*	*0.2*	*0.5*	*1.6*	*2.9*	*2.7*	*1.2*	*2.2*	*2.8*	*7.0*	*Caraïbes*
6.7	4.9	4.1	2.9	2.4	2.5	2.1	-3.2	0.4	10.8	1.8	Anguilla
8.4	4.5	3.6	1.0	1.3	1.7	2.7	0.8	3.7	5.7	1.6	Antigua-et-Barbuda
9.8	5.9	4.2	1.7	0.6	0.1	-1.7	-5.5	-1.5	0.9	1.4	Aruba
1.2	0.1	0.3	1.1	1.2	1.5	0.5	0.9	0.2	0.6	1.5	Bahamas
0.8	0.3	0.6	1.5	1.3	1.5	1.1	0.1	1.6	3.3	2.7	Barbade
1.8	3.4	3.5	5.2	4.3	4.1	0.0	-4.9	-8.4	9.1	7.8	Îles Vierges britanniques
4.8	3.8	2.9	2.9	1.3	-0.1	-0.9	-1.0	-0.5	-0.5	-0.6	Îles Caïmanes
2.6	-1.5	-0.5	-1.2	1.2	3.9	4.5	1.5	3.6	5.2	11.7	Cuba
5.9	3.8	3.0	2.0	1.3	0.8	1.1	-3.9	2.4	7.0	2.8	Dominique
0.7	2.1	2.5	4.7	4.0	3.6	1.1	2.8	-3.4	0.4	7.6	République dominicaine
5.2	4.0	3.5	3.1	2.5	2.6	-0.3	0.4	6.3	-5.0	0.2	Grenade
-2.0	-2.8	-2.5	-2.7	-2.0	-1.1	-2.4	-2.2	-1.1	-5.3	-0.1	Haïti
0.5	0.7	0.5	-0.4	-0.1	0.0	0.6	0.4	1.5	0.3	0.1	Jamaïque
3.9	2.7	2.2	0.9	0.9	0.7	-2.7	2.1	-6.7	-2.5	-5.6	Montserrat
-1.4	1.0	0.9	2.1	1.2	0.0	0.3	0.0	0.6	0.1	-0.3	Antilles néerlandaises
7.0	5.0	4.2	3.8	2.8	1.9	1.4	-0.3	-0.6	5.3	2.7	Saint-Kitts-et-Nevis
5.8	3.4	2.5	1.2	0.7	0.5	1.5	0.6	2.0	5.1	3.9	Sainte-Lucie
5.1	4.9	4.4	4.5	3.6	2.8	3.1	3.1	3.5	4.3	3.0	Saint-Vincent-et-les Grenadines
-4.6	-0.6	1.3	3.9	5.5	7.2	7.5	3.7	13.0	6.1	6.3	Trinité-et-Tobago
2.3	2.1	2.2	3.3	2.8	2.6	2.6	-4.7	3.2	6.0	9.7	Îles Turques et Caïques
-0.9	*0.5*	*0.8*	*1.3*	*1.4*	*1.9*	*0.9*	*-0.2*	*0.6*	*3.0*	*1.8*	*Amérique centrale*
2.1	2.5	2.5	1.1	1.8	2.5	3.1	2.2	6.6	2.2	0.8	Belize
0.3	1.7	1.9	2.7	2.3	2.1	2.0	0.8	4.4	2.3	2.3	Costa Rica

Pour les sources et les notes, se reporter à la fin du tableau.

8.2.1 Annual average growth rates of total and per capita real gross domestic product of countries and geographical regions

Region, country or territory	Total real product / Produit réel total Percentage										
	80 -90	80 -00	80 -05	90 -00	90 -05	95 -05	00 -05	01 -02	02 -03	03 -04	04 -05
El Salvador	0.6	3.1	3.2	4.8	3.7	2.5	1.9	2.2	1.8	1.5	2.1
Guatemala	0.8	2.9	3.1	4.1	3.6	3.2	2.5	2.2	2.1	2.7	3.2
Honduras	2.7	3.1	3.1	3.2	3.2	3.1	3.6	2.7	3.5	5.0	4.2
Mexico	1.1	2.4	2.5	3.1	3.0	3.4	1.9	0.8	1.4	4.2	2.8
Nicaragua	-1.9	0.2	1.1	3.7	3.7	3.8	3.0	0.8	2.5	5.1	4.0
Panama	–	–	–	4.7	4.2	4.0	4.2	2.2	4.2	7.6	5.5
South America	**1.8**	**2.5**	**2.4**	**3.3**	**2.6**	**1.8**	**2.5**	**-1.1**	**2.2**	**6.4**	**5.0**
Argentina	-0.4	2.1	1.8	4.0	2.1	0.7	2.2	-10.9	8.8	9.0	9.2
Bolivia	-0.2	2.4	2.7	4.0	3.4	2.8	2.7	2.4	2.8	3.6	2.7
Brazil	2.8	2.4	2.3	2.9	2.6	2.1	2.3	1.9	0.5	4.9	3.3
Chile	3.1	5.9	5.5	6.6	5.2	3.6	4.2	2.2	3.7	6.1	5.9
Colombia	3.6	3.6	3.2	2.9	2.5	1.7	3.2	1.9	4.1	4.0	4.0
Ecuador	2.0	2.5	2.5	2.2	2.5	2.5	4.5	4.2	3.6	7.6	0.7
Guyana	-3.1	1.4	1.7	5.4	3.4	1.2	0.3	1.1	-0.6	1.5	-2.8
Paraguay	2.6	2.9	2.5	2.2	1.6	0.8	2.6	0.0	3.8	4.1	2.7
Peru	-0.3	1.3	1.8	4.7	3.9	2.8	4.0	4.9	4.0	4.8	5.5
Suriname	0.9	0.6	1.1	0.7	1.9	3.2	5.0	2.1	5.4	7.8	5.1
Uruguay	1.0	2.7	2.1	3.4	1.5	0.1	0.9	-11.2	2.4	11.9	6.4
Venezuela (Bolivarian Republic of)	0.7	1.9	1.6	1.6	1.0	0.4	1.3	-8.9	-7.7	17.9	9.3
Developing economies: Asia	**5.7**	**6.1**	**6.0**	**6.2**	**5.9**	**5.5**	**6.3**	**6.0**	**6.6**	**7.6**	**7.0**
Eastern Asia	**9.1**	**8.5**	**8.1**	**7.9**	**7.4**	**6.6**	**7.1**	**7.4**	**7.0**	**8.2**	**7.4**
China	10.3	10.1	9.9	10.6	9.8	8.8	9.6	9.1	10.0	10.1	9.9
China, Hong Kong SAR	7.1	5.7	5.1	4.1	3.8	3.3	3.8	1.8	3.1	8.2	4.6
China, Macao SAR	7.5	5.5	5.4	2.2	4.0	5.3	12.9	10.1	14.2	28.6	2.5
China, Taiwan Province of	8.5	7.5	6.6	6.4	5.1	4.1	3.4	4.2	3.4	6.1	3.8
Korea, Dem. People's Rep. of	2.3	-1.0	-0.7	-2.8	-0.9	1.0	1.4	1.2	1.8	0.0	0.9
Korea, Republic of	9.0	7.7	7.0	5.8	5.3	4.5	4.6	7.0	3.1	4.7	4.0
Mongolia	5.7	1.6	1.9	1.0	2.4	3.8	5.9	4.0	5.6	10.7	7.0
Southern Asia	**4.7**	**4.9**	**5.0**	**5.1**	**5.3**	**5.5**	**6.5**	**4.8**	**8.0**	**6.8**	**7.9**
Afghanistan	-1.6	-2.1	-1.5	-1.1	-0.1	1.1	13.3	29.7	18.6	8.0	13.8
Bangladesh	3.9	4.4	4.6	4.9	5.1	5.3	5.5	5.3	6.3	5.4	5.5
Bhutan	7.5	6.2	6.4	5.6	6.5	7.5	7.9	7.1	6.8	8.7	8.8
India	5.8	5.7	5.7	6.0	6.0	5.9	6.7	4.1	8.6	7.1	8.7
Iran, Islamic Republic of	1.7	2.9	3.5	3.0	4.1	5.2	6.9	7.8	8.0	6.5	5.9
Maldives	11.9	9.7	8.9	7.8	7.2	6.9	6.3	6.1	9.2	9.6	-0.2
Nepal	4.6	4.9	4.7	4.9	4.4	3.8	2.6	-0.6	3.4	3.4	2.5
Pakistan	6.1	4.9	4.5	3.5	3.6	3.6	4.8	3.2	5.0	6.4	7.8
Sri Lanka	4.0	4.6	4.5	5.3	4.7	4.2	4.3	4.0	5.9	5.4	6.2
South-Eastern Asia	**5.3**	**6.0**	**5.5**	**5.0**	**4.4**	**3.3**	**5.0**	**4.8**	**5.4**	**6.2**	**5.4**
Brunei Darussalam	-0.7	0.6	1.0	1.3	1.8	2.1	2.9	2.8	3.8	1.7	3.0
Cambodia	6.3	6.4	6.5	6.4	6.7	7.1	6.5	5.2	7.0	7.7	7.0
Indonesia	5.9	6.0	5.2	4.2	3.5	2.2	4.7	4.4	4.7	5.1	5.6
Lao People's Dem. Rep.	5.1	5.8	5.9	6.5	6.3	6.1	6.3	5.9	5.8	6.9	7.3
Malaysia	5.2	6.9	6.4	7.0	5.7	4.1	4.8	4.4	5.4	7.1	5.3
Myanmar	0.6	3.1	4.8	7.0	8.5	9.8	9.6	12.0	13.8	5.0	4.5
Philippines	1.0	2.3	2.8	3.3	3.6	3.9	4.7	4.4	4.5	6.0	5.1
Singapore	6.7	7.7	7.0	7.7	6.2	4.6	4.2	4.0	2.9	8.7	6.4
Thailand	7.6	7.2	6.2	4.2	3.8	2.5	5.4	5.3	7.0	6.2	4.5
Timor-Leste	–	1.4	0.2	1.4	0.2	-2.4	-0.2	-6.7	-6.2	1.8	3.2
Viet Nam	5.5	6.5	6.7	7.9	7.5	6.9	7.5	7.1	7.3	7.8	8.4
Western Asia	**1.6**	**2.9**	**3.1**	**4.0**	**3.7**	**3.6**	**4.4**	**3.7**	**4.1**	**8.3**	**6.0**
Bahrain	-0.1	3.2	3.8	4.8	4.9	4.8	5.9	5.2	7.2	5.4	7.1
Iraq	1.3	-1.2	-0.2	6.9	4.3	3.8	-6.5	-5.7	-44.3	46.5	2.6
Jordan	1.4	2.6	3.1	4.7	4.7	4.4	5.6	5.7	4.1	7.7	5.0
Kuwait	0.4	2.4	2.9	7.0	5.3	3.1	6.5	5.1	13.4	6.2	3.2
Lebanon	-1.6	0.3	0.9	6.0	4.1	2.1	2.2	-1.3	3.0	5.0	1.0
Palestinian territory	3.5	5.3	4.6	6.0	3.8	2.5	1.4	-3.8	8.5	2.0	4.9
Oman	7.7	5.8	5.3	4.5	4.2	3.8	4.0	2.6	2.0	5.6	3.8
Qatar	1.7	3.7	4.7	6.4	6.9	8.0	7.5	7.3	5.9	11.2	6.5
Saudi Arabia	-1.3	1.7	2.0	2.1	2.4	2.8	4.1	0.1	7.7	5.2	6.0
Syrian Arab Republic	0.6	3.5	3.7	6.3	4.8	3.1	3.3	5.9	1.1	2.0	3.5
Turkey	5.3	4.5	4.1	3.8	3.4	3.2	5.2	7.9	5.8	8.9	7.4
United Arab Emirates	-1.5	3.1	4.0	5.4	5.8	6.1	6.4	1.8	11.9	7.4	5.6
Yemen	–	–	–	6.6	6.0	5.3	3.9	3.5	3.8	3.9	3.8
Developing economies: Oceania	**3.7**	**3.6**	**3.3**	**2.9**	**2.6**	**2.3**	**2.3**	**2.5**	**2.5**	**2.4**	**2.2**
Cook Islands	7.0	4.2	4.0	1.5	2.8	4.1	4.4	2.6	8.0	5.6	-1.0
Fiji	1.7	2.5	2.5	2.7	2.5	2.3	2.6	3.2	1.0	5.3	0.7
French Polynesia	5.8	3.5	3.3	1.9	2.6	3.5	3.5	4.4	4.0	3.5	3.4

For sources and notes, see end of table.

Per capita real product / Produit réel par habitant En pourcentage											Régions, pays ou territoires
80-90	80-00	80-05	90-00	90-05	95-05	00-05	01-02	02-03	03-04	04-05	
-0.4	1.5	1.5	2.7	1.8	0.8	0.4	0.7	0.4	0.1	0.7	El Salvador
-1.6	0.5	0.7	1.8	1.2	0.8	0.0	-0.2	-0.4	0.2	0.6	Guatemala
-0.3	0.4	0.6	0.8	0.9	1.0	1.6	0.7	1.5	3.0	2.1	Honduras
-0.8	0.5	0.8	1.3	1.4	2.1	1.0	-0.1	0.6	3.3	1.9	Mexique
-4.2	-2.1	-1.0	1.5	1.8	2.2	1.6	-0.6	1.2	3.8	2.7	Nicaragua
—	—	—	2.6	2.2	2.0	2.3	0.3	2.3	5.7	3.7	Panama
-0.2	*0.6*	*0.6*	*1.7*	*1.0*	*0.4*	*1.1*	*-2.5*	*0.8*	*5.0*	*3.6*	*Amerique du Sud*
-1.9	0.7	0.5	2.8	1.0	-0.4	1.2	-11.8	7.8	8.0	8.1	Argentine
-2.4	0.2	0.4	1.7	1.2	0.7	0.7	0.4	0.8	1.6	0.8	Bolivie
0.6	0.6	0.6	1.3	1.1	0.6	0.9	0.5	-0.9	3.5	1.9	Brésil
1.4	4.1	3.9	4.9	3.7	2.4	3.0	1.0	2.6	4.9	4.8	Chili
1.5	1.6	1.3	1.1	0.7	0.0	1.6	0.4	2.5	2.5	2.5	Colombie
-0.6	0.2	0.5	0.4	0.9	1.1	3.3	3.0	2.4	6.4	-0.4	Équateur
-2.7	1.6	1.9	5.3	3.3	1.2	0.2	0.9	-0.9	1.4	-2.9	Guyana
-0.3	0.3	0.0	-0.1	-0.6	-1.3	0.6	-2.0	1.8	2.1	0.8	Paraguay
-2.6	-0.7	0.0	3.0	2.4	1.5	2.8	3.6	2.7	3.6	4.3	Pérou
-0.3	-0.4	0.2	-0.1	1.1	2.3	4.3	1.3	4.7	7.1	4.5	Suriname
0.3	2.0	1.5	2.7	1.0	-0.2	0.9	-11.2	2.5	11.9	6.3	Uruguay
-1.9	-0.5	-0.7	-0.5	-1.0	-1.5	-0.5	-10.5	-9.4	15.8	7.4	Venezuela (République bolivarienne du)
3.7	**4.3**	**4.3**	**4.5**	**4.3**	**4.0**	**5.0**	**4.6**	**5.3**	**6.3**	**5.7**	**Économies en développement : Asie**
7.6	*7.1*	*6.8*	*6.9*	*6.4*	*5.8*	*6.4*	*6.7*	*6.3*	*7.5*	*6.8*	*Asie orientale*
8.8	8.8	8.7	9.5	8.9	8.0	8.8	8.3	9.3	9.4	9.2	Chine
5.8	4.3	3.7	2.4	2.3	2.0	2.6	0.6	2.0	7.0	3.5	Chine, Hong Kong RAS
3.2	2.5	2.8	0.5	2.5	3.8	11.3	8.5	12.5	26.9	1.3	Chine, Macao RAS
7.0	6.3	5.6	5.4	4.3	3.4	3.0	3.7	3.0	5.7	3.4	Chine, Taiwan Province de
0.7	-2.4	-2.0	-4.1	-2.0	0.2	0.8	0.6	1.2	-0.5	0.5	Corée, Rép. populaire dém. de
7.7	6.6	6.0	4.8	4.6	3.9	4.1	6.4	2.6	4.3	3.6	Corée, République de
2.7	-0.4	0.2	0.0	1.5	3.0	5.0	3.2	4.6	9.7	6.0	Mongolie
2.3	*2.6*	*2.8*	*3.0*	*3.3*	*3.6*	*4.7*	*3.0*	*6.2*	*5.1*	*6.2*	*Asie méridionale*
-0.2	-4.7	-4.5	-5.9	-4.2	-1.9	9.1	25.1	13.9	3.7	9.3	Afghanistan
1.4	2.0	2.3	2.8	3.0	3.3	3.5	3.2	4.3	3.4	3.6	Bangladesh
4.6	5.1	5.1	5.5	5.3	4.8	5.0	4.1	3.9	6.0	6.4	Bhoutan
3.4	3.5	3.6	3.9	4.0	4.1	5.0	2.4	6.9	5.4	7.0	Inde
-2.0	0.3	1.2	1.4	2.8	4.1	5.9	6.8	7.1	5.5	4.7	Iran, Rép. islamique d'
8.4	6.6	6.1	5.3	5.1	5.1	4.7	4.5	7.6	7.9	-1.8	Maldives
2.2	2.4	2.2	2.4	1.9	1.5	0.5	-2.7	1.3	1.3	0.5	Népal
2.4	1.8	1.6	1.0	1.2	1.5	3.0	1.3	3.1	4.6	5.9	Pakistan
2.7	3.4	3.5	4.3	3.9	3.7	3.9	3.6	5.5	5.0	5.8	Sri Lanka
3.1	*4.0*	*3.6*	*3.3*	*2.8*	*1.8*	*3.5*	*3.3*	*3.9*	*4.8*	*4.0*	*Asie du Sud-Est*
-3.5	-2.1	-1.6	-1.3	-0.7	-0.3	0.6	0.5	1.5	-0.6	0.8	Brunéi Darussalam
2.3	2.9	3.3	3.5	4.2	4.9	4.7	3.4	5.2	5.9	5.2	Cambodge
3.9	4.2	3.6	2.7	2.1	0.8	3.3	3.0	3.3	3.7	4.3	Indonésie
2.2	2.9	3.3	3.9	4.0	4.1	4.6	4.2	4.1	5.3	5.6	Rép. dém. populaire lao
2.4	4.1	3.8	4.4	3.3	1.9	2.8	2.3	3.4	5.2	3.4	Malaisie
-1.3	1.5	3.3	5.6	7.2	8.7	8.7	11.0	12.9	4.1	3.6	Myanmar
-1.4	0.0	0.5	1.1	1.4	1.7	2.5	2.3	2.3	3.9	3.0	Philippines
4.3	5.0	4.4	4.6	3.5	2.4	2.7	2.4	1.5	7.4	5.1	Singapour
6.0	5.8	4.9	3.1	2.7	1.6	4.6	4.5	6.3	5.4	3.7	Thaïlande
—	0.6	-1.5	0.6	-1.5	-4.6	-5.5	-11.6	-11.9	-4.1	-2.0	Timor-Leste
3.1	4.3	4.7	6.0	5.7	5.4	5.9	5.5	5.8	6.2	6.9	Viet Nam
-1.4	*0.1*	*0.4*	*1.4*	*1.3*	*1.3*	*2.2*	*1.5*	*1.9*	*6.0*	*3.8*	*Asie occidentale*
-3.5	0.0	0.7	2.0	2.3	2.4	3.7	2.9	4.8	3.2	4.9	Bahreïn
-1.4	-4.0	-3.0	3.7	1.4	1.2	-8.5	-7.9	-45.5	43.5	0.6	Iraq
-2.3	-1.6	-0.7	0.7	1.3	1.9	2.6	2.9	1.0	4.4	1.7	Jordanie
-4.2	0.9	0.9	6.9	3.0	-1.8	2.5	0.8	9.3	2.7	0.0	Koweït
-2.1	-1.4	-0.8	3.5	2.1	0.7	1.0	-2.6	1.7	3.7	-0.2	Liban
-0.4	1.3	0.7	2.0	0.0	-1.1	-2.1	-7.2	4.7	-1.5	1.4	Territoire palestinien
3.1	2.1	2.2	1.7	2.2	2.4	3.2	1.8	1.4	4.8	2.6	Oman
-5.4	-0.8	0.3	3.7	3.3	3.5	2.1	1.4	0.1	5.7	2.2	Qatar
-6.4	-2.0	-1.4	-0.3	-0.1	0.2	1.5	-2.4	5.0	2.6	3.5	Arabie saoudite
-2.9	0.5	0.7	3.6	2.1	0.5	0.6	3.1	-1.6	-0.7	0.7	République arabe syrienne
3.1	2.5	2.2	2.0	1.7	1.6	3.8	6.4	4.4	7.5	6.0	Turquie
-7.2	-2.5	-1.6	-0.3	0.2	0.7	1.5	-3.3	6.7	2.8	1.5	Émirats arabes unis
—	—	—	2.5	2.3	2.1	0.9	0.5	0.7	0.8	0.7	Yémen
1.3	**1.3**	**1.0**	**0.6**	**0.3**	**0.1**	**0.2**	**0.3**	**0.4**	**0.3**	**0.2**	**Économies en développement : Océanie**
6.9	4.5	4.8	2.5	4.7	6.9	7.3	5.4	10.9	8.4	1.6	Îles Cook
0.4	1.4	1.5	1.6	1.6	1.5	1.9	2.5	0.4	4.6	0.1	Fidji
3.2	1.2	1.2	0.0	0.8	1.8	1.9	2.7	2.3	2.0	1.9	Polynésie française

Pour les sources et les notes, se reporter à la fin du tableau.

8.2.1 Annual average growth rates of total and per capita real gross domestic product of countries and geographical regions

Region, country or territory	Total real product / Produit réel total Percentage										
	80 -90	80 -00	80 -05	90 -00	90 -05	95 -05	C0 -05	01 -02	02 -03	03 -04	04 -05
Kiribati	0.0	-3.9	-2.9	0.8	0.8	1.2	2.5	-0.2	2.3	8.9	5.6
Marshall Islands	8.2	3.3	2.1	-2.1	-1.2	-0.8	1.7	4.0	2.0	1.5	0.8
Micronesia, Federated States of	4.4	3.0	2.3	0.4	0.5	0.2	1.1	2.9	4.3	-3.5	1.4
Nauru	4.4	-1.6	-1.9	-5.8	-3.6	-1.2	0.3	0.8	0.0	0.0	0.0
New Caledonia	5.4	4.5	3.6	1.6	1.1	0.4	0.3	1.6	0.6	-1.1	0.2
Palau, Pacific Islands (former)	1.1	1.4	1.5	1.6	1.7	1.3	2.0	1.1	1.5	2.0	2.0
Papua New Guinea	1.9	4.0	3.8	5.0	3.9	2.8	2.5	2.0	2.7	2.5	2.8
Samoa	1.0	1.2	1.8	2.6	3.1	3.5	3.2	1.3	3.5	3.5	2.5
Solomon Islands	2.3	3.2	2.0	2.1	-0.1	-2.3	1.3	-2.7	5.6	5.5	4.0
Tonga	3.9	2.5	2.5	2.2	2.4	2.4	2.4	3.2	2.7	1.3	2.5
Tuvalu	1.2	3.5	3.6	3.5	3.6	3.8	5.9	5.5	2.0	6.9	4.8
Vanuatu	4.5	4.1	3.3	3.8	2.2	0.7	0.1	-4.9	2.4	3.0	2.8
Economies in transition: Asia	_	_	_	_	_	**6.3**	**8.4**	**7.3**	**8.1**	**8.7**	**9.4**
Armenia	_	_	_	_	_	8.5	12.3	13.2	14.0	10.1	13.9
Azerbaijan	_	_	_	_	_	10.7	12.4	10.6	11.2	10.2	24.3
Georgia	_	_	_	_	_	5.7	7.5	5.5	11.1	6.3	9.3
Kazakhstan	_	_	_	_	_	6.8	10.1	9.8	9.3	9.6	9.4
Kyrgyzstan	_	_	_	_	_	4.6	4.0	0.0	7.0	7.0	-0.6
Tajikistan	_	_	_	_	_	6.3	9.7	9.5	10.2	10.6	7.5
Turkmenistan	_	_	_	_	_	4.6	4.0	0.3	3.3	5.0	9.6
Uzbekistan	_	_	_	_	_	4.5	5.2	4.2	4.5	7.7	5.0
Economies in transition: Europe	**-0.2**	**-7.0**	**-4.9**	**-5.2**	**-0.7**	**4.1**	**6.0**	**4.7**	**6.7**	**7.4**	**5.9**
Albania	1.5	-0.2	1.3	3.2	4.7	5.8	5.8	4.3	5.7	6.7	6.0
Belarus	_	_	_	_	_	6.6	7.5	5.0	7.0	11.4	9.2
Bosnia and Herzegovina (1)	_	_	_	_	_	9.5	1.9	1.6	0.6	0.9	5.4
Bulgaria	3.4	-0.6	0.0	-1.8	0.7	2.9	5.0	4.9	4.5	5.6	6.0
Croatia	_	_	_	_	_	3.6	4.3	5.2	4.3	3.8	3.6
Macedonia, TFYR	_	_	_	_	_	1.8	1.2	0.9	2.8	1.8	3.8
Moldova, Republic of	_	_	_	_	_	2.4	7.1	7.8	6.6	7.4	7.1
Romania	1.1	-1.3	-0.5	-0.6	1.1	2.1	5.8	5.1	5.2	8.4	4.1
Russian Federation	_	_	_	_	_	4.4	6.2	4.7	7.3	7.1	6.4
Serbia and Montenegro	_	_	_	_	_	0.9	4.9	3.9	2.1	8.5	6.1
Yugoslavia, SFR (former)	5.9	_	_	_	_	_	_	_	_	_	_
USSR (former)	-0.7	_	_	_	_	_	_	_	_	_	_
Ukraine	_	_	_	_	_	3.8	8.1	5.2	9.6	12.1	2.6

Sources:
- UN DESA Population Division
- UN DESA Statistics Division

Notes:

(1)   GDP data include the Federation of Bosnia and Herzegovina only. Data for the Republika Srpska are excluded.

Per capita real product / Produit réel par habitant En pourcentage											Régions, pays ou territoires
80 -90	80 -00	80 -05	90 -00	90 -05	95 -05	00 -05	01 -02	02 -03	03 -04	04 -05	
-2.8	-6.0	-4.9	-0.7	-0.8	-0.6	0.7	-2.0	0.4	6.9	3.8	Kiribati
3.4	0.5	-0.2	-2.9	-2.2	-1.8	-0.1	2.5	0.2	-0.5	-1.3	Îles Marshall
1.5	0.9	0.7	-0.7	-0.2	0.0	0.6	2.4	3.6	-4.2	0.7	Micronésie, États fédérés de
2.3	-3.2	-3.2	-6.7	-4.1	-1.3	0.1	0.7	-0.2	-0.2	-0.2	Nauru
3.6	2.4	1.4	-0.8	-1.0	-1.5	-1.4	-0.2	-1.1	-2.7	-1.4	Nouvelle-Calédonie
-0.9	-0.9	-0.7	-1.1	-0.5	-0.3	1.2	0.1	0.7	1.4	1.5	Palaos, Îles du Pacifique (anc.)
-0.6	1.4	1.2	2.3	1.2	0.2	0.1	-0.5	0.2	0.1	0.5	Papouasie-Nouvelle-Guinée
0.6	0.5	1.0	1.6	2.2	2.6	2.5	0.6	2.8	2.9	1.7	Samoa
-0.9	0.2	-0.9	-0.7	-2.8	-4.8	-1.2	-5.2	3.0	2.9	1.5	Îles Salomon
4.2	2.3	2.2	1.8	2.1	2.3	2.1	3.0	2.5	1.0	2.1	Tonga
-0.4	2.3	2.5	2.7	2.9	3.1	5.4	5.0	1.5	6.4	4.4	Tuvalu
2.1	1.5	0.8	1.4	-0.2	-1.5	-2.4	-7.3	-0.2	0.3	0.2	Vanuatu
–	–	–	–	–	5.6	7.5	6.5	7.2	7.7	8.4	**Économies en transition : Asie**
–	–	–	–	–	9.1	12.7	13.7	14.5	10.5	14.3	Arménie
–	–	–	–	–	9.9	11.8	10.0	10.7	9.6	23.6	Azerbaïdjan
–	–	–	–	–	7.0	8.7	6.7	12.3	7.4	10.4	Géorgie
–	–	–	–	–	7.4	9.7	9.6	8.8	8.9	8.7	Kazakhstan
–	–	–	–	–	3.2	3.0	-1.0	6.0	6.0	-1.6	Kirghizistan
–	–	–	–	–	5.0	8.5	8.3	8.9	9.3	6.1	Tadjikistan
–	–	–	–	–	3.2	2.5	-1.2	1.8	3.5	8.1	Turkménistan
–	–	–	–	–	3.0	3.7	2.7	2.9	6.2	3.5	Ouzbékistan
-1.0	-5.6	-3.6	-3.0	0.7	4.6	6.6	5.2	7.2	7.9	6.5	**Économies en transition : Europe**
-0.7	-0.8	0.8	4.0	5.1	5.8	5.3	3.9	5.1	6.0	5.4	Albanie
					7.1	8.1	5.5	7.5	12.0	9.8	Bélarus
					7.7	1.3	0.7	0.2	0.7	5.1	Bosnie-Herzégovine (1)
3.4	0.0	0.7	-0.8	1.6	3.7	5.7	5.6	5.1	6.2	6.7	Bulgarie
–	–	–	–	–	3.9	4.1	5.0	3.9	3.4	3.3	Croatie
–	–	–	–	–	1.4	0.9	0.6	2.6	1.6	3.6	Macédoine, LERY
–	–	–	–	–	3.7	8.5	9.3	8.1	8.8	8.4	Moldova, République de
0.7	-1.3	-0.4	-0.1	1.6	2.6	6.3	5.6	5.7	8.9	4.5	Roumanie
–	–	–	–	–	4.8	6.8	5.2	7.9	7.7	7.0	Fédération de Russie
–	–	–	–	–	1.3	5.6	4.6	2.8	9.2	6.6	Serbie-et-Monténégro
5.3	–	–	–	–	–	–	–	–	–	–	Yougoslavie, RSF (anc.)
-1.6	–	–	–	–	–	–	–	–	–	–	URSS (anc.)
–	–	–	–	–	4.7	9.0	6.1	10.5	13.0	3.4	Ukraine

Sources :
- ONU DAES Division de la population
- ONU DAES Division de statistique

Notes :

(1)   Y compris le PIB de la Fédération de Bosnie-Herzégovine seulement. Non compris le PIB de la Republika Srpska.

8.2.2 Annual average growth rates of total and per capita real gross domestic product of economic groupings

Region, country or territory	Total real product / Produit réel total Percentage										
	80 - 90	80 - 00	80 - 05	90 - 00	90 - 05	95 - 05	00 - 05	01 - 02	02 - 03	03 - 04	04 - 05
DEVELOPING ECONOMIES	**3.9**	**4.5**	**4.5**	**4.9**	**4.7**	**4.5**	**5.2**	**4.1**	**5.4**	**6.9**	**6.3**
Developing economies excluding China	3.4	3.8	3.8	4.1	3.9	3.6	4.2	3.1	4.4	6.2	5.3
Developing economies excluding LDCs	4.0	4.5	4.6	5.0	4.8	4.5	5.2	4.1	5.4	6.9	6.3
High-income countries	3.0	4.2	4.1	4.5	4.0	3.5	3.6	1.7	4.1	6.2	4.8
Middle-income countries	3.2	3.1	3.1	3.3	3.3	3.1	4.0	4.0	3.8	5.7	4.7
Low-income countries	5.8	6.1	6.2	6.7	6.6	6.4	7.4	6.3	7.5	8.4	8.4
Heavily indebted poor countries	2.2	2.3	2.7	3.0	3.6	4.1	4.5	3.6	3.7	5.7	5.2
Landlocked countries	2.5	6.3	5.9	6.4	5.3	4.3	5.5	4.5	4.7	7.0	6.3
Small island developing states	1.4	2.4	2.8	3.5	3.6	3.7	3.7	2.3	5.1	3.9	3.5
Least developed countries	*2.4*	*2.6*	*3.2*	*3.6*	*4.4*	*5.2*	*5.9*	*5.7*	*5.5*	*6.5*	*6.3*
Africa and Haiti	2.2	2.1	2.7	2.7	3.8	4.9	5.8	5.4	4.2	7.3	7.0
Asia	2.8	3.5	4.0	5.0	5.4	5.7	6.0	6.3	7.4	5.3	5.4
Islands	4.3	4.6	4.3	4.1	3.7	3.3	3.6	1.8	4.1	5.0	3.3
Major petroleum exporters	*1.5*	*2.7*	*2.9*	*3.1*	*3.4*	*3.5*	*4.9*	*2.9*	*5.0*	*7.1*	*5.8*
Africa	2.0	1.5	2.0	1.3	2.6	4.0	5.9	3.9	9.6	5.7	6.0
America	0.2	1.7	1.6	1.9	1.5	1.2	2.2	-7.0	-4.6	15.4	8.7
Asia	1.5	3.2	3.4	3.8	3.8	3.6	4.8	3.6	4.6	6.7	5.4
Major exporters of manufactured goods	*5.5*	*5.7*	*5.6*	*5.9*	*5.6*	*5.2*	*5.7*	*5.4*	*5.7*	*7.2*	*6.5*
America	2.1	2.4	2.4	3.0	2.7	2.6	2.2	1.5	0.9	4.6	3.1
Asia	7.5	7.3	7.0	7.0	6.5	5.9	6.7	6.5	7.0	7.9	7.4
Emerging economies	*3.7*	*4.2*	*4.0*	*4.5*	*3.8*	*3.2*	*3.3*	*2.4*	*3.0*	*5.6*	*4.3*
America	1.6	2.4	2.4	3.4	2.8	2.3	2.3	-0.4	2.3	5.4	4.3
Asia	8.2	7.5	6.7	6.0	5.2	4.1	4.3	5.6	3.8	5.7	4.3
Newly industrialized economies	*7.2*	*6.8*	*6.1*	*5.4*	*4.7*	*3.8*	*4.4*	*5.1*	*3.9*	*5.9*	*4.5*
First tier	8.4	7.4	6.6	5.9	5.1	4.2	4.1	5.3	3.2	5.8	4.2
Second tier	5.3	5.9	5.3	4.5	4.0	2.8	4.9	4.6	5.5	5.9	5.2
Developing economies: Africa	**2.6**	**2.3**	**2.6**	**2.4**	**3.1**	**3.8**	**4.7**	**3.6**	**5.4**	**5.3**	**4.9**
Northern Africa excluding Sudan	2.6	2.4	2.7	2.8	3.4	3.9	4.9	3.1	7.8	4.9	4.4
Sub-Saharan Africa	2.5	2.2	2.5	2.2	3.0	3.7	4.5	3.9	4.0	5.6	5.1
Sub-Saharan Africa excluding South Africa	3.2	2.6	2.9	2.3	3.2	4.1	5.0	4.0	4.5	6.1	5.6
Developing economies: America	**1.7**	**2.4**	**2.4**	**3.2**	**2.7**	**2.3**	**2.4**	**-0.4**	**2.1**	**5.7**	**4.6**
Central America and Greater Carribean Islands excluding Puerto Rico	1.3	2.2	2.4	3.0	3.0	3.5	2.2	1.1	1.7	4.1	3.7
Central America and Greater Carribean Islands excluding Mexico and Puerto Rico	2.1	1.6	2.1	2.6	3.1	3.8	3.4	2.3	2.8	4.0	6.6
South America and Central America	1.6	2.5	2.4	3.3	2.7	2.3	2.4	-0.5	2.1	5.8	4.4
South America excluding Brazil	0.7	2.6	2.4	3.8	2.6	1.5	2.7	-4.9	4.4	8.3	7.1
Developing economies: Asia	**5.7**	**6.1**	**6.0**	**6.2**	**5.9**	**5.5**	**6.3**	**6.0**	**6.6**	**7.6**	**7.0**
Eastern and South-Eastern Asia excluding China	7.0	6.6	6.0	5.3	4.7	3.8	4.4	5.1	4.1	5.9	4.5
Southern Asia excluding India	3.2	3.6	3.9	3.5	4.1	4.7	6.0	6.0	6.9	6.2	6.3

Sources:
- UN DESA Population Division
- UN DESA Statistics Division

410

			Per capita real product / Produit réel par habitant En pourcentage								Régions, pays ou territoires
80 - 90	80 - 00	80 - 05	90 - 00	90 - 05	95 - 05	00 - 05	01 - 02	02 - 03	03 - 04	04 - 05	
1.8	2.5	2.6	3.1	3.0	2.9	3.7	2.6	3.9	5.4	4.8	ÉCONOMIES EN DÉVELOPPEMENT
0.9	1.6	1.6	2.0	1.9	1.8	2.5	1.3	2.6	4.4	3.6	Économies en développement sans la Chine
1.9	2.6	2.8	3.3	3.2	3.0	3.8	2.7	4.1	5.6	4.9	Économies en développement sans les PMA
1.0	2.4	2.4	2.9	2.5	2.1	2.5	0.5	3.0	5.1	3.7	Pays à revenu élevé
0.8	1.1	1.2	1.6	1.6	1.5	2.6	2.5	2.4	4.2	3.3	Pays à revenu intermédiaire
3.7	4.1	4.3	4.8	4.9	4.8	5.8	4.7	6.0	6.8	6.9	Pays à revenu faible
-0.7	-0.6	-0.1	0.2	0.8	1.4	1.9	1.0	1.1	3.0	2.5	Pays pauvres très endettés
-0.2	1.6	1.7	1.7	1.8	2.0	3.2	2.2	2.4	4.7	3.9	Pays sans littoral
-0.4	0.7	1.0	1.7	1.8	2.0	1.8	0.5	3.2	2.0	1.7	Petits états insulaires en développement
-0.2	*0.0*	*0.6*	*0.9*	*1.8*	*2.6*	*3.3*	*3.2*	*2.9*	*3.9*	*3.8*	*Pays les moins avancés*
-0.6	-0.7	-0.1	-0.1	1.0	2.0	3.0	2.6	1.5	4.4	4.1	Afrique et Haïti
0.6	1.1	1.7	2.6	3.1	3.6	4.0	4.2	5.3	3.3	3.4	Asie
1.7	2.1	1.9	2.1	1.5	1.0	0.4	-1.2	0.7	1.6	0.2	Îles
-1.2	*0.3*	*0.7*	*1.0*	*1.3*	*1.6*	*2.9*	*1.0*	*3.1*	*5.1*	*3.9*	*Principaux exportateurs de pétrole*
-0.9	-1.3	-0.7	-1.3	0.1	1.5	3.5	1.5	7.1	3.3	3.6	Afrique
-2.3	-0.6	-0.6	-0.1	-0.4	-0.6	0.4	-8.6	-6.2	13.5	6.9	Amérique
-1.1	1.0	1.3	2.0	2.0	1.9	3.2	1.9	3.0	5.1	3.8	Asie
3.6	*4.0*	*4.0*	*4.3*	*4.1*	*3.9*	*4.5*	*4.2*	*4.5*	*6.0*	*5.4*	*Principaux exportateurs d'articles manufacturés*
0.1	0.6	0.7	1.3	1.2	1.2	0.9	0.2	-0.3	3.4	1.9	Amérique
5.6	5.6	5.4	5.4	5.1	4.6	5.5	5.3	5.8	6.7	6.3	Asie
1.8	*2.6*	*2.5*	*2.9*	*2.4*	*1.9*	*2.2*	*1.3*	*2.0*	*4.5*	*3.2*	*Économies émergentes*
-0.4	0.6	0.7	1.7	1.3	1.0	1.1	-1.6	1.1	4.2	3.1	Amérique
6.5	6.0	5.4	4.6	4.0	3.1	3.5	4.7	3.0	4.9	3.5	Asie
5.2	*5.0*	*4.5*	*3.8*	*3.2*	*2.4*	*3.0*	*3.7*	*2.6*	*4.5*	*3.2*	*Économies nouvellement industrialisées*
7.0	6.2	5.5	4.8	4.2	3.4	3.5	4.6	2.6	5.3	3.7	Premier tier
3.2	4.0	3.5	2.9	2.4	1.3	3.4	3.1	4.0	4.4	3.7	Deuxième tier
-0.3	*-0.5*	*-0.1*	*-0.1*	*0.6*	*1.4*	*2.3*	*1.2*	*2.9*	*2.9*	*2.5*	*Économies en développement : Afrique*
0.1	0.3	0.7	1.0	1.6	2.3	3.3	1.5	6.1	3.3	2.8	Afrique septentrionale sans le Soudan
-0.4	-0.7	-0.3	-0.5	0.3	1.1	2.0	1.3	1.5	3.0	2.6	Afrique subsaharienne
0.2	-0.3	0.0	-0.5	0.5	1.4	2.3	1.4	1.9	3.4	2.9	Afrique sub-saharienne sans l'Afrique du Sud
-0.3	*0.5*	*0.6*	*1.5*	*1.1*	*0.9*	*1.1*	*-1.7*	*0.8*	*4.4*	*3.3*	*Économies en développement : Amérique*
-0.6	0.4	0.7	1.2	1.4	2.0	1.1	-0.1	0.6	3.0	2.5	Amérique centrale et Grandes Antilles sans Porto Rico
0.3	-0.2	0.3	0.8	1.4	2.1	1.9	0.8	1.3	2.4	5.1	Amérique centrale et Grandes Antilles sans le Mexique et Porto Rico
-0.4	0.6	0.7	1.6	1.1	0.8	1.0	-1.9	0.8	4.4	3.1	Amérique du Sud et Amérique centrale
-1.3	0.7	0.6	2.1	1.0	0.0	1.3	-6.2	3.0	6.8	5.7	Amérique du Sud sans le Brésil
3.7	*4.3*	*4.3*	*4.5*	*4.3*	*4.0*	*5.0*	*4.6*	*5.3*	*6.3*	*5.7*	*Économies en développement : Asie*
4.9	4.8	4.3	3.7	3.2	2.4	3.1	3.8	2.8	4.6	3.3	Asie orientale et Asie du Sud-Est sans la Chine
0.4	1.1	1.4	1.3	2.0	2.7	4.1	4.1	5.0	4.4	4.5	Asie méridionale sans l'Inde

Sources :
- ONU DAES Division de la population
- ONU DAES Division de statistique

411

8.3.1 Nominal gross domestic product by type of expenditure and by kind of economic activity of countries and geographical regions

8.3.1 Produit intérieur brut nominal par catégories de dépenses et par branches d'activité économique des pays et des régions géographiques

Region, country or territory / Régions, pays ou territoires	Year / Année	Total GDP (millions of dollars) / PIB total (millions de dollars)	GDP by type of expenditure (1) / PIB par catégories de dépense (1)					GDP by kind of economic activity (2) / PIB par branches d'activité économique (2)			
			Final consumption / Consommation finale		Gross capital formation / Formation brute de capital	Exports / Exportations / Of goods and services	Less imports / Moins les importations / Des biens et services	Agriculture (3)	Industry (4) / Industrie (4)		Services (5)
			Government / Administration publique	Household / Ménages					Total	Manufacturing / Activités de fabrication	
			Percentage / En pourcentage								
WORLD - MONDE	1990	22 059 825	17.3	59.5	23.5	19.6	19.9	6.0	33.5	22.5	60.5
	1995	29 556 282	16.8	60.1	22.6	21.8	21.4	4.4	30.6	20.6	65.0
	2000	31 678 619	16.3	61.3	22.3	25.2	25.1	3.8	29.1	19.3	67.1
	2005	44 475 204	18.1	60.7	21.0	28.3	28.1	3.9	28.3	17.8	67.8
DEVELOPED ECONOMIES - ÉCONOMIES DÉVELOPPÉES	1990	17 304 955	17.9	59.7	22.9	18.2	18.7	2.7	31.8	21.4	65.4
	1995	23 287 869	17.6	60.4	21.4	19.5	18.8	2.2	29.2	19.8	68.6
	2000	24 577 132	17.0	62.1	21.7	21.9	22.6	1.8	26.9	18.2	71.3
	2005	33 314 361	19.6	62.4	19.4	24.0	25.4	1.6	24.9	15.9	73.5
DEVELOPING ECONOMIES - ÉCONOMIES EN DÉVELOPPEMENT	1990	3 810 973	13.9	59.7	25.0	25.0	24.0	14.9	35.9	22.1	49.2
	1995	5 653 956	13.5	59.4	27.5	30.6	31.2	12.8	35.9	22.8	51.3
	2000	6 659 394	13.8	58.6	24.6	36.4	33.6	10.8	36.7	22.9	52.5
	2005	9 962 981	13.3	55.9	26.0	41.1	36.9	10.5	37.8	23.5	51.7
ECONOMIES IN TRANSITION - ÉCONOMIES EN TRANSITION	1990	943 896	19.8	53.6	28.9	24.1	26.7	19.1	45.1	34.6	35.7
	1995	614 457	19.3	56.5	24.3	32.3	32.3	11.4	36.8	27.5	51.8
	2000	442 093	16.2	54.0	19.4	44.7	34.3	10.5	36.4	27.0	53.1
	2005	1 197 861	17.0	53.1	22.3	38.8	32.2	8.1	36.7	18.7	55.3
Developed economies: America - Économies développées : Amérique	1990	6 365 714	17.5	65.7	18.0	11.4	12.6	2.0	27.8	18.2	70.2
	1995	7 971 882	15.8	66.9	18.2	13.3	14.2	1.6	26.2	17.8	72.2
	2000	10 551 983	14.7	68.0	20.5	14.0	17.1	1.4	24.1	16.1	74.4
	2005	13 678 531	19.0	68.9	16.9	13.2	18.0	1.1	21.4	12.7	77.5
Bermuda - Bermudes	1990	2 023	12.5	69.1	16.4	47.5	43.7	0.8	10.4	2.4	88.9
	1995	2 577	11.8	64.3	14.0	45.5	36.0	0.8	10.4	2.4	88.8
	2000	3 522	10.9	51.5	20.1	47.3	34.4	0.7	11.0	2.4	88.4
	2005	4 090	11.0	51.8	19.2	47.1	34.2	0.7	9.9	2.0	89.4
Canada	1990	574 204	22.5	56.2	21.2	26.0	26.0	2.9	31.3	16.9	65.8
	1995	581 664	21.5	56.4	19.0	37.7	34.6	2.9	30.7	18.4	66.4
	2000	714 453	18.8	54.8	20.5	46.1	40.3	2.3	33.2	19.2	64.5
	2005	1 131 760	19.3	55.4	21.5	37.9	34.1	2.3	31.8	18.3	65.9
United States - États-Unis	1990	5 789 487	17.0	66.7	17.6	10.0	11.3	1.9	27.5	18.3	70.6
	1995	7 387 641	15.3	67.7	18.1	11.4	12.6	1.5	25.8	17.8	72.6
	2000	9 834 008	14.4	68.9	20.5	11.7	15.4	1.4	23.5	15.9	75.1
	2005	12 542 682	19.0	70.1	16.5	11.0	16.6	1.0	20.5	12.2	78.5
Developed economies: Asia - Économies développées : Asie	1990	3 052 658	13.7	53.0	32.4	11.0	10.1	2.5	38.1	25.9	59.4
	1995	5 301 247	15.5	55.4	27.9	9.6	8.3	1.9	33.1	22.4	65.1
	2000	4 770 639	17.2	56.3	25.1	11.7	10.3	1.7	30.9	21.2	67.4
	2005	4 688 598	18.2	57.4	23.1	15.1	13.8	1.7	29.4	20.2	68.9
Israel - Israël	1990	56 923	28.5	55.0	19.8	31.0	34.9	3.0	25.6	18.5	71.5
	1995	94 588	28.0	55.2	25.1	29.1	37.3	2.1	26.1	16.9	71.8
	2000	121 023	26.6	53.3	20.6	37.9	38.5	1.6	24.6	17.6	73.8
	2005	129 648	26.9	56.2	17.2	43.8	44.1	1.7	22.6	15.5	75.7
Japan - Japon	1990	2 995 736	13.4	53.0	32.6	10.6	9.6	2.5	38.4	26.0	59.2
	1995	5 206 658	15.2	55.4	28.0	9.2	7.8	1.9	33.2	22.4	64.9
	2000	4 649 615	16.9	56.4	25.2	11.0	9.6	1.7	31.1	21.3	67.2
	2005	4 558 950	18.0	57.4	23.2	14.3	12.9	1.6	29.6	20.3	68.8
Developed economies: Europe - Économies développées : Europe	1990	7 532 437	20.0	57.4	23.2	26.8	27.3	3.4	32.7	22.6	63.8
	1995	9 569 362	20.2	57.8	20.3	30.0	28.3	2.7	29.6	20.3	67.6
	2000	8 802 179	19.6	58.4	21.3	36.6	35.9	2.2	28.1	19.3	69.6
	2005	14 128 179	20.6	58.0	20.2	37.7	36.5	2.0	27.3	18.2	70.7
Andorra - Andorre	1990	1 371	16.2	60.9	27.3	15.7	19.7	5.5	33.0	21.7	61.5
	1995	1 554	18.1	60.0	21.9	22.4	22.4	1.0	17.4	5.2	81.6
	2000	1 360	17.2	59.7	26.3	29.0	32.2	0.9	17.3	4.5	81.8
	2005	3 091	17.8	57.7	29.7	25.4	30.6	3.3	29.5	15.9	67.2

For sources and notes, see end of table.

Pour les sources et les notes, se reporter à la fin du tableau.

8.3.1 Nominal gross domestic product by type of expenditure and by kind of economic activity of countries and geographical regions

8.3.1 Produit intérieur brut nominal par catégories de dépenses et par branches d'activité économique des pays et des régions géographiques

Region, country or territory / Régions, pays ou territoires	Year / Année	Total GDP (millions of dollars) / PIB total (millions de dollars)	GDP by type of expenditure (1) / PIB par catégories de dépense (1)					GDP by kind of economic activity (2) / PIB par branches d'activité économique (2)			
			Final consumption / Consommation finale		Gross capital formation / Formation brute de capital	Exports / Exportations	Less imports / Moins les importations	Agri-culture (3)	Industry (4) / Industrie (4)		Services (5)
			Government / Administration publique	Household / Ménages		Of goods and services / Des biens et services			Total	Manu-facturing / Activités de fabrication	
			Percentage / En pourcentage								
Austria - Autriche	1990	164 988	18.7	56.9	23.9	37.7	36.8	4.0	31.8	21.4	64.2
	1995	239 576	20.1	57.1	23.4	35.1	35.4	2.7	30.4	19.3	66.9
	2000	193 838	18.4	56.8	23.4	45.4	44.1	2.1	30.9	20.3	67.0
	2005	306 065	17.7	55.5	21.2	53.2	47.8	1.6	29.7	19.4	68.6
Belgium - Belgique	2005	370 815	23.1	53.2	21.4	87.1	84.8	1.0	24.0	16.8	74.9
Belgium-Luxembourg - Belgique-Luxembourg	1990	215 359	19.7	54.8	22.4	71.4	68.7	2.3	30.7	22.5	67.0
	1995	305 002	21.2	53.4	20.0	70.4	64.9	1.5	27.9	19.8	70.7
	2000	252 203	20.8	52.9	21.9	89.9	85.5	1.3	26.3	18.6	72.4
Cyprus - Chypre	1990	5 777	14.8	61.2	26.8	55.5	57.6	6.9	25.9	14.3	67.2
	1995	9 168	13.7	64.8	21.8	50.2	50.5	5.1	22.8	12.1	72.0
	2000	9 124	16.4	65.4	18.7	54.7	55.1	3.6	19.5	10.2	76.9
	2005	16 723	18.1	64.5	21.3	47.3	51.2	3.4	19.9	9.3	76.7
Czechoslovakia (former) - Tchécoslovaquie (anc.)	1990	53 350	24.2	50.1	26.1	37.5	38.3	8.4	49.5	24.5	42.1
Czech Republic - République tchèque	1995	55 262	21.7	50.1	32.5	50.7	55.0	4.6	39.9	23.2	55.5
	2000	55 703	22.1	52.2	28.8	64.5	67.5	3.9	38.5	26.2	57.6
	2005	122 345	22.4	49.1	26.4	72.8	70.7	3.0	37.8	25.6	59.2
Denmark - Danemark	1990	135 839	25.1	50.3	19.9	37.2	32.6	4.0	25.6	17.4	70.4
	1995	181 985	25.2	51.2	19.5	37.6	33.5	3.5	25.1	17.1	71.5
	2000	160 082	25.1	47.7	21.2	46.6	40.6	2.6	26.8	16.2	70.6
	2005	258 718	25.9	48.5	20.9	48.6	43.9	2.1	23.9	13.3	74.0
Estonia - Estonie	1995	4 359	27.2	55.3	26.6	68.4	76.0	8.1	29.2	17.9	62.6
	2000	5 477	20.2	56.9	27.8	88.4	92.0	5.5	26.5	16.7	68.0
	2005	12 762	18.3	54.7	32.2	85.3	90.5	4.4	28.2	17.9	67.4
Finland - Finlande	1990	138 238	21.5	50.7	28.8	22.4	24.2	6.2	33.0	22.4	60.8
	1995	130 913	22.7	51.8	18.0	36.3	28.7	4.5	32.5	25.0	63.0
	2000	120 563	20.6	50.0	20.5	42.7	33.7	3.8	33.7	26.2	62.5
	2005	193 155	22.5	52.4	20.2	38.7	35.2	2.9	31.3	22.9	65.8
France	1990	1 239 858	21.7	57.3	22.3	21.3	22.7	3.8	26.6	18.0	69.7
	1995	1 570 990	23.6	56.6	18.6	22.8	21.6	3.3	24.5	16.5	72.2
	2000	1 328 689	22.9	55.7	20.5	28.6	27.7	2.8	22.9	16.0	74.3
	2005	2 127 781	23.7	57.1	20.2	26.1	27.1	2.2	20.9	13.3	76.9
Germany - Allemagne	1990	1 707 359	19.6	57.4	23.5	24.6	24.8	1.7	37.6	28.2	60.7
	1995	2 522 624	19.6	57.7	22.2	24.0	23.5	1.3	32.1	22.6	66.6
	2000	1 900 220	19.0	58.9	21.8	33.4	33.0	1.3	30.3	22.9	68.5
	2005	2 794 856	18.6	59.3	17.2	40.1	35.1	0.9	29.7	23.5	69.4
Greece - Grèce	1990	85 931	14.8	72.8	22.7	17.7	27.8	10.2	26.2	15.1	63.6
	1995	120 159	15.0	74.3	18.5	17.2	24.9	9.9	22.4	13.0	67.7
	2000	115 997	17.4	70.2	23.4	25.0	35.9	7.3	22.0	12.0	70.7
	2005	225 201	16.4	67.1	23.8	20.8	28.0	5.2	20.8	10.9	74.0
Hungary - Hongrie	1990	36 385	22.5	48.7	22.6	36.3	29.9	10.5	36.0	25.0	53.5
	1995	45 008	24.3	54.4	21.9	44.3	44.5	6.8	31.0	22.6	62.2
	2000	47 035	21.4	52.7	29.9	74.0	78.0	4.3	33.2	24.1	62.6
	2005	109 239	23.6	54.9	23.7	66.4	68.5	4.9	32.8	24.6	62.3
Iceland - Islande	1990	6 367	19.9	59.8	19.0	33.7	32.4	11.3	29.6	16.2	59.1
	1995	7 013	22.1	58.0	16.4	35.6	31.9	11.0	27.6	15.8	61.4
	2000	8 628	23.5	61.0	22.9	33.8	41.2	8.5	25.2	13.5	66.3
	2005	15 814	24.7	60.2	28.6	31.5	45.0	7.7	24.4	12.9	67.9
Ireland - Irlande	1990	47 856	16.2	59.3	20.8	56.7	51.8	8.9	35.1	28.1	56.0
	1995	67 106	16.3	54.3	18.2	76.2	64.4	7.0	38.0	30.1	55.0
	2000	96 166	13.8	47.2	25.1	98.6	85.0	3.4	42.5	33.4	54.0
	2005	201 763	15.8	43.9	26.9	80.4	67.2	2.5	39.0	29.2	58.5

For sources and notes, see end of table.

Pour les sources et les notes, se reporter à la fin du tableau.

8.3.1 Nominal gross domestic product by type of expenditure and by kind of economic activity of countries and geographical regions

8.3.1 Produit intérieur brut nominal par catégories de dépenses et par branches d'activité économique des pays et des régions géographiques

Region, country or territory / Régions, pays ou territoires	Year / Année	Total GDP (millions of dollars) / PIB total (millions de dollars)	GDP by type of expenditure (1) / PIB par catégories de dépense (1)					GDP by kind of economic activity (2) / PIB par branches d'activité économique (2)			
			Final consumption / Consommation finale		Gross capital formation / Formation brute de capital	Exports / Exportations — Of goods and services / Des biens et services	Less imports / Moins les importations	Agriculture (3)	Industry (4) / Industrie (4)		Services (5)
			Government / Administration publique	Household / Ménages					Total	Manufacturing / Activités de fabrication	
			Percentage / En pourcentage								
Italy - Italie	1990	1 133 465	20.1	57.3	22.3	19.2	19.0	3.5	32.1	23.3	64.4
	1995	1 126 077	18.0	58.4	19.8	25.7	21.9	3.3	30.3	22.2	66.4
	2000	1 097 343	18.4	59.9	20.7	27.1	26.1	2.8	28.4	21.0	68.8
	2005	1 762 475	20.3	58.9	20.9	26.3	26.4	2.3	26.9	18.4	70.9
Latvia - Lettonie	1995	4 890	24.4	63.5	14.3	42.7	44.9	9.0	29.8	20.2	61.2
	2000	7 726	21.0	63.0	23.6	41.8	49.4	4.5	23.3	13.4	72.2
	2005	15 244	18.8	61.8	33.0	48.3	63.0	4.3	22.4	13.4	73.3
Lithuania - Lituanie	1995	6 392	21.9	66.8	22.4	49.9	61.0	11.4	33.1	20.2	55.5
	2000	11 462	21.6	64.9	19.8	44.6	50.9	7.8	29.6	19.3	62.5
	2005	24 864	17.4	65.3	24.3	56.3	63.3	6.4	31.4	19.6	62.2
Luxembourg	2005	36 468	16.6	39.7	21.4	158.1	135.8	0.4	16.3	9.1	83.3
Malta - Malte	1990	2 458	18.9	65.0	27.7	78.5	91.1	3.6	29.5	23.2	66.9
	1995	3 449	22.0	63.3	26.5	86.4	98.9	2.9	27.3	20.8	69.7
	2000	3 793	19.7	64.5	25.9	94.6	104.7	2.3	29.6	23.6	68.1
	2005	5 573	21.7	65.7	23.1	71.2	81.7	2.5	25.5	19.3	72.0
Netherlands - Pays-Bas	1990	307 381	22.6	50.1	23.1	56.2	52.1	4.2	28.9	18.3	66.9
	1995	432 563	23.2	49.6	20.8	59.3	52.9	3.4	26.8	17.3	69.8
	2000	386 510	21.9	50.4	22.1	69.6	63.9	2.6	24.9	15.4	72.5
	2005	624 187	24.0	48.6	19.2	71.2	63.0	2.1	24.1	14.2	73.8
Norway - Norvège	1990	116 107	21.2	49.1	23.1	40.4	33.9	3.4	33.9	12.5	62.7
	1995	147 975	21.6	49.3	22.9	38.0	31.7	3.0	34.1	13.3	62.9
	2000	166 905	19.1	42.6	21.0	46.7	29.4	2.1	41.8	10.7	56.1
	2005	295 513	20.4	41.8	20.6	45.3	28.1	1.6	42.3	12.1	56.2
Poland - Pologne	1990	63 084	21.0	47.5	23.9	26.8	20.1	8.3	50.1	30.6	41.6
	1995	135 905	19.0	60.4	18.4	23.7	21.5	6.5	36.8	22.2	56.8
	2000	166 561	18.0	63.9	24.7	27.8	34.4	3.6	33.7	19.9	62.7
	2005	290 006	17.5	63.7	18.9	38.5	38.6	2.7	31.8	19.4	65.5
Portugal	1990	75 278	15.6	64.2	26.7	31.2	37.9	8.5	26.7	18.2	64.8
	1995	112 958	17.9	65.2	23.3	28.6	35.0	5.7	28.4	18.6	65.9
	2000	112 650	19.3	63.9	27.7	29.8	40.6	3.8	27.6	17.1	68.6
	2005	183 300	21.1	65.5	22.3	28.5	37.4	2.8	24.6	15.5	72.6
San Marino - Saint-Marin	1990	565	14.0	64.2	23.4	268.5	269.1	3.5	32.1	23.3	64.4
	1995	692	9.5	68.5	18.0	236.7	232.7	3.3	30.3	22.2	66.4
	2000	774	12.9	42.5	50.3	193.8	199.5	2.8	28.4	21.0	68.8
	2005	1 315	12.2	40.2	55.3	183.9	191.5	2.3	26.9	18.4	70.9
Slovakia - Slovaquie	1995	19 402	20.5	52.1	24.8	58.3	55.8	5.9	38.1	27.1	55.9
	2000	20 291	19.8	56.5	26.1	70.8	73.3	4.6	33.8	23.3	61.6
	2005	46 417	18.2	57.3	28.8	78.7	83.1	4.1	31.6	21.2	64.3
Slovenia - Slovénie	1995	20 019	19.7	59.6	22.5	51.7	53.6	4.2	35.8	26.8	60.0
	2000	19 098	19.8	57.1	26.7	56.1	59.7	3.2	36.5	26.8	60.4
	2005	34 030	19.6	55.4	25.3	64.8	65.2	2.9	35.8	26.5	61.3
Spain - Espagne	1990	526 441	16.2	60.9	27.3	15.7	19.7	5.5	33.0	21.7	61.5
	1995	596 755	18.1	60.0	21.9	22.4	22.4	4.5	29.4	19.5	66.1
	2000	580 673	17.2	59.7	26.3	29.0	32.2	4.4	29.2	18.6	66.4
	2005	1 124 612	17.8	57.7	29.7	25.4	30.6	3.3	29.5	15.9	67.2
Sweden - Suède	1990	242 179	27.2	49.2	23.3	29.8	29.7	3.3	30.5	20.1	66.2
	1995	250 641	27.0	49.5	17.0	39.2	32.7	2.7	30.3	22.3	67.0
	2000	242 003	26.4	49.4	18.3	45.9	40.0	1.9	28.6	22.0	69.5
	2005	357 683	27.2	48.0	17.1	48.6	40.9	1.1	28.2	20.5	70.7
Switzerland - Suisse	1990	237 236	11.1	57.0	30.5	35.7	34.4	2.8	31.3	20.8	65.9
	1995	317 236	11.7	59.8	23.4	35.4	30.3	2.0	29.8	20.0	68.2
	2000	248 527	11.1	60.0	23.2	45.7	40.0	1.5	26.8	18.8	71.7
	2005	369 369	11.4	60.3	21.5	47.9	41.1	1.2	26.5	18.4	72.3

For sources and notes, see end of table.

Pour les sources et les notes, se reporter à la fin du tableau.

8.3.1 Nominal gross domestic product by type of expenditure and by kind of economic activity of countries and geographical regions

8.3.1 Produit intérieur brut nominal par catégories de dépenses et par branches d'activité économique des pays et des régions géographiques

Region, country or territory / Régions, pays ou territoires	Year / Année	Total GDP (millions of dollars) / PIB total (millions de dollars)	GDP by type of expenditure (1) / PIB par catégories de dépense (1)					GDP by kind of economic activity (2) / PIB par branches d'activité économique (2)			
			Final consumption / Consommation finale		Gross capital formation / Formation brute de capital	Exports / Exportations	Less imports / Moins les importations	Agriculture (3)	Industry (4) / Industrie (4)		Services (5)
			Government / Administration publique	Household / Ménages	Formation brute de capital	Of goods and services / Des biens et services			Total	Manufacturing / Activités de fabrication	
			Percentage / En pourcentage								
United Kingdom - Royaume-Uni	1990	989 564	19.8	62.6	20.2	24.0	26.6	1.8	34.0	22.4	64.2
	1995	1 133 690	19.5	64.0	17.0	28.3	28.8	1.8	30.9	21.1	67.3
	2000	1 442 777	18.8	65.7	17.5	28.0	30.1	1.0	27.2	17.4	71.8
	2005	2 198 796	21.8	65.3	16.8	26.1	30.0	..	..	..	..
Developed economies: Oceania - Économies développées : Océanie	1990	354 146	18.8	59.0	22.0	17.9	18.1	4.2	28.7	14.2	67.1
	1995	445 378	18.2	59.1	22.9	20.5	20.7	4.3	28.0	15.1	67.7
	2000	452 331	18.1	59.6	22.0	24.0	23.7	4.5	25.9	13.1	69.6
	2005	819 053	18.2	57.9	25.9	20.2	22.4	4.3	26.0	13.0	69.6
Australia - Australie	1990	310 528	18.7	58.8	22.3	16.7	16.8	3.8	29.0	13.6	67.1
	1995	384 096	18.3	59.2	22.8	19.2	19.5	3.8	28.3	14.6	67.9
	2000	399 658	18.2	59.6	22.1	22.4	22.3	4.0	26.1	12.7	70.0
	2005	709 446	18.2	57.7	26.2	19.0	21.1	3.7	26.3	12.5	69.9
New Zealand - Nouvelle-Zélande	1990	43 618	19.2	61.1	19.5	27.0	26.8	6.7	26.8	18.0	66.5
	1995	61 282	17.5	58.4	23.3	29.0	28.2	7.2	25.9	17.9	66.9
	2000	52 673	17.5	59.2	21.6	35.5	33.8	8.6	24.4	16.3	66.9
	2005	109 607	18.5	59.5	24.5	28.0	30.5	8.1	24.2	16.0	67.7
Developing economies: Africa - Économies en développement : Afrique	1990	508 443	15.4	64.1	19.8	28.0	26.2	18.2	38.1	16.7	43.7
	1995	531 146	15.3	68.7	18.4	26.7	30.1	17.8	34.4	15.2	47.8
	2000	599 779	14.4	62.2	17.1	33.4	27.1	16.6	37.0	13.0	46.4
	2005	947 747	14.3	60.8	19.2	37.9	31.8	16.7	36.8	12.0	46.5
Eastern Africa - Afrique orientale	1990	55 962	15.9	74.0	18.8	19.1	27.3	33.7	22.6	15.1	43.8
	1995	55 521	14.2	76.8	19.0	26.1	35.7	34.2	18.8	11.5	46.9
	2000	63 636	13.8	77.8	18.7	22.5	32.4	33.9	17.6	10.4	48.4
	2005	88 110	14.9	76.9	21.8	26.4	39.4	32.8	19.1	10.1	48.1
Burundi	1990	1 148	19.5	83.0	15.8	8.0	26.2	52.4	21.1	16.8	26.5
	1995	1 003	10.6	90.0	12.3	17.1	30.4	48.2	19.2	12.1	32.6
	2000	711	11.7	89.5	9.9	10.3	23.7	40.4	18.8	13.1	40.8
	2005	845	17.9	89.2	12.7	12.2	34.9	40.7	18.8	13.1	40.6
Comoros - Comores	1990	250	24.5	78.7	19.7	14.3	37.1	40.4	8.1	4.1	51.5
	1995	232	22.3	83.1	19.5	19.8	44.6	39.9	11.7	4.1	48.5
	2000	204	13.3	88.3	13.1	15.1	27.0	39.9	11.7	4.1	48.5
	2005	380	12.6	91.8	10.9	15.0	30.4	40.0	11.6	4.1	48.4
Djibouti	1990	457	33.6	67.2	27.1	81.4	109.3	3.1	22.0	3.6	74.9
	1995	510	35.4	62.6	18.7	39.2	55.8	3.2	15.4	2.9	81.3
	2000	553	25.8	82.1	12.2	44.0	63.6	3.5	15.2	3.0	81.3
	2005	705	25.9	78.6	13.5	44.4	61.5	3.5	15.6	3.1	80.9
Ethiopia (former) - Éthiopie (anc.)	1990	8 128	19.2	72.9	12.5	7.7	12.2	41.1	16.4	11.1	42.5
Eritrea - Érythrée	1995	598	57.8	80.0	22.9	22.5	83.2	11.2	22.7	14.4	66.2
	2000	634	63.8	70.9	31.9	15.1	81.8	15.1	23.0	11.2	61.9
	2005	1 077	39.6	88.4	23.7	9.1	60.7	14.8	23.8	11.1	61.4
Ethiopia - Éthiopie	1995	5 502	10.8	82.5	16.4	14.3	24.1	55.1	10.0	6.2	34.9
	2000	6 473	23.8	75.3	15.9	15.1	30.0	46.4	10.2	6.3	43.4
	2005	9 297	23.4	72.8	26.7	18.0	39.9	43.9	11.1	6.9	45.1
Kenya	1990	11 104	17.9	70.1	17.9	20.1	24.5	29.7	21.0	14.1	49.3
	1995	11 772	14.1	77.3	16.1	25.2	30.3	32.3	17.9	12.1	49.7
	2000	12 705	15.1	78.3	17.4	22.2	30.2	32.5	17.3	11.5	50.2
	2005	19 184	16.9	79.6	19.5	26.9	42.9	27.7	17.3	10.9	55.0
Madagascar	1990	3 080	8.0	86.0	17.0	15.9	26.9	28.6	12.8	11.6	58.6
	1995	3 160	6.2	89.9	11.3	24.1	31.4	32.3	14.8	13.5	52.8
	2000	3 878	6.8	85.5	15.0	30.7	33.0	30.0	16.7	14.9	53.4
	2005	4 950	8.4	81.7	24.8	31.2	46.1	29.4	16.9	14.9	53.7

For sources and notes, see end of table.

Pour les sources et les notes, se reporter à la fin du tableau.

8.3.1 Nominal gross domestic product by type of expenditure and by kind of economic activity of countries and geographical regions

8.3.1 Produit intérieur brut nominal par catégories de dépenses et par branches d'activité économique des pays et des régions géographiques

Region, country or territory / Régions, pays ou territoires	Year / Année	Total GDP (millions of dollars) PIB total (millions de dollars)	GDP by type of expenditure (1) PIB par catégories de dépense (1)					GDP by kind of economic activity (2) PIB par branches d'activité économique (2)			
			Final consumption Consommation finale		Gross capital formation Formation brute de capital	Exports Exportations	Less imports Moins les importations	Agriculture (3)	Industry (4) Industrie (4)		Services (5)
			Government Administration publique	Household Ménages		Of goods and services Des biens et services			Total	Manufacturing Activités de fabrication	
			Percentage / En pourcentage								
Malawi	1990	1 752	16.2	91.6	17.1	25.3	36.2	45.0	28.9	19.5	26.1
	1995	1 423	20.6	76.1	17.1	33.0	46.7	30.4	19.6	15.8	50.0
	2000	1 744	14.6	81.1	14.5	25.1	35.3	39.5	17.9	12.9	42.5
	2005	2 140	16.1	92.7	11.3	25.7	45.7	39.6	16.5	11.5	43.9
Mauritius - Maurice	1990	2 588	12.7	64.6	30.3	66.8	74.3	12.1	33.7	25.9	54.3
	1995	4 042	13.1	63.7	25.6	58.6	61.1	10.0	30.9	22.2	59.1
	2000	4 552	13.0	61.9	25.6	61.8	62.4	6.5	29.8	22.4	63.7
	2005	6 288	13.4	67.4	24.4	61.5	65.1	5.2	25.9	18.5	69.0
Mozambique	1990	2 708	12.0	102.3	19.7	6.1	38.3	37.1	18.4	11.7	44.5
	1995	2 291	9.7	99.4	30.6	12.6	52.4	33.9	14.2	7.4	51.9
	2000	3 832	11.5	80.1	33.5	12.7	37.8	23.6	24.1	12.0	52.3
	2005	6 682	12.8	65.8	24.1	33.6	36.3	21.8	25.3	12.7	52.8
Rwanda	1990	2 541	10.2	84.4	13.9	5.7	14.1	43.6	23.6	15.8	32.8
	1995	1 283	9.2	100.6	13.5	5.8	29.1	44.0	16.0	10.2	40.0
	2000	1 732	8.9	90.2	18.0	6.3	23.4	40.7	19.7	10.0	39.7
	2005	2 118	13.8	87.2	21.5	9.5	31.4	42.1	19.9	9.3	38.0
Seychelles	1990	369	27.7	52.0	24.6	62.5	66.7	5.7	19.1	11.9	75.2
	1995	508	27.7	51.0	30.1	54.0	62.7	4.5	24.4	13.6	71.1
	2000	618	26.2	38.2	35.1	83.4	85.9	3.0	31.0	20.5	66.0
	2005	699	23.0	84.7	11.7	96.8	116.2	3.0	30.9	19.2	66.1
Somalia - Somalie	1990	994	10.3	71.0	23.6	0.9	5.7	69.3	6.0	2.0	24.7
	1995	1 122	8.5	72.2	20.7	0.3	1.7	60.1	7.3	2.5	32.6
	2000	2 070	8.6	72.4	20.4	0.3	1.7	60.1	7.3	2.5	32.6
	2005	2 182	8.7	72.4	20.3	0.3	1.7	60.1	7.3	2.5	32.6
Uganda - Ouganda	1990	3 652	9.7	82.0	14.7	6.9	17.7	52.8	12.5	6.4	34.7
	1995	6 046	11.6	77.4	16.8	10.9	19.4	46.5	16.0	7.9	37.5
	2000	5 734	13.7	80.6	18.9	10.7	23.6	36.9	20.1	9.3	43.0
	2005	9 115	14.2	76.2	22.7	13.2	26.3	33.4	21.1	9.4	45.4
United Republic of Tanzania - République-Unie de Tanzanie	1990	4 683	10.3	76.0	35.0	11.8	33.5	44.2	15.3	8.3	40.6
	1995	5 404	15.3	83.9	19.8	24.1	41.5	44.9	14.1	6.9	41.0
	2000	9 331	6.6	83.4	17.6	14.6	23.0	43.7	15.3	7.3	41.0
	2005	12 937	7.3	80.3	22.2	22.9	30.4	44.9	16.6	6.7	38.5
Zambia - Zambie	1990	3 742	19.0	64.4	17.3	35.9	36.6	20.6	51.3	36.1	28.1
	1995	3 471	15.5	72.3	15.9	36.1	39.8	17.3	33.6	10.6	49.1
	2000	3 239	9.5	82.2	18.7	21.1	31.4	21.0	23.8	10.8	55.2
	2005	7 315	13.3	69.0	25.6	16.3	25.0	21.6	28.5	10.9	49.8
Zimbabwe	1990	8 767	19.4	63.1	17.4	22.9	22.8	16.1	32.4	22.3	51.5
	1995	7 153	17.9	59.3	25.4	38.0	40.7	14.9	28.5	21.4	56.6
	2000	5 628	16.4	70.7	13.1	32.7	32.9	20.2	16.5	11.7	63.3
	2005	2 198	26.3	91.9	4.5	61.4	84.1	16.7	36.8	23.3	46.6
Middle Africa - Afrique centrale	*1990*	*45 106*	*16.5*	*66.5*	*13.8*	*31.2*	*27.8*	*20.6*	*34.6*	*11.6*	*44.7*
	1995	*29 500*	*16.8*	*59.1*	*19.0*	*42.2*	*37.2*	*25.1*	*38.1*	*11.5*	*36.8*
	2000	*35 466*	*17.8*	*47.8*	*18.0*	*52.1*	*35.7*	*19.0*	*49.8*	*8.9*	*31.2*
	2005	*78 325*	*13.4*	*52.2*	*16.3*	*58.5*	*40.6*	*16.8*	*52.8*	*9.0*	*30.4*
Angola	1990	10 295	28.6	44.8	11.7	39.0	23.7	18.0	40.8	4.9	41.2
	1995	4 994	52.3	21.9	27.9	76.2	78.2	7.4	67.4	4.0	25.2
	2000	9 130	42.5	15.6	15.1	89.6	62.8	5.7	73.1	2.9	21.2
	2005	28 853	22.3	49.2	11.3	78.8	61.6	7.6	67.2	3.6	25.2
Cameroon - Cameroun	1990	14 310	11.4	76.7	15.0	17.9	21.1	18.2	32.9	19.2	48.9
	1995	9 074	8.7	72.2	13.3	23.6	17.8	23.5	31.1	21.5	45.4
	2000	9 287	9.5	70.2	16.7	23.3	19.7	22.0	35.5	20.7	42.5
	2005	16 823	10.0	69.5	16.2	20.9	17.6	22.1	32.5	20.5	45.3

For sources and notes, see end of table.

Pour les sources et les notes, se reporter à la fin du tableau.

8.3.1 Nominal gross domestic product by type of expenditure and by kind of economic activity of countries and geographical regions

8.3.1 Produit intérieur brut nominal par catégories de dépenses et par branches d'activité économique des pays et des régions géographiques

Region, country or territory / Régions, pays ou territoires	Year / Année	Total GDP (millions of dollars) PIB total (millions de dollars)	GDP by type of expenditure (1) PIB par catégories de dépense (1)					GDP by kind of economic activity (2) PIB par branches d'activité économique (2)			
			Final consumption Consommation finale		Gross capital formation Formation brute de capital	Exports Exportations	Less imports Moins les importations	Agriculture (3)	Industry (4) Industrie (4)		Services (5)
			Government Administration publique	Household Ménages		Of goods and services Des biens et services			Total	Manufacturing Activités de fabrication	
			Percentage / En pourcentage								
Central African Republic - République centrafricaine	1990	1 297	14.9	85.7	12.3	14.8	27.6	43.0	16.8	9.5	40.2
	1995	1 058	14.7	80.4	13.8	15.2	25.8	41.8	18.1	10.2	40.1
	2000	906	15.3	83.4	9.1	13.3	22.2	51.2	17.6	9.9	31.2
	2005	1 325	8.6	93.9	5.6	13.0	21.5	52.2	19.0	10.7	28.8
Chad - Tchad	1990	1 539	21.3	96.3	10.1	18.2	45.9	38.3	19.3	16.2	42.4
	1995	1 444	16.1	87.3	10.3	23.3	37.2	37.6	16.8	14.3	45.6
	2000	1 386	7.6	86.9	23.3	16.9	34.7	39.9	14.5	12.1	45.6
	2005	4 942	5.0	44.3	25.1	63.9	38.4	33.5	22.6	19.2	43.9
Congo	1990	2 799	13.8	62.4	15.9	53.7	45.8	12.9	40.6	10.9	46.5
	1995	2 116	13.0	49.4	36.6	64.7	63.6	10.5	44.9	12.3	44.7
	2000	3 220	11.1	27.7	19.7	81.8	40.3	5.4	73.9	3.6	20.7
	2005	5 528	13.2	35.6	23.5	74.7	47.0	6.1	67.0	5.4	26.9
Dem. Rep. of the Congo - Rép. dém. du Congo	1990	9 187	13.0	77.9	9.1	31.8	31.8	31.0	29.0	10.2	40.0
	1995	5 643	4.9	79.3	11.0	28.5	23.7	57.0	17.0	6.0	26.0
	2000	5 256	7.5	81.7	11.0	6.5	6.7	50.0	20.3	4.8	29.7
	2005	7 212	6.5	82.8	12.4	21.4	23.1	52.0	21.4	5.2	26.6
Equatorial Guinea - Guinée équatoriale	1990	133	11.4	69.2	54.4	31.8	66.8	61.9	10.6	1.6	27.6
	1995	166	13.0	41.2	79.2	55.9	89.3	55.3	28.2	1.0	16.5
	2000	1 216	4.7	18.1	61.3	105.1	89.2	8.3	88.1	0.2	3.7
	2005	5 651	2.0	11.2	26.4	99.8	38.7	5.0	91.2	4.2	3.8
Gabon	1990	5 489	13.4	49.7	21.7	46.0	30.9	7.3	43.0	6.8	49.7
	1995	4 959	11.8	41.3	23.3	59.4	35.7	8.0	52.4	7.6	39.6
	2000	5 019	9.7	32.0	21.6	69.7	33.0	6.4	53.2	7.8	40.4
	2005	7 919	8.5	37.1	22.5	61.7	29.9	7.8	56.2	8.2	36.1
São Tome and Principe - Sao Tomé-et-Principe	1990	58	27.6	114.8	15.6	14.5	72.5	27.6	17.9	4.3	54.5
	1995	45	27.6	83.8	68.1	20.6	100.1	26.4	19.6	5.0	53.9
	2000	46	31.6	80.2	35.8	33.4	81.0	20.5	17.0	4.4	62.5
	2005	73	36.2	80.1	33.6	35.8	85.5	18.0	15.4	3.9	66.5
Northern Africa - Afrique septentrionale	*1990*	*184 653*	*15.5*	*61.8*	*26.2*	*27.1*	*30.2*	*15.2*	*39.0*	*13.6*	*45.8*
	1995	*201 224*	*14.7*	*67.6*	*20.8*	*24.3*	*28.1*	*16.3*	*36.2*	*14.3*	*47.5*
	2000	*252 983*	*14.2*	*62.1*	*19.9*	*29.0*	*25.1*	*13.7*	*39.4*	*13.0*	*46.9*
	2005	*346 013*	*12.6*	*56.1*	*24.3*	*38.5*	*30.6*	*13.6*	*41.4*	*11.7*	*45.0*
Algeria - Algérie	1990	61 891	16.2	56.6	28.9	23.4	25.1	11.9	48.3	11.6	39.8
	1995	42 066	17.0	55.6	31.6	26.6	30.7	10.3	47.9	8.9	41.8
	2000	54 790	13.6	41.6	23.5	42.1	20.7	8.8	56.7	6.0	34.5
	2005	102 257	7.2	38.5	32.1	46.3	24.1	8.3	53.3	6.1	38.4
Egypt - Égypte	1990	39 412	8.6	71.5	28.3	27.4	33.8	16.2	34.0	18.6	49.8
	1995	68 653	10.4	76.9	16.6	20.8	26.6	17.3	31.6	17.7	51.1
	2000	99 601	11.1	76.8	17.7	19.1	24.7	14.1	31.4	16.9	54.5
	2005	101 406	12.0	78.9	18.6	20.7	26.9	13.4	32.3	16.4	54.3
Libyan Arab Jamahiriya - Jamahiriya arabe libyenne	1990	28 905	24.4	48.4	18.6	39.7	31.1	8.7	46.0	6.3	45.4
	1995	25 540	22.3	58.8	12.2	29.2	22.4	8.7	46.4	7.0	44.9
	2000	34 265	20.6	46.4	13.0	35.2	15.3	8.1	53.7	5.0	38.2
	2005	37 173	11.6	20.9	20.3	80.0	32.9	4.6	68.1	2.6	27.4
Morocco - Maroc	1990	25 824	15.5	64.6	25.2	24.6	29.9	18.6	34.1	19.4	47.2
	1995	32 985	17.8	68.5	20.7	22.9	29.6	15.2	34.2	19.0	50.6
	2000	33 335	19.1	63.8	23.7	26.2	32.8	14.3	32.9	18.1	52.8
	2005	51 461	21.6	63.5	24.6	33.0	42.8	16.0	31.4	17.3	52.6
Sudan - Soudan	1990	16 307	12.8	76.3	25.6	9.8	24.5	30.3	17.0	9.4	52.7
	1995	13 950	5.8	78.2	19.6	3.3	7.4	50.9	13.0	8.1	36.1
	2000	11 549	7.7	76.9	17.9	15.5	18.0	46.4	21.4	7.5	32.2
	2005	24 667	15.8	65.3	20.9	21.0	23.2	45.6	24.3	8.1	30.1

For sources and notes, see end of table.

Pour les sources et les notes, se reporter à la fin du tableau.

8.3.1 Nominal gross domestic product by type of expenditure and by kind of economic activity of countries and geographical regions

8.3.1 Produit intérieur brut nominal par catégories de dépenses et par branches d'activité économique des pays et des régions géographiques

Region, country or territory / Régions, pays ou territoires	Year / Année	Total GDP (millions of dollars) PIB total (millions de dollars)	GDP by type of expenditure (1) PIB par catégories de dépense (1)					GDP by kind of economic activity (2) PIB par branches d'activité économique (2)			
			Final consumption Consommation finale		Gross capital formation Formation brute de capital	Exports Exportations	Less imports Moins les importations	Agriculture (3)	Industry (4) Industrie (4)		Services (5)
			Government Administration publique	Household Ménages		Of goods and services Des biens et services			Total	Manufacturing Activités de fabrication	
			Percentage / En pourcentage								
Tunisia - Tunisie	1990	12 314	16.4	63.6	27.1	43.6	50.6	17.1	32.4	18.4	50.4
	1995	18 030	16.3	62.9	24.7	44.9	48.8	12.6	32.5	21.0	54.9
	2000	19 444	15.6	60.7	27.3	44.5	48.2	13.8	31.9	20.4	54.3
	2005	29 049	16.0	62.8	24.5	44.1	48.7	12.8	30.2	19.5	57.0
Southern Africa - Afrique australe	*1990*	*119 332*	*20.0*	*60.5*	*18.8*	*26.0*	*21.7*	*4.9*	*40.7*	*22.9*	*54.4*
	1995	*161 337*	*18.9*	*62.2*	*18.7*	*24.5*	*24.5*	*4.2*	*35.2*	*20.7*	*60.6*
	2000	*143 427*	*18.8*	*62.2*	*16.3*	*30.0*	*27.2*	*3.6*	*32.4*	*18.4*	*63.9*
	2005	*257 729*	*20.6*	*62.7*	*18.1*	*28.6*	*29.9*	*3.9*	*32.6*	*18.8*	*63.6*
Botswana	1990	3 489	24.0	31.8	38.0	56.4	50.1	4.9	61.1	5.2	34.0
	1995	4 423	28.9	34.7	25.7	49.5	38.9	4.1	49.6	5.3	46.2
	2000	4 889	30.2	31.4	20.4	61.4	41.8	2.8	48.8	5.2	48.4
	2005	8 850	32.3	27.1	29.9	43.6	33.8	2.5	49.0	4.4	48.5
Lesotho	1990	618	14.0	138.2	53.0	16.7	121.9	21.4	30.2	12.6	48.3
	1995	933	17.9	120.4	60.5	21.3	120.2	17.2	38.0	15.4	44.7
	2000	859	19.1	101.3	42.2	29.8	92.4	17.8	39.5	16.2	42.7
	2005	1 335	24.6	104.4	39.1	51.8	123.0	17.1	40.0	18.9	42.9
Namibia - Namibie	1990	2 340	30.8	50.7	33.8	52.1	67.7	11.9	38.6	14.0	49.5
	1995	3 503	30.2	56.6	21.7	49.5	55.7	12.0	27.6	12.9	60.4
	2000	3 414	28.8	59.9	19.5	45.6	51.2	10.8	28.0	11.0	61.2
	2005	6 130	24.7	55.9	25.6	40.9	44.5	10.6	29.8	11.6	59.6
South Africa - Afrique du Sud	1990	112 014	19.7	61.0	17.7	24.2	18.8	4.6	40.1	23.6	55.3
	1995	151 113	18.3	62.6	18.2	22.8	22.1	3.9	34.8	21.2	61.3
	2000	132 878	18.1	63.0	15.9	27.9	24.9	3.3	31.8	19.0	64.9
	2005	238 825	19.9	63.9	17.4	27.1	28.3	3.6	31.9	19.4	64.6
Swaziland	1990	871	18.4	79.2	19.4	73.4	88.9	12.6	42.0	34.3	45.4
	1995	1 364	19.2	79.5	19.9	74.7	93.4	15.0	43.3	35.6	41.6
	2000	1 388	20.0	75.4	19.9	80.6	96.0	15.2	43.7	35.1	41.1
	2005	2 588	33.0	60.3	18.7	80.2	90.7	13.5	45.1	36.7	41.4
Western Africa - Afrique occidentale	*1990*	*103 390*	*9.1*	*66.0*	*12.5*	*35.3*	*22.9*	*28.5*	*43.9*	*18.7*	*27.6*
	1995	*83 564*	*10.3*	*81.9*	*11.3*	*31.5*	*39.7*	*32.4*	*38.6*	*11.1*	*29.0*
	2000	*104 266*	*8.3*	*58.0*	*9.9*	*49.4*	*25.7*	*28.4*	*45.8*	*9.1*	*25.8*
	2005	*177 569*	*8.9*	*62.9*	*10.6*	*46.7*	*29.0*	*31.6*	*36.0*	*6.0*	*32.3*
Benin - Bénin	1990	1 845	13.2	80.4	14.2	20.4	28.2	35.4	12.7	7.5	51.9
	1995	2 170	14.4	73.2	21.4	27.4	36.4	35.4	14.3	8.6	50.3
	2000	2 359	12.6	73.1	18.7	25.4	29.7	38.5	14.2	9.0	47.3
	2005	4 378	11.9	76.2	18.9	21.4	28.4	36.2	15.0	8.9	48.8
Burkina Faso	1990	3 120	21.5	72.7	18.8	10.9	23.9	28.6	20.8	14.2	50.6
	1995	2 665	23.1	66.7	21.4	12.6	23.8	31.4	18.9	12.0	49.7
	2000	2 415	24.3	66.6	26.5	9.8	27.2	34.6	17.9	11.1	47.4
	2005	5 397	22.4	69.1	22.7	9.6	23.9	26.9	20.2	13.3	52.9
Cape Verde - Cap-Vert	1990	308	18.9	88.9	43.6	17.1	68.6	15.2	22.6	7.9	62.3
	1995	491	22.8	86.3	40.8	16.6	66.5	14.6	20.4	7.3	65.1
	2000	539	18.9	86.7	30.7	20.9	57.3	13.9	16.5	5.6	69.7
	2005	1 038	25.0	82.3	22.5	31.9	61.6	11.5	15.6	4.6	72.9
Côte d'Ivoire	1990	11 893	20.7	69.1	6.1	28.8	24.6	29.7	24.0	19.8	46.3
	1995	11 105	16.9	64.1	14.1	37.0	32.1	29.7	24.9	20.2	45.4
	2000	10 682	15.5	67.2	11.3	39.8	33.8	27.6	30.5	25.0	41.9
	2005	16 785	15.7	67.5	12.0	40.2	35.2	27.3	23.6	17.8	49.1
Gambia - Gambie	1990	333	14.5	82.1	17.9	43.2	57.7	22.2	11.0	5.6	66.8
	1995	382	13.7	90.2	20.2	48.9	73.0	30.0	13.4	6.1	56.7
	2000	421	13.7	77.8	17.4	48.0	56.8	35.8	13.1	5.4	51.1
	2005	480	16.2	75.2	24.4	48.1	63.9	32.2	14.0	5.4	53.8

For sources and notes, see end of table.

Pour les sources et les notes, se reporter à la fin du tableau.

8.3.1 Nominal gross domestic product by type of expenditure and by kind of economic activity of countries and geographical regions

8.3.1 Produit intérieur brut nominal par catégories de dépenses et par branches d'activité économique des pays et des régions géographiques

Region, country or territory / Régions, pays ou territoires	Year / Année	Total GDP (millions of dollars) / PIB total (millions de dollars)	GDP by type of expenditure (1) / PIB par catégories de dépense (1)					GDP by kind of economic activity (2) / PIB par branches d'activité économique (2)			
			Final consumption / Consommation finale		Gross capital formation / Formation brute de capital	Exports / Exportations	Less imports / Moins les importations	Agriculture (3)	Industry (4) / Industrie (4)		Services (5)
			Government / Administration publique	Household / Ménages		Of goods and services / Des biens et services			Total	Manufacturing / Activités de fabrication	
			Percentage / En pourcentage								
Ghana	1990	6 226	10.9	85.5	12.3	15.4	24.0	42.0	27.4	10.3	30.6
	1995	6 458	12.1	76.2	20.0	24.5	32.8	42.7	26.7	10.3	30.6
	2000	4 978	7.8	86.7	24.0	49.0	67.5	36.0	25.4	9.4	38.6
	2005	10 393	11.4	79.6	23.3	40.5	54.8	36.7	24.9	9.3	38.4
Guinea - Guinée	1990	2 818	8.8	75.9	17.0	28.3	30.0	23.8	33.3	4.6	42.9
	1995	3 923	7.4	85.1	12.6	17.5	22.6	21.5	33.1	4.9	45.4
	2000	3 134	6.5	73.7	21.5	18.6	22.1	21.6	33.8	3.8	44.5
	2005	3 058	5.4	83.1	16.4	27.4	32.7	23.8	35.8	4.3	40.4
Guinea-Bissau - Guinée-Bissau	1990	233	11.4	100.9	14.7	12.0	39.0	44.6	18.2	..	37.2
	1995	248	6.4	94.8	22.3	11.7	35.1	54.8	15.3	..	29.8
	2000	215	17.6	71.5	15.1	31.8	36.0	58.8	12.3	..	28.9
	2005	298	16.9	78.6	20.4	30.9	46.7	56.8	12.9	..	30.3
Liberia - Libéria	1990	384	13.0	69.8	10.8	34.3	27.8	53.4	16.5	11.2	30.0
	1995	135	13.0	69.6	10.8	35.7	29.0	80.5	5.2	2.7	14.3
	2000	561	14.1	82.5	6.9	26.8	30.2	72.0	11.6	9.5	16.4
	2005	561	10.7	91.6	9.0	29.3	40.7	68.9	10.2	7.3	20.9
Mali	1990	2 510	15.2	79.0	22.2	17.3	33.7	47.8	13.5	8.1	38.8
	1995	2 721	19.3	72.4	25.3	19.5	36.4	49.5	18.7	10.5	31.8
	2000	2 670	16.4	74.6	19.7	24.1	34.7	41.6	20.6	11.5	37.9
	2005	5 181	14.3	73.7	20.3	25.0	33.3	35.9	27.1	15.2	37.0
Mauritania - Mauritanie	1990	1 022	16.6	78.3	19.5	43.4	57.8	28.9	30.3	13.3	40.9
	1995	1 058	21.9	58.2	20.4	47.6	48.1	26.4	31.3	13.7	42.2
	2000	928	21.2	73.0	15.7	42.5	52.4	21.8	31.2	13.7	47.1
	2005	1 672	20.7	74.2	16.1	42.6	53.6	21.1	29.4	12.9	49.5
Niger	1990	2 506	17.2	74.1	12.8	16.8	20.9	35.3	16.2	7.3	48.6
	1995	1 672	15.8	77.7	14.3	20.0	27.9	35.1	15.4	6.9	49.6
	2000	1 666	19.0	75.2	13.9	19.2	27.3	38.8	13.2	6.7	47.9
	2005	3 245	17.0	75.0	19.3	18.4	29.8	44.3	12.4	6.1	43.3
Nigeria - Nigéria	1990	61 873	4.4	59.6	11.9	43.2	19.1	26.4	58.7	22.8	14.9
	1995	43 881	6.2	89.8	5.8	34.7	45.7	32.3	51.3	10.2	16.4
	2000	67 359	5.2	49.1	5.4	58.9	13.6	26.8	57.1	7.0	16.1
	2005	113 461	5.5	56.3	6.1	55.4	23.3	32.5	43.4	2.8	24.1
Senegal - Sénégal	1990	5 698	14.7	76.4	13.8	25.4	30.3	19.9	18.7	13.1	61.4
	1995	4 476	12.4	79.0	16.7	32.1	40.2	20.2	19.8	13.4	60.0
	2000	4 374	14.0	72.9	22.9	29.7	39.6	19.6	19.8	12.1	60.6
	2005	8 274	16.0	75.4	22.1	27.9	40.8	14.7	20.1	12.3	65.2
Sierra Leone	1990	992	10.4	77.9	11.9	25.4	25.7	35.3	19.6	8.7	45.1
	1995	871	8.8	86.2	5.5	19.8	20.4	42.4	38.3	9.2	19.3
	2000	636	10.1	85.9	6.5	17.3	19.7	57.4	27.9	3.5	14.6
	2005	1 162	13.0	84.8	20.6	25.7	44.4	50.9	22.6	3.0	26.5
Togo	1990	1 628	14.2	71.1	26.6	33.5	45.3	33.8	22.5	6.2	43.7
	1995	1 309	12.1	76.7	16.1	32.4	37.4	37.8	22.2	6.1	40.1
	2000	1 329	10.2	92.0	17.8	30.7	50.7	34.2	17.8	4.9	47.9
	2005	2 187	9.3	87.2	18.5	33.7	48.7	40.0	21.1	5.8	38.8
Developing economies: America - Économies en développement : Amérique	**1990**	**1 123 193**	**13.9**	**63.1**	**21.1**	**16.6**	**14.8**	**8.0**	**33.2**	**22.3**	**58.8**
	1995	**1 720 950**	**15.5**	**63.8**	**21.5**	**16.7**	**17.7**	**8.0**	**31.8**	**20.1**	**60.2**
	2000	**2 009 383**	**14.9**	**64.8**	**21.2**	**21.6**	**22.5**	**6.5**	**31.8**	**19.2**	**61.7**
	2005	**2 486 993**	**14.7**	**62.5**	**21.0**	**25.9**	**24.1**	**7.3**	**32.4**	**19.0**	**60.3**
Caribbean - Caraïbes	*1990*	*60 260*	*22.4*	*59.2*	*23.8*	*40.1*	*45.8*	*9.8*	*23.9*	*11.6*	*66.3*
	1995	*71 162*	*20.9*	*63.3*	*18.2*	*33.4*	*36.5*	*7.0*	*26.0*	*15.2*	*66.9*
	2000	*89 519*	*20.7*	*64.5*	*19.9*	*36.6*	*41.5*	*6.7*	*26.2*	*13.7*	*67.2*
	2005	*125 729*	*22.4*	*61.6*	*18.0*	*34.9*	*37.0*	*5.7*	*24.9*	*12.6*	*69.4*

For sources and notes, see end of table.

Pour les sources et les notes, se reporter à la fin du tableau.

8.3.1 Nominal gross domestic product by type of expenditure and by kind of economic activity of countries and geographical regions

8.3.1 Produit intérieur brut nominal par catégories de dépenses et par branches d'activité économique des pays et des régions géographiques

Region, country or territory / Régions, pays ou territoires	Year / Année	Total GDP (millions of dollars) / PIB total (millions de dollars)	GDP by type of expenditure (1) / PIB par catégories de dépense (1)					GDP by kind of economic activity (2) / PIB par branches d'activité économique (2)			
			Final consumption / Consommation finale		Gross capital formation / Formation brute de capital	Exports / Exportations	Less imports / Moins les importations	Agriculture (3)	Industry (4) / Industrie (4)		Services (5)
			Government / Administration publique	Household / Ménages		Of goods and services / Des biens et services			Total	Manufacturing / Activités de fabrication	
			Percentage / En pourcentage								
Anguilla	1990	54	13.4	51.6	40.8	75.6	79.7	4.9	21.0	0.7	74.1
	1995	75	17.6	77.5	29.0	76.0	100.1	3.5	16.5	0.7	80.0
	2000	108	17.1	90.2	43.4	64.2	114.9	2.4	19.0	1.2	78.5
	2005	157	17.1	84.3	33.7	62.7	97.9	2.5	18.5	1.2	79.0
Antigua and Barbuda - Antigua-et-Barbuda	1990	392	18.0	47.6	32.4	89.0	87.0	4.0	19.0	3.2	77.0
	1995	494	21.4	50.5	36.9	81.4	90.1	3.6	17.2	2.2	79.2
	2000	665	22.3	34.3	48.0	70.3	74.9	3.6	18.3	2.1	78.1
	2005	856	22.4	35.3	50.2	63.5	71.3	3.5	19.3	2.1	77.2
Aruba	1990	828	13.3	45.5	30.6	80.1	69.2	0.6	16.1	1.4	83.3
	1995	1 321	20.0	50.5	31.1	84.9	86.5	0.5	15.6	2.7	83.9
	2000	1 859	22.0	50.0	24.6	74.4	71.0	0.4	16.0	3.8	83.6
	2005	2 258	26.6	52.4	31.6	63.2	73.8	0.4	15.7	3.5	83.9
Bahamas	1990	3 166	12.9	62.8	29.4	54.2	56.0	2.3	14.6	3.9	83.1
	1995	3 429	13.9	68.1	27.7	49.5	54.9	2.8	13.8	3.5	83.4
	2000	5 004	13.6	67.1	38.6	47.2	63.4	2.4	16.6	3.9	81.0
	2005	5 870	14.9	67.8	32.8	49.1	61.7	2.4	16.0	4.4	81.6
Barbados - Barbade	1990	1 720	20.2	63.6	18.8	49.1	51.7	5.4	18.3	8.0	76.3
	1995	1 871	20.1	61.6	15.2	58.2	55.0	6.3	15.6	6.7	78.2
	2000	2 559	21.2	66.9	18.5	50.5	57.0	4.3	16.3	6.4	79.4
	2005	2 996	21.2	70.2	20.3	49.9	60.7	3.9	16.2	6.7	79.9
British Virgin Islands - Îles Vierges britanniques	1990	108	13.6	45.4	25.5	100.4	85.0	2.7	11.6	2.9	85.7
	1995	397	13.9	49.9	25.4	92.2	81.4	1.8	13.3	3.6	84.9
	2000	784	10.5	40.5	23.2	104.3	78.6	1.1	11.4	3.4	87.5
	2005	972	9.2	37.1	22.4	108.8	77.7	0.9	10.7	2.7	88.4
Cayman Islands - Îles Caïmanes	1990	708	14.2	62.5	21.4	64.1	58.5	0.3	14.6	1.5	85.0
	1995	960	14.6	63.2	22.2	62.0	60.2	0.4	14.8	1.7	84.8
	2000	1 323	14.6	63.3	22.4	61.9	61.1	0.4	14.9	1.8	84.8
	2005	1 593	14.6	63.4	22.4	61.9	61.3	0.4	14.9	1.8	84.7
Cuba	1990	30 914	31.0	53.9	24.8	30.2	40.9	10.4	19.3	10.0	70.2
	1995	32 838	30.8	56.8	12.8	11.3	13.6	6.2	25.0	18.1	68.8
	2000	32 685	34.2	56.8	11.7	13.2	15.8	6.2	24.2	15.5	69.6
	2005	46 932	37.5	54.7	9.4	12.4	14.0	4.4	21.0	12.6	74.6
Dominica - Dominique	1990	167	20.3	64.1	40.8	50.1	75.3	24.1	17.1	6.6	58.8
	1995	219	20.8	63.8	31.5	50.9	67.0	17.3	20.1	6.8	62.7
	2000	269	22.6	64.0	27.7	53.7	68.0	16.7	21.6	8.1	61.8
	2005	283	18.7	73.5	25.0	49.5	66.6	16.4	20.3	7.5	63.3
Dominican Republic - République dominicaine	1990	7 074	2.7	79.4	21.6	43.7	47.2	13.3	31.5	21.6	55.3
	1995	11 935	5.1	78.8	19.5	47.5	50.9	10.1	30.3	19.6	59.6
	2000	19 772	8.4	77.8	23.8	44.9	54.9	9.8	31.0	18.9	59.1
	2005	29 101	9.8	74.0	19.9	34.0	37.7	9.9	26.3	16.6	63.8
Grenada - Grenade	1990	221	21.6	62.1	38.1	42.5	64.3	12.6	17.0	6.2	70.4
	1995	277	16.5	67.6	32.0	44.7	60.7	9.6	19.0	6.2	71.4
	2000	410	14.3	59.7	43.8	57.6	75.3	7.2	22.5	7.1	70.3
	2005	454	16.7	70.6	38.0	46.8	72.1	8.2	21.6	6.2	70.2
Haiti - Haïti	1990	2 614	8.0	81.3	14.3	18.1	21.7	35.8	22.6	15.5	41.6
	1995	2 334	7.8	100.5	13.8	10.9	33.0	33.2	18.0	7.5	48.8
	2000	3 515	8.8	97.1	12.9	13.8	31.7	27.2	16.1	7.8	56.7
	2005	3 884	5.8	105.7	12.9	14.7	37.0	26.8	16.3	8.0	57.0
Jamaica - Jamaïque	1990	4 271	14.0	62.3	27.7	51.7	55.8	6.0	40.4	18.4	53.5
	1995	5 796	11.1	70.4	28.8	50.7	61.0	8.4	34.5	15.1	57.0
	2000	7 889	15.8	68.8	26.8	43.1	54.5	6.3	29.6	13.0	64.1
	2005	10 063	11.0	72.4	32.9	40.5	57.5	5.8	30.2	13.0	64.0

For sources and notes, see end of table.

Four les sources et les notes, se reporter à la fin du tableau.

8.3.1 Nominal gross domestic product by type of expenditure and by kind of economic activity of countries and geographical regions

8.3.1 Produit intérieur brut nominal par catégories de dépenses et par branches d'activité économique des pays et des régions géographiques

Region, country or territory / Régions, pays ou territoires	Year / Année	Total GDP (millions of dollars) / PIB total (millions de dollars)	GDP by type of expenditure (1) / PIB par catégories de dépense (1)					GDP by kind of economic activity (2) / PIB par branches d'activité économique (2)			
			Final consumption / Consommation finale		Gross capital formation / Formation brute de capital	Exports / Exportations	Less imports / Moins les importations	Agriculture (3)	Industry (4) / Industrie (4)		Services (5)
			Government / Administration publique	Household / Ménages	Formation brute de capital	Of goods and services / Des biens et services			Total	Manufacturing / Activités de fabrication	
			Percentage / En pourcentage								
Montserrat	1990	67	17.7	61.6	73.4	28.6	81.4	2.5	37.6	2.3	60.0
	1995	60	22.7	61.8	35.4	61.2	81.1	5.4	13.0	3.0	81.6
	2000	35	50.8	62.4	46.6	48.7	108.6	1.3	20.6	0.7	78.1
	2005	42	51.6	71.5	50.8	43.2	117.2	1.2	24.7	0.6	74.1
Netherlands Antilles - Antilles néerlandaises	1990	1 980	40.7	40.1	29.8	82.8	92.8	0.6	15.2	7.4	84.1
	1995	2 571	25.6	62.6	24.2	76.7	90.1	0.7	16.5	7.7	82.8
	2000	2 798	23.2	52.5	28.5	82.5	86.7	0.6	14.1	6.2	85.3
	2005	3 204	24.2	55.8	23.3	90.2	93.4	0.8	14.1	5.7	85.1
Saint Kitts and Nevis - Saint-Kitts-et-Nevis	1990	159	18.0	57.9	55.4	51.7	83.1	6.1	27.4	12.1	66.5
	1995	230	20.4	56.5	46.5	51.5	74.9	5.0	23.5	10.0	71.6
	2000	329	21.1	59.3	49.6	45.6	75.5	2.6	27.1	9.8	70.3
	2005	453	31.9	36.7	45.0	53.5	67.1	2.9	27.1	9.5	70.0
Saint Lucia - Sainte-Lucie	1990	432	14.6	70.9	23.7	66.0	75.3	13.1	16.1	7.4	70.8
	1995	571	16.8	60.0	23.8	67.4	68.0	8.6	17.2	6.2	74.2
	2000	707	22.5	61.8	25.7	53.1	63.1	6.6	17.5	4.5	75.9
	2005	851	22.5	68.8	20.1	54.8	67.3	5.5	16.5	4.5	78.0
Saint Vincent and the Grenadines - Saint-Vincent-et-les Grenadines	1990	198	20.9	68.4	31.0	65.8	76.8	20.0	21.7	8.1	58.3
	1995	264	20.2	64.0	30.2	51.6	66.1	13.3	23.6	8.0	63.1
	2000	335	19.4	59.6	27.3	53.5	59.9	10.1	22.6	5.7	67.3
	2005	428	19.7	65.3	40.0	44.0	69.0	8.9	23.2	5.8	67.9
Trinidad and Tobago - Trinité-et-Tobago	1990	5 068	16.2	54.7	13.8	49.1	33.5	2.6	46.4	13.8	51.0
	1995	5 329	15.9	48.8	20.8	53.8	39.2	1.9	41.7	16.5	56.3
	2000	8 154	12.0	57.1	17.0	59.2	45.3	1.3	44.3	16.8	54.5
	2005	14 763	15.1	42.1	17.0	71.2	48.2	1.0	44.9	17.1	54.1
Turks and Caicos Islands - Îles Turques et Caïques	1990	119	27.6	51.0	30.8	62.2	71.9	1.3	16.4	4.4	82.3
	1995	191	25.7	57.0	32.9	64.1	79.7	1.3	16.4	4.3	82.3
	2000	319	15.2	30.8	26.3	78.5	50.8	1.5	15.6	3.5	82.9
	2005	570	17.1	38.2	39.0	64.8	59.2	1.3	19.8	2.4	78.9
Central America - Amérique centrale	*1990*	*295 544*	*9.0*	*70.2*	*22.5*	*20.5*	*22.1*	*9.0*	*27.5*	*20.2*	*63.4*
	1995	*338 845*	*10.4*	*68.4*	*19.9*	*31.6*	*30.3*	*7.0*	*26.2*	*19.4*	*66.8*
	2000	*651 545*	*11.1*	*68.0*	*23.4*	*31.8*	*34.4*	*5.2*	*27.4*	*19.8*	*67.4*
	2005	*866 788*	*11.4*	*69.5*	*21.7*	*30.6*	*33.2*	*5.1*	*25.4*	*17.4*	*69.5*
Belize	1990	405	14.4	60.4	26.1	60.3	61.3	20.7	25.4	14.9	53.8
	1995	620	14.3	71.9	21.7	48.0	49.1	16.6	19.2	10.5	64.2
	2000	832	12.9	74.0	31.7	53.0	73.6	16.3	20.7	10.7	62.9
	2005	1 105	13.9	77.4	24.2	51.8	67.2	15.2	18.9	9.7	65.9
Costa Rica	1990	7 254	15.0	74.9	19.6	29.9	39.0	12.1	29.3	22.0	58.6
	1995	11 716	13.5	71.1	18.2	37.6	40.4	13.3	28.7	21.2	58.0
	2000	15 947	13.3	67.0	16.9	48.6	45.8	9.1	31.0	24.5	59.9
	2005	19 818	13.9	66.0	24.2	49.0	53.1	8.6	28.6	21.0	62.8
El Salvador	1990	4 801	9.9	88.9	13.9	18.6	31.2	17.1	26.8	21.8	56.1
	1995	9 501	8.6	87.4	20.0	21.6	37.8	14.0	28.7	22.3	57.3
	2000	13 134	10.2	87.9	16.9	27.4	42.4	10.0	30.3	23.6	59.7
	2005	16 980	10.5	88.9	16.4	26.7	42.5	10.1	29.3	22.7	60.5
Guatemala	1990	7 650	6.8	83.6	13.6	19.7	23.7	25.9	19.8	15.1	54.3
	1995	14 656	5.5	85.6	15.1	19.3	25.4	24.2	19.7	14.1	56.2
	2000	19 289	7.0	83.9	17.8	20.2	29.0	22.8	19.8	13.2	57.4
	2005	31 923	5.9	89.2	19.3	15.6	29.9	22.8	18.9	12.6	58.3
Honduras	1990	3 049	12.9	66.8	23.0	37.2	39.9	22.4	26.4	16.3	51.2
	1995	3 960	9.3	63.5	31.6	43.7	48.1	21.5	30.7	17.8	47.8
	2000	6 025	12.5	70.6	30.7	41.3	55.2	16.2	31.6	19.6	52.2
	2005	8 374	13.6	76.5	30.1	41.0	61.2	13.9	31.2	20.1	54.9

For sources and notes, see end of table.

Pour les sources et les notes, se reporter à la fin du tableau.

8.3.1 Nominal gross domestic product by type of
expenditure and by kind of economic activity
of countries and geographical regions

8.3.1 Produit intérieur brut nominal par catégories de
dépenses et par branches d'activité économique
des pays et des régions géographiques

Region, country or territory / Régions, pays ou territoires	Year / Année	Total GDP (millions of dollars) / PIB total (millions de dollars)	GDP by type of expenditure (1) / PIB par catégories de dépense (1)					GDP by kind of economic activity (2) / PIB par branches d'activité économique (2)			
			Final consumption / Consommation finale		Gross capital formation	Exports / Expor-tations	Less imports / Moins les impor-tations	Agri-culture (3)	Industry (4) / Industrie (4)		Services (5)
			Government / Administra-tion publique	Household / Ménages	Formation brute de capital	Of goods and services / Des biens et services			Total	Manu-facturing / Activités de fabrication	
			Percentage / En pourcentage								
Mexico - Mexique	1990	262 710	8.4	69.6	23.1	18.6	19.7	7.8	28.1	20.6	64.1
	1995	286 166	10.5	67.1	19.8	30.4	27.8	5.2	26.5	19.8	68.3
	2000	580 792	11.2	67.1	23.8	31.0	33.0	4.0	27.7	20.1	68.3
	2005	768 437	11.5	68.3	21.8	29.9	31.5	3.8	25.6	17.5	70.6
Nicaragua	1990	3 598	33.5	66.3	20.5	25.7	46.1	30.0	21.5	16.9	48.5
	1995	3 185	14.9	78.6	22.0	19.1	34.7	22.8	26.6	18.2	50.5
	2000	3 907	12.3	84.7	30.4	24.1	51.5	20.1	27.2	16.4	52.7
	2005	4 910	11.1	89.1	29.4	28.0	57.6	18.6	28.0	17.9	53.4
Panama	1990	6 077	15.7	63.5	14.7	77.9	70.5	9.0	17.7	13.3	73.2
	1995	9 042	13.1	57.4	26.5	90.5	87.8	7.4	19.9	12.5	72.7
	2000	11 621	13.2	59.9	24.1	72.6	69.8	7.0	18.5	9.7	74.5
	2005	15 241	13.9	62.3	19.2	68.8	64.2	7.4	16.7	8.4	75.9
South America - Amérique du Sud	*1990*	*767 389*	*15.1*	*60.7*	*20.3*	*13.2*	*9.5*	*7.5*	*35.8*	*23.8*	*56.6*
	1995	*1 310 943*	*16.6*	*62.7*	*22.1*	*12.0*	*13.4*	*8.4*	*33.5*	*20.5*	*58.1*
	2000	*1 268 319*	*16.4*	*63.1*	*20.2*	*15.3*	*15.0*	*7.2*	*34.4*	*19.2*	*58.4*
	2005	*1 494 475*	*16.0*	*58.6*	*20.8*	*22.4*	*17.7*	*8.7*	*36.9*	*20.5*	*54.4*
Argentina - Argentine	1990	141 353	12.9	67.3	14.0	10.4	4.6	8.0	35.6	26.5	56.4
	1995	258 096	13.3	68.6	18.5	9.7	10.1	5.7	28.0	18.4	66.3
	2000	284 346	13.8	69.3	17.5	11.0	11.6	5.0	27.6	17.5	67.4
	2005	183 310	11.9	61.3	21.2	24.6	19.1	9.4	35.6	23.2	55.0
Bolivia - Bolivie	1990	4 868	11.8	76.9	12.5	22.8	23.9	16.4	34.2	18.2	49.4
	1995	6 715	13.6	75.8	15.2	22.6	27.2	16.4	32.1	18.4	51.5
	2000	8 398	14.5	76.4	18.1	18.3	27.3	14.3	28.3	14.6	57.4
	2005	9 728	13.3	65.4	15.6	34.3	29.0	15.0	31.1	14.4	53.9
Brazil - Brésil	1990	438 228	16.9	58.4	22.9	7.8	6.1	6.0	34.3	24.1	59.7
	1995	704 169	19.6	59.9	22.3	7.7	9.5	8.5	34.5	22.5	57.1
	2000	601 732	19.1	60.9	21.5	10.7	12.2	7.7	36.1	21.6	56.3
	2005	799 413	18.6	57.0	20.6	16.5	12.7	9.1	36.7	22.6	54.2
Chile - Chili	1990	33 507	10.4	60.1	25.6	33.1	29.4	7.1	41.2	18.0	51.7
	1995	72 065	10.5	60.8	26.3	29.2	26.9	6.1	40.8	19.0	53.1
	2000	75 196	12.5	63.8	21.9	31.6	29.7	5.9	37.0	18.7	57.1
	2005	111 339	11.1	58.0	23.2	43.2	35.5	5.7	40.2	18.8	54.1
Colombia - Colombie	1990	47 743	11.4	63.8	22.2	18.6	16.0	18.2	32.6	18.0	49.1
	1995	92 503	14.9	65.7	25.8	14.5	21.0	14.4	30.1	15.2	55.5
	2000	83 766	21.2	63.0	13.7	21.5	19.4	13.5	29.2	15.2	57.3
	2005	121 877	19.9	61.8	20.8	21.4	23.9	12.4	30.5	15.1	57.2
Ecuador - Équateur	1990	11 248	13.0	67.0	17.0	31.4	28.6	13.9	39.5	20.1	46.6
	1995	20 196	12.5	68.5	21.6	25.7	28.3	17.6	26.2	11.9	56.2
	2000	15 934	9.8	64.0	20.1	37.1	31.0	11.5	37.6	5.5	50.9
	2005	33 062	8.6	63.6	27.1	29.1	28.4	7.6	35.5	5.5	56.9
Guyana	1990	396	13.6	60.9	42.3	55.1	78.5	43.2	19.7	5.2	37.0
	1995	622	16.0	46.3	45.4	-7.7	..	48.8	25.1	3.8	26.1
	2000	713	27.5	49.9	38.5	-15.9	..	36.1	24.1	3.2	39.9
	2005	786	28.2	72.0	33.9	-34.2	..	30.3	24.7	8.0	45.0
Paraguay	1990	4 904	6.2	77.2	22.9	33.2	39.5	27.8	25.6	17.3	46.6
	1995	8 066	10.0	75.8	26.0	59.4	71.2	22.8	25.7	18.0	51.5
	2000	7 095	12.7	79.2	18.8	38.1	48.8	18.5	24.8	17.2	56.7
	2005	7 684	10.7	69.5	22.0	37.0	39.1	20.2	24.6	16.7	55.3
Peru - Pérou	1990	29 281	11.3	70.2	18.1	15.1	14.5	7.7	30.5	19.5	61.8
	1995	53 635	9.8	71.1	24.8	12 5	18.2	8.8	31.0	16.8	60.2
	2000	53 131	10.6	71.0	20.2	16 1	18.0	8.5	30.0	15.9	61.4
	2005	76 607	10.2	67.0	19.7	24 1	19.4	7.6	31.3	15.9	61.1

For sources and notes, see end of table.

Pour les sources et les notes, se reporter à la fin du tableau.

8.3.1 Nominal gross domestic product by type of expenditure and by kind of economic activity of countries and geographical regions

8.3.1 Produit intérieur brut nominal par catégories de dépenses et par branches d'activité économique des pays et des régions géographiques

Region, country or territory / Régions, pays ou territoires	Year / Année	Total GDP (millions of dollars) PIB total (millions de dollars)	GDP by type of expenditure (1) / PIB par catégories de dépense (1)					GDP by kind of economic activity (2) / PIB par branches d'activité économique (2)			
			Final consumption / Consommation finale		Gross capital formation / Formation brute de capital	Exports / Exportations	Less imports / Moins les importations	Agriculture (3)	Industry (4) / Industrie (4)		Services (5)
			Government / Administration publique	Household / Ménages		Of goods and services / Des biens et services			Total	Manufacturing / Activités de fabrication	
			Percentage / En pourcentage								
Suriname	1990	467	24.4	53.8	20.8	27.4	26.6	10.1	27.3	12.0	62.6
	1995	691	25.3	63.7	15.3	22.9	27.2	18.3	38.3	16.0	43.4
	2000	775	37.5	63.6	12.4	19.7	33.2	12.5	28.7	16.3	58.8
	2005	1 503	31.2	55.3	33.2	40.6	60.3	9.8	32.8	16.2	57.4
Uruguay	1990	8 366	13.9	69.1	11.0	26.2	20.1	10.7	30.2	24.8	59.1
	1995	19 298	11.8	72.9	15.4	19.0	19.1	8.4	28.1	19.1	63.6
	2000	20 086	13.2	74.5	14.0	19.3	21.0	5.9	26.0	16.1	68.1
	2005	16 792	11.2	73.5	13.2	29.8	27.6	9.2	30.8	21.9	60.0
Venezuela (Bolivarian Republic of) - Venezuela (République bolivarienne du)	1990	47 028	16.8	46.6	13.4	40.6	20.4	5.9	57.3	27.1	36.8
	1995	74 889	14.8	54.1	23.8	27.9	22.1	5.9	47.1	23.4	47.0
	2000	117 148	12.4	51.7	24.2	29.7	18.1	4.1	48.4	19.3	47.5
	2005	132 373	12.8	52.7	19.4	33.5	18.4	4.2	48.8	17.4	47.0
Developing economies: Asia - Économies en développement : Asie	1990	2 168 131	13.5	57.0	28.2	28.7	28.2	17.9	36.9	23.3	45.2
	1995	3 386 090	12.2	55.7	32.1	38.2	38.2	14.4	38.3	25.4	47.4
	2000	4 036 872	13.2	55.0	27.4	44.2	40.0	11.9	39.0	26.0	49.0
	2005	6 508 128	12.6	52.7	28.9	47.5	42.5	10.7	39.9	26.8	49.4
Eastern Asia - Asie orientale	1990	909 162	12.4	50.8	32.3	29.4	26.9	15.4	39.9	31.5	44.7
	1995	1 649 670	11.5	51.3	36.5	38.8	38.4	11.4	40.9	31.9	47.7
	2000	2 098 447	12.6	52.0	32.1	43.2	40.4	9.7	40.1	33.0	50.2
	2005	3 312 024	12.6	48.2	35.6	47.1	44.0	9.4	41.1	34.4	49.5
China - Chine	1990	382 996	12.3	49.7	35.2	2.8	..	26.6	40.9	36.4	32.6
	1995	700 606	11.4	46.1	40.8	21.0	19.3	19.8	47.2	41.0	33.1
	2000	1 079 191	13.1	48.0	36.4	25.9	23.4	14.8	45.9	40.4	39.3
	2005	1 981 648	12.2	43.3	41.9	33.0	30.5	13.1	45.7	40.2	41.3
China, Hong Kong SAR - Chine, Hong Kong RAS	1990	76 890	7.2	57.1	27.0	130.6	122.0	0.2	24.4	16.7	75.4
	1995	144 230	8.4	62.0	34.1	143.2	147.6	0.1	15.2	7.7	84.7
	2000	168 754	9.1	58.9	27.5	143.6	139.1	0.1	13.3	5.4	86.6
	2005	172 649	9.0	58.9	20.9	197.5	186.3	0.1	9.3	3.3	90.6
China, Macao SAR - Chine, Macao RAS	1990	3 263	8.8	36.7	25.0	96.9	67.4	..	23.8	16.5	76.2
	1995	6 945	8.4	33.6	29.5	74.2	45.7	..	15.6	7.6	84.4
	2000	6 102	12.3	40.2	11.6	100.4	64.6	..	14.8	9.5	85.2
	2005	10 992	7.9	28.7	23.4	98.3	58.3	..	12.8	7.1	87.2
China, Taiwan Province of - Chine, Taiwan Province de	1990	166 281	17.2	54.8	23.1	46.8	41.8	4.1	40.5	32.7	55.4
	1995	274 698	14.2	58.8	25.3	48.0	46.3	3.4	35.4	27.2	61.2
	2000	321 187	13.9	60.7	23.3	52.4	50.2	2.0	31.2	25.4	66.7
	2005	344 981	13.5	62.5	21.0	62.8	59.8	1.8	29.6	24.6	68.6
Korea, Dem. People's Rep. of - Corée, Rép. populaire dém. de	1990	14 702	..	..	..	7.5	11.8	27.4	54.6	31.8	18.0
	1995	4 849	..	..	..	3.8	5.7	27.6	42.0	22.5	30.3
	2000	10 608	..	..	..	4.2	10.0	30.4	37.1	17.7	32.4
	2005	12 260	..	..	..	5.5	11.0	28.1	39.7	18.3	32.2
Korea, Republic of - Corée, République de	1990	263 776	11.8	50.9	37.5	28.0	29.0	8.9	41.6	27.3	49.5
	1995	517 116	11.2	52.3	37.7	28.8	29.9	6.3	41.9	27.6	51.8
	2000	511 659	12.1	54.0	31.0	40.8	37.7	4.9	40.7	29.4	54.4
	2005	787 627	14.1	52.6	30.1	42.5	40.0	3.3	40.3	28.4	56.3
Mongolia - Mongolie	1990	1 254	29.8	62.2	34.3	21.4	42.4	15.2	40.6	13.1	44.2
	1995	1 227	13.3	63.6	31.7	48.0	49.2	37.6	27.2	11.9	35.1
	2000	946	17.7	71.9	36.2	64.9	81.6	32.7	23.1	5.1	44.2
	2005	1 867	17.6	71.7	35.8	66.3	84.0	26.1	26.3	5.4	47.6
Southern Asia - Asie méridionale	1990	520 038	11.3	69.2	23.0	9.3	12.9	28.1	27.4	16.0	44.4
	1995	619 778	11.3	65.6	23.6	13.5	14.1	25.8	28.7	16.6	45.5
	2000	723 057	11.7	65.2	22.4	15.9	16.3	22.7	28.4	15.7	48.9
	2005	1 231 100	11.3	65.0	22.5	18.2	19.1	18.0	29.5	16.0	52.5

For sources and notes, see end of table.

Pour les sources et les notes, se reporter à la fin du tableau.

8.3.1 Nominal gross domestic product by type of expenditure and by kind of economic activity of countries and geographical regions

8.3.1 Produit intérieur brut nominal par catégories de dépenses et par branches d'activité économique des pays et des régions géographiques

Region, country or territory / Régions, pays ou territoires	Year / Année	Total GDP (millions of dollars) / PIB total (millions de dollars)	GDP by type of expenditure (1) / PIB par catégories de dépense (1)					GDP by kind of economic activity (2) / PIB par branches d'activité économique (2)			
			Final consumption / Consommation finale		Gross capital formation / Formation brute de capital	Exports / Exportations	Less imports / Moins les importations	Agriculture (3)	Industry (4) / Industrie (4)		Services (5)
			Government / Administration publique	Household / Ménages		Of goods and services / Des biens et services			Total	Manufacturing / Activités de fabrication	
			Percentage / En pourcentage								
Afghanistan	1990	3 622	5.6	83.9	13.4	11.5	14.4	35.7	23.7	20.6	40.6
	1995	3 236	7.0	101.7	14.2	24.6	47.6	65.7	10.5	5.4	23.8
	2000	2 963	8.5	119.5	15.1	37.7	80.8	57.0	23.2	16.9	19.8
	2005	6 504	8.8	119.8	16.3	36.4	81.3	35.1	27.3	18.8	37.6
Bangladesh	1990	31 830	4.4	83.3	16.4	6.7	12.3	30.8	21.4	13.4	47.7
	1995	41 294	4.4	80.7	20.0	11.1	18.7	25.7	24.9	15.4	49.5
	2000	48 626	4.5	77.5	23.1	15.4	21.5	24.1	25.9	15.6	50.0
	2005	64 058	5.2	75.9	23.6	14.9	20.8	21.9	26.5	16.0	51.6
Bhutan - Bhoutan	1990	285	15.7	52.4	35.9	28.3	32.3	42.7	25.0	8.1	32.3
	1995	295	12.3	41.6	46.7	36.9	37.5	34.0	34.8	10.9	31.2
	2000	447	19.1	38.3	60.5	29.8	47.7	28.2	37.9	8.4	33.9
	2005	917	14.7	35.3	69.1	26.5	45.6	22.3	48.8	6.3	28.9
India - Inde	1990	324 250	11.8	67.2	25.2	7.2	8.6	31.5	27.7	17.2	40.8
	1995	366 364	10.8	64.0	26.5	11.0	12.2	28.2	28.1	18.1	43.6
	2000	464 937	12.6	64.8	22.6	13.3	14.2	24.6	26.6	15.9	48.8
	2005	800 783	11.9	63.8	23.5	14.9	16.1	19.0	27.4	15.9	53.6
Iran, Islamic Republic of - Iran, Rép. islamique d'	1990	95 903	11.3	70.3	19.9	13.2	24.4	16.6	30.1	12.7	53.3
	1995	116 203	15.3	58.6	17.5	19.1	11.5	17.3	35.3	14.4	47.5
	2000	112 695	12.5	52.7	24.0	23.4	15.5	11.7	39.8	15.5	48.4
	2005	216 713	13.3	55.4	21.1	30.6	24.4	11.0	40.0	15.4	48.9
Maldives	1990	215	17.2	35.9	31.5	92.0	76.5	17.7	15.5	8.7	66.8
	1995	399	16.8	36.5	31.3	92.7	77.2	11.0	13.0	7.6	76.0
	2000	624	22.9	32.9	26.3	89.5	71.6	8.4	14.5	7.7	77.1
	2005	770	29.7	62.4	26.9	69.3	88.2	9.1	17.2	7.3	73.7
Nepal - Népal	1990	3 521	8.7	83.5	18.4	10.5	21.1	50.6	15.9	6.0	33.5
	1995	4 224	9.2	75.9	25.2	24.2	34.6	40.8	22.2	9.3	37.0
	2000	5 338	8.9	75.9	24.3	23.3	32.4	39.6	21.5	9.2	38.9
	2005	7 412	10.1	77.7	26.1	16.4	30.2	38.3	21.3	7.8	40.4
Pakistan	1990	52 207	12.2	68.9	20.7	12.7	14.2	26.9	25.2	16.4	47.9
	1995	74 401	10.8	73.2	20.7	12.7	16.4	26.7	23.7	15.0	49.6
	2000	70 709	8.7	75.2	17.4	13.6	14.8	26.2	22.6	14.8	51.2
	2005	110 017	7.8	80.0	16.8	15.3	19.9	21.6	25.1	18.2	53.3
Sri Lanka	1990	8 204	12.7	75.2	20.5	29.5	37.3	25.6	29.4	18.6	45.0
	1995	13 363	14.2	71.2	25.3	34.7	44.0	20.6	29.7	18.5	49.7
	2000	16 717	13.7	70.9	25.4	38.2	48.4	17.6	29.9	19.5	52.5
	2005	23 927	7.5	75.2	24.4	33.2	41.0	15.5	29.8	18.4	54.7
South-Eastern Asia - Asie du Sud-Est	*1990*	*354 303*	*11.0*	*57.1*	*32.3*	*50.6*	*51.1*	*17.0*	*36.7*	*22.5*	*46.3*
	1995	*676 101*	*10.4*	*56.0*	*34.6*	*60.6*	*62.0*	*14.4*	*38.2*	*24.6*	*47.4*
	2000	*594 296*	*10.7*	*55.0*	*24.6*	*85.6*	*75.3*	*12.1*	*40.4*	*27.2*	*47.5*
	2005	*882 071*	*11.0*	*56.7*	*23.1*	*86.3*	*77.8*	*11.7*	*41.8*	*27.8*	*46.5*
Brunei Darussalam - Brunéi Darussalam	1990	3 591	11.7	11.4	9.9	105.6	38.6	2.3	53.6	8.8	44.1
	1995	5 217	11.2	10.9	9.4	90.3	26.3	2.5	42.8	..	54.7
	2000	4 316	11.3	10.8	9.4	96.6	29.3	2.6	46.6	..	50.8
	2005	6 280	11.3	10.9	9.4	97.1	29.5	3.2	45.3	..	51.5
Cambodia - Cambodge	1990	1 698	7.2	90.4	8.3	2.4	8.4	50.1	11.7	7.3	38.2
	1995	3 309	5.1	90.9	13.4	32.7	43.9	51.4	12.9	7.4	35.7
	2000	3 668	5.2	88.8	16.9	49.8	61.7	37.9	23.0	16.9	39.1
	2005	5 397	5.2	82.5	22.2	59.5	73.2	35.2	26.3	19.4	38.5
Indonesia - Indonésie	1990	125 720	8.8	58.9	30.7	25.3	23.7	19.4	39.1	20.7	41.5
	1995	222 082	7.8	61.6	31.9	26.3	27.6	17.1	41.8	24.1	41.1
	2000	165 021	6.5	61.7	22.2	41.0	30.5	15.6	45.9	27.7	38.5
	2005	281 276	8.2	65.4	22.2	33.5	29.2	13.4	45.8	28.1	40.8

For sources and notes, see end of table.

Pour les sources et les notes, se reporter à la fin du tableau.

424

8.3.1 Nominal gross domestic product by type of expenditure and by kind of economic activity of countries and geographical regions

8.3.1 Produit intérieur brut nominal par catégories de dépenses et par branches d'activité économique des pays et des régions géographiques

Region, country or territory / Régions, pays ou territoires	Year / Année	Total GDP (millions of dollars) PIB total (millions de dollars)	Final consumption / Consommation finale — Government / Administration publique	Final consumption — Household / Ménages	Gross capital formation / Formation brute de capital	Exports / Exportations — Of goods and services / Des biens et services	Less imports / Moins les importations — Of goods and services / Des biens et services	Agriculture / Agriculture (3)	Industry (4) / Industrie (4) — Total	Industry — Manufacturing / Activités de fabrication	Services (5)
			Percentage / En pourcentage								
Lao People's Dem. Rep. - Rép. dém. populaire lao	1990	866	9.5	92.1	11.3	11.8	24.7	61.2	14.5	10.0	24.3
	1995	1 778	9.7	93.0	11.3	23.2	37.3	55.0	19.0	14.1	26.0
	2000	1 733	8.9	85.0	10.4	30.1	34.4	52.5	22.9	17.0	24.6
	2005	2 872	8.3	78.8	16.7	27.6	31.4	46.0	27.9	21.0	26.1
Malaysia - Malaisie	1990	44 025	13.8	51.8	32.4	74.5	72.4	15.0	41.5	23.8	43.5
	1995	88 833	12.4	47.9	43.6	94.1	98.0	12.7	40.5	25.8	46.8
	2000	90 320	10.4	42.4	27.3	124.4	104.5	8.4	48.4	31.1	43.1
	2005	130 770	12.9	43.6	19.9	123.4	99.9	8.3	49.9	29.5	41.8
Myanmar	1990	5 179	88.3	..	13.4	1.9	3.6	57.3	10.5	7.8	32.2
	1995	7 761	86.6	..	14.2	0.8	1.7	60.0	9.9	6.9	30.1
	2000	7 275	87.7	..	12.4	0.5	0.6	57.2	9.7	7.2	33.1
	2005	10 938	88.6	..	11.4	0.1	0.1	56.8	10.9	7.9	32.4
Philippines	1990	44 312	10.1	71.2	24.2	27.5	33.3	21.9	34.5	24.8	43.6
	1995	74 120	11.4	74.1	22.5	36.4	44.2	21.6	32.1	23.0	46.3
	2000	75 031	13.2	70.4	19.5	56.1	54.1	16.0	31.5	22.5	52.6
	2005	97 653	9.7	70.1	15.7	46.4	47.1	14.4	32.6	23.7	53.0
Singapore - Singapour	1990	36 901	10.1	46.1	36.4	182.9	176.1	0.3	32.7	25.5	67.0
	1995	83 932	8.5	41.3	34.2	187.7	171.7	0.1	33.7	25.0	66.1
	2000	92 717	10.8	42.2	33.3	195.6	182.0	0.1	33.5	26.2	66.4
	2005	116 775	10.6	41.9	18.6	243.0	213.1	0.1	32.5	27.3	67.4
Thailand - Thaïlande	1990	85 361	9.4	56.5	41.3	34.1	41.6	14.4	35.9	24.9	49.7
	1995	168 019	9.9	53.2	42.1	41.8	48.6	10.8	40.2	28.7	49.0
	2000	122 725	11.3	56.1	22.8	66.8	58.1	10.0	40.7	32.2	49.3
	2005	176 602	11.8	56.9	31.6	73.7	75.2	11.1	43.5	34.0	45.4
Timor-Leste	1990	179	15.0	81.1	35.0	-31.1	..	29.5	25.4	2.9	45.1
	1995	315	15.0	81.1	35.0	-31.1	..	29.4	25.5	3.2	45.1
	2000	316	53.8	65.1	41.3	-60.2	..	25.8	18.5	2.8	55.8
	2005	354	51.2	61.3	28.4	-40.9	..	31.6	14.9	3.7	53.5
Viet Nam	1990	6 472	7.5	89.6	14.4	26.4	35.7	39.8	23.3	12.6	36.8
	1995	20 736	8.2	73.6	27.1	32.8	41.9	27.2	28.8	15.0	44.1
	2000	31 173	6.4	66.5	29.6	55.0	57.5	24.5	36.7	18.6	38.7
	2005	53 153	6.2	63.6	35.5	69.0	73.3	20.9	41.0	20.7	38.1
Western Asia - Asie occidentale	*1990*	*384 628*	*21.1*	*54.9*	*21.8*	*33.0*	*31.0*	*11.7*	*42.2*	*13.8*	*46.2*
	1995	*440 541*	*18.6*	*57.3*	*23.7*	*36.0*	*34.7*	*10.2*	*41.5*	*14.7*	*48.4*
	2000	*621 072*	*19.1*	*53.3*	*20.0*	*40.9*	*32.6*	*7.9*	*45.6*	*12.1*	*46.5*
	2005	*1 082 933*	*15.4*	*49.2*	*20.4*	*50.3*	*35.6*	*6.5*	*45.3*	*13.2*	*48.2*
Bahrain - Bahreïn	1990	4 293	25.2	32.4	20.0	122.0	99.7	0.9	41.5	15.2	57.6
	1995	5 848	20.9	53.0	14.6	82.0	70.5	0.8	35.8	16.0	63.4
	2000	7 971	17.6	47.1	10.3	89.4	64.4	0.7	40.0	10.3	59.4
	2005	13 348	14.4	40.3	23.0	93.4	71.1	0.6	38.1	10.4	61.3
Iraq	1990	29 980	26.4	50.5	22.5	18.5	17.8	18.9	30.0	8.4	51.1
	1995	6 187	22.4	74.7	3.1	1.8	2.1	18.9	30.0	8.4	51.1
	2000	20 969	19.1	75.8	6.2	10.4	11.5	4.6	84.6	0.9	10.8
	2005	33 379	19.2	75.9	6.0	10.1	11.2	8.3	72.3	1.3	19.4
Jordan - Jordanie	1990	4 020	24.9	74.1	31.9	61.9	92.7	7.5	30.9	17.0	61.7
	1995	6 732	23.6	64.6	33.0	51.7	72.9	4.3	27.5	13.9	68.3
	2000	8 461	23.7	80.6	22.4	41.8	68.5	2.3	24.4	14.8	73.3
	2005	12 535	23.2	90.8	23.8	49.7	87.6	2.5	25.6	15.9	71.9
Kuwait - Koweït	1990	18 471	38.6	58.6	15.9	44.8	57.8	0.9	51.7	11.5	47.4
	1995	26 554	33.0	41.3	15.1	53.6	43.0	0.4	52.8	11.1	46.7
	2000	37 718	21.5	41.5	10.7	56.5	30.1	0.3	57.2	6.7	42.5
	2005	74 214	16.7	31.5	11.8	66.1	26.4	0.4	53.9	7.1	45.7

For sources and notes, see end of table.

Pour les sources et les notes, se reporter à la fin du tableau.

8.3.1 Nominal gross domestic product by type of expenditure and by kind of economic activity of countries and geographical regions

8.3.1 Produit intérieur brut nominal par catégories de dépenses et par branches d'activité économique des pays et des régions géographiques

Region, country or territory — Régions, pays ou territoires	Year Année	Total GDP (millions of dollars) PIB total (millions de dollars)	GDP by type of expenditure (1) PIB par catégories de dépense (1)					GDP by kind of economic activity (2) PIB par branches d'activité économique (2)			
			Final consumption Consommation finale		Gross capital formation Formation brute de capital	Exports Exportations	Less imports Moins les importations	Agriculture (3)	Industry (4) Industrie (4)		Services (5)
			Government Administration publique	Household Ménages		Of goods and services Des biens et services			Total	Manufacturing Activités de fabrication	
			Percentage / En pourcentage								
Lebanon - Liban	1990	2 812	25.1	123.3	28.7	22.2	99.2	8.8	21.2	12.6	70.0
	1995	10 965	9.9	107.7	36.3	11.0	64.9	11.7	30.8	16.3	57.5
	2000	16 679	17.6	85.6	20.3	13.6	37.1	6.4	20.9	12.0	72.7
	2005	21 184	17.5	84.5	17.4	16.1	35.4	5.8	19.5	10.7	74.7
Palestinian territory - Territoire palestinien	1990	1 936	11.8	112.1	30.3	27.5	81.7	14.2	28.8	17.5	57.0
	1995	3 220	18.5	98.2	35.4	15.5	67.6	12.9	31.3	19.5	55.8
	2000	4 116	27.0	95.5	32.6	16.0	71.1	11.4	24.0	15.2	64.6
	2005	4 179	30.2	97.2	25.8	12.3	65.5	8.0	17.4	12.1	74.6
Oman	1990	11 685	26.6	41.4	12.3	47.2	27.6	2.6	53.4	2.9	44.0
	1995	13 803	27.5	49.0	15.0	44.0	35.6	2.7	45.8	4.6	51.5
	2000	19 868	20.7	40.2	11.9	59.2	32.0	1.9	56.1	5.3	42.0
	2005	30 269	20.2	44.8	17.8	59.5	42.3	1.9	53.6	7.6	44.5
Qatar	1990	7 360	32.9	27.8	18.0	53.5	32.1	0.8	55.7	12.7	43.6
	1995	8 138	31.9	32.1	35.1	44.3	43.3	1.0	52.1	8.2	46.9
	2000	17 760	19.7	15.2	20.2	67.3	22.3	0.4	69.5	5.3	30.1
	2005	42 113	12.0	17.3	35.6	68.8	33.7	0.1	74.1	8.3	25.7
Saudi Arabia - Arabie saoudite	1990	104 531	31.8	39.8	21.1	46.8	39.4	6.5	53.2	8.2	40.3
	1995	127 641	25.7	40.4	20.7	43.7	30.5	6.6	53.0	9.0	40.4
	2000	188 442	26.0	36.5	18.7	43.7	24.9	4.9	53.6	9.6	41.5
	2005	314 021	19.1	29.4	17.3	61.6	27.5	4.7	53.5	10.1	41.8
Syrian Arab Republic - République arabe syrienne	1990	11 152	14.3	68.7	16.5	28.3	28.0	28.3	24.2	5.5	47.6
	1995	13 538	13.4	66.2	27.2	31.0	37.9	28.2	18.1	6.2	53.7
	2000	19 651	12.4	63.4	17.3	36.1	29.2	24.8	33.3	1.5	41.9
	2005	25 812	14.5	63.1	20.5	35.6	33.9	24.6	29.6	4.1	45.8
Turkey - Turquie	1990	150 676	11.0	68.6	24.3	13.3	17.6	17.6	32.1	22.2	50.3
	1995	169 319	10.8	70.3	25.5	19.9	24.4	15.7	31.9	22.6	52.4
	2000	199 264	14.1	71.5	24.5	24.0	31.5	14.2	28.7	19.3	57.1
	2005	362 614	13.1	67.4	24.8	27.4	34.0	10.5	30.3	21.2	59.2
United Arab Emirates - Émirats arabes unis	1990	33 780	16.3	38.6	20.4	65.4	40.8	1.6	62.2	7.2	36.2
	1995	42 807	16.4	47.9	29.7	69.0	63.0	2.8	51.0	10.2	46.1
	2000	70 522	15.4	43.5	23.2	73.7	55.8	3.5	54.8	13.3	41.8
	2005	133 757	10.0	46.0	20.0	84.9	59.8	2.9	51.5	13.1	45.6
Yemen - Yémen	1990	3 930	17.0	72.1	15.2	13.9	19.5	25.6	25.7	8.3	48.7
	1995	5 789	14.3	83.0	21.8	21.7	41.9	20.1	31.0	12.7	48.9
	2000	9 652	13.6	60.3	18.9	41.3	34.1	13.8	45.3	5.1	41.0
	2005	15 508	15.0	62.9	16.9	44.0	38.8	13.7	42.6	5.5	43.7
Developing economies: Oceania - Économies en développement : Océanie	**1990**	**11 207**	**31.4**	**60.4**	**23.2**	**30.3**	**45.4**	**14.9**	**22.6**	**7.9**	**62.5**
	1995	**15 769**	**28.3**	**56.1**	**20.4**	**35.7**	**39.2**	**16.5**	**22.4**	**7.6**	**61.1**
	2000	**13 361**	**28.6**	**59.6**	**20.0**	**33.6**	**41.9**	**15.2**	**24.7**	**9.1**	**60.1**
	2005	**20 114**	**27.8**	**61.7**	**19.3**	**31.4**	**43.1**	**15.6**	**23.7**	**8.5**	**60.7**
Cook Islands - Îles Cook	1990	59	42.9	107.3	21.0	4.7	76.0	11.3	8.2	4.2	80.5
	1995	93	27.8	69.5	13.6	47.7	58.7	9.5	7.6	2.9	83.0
	2000	81	22.3	55.9	10.9	95.0	84.2	13.0	8.1	3.4	78.9
	2005	183	22.2	55.5	10.9	73.9	62.5	12.5	8.3	3.6	79.2
Fiji - Fidji	1990	1 337	17.5	69.0	18.3	62.3	67.2	18.7	20.4	10.5	60.9
	1995	1 990	15.9	74.0	13.6	54.7	58.3	18.8	22.8	13.1	58.3
	2000	1 686	17.2	70.6	17.2	65.1	70.2	16.5	21.5	13.5	62.0
	2005	2 998	15.2	83.4	19.0	55.0	72.6	13.7	21.0	12.6	65.4
French Polynesia - Polynésie française	1990	2 930	40.4	61.9	20.0	9.4	31.7	4.5	15.3	7.3	80.2
	1995	3 750	41.5	57.8	15.3	12.5	27.0	4.1	13.3	6.3	82.6
	2000	3 242	42.1	49.7	13.2	20.9	26.0	4.0	14.5	6.5	81.5
	2005	5 388	44.5	48.7	12.9	20.7	26.9	3.4	14.4	6.6	82.1

For sources and notes, see end of table.

Pour les sources et les notes, se reporter à la fin du tableau.

8.3.1 Nominal gross domestic product by type of expenditure and by kind of economic activity of countries and geographical regions

8.3.1 Produit intérieur brut nominal par catégories de dépenses et par branches d'activité économique des pays et des régions géographiques

Region, country or territory / Régions, pays ou territoires	Year / Année	Total GDP (millions of dollars) / PIB total (millions de dollars)	GDP by type of expenditure (1) / PIB par catégories de dépense (1)					GDP by kind of economic activity (2) / PIB par branches d'activité économique (2)			
			Final consumption / Consommation finale		Gross capital formation / Formation brute de capital	Exports / Exportations	Less imports / Moins les importations	Agriculture (3)	Industry (4) / Industrie (4)		Services (5)
			Government / Administration publique	Household / Ménages		Of goods and services / Des biens et services			Total	Manufacturing / Activités de fabrication	
			Percentage / En pourcentage								
Kiribati	1990	28	52.8	89.6	93.1	11.6	147.2	18.6	7.6	1.2	73.8
	1995	41	45.4	76.9	53.3	14.5	90.1	11.1	5.8	1.4	83.1
	2000	47	36.1	61.2	43.2	26.6	67.0	7.3	10.1	0.8	82.6
	2005	72	36.4	61.8	43.7	30.4	72.2	8.6	13.2	0.8	78.2
Marshall Islands - Îles Marshall	1990	69	50.2	97.6	88.4	11.0	147.2	13.9	12.9	1.0	73.2
	1995	105	54.2	91.0	56.3	12.5	114.0	14.9	15.0	2.6	70.0
	2000	99	54.1	91.1	56.8	12.4	114.5	10.0	19.2	4.6	70.8
	2005	111	54.1	91.1	56.8	12.4	114.5	10.0	19.1	4.4	70.9
Micronesia, Federated States of - Micronésie, États fédérés de	1990	146	58.3	83.9	37.7	3.4	84.3	17.6	3.7	1.3	78.7
	1995	209	58.3	83.9	37.7	3.4	84.3	17.6	3.7	1.3	78.7
	2000	214	58.3	83.9	37.7	3.4	84.3	17.6	3.7	1.3	78.7
	2005	239	58.3	83.9	37.7	3.4	84.3	17.6	3.7	1.3	78.7
Nauru	1990	51	52.8	89.6	93.1	11.6	147.2	18.6	7.6	1.2	73.8
	1995	41	45.4	76.9	53.3	14.5	90.1	11.1	5.8	1.4	83.1
	2000	33	36.1	61.2	43.2	26.6	67.0	7.3	10.1	0.8	82.6
	2005	55	36.4	61.8	43.7	30.4	72.2	8.6	13.2	0.8	78.2
New Caledonia - Nouvelle-Calédonie	1990	2 529	32.6	57.3	23.3	22.0	35.4	2.0	24.9	6.4	73.1
	1995	3 628	33.3	56.0	24.1	19.1	26.2	1.8	22.0	6.0	76.2
	2000	3 003	33.2	55.8	24.2	16.4	28.8	2.0	25.0	10.4	73.0
	2005	4 341	33.2	55.8	24.2	15.5	29.1	2.0	25.1	10.5	72.9
Palau, Pacific Islands (former) - Palaos, Îles du Pacifique (anc.)	1990	77	39.3	65.1	17.0	25.4	46.8	25.9	15.5	0.7	58.6
	1995	95	48.0	79.6	21.3	14.6	63.5	5.9	9.4	0.9	84.7
	2000	117	57.2	110.2	31.2	9.8	108.4	4.1	12.3	1.5	83.6
	2005	123	49.7	83.7	42.4	16.7	92.5	4.1	12.7	1.5	83.3
Papua New Guinea - Papouasie-Nouvelle-Guinée	1990	3 286	26.2	51.6	24.0	43.0	45.4	29.7	31.2	9.2	39.0
	1995	4 840	17.1	42.7	21.9	59.3	41.1	35.1	33.3	8.3	31.6
	2000	3 864	16.2	60.1	21.3	43.9	41.5	31.7	39.2	9.9	29.1
	2005	5 330	12.3	61.7	20.0	40.7	44.5	38.2	36.9	7.7	24.9
Samoa	1990	201	28.6	84.9	20.8	29.0	63.3	20.5	28.8	19.2	50.6
	1995	200	24.6	80.6	19.4	32.9	57.6	18.4	29.4	19.2	52.2
	2000	231	24.0	86.2	13.1	30.6	53.9	16.5	25.6	14.6	57.8
	2005	406	23.1	91.6	11.7	30.0	56.4	13.7	26.5	15.3	59.8
Solomon Islands - Îles Salomon	1990	208	31.1	57.4	20.1	46.5	56.8	45.5	7.9	3.7	46.6
	1995	365	32.9	48.9	19.2	57.7	58.8	44.7	9.9	5.8	45.3
	2000	338	31.8	48.5	19.6	59.1	59.1	44.5	10.1	5.9	45.4
	2005	299	31.9	48.5	19.6	59.1	59.1	44.5	10.1	5.9	45.4
Tonga	1990	124	19.1	93.6	18.5	33.9	65.1	35.1	14.4	6.1	50.4
	1995	156	19.7	107.1	22.2	20.2	69.2	23.7	11.1	3.4	65.2
	2000	148	14.9	103.4	19.2	15.7	54.0	28.6	16.7	5.3	54.6
	2005	214	13.0	116.3	15.8	20.6	64.0	27.9	15.2	4.5	56.9
Tuvalu	1990	10	52.8	102.9	93.1	11.6	147.2	25.6	14.5	3.1	59.8
	1995	12	54.2	91.1	56.3	12.6	114.0	24.0	14.0	3.9	62.0
	2000	12	54.2	91.1	54.7	12.6	114.0	17.3	13.1	3.2	69.7
	2005	26	54.2	91.1	55.8	12.6	114.0	16.5	13.7	3.4	69.8
Vanuatu	1990	153	28.2	62.9	43.2	46.4	76.6	20.0	13.5	5.9	66.5
	1995	243	25.4	46.9	31.9	44.2	53.6	15.6	11.6	4.4	72.8
	2000	245	23.1	57.6	22.1	43.0	56.7	14.9	8.9	4.2	76.3
	2005	329	22.9	61.2	20.4	42.8	58.7	14.5	8.5	3.4	77.0
Economies in transition: Asia - Économies en transition : Asie	**1995**	**46 007**	**15.5**	**67.0**	**24.0**	**41.0**	**46.3**	**23.5**	**30.7**	**23.2**	**45.8**
	2000	**48 676**	**14.4**	**63.4**	**20.8**	**46.5**	**44.3**	**20.4**	**34.5**	**17.5**	**45.1**
	2005	**102 997**	**13.5**	**54.0**	**27.9**	**51.2**	**46.1**	**14.4**	**38.0**	**15.9**	**47.6**
Armenia - Arménie	1995	1 287	11.2	106.3	18.4	23.9	62.2	40.8	31.0	24.4	28.2
	2000	1 912	11.8	97.1	18.6	23.4	50.5	25.2	35.0	23.9	39.8
	2005	4 868	11.2	77.7	28.3	27.0	40.0	20.4	43.8	20.5	35.8

For sources and notes, see end of table.

Pour les sources et les notes, se reporter à la fin du tableau.

427

8.3.1 Nominal gross domestic product by type of expenditure and by kind of economic activity of countries and geographical regions

8.3.1 Produit intérieur brut nominal par catégories de dépenses et par branches d'activité économique des pays et des régions géographiques

Region, country or territory / Régions, pays ou territoires	Year / Année	Total GDP (millions of dollars) PIB total (millions de dollars)	GDP by type of expenditure (1) / PIB par catégories de dépense (1)					GDP by kind of economic activity (2) / PIB par branches d'activité économique (2)			
			Final consumption / Consommation finale		Gross capital formation / Formation brute de capital	Exports / Exportations	Less imports / Moins les importations	Agriculture (3)	Industry (4) / Industrie (4)		Services (5)
			Government / Administration publique	Household / Ménages		Of goods and services / Des biens et services			Total	Manufacturing / Activités de fabrication	
			Percentage / En pourcentage								
Azerbaijan - Azerbaïdjan	1995	3 079	12.8	84.3	23.8	32.5	53.4	26.9	32.9	12.2	40.2
	2000	5 273	15.2	64.4	20.7	40.2	38.4	17.0	45.1	5.6	37.9
	2005	12 561	9.8	40.1	45.7	62.9	56.4	10.0	61.9	7.8	28.2
Georgia - Géorgie	1995	2 721	8.0	83.2	24.0	14.0	28.5	44.4	12.7	10.3	43.0
	2000	3 044	8.6	90.9	26.7	23.1	39.8	21.3	22.2	13.0	56.4
	2005	6 490	14.7	69.8	27.8	31.2	46.5	20.3	23.7	13.5	55.9
Kazakhstan	1995	20 547	13.6	71.1	23.3	39.0	43.5	12.8	31.2	24.4	56.0
	2000	18 292	12.1	61.9	18.1	56.6	49.1	8.6	40.1	17.5	51.3
	2005	56 088	13.4	50.6	26.2	54.3	44.1	8.1	37.4	14.8	54.6
Kyrgyzstan - Kirghizistan	1995	1 492	19.5	75.0	18.3	29.5	42.4	43.1	20.1	13.6	36.8
	2000	1 370	20.0	65.7	20.0	41.8	47.6	36.6	31.3	19.4	32.1
	2005	2 441	18.9	80.9	15.6	38.6	58.2	34.1	20.9	14.1	45.0
Tajikistan - Tadjikistan	1995	1 230	10.9	60.5	28.7	112.0	121.2	35.9	36.4	33.3	27.7
	2000	870	8.5	73.2	11.6	85.1	74.9	29.4	29.7	26.0	41.0
	2005	2 342	8.8	82.7	14.8	63.5	68.9	27.8	31.1	26.7	41.1
Turkmenistan - Turkménistan	1995	2 188	8.4	60.6	33.6	142.5	145.0	16.9	64.8	58.8	18.3
	2000	4 157	14.5	35.3	35.4	97.2	82.4	22.9	41.8	35.0	35.2
	2005	5 826	12.9	47.0	29.6	76.0	65.5	22.8	42.8	35.8	34.4
Uzbekistan - Ouzbékistan	1995	13 465	22.3	50.6	24.2	31.6	28.7	31.4	28.1	20.2	40.5
	2000	13 759	18.7	61.9	19.6	26.5	26.7	34.9	22.8	15.8	42.3
	2005	12 381	17.9	58.2	21.3	33.3	30.7	33.4	23.2	17.3	43.4
Economies in transition: Europe - Économies en transition : Europe	**1990**	**943 896**	**19.8**	**53.6**	**28.9**	**24.1**	**26.7**	**18.5**	**45.6**	**35.1**	**35.9**
	1995	**568 450**	**19.6**	**55.7**	**24.3**	**31.5**	**31.2**	**10.4**	**37.3**	**27.9**	**52.2**
	2000	**393 416**	**16.4**	**52.9**	**19.2**	**44.5**	**33.0**	**9.3**	**36.6**	**28.2**	**54.1**
	2005	**1 094 864**	**17.3**	**53.0**	**21.8**	**37.6**	**30.8**	**7.4**	**36.5**	**19.0**	**56.1**
Albania - Albanie	1990	2 184	10.2	72.7	24.4	14.9	22.2	40.2	43.8	..	16.0
	1995	2 479	13.3	88.4	17.6	12.2	33.8	54.6	22.0	..	23.4
	2000	3 709	10.6	67.5	41.7	17.5	37.3	25.5	15.7	4.7	58.8
	2005	8 538	10.9	63.2	47.5	21.2	42.7	22.9	21.3	5.0	55.8
Bosnia and Herzegovina - Bosnie-Herzégovine (6)	1995	2 043	27.2	103.9	20.0	20.4	71.5	14.4	28.7	12.7	56.9
	2000	4 527	22.8	88.2	21.2	27.8	60.0	13.4	28.9	12.8	57.7
	2005	9 132	23.5	91.6	20.1	25.0	60.2	11.4	26.6	12.4	62.0
Belarus - Bélarus	1995	13 845	20.6	59.1	24.8	49.7	54.1	16.8	39.0	33.2	44.2
	2000	10 418	19.5	56.9	25.4	69.2	72.4	13.9	40.0	32.7	46.1
	2005	29 566	21.7	53.7	27.7	65.0	70.4	10.6	39.2	32.1	50.2
Bulgaria - Bulgarie	1990	20 726	7.2	66.8	30.4	33.1	37.5	18.3	50.9	35.8	30.8
	1995	13 106	15.3	70.7	15.7	44.7	46.3	13.4	32.4	22.3	54.3
	2000	12 600	17.9	69.2	18.3	55.7	61.1	13.9	30.1	17.8	56.0
	2005	26 419	19.2	69.4	25.3	62.0	75.9	11.5	29.6	18.1	58.9
Croatia - Croatie	1995	18 811	28.2	65.1	17.6	38.6	49.5	10.4	33.4	23.6	56.3
	2000	18 428	24.8	60.1	20.2	47.1	52.3	8.8	29.3	21.0	61.9
	2005	36 947	20.4	57.0	31.3	47.1	55.8	6.7	29.5	23.2	63.8
Macedonia, TFYR - Macédoine, LERY	1995	4 475	18.6	70.4	20.8	33.0	42.8	12.6	31.2	20.4	56.2
	2000	3 587	18.2	74.4	22.3	48.6	63.5	11.7	32.9	20.2	55.4
	2005	5 651	20.3	76.2	22.4	40.2	58.5	12.7	29.4	17.9	57.9
Moldova, Republic of - Moldova, République de	1995	1 766	25.9	57.0	24.9	60.1	67.9	32.2	31.4	25.1	36.4
	2000	1 288	14.7	88.4	23.9	49.6	76.6	28.3	21.2	15.8	50.6
	2005	2 917	15.5	92.9	29.8	53.1	91.3	16.7	23.9	16.9	59.4
Romania - Roumanie	1990	38 242	13.3	65.9	30.2	16.7	26.2	23.2	48.7	39.0	28.1
	1995	35 478	13.7	67.6	24.3	27.6	33.2	20.7	41.4	27.8	37.9
	2000	37 025	16.1	70.1	19.5	32.9	38.5	12.4	35.9	24.5	51.7
	2005	98 566	19.6	68.1	22.7	33.0	43.4	13.9	48.1	31.1	38.0

For sources and notes, see end of table.   Pour les sources et les notes, se reporter à la fin du tableau.

428

8.3.1 Nominal gross domestic product by type of expenditure and by kind of economic activity of countries and geographical regions

8.3.1 Produit intérieur brut nominal par catégories de dépenses et par branches d'activité économique des pays et des régions géographiques

Region, country or territory / Régions, pays ou territoires	Year / Année	Total GDP (millions of dollars) / PIB total (millions de dollars)	GDP by type of expenditure (1) / PIB par catégories de dépense (1)					GDP by kind of economic activity (2) / PIB par branches d'activité économique (2)			
			Final consumption / Consommation finale		Gross capital formation / Formation brute de capital	Exports / Expor-tations	Less imports / Moins les impor-tations	Agri-culture (3)	Industry (4) / Industrie (4)		Services (5)
			Government / Administra-tion publique	Household / Ménages		Of goods and services / Des biens et services			Total	Manu-facturing / Activités de fabrication	
			Percentage / En pourcentage								
Serbia and Montenegro - Serbie-et-Monténégro	1995	28 673	27.0	68.5	15.0	22.5	33.1	19.4	37.9	25.2	42.7
	2000	10 855	23.5	77.1	11.4	15.3	28.2	19.9	33.6	22.5	46.5
	2005	29 493	28.6	76.6	15.4	21.6	41.9	14.6	27.9	16.5	57.4
Russian Federation - Fédération de Russie	1995	399 166	19.1	52.1	25.4	29.3	25.9	7.6	37.0	27.9	55.5
	2000	259 718	15.1	46.2	18.7	44.1	24.0	6.7	37.9	31.4	55.4
	2005	765 968	16.0	48.0	20.8	35.2	21.4	5.4	37.1	17.4	57.5
USSR (former) - URSS (anc.)	1990	776 920	19.8	50.9	30.5	21.9	23.3	19.5	45.6	36.1	34.8
Yugoslavia, SFR (former) - Yougoslavie, RSF (anc.)	1990	105 824	24.8	66.1	16.0	41.7	49.1	14.5	37.4	19.7	48.1
Ukraine	1995	48 608	21.3	55.1	26.7	47.1	50.2	15.0	41.3	33.8	43.7
	2000	31 262	18.6	56.6	19.7	62.4	57.4	16.8	37.6	21.3	45.5
	2005	81 669	19.5	58.2	21.8	51.9	51.4	13.0	32.3	19.8	54.7

Sources:
- UN DESA Statistics Division

Notes:

(1) The breakdown in shares might not add-up to 100 percent due to statistical discrepancies.

(2) Refers to Total Value Added.

(3) Includes agriculture, hunting, forestry and fishing (ISIC Rev.3 divisions 01-05).

(4) Includes mining and quarrying, manufacturing, electricity, gas and water supply, and construction (ISIC Rev.3 divisions 10-45).

(5) Include all other economic activities (ISIC Rev.3 divisions 50-99).

(6) GDP data include the Federation of Bosnia and Herzegovina only. Data for the Republika Srpska are excluded.

Sources :
- ONU DAES Division de statistique

Notes :

(1) La somme des pourcentages du PIB peut ne pas être égale à 100 à cause des écarts statistiques.

(2) Renvoie à la Valeur Ajoutée Totale.

(3) Inclut agriculture, chasse, sylviculture et pêche (CITI Rev.3 divisions 01-05).

(4) Inclut les activités extractives, les activités de fabrication, la production et distribution d'électricité, de gaz et d'eau et la construction (CITI Rev.3 divisions 10-45).

(5) Incluent toutes les autres activités économiques (CITI Rev.3 divisions 50-99).

(6) Y compris le PIB de la Fédération de Bosnie-Herzégovine seulement. Non compris le PIB de la Republika Srpska.

8.3.2 Nominal gross domestic product by type of expenditure and by kind of economic activity of economic groupings

8.3.2 Produit intérieur brut nominal par catégories de dépenses et par branches d'activité économique des groupements économiques

Economic grouping / Groupements économiques	Year / Année	Total GDP (millions of dollars) / PIB total (millions de dollars)	Final consumption / Consommation finale: Government / Administration publique	Household / Ménages	Gross capital formation / Formation brute de capital	Exports / Exportations: Of goods and services / Des biens et services	Less imports / Moins les importations	Agriculture (3)	Industry (4) / Industrie (4): Total	Manufacturing / Activités de fabrication	Services (5)
DEVELOPING ECONOMIES - ÉCONOMIES EN DÉVELOPPEMENT	1990	3 810 973	13.9	59.7	25.0	25.0	24.0	14.9	35.9	22.1	49.2
	1995	5 653 956	13.5	59.4	27.5	30.6	31.2	12.8	35.9	22.8	51.3
	2000	6 659 394	13.8	58.6	24.6	36.4	33.6	10.8	36.7	22.9	52.5
	2005	9 962 981	13.3	55.9	26.0	41.1	36.9	10.5	37.8	23.5	51.7
Developing economies excluding China - Économies en développement sans la Chine	1990	3 427 779	14.1	60.9	23.8	27.5	26.7	13.5	35.3	20.4	51.2
	1995	4 953 086	13.8	61.3	25.7	31.9	32.9	11.7	34.2	20.0	54.1
	2000	5 579 867	14.0	60.7	22.3	38.4	35.5	9.9	34.7	18.9	55.4
	2005	7 980 905	13.6	59.1	22.0	43.2	38.4	9.7	35.5	18.7	54.8
Developing economies excluding LDCs - Économies en développement sans les PMA	1990	3 660 270	13.8	59.1	25.3	25.4	24.1	14.1	36.5	22.5	49.4
	1995	5 499 697	13.5	58.9	27.8	30.9	31.3	12.1	36.4	23.2	51.6
	2000	6 482 298	13.8	58.3	24.7	36.8	33.7	10.2	37.1	23.2	52.7
	2005	9 672 078	13.3	55.5	26.1	41.5	36.9	9.9	38.1	24.0	52.0
High-income countries - Pays à revenu élevé	1990	1 276 432	14.7	56.1	24.7	42.2	38.1	6.2	39.0	22.0	54.8
	1995	2 029 702	13.4	57.3	27.1	46.7	44.6	4.8	35.7	20.4	59.6
	2000	2 607 559	13.7	57.6	24.0	50.0	45.1	3.7	35.1	19.5	61.2
	2005	3 363 222	13.3	54.2	22.7	60.7	50.9	3.4	36.7	18.9	59.8
Middle-income countries - Pays à revenu intermédiaire	1990	1 267 658	14.8	62.1	24.3	19.9	21.6	11.0	34.4	20.9	54.6
	1995	1 883 670	16.0	61.9	24.8	22.4	25.2	11.1	34.2	20.8	54.7
	2000	1 814 272	16.0	62.0	21.3	29.4	28.7	9.9	35.1	19.7	55.0
	2005	2 717 769	15.8	60.2	22.0	33.3	31.7	9.7	35.7	19.9	54.6
Low-income countries - Pays à revenu faible	1990	1 266 884	12.2	61.0	26.0	12.8	12.4	27.6	34.4	23.4	38.0
	1995	1 740 584	11.1	59.1	30.9	20.6	22.1	23.6	37.9	27.7	38.4
	2000	2 237 563	12.2	57.1	28.0	26.3	24.0	19.1	39.7	28.8	41.2
	2005	3 881 991	11.6	54.5	31.5	29.7	28.3	16.5	40.0	29.5	43.5
Heavily indebted poor countries - Pays pauvres très endettés	1990	137 429	14.4	76.8	16.4	19.8	27.3	32.1	23.5	13.4	44.4
	1995	126 591	11.9	76.6	18.0	22.5	29.2	36.6	21.3	11.5	42.2
	2000	136 862	12.1	76.2	19.1	23.6	31.0	33.5	23.3	11.3	43.2
	2005	220 213	13.2	73.0	20.6	27.2	33.9	32.8	23.8	11.3	43.4
Landlocked countries - Pays sans littoral	1990	65 000	15.5	74.1	17.9	20.4	27.6	31.3	31.9	20.5	36.9
	1995	117 230	15.4	70.9	21.9	35.4	43.3	27.7	27.5	17.4	44.8
	2000	118 867	15.5	70.6	19.6	36.0	41.5	25.8	28.1	14.3	46.1
	2005	207 951	15.1	63.2	25.1	41.0	44.0	21.2	32.2	14.3	46.6
Small island developing states - Petits états insulaires en développement	1990	25 448	18.0	61.1	24.7	51.2	54.5	11.1	30.7	12.4	58.2
	1995	32 812	16.4	60.5	24.8	52.9	54.1	12.6	28.4	11.9	59.0
	2000	40 255	16.5	63.1	25.6	51.0	56.0	8.5	29.1	12.0	62.4
	2005	56 821	16.0	62.5	24.5	53.7	57.9	8.4	30.0	12.0	61.6
Least developed countries - Pays les moins avancés	*1990*	*150 505*	*15.3*	*74.7*	*17.1*	*15.8*	*23.1*	*34.1*	*21.7*	*11.1*	*44.2*
	1995	*153 994*	*14.7*	*75.3*	*18.9*	*18.5*	*28.3*	*36.7*	*21.1*	*10.3*	*42.2*
	2000	*176 761*	*14.6*	*71.6*	*19.8*	*23.3*	*29.8*	*32.5*	*25.1*	*10.1*	*42.5*
	2005	*290 475*	*15.1*	*68.9*	*20.4*	*29.6*	*34.2*	*29.7*	*28.9*	*10.2*	*41.4*
Africa and Haiti - Afrique et Haïti	1990	97 965	15.5	75.0	17.6	19.9	27.9	33.1	22.7	10.6	44.2
	1995	83 966	14.0	77.3	18.5	21.8	31.8	39.0	20.4	8.3	40.7
	2000	94 454	15.0	72.9	18.7	25.4	32.0	35.2	24.3	7.9	40.5
	2005	173 122	14.7	68.4	19.7	35.0	37.5	31.4	30.2	8.2	38.4
Asia - Asie	1990	50 931	14.6	74.2	15.7	7.4	12.9	36.2	20.0	12.1	43.9
	1995	67 685	15.3	73.0	19.1	13.8	22.9	34.2	22.1	12.9	43.7
	2000	79 704	13.9	70.3	21.0	20.5	26.3	29.4	26.3	13.2	44.2
	2005	113 606	15.2	69.5	21.4	21.3	28.3	27.2	27.2	13.5	45.6
Islands - Îles	1990	1 610	23.9	73.3	31.6	29.2	57.7	26.8	17.4	7.3	55.8
	1995	2 343	23.3	66.2	31.0	34.1	55.2	23.8	17.0	6.8	59.2
	2000	2 603	26.9	63.0	26.2	35.2	52.1	20.2	15.1	6.2	64.7
	2005	3 747	28.0	73.3	22.0	33.8	58.1	19.1	15.5	6.1	65.3

For sources and notes, see end of table.

Pour les sources et les notes, se reporter à la fin du tableau.

8.3.2 Nominal gross domestic product by type of expenditure and by kind of economic activity of economic groupings

8.3.2 Produit intérieur brut nominal par catégories de dépenses et par branches d'activité économique des groupements économiques

Economic grouping / Groupements économiques	Year Année	Total GDP (millions of dollars) PIB total (millions de dollars)	GDP by type of expenditure (1) / PIB par catégories de dépense (1)					GDP by kind of economic activity (2) / PIB par branches d'activité économique (2)			
			Final consumption Consommation finale		Gross capital formation Formation brute de capital	Exports Exportations	Less imports Moins les importations	Agriculture (3)	Industry (4) Industrie (4)		Services (5)
			Government Administration publique	Household Ménages		Of goods and services / Des biens et services			Total	Manufacturing Activités de fabrication	
			Percentage / En pourcentage								
Major petroleum exporters - Principaux exportateurs de pétrole	*1990*	*675 726*	*17.5*	*53.5*	*21.3*	*34.8*	*28.8*	*13.2*	*45.5*	*14.0*	*41.3*
	1995	*800 151*	*16.0*	*55.7*	*23.4*	*34.1*	*30.0*	*12.6*	*44.7*	*15.3*	*42.7*
	2000	*976 467*	*15.3*	*47.9*	*19.2*	*43.9*	*26.5*	*9.2*	*51.4*	*13.4*	*39.5*
	2005	*1 632 219*	*12.9*	*47.0*	*19.3*	*50.9*	*30.5*	*9.1*	*50.1*	*13.0*	*40.9*
Africa - Afrique	1990	171 252	14.0	55.5	19.6	35.4	24.4	16.8	50.8	14.1	32.4
	1995	123 555	15.4	66.3	18.0	34.0	37.0	17.6	49.7	8.8	32.7
	2000	173 783	13.1	43.6	13.9	51.3	21.8	15.3	57.3	6.0	27.3
	2005	295 190	8.7	44.1	18.2	58.2	29.2	17.0	53.1	4.2	29.9
America - Amérique	1990	54 076	17.7	47.1	14.1	43.0	24.3	5.4	54.8	25.2	39.8
	1995	82 789	15.2	54.0	23.6	31.1	25.3	5.5	45.8	22.5	48.7
	2000	128 100	12.7	52.1	23.8	32.8	21.3	3.8	47.4	18.9	48.7
	2005	150 340	13.3	51.7	19.3	38.4	22.9	3.8	47.7	17.1	48.5
Asia - Asie	1990	450 399	18.9	53.6	22.8	33.6	31.0	12.8	42.5	12.6	44.7
	1995	593 806	16.2	53.8	24.6	34.5	29.3	12.5	43.5	15.7	43.9
	2000	674 585	16.3	48.2	19.7	44.2	28.7	8.6	50.6	14.2	40.8
	2005	1 186 689	13.8	47.2	19.6	50.7	31.8	7.8	49.6	14.7	42.6
Major exporters of manufactured goods - Principaux exportateurs d'articles manufacturés	*1990*	*2 276 405*	*12.5*	*58.8*	*28.4*	*23.3*	*22.8*	*14.5*	*34.9*	*25.7*	*50.6*
	1995	*3 577 570*	*12.8*	*56.8*	*31.0*	*33.2*	*33.8*	*12.1*	*36.4*	*26.7*	*51.5*
	2000	*4 308 308*	*13.3*	*57.7*	*27.7*	*38.8*	*37.4*	*10.3*	*36.0*	*27.2*	*53.7*
	2005	*6 539 953*	*13.1*	*55.1*	*29.1*	*42.0*	*39.8*	*9.8*	*36.8*	*28.0*	*53.4*
America - Amérique	1990	700 937	13.7	62.6	23.0	11.9	11.2	6.6	32.2	22.9	61.2
	1995	990 334	17.0	62.0	21.6	14.3	14.8	7.5	32.1	21.7	60.4
	2000	1 182 524	15.2	63.9	22.6	20.6	22.4	5.9	32.0	20.8	62.1
	2005	1 567 851	15.1	62.5	21.2	23.1	21.9	6.5	31.4	20.2	62.1
Asia - Asie	1990	1 575 467	12.0	57.2	30.8	28.4	28.0	18.4	36.1	27.0	45.5
	1995	2 587 236	11.2	54.8	34.6	40.5	41.0	13.8	38.0	28.5	48.1
	2000	3 125 784	12.6	55.4	29.6	45.6	43.0	11.8	37.4	29.4	50.8
	2005	4 972 102	12.4	52.7	31.6	48.0	45.4	10.7	38.4	30.3	51.0
Emerging economies - Économies émergentes	*1990*	*1 501 423*	*13.2*	*59.1*	*26.3*	*26.3*	*25.1*	*7.3*	*35.6*	*25.1*	*57.1*
	1995	*2 506 727*	*13.8*	*58.7*	*27.8*	*31.4*	*31.8*	*6.7*	*35.1*	*23.7*	*58.1*
	2000	*2 733 804*	*13.7*	*60.6*	*24.2*	*38.8*	*37.2*	*5.2*	*34.1*	*23.5*	*60.7*
	2005	*3 495 861*	*13.9*	*58.5*	*23.6*	*45.8*	*41.9*	*5.5*	*35.0*	*23.8*	*59.5*
America - Amérique	1990	905 079	13.4	63.5	21.5	12.5	10.9	6.9	33.0	23.2	60.2
	1995	1 374 131	15.7	63.5	21.4	14.1	14.7	7.1	31.8	20.7	61.1
	2000	1 595 197	14.7	65.1	21.6	19.3	20.7	5.8	31.4	20.0	62.8
	2005	1 939 106	14.4	62.3	21.2	24.4	22.3	6.8	32.3	20.2	60.9
Asia - Asie	1990	596 344	13.0	52.5	33.6	47.1	46.7	8.1	39.9	28.2	52.0
	1995	1 132 597	11.6	52.8	35.5	52.3	52.5	6.2	39.2	27.3	54.6
	2000	1 138 608	12.3	54.2	27.8	66.1	60.5	4.4	37.9	28.4	57.7
	2005	1 556 755	13.3	53.8	26.5	72.4	66.4	4.0	38.3	28.1	57.7
Newly industrialized economies - Économies nouvellement industrialisées	*1990*	*843 265*	*11.7*	*54.9*	*32.1*	*50.4*	*49.4*	*9.9*	*38.1*	*25.8*	*52.0*
	1995	*1 573 028*	*10.8*	*55.9*	*34.3*	*56.2*	*57.3*	*8.0*	*37.0*	*24.8*	*54.9*
	2000	*1 547 413*	*11.4*	*56.3*	*26.8*	*71.4*	*65.5*	*5.8*	*35.8*	*25.5*	*58.4*
	2005	*2 108 332*	*12.1*	*56.5*	*25.0*	*76.2*	*70.3*	*5.5*	*36.7*	*25.9*	*57.8*
First tier - Premier tier	1990	543 848	12.7	52.6	31.5	58.7	56.0	5.5	38.1	27.4	56.4
	1995	1 019 975	11.4	54.5	33.5	63.2	62.6	4.1	35.5	24.4	60.4
	2000	1 094 316	12.1	55.7	28.4	73.2	69.2	2.8	32.8	24.1	64.4
	2005	1 422 031	13.0	54.9	25.8	82.7	76.8	2.3	33.0	24.2	64.8
Second tier - Deuxième tier	1990	299 417	9.9	59.0	33.0	35.4	37.4	17.8	38.0	22.9	44.2
	1995	553 053	9.7	58.5	35.6	43.3	47.5	15.2	39.8	25.5	45.0
	2000	453 097	9.7	57.8	23.0	67.1	56.6	12.7	42.7	28.7	44.5
	2005	686 301	10.3	59.7	23.3	62.8	57.0	12.0	44.2	29.1	43.9

For sources and notes, see end of table.

Pour les sources et les notes, se reporter à la fin du tableau.

8.3.2 Nominal gross domestic product by type of expenditure and by kind of economic activity of economic groupings

8.3.2 Produit intérieur brut nominal par catégories de dépenses et par branches d'activité économique des groupements économiques

Economic grouping / Groupements économiques	Year / Année	Total GDP (millions of dollars) PIB total (millions de dollars)	GDP by type of expenditure (1) / PIB par catégories de dépense (1)					GDP by kind of economic activity (2) / PIB par branches d'activité économique (2)			
			Final consumption / Consommation finale		Gross capital formation / Formation brute de capital	Exports / Exportations	Less imports / Moins les importations	Agriculture (3)	Industry (4) / Industrie (4)		Services (5)
			Government / Administration publique	Household / Ménages	Formation brute de capital	Of goods and services / Des biens et services			Total	Manufacturing / Activités de fabrication	
			Percentage / En pourcentage									
Developing economies: Africa -	**1990**	**508 443**	**15.4**	**64.1**	**19.8**	**28.0**	**26.2**	**18.2**	**38.1**	**16.7**	**43.7**
Économies en développement : Afrique	**1995**	**531 146**	**15.3**	**68.7**	**18.4**	**26.7**	**30.1**	**17.8**	**34.4**	**15.2**	**47.8**
	2000	**599 779**	**14.4**	**62.2**	**17.1**	**33.4**	**27.1**	**16.6**	**37.0**	**13.0**	**46.4**
	2005	**947 747**	**14.3**	**60.8**	**19.2**	**37.9**	**31.8**	**16.7**	**36.8**	**12.0**	**46.5**
Northern Africa excluding Sudan -	1990	168 346	15.7	60.4	26.3	28.8	30.8	13.8	41.1	14.0	45.1
Afrique septentrionale sans le Soudan	1995	187 274	15.4	66.8	20.9	25.9	29.6	13.7	38.0	14.7	48.4
	2000	241 434	14.5	61.4	20.0	29.6	25.5	12.1	40.3	13.3	47.6
	2005	321 346	12.3	55.4	24.6	39.8	31.2	11.1	42.7	12.0	46.1
Sub-Saharan Africa - Afrique subsaharienne	1990	340 097	15.2	65.9	16.5	27.6	23.9	20.4	36.6	18.1	42.9
	1995	343 872	15.3	69.7	17.0	27.1	30.4	20.1	32.5	15.4	47.5
	2000	358 344	14.4	62.8	15.1	36.0	28.2	19.8	34.8	12.8	45.5
	2005	626 401	15.4	63.5	16.4	36.9	32.1	19.7	33.7	12.1	46.6
Sub-Saharan Africa excluding South Africa -	1990	228 083	13.0	68.4	16.0	29.3	26.5	27.7	35.0	15.5	37.3
Afrique sub-saharienne sans l'Afrique du Sud	1995	192 759	13.0	75.3	16.1	30.5	36.9	32.0	30.8	11.1	37.2
	2000	225 467	12.2	62.7	14.6	40.8	30.2	28.7	36.4	9.5	35.0
	2005	387 576	12.6	63.3	15.8	42.9	34.4	28.8	34.7	7.9	36.5
Developing economies: America -	**1990**	**1 123 193**	**13.9**	**63.1**	**21.1**	**16.6**	**14.8**	**8.0**	**33.2**	**22.3**	**58.8**
Économies en développement : Amérique	**1995**	**1 720 950**	**15.5**	**63.8**	**21.5**	**16.7**	**17.7**	**8.0**	**31.8**	**20.1**	**60.2**
	2000	**2 009 383**	**14.9**	**64.8**	**21.2**	**21.6**	**22.5**	**6.5**	**31.8**	**19.2**	**61.7**
	2005	**2 486 993**	**14.7**	**62.5**	**21.0**	**25.9**	**24.1**	**7.3**	**32.4**	**19.0**	**60.3**
Central America and Greater Carribean Islands	1990	340 416	11.0	68.9	22.7	22.2	24.7	9.4	26.9	19.1	63.7
excluding Puerto Rico - Amérique centrale et	1995	391 748	11.9	68.0	19.4	30.6	30.0	7.2	26.3	19.2	66.5
Grandes Antilles sans Porto Rico	2000	715 406	12.1	67.9	22.9	31.4	34.3	5.5	27.3	19.4	67.2
	2005	956 768	12.6	69.1	21.2	29.8	32.7	5.3	25.2	17.0	69.5
Central America and Greater Carribean Islands	1990	77 706	19.7	66.5	21.0	34.4	41.8	14.5	23.2	14.6	62.3
excluding Mexico and Puerto Rico -	1995	105 583	16.0	70.4	18.2	31.0	36.1	12.6	25.7	17.5	61.8
Amérique centrale et Grandes Antilles sans	2000	134 615	16.4	71.6	19.0	33.2	40.1	11.4	25.9	16.8	62.8
le Mexique et Porto Rico	2005	188 331	17.1	72.4	18.5	29.4	37.5	11.0	23.6	15.0	65.4
South America and Central America -	1990	1 062 933	13.4	63.3	20.9	15.2	13.0	7.9	33.7	22.9	58.4
Amérique du Sud et Amérique centrale	1995	1 649 788	15.3	63.8	21.6	16.0	16.8	8.1	32.0	20.3	59.9
	2000	1 919 864	14.6	64.8	21.3	20.9	21.6	6.5	32.1	19.4	61.4
	2005	2 361 263	14.3	62.6	21.1	25.4	23.4	7.4	32.8	19.4	59.8
South America excluding Brazil -	1990	329 161	12.8	63.7	16.8	20.4	14.1	9.8	38.2	23.4	52.0
Amérique du Sud sans le Brésil	1995	606 775	13.0	65.9	21.8	16.9	17.8	8.3	32.5	18.2	59.3
	2000	666 586	14.0	65.2	18.9	19.6	17.6	6.8	32.9	17.2	60.3
	2005	695 062	13.1	60.4	21.0	29.2	23.5	8.3	37.2	18.1	54.5
Developing economies: Asia -	**1990**	**2 168 131**	**13.5**	**57.0**	**28.2**	**28.7**	**28.2**	**17.9**	**36.9**	**23.3**	**45.2**
Économies en développement : Asie	**1995**	**3 386 090**	**12.2**	**55.7**	**32.1**	**38.2**	**38.2**	**14.4**	**38.3**	**25.4**	**47.4**
	2000	**4 036 872**	**13.2**	**55.0**	**27.4**	**44.2**	**40.0**	**11.9**	**39.0**	**26.0**	**49.0**
	2005	**6 508 128**	**12.6**	**52.7**	**28.9**	**47.5**	**42.5**	**10.7**	**39.9**	**26.8**	**49.4**
Eastern and South-Eastern Asia excluding China -	1990	880 469	11.9	53.8	31.1	49.5	48.3	10.8	38.1	25.5	51.1
Asie orientale et Asie du Sud-Est sans la Chine	1995	1 625 165	11.1	55.6	33.8	55.6	56.5	8.8	36.7	24.4	54.5
	2000	1 613 551	11.5	55.8	26.5	70.4	64.6	6.7	35.7	25.1	57.6
	2005	2 212 447	12.3	55.9	25.0	75.3	69.5	6.4	36.7	25.5	56.9
Southern Asia excluding India -	1990	195 788	10.3	72.7	19.5	12.7	20.1	22.9	27.0	14.0	50.1
Asie méridionale sans l'Inde	1995	253 414	12.0	67.9	19.4	17.0	16.8	22.5	29.5	14.7	48.0
	2000	258 120	9.9	65.9	22.1	20.5	19.9	19.4	31.4	15.4	49.2
	2005	430 317	10.3	67.2	20.7	24.4	24.7	16.4	33.3	16.2	50.4

8.3.2 Nominal gross domestic product by type of expenditure and by kind of economic activity of economic groupings

8.3.2 Produit intérieur brut nominal par catégories de dépenses et par branches d'activité économique des groupements économiques

Sources:
- UN DESA Statistics Division

Notes:

(1) The breakdown in shares might not add-up to 100 percent due to statistical discrepancies.

(2) Refers to Total Value Added.

(3) Includes agriculture, hunting, forestry and fishing (ISIC Rev.3 divisions 01-05).

(4) Includes mining and quarrying, manufacturing, electricity, gas and water supply, and construction (ISIC Rev.3 divisions 10-45).

(5) Include all other economic activities (ISIC Rev.3 divisions 50-99).

Sources :
- ONU DAES Division de statistique

Notes :

(1) La somme des pourcentages du PIB peut ne pas être égale à 100 à cause des écarts statistiques.

(2) Renvoie à la Valeur Ajoutée Totale.

(3) Inclut agriculture, chasse, sylviculture et pêche (CITI Rev.3 divisions 01-05).

(4) Inclut les activités extractives, les activités de fabrication, la production et distribution d'électricité, de gaz et d'eau et la construction (CITI Rev.3 divisions 10-45).

(5) Incluent toutes les autres activités économiques (CITI Rev.3 divisions 50-99).

Region, country or territory / Régions, pays ou territoires	Year / Année	Population		Total labour force / Main d'œuvre totale		Agriculture labour force / Main d'œuvre dans l'agriculture	
		Total (thousands) / Total (milliers)	Urban population (% of total population) / Population urbaine (en % de la population totale)	Total (thousands) / Total (milliers)	Female labour (% of total labour force) / Main d'œuvre féminine (en % de la main d'œuvre totale)	Total (thousands) / Total (milliers)	Female labour (% of total agriculture labour force) / Main d'œuvre féminine (en % de la main d'œuvre totale dans l'agriculture)
		(1)	(2)	(3)	(4)	(5)	(6)
WORLD - MONDE	1990	5 294 879	43.1	2 405 548	39.8	1 220 515	42.7
	2000	6 124 123	46.8	2 818 382	39.8	1 317 867	43.7
	2004	6 436 826	48.4	3 003 499	40.0	1 347 283	43.9
	2006	6 592 900	49.2	3 096 808	..	..	..
DEVELOPED ECONOMIES - ÉCONOMIES DÉVELOPPÉES	1990	878 398	73.4	429 414	42.3	27 668	37.2
	2000	941 802	75.8	467 279	44.0	20 981	36.6
	2004	965 245	76.5	479 695	44.6	18 336	36.2
	2006	976 183	76.8	485 467	..	..	..
DEVELOPING ECONOMIES - ÉCONOMIES EN DÉVELOPPEMENT	1990	4 068 994	34.7	1 803 721	38.4	1 159 867	42.9
	2000	4 846 278	40.0	2 193 632	38.4	1 271 626	43.9
	2004	5 138 632	42.2	2 363 482	38.6	1 305 735	44.2
	2006	5 285 055	43.2	2 449 990	..	..	..
ECONOMIES IN TRANSITION - ÉCONOMIES EN TRANSITION	1990	347 486	63.4	172 412	47.5	32 898	40.0
	2000	336 042	62.7	157 471	47.4	25 158	36.7
	2004	332 949	62.4	160 322	47.8	23 103	35.3
	2006	331 662	62.3	161 351	..	..	..
Developed economies: America - Économies développées : Amérique	1990	287 448	75.2	148 132	44.3	4 196	22.6
	2000	319 506	79.1	166 469	45.8	3 449	26.2
	2004	332 851	80.3	173 535	46.2	3 172	27.6
	2006	339 515	80.8	177 301	..	..	..
Bermuda - Bermudes	1990	60	100.3	..	..	1	0.0
	2000	63	100.2	..	..	1	0.0
	2004	64	101.0	..	..	1	0.0
	2006	64	..	..	..	..	..
Canada	1990	27 701	76.6	14 665	44.1	494	32.2
	2000	30 689	79.4	16 224	45.7	391	42.2
	2004	31 955	80.8	17 371	46.2	353	46.2
	2006	32 577	81.4	17 901	..	..	..
Greenland - Groenland	1990	56	79.2	..	..	1	0.0
	2000	56	81.8	..	..	1	0.0
	2004	57	82.4	..	..	1	0.0
	2006	58	..	..	..	..	..
Saint Pierre and Miquelon - Saint-Pierre-et-Miquelon	1990	6	79.6	..	..	0	..
	2000	6	79.1	..	..	0	..
	2004	6	..	..	..	0	..
	2006	6	..	..	..	..	..
United States - États-Unis	1990	259 625	75.1	133 467	44.3	3 700	21.3
	2000	288 691	79.1	150 244	45.8	3 056	24.2
	2004	300 769	80.3	156 164	46.2	2 817	25.2
	2006	306 810	80.8	159 400	..	..	..
Developed economies: Asia - Économies développées : Asie	1990	128 051	64.0	65 502	40.6	4 742	45.2
	2000	133 118	66.4	70 077	40.7	2 840	43.0
	2004	134 372	66.9	69 613	41.2	2 238	42.0
	2006	134 763	67.3	69 066	..	..	..
Israel - Israël	1990	4 514	90.3	1 597	40.6	73	20.5
	2000	6 084	91.5	2 373	45.6	70	20.0
	2004	6 574	92.1	2 594	46.8	66	19.7
	2006	6 810	92.3	2 706	..	..	..
Japan - Japon	1990	123 537	63.1	63 905	40.6	4 669	45.6
	2000	127 034	65.2	67 705	40.6	2 770	43.6
	2004	127 798	65.6	67 020	41.0	2 172	42.7
	2006	127 953	65.9	66 361	..	..	..
Developed economies: Europe - Économies développées : Europe	1990	442 615	74.4	205 770	41.5	18 098	38.8
	2000	466 185	75.6	219 326	43.6	14 075	37.9
	2004	473 890	75.9	224 360	44.3	12 323	37.2
	2006	477 234	76.0	226 540	..	..	..

For sources and notes, see end of table.

Pour les sources et les notes, se reporter à la fin du tableau.

Region, country or territory / Régions, pays ou territoires	Year / Année	Population		Total labour force / Main d'œuvre totale		Agriculture labour force / Main d'œuvre dans l'agriculture	
		Total (thousands) / Total (milliers)	Urban population (% of total population) / Population urbaine (en % de la population totale)	Total (thousands) / Total (milliers)	Female labour (% of total labour force) / Main d'œuvre féminine (en % de la main d'œuvre totale)	Total (thousands) / Total (milliers)	Female labour (% of total agriculture labour force) / Main d'œuvre féminine (en % de la main d'œuvre totale dans l'agriculture)
		(1)	(2)	(3)	(4)	(5)	(6)
Andorra - Andorre	1990	53	94.7	..	..	3	33.3
	2000	66	91.8	..	..	3	33.3
	2004	72	83.0	..	..	3	33.3
	2006	74	..	..	..	..	..
Austria - Autriche	1990	7 729	65.8	3 558	40.8	276	46.7
	2000	8 111	65.7	3 917	43.1	192	43.8
	2004	8 253	65.1	3 943	44.4	162	43.2
	2006	8 327	64.9	3 976	..	..	..
Belgium - Belgique	2004	10 360	97.6	4 453	43.3	67	28.4
	2006	10 430	97.4	4 488	..	..	..
Belgium-Luxembourg - Belgique-Luxembourg	1990	10 315	96.3	4 108	38.8	112	26.8
	2000	10 630	97.9	4 636	42.7	81	28.4
Cyprus - Chypre	1990	681	65.0	324	37.7	44	43.2
	2000	786	68.8	370	41.2	33	39.4
	2004	827	69.2	406	44.5	29	37.9
	2006	846	69.6	421	..	..	..
Czechoslovakia (former) - Tchécoslovaquie (anc.)	1990	15 559	68.9	8 049	47.0	933	38.0
Czech Republic - République tchèque	2000	10 220	74.4	5 181	44.4	472	31.6
	2004	10 195	74.7	5 189	44.9	413	28.8
	2006	10 189	74.8	5 196	..	..	..
Denmark - Danemark	1990	5 140	84.8	2 912	46.1	162	24.1
	2000	5 335	85.2	2 864	46.6	111	24.3
	2004	5 403	85.6	2 851	46.6	93	24.7
	2006	5 430	85.9	2 846	..	..	..
Estonia - Estonie	2000	1 370	69.2	669	48.8	83	32.5
	2004	1 348	68.8	655	49.3	74	29.7
	2006	1 340	68.9	656	..	..	..
Faeroe Islands - Îles Féroé	1990	47	29.6	..	..	1	0.0
	2000	46	36.6	..	..	1	0.0
	2004	48	38.4	..	..	1	0.0
	2006	49	..	..	..	..	..
Finland - Finlande	1990	4 986	61.4	2 574	47.3	216	35.2
	2000	5 176	61.1	2 599	47.7	143	35.7
	2004	5 231	60.9	2 649	47.8	118	35.6
	2006	5 261	60.9	2 662	..	..	..
France	1990	58 237	74.4	25 420	43.3	1 409	34.9
	2000	60 915	76.3	27 071	45.4	936	33.8
	2004	62 446	76.5	27 610	45.8	777	33.2
	2006	63 195	76.6	27 722	..	..	..
Germany - Allemagne	1990	79 433	85.3	38 304	40.5	1 588	42.6
	2000	82 309	87.6	40 464	43.7	1 013	38.7
	2004	82 628	88.3	40 920	44.9	841	37.3
	2006	82 641	88.7	41 217	..	..	..
Gibraltar	1990	27	100.6	..	..	2	50.0
	2000	27	102.3	..	..	1	0.0
	2004	29	..	..	..	1	0.0
	2006	29	..	..	..	..	..
Greece - Grèce	1990	10 161	58.8	4 185	36.1	963	44.7
	2000	10 975	60.1	4 894	39.2	797	48.2
	2004	11 079	61.2	5 095	40.5	707	49.4
	2006	11 123	61.8	5 211	..	..	..
Holy See - Saint-Siège	1990	1	..	..	..	0	..
	2000	1	..	..	..	0	..
	2004	1	..	..	..	0	..
	2006	1	..	..	..	..	..

For sources and notes, see end of table.

Pour les sources et les notes, se reporter à la fin du tableau.

Region, country or territory / Régions, pays ou territoires	Year / Année	Population		Total labour force / Main d'œuvre totale		Agriculture labour force / Main d'œuvre dans l'agriculture	
		Total (thousands) / Total (milliers)	Urban population (% of total population) / Population urbaine (en % de la population totale)	Total (thousands) / Total (milliers)	Female labour (% of total labour force) / Main d'œuvre féminine (en % de la main d'œuvre totale)	Total (thousands) / Total (milliers)	Female labour (% of total agriculture labour force) / Main d'œuvre féminine (en % de la main d'œuvre totale dans l'agriculture)
		(1)	(2)	(3)	(4)	(5)	(6)
Hungary - Hongrie	1990	10 365	62.0	4 531	44.5	721	30.5
	2000	10 214	64.1	4 235	44.5	513	26.3
	2004	10 113	65.6	4 215	45.0	437	24.5
	2006	10 058	66.4	4 207	..	..	..
Iceland - Islande	1990	255	90.6	142	45.6	16	18.8
	2000	281	92.5	165	47.0	13	15.4
	2004	293	92.6	173	46.7	12	16.7
	2006	298	92.8	178	..	..	..
Ireland - Irlande	1990	3 515	56.9	1 335	34.3	188	6.9
	2000	3 804	59.1	1 757	40.7	164	6.7
	2004	4 068	60.3	2 011	42.5	153	6.5
	2006	4 221	60.5	2 130	..	..	..
Italy - Italie	1990	56 719	66.7	23 915	37.1	2 101	38.6
	2000	57 692	67.2	23 837	38.3	1 352	41.2
	2004	58 475	66.9	24 182	39.6	1 099	41.9
	2006	58 779	66.9	24 279	..	..	..
Latvia - Lettonie	2000	2 379	66.7	1 092	49.0	153	32.7
	2004	2 315	66.1	1 096	48.6	135	29.6
	2006	2 289	65.9	1 098	..	..	..
Lithuania - Lituanie	2000	3 503	66.9	1 681	48.7	218	28.4
	2004	3 440	66.7	1 629	49.2	183	25.7
	2006	3 408	66.8	1 628	..	..	..
Luxembourg	2004	452	93.5	202	41.6	3	33.3
	2006	461	94.5	209	..	..	..
Malta - Malte	1990	360	87.6	127	23.6	3	0.0
	2000	389	91.6	153	28.9	2	0.0
	2004	400	91.8	166	32.6	2	0.0
	2006	405	92.0	172	..	..	..
Netherlands - Pays-Bas	1990	14 952	60.0	6 932	39.1	315	28.6
	2000	15 924	64.2	8 128	42.9	248	30.6
	2004	16 264	66.2	8 529	44.0	221	31.7
	2006	16 379	67.2	8 665	..	..	..
Norway - Norvège	1990	4 241	72.0	2 217	44.7	134	27.6
	2000	4 489	76.1	2 411	46.6	106	34.0
	2004	4 609	79.4	2 503	47.2	95	35.8
	2006	4 669	80.8	2 542	..	..	..
Poland - Pologne	1990	38 111	60.7	18 584	45.9	5 144	45.5
	2000	38 433	62.0	17 567	45.7	4 334	41.9
	2004	38 247	62.4	17 508	45.7	3 988	40.0
	2006	38 140	62.7	17 499	..	..	..
Portugal	1990	9 983	46.7	4 836	42.8	860	50.6
	2000	10 227	53.0	5 223	45.4	650	56.6
	2004	10 472	55.0	5 473	46.3	570	58.9
	2006	10 579	56.0	5 582	..	..	..
San Marino - Saint-Marin	1990	24	91.1	..	..	1	100.0
	2000	27	92.8	..	..	1	0.0
	2004	30	91.1	..	..	1	0.0
	2006	31	..	..	..	..	..
Slovakia - Slovaquie	2000	5 388	56.9	2 611	45.6	268	30.2
	2004	5 387	57.9	2 670	45.2	244	27.5
	2006	5 388	58.4	2 693	..	..	..
Slovenia - Slovénie	2000	1 984	50.4	963	46.2	20	50.0
	2004	1 997	50.0	1 008	46.1	13	46.2
	2006	2 001	50.0	1 020	..	..	..

For sources and notes, see end of table.

Pour les sources et les notes, se reporter à la fin du tableau.

Region, country or territory / Régions, pays ou territoires	Year / Année	Population		Total labour force / Main d'œuvre totale		Agriculture labour force / Main d'œuvre dans l'agriculture	
		Total (thousands) / Total (milliers)	Urban population (% of total population) / Population urbaine (en % de la population totale)	Total (thousands) / Total (milliers)	Female labour (% of total labour force) / Main d'œuvre féminine (en % de la main d'œuvre totale)	Total (thousands) / Total (milliers)	Female labour (% of total agriculture labour force) / Main d'œuvre féminine (en % de la main d'œuvre totale dans l'agriculture)
		(1)	(2)	(3)	(4)	(5)	(6)
Spain - Espagne	1990	38 851	76.2	16 179	34.4	1 892	30.4
	2000	40 229	77.2	18 661	39.5	1 333	32.8
	2004	42 795	76.3	20 304	40.8	1 113	33.2
	2006	43 887	75.9	20 949	..	..	..
Sweden - Suède	1990	8 559	83.1	4 745	47.7	204	28.4
	2000	8 868	83.4	4 609	47.3	151	32.5
	2004	8 998	83.5	4 672	47.4	131	34.4
	2006	9 078	83.4	4 705	..	..	..
Switzerland - Suisse	1990	6 863	68.2	3 744	40.4	201	30.3
	2000	7 296	66.5	4 003	45.0	160	34.4
	2004	7 426	65.9	4 073	46.4	143	36.4
	2006	7 490	65.5	4 097	..	..	..
United Kingdom - Royaume-Uni	1990	57 449	87.7	29 050	44.0	609	20.4
	2000	59 091	88.4	29 558	45.5	523	22.6
	2004	60 191	88.2	30 170	45.9	494	23.5
	2006	60 739	88.1	30 492	.	..	..
Developed economies: Oceania - Économies développées : Océanie	**1990**	**20 284**	**85.0**	**10 011**	**41.6**	**632**	**29.3**
	2000	**22 993**	**89.5**	**11 407**	**44.6**	**617**	**35.8**
	2004	**24 131**	**90.5**	**12 186**	**45.4**	**603**	**38.3**
	2006	**24 670**	**90.9**	**12 560**	**..**	**..**	**..**
Australia - Australie	1990	16 873	85.1	8 353	41.3	464	28.9
	2000	19 139	90.4	9 498	44.4	447	36.9
	2004	20 081	91.7	10 107	45.3	436	39.9
	2006	20 530	92.2	10 408	.	..	..
New Zealand - Nouvelle-Zélande	1990	3 411	84.7	1 658	43.1	168	30.4
	2000	3 854	84.9	1 909	45.4	170	32.9
	2004	4 050	84.6	2 079	46.4	167	34.1
	2006	4 140	84.5	2 152	..	..	..
Developing economies: Africa - Économies en développement : Afrique	**1990**	**636 817**	**31.7**	**246 032**	**40.3**	**165 450**	**46.7**
	2000	**820 235**	**36.6**	**321 500**	**39.8**	**197 294**	**47.9**
	2004	**900 345**	**38.5**	**354 732**	**39.7**	**209 666**	**48.1**
	2006	**942 504**	**39.4**	**372 729**	**..**	**..**	**..**
Eastern Africa - Afrique orientale	*1990*	*196 640*	*19.0*	*87 714*	*47.5*	*76 577*	*49.7*
	2000	*256 570*	*23.8*	*114 652*	*47.1*	*94 621*	*49.8*
	2004	*284 417*	*25.8*	*126 805*	*46.9*	*101 666*	*49.5*
	2006	*299 306*	*26.7*	*133 521*	*..*	*..*	*..*
Burundi	1990	5 692	6.2	2 799	52.6	2 765	52.4
	2000	6 668	8.7	3 111	53.0	2 953	53.2
	2004	7 566	9.9	3 657	52.2	3 355	52.9
	2006	8 173	10.5	4 015	..	..	..
Comoros - Comores	1990	527	27.9	208	42.7	184	50.5
	2000	699	33.2	287	40.5	244	50.8
	2004	778	35.6	325	40.2	270	50.7
	2006	818	36.9	345	..	..	..
Djibouti	1990	561	75.0	217	40.8	219	49.3
	2000	730	80.5	280	39.9	260	49.2
	2004	790	83.0	308	39.4	272	48.9
	2006	819	83.7	322	..	..	..
Ethiopia (former) - Éthiopie (anc.)	1990	54 306	12.8	23 777	44.8	19 869	42.4
Eritrea - Érythrée	2000	3 634	18.1	1 451	41.5	1 397	50.3
	2004	4 354	19.8	1 717	41.2	1 603	50.2
	2006	4 692	20.7	1 855	..	..	..
Ethiopia - Éthiopie	2000	69 388	14.7	30 160	44.9	23 568	41.0
	2004	76 995	15.6	33 423	44.9	25 553	40.5
	2006	81 021	16.1	35 279	..	..	..

For sources and notes, see end of table.

Pour les sources et les notes, se reporter à la fin du tableau.

Region, country or territory / Régions, pays ou territoires	Year / Année	Population		Total labour force / Main d'œuvre totale		Agriculture labour force / Main d'œuvre dans l'agriculture	
		Total (thousands) / Total (milliers)	Urban population (% of total population) / Population urbaine (en % de la population totale)	Total (thousands) / Total (milliers)	Female labour (% of total labour force) / Main d'œuvre féminine (en % de la main d'œuvre totale)	Total (thousands) / Total (milliers)	Female labour (% of total agriculture labour force) / Main d'œuvre féminine (en % de la main d'œuvre totale dans l'agriculture)
		(1)	(2)	(3)	(4)	(5)	(6)
Kenya	1990	23 447	24.7	9 830	46.0	8 910	49.7
	2000	31 252	35.2	13 631	44.3	11 910	50.0
	2004	34 675	39.1	15 115	43.9	12 570	49.8
	2006	36 553	41.1	15 905	..	..	..
Madagascar	1990	12 033	23.6	5 364	49.2	4 542	50.5
	2000	16 187	26.0	7 329	48.7	5 666	49.9
	2004	18 135	26.7	8 329	48.4	6 220	49.6
	2006	19 159	27.2	8 856	..	..	..
Malawi	1990	9 446	11.7	4 454	50.3	4 099	54.3
	2000	11 623	14.9	5 383	49.9	4 574	55.9
	2004	12 894	16.4	5 810	49.8	4 777	56.4
	2006	13 571	17.1	6 063	..	..	..
Mauritius - Maurice	1990	1 057	40.5	460	33.9	72	26.4
	2000	1 186	42.7	529	34.2	61	24.6
	2004	1 231	43.6	562	35.3	56	23.2
	2006	1 252	44.2	576	..	..	..
Mozambique	1990	13 544	20.9	6 330	54.0	5 743	58.7
	2000	18 194	31.6	8 569	53.7	7 591	59.6
	2004	20 078	35.6	9 132	53.6	8 065	59.7
	2006	20 971	37.6	9 452	..	..	..
Rwanda	1990	7 294	5.2	3 071	51.0	3 239	52.1
	2000	8 176	13.3	3 600	51.9	3 731	55.6
	2004	9 052	19.6	4 080	51.4	4 067	55.1
	2006	9 464	23.0	4 296	..	..	..
Seychelles	1990	72	50.0	..	..	28	50.0
	2000	81	48.1	.	..	30	50.0
	2004	85	51.8	..	..	30	50.0
	2006	86	..	..	..	..	..
Somalia - Somalie	1990	6 717	29.2	2 839	39.9	2 356	50.3
	2000	7 055	33.1	3 014	39.4	2 665	50.5
	2004	7 954	35.4	3 413	39.3	3 028	50.4
	2006	8 445	36.7	3 633	..	..	..
Uganda - Ouganda	1990	17 841	11.1	7 813	47.4	7 446	50.0
	2000	24 690	11.8	10 157	48.0	9 076	49.9
	2004	28 028	12.2	11 483	48.2	9 953	49.6
	2006	29 899	12.5	12 254	..	..	..
United Republic of Tanzania - République-Unie de Tanzanie	1990	25 494	22.3	12 817	50.2	11 255	53.7
	2000	33 849	33.1	17 315	49.8	14 244	54.0
	2004	37 508	36.6	18 913	49.5	15 214	54.0
	2006	39 459	38.1	19 776	..	..	..
Zambia - Zambie	1990	8 122	40.6	3 475	43.2	2 645	48.9
	2000	10 451	36.0	4 498	42.7	3 048	48.3
	2004	11 270	36.8	4 855	42.3	3 078	47.6
	2006	11 696	37.4	5 052	..	..	..
Zimbabwe	1990	10 487	29.2	4 260	47.2	3 205	52.5
	2000	12 656	33.5	5 337	45.1	3 603	53.6
	2004	13 025	35.1	5 684	44.3	3 555	53.2
	2006	13 228	36.0	5 843	..	..	..
Middle Africa - Afrique centrale	*1990*	*73 632*	*30.4*	*29 238*	*42.9*	*21 677*	*51.0*
	2000	*97 765*	*34.4*	*38 801*	*42.4*	*25 634*	*51.8*
	2004	*109 319*	*36.3*	*42 939*	*42.4*	*27 230*	*52.0*
	2006	*115 760*	*37.3*	*45 334*	*..*	*..*	*..*
Angola	1990	10 534	26.1	4 545	46.4	3 297	53.4
	2000	13 930	33.2	6 079	46.0	4 088	53.7
	2004	15 636	36.1	6 825	45.8	4 521	53.7
	2006	16 557	37.6	7 250	..	..	..

For sources and notes, see end of table.

Pour les sources et les notes, se reporter à la fin du tableau.

Region, country or territory / Régions, pays ou territoires	Year / Année	Population		Total labour force / Main d'œuvre totale		Agriculture labour force / Main d'œuvre dans l'agriculture	
		Total (thousands) / Total (milliers)	Urban population (% of total population) / Population urbaine (en % de la population totale)	Total (thousands) / Total (milliers)	Female labour (% of total labour force) / Main d'œuvre féminine (en % de la main d'œuvre totale)	Total (thousands) / Total (milliers)	Female labour (% of total agriculture labour force) / Main d'œuvre féminine (en % de la main d'œuvre totale dans l'agriculture)
		(1)	(2)	(3)	(4)	(5)	(6)
Cameroon - Cameroun	1990	12 239	38.4	4 411	41.5	3 255	44.0
	2000	15 861	45.9	5 747	40.1	3 692	45.3
	2004	17 409	48.1	6 177	39.8	3 728	45.3
	2006	18 175	49.0	6 426	..	..	..
Central African Republic - République centrafricaine	1990	3 008	37.4	1 350	47.1	1 151	51.2
	2000	3 864	40.3	1 704	46.6	1 271	51.5
	2004	4 123	41.8	1 800	46.2	1 264	51.2
	2006	4 265	42.5	1 856	..	..	..
Chad - Tchad	1990	6 113	20.8	2 348	46.0	2 279	48.4
	2000	8 465	23.1	3 169	46.2	2 706	50.8
	2004	9 810	24.4	3 566	46.8	2 870	51.8
	2006	10 468	25.1	3 766	..	..	..
Congo	1990	2 422	49.5	960	41.5	503	60.4
	2000	3 203	56.0	1 406	40.7	570	60.5
	2004	3 530	59.3	1 466	40.3	576	60.1
	2006	3 689	61.2	1 546	..	..	..
Dem. Rep. of the Congo - Rép. dém. du Congo	1990	37 942	27.8	15 051	41.6	10 826	52.5
	2000	50 689	29.9	19 944	41.3	12 921	52.9
	2004	56 918	31.6	22 282	41.2	13 880	53.1
	2006	60 644	32.6	23 628	..	..	..
Equatorial Guinea - Guinée équatoriale	1990	340	35.9	140	35.9	113	42.5
	2000	431	47.1	177	36.6	133	45.1
	2004	473	51.1	193	36.7	143	46.2
	2006	496	52.9	201	..	..	..
Gabon	1990	918	71.1	398	43.9	218	50.5
	2000	1 182	87.6	534	43.5	210	49.0
	2004	1 270	90.7	583	43.4	201	48.3
	2006	1 311	92.0	611	..	..	..
São Tome and Principe - Sao Tomé-et-Principe	1990	116	36.7	34	33.4	35	51.4
	2000	140	37.5	42	29.6	43	51.2
	2004	150	38.6	48	29.3	47	51.1
	2006	155	39.3	51	..	..	..
Northern Africa - Afrique septentrionale	*1990*	*143 963*	*44.8*	*43 212*	*24.7*	*20 970*	*40.8*
	2000	*174 435*	*48.5*	*56 141*	*24.5*	*23 754*	*45.3*
	2004	*186 424*	*50.3*	*63 023*	*25.1*	*24 725*	*46.9*
	2006	*192 793*	*51.2*	*66 569*	*..*	*..*	*..*
Algeria - Algérie	1990	25 283	51.4	7 227	22.6	1 824	46.3
	2000	30 506	57.1	11 069	28.0	2 525	50.9
	2004	32 366	59.4	12 945	30.1	2 800	52.1
	2006	33 351	60.5	13 883	..	..	..
Egypt - Égypte	1990	55 137	43.9	16 577	26.3	7 577	41.7
	2000	66 529	42.6	20 009	21.7	8 354	47.2
	2004	71 550	42.8	22 277	21.8	8 594	48.8
	2006	74 166	43.1	23 484	..	..	..
Libyan Arab Jamahiriya - Jamahiriya arabe libyenne	1990	4 364	79.5	1 257	17.3	139	46.8
	2000	5 346	84.6	1 918	23.8	108	62.0
	2004	5 799	85.7	2 249	26.3	94	67.0
	2006	6 039	86.2	2 429	..	..	..
Morocco - Maroc	1990	24 808	48.2	7 779	23.7	4 073	48.8
	2000	28 827	56.2	10 459	25.5	4 250	54.1
	2004	30 152	59.8	11 350	25.4	4 296	56.8
	2006	30 853	61.5	11 863	..	..	..
Sudan - Soudan	1990	25 933	26.8	7 810	26.0	6 526	32.8
	2000	33 349	35.6	9 225	25.1	7 537	36.6
	2004	36 145	39.2	10 288	24.8	7 925	38.1
	2006	37 707	40.9	10 761	..	..	..

For sources and notes, see end of table.   Pour les sources et les notes, se reporter à la fin du tableau.

Region, country or territory / Régicns, pays ou territoires	Year / Année	Population		Total labour force / Main d'œuvre totale		Agriculture labour force / Main d'œuvre dans l'agriculture	
		Total (thousands) Total (milliers)	Urban population (% of total population) Population urbaine (en % de la population totale)	Total (thousands) Total (milliers)	Female labour (% of total labour force) Main d'œuvre féminine (en % de la main d'œuvre totale)	Total (thousands) Total (milliers)	Female labour (% of total agriculture labour force) Main d'œuvre féminine (en % de la main d'œuvre totale dans l'agriculture)
		(1)	(2)	(3)	(4)	(5)	(6)
Tunisia - Tunisie	1990	8 219	58.0	2 462	21.5	798	43.5
	2000	9 564	62.8	3 327	25.4	941	42.5
	2004	9 996	64.0	3 765	27.2	974	41.8
	2006	10 215	64.7	3 986	..	..	..
Western Sahara - Sahara occidental	1990	221	87.5	99	32.7	33	36.4
	2000	315	88.3	135	32.2	39	41.0
	2004	416	74.4	148	31.5	42	42.9
	2006	462	72.7	162	..	..	..
Southern Africa - Afrique australe	*1990*	*41 828*	*46.5*	*16 875*	*41.9*	*2 839*	*35.6*
	2000	*51 950*	*52.6*	*21 490*	*39.4*	*2 804*	*36.2*
	2004	*54 430*	*53.7*	*21 961*	*38.8*	*2 624*	*36.2*
	2006	*55 316*	*54.2*	*22 011*	*..*	*..*	*..*
Botswana	1990	1 367	44.2	514	45.2	268	55.2
	2000	1 729	50.9	625	43.9	349	56.4
	2004	1 815	50.7	619	42.0	352	56.8
	2006	1 858	50.2	613	..	..	..
Lesotho	1990	1 601	17.1	605	46.5	246	58.1
	2000	1 886	16.7	647	45.3	279	58.4
	2004	1 966	16.5	637	44.7	277	58.5
	2006	1 995	16.5	632	..	..	..
Namibia - Namibie	1990	1 417	26.2	446	44.2	283	45.6
	2000	1 879	31.1	607	44.3	313	43.5
	2004	1 994	33.2	639	43.7	306	42.2
	2006	2 047	34.1	656	..	..	..
South Africa - Afrique du Sud	1990	36 577	49.2	15 054	41.6	1 931	27.8
	2000	45 398	55.7	19 310	39.0	1 742	26.4
	2004	47 541	57.0	19 759	38.4	1 570	25.7
	2006	48 282	57.5	19 800	..	..	..
Swaziland	1990	865	22.9	254	38.1	111	50.5
	2000	1 058	22.4	301	34.4	121	48.8
	2004	1 114	22.0	307	33.1	119	47.1
	2006	1 134	21.9	309	..	..	..
Western Africa - Afrique occidentale	*1990*	*180 754*	*32.3*	*68 994*	*39.6*	*43 387*	*42.9*
	2000	*239 515*	*39.2*	*90 417*	*39.1*	*50 481*	*44.1*
	2004	*265 755*	*41.6*	*100 005*	*38.8*	*53 421*	*44.4*
	2006	*279 329*	*42.7*	*105 294*	*..*	*..*	*..*
Benin - Bénin	1990	5 179	34.5	2 009	40.8	1 334	49.6
	2000	7 227	42.1	2 793	39.3	1 521	48.7
	2004	8 224	45.1	3 186	38.5	1 583	48.0
	2006	8 760	46.6	3 408	..	..	..
Burkina Faso	1990	8 871	13.0	3 798	46.3	4 155	49.8
	2000	11 882	15.9	4 904	47.0	5 219	49.2
	2004	13 507	17.2	5 636	46.7	5 747	48.8
	2006	14 359	18.0	6 028	..	..	..
Cape Verde - Cap-Vert	1990	355	44.1	113	38.4	38	39.5
	2000	451	53.3	144	34.6	40	37.5
	2004	495	56.8	130	33.8	40	37.5
	2006	519	58.4	139	..	..	..
Côte d'Ivoire	1990	12 780	39.5	4 606	30.2	2 917	37.8
	2000	17 049	42.8	6 147	29.3	3 135	39.8
	2004	18 275	44.3	6 665	29.3	3 107	40.0
	2006	18 914	45.1	6 939	..	..	..
Gambia - Gambie	1990	962	24.2	394	43.4	383	50.4
	2000	1 384	24.9	562	42.1	522	51.1
	2004	1 571	24.6	639	41.7	577	51.5
	2006	1 663	24.5	676	..	..	..

For sources and notes, see end of table.

Pour les sources et les notes, se reporter à la fin du tableau.

Region, country or territory / Régions, pays ou territoires	Year / Année	Population		Total labour force / Main d'œuvre totale		Agriculture labour force / Main d'œuvre dans l'agriculture	
		Total (thousands) / Total (milliers)	Urban population (% of total population) / Population urbaine (en % de la population totale)	Total (thousands) / Total (milliers)	Female labour (% of total labour force) / Main d'œuvre féminine (en % de la main d'œuvre totale)	Total (thousands) / Total (milliers)	Female labour (% of total agriculture labour force) / Main d'œuvre féminine (en % de la main d'œuvre totale dans l'agriculture)
		(1)	(2)	(3)	(4)	(5)	(6)
Ghana	1990	15 579	36.2	6 709	48.8	4 208	47.0
	2000	20 148	43.3	8 658	48.5	5 471	46.2
	2004	22 057	45.1	9 556	48.1	6 021	45.7
	2006	23 008	45.9	10 055	..	..	..
Guinea - Guinée	1990	6 033	26.1	2 993	46.2	2 671	50.0
	2000	8 203	33.5	3 992	46.4	3 365	49.9
	2004	8 833	37.2	4 326	46.5	3 497	49.7
	2006	9 181	39.0	4 513	..	..	..
Guinea-Bissau - Guinée-Bissau	1990	1 017	23.7	412	40.3	391	45.5
	2000	1 370	31.4	552	41.0	491	47.0
	2004	1 549	34.6	618	40.9	540	47.6
	2006	1 646	36.1	654	..	..	..
Liberia - Libéria	1990	2 137	42.0	787	39.5	610	46.4
	2000	3 071	44.8	1 128	39.7	766	45.8
	2004	3 348	45.8	1 184	39.8	863	45.4
	2006	3 579	45.5	1 218	..	..	..
Mali	1990	7 669	27.6	3 760	46.0	3 860	48.1
	2000	10 004	35.2	4 821	46.5	4 562	47.2
	2004	11 265	38.4	5 322	47.3	4 920	46.5
	2006	11 968	40.0	5 600	..	..	..
Mauritania - Mauritanie	1990	1 945	45.9	805	40.6	511	50.5
	2000	2 566	59.5	1 033	40.7	627	52.2
	2004	2 882	65.2	1 167	40.4	689	52.8
	2006	3 044	67.9	1 238	..	..	..
Niger	1990	7 822	17.4	3 565	42.6	3 239	46.8
	2000	11 124	21.8	5 017	42.0	4 352	47.9
	2004	12 808	23.9	5 739	41.9	4 928	48.4
	2006	13 737	25.0	6 139	..	..	..
Nigeria - Nigéria	1990	94 454	33.6	32 712	36.2	14 612	35.5
	2000	124 773	41.6	42 561	35.5	15 152	37.4
	2004	138 001	44.3	46 701	34.9	15 159	38.1
	2006	144 720	45.6	49 027	..	..	..
Saint Helena - Sainte-Hélène	1990	5	36.7	..	..	1	100.0
	2000	6	33.6	..	..	1	0.0
	2004	6	..	..	..	1	0.0
	2006	6	..	..	..	..	..
Senegal - Sénégal	1990	7 896	40.4	3 117	43.4	2 482	47.9
	2000	10 334	47.5	4 071	42.6	3 084	48.1
	2004	11 472	50.0	4 480	42.4	3 369	47.9
	2006	12 072	51.2	4 715	..	..	..
Sierra Leone	1990	4 087	29.9	1 694	38.5	1 026	42.4
	2000	4 521	36.6	1 930	38.5	1 022	45.4
	2004	5 390	39.1	2 276	38.4	1 153	46.8
	2006	5 743	40.5	2 425	..	..	..
Togo	1990	3 961	28.5	1 520	38.5	949	39.3
	2000	5 403	33.1	2 104	37.4	1 151	41.1
	2004	6 071	35.2	2 351	37.0	1 227	42.0
	2006	6 410	36.4	2 490	..	..	..
Developing economies: America - Économies en développement : Amérique	1990	439 876	71.0	171 546	34.1	44 629	16.9
	2000	518 242	75.4	228 519	33.8	43 835	17.3
	2004	546 089	77.5	249 933	40.2	43 009	17.4
	2006	560 044	78.4	260 440	..	..	..
Caribbean - Caraïbes	1990	30 074	55.1	11 882	37.1	3 963	26.5
	2000	33 976	56.7	14 143	38.3	3 956	27.9
	2004	35 400	57.3	15 023	38.7	3 923	28.2
	2006	36 081	57.3	15 506	..	..	..

For sources and notes, see end of table.

Pour les sources et les notes, se reporter à la fin du tableau.

Region, country or territory / Régions, pays ou territoires	Year / Année	Population		Total labour force / Main d'œuvre totale		Agriculture labour force / Main d'œuvre dans l'agriculture	
		Total (thousands) / Total (milliers)	Urban population (% of total population) / Population urbaine (en % de la population totale)	Total (thousands) / Total (milliers)	Female labour (% of total labour force) / Main d'œuvre féminine (en % de la main d'œuvre totale)	Total (thousands) / Total (milliers)	Female labour (% of total agriculture labour force) / Main d'œuvre féminine (en % de la main d'œuvre totale dans l'agriculture)
		(1)	(2)	(3)	(4)	(5)	(6)
Anguilla	1990	9	99.7	..	..	1	0.0
	2000	11	97.9	..	..	1	0.0
	2004	12	..	..	..	1	0.0
	2006	12	..	..	..	..	..
Antigua and Barbuda - Antigua-et-Barbuda	1990	62	35.5	..	..	8	25.0
	2000	77	37.8	..	..	8	25.0
	2004	82	..	..	..	7	28.6
	2006	84	..	..	..	..	..
Aruba	1990	64	51.8	..	..	8	25.0
	2000	90	47.6	..	..	10	30.0
	2004	101	45.7	..	..	10	30.0
	2006	104	..	..	..	..	..
Bahamas	1990	255	83.5	119	45.4	7	14.3
	2000	303	88.0	145	49.2	6	16.7
	2004	319	89.6	154	49.7	5	0.0
	2006	327	90.3	159	..	..	..
Barbados - Barbade	1990	271	42.5	130	46.6	9	44.4
	2000	286	46.5	149	48.1	6	50.0
	2004	291	48.4	154	47.4	5	40.0
	2006	293	49.4	156	..	..	..
British Virgin Islands - Îles Vierges britanniques	1990	17	..	.	..	2	50.0
	2000	21	..	.	..	2	50.0
	2004	22	..	..	..	2	50.0
	2006	22	..	..	..	..	..
Cayman Islands - Îles Caïmanes	1990	26	98.9	..	..	3	33.3
	2000	40	99.4	..	..	4	25.0
	2004	45	98.5	..	..	4	25.0
	2006	46	..	..	..	..	..
Cuba	1990	10 605	73.2	4 545	34.8	870	16.6
	2000	11 142	75.1	5 249	36.8	784	18.5
	2004	11 247	75.8	5 347	37.2	727	18.8
	2006	11 267	76.3	5 402	..	..	..
Dominica - Dominique	1990	69	71.2	..	..	9	22.2
	2000	68	80.4	..	..	8	25.0
	2004	68	76.2	..	..	8	25.0
	2006	68	..	..	..	..	..
Dominican Republic - République dominicaine	1990	7 295	53.7	2 630	29.7	688	10.3
	2000	8 744	55.0	3 386	33.7	603	15.4
	2004	9 325	56.1	3 751	35.3	561	18.0
	2006	9 615	56.8	3 949	..	..	..
Grenada - Grenade	1990	96	32.3	..	..	10	30.0
	2000	100	30.9	..	..	9	22.2
	2004	105	31.0	..	..	8	25.0
	2006	106	..	..	..	..	..
Haiti - Haïti	1990	7 110	28.5	2 642	43.3	1 973	36.6
	2000	8 573	33.0	3 207	41.8	2 156	35.0
	2004	9 149	35.0	3 571	41.7	2 232	34.1
	2006	9 446	36.1	3 763	..	..	..
Jamaica - Jamaïque	1990	2 369	51.5	1 113	46.8	276	27.9
	2000	2 589	52.0	1 165	44.8	264	29.2
	2004	2 665	51.6	1 162	43.7	261	29.5
	2006	2 699	51.6	1 171	..	..	..
Montserrat	1990	11	9.3	..	..	1	0.0
	2000	5	0.0	..	..	0	..
	2004	5	..	..	..	0	..
	2006	6	..	..	..	..	..

For sources and notes, see end of table.

Pour les sources et les notes, se reporter à la fin du tableau.

Region, country or territory / Régions, pays ou territoires	Year / Année	Population		Total labour force / Main d'œuvre totale		Agriculture labour force / Main d'œuvre dans l'agriculture	
		Total (thousands) / Total (milliers)	Urban population (% of total population) / Population urbaine (en % de la population totale)	Total (thousands) / Total (milliers)	Female labour (% of total labour force) / Main d'œuvre féminine (en % de la main d'œuvre totale)	Total (thousands) / Total (milliers)	Female labour (% of total agriculture labour force) / Main d'œuvre féminine (en % de la main d'œuvre totale dans l'agriculture)
		(1)	(2)	(3)	(4)	(5)	(6)
Netherlands Antilles - Antilles néerlandaises	1990	191	68.3	88	44.1	1	0.0
	2000	181	67.2	81	46.5	0	..
	2004	184	68.6	82	46.1	0	..
	2006	189	68.6	83	..	..	..
Saint Kitts and Nevis - Saint-Kitts-et-Nevis	1990	41	34.4	..	..	5	20.0
	2000	46	28.2	..	..	4	25.0
	2004	49	..	..	..	4	25.0
	2006	50	..	..	..	..	..
Saint Lucia - Sainte-Lucie	1990	138	26.7	55	39.0	14	28.6
	2000	153	29.7	69	41.1	15	26.7
	2004	159	30.9	75	41.3	15	26.7
	2006	163	31.6	78	..	..	..
Saint Vincent and the Grenadines - Saint-Vincent-et-les Grenadines	1990	109	40.6	42	36.3	12	25.0
	2000	116	54.8	51	39.1	12	25.0
	2004	118	59.4	55	40.5	12	25.0
	2006	120	61.4	58	..	..	..
Trinidad and Tobago - Trinité-et-Tobago	1990	1 224	68.6	469	36.1	52	17.3
	2000	1 301	73.2	589	39.0	50	16.0
	2004	1 319	74.8	620	38.9	48	16.7
	2006	1 328	75.5	634	..	..	..
Turks and Caicos Islands - Îles Turques et Caïques	1990	12	43.3	..	..	1	0.0
	2000	19	42.4	..	..	2	50.0
	2004	24	..	..	..	2	50.0
	2006	25	..	..	..	..	..
United States Virgin Islands - Îles Vierges américaines	1990	103	88.0	48	45.2	13	30.8
	2000	110	93.0	52	46.0	12	25.0
	2004	111	94.2	52	46.4	11	27.3
	2006	111	94.7	52	..	..	..
Central America - Amérique centrale	*1990*	*112 724*	*66.0*	*39 768*	*30.5*	*12 466*	*11.2*
	2000	*135 587*	*68.7*	*53 548*	*33.4*	*13 007*	*11.7*
	2004	*142 104*	*70.9*	*58 239*	*34.8*	*13 108*	*11.8*
	2006	*145 602*	*71.8*	*60 656*	*..*	*..*	*..*
Belize	1990	186	48.1	60	27.2	20	5.0
	2000	245	47.5	89	31.6	25	4.0
	2004	269	47.5	104	33.7	28	3.6
	2006	282	47.7	111	..	..	..
Costa Rica	1990	3 076	53.6	1 155	27.6	307	6.8
	2000	3 929	59.0	1 593	30.9	324	9.0
	2004	4 253	61.2	1 890	34.5	327	10.1
	2006	4 399	62.2	2 022	..	..	..
El Salvador	1990	5 110	49.2	1 961	41.2	709	6.1
	2000	6 195	59.2	2 503	38.1	775	7.6
	2004	6 576	61.5	2 714	39.6	782	8.2
	2006	6 762	62.6	2 831	..	..	..
Guatemala	1990	8 908	41.1	2 869	24.7	1 569	7.1
	2000	11 229	44.9	3 566	30.3	1 916	8.0
	2004	12 397	46.4	3 959	31.1	2 089	8.3
	2006	13 029	47.2	4 195	..	..	..
Honduras	1990	4 891	40.1	1 611	27.7	693	16.6
	2000	6 196	46.0	2 494	33.7	769	19.9
	2004	6 702	48.4	2 999	37.0	789	21.4
	2006	6 969	49.5	3 265	..	..	..
Mexico - Mexique	1990	84 002	72.7	29 915	30.6	8 531	12.4
	2000	99 735	75.0	40 300	33.6	8 551	12.7
	2004	103 333	77.5	43 176	34.8	8 453	12.5
	2006	105 342	78.5	44 624	..	..	..

For sources and notes, see end of table.

Pour les sources et les notes, se reporter à la fin du tableau.

Region, country or territory / Régions, pays ou territoires	Year / Année	Population		Total labour force / Main d'œuvre totale		Agriculture labour force / Main d'œuvre dans l'agriculture	
		Total (thousands) / Total (milliers)	Urban population (% of total population) / Population urbaine (en % de la population totale)	Total (thousands) / Total (milliers)	Female labour (% of total labour force) / Main d'œuvre féminine (en % de la main d'œuvre totale)	Total (thousands) / Total (milliers)	Female labour (% of total agriculture labour force) / Main d'œuvre féminine (en % de la main d'œuvre totale dans l'agriculture)
		(1)	(2)	(3)	(4)	(5)	(6)
Nicaragua	1990	4 141	50.7	1 272	30.1	392	9.9
	2000	5 108	54.5	1 730	29.8	396	10.1
	2004	5 394	57.5	1 967	29.7	392	10.2
	2006	5 532	59.2	2 103	..	..	..
Panama	1990	2 411	53.7	925	32.5	245	4.1
	2000	2 950	56.2	1 273	35.4	251	3.6
	2004	3 175	57.4	1 430	38.3	248	3.6
	2006	3 288	58.1	1 504	..	..	..
South America - Amérique du Sud	*1990*	*297 077*	*74.5*	*119 896*	*34.9*	*28 200*	*18.1*
	2000	*348 679*	*79.8*	*160 827*	*40.6*	*26 872*	*18.4*
	2004	*368 584*	*81.9*	*176 670*	*42.2*	*25 978*	*18.6*
	2006	*378 361*	*82.9*	*184 279*	*..*	*..*	*..*
Argentina - Argentine	1990	32 581	87.0	13 006	34.4	1 482	6.7
	2000	36 896	89.5	16 233	40.0	1 464	8.0
	2004	38 372	90.4	17 943	42.4	1 455	8.6
	2006	39 134	90.7	18 762	..	..	..
Bolivia - Bolivie	1990	6 669	55.6	2 511	39.2	1 249	35.5
	2000	8 317	61.9	3 553	43.2	1 497	35.5
	2004	9 009	63.9	4 029	43.5	1 619	35.4
	2006	9 354	64.8	4 286	..	..	..
Brazil - Brésil	1990	149 522	74.6	62 430	35.1	15 232	20.4
	2000	174 161	81.0	83 387	41.2	13 211	19.6
	2004	184 318	83.5	89 910	42.5	12 134	19.2
	2006	189 323	84.6	92 810	..	..	..
Chile - Chili	1990	13 179	83.3	5 002	30.5	938	9.5
	2000	15 412	85.9	6 081	33.4	980	11.7
	2004	16 124	87.3	6 437	34.7	989	12.8
	2006	16 465	88.0	6 597	..	..	..
Colombia - Colombie	1990	34 875	68.9	14 083	36.9	3 696	17.5
	2000	41 683	75.7	19 435	42.4	3 719	19.3
	2004	44 317	78.0	21 743	44.0	3 666	19.9
	2006	45 558	79.1	22 913	..	..	..
Ecuador - Équateur	1990	10 272	55.1	3 682	27.8	1 201	11.9
	2000	12 306	60.3	5 584	40.5	1 249	14.6
	2004	12 917	62.9	6 173	42.0	1 242	15.9
	2006	13 202	64.3	6 533	..	..	..
Falkland Islands (Malvinas) - Îles Falkland (Malvinas)	1990	2	49.9	..	..	0	..
	2000	3	103.5	..	..	0	..
	2004	3	..	..	..	0	..
	2006	3	..	..	..	..	..
Guyana	1990	731	33.1	268	32.8	58	12.1
	2000	734	36.7	312	36.3	56	10.7
	2004	739	38.6	326	36.7	54	9.3
	2006	739	39.7	332	..	..	..
Paraguay	1990	4 248	48.4	1 649	38.4	595	5.4
	2000	5 349	56.6	2 390	41.3	706	5.0
	2004	5 793	60.1	2 775	43.1	756	4.8
	2006	6 016	61.9	2 977	..	..	..
Peru - Pérou	1990	21 762	68.9	8 507	36.9	2 654	16.9
	2000	25 663	73.6	11 558	40.0	2 965	19.5
	2004	26 959	75.9	12 930	41.6	3 074	20.4
	2006	27 589	77.1	13 736	..	..	..
Suriname	1990	402	65.4	134	36.1	28	21.4
	2000	436	73.7	143	36.9	30	23.3
	2004	450	76.1	150	34.8	31	25.8
	2006	455	77.2	155	..	..	..

For sources and notes, see end of table.

Pour les sources et les notes, se reporter à la fin du tableau.

Region, country or territory / Régions, pays ou territoires	Year / Année	Population		Total labour force / Main d'œuvre totale		Agriculture labour force / Main d'œuvre dans l'agriculture	
		Total (thousands) / Total (milliers)	Urban population (% of total population) / Population urbaine (en % de la population totale)	Total (thousands) / Total (milliers)	Female labour (% of total labour force) / Main d'œuvre féminine (en % de la main d'œuvre totale)	Total (thousands) / Total (milliers)	Female labour (% of total agriculture labour force) / Main d'œuvre féminine (en % de la main d'œuvre totale dans l'agriculture)
		(1)	(2)	(3)	(4)	(5)	(6)
Uruguay	1990	3 106	89.0	1 379	39.9	193	10.9
	2000	3 318	92.6	1 623	42.7	190	12.1
	2004	3 324	96.0	1 727	43.9	189	12.7
	2006	3 331	97.5	1 779	..	..	..
Venezuela (Bolivarian Republic of) - Venezuela (République bolivarienne du)	1990	19 731	84.0	7 247	31.8	874	4.8
	2000	24 402	87.0	10 528	36.8	805	5.3
	2004	26 260	88.0	12 475	40.3	769	5.5
	2006	27 191	88.4	13 394	..	..	..
Developing economies: Asia - Économies en développement : Asie	1990	2 985 852	30.1	1 383 595	38.6	947 777	43.5
	2000	3 499 689	35.6	1 640 396	38.1	1 028 128	44.3
	2004	3 683 371	37.9	1 755 254	38.1	1 050 511	44.5
	2006	3 773 332	39.0	1 813 070	..	..	..
Eastern Asia - Asie orientale	*1990*	*1 220 374*	*30.1*	*694 191*	*44.6*	*500 909*	*47.3*
	2000	*1 349 261*	*38.1*	*783 240*	*44.5*	*517 137*	*47.7*
	2004	*1 386 187*	*41.8*	*815 057*	*44.4*	*515 459*	*47.7*
	2006	*1 402 837*	*43.6*	*830 081*	*..*	*..*	*..*
China - Chine	1990	1 128 790	28.0	661 448	44.8	493 124	47.4
	2000	1 247 777	36.5	745 715	44.7	511 001	47.7
	2004	1 282 336	40.4	775 430	44.6	510 010	47.7
	2006	1 298 049	42.3	789 652	..	..	..
China, Hong Kong SAR - Chine, Hong Kong RAS	1990	5 704	99.5	2 852	36.3	..	..
	2000	6 662	99.6	3 375	42.4	..	..
	2004	6 982	99.7	3 648	45.9	..	..
	2006	7 132	99.8	3 773	..	..	..
China, Macao SAR - Chine, Macao RAS	1990	372	98.7	160	40.6	..	..
	2000	441	99.4	224	44.7	..	..
	2004	468	96.7	252	46.6	..	..
	2006	478	96.0	266	..	..	..
China, Taiwan Province of - Chine, Taiwan Province de (7)	1990	20 279	..	..	..	..	..
	2000	22 185	..	..	..	..	..
	2004	22 647	..	..	..	..	..
	2006	22 815	..	..	..	..	..
Korea, Dem. People's Rep. of - Corée, Rép. populaire dém. de	1990	20 143	57.1	9 720	39.3	3 904	48.1
	2000	22 946	57.4	10 323	38.8	3 439	46.4
	2004	23 514	58.5	10 623	38.6	3 202	45.8
	2006	23 708	59.1	10 775	..	..	..
Korea, Republic of - Corée, République de	1990	42 869	73.8	19 128	39.3	3 555	43.9
	2000	46 780	79.6	22 501	40.3	2 387	45.1
	2004	47 684	80.5	23 889	40.8	1 944	45.5
	2006	48 050	80.9	24 341	..	..	..
Mongolia - Mongolie	1990	2 216	57.0	884	41.0	326	43.9
	2000	2 470	57.2	1 101	40.3	310	44.5
	2004	2 557	58.1	1 215	40.2	303	44.9
	2006	2 605	58.8	1 274	..	..	..
Southern Asia - Asie méridionale	*1990*	*1 192 558*	*26.1*	*449 785*	*29.4*	*306 695*	*37.3*
	2000	*1 460 857*	*28.4*	*552 958*	*29.0*	*353 749*	*39.0*
	2004	*1 562 099*	*29.4*	*604 850*	*29.5*	*372 798*	*39.5*
	2006	*1 612 841*	*30.0*	*632 261*	*..*	*..*	*..*
Afghanistan	1990	12 659	21.0	5 007	28.4	3 970	40.9
	2000	20 737	25.1	8 001	28.4	5 843	43.9
	2004	24 076	28.2	9 724	29.0	6 655	45.2
	2006	26 088	29.6	10 708	..	..	..
Bangladesh	1990	113 049	18.2	46 940	40.1	34 744	46.8
	2000	139 434	21.4	57 239	37.6	38 530	50.0
	2004	150 528	22.8	62 399	37.0	39 723	51.4
	2006	155 991	23.5	65 344	..	..	..

For sources and notes, see end of table.

Pour les sources et les notes, se reporter à la fin du tableau.

Region, country or territory / Régions, pays ou territoires	Year / Année	Population		Total labour force / Main d'œuvre totale		Agriculture labour force / Main d'œuvre dans l'agriculture	
		Total (thousands) Total (milliers)	Urban population (% of total population) Population urbaine (en % de la population totale)	Total (thousands) Total (milliers)	Female labour (% of total labour force) Main d'œuvre féminine (en % de la main d'œuvre totale)	Total (thousands) Total (milliers)	Female labour (% of total agriculture labour force) Main d'œuvre féminine (en % de la main d'œuvre totale dans l'agriculture)
		(1)	(2)	(3)	(4)	(5)	(6)
Bhutan - Bhoutan	1990	547	16.4	576	28.9	792	41.0
	2000	559	26.7	688	30.6	933	41.5
	2004	623	29.9	809	35.1	1 055	41.6
	2006	649	32.1	883	..	..	..
India - Inde	1990	860 195	25.2	329 760	28.7	229 417	36.2
	2000	1 046 235	27.0	398 363	28.0	263 369	37.1
	2004	1 116 985	27.7	430 445	28.3	276 687	37.3
	2006	1 151 751	28.2	446 883	..	..	..
Iran, Islamic Republic of - Iran, Rép. islamique d'	1990	56 674	56.3	16 264	20.2	5 405	27.3
	2000	66 125	64.6	22 787	29.5	6 168	38.5
	2004	68 669	67.5	26 952	33.0	6 602	43.3
	2006	70 270	68.8	29 141	..	..	..
Maldives	1990	216	25.9	58	19.4	29	34.5
	2000	273	29.2	90	32.9	28	35.7
	2004	291	32.3	112	37.9	27	37.0
	2006	300	33.9	123	..	..	..
Nepal - Népal	1990	19 114	8.9	7 122	37.9	8 369	40.8
	2000	24 419	13.7	9 178	40.1	10 388	41.7
	2004	26 554	15.5	10 227	40.4	11 419	42.0
	2006	27 641	16.3	10 837	..	..	..
Pakistan	1990	112 991	30.2	36 469	23.3	20 561	34.1
	2000	144 360	32.7	48 238	24.8	24 652	40.4
	2004	155 333	34.3	55 413	26.5	26 682	42.6
	2006	160 943	35.2	59 375	..	..	..
Sri Lanka	1990	17 114	22.1	7 591	34.8	3 408	32.4
	2000	18 714	22.4	8 374	31.5	3 838	33.9
	2004	19 040	22.7	8 769	30.5	3 948	34.4
	2006	19 207	22.9	8 967	..	..	..
South-Eastern Asia - Asie du Sud-Est	*1990*	*440 574*	*31.5*	*196 761*	*41.9*	*121 579*	*42.6*
	2000	*519 996*	*39.5*	*247 707*	*41.5*	*136 356*	*43.3*
	2004	*550 201*	*42.7*	*270 313*	*41.8*	*140 821*	*43.9*
	2006	*565 105*	*44.3*	*281 993*	*..*	*..*	*..*
Brunei Darussalam - Brunéi Darussalam	1990	257	65.8	110	32.1	2	50.0
	2000	333	73.9	147	34.4	1	0.0
	2004	366	76.9	160	34.1	1	0.0
	2006	382	78.2	167	..	..	..
Cambodia - Cambodge	1990	9 698	12.7	4 381	52.5	3 418	57.1
	2000	12 780	16.9	5 848	51.8	4 529	55.6
	2004	13 720	19.3	6 615	51.5	5 001	54.9
	2006	14 197	20.6	7 016	..	..	..
Indonesia - Indonésie	1990	182 847	30.3	76 615	38.5	44 086	39.0
	2000	211 693	41.5	98 742	37.8	49 309	42.2
	2004	223 225	46.1	106 278	37.8	50 531	43.4
	2006	228 864	48.3	110 432	..	..	..
Lao People's Dem. Rep. - Rép. dém. populaire lao	1990	4 076	15.6	1 544	41.3	1 585	48.3
	2000	5 224	19.5	2 023	40.8	2 007	48.5
	2004	5 574	22.0	2 286	40.7	2 223	48.6
	2006	5 759	23.3	2 427	..	..	..
Malaysia - Malaisie	1990	18 103	49.1	7 122	34.8	1 985	32.7
	2000	23 274	61.1	9 634	35.3	1 844	28.5
	2004	25 191	63.7	10 735	35.6	1 740	26.7
	2006	26 114	64.9	11 288	..	..	..
Myanmar	1990	40 147	25.2	20 000	44.6	15 320	45.9
	2000	45 884	29.1	24 832	44.8	17 950	45.9
	2004	47 565	31.5	26 900	44.9	18 897	45.9
	2006	48 379	32.9	27 954	..	..	..

For sources and notes, see end of table.   Pour les sources et les notes, se reporter à la fin du tableau.

Region, country or territory / Régions, pays ou territoires	Year / Année	Population		Total labour force / Main d'œuvre totale		Agriculture labour force / Main d'œuvre dans l'agriculture	
		Total (thousands) / Total (milliers)	Urban population (% of total population) / Population urbaine (en % de la population totale)	Total (thousands) / Total (milliers)	Female labour (% of total labour force) / Main d'œuvre féminine (en % de la main d'œuvre totale)	Total (thousands) / Total (milliers)	Female labour (% of total agriculture labour force) / Main d'œuvre féminine (en % de la main d'œuvre totale dans l'agriculture)
		(1)	(2)	(3)	(4)	(5)	(6)
Philippines	1990	61 226	48.7	23 439	36.6	11 001	24.6
	2000	76 213	58.2	30 761	37.4	12 408	24.5
	2004	82 868	60.9	35 916	39.4	12 942	24.5
	2006	86 264	62.0	38 294	..	..	..
Singapore - Singapour	1990	3 016	100.0	1 541	38.7	6	16.7
	2000	4 017	100.0	2 059	40.0	3	0.0
	2004	4 274	100.0	2 176	39.8	2	0.0
	2006	4 382	99.9	2 238	..	..	..
Thailand - Thaïlande	1990	54 291	29.6	30 442	46.6	19 929	47.8
	2000	60 666	31.5	33 586	45.5	20 484	47.1
	2004	62 565	32.8	35 293	46.0	20 185	46.6
	2006	63 444	33.5	36 136	..	..	..
Timor-Leste	1990	740	7.8	284	37.0	322	49.7
	2000	819	6.6	256	34.9	294	47.3
	2004	1 013	6.7	351	37.1	363	48.2
	2006	1 114	7.1	413	..	..	..
Viet Nam	1990	66 173	20.3	31 284	48.4	23 925	49.6
	2000	79 094	24.2	39 770	48.5	27 527	49.3
	2004	83 839	26.0	43 603	48.5	28 936	49.1
	2006	86 206	27.0	45 628	..	..	..
Western Asia - Asie occidentale	*1990*	*132 346*	*60.5*	*42 857*	*24.1*	*18 594*	*47.5*
	2000	*169 574*	*64.6*	*56 491*	*23.2*	*20 886*	*55.4*
	2004	*184 883*	*66.2*	*65 035*	*23.8*	*21 433*	*58.3*
	2006	*192 550*	*66.9*	*68 734*	*..*	*..*	*..*
Bahrain - Bahreïn	1990	493	88.2	220	16.8	4	0.0
	2000	650	92.6	311	18.3	3	0.0
	2004	710	90.8	332	18.6	3	0.0
	2006	739	90.3	343	..	..	..
Iraq	1990	18 515	69.7	4 726	16.8	712	39.6
	2000	25 052	67.9	6 963	19.2	643	50.2
	2004	27 456	68.5	8 063	20.0	609	53.9
	2006	28 506	69.2	8 646	..	..	..
Jordan - Jordanie	1990	3 254	72.2	773	18.8	123	46.3
	2000	4 799	81.5	1 569	22.7	188	63.8
	2004	5 371	82.0	1 849	24.1	195	69.2
	2006	5 729	81.0	1 988	..	..	..
Kuwait - Koweït	1990	2 143	94.9	859	21.8	11	0.0
	2000	2 228	96.1	1 165	22.3	13	0.0
	2004	2 617	95.9	1 405	24.7	15	0.0
	2006	2 779	96.0	1 505	..	..	..
Lebanon - Liban	1990	2 974	76.7	942	31.7	62	37.1
	2000	3 772	78.0	1 265	29.4	47	38.3
	2004	3 965	78.4	1 374	30.0	40	40.0
	2006	4 055	78.7	1 443	..	..	..
Palestinian territory - Territoire palestinien	1990	2 154	66.0	430	12.0	..	..
	2000	3 149	70.0	656	13.0	..	..
	2004	3 636	70.6	756	13.1	..	..
	2006	3 889	71.0	810	..	..	..
Oman	1990	1 843	62.1	567	11.1	256	4.3
	2000	2 402	77.2	912	12.7	353	5.1
	2004	2 479	79.9	941	15.6	362	6.1
	2006	2 546	81.2	983	..	..	..
Qatar	1990	467	89.3	256	10.5	7	0.0
	2000	617	89.9	320	14.5	4	0.0
	2004	764	93.7	447	13.7	3	0.0
	2006	821	94.5	488	..	..	..

For sources and notes, see end of table.

Pour les sources et les notes, se reporter à la fin du tableau.

Region, country or territory / Régions, pays ou territoires	Year / Année	Population		Total labour force / Main d'œuvre totale		Agriculture labour force / Main d'œuvre dans l'agriculture	
		Total (thousands) / Total (milliers)	Urban population (% of total population) / Population urbaine (en % de la population totale)	Total (thousands) / Total (milliers)	Female labour (% of total labour force) / Main d'œuvre féminine (en % de la main d'œuvre totale)	Total (thousands) / Total (milliers)	Female labour (% of total agriculture labour force) / Main d'œuvre féminine (en % de la main d'œuvre totale dans l'agriculture)
		(1)	(2)	(3)	(4)	(5)	(6)
Saudi Arabia - Arabie saoudite	1990	16 256	78.8	5 098	11.4	1 031	7.2
	2000	20 807	89.0	6 716	13.5	730	8.9
	2004	23 047	91.5	7 668	14.9	633	9.2
	2006	24 175	92.6	8 184	..	..	..
Syrian Arab Republic - République arabe syrienne	1990	12 721	49.4	3 670	26.2	1 178	51.6
	2000	16 511	51.0	6 036	29.3	1 493	61.2
	2004	18 389	50.7	7 280	30.4	1 636	65.1
	2006	19 408	50.7	7 880	..	..	..
Turkey - Turquie	1990	57 345	59.2	21 402	29.4	12 994	53.2
	2000	68 158	64.8	23 877	26.2	14 513	61.3
	2004	72 025	67.0	26 669	26.4	14 854	64.2
	2006	73 922	68.0	27 460	..	..	..
United Arab Emirates - Émirats arabes unis	1990	1 867	82.8	953	9.8	84	0.0
	2000	3 247	84.6	1 875	12.4	75	0.0
	2004	3 947	92.6	2 558	13.1	67	0.0
	2006	4 248	93.9	2 812	..	..	..
Yemen - Yémen	1990	12 314	20.9	2 963	27.4	2 132	39.9
	2000	18 182	24.4	4 824	27.0	2 824	42.9
	2004	20 478	25.8	5 694	27.7	3 016	44.0
	2006	21 732	26.6	6 190	..	..	..
Developing economies: Oceania - Économies en développement : Océanie	**1990**	**6 449**	**23.3**	**2 549**	**43.7**	**2 011**	**43.4**
	2000	**8 113**	**23.9**	**3 217**	**45.0**	**2 369**	**46.2**
	2004	**8 828**	**23.7**	**3 562**	**44.9**	**2 549**	**47.0**
	2006	**9 176**	**21.3**	**3 752**	**..**	**..**	**..**
American Samoa - Samoa américaines	1990	47	80.7	..	..	8	25.0
	2000	57	89.4	..	..	8	25.0
	2004	63	82.7	.	..	8	37.5
	2006	65	..	..	..	..	..
Cook Islands - Îles Cook	1990	18	56.3	..	..	3	33.3
	2000	16	75.1	..	..	2	50.0
	2004	14	..	..	..	2	50.0
	2006	14	..	..	..	..	..
Fiji - Fidji	1990	724	41.6	289	37.6	115	14.8
	2000	802	50.0	354	38.0	129	19.4
	2004	823	53.6	380	38.3	134	21.6
	2006	833	55.3	393	..	..	..
French Polynesia - Polynésie française	1990	195	56.1	78	37.2	34	29.4
	2000	236	52.7	99	37.8	34	32.4
	2004	252	52.2	109	38.2	34	32.4
	2006	259	52.1	114	..	..	..
Guam	1990	134	90.8	63	35.3	21	23.8
	2000	155	93.3	72	38.6	20	25.0
	2004	166	94.3	77	38.8	21	23.8
	2006	171	94.9	80	..	..	..
Kiribati	1990	72	34.8	..	..	9	22.2
	2000	84	46.4	..	..	10	20.0
	2004	90	50.3	..	..	10	20.0
	2006	94	..	..	..	..	..
Marshall Islands - Îles Marshall	1990	47	65.6	..	..	6	16.7
	2000	52	65.2	..	..	6	16.7
	2004	56	73.3	..	..	6	16.7
	2006	58	..	..	..	..	..
Micronesia, Federated States of - Micronésie, États fédérés de	1990	96	26.4	..	..	11	27.3
	2000	107	28.3	..	..	12	25.0
	2004	109	29.7	..	..	12	25.0
	2006	111	30.6	..	..	..	..

For sources and notes, see end of table.   Pour les sources et les notes, se reporter à la fin du tableau.

Region, country or territory Régions, pays ou territoires	Year Année	Population		Total labour force Main d'œuvre totale		Agriculture labour force Main d'œuvre dans l'agriculture	
		Total (thousands) Total (milliers)	Urban population (% of total population) Population urbaine (en % de la population totale)	Total (thousands) Total (milliers)	Female labour (% of total labour force) Main d'œuvre féminine (en % de la main d'œuvre totale)	Total (thousands) Total (milliers)	Female labour (% of total agriculture labour force) Main d'œuvre féminine (en % de la main d'œuvre totale dans l'agriculture)
		(1)	(2)	(3)	(4)	(5)	(6)
Nauru	1990	9	98.4	..	..	1	0.0
	2000	10	119.5	..	..	1	0.0
	2004	10	..	..	..	1	0.0
	2006	10	..	..	..	..	..
New Caledonia - Nouvelle-Calédonie	1990	171	59.5	69	37.5	37	45.9
	2000	215	60.8	89	37.2	41	46.3
	2004	230	62.0	97	37.0	42	45.2
	2006	238	62.7	100	..	..	..
Niue - Nioué	1990	2	44.3	..	..	0	..
	2000	2	53.3	..	..	0	..
	2004	2	..	..	..	0	..
	2006	2	..	..	..	..	..
Northern Mariana Islands - Îles Mariannes du Nord	1990	44	91.4	..	..	6	16.7
	2000	69	94.2	..	..	8	25.0
	2004	78	92.8	..	..	9	22.2
	2006	82	..	..	..	..	..
Palau, Pacific Islands (former) - Palaos, Îles du Pacifique (anc.)	1990	15	73.7	..	..	2	50.0
	2000	19	67.4	..	..	2	50.0
	2004	20	69.5	..	..	2	50.0
	2006	20	..	..	..	..	..
Papua New Guinea - Papouasie-Nouvelle-Guinée	1990	4 131	13.1	1 771	46.4	1 564	46.0
	2000	5 381	13.0	2 244	47.8	1 866	48.7
	2004	5 935	12.8	2 504	47.6	2 019	49.4
	2006	6 202	12.8	2 649	..	..	..
Pitcairn	1990	0	..	..	..	..	..
	2000	0	..	..	..	..	..
	2004	0	..	..	..	..	..
	2006	0	..	..	..	..	..
Samoa	1990	161	21.5	56	31.5	24	33.3
	2000	177	22.1	63	32.1	21	33.3
	2004	183	22.5	65	31.9	20	35.0
	2006	185	22.7	65	..	..	..
Solomon Islands - Îles Salomon	1990	314	13.8	118	39.3	125	52.8
	2000	415	15.8	166	38.8	163	53.4
	2004	461	16.9	189	38.6	181	53.6
	2006	484	17.6	201	..	..	..
Tokelau - Tokélaou	1990	2	..	..	..	0	..
	2000	2	..	..	..	0	..
	2004	1	..	..	..	0	..
	2006	1	..	..	..	..	..
Tonga	1990	95	31.2	33	32.6	15	33.3
	2000	98	33.4	37	37.8	12	33.3
	2004	99	34.7	39	37.8	12	33.3
	2006	100	35.3	40	..	..	..
Tuvalu	1990	9	42.4	..	..	1	0.0
	2000	10	49.1	..	..	1	0.0
	2004	10	..	..	..	1	0.0
	2006	10	..	..	..	..	..
Vanuatu	1990	149	18.5	71	46.3	27	48.1
	2000	190	21.9	92	46.6	31	48.4
	2004	210	23.0	104	46.7	33	45.5
	2006	221	23.5	110	..	..	..
Wallis and Futuna Islands - Îles Wallis et Futuna	1990	14	..	..	..	2	50.0
	2000	15	..	..	..	2	50.0
	2004	15	..	..	..	2	50.0
	2006	15	..	..	..	..	..

For sources and notes, see end of table.

Pour les sources et les notes, se reporter à la fin du tableau.

Region, country or territory Régions, pays ou territoires	Year Année	Population		Total labour force Main d'œuvre totale		Agriculture labour force Main d'œuvre dans l'agriculture	
		Total (thousands) Total (milliers) (1)	Urban population (% of total population) Population urbaine (en % de la population totale) (2)	Total (thousands) Total (milliers) (3)	Female labour (% of total labour force) Main d'œuvre féminine (en % de la main d'œuvre totale) (4)	Total (thousands) Total (milliers) (5)	Female labour (% of total agriculture labour force) Main d'œuvre féminine (en % de la main d'œuvre totale dans l'agriculture) (6)
Economies in transition: Asia - Économies en transition : Asie	2000	71 244	44.2	30 810	46.0	8 052	43.1
	2004	73 551	43.2	33 085	46.2	8 029	42.7
	2006	74 941	42.9	34 459	..	..	..
Armenia - Arménie	2000	3 082	65.0	1 300	47.8	204	22.1
	2004	3 027	64.2	1 278	49.0	188	19.1
	2006	3 010	63.9	1 284	..	..	..
Azerbaijan - Azerbaïdjan	2000	8 143	50.5	3 711	46.7	959	52.1
	2004	8 306	50.2	4 039	47.4	979	52.4
	2006	8 406	50.2	4 246	..	..	..
Georgia - Géorgie	2000	4 720	52.7	2 356	46.2	527	40.2
	2004	4 517	51.7	2 281	43.9	468	38.7
	2006	4 433	51.3	2 237	..	..	..
Kazakhstan	2000	14 954	56.1	7 608	48.6	1 340	28.1
	2004	15 107	54.9	7 868	49.4	1 246	26.1
	2006	15 314	54.2	8 043	..	..	..
Kyrgyzstan - Kirghizistan	2000	4 946	34.4	2 091	44.7	555	37.7
	2004	5 153	34.1	2 269	44.2	559	36.0
	2006	5 259	34.1	2 368	..	..	..
Tajikistan - Tadjikistan	2000	6 173	25.7	1 971	42.5	810	50.6
	2004	6 467	24.3	2 110	43.6	832	51.4
	2006	6 640	23.8	2 197	..	..	..
Turkmenistan - Turkménistan	2000	4 502	44.8	1 915	46.1	683	51.4
	2004	4 766	45.5	2 136	46.6	728	51.6
	2006	4 899	46.1	2 258	..	..	..
Uzbekistan - Ouzbékistan	2000	24 724	37.3	9 858	44.3	2 974	46.0
	2004	26 209	36.5	11 103	44.6	3 029	45.2
	2006	26 981	36.3	11 825	..	..	..
Economies in transition: Europe - Économies en transition : Europe	1990	347 486	63.4	172 412	47.5	32 898	40.0
	2000	264 798	67.6	126 661	47.8	17 106	33.7
	2004	259 398	67.8	127 237	48.2	15 074	31.3
	2006	256 721	67.9	126 892	..	..	..
Albania - Albanie	1990	3 289	36.1	1 564	40.2	857	44.3
	2000	3 080	41.7	1 347	41.7	751	43.8
	2004	3 134	44.0	1 352	42.1	745	43.4
	2006	3 172	45.2	1 368	..	..	..
Bosnia and Herzegovina - Bosnie-Herzégovine	2000	3 787	43.6	1 966	45.7	96	52.1
	2004	3 905	44.9	2 043	47.8	73	52.1
	2006	3 926	45.7	2 065	..	..	..
Belarus - Bélarus	2000	10 052	69.6	4 770	48.8	700	25.4
	2004	9 848	71.0	4 771	49.2	606	22.4
	2006	9 742	71.7	4 762	..	..	..
Bulgaria - Bulgarie	1990	8 819	65.6	4 436	48.0	597	46.6
	2000	8 003	68.7	3 208	46.6	295	39.3
	2004	7 795	70.0	3 153	46.2	222	36.0
	2006	7 693	70.7	3 065	..	..	..
Croatia - Croatie	2000	4 506	57.7	1 994	44.2	177	35.6
	2004	4 540	59.4	1 999	44.8	134	33.6
	2006	4 556	60.3	1 999	..	..	..
Moldova, Republic of - Moldova, République de	2000	4 145	47.2	2 056	48.2	496	33.7
	2004	3 925	49.6	2 140	47.8	438	30.4
	2006	3 833	50.9	2 177	..	..	..
Macedonia, TFYR - Macédoine, LERY	2000	2 009	59.4	831	38.9	120	39.2
	2004	2 030	59.6	859	39.1	99	38.4
	2006	2 036	59.8	859	..	..	..

For sources and notes, see end of table.

Pour les sources et les notes, se reporter à la fin du tableau.

Region, country or territory Régions, pays ou territoires	Year Année	Population		Total labour force Main d'œuvre totale		Agriculture labour force Main d'œuvre dans l'agriculture	
		Total (thousands) Total (milliers)	Urban population (% of total population) Population urbaine (en % de la population totale)	Total (thousands) Total (milliers)	Female labour (% of total labour force) Main d'œuvre féminine (en % de la main d'œuvre totale)	Total (thousands) Total (milliers)	Female labour (% of total agriculture labour force) Main d'œuvre féminine (en % de la main d'œuvre totale dans l'agriculture)
		(1)	(2)	(3)	(4)	(5)	(6)
Romania - Roumanie	1990	23 207	53.2	10 965	44.3	2 551	51.3
	2000	22 138	54.5	11 454	46.0	1 624	47.5
	2004	21 726	54.8	10 433	46.0	1 338	45.6
	2006	21 532	55.1	10 201	..	..	..
Russian Federation - Fédération de Russie	2000	147 423	72.9	71 319	48.5	8 186	29.4
	2004	144 696	72.9	73 217	49.0	7 374	27.2
	2006	143 221	73.0	73 337	..	..	..
Serbia and Montenegro - Serbie-et-Monténégro	2000	10 801	50.4	4 868	40.6	1 008	42.0
	2004	10 517	52.1	5 057	41.7	857	40.0
	2006	10 452	52.8	5 183	..	..	..
Ukraine	2000	48 854	67.5	22 847	48.9	3 653	33.1
	2004	47 282	66.9	22 214	49.1	3 188	30.4
	2006	46 557	66.6	21 866	..	..	..
USSR (former) - URSS (anc.)	1990	289 353	65.6	144 579	48.2	26 669	38.2
Yugoslavia, SFR (former) - Yougoslavie, RSF (anc.)	1990	22 817	49.9	10 868	42.6	2 224	45.0

Sources:
- UN DESA Population Division, *World Population Prospects: The 2004 Revision*
- UN DESA Population Division, *World Population Prospects: The 2006 Revision*
- UN DESA Population Division, *World Urbanization Prospects: The 2005 Revision*
- ILO, online database
- FAO, online database
- World Bank, *World development indicators* online

Notes:

(1)   Total Population: de facto population in a country, area or region as of 1 July of the year indicated.

(2)   Urban population as % of total population: population living in areas classified as urban according to the criteria used by each area or country. Data refer to 1st July of the year indicated.

(3)   Total labour force: comprises all persons over age 15 of both sexes.

(4)   Female labour force as % of total labour force: comprises all persons of sex feminine over age 15.

(5)   Total labour force in agriculture: is that part (male and female) of the total labour force engaged in or seeking work agriculture, hunting, fishing and forestry. These estimates are related neither to the agriculture nor to the rural population.

(6)   Female labour force as % of total agriculture labour force: is that part (female) of the total labour force engaged or seeking work in agriculture, hunting, fishing and forestry.

(7)   National Source.

Sources :
- ONU DAES Division de la population, *World Population Prospects: The 2004 Revision*
- ONU DAES Division de la population, *World Population Prospects: The 2006 Revision*
- ONU DAES Division de la population, *World Urbanization Prospects: The 2005 Revision*
- BIT, base de données en ligne
- FAO, base de données en ligne
- Banque mondiale, *World development indicators* en ligne

Notes :

(1)   Population totale : de facto la population dans un pays ou région au 1er juillet de l'année indiquée.

(2)   Population urbaine en % de la population totale : la population au 1er juillet vivant dans une région classée comme urbaine selon les critères définis par une région ou un pays.

(3)   Main-d'œuvre totale : toutes les personnes (hommes et femmes) de 15 ans et plus.

(4)   Main-d'œuvre féminine en % de la main d'œuvre totale : toutes les personnes de sexe féminin de 15 ans et plus.

(5)   Main-d'œuvre totale en agriculture : la part (hommes et femmes) du total de la main d'œuvre qui travaille ou cherche du travail dans l'agriculture, la chasse, la pêche et la sylviculture. Ces estimations ne sont reliées ni à l'agriculture ni à la population rurale.

(6)   Main-d'œuvre totale féminine en % du total de la main-d'œuvre en agriculture : la part (femmes) du total de la main d'œuvre qui travaille ou cherche du travail dans l'agriculture, la chasse, la pêche et la sylviculture.

(7)   Sources nationales.

Economic grouping / Groupements économiques	Year / Année	Population Total (thousands) / Total (milliers) (1)	Population Urban population (% of total population) / Population urbaine (en % de la population totale) (2)	Total labour force Total (thousands) / Main d'œuvre totale Total (milliers) (3)	Total labour force Female labour (% of total labour force) / Main d'œuvre féminine (en % de la main d'œuvre totale) (4)	Agriculture labour force Total (thousands) / Main d'œuvre dans l'agriculture Total (milliers) (5)	Agriculture labour force Female labour (% of total agriculture labour force) / Main d'œuvre féminine (en % de la main d'œuvre totale dans l'agriculture) (6)
DEVELOPING ECONOMIES - ÉCONOMIES EN DÉVELOPPEMENT	1990	4 068 994	34.7	1 803 721	38.4	1 159 867	42.9
	2000	4 846 278	40.0	2 193 632	38.4	1 271 626	43.9
	2004	5 138 632	42.2	2 363 482	38.6	1 305 735	44.2
	2006	5 285 055	43.2	2 449 990	..	..	..
Developing economies excluding China - Économies en développement sans la Chine	1990	2 940 101	37.3	1 142 231	34.7	666 731	39.6
	2000	3 598 391	41.2	1 447 866	35.2	760 613	41.4
	2004	3 856 183	42.8	1 587 997	35.6	795 713	41.9
	2006	3 986 893	43.6	1 660 280	..	..	..
Developing economies excluding LDCs - Économies en développement sans les PMA	1990	3 543 412	36.8	1 581 902	37.8	976 531	42.1
	2000	4 166 715	42.4	1 907 882	37.8	1 051 189	43.0
	2004	4 389 949	44.8	2 046 216	38.0	1 069 352	43.2
	2006	4 499 491	45.9	2 115 282	..	..	..
High-income countries - Pays à revenu élevé	1990	258 702	72.2	91 610	31.9	17 446	18.0
	2000	302 830	76.0	118 899	34.6	15 986	17.0
	2004	316 891	77.8	130 279	35.9	15 287	16.4
	2006	323 898	78.5	135 585	..	..	..
Middle-income countries - Pays à revenu intermédiaire	1990	630 318	57.2	240 329	33.8	88 515	36.2
	2000	748 302	62.5	310 849	36.2	92 314	39.8
	2004	791 527	64.4	341 564	37.1	92 479	41.2
	2006	813 149	65.3	356 247	..	..	..
Low-income countries - Pays à revenu faible	1990	3 179 754	27.2	1 471 683	39.6	1 053 873	43.9
	2000	3 794 831	32.7	1 763 749	39.1	1 163 287	44.6
	2004	4 029 798	35.0	1 891 491	39.0	1 197 927	44.8
	2006	4 147 547	36.2	1 957 996	..	..	..
Heavily indebted poor countries - Pays pauvres très endettés	1990	377 383	24.3	156 505	43.6	130 188	47.0
	2000	498 815	29.1	206 388	43.7	158 602	47.5
	2004	552 649	31.0	229 297	43.6	170 758	47.5
	2006	581 496	32.0	241 961	..	..	..
Landlocked countries - Pays sans littoral	1990	200 035	18.7	85 135	43.9	75 463	46.0
	2000	333 418	26.6	141 710	44.4	99 237	45.8
	2004	364 414	27.4	157 485	44.4	106 943	45.7
	2006	381 324	27.8	166 404	..	..	..
Small island developing states - Petits états insulaires en développement	1990	13 538	33.9	5 424	42.3	3 010	42.2
	2000	16 034	34.6	6 473	42.8	3 376	44.3
	2004	17 224	34.2	7 058	42.7	3 637	45.3
	2006	17 809	32.9	7 391	..	..	..
Least developed countries - Pays les moins avancés	*1990*	*525 473*	*20.7*	*221 777*	*43.0*	*183 324*	*47.4*
	2000	*679 447*	*24.9*	*285 699*	*42.4*	*220 425*	*48.4*
	2004	*748 564*	*26.9*	*317 211*	*42.2*	*236 371*	*48.6*
	2006	*785 444*	*27.9*	*334 650*	*..*	*..*	*..*
Africa and Haiti - Afrique et Haïti	1990	311 210	22.1	132 302	44.8	112 200	48.4
	2000	408 970	26.7	171 926	44.6	136 546	48.9
	2004	455 764	28.7	191 204	44.5	147 390	48.8
	2006	481 108	29.8	201 813	..	..	..
Asia - Asie	1990	211 604	18.7	88 534	40.4	70 330	45.8
	2000	267 219	22.3	112 633	39.0	83 004	47.6
	2004	289 119	24.0	124 654	38.8	87 989	48.3
	2006	300 436	25.0	131 360	..	..	..
Islands - Îles	1990	2 660	22.4	942	37.9	794	48.5
	2000	3 258	26.1	1 141	37.3	875	48.1
	2004	3 681	26.9	1 353	37.9	992	48.6
	2006	3 900	26.3	1 477	..	..	..

For sources and notes, see end of table.   Pour les sources et les notes, se reporter à la fin du tableau.

Economic grouping / Groupements économiques	Year / Année	Population		Total labour force / Main d'œuvre totale		Agriculture labour force / Main d'œuvre dans l'agriculture	
		Total (thousands) / Total (milliers)	Urban population (% of total population) / Population urbaine (en % de la population totale)	Total (thousands) / Total (milliers)	Female labour (% of total labour force) / Main d'œuvre féminine (en % de la main d'œuvre totale)	Total (thousands) / Total (milliers)	Female labour (% of total agriculture labour force) / Main d'œuvre féminine (en % de la main d'œuvre totale dans l'agriculture)
		(1)	(2)	(3)	(4)	(5)	(6)
Major petroleum exporters -	*1990*	*465 515*	*42.6*	*167 203*	*33.0*	*76 428*	*37.7*
Principaux exportateurs de pétrole	*2000*	*572 670*	*50.8*	*225 565*	*33.9*	*85 124*	*41.6*
	2004	*616 512*	*53.9*	*251 723*	*34.4*	*87 646*	*43.1*
	2006	*638 846*	*55.3*	*265 629*	*..*	*..*	*..*
Africa - Afrique	1990	137 975	38.3	47 100	34.8	20 593	40.2
	2000	178 939	45.4	63 568	35.0	22 653	42.6
	2004	196 602	47.9	70 768	35.0	23 351	43.6
	2006	205 667	49.1	74 746	..	..	..
America - Amérique	1990	21 145	83.0	7 804	32.2	927	5.5
	2000	25 884	86.2	11 197	37.0	855	6.0
	2004	27 764	87.2	13 177	40.3	817	6.1
	2006	28 708	87.7	14 111	..	..	..
Asia - Asie	1990	306 396	41.7	112 300	32.4	54 908	37.3
	2000	367 847	50.9	150 800	33.2	61 616	41.7
	2004	392 147	54.5	167 777	33.8	63 478	43.5
	2006	404 471	56.1	176 772	..	..	..
Major exporters of manufactured goods -	*1990*	*2 485 343*	*33.6*	*1 189 477*	*38.9*	*795 774*	*43.0*
Principaux exportateurs d'articles manufacturés	*2000*	*2 875 863*	*39.1*	*1 393 607*	*38.8*	*847 771*	*43.5*
	2004	*3 011 213*	*41.4*	*1 477 288*	*38.9*	*858 951*	*43.5*
	2006	*3 076 589*	*42.5*	*1 517 498*	*..*	*..*	*..*
America - Amérique	1990	233 524	73.9	92 345	33.6	23 763	17.6
	2000	273 895	78.8	123 687	38.7	21 762	16.9
	2004	287 656	81.3	133 087	40.0	20 587	16.4
	2006	294 665	82.4	137 433	..	..	..
Asia - Asie	1990	2 251 820	29.4	1 097 132	39.4	772 011	43.8
	2000	2 601 968	34.9	1 269 921	38.8	826 009	44.2
	2004	2 723 557	37.2	1 344 201	38.7	838 364	44.1
	2006	2 781 923	38.3	1 380 065	..	..	..
Emerging economies - Économies émergentes	*1990*	*439 605*	*65.2*	*177 092*	*36.7*	*54 312*	*30.5*
	2000	*508 787*	*69.9*	*225 390*	*39.8*	*51 889*	*30.3*
	2004	*531 471*	*71.9*	*242 540*	*40.9*	*49 976*	*30.1*
	2006	*542 658*	*72.9*	*250 532*	*..*	*..*	*..*
America - Amérique	1990	301 046	75.4	118 859	33.8	28 837	16.7
	2000	351 865	79.9	157 559	38.8	27 171	16.5
	2004	369 109	82.1	170 447	40.2	26 105	16.3
	2006	377 853	83.1	176 528	..	..	..
Asia - Asie	1990	138 559	43.0	58 233	42.6	25 475	46.1
	2000	156 921	47.5	67 831	42.1	24 718	45.5
	2004	162 361	48.8	72 093	42.5	23 871	45.1
	2006	164 805	49.4	74 004	..	..	..
Newly industrialized economies -	*1990*	*388 336*	*38.8*	*161 138*	*39.6*	*80 562*	*39.3*
Économies nouvellement industrialisées	*2000*	*451 490*	*47.3*	*200 708*	*39.3*	*86 435*	*40.6*
	2004	*475 436*	*50.4*	*217 935*	*39.8*	*87 344*	*41.1*
	2006	*487 065*	*51.8*	*226 502*	*..*	*..*	*..*
First tier - Premier tier	1990	71 869	56.1	23 521	38.9	3 561	43.9
	2000	79 644	60.1	27 936	40.5	2 390	45.1
	2004	81 587	60.8	29 714	41.3	1 946	45.5
	2006	82 380	61.1	30 352	..	..	..
Second tier - Deuxième tier	1990	316 467	34.8	137 617	39.7	77 001	39.1
	2000	371 845	44.5	172 773	39.1	84 045	40.5
	2004	393 849	48.2	188 222	39.5	85 398	41.0
	2006	404 686	50.0	196 150	..	..	..

For sources and notes, see end of table.

Pour les sources et les notes, se reporter à la fin du tableau.

Economic grouping / Groupements économiques	Year / Année	Population		Total labour force / Main d'œuvre totale		Agriculture labour force / Main d'œuvre dans l'agriculture	
		Total (thousands) / Total (milliers)	Urban population (% of total population) / Population urbaine (en % de la population totale)	Total (thousands) / Total (milliers)	Female labour (% of total labour force) / Main d'œuvre féminine (en % de la main d'œuvre totale)	Total (thousands) / Total (milliers)	Female labour (% of total agriculture labour force) / Main d'œuvre féminine (en % de la main d'œuvre totale dans l'agriculture)
		(1)	(2)	(3)	(4)	(5)	(6)
Developing economies: Africa - **Économies en développement : Afrique**	**1990**	**636 817**	**31.7**	**246 032**	**40.3**	**165 450**	**46.7**
	2000	**820 235**	**36.6**	**321 500**	**39.8**	**197 294**	**47.9**
	2004	**900 345**	**38.5**	**354 732**	**39.7**	**209 666**	**48.1**
	2006	**942 504**	**39.4**	**372 729**	**..**	**..**	**..**
Northern Africa excluding Sudan - Afrique septentrionale sans le Soudan	1990	117 809	48.7	35 302	24.3	14 411	44.4
	2000	140 771	51.5	46 781	24.4	16 178	49.4
	2004	149 863	52.9	52 586	25.2	16 758	51.1
	2006	154 624	53.6	55 645	..	..	..
Sub-Saharan Africa - Afrique subsaharienne	1990	519 007	27.9	210 730	43.0	151 039	46.9
	2000	679 464	33.6	274 719	42.5	181 116	47.7
	2004	750 482	35.6	302 146	42.2	192 908	47.8
	2006	787 880	36.6	317 084	..	..	..
Sub-Saharan Africa excluding South Africa - Afrique sub-saharienne sans l'Afrique du Sud	1990	482 430	26.3	195 675	43.1	149 108	47.2
	2000	634 066	32.0	255 409	42.7	179 374	47.9
	2004	702 941	34.1	282 387	42.5	191 338	48.0
	2006	739 597	35.2	297 283	..	..	..
Developing economies: America - **Économies en développement : Amérique**	**1990**	**439 876**	**71.0**	**171 546**	**34.1**	**44 629**	**16.9**
	2000	**518 242**	**75.4**	**228 519**	**38.8**	**43 835**	**17.3**
	2004	**546 089**	**77.5**	**249 933**	**40.2**	**43 009**	**17.4**
	2006	**560 044**	**78.4**	**260 440**	**..**	**..**	**..**
Central America and Greater Carribean Islands excluding Puerto Rico - Amérique centrale et Grandes Antilles sans Porto Rico	1990	140 103	63.7	50 699	31.9	16 273	14.8
	2000	166 634	66.3	66 556	34.3	16 814	15.4
	2004	174 490	68.3	72 070	35.5	16 889	15.5
	2006	178 628	69.1	74 941	..	..	..
Central America and Greater Carribean Islands excluding Mexico and Puerto Rico - Amérique centrale et Grandes Antilles sans le Mexique et Porto Rico	1990	56 100	50.2	20 784	33.7	7 742	17.5
	2000	66 900	53.5	26 256	35.4	8 263	18.3
	2004	71 152	54.9	28 894	36.5	8 436	18.5
	2006	73 286	55.6	30 318	..	..	..
South America and Central America - Amérique du Sud et Amérique centrale	1990	409 802	72.1	159 664	33.8	40 666	16.0
	2000	484 266	76.7	214 375	38.8	39 879	16.2
	2004	510 688	78.9	234 910	40.3	39 086	16.3
	2006	523 963	79.8	244 934	..	..	..
South America excluding Brazil - Amérique du Sud sans le Brésil	1990	147 556	74.3	57 466	34.8	12 968	15.3
	2000	174 519	78.6	77 441	39.9	13 661	17.2
	2004	184 266	80.3	86 760	41.8	13 844	18.0
	2006	189 038	81.2	91 469	..	..	..
Developing economies: Asia - **Économies en développement : Asie**	**1990**	**2 985 852**	**30.1**	**1 383 595**	**38.6**	**947 777**	**43.5**
	2000	**3 499 689**	**35.6**	**1 640 396**	**38.1**	**1 028 128**	**44.3**
	2004	**3 683 371**	**37.9**	**1 755 254**	**38.1**	**1 050 511**	**44.5**
	2006	**3 773 332**	**39.0**	**1 813 070**	**..**	**..**	**..**
Eastern and South-Eastern Asia excluding China - Asie orientale et Asie du Sud-Est sans la Chine	1990	532 158	35.6	229 504	41.5	129 364	42.8
	2000	621 480	42.5	285 232	41.3	142 492	43.7
	2004	654 052	45.3	309 941	41.7	146 270	44.0
	2006	669 892	46.6	322 422	..	..	..
Southern Asia excluding India - Asie méridionale sans l'Inde	1990	332 363	28.6	120 026	31.3	77 278	40.4
	2000	414 622	32.0	154 595	31.7	90 380	44.5
	2004	445 114	33.6	174 405	32.5	96 111	46.0
	2006	461 090	34.4	185 379	..	..	..

For sources and notes, see next page.

Pour les sources et les notes, se reporter à la page suivante.

Sources:
- UN DESA Population Division, *World Population Prospects: The 2004 Revision*
- UN DESA Population Division, *World Population Prospects: The 2006 Revision*
- UN DESA Population Division, *World Urbanization Prospects: The 2005 Revision*
- ILO, online database
- FAO, online database
- World Bank, *World development indicators* online

Notes:

(1) Total Population: de facto population in a country, area or region as of 1 July of the year indicated.

(2) Urban population as % of total population: population living in areas classified as urban according to the criteria used by each area or country. Data refer to 1st July of the year indicated.

(3) Total labour force: comprises all persons over age 15 of both sexes.

(4) Female labour force as % of total labour force: comprises all persons of sex feminine over age 15.

(5) Total labour force in agriculture: is that part (male and female) of the total labour force engaged in or seeking work agriculture, hunting, fishing and forestry. These estimates are related neither to the agriculture nor to the rural population.

(6) Female labour force as % of total agriculture labour force: is that part (female) of the total labour force engaged or seeking work in agriculture, hunting, fishing and forestry.

Sources :
- ONU DAES Division de la population, *World Population Prospects: The 2004 Revision*
- ONU DAES Division de la population, *World Population Prospects: The 2006 Revision*
- ONU DAES Division de la population, *World Urbanization Prospects: The 2005 Revision*
- BIT, base de données en ligne
- FAO, base de données en ligne
- Banque mondiale, *World development indicators* en ligne

Notes :

(1) Population totale : de facto la population dans un pays ou région au 1er juillet de l'année indiquée.

(2) Population urbaine en % de la population totale : la population au 1er juillet vivant dans une région classée comme urbaine selon les critères définis par une région ou un pays.

(3) Main-d'œuvre totale : toutes les personnes (hommes et femmes) de 15 ans et plus.

(4) Main-d'œuvre féminine en % de la main d'œuvre totale : toutes les personnes de sexe féminin de 15 ans et plus.

(5) Main-d'œuvre totale en agriculture : la part (hommes et femmes) du total de la main d'œuvre qui travaille ou cherche du travail dans l'agriculture, la chasse, la pêche et la sylviculture. Ces estimations ne sont reliées ni à l'agriculture ni à la population rurale.

(6) Main-d'œuvre totale féminine en % du total de la main-d'œuvre en agriculture : la part (femmes) du total de la main d'œuvre qui travaille ou cherche du travail dans l'agriculture, la chasse, la pêche et la sylviculture.

Region, country or territory / Régions, pays ou territoires	Year / Année	Population growth rate / Taux d'accroissement de la population	Natural increase rate per 1000 inhabitants / Taux d'évolution naturel pour 1000 habitants	Net migration rate per 1000 inhabitants / Taux net de migration pour 1000 habitants	Crude birth rate per 1000 inhabitants / Taux de natalité brut pour 1000 habitants	Crude death rate per 1000 inhabitants / Taux de mortalité brut pour 1000 habitants	Infant mortality rate per 1000 live births / Taux de mortalité infantile pour 1000 naissances vivantes	Life expectancy at birth / Espérance de vie à la naissance
		(1)	(2)	(3)	(4)	(5)	(6)	(7)
WORLD - MONDE	**1990 - 1995**	**1.54**	**15.05**	**0.00**	**24.57**	**9.52**	**66.29**	**64**
	1995 - 2000	**1.37**	**13.35**	**0.00**	**22.50**	**9.15**	**62.02**	**65**
	2000 - 2005	**1.24**	**12.09**	**0.00**	**21.12**	**9.03**	**57.43**	**65**
DEVELOPED ECONOMIES - ÉCONOMIES DÉVELOPPÉES	1990 - 1995	0.86	3.52	2.83	12.80	9.28	7.59	76
	1995 - 2000	0.54	2.80	2.67	11.85	9.04	6.44	77
	2000 - 2005	0.61	2.47	2.92	11.47	9.00	5.70	79
DEVELOPING ECONOMIES - ÉCONOMIES EN DÉVELOPPEMENT	1990 - 1995	1.85	18.67	-0.46	28.13	9.46	73.18	61
	1995 - 2000	1.65	16.63	-0.46	25.61	8.99	68.07	62
	2000 - 2005	1.45	14.91	-0.47	23.73	8.82	63.06	63
ECONOMIES IN TRANSITION - ÉCONOMIES EN TRANSITION	1990 - 1995	-0.48	2.34	-1.86	14.35	12.01	37.81	67
	1995 - 2000	-0.19	-0.68	-1.11	11.90	12.59	36.52	66
	2000 - 2005	-0.23	-1.11	-1.44	12.08	13.19	33.72	66
Developed economies: America - Économies développées : Amérique	**1990 - 1995**	**1.08**	**6.82**	**3.98**	**15.57**	**8.75**	**7.73**	**75**
	1995 - 2000	**1.04**	**5.92**	**4.48**	**14.16**	**8.25**	**7.38**	**77**
	2000 - 2005	**1.02**	**5.48**	**4.21**	**13.77**	**8.29**	**6.82**	**78**
Bermuda - Bermudes	1990 - 1995	0.54	..	..	..	..	..	..
	1995 - 2000	0.46	..	..	..	..	..	..
	2000 - 2005	0.41	..	..	..	..	..	..
Canada	1990 - 1995	1.12	6.73	4.51	13.79	7.06	6.31	78
	1995 - 2000	0.92	4.36	4.89	11.59	7.23	5.70	79
	2000 - 2005	1.00	3.37	6.67	10.55	7.18	5.09	80
Greenland - Groenland	1990 - 1995	0.02	..	..	..	..	..	..
	1995 - 2000	0.23	..	..	..	..	..	..
	2000 - 2005	0.43	..	..	..	..	..	..
Saint Pierre and Miquelon - Saint-Pierre-et-Miquelon	1990 - 1995	0.07	..	..	..	..	..	..
	1995 - 2000	0.05	..	..	..	..	..	..
	2000 - 2005	0.07	..	..	..	..	..	..
United States - États-Unis	1990 - 1995	1.07	6.83	3.93	15.76	8.93	7.86	75
	1995 - 2000	1.05	6.08	4.44	14.44	8.36	7.52	77
	2000 - 2005	1.02	5.71	3.95	14.12	8.41	6.96	77
Developed economies: Asia - Économies développées : Asie	**1990 - 1995**	**0.43**	**3.19**	**1.13**	**10.21**	**7.02**	**4.75**	**79**
	1995 - 2000	**0.34**	**2.60**	**0.84**	**10.14**	**7.53**	**4.01**	**80**
	2000 - 2005	**0.22**	**1.89**	**0.64**	**9.77**	**7.89**	**3.48**	**82**
Israel - Israël	1990 - 1995	3.49	15.20	19.60	21.50	6.30	8.71	77
	1995 - 2000	2.48	15.17	9.62	21.49	6.31	6.19	78
	2000 - 2005	1.90	15.06	4.94	20.73	5.67	5.07	80
Japan - Japon	1990 - 1995	0.31	2.71	0.40	9.74	7.03	4.40	80
	1995 - 2000	0.25	2.03	0.44	9.61	7.58	3.79	81
	2000 - 2005	0.14	1.22	0.42	9.22	7.99	3.30	82
Developed economies: Europe - Économies développées : Europe	**1990 - 1995**	**0.81**	**1.28**	**2.50**	**11.64**	**10.35**	**8.21**	**76**
	1995 - 2000	**0.22**	**0.59**	**1.87**	**10.69**	**10.11**	**6.27**	**77**
	2000 - 2005	**0.40**	**0.37**	**2.58**	**10.29**	**9.92**	**5.30**	**78**
Andorra - Andorre	1990 - 1995	4.07	..	..	..	..	..	..
	1995 - 2000	0.54	..	..	..	..	..	..
	2000 - 2005	2.01	..	..	..	..	..	..
Austria - Autriche	1990 - 1995	0.80	1.40	6.64	11.84	10.44	6.97	76
	1995 - 2000	0.16	0.12	1.12	10.13	10.02	5.95	78
	2000 - 2005	0.44	-0.17	2.46	9.43	9.60	4.78	79
Belgium - Belgique	2000 - 2005	0.40	0.93	1.29	10.89	9.96	4.11	79
Belgium-Luxembourg - Belgique-Luxembourg	1990 - 1995	0.34	1.77	2.01	12.16	10.39	6.85	77
	1995 - 2000	0.26	1.48	2.24	11.31	9.83	4.95	78
Cyprus - Chypre	1990 - 1995	1.43	9.79	4.50	17.50	7.71	7.80	77
	1995 - 2000	1.46	6.96	7.63	14.02	7.06	6.56	78
	2000 - 2005	1.23	4.94	7.14	12.14	7.19	6.22	79
Czechoslovakia (former) - Tchécoslovaquie (anc.)	1990 - 1995	..	1.09	0.60	12.22	11.13	10.38	(a)72
Czech Republic - République tchèque	1995 - 2000	-0.17	-2.24	1.00	8.76	11.00	7.52	74
	2000 - 2005	-0.06	-1.91	0.98	8.87	10.78	5.59	75

For sources and notes, see end of table.

Pour les sources et les notes, se reporter à la fin du tableau.

Region, country or territory / Régions, pays ou territoires	Year / Année	Population growth rate / Taux d'accroissement de la population	Natural increase rate per 1000 inhabitants / Taux d'évolution naturel pour 1000 habitants	Net migration rate per 1000 inhabitants / Taux net de migration pour 1000 habitants	Crude birth rate per 1000 inhabitants / Taux de natalité brut pour 1000 habitants	Crude death rate per 1000 inhabitants / Taux de mortalité brut pour 1000 habitants	Infant mortality rate per 1000 live births / Taux de mortalité infantile pour 1000 naissances vivantes	Life expectancy at birth / Espérance de vie à la naissance
		(1)	(2)	(3)	(4)	(5)	(6)	(7)
Denmark - Danemark	1990 - 1995	0.34	1.14	2.25	12.95	11.81	6.63	75
	1995 - 2000	0.41	1.07	3.16	12.59	11.52	5.94	76
	2000 - 2005	0.30	1.13	2.25	11.94	10.81	5.03	77
Estonia - Estonie	1990 - 1995	-1.70	-2.62	-15.50	11.16	13.78	16.72	69
	1995 - 2000	-0.98	-4.77	-6.59	9.12	13.89	11.91	70
	2000 - 2005	-0.38	-4.04	-1.48	9.68	13.71	9.53	71
Faeroe Islands - Îles Féroé	1990 - 1995	-1.45	..	..	..	..	..	..
	1995 - 2000	1.05	..	..	..	..	..	..
	2000 - 2005	0.76	..	..	..	..	..	..
Finland - Finlande	1990 - 1995	0.48	3.13	1.69	12.97	9.84	5.03	76
	1995 - 2000	0.26	1.88	0.79	11.50	9.62	4.49	77
	2000 - 2005	0.27	1.20	1.58	10.75	9.55	3.97	78
France	1990 - 1995	0.54	3.92	1.46	13.00	9.08	6.80	77
	1995 - 2000	0.36	3.21	0.74	12.66	9.45	5.18	78
	2000 - 2005	0.62	3.34	0.98	12.67	9.32	4.56	79
Germany - Allemagne	1990 - 1995	0.55	-1.14	6.69	10.06	11.20	6.41	76
	1995 - 2000	0.16	-1.10	2.77	9.49	10.59	5.03	77
	2000 - 2005	0.08	-1.83	2.67	8.51	10.34	4.56	79
Gibraltar	1990 - 1995	0.34	..	..	..	..	..	..
	1995 - 2000	0.05	..	..	..	..	..	..
	2000 - 2005	1.22	..	..	..	..	..	..
Greece - Grèce	1990 - 1995	0.95	0.52	9.03	10.05	9.52	8.08	77
	1995 - 2000	0.59	0.32	5.55	9.66	9.34	6.72	78
	2000 - 2005	0.23	-0.62	3.24	9.28	9.90	6.48	78
Holy See - Saint-Siège	1990 - 1995	0.28	..	..	..	..	..	..
	1995 - 2000	0.15	..	..	..	..	..	..
	2000 - 2005	-0.10	..	..	..	..	..	..
Hungary - Hongrie	1990 - 1995	-0.07	-2.64	1.95	11.66	14.30	13.55	70
	1995 - 2000	-0.22	-3.96	1.95	9.87	13.82	10.31	71
	2000 - 2005	-0.25	-3.50	0.98	9.46	12.97	8.32	73
Iceland - Islande	1990 - 1995	0.97	10.66	-0.95	17.40	6.74	4.84	79
	1995 - 2000	0.99	8.75	1.31	15.49	6.74	3.81	79
	2000 - 2005	1.02	8.01	1.23	14.35	6.35	3.15	81
Ireland - Irlande	1990 - 1995	0.53	5.36	-0.07	14.20	8.84	6.97	75
	1995 - 2000	1.05	5.61	4.79	14.19	8.59	6.18	76
	2000 - 2005	1.71	7.68	9.76	15.28	7.61	5.48	78
Italy - Italie	1990 - 1995	0.20	0.03	2.01	9.69	9.66	7.56	77
	1995 - 2000	0.14	-0.65	2.09	9.22	9.87	5.86	79
	2000 - 2005	0.33	-0.77	2.07	9.20	9.97	5.15	80
Latvia - Lettonie	1990 - 1995	-1.35	-3.17	-13.39	11.29	14.46	19.23	68
	1995 - 2000	-0.91	-5.64	-4.59	7.96	13.60	16.35	70
	2000 - 2005	-0.66	-4.63	-1.03	8.79	13.42	10.27	71
Lithuania - Lituanie	1990 - 1995	-0.37	1.64	-5.44	13.48	11.84	15.76	70
	1995 - 2000	-0.71	-1.12	-6.10	10.60	11.72	13.26	71
	2000 - 2005	-0.45	-2.80	-1.15	9.04	11.84	9.67	72
Luxembourg	2000 - 2005	0.89	4.49	8.70	12.65	8.15	5.31	78
Malta - Malte	1990 - 1995	0.96	6.70	2.87	14.20	7.50	8.97	76
	1995 - 2000	0.58	4.43	2.86	12.23	7.80	8.08	77
	2000 - 2005	0.69	2.18	2.77	10.12	7.94	7.37	78
Netherlands - Pays-Bas	1990 - 1995	0.67	4.17	2.50	12.90	8.73	6.16	77
	1995 - 2000	0.59	3.54	2.05	12.37	8.83	4.89	78
	2000 - 2005	0.50	3.13	1.86	12.08	8.95	4.41	78
Norway - Norvège	1990 - 1995	0.55	3.51	1.98	14.06	10.55	6.01	77
	1995 - 2000	0.59	3.42	3.05	13.40	9.97	5.43	78
	2000 - 2005	0.66	2.62	2.57	12.25	9.63	4.17	79

For sources and notes, see end of table.   Pour les sources et les notes, se reporter à la fin du tableau.

Region, country or territory / Régions, pays ou territoires	Year / Année	Population growth rate / Taux d'accroissement de la population	Natural increase rate per 1000 inhabitants / Taux d'évolution naturel pour 1000 habitants	Net migration rate per 1000 inhabitants / Taux net de migration pour 1000 habitants	Crude birth rate per 1000 inhabitants / Taux de natalité brut pour 1000 habitants	Crude death rate per 1000 inhabitants / Taux de mortalité brut pour 1000 habitants	Infant mortality rate per 1000 live births / Taux de mortalité infantile pour 1000 naissances vivantes	Life expectancy at birth / Espérance de vie à la naissance
		(1)	(2)	(3)	(4)	(5)	(6)	(7)
Poland - Pologne	1990 - 1995	0.25	2.93	-0.40	13.19	10.26	14.84	72
	1995 - 2000	-0.08	0.65	-0.37	10.59	9.94	11.12	73
	2000 - 2005	-0.12	-0.21	-0.42	9.49	9.70	8.88	74
Portugal	1990 - 1995	0.09	1.08	-0.14	11.32	10.24	9.62	75
	1995 - 2000	0.39	0.39	3.46	11.16	10.77	6.58	76
	2000 - 2005	0.58	0.38	4.83	10.91	10.53	5.54	77
San Marino - Saint-Marin	1990 - 1995	1.24	..	..	..	..	..	..
	1995 - 2000	0.95	..	..	..	..	..	..
	2000 - 2005	2.29	..	..	..	..	..	..
Slovakia - Slovaquie	1995 - 2000	0.09	1.01	0.35	10.83	9.82	9.35	73
	2000 - 2005	0.00	-0.16	0.19	9.54	9.70	7.86	74
Slovenia - Slovénie	1990 - 1995	0.39	-0.02	3.88	10.09	10.11	7.44	73
	1995 - 2000	0.20	-0.53	0.81	9.14	9.67	6.08	75
	2000 - 2005	0.16	-1.02	1.02	8.81	9.82	5.57	76
Spain - Espagne	1990 - 1995	0.27	0.59	2.52	9.77	9.18	7.07	77
	1995 - 2000	0.42	0.60	3.35	9.48	8.88	5.35	78
	2000 - 2005	1.52	1.54	9.67	10.35	8.82	4.48	79
Sweden - Suède	1990 - 1995	0.62	2.70	3.47	13.59	10.89	5.11	78
	1995 - 2000	0.09	-0.22	1.36	10.34	10.57	4.69	79
	2000 - 2005	0.38	0.15	3.51	10.59	10.44	3.40	80
Switzerland - Suisse	1990 - 1995	0.86	2.57	2.31	12.05	9.49	5.91	78
	1995 - 2000	0.36	2.37	2.25	10.99	8.62	4.92	79
	2000 - 2005	0.44	1.24	1.10	9.69	8.45	4.48	80
United Kingdom - Royaume-Uni	1990 - 1995	0.25	1.84	1.34	13.24	11.40	7.86	76
	1995 - 2000	0.31	1.46	1.98	12.28	10.82	6.20	77
	2000 - 2005	0.46	1.05	2.32	11.37	10.31	5.34	78
Developed economies: Oceania - Économies développées : Océanie	**1990 - 1995**	**1.39**	**8.12**	**4.51**	**15.22**	**7.10**	**7.08**	**77**
	1995 - 2000	**1.12**	**6.89**	**4.79**	**13.84**	**6.96**	**6.32**	**79**
	2000 - 2005	**1.19**	**6.11**	**4.94**	**12.97**	**6.86**	**5.24**	**80**
Australia - Australie	1990 - 1995	1.37	7.78	4.48	14.73	6.95	6.89	78
	1995 - 2000	1.15	6.71	5.51	13.51	6.80	6.17	79
	2000 - 2005	1.19	5.95	5.10	12.69	6.74	5.14	80
New Zealand - Nouvelle-Zélande	1990 - 1995	1.48	9.51	4.47	17.10	7.59	7.87	76
	1995 - 2000	0.96	7.51	1.07	14.99	7.48	6.99	78
	2000 - 2005	1.22	6.72	4.00	13.99	7.27	5.66	79
Developing economies: Africa - Économies en développement : Afrique	**1990 - 1995**	**2.61**	**26.35**	**-0.39**	**41.33**	**14.98**	**102.13**	**51**
	1995 - 2000	**2.45**	**24.06**	**-0.37**	**39.21**	**15.15**	**98.63**	**50**
	2000 - 2005	**2.32**	**22.55**	**-0.54**	**38.03**	**15.48**	**93.92**	**49**
Eastern Africa - Afrique orientale	***1990 - 1995***	***2.57***	***27.67***	***-1.92***	***44.85***	***17.17***	***104.33***	***47***
	1995 - 2000	***2.75***	***25.60***	***0.83***	***42.92***	***17.32***	***97.96***	***46***
	2000 - 2005	***2.57***	***24.05***	***-0.16***	***41.35***	***17.31***	***92.43***	***46***
Burundi	1990 - 1995	1.85	24.98	-8.45	46.07	21.09	122.69	42
	1995 - 2000	1.32	23.00	-12.65	43.22	20.22	116.77	42
	2000 - 2005	3.29	24.79	5.46	43.65	18.86	105.55	43
Comoros - Comores	1990 - 1995	2.85	29.47	-1.06	39.34	9.87	81.54	58
	1995 - 2000	2.82	29.99	-1.84	38.51	8.52	68.04	61
	2000 - 2005	2.65	29.09	-2.67	36.53	7.44	58.10	63
Djibouti	1990 - 1995	2.15	27.68	-10.29	41.74	14.06	110.19	51
	1995 - 2000	3.13	25.86	6.13	39.04	13.17	102.39	52
	2000 - 2005	1.94	23.43	-2.60	36.15	12.73	93.07	53
Ethiopia (former) - Éthiopie (anc.)	1990 - 1995	..	29.47	1.84	47.24	17.77	111.78	47
Eritrea - Érythrée	1995 - 2000	2.74	28.14	-0.53	40.93	12.79	75.34	52
	2000 - 2005	4.12	28.39	14.07	39.95	11.56	63.81	54
Ethiopia - Éthiopie	1995 - 2000	2.81	27.10	-0.24	44.27	17.16	106.37	47
	2000 - 2005	2.59	25.14	-0.42	41.67	16.53	99.39	48

For sources and notes, see end of table.

Pour les sources et les notes, se reporter à la fin du tableau.

458

Region, country or territory / Régions, pays ou territoires	Year / Année	Population growth rate / Taux d'accroissement de la population	Natural increase rate per 1000 inhabitants / Taux d'évolution naturel pour 1000 habitants	Net migration rate per 1000 inhabitants / Taux net de migration pour 1000 habitants	Crude birth rate per 1000 inhabitants / Taux de natalité brut pour 1000 habitants	Crude death rate per 1000 inhabitants / Taux de mortalité brut pour 1000 habitants	Infant mortality rate per 1000 live births / Taux de mortalité infantile pour 1000 naissances vivantes	Life expectancy at birth / Espérance de vie à la naissance
		(1)	(2)	(3)	(4)	(5)	(6)	(7)
Kenya	1990 - 1995	3.10	28.22	1.75	38.52	10.29	64.15	57
	1995 - 2000	2.65	24.07	-0.15	37.45	13.38	64.14	50
	2000 - 2005	2.60	23.27	-1.30	38.77	15.50	66.31	47
Madagascar	1990 - 1995	2.95	29.35	-0.09	43.73	14.38	97.26	52
	1995 - 2000	2.98	29.89	-0.04	42.96	13.07	86.44	54
	2000 - 2005	2.83	27.71	0.00	39.70	11.99	79.34	55
Malawi	1990 - 1995	1.32	30.38	-17.07	49.97	19.59	133.64	45
	1995 - 2000	2.83	26.86	-0.93	48.11	21.25	120.73	42
	2000 - 2005	2.58	22.82	-0.33	44.59	21.77	110.71	40
Mauritius - Maurice	1990 - 1995	1.25	13.74	-1.28	20.43	6.69	19.73	70
	1995 - 2000	1.06	10.93	-0.35	17.62	6.70	18.26	71
	2000 - 2005	0.91	9.70	0.00	16.41	6.71	15.37	72
Mozambique	1990 - 1995	3.26	24.24	8.88	44.62	20.38	132.31	44
	1995 - 2000	2.64	23.48	0.89	42.91	19.44	114.50	44
	2000 - 2005	2.42	20.18	-0.21	40.37	20.20	101.37	42
Rwanda	1990 - 1995	-5.13	1.82	-54.69	43.71	41.89	130.99	24
	1995 - 2000	7.41	18.08	58.74	41.44	23.37	118.98	37
	2000 - 2005	2.43	22.70	1.06	40.99	18.30	111.34	44
Seychelles	1990 - 1995	1.00	..	..	..	..	..	..
	1995 - 2000	1.39	..	..	..	..	..	..
	2000 - 2005	1.06	..	..	..	..	..	..
Somalia - Somalie	1990 - 1995	-1.46	22.21	-33.37	45.74	23.53	156.54	40
	1995 - 2000	2.45	27.45	-6.43	47.73	20.28	142.54	44
	2000 - 2005	3.00	27.46	4.46	45.82	18.36	125.44	46
Uganda - Ouganda	1990 - 1995	3.48	31.04	1.40	49.78	18.74	89.64	44
	1995 - 2000	3.01	30.82	-0.58	49.58	18.77	84.63	43
	2000 - 2005	3.18	34.05	-0.11	50.17	16.12	80.42	47
United Republic of Tanzania - République-Unie de Tanzanie	1990 - 1995	3.19	29.21	4.21	43.09	13.88	106.19	52
	1995 - 2000	2.48	24.84	-1.27	40.57	15.73	104.11	48
	2000 - 2005	2.56	21.61	-1.91	38.45	16.84	103.94	46
Zambia - Zambie	1990 - 1995	2.62	26.54	-0.16	45.70	19.16	100.11	43
	1995 - 2000	2.42	20.86	1.70	42.98	22.13	98.84	39
	2000 - 2005	1.88	18.44	-1.16	41.26	22.82	94.70	37
Zimbabwe	1990 - 1995	2.34	25.67	-3.25	36.13	10.46	50.74	56
	1995 - 2000	1.42	14.75	-2.05	32.09	17.34	55.27	44
	2000 - 2005	0.72	7.26	-0.78	30.00	22.74	61.42	37
Middle Africa - Afrique centrale	*1990 - 1995*	*3.26*	*28.83*	*3.67*	*48.06*	*19.22*	*117.14*	*46*
	1995 - 2000	*2.41*	*26.34*	*-3.05*	*46.93*	*20.59*	*121.70*	*43*
	2000 - 2005	*2.81*	*26.81*	*0.06*	*46.97*	*20.16*	*116.25*	*43*
Angola	1990 - 1995	3.13	28.13	2.51	52.43	24.29	152.53	40
	1995 - 2000	2.46	25.74	-1.84	48.87	23.13	147.08	40
	2000 - 2005	2.89	26.27	1.95	48.54	22.27	137.36	41
Cameroon - Cameroun	1990 - 1995	2.77	26.55	-0.09	40.94	14.38	90.96	52
	1995 - 2000	2.41	22.08	0.00	37.79	15.71	93.95	49
	2000 - 2005	2.30	18.64	0.17	35.88	17.24	93.66	46
Central African Republic - République centrafricaine	1990 - 1995	2.74	23.54	2.33	41.52	17.99	103.20	47
	1995 - 2000	2.27	19.56	0.63	39.80	20.24	100.33	42
	2000 - 2005	1.63	15.63	-2.30	37.77	22.14	98.00	39
Chad - Tchad	1990 - 1995	3.14	29.32	0.60	48.37	19.05	116.73	46
	1995 - 2000	3.37	28.39	2.61	48.06	19.66	115.37	45
	2000 - 2005	3.62	28.11	6.03	48.24	20.13	114.28	44
Congo	1990 - 1995	2.85	30.95	1.05	43.93	12.99	73.44	53
	1995 - 2000	2.74	30.26	2.62	44.06	13.80	71.51	51
	2000 - 2005	2.39	30.93	-0.75	44.11	13.18	71.14	52
Dem. Rep. of the Congo - Rép. dém. du Congo	1990 - 1995	3.56	29.12	5.84	48.59	19.47	118.07	45
	1995 - 2000	2.23	27.20	-5.94	48.99	21.79	127.71	42
	2000 - 2005	2.95	29.06	-1.20	49.45	20.39	120.48	43

For sources and notes, see end of table.
Pour les sources et les notes, se reporter à la fin du tableau.

459

Region, country or territory / Régions, pays ou territoires	Year / Année	Population growth rate / Taux d'accroissement de la population	Natural increase rate per 1000 inhabitants / Taux d'évolution naturel pour 1000 habitants	Net migration rate per 1000 inhabitants / Taux net de migration pour 1000 habitants	Crude birth rate per 1000 inhabitants / Taux de natalité brut pour 1000 habitants	Crude death rate per 1000 inhabitants / Taux de mortalité brut pour 1000 habitants	Infant mortality rate per 1000 live births / Taux de mortalité infantile pour 1000 naissances vivantes	Life expectancy at birth / Espérance de vie à la naissance
		(1)	(2)	(3)	(4)	(5)	(6)	(7)
Equatorial Guinea - Guinée équatoriale	1990 - 1995	2.35	24.07	0.00	43.41	19.35	118.29	46
	1995 - 2000	2.39	23.96	0.00	43.03	19.07	109.45	46
	2000 - 2005	2.34	22.96	0.00	42.93	19.97	101.74	43
Gabon	1990 - 1995	2.80	27.24	3.85	38.33	11.09	57.87	60
	1995 - 2000	2.26	23.25	2.40	34.30	11.04	57.34	58
	2000 - 2005	1.75	19.09	-2.26	31.59	12.50	57.02	55
São Tome and Principe - Sao Tomé-et-Principe	1990 - 1995	1.94	25.87	-8.19	35.46	9.59	85.27	62
	1995 - 2000	1.82	25.70	-7.49	34.79	9.09	84.08	62
	2000 - 2005	1.71	25.45	-2.70	34.21	8.76	81.67	63
Northern Africa - Afrique septentrionale	*1990 - 1995*	*2.04*	*21.92*	*-1.48*	*30.16*	*8.24*	*66.80*	*63*
	1995 - 2000	*1.80*	*19.70*	*-1.44*	*26.86*	*7.16*	*55.00*	*65*
	2000 - 2005	*1.66*	*19.10*	*-1.62*	*25.85*	*6.75*	*45.14*	*67*
Algeria - Algérie	1990 - 1995	2.23	22.69	-0.43	28.77	6.08	54.32	68
	1995 - 2000	1.53	16.19	-1.26	21.59	5.40	48.72	69
	2000 - 2005	1.48	15.74	-0.63	20.77	5.03	37.96	71
Egypt - Égypte	1990 - 1995	1.91	21.05	-2.05	28.94	7.89	66.99	64
	1995 - 2000	1.85	20.42	-1.56	26.88	6.46	48.48	68
	2000 - 2005	1.82	20.37	-1.27	26.33	5.96	36.87	70
Libyan Arab Jamahiriya - Jamahiriya arabe libyenne	1990 - 1995	2.04	20.29	0.44	24.82	4.53	30.67	69
	1995 - 2000	2.02	19.33	0.40	23.27	3.95	22.98	72
	2000 - 2005	2.03	19.26	0.36	23.26	4.00	19.12	73
Morocco - Maroc	1990 - 1995	1.66	20.18	-2.32	27.30	7.12	59.32	66
	1995 - 2000	1.35	17.97	-2.13	24.19	6.21	47.54	68
	2000 - 2005	1.12	17.45	-2.64	23.28	5.83	38.45	70
Sudan - Soudan	1990 - 1995	2.57	24.86	-1.14	37.84	12.98	90.49	53
	1995 - 2000	2.46	24.14	-1.33	35.90	11.76	80.67	55
	2000 - 2005	2.02	22.27	-3.00	33.50	11.23	72.64	56
Tunisia - Tunisie	1990 - 1995	1.76	18.14	-0.52	24.13	5.99	36.58	70
	1995 - 2000	1.27	13.09	-0.43	18.61	5.51	27.95	72
	2000 - 2005	1.10	11.37	-0.41	16.80	5.43	22.55	73
Western Sahara - Sahara occidental	1990 - 1995	3.20	23.51	10.88	33.42	9.91	76.78	59
	1995 - 2000	3.93	21.55	7.16	30.16	8.61	64.70	61
	2000 - 2005	6.68	19.88	6.24	27.53	7.65	54.38	64
Southern Africa - Afrique australe	*1990 - 1995*	*2.50*	*20.93*	*4.50*	*29.21*	*8.29*	*48.15*	*62*
	1995 - 2000	*1.83*	*15.83*	*1.33*	*26.33*	*10.49*	*45.68*	*57*
	2000 - 2005	*1.10*	*7.50*	*-0.01*	*24.41*	*16.91*	*44.51*	*48*
Botswana	1990 - 1995	2.72	25.53	-0.96	32.04	6.50	46.83	64
	1995 - 2000	1.98	17.27	-0.83	29.77	12.50	51.11	52
	2000 - 2005	1.20	1.92	-0.68	26.92	24.99	51.83	37
Lesotho	1990 - 1995	1.46	22.37	-10.23	33.23	10.86	75.94	58
	1995 - 2000	1.81	15.09	-4.14	30.18	15.09	69.79	49
	2000 - 2005	0.99	4.83	-4.02	28.48	23.64	66.74	37
Namibia - Namibie	1990 - 1995	3.12	32.85	0.46	41.54	8.69	55.51	62
	1995 - 2000	2.52	25.13	2.27	35.07	9.94	50.37	58
	2000 - 2005	1.44	14.50	-0.56	29.13	14.63	44.78	49
South Africa - Afrique du Sud	1990 - 1995	2.53	19.77	5.71	27.82	8.05	45.54	62
	1995 - 2000	1.79	15.32	1.67	25.38	10.06	43.17	58
	2000 - 2005	1.09	7.62	0.22	23.83	16.21	42.36	49
Swaziland	1990 - 1995	2.06	27.69	-8.41	38.62	10.92	74.67	56
	1995 - 2000	1.98	16.59	-2.43	33.07	16.49	74.80	45
	2000 - 2005	1.22	2.99	-1.17	29.65	26.66	73.49	33
Western Africa - Afrique occidentale	*1990 - 1995*	*2.86*	*28.69*	*-0.66*	*46.44*	*17.75*	*119.67*	*48*
	1995 - 2000	*2.77*	*26.66*	*-0.14*	*44.38*	*17.73*	*116.68*	*47*
	2000 - 2005	*2.58*	*24.96*	*-0.51*	*42.65*	*17.69*	*113.28*	*46*

For sources and notes, see end of table.   Pour les sources et les notes, se reporter à la fin du tableau.

Region, country or territory / Régions, pays ou territoires	Year / Année	Population growth rate / Taux d'accroissement de la population	Natural increase rate per 1000 inhabitants / Taux d'évolution naturel pour 1000 habitants	Net migration rate per 1000 inhabitants / Taux net de migration pour 1000 habitants	Crude birth rate per 1000 inhabitants / Taux de natalité brut pour 1000 habitants	Crude death rate per 1000 inhabitants / Taux de mortalité brut pour 1000 habitants	Infant mortality rate per 1000 live births / Taux de mortalité infantile pour 1000 naissances vivantes	Life expectancy at birth / Espérance de vie à la naissance
		(1)	(2)	(3)	(4)	(5)	(6)	(7)
Benin - Bénin	1990 - 1995	3.63	32.25	3.69	46.31	14.06	114.82	54
	1995 - 2000	3.04	30.62	-0.87	43.93	13.31	109.04	54
	2000 - 2005	3.22	29.24	2.53	42.10	12.86	104.11	54
Burkina Faso	1990 - 1995	2.93	31.10	--2.78	49.68	18.59	124.38	47
	1995 - 2000	2.91	29.93	-2.28	48.27	18.34	121.97	46
	2000 - 2005	3.19	29.96	1.63	47.14	17.18	119.98	47
Cape Verde - Cap-Vert	1990 - 1995	2.42	28.77	-4.55	36.28	7.52	44.96	66
	1995 - 2000	2.33	25.59	-2.35	31.67	6.08	36.78	69
	2000 - 2005	2.35	25.57	-2.09	30.89	5.32	29.70	70
Côte d'Ivoire	1990 - 1995	3.18	27.69	2.92	42.55	14.85	111.35	50
	1995 - 2000	2.58	23.24	1.91	39.18	15.94	114.28	47
	2000 - 2005	1.72	20.52	-4.26	37.54	17.02	116.66	46
Gambia - Gambie	1990 - 1995	3.72	26.25	8.78	40.95	14.70	100.18	51
	1995 - 2000	3.55	25.61	7.40	38.76	13.14	87.93	54
	2000 - 2005	3.11	24.01	4.40	36.03	12.02	77.53	55
Ghana	1990 - 1995	2.76	26.57	0.48	37.69	11.11	73.49	57
	1995 - 2000	2.38	23.34	-0.55	34.03	10.70	67.14	57
	2000 - 2005	2.24	21.29	0.11	32.08	10.80	61.92	57
Guinea - Guinée	1990 - 1995	3.88	27.87	10.19	44.92	17.06	133.06	49
	1995 - 2000	2.27	28.48	-5.69	43.70	15.23	118.27	52
	2000 - 2005	1.86	28.42	-6.71	42.20	13.78	106.09	54
Guinea-Bissau - Guinée-Bissau	1990 - 1995	3.17	27.90	3.63	49.97	22.07	138.75	43
	1995 - 2000	2.80	29.28	-1.68	50.06	20.78	128.50	44
	2000 - 2005	3.06	29.75	0.16	49.75	20.01	119.17	45
Liberia - Libéria	1990 - 1995	0.06	26.94	-26.43	49.98	23.04	169.61	41
	1995 - 2000	7.19	28.34	42.64	49.68	21.34	154.00	42
	2000 - 2005	2.28	29.13	-15.41	49.79	20.66	138.42	42
Mali	1990 - 1995	2.60	31.79	-5.47	50.80	19.01	140.87	47
	1995 - 2000	2.71	32.74	-5.21	51.17	18.43	135.07	47
	2000 - 2005	2.98	31.88	-2.13	49.70	17.82	132.10	48
Mauritania - Mauritanie	1990 - 1995	2.69	26.27	-1.36	42.43	16.16	109.55	49
	1995 - 2000	2.85	27.07	0.80	42.58	15.52	104.38	50
	2000 - 2005	2.88	27.60	2.10	41.80	14.20	96.56	52
Niger	1990 - 1995	3.43	31.56	0.11	56.40	24.84	172.55	41
	1995 - 2000	3.61	34.25	-0.11	57.16	22.91	159.31	43
	2000 - 2005	3.52	33.95	-0.16	55.11	21.16	151.37	44
Nigeria - Nigéria	1990 - 1995	2.87	27.67	-0.20	46.11	18.44	117.32	46
	1995 - 2000	2.70	24.90	-0.17	43.89	18.99	116.25	45
	2000 - 2005	2.50	22.63	-0.27	42.02	19.39	113.65	43
Saint Helena - Sainte-Hélène	1990 - 1995	-0.96	..	..	..	..	..	..
	1995 - 2000	2.73	..	..	..	..	..	..
	2000 - 2005	1.46	..	..	..	..	..	..
Senegal - Sénégal	1990 - 1995	2.74	29.06	-2.34	42.18	13.13	90.68	54
	1995 - 2000	2.64	27.20	-2.06	39.56	12.36	86.28	55
	2000 - 2005	2.60	25.73	-1.82	37.43	11.69	83.12	56
Sierra Leone	1990 - 1995	0.27	21.34	-18.50	47.47	26.14	182.19	38
	1995 - 2000	1.75	22.32	-5.10	46.95	24.63	174.22	40
	2000 - 2005	4.23	23.05	17.47	46.72	23.67	162.42	41
Togo	1990 - 1995	2.62	31.77	-5.77	43.12	11.35	98.90	58
	1995 - 2000	3.59	29.32	5.17	41.24	11.92	95.65	56
	2000 - 2005	2.88	27.28	-0.12	39.54	12.27	91.75	54
Developing economies: America - Économies en développement : Amérique	**1990 - 1995**	**1.71**	**19.06**	**-1.67**	**25.78**	**6.72**	**39.79**	**68**
	1995 - 2000	**1.56**	**17.49**	**-1.69**	**23.70**	**6.20**	**32.80**	**70**
	2000 - 2005	**1.30**	**15.83**	**-1.50**	**21.93**	**6.10**	**26.83**	**71**
Caribbean - Caraïbes	*1990 - 1995*	*1.30*	*14.67*	*-3.83*	*23.57*	*8.90*	*47.66*	*65*
	1995 - 2000	*1.14*	*13.10*	*-3.36*	*21.62*	*8.52*	*40.50*	*66*
	2000 - 2005	*1.01*	*12.14*	*-3.21*	*20.66*	*8.52*	*36.41*	*66*

For sources and notes, see end of table.

Pour les sources et les notes, se reporter à la fin du tableau.

8.5.1 Demographic indicators of economies and geographical regions

8.5.1 Indicateurs démographiques des pays et des régions géographiques

Region, country or territory / Régions, pays ou territoires	Year / Année	Population growth rate / Taux d'accroissement de la population (1)	Natural increase rate per 1000 inhabitants / Taux d'évolution naturel pour 1000 habitants (2)	Net migration rate per 1000 inhabitants / Taux net de migration pour 1000 habitants (3)	Crude birth rate per 1000 inhabitants / Taux de natalité brut pour 1000 habitants (4)	Crude death rate per 1000 inhabitants / Taux de mortalité brut pour 1000 habitants (5)	Infant mortality rate per 1000 live births / Taux de mortalité infantile pour 1000 naissances vivantes (6)	Life expectancy at birth / Espérance de vie à la naissance (7)
Anguilla	1990 - 1995	2.66	..	..	..	..	..	..
	1995 - 2000	1.71	..	..	..	..	..	..
	2000 - 2005	1.74	..	..	..	..	..	..
Antigua and Barbuda - Antigua-et-Barbuda	1990 - 1995	1.86	..	..	..	..	..	..
	1995 - 2000	2.44	..	..	..	..	..	..
	2000 - 2005	1.57	..	..	..	..	..	..
Aruba	1990 - 1995	5.32	..	..	..	..	..	..
	1995 - 2000	1.67	..	..	..	..	..	..
	2000 - 2005	2.60	..	..	..	..	..	..
Bahamas	1990 - 1995	1.88	16.70	1.50	23.71	7.01	19.24	68
	1995 - 2000	1.56	14.00	1.38	21.37	7.37	16.76	68
	2000 - 2005	1.29	12.57	1.28	19.77	7.20	14.03	69
Barbados - Barbade	1990 - 1995	0.63	4.72	-0.96	14.29	9.57	14.12	75
	1995 - 2000	0.46	4.01	-0.95	12.98	8.97	12.73	75
	2000 - 2005	0.38	3.52	-0.93	12.25	8.73	10.97	75
British Virgin Islands - Îles Vierges britanniques	1990 - 1995	2.24	..	..	..	..	..	..
	1995 - 2000	2.12	..	..	..	..	..	..
	2000 - 2005	1.41	..	..	..	..	..	..
Cayman Islands - Îles Caïmanes	1990 - 1995	4.46	..	..	..	..	..	..
	1995 - 2000	4.04	..	..	..	..	..	..
	2000 - 2005	2.50	..	..	..	..	..	..
Cuba	1990 - 1995	0.60	8.04	-1.87	15.08	7.04	15.36	74
	1995 - 2000	0.38	6.51	-1.82	13.24	6.73	10.61	76
	2000 - 2005	0.21	5.44	-2.86	12.44	7.00	6.45	77
Dominica - Dominique	1990 - 1995	-0.03	..	..	..	..	..	..
	1995 - 2000	-0.08	..	..	..	..	..	..
	2000 - 2005	-0.18	..	..	..	..	..	..
Dominican Republic - République dominicaine	1990 - 1995	1.88	21.74	-5.96	28.23	6.49	47.58	66
	1995 - 2000	1.75	19.39	-4.52	25.75	6.36	41.07	67
	2000 - 2005	1.59	17.95	-3.26	24.46	6.52	34.99	67
Grenada - Grenade	1990 - 1995	0.51	..	..	..	..	..	..
	1995 - 2000	0.42	..	..	..	..	..	..
	2000 - 2005	0.94	..	..	..	..	..	..
Haiti - Haïti	1990 - 1995	1.94	17.64	-2.95	33.43	15.79	82.52	48
	1995 - 2000	1.80	17.03	-2.74	31.63	14.60	67.76	50
	2000 - 2005	1.62	16.86	-2.55	30.45	13.59	62.08	51
Jamaica - Jamaïque	1990 - 1995	0.96	17.75	-8.24	24.84	7.09	18.50	72
	1995 - 2000	0.82	15.81	-7.89	22.87	7.06	15.41	72
	2000 - 2005	0.71	12.70	-7.64	20.30	7.60	15.19	71
Montserrat	1990 - 1995	-0.95	..	..	..	..	..	..
	1995 - 2000	-14.49	..	..	..	..	..	..
	2000 - 2005	2.54	..	..	..	..	..	..
Netherlands Antilles - Antilles néerlandaises	1990 - 1995	0.00	13.19	-17.33	19.77	6.58	15.98	75
	1995 - 2000	-1.08	10.63	-22.85	17.32	6.69	14.97	75
	2000 - 2005	0.62	7.81	0.00	14.77	6.96	13.45	76
Saint Kitts and Nevis - Saint-Kitts-et-Nevis	1990 - 1995	1.14	..	..	..	..	..	..
	1995 - 2000	1.33	..	..	..	..	..	..
	2000 - 2005	1.30	..	..	..	..	..	..
Saint Lucia - Sainte-Lucie	1990 - 1995	1.19	19.22	-4.99	26.17	6.94	16.65	71
	1995 - 2000	0.88	12.25	-3.53	19.22	6.98	17.55	72
	2000 - 2005	1.09	11.83	-3.81	18.80	6.98	14.98	72
Saint Vincent and the Grenadines - Saint-Vincent-et-les Grenadines	1990 - 1995	0.65	16.62	-10.11	23.60	6.98	30.79	70
	1995 - 2000	0.52	13.93	-8.74	20.76	6.83	28.70	70
	2000 - 2005	0.54	13.79	-8.51	20.54	6.75	25.60	71
Trinidad and Tobago - Trinité-et-Tobago	1990 - 1995	0.75	11.01	-3.88	17.60	6.58	17.46	71
	1995 - 2000	0.48	7.14	-3.15	14.08	6.94	15.49	71
	2000 - 2005	0.35	6.26	-3.09	14.20	7.94	13.61	70

For sources and notes, see end of table.

Pour les sources et les notes, se reporter à la fin du tableau.

Region, country or territory Régions, pays ou territoires	Year Année	Population growth rate Taux d'accroissement de la population (1)	Natural increase rate per 1000 inhabitants Taux d'évolution naturel pour 1000 habitants (2)	Net migration rate per 1000 inhabitants Taux net de migration pour 1000 habitants (3)	Crude birth rate per 1000 inhabitants Taux de natalité brut pour 1000 habitants (4)	Crude death rate per 1000 inhabitants Taux de mortalité brut pour 1000 habitants (5)	Infant mortality rate per 1000 live births Taux de mortalité infantile pour 1000 naissances vivantes (6)	Life expectancy at birth Espérance de vie à la naissance (7)
Turks and Caicos Islands - Îles Turques et Caïques	1990 - 1995	5.67	..	..	..	..	..	..
	1995 - 2000	4.16	..	..	..	..	..	..
	2000 - 2005	5.19	..	..	..	..	..	..
United States Virgin Islands - Îles Vierges américaines	1990 - 1995	0.72	18.17	-10.95	23.45	5.29	13.75	75
	1995 - 2000	0.65	11.95	-5.43	17.17	5.22	12.17	77
	2000 - 2005	0.16	8.84	-7.18	14.58	5.75	9.73	78
Central America - Amérique centrale	*1990 - 1995*	*1.92*	*24.03*	*-3.91*	*29.60*	*5.57*	*36.99*	*70*
	1995 - 2000	*1.78*	*21.48*	*-3.82*	*26.47*	*4.98*	*30.94*	*72*
	2000 - 2005	*1.17*	*19.03*	*-3.38*	*23.87*	*4.84*	*24.79*	*74*
Belize	1990 - 1995	2.85	29.28	-1.00	34.37	5.09	33.92	72
	1995 - 2000	2.67	25.68	-0.88	30.55	4.88	32.91	73
	2000 - 2005	2.38	22.24	-0.78	27.34	5.10	30.80	72
Costa Rica	1990 - 1995	2.44	20.57	3.81	24.70	4.13	14.95	76
	1995 - 2000	2.46	17.63	6.89	21.45	3.81	12.14	77
	2000 - 2005	1.93	15.23	4.07	19.11	3.88	10.60	78
El Salvador	1990 - 1995	1.94	22.84	-2.12	29.57	6.73	40.91	67
	1995 - 2000	1.91	21.76	-1.27	27.72	5.96	32.48	70
	2000 - 2005	1.47	19.40	-1.16	25.25	5.85	26.87	71
Guatemala	1990 - 1995	2.32	30.47	-7.63	38.94	8.47	55.42	62
	1995 - 2000	2.31	30.02	-7.38	37.36	7.35	46.42	65
	2000 - 2005	2.48	29.16	-5.05	35.81	6.65	39.03	67
Honduras	1990 - 1995	2.60	30.44	-1.53	37.12	6.69	43.80	66
	1995 - 2000	2.13	27.20	-0.66	33.45	6.25	36.51	67
	2000 - 2005	1.96	23.78	-0.88	29.94	6.16	32.11	68
Mexico - Mexique	1990 - 1995	1.78	22.69	-4.07	27.76	5.07	33.65	72
	1995 - 2000	1.65	19.86	-4.15	24.41	4.55	28.24	74
	2000 - 2005	0.89	17.27	-3.86	21.73	4.46	21.51	75
Nicaragua	1990 - 1995	2.38	29.73	-5.22	36.05	6.32	49.59	66
	1995 - 2000	1.82	26.99	-6.57	32.45	5.45	36.35	68
	2000 - 2005	1.34	24.05	-3.83	29.08	5.03	30.30	70
Panama	1990 - 1995	2.04	20.02	0.64	25.34	5.32	27.31	72
	1995 - 2000	1.99	19.31	0.79	24.37	5.06	23.85	74
	2000 - 2005	1.82	17.86	0.52	22.89	5.03	20.89	75
South America - Amérique du Sud	*1990 - 1995*	*1.68*	*17.60*	*-0.60*	*24.54*	*6.95*	*40.34*	*68*
	1995 - 2000	*1.52*	*16.37*	*-0.71*	*22.82*	*6.45*	*32.94*	*70*
	2000 - 2005	*1.37*	*14.92*	*-0.61*	*21.29*	*6.37*	*26.87*	*71*
Argentina - Argentine	1990 - 1995	1.34	13.08	0.30	21.27	8.19	24.59	72
	1995 - 2000	1.15	12.05	-0.56	19.73	7.68	21.72	73
	2000 - 2005	0.98	10.32	-0.53	18.02	7.70	16.31	74
Bolivia - Bolivie	1990 - 1995	2.30	25.81	-2.83	35.80	9.99	75.79	60
	1995 - 2000	2.12	23.67	-2.53	32.59	8.92	67.22	62
	2000 - 2005	1.98	22.07	-2.29	30.25	8.18	56.52	64
Brazil - Brésil	1990 - 1995	1.56	15.66	-0.24	22.64	6.98	44.00	67
	1995 - 2000	1.50	15.05	-0.16	21.61	6.56	34.63	69
	2000 - 2005	1.40	14.08	-0.14	20.66	6.58	27.98	70
Chile - Chili	1990 - 1995	1.77	16.34	1.31	21.88	5.53	14.54	74
	1995 - 2000	1.37	12.84	0.81	18.02	5.18	11.78	76
	2000 - 2005	1.11	10.77	0.38	15.73	4.97	8.60	78
Colombia - Colombie	1990 - 1995	1.85	20.53	-1.09	26.97	6.45	35.34	68
	1995 - 2000	1.71	18.74	-0.99	24.45	5.71	30.57	71
	2000 - 2005	1.51	16.78	-0.91	22.22	5.44	26.03	72
Ecuador - Équateur	1990 - 1995	2.08	21.68	-0.92	27.54	5.85	45.34	70
	1995 - 2000	1.54	20.41	-5.06	25.60	5.20	34.14	72
	2000 - 2005	1.19	18.37	-3.92	23.31	4.94	25.91	74
Falkland Islands (Malvinas) - Îles Falkland (Malvinas)	1990 - 1995	4.05	..	..	..	..	..	..
	1995 - 2000	3.34	..	..	..	..	..	..
	2000 - 2005	0.52	..	..	..	..	..	..

For sources and notes, see end of table.

Pour les sources et les notes, se reporter à la fin du tableau.

Region, country or territory Régions, pays ou territoires	Year Année	Population growth rate Taux d'accroissement de la population	Natural increase rate per 1000 inhabitants Taux d'évolution naturel pour 1000 habitants	Net migration rate per 1000 inhabitants Taux net de migration pour 1000 habitants	Crude birth rate per 1000 inhabitants Taux de natalité brut pour 1000 habitants	Crude death rate per 1000 inhabitants Taux de mortalité brut pour 1000 habitants	Infant mortality rate per 1000 live births Taux de mortalité infantile pour 1000 naissances vivantes	Life expectancy at birth Espérance de vie à la naissance
		(1)	(2)	(3)	(4)	(5)	(6)	(7)
Guyana	1990 - 1995	0.23	14.58	-13.69	24.52	9.94	62.68	60
	1995 - 2000	-0.12	13.92	-10.84	23.82	9.90	56.61	60
	2000 - 2005	0.14	12.72	-10.70	21.86	9.14	50.36	63
Paraguay	1990 - 1995	2.44	28.06	-1.11	34.09	6.02	43.24	69
	1995 - 2000	2.17	25.89	-0.97	31.29	5.40	39.69	70
	2000 - 2005	1.97	24.53	-0.86	29.58	5.05	36.83	71
Peru - Pérou	1990 - 1995	1.84	22.23	-3.95	29.20	6.97	56.17	66
	1995 - 2000	1.46	19.81	-2.81	26.19	6.39	43.70	68
	2000 - 2005	1.22	17.18	-2.23	23.28	6.10	34.43	70
Suriname	1990 - 1995	0.66	16.14	-9.90	22.91	6.77	34.39	68
	1995 - 2000	0.96	16.69	-7.54	23.71	7.01	29.29	68
	2000 - 2005	0.72	14.14	-7.25	21.28	7.14	26.48	69
Uruguay	1990 - 1995	0.71	8.39	-1.27	18.19	9.81	19.88	73
	1995 - 2000	0.61	8.50	-0.98	17.64	9.14	17.58	74
	2000 - 2005	0.05	7.74	-0.59	16.83	9.10	13.79	75
Venezuela (Bolivarian Republic of) - Venezuela (République bolivarienne du)	1990 - 1995	2.25	22.12	0.38	26.95	4.83	23.51	71
	1995 - 2000	2.00	19.70	0.34	24.49	4.78	20.78	72
	2000 - 2005	1.82	17.91	0.31	22.86	4.95	17.89	73
Developing economies: Asia - Économies en développement : Asie	**1990 - 1995**	**1.70**	**16.93**	**-0.29**	**25.59**	**8.66**	**68.01**	**63**
	1995 - 2000	**1.48**	**14.79**	**-0.29**	**22.79**	**8.00**	**61.57**	**65**
	2000 - 2005	**1.27**	**12.94**	**-0.29**	**20.58**	**7.64**	**55.27**	**67**
Eastern Asia - Asie orientale	*1990 - 1995*	*1.10*	*11.03*	*-0.18*	*18.34*	*7.30*	*47.51*	*70*
	1995 - 2000	*0.91*	*9.07*	*-0.27*	*16.04*	*6.97*	*41.11*	*71*
	2000 - 2005	*0.66*	*6.69*	*-0.26*	*13.52*	*6.82*	*35.61*	*72*
China - Chine	1990 - 1995	1.10	(b)11.00	(b)-0.22	(b)18.31	(b)7.31	(b)48.87	(b)68
	1995 - 2000	0.91	(b)9.08	(b)-0.31	(b)16.04	(b)6.96	(b)42.10	(b)70
	2000 - 2005	0.67	(b)6.77	(b)-0.30	(b)13.56	(b)6.79	(b)36.29	(b)71
China, Hong Kong SAR - Chine, Hong Kong RAS	1990 - 1995	1.68	6.12	10.09	11.73	5.60	5.09	78
	1995 - 2000	1.42	4.69	9.36	9.83	5.14	4.19	80
	2000 - 2005	1.15	3.04	8.77	8.33	5.29	3.86	82
China, Macao SAR - Chine, Macao RAS	1990 - 1995	2.02	12.37	8.36	16.89	4.51	10.17	77
	1995 - 2000	1.38	6.68	7.66	10.89	4.21	9.22	79
	2000 - 2005	1.40	2.93	4.43	7.28	4.35	8.15	80
China, Taiwan Province of - Chine, Taiwan Province de (8)	1990 - 1995	0.95	..	..	..	..	..	..
	1995 - 2000	0.84	..	..	..	..	..	..
	2000 - 2005	0.49	..	..	..	..	..	..
Korea, Dem. People's Rep. of - Corée, Rép. populaire dém. de	1990 - 1995	1.50	12.10	0.00	20.98	8.88	39.56	65
	1995 - 2000	1.10	8.82	0.00	18.89	10.06	45.07	63
	2000 - 2005	0.58	5.64	0.00	16.37	10.73	46.11	63
Korea, Republic of - Corée, République de	1990 - 1995	0.97	10.25	-0.52	15.90	5.65	12.52	72
	1995 - 2000	0.77	8.07	-0.35	13.53	5.46	8.17	75
	2000 - 2005	0.46	4.73	-0.34	10.26	5.54	4.36	77
Mongolia - Mongolie	1990 - 1995	1.51	20.26	-5.21	29.13	8.88	69.72	61
	1995 - 2000	0.66	16.21	-7.37	24.29	8.08	66.99	62
	2000 - 2005	0.88	15.49	-3.89	22.75	7.26	58.98	64
Southern Asia - Asie méridionale	*1990 - 1995*	*2.17*	*21.41*	*-0.47*	*31.88*	*10.46*	*85.73*	*63*
	1995 - 2000	*1.89*	*18.98*	*-0.42*	*28.37*	*9.39*	*78.19*	*65*
	2000 - 2005	*1.66*	*17.13*	*-0.41*	*25.88*	*8.75*	*70.08*	*66*
Afghanistan	1990 - 1995	7.32	31.18	37.57	51.67	20.49	147.64	46
	1995 - 2000	2.55	31.19	-3.58	51.54	20.35	146.65	46
	2000 - 2005	3.79	29.76	15.97	49.35	19.58	147.67	46
Bangladesh	1990 - 1995	2.22	22.98	-0.47	34.12	11.14	87.99	56
	1995 - 2000	1.98	20.80	-0.49	29.90	9.10	73.07	60
	2000 - 2005	1.89	19.59	-0.52	27.55	7.97	59.58	63
Bhutan - Bhoutan	1990 - 1995	-1.53	25.04	-14.22	37.27	12.23	83.15	56
	1995 - 2000	1.94	22.90	-0.55	32.97	10.07	68.68	60
	2000 - 2005	2.63	21.89	0.00	30.61	8.72	56.32	63

For sources and notes, see end of table.

Pour les sources et les notes, se reporter à la fin du tableau.

Region, country or territory Régions, pays ou territoires	Year Année	Population growth rate Taux d'accroissement de la population	Natural increase rate per 1000 inhabitants Taux d'évolution naturel pour 1000 habitants	Net migration rate per 1000 inhabitants Taux net de migration pour 1000 habitants	Crude birth rate per 1000 inhabitants Taux de natalité brut pour 1000 habitants	Crude death rate per 1000 inhabitants Taux de mortalité brut pour 1000 habitants	Infant mortality rate per 1000 live births Taux de mortalité infantile pour 1000 naissances vivantes	Life expectancy at birth Espérance de vie à la naissance
		(1)	(2)	(3)	(4)	(5)	(6)	(7)
India - Inde	1990 - 1995	2.08	19.82	-0.32	30.36	10.55	85.62	59
	1995 - 2000	1.84	17.92	-0.29	27.41	9.49	77.15	61
	2000 - 2005	1.62	15.88	-0.27	24.76	8.88	68.63	63
Iran, Islamic Republic of - Iran, Rép. islamique d'	1990 - 1995	1.86	24.08	-5.08	30.61	6.54	54.67	66
	1995 - 2000	1.22	13.98	-1.42	19.50	5.52	46.35	68
	2000 - 2005	0.97	13.33	-4.06	18.60	5.27	33.91	70
Maldives	1990 - 1995	2.78	30.92	0.00	39.98	9.06	66.33	61
	1995 - 2000	1.93	28.34	0.00	35.80	7.46	53.61	64
	2000 - 2005	1.57	25.18	0.00	31.50	6.32	43.69	66
Nepal - Népal	1990 - 1995	2.51	26.17	-0.99	38.06	11.90	89.97	56
	1995 - 2000	2.39	24.70	-0.86	34.48	9.78	75.04	59
	2000 - 2005	2.08	21.74	-0.78	30.45	8.71	65.06	61
Pakistan	1990 - 1995	2.46	28.92	-4.44	38.81	9.88	88.85	61
	1995 - 2000	2.44	25.05	-0.06	34.33	9.28	84.98	61
	2000 - 2005	1.82	22.99	-2.43	31.38	8.39	79.25	63
Sri Lanka	1990 - 1995	1.10	13.84	-1.98	19.75	5.91	23.40	71
	1995 - 2000	0.69	11.73	-1.65	17.44	5.72	19.92	73
	2000 - 2005	0.43	10.40	-1.57	16.41	6.01	17.13	74
South-Eastern Asia - Asie du Sud-Est	*1990 - 1995*	*1.77*	*18.69*	*-0.62*	*26.67*	*7.99*	*54.88*	*64*
	1995 - 2000	*1.55*	*15.78*	*-0.55*	*23.10*	*7.33*	*47.60*	*66*
	2000 - 2005	*1.40*	*14.47*	*-0.62*	*21.59*	*7.12*	*40.38*	*67*
Brunei Darussalam - Brunéi Darussalam	1990 - 1995	2.76	24.97	2.55	28.15	3.18	7.93	74
	1995 - 2000	2.45	22.26	2.24	25.12	2.86	6.69	75
	2000 - 2005	2.29	20.83	1.99	23.60	2.77	6.06	76
Cambodia - Cambodge	1990 - 1995	3.23	27.21	3.68	39.62	12.41	110.29	55
	1995 - 2000	2.29	21.18	1.66	32.31	11.13	104.65	55
	2000 - 2005	1.76	19.94	-0.15	30.78	10.84	94.55	56
Indonesia - Indonésie	1990 - 1995	1.53	15.87	-0.77	24.16	8.29	59.46	63
	1995 - 2000	1.40	14.25	-0.89	21.89	7.64	50.77	65
	2000 - 2005	1.31	13.53	-0.93	20.98	7.45	42.73	67
Lao People's Dem. Rep. - Rép. dém. populaire lao	1990 - 1995	2.81	25.57	-0.46	41.35	15.78	105.28	51
	1995 - 2000	2.15	24.06	-0.27	38.15	14.10	96.89	52
	2000 - 2005	1.62	23.29	-0.24	35.88	12.59	88.35	54
Malaysia - Malaisie	1990 - 1995	2.58	23.94	2.41	29.06	5.12	14.73	71
	1995 - 2000	2.45	20.71	3.60	25.48	4.77	12.14	72
	2000 - 2005	1.95	18.20	1.24	22.85	4.65	10.16	73
Myanmar	1990 - 1995	1.44	18.17	-0.59	29.71	11.55	89.79	57
	1995 - 2000	1.24	13.73	0.26	24.04	10.31	85.63	59
	2000 - 2005	0.89	11.10	0.29	20.83	9.73	75.69	60
Philippines	1990 - 1995	2.27	25.30	-2.78	31.58	6.27	43.25	66
	1995 - 2000	2.11	22.95	-2.50	28.43	5.49	35.23	69
	2000 - 2005	2.08	20.62	-2.27	25.68	5.06	28.68	70
Singapore - Singapour	1990 - 1995	2.85	13.04	15.40	17.90	4.87	5.64	76
	1995 - 2000	2.88	9.15	19.64	13.96	4.81	3.93	77
	2000 - 2005	1.49	5.18	9.59	10.11	4.93	3.06	79
Thailand - Thaïlande	1990 - 1995	1.16	13.40	-0.31	19.39	5.99	29.68	69
	1995 - 2000	1.06	10.65	-0.29	17.29	6.63	23.78	69
	2000 - 2005	0.76	9.05	-0.16	16.31	7.26	19.87	70
Timor-Leste	1990 - 1995	2.77	21.26	5.79	36.80	15.54	134.72	48
	1995 - 2000	-0.76	18.99	-50.97	31.13	12.15	116.38	53
	2000 - 2005	5.31	34.74	19.17	47.36	12.62	89.42	55
Viet Nam	1990 - 1995	2.05	20.93	-0.78	28.45	7.53	43.24	66
	1995 - 2000	1.51	15.13	-0.53	21.58	6.44	36.97	69
	2000 - 2005	1.45	14.26	-0.49	20.38	6.13	29.91	70
Western Asia - Asie occidentale	*1990 - 1995*	*2.58*	*24.88*	*1.42*	*32.11*	*7.24*	*54.39*	*65*
	1995 - 2000	*2.37*	*23.56*	*1.54*	*30.27*	*6.71*	*52.10*	*66*
	2000 - 2005	*2.14*	*21.60*	*1.48*	*27.95*	*6.35*	*48.99*	*67*

For sources and notes, see end of table. Pour les sources et les notes, se reporter à la fin du tableau.

Region, country or territory Régions, pays ou territoires	Year Année	Population growth rate Taux d'accroissement de la population	Natural increase rate per 1000 inhabitants Taux d'évolution naturel pour 1000 habitants	Net migration rate per 1000 inhabitants Taux net de migration pour 1000 habitants	Crude birth rate per 1000 inhabitants Taux de natalité brut pour 1000 habitants	Crude death rate per 1000 inhabitants Taux de mortalité brut pour 1000 habitants	Infant mortality rate per 1000 live births Taux de mortalité infantile pour 1000 naissances vivantes	Life expectancy at birth Espérance de vie à la naissance
		(1)	(2)	(3)	(4)	(5)	(6)	(7)
Bahrain - Bahreïn	1990 - 1995	3.17	22.74	11.14	26.37	3.63	19.63	72
	1995 - 2000	2.36	18.41	9.55	21.63	3.22	16.58	73
	2000 - 2005	2.18	15.62	0.00	18.84	3.22	13.98	74
Iraq	1990 - 1995	3.11	29.37	1.69	38.96	9.59	68.96	59
	1995 - 2000	2.94	28.30	1.19	38.32	10.03	90.66	59
	2000 - 2005	2.22	25.93	1.78	35.66	9.73	94.69	59
Jordan - Jordanie	1990 - 1995	5.59	28.61	26.23	34.40	5.79	33.87	69
	1995 - 2000	2.18	28.03	1.51	32.63	4.61	27.75	70
	2000 - 2005	2.89	23.64	3.75	27.81	4.17	24.18	71
Kuwait - Koweït	1990 - 1995	-4.34	18.60	-65.21	20.70	2.10	14.53	75
	1995 - 2000	5.12	19.06	35.36	20.90	1.84	11.63	76
	2000 - 2005	3.84	17.67	19.53	19.47	1.80	10.31	77
Lebanon - Liban	1990 - 1995	3.20	17.39	12.03	24.74	7.35	32.00	69
	1995 - 2000	1.55	15.28	-1.83	22.26	6.99	27.10	71
	2000 - 2005	1.23	12.27	-2.01	18.99	6.72	23.44	72
Palestinian territory - Territoire palestinien	1990 - 1995	3.89	39.58	-0.47	46.64	7.06	27.33	70
	1995 - 2000	3.70	37.52	0.75	42.67	5.16	24.74	71
	2000 - 2005	3.55	35.17	-2.38	39.48	4.31	21.13	72
Oman	1990 - 1995	3.28	30.77	2.49	34.36	3.59	25.41	71
	1995 - 2000	2.02	26.39	-3.46	29.49	3.10	19.38	73
	2000 - 2005	0.85	22.76	-12.78	25.59	2.83	16.20	74
Qatar	1990 - 1995	2.35	17.80	5.68	21.20	3.40	17.25	70
	1995 - 2000	3.19	17.88	10.60	21.21	3.33	13.69	72
	2000 - 2005	5.11	15.93	42.28	19.09	3.17	11.66	73
Saudi Arabia - Arabie saoudite	1990 - 1995	2.32	29.98	-3.71	34.58	4.60	32.85	69
	1995 - 2000	2.62	27.16	0.75	31.22	4.06	26.56	71
	2000 - 2005	2.53	24.65	2.17	28.52	3.86	22.54	72
Syrian Arab Republic - République arabe syrienne	1990 - 1995	2.77	28.14	-0.44	32.71	4.57	32.21	69
	1995 - 2000	2.45	26.46	-0.38	30.32	3.86	23.63	72
	2000 - 2005	2.70	25.22	-0.34	28.74	3.52	18.52	73
Turkey - Turquie	1990 - 1995	1.80	17.51	0.24	24.70	7.19	54.96	66
	1995 - 2000	1.66	16.75	0.41	23.39	6.64	45.57	68
	2000 - 2005	1.36	14.73	-0.71	21.36	6.63	41.78	69
United Arab Emirates - Émirats arabes unis	1990 - 1995	5.28	21.07	31.60	23.36	2.29	16.57	74
	1995 - 2000	5.79	17.25	39.91	18.89	1.64	11.21	76
	2000 - 2005	4.68	14.92	49.59	16.26	1.34	8.83	78
Yemen - Yémen	1990 - 1995	4.63	37.29	9.76	49.38	12.08	91.57	56
	1995 - 2000	3.16	33.92	-0.61	44.47	10.55	80.96	58
	2000 - 2005	2.97	32.84	-1.05	41.70	8.86	69.78	60
Developing economies: Oceania - Économies en développement : Océanie	**1990 - 1995**	**2.34**	**24.30**	**-1.72**	**34.68**	**10.38**	**66.19**	**57**
	1995 - 2000	**2.25**	**22.94**	**-1.96**	**32.62**	**9.68**	**62.74**	**58**
	2000 - 2005	**2.08**	**19.97**	**-1.53**	**28.88**	**8.91**	**58.91**	**59**
American Samoa - Samoa américaines	1990 - 1995	2.22	..	..	..	..	..	..
	1995 - 2000	1.61	..	..	..	..	..	..
	2000 - 2005	2.31	..	..	..	..	..	..
Cook Islands - Îles Cook	1990 - 1995	0.33	..	..	..	..	..	..
	1995 - 2000	-2.46	..	..	..	..	..	..
	2000 - 2005	-2.67	..	..	..	..	..	..
Fiji - Fidji	1990 - 1995	1.19	21.23	-9.33	27.50	6.27	33.93	67
	1995 - 2000	0.86	19.66	-8.82	25.85	6.19	26.28	67
	2000 - 2005	0.65	17.31	-8.39	23.56	6.25	21.82	68
French Polynesia - Polynésie française	1990 - 1995	1.99	20.37	-0.52	25.41	5.04	12.06	70
	1995 - 2000	1.80	16.58	1.42	21.36	4.79	9.65	72
	2000 - 2005	1.59	14.49	2.13	19.32	4.82	8.78	73
Guam	1990 - 1995	1.67	21.26	-4.58	25.96	4.69	14.17	73
	1995 - 2000	1.28	20.94	-7.90	25.57	4.63	10.50	74
	2000 - 2005	1.66	17.54	0.00	22.26	4.72	9.95	75

For sources and notes, see end of table.

Pour les sources et les notes, se reporter à la fin du tableau.

Region, country or territory / Régions, pays ou territoires	Year / Année	Population growth rate / Taux d'accroissement de la population	Natural increase rate per 1000 inhabitants / Taux d'évolution naturel pour 1000 habitants	Net migration rate per 1000 inhabitants / Taux net de migration pour 1000 habitants	Crude birth rate per 1000 inhabitants / Taux de natalité brut pour 1000 habitants	Crude death rate per 1000 inhabitants / Taux de mortalité brut pour 1000 habitants	Infant mortality rate per 1000 live births / Taux de mortalité infantile pour 1000 naissances vivantes	Life expectancy at birth / Espérance de vie à la naissance
		(1)	(2)	(3)	(4)	(5)	(6)	(7)
Kiribati	1990 - 1995	1.45	..	..	..	..	..	..
	1995 - 2000	1.68	..	..	..	..	..	..
	2000 - 2005	1.81	..	..	..	..	..	..
Marshall Islands - Îles Marshall	1990 - 1995	1.51	..	..	..	..	..	..
	1995 - 2000	0.44	..	..	..	..	..	..
	2000 - 2005	1.68	..	..	..	..	..	..
Micronesia, Federated States of - Micronésie, États fédérés de	1990 - 1995	2.15	25.83	-4.39	32.24	6.41	42.61	66
	1995 - 2000	-0.02	25.19	-25.42	31.48	6.29	40.14	67
	2000 - 2005	0.55	24.63	-18.38	30.85	6.23	38.31	68
Nauru	1990 - 1995	1.71	..	..	..	..	..	..
	1995 - 2000	0.15	..	..	..	..	..	..
	2000 - 2005	0.14	..	..	..	..	..	..
New Caledonia - Nouvelle-Calédonie	1990 - 1995	2.42	18.36	5.84	23.84	5.48	11.01	71
	1995 - 2000	2.15	16.52	5.23	21.44	4.93	7.67	74
	2000 - 2005	1.71	14.33	4.73	19.23	4.90	6.49	75
Niue - Nioué	1990 - 1995	-0.11	..	..	..	..	..	..
	1995 - 2000	-3.59	..	..	..	..	..	..
	2000 - 2005	-2.80	..	..	..	..	..	..
Northern Mariana Islands - Îles Mariannes du Nord	1990 - 1995	5.52	..	..	..	..	..	..
	1995 - 2000	3.57	..	..	..	..	..	..
	2000 - 2005	3.02	..	..	..	..	..	..
Palau, Pacific Islands (former) - Palaos, Îles du Pacifique (anc.)	1990 - 1995	2.66	..	..	..	..	..	..
	1995 - 2000	2.45	..	..	..	..	..	..
	2000 - 2005	0.86	..	..	..	..	..	..
Papua New Guinea - Papouasie-Nouvelle-Guinée	1990 - 1995	2.62	26.06	0.00	38.87	12.81	79.03	52
	1995 - 2000	2.67	24.50	0.00	36.31	11.81	75.58	54
	2000 - 2005	2.41	21.04	0.00	31.73	10.69	71.41	55
Pitcairn	1990 - 1995	-1.27	..	..	..	..	..	..
	1995 - 2000	-1.01	..	..	..	..	..	..
	2000 - 2005	-2.97	..	..	..	..	..	..
Samoa	1990 - 1995	0.84	24.20	-15.81	31.06	6.86	38.68	66
	1995 - 2000	1.07	26.90	-16.23	33.10	6.20	29.64	68
	2000 - 2005	0.71	23.74	-15.45	29.44	5.70	26.39	70
Solomon Islands - Îles Salomon	1990 - 1995	2.86	27.60	0.00	35.76	8.16	37.85	61
	1995 - 2000	2.76	28.06	0.00	35.91	7.85	36.15	61
	2000 - 2005	2.57	26.33	0.00	33.58	7.25	34.41	62
Tokelau - Tokélaou	1990 - 1995	-1.61	..	..	..	..	..	..
	1995 - 2000	0.52	..	..	..	..	..	..
	2000 - 2005	-1.59	..	..	..	..	..	..
Tonga	1990 - 1995	0.60	23.40	-18.26	29.48	6.08	25.61	70
	1995 - 2000	0.14	21.26	-14.51	27.10	5.84	23.60	71
	2000 - 2005	0.26	18.31	-14.12	24.22	5.91	21.45	72
Tuvalu	1990 - 1995	0.80	..	..	..	..	..	..
	1995 - 2000	0.75	..	..	..	..	..	..
	2000 - 2005	0.50	..	..	..	..	..	..
Vanuatu	1990 - 1995	2.84	29.40	-1.08	36.46	7.06	41.13	65
	1995 - 2000	1.94	27.42	-6.26	34.07	6.65	39.97	66
	2000 - 2005	2.54	25.73	-5.96	31.40	5.67	35.71	68
Wallis and Futuna Islands - Îles Wallis et Futuna	1990 - 1995	0.67	..	..	..	..	..	..
	1995 - 2000	0.78	..	..	..	..	..	..
	2000 - 2005	0.24	..	..	..	..	..	..
Economies in transition: Asia - Économies en transition : Asie	**1990 - 1995**	..	**18.71**	**-10.49**	**26.96**	**8.26**	**64.62**	**66**
	1995 - 2000	**0.51**	**13.61**	**-8.11**	**21.79**	**8.18**	**66.62**	**65**
	2000 - 2005	**0.82**	**12.14**	**-4.92**	**20.37**	**8.23**	**64.01**	**66**
Armenia - Arménie	1990 - 1995	-1.88	10.77	-29.54	19.09	8.32	42.71	69
	1995 - 2000	-0.92	5.07	-14.27	13.50	8.42	37.51	70
	2000 - 2005	-0.42	2.25	-6.56	11.10	8.85	31.39	71

For sources and notes, see end of table.

Pour les sources et les notes, se reporter à la fin du tableau.

8.5.1 Demographic indicators of economies and geographical regions

8.5.1 Indicateurs démographiques des pays et des régions géographiques

Region, country or territory — Régions, pays ou territoires	Year — Année	Population growth rate — Taux d'accroissement de la population	Natural increase rate per 1000 inhabitants — Taux d'évolution naturel pour 1000 habitants	Net migration rate per 1000 inhabitants — Taux net de migration pour 1000 habitants	Crude birth rate per 1000 inhabitants — Taux de natalité brut pour 1000 habitants	Crude death rate per 1000 inhabitants — Taux de mortalité brut pour 1000 habitants	Infant mortality rate per 1000 live births — Taux de mortalité infantile pour 1000 naissances vivantes	Life expectancy at birth — Espérance de vie à la naissance
		(1)	(2)	(3)	(4)	(5)	(6)	(7)
Azerbaijan - Azerbaïdjan	1990 - 1995	1.55	18.54	-3.09	26.08	7.54	79.48	66
	1995 - 2000	0.88	12.03	-3.20	18.89	6.85	82.53	66
	2000 - 2005	0.51	8.89	-2.42	15.84	6.95	77.11	67
Georgia - Géorgie	1990 - 1995	-1.63	5.05	-21.35	14.81	9.76	42.03	70
	1995 - 2000	-1.28	1.54	-14.36	11.76	10.22	42.38	70
	2000 - 2005	-1.07	0.10	-10.79	11.17	11.07	40.32	70
Kazakhstan	1990 - 1995	-0.75	10.82	-18.65	19.83	9.02	56.44	65
	1995 - 2000	-1.25	6.31	-17.09	16.87	10.56	61.88	63
	2000 - 2005	0.34	5.25	-8.04	16.07	10.82	61.68	63
Kyrgyzstan - Kirghizistan	1990 - 1995	0.88	20.77	-12.16	28.87	8.10	62.29	66
	1995 - 2000	1.49	16.40	-1.13	24.16	7.76	60.33	66
	2000 - 2005	1.01	15.14	-2.94	22.61	7.47	55.51	67
Tajikistan - Tadjikistan	1990 - 1995	1.70	28.16	-11.31	37.16	9.00	92.01	63
	1995 - 2000	1.34	24.62	-11.57	32.72	8.10	91.03	63
	2000 - 2005	1.19	21.89	-10.90	29.50	7.60	89.58	64
Turkmenistan - Turkménistan	1990 - 1995	2.68	24.17	2.54	32.54	8.37	73.88	63
	1995 - 2000	1.42	16.52	-2.30	24.49	7.96	78.59	63
	2000 - 2005	1.42	14.62	-0.43	22.89	8.27	77.12	62
Uzbekistan - Ouzbékistan	1990 - 1995	2.22	25.27	-3.13	32.62	7.35	59.51	66
	1995 - 2000	1.52	18.51	-3.36	25.24	6.72	60.22	67
	2000 - 2005	1.46	16.91	-2.34	23.67	6.76	57.37	66
Economies in transition: Europe - Économies en transition : Europe	**1990 - 1995**	**-5.06**	**-1.77**	**0.31**	**11.19**	**12.95**	**21.61**	**68**
	1995 - 2000	**-0.38**	**-4.44**	**0.73**	**9.31**	**13.74**	**18.01**	**67**
	2000 - 2005	**-0.52**	**-4.77**	**-0.47**	**9.79**	**14.56**	**16.28**	**67**
Albania - Albanie	1990 - 1995	-0.87	16.62	-26.36	22.88	6.26	33.18	72
	1995 - 2000	-0.45	12.65	-17.25	18.86	6.21	29.82	73
	2000 - 2005	0.47	10.85	-6.46	17.23	6.38	25.43	74
Bosnia and Herzegovina - Bosnie-Herzégovine	1990 - 1995	-4.61	5.79	-51.76	12.87	7.08	18.35	72
	1995 - 2000	2.03	4.24	19.27	11.89	7.64	15.12	73
	2000 - 2005	0.66	1.03	2.06	9.68	8.65	13.90	74
Belarus - Bélarus	1990 - 1995	0.01	-0.62	0.29	11.79	12.41	14.60	70
	1995 - 2000	-0.42	-4.63	0.28	9.10	13.73	15.10	68
	2000 - 2005	-0.52	-5.33	-0.20	9.17	14.50	14.82	68
Bulgaria - Bulgarie	1990 - 1995	-1.08	-2.65	-7.26	10.15	12.80	16.06	71
	1995 - 2000	-0.87	-6.14	-1.23	8.16	14.30	15.67	71
	2000 - 2005	-0.66	-5.62	-1.27	8.67	14.28	13.12	72
Croatia - Croatie	1990 - 1995	0.66	-0.04	6.65	10.67	10.71	11.32	73
	1995 - 2000	-0.71	-0.59	-6.54	10.47	11.07	9.19	74
	2000 - 2005	0.20	-2.39	4.42	9.10	11.49	7.58	75
Moldova, Republic of - Moldova, République de	1990 - 1995	-0.04	4.39	-5.55	15.47	11.08	30.88	67
	1995 - 2000	-1.10	0.27	-3.25	11.99	11.71	28.36	66
	2000 - 2005	-1.34	-1.36	-1.89	10.10	11.47	26.48	67
Macedonia, TFYR - Macédoine, LERY	1990 - 1995	0.56	8.43	-2.84	16.40	7.97	28.44	72
	1995 - 2000	0.46	5.14	-0.50	13.38	8.24	19.91	73
	2000 - 2005	0.24	3.42	-0.99	11.84	8.42	16.13	74
Romania - Roumanie	1990 - 1995	-0.46	0.03	-4.61	11.40	11.37	25.86	69
	1995 - 2000	-0.49	-1.91	-3.13	10.21	12.12	22.18	70
	2000 - 2005	-0.47	-2.33	-1.37	9.86	12.19	18.82	71
Serbia and Montenegro - Serbie-et-Monténégro	1990 - 1995	..	3.73	3.87	13.77	10.04	19.42	72
	1995 - 2000	-0.03	1.83	-1.89	12.20	10.37	14.67	72
	2000 - 2005	-0.62	1.10	-1.90	11.76	10.66	13.21	73
Russian Federation - Fédération de Russie	1990 - 1995	0.07	-2.75	2.51	10.59	13.34	22.48	67
	1995 - 2000	-0.23	-5.33	3.12	8.89	14.22	17.65	66
	2000 - 2005	-0.48	-5.19	0.55	10.13	15.32	16.26	65
Ukraine	1990 - 1995	-0.20	-3.71	2.31	11.15	14.86	18.36	67
	1995 - 2000	-0.87	-6.82	-2.78	8.58	15.40	17.19	67
	2000 - 2005	-0.81	-8.10	-2.93	8.22	16.32	15.62	66

For sources and notes, see next page.

Pour les sources et les notes, se reporter à la page suivante.

Sources:
- UN DESA Population Division, *World Population Prospects: The 2004 Revision*
- UN DESA Population Division, *World Population Prospects: The 2006 Revision*
- UNCTAD secretariat calculations

Notes:

(a) Czech Republic data

(b) Including Taïwan

(1) Population growth rate: Average exponential rate of growth of the population over a given period. It is calculated as $\ln(P_t/P_0)/t$ where t is the length of the period. It is expressed as a percentage.

(2) Natural increase rate per 1000 inhabitants: Crude birth rate minus the crude death rate.

(3) Net migration rate per 1000 inhabitants: Net number of migrants over a given period divided by the person-years lived by the population over that period. It is expressed as net number of migrants per 1000 population.

(4) Crude birth rate per 1000 inhabitants: Number of births over a given period divided by the person-years lived by the population over that period. It is expressed as number of births per 1000 population.

(5) Crude death rate per 1000 inhabitants: Number of deaths over a given period divided by the person-years lived by the population over that period. It is expressed as number of deaths per 1000 population.

(6) Infant mortality rate per 1000 live births: The number of deaths under one year of age in a given period of time divided by the number of live-births in the same period. It is expressed as number of deaths under one year per 1000 births.

(7) Life expectancy at birth: The average number of years a newborn infant would to be expected to live if current mortality trends were to continue for the rest of that person's life.

(8) National source.

Sources :
- ONU DAES Division de la population, *World Population Prospects: The 2004 Revision*
- ONU DAES Division de la population, *World Population Prospects: The 2006 Revision*
- Calculs du secrétariat de la CNUCED

Notes :

(a) Données de la République Tchèque

(b) Y compris Taïwan

(1) Taux d'accroissement de la population : le taux exponentiel d'accroissement de la population pour une période donnée, calculé comme $\ln(P_t/P_0)/t$, où le t est la longueur de la période, et exprimé en pourcentage.

(2) Taux d'évolution naturelle pour 1000 habitants : le taux de natalité brut moins le taux de mortalité brut.

(3) Taux net de migration pour 1000 habitants : le rapport entre le nombre net des migrants pour une période donnée et l'effectif de la population vivant durant la période considérée. Il est exprimé en nombre net des migrants pour 1000 habitants.

(4) Taux de natalité brut pour 1000 habitants : le rapport entre le nombre de naissances vivantes pour une période donnée et l'effectif de la population durant la période considérée. Il est exprimé en nombre de naissances pour 1000 habitants.

(5) Taux de mortalité brut pour 1000 habitants : c'est le rapport entre le nombre de décès pour une période donnée et l'effectif de la population durant la période considérée. Il est exprimé en nombre de décès pour 1000 habitants.

(6) Taux de mortalité infantile pour 1000 naissances vivantes : il est défini par le nombre des décès d'enfants âgés de moins d'un an pour une période donnée, rapporté au nombre de naissances vivantes durant la période considérée. Il est exprimé en nombre de décès d'enfants âgés de moins d'un an pour 1000 naissances.

(7) Espérance de vie à la naissance : nombre moyen d'années à vivre pour un nouveau-né soumis aux conditions de mortalité de l'année de sa naissance.

(8) Sources nationales.

Economic grouping / Groupements économiques	Year / Année	Population growth rate / Taux d'accroissement de la population	Natural increase rate per 1000 inhabitants / Taux d'évolution naturel pour 1000 habitants	Net migration rate per 1000 inhabitants / Taux net de migration pour 1000 habitants	Crude birth rate per 1000 inhabitants / Taux de natalité brut pour 1000 habitants	Crude death rate per 1000 inhabitants / Taux de mortalité brut pour 1000 habitants	Infant mortality rate per 1000 live births / Taux de mortalité infantile pour 1000 naissances vivantes	Life expectancy at birth / Espérance de vie à la naissance
		(1)	(2)	(3)	(4)	(5)	(6)	(7)
DEVELOPING ECONOMIES -	**1990 - 1995**	**1.85**	**18.67**	**-0.46**	**28.13**	**9.46**	**73.18**	**61**
ÉCONOMIES EN DÉVELOPPEMENT	**1995 - 2000**	**1.65**	**16.63**	**-0.46**	**25.61**	**8.99**	**68.07**	**62**
	2000 - 2005	**1.45**	**14.91**	**-0.47**	**23.73**	**8.82**	**63.06**	**63**
Developing economies excluding China -	1990 - 1995	2.13	21.51	-0.55	31.72	10.22	78.66	59
Économies en développement sans la Chine	1995 - 2000	1.91	19.29	-0.51	28.96	9.67	73.40	60
	2000 - 2005	1.72	17.67	-0.52	27.14	9.47	67.76	61
Developing economies excluding LDCs -	1990 - 1995	1.72	17.48	-0.62	25.95	8.47	64.06	..
Économies en développement sans les PMA	1995 - 2000	1.52	15.31	-0.44	23.31	8.01	58.26	..
	2000 - 2005	1.29	13.40	-0.59	21.29	7.89	52.75	..
High-income countries - Pays à revenu élevé	1990 - 1995	1.61	17.07	-1.18	22.28	5.20	26.61	72
	1995 - 2000	1.54	15.02	-0.32	19.85	4.82	22.27	74
	2000 - 2005	1.12	12.93	-0.13	17.70	4.77	17.62	75
Middle-income countries -	1990 - 1995	1.84	19.61	-0.79	26.53	6.92	47.37	66
Pays à revenu intermédiaire	1995 - 2000	1.59	17.02	-0.70	23.52	6.51	38.47	68
	2000 - 2005	1.39	15.36	-1.09	22.17	6.81	31.86	68
Low-income countries - Pays à revenu faible	1990 - 1995	1.87	18.62	-0.33	28.93	10.31	80.83	60
	1995 - 2000	1.67	16.68	-0.42	26.50	9.82	76.11	61
	2000 - 2005	1.49	14.98	-0.37	24.53	9.55	71.34	62
Heavily indebted poor countries -	1990 - 1995	2.92	27.83	-1.08	44.72	16.89	109.65	48
Pays pauvres très endettés	1995 - 2000	2.66	26.38	-0.42	42.91	16.53	104.90	48
	2000 - 2005	2.56	25.26	-0.60	41.24	15.98	99.33	48
Landlocked countries - Pays sans littoral	1990 - 1995	7.99	25.93	-2.12	41.49	15.56	104.58	50
	1995 - 2000	2.23	23.72	-1.45	39.10	15.38	102.35	50
	2000 - 2005	2.23	22.56	0.20	37.76	15.19	98.96	50
Small island developing states -	1990 - 1995	1.83	20.70	-2.75	29.98	9.28	59.32	61
Petits états insulaires en développement	1995 - 2000	1.55	19.06	-5.52	27.74	8.68	54.78	62
	2000 - 2005	1.77	17.94	-1.66	26.38	8.45	51.26	63
Least developed countries -	***1990 - 1995***	***2.69***	***26.22***	***0.65***	***42.03***	***15.81***	***110.00***	***49***
Pays les moins avancés	***1995 - 2000***	***2.45***	***24.65***	***-0.54***	***39.62***	***14.98***	***104.10***	***50***
	2000 - 2005	***2.42***	***23.68***	***0.29***	***37.93***	***14.25***	***97.32***	***51***
Africa and Haiti - Afrique et Haïti	1990 - 1995	2.72	28.02	-1.04	46.49	18.47	117.00	46
	1995 - 2000	2.74	26.93	-0.42	45.03	18.09	111.88	46
	2000 - 2005	2.71	26.18	-0.30	43.58	17.40	105.57	47
Asia - Asie	1990 - 1995	2.64	24.45	3.25	36.86	12.41	97.04	55
	1995 - 2000	2.03	21.94	-0.57	32.73	10.79	88.16	57
	2000 - 2005	1.96	20.50	1.20	30.37	9.87	79.43	59
Islands - Îles	1990 - 1995	2.57	25.87	-0.53	36.19	10.32	80.93	62
	1995 - 2000	1.49	24.98	-15.27	33.50	8.51	66.62	64
	2000 - 2005	3.05	28.38	2.55	36.46	8.09	59.15	65
Major petroleum exporters -	***1990 - 1995***	***2.18***	***22.63***	***-0.81***	***32.77***	***10.14***	***76.69***	***59***
Principaux exportateurs de pétrole	***1995 - 2000***	***1.96***	***19.50***	***-0.23***	***29.31***	***9.81***	***74.91***	***59***
	2000 - 2005	***1.83***	***18.43***	***-0.32***	***28.18***	***9.75***	***70.12***	***60***
Africa - Afrique	1990 - 1995	2.75	26.97	0.05	43.19	16.23	109.99	49
	1995 - 2000	2.45	23.58	-0.42	40.01	16.43	109.60	48
	2000 - 2005	2.34	22.01	-0.16	38.68	16.67	105.85	47
America - Amérique	1990 - 1995	2.14	21.65	0.00	26.65	5.00	23.24	71
	1995 - 2000	1.90	19.17	-0.01	24.13	4.95	20.59	72
	2000 - 2005	1.74	17.44	0.15	22.59	5.15	17.74	73
Asia - Asie	1990 - 1995	1.92	20.77	-1.25	28.54	7.77	57.66	63
	1995 - 2000	1.73	17.63	-0.16	24.73	7.10	52.72	65
	2000 - 2005	1.59	16.80	-0.44	23.59	6.80	45.88	67
Major exporters of manufactured goods -	***1990 - 1995***	***1.55***	***15.41***	***-0.38***	***23.66***	***8.25***	***63.04***	***65***
Principaux exportateurs d'articles	***1995 - 2000***	***1.37***	***13.62***	***-0.39***	***21.28***	***7.66***	***55.83***	***66***
manufacturés	***2000 - 2005***	***1.14***	***11.56***	***-0.42***	***18.95***	***7.38***	***49.35***	***68***
America - Amérique	1990 - 1995	1.64	18.35	-1.64	24.69	6.34	39.74	68
	1995 - 2000	1.55	16.93	-1.63	22.81	5.87	32.11	70
	2000 - 2005	1.22	15.34	-1.51	21.19	5.85	25.54	72

For sources and notes, see end of table.

Pour les sources et les notes, se reporter à la fin du tableau.

Economic grouping Groupements économiques	Year Année	Population growth rate Taux d'accroissement de la population	Natural increase rate per 1000 inhabitants Taux d'évolution naturel pour 1000 habitants	Net migration rate per 1000 inhabitants Taux net de migration pour 1000 habitants	Crude birth rate per 1000 inhabitants Taux de natalité brut pour 1000 habitants	Crude death rate per 1000 inhabitants Taux de mortalité brut pour 1000 habitants	Infant mortality rate per 1000 live births Taux de mortalité infantile pour 1000 naissances vivantes	Life expectancy at birth Espérance de vie à la naissance
		(1)	(2)	(3)	(4)	(5)	(6)	(7)
Asia - Asie	1990 - 1995	1.54	15.11	-0.25	23.55	8.45	65.59	61
	1995 - 2000	1.35	13.27	-0.26	21.12	7.85	58.53	63
	2000 - 2005	1.13	11.16	-0.30	18.71	7.55	52.23	65
Emerging economies -	*1990 - 1995*	*1.52*	*16.11*	*-0.89*	*22.16*	*6.04*	*34.43*	*69*
Économies émergentes	*1995 - 2000*	*1.40*	*14.40*	*-0.79*	*20.16*	*5.76*	*27.93*	*71*
	2000 - 2005	*1.08*	*12.64*	*-0.87*	*18.44*	*5.81*	*22.38*	*72*
America - Amérique	1990 - 1995	1.62	18.01	-1.47	24.57	6.56	38.76	69
	1995 - 2000	1.49	16.47	-1.50	22.55	6.08	31.42	71
	2000 - 2005	1.19	14.77	-1.38	20.80	6.03	24.89	72
Asia - Asie	1990 - 1995	1.30	11.97	0.39	16.88	4.91	20.67	71
	1995 - 2000	1.19	9.80	0.78	14.86	5.06	16.19	72
	2000 - 2005	0.83	7.82	0.27	13.12	5.30	13.41	73
Newly industrialized economies -	*1990 - 1995*	*1.57*	*15.95*	*-0.52*	*22.71*	*6.76*	*45.10*	*..*
Économies nouvellement industrialisées	*1995 - 2000*	*1.44*	*14.06*	*-0.42*	*20.43*	*6.37*	*37.94*	*..*
	2000 - 2005	*1.28*	*12.67*	*-0.60*	*18.96*	*6.29*	*32.13*	*..*
First tier - Premier tier	1990 - 1995	1.11	7.20	1.18	11.24	4.04	11.41	..
	1995 - 2000	0.95	5.61	1.52	9.50	3.89	7.53	..
	2000 - 2005	0.58	3.30	1.04	7.25	3.95	4.22	..
Second tier - Deuxième tier	1990 - 1995	1.68	17.92	-0.91	25.29	7.37	48.48	..
	1995 - 2000	1.55	15.92	-0.85	22.83	6.91	40.72	..
	2000 - 2005	1.42	14.66	-0.95	21.45	6.79	34.13	..
Developing economies: Africa -	**1990 - 1995**	**2.61**	**26.35**	**-0.39**	**41.33**	**14.98**	**102.13**	**51**
Économies en développement : Afrique	**1995 - 2000**	**2.45**	**24.06**	**-0.37**	**39.21**	**15.15**	**98.63**	**50**
	2000 - 2005	**2.32**	**22.55**	**-0.54**	**38.03**	**15.48**	**93.92**	**49**
Northern Africa excluding Sudan -	1990 - 1995	1.92	21.18	-1.58	28.33	7.15	59.65	66
Afrique septentrionale sans le Soudan	1995 - 2000	1.64	18.62	-1.48	24.70	6.08	46.37	68
	2000 - 2005	1.56	18.31	-1.31	23.98	5.68	36.07	70
Sub-Saharan Africa - Afrique subsaharienne	1990 - 1995	2.77	27.52	-0.12	44.25	16.74	108.25	48
	1995 - 2000	2.62	25.23	-0.13	42.35	17.11	105.23	47
	2000 - 2005	2.48	23.44	-0.38	40.96	17.53	101.00	46
Sub-Saharan Africa excluding South Africa -	1990 - 1995	2.78	28.09	-0.57	45.48	17.40	111.23	47
Afrique sub-saharienne sans l'Afrique du Sud	1995 - 2000	2.68	25.97	-0.27	43.61	17.64	107.96	46
	2000 - 2005	2.57	24.56	-0.42	42.18	17.62	103.35	46
Developing economies: America -	**1990 - 1995**	**1.71**	**19.06**	**-1.67**	**25.78**	**6.72**	**39.79**	**68**
Économies en développement : Amérique	**1995 - 2000**	**1.56**	**17.49**	**-1.69**	**23.70**	**6.20**	**32.80**	**70**
	2000 - 2005	**1.30**	**15.83**	**-1.50**	**21.93**	**6.10**	**26.83**	**71**
Central America and Greater Carribean Islands	1990 - 1995	1.80	22.34	-3.89	28.60	6.26	39.03	69
excluding Puerto Rico - Amérique centrale et	1995 - 2000	1.67	20.05	-3.73	25.73	5.68	32.70	71
Grandes Antilles sans Porto Rico	2000 - 2005	1.15	17.90	-3.37	23.44	5.54	26.89	72
Central America and Greater Carribean Islands	1990 - 1995	1.84	21.50	-3.56	29.49	7.99	46.84	65
excluding Mexico and Puerto Rico -	1995 - 2000	1.69	20.11	-3.03	27.46	7.35	38.79	67
Amérique centrale et Grandes Antilles sans le Mexique et Porto Rico	2000 - 2005	1.53	18.70	-2.59	25.82	7.12	33.79	68
South America and Central America -	1990 - 1995	1.74	19.38	-1.51	25.94	6.57	39.28	68
Amérique du Sud et Amérique centrale	1995 - 2000	1.60	17.80	-1.57	23.84	6.04	32.32	70
	2000 - 2005	1.32	16.08	-1.39	22.02	5.94	26.23	72
South America excluding Brazil -	1990 - 1995	1.80	19.43	-0.96	26.29	6.86	37.14	69
Amérique du Sud sans le Brésil	1995 - 2000	1.55	17.56	-1.25	23.86	6.30	31.41	71
	2000 - 2005	1.34	15.67	-1.07	21.78	6.11	25.81	72
Developing economies: Asia -	**1990 - 1995**	**1.70**	**16.93**	**-0.29**	**25.59**	**8.66**	**68.01**	**63**
Économies en développement : Asie	**1995 - 2000**	**1.48**	**14.79**	**-0.29**	**22.79**	**8.00**	**61.57**	**65**
	2000 - 2005	**1.27**	**12.94**	**-0.29**	**20.58**	**7.64**	**55.27**	**67**
Eastern and South-Eastern Asia excluding China	1990 - 1995	1.66	16.95	-0.46	24.46	7.51	51.99	..
Asie orientale et Asie du Sud-Est sans la Chine	1995 - 2000	1.44	14.24	-0.41	21.24	6.99	45.44	..
	2000 - 2005	1.26	12.80	-0.47	19.66	6.86	39.06	..
Southern Asia excluding India -	1990 - 1995	2.42	25.53	-0.86	35.78	10.25	85.97	..
Asie méridionale sans l'Inde	1995 - 2000	2.01	21.64	-0.76	30.78	9.14	80.52	..
	2000 - 2005	1.77	20.26	-0.78	28.68	8.42	73.19	..

For sources and notes, see end of table.   Pour les sources et les notes, se reporter à la fin du tableau.

Sources:
- UN DESA Population Division, *World Population Prospects: The 2004 Revision*
- UN DESA Population Division, *World Population Prospects: The 2006 Revision*
- UNCTAD secretariat calculations

Notes:

(1) Population growth rate: Average exponential rate of growth of the population over a given period. It is calculated as ln(Pt/P0)/t where t is the length of the period. It is expressed as a percentage.

(2) Natural increase rate per 1000 inhabitants: Crude birth rate minus the crude death rate.

(3) Net migration rate per 1000 inhabitants: Net number of migrants over a given period divided by the person- years lived by the population over that period. It is expressed as net number of migrants per 1000 population.

(4) Crude birth rate per 1000 inhabitants: Number of births over a given period divided by the person-years lived by the population over that period. It is expressed as number of births per 1000 population.

(5) Crude death rate per 1000 inhabitants: Number of deaths over a given period divided by the person-years lived by the population over that period. It is expressed as number of deaths per 1000 population.

(6) Infant mortality rate per 1000 live births: The number of deaths under one year of age in a given period of time divided by the number of live-births in the same period. It is expressed as number of deaths under one year per 1000 births.

(7) Life expectancy at birth: The average number of years a newborn infant would to be expected to live if current mortality trends were to continue for the rest of that person's life.

Sources :
- ONU DAES Division de la population, *World Population Prospects: The 2004 Revision*
- ONU DAES Division de la population, *World Population Prospects: The 2006 Revision*
- Calculs du secrétariat de la CNUCED

Notes :

(1) Taux d'accroissement de la population : le taux exponentiel d'accroissement de la population pour une période donnée, calculé comme ln(Pt/P0)/t, où le t est la longueur de la période, et exprimé en pourcentage.

(2) Taux d'évolution naturelle pour 1000 habitants : le taux de natalité brut moins le taux de mortalité brut.

(3) Taux net de migration pour 1000 habitants : le rapport entre le nombre net des migrants pour une période donnée et l'effectif de la population vivant durant la période considérée. Il est exprimé en nombre net des migrants pour 1000 habitants.

(4) Taux de natalité brut pour 1000 habitants : le rapport entre le nombre de naissances vivantes pour une période donnée et l'effectif de la population durant la période considérée. Il est exprimé en nombre de naissances pour 1000 habitants.

(5) Taux de mortalité brut pour 1000 habitants : c'est le rapport entre le nombre de décès pour une période donnée et l'effectif de la population durant la période considérée. Il est exprimé en nombre de décès pour 1000 habitants.

(6) Taux de mortalité infantile pour 1000 naissances vivantes : il est défini par le nombre des décès d'enfants âgés de moins d'un an pour une période donnée, rapporté au nombre de naissances vivantes durant la période considérée. Il est exprimé en nombre de décès d'enfants âgés de moins d'un an pour 1000 naissances.

(7) Espérance de vie à la naissance : nombre moyen d'années à vivre pour un nouveau-né soumis aux conditions de mortalité de l'année de sa naissance.